Lecture Notes in Computer Science 7211

Commenced Publication in 1973

Advanced Research in Computing and Software Science

Subline of Lectures Notes in Computer Science

Helmut Seidl (Ed.)

Programming Languages and Systems

21st European Symposium on Programming, ESOP 2012
Held as Part of the European Joint Conferences
on Theory and Practice of Software, ETAPS 2012
Tallinn, Estonia, March 24 – April 1, 2012
Proceedings

Springer

Volume Editor

Helmut Seidl
Technische Universität München
Institut für Informatik, 12
Boltzmannstrasse 3
85748 Garching, Germany
E-mail: seidl@cs.tum.edu

ISSN 0302-9743 e-ISSN 1611-3349
ISBN 978-3-642-28868-5 ISBN 978-3-642-28869-2 (eBook)
DOI 10.1007/978-3-642-28869-2
Springer Heidelberg Dordrecht London New York

Library of Congress Control Number: 2012932858

CR Subject Classification (1998): D.2, F.3, C.2, D.3, F.4.1, H.4, D.1

LNCS Sublibrary: SL 2 – Programming and Software Engineering

Typesetting: Camera-ready by author, data conversion by Scientific Publishing Services, Chennai, India

Printed on acid-free paper

Springer is part of Springer Science+Business Media (www.springer.com)

Foreword

ETAPS 2012 is the fifteenth instance of the European Joint Conferences on Theory and Practice of Software. ETAPS is an annual federated conference that was established in 1998 by combining a number of existing and new conferences. This year it comprised six sister conferences (CC, ESOP, FASE, FOSSACS, POST, TACAS), 21 satellite workshops (ACCAT, AIPA, BX, BYTECODE, CMCS, DICE, FESCA, FICS, FIT, GRAPHITE, GT-VMT, HAS, IWIGP, LDTA, LINEARITY, MBT, MSFP, PLACES, QAPL, VSSE and WRLA), and eight invited lectures (excluding those specific to the satellite events).

The six main conferences received this year 606 submissions (including 21 tool demonstration papers), 159 of which were accepted (6 tool demos), giving an overall acceptance rate just above 26%. Congratulations therefore to all the authors who made it to the final programme! I hope that most of the other authors will still have found a way to participate in this exciting event, and that you will all continue to submit to ETAPS and contribute to making it the best conference on software science and engineering.

The events that comprise ETAPS address various aspects of the system development process, including specification, design, implementation, analysis, security and improvement. The languages, methodologies and tools that support these activities are all well within its scope. Different blends of theory and practice are represented, with an inclination towards theory with a practical motivation on the one hand and soundly based practice on the other. Many of the issues involved in software design apply to systems in general, including hardware systems, and the emphasis on software is not intended to be exclusive.

ETAPS is a confederation in which each event retains its own identity, with a separate Programme Committee and proceedings. Its format is open-ended, allowing it to grow and evolve as time goes by. Contributed talks and system demonstrations are in synchronised parallel sessions, with invited lectures in plenary sessions. Two of the invited lectures are reserved for 'unifying' talks on topics of interest to the whole range of ETAPS attendees. The aim of cramming all this activity into a single one-week meeting is to create a strong magnet for academic and industrial researchers working on topics within its scope, giving them the opportunity to learn about research in related areas, and thereby to foster new and existing links between work in areas that were formerly addressed in separate meetings.

This year, ETAPS welcomes a new main conference, *Principles of Security and Trust*, as a candidate to become a permanent member conference of ETAPS. POST is the first addition to our main programme since 1998, when the original five conferences met in Lisbon for the first ETAPS event. It combines the practically important subject matter of security and trust with strong technical connections to traditional ETAPS areas.

A step towards the consolidation of ETAPS and its institutional activities has been undertaken by the Steering Committee with the establishment of *ETAPS e.V.*, a non-profit association under German law. ETAPS e.V. was founded on April 1st, 2011 in Saarbrücken, and we are currently in the process of defining its structure, scope and strategy.

ETAPS 2012 was organised by the *Institute of Cybernetics at Tallinn University of Technology*, in cooperation with

- ▷ European Association for Theoretical Computer Science (EATCS)
- ▷ European Association for Programming Languages and Systems (EAPLS)
- ▷ European Association of Software Science and Technology (EASST)

and with support from the following sponsors, which we gratefully thank:

> INSTITUTE OF CYBERNETICS AT TUT; TALLINN UNIVERSITY OF TECHNOLOGY (TUT); ESTONIAN CENTRE OF EXCELLENCE IN COMPUTER SCIENCE (EXCS) FUNDED BY THE EUROPEAN REGIONAL DEVELOPMENT FUND (ERDF); ESTONIAN CONVENTION BUREAU; and MICROSOFT RESEARCH.

The organising team comprised:

General Chair:	*Tarmo Uustalu*
Satellite Events:	*Keiko Nakata*
Organising Committee:	*James Chapman, Juhan Ernits, Tiina Laasma, Monika Perkmann* and their colleagues in the *Logic and Semantics* group and *administration* of the *Institute of Cybernetics*

The ETAPS portal at http://www.etaps.org is maintained by *RWTH Aachen University*.

Overall planning for ETAPS conferences is the responsibility of its Steering Committee, whose current membership is:

Vladimiro Sassone (Southampton, Chair), Roberto Amadio (Paris 7), Gilles Barthe (IMDEA-Software), David Basin (Zürich), Lars Birkedal (Copenhagen), Michael O'Boyle (Edinburgh), Giuseppe Castagna (CNRS Paris), Vittorio Cortellessa (L'Aquila), Koen De Bosschere (Gent), Pierpaolo Degano (Pisa), Matthias Felleisen (Boston), Bernd Finkbeiner (Saarbrücken), Cormac Flanagan (Santa Cruz), Philippa Gardner (Imperial College London), Andrew D. Gordon (MSR Cambridge and Edinburgh), Daniele Gorla (Rome), Joshua Guttman (Worcester USA), Holger Hermanns (Saarbrücken), Mike Hinchey (Lero, the Irish Software Engineering Research Centre), Ranjit Jhala (San Diego), Joost-Pieter Katoen (Aachen), Paul Klint (Amsterdam), Jens Knoop (Vienna), Barbara König (Duisburg), Juan de Lara (Madrid), Gerald Lüttgen (Bamberg), Tiziana Margaria (Potsdam), Fabio Martinelli (Pisa), John Mitchell (Stanford), Catuscia Palamidessi (INRIA Paris), Frank Pfenning (Pittsburgh), Nir Piterman (Leicester), Don Sannella (Edinburgh), Helmut Seidl (TU Munich),

Scott Smolka (Stony Brook), Gabriele Taentzer (Marburg), Tarmo Uustalu (Tallinn), Dániel Varró (Budapest), Andrea Zisman (London), and Lenore Zuck (Chicago).

I would like to express my sincere gratitude to all of these people and organisations, the Programme Committee Chairs and PC members of the ETAPS conferences, the organisers of the satellite events, the speakers themselves, the many reviewers, all the participants, and Springer-Verlag for agreeing to publish the ETAPS proceedings in the ARCoSS subline.

Finally, I would like to thank the Organising Chair of ETAPS 2012, Tarmo Uustalu, and his Organising Committee, for arranging to have ETAPS in the most beautiful surroundings of Tallinn.

January 2012

Vladimiro Sassone
ETAPS SC Chair

Preface

This volume contains the papers presented at ESOP 2012, the 21st European Symposium on Programming, held March 26–28, 2012, in Tallinn, Estonia.

ESOP is an annual conference devoted to fundamental issues in the specification, design, analysis, and implementation of programming languages and systems. ESOP 2012 was the 21st edition in the series. The Programme Committee (PC) invited papers on all aspects of programming language research including: programming paradigms and styles, methods and tools to write and specify programs and languages, methods and tools for reasoning about programs, methods and tools for implementation, and concurrency and distribution.

Following previous editions, we maintained the page limit of 20 pages, and a rebuttal process of 72 hours during which the authors could respond to the reviews of their submissions. Like last year, PC submissions were not allowed. We received 106 abstracts and in the end got 92 full submissions; four submissions were withdrawn. The remaining 88 submissions were assigned to 3 to 4 PC members; eventually the PC selected 28 papers for publication. These proceedings consist of an invited paper by Bjarne Stroustrup and of the 28 selected papers.

I would like to thank the PC and the subreviewers for their dedicated work in the paper selection process, and all authors who submitted their work to the conference. I would also like to thank the 2012 Organizing Committee, chaired by Tarmo Uustalu, and the Steering Committee, chaired by Vladimiro Sassone, for coordinating the organization of ETAPS 2012. Finally, I would like to thank Andrei Voronkov, whose EasyChair system proved (once more) invaluable throughout the whole process.

January 2012 Helmut Seidl

Organization

Program Chair

Helmut Seidl	TU München, Germany

Program Committee

Andreas Abel	Ludwig-Maximilians-University Munich, Germany
Chandra Boyapati	University of Michigan, USA
Witold Charatonik	Wroclaw University, Wroclaw, Poland
Kostas Chatzikokolakis	Ecole Polytechnique de Paris, France
Dave Clarke	K.U. Leuven, Belgium
Philippa Gardner	Imperial College, London, UK
Sebastian Hack	Saarland University, Germany
Suresh Jagannathan	Purdue University, USA
Somesh Jha	University of Wisconsin, USA
Patrick Lam	University of Waterloo, Canada
Isabella Mastroeni	Università di Verona, Italy
Matthew Might	University of Utah, USA
Anders Moeller	Aarhus University, Denmark
David Monniaux	CNRS / VERIMAG, France
Flemming Nielson	Technical University of Denmark
German Puebla	Technical University of Madrid, Spain
Sylvie Putot	CEA-LIST (Commissariat à l'Energie Atomique), France
Sriram Rajamani	Microsoft Research India
Noam Rinetzky	Queen Mary University of London, UK
Xavier Rival	INRIA / ENS (Paris), France
Christian Schallhart	Oxford University, UK
David Schmidt	Kansas State University, USA
Harald Sondergaard	The University of Melbourne, Australia
Ian Stark	University of Edinburgh, UK
Elena Zucca	DISI - University of Genoa, Italy

Additional Reviewers

Alglave, Jade
Allwood, Tristian
Alvim, Mario
Ancona, Davide
Andres, Miguel E.
Beringer, Lennart
Besson, Frédéric
Biernacki, Dariusz
Birkedal, Lars

Blanc, Benjamin
Boesche, Klaas
Bouissou, Olivier
Boulmé, Sylvain
Brady, Edwin
Chang, Bor-Yuh Evan
Chapman, James
Dal Lago, Ugo
Davidson, Drew
De Nivelle, Hans
Delzanno, Giorgio
Di Pierro, Alessandra
Dinsdale-Young, Thomas
Feret, Jérôme
Ferrara, Pietro
Florido, Mario
Fredrikson, Matt
Furche, Tim
Gaiser, Andreas
Genaim, Samir
Giacobazzi, Roberto
Giannini, Paola
Giuca, Matthew
Giunti, Marco
Gonnord, Laure
Gopan, Denis
Gotsman, Alexey
Grund, Daniel
Harris, William
Herz, Alexander
Horsfall, Ben
Huisman, Marieke
Jeannet, Bertrand
Jonsson, Peter
Kameyama, Yukiyoshi
Kinder, Johannes
King, Andy
Krauss, Alexander
Lal, Akash
Laviron, Vincent
Leißa, Roland
Lenglet, Sergueï
Leucker, Martin
Lhotak, Ondrej
Lienhardt, Michael
Lochbihler, Andreas
Luchaup, Daniel
Mackie, Ian
Mallon, Christoph
Manevich, Roman
Maranget, Luc
Marpons, Guillem
Marron, Mark
Mauborgne, Laurent
Midtgaard, Jan
Miller, Dale
Milushev, Dimiter
Mimram, Samuel
Moy, Matthieu
Muschevici, Radu
Nakata, Keiko
Navas, Jorge A.
Nori, Aditya
Östlund, Johan
Owens, Scott
Padovani, Luca
Patrignani, Marco
Paulin-Mohring, Christine
Pena, Ricardo
Perin, Michael
Petersen, Rasmus L.
Petter, Michael
Pope, Bernard.
Proenca, Jose
Rajan, Ajitha
Rajan, Kaushik
Ramalingam, Ganesan
Ramananandro, Tahina
Reps, Thomas
Sagiv, Mooly
Scherer, Gabriel
Schneider, Sigurd
Segala, Roberto
Senellart, Pierre
Sergey, Ilya
Shkaravska, Olha
Sieczkowski, Filip
Simon, Axel
Somogyi, Zoltan
Song, Lei
Sotin, Pascal
Stark, Ian
Streit, Kevin
Strichman, Ofer
Stuckey, Peter
Sulzmann, Martin
Suter, Philippe
Terepeta, Michał
Thakur, Aditya
Toubhans, Antoine
Truderung, Tomasz
Vafeiadis, Viktor
Valencia, Frank
Vaswani, Kapil
Vechev, Martin
Verbrugge, Clark
Villard, Jules
Villard, Julles
Vytiniotis, Dimitrios
Wadler, Philip
Wasowski, Andrzej
Weirich, Stephanie
Witkowski, Piotr
Wright, Adam
Zanardini, Damiano
Zappa Nardelli, Francesco
Zerny, Ian

Table of Contents

Foundations of C++

Bjarne Stroustrup

Texas A&M University
bs@cs.tamu.edu

Abstract. C++ is a large and complicated language. People get lost in details. However, to write good C++ you only need to understand a few fundamental techniques – the rest is indeed details. This paper presents fundamental examples and explains the principles behind them. Among the issues touched upon are type safety, resource management, compile-time computation, error-handling, concurrency, performance, object-oriented programming, and generic programming. The presentation relies on and introduces a few features from the recent ISO C++ standard, C++11, that simplify the discussion of C++ fundamentals and modern style.

Keywords: C++, programming style, fundamental techniques.

1 Introduction

A programming language – any programming language – has a few fundamental constructs, techniques, and underlying models. Understand those and you have a good idea of what can be expressed in the language, and how. In addition, most languages – and especially older languages that are maintained with a concern for compatibility – provides a host of "incidental" features that can distract from understanding and complicate use. Here, I will briefly present most of the key concepts of C++. Naturally, my presentation will not be complete in either features offered or their details. That's what textbooks and standards are for. So, with the caveat that there is always much more that could be said, here we go!

C++ is defined by its ISO Standard [1]. A detailed description can be found in [2], a tutorial for beginners in [3], and a list of language and library features added for C++11 in [4].

I assume that you know about traditional naming and lexical scoping so I don't waste time on such topics. Similarly, I assume that you are at least superficially acquainted with C/C++ syntax and linkage conventions.

H. Seidl (Ed.): ESOP 2012, LNCS 7211, pp. 1–25, 2012.

2 Ideals

The aim of C++ is to help in classical systems programming tasks. It supports the use of light-weight abstraction for resource-constrained and often mission-critical infrastructure applications. By "light-weight abstraction," I mean abstractions that do not impose space or time overheads in excess of what would be imposed by careful hand coding of a particular example of the abstraction. The aim is to allow a programmer to work at the highest feasible level of abstraction by providing

- A simple and direct mapping to hardware
- Zero-overhead abstraction mechanisms

The aim is to support a type-rich style of programming. In particular, C++ supports type-safe programming with a non-trivial set of types.

Naturally, not every application meets these ideals. In particular, a programmer can choose to write a low-level-C style and/or violate every rule of good programming. That is not my topic here.

3 Memory and Objects

C++ maps directly onto hardware. Its basic types (such as, **char**, **int**, and **double**) map directly into memory entities (such as, bytes and words), most arithmetic and logical operations provided by processors are available for those types. Pointers, arrays, and references directly reflect the addressing hardware. There is no "abstract", "virtual" or mathematical model between the C++ programmer's expressions and the machine's facilities. Memory is seen as sequences of bytes. A typed object is given a location in memory (a sequence of bytes) and values are placed in such objects. Sequences of objects are dealt with as arrays, typically accessed through pointers holding machine addresses. Often, code manipulates sequence of objects defined by a pointer to the beginning of an array and a pointer to one-beyond-the-end of an array:

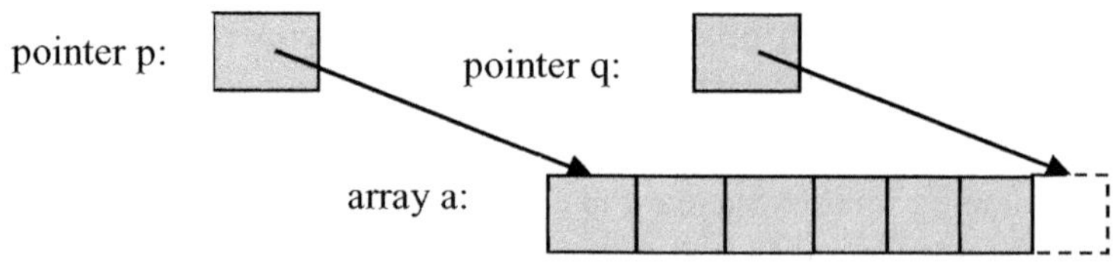

That is, the array **a** can be seen as a half-open sequence of elements [**p**:**q**). The flexibility of forming such addresses by the user and by code generators can be important.

User-defined types are created by simple composition. Consider a simple type **Point**:

```
class Point { int x; int y; /* … */ };

Point xy {1,2};                          // named and scoped object

Point* p = new Point{1,2};      // free store (dynamic, heap) object
```

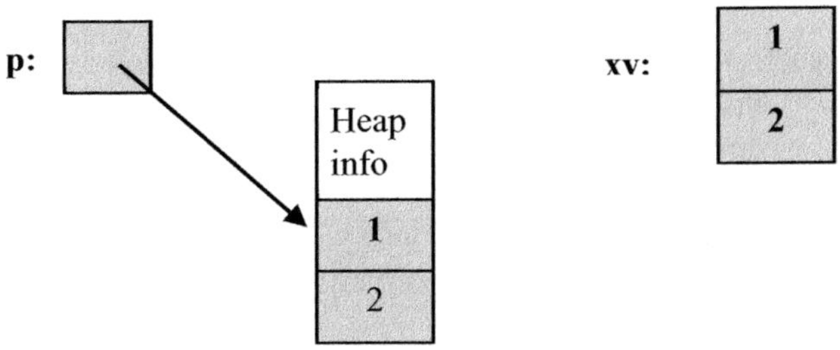

A **Point** is simply the concatenation of its data members, so the size of the **Point xy** is simply two times the size of an **int**. Named objects (of any built-in or user-defined type) are allocated statically or on the stack. Only if we explicitly allocate an (unnamed) **Point** on the free store (the heap), as done for the **Point** pointed to by **p**, do we incur memory overhead (and allocation overhead). Such very simple user-defined types are critical to type-rich programming and very common

Similarly, basic inheritance simply involves the concatenation of members of the base and derived classes:

```
class X { int b; }

class Y : public X { int d; };
```

Only when we add virtual functions (C++'s variant of run-time dispatch supplying run-time polymorphism), do we need to add supporting data structures, and those are just tables of functions:

```
class Shape {                          // a base class; an interface

public:
        virtual void draw() = 0;
        virtual Point center() const = 0;
        // ...
};

Class Circle : public Shape {          // a derived class
        Point c;
        double radius;
public:
        void draw() { /* draw the circle */ }
        Point center() const { return c; }
        // ...
};

Shape* p = new Circle{Point{1,2},3.4};
```

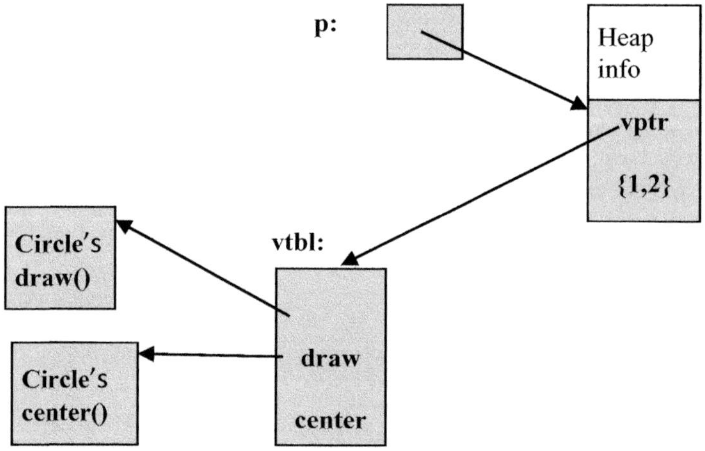

What you see is what you get. For more details see [5]. In general, C++ implementations obey the zero-overhead principle: What you don't use, you don't pay for [6]. And further: What you do use, you couldn't hand code any better.

Please note that not every language provides such simple mappings to hardware and obeys these simple rules. Consider the C++ layout of an array of objects of a user-defined type:

```
class complex { double re, im; /* ... */ };
complex a[ ] = { {1,2}, {3,4} };
```

The likely size is **4*sizeof(double)** which is likely to be 8 words (assuming a 32-bit word). Compare this with a more typical layout from a "pure object-oriented language" where each user-defined object is allocated separately on the heap and accessed through a reference:

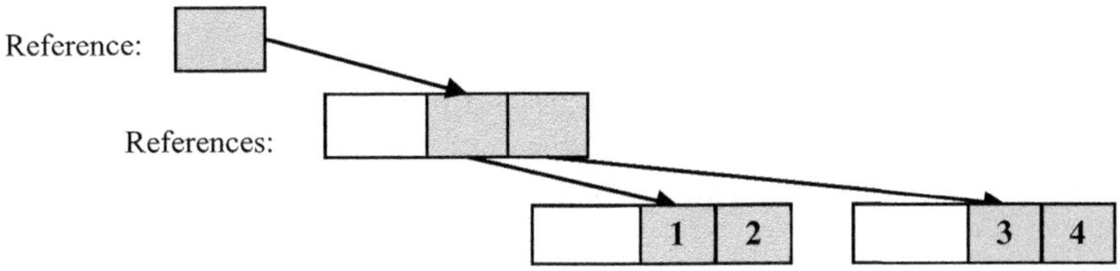

Here, **3*sizeof(reference)+3*sizeof(heap_overhead)+4*sizeof(double)** is the likely size. Assuming a reference to be one word and the heap overhead to be two words, we get a likely size of 19 words to compare to C++'s 8 words. This memory overhead comes with a run-time overhead from allocation and indirect access to elements. That indirect access to memory typically causes problems with cache utilization and limits ROMability.

Memory is turned into an object containing a value of some type by a constructor [6,7]. This operation is reversed by a destructor: after a destructor is run the object no longer exist and its former location is simply memory again. The meaning of constructors and destructors for built-in types and simple aggregates are language defined. For more complex types, the programmer can define constructors and destructors.

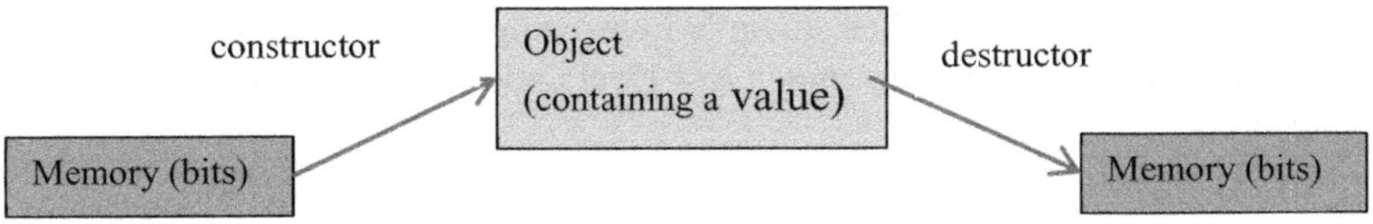

4 Compile-Time Computation

Sometimes, we prefer a computation be done at compile-time. The reasons vary, for example:

- *Efficiency*: To pre-calculate a value (often a size). For simple cases, that is done by an optimizer. Examples include object and array sizes and table values.
- *Type-safety*: To compute a type at compile time.
- *Simplify concurrency*: you can't have a race condition on a constant.

In C++11, we can do type-rich computation at compile time. Consider a simple distance calculation:

```
constexpr double d = dist(NewYork,Boston);
```

Here, I assume that the city names are 2D grid points and that **dist()** computes the distance between them. The **constexpr** keyword is C++'s way of requesting compile-time evaluation. The code doing the calculation might look like this:

```
struct City { double   x, y };
constexpr double csqrt(double) { /* calculate square root */ }
constexpr double square(double d) { return d*d; }
constexpr double dist(City c1, City c2)
        { return csqrt(square(abs(c1.x-c2.x))+square(abs(c1.y-c2.y))); }
```

I had to define my own **csqrt()** because the standard library **sqrt()** isn't designed to work at compile time; **constexpr** is C++'s way of requiring that a function is executable at compile-time. If I wanted to, I could add unit checking [8,9]:

```
constexpr Distance d = dist_in_km(NewYork,Boston);
```

Various forms of user-specified compile-time computation are essential in critical embedded systems applications, much low-level code, and many high-end numerical applications.

5 Error Handling

Errors that cannot be handled locally are reported by throwing an exception. An exception is a value of some type, usually a user-defined type. Code that is interested in handling a type of exception provides a handler (catch-clause) for it. For example:

```
void do_task(int i)
{
        if (i==0) throw std::runtime_error{"do_task() of zero"};
        if (i<0) throw Bad_arg{i};
        // do the task and return normally
}

void task_master(int i)
{
        try {
                do_task(i);
                // ...
        }
        catch (Bad_arg a) {
                cout << "do_task() of negative" << a.val << "\n";
        }
}
```

Code that cannot perform its required task throws an exception and that code that requests a task to be done provides a handler for the kinds of errors it is prepared to handle. If an exception that the requestor has not expressed interest in is thrown, the requestor itself fails.

Exceptions can – and often do – carry information. A catch-clause is associated with a try-block. An exception propagated up the call stack until caught. An uncaught exception causes program termination. A thread can transfer a thrown exception (that it is not willing to handle) to another (calling) thread.

For hard-real-time programming (and only for that), this exception-based error handling must be abandoned for a lower-level error-handling style. The reason is that it is hard to provide good real-time guarantees for exception propagation.

6 Containers

How do you store a lot of data? We place it in user-defined containers, such as vectors, lists, and maps. The archetypical C++ container is the vector. Here is a simple first **Vector**:

```
template<typename T>                    // T is the element type
class Vector {
public:
    Vector(int  n);                     // constructor: initialize to n  elements
    Vector(initializer_list<T>) ;       // constructor: initialize with element list
    ~Vector();                          // destructor: deallocate elements
    int size() ;                        // number of elements
    T& operator[](int i);               // access the ith element
    void push_back(const T& x);         //add x as a new element at the end
T* begin();                             //fist element
    T* end();                           // one-beyond-last element
private:
    int sz;                             // number of elements
    T* elem;                            // pointer to sz elements of type T
};
```

T* means "pointer to **T**" and **T&** means "reference to **T**." Given that declaration, we can allocate and manipulate elements of an arbitrary type, **T**:

```
void f(Vector<string>& vs)
{
        Vector<int> sizes;
        for (auto   x : vs)             // loop through all elements of vs
             sizes.push_back(x.size());
        if (0<vs.size())
             vs[0] = "Whatever!";
          // ...
}
```

The range-for loop uses **Vector**'s **begin()** and **end()** members to determine its range. We might call **f()** like this:

```
int main()
{
       f({"Wheeler", "Wilkes", "Radcliffe", "Appleton","Rutherford"});
       Vector<string> places(10);
       places[2] = "Cambridge";
       f(v);
}
```

The declaration of **Vector** separates the class into two parts, the **public** interface and the **private** implementation (so far, just a representation). The implementation of the **Vector** consists of the definitions of the member functions. In particular, the constructors and the destructor manage a **Vector**'s resource, its elements:

```
template<typename T>
Vector<T>::Vector(int n) // make a vector with n elements of default value
    :sz(n)
{
    if (sz<0) throw std::runtime_error{"negative Vector size"};
    elem = new T[sz];      // sz uninitialized memory slots
    std::uninitialized_fill(elem,elem+sz,T{});      // initialize to default
}
```

The standard technique is to throw an exception if a constructor cannot establish its invariant. Here the invariant is that **elem** points to **sz** elements of type **T** allocated on the free store. The **std::** is used to indicate facilities provided by the ISO C++ standard library (so we don't have to do it ourselves). A constructor handling **{}** lists is defined as taking an argument of the standard-library type **initializer_list**:

```
template<typename T>
Vector<T>::Vector(std::initializer_list<T> lst)    // elemens from the list
    :sz{lst.size()}, elem{new T[sz]}
{
    std::uninitialized_copy(lst.begin(), lst.end(), elem);
}
```

The destructor releases resources acquired:

```
template<typename T>
Vector<T>::~Vector()
{
     delete[] elem;
}
```

This **Vector** is pretty basic, but is illustrates several fundamental C++ techniques and their supporting language features. Containers and resource management are not built into the language or into a run-time support system. Instead, only the minimal facilities for dealing with objects and fixed-sized sequences of objects in memory are "built-in." Everything else is "user-defined" and often provided by libraries written in C++. The standard library **vector**, **map**, **set**, and **list** are examples of containers built using the techniques presented here:

- classes for separating interfaces from implementations,
- constructors for establishing invariants, including acquiring resources,
- destructors for releasing resources,
- templates for parameterizing types and algorithms with types
- mapping of source language features to user-defined code specifying their meaning, e.g. [] for subscripting, the **for**-loop, **new/delete** for construction/destruction on the free store, and the **{}** lists.
- use of half-open sequences, e.g. [**begin()**:**end()**), to define for-loops and general algorithms.
- Use of standard-library facilities to simplify specification and implementation

Importantly, this abstraction from "memory" to "containers of objects" carries no overheads beyond the code necessarily executed for memory management, initialization, and error checking.

Note that

- There is no data stored in a **Vector** object beyond the two named members
- There is no requirement that the element type should be part of a hierarchy. The only requirements on a template argument are imposed by its use; this is "duck typing."
- The operations on a **Vector** are not required to be dynamically resolved (virtual). Simple operations, such as **size()** and **[]**, are typically inlined.

In other words, these language features and techniques ("abstraction mechanisms") are light weight, aimed for use in demanding systems programming and infrastructure implementation tasks. I could, of course, have built a few key abstractions, such as **vector** and **string**, into the language. The reason not to do that is to allow the programmer to define a much larger and varied set of abstractions without losing the flexibility and efficiency needed for the most demanding systems programming tasks.

7 Copy and Move

To complete a class, we have to consider if and how objects can be copied and moved around. As defined above, **Vector** cannot be copied:

```
Vector capitals { "Helsinki", "København", "Riga", "Tallinn" };
Vector c2 = capitals;      // error: no copy defined for Vector
```

By default, you can copy only objects with "simple representations." When I defined a destructor for **Vector**, I implied that I did not consider the representation **Vector** simple: the **elem** pointer represents ownership. Let us define copy:

```
template<typename T>
Vector<T>::Vector(const Vector& v)      // copy constructor
   : sz{v.sz}, elem{new T[v.sz]}
{
   std::uninitialized_copy(v.begin(),v.end(), elem);
}
```

This defines copy initialization. In addition, we can define assignment of one **Vector** by another:

```
template<typename T>
Vector<T> Vector<T>::operator=(Vector<T>& v)    // copy assignment
{
    Vector<T> tmp {v}; // copy v
    delete[] elem;
    elem = tmp.elem;    // "steal" tmp's representation
    tmp.elem = nullptr;
    sz = tmp.elem;
    tmp.sz = 0;
    return *this;
}
```

I chose to have "copy" mean "copy all elements" because that is the intuitive meaning of assignment, fits best with classical mathematical notions, and is what the C++ standard provides for containers.

Copying elements can be costly for large containers, so choosing copy semantics implies a logical or a performance problem. How do we get a **Vector** out of a function? Consider:

```
Vector<int*> find_all(Vector<int>& v, int val)
        // find all occurrences of val in v
{
    Vector<int*> res;
    for (int& x : v)
        if (x==val)
            res.push_back(&x);    // add the address of the element to res
    return res;
}
```

The member function **push_back()** is one of the most useful standard-library container functions. It adds an element to the end of a container, increasing the container's size by one. Here, I have omitted its definition here to avoid getting side tracked. The **find_all** algorithm can be use like this:

```
void  test()
{
    Vector<int> lst { 1,2,3,1,2,3,4,1,2,3,4,5 };
    for (int* p :  find_all(lst,3))
        cout << "address: " << p << ", value: " << *p << "\n";
        // ...
}
```

This should work, and it does, but the cost involved in copying the elements out of **find_all()** can be significant. In particular, I might use something like **find_all()** to locate large numbers of elements in **Vector**s of millions of elements. This makes people search for alternatives to returning a container "by value," such as passing a vector to be filled as an argument, returning a pointer to a result stored on the free store, or plugging in a garbage collector. These alternatives all have serious logical or performance problems. Fortunately, there is a much simpler and more general solution: Note that I didn't want to copy anything; I just wanted to transfer (move) the result vector out of **find_all()**. We can define move operations in a way very similar to the way we define copy operations. Move operations "steal" the representation of an object, leaving behind an "empty" object:

```
template<typename T>
Vector<T>::Vector(const Vector&& v)           // move constructor
    : sz{v.sz}, elem{v.elem}               // grab v's elements
{
    v.elem = nullptr;              // make v empty
    v.sz = 0;
}
```

```
template<typename T>
Vector<T> Vector<T>::operator=(Vector<T>&& v) // move assignment
{
    delete[] elem;          // delete old elements
    elem = v.elem;          // grab v's elements
    sz = v.sz;
    v.elem = nullptr;       // make v empty
    v.sz = 0;
    return *this;
}
```

The **&&** means "rvalue reference" and the effect is that only rvalues can be used as arguments to move operations. Rvalues are objects that will not be used again, such as a local variable used as the return value.

By using the move constructor rather than the copy constructor to return the value from **find_all()**, that return is efficient even if the returned **Vector** happens to have a million elements.

For this to work, we have to declare the copy and move operations in the definition of **Vector**:

```
template<typename T>  // T is the element type
class Vector {
public:
    // ...
    Vector(const Vector&);                // copy constructor
    Vector(Vector&&);                     // move constructor
    Vector& operator=(const Vector&);     // copy assignment
    Vector& operator=(Vector&&);          // move assignment
    // ...
};
```

If a class provides both move and copy operations, move is preferred for rvalues and copy for lvalues [10]. All the standard library containers, including **vector** and **string**, have both copy and move operations. This implies that for real program, all the moderately clever and complicated code in the last two sections have already been done for the programmer. What is left is the much simpler use of **vector**, etc.

8 RAII

Systems manipulate resources. We must manage many kinds of resources, such as files, sockets, locks, threads, and database transactions. A resource is anything that a program acquires from another part of the system and must (explicitly or implicitly) release back to its owner after use. An unused and unreleased resource is called a leak. Memory is an important example of a resource. If resources are not properly released, the system's performance will suffer and eventually a long-running system will fail for lack of usable memory. How do we prevent resource leaks?

The constructor/destructor technique used for **Vector** generalizes to any scoped use of a resource and the move technique handles transfers of ownership between scopes. The key idea is that a resource is always owned by a local (scoped) object. Such a local object is sometimes called a resource handle (e.g. file handle), an owner, or simply an interface (e.g., a **Vector** is the interface to its elements). The handle's constructor acquires the resource and the handle's destructor releases it. Consider a standard-library lock used to ensure exclusive access to some shared data:

```
std::mutex m;   // a system resource
int sh;         // shared data

void f()
{
    // ...
    std::unique_lock lck(m);      // grab (acquire) the mutex
    sh+=1;                        // manipulate shared data
}                                 // implicitly release the mutex
```

This technique is usually called RAII ("Resource Acquisition Is Initialization") and is widely used in modern C++.

Looking at a simple example, it is tempting to think that a pair of **lock()/unlock()** functions would be as good or better than using an object of the manager type **unique_lock**. In practice, it is not so. A handler has a destructor, so you cannot forget the release operation. But how could anyone forget something as simple as and **unlock()**? Or forget an **fclose()**, a **free()**, or a **delete**? Well, people do, so resource leaks in undisciplined code are common (in any language). There are several reasons, including:

- Often, a resource doesn't look like a resource. For example, a **File*** is just a pointer to the compiler and a casual reader and nothing (except the manual) says that **fclose()** must be called to avoid the leak of a file handle.
- Often, several resources need to be acquired and their patterns of acquisition and release vary.
- Error handling typically requires that a resource is released only if acquired and that related resources are released in some specific order.
- Complex control structures (especially when several functions are involved) obscure acquisition and release patterns.

Consider a simple example:

```
// unsafe, naïve use:
void f(const char* p)
{
    FILE* f = fopen(p,"r");     // acquire
    // use f
    fclose(f);                  // release
}
```

This seems innocent enough, but if the "*use f*" code contains a return statement, a C-style **longjmp()**, or an exception **throw**, we never get to the **fclose()** and we have a leak. This can easily happen if the "*use f*" code is long or complicated. People often try to compensate with code that catches exceptions:

```
// naïve fix:
void f(const char* p)
{
    FILE* f = 0;
    try {
        f = fopen(p, "r");
        // use f
    }
    catch (...) { // handle every exception
        if (f) fclose(f);
        throw; // re-throw; let a caller handle this exception
    }
    if (f) fclose(f);
}
```

It is easy to devise a prettier syntax (e.g., Java's **finally**), but the fundamental problem is that any variant of this technique requires the programmer's attention in each place a resource is used. We may open files in dozens of places in a program and in each place the programmer has to remember that **fopen()** acquires a file, be prepared to deal with a failure, and remember to release it. Using return values to handle errors, rather than exceptions, doesn't reduce the complexity.

The solution is to explicitly represent the file handle as a resource:

```
class File_handle {          // belongs in some support library
    FILE* p;
public:
    File_handle(const char* pp, const char* r)
        { p = fopen(pp,r); if (p==0) throw File_error{pp,r}; }
    File_handle(const string& s, const char* r)
        { p = fopen(s.c_str(),r); if (p==0) throw File_error{pp,r}; }

    ~File_handle() { fclose(p); }          // destructor: close file

    // copy and/or move operations
    // access functions
};
```

Now we can simplify the original code to:

```
void f(string s)
{
    File_handle fh {s, "r"};
    // use fh
}
```

The handle class, here **File_handle**, needs only be defined once and put in a library. For example, **unique_lock**, the handle for **mutex**es, is defined in the standard library.

Using such handles, multiple resources are released in the reverse order of acquisition. That is almost always correct. Acquiring a few resources, but failing to acquire all that are needed is handled correctly without programmer intervention. That is crucial for errors in constructors of complex data structures, such as objects from a complex class hierarchy or elements of a container.

Generally, a handle can be moved, but not copied, so move operations need to be provided. For example:

```
class File_handle {          // belongs in some support library
    FILE* p;
public:
    // ...

    // move operations:
    File_handle(File_handle&& h) : p{h.p}   { h.p=nullptr; }
    File_handle& operator=(File_handle&& h) { p=h.p;   h.p=nullptr; }

    // access functions
};
```

Given that, we can pass a **File_handle** around (cheaply).

Memory is not the only resource, so a simply adding a garbage collector is not a solution, at least not a complete solution.

9 Class Hierarchies

C++ allows for the definition and use of class hierarchies. The scheme is fairly conventional, but general. It allows for multiple inheritance both of interface classes (abstract classes) and of classes with implementation. The layout of objects is minimal and obvious. The mechanism for virtual function calls is minimal, obvious, and runs in constant time. The resulting compactness, speed, and predictability are essential for many real-time uses. The (classical) **Circle**-and-**Shape** example from "Memory and Objects" is fairly typical. A class can be derived from another (as **Circle** was from **Shape**). The resulting class is called a derived class and – if publicly derived – is a subtype of the other class, called its base.

The protection model is that

- **public** members and bases of a class can be accessed by all
- **protected** members and bases of a class can be accessed only by members of a derived class
- **private** members and bases of a class can be accessed only by members of that class

To avoid confusion and maintenance problems, I recommend using **protected** only for functions and bases.

Abstract classes, like **Shape**, provide the most stable interfaces because they reveal very little about implementation details (such as object sizes), which are supplied in derived classes, such as **Circle**.

C++ does not provide a universal base class. I consider such a class an unnecessary implementation-oriented artifact that imposes avoidable space and time overheads. Also, a universal "Object" base encourages underspecified (overly general) interfaces that let errors that could be detected at compile time through to run time. Typically, C++ uses parameterization where another language might use a common base class and require implicit or explicit type conversion to determine the exact derived class.

10 Algorithms

A function template that implements an algorithm for a variety of types is conventionally called an algorithm. The C++ standard library provides many algorithms, such as **sort()** and **find()**. For example:

```
void f(vector<int>& v, list<string>& lst)
{
    std::sort(v.begin(),v.end());

    // find "Aarhus" in lst:
    auto p = std::find(lst.begin(),lst.end(),"Aarhus");
    if (p!=lst.end()) {         // found: *p=="Aarhus"
                // ...
    }
    else {                      // not found *p!="Aarhus"
                // ...
    }
      // ...
}
```

Standard-library algorithms, such as **sort()** and **find()**, take half-open sequences of elements, presented as a pair of iterators, as arguments. An iterator is something that points to an element of a sequence. To get to the next element of a sequence, we use ++ and to access the element pointed to, we use *.

Note that I did not name the type of **p**. Instead, I said **auto**, which gives a variable the type of its initializer. This is often a useful shorthand and can be a significant help in generic programming. Here, it saved me from typing **list<string>::iterator**. Interestingly, **auto** is the oldest feature of C++11: I implemented it in 1983, but had to take it out for reasons of C compatibility.

We could implement **find** like this:

```
template<typename Iter, typename Value>
Iter find(Iter first, Iter last, Value val)
{
    while (first!=last && *first!=val)
        ++first;
    return first;
}
```

That is, **find()** compares **val** to each element in the sequence until it finds one that is equal. If you like the terse C-style syntax, you'll find the body of **find()** beautiful. If not, you should still appreciate that **find()** works for a wide variety of data structures and a wide variety of element types with no overhead compared to hand-crafted code for a specific container and value pair. Returning the end of the sequence to indicate "not found" is a standard-library convention.

Algorithms are typically rendered much more useful by parameterizing them with operations. For example, **find()** would be much more useful if instead of simply finding an element of a given value, it found an element that met some user-supplied criterion. The "find" that does that is called **find_if()**. For example:

```
void g(vector< string>& vs)
{
    auto p = std::find_if(vs.begin(),vs.end(),Less_than{"Griffin"});
    if (p!=vs.end()) {         // found: *p<"Griffin"
          // ...
    }
    else {                     // not found *p>="Griffin"
          // ...
    }
    // ...
}
```

Less_than is a function object; that is, an object of type **Less_than** can be called like a function. We can define **find_if()** similarly to **find()**; we just replace the comparison with a call of the predicate:

```
template<typename Iter, typename Value>
Iter find_if(Iter first, Iter last, Predicate p)
{
      while (first!=last && !p(*first))
            ++first;
      return first;
}
```

That is, **find_if** calls the predicate for each element in the sequence. In our example, **p(*first)** means **Less_than{"Griffin"}(*first)** which in turn means ***first<"Griffin"**, assuming that **Less_than** has an obvious definition, such as:

```
struct Less_than {
    String s;
    Less_than(const string& ss) :s{ss} {}   // the value to compare against
    bool operator(const string& v) const { return v<s; } // the comparison
};
```

The general function-object notation can be verbose, but we can let the language write the function object for us by using the lambda notation:

```
auto p = std::find_if(vs.begin(),vs.end(),
                              [](const string& v) { return v<"Griffin"; } );
```

Function objects (incl. lambdas) are very efficient and general because they are easily inlined and can carry information. In particular, simple function objects tend to significantly outperform indirect calls to simple functions. They are the basic parameterization mechanism of the standard library.

If the sequence notation gets too cumbersome, we can define algorithms over containers. For example:

```
namespace MySTL {
        template<class C>
        void sort(C& c) { std::sort(c.begin(),c.end(); }
        // ...
}
```

Given that, I can write **sort(v)** for a container **v**, rather than **sort(v.begin(),v.end())**. Notation matters more than we usually like to believe.

Templates are the language-technical basis for generic programming in C++. Similarly, class hierarchies are the language-technical basis for Object-oriented programming in C++. These two programming styles ("paradigms", if you must) are not meant to be disjoint. Rather, they are meant to be used in combination. For example, **vector<Shape*>** is a container of a run-time polymorphic type. Any use will necessarily involve both generic and object-oriented techniques. For example, consider this variant of the classical "draw all shapes example":

```
template<typename Cont>
void draw_all(Cont& c)
{
     for_each(c.begin(),c.end(), [](Shape* p) { p->draw(); }
}
```

Much of the distinction between object-oriented programming and generic programming is an illusion based on a focus on language features and incomplete support for a synthesis of techniques.

11 Type Functions

Templates, as used to parameterize vector with its element type in "Containers," can be seen as generators. A function template generates functions and a class template generates classes. Thus a template can be understood as a function from a set of arguments to a function or a type. For example, **vector<T>** is a function that produces a **vector** of **T**s from the type **T**. The evaluation of such a type function is called template instantiation. Template instantiation is Turing complete [11]. Template arguments are typically types or integers.

This view of templates as type functions gains great practical importance when applied to functions that associate properties to types. For example, elements in a container have a type. We would like to name that type for every data structure we consider a container, independently of whether its designer planned for that. For starters, we can define a **struct** that defines a name **value_type** for every container that has a member type called **value_type**:

```
template<typename Cont>
struct container_traits {
    using value_type = typename Cont::value_type;
    // ...
};


template<typename T>
using Value_type = typename container_traits<T>::value_type;
```

For example, **Value_type<std::vector<int>>** is **int**. Given **container_traits**, we can define **Value_type** for types that do not have a member called **value_type**. For example, for any pointer, **T***, the value type is **T**:

```
template<typename T>
struct container_traits<T*> {
    using value_type = T;
    // ...
};
```

Technically, this is a specialization of **container_traits** for pointers. Specialization is the language-technical basis for template metaprogramming [12]. Now, **Value_type<int*>** is **int**. We have provided a type function **Value_type** that provides the type of a contained element for every data structure we consider a container. As a user, the implementation details are immaterial, and we can just write

```
Value_type<X> a;
```

Traits are widely used in the implementation of the standard library.

There is an obvious weakness in my description of **container_traits**: I said "a type that I consider a container" rather than precisely specifying the requirements for being a container. In other words, the arguments to a template are unconstrained and only their instantiations are type checked. This is "Duck tying" ("if it walks like a duck and quacks like a duck, it's a duck") and leads to late (link-time) type checking and appallingly poor error messages.

Designing a system of requirements (called a concept in C++) is still a research topic. A concept design for C++0x [13] failed to meet the needs of C++'s large and diverse user community and concepts is an area of active research [14-17]. The demands of compile-time efficiency (within a few percent of unconstrained templates), run-time efficiency (no slower than templates with unconstrained arguments), ease of use by non-experts, no verbosity, ability to handle type conversion, ability to interoperate with unconstrained templates, and ease of conversion of pre-concept C++ programs makes this a challenging task.

12 Concurrency

C++ must support the forms of concurrency offered by the hardware and operating system on which it runs. Something else may make it a better platform for specific applications, but not supporting "the system's" notion of concurrency would disqualify C++ as a systems programming language. Consequently, ISO standard C++ supports a conventional threads-and-locks model of concurrency. I consider threads-and-locks an unfortunate low-level view, but higher level concurrency models can be efficiently built as libraries on top of what the standard offers. C++ provides support for lock-free programming for cases where you have to get really close to the hardware [18].

What the standard offers differs from earlier C and C++ thread implementations in being type safe. Consider a simple example of a function, **f**, and a function object, **F**, being run on separate threads:

```
void f(vector<double>&);          // function

struct F {                        // function object
    vector<double>& v;
    F(vector<double>& vv) :v{vv} { }
    void operator()();
};

void code(vector<double>& vec1, vector<double>& vec2)
{
    std::thread t1 {f,vec1};      // f(vec1)
    std::thread t2 {F{vec2}};     // F{vec2}()
    t1.join();
    t2.join();
    // use vec1 and vec2
}
```

For simplicity, I have assumed that **f** and **F** modify their arguments. Note how **t1**'s constructor takes the function to be called followed by its arguments. It will accept any function as long as its arguments type checks using what is called variadic templates. However, here the simplicity of the interface is more important than the implementation technology.

I consider that style of concurrency clumsy, with endless opportunity for confusion and avoidable overheads. However, It does not require regression to type-unsafe the C-style **void**** and macros common in older threads programming and is supported with a variety of synchronization mechanisms (e.g., mutexes, locks, condition variables).

In addition, the standard library supports **futures** to enable a style of concurrency without explicit use of threads and locks. For example:

```
double comp(vector<double>& v)          // spawn many tasks
{
    auto b = v.begin();
    auto sz = v.size();

    auto f0 = std::async(std::accumulate, b, b+sz/4, 0.0);
    auto f1 = std::async(std::accumulate, b+sz/4, b+sz/2, 0.0);
    auto f2 = std::async(std::accumulate, b+sz/2, b+sz*3/4, 0.0);
    auto f3 = std::async(std::accumulate, b+sz*3/4, v.end(), 0.0);

    return f0.get()+f1.get()+f2.get()+f3.get();
}
```

Here, the "thread launcher" **std::async** launches threads as needed to evaluate **std::accumulate**. Each call of **async** returns a handle, called a **future**, from which the result can be obtained by a call of **get()**. If a task launched by **async** hasn't completed by the call of **get()**, the calling thread waits. This programming model is much cleaner than the more general threads-and-locks model for the independent tasks for which it is intended.

13 Type Safety

C++ is not guaranteed to be statically type safe. A language designed for general and performance critical systems programming with the ability to manipulate hardware cannot be. It provides facilities for manipulating hardware at a low level that can easily be misused to break the type system. Examples are untagged unions, explicit type conversions (casts), arrays without (guaranteed) range checks, and the ability to deallocate a free store (heap) object while holding on to a pointer allowing for post-allocation access. It would be nice to isolate the type violations in a few clearly delimited sections of code, but history precludes that. Don't use these facilities outside the implementation of higher-level facilities (such as **vector**). The ISO C++ standard library contains a rich set of such abstractions (e.g., **string**, **vector**, **map**, **set**, and **thread**), so that you don't have to define them yourself.

14 Challenges

Obviously, C++ is not perfect. For the future, we face several challenges:

- How to make programmers prefer modern C++ styles over low-level (C-style) code, which is far more error-prone and harder to maintain, yet no more efficient.
- How to make C++ a better language given the Draconian constraints of C and C++ compatibility.
- How to improve and complete the techniques and models (incompletely and imperfectly) embodied in C++.

In particular, I would like to:

- Close more type loopholes (in particular, find a way to prevent misuses of **delete** without spoiling RAII)
- Simplify concurrent programming (in particular, provide some higher-level concurrency models as libraries)
- Simplify generic programming (in particular, introduce simple and effective concepts)
- Simplify programming using class hierarchies (in particular, eliminate use of the visitor pattern)
- Provide better support for combinations of object-oriented and generic programming styles.
- Make exceptions usable for hard-real-time projects (that will most likely be a tool rather than a language change)
- Find a good way of using multiple address spaces (as needed for distributed computing); this would most likely involve defining a more general module mechanism that would also address dynamic linking, and more.
- Provide many more domain-specific libraries
- Develop a more precise and formal specification of C++ (e.g. see [19,8,7])

Inside C++ is a smaller, cleaner, and even more powerful language struggling to get out. And no, that language is not C, C#, D, Haskell, Java, ML, Lisp, Scala, Smalltalk, or whatever. Whatever that language is, it must be better than C++ at light-weight abstraction in even the most demanding infrastructure applications.

References

1. ISO/IEC JTC1 SC22 WG21 N3092: Programming Languages — C++
2. Stroustrup, B.: The C++ Programming Language (Special Edition). Addison Wesley, Reading (2000) ISBN 0-201-70073-5
3. Stroustrup, B.: Programming – Principles and Practice Using C++. Addison-Wesley (December 2008) ISBN 978-0321543721
4. Stroustrup, B.: The C++11 FAQ, `http://www.research.att.com/~bs/C++11FAQ.html`

5. Stroustrup, B.: Abstraction and the C++ Machine Model. In: Wu, Z., Chen, C., Guo, M., Bu, J. (eds.) ICESS 2004. LNCS, vol. 3605, pp. 1–13. Springer, Heidelberg (2005)
6. Stroustrup, B.: The Design and Evolution of C++. Addison Wesley (March 1994) ISBN 0-201-54330-3
7. Ramananandro, T., Dos Reis, G., Leroy, X.: A Mechanized Semantics for C++ Object Construction and Destruction with Applications to Resource Management. In: POPL 2012, Philadelphia (Pennsylvania), USA (January 2012)
8. Dos Reis, G., Stroustrup, B.: General Constant Expressions for System Programming Languages. In: The 25th ACM Symposium On Applied Computing, SAC 2010 (March 2010)
9. Stroustrup, B.: Software Development for Infrastructure. IEEE Computer (January 2012)
10. Barron, D.W., et al.: The main features of CPL. The Computer Journal 6(2), 134 (1963)
11. Velthuizen, T.L.: C++ Templates are Turing Complete. University of Indiana Technical Report (2003)
12. Veldhuizen, T.: Using C++ template metaprograms. C++ Report 7(4) (May 1995)
13. Gregor, D., Jarvi, J., Siek, J., Stroustrup, B., Dos Reis, G., Lumsdaine, A.: Concepts: Linguistic Support for Generic Programming in C++. In: OOPSLA 2006 (October 2006)
14. Dos Reis, G., Stroustrup, B.: Specifying C++ Concepts. In: POPL 2006 (January 2006)
15. Sutton, A., Stroustrup, B.: Design of Concept Libraries for C++. In: Proc. International Conference on Software Language Engineering, SLE 2011 (July 2011)
16. Stepanov, A., McJones, P.: Elements of Programming. Addison-Wesley Professional, June 19 (2009) ISBN-13: 978-0321635372
17. Stroustrup, B., Sutton, A. (eds.): A Concept Design for the STL. WG21 Technical Report N3351=12-0041 (January 2012)
18. Williams, A.: C++ Concurrency in Action – Practical Multithreading. Manning Publications (2012) ISBN: 1933988770
19. Dos Reis, G., Stroustrup, B.: A formalism for C++. N1885 (October 2005)

What's Decidable about Weak Memory Models?*

Mohamed Faouzi Atig[1], Ahmed Bouajjani[2],
Sebastian Burckhardt[3], and Madanlal Musuvathi[3]

[1] Uppsala University, Sweden
mohamed_faouzi.atig@it.uu.se
[2] LIAFA, Univ. Paris Diderot & CNRS, France
abou@liafa.jussieu.fr
[3] Microsoft Research Redmond, USA
{sburckha,madanm}@microsoft.com

Abstract. We investigate the decidability of the state reachability problem in finite-state programs running under weak memory models. In [3], we have shown that this problem is decidable for TSO and its extension with the write-to-write order relaxation, but beyond these models nothing is known to be decidable. Moreover, we have shown that relaxing the program order by allowing reads or writes to overtake reads leads to undecidability. In this paper, we refine these results by sharpening the (un)decidability frontiers on both sides. On the positive side, we introduce a new memory model NSW (for non-speculative writes) that extends TSO with the write-to-write relaxation, the read-to-read relaxation, and support for partial fences. We present a backtrack-free operational model for NSW, and prove that it does not allow causal cycles (thus barring pathological out-of-thin-air effects). On the negative side, we show that adding the read-to-write relaxation to TSO causes undecidability, and that adding non-atomic writes to NSW also causes undecidability. Our results establish that NSW is the first known hardware-centric memory model that is relaxed enough to permit both delayed execution of writes and early execution of reads for which the reachability problem is decidable.

1 Introduction

The memory consistency model (or simply, the memory model) of a shared-memory multiprocessor is a low-level programming abstraction that defines when and in what order writes performed by one processor become visible to other processors. The simplest memory model, sequential consistency [16], requires that the operations performed by the processors should appear as if these operations are interleaved in a consistent global order. Despite its simplicity and appeal, most contemporary hardware platforms support weak (relaxed) memory models for performance reasons [2,13].

The effects of weak memory models can be counterintuitive and difficult to understand even for very small programs. Not surprisingly, relaxed memory models are an active research area today. Much progress has been made to aid programmers, in the form of verification or model-checking algorithms [8,15,26,4], testing tools [11,18], analyses

* Extended version with proofs at http://user.it.uu.se/%7Emohat117/esop12.pdf

H. Seidl (Ed.): ESOP 2012, LNCS 7211, pp. 26–46, 2012.

that check whether programs are exposed to specific relaxations [7,9,20], fence insertion tools [14,15,17], verified compilation [10,24,23], and formal models that closely approximate commercial multiprocessors [21,22,25].

Nevertheless, many foundational questions about weak memory models remain. For instance, given a finite-state concurrent program under weak memory model, what is the complexity of deciding if a particular erroneous state can be reached? What is the most relaxed model for which the safety verification problem is decidable? Understanding the answers to these questions is crucial for model checking safety properties of programs under a relaxed memory model and for checking if a program exhibits the same behavior under different memory models.

$\mathsf{w} \to \mathsf{r}$ (Write-to-read order). The effect of a write may be delayed past a subsequent read. This relaxation enables the use of per-processor *write buffers*. Specifically, when executing a write, a processor may buffer the value to be written in its local buffer and continue executing before the buffered value becomes globally visible.

$\mathsf{w} \to \mathsf{w}$ (Write-to-write order). A processor may swap the order of two writes. For instance, if using a write buffer as described above, writes may exit the buffer in a different order than they entered.

$\mathsf{r} \to \mathsf{r/w}$ (Read-to-read/write order). A processor may change the order of a read and a subsequent read or write. This enables out-of-order execution techniques that help to hide latency of memory accesses. We further distinguish between $\mathsf{r} \to \mathsf{r}$ (read-to-read) and $\mathsf{r} \to \mathsf{w}$ (read-to-write) relaxations.

RLWE (Read local writes early). A processor may read its own writes even if they are not globally visible yet (i.e. before the exit the buffer). For example, if a processor executes a read from a location for which there are pending writes in the local buffer, it can immediately forward the value of the last such write from the buffer to the read.

RRWE (Read remote writes early). A processor may read other processors' writes even if they are not globally visible yet. For example, a write in a local buffer may be directly forwarded to some remote processors before it exits the buffer.

RWF (read-read and write-write fences). A processor may issue a read-read (write-write) fence to prevent reordering of reads (writes) that precede the fence with reads (writes) that succeed it.

Fig. 1. Definition Acronyms that represent relaxations/features, following the terminology in [2]

In prior work [3], we have presented some early decidability results for relaxed memory models. In this paper, we refine these results with a precise study of relaxations that lead to the undecidability of memory models. Fig. 1 describes the relaxations studied in this paper and Fig. 2 summarizes our results.

Memory Model	Name	Reach. Problem
$\{\mathsf{w} \to \mathsf{r}$, RLWE$\}$	TSO	decidable [3]
TSO$\cup\{\mathsf{w} \to \mathsf{w}\}$	-	decidable [3]
TSO$\cup\{\mathsf{w} \to \mathsf{w}$, RWF$\}$	PSO	decidable **[new]**
PSO$\cup\{\mathsf{r} \to \mathsf{r}\}$	NSW	decidable **[new]**
TSO$\cup\{\mathsf{r} \to \mathsf{r/w}\}$	-	undecidable [3]
TSO$\cup\{\mathsf{r} \to \mathsf{w}\}$	-	undecidable **[new]**
NSW$\cup\{$RRWE$\}$	-	undecidable **[new]**

Fig. 2. Summary of previously known and unknown results about the decidability of the reachability problem on weak memory models. The acronyms are defined in Fig. 1.

Our results show (perhaps surprisingly) that relaxations that are commonly considered as counter-intuitive by programmers coincide with those that lead to undecidability. For instance, we show that adding the read-to-write relaxation to TSO (total store order) results in an undecidable memory model. In such a relaxation, a processor eagerly makes a write visible to other processors before a prior read has completed. Such speculative writes can result in causal cycles, a well known memory model hazard [12,19]. On the other hand, a memory model that avoids this relaxation but otherwise remains general by allowing read-to-read, write-to-read, and write-to-write relaxations together with read-read and write-write fences is actually decidable. We call this memory model NSW (non speculative writes) and study its properties. Finally, we show that adding non-atomic writes to NSW leads to undecidability. Such non-atomic writes can lead to counter-intuitive IRIW (independent reads of independent writes) effects [6].

Along the same vein, we show that NSW, which is the most relaxed model known to be decidable, exhibits the following desirable properties:

- NSW enables significant optimizations; specifically, (1) it permits a write to be moved down (later) in the program execution past any other read or write (by delaying it in a buffer), and (2) it permits reads to be moved up (earlier) in the program execution, before any read or write (even before a read on whose value it depends).
- The performance impact of prohibiting the read-to-write relaxation (which is the only ordering relaxation remaining in NSW) can be ameliorated by write buffers: even if we disallow writes to become visible to other processors (i.e. exit the write buffer) before all preceding reads have completed, we may still allow writes to enter into the buffer while older reads are still pending.
- Since NSW does not permit writes to become visible to other processors before all older loads by the same processor have completed, causal cycles and out-of-thin-air behaviors are impossible. We formalize and prove this fact in Section 3.6.
- In operational memory models, reordering of dependent memory accesses is usually modeled by nondeterministically guessing the read value and validating it later. In some sense, such models are not very constructive as they may require backtracking if a guess can not be validated later on. We discovered a way to eliminate all such guesses from our operational model for NSW, obtaining an alternative operational model that is backtrack-free (Section 5).
- The relaxations in NSW do not depend on any notion of data/control-dependencies. Not only does this greatly simplify the formalism, but it also avoids subtle soundness problems with compiler optimizations that may break dependencies [5].

To establish that the state reachability problem for NSW is decidable, we proceed in two steps. First, we define an operational model for NSW where reads do not need to be stored, but still allowing the precise simulation of all their possible reorderings due to the read-to-read relaxation (section 5). The key idea for tackling this issue consists, roughly speaking, in using a buffer storing the history of all the past memory states, in addition to informations about the most recent value read by each process on each variable. The whole model has actually three levels of buffers, each of them related to one of the considered relaxations (write-to-write, write-to-read, and finally read-to-read). We think that this step has its own interest from the point of view of modeling and of understanding the effects of each of the considered relaxations, regardless from the decidability issue. Then, in a second step (section 6), we prove that the defined operational model can be transformed, while preserving state reachability, into a system that is monotonic w.r.t. a well quasi-ordering on the set of its configurations. This allows to deduce that the model has a decidable state reachability problem, using [1]. Both steps are nontrivial and are based on new and quite subtle constructions.

2 Preliminary Definitions and Notations

Let $k \in \mathbb{N}$ such that $k \geq 1$. Then, we denote by $[k]$ the set $\{1,\ldots,k\}$. Let Σ be a finite alphabet. We denote by Σ^* the set of all *words* over Σ, and by ε the empty word. The length of a word $w \in \Sigma^*$ is denoted by $length(w)$. (We assume that $length(\varepsilon) = 0$.) For every $i \in [length(w)]$, let $w(i)$ denote the symbol at position i in w. For $a \in \Sigma$ and $w \in \Sigma^*$, we write $a \in w$ if a appears in w, i.e., $\exists i \in [length(w)]$ such that $a = w(i)$.

Given a sub-alphabet $\Theta \subseteq \Sigma$ and a word $u \in \Sigma^*$, we denote by $u|_\Theta$ the *projection* of u over Θ, i.e., the word obtained from u by erasing all the symbols that are not in Θ.

Let $k \geq 1$ be an integer and E be a set. Let $\mathbf{e} = (e_1,\ldots,e_k) \in E^k$ be a k-dim vector over E. For every $i \in [k]$, we use $\mathbf{e}[i]$ to denote the i-th component of $\mathbf{e}$ (i.e., $\mathbf{e}[i] = e_i$). For every $j \in [k]$ and $e' \in E$, we denote by $\mathbf{e}[j \leftarrow e']$ the k-dim vector $\mathbf{e}'$ over E defined as follows: $\mathbf{e}'[j] = e'$ and $\mathbf{e}'[l] = \mathbf{e}[l]$ for all $l \neq j$.

Let E and F be two sets. We denote by $[E \rightarrow F]$ the set of all mappings from E to F. Assume that E is finite and that $E = \{e_1,\ldots,e_k\}$ for some integer $k \geq 1$. Then, we sometimes identify a mapping $\mathbf{g} \in [E \rightarrow F]$ with a k-dim vector over F.

3 Weak Memory Models

3.1 Shared Memory Concurrent Systems

Let D be a finite data domain, and $X = \{x_1,\ldots,x_m\}$ a finite set of variables valued in D. Let M denote the set D^m, i.e., the set of all possible valuations of the variables in X.

For a given finite set of process identities I, let $\Omega(I,X,D)$ be the set of operations of the form: (1) *"no operation"*: nop, (2) *read*: $\mathsf{r}(i,j,d)$, (3) *write*: $\mathsf{w}(i,j,d)$, (4) *atomic read-write* : $\mathsf{arw}(i,j,d,d')$, (5) *read_fence*: $\mathsf{rfence}(i)$, and (6) *write_fence*: $\mathsf{wfence}(i)$, where $i \in I$, $j \in [m]$, and $d,d' \in D$. Intuitively, $\mathsf{r}(i,j,d)$ (resp. $\mathsf{w}(i,j,d)$) means that process i reads (resp. writes) the data d from (resp. to) the variable x_j. The semantics of atomic read-writes and of read/write_fences will be explained in section 3.2.

A *concurrent system* over D and X is a tuple $\mathcal{N} = (\mathcal{P}_1,\ldots,\mathcal{P}_n)$ such that for every $i \in [n]$, $\mathcal{P}_i = (P_i,\Delta_i)$ is a finite-state process where (1) P_i is a finite set of control states, and (2) $\Delta_i \subseteq P_i \times \Omega(\{i\},X,D) \times P_i$ is a finite set of labeled transitions.

Let $\mathbf{P} = P_1 \times \ldots \times P_n$. For convenience, we write $p \xrightarrow{op}_i p'$ instead of $(p,op,p') \in \Delta_i$, for any $p,p' \in P_i$ and $op \in \Omega(\{i\},X,D)$. We denote by $\Omega(\mathcal{N}) \subseteq \Omega([n],X,D)$ the set of operations used in $\mathcal{N}$. Given an operation $\omega = op(i,j,d)$ with $op \in \{\mathsf{r},\mathsf{w}\}$, $i \in [n]$, $j \in [m]$, and $d \in D$, let $proc(\omega) = i$, $var(\omega) = j$, and $data(\omega) = d$.

3.2 Memory Models

The executions of a concurrent system are obtained by interleaving the operations issued by its different processes. In the Sequential Consistency (SC) model, the order between operations of a same process is preserved. Relaxations of this program order lead to the definition of various weak memory models. However, fences (i.e., barriers) can be used to impose the serialization of some operations at some execution points. An operation $\mathsf{arw}(i,j,d,d')$ is equivalent to the atomic execution of the sequence $\mathsf{r}(i,j,d);\mathsf{w}(i,j,d')$, with the additional assumption that this operation is never reordered with any other operation of the same process. Therefore, this operation can emulate a full fence, i.e., a fence such that any two operations by the same process occurring before and after (in program order) the full fence cannot be swapped. The operation $\mathsf{wfence}(i)$ (resp. $\mathsf{rfence}(i)$) is a fence for writes (resp. reads) only, i.e., writes (resp. reads) that occur before and after a write_fence (resp. read_fence) cannot be swapped.

3.3 A Semantics Based on Rewrite Rules

We consider memory models corresponding to a set of program order relaxations defined by permutation rules between the operations. Given read/write operations $op_1, op_2 \in \{\mathsf{w},\mathsf{r}\}$, relaxing the **op₁ to op₂** order consists in allowing that operations of the class op_2 are allowed to overtake operations of the class op_1 in a computation, provided that these operations are issued by the same process, and that they are acting on *different* variables. This corresponds to defining a set of rewrite rules:

$$op_1(i,j,d)op_2(i,k,d') \hookrightarrow op_2(i,k,d')op_1(i,j,d) \tag{1}$$

for any $i \in [n]$, $j,k \in [m]$, $j \neq k$, and $d,d' \in D$.

In addition to permutations between reads and writes, we consider that reads and write_fences issued by the same process can always be swapped, and the same holds concerning writes and read_fences. Then, we consider the following set of rewrite rules RWF defining the semantics of read/write fences: For any $i \in [n]$, $j \in [m]$, $d \in D$,

$$\begin{aligned} \mathsf{wfence}(i)\mathsf{r}(i,j,d) &\hookrightarrow \mathsf{r}(i,j,d)\mathsf{wfence}(i) \\ \mathsf{r}(i,j,d)\mathsf{wfence}(i) &\hookrightarrow \mathsf{wfence}(i)\mathsf{r}(i,j,d) \\ \mathsf{rfence}(i)\mathsf{w}(i,j,d) &\hookrightarrow \mathsf{w}(i,j,d)\mathsf{rfence}(i) \\ \mathsf{w}(i,j,d)\mathsf{rfence}(i) &\hookrightarrow \mathsf{rfence}(i)\mathsf{w}(i,j,d) \end{aligned} \tag{2}$$

We also consider the following set RLWE (Read Local Write Early) of rewrite rules:

$$\mathsf{w}(i,j,d)\mathsf{r}(i,j,d) \hookrightarrow \mathsf{w}(i,j,d) \tag{3}$$

for any $i \in [n]$, $j \in [m]$, $d \in D$. These rules say that a read that occurs after a write of the same value on the same variable by the same process can be validated immediately.

Then, we consider that a memory model M is defined by the choice of a set of rewrite rules defining the allowed relaxations of the program order. For instance, we define in this framework the two well known models TSO and PSO as follows:

$$\begin{aligned} \mathsf{TSO} &= \mathsf{RWF} \cup \mathsf{RLWE} \cup \{\mathsf{w} \to \mathsf{r}\} \\ \mathsf{PSO} &= \mathsf{RWF} \cup \mathsf{RLWE} \cup \{\mathsf{w} \to \mathsf{r}, \mathsf{w} \to \mathsf{w}\} \end{aligned}$$

Clearly, TSO can be simulated under PSO by inserting a wfence before each write operation. Notice that using read_fences in TSO and PSO is not relevant since reads cannot be swapped in these models. Similarly, using write_fences in TSO is not relevant. But the possibility of using write_fences in PSO is important. Without write_fences, it is not possible to simulate TSO under PSO.

Given a process $\mathcal{P}_i$ of $\mathcal{N}$, and two control states $p, p' \in P_i$, a computation trace of $\mathcal{P}_i$ from p to p' is a finite sequence $\tau = \omega_0 \cdots \omega_{\ell-1} \in \Omega(\{i\}, X, D)^*$ such that there are $p_0 \cdots p_\ell \in P_i^*$ such that $p = p_0$, $p' = p_\ell$, and for every $j \in \{0, \ldots, \ell-1\}$, $(p_j, \omega_i, p_{j+1}) \in \Delta_i$. The set of computation traces of $\mathcal{P}_i$ from p to p' is denoted by $\mathcal{T}(\mathcal{P}_i, p, p')$.

Let R be a set of rewrite rules over traces defining a memory model M. Given a rewrite rule $\rho = \alpha \hookrightarrow \beta$, where $\alpha, \beta \in \Omega(\mathcal{N})^*$, and a computation trace $\tau \in \Omega(\mathcal{N})^*$, we define a rewriting relation $\hookrightarrow_\rho$ between traces as follows: $\tau \hookrightarrow_\rho \tau'$ if $\tau = \tau_1 \alpha \tau_2$ and $\tau' = \tau_1 \beta \tau_2$ for some $\tau_1, \tau_2 \in \Omega(\mathcal{N})^*$. As usual, $\hookrightarrow_\rho^*$ denotes the reflexive-transitive closure of $\hookrightarrow_\rho$. These definitions are generalized in the obvious way to sets of rules and sets of computation traces. Given a set of rewrite rules R, the closure of a set of traces T, denoted by $[T]_R$, is the smallest set containing T and which is closed under the application of the rules in R, i.e., $[T]_R = \{\tau' \in \Omega(\mathcal{N})^* \ : \ \tau \in T \wedge \tau \hookrightarrow_R^* \tau'\}$.

Given two traces τ_1 and τ_2, the shuffle of the two traces is the set of traces obtained by interleaving the elements of τ_1 and τ_2 while preserving the original order between elements of each trace. Formally, the operator $\|$ is defined inductively as follows: (1) $\varepsilon \| \tau = \tau \| \varepsilon = \tau$, and (2) $\omega_1 \tau_1 \| \omega_2 \tau_2 = \omega_1(\tau_1 \| \omega_2 \tau_2) \cup \omega_2(\omega_1 \tau_1 \| \tau_2)$ for every $\omega_1, \omega_2 \in \Omega(\mathcal{N})$, and for every $\tau, \tau_1, \tau_2 \in \Omega(\mathcal{N})^*$. The definition can be extended in a straightforward manner to a finite number of traces.

Given two vectors of control states $\mathbf{p}, \mathbf{p}' \in \mathbf{P}$, the set of computation traces in $\mathcal{N}$ from $\mathbf{p}$ to $\mathbf{p}'$ in the memory model M (defined by R), denoted by $\mathcal{T}_{\mathsf{M}}(\mathcal{N}, \mathbf{p}, \mathbf{p}')$, is defined by

$$[\mathcal{T}(\mathcal{P}_1, \mathbf{p}[1], \mathbf{p}'[1])]_R \parallel \ldots \parallel [\mathcal{T}(\mathcal{P}_n, \mathbf{p}[n], \mathbf{p}'[n])]_R$$

We define a relation $[\,\rangle$ between memory states corresponding to the execution of operations in $\Omega(\mathcal{N})$. Given $\mathbf{d}, \mathbf{d}' \in M$, we have, for every $i \in [n]$ and for every $j \in [m]$:

- $\mathbf{d}[\mathsf{w}(i,j,d)\rangle \mathbf{d}'$ if $\mathbf{d}' = \mathbf{d}[j \leftarrow d]$,
- $\mathbf{d}[\mathsf{r}(i,j,d)\rangle \mathbf{d}'$ if $\mathbf{d}[j] = d$ and $\mathbf{d} = \mathbf{d}'$,
- $\mathbf{d}[\mathsf{arw}(i,j,d,d')\rangle \mathbf{d}'$ if $\mathbf{d}[j] = d$ and $\mathbf{d}' = \mathbf{d}[j \leftarrow d']$,
- $\mathbf{d}[op\rangle \mathbf{d}'$ with $op \in \{\mathsf{nop}, \mathsf{wfence}(i), \mathsf{rfence}(i)\}$, if $\mathbf{d} = \mathbf{d}'$.

We extend this definition to sequences of operations, and therefore to computation traces. A *state* of $\mathcal{N}$ is a pair $\langle \mathbf{p}, \mathbf{d} \rangle$ where $\mathbf{p} \in \mathbf{P}$ and $\mathbf{d} \in M$. For a given memory model M, we define a reachability relation $Reach_{\mathcal{N}}^{\mathsf{M}}$ between states of $\mathcal{N}$ as follows. Let $s = \langle \mathbf{p}, \mathbf{d} \rangle$ and $s' = \langle \mathbf{p}', \mathbf{d}' \rangle$ be two states of $\mathcal{N}$. We consider that $Reach_{\mathcal{N}}^{\mathsf{M}}(s, s')$ holds if there exists a trace $\tau \in \mathcal{T}_{\mathsf{M}}(\mathcal{N}, \mathbf{p}, \mathbf{p}')$ such that $\mathbf{d}[\tau\rangle \mathbf{d}'$.

3.4 The State Reachability Problem

The state reachability problem for a memory model M consists in, given a concurrent system $\mathcal{N}$ and two states s and s' of $\mathcal{N}$, checking whether $Reach_{\mathcal{N}}^{\mathsf{M}}(s, s')$ holds. We have:

Theorem 1 ([3]). *The state reachability problem for* TSO *is decidable.*

We also proved in [3] the decidability of the state reachability problem for a model with both $\mathsf{w} \rightarrow \mathsf{w}$ and $\mathsf{w} \rightarrow \mathsf{r}$ relaxations, but without considering write_fences. Therefore, the so-called PSO in [3] is incomparable with TSO (since write_fences are necessary to simulate TSO under that model), and is strictly less expressive (w.r.t. the set of computation traces) than the PSO as defined in this paper. We show also in [3] that the state reachability problem is undecidable for the model where all four read/write relaxations are considered. We prove, using a reduction of Post's Correspondence Problem, the following stronger result:

Theorem 2. *The state reachability problem for* $\mathsf{TSO} \cup \{\mathsf{r} \rightarrow \mathsf{w}\}$ *is undecidable.*

3.5 NSW: A Model with Non Speculative Writes

We have seen in Section 3.4 that including the $\mathsf{r} \rightarrow \mathsf{w}$ relaxation to TSO results in a memory model with an undecidable state reachability problem. Motivated by this, we introduce a memory model called NSW (for Non Speculative Writes) obtained by discarding this relaxation, i.e., by considering the following set of rules:

$$\mathsf{NSW} = \mathsf{RLWE} \cup \mathsf{RWF} \cup \{\mathsf{w} \rightarrow \mathsf{r},\ \mathsf{w} \rightarrow \mathsf{w},\ \mathsf{r} \rightarrow \mathsf{r}\}$$

Clearly, the NSW model subsumes TSO and PSO, and since it allows out-of-order reads, it is actually a strictly more relaxed model than PSO. Notice that PSO can be simulated under NSW by inserting a rfence after each read operation. We show later that the state reachability problem problem for NSW is decidable. In the next section, we discuss another desirable property of the NSW memory model.

3.6 Absence of Causality Cycles in NSW

Let po denote the *program order* relation corresponding to the order in which operations of each thread are issued by the program. Then, one can define a dependency relation between operations of a same process that reflects the data and control dependencies. We adopt here a conservative definition by considering that all operations occurring after a read operation, in the program order, are dependent from that read. Formally, this corresponds to the following dependency relation.

$$\mathsf{dep} = \mathsf{po} \cap (\{\mathsf{r}\} \times \{\mathsf{r}, \mathsf{w}, \mathsf{arw}\}) \tag{4}$$

Second, we define a *read-from* relation, denoted rf, that associates with each read event of the computation a write event such that $\mathsf{w}(i,k,d) \rightarrow_{\mathsf{rf}} \mathsf{r}(j,k,d)$ if the $\mathsf{r}(j,k,d)$ operation issued by process $\mathcal{P}_j$ takes the value d that has been written by the operation $\mathsf{w}(i,k,d)$ issued by process $\mathcal{P}_i$ on the variable x_k. Then, the causality relation corresponding to the considered computation is defined by $\mathsf{c} = \mathsf{dep} \cup \mathsf{rf}$.

$x = y = 0$	
$\mathcal{P}_1$	$\mathcal{P}_2$
(1) $\mathsf{r}(x,1)$	(3) $\mathsf{r}(y,1)$
(2) $\mathsf{w}(y,1)$	(4) $\mathsf{w}(x,1)$
$x = y = 1$	

It can be seen that under the model SC $\cup \{\mathsf{r} \rightarrow \mathsf{w}\}$, there are programs having computations with a cyclic causality relation. An example of such a program is given on the right. It is clear that under the SC model, the four operations of this program cannot belong to a same computation from $x = y = 0$ to $x = y = 1$. However, using the $\mathsf{r} \rightarrow \mathsf{w}$ relaxation, it is possible by permuting (1) and (2), to execute the four operations in the following order (2),(3),(4),(1). This computation contains the causality cycle: (2) $\rightarrow_{\mathsf{rf}}$ (3) $\rightarrow_{\mathsf{dep}}$ (4) $\rightarrow_{\mathsf{rf}}$ (1) $\rightarrow_{\mathsf{dep}}$ (2). We prove that by discarding the $\mathsf{r} \rightarrow \mathsf{w}$ relaxation, NSW avoids causal cycles.

Theorem 3. *Every computation of any concurrent system under the* NSW *model has an acyclic causality relation.*

Notice that since this theorem relies on the conservative definition of dependency given above (4), it also holds for any refinement of the dependency relation.

4 An Operational Model for NSW

We provide an operational model for NSW where configurations are formed by a vector of control states, one per process, a memory state giving the valuation of the shared variables, and an *event structure* where pending operations, issued by the different processes but not yet executed, are stored. This event structure defines a partial order between these operations reflecting the constraints imposed by the memory model on the order of their execution. We start by defining the notion of event structure. Then, we define a first operational model where the stored operations can be reads, writes, or write_fences. (Nop's, atomic read-writes, and read_fences do not need to be stored.)

4.1 Event Structures

Let $\mathcal{E}$ be an enumerable set of of events. An *event structure* over an alphabet Σ is a tuple $\mathcal{S} = (E, \rightsquigarrow, \lambda)$ where E is a finite subset of $\mathcal{E}$, $\rightsquigarrow \subseteq E \times E$ is a partial order over E, and $\lambda : E \rightarrow \Sigma$ is a mapping associating with each event a symbol in Σ.

Given an event $e \in \mathcal{E} \setminus E$ and a symbol $a \in \Sigma$, we denote by $\mathcal{S} \lhd [e \leftarrow a]$ the structure $(E \cup \{e\}, \rightsquigarrow, \lambda')$ such that $\lambda'(e) = a$ and $\lambda'(e') = \lambda(e')$ for all $e' \in E$. Given an event $e \in E$, we denote by $\mathcal{S} \rhd e$ the structure $(E' = E \setminus \{e\}, \rightsquigarrow|_{E'}, \lambda|_{E'})$. Moreover, given $e, e' \in E$, we denote by $\mathcal{S} \oplus e \rightsquigarrow e'$ the event structure $(E, (\rightsquigarrow \cup \{(e,e')\})^*, \lambda)$. These notations can be generalized to sets (of events and transitions) in the obvious way.

Given a concurrent system $\mathcal{N} = (\mathcal{P}_1, \ldots, \mathcal{P}_n)$, an *event structure* $\mathcal{S}$ over $\mathcal{N}$ is an event structure over $\Omega(\mathcal{N})$. Given $i \in [n]$ and $j \in [m]$, let $E_{(i,j)} = \{e \in E \;:\; \exists d \in D.\ \exists op \in \{\mathsf{w}, \mathsf{r}\}.\ \lambda(e) = op(i,j,d)\}$. An event structure over $\Omega(N)$ is *well-formed* if, for every i and j, the relation $\rightsquigarrow |_{E_{(i,j)}}$ is a total order. We assume in the rest of the paper that all event structures over $\mathcal{N}$ are well-formed. This condition corresponds to the fact that read/write operations on the same variable should not be reordered.

Let $\widehat{E}_{(i,j)} = E_{(i,j)} \cup \{e \in E \;:\; \lambda(e) = \mathsf{wfence}(i)\}$. For every $i \in [n]$ and $j \in [m]$, let $RE(i,j) = \{e \in E \;:\; \exists d \in D.\ \lambda(e) = \mathsf{r}(i,j,d)\}$, and let $WE(i,j) = \{e \in E \;:\; \exists d \in D.\ \lambda(e) = \mathsf{w}(i,j,d)\}$. For every $e \in E$, we use $data(e)$ to denote $data(\lambda(e))$.

4.2 An Operational Model with Stored Reads

We associate with the concurrent system $\mathcal{N}$ a transition system $(Conf_{\mathcal{N}}, \Rightarrow_{\mathcal{N}})$ where $Conf_{\mathcal{N}}$ is a set of configurations, and $\Rightarrow_{\mathcal{N}} \subseteq Conf_{\mathcal{N}} \times Conf_{\mathcal{N}}$ is a transition relation between configurations. A *configuration* of $\mathcal{N}$ (an element of $Conf_{\mathcal{N}}$) is any triple $(\mathbf{p}, \mathbf{d}, \mathcal{S})$ where $\mathbf{p} \in \mathbf{P}$, $\mathbf{d} \in M$, and $\mathcal{S}$ is an event structure over $\mathcal{N}$. The transition relation $\Rightarrow_{\mathcal{N}}$ is the smallest relation such that for every $\mathbf{p}, \mathbf{p}' \in \mathbf{P}$, for every $\mathbf{d}, \mathbf{d}' \in M$, and for every $\mathcal{S} = (E, \rightsquigarrow, \lambda)$, $\mathcal{S}' = (E', \rightsquigarrow', \lambda')$ two event structures over $\mathcal{N}$, we have $(\mathbf{p}, \mathbf{d}, \mathcal{S}) \Rightarrow_{\mathcal{N}} (\mathbf{p}', \mathbf{d}', \mathcal{S}')$ if there is an $i \in [n]$, and there are $p, p' \in P_i$, such that $\mathbf{p}[i] = p$, $\mathbf{p}' = \mathbf{p}[i \leftarrow p']$, and one of the following cases hold:

1. Nop: $p \xrightarrow{\mathsf{nop}}_i p'$, $\mathbf{d} = \mathbf{d}'$, and $\mathcal{S} = \mathcal{S}'$.
2. Write: $p \xrightarrow{\mathsf{w}(i,j,d)}_i p'$, $\mathbf{d} = \mathbf{d}'$, and $\exists e \in \mathcal{E} \setminus E$ such that $\mathcal{S}' = ((\mathcal{S} \lhd [e \leftarrow \mathsf{w}(i,j,d)]) \oplus \{e' \rightsquigarrow e : e' \in max(\widehat{E}_{(i,j)})\}$.
3. RLWE: $p \xrightarrow{\mathsf{r}(i,j,d)}_i p'$, $\mathbf{d} = \mathbf{d}'$, $\mathcal{S}' = \mathcal{S}$, $WE(i,j) \neq \emptyset$ with $e_m = max(WE(i,j))$, $\nexists e \in RE(i,j).\ e_m \rightsquigarrow e$, and $data(e_m) = d$.
4. Read: $p \xrightarrow{\mathsf{r}(i,j,d)}_i p'$, $\mathbf{d} = \mathbf{d}'$, either $WE(i,j) = \emptyset$ or $data(max(WE(i,j))) \neq d$, and $\exists e, f \in \mathcal{E} \setminus E$ such that $\mathcal{S}' = ((\mathcal{S} \lhd \{[e \leftarrow \mathsf{r}(i,j,d)], [f \leftarrow \mathsf{wfence}(i)]\}) \oplus (\{e' \rightsquigarrow e : e' \in max(E_{(i,j)})\} \cup \{e \rightsquigarrow f\}))$.
5. ARW: $p \xrightarrow{\mathsf{arw}(i,j,d,d')}_i p'$, $\bigcup_{\ell=1}^{m} \widehat{E}_{(i,\ell)} = \emptyset$, $\mathbf{d}[j] = d$, $\mathbf{d}' = \mathbf{d}[j \leftarrow d']$, and $\mathcal{S} = \mathcal{S}'$.
6. Read fence: $p \xrightarrow{\mathsf{rfence}(i)}_i p'$, $\bigcup_{j=1}^{m} RE(i,j) = \emptyset$, $\mathbf{d} = \mathbf{d}'$, and $\mathcal{S} = \mathcal{S}'$.
7. Write fence: $p \xrightarrow{\mathsf{wfence}(i)}_i p'$, $\mathbf{d} = \mathbf{d}'$, and $\exists e \in \mathcal{E} \setminus E$ such that $\mathcal{S}' = ((\mathcal{S} \lhd [e \leftarrow \mathsf{wfence}(i)]) \oplus \{e' \rightsquigarrow e : \exists k.\ 1 \leq k \leq m \text{ and } e' \in max(\widehat{E}_{(i,k)})\})$.
8. Memory update: $\mathbf{p} = \mathbf{p}'$, and there is an event e such that e is a minimal of $\rightsquigarrow$, $\lambda(e) = \mathsf{w}(i,j,d)$ for some $d \in D$, $\mathbf{d}' = \mathbf{d}[j \leftarrow d]$, and $\mathcal{S}' = \mathcal{S} \rhd e$.
9. Read validation: $\mathbf{p} = \mathbf{p}'$, $\mathbf{d}' = \mathbf{d}$, and there is an event e such that e is a minimal of $\rightsquigarrow$, $\lambda(e) = \mathsf{r}(i,j,d)$, $\mathbf{d}[j] = d$, and $\mathcal{S}' = \mathcal{S} \rhd e$.
10. Write fence elimination: $\mathbf{p} = \mathbf{p}'$, $\mathbf{d}' = \mathbf{d}$, and there is an event e such that e is a minimal of $\rightsquigarrow$, $\lambda(e) = \mathsf{wfence}(i)$, and $\mathcal{S}' = \mathcal{S} \rhd e$.

Let us explain each case. A write operation $\mathsf{w}(i,j,d)$ is simply added to the structure by introducing a new event e labelled with this operation, which is inserted after all write_fences issued by $\mathcal{P}_i$ as well as all the write/read operations of $\mathcal{P}_i$ on x_j.

A read operation $\mathsf{r}(i,j,d)$ can be validated immediately (point 3) if $\mathcal{S}$ still contain a write of $\mathcal{P}_i$ on x_j (and there is no read of $\mathcal{P}_i$ on x_i after this write), and the last of such an operation writes precisely the value d on x_j. Otherwise, (in point 4) a read operation $\mathsf{r}(i,j,d)$ is simply added to the structure $\mathcal{S}$ after all reads/writes of $\mathcal{P}_i$ on x_j. Notice, that the event associated with this read operation is not ordered w.r.t. write_fences that are maximal in $\mathcal{S}$ (i.e., the read is allowed to overtake such write_fences). Moreover, a new write_fence is inserted after the read. This ensures that, as long as this read has not been validated, it cannot be overtaken by any write.

An atomic read-write operation, which acts as a fence on all operations of the process $\mathcal{P}_i$, can be executed only when all events before it have been executed. A read_fence issued by $\mathcal{P}_i$ is executed immediately (it is not stored in $\mathcal{S}$) if there is no reads in $\mathcal{S}$ issued by $\mathcal{P}_i$. A write_fence is inserted in $\mathcal{S}$ after all the events issued by $\mathcal{P}_i$.

Writes are removed from $\mathcal{S}$ and used to update the main memory when these operations correspond to minimal events of $\mathcal{S}$. Similarly, reads are validated w.r.t. the main memory and removed from $\mathcal{S}$ if they correspond to minimal events. Finally, a write_fence can simply be removed from $\mathcal{S}$ when it becomes minimal.

Let $\mathcal{S}_0$ denote the empty event structure. Then, we have:

Theorem 4. *For every states s and s', we have $Reach_{\mathcal{N}}^{\mathsf{NSW}}(s,s')$ iff $(s,\mathcal{S}_0) \Rightarrow_{\mathcal{N}}^{*} (s',\mathcal{S}_0)$.*

5 From Event Structures to FIFO Buffers

We provide in this section a model for NSW using FIFO buffers where reads and fences are never stored. We proceed in two steps. First, we provide an alternative operational model for NSW where reads can be immediately validated using informations about the sequence of states that the memory had in the past. The history of the memory states is stored in an additional FIFO buffer. Then, we show that it is also possible to get rid of wfences by converting event structures into two-level structures of write buffers.

5.1 Eliminating Reads from Event Structures

We present hereafter a new operational model where reads are validated using an additional buffer storing memory states, called *history buffer*. The idea is the following. Consider a read operation $\mathsf{r}(i,j,d)$ issued by process $\mathcal{P}_i$ that can be validated during a computation from a write operation $\mathsf{w}(k,j,d)$ issued by process $\mathcal{P}_k$. Then, if at the moment $\mathsf{r}(i,j,d)$ is issued $\mathsf{w}(k,j,d)$ has not yet been issued, it is actually possible for $\mathcal{P}_i$ to wait until $\mathcal{P}_k$ produces $\mathsf{w}(k,j,d)$. The reason is that issuing $\mathsf{w}(k,j,d)$ by $\mathcal{P}_k$ can't depend from the actions of $\mathcal{P}_i$ after $\mathsf{r}(i,j,d)$, because otherwise, this would mean that there is a read by $\mathcal{P}_k$ before $\mathsf{w}(k,j,d)$ which needs (i.e., is causally dependent from) a write of $\mathcal{P}_i$ occurring after $\mathsf{r}(i,j,d)$. But this would imply the existence of a causality cycle, which contradicts the fact that such cycle do not exist in NSW computations due to the fact that writes cannot overtake reads (see Thm. 3). Therefore, it is always possible to consider computations where reads are validated w.r.t. writes that have been issued in the past. However, since some actions must exit the event structure of the system configuration (due to fences), we need to maintain the history of all past memory states in a buffer.

Then, we use a buffer such that the last element represents actually the current state of the memory, and where the other elements represent the precedent states of the memory in the order they have been produced. Notice that a history buffer is never empty since it must contain at least one element representing the state of the memory.

Now, since reads can be swapped, their validation can use writes that might be issued in a different order. However, reads by the same process on a same variable must be done in a coherent way, i.e., they should read from states occurring in the same order. To ensure that, we introduce pointers $\pi(i,j)$ on the history buffer defining for each process $\mathcal{P}_i$ and each variable x_j the oldest memory state that can be observed. Then, to validate a read on x_j by $\mathcal{P}_i$, we should find a memory state that occurs after $\pi(i,j)$ in the buffer where x_j has the right value. Actually, to simplify the construction, we allow that a pointer can move in a nondeterministic way toward the tail of the buffer (i.e., the most recent element). Then, to validate an operation $\mathsf{r}(i,j,d)$, we simply require that the value of x_j in the element pointed by $\pi(i,j)$ is precisely d. Also, when a write event

$\mathsf{w}(i,j,d)$ exits the event structure and is used to update the memory, the pointer $\pi(i,j)$ is moved to the last element of the history buffer (i.e., the current state of the memory) since this is the only value of x_j that is visible to $\mathcal{P}_i$.

Notice that the relevant part of the history buffer at any moment is formed by the elements between the last element (current state of the memory) and the oldest element that is pointed by π.

To give the formal description of our model, we need to introduce some definitions concerning buffers and their manipulation. An event structure $(E,\rightsquigarrow,\lambda)$ is *totally ordered* when $\rightsquigarrow$ is a total order. We use such structures to encode FIFO buffers. Given a buffer $\mathcal{B}=(E,\rightsquigarrow,\lambda)$ over an alphabet Σ, and a symbol $a\in\Sigma$, let $add(\mathcal{B},a)$ be the buffer $(E',\rightsquigarrow',\lambda')$ such that (1) $E'=E\cup\{e\}$ for some $e\in\mathcal{E}\setminus E$, (2) if $E=\emptyset$ then $\rightsquigarrow'=\{(e,e)\}$, otherwise $\rightsquigarrow'=(\rightsquigarrow\cup\{(max(E),e)\})^*$, and (3) $\lambda'=\lambda\cup[e\mapsto a]$. Then, if $\lambda(min(B))=a$, let $remove(\mathcal{B},a)$ be the buffer $(E',\rightsquigarrow',\lambda')$ such that (1) $E'=E\setminus\{min(E)\}$, (2) $\rightsquigarrow'=\rightsquigarrow|_{E'}$, and (3) $\lambda'=\lambda|_{E'}$. We also define the predicate *Empty* which is true when the buffer has an empty set of events. When the buffer $\mathcal{B}$ is not empty, we denote by $tail(\mathcal{B})$ (resp. $head(\mathcal{B})$) the element $\lambda(max(E))$ (resp. $\lambda(min(E))$).

Given a concurrent system $\mathcal{N}$, a *history buffer* of memory states is a tuple $\mathcal{H}=(E,\rightsquigarrow,\lambda,\pi)$ where $(E,\rightsquigarrow,\lambda)$ is a buffer over M (the set of all memory states) such that $E\neq\emptyset$, and $\pi:[n]\times[m]\rightarrow E$ is a mapping associating with each process and each variable an event in E. We say that a history buffer is *unitary* if $\mathcal{H}$ is reduced to a singleton (i.e., $\pi(i,j)=max(E)$ for all $i\in[n]$ and $j\in[m]$).

Then, we are ready to define the transition system of the new model. A configuration is a tuple $\langle\mathbf{p},\mathcal{S},\mathcal{H}\rangle$ where, as in the previous model $\mathbf{p}\in\mathbf{P}$ is a vector of control states of each of the processes and $\mathcal{S}$ is an event structure, and where $\mathcal{H}$ is a history buffer over M. The new transition relation $\Rrightarrow_{\mathcal{N}}$ is the smallest relation s.t. for every $\mathbf{p},\mathbf{p}'\in\mathbf{P}$, $\mathcal{S}=(E,\rightsquigarrow,\lambda),\mathcal{S}'=(E',\rightsquigarrow',\lambda')$ two event structures over $\mathcal{N}$, and $\mathcal{H}=(\mathcal{B},\pi)$ and $\mathcal{H}'=(\mathcal{B}',\pi')$ two history buffers over M, where $\mathcal{B}=(H,\rightsquigarrow_H,\lambda_H)$ and $\mathcal{B}'=(H',\rightsquigarrow_{H'},\lambda_{H'})$ are two buffers over M, we have $\langle\mathbf{p},\mathcal{S},\mathcal{H}\rangle\Rrightarrow_{\mathcal{N}}\langle\mathbf{p}',\mathcal{S}',\mathcal{H}'\rangle$ if there is an $i\in[n]$, and there are $p,p'\in P_i$, such that $\mathbf{p}[i]=p$, $\mathbf{p}'=\mathbf{p}[i\leftarrow p']$, and one of the following cases holds:

1. Nop: $p\xrightarrow{\mathsf{nop}}_i p'$, $\mathcal{S}=\mathcal{S}'$, and $\mathcal{H}=\mathcal{H}'$.
2. Write: $p\xrightarrow{\mathsf{w}(i,j,d)}_i p'$, $\mathcal{H}=\mathcal{H}'$, and $\exists e\in\mathcal{E}\setminus E$ such that $\mathcal{S}'=((\mathcal{S}\lhd[e\leftarrow\mathsf{w}(i,j,d)])\oplus\{e'\rightsquigarrow e:e'\in max(\widehat{E}_{(i,j)})\}$.
3. Write fence: $p\xrightarrow{\mathsf{wfence}(i)}_i p'$, $\mathcal{H}=\mathcal{H}'$, and $\exists e\in\mathcal{E}\setminus E$ such that $\mathcal{S}'=((\mathcal{S}\lhd[e\leftarrow\mathsf{wfence}(i)])\oplus\{e'\rightsquigarrow e:\exists k.\ 1\leq k\leq m \text{ and } e'\in max(\widehat{E}_{(i,k)})\})$.
4. RLWE: $p\xrightarrow{\mathsf{r}(i,j,d)}_i p'$, $\mathcal{S}=\mathcal{S}'$, $\mathcal{H}=\mathcal{H}'$, $WE(i,j)\neq\emptyset$, and $data(max(WE(i,j)))=d$.
5. Move pointer: $\mathbf{p}=\mathbf{p}'$, $\mathcal{S}=\mathcal{S}'$, $\mathcal{B}=\mathcal{B}'$, and $\exists j\in[m].\ \exists e\in H.\ \pi(i,j)\rightsquigarrow_H e$ and $\pi'=\pi[(i,j)\leftarrow e]$.
6. Read: $p\xrightarrow{\mathsf{r}(i,j,d)}_i p'$, $\mathcal{S}=\mathcal{S}'$, $\mathcal{H}=\mathcal{H}'$, $WE(i,j)=\emptyset$, and $\exists\mathbf{d}\in M$ such that $\lambda_H(\pi(i,j))=\mathbf{d}$ and $\mathbf{d}[j]=d$.
7. Read fence: $p\xrightarrow{\mathsf{rfence}(i)}_i p'$, $\mathcal{S}=\mathcal{S}'$, $\mathcal{H}=\mathcal{H}'$, and $\pi(i,j)=max(H)$ for every $j\in[m]$.
8. ARW: $p\xrightarrow{\mathsf{arw}(i,j,d,d')}_i p'$, $\mathcal{S}=\mathcal{S}'$, $\bigcup_{\ell=1}^m\widehat{E}_{(i,\ell)}=\emptyset$, $\pi(i,\ell)=max(H)$ for every $\ell\in[m]$, there is a $\mathbf{d}=tail(\mathcal{B})$ such that $\mathbf{d}[j]=d$ and $\mathcal{B}'=add(\mathcal{B},\mathbf{d}[j\leftarrow d'])$, and $\pi'=\pi[(i,\ell)\leftarrow max(H')]_{\ell\in[m]}$.

9. Memory update: $\mathbf{p} = \mathbf{p}'$, $\exists e \in min(E)$ such that $\lambda(e) = \mathsf{w}(i,j,d)$ for some $j \in [m]$ and $d \in D$, $\mathcal{S}' = \mathcal{S} \rhd e$, $\mathcal{B}' = add(\mathcal{B}, \mathbf{d})$ where $\mathbf{d} = tail(H)[j \leftarrow d]$, and $\pi' = \pi[(i,j) \leftarrow max(H')]$.
10. Write fence elimination: $\mathbf{p} = \mathbf{p}'$, $\mathcal{H} = \mathcal{H}'$, $\mathbf{d}' = \mathbf{d}$, and $\exists e \in min(E)$ such that $\lambda(e) = \mathsf{wfence}(i)$, and $\mathcal{S}' = \mathcal{S} \rhd e$.

Theorem 5. *Let $s = (\mathbf{p}, \mathbf{d})$ and $s' = (\mathbf{p}', \mathbf{d}')$ be two states of $\mathcal{N}$, and let $\mathcal{H}$ and $\mathcal{H}'$ be two unitary history buffers over M such that $tail(\mathcal{H}) = \mathbf{d}$ and $tail(\mathcal{H}') = \mathbf{d}'$. Then, $(s, \mathcal{S}_\emptyset) \Rightarrow^*_{\mathcal{N}} (s', \mathcal{S}_\emptyset)$ if and only if $\langle \mathbf{p}, \mathcal{S}_\emptyset, \mathcal{H} \rangle \Rrightarrow^*_{\mathcal{N}} \langle \mathbf{p}', \mathcal{S}_\emptyset, \mathcal{H}' \rangle$.*

5.2 Eliminating Write Fences from Event Structures

We show in this section that we can avoid storing write_fences and to convert event structures into write buffers. The idea is the following. We observe that the projection of the event structure on the events of a same process is, roughly speaking, a sequence of partial orders, each of these partial orders corresponding to the set of write events occurring between two successive write_fences. These partial order have also the property that they are unions of m total orders, each of them corresponding to the set of writes to a same variable. These total orders can naturally be manipulated using m FIFO buffers $WB_{(i,1)}, \ldots, WB_{(i,m)}$. Then, to simulate the whole sequence of partial orders corresponding the events of a process, we need to reuse the same buffers after each write_fence, while ensuring that all writes occurring before the write_fence are executed before all those occurring after it. The solution for that is to introduce for each process $\mathcal{P}_i$ an additional buffer $WB_{(i,m+1)}$ used to flush the buffers $WB_{(i,1)}, \ldots, WB_{(i,m)}$ after each write_fence without imposing that their content is directly written in the memory.

Then, the architecture of our model is as follows. Each process $\mathcal{P}_i$ has two levels of buffers, a first level with m write buffers storing the writes for each variable, and a second level with one buffer used to serialize the writes before committing them to the main memory. Then, we have the history buffer, the last element of which represents the current state of the memory, and the rest of its elements represent the history of all past memory states. Pointers on this buffer allow to each process to know what is the oldest value it can read on each variable.

We give hereafter the formal definition of our model. A configuration in this model is a tuple of the form $\langle \mathbf{p}, (WB_{(i,j)})_{i \in [n]}^{j \in [m+1]}, \mathcal{H} \rangle$ where $\mathbf{p} \in \mathbf{P}$, for every $i \in [n]$ and every $j \in [m+1]$, $WB_{(i,j)}$ is a write buffer, and $\mathcal{H}$ is a history buffer over M. Then, we define the transition relation $\rightarrow_{\mathcal{N}}$ between configurations as the smallest relation such that for every $\mathbf{p}, \mathbf{p}' \in \mathbf{P}$, for every two vectors of store buffers $(WB_{(i,j)})_{i \in [n]}^{j \in [m+1]}$ and $(WB'_{(i,j)})_{i \in [n]}^{j \in [m+1]}$, where $WB_{(i,j)} = (B_{(i,j)}, \rightsquigarrow_{(i,j)}, \lambda_{(i,j)})$ and $WB'_{(i,j)} = (B'_{(i,j)}, \rightsquigarrow'_{(i,j)}, \lambda'_{(i,j)})$ for all i and j, and for every two history buffers $\mathcal{H} = (\mathcal{B}, \pi)$ and $\mathcal{H}' = (\mathcal{B}', \pi')$, where $\mathcal{B} = (H, \rightsquigarrow_H, \lambda_H)$ and $\mathcal{B}' = (H', \rightsquigarrow_{H'}, \lambda_{H'})$ are two buffers over M, we have $\langle \mathbf{p}, (WB_{(i,j)})_{i \in [n]}^{j \in [m+1]}, \mathcal{H} \rangle \rightarrow_{\mathcal{N}} \langle \mathbf{p}', (WB'_{(i,j)})_{i \in [n]}^{j \in [m+1]}, \mathcal{H}' \rangle$ if there are $i \in [n]$, and $p, p' \in P_i$, such that $\mathbf{p}[i] = p$, $\mathbf{p}' = \mathbf{p}[i \leftarrow p']$, $WB_{(k,j)} = WB_{(k,j)}$ for every $k \in [n] \setminus \{i\}$ and every $j \in [m+1]$, and one of the following cases holds:

1. Nop: $p \xrightarrow{\text{nop}}_i p'$, $WB_{(i,j)} = WB'_{(i,j)}$ for every $j \in [m+1]$, and $\mathcal{H} = \mathcal{H}'$.
2. Write: $p \xrightarrow{\mathsf{w}(i,j,d)}_i p'$, $\mathcal{H} = \mathcal{H}'$, $WB_{(i,k)} = WB'_{(i,k)}$ for every $k \in ([m+1] \setminus \{j\}$, and $WB'_{(i,j)} = add(WB_{(i,j)}, \mathsf{w}(i,j,d))$.
3. Write fence: $p \xrightarrow{\mathsf{wfence}(i)}_i p'$, $Empty(WB_{(i,j)})$ for all $j \in [m]$, $WB_{(i,s)} = WB'_{(i,s)}$ for all $s \in [m+1]$, and $\mathcal{H} = \mathcal{H}'$.
4. Transfer write: $p = p'$, $\mathcal{H} = \mathcal{H}'$, $\exists j \in [m]$. $WB_{(i,k)} = WB'_{(i,k)}$ for every $k \in ([m] \setminus \{j\})$, and $\exists \omega = head(WB_{(i,j)})$. $WB'_{(i,j)} = remove(WB_{(i,j)}, \omega)$ and $WB'_{(i,m+1)} = add(WB_{(i,m+1)}, \omega)$.
5. RLWE from $WB_{(i,j)}$, $j \in [m]$: $p \xrightarrow{\mathsf{r}(i,j,d)}_i p'$, $\mathcal{H} = \mathcal{H}'$, $WB_{(i,k)} = WB'_{(i,k)}$ for every $k \in [m+1]$, and $data(tail(WB_{(i,j)})) = d$.
6. RLWE from $WB_{(i,m+1)}$: $p \xrightarrow{\mathsf{r}(i,j,d)}_i p'$, $\mathcal{H} = \mathcal{H}'$, $WB_{(i,k)} = WB'_{(i,k)}$ for every $k \in [m+1]$, $Empty(WB_{(i,j)})$, the set $W_{(i,m+1)} = \{e \in B_{(i,m+1)} : \exists d' \in D.\ \lambda_{(i,m+1)}(e) = \mathsf{w}(i,j,d')\}$ is not empty, and $data(max(W_{(i,m+1)}) = d$.
7. Read: $p \xrightarrow{\mathsf{r}(i,j,d)}_i p'$, $\mathcal{H} = \mathcal{H}'$, $WB_{(i,k)} = WB'_{(i,k)}$ for every $k \in [m+1]$, $Empty(WB_{(i,j)})$, the set $W_{(i,m+1)}$ defined above is empty, and $\exists \mathbf{d} \in M$ such that $\lambda_H(\pi(i,j)) = \mathbf{d}$ and $\mathbf{d}[j] = d$.
8. Move pointer: $\mathbf{p} = \mathbf{p}'$, $\mathcal{B} = \mathcal{B}'$, $WB_{(i,k)} = WB'_{(i,k)}$ for every $k \in [m+1]$, and $\exists j \in [m]$. $\exists e \in H.\ \pi(i,j) \rightsquigarrow_H e$ and $\pi' = \pi[(i,j) \leftarrow e]$.
9. ARW: $p \xrightarrow{\mathsf{arw}(i,j,d,d')}_i p'$, $Empty(WB_{(i,j)})$ and $Empty(WB'_{(i,j)})$ for every $j \in [m+1]$, $\pi(i,\ell) = max(H)$ for every $\ell \in [m]$, there is a $\mathbf{d} = tail(\mathcal{B})$ such that $\mathbf{d}[j] = d$ and $\mathcal{B}' = add(\mathcal{B}, \mathbf{d}[j \leftarrow d'])$, and $\pi' = \pi[(i,\ell) \leftarrow max(H')]_{\ell \in [m]}$.
10. Read fence: $p \xrightarrow{\mathsf{rfence}(i)}_i p'$, $WB_{(i,k)} = WB'_{(i,k)}$ for every $k \in [m+1]$, $\mathcal{H} = \mathcal{H}'$, and $\pi(i,\ell) = max(H)$ for every $\ell \in [m]$.
11. Memory update: $\mathbf{p} = \mathbf{p}'$, $WB_{(i,k)} = WB'_{(i,k)}$ for every $k \in [m]$, $head(WB_{(i,m+1)}) = \mathsf{w}(i,j,d)$ for some $j \in [m]$ and $d \in D$, $WB'_{(i,m+1)} = remove(WB_{(i,m+1)}, \mathsf{w}(i,j,d))$, $\mathcal{B}' = add(\mathcal{B}, \mathbf{d})$ where $\mathbf{d} = tail(H)[j \leftarrow d]$, and $\pi' = \pi[(i,j) \leftarrow max(H')]$.

Theorem 6. *Let $s = (\mathbf{p}, \mathbf{d})$ and $s' = (\mathbf{p}', \mathbf{d}')$ be two states of $\mathcal{N}$, and let $\mathcal{H}$ and $\mathcal{H}'$ be two unitary history buffers over M such that $tail(\mathcal{H}) = \mathbf{d}$ and $tail(\mathcal{H}') = \mathbf{d}'$. Then, $(s, \mathcal{S}_0) \Rightarrow^*_{\mathcal{N}} (s', \mathcal{S}_0)$ if and only if $\langle \mathbf{p}, \overline{\mathcal{S}_0}, \mathcal{H} \rangle \rightarrow^*_{\mathcal{N}} \langle \mathbf{p}', \overline{\mathcal{S}_0}, \mathcal{H}' \rangle$, where $\overline{\mathcal{S}_0}$ denotes an $[n] \times [m+1]$-dim vector of empty write buffers.*

It is worth noting that for PSO, i.e., when read_fences are systematically inserted after reads, the operational model we define has always a history buffer of size 1 (i.e., reduced to the memory state). Notice that still we need two levels of write buffers for PSO due to the use of write_fences. For TSO, write buffers for each variable ($WB_{(i,j)}$ for $j \in [m]$) are not needed since writes are immediately followed by write_fences. This coincides with the operational model defined, e.g., in [3].

6 The State Reachability Problem of NSW

We show hereafter that the state reachability problem of NSW is decidable. For that, we use the framework defined in [1] which establishes that state reachability can be solved using backward reachability analysis in the following case: Given a well quasi-ordering (WQO) $\preceq$ on configurations[1], if the system is monotonic w.r.t. $\preceq$, i.e., larger configurations w.r.t. $\preceq$ can always simulate smaller ones, then backward reachability in this system is guaranteed to terminate if it starts from $\preceq$-upward closed sets, i.e., sets that whenever they contain a configuration c, they also contain all $\preceq$-larger one than c.

To define such ordering, we observe that a value in the memory written by some process might be overwritten by other write operations by the same process before any other process has had time to read it. Therefore, the effect of a write operation sent by a process to its store buffer may never be used, and this would suggest that we should define $\preceq$ to reflect the subword relation between the buffer contents. However, this intuition cannot be exploited directly. As we will see below, NSW's are not monotonic in general w.r.t. such as subword-based relation. To circumvent this problem, we introduce another model called NSW$^+$ obtained from the NSW, where, roughly, serialization buffers $W_{(i,m+1)}$ contain memory states (corresponding to cumulated effects of write operations) instead of write operations and we associate one history buffer per process, and we show that (1) the state reachability problem in a given NSW is reducible to the one in its corresponding NSW$^+$, and (2) every NSW$^+$ is monotonic w.r.t. a subword-based relation on buffers. Notice that the translation from NSW to NSW$^+$ preserves reachability but the resulting model from this translation is not bisimilar to the original one (and therefore monotonicity can not be transferred).

Informal Introduction to NSW$^+$: We explain hereafter how a NSW$^+$ model is defined starting from a given NSW. Let us first see why NSW's are not monotonic w.r.t. the subword relation, i.e., considering that the buffers in NSW are *lossy* is not sound. More precisely, while it can be shown that it is possible to consider safely that the write buffers $WB_{(i,j)}$ for all $i \in [n]$ and $j \in [m]$ as well as the history buffer are lossy, the serialization buffers $WB_{(i,m+1)}$ for $i \in [n]$ cannot be simply turned to lossy buffers. Consider first a sequence of write operations $\mathsf{w}(i,j,d')\mathsf{w}(i,j,d)$ in the write buffer $WB_{(i,j)}$, for some $j \in [m]$, where $\mathsf{w}(i,j,d)$ is the oldest operation. Since both operations are on the same variable x_j, losing the operation $\mathsf{w}(i,j,d)$, i.e., replacing this sequence by just $\mathsf{w}(i,j,d')$, yields a valid computation corresponding to compaction of the two operations. Indeed, it is possible to overwrite the value d by d' before that any process is able to read d. Therefore, it is possible to lose any operation in a write buffer corresponding to a variable, except the last operation. This is especially important for the read-local-write-early operation. Then, by considering the last symbol in each write buffer $WB_{(i,j)}$ as a strong symbol (can not be lost), and turning $WB_{(i,j)}$ to a lossy channel does not introduce computations that are not possible in the original program. Observe that the number of possible such strong symbols is finite (one per write buffer $WB_{(i,j)}$).

Consider now a sequence of memory states $\mathbf{d} \cdot \mathbf{d}'$ in the history buffer $\mathcal{H}$, where $\mathbf{d}'$ is the oldest state. Then, losing the memory state $\mathbf{d}'$ in $\mathcal{M}_i$ is similar to considering that

[1] Recall that a well quasi-ordering $\preceq$ over a set E is an ordering such that for every infinite sequence $e_1, e_2, \ldots$ of elements of E, there exist two integers $i < j$ such that $e_i \preceq e_j$.

this state has not been observed by $\mathcal{P}_i$. This is perfectly valid since processes observe the states of the memory in an asynchronous way, and therefore they may miss some states. However, memory states in $\mathcal{H}$ that are pointed by some pointer $\pi(i,j)$ should not be lost, and they must be considered as strong symbol. Indeed, without these pointed states, reads cannot be validated. In addition, we also should not lose the tail of $\mathcal{H}$ (which corresponds to the current memory state) since it is used to compute the next memory state. Then, pointed elements as well as the last element of the history buffer must be considered as strong symbols (again the number of such symbols is finite).

It remains to consider the case of the serialization write buffer $WB_{(i,m+1)}$. Consider a sequence of operations $\mathsf{w}(i,j,d')\mathsf{w}(i,k,d)$ in $WB_{(i,m+1)}$. Since these two operations are on different variables, losing $\mathsf{w}(i,k,d)$ does not correspond to the compaction of the two operations. To encode the compaction (or the summary) of such a sequence of operations, we need to use a vector of values defining the last written value to each variable by the operations in the sequence. Then, an idea is to replace the content of $WB_{(i,m+1)} = \omega_\ell \cdots \omega_1$ by the sequence of summaries $\sigma_\ell \cdots \sigma_1$ where σ_i is the summary of the sequence $\omega_i \cdots \omega_1$. For instance, in our example, the sequence of summaries is $(x_j = d', x_k = d)(x_k = d)$. Then, losing $(x_k = d)$ does not correspond to losing the effect of the operation $\mathsf{w}(i,k,d)$ since this effect is still visible in $(x_j = d', x_k = d)$. Assume now that $(x_k = d)$ has not been lost and has been updated to the main memory. This value of x_k in the main memory can be over-written by a write operation $(x_k = d'')$ $(d'' \neq d)$ of a different process from $\mathcal{P}_i$. Then, when the system decides to update $(x_j = d', x_k = d)$ to the main memory, we should not reset the value of x_k to d (since the write operation $(x_k = d)$ has already taken effect). This shows that $WB_{(i,m+1)}$ (under NSW^+) must contain a *valid* sequence of memory states (that will be used to update the memory in the future). Then, we can formulate a similar argument as in the case of the history buffer to allow some of the memory states in $WB_{(i,m+1)}$ to be lost.

However, in order to have a valid sequence of memory states, the serialization buffer $WB_{(i,m+1)}$ under NSW^+ should simulate the contributions of the other processes. Therefore, it has to insert in $WB_{(i,m+1)}$ the memory states resulting from writes performed by other processes. This implies that the system should guess in advance in which order the write operations will be updated to the main memory. This is performed under NSW^+ as follows: (1) a write is removed from some write buffer $WB_{(k,j)}$ (chosen nondeterministically), (2) a new memory state is then computed from the last state added to $WB_{(k,m+1)}$, and (3) this new state is added to *all* the serialization buffers. Observe that a memory state in $WB_{(i,m+1)}$ resulting from a write operation of a process $\mathcal{P}_k$ (with $k \neq j$) should not be detected by $\mathcal{P}_i$ (since it has not been yet committed to the main memory).

Observe that the execution of each process is totally determined by the sequence of memory states and its local configuration (i.e., its control state, its store buffer contents, and its serialization buffer content). Therefore, under NSW^+, each process $\mathcal{P}_i$ has its own private copy of the history buffer $\mathcal{H}_i$ (without any need of synchronization with the other threads) since it has already the sequence of memory states in its serialization buffer. Now, if a memory state is at the head of the serialization buffer $WB_{(i,m+1)}$ of the process $\mathcal{P}_i$, then this state will be removed from all this buffer and one copy is transferred to its history buffer $\mathcal{H}_i$.

Formal definition of NSW$^+$: A configuration of NSW$^+$ is a tuple of the form $\langle \mathbf{p}, (WB_{(i,j)})_{i\in[n]}^{j\in[m+1]}, (\mathcal{H}_i)_{i\in[n]}\rangle$ where $\mathbf{p}$ and $(WB_{(i,j)})_{i\in[n]}^{j\in[m]}$ are defined as in the previous section, $(WB_{(i,m+1)})_{i\in[n]}$ are write buffers over $F = \{\mathsf{w}(i,j,\mathbf{d}) : j \in [m] \wedge \mathbf{d} \in M\}$, and $\mathcal{H}_i$ are history buffers over M. Then, we define the transition relation $\mapsto_{\mathcal{N}}$ as the smallest relation such that for every $\mathbf{p},\mathbf{p}' \in \mathbf{P}$, for every two vectors of buffers $(WB_{(i,j)})_{i\in[n]}^{j\in[m+1]}$ and $(WB'_{(i,j)})_{i\in[n]}^{j\in[m+1]}$, where $WB_{(i,j)} = (B_{(i,j)}, \rightsquigarrow_{(i,j)}, \lambda_{(i,j)})$ and $WB'_{(i,j)} = (B'_{(i,j)}, \rightsquigarrow'_{(i,j)}, \lambda'_{(i,j)})$ for all $i \in [n]$ and $j \in [m+1]$, and for every two vectors of history buffers $(\mathcal{H}_i = (\mathcal{B}_i, \pi_i))_{i\in[n]}$ and $(\mathcal{H}'_i = (\mathcal{B}'_i, \pi'_i))_{i\in[n]}$, where $\mathcal{B}_i = (H_i, \rightsquigarrow_{H_i}, \lambda_{H_i})$ and $\mathcal{B}'_i = (H'_i, \rightsquigarrow_{H'_i}, \lambda_{H'_i})$ are two buffers over M for all $i \in [n]$, we have $\langle \mathbf{p}, (WB_{(i,j)})_{i\in[n]}^{j\in[m+1]}, (\mathcal{H}_i)_{i\in[n]}\rangle \rightarrow_{\mathcal{N}} \langle \mathbf{p}', (WB'_{(i,j)})_{i\in[n]}^{j\in[m+1]}, (\mathcal{H}'_i)_{i\in[n]}\rangle$ if there are $i \in [n]$, and $p, p' \in P_i$, such that $\mathbf{p}[i] = p$, $\mathbf{p}' = \mathbf{p}[i \leftarrow p']$, $\mathcal{H}_k = \mathcal{H}'_k$ for all $k \in [n] \setminus \{i\}$, and one of the following cases holds:

1. Nop: $p \xrightarrow{\mathsf{nop}}_i p'$, $WB_{(k,j)} = WB'_{(k,j)}$ for all $k \in [n]$ and $j \in [m+1]$, and $\mathcal{H}_i = \mathcal{H}'_i$.
2. Write: $p \xrightarrow{\mathsf{w}(i,j,d)}_i p'$, $\mathcal{H}_i = \mathcal{H}'_i$, $WB_{(k,\ell)} = WB'_{(k,\ell)}$ for every $(k,\ell) \in ([n] \times [m+1]) \setminus \{(i,j)\}$, and $WB'_{(i,j)} = add(WB_{(i,j)}, \mathsf{w}(i,j,d))$.
3. Write fence: $p \xrightarrow{\mathsf{wfence}(i)}_i p'$, $Empty(WB_{(i,j)})$ for all $j \in [m]$, $WB_{(k,\ell)} = WB'_{(k,\ell)}$ for all $k \in [n]$ and $\ell \in [m+1]$, and $\mathcal{H}_i = \mathcal{H}'_i$.
4. Transfer write: $p = p'$, $\mathcal{H}_i = \mathcal{H}'_i$, $\exists j \in [m].\ WB_{(k,\ell)} = WB'_{(k,\ell)}$ for all $(k,\ell) \in ([n] \times [m] \setminus \{(i,j)\})$, and $\exists \omega = head(WB_{(i,j)}).\ WB'_{(i,j)} = remove(WB_{(i,j)}, \omega)$ and for every $k \in [n]$, $WB'_{(k,m+1)} = add(WB_{(k,m+1)}, \mathsf{w}(i,j,\mathbf{d}'))$ where $\mathbf{d}[\omega\rangle\mathbf{d}'$ and if $Empty(WB_{(i,m+1)})$ then $\mathbf{d} = tail(\mathcal{B}_i)$ else $\mathsf{w}(t,\ell,\mathbf{d}) = tail(WB_{(i,m+1)})$ with $t \in [n]$ and $\ell \in [m]$.
5. RLWE from $WB_{(i,j)}$, $j \in [m]$: $p \xrightarrow{\mathsf{r}(i,j,d)}_i p'$, $\mathcal{H}_i = \mathcal{H}'_i$, $WB_{(k,\ell)} = WB'_{(k,\ell)}$ for all $k \in [n]$ and $\ell \in [m+1]$, and $data(tail(WB_{(i,j)})) = d$.
6. RLWE from $WB_{(i,m+1)}$: $p \xrightarrow{\mathsf{r}(i,j,d)}_i p'$, $\mathcal{H}_i = \mathcal{H}'_i$, $WB_{(k,\ell)} = WB'_{(k,\ell)}$ for all $(k,\ell) \in [n] \times [m+1]$, $Empty(WB_{(i,j)})$, the set $W_{(i,m+1)} = \{e \in B_{(i,m+1)} : \exists \mathbf{d}' \in M.\ \lambda_{(i,m+1)}(e) = \mathsf{w}(i,j,\mathbf{d}')\}$ is not empty, and $\lambda_{(i,m+1)}(max(W_{(i,m+1)})) = \mathsf{w}(i,j,\mathbf{d})$ such that $\mathbf{d}[j] = d$.
7. Read: $p \xrightarrow{\mathsf{r}(i,j,d)}_i p'$, $\mathcal{H}_i = \mathcal{H}'_i$, $WB_{(k,\ell)} = WB'_{(k,\ell)}$ for every $(k,\ell) \in [n] \times [m+1]$, $Empty(WB_{(i,j)})$, the set $W_{(i,m+1)}$ defined above is empty, and $\exists \mathbf{d} \in M$ such that $\lambda_{H_i}(\pi_i(i,j)) = \mathbf{d}$ and $\mathbf{d}[j] = d$.
8. Move pointer: $\mathbf{p} = \mathbf{p}'$, $\mathcal{B}_i = \mathcal{B}'_i$, $WB_{(k,\ell)} = WB'_{(k,\ell)}$ for every $(k,\ell) \in [n] \times [m+1]$, and $\exists j \in [m].\ \exists e \in H_i.\ \pi_i(i,j) \rightsquigarrow_{H_i} e$ and $\pi'_i = \pi_i[(k,j) \leftarrow e]_{k\in[n]}$.
9. ARW: $p \xrightarrow{\mathsf{arw}(i,j,d,d')}_i p'$, $WB_{(k,\ell)} = WB'_{(k,\ell)}$ for all $(k,\ell) \in [n] \times [m]$, $Empty(WB_{(i,j)})$ and $Empty(WB'_{(i,j)})$ for every $j \in [m+1]$, $\pi_i(i,\ell) = max(H_i)$ for every $\ell \in [m]$, there is a $\mathbf{d} = tail(\mathcal{B}_i)$ such that $WB'_{(k',m+1)} = add(WB_{(k',m+1)}, \mathsf{w}(i,j,\mathbf{d}'))$ for all $k' \in ([n] \setminus \{i\})$, $\mathbf{d}[j] = d$, $\mathcal{B}'_i = add(\mathcal{B}_i, \mathbf{d}')$, and $\pi'_i = \pi_i[(k,\ell) \leftarrow max(H'_i)]_{k\in[n],\ell\in[m]}$ where $\mathbf{d}' = \mathbf{d}[j \leftarrow d']$.

10. Read fence: $p \xrightarrow{\mathsf{rfence}(i)}_i p'$, $WB_{(k,\ell)} = WB'_{(k,\ell)}$ for every $(k,\ell) \in [n] \times [m+1]$, $\mathcal{H}_i = \mathcal{H}'_i$, and $\pi_i(i,\ell) = max(H_i)$ for every $\ell \in [m]$.
11. Memory update: $\mathbf{p} = \mathbf{p}'$, $WB_{(k,\ell)} = WB'_{(k,\ell)}$ for every $(k,\ell) \in ([n] \times [m] \setminus \{(i,m+1)\})$, there exist $t \in [n]$, $j \in [m]$ and $\mathbf{d} \in M$ such that $head(WB_{(i,m+1)}) = \mathsf{w}(t,j,\mathbf{d})$, $WB'_{(i,m+1)} = remove(WB_{(i,m+1)}, \mathsf{w}(t,j,\mathbf{d}))$, $\mathcal{B}'_i = add(\mathcal{B}_i, \mathbf{d})$, and $\pi'_i = \pi_i[(k,j) \leftarrow max(H'_i)]_{k\in[n]}$ if $t = i$, otherwise $\pi'_i = \pi_i$.

We prove that the state reachability problem for a concurrent system $\mathcal{N}$ under NSW can be reduced to its corresponding one for $\mathcal{N}$ under NSW$^+$.

Theorem 7. *Let $s = (\mathbf{p},\mathbf{d})$ and $s' = (\mathbf{p}',\mathbf{d}')$ be two states of $\mathcal{N}$, and let $\mathcal{H}$ and $\mathcal{H}'$ be two unitary history buffers over M such that $tail(\mathcal{H}) = \mathbf{d}$ and $tail(\mathcal{H}') = \mathbf{d}'$. Then, $\langle \mathbf{p}, \overline{S_\emptyset}, \mathcal{H}\rangle \rightarrow^*_{\mathcal{N}} \langle \mathbf{p}', \overline{S_\emptyset}, \mathcal{H}'\rangle$ iff $\langle \mathbf{p}, \overline{S'_\emptyset}, \mathcal{H},\ldots,\mathcal{H}\rangle \mapsto^*_{\mathcal{N}} \langle \mathbf{p}', \overline{S'_\emptyset}, \mathcal{H}',\ldots,\mathcal{H}'\rangle$ where $\overline{S_\emptyset}$ and $\overline{S'_\emptyset}$ denotes an $[n]\times[m+1]$-dim vector of empty buffers.*

The state reachability problem for NSW$^+$: We show in the following that the state reachability problem is decidable for the NSW$^+$ model. As mentioned earlier, we establish this fact by proving that NSW$^+$'s are monotonic w.r.t. a particular WQO $\preceq$.

Let $\mathcal{N}$ be an NSW$^+$, and let us define the relation $\preceq$ on the configurations of $\mathcal{N}$. Consider two configurations $c = \langle \mathbf{p}, (WB_{(i,j)})_{i\in[n]}^{j\in[m+1]}, (\mathcal{H}_k)_{k\in[n]}\rangle$ and $c' = \langle \mathbf{p}', (WB'_{(i,j)})_{i\in[n]}^{j\in[m+1]}, (\mathcal{H}'_k)_{k\in[n]}\rangle$, where $WB_{(i,j)} = (B_{(i,j)}, \rightsquigarrow_{(i,j)}, \lambda_{(i,j)})$ and $WB'_{(i,j)} = (B'_{(i,j)}, \rightsquigarrow'_{(i,j)}, \lambda'_{(i,j)})$ for all i and j, and $\mathcal{H}_k = (\mathcal{B}_k, \pi_k)$ and $\mathcal{H}'_k = (\mathcal{B}'_k, \pi'_k)$ with $\mathcal{B}_k = (H_k, \rightsquigarrow_{H_k}, \lambda_{H_k})$ and $\mathcal{B}'_k = (H'_k, \rightsquigarrow_{H'_k}, \lambda_{H'_k})$ for all $k \in [n]$. Then, we consider that $c \preceq c'$ if

1. c and c' have the same vector of control states, i.e., $\mathbf{p} = \mathbf{p}'$,
2. the content of $WB_{(i,j)}$ is a subword of the content $WB'_{(i,j)}$, while the sequences of operations in $WB_{(i,j)}$ and $WB'_{(i,j)}$ corresponding the last operations performed every process on each of the variables are the same, i.e., for every $i \in [n]$ and $j \in [m+1]$, there is an injection $g_{(i,j)}$ from $B_{(i,j)}$ to $B'_{(i,j)}$ such that: (a) for every $e_1, e_2 \in B_{(i,j)}$, $\lambda'_{(i,j)}(g_{(i,j)}(e_1)) = \lambda_{(i,j)}(e_1)$ and $e_1 \rightsquigarrow_{(i,j)} e_2$ implies $g_{(i,j)}(e_1) \rightsquigarrow_{(i,j)} g_{(i,j)}(e_2)$, and (b) for every $k \in [n]$ and $\ell \in [m]$, if $E_{(k,\ell)} = \{e \in B_{(i,j)} : \lambda_{(i,j)}(e) \in \{\mathsf{w}(k,\ell,\mathbf{d}'), \mathsf{w}(k,\ell,d') \mid \mathbf{d}' \in M, d' \in D\}\}$ and $E'_{(k,\ell)} = \{e \in B'_{(i,j)} : \lambda'_{(i,j)}(e) \in \{\mathsf{w}(k,\ell,\mathbf{d}'), \mathsf{w}(k,\ell,d') \mid \mathbf{d}' \in M, d' \in D\}\}$, then $g_{(i,j)}(max(E_{(k,\ell)})) = max(E'_{(k,\ell)})$,
3. the content of $\mathcal{H}_k$ is a subword of the content $\mathcal{H}'_k$, while the last memory states added to $\mathcal{H}_k$ and $\mathcal{H}'_k$ are the same, and the memory states pointed by $\pi_k(i,j)$ and by $\pi'_k(i,j)$ are equal for every i and j, i.e., for every $k \in [n]$ there is an injection g_k from H_k to H'_k such that: (a) for every $e_1, e_2 \in H_k$, $\lambda_{H'_k}(g_k(e_1)) = \lambda_{H_k}(e_1)$ and $e_1 \rightsquigarrow_{H_k} e_2$ implies $g_k(e_1) \rightsquigarrow_{H'_k} g_k(e_2)$, (b) for every $i \in [n]$ and $j \in [m]$, $g_k(\pi_k(i,j)) = \pi'_k(i,j)$, and (c) $g_k(max(H_k)) = max(H'_k)$.

By Higman's lemma (the subword relation is a well quasi-ordering) and standard composition properties of well quasi-orderings, it is easy to prove the following fact.

Lemma 8 (WQO). *The relation $\preceq$ is a WQO on the set of NSW$^+$-configurations of $\mathcal{N}$.*

Then, we can prove the following important fact:

Lemma 9 (Monotonicity). *For every configurations c_1, c_2, c'_1 of a $\mathcal{N}$ such that $c_1 \mapsto_{\mathcal{N}} c_2$ and $c_1 \preceq c'_1$, there exists a configuration c'_2 such that $c'_1 \mapsto^*_{\mathcal{N}} c'_2$ and $c_2 \preceq c'_2$.*

From [1], we know that in order to show the decidability of the state reachability problem for NSW^+, we only need to show that:

Lemma 10 (Effectiveness). *Given a finite set M of $\preceq$-minimals of a $\preceq$-upward closed set C, the (finite) set of $\preceq$-minimals of $pre_{\mathcal{N}}(C)$ is effectively computable from M.*

Then, from the three lemmas above and [1], we deduce the following fact:

Theorem 11. *The state reachability problem for* NSW^+ *is decidable.*

As a corollary of Theorem 7 and Theorem 11, we obtain our main result:

Corollary 12. *The state reachability problem for* NSW *is decidable.*

7 Nonatomic Writes Cause Undecidability

So far, we have considered only models that do not contain the RRWE (read remote writes early) relaxation. In this section, we show that adding RRWE to NSW makes the reachability problem undecidable. The RRWE relaxation allows a processor to read other processors' writes even if they are not globally visible yet. This makes writes non-atomic and can be detected by the IRIW litmus test (Fig. 3). IRIW is not possible in NSW as defined earlier. However, if we change the model to allow a read operation of $\mathcal{P}_i$ from a variable x_j to be validated by the last write issued by $\mathcal{P}_k$ (with $k \neq i$) on x_j, although this write has not been yet committed, it becomes possible.

$x = y = 0$			
$\mathcal{P}_1$	$\mathcal{P}_2$	$\mathcal{P}_3$	$\mathcal{P}_4$
(1) r$(x,1)$	(4) r$(y,1)$	(7) w$(x,1)$	(8) w$(y,1)$
(2) rfence	(5) rfence		
(3) r$(y,0)$	(6) r$(x,0)$		
$x = y = 1$			

Fig. 3. The IRIW (Independent Reads of Independent Writes) Litmus Test. $\mathcal{P}_3$ writes 1 to x and $\mathcal{P}_4$ writes 1 to y. In parallel, $\mathcal{P}_1$ observes that x has been modified before y, whereas $\mathcal{P}_2$ observes that y is modified before x.

An Operational Model An operational model for NSW with the RRWE relaxation can be defined as an extension of the one defined in Sec. 4. The idea is to add to the event structure $\mathcal{S} = (E, \rightsquigarrow, \lambda)$ a mapping $\sigma : [n] \times [m] \to E \cup \{\perp\}$, with $\perp \notin E$, that associates with each process and variable, either a pointer on some event of the structure, or $\perp$ when it is not defined. The pointer $\sigma(i, j)$ defines an event e such that every future read operation of $\mathcal{P}_i$ on the variable x_j should not take its value from a write event that is $\rightsquigarrow$-smaller than e. The intuition is that the validation of successive reads by the same process on a same variable should be done in a coherent way, i.e., the writes from which they read their values should occur in the same order. If $\sigma(i, j)$ points to some event e in the event structure, then e corresponds to the write event from which the last read performed by the process $\mathcal{P}_i$ on the variable x_j took its value. The fact that $\sigma(i, j) = \perp$ means that either $\mathcal{P}_i$ has never read a value from x_j, or the last write operation on x_j (issued by some other process) that has validated a read of $\mathcal{P}_i$ has already been updated.

Then, to validate a read operation of $\mathcal{P}_i$ on x_j using the RRWE, an event e must be found such that (1) e does not occur before the event $e' = \sigma(i,j)$ or any read/write event of P_i on x_j, and (2) e is the last write operation on x_j of $\mathcal{P}_k$ different from $\mathcal{P}_i$. If this is the case, then $\sigma(i,j)$ is updated to e and constraints are added to ensure that (i) e should be executed after the event e' and any read/write event of P_i on x_j, and (ii) e should be executed before all writes/reads by $\mathcal{P}_i$ on x_j coming after the validated read operation. When a write event is executed and exits the event structure $\mathcal{S}$, if this write event is pointed by $\sigma(i,j)$, then $\sigma(i,j)$ is set to $\perp$. $\mathcal{P}_i$ can perform a RLWE on x_j only if the event associated to the last write operation of P_i on x_j does not occur before $\sigma(i,j)$.

An atomic read-write operation $\mathsf{arw}(i,j,d,d')$ can be executed only when no pending reads on the same variable still exist in the structure $\mathcal{S}$, i.e., $\sigma(i,j) = \perp$. The reason is that operations on the same variable cannot be reordered. Finally, all the other operations are defined as in Sec. 4 while keeping the pointers unchanged.

As an example, consider the IRIW litmus test (Fig. 3). Starting from$(x = 0, y = 0)$ and an empty event structure $\mathcal{S}$, the execution of the writes (7) and (8) by $\mathcal{P}_3$ and $\mathcal{P}_4$ adds two events e_1 and e_2 to $\mathcal{S}$ labeled by $\mathsf{w}(3,x,1)$ and $\mathsf{w}(4,y,1)$, respectively. Then, $\mathcal{P}_1$ and $\mathcal{P}_2$ can execute their reads (1) and (4) that are validated using the RRWE relaxation, and set the pointers $\sigma(1,x)$ and $\sigma(2,y)$ to e_1 and e_2. At this point, (2) and (5) can be executed, and then, the reads (3) and (6) can be validated w.r.t. the content of the main memory. Finally, the writes corresponding to e_1 and e_2 in $\mathcal{S}$ are committed to the main memory, and this yields the memory state $(x = 1, y = 1)$.

We can prove by a reduction of Post's Correspondance Problem the following fact:

Theorem 13. *The state reachability problem for* $\mathsf{NSW} \cup \{\mathsf{RRWE}\}$ *is undecidable.*

8 Conclusion and Future Work

We have sharpened the decidability boundary of the reachability problem for weak memory models by (1) introducing a model NSW which supports many important relaxations (delay writes, perform reads early, allow partial fences) yet has a decidable reachability problem, and (2) showing that the read-write relaxation and the non-atomic-stores-relaxation are problematic (cause non-decidability) if added to TSO or NSW, respectively. Besides decidability, our work contributes in clarifying the effects and the power of common relaxations existing in weak memory models. It provides an insight on the formal models needed to reason about these relaxations, which can be useful for other formal algorithmic verification approaches, including approximate analyses. Notice that the models we introduce in Sections 4 and 5 can be also considered in the case of an infinite data domain, and the relationship between them still holds in the same manner. It is only when we address the decidability issue that we need to restrict ourselves to a finite data domain.

Future work may address the question of further sharpening the boundary by considering finer distinctions of the $\mathsf{r} \rightarrow \mathsf{w}$ relaxation, say by making it conditional on the absence of control- or data-dependencies. Moreover, we would like to explore the effect of non-atomic stores in more detail, such as whether it causes undecidability in weaker forms (e.g. if caused by static memory hierarchies) or if added to TSO rather than NSW.

Acknowledgements. Partially supported by the project ANR-09-SEGI-016 Veridyc.

References

1. Abdulla, P.A., Cerans, K., Jonsson, B., Tsay, Y.K.: General decidability theorems for infinite-state systems. In: LICS, pp. 313–321 (1996)
2. Adve, S., Gharachorloo, K.: Shared memory consistency models: a tutorial. Computer 29(12), 66–76 (1996)
3. Atig, M.F., Bouajjani, A., Burckhardt, S., Musuvathi, M.: On the verification problem for weak memory models. In: POPL, pp. 7–18. ACM (2010)
4. Atig, M.F., Bouajjani, A., Parlato, G.: Getting Rid of Store-Buffers in TSO Analysis. In: Gopalakrishnan, G., Qadeer, S. (eds.) CAV 2011. LNCS, vol. 6806, pp. 99–115. Springer, Heidelberg (2011)
5. Boehm, H.: WG21/N2176 memory model rationales (March 2007), http://open-std.org/jtc1/sc22/wg21/docs/papers/2007/n2176.html#dependencies
6. Boehm, H., Adve, S.: Foundations of the C++ concurrency memory model. In: PLDI, pp. 68–78 (2008)
7. Bouajjani, A., Meyer, R., Möhlmann, E.: Deciding Robustness against Total Store Ordering. In: Aceto, L., Henzinger, M., Sgall, J. (eds.) ICALP 2011, Part II. LNCS, vol. 6756, pp. 428–440. Springer, Heidelberg (2011
8. Burckhardt, S., Alur, R., Martin, M.: CheckFence: Checking consistency of concurrent data types on relaxed memory models. In: PLDI, pp. 12–21 (2007)
9. Burckhardt, S., Musuvathi, M.: Effective Program Verification for Relaxed Memory Models. In: Gupta, A., Malik, S. (eds.) CAV 2008. LNCS, vol. 5123, pp. 107–120. Springer, Heidelberg (2008); 2008 Extended Version as Tech Report MSR-TR-2008-12, Microsoft Research
10. Burckhardt, S., Musuvathi, M., Singh, V.: Verifying Local Transformations on Relaxed Memory Models. In: Gupta, R. (ed.) CC 2010. LNCS, vol. 6011, pp. 104–123. Springer, Heidelberg (2010)
11. Burnim, J., Sen, K., Stergiou, C.: Testing concurrent programs on relaxed memory models. Tech. Rep. UCB/EECS-2010-32, EECS Department, University of California, Berkeley (March 2010), http://www.eecs.berkeley.edu/Pubs/TechRpts/2010/EECS-2010-32.html
12. Chen, C., Chen, W., Sreedhar, V., Barik, R., Sarkar, V., Gao, G.: Establishing causality as a desideratum for memory models and transformations of parallel programs. Tech. rep., University of Delaware (2010)
13. Gharachorloo, K., Gupta, A., Hennessy, J.: Performance evaluation of memory consistency models for shared-memory multiprocessors. In: ASPLOS 1991, pp. 245–257 (1991)
14. Kuperstein, M., Vechev, M., Yahav, E.: Automatic inference of memory fences. In: FMCAD, pp. 111–119 (October 2010)
15. Kuperstein, M., Vechev, M., Yahav, E.: Partial-coherence abstractions for relaxed memory models. In: PLDI, San Jose, CA (June 2011)
16. Lamport, L.: How to make a multiprocessor computer that correctly executes multiprocess programs. IEEE Trans. Comp. C-28(9), 690–691 (1979)
17. Linden, A., Wolper, P.: A Verification-Based Approach to Memory Fence Insertion in Relaxed Memory Systems. In: Groce, A., Musuvathi, M. (eds.) SPIN 2011. LNCS, vol. 6823, pp. 144–160. Springer, Heidelberg (2011)
18. Mador-Haim, S., Alur, R., Martin, M.M.K.: Generating Litmus Tests for Contrasting Memory Consistency Models. In: Touili, T., Cook, B., Jackson, P. (eds.) CAV 2010. LNCS, vol. 6174, pp. 273–287. Springer, Heidelberg (2010)

19. Manson, J., Pugh, W., Adve, S.: The java memory model. In: POPL, pp. 378–391 (2005)
20. Owens, S.: Reasoning about the Implementation of Concurrency Abstractions on x86-TSO. In: D'Hondt, T. (ed.) ECOOP 2010. LNCS, vol. 6183, pp. 478–503. Springer, Heidelberg (2010)
21. Owens, S., Sarkar, S., Sewell, P.: A Better x86 Memory Model: x86-TSO. In: Berghofer, S., Nipkow, T., Urban, C., Wenzel, M. (eds.) TPHOLs 2009. LNCS, vol. 5674, pp. 391–407. Springer, Heidelberg (2009)
22. Sarkar, S., Sewell, P., Alglave, J., Maranget, L., Williams, D.: Understanding POWER multiprocessors. In: PLDI, San Jose, CA (June 2011)
23. Sevcik, J.: Safe optimisations for shared-memory concurrent programs. In: PLDI, pp. 306–316 (2011)
24. Sevcik, J., Vafeiadis, V., Nardelli, F.Z., Jagannathan, S., Sewell, P.: Relaxed-memory concurrency and verified compilation. In: POPL, pp. 43–54 (2011)
25. Sewell, P., Sarkar, S., Owens, S., Nardelli, F., Myreen, M.: x86-TSO: A rigorous and usable programmer's model for x86 multiprocessors. Commun. ACM 53 (2010)
26. Yang, Y., Gopalakrishnan, G., Lindstrom, G.: UMM: an operational memory model specification framework with integrated model checking capability. Concurrency and Computation: Practice and Experience 17(5-6), 465–487 (2005)

A Formally Verified SSA-Based Middle-End*

Static Single Assignment Meets CompCert

Gilles Barthe[1], Delphine Demange[2], and David Pichardie[3]

[1] IMDEA Software Institute, Madrid, Spain
[2] ENS Cachan Bretagne / IRISA, Rennes, France
[3] INRIA, Centre Rennes - Bretagne Atlantique, Rennes, France

Abstract. CompCert is a formally verified compiler that generates compact and efficient PowerPC, ARM and x86 code for a large and realistic subset of the C language. However, CompCert foregoes using Static Single Assignment (SSA), an intermediate representation that allows for writing simpler and faster optimizers, and is used by many compilers. In fact, it has remained an open problem to verify formally a SSA-based compiler middle-end. We report on a formally verified, SSA-based, middle-end for CompCert. Our middle-end performs conversion from CompCert intermediate form to SSA form, optimization of SSA programs, including Global Value Numbering, and transforming out of SSA to intermediate form. In addition to provide the first formally verified SSA-based middle-end, we address two problems raised by Leroy [13]: giving a simple and intuitive formal semantics to SSA, and leveraging the global properties of SSA to reason locally about program optimizations.

1 Introduction

Static Single Assignment. Static single assignment (SSA) form [7] is an intermediate representation where variables are statically assigned exactly once. Thanks to the considerable strength of this property, the SSA form simplifies the definition of many optimizations, and improves their efficiency, as well as the quality of their results. It is therefore not surprising that many modern compilers, including GCC and LLVMC [14], rely heavily on SSA form, and that there is a vast body of work on SSA. However, the simplicity of SSA form is deceptive, and designing a correct SSA-based middle-end compiler has been fraught with difficulties. In fact, it has been a significant challenge to design efficient, semantics-preserving, algorithms for converting programs into SSA form, or optimizing SSA programs, or even transforming programs out of SSA form.

Verified Compilers. Compiler correctness aims at giving a rigorous proof that a compiler preserves the behavior of programs. After 40 years of a rich history, the field is entering into a new dimension, with the advent of realistic and

* Partially funded by Spanish project TIN2009-14599 DESAFIOS 10, and Madrid Regional project S2009TIC-1465 PROMETIDOS, and French project ANR Verasco, FNRAE ASCERT and Bretagne Regional project CertLogS.

H. Seidl (Ed.): ESOP 2012, LNCS 7211, pp. 47–66, 2012.

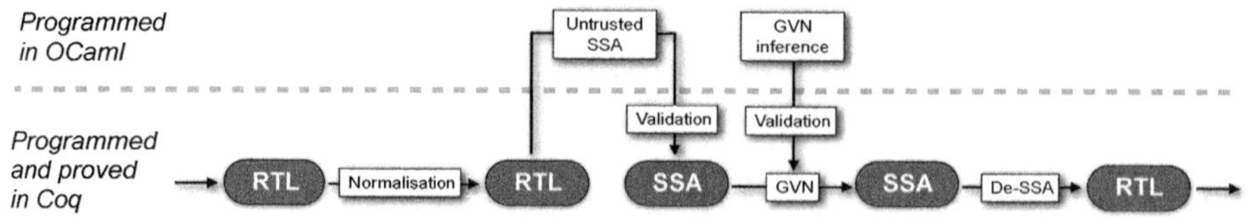

Fig. 1. The SSA Middle-end

mechanically verified compilers. This new generation of compilers was initiated with CompCert [13], a compiler that is programmed and verified in the Coq proof assistant and generates compact and efficient assembly code for a large fragment of the C language. Leroy's CompCert has been rightfully acclaimed as a *tour de force*, but it foregoes relying on an SSA-based middle end. In [13], Leroy reports:

> Since the beginning of CompCert we have been considering using SSA-based intermediate languages, but were held off by two difficulties. First, the dynamic semantics for SSA is not obvious to formalize. Second, the SSA property is global to the code of a whole function and not straightforward to exploit locally within proofs.

add adds: "A typical SSA-based optimization that interests us is global value numbering". However verifying GVN is a significant challenge, and its formal verification has remained beyond current state-of-the-art in certified compilers.

Static Single Assignment Meets Verified Compilers. The thesis of our work is that a compiler can be realistic, verified and still rely on a SSA form. To support our thesis, we provide the first verified SSA-based middle-end. Rather than programming and proving a verified compiler from scratch, we have programmed and verified a SSA-based middle-end compiler that can be plugged into CompCert at the level of RTL. Fig. 1 describes the overall architecture. Our middle-end performs four phases: (i) normalization of RTL program; (ii) transformation from RTL form into SSA form; (iii) optimization of programs in SSA form, including Global Value Numbering (GVN) [1]; (iv) transformation of programs from SSA form to RTL form; and relies on CompCert for the transformation from C to RTL programs prior to SSA conversion, and from RTL programs to assembly code after conversion out of SSA—our point is to program a realistic and verified SSA-based middle-end, rather than to demonstrate that SSA-based optimizations dramatically improve the efficiency of generated code.

We validate our compiler middle-end with a mix of techniques directly inherited from CompCert. We resort to translation validation [19,18]—increasingly favored by CompCert [24,25]—for converting programs into SSA form and for GVN. Specifically, we program in Coq verified checkers that validate *a posteriori* results of untrusted computations, and we implement in OCaml efficient algorithms for these computations; we rely on Cytron *et al* algorithm [7] for computing minimal SSA form, and on Alpern *et al* iteration strategy [1] for computing a numbering in GVN. In contrast, the normalization of the RTL program, and the conversion out of SSA are directly programmed and proved in Coq. In addition, our work addresses the two issues raised by Leroy [13]. First, we give a simple and intuitive operational semantics for SSA; the semantics follows the informal description given in [7], and does not require any artificial state instrumentation. Second, we define on SSA programs two global properties, called strictness and equational form, allowing to conclude reasonably directly that the substitutions performed by GVN and other optimizations are sound.

Summarizing, our work provides the first verified SSA-based middle-end, the first formal proof of an SSA-based optimization, as well as an intuitive semantics for SSA. It thus serves as a good starting point for further studies of verified and realistic SSA-based compilers.

Contents. The paper is organized as follows: Section 2 provides a brief primer on SSA and CompCert. Section 3 defines the SSA language used by our middle-end. Conversion to and out of SSA forms are presented in Section 4 and 5 respectively. Section 6 presents SSA-based optimizations. We conclude with experimental results in Section 7 and related work in Section 8.

Throughout the paper, we use Coq syntax for our definitions and results. Statements occasionally involve some notions that are not introduced formally. In such cases, names are generally chosen to be self-explanatory (for instance, `not_wrong_program`); in other cases, we forego giving precise definitions as they are not needed to understand the paper (for instance, the types `chunk` and `addressing` are unspecified in the definition of state). Our formalization makes an extensive use of inductive definitions, which are introduced in Coq using the keyword **`Inductive`**. Inductive definitions are used both for introducing new datatypes, e.g. the type of RTL instructions in Fig. 4, and for introducing inductive relations, e.g. the operational semantics of RTL instructions in Fig. 4. In the latter case, the declarations are written according to the pattern `Inductive R : A →B →Prop := | Rule1: ∀ a b, ... →R a b | Rule2:....`

2 Background

Static Single Assignment Form. is an intermediate representation in which variables are statically assigned exactly once, thus making explicit in the program syntax the link between the program point where a variable is defined and read.

Converting into SSA Form is easy for straighline code: one simply tags each variable definition with an index, and each variable use with the index corresponding to the last definition of this variable. For example, $[x := 1; y := x + 1; x := y - 1; y := x]$ is transformed into $[x_0 := 1; y_0 := x_0 + 1; x_1 := y_0 - 1; y_1 := x_1]$. The transformation is semantics-preserving, in the sense that the final values of x and y in the first snippet coincide with the final values of x_1 and y_1 in the second snippet. On the other hand, one cannot transform arbitrary programs into semantically equivalent programs in SSA form solely by tagging variables:

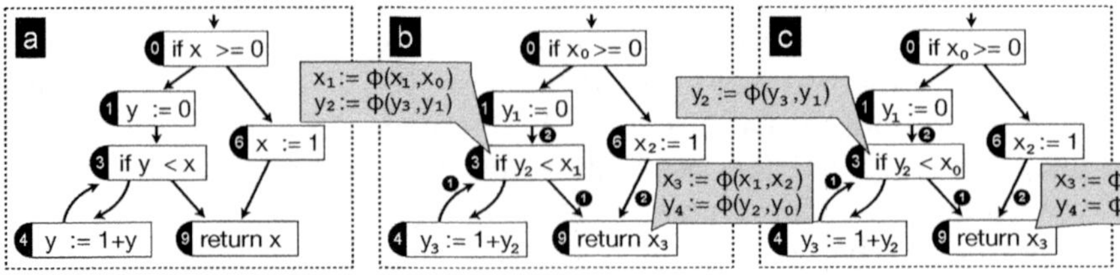

Fig. 2. Example programs. Programs b), c) are SSA forms of a). Programs b) is in naive form and c) in minimal form.

one must insert *ϕ-functions* to handle branching statements. Fig. 2 shows a program a), and a program b) that corresponds to a SSA form of a). In program a), the value of variable x read at node 9 either comes from the definition of x at entry or at node 6. In program b), these two definitions of x are renamed into the unique definition of x_0 and x_2 and merged together by the ϕ-function of x_3 at entry of node 9. The precise meaning of a ϕ-block depends on the numbering convention of the predecessor nodes of each junction point. In Fig. 2 b) we make explicit this numbering by labelling the CFG edges. For example, node 3 is the first predecessor of point 9 and node 6 is the second one. The semantics of ϕ-functions is given in the seminal paper by Cytron *et al* [7]:

"If control reaches node j from its kth predecessor, then the run-time support remembers k while executing the ϕ-functions in j. The value of $\phi(x_1, x_2, \ldots)$ is just the value of the kth operand. Each execution of a ϕ-function uses only one of the operands, but which one depends on the flow of control just before entering j. "

There may be several SSA forms for a single control-flow graph program; Fig. 2 b) and c) gives alternative SSA forms for program a). As the number of ϕ-functions directly impacts the quality of the subsequent optimizations—as well as the size of the SSA form—it is important that SSA generators for real compilers produce a SSA form with a minimal number of ϕ-functions. Implementations of minimal SSA generally rely on the notion of *dominance frontier* to choose where to insert ϕ-functions. A node i in a CFG dominates another node j if every path from then entry of the CFG to j contains i. The dominance is said to be strict if additionally $i \neq j$. A tree can encode the dominance relation between the nodes of the CFG. For a node i of a CFG, the *dominance frontier* $DF(i)$ of i is defined as the set of nodes j such that i dominates at least one predecessor of j in the CFG but does not strictly dominates j itself. The notion is extended to a set of nodes S with $DF(S) = \bigcup_{i \in S} DF(i)$. The *iterated dominance frontier* $DF^+(S)$ of a set of nodes S is $\lim_{i \to \infty} DF^i(S)$, where $DF^1(S) = DF(S)$ and $DF^{i+1}(S) = DF(S \cup DF^i(S))$. Formally, a program is in *minimal-SSA* form when a ϕ-function of an instance x_i of an original variable x appears in a junction point j iff j belongs to the iterated dominance frontier of the set of definition nodes of x in the original program. For instance, program c) in Fig. 2 is in minimal-SSA form. However, one can achieve more compact SSA forms by observing that, at any junction point, dead variables need not be defined by a ϕ-function. The intuition is captured by the notion of *pruned-SSA* form: a program is in

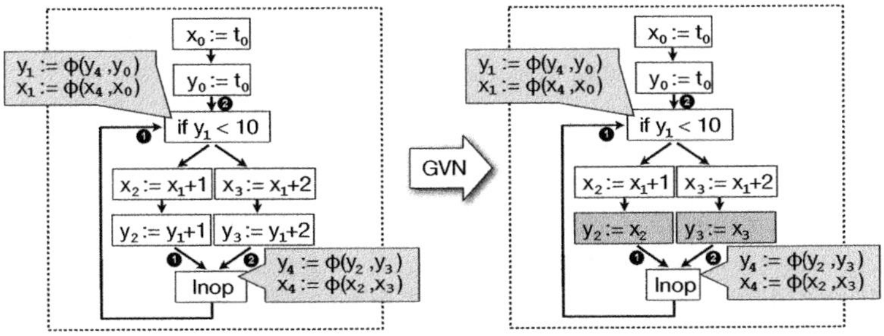

Fig. 3. Common sub-expression elimination (CSE) using GVN

pruned-SSA form if it is in minimal-SSA form and for each ϕ-function of an instance x_i of an original variable x at a junction point j, x is live at j in the original program (there is a path from j to a use of x that does not redefine x).

SSA-Based Optimizations. The SSA form simplifies the definition of many common optimizations; for instance, copy propagation algorithms can just walk through a SSA program, identify statements of the form $x := y$, and replace every use of x by y. Furthermore, several optimizations are naturally formulated on SSA. One typical SSA-based optimization is *Global Value Numbering* (GVN) [1], which assigns to variables an identifying number such that variables with the same number will hold equal values at execution time. The effectiveness of GVN lies in its ability to compute efficiently numberings that identify as many variables as possible. Advanced algorithms [1,5] allow to compute efficiently such numberings. We briefly explain one such numbering in Section 6.

Fig. 3 illustrates how GVN can be used to eliminate redundant computation. The left program is the original code; in this program, for each i, x_i and y_i are assigned the same value number. Hence, the evaluation of y_1+1 (resp. y_1+2) is a redundant computation when assigning y_2 (resp. y_3), and one can transform the program into the semantically equivalent one shown on the right of the figure. The strength of the analysis lies in its ability to reason about ϕ-functions, which allows it to infer the equality $x_2 = y_2$. This is only possible because numbering is global to the whole program; in fact, any block-local analysis would fail to discover the equality $x_2 = y_2$.

CompCert. is a realistic formally verified compiler that generates PowerPC, ARM or x86 code from source programs written in a large subset of C. CompCert formalizes the operational semantics of dozen intermediate languages, and proves for each phase a semantics preservation theorem. Preservation theorems are expressed in terms of program behaviors, i.e. finite or infinite traces of external function calls (a.k.a. events) that are performed during the execution of the program, and claim that individual compilation phases preserve behaviors. A consequence of the theorems is that for any C program p that does not go wrong, and target program tp output by the successful compilation of p by the compiler compcert_compiler, the set of behaviors of p contains all behaviors of the target program tp. The formal theorem is:

```
Theorem compcert_compiler_correct: ∀ (p: C.program) (tp: Asm.program),
  (not_wrong_program p ∧ compcert_compiler p = OK tp) →
  (∀ beh, exec_asm_program tp beh → exec_C_program p beh).
```

This paper focuses on the CompCert middle-end where most of the existing optimisations are performed (currently: constant propagation, removal of redundant cast, tail call detection, local value numbering and a register allocation phase that includes copy propagation). These operate on a Register Transfer Language (RTL), whose syntax and semantics is given in Fig. 4. A RTL program is defined as a set of global variables, a set of functions, and an entry node. Functions are modelled as records that include a function signature fn_sig, a CFG fn_code of instructions over pseudo-registers. The CFG is not a basic-block graph: it partially maps each CFG node to a single instruction, and we stick to this important design choice of CompCert. As explained by Knoop *et al* [10], it allows for simpler implementations of code manipulations and simplifies correctness proofs of analyses or transformations, without impacting too much their efficiency.

The RTL instruction set includes arithmetic operations (Iop), memory loads (Iload) and stores (Istore), function calls (Icall), conditional (Icond) and unconditional jumps (Inop), and a return statement (Ireturn)— for brevity, we do not discuss here jumptables and other kinds of function calls: call to a function pointer stored in a register, tail calls, and built-in functions. All instructions take as last argument a node pc denoting the next instruction to be executed; additionally, all instructions but Inop take as arguments pseudo-registers of type reg, memory chunks, and addressing modes.

The type of states is defined as the tagged union of regular states, call states and return states (Fig. 4). We focus on regular states, as we only expose here the intra-procedural part of the language. A regular semantic state (State) is a tuple that contains a call stack (representing the current pending function calls), the current function description and stack pointer (to the stack data block, a part of the global memory where variables dereferenced in the C source program reside), the current program point, the registers state (a mapping of local variables to values) and the global memory. The semantics also includes a global environment mapping function names and global variables to memory addresses; it is never modified during a program execution, and thus ommitted in our presentation.

The operational behavior of programs is modelled by the relation step between two semantic states (see Fig. 4), and a trace of events; all instructions except function calls do not emit any event, hence the transitions that they induced are tagged by the empty event trace ϵ. We briefly comment on the rules: (Inop pc′) branches to the next program point pc′. (Iop op args res pc′) performs the arithmetic operation op over the values of registers args (written rs##args), stores the result in res (written rs#res ← v), and branches to pc′. The instruction (Iload chk addr args res pc′) loads a chk memory quantity from the address determined by the addressing mode addr and the values of the args registers, stores the quantity just read into res, and branches to pc′.

```
Inductive instr  :=
  | Inop (pc: node)
  | Iop (op: operation) (args: list reg) (res: reg) (pc: node)
  | Iload (chk:chunk) (addr:addressing) (args: list reg) (res: reg) (pc: node)
  | Istore (chk:chunk) (addr:addressing) (args:list reg) (src: reg) (pc: node)
  | Icall (sig: signature) (fn:ident) (args: list reg) (res: reg) (pc: node)
  | Icond (cond: condition) (args: list reg) (ifso ifnot: node)
  | Ireturn (or: option reg).

Inductive state :=
 | State (stack: list stackframe) (* call stack *)
         (f: function)            (* current function *)
         (sp: val)                (* stack pointer *)
         (pc: node)               (* current program point *)
         (rs: regset)             (* register state *)
         (m: mem)                 (* memory state *)
 | Callstate (stack: list stackframe) (f: fundef) (args: list val) (m: mem)
 | Returnstate (stack: list stackframe) (v: val) (m: mem).

Inductive step: state → trace → state → Prop :=
 | ex_Inop: ∀ s f sp pc rs m pc',
     fn_code f pc = Some(Inop pc') →
     step (State s f sp pc rs m) ε (State s f sp pc' rs m)
 | ex_Iop: ∀ s f sp pc rs m pc' op args res v,
     fn_code f pc = Some(Iop op args res pc') →
     eval_operation sp op (rs##args) m = Some v →
     step (State s f sp pc rs m) ε (State s f sp pc' (rs#res←v) m)
 | ex_Iload: ∀ s f sp pc rs m pc' chk addr args res a v,
     fn_code f pc = Some(Iload chk addr args res pc') →
     eval_addressing sp addr (rs##args) = Some a →
     Mem.loadv chk m a = Some v →
     step (State s f sp pc rs m) ε (State s f sp pc' (rs#res←v) m)
```

Fig. 4. Syntax and semantics of RTL (excerpt)

3 The SSA Language

We describe the syntax and operational semantics of the language SSA that provides the SSA form of RTL programs. We equip the notion of SSA program with a *well-formedness* predicate capturing essential properties of SSA forms.

SSA Programs. Our definition of SSA program distinguishes between RTL-like instructions and ϕ-functions; the distinction avoids the need for unwieldy mappings between program points when converting to SSA, and allows for a smooth integration in CompCert. Fig. 5 introduces the syntax of SSA. SSA functions operate on indexed registers of type `SSA.reg` = `RTL.reg` ∗ `idx`, and include an additional field `fn_phicode` mapping junction points to ϕ-blocks. The latter are modelled as lists of ϕ-functions of the form (`Iphi args res`), where `res` is an indexed register, and `args` a list of indexed registers.

Next, we define structural constraints that allow giving an intuitive semantics to SSA programs. First, we require that the domain of the function `fn_phicode` be the set of junction points. Second, we require that all ϕ-functions in a ϕ-block have the same number of arguments as the number of predecessors of that block. Third, we require that all predecessors of a junction point be (`Inop pc`) instructions. This is a mild constraint, that can be ensured systematically on RTL programs through normalization, and that will carry over to their SSA forms. Fig. 6 shows the RTL program from Fig. 2 after normalization.

Finally, we consider two essential properties of SSA forms: unique definitions and strictness. The unique definitions property states that each register is uniquely defined, whereas the strictness property states that each variable use is dominated by the (unique) definition of that variable. While the two properties are closely related, none implies the other; the program $[y_0 := x_0; x_0 := 1]$ satisfies the unique definitions property but is not in strict form whereas the program $[x_0 := 1; x_0 := 2; y_0 := x_0]$ is strict but does not satisfy the unique definitions property. To formalize these properties, one first defines the type of paths in a CFG, and predicates `dom` and `sdom` for dominance and strict dominance. Then, one must define the two predicates `def`, `use` of type `SSA.function` → `SSA.reg` → `node` → `Prop` such that proposition `def f x pc` (respectively `use f x pc`) holds iff the register `x` is defined (resp. used) at node `pc` in the (RTL-like or ϕ-) code of the function `f`. The definition of `use` is complex because variables may be used in ϕ-functions: the widely adopted convention is to view ϕ-functions as lazily evaluated, their ith argument thus being used at the ith predecessor of the instruction. For example, in the SSA program of Fig. 6, variable $\mathtt{x}_2$ is defined at node 6 and used at node 8, the 2nd predecessor of the junction point 9 where $\mathtt{x}_2$ appears as 2nd argument of the ϕ-function. A use in the regular code is more straightforward: a variable is used by an instruction if it appears on its right-hand side. Using `def` and `use`, one can then state the unique definition and strictness properties, and well-formedness. Formally, we say that a SSA function is well-formed if it satisfies the following predicate:

```
Record wf_ssa_function (f:SSA.function) : Prop := {
  fn_ssa:           unique_def f;
  fn_strict:        ∀ x u d, use f x u → def f x d → dom f d u;
  fn_wf_block:      block_nb_args f;
  fn_block_at_jp:   ∀ jp, join_point jp f ↔ fn_phicode f jp ≠ None;
  fn_normalized:    ∀ jp pc, join_point jp f → In jp (succs f pc) →
                              fn_code f pc = Some (Inop jp);}.
```

where predicates `unique_def` and `block_nb_args` respectively capture that a function satisfies the unique definitions property and the structural constraint about arguments. In the sequel, we show that conversion to SSA yields well-formed programs. Besides, our SSA-based optimizations will assume that the input SSA programs are well-formed; in turn, we prove for each of them that output programs are well-formed.

Semantics. The notion of SSA state is similar to the notion of RTL state, except that the type of registers and current function are modified into `SSA.reg` and `SSA.function` respectively. The small-step operational semantics is defined on SSA programs that satisfy the structural constraints introduced in the previous paragraph. Formally, we define `SSA.step` as a relation between pairs of (SSA) states and a trace of events. The definition follows the one of `RTL.step`, except for instructions of the form (`Inop pc'`), where one distinguishes whether `pc'` is a junction point or not. In the latter case, the semantics coincide with the RTL

```
Inductive instr := ...

Inductive phiinstr :=
  | Iphi (args: list SSA.reg)
         (res: SSA.reg).

Definition phiblock:= list phiinstr.
```

```
Record function := {
  fn_sig: signature;            signature
  fn_params: list SSA.reg;      parameters
  fn_stacksize: Z;   activation record size
  fn_code: code;                code graph
  fn_phicode: phicode;          φ-blocks graph
  fn_entrypoint: node}.         entry node
```

```
Inductive step: SSA.state → trace → SSA.state → Prop :=
  | ex_Inop_njp: ∀ s f sp pc rs m pc',
     fn_code f pc = Some(Inop pc') →
     ¬ join_point pc' f →
     step (State s f sp pc rs m) ϵ (State s f sp pc' rs m)
  | ex_Inop_jp: ∀ s f sp pc rs m pc' phib k,
     fn_code f pc = Some(Inop pc') →
     join_point pc' f →
     fn_phicode f pc' = Some phib →
     index_pred f pc pc' = Some k →
     step (State s f sp pc rs m) ϵ (State s f sp pc' (phistore k rs phib) m)

Fixpoint phistore k rs phib : nat → SSA.regset → phiblock → SSA.regset :=
  match phib with
    | nil => rs
    | (Iphi args res)::phib =>
      match nth_error args k with
        | None => rs
        | Some arg => (phistore k rs phib)#res ← (rs#arg)
      end end.
```

Fig. 5. Syntax and semantics of SSA (excerpt)

semantics, i.e. the program point is updated in the semantic state. If on the contrary pc′ is a junction point, then one executes the ϕ-block attached to pc′ before the control flows to pc′. Executing ϕ-blocks on the way to pc′ avoids the need to instrument the semantics of SSA with the predecessor program point, and crisply captures the intuitive meaning given to ϕ-blocks by Cytron *et al* (see Section 2). Note in particular that the normalization ensures the predecessor of a junction point is an `Inop` instruction. This greatly simplifies the definition of the semantics, and subsequently the proofs about SSA programs.

Following conventional practice, ϕ-blocks are given a parallel (big-step) semantics. This is formally embedded in the rule for `phistore` (Fig. 5). When reaching a join point pc′ from its kth predecessor, we update the register set `rs` for each register `res` assigned in the ϕ-block `phib` with the value of register `arg` in `rs` (written `rs#arg`), where `arg` is the kth operand in the ϕ-function of `res` (written `nth_error args k = Some arg`). With the same notations, `phistore` satisfies, on well-formed SSA functions, a *parallel assignment* property:

```
∀ arg res, In (Iphi args res) phib →
   nth_error args k = Some arg → (phistore k rs phib)#res = rs#arg
```

4 Translation Validation of SSA Generation

Modern compilers typically follow the algorithm by Cytron *et al* [7] to generate a minimal SSA form of programs in almost linear time w.r.t. the size of the program.

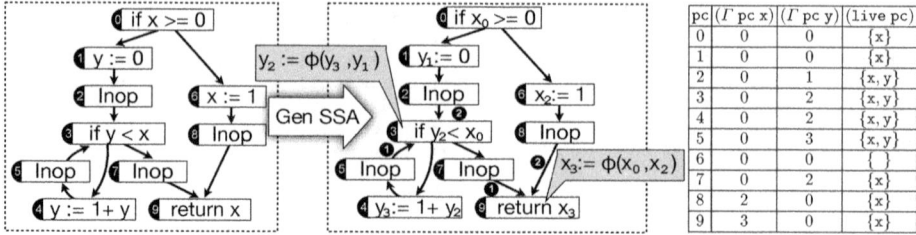

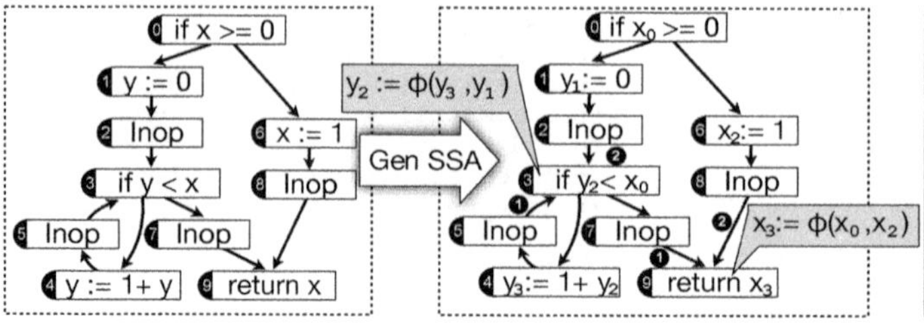

pc	(Γ pc x)	(Γ pc y)	(live pc)
0	0	0	{x}
1	0	0	{x}
2	0	1	{x, y}
3	0	2	{x, y}
4	0	2	{x, y}
5	0	3	{x, y}
6	0	0	{ }
7	0	2	{x}
8	2	0	{x}
9	3	0	{x}

Fig. 6. A RTL program, its pruned SSA form and the corresponding type information

The algorithm proceeds in four steps: (i) it computes the dominator tree of the CFG using the Lengauer and Tarjan algorithm [12]; (ii) it builds the dominance frontier using a bottom-up traversal of the dominator tree; (iii) for each variable, it places ϕ-functions using iterated dominance frontier; (iv) at last, it uses a top-down traversal of the dominator tree to rename each def and use of RTL variables with correct indexes. Programming efficiently the algorithm in Coq and proving formally its correctness is a significant challenge—even verifying formally Step (i) requires to formalize a substantial amount of graph theory. Instead, we provide a new validation algorithm that checks in linear time that a SSA program is a correct SSA form of an input RTL program. The algorithm is complete w.r.t. minimal SSA form, and can be enhanced by a liveness analysis to handle pruned and semi-pruned SSA forms. In order to be used in a certified compiler chain, we also show that our validator preserves behaviors.

Translation validation of SSA conversion is performed in two passes. The first pass performs a structural verification on programs: given a RTL function `f` and a SSA function `tf`, it verifies that `tf` satisfies all clauses of well-formedness except strictness, and that the code of `f` can be recovered from its SSA form `tf` simply by erasing ϕ-blocks and variable indices—the latter property is captured formally by the proposition `structural_spec f tf`. The second pass relies on a type system to ensure strictness and semantics-preservation. Overall the pseudo-code of the validator is:

```
let SSA_validator (f: RTL.function) (tf: SSA.function): bool :=
  if     (check_blocks_are_wf tf)          (* ensures block_are_wf tf *)
     && (check_blocks_are_at_jp tf)        (* ensures block_at_jp tf *)
     && (check_normalized tf)              (* ensures normalization *)
     && (check_unique_def tf)              (* ensures unique_def tf *)
     && (check_structural_spec f tf)       (* ensures structural_spec f tf *)
  then (is_well_typed f tf) else false
```

where `is_well_typed f tf` is the predicate stating that the function is well-typed w.r.t. our type system for SSA form.

Type System. The basic idea of our type system is to track for each variable its *last* definition; this is achieved by assigning to all program points a local typing, i.e., an element of `ltype` = `RTL.reg` $\rightarrow$ `idx`; we let γ range over local typings. Then, the global typing of an SSA function `tf` is an element of `gtype` = `node` $\rightarrow$ `RTL.reg` $\rightarrow$ `idx`; we let Γ range over global typings. The type

```
Definition use_ok (uses:list SSA.reg)(γ:ltype):= ∀ r i, In (r,i) uses→ γ r=i.

Inductive wt_instr: ltype → SSA.instr → ltype → Prop :=
| wt_Inop: ∀ γ s, {γ} Inop s {γ}
| wt_Istore: ∀ γ chk addr args s src,
      use_ok (src::args) γ → {γ} Istore chk addr args src s {γ}
| wt_Icond: ∀ γ cond args s1 s2,
      use_ok args γ → {γ} Icond cond args s1 s2 {γ}
| wt_Ireturn_some: ∀ γ r, use_ok [r] γ → {γ} Ireturn (Some r) {γ}
| wt_Ireturn_none: ∀ γ, {γ} Ireturn None {γ}
| wt_Iop: ∀ γ op args s r i,
      use_ok args γ  → i ≠ dft → {γ} Iop op args (r,i) s {γ[r ← i]}
| wt_Iload: ∀ γ chk addr args s r i,
      use_ok args γ → i ≠ dft → {γ} Iload chk addr args (r,i) s {γ[r ← i]}
| wt_Icall: ∀ γ sig args s id r i,
      use_ok args γ → i ≠ dft → {γ} Icall sig id args (r,i) s {γ[r ← i]}
```

Fig. 7. Typing rules for instructions

system is structured in three layers. The lowest layer checks that RTL-like instructions make a correct use of variables. The middle layer checks that CFG edges are well-typed. Finally, the third layer of the type system defines the notion of well-typed function. Throughout this section, we use Fig. 6 as a running example (an RTL program, its pruned SSA form and its type mapping).

Liveness. As explained in Section 2, liveness information can be used to minimize the number of ϕ-functions in a SSA program; specifically, ϕ-blocks only need to assign live variables (in Fig. 6, the variable y is live at node 3, and x is live at node 9). Hence, our type system is parametrized by a function `live` that models a liveness analysis. Formally, we require that the `live` function satisfy two properties (for a function `f`, their conjunction is denoted by (`wf_live f live`)): (i) if a variable is used at a program point, then it should be live at this point and (ii) a variable that is live at a given program point is, at the predecessor point, either live or assigned.

Our type system is able to handle different SSA forms through appropriate instantiations of `live`. Our formalization provides support for minimal SSA and pruned SSA forms, respectively by defining `live` respectively as the trivial over-approximation (for each point, it is the set of all the RTL variables), and the result of a standard liveness analysis. One could also support semi-pruned forms, by instantiating `live` as the result of the block-local liveness analysis of [4].

The Type System for Instructions checks that RTL-like instructions make of correct use of variables, and that they do not redefine parameters; its formal definition is given in Fig. 7. Judgments are of the form $\{\gamma\}$ `ins` $\{\gamma'\}$; intuitively, the judgment is valid if each variable `x` is used in `ins` with the index (γ `x`), and γ' maps each variable to its last definition after execution of `ins`. The typing rules are formalized as an inductive relation `wt_instr`; we briefly comment on some rules. Several rules correspond to instructions that do not define variables, so the input and output local typings are equal. For such rules, one simply checks that the instruction makes a correct use of the variables (through `use_ok`). The typing rule for (`Inop pc`) states that for every local typing γ, (`Inop pc`) makes a correct use of variables. The typing rule for `Icond` checks that the variables used in the guard are consistent with the local typing input (in Fig. 6, the uses of x_0 and y_2 at node 3 are consistent with the intput local typing: $(\Gamma\ 3\ \mathtt{x}) = 0$ and $(\Gamma\ 3\ \mathtt{y}) = 2$). In the case of the instruction Iop, which defines the variable (r, i), the output local typing is $\gamma[\mathtt{r} \leftarrow \mathtt{i}]$, i.e. the input local typing updated for the initial variable r. From this program node onwards, the new version for r is the one indexed with i, and this is the one that should be used later on, until another version for r is defined (in Fig. 6, the definition of x_2 at node 6 makes the local typing change for variable x between nodes 6 and 8). Note that each time a variable is defined, we demand its index to be different from the index dft assigned to parameters at the onset of the program (in the example, the default index is 0). This prevents that a parameter is redefined during execution, which would violate the unique definition property.

Typing Rules for Edges and Functions. The typing rules for edges ensure that ϕ-blocks make a correct use of definitions w.r.t. a global typing Γ. There are two rules—modelled by the clauses of the inductive relation wt_edge in Fig. 8. The first rule considers the case where the edge does not end in a junction point; in this case, typing the edge is equivalent to typing the corresponding instruction. The second rule considers the case where the edge ends in a junction point: the typing rule checks the ϕ-block attached to it—structural constraints impose that the instruction is an Inop, so we do not need to type-check the instruction. Hypothesis USES ensures the ϕ-arguments args passed to ϕ-functions are consistent w.r.t. all incoming local typings: its kth argument should be the version of the initial variable brought by the kth predecessor of the join point (we omit the formal definition of phiuse_ok). Hypothesis ASSIG ensures the ϕ-block is compatible with the output local typing; Hypothesis NASSIG ensures that variables not assigned in the ϕ-block are either dead, or the incoming indices are the same. In Fig. 6, the ϕ-function for x makes correct uses of it because its first argument x_0 matches $(\Gamma\ 7\ \mathtt{x}) = 0$ and x_2 matches $(\Gamma\ 8\ \mathtt{x}) = 2$. The local typing at node 9 takes into account the definition of x_3 in the block by setting $(\Gamma\ 9\ \mathtt{x})$ to 3. Moreover, no ϕ-function is required for y at node 9 since $\mathtt{y} \notin (\mathtt{live}\ 9)$, and no ϕ-function is required for x at node 3, since $(\Gamma\ 2\ \mathtt{x}) = (\Gamma\ 5\ \mathtt{x})$.

Finally, a function is well-typed w.r.t. global typing Γ if the local typing induced by Γ at the entry node fn_entrypoint is consistent with the parameters, and all edges and return instructions are well-typed.[1]

Implementation. For the sake of clarity, we have described a non-executable type checker which assumes that structural constraints are satisfied. The Coq implementation of the type system is in fact a bit more complex. In particular, it performs type inference rather than type checking; for efficiency reasons, the algorithm performs a single, linear scan of the program, and checks the list of arguments of ϕ-functions only once per junction point, rather than once per incoming edge for a given join point. On the benchmarks given in Section 7, our efficient implementation is ten times faster than a naive type checker derived from the non-executable type system.

[1] Return instructions do not correspond to any edge.

```
Inductive wt_edge (f:SSA.function)(Γ:gtype)(live:Regset.t):node→ node → Prop:=
| wt_edge_not_jp: ∀ i j ins
(NOTJP : fn_code f i = Some ins ∧ fn_phicode f j = None)
(WTI :   {Γ i} ins {Γ j}),
(wt_edge f Γ live i j)

| wt_edge_jp: ∀ i j ins block
(JP:  fn_code f i = Some ins ∧ fn_phicode f j = Some block)
(USES:∀ args r k, In (Iphi args (r,k)) block → phiuse_ok r args (preds f j) Γ)
(ASSIG: ∀ r k, assigned (r,k) block → r ∈ live ∧ (Γ j r) = k ∧ k ≠ dft)
(NASSIG: ∀ r, (∀ k, ¬ (assigned (r,k) block)) → (Γ i r = Γ j r) ∨ r ∉ live),
(wt_edge f Γ live i j).

Definition wt_function (f:SSA.function)(Γ:gtype)(live:node→ Regset.t):Prop:=
(∀ i j, is_edge f i j → wt_edge f Γ (live j) i j)
∧ (∀ i or, fn_code f i = Some (Ireturn or) → {Γ i} Ireturn or {Γ i})
∧ (∀ p, In p (fn_params f) → ∃ r, p = (r, Γ (fn_entrypoint f) r)).
```

Fig. 8. Typing rules for edges and functions

Properties of the Validator

Strictness. All SSA programs accepted by the type system are strict. It follows that only well-formed SSA functions will be accepted by the validator.

```
Theorem wt_strict: ∀ f tf Γ live,
wf_live f live → wt_function tf Γ live →
∀ (xi : SSA.reg) (u d : node), use tf xi u → def tf xi d → dom tf d u.
```

The proof of `wt_strict` relies on two auxiliary lemmas about local typings in well-typed functions. The first lemma states that if a variable (x, i) is used at node pc, then it must be that (Γ pc x = i). The second lemma states that whenever (Γ pc x = i), the definition point of variable (x, i) dominates pc.

Soundness. The validator is sound in the sense that if it accepts a RTL program `f` and an SSA form `tf`, then all behaviors of `tf` are also behaviors of `f`. Since CompCert already shows the general result that a lock-step forward simulation implies preservation of behaviors, it is sufficient to exhibit such a simulation:

```
Theorem validator_correct : ∀ (prog:RTL.program) (tprog:SSA.program),
SSA_validator prog tprog = true →
 ∀ s1 t s2, RTL.step s1 t s2 →
   ∀ s1', s1 ≃ s1' → ∃ s2', SSA.step s1' t s2' ∧ s2 ≃ s2'.
```

where the binary relation ≃ between semantic states of RTL and SSA carries the invariants needed for proving behavior preservation. For instance, two regular states are related by ≃ if their memory states, stack pointers, and program counters are equal, their function descriptions are suitably related, e.g. by `structural_spec`, and their register states `rs` and `rs'` agree, i.e. satisfy (agree (Γ pc) rs rs′ (live pc)), where

```
Definition agree (γ:ltype) (rs:RTL.regset) (rs':SSA.regset) (live:Regset.t):=
  ∀ r, r ∈ live → rs#r  = rs'#(r, γ r).
```

Agreement is at the heart of the proof. It captures the semantics of local typings by making explicit how, at a given program point, variables of `f` should be interpreted in terms of the new variables in `tf`. The definition of $\simeq$ is completed by defining equivalence of stackframes; this relation basically lifts to the callstack all the invariants enforced by $\simeq$ (see [6] for the formal definition of $\simeq$).

Completeness. An essential property of our type system is that it accepts all the SSA programs that are output by the algorithm by Cytron *et al* [7]. The idea of the proof is as follows (provided in [6]). First, one defines for each RTL normalized program `f` a global typing Γ. Second, we show that all instructions of the program `tf` output by our implementation are typable. Then, we show that all edges are typable if we omit the constraints about correct use; the proof relies crucially on the fixpoint characterization of the iterated dominance frontier, as given in work of Cytron *et al* [7]. Finally, one shows that all constraints about correct use are satisfied, and hence the program `tf` is typable with Γ.

5 Conversion out of SSA

We have programed and verified a simple de-SSA algorithm that transforms SSA programs into RTL programs—so that they can be further processed by CompCert back end. The idea is to substitute each ϕ-function with one variable copy at each predecessor of junction points. Thanks to the single-instruction graph of RTL, replacing ϕ-functions with copies ensures soundness of the transformation, since critical edges are automatically splitted by code insertion—a critical edge is an edge whose entry has several successors and exit has several predecessors (see [4]). Pleasingly, the representation of programs inherited from CompCert deflates the penalty cost of splitting edges—on the contrary, algorithms that operate on *basic-block graphs* carefully avoid edge splitting, at the cost of making de-SSA algorithms significantly more complex. On the negative side, our current implementation of de-SSA fails on SSA programs with non-parallel ϕ-blocks, i.e. in which some variable is both used and defined. Minor future work includes making de-SSA total, reusing the formalization of the parallel moves algorithm [20]—which transforms a set of parallel moves into an equivalent sequence of elementary moves (using additional temporaries), and that is already used in CompCert. Concerning the correctness of the transformation, we proceed by giving a forward simulation between the SSA program and the RTL program after de-SSA. The simulation requires the RTL program to perform several steps to simulate a (big-step) execution of a ϕ-block by the initial SSA program.

6 Validation of SSA-Based Optimizations

In this section, we introduce the *equation lemma* that supports the view of programs in SSA form as *systems of equations*. We then illustrate how to reason about a simple SSA-based optimization, namely copy propagation. Finally, we formalize and prove correct a GVN optimization.

Equation Lemma. The SSA representation provides an intuitive reading of programs: one can view the unique definition of a variable as an equation, and by extension one can view SSA programs as systems of equations. For instance, the definitions of x_3 and y_1 respectively induce the two equations $x_3 = y_1 + 1$ and $y_1 = x_3 + 1$. There is however a pitfall: the two equations entail $x_3 = x_3 + 2$, and thus are inconsistent. In fact, equations are only valid at program nodes dominated by the definition that induce them, as captured formally by the *equation-lemma* of SSA:

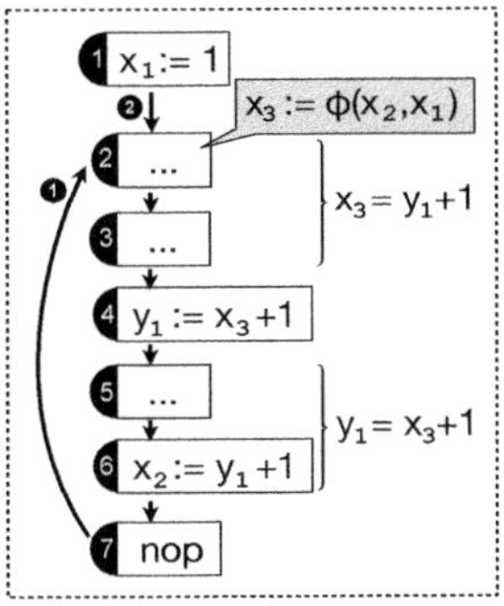


```
Lemma equation_lemma : ∀ prog d op args x succ f m rs sp pc s,
    wf_ssa_program prog →
      reachable prog (State s f sp pc rs m) →
      fn_code f d  = Some (Iop op args x succ) →
      sdom f d pc →
      eval_operation sp op (rs##args) m = Some (rs#x).
```

where `reachable` is a predicate that defines reachable states. In practice, it is often convenient to rely on a corollary that proves the validity of the defining equation of x at program points where x is used – thus avoiding reasoning on the dominance relation. The formal statement of the corollary is obtained by replacing the hypothesis `sdom f d pc` by the hypothesis `use f x pc`; the proof of the corollary intensively uses the strictness property of well-formed SSA programs.

We conclude with a succinct account of applying the corollary to prove the soundness of copy propagation (CP)—recall that CP will search for copies x := y and replace every use of x by a use of y. Suppose pc is a program point where such a replacement has been done. Every time pc is reached during the program execution, we are able to derive, using the corollary, that `rs#y` = `rs#x`, where `rs` is the current register state because (i) y is the right hand side of the definition of x and (ii) pc was a use point of x in the initial program. On non-SSA forms, the reasoning is more involved since one has to prove that the reaching definition for x is unique at pc, and that no redefinition of y can occur in between.

Global Value Numbering. Our implementation of GVN is made of two components. The first one is an efficient but untrusted analysis, written in OCaml, for computing numberings of SSA programs. From an abstract interpretation point of view, the analysis—which follows [1]—computes a fixpoint in the abstract domain of congruence partitions, where partitions are modelled as mappings $\mathcal{N}$: `reg` → `reg` that map a register to the canonical register of its equivalence class, and ordered w.r.t. reverse inclusion of equivalence kernels—recall that the equivalence kernel of $\mathcal{N}$ is the relation $\sim$ defined by x $\sim$ y if and only if $\mathcal{N}\ x = \mathcal{N}\ y$. Viewing the result of the analysis as a post-fixpoint is the key to our second component, a validator that checks whether a numbering $\mathcal{N}$ is indeed a post-fixpoint of the analysis on a program p, and if so returns an optimized SSA program tp. The validator is programmed in Coq, and is accompanied with a proof that optimized programs preserve the behaviors of the original programs.

```
Inductive ≡^𝒩 : reg → reg → Prop :=
| GVN_refl : ∀ x, ≡^𝒩 x x
| GVN_Iop : ∀ x y pc1 pc2 op args1 args2 pc1' pc2'
    fn_code f pc1 = Some(Iop op args1 x pc1') → same_number 𝒩 args1 args2 →
    fn_code f pc2 = Some(Iop op args2 y pc2') → ≡^𝒩 x y
| GVN_Phi : ∀ x y pc args_x args_y
    fn_phicode f pc = Some phib → same_number 𝒩 args_x args_y →
    (Iphi args_x x) ∈ phib → (Iphi args_y y) ∈ phib → ≡^𝒩 x y.

Definition GVN_spec (𝒩:reg → reg) : Prop :=
(∀ x y, 𝒩 x = 𝒩 y → param f x → param f y→ x=y)∧(∀ x y, 𝒩 x = 𝒩 y → ≡^𝒩 x y).
```

Fig. 9. Valid numbering

The notion of valid numbering is formally defined in Fig. 9. First, we define for each numbering $\mathcal{N}$ the relation $\equiv^{\mathcal{N}}$ as the smallest reflexive relation identifying: (i) registers whose assignments share the same operator and corresponding arguments are equivalent w.r.t. $\mathcal{N}$ (predicate `same_number`); (ii) registers that are defined in the same ϕ-block with equivalent arguments.Then, for a numbering $\mathcal{N}$ to be valid (see `GVN_spec`), its equivalence kernel must not contain a pair of distinct function parameters and it must moreover be included in $\equiv^{\mathcal{N}}$. The latter ensures the intended post-fixpoint property.

The crux of the correctness proof of the GVN validator is the correctness lemma for a valid numbering: if $\mathcal{N}$ is a valid numbering for `f`, and `rs` is a register state that can be reached at node `pc`, and `x` and `y` are two registers whose definition strictly dominate `pc`, then $\mathcal{N}$ `x` $=$ $\mathcal{N}$ `y` entails that `rs` holds equal values for `x` and `y`:

```
Lemma valid_numbering_correct : ∀ prog s sp pc rs m,
   wf_ssa_program prog → GVN_spec 𝒩→
     reachable prog (State s f sp pc rs m) → gamma 𝒩 pc rs.
```

where gamma is defined by

```
Definition gamma (𝒩:reg → reg) (pc:node) (rs: regset) : Prop :=
 ∀ x y: reg, def_sdom f x pc → def_sdom f y pc → 𝒩 x = 𝒩 y → rs#x = rs#y.
```

and `def_sdom f x pc` states that the definition of `x` in `f` strictly dominates `pc`. Let us illustrate this property with Fig. 3; registers x_2 and y_2 share the same numbering; they are indeed equal just after the assignment of y_2 but not before.

Next, we describe the Coq implementation for optimizing SSA programs. The implementation takes as input a numbering $\mathcal{N}$, and a partial mapping `crep` that takes as input a register `x` and node `pc` and returns, if it exists, a register `y` such that `x` and `y` are related by the equivalence kernel of $\mathcal{N}$, and the definition of `y` strictly dominates `pc`. For efficiency reasons, we do not check the correctness of `crep` a priori, but lazily during the construction of the optimized program. The optimizer proceeds as follows: first, it checks whether $\mathcal{N}$ satisfies the predicate `GVN_spec`. Then, for each assignment (`Iop op args x pc`) of the original SSA program, the optimizer checks whether `crep` provides a canonical representative `y` for `x` at node `pc`. If so, it checks whether the definition of `y` strictly dominates `pc`; this is achieved by means of a dominance analysis, computed directly inside

Coq with a standard dataflow framework *a la* Kildall. Provided `y` is validated, we can safely replace the previous instruction by a move from `y` to `x`.

We conclude by commenting briefly on the soundness proof of the transformation. It follows a standard forward simulation proof where the correctness of the numbering is proved at the same time as the simulation itself. Noticeably, the CFG normalization turned out to be extremely valuable for this proof. Indeed, consider a step from node pc to node pc′: we have to prove that (`gamma` $\mathcal{N}$ pc′ `rs`) holds, asumming (`gamma` $\mathcal{N}$ pc `rs`). We reason by case analysis: if the instruction at pc is not an `Inop` instruction, we know by normalization that pc′ is not a junction point. In this case, (`def_sdom f x pc′`) is equivalent to (`def_sdom f x pc`) ∨ (`def f x pc`) which is particularly useful to exploit the hypothesis that (`gamma` $\mathcal{N}$ `pc rs`) holds.

7 Implementation and Experimental Results

We have plugged in Compcert 1.8.2 our SSA middle-end made of (i) a Coq normalization (ii) an Ocaml SSA generator and its Coq validator; (iii) an Ocaml GVN inference tool and its Coq validator; (iv) a Coq de-SSA transformation. Our formal development adds 15.000 lines of Coq code and 1.000 lines of Ocaml to the 80.000 lines of Coq and 1.000 lines of Ocaml provided in CompCert. It does not add any axioms to CompCert. We use the Coq extraction mechanism to obtain a SSA-based certified compiler, that we evaluate experimentally using the CompCert benchmarks. These include around 75.000 lines of C code, and fall into three categories of programs (from 20 to 5.000 LoC): small computation kernels, a raytracer, and the theorem prover Spass[2]. Below we briefly comment on three key points: efficiency of the SSA validator; effectiveness of the GVN optimizer; efficiency of generated code.

SSA Validator. In order to be practical, validators must be more efficient than state-of-the-art implementations of the transformations that they validate. At first sight, this criterion may seem too demanding for SSA, since generation into SSA form is performed in almost linear time. However, experimental results are surprisingly good: overall converting a program into SSA form takes approximately twice longer than type-checking the output program. In more detail, the times for SSA generation—specialized to pruned SSA—distribute as follows: (i) 9% for normalization of RTL; (ii) 37% for liveness analysis of RTL (the liveness analysis is provided in the CompCert distribution); (iii) 35% for conversion to SSA using the untrusted OCaml implementation (based on state-of-the-art algorithms); (iv) 19% for validation using the verified validator. This distribution appears to be uniform on all benchmarks except on the biggest functions where the liveness analysis exhibits a non-linear complexity.

GVN Optimizer. We measure the effectiveness of our GVN analyzer by performing a GVN-based CSE right after (Local Value Numbering) LVN-based CSE

[2] Spass is the largest (69.073 LoC), we only use it to evaluate the compilation time.

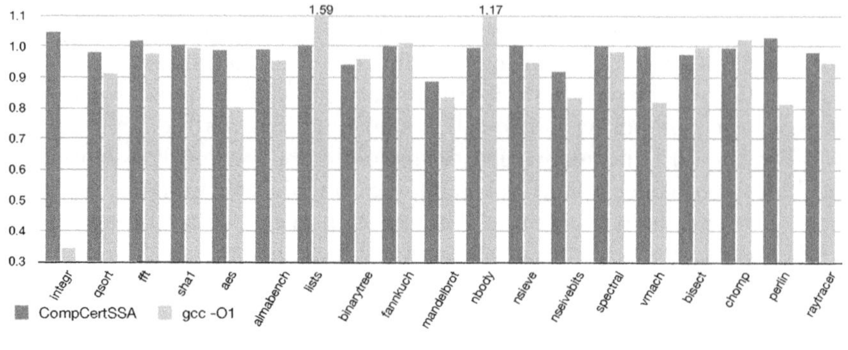

Fig. 10. Execution times of generated code

implemented by CompCert, counting how many additional `Iop` instructions are optimized by this additional CSE phase. To keep the comparison fair, we allow CompCert CSE to optimize around function calls—this is disabled in CompCert to keep the register pressure low. The overall improvement is significative: our global CSE optimizes an additional 25% of `Iop`.

Generated Code. To assess the efficiency of the generated code, we have compiled the benchmarks with three compilers: CompCert, our version of CompCert extended with a SSA middle-end (CompCertSSA), and `gcc -O1`. Fig. 10 gives the execution times *relative* to Compcert (shorter bars mean faster) on PowerPC. The test suite is too small to draw definite conclusions, but the results are encouraging. Our version of CompCert performs slightly better than CompCert. We expect that performance improves significantly by enhancing our middle-end with additional optimizations, and by relying on an SSA-based register allocator.

8 Related Work

Machine-Checked Formalizations. Blech *et al* [3] use the Isabelle/HOL proof assistant to verify the generation of machine code from a representation of SSA programs that relies on term graphs. While graph-based representations may be useful for the untrusted parts of our compiler, they increase the complexity of the formal SSA semantics, and make it a greater challenge to verify SSA-based optimizations. They do not provide an algorithm to convert into SSA form, and leave as future work proving the correctness of SSA-based optimizations. Mansky and Gunter [15] use Isabelle/HOL to formalize and verify the conversion of CFG programs into SSA form. However, their transformation may yield non-minimal SSA, and does not aim extraction into efficient code. Moreover, it is not clear whether their semantics of SSA can be used to reason about optimizations. Zhao *et al* [26] formalize the LLVM intermediate representation in Coq. They define and relate several formal semantics of LLVM, including a static and dynamic semantics. They show how simple code motions can be validated with a simulation relation based on symbolic evaluation, and plan to extend the method to other transformations such as dead code elimination or constant propagation. Finally, there are several machine-checked accounts of Continuation Passing Style translations, e.g. [8], closely related to conversion to SSA form [2].

Translation Validation and Type Systems. Menon *et al* [17] propose a type system that can be used to verify memory safety of programs in SSA form, but their system does not enforce the SSA property. Matsuno and Ohori [16] define a type system equivalent to SSA: every typable program is given a type annotation makeing explicit def-use relations. Their type system is similar to ours except they type check one program w.r.t. annotations while we type check a pair of a RTL and a SSA program. They show that common optimizations such as dead code elimination and CSE are type-preserving. But they do not prove the semantics preservation of the optimizations. Stepp *et al* [21] report on a translation validator for LLVM. Their validator uses Equality Saturation [22], which views optimizations as equality analyses. Their tool does not validate GVN. Tristan *et al* [23] independently report on an a translation validator for LLVM's inter-procedural optimizations. This tool supports GVN, but is currently not certified.

9 Conclusion and Future Work

Our work shows that verified and realistic compilers can rely on a SSA-based middle-end that implements state-of-the-art algorithms, and opens the way for a new generation of verified compilers based on SSA. A priority for further work is to achieve a tighter integration of our middle-end into CompCert. There are three immediate objectives: (i) enhancing our SSA middle-end to handle memory aliases as done by CompCert RTL-based middle-end, (ii) implementing a SSA-based register allocator [9], and (iii) verifying more SSA-based optimizations, including lazy code motion [11]—we expect that our implementation of GVN will provide significant leverage there. Eventually, it should be possible to shift all CompCert optimisations into the SSA middle-end. In the longer term, it would be appealing to apply our methods to LLVM, building on [23,21,26].

Acknowledgments. We thank Xavier Leroy for his thoughtful feedback.

References

1. Alpern, B., Wegman, M.N., Zadeck, F.K.: Detecting equality of variables in programs. In: POPL 1988. ACM (1988)
2. Appel, A.W.: SSA is functional programming. SIGPLAN Notices 33 (1998)
3. Blech, J.O., Glesner, S., Leitner, J., Mülling, S.: Optimizing code generation from SSA form: A comparison between two formal correctness proofs in Isabelle/HOL. In: COCV 2005. ENTCS. Elsevier (2005)

4. Briggs, P., Cooper, K.D., Harvey, T.J., Simpson, L.T.: Practical improvements to the construction and destruction of static single assignment form. In: SPE (1998)
5. Briggs, P., Cooper, K.D., Simpson, L.T.: Value numbering. In: SPE (1997)
6. Companion web page, `http://www.irisa.fr/celtique/ext/compcertSSA`
7. Cytron, R., Ferrante, J., Rosen, B.K., Wegman, M.N., Zadeck, F.K.: Efficiently computing static single assignment form and the control dependence graph. In: ACM TOPLAS (1991)
8. Dargaye, Z., Leroy, X.: Mechanized Verification of CPS Transformations. In: Dershowitz, N., Voronkov, A. (eds.) LPAR 2007. LNCS (LNAI), vol. 4790, pp. 211–225. Springer, Heidelberg (2007)
9. Hack, S., Grund, D., Goos, G.: Register Allocation for Programs in SSA-Form. In: Mycroft, A., Zeller, A. (eds.) CC 2006. LNCS, vol. 3923, pp. 247–262. Springer, Heidelberg (2006)
10. Knoop, J., Koschützki, D., Steffen, B.: Basic-Block Graphs: Living Dinosaurs? In: Koskimies, K. (ed.) CC 1998. LNCS, vol. 1383, pp. 65–79. Springer, Heidelberg (1998)
11. Knoop, J., Rüthing, O., Steffen, B.: Lazy code motion. In: PLDI 1992 (1992)
12. Lengauer, T., Tarjan, R.E.: A fast algorithm for finding dominators in a flowgraph. In: ACM TOPLAS (1979)
13. Leroy, X.: A formally verified compiler back-end. JAR 43(4) (2009)
14. The LLVM compiler infrastructure, `http://llvm.org/`
15. Mansky, W., Gunter, E.: A Framework for Formal Verification of Compiler Optimizations. In: Kaufmann, M., Paulson, L.C. (eds.) ITP 2010. LNCS, vol. 6172, pp. 371–386. Springer, Heidelberg (2010)
16. Matsuno, Y., Ohori, A.: A type system equivalent to static single assignment. In: PPDP 2006. ACM (2006)
17. Menon, V., Glew, N., Murphy, B.R., McCreight, A., Shpeisman, T., Adl-Tabatabai, A.R., Petersen, L.: A verifiable SSA program representation for aggressive compiler optimization. In: POPL 2006, ACM (2006)
18. Necula, G.: Translation validation for an optimizing compiler. In: PLDI 2000. ACM (2000)
19. Pnueli, A., Siegel, M.D., Singerman, E.: Translation Validation. In: Steffen, B. (ed.) TACAS 1998. LNCS, vol. 1384, pp. 151–166. Springer, Heidelberg (1998)
20. Rideau, L., Serpette, B.P., Leroy, X.: Tilting at windmills with Coq: Formal verification of a compilation algorithm for parallel moves. In: JAR (2008)
21. Stepp, M., Tate, R., Lerner, S.: Equality-Based Translation Validator for LLVM. In: Gopalakrishnan, G., Qadeer, S. (eds.) CAV 2011. LNCS, vol. 6806, pp. 737–742. Springer, Heidelberg (2011)
22. Tate, R., Stepp, M., Tatlock, Z., Lerner, S.: Equality saturation: a new approach to optimization. In: POPL 2009. ACM (2009)
23. Tristan, J.B., Govereau, P., Morrisett, G.: Evaluating value-graph translation validation for LLVM. In: PLDI 2011. ACM (2011)
24. Tristan, J.B., Leroy, X.: Verified validation of lazy code motion. In: PLDI 2009. ACM (2009)
25. Tristan, J.B., Leroy, X.: A simple, verified validator for software pipelining. In: POPL 2010. ACM (2010)
26. Zhao, J., Zdancewic, S., Nagarakatte, S., Martin, M.: Formalizing the LLVM intermediate representation for verified program transformation. In: POPL 2012. ACM (2012)

Eventually Consistent Transactions

Sebastian Burckhardt[1], Daan Leijen[1], Manuel Fähndrich[1], and Mooly Sagiv[2]

[1] Microsoft Research
[2] Tel-Aviv University

Abstract. When distributed clients query or update shared data, eventual consistency can provide better availability than strong consistency models. However, programming and implementing such systems can be difficult unless we establish a reasonable consistency model, i.e. some minimal guarantees that programmers can understand and systems can provide effectively.

To this end, we propose a novel consistency model based on *eventually consistent transactions*. Unlike serializable transactions, eventually consistent transactions are ordered by two order relations (visibility and arbitration) rather than a single order relation. To demonstrate that eventually consistent transactions can be effectively implemented, we establish a handful of simple operational rules for managing replicas, versions and updates, based on graphs called *revision diagrams*. We prove that these rules are sufficient to guarantee correct implementation of eventually consistent transactions. Finally, we present two operational models (single server and server pool) of systems that provide eventually consistent transactions.

1 Introduction

Eventual Consistency [17] is a well-known workaround to the fundamental problem of providing CAP [9] (consistency, availability, and partition tolerance) to clients that perform queries and updates against shared data in a distributed system. It weakens traditional consistency guarantees (such as linearizability) in order to allow clients to perform updates against any replica, at any time. Eventually consistent systems guarantee that all updates are eventually delivered to all replicas, and that they are applied in a consistent order.

Eventual consistency is popular with system builders. One reason is that it allows temporarily disconnected replicas to remain fully available to clients. This is particularly useful for implementing clients on mobile devices [20]. Another reason is that it does not require updates to be immediately performed on all server replicas, thus improving scalability. In more theoretical terms, the benefit of eventual consistency can be understood as its ability to *delay* consensus [16].

However, eventual consistency is a weak consistency model that breaks with traditional approaches (e.g. serializable operations) and thus requires developers to be more careful. The essential problem is that updates are not immediately applied globally, thus the conditions under which they are applied are subject to change, which can easily break data invariants. Many eventually consistent systems address this issue by providing higher-level data types to programmers. Still, the semantic details often remain

H. Seidl (Ed.): ESOP 2012, LNCS 7211, pp. 67–86, 2012.

sketchy. Experience has shown that ad-hoc approaches to the semantics and implementation of such systems can lead to surprising behaviors (e.g. a shopping cart where deleted items reappear [7]). To take eventual consistency to its full potential, we need answers to the following questions:

- How can we provide consistency guarantees that are as strong as possible without forsaking lazy consensus?
- How can we effectively understand and implement systems that provide those guarantees?

In this paper, we propose a two-pronged solution that addresses both questions, based on (1) a notion of transactions for eventual consistency, and (2) a general implementation technique based on revision diagrams.

Eventually consistent transactions differ significantly from traditional transactions, as they are not serializable. Nevertheless, they uphold traditional atomicity and isolation guarantees. Even better, they exhibit some strong properties that simplify the life of programmers and are not typically offered by traditional transactions: (1) transactions cannot fail and never roll back, and (2) all code, even long-running tasks, can run inside transactions without compromising performance.

We first present an abstract, concise specification of eventually consistent transactions. This formalization uses mathematical techniques (sets of events, partial orders, and equivalence relations) that are commonly used in research on relaxed memory models and transactional memory. Our definition provides immediate insight on how eventual consistency is related to strong consistency: the only difference is that eventual consistency uses two separate order relations (visibility order and arbitration order) rather than a single order over transactions.

We then proceed to describe a more concrete and operational implementation technique based on *revision diagrams* [6]. Revision diagrams provide implementors with a simple set of rules for managing updates and replicas. Revision diagrams make the fork and join of versions explicit, which determines the visibility and arbitration of transactions. We prove a theorem that guarantees that any system following the revision diagram rules provides eventually consistent transactions according to the abstract definition. We also illustrate the use of revision diagrams by presenting two simple system models (one using a single server, and one using a server pool).

Overall, we make the following contributions:

- We introduce a notion of *eventually consistent transactions* and give a concise and abstract definition.
- We present a systematic approach for building systems that support such transactions, based on *revision diagrams*. We present a precise, operational definition of revision diagrams.
- We prove a theorem stating that the revision diagram rules are sufficient to guarantee eventual consistency. The proof is nontrivial as it depends on deep structural properties of revision diagrams.
- We illustrate the use of revision diagrams by presenting two operational system models, using a single server and a server pool, respectively.

2 Formulation

To get started, we need to establish some precise terminology. Perhaps the very first question is: what is a database? At a high abstraction level, databases are no different than abstract data types, which are semantically defined by the operations they support to update them and retrieve data. Taking cues from common definitions of abstract data types, we define:

Definition 1. *A* query-update *interface is a tuple* (Q, V, U) *where* Q *is an abstract set of query operations,* V *is an abstract set of values returned by queries, and* U *is an abstract set of update operations.*

Note that the sets of queries, query results, and updates are not required to be finite (and usually are not). Query-update interfaces can apply in various scenarios, where they may describe abstract data types, relational databases, or simple random-access memory, for example. For databases, queries are typically defined recursively by a query language.

Example 1. Consider random-access memory that supports loads and stores of bytes in a 64-bit address space $A = \{a \in \mathbb{N} \mid 0 < a \leq 2^{64}\}$. For that example we define $Q = \{\mathit{load}(a) \mid a \in A\}$, $V = \{v \in \mathbb{N} \mid 0 < v \leq 2^8\}$ and $U = \{\mathit{store}(a, v) \mid a \in A \text{ and } v \in V\}$.

This example is excellent for illustration purposes (we will revisit it throughout), and it provides an explicit connection between our results and previous work on relaxed memory models and transactional memory. Of course, most databases also fit in this abstract interface where the queries are SQL queries and the update operations are SQL updates like insertion and deletion.

So far, our interfaces have no inherent meaning. The most direct way to define the semantics of queries and updates is to relate them to some notion of state:

Definition 2. *A* query-update automaton *(QUA) for the interface* (Q, V, U) *is a tuple* (S, s_0) *where* S *is a set of states with (1) an initial state* $s_0 \in S$*, (2) an interpretation* $q^\#$ *of each query* $q \in Q$ *as a function* $S \to V$*, and (3) an interpretation* $u^\#$ *of each update operation* $u \in U$ *as a a function* $S \to S$*.*

Example 2. The random-access memory interface described in Example 1 above can be represented by a QUA (S, s_0) where S is the set of total functions $A \to V$, and where s_0 is the constant function that maps all locations to zero, and where $\mathit{load}(a)^\#(s) = s(a)$ and $\mathit{store}(a, v)^\#(s) = s[a \mapsto v]$.

QUAs can naturally support abstract data types (e.g. collections, or even entire documents) that offer higher-level operations (queries and updates) beyond just loads and stores. Such data types are often important when programming against a weak consistency model [18], since they can ensure that the data representation remains intact when handling concurrent and potentially conflicting updates.

The following two characteristics of QUAs are important to understand how they relate to other definitions of abstract data types:

- There is a strict separation between query and update operations: it is not possible for an operation to both update the data *and* return information to the caller.
- All updates are total functions. It is thus not possible for an update to 'fail'; however, it is of course possible to define updates to have no effect in the case some precondition is not satisfied.

For instance, in our formalization, we would not allow a classic stack abstract data type with a pop operation for two reasons, (1) pop both removes the top element of the stack and returns it, so it is neither an update nor a query, and (2) pop is not total, i.e. it can not be applied to the empty stack.

This restriction is crucial to enable eventual consistency, where the sequencing and application of updates may be delayed, and updates may thus be applied to a different state than the one in which they were originally issued by the program.

2.1 Clients and Transactions

Things become more interesting and challenging once we consider a distributed system. We call the participants of our system *clients*. Clients typically reside on physically distinct devices, but are not required to do so. When clients in a distributed system issue queries and updates against some shared QUA, we need to define what consistency programmers can expect. This consistency model should also address the semantics of *transactions*, which provide clients with the ability to perform several updates as an atomic "bundle".

We formally represent this scenario by defining a set C of clients. Each client, at its own speed, issues a sequence of transactions. Supposedly, each client runs some form of program (the details of which we leave unspecified for simplicity and generality). This program determines when to begin and end a transaction, and what operations to perform in each transaction, which may depend on various factors, such as the results returned by queries, or external factors such as user inputs.

For uniformness, we require that all operations are part of a transaction. This assumption comes at no loss of generality: a device that does not care about transactions can simply issue each operation in its own transaction.

Since all operations are inside transactions, we need not distinguish between the end of a transaction and the beginning of a transaction. Formally, we can thus represent the activities on a device as a stream of operations (queries or updates) interrupted by special yield operations that mark the transaction boundary.[1]

We can thus fully describe the interaction between programs executing on the clients and the database by the following three types of operations:

1. Updates $u \in U$ issued by the program,
2. Pairs (q, v) representing a query $q \in Q$ issued by the program, together with a response $v \in V$ by the database system,
3. The yield operations issued by the program.

[1] We call this operation yield() since it is semantically similar to a yield we may encounter on a uniprocessor performing cooperative multittasking: such a yield marks locations where other threads may read and modify the current state of the data, while at all other locations, only the current thread may read or modify the state.

Definition 3. *A history H for a set C of clients and a query-update interface (Q, V, U) is a map H which maps each client $c \in C$ to a finite or infinite sequence $H(c)$ of operations from the alphabet $\Sigma = U \cup (Q \times V) \cup \{\textit{yield}\}$.*

Note that our history does not a priori include a global ordering of events, since such an order is not always meaningful when working with relaxed consistency models. Rather, the existence of certain orderings, subject to certain conditions, is what determines whether a history satisfies a consistency model or not.

Notation and Terminology. To reason about a history H, it is helpful to introduce the following auxiliary terminology. We let E_H be the set of all *events* in H, by which we mean all occurrences of operations in $\Sigma \setminus \{\text{yield}\}$ in the sequences $H(c)$ (we consider yield to be just a marker within the operation sequence, but not an event).

For a client c, we call a maximal nonempty contiguous subsequence of events in $H(c)$ that does not contain yield a *transaction* of c. We call a transaction *committed* if it is succeeded by a yield operation, and uncommitted otherwise. We let T_H be the set of all transactions of all clients, and $\textit{committed}(T_H) \subseteq T_H$ the subset of all committed transactions. For an event e, we let $\textit{trans}(e) \in T_H$ be the transaction that contains e. Moreover, we let $\textit{committed}(E_H) \subseteq E_H$ be the subset of events that are contained in committed transactions. We conclude by giving definitions related to ordering events and transactions:

- *Program order*. For a given history H, we define a partial order $<_p$ over events in H such that $e <_p e'$ iff e appears before e' in some sequence $H(c)$.
- *Apply in order*. For a history H, for a state $s \in S$, for a subset of events $E' \subset E_H$, and for a total order $<$ over the events in E', we let $\textit{apply}(E', <, s)$ be the state obtained by applying all updates appearing in E' to the state s, in the order specified by $<$.
- *Factoring*. We define an equivalence relation $\sim_t$ (same-transaction) over events such that $e \sim_t e'$ iff $\textit{trans}(e) = \textit{trans}(e')$. For any partial order $\prec$ over events, we say that $\prec$ *factors* over $\sim_t$ iff for any events x and y from different transactions, $x \prec y$ implies $x' \prec y'$ for any x, y such that $x \sim_t x'$ and $y \sim_t y'$. This is an important property to have for any ordering $\prec$, since if $\prec$ factors over $\sim_t$, it induces a corresponding partial order on the transactions.

2.2 Sequential Consistency

Sequential consistency posits that the observed behavior must be consistent with an interleaving of the transactions by the various devices. We formalize this interleaving as a partial order over events (rather than a total order as more commonly used) since some events are not instantly ordered by the system; for example, the relative order of operations in uncommitted transactions may not be fully determined yet.

Definition 4. *A history H is* sequentially consistent *if there exists a partial order $<$ over the events in E_H that satisfies the following conditions for all events $e_1, e_2, e \in E_H$:*

- *(compatible with program order) if* $e_1 <_p e_2$ *then* $e_1 < e_2$
- *(total order on past events) if* $e_1 < e$ *and* $e_2 < e$ *then either* $e_1 < e_2$ *or* $e_2 < e_1$.
- *(consistent query results) for all* $(q, v) \in E_H$, $v = q^\#(apply(\{e \in (H) \mid e < q\}, <, s_0))$. *This simply says that a query returns the state as it results from applying all past updates to the initial state.*
- *(atomicity)* $<$ *factors over* $\sim_t$.
- *(isolation) if* $e_1 \notin committed(E_H)$ *and* $e_1 < e_2$, *then* $e_1 <_p e_2$. *That is, events in uncommitted transactions precede only events on the same client.*
- *(eventual delivery) for all committed transactions* $t \in committed(T_H)$, *there exist only finitely many transactions* $t' \in T_H$ *such that* $t \not< t'$.

Sequential consistency fundamentally limits availability in the presence of network partitions. The reason is that any query issued by some transaction t *must* see the effect of all updates that occur in transactions that are globally ordered before t, even if on a remote device. Thus we cannot conclusively commit transactions in the presence of network partitions.

2.3 Eventual Consistency

Eventual consistency relaxes sequential consistency by allowing queries in a transaction t to see only a subset of all transactions that are globally ordered before t. It does so by distinguishing between a visibility order (a partial order that defines what updates are visible to a query), and an arbitration order (a partial order that determines the relative order of updates).

Definition 5. *A history* H *is* eventually consistent *if there exist two partial orders* $<_v$ *(the visibility order) and* $<_a$ *(the arbitration order) over events in* H, *such that the following conditions are satisfied for all events* $e_1, e_2, e \in E_H$:

- *(arbitration extends visibility) if* $e_1 <_v e_2$ *then* $e_1 <_a e_2$.
- *(total order on past events) if* $e_1 <_v e$ *and* $e_2 <_v e$, *then either* $e_1 <_a e_2$ *or* $e_2 <_a e_1$.
- *(compatible with program order) if* $e_1 <_p e_2$ *then* $e_1 <_v e_2$.
- *(consistent query results) for all* $(q, v) \in E_H$, $v = q^\#(apply(\{e \in H) \mid e <_v q\}, <_a, s_0))$. *This says that a query returns the state as it results from applying all preceding* visible *updates (as determined by the visibility order) to the initial state, in the order given by the arbitration order.*
- *(atomicity) Both* $<_v$ *and* $<_a$ *factor over* $\sim_t$.
- *(isolation) if* $e_1 \notin committed(E_H)$ *and* $e_1 <_v e_2$, *then* $e_1 <_p e_2$. *That is, events in uncommitted transactions are visible only to later events by the same client.*
- *(eventual delivery) for all committed transactions* $t \in committed(T_H)$, *there exist only finitely many transactions* $t' \in T_H$ *such that* $t \not<_v t'$.

The reason why eventual consistency can tolerate temporary network partitions is that the arbitration order can be constructed incrementally, i.e. may remain only partially determined for some time after a transaction commits. This allows conflicting updates to be committed even in the presence of network partitions.

Note that eventual consistency is a weaker consistency model than sequential consistency. We can prove this statement as follows.

Lemma 1. *A sequentially consistent history is eventually consistent.*

Proof. Given a history H that is sequentially consistent, we know there exists a partial order $<$ satisfying all conditions. Now define $<_v = <_a = <$; then all conditions for eventual consistency follow easily.

2.4 Eventual Consistency in Related Work

Eventual consistency across the literature uses a variety of techniques to propagate updates (e.g. general causally-ordered broadcast [18,19], or pairwise anti-entropy [15]). All of these techniques are particular implementations that specialize our general definition of visibility as a partial order. As for the arbitration order, we found that two main approaches prevail. The most common one is to use (logical or actual) *timestamps*: Timestamps provide a simple way to arbitrate events. Another approach (sometimes combined with timestamps) is to make updates *commutative*, which makes arbitration unnecessary (i.e. we can pick an arbitrary serialization of the visibility order to satisfy the conditions in Def. 5).

We show in the next section (Section 3) how to arbitrate updates without using timestamps or requiring commutativity, a feature that sets our work apart. We prefer to not use timestamps because they exhibit the *write stabilization* problem [20], i.e. the inability to finalize the effect of updates while older updates may still linger in disconnected network partitions. Consider, for example, a mobile user called Robinson performing an important update, but getting stranded on a disconnected island before transmitting it. When Robinson reconnects after years of exile, Robinson's update is older than (and may thus alter the effect of) all the updates committed by other users in the meantime. So either (1) none of these updates can stabilize until Robinson returns, or (2) after some timeout we give up on Robinson and discard his update. Clearly, neither of these solutions is satisfactory. A better solution is to abandon time stamps and instead use an arbitration order that simply orders Robinson's update *after* all the other updates. In fact, this is the outcome we achieve when using revision diagrams, as explained in Section 3.

3 Revision Consistency

Our definition of eventual consistency (Def. 5) is concise and general. By itself, it is however not very constructive, insofar that it does not give practical guidelines as to how a system can efficiently and correctly construct the necessary ordering (visibility and arbitration). We now proceed to describe a more specific implementation technique for eventually consistent systems, based on the notion of *revision diagrams* introduced in [6].

Revision diagrams show an extended history not only of the queries, updates, and transactions by each client, but also of the forking and joining of *revisions*, which are logical replicas of the state (Fig. 1). A client works with one revision at a time, and can perform operations (queries and updates) on it. Since different clients work with different revisions, clients can perform both queries and updates concurrently and in isolation (i.e. without creating race conditions). Reconciliation happens during *join* operations. When a revision *joins* another revision, it replays all the updates performed in the joined revision at the join point.[2] After a revision is joined, no more operations can be performed on it (i.e. clients may need to fork new revisions to keep enough revisions available).

3.1 Revision Diagrams

Revision diagrams are directed graphs constructed from three types of edges (successor, fork, and join edges, or s-, f- and j-edges for short), and five types of vertices (start, fork, join, update, and query vertices). A start vertex represents the beginning of a revision, s-edges represent successors within a revision, and fork/join edges represent the forking and joining of revisions.

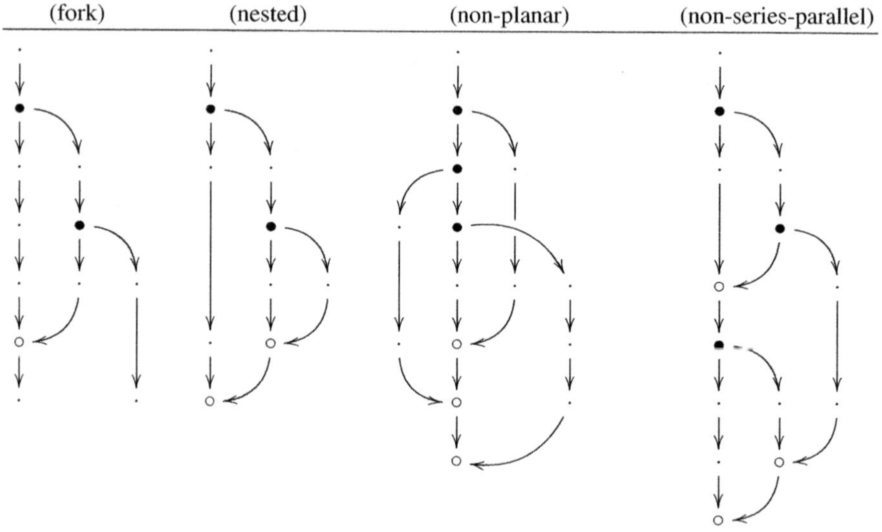

Fig. 1. Examples of Valid Revision Diagrams

We pictorially represent revision diagrams using the following conventions

- Use · for start, query, and update vertices
- Use • and ∘ for fork and join vertices, respectively
- Use vertical down-arrows for s-edges
- Use horizontal-to-vertical curved arrows for f-edges
- Use vertical-to-horizontal curved arrows for j-edges

A vertex x has a s-path (i.e. a path contanining only s-edges) to vertex y if and only if they are part of the same revision. Since all s-edges are vertical in our pictures,

[2] This replay operation is *conceptual*. Rather than replaying a potentially unbounded log, actual implementations can often use much more space- and time-efficient merge functions, as explained in Section 4.

vertices belonging to the same revision are always aligned vertically. For any vertex x we let $S(x)$ be the start vertex of the revision that x belongs to. For any vertex x whose start vertex $S(x)$ is not the root, we define $F(x)$ to be the fork vertex such that $F(x) \xrightarrow{f} S(x)$ (i.e. the fork vertex that started the revision x belongs to). We call a vertex with no outgoing s- or j-edges a *terminal*; terminals are the last operation in a revision that can still perform operations (has not been joined yet), and thus represent potential extension points of the graph.

We now give a formal, constructive definition for revision diagrams.

Definition 6. *A* revision diagram *is a directed graph constructed by applying a (possibly empty or infinite) sequence of the following construction steps (see Fig 2(a)) to a single initial start vertex (called the root):*

Query. *Choose some terminal* t*, create a new query vertex* x*, and add an edge* $t \xrightarrow{s} x$.
Update. *Choose some terminal* t*, create a new update vertex* x*, and add an edge* $t \xrightarrow{s} x$.
Fork. *Choose some terminal* t*, create a new fork vertex* x *and a new start vertex* y*, and add edges* $t \xrightarrow{s} x$ *and* $x \xrightarrow{f} y$.
Join. *Choose two terminals* t, t' *satisfying the* ***join condition*** $F(t') \rightarrow^* t$*, then create a new join vertex* x *and add edges* $t \xrightarrow{s} x$ *and* $t' \xrightarrow{j} x$.

The join condition expresses that the terminal t (the "joiner") must be reachable from the *fork* vertex that started the revision that contains t' (the "joinee"). This condition makes revision diagrams more restricted than general task graphs. See Fig 2(b) for some examples of invalid diagrams where the join condition does not hold at construction of the join nodes.

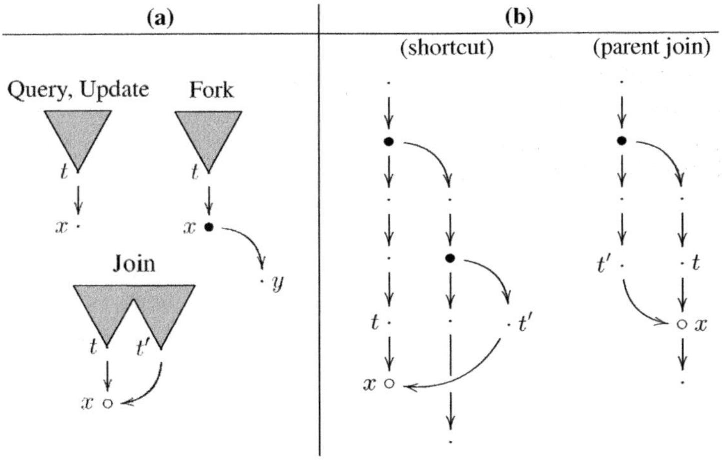

Fig. 2. (a) (left) Visualization of the construction rules for revision diagrams in Def. 6. **(b)** (right) Examples of *invalid* revision diagrams. Both diagrams are not possible since they violate the join property at the creation of the join node x. Note that in the right diagram, $F(t')$ is undefined on the main revision and therefore $F(t') \rightarrow^* t$ does not hold.

The join condition has some important, not immediately obvious consequences. For example, it implies that revision diagrams are always semilattices (for a proof of this nontrivial fact see [6]). Also, it ensures some diagram properties (Lemmas 2 and 3) that we need to prove our main result (Thm. 1). Futhermore, it still allows more general graphs than strict series-parallel graphs [21], which allow only the recursive serial and parallel composition of tasks (and are also called fork-join concurrency in some contexts, which is potentially misleading). For instance, the right-most revision diagram in Fig. 1 is not a series-parallel graph but it is a valid revision diagram. While series-parallel graphs are easier to work with than revision diagrams, they are not flexible enough for our purpose, since they would enforce too much synchronization between participants.

Also, note that fork and the join are fundamentally asymmetric: the revision that initiates the fork (the "forker") continues to exist after the fork, but also starts a new revision (the "forkee"), and similarly, the revision that initiates the join (the "joiner") can continue to perform operations after the join, but ends the joined revision (the "joinee").

3.2 Graph Properties

We now examine some properties of the revision diagrams, for better visualization, and because we need some technical properties in our later proofs. Most statements are easily proved by induction over the construction rules in Def. 6; if not, we mention how to prove them.

Revision diagrams are connected, and all vertices are reachable from the root vertex. There can be multiple paths from the root to a given vertex, but exactly one of those is free of j-edges.

Definition 7. *For any vertex v in a revision diagram, let the* root-path *of v be the unique path from the root to v that does not contain j-edges.*

The join condition does not make revision diagrams necessarily planar, i.e. when drawing revision diagrams, it is not always possible to avoid crossing lines (see the third diagram in Fig. 1 for an example). However, it is always possible to choose horizontal coordinates for the vertices such that (1) vertices in the same revisions are vertically aligned, and (2) revisions are horizontally arranged such that forkers are left of forkees, and (3) joiners are left of joinees. The existence of such an order is not immediately obvious; for example, such a layout is not possible for the incorrect revision diagram at the right in Fig. 2(b). The following lemma formalizes the claims (1,2,3) above (where the preorder $\leq_l$ corresponds to a relation on vertices that compares their horizontal coordinates):

Lemma 2. *[Layout Preorder] In any revision diagram, there exists a preorder $\leq_l$ on vertices*[3] *such that*

$$S(x) = S(y) \quad \Leftrightarrow \quad (x \leq_l y) \wedge (y \leq_l x) \tag{1}$$

$$x \xrightarrow{f} y \quad \Rightarrow \quad x \leq_l y \tag{2}$$

$$x \xrightarrow{j} y \quad \Rightarrow \quad y \leq_l x \tag{3}$$

[3] A *preorder* is a reflexive transitive binary relation. Unlike partial orders, preorders are not necessarily antisymmetric, i.e. they may contain cycles.

We include the proof in the full version [4]. For proving our main result later on, we need to establish another basic fact about revision diagrams. We call a path *direct* if all of its f-edges (if any) appear after all of its j-edges (if any). The following lemma (which appears as a theorem in [6], and for which we include a proof in [4] as well) shows that we can always choose direct paths:

Lemma 3 (Direct Paths.). *Let x, y be vertices in a revision diagram. If $x \rightarrow^* y$, there exists a direct path from x to y.*

3.3 Query and Update Semantics

We now proceed to explain how to determine the results of a query in a revision diagram. The basic idea is to (1) return a result that is consistent with applying all the updates along the root path, and (2) if there are join vertices along that path, they summarize the effect of *all* updates by the joined revision.

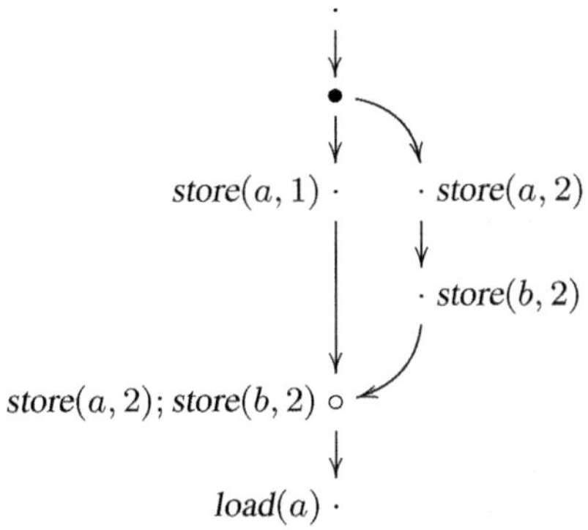

Fig. 3. A labeled revision diagram. The *path-result* of the bottom vertex is now the query applied to its root-path: $\mathit{load}(a)^\#(\mathit{store}(b,2)^\#(\mathit{store}(a,2)^\#(\mathit{store}(a,1)^\#(s_0)))) = 2$.

For example, consider the diagram in Fig. 3. This is an example of a revision diagram labeled with the operations of the random access memory example described in Example 2. The join vertex is labeled with the composition of all update operations of the joinee. The *path-result* of the final query node $\mathit{load}(a)$ can now be evaluated by applying to the composition of all update operations along the root-path: $\mathit{load}(a)^\#(\mathit{store}(b,2)^\#(\mathit{store}(a,2)^\#(\mathit{store}(a,1)^\#(s_0)))) = 2$.

We can define this more formally. To reduce the verbosity of our definitions, we assume a fixed query-update interface (Q, V, U) and QUA (S, s_0) for the rest of this section.

Definition 8. *For any vertex x, we let the* effect *of x be a function $x^\circ : S \rightarrow S$ defined inductively as follows:*

- *If x is a start, fork, or query vertex, the effect is a no-op, i.e. $x^\circ(s) = s$.*
- *If x is an update vertex for the update operation u, then the effect is that update, i.e. $x^\circ(s) = u^\#(s)$.*

– *If x is a join vertex, then the effect is the composition of all effects in the joined revision, i.e. if $y_1, \ldots, y_n$ is the sequence of vertices in the joined revision (i.e. y_1 is a start vertex, $y_i \xrightarrow{s} y_{i+1}$ for all $1 \leq i < n$, and $y_n \xrightarrow{j} x$), then $x^\circ(s) = y_n^\circ(y_{n-1}^\circ(\cdots y_1^\circ(s)))$.*

We can then define the expected query result as follows.

Definition 9. *Let x be a query vertex with query q, and let $(y_1, \ldots, y_n, x)$ be the root path of x. Then define the* path*-result of x as $q^\#(y_n^\circ(y_{n-1}^\circ(\cdots y_1^\circ(s_0))))$.*

3.4 Revision Diagrams and Histories

We can naturally relate histories to revision diagrams by associating each query event $(q, v) \in E_H$ with a query vertex, and each update event $u \in E_H$ with a update vertex. The intention is to validate the query results in the history using the path results, and to keep transactions atomic and isolated by ensuring that their events form contiguous sequences within a revision.

Definition 10. *We call a revision diagram a* witness *for the history H if it satisfies the following conditions:*

1. *For all query events (q, v) in E_H, the value v matches the path-result of the query vertex.*
2. *If x, y are two successive non-*yield *operations in $H(c)$ for some c, then they must be connected by a s-edge.*
3. *If x is the last event of $H(c)$ for some c and not a* yield*, then it must be a terminal.*
4. *If x, y are two operations preceding and succeeding some* yield *in $H(c)$ for some c, then there must exist a path from x to y. In other words, the beginning of a transaction must be reachable from the end of the previous transaction.*

We call a history H revision-consistent *if there exists a witness revision diagram.*

To ensure eventual delivery of updates, we need to somehow make sure there are enough forks and joins. To formulate a liveness condition on infinite histories, we define "neglected vertices" as follows:

Definition 11. *We call a vertex x in a revision diagram* neglected *if there exists an infinite number of vertices y such that there is no path from x to y.*

We are now ready to state and prove our main result.

Theorem 1. *Let H be a history. If there exists a witness diagram for H such that no committed events are neglected, then H is eventually consistent.*

Note that this theorem gives us a solid basis for implementing eventually consistent transactions: an implementation can be based on dynamically constructing a witness revision diagram and as a consequence guarantee eventual consistent transactions. Moreover, as we will see in Section 4, implementations do not need to actually construct such witness diagrams at runtime but can rely on efficient state-based implementations.

The proof of our Theorem (in Section 3.5 below) constructs partial orders $<_v, <_a$ from the revision diagram by (1) specifying $x <_v y$ iff there is a path from x to y in the revision diagram, and (1) specifying $<_a$ to order all events in a joined revision to occur in between the joiner terminal and the join vertex. Note that the converse of Thm. 1 is not true, not even if restricted to finite histories (we include a finite counterexample in the full version [4]). Also Note that the most difficult part of the proof is the safety, not the liveness, since the proof that $<_a$ is a partial order extending $<_v$ depends on the join condition in a nontrivial way.

3.5 Proof of Thm 1

We devote the rest of this section to this proof, which requires some deeper insight into structural properties of revision diagrams. First, however, we need some definitions, notations, and lemmas.

A revision diagrams is a connected graph. However, if we remove all f-edges from the picture, it may decompose into several components. We define a *join-component* to be a maximal component connected by s and j edges only. We say $x \sim_j y$ if they are in the same join component, and let $J(x) = \{y \mid x \sim_j y\}$. It is easy to see that each join-component contains exactly one terminal. For a vertex x, we let $T(x)$ be the terminal of $J(x)$ (note that $T(x)$ is the unique terminal reachable from x by a path containing j and s edges only).

Definition 12. *Define the binary relation $\rightarrow_a$ on vertices by adding the following edges during the construction of a revision diagram as in Def. 6:*

- ***(Query, Update, Fork)*** *for all $y \in J(t)$, add $y \rightarrow_a x$*
- ***(Join)*** *for all $y \in J(t)$ and $y' \in J(t')$, add edges $y \rightarrow_a x$, $y' \rightarrow_a x$, and $y \rightarrow_a y'$.*

Lemma 4. *For any revision diagram, $\rightarrow_a$ as defined above is a partial order over all vertices in the diagram satisfying (1) when restricted to any one join-component, $\rightarrow_a$ is a total order (2) $\rightarrow_a$ does not cross join-components.*

Lemma 5. *For vertices x, y in a revision diagram and a preorder $\leq_l$ as guaranteed by Lemma 2, $x \rightarrow^* y$ implies $T(x) \leq_l T(y)$.*

We include proofs for both lemmas in [4]. The first one is a simple induction, the second one is a bit more intricate and uses the path properties guaranteed by Lemma 3 and the layout preorder guaranteed by Lemma 2.

We are now ready to prove Theorem 1. Given a history H and a witness revision diagram, define two binary relations

$$<_v = \rightarrow^* \quad \text{and} \quad <_a = (<_v \cup \rightarrow_a)^*.$$

By Lemma 6 below, $<_a$ and $<_v$ are partial orders. We can then prove the remaining claims as follows:

- (arbitration extends visibility) By Lemma 6 below.

- (total order on past events) if $e_1 <_v e$ and $e_2 <_v e$, then by Lemma 3 there exist direct paths for $e_1 \to^* e$ and for $e_2 \to^* e$. If either path is a prefix of the other, e_1 and e_2 are ordered by $<_v$ and thus by $<_a$. If not, they must combine in a join vertex, implying that $e_1 \sim_j e_2$, which implies (by Lemma 4) that they are ordered by $<_a$.
- (compatible with program order) By conditions 2 and 4 of Def. 10.
- (consistent query results) We can show inductively (over Def. 6) that for any vertex x, the combined effect of the vertices on the root path (as in Def. 8) to x is equal to the combined effect of all updates $\{x' \mid x' <_v x\}$ ordered by $<_a$. This is trivial for all but the join case. In the join case, Def. 12 orders all all updates in the joinee after updates in the joiner which is consistent with interpreting them as an effect of the join vertex.
- (atomicity) By condition 2 we know there can be no intervening forks or joins. This implies that both $\to$ and $<_a$ factor over $\sim_t$.
- (isolation) By condition 3.
- (eventual delivery) Assume the condition is violated. Then there exists a committed transaction $t \in \mathit{committed}(T_H)$ and an infinite number of transactions $t_1, t_2, \ldots$ such that for all $i, t \not<_v t_i$. Since transactions can not be empty, we can pick vertices $x \in t$ and $x_i \in t_i$, with $x \not<_v x_i$ for all i. But that implies that x is neglected, contradicting the condition in the theorem.

The only thing left to prove is the lemma below, which arguably contains the most interesting part of the proof. In particular, it shows how consequences of the join condition (specifically, Lemmas 2 and 5) are used in the construction of an arbitration order $<_a$ that satisfies $<_v \subseteq <_a$ as required for eventual consistency.

Lemma 6. *Given some revision diagram, define binary relations* $<_v = \to^*$ *and* $<_a = (<_v \cup \to_a)^*$. *Then both* $<_v$ *and* $<_a$ *are partial orders, and* $<_v \subseteq <_a$.

Proof. Clearly, $<_v$ is a partial order (since revision diagrams are acyclic) and $<_v \subseteq <_a$. The interesting part is to show that $<_a$ is antisymmetric (i.e. $x <_a y$ and $y <_a x$ implies $x = y$). We prove this by showing that $(\to_a \cup \to)$ is acyclic. Consider some minimal cycle. Since $\to_a$ is transitive, and both $\to_a$ and $\to$ are acyclic on their own, it must be of the following form (where $n \geq 1$):

$$x_1 \to^* y_1 \to_a x_2 \to^* y_2 \to_a \ldots \to_a x_n \to^* y_n \to_a x_1$$

By Lemma 4 this implies

$$x_1 \to^* y_1 \sim_j x_2 \to^* y_2 \sim_j \ldots \to_a x_n \to^* y_n \sim_j x_1$$

using the preorder guaranteed by Lemma 2 and Lemma 5, we get

$$T(x_1) \leq_l T(y_1) = T(x_2) \leq_l T(y_2) \ldots T(x_n) \leq_l T(y_n) = T(x_1)$$

But by Lemma 2 such an $\leq_l$-cycle implies that all vertices are in the same revision which is a contradiction.

4 System Implementation

Revision diagrams can help to develop efficient implementations since they provide a solid abstraction that decouples the consistency model from actual implementation choices. In this section, we describe some implementation techniques that are likely to be useful for that purpose. We present three sketches of client-server systems that implement eventual consistency.

It is usually not necessary for implementations to store the actual revision diagram. Rather, we found it highly convenient to work with state representations that can directly provide fork and join operations.

Definition 13. *A* fork-join QUA *(FJ-QUA) for a query-update interface* (Q, V, U) *is a tuple* (Σ, σ_0, f, j) *where (1)* (Σ, σ_0) *is a QUA over* (Q, V, U)*, (2)* $f : \Sigma \to \Sigma \times \Sigma$*, and (3)* $j : \Sigma \times \Sigma \to \Sigma$.

If we have a fork-join QUA, we can simply associate a Σ-state with each revision, and then perform all queries and updates locally on that state, without communicating with other revisions. The join function of the FJ-QUA, if implemented correctly, guarantees that all updates are applied at the join time. We can state this more formally as follows.

Definition 14. *For a FJ-QUA* (Σ, σ_0, f, j) *and a revision diagram over the same interface* (Q, V, U)*, define the state* $\sigma(x)$ *of each vertex* x *inductively by setting* $\sigma(r) = \sigma_0$ *for the initial vertex* r*, and (for the construction rules as they appear in Def. 6)*

- *(Query) Let* $\sigma(x) = \sigma(t)$
- *(Update) Let* $\sigma(x) = u^{\#}(\sigma(t))$
- *(Fork) Let* $(\sigma(x), \sigma(y)) = f(\sigma(t))$
- *(Join) Let* $\sigma(x) = j(\sigma(t), \sigma(t'))$

Definition 15. *A FJ-QUA* (Σ, σ_0, f, j) implements *the QUA* (S, s_0) *over the same interface if and only if for all revision diagrams, for all vertices* x*, the locally computed state* $\sigma(x)$ *(as in Def. 14) matches the path result (as in Def. 9).*

Example 3. Consider the QUA representing random access memory as defined in Example 2. We can implement this QUA using an FJ-QUA that maintains a "write-set" as follows:

$$\begin{aligned}
\Sigma &= S \times \mathcal{P}(A) \\
\sigma_0 &= (s_0, \emptyset) \\
\mathsf{load}(a)^{\#}(s, W) &= s(a) \\
\mathsf{store}(a, v)^{\#}(s, W) &= (s[a \mapsto v], W \cup \{a\}) \\
f(s, W) &= ((s, W), (s, \emptyset)) \\
j((s_1, W_1), (s_2, W_2)) &= (s', W_1 \cup W_2) \quad \text{where } s'(a) = \begin{cases} s_1(a) \text{ if } a \notin W_2 \\ s_2(a) \text{ if } a \in W_2 \end{cases}
\end{aligned}$$

The write set (together with the current state) provides sufficient information to conceptually replay all updates during join (since only the last written value matters). Note that the write set gets cleared on forks.

Since we can store a log of updates inside Σ, it is always possible to provide an FJ-QUA for any QUA (we show this construction in detail in the full version [4]). However, more space-effective implementations are often possible for QUAs since logs are typically compressible. We include several finite-state examples of FJ-QUAs in [4] as well.

4.1 System Models

If we have a FJ-QUA, we can implement eventually consistent systems quite easily. We now present two models that demonstrate this principle.

4.2 Single Synchronous Server Model

We first present a model using a single server. We define the set of devices $I = C \cup \{s\}$ where C is the set of clients and s is the single server. We store on each device i a state from the FJ-QUA, that is, we define $R : I \rightharpoonup \Sigma$. To keep the transition rules simple, we use the notation $R[i \mapsto \sigma]$ to denote the map R modified by mapping i to σ, and we let $R(c \mapsto \sigma)$ be a pattern that matches R, c, and σ such that $R(c) = \sigma$. Each client can perform updates and queries while reading and writing only the local state:

$$\text{UPDATE}(c,u)\text{:}\quad \frac{\sigma' = u^{\#}(\sigma)}{R(c \mapsto \sigma) \to R[c \mapsto \sigma']} \qquad\qquad \text{QUERY}(c,q,v)\text{:}\quad \frac{q^{\#}(\sigma) = v}{R(c \mapsto \sigma) \to R}$$

As for synchronization, all we need is two rules, one to create a new client (forking the server state), and one to perform the yield on the client (joining the client state into the server, then forking a fresh client state from the server):

$$\text{SPAWN}(c)\text{:}\quad \frac{c \notin dom\, R \qquad f(\sigma) = (\sigma_1, \sigma_2)}{R(s \mapsto \sigma) \to R[s \mapsto \sigma_1][c \mapsto \sigma_2]} \qquad \text{YIELD}(c)\text{:}\quad \frac{j(\sigma_1, \sigma_2) = \sigma_3 \qquad f(\sigma_3) = (\sigma_4, \sigma_5)}{R(s \mapsto \sigma_1)(c \mapsto \sigma_2) \to R[s \mapsto \sigma_4][c \mapsto \sigma_5]}$$

Thanks to Theorem 1, we can precisely argue why this system is eventually consistent. By induction over the transitions, we can show that each state σ appearing in R corresponds to a terminal in the revision diagram, and each transition rule manipulates those terminals (applying fork, join, update or query) in accordance with the revision diagram construction rules. In particular, the join condition is always satisfied since all forks and joins are performed by the same server revision. Transactions are not interrupted by forks or joins, and no vertices are neglected: each yield creates a path from the freshly committed vertices into the server revision, from where it must be visible to any new clients, and to any client that performs an infinite number of yields.

An interesting observation is that, if the fork does not modify the left component (i.e. for all $\sigma \in \Sigma$, $f(\sigma) = (\sigma, \sigma')$ for some σ'), the server is effectively stateless, in the sense that it does not store any information about the client. This is a highly desirable characteristics for scalability, and in our experience it is well worth to go through some extra length in defining FJ-QUAs that have this property.

4.3 Server Pool Model

The single server model still suffers some drawbacks. For one, clients performing a yield access both server and client state. This means clients block if they have no connection. Also, a single server may not scale to large numbers of clients.

We can fix both of these issues by using a *server pool* rather than a single server, i.e. we let the set of devices be $I = C \cup S$ where S is a set of server identifiers. Using multiple servers not only improves scalability, but it helps with disconnected operation as well: if we keep one server next to each client (e.g. on the same mobile device), we can guarantee that the client does not block on yield. Servers themselves can perform a sync operation (at any convenient time) to exchange state with other servers.

However, we need to keep additional information in each device to ensure that the join condition is maintained. We do so by (1) storing on each client c a pair (σ, n) where σ is the revision state as before, and n is a counter indicating the current transaction, and (2) storing on each server s a triple (σ, J, L) where σ is the revision state as before, J is the set of servers that s may join, and L is a vectorclock (a partial function $(I \rightarrow \mathbb{N})$) indicating for each client the latest transaction of c that s may join.

The transitions that involve the client are then as follows:

UPDATE(c, u):
$$\frac{\sigma' = u^{\#}(\sigma)}{R(c \mapsto (\sigma, n)) \rightarrow R[c \mapsto (\sigma', n)]}$$

QUERY(c, q, v):
$$\frac{q^{\#}(\sigma) = v}{R(c \mapsto (\sigma, L)) \rightarrow R}$$

SPAWN(c):
$$\frac{c \notin dom\, R \qquad f(\sigma) = (\sigma_1, \sigma_2) \qquad L' = L[c \mapsto 0]}{R(s \mapsto (\sigma, J, L)) \rightarrow R[s \mapsto (\sigma_1, J, L')][c \mapsto (\sigma_2, 0)]}$$

YIELD(s, c):
$$\frac{L(c) = n \qquad L' = L[c \mapsto n+1] \qquad j(\sigma_1, \sigma_2) = \sigma_3 \qquad f(\sigma_3) = (\sigma_4, \sigma_5)}{R(s \mapsto (\sigma_1, J, L))(c \mapsto (\sigma_2, n)) \rightarrow R[s \mapsto (\sigma_4, J, L')][c \mapsto (\sigma_5, n+1)]}$$

The servers can perform forks and joins without involving clients. On joins, servers join the state, take the union of the sets J of joinable servers, and merge the vector clocks (defined as taking the pointwise maximum).

FORK(s_1, s_2):
$$\frac{s_2 \notin dom\, R \qquad f(\sigma) = (\sigma_1, \sigma_2) \qquad J' = J \cup \{s_2\}}{R(s_1 \mapsto (\sigma, J, L)) \rightarrow R[s_1 \mapsto (\sigma_1, J', L)][s_2 \mapsto (\sigma_2, J, L)]}$$

JOIN(s_1, s_2):
$$\frac{s_2 \in J_1 \qquad \sigma' = j(\sigma_1, \sigma_2) \qquad J' = J_1 \cup J_2 \qquad L' = merge(L_1, L_2)}{R(s_1 \mapsto (\sigma_1, J_1, L_1))(s_2 \mapsto (\sigma_2, J_2, L_2)) \rightarrow R[s_1 \mapsto (\sigma', J', L')][s_2 \mapsto \bot]}$$

Again, we can use Theorem 1 to reason that finite executions of this system are eventually consistent (for infinite executions we need additional fairness guarantees as discussed below). Again, all states σ stored in R correspond to terminals in a revision diagram and are manipulated according to the rules. This time, the join condition is satisfied because of the following invariants: (1) if the set J of server s_1 contains s_2, then s_1's terminal is reachable from the fork vertex that forked s_2's revision, and (2) if $L(c) = n$ for server s, and client c's transaction counter is n, then s' terminal is reachable from the fork vertex that forked c's revision.

Since the transition rules do not contain any guarantees that force servers to synchronize with each other, it is possible to construct infinite executions that violate eventual consistency. Actual implementations would thus likely add a mechanism to guarantee that updates eventually reach the main revision, and that clients that perform an infinite sequence of transactions receive versions from the main revision infinitely often.

5 Related Work

For a high-level comparison of our work with various notions of eventual consistency appearing in the literature, see Section 2.4. Briefly stated, our work is set apart by its unique use of *revision diagrams* to determine both arbitration and visibility, rather than separately using a causally consistent partial order for visibility, and timestamps for arbitration.

There is of course a large body of work on transactions. Most academic work considers strong consistency (serializable transactions) only, and is thus not directly applicable to eventual consistency. Nevertheless there are some similarities, to pick a few:

- [10] provides insight on the limitations of serializable transactions, and proposes similar workarounds as used by eventual consistency (timestamps and commutative updates). However, transactions remain tentative during disconnection.
- Snapshot isolation [8] relaxes the consistency model, but transactions can still fail, and can not commit in the presence of network partitions.
- Coarse-grained transactions [11,14] share with our work the use of abstract data types to facilitate concurrent transactions.
- Automatic Mutual Exclusion [1], like our work, uses yield statements to separate transactions.

Previous work on revisions [2,6,3,5] introduces revision diagrams and conflict resolution. In this paper we feature a simpler, more direct definition using graph construction rules. Also, we pursue a different goal (eventually consistent transactions in a distributed system, rather than deterministic parallel programming). In particular, eventually consistent transactions exhibit pervasive nondeterminism caused by factors that are by definition outside the control of the system, such as network partitions. Also, this paper is the first to give a single, simple formalization of merge functions (FJ-QUAS are optimized implementations of QUAs).

Research on *persistent data types* [13] is related to our definition of FJ-QUAs insofar it concerns itself with efficient implementations of data types that permit retrieval and mutations of past versions. However, it does not concern itself with apects related to transactions or distribution.

Prior work on *operational transformations* [19] can be understood as a specialized form of eventual consistency where updates are applied to different replicas in different orders, but are themselves modified in such a way as to guarantee convergence. This specialized formulation can provide highly efficient broadcast-based real-time collaboration, but poses significant implementation challenges [12].

If we consider transactions with single elements only, it is sensible to compare our work with related work on conflict-free replicated data types (CRDTs) [18] and Bayou's weakly consistent replication [20].

- Our definition is strictly more general than CRDTs [18] in the following sense: From any state-based CRDT we can obtain a FJ-QUA by using the same state and initial state, the same query and update functions, a fork function that creates a new replica and then merges the forker state, and a join function that uses the merge. Note that the definition of strong eventual consistency in [18], just like ours, requires that updates can be applied to any state.
- In Bayou [20], and in the Concurrent Revisions work[6], users can specify how to resolve conflicting updates by writing custom merge functions. At first sight, this may appear more general that QUAs. However, by performing a simple automatic transformation of the QUA and the client program, we can support merge functions for conflict resolution purposes. The reason is that QUAs already allow updates to perform any desired total function. We describe this transformation in the full version [4].

6 Conclusion and Future Work

We have proposed *eventually consistent transactions* as a consistency model that (1) generalizes earlier definitions of eventual consistency and (2) shows how to make some strong guarantees (transactions never fail, all code runs in transactions) to compensate for weak consistency. We have shown that revision diagrams provide a convenient way to build correct implementations of eventual consistency, by relying on just a handful of simple rules that are easily visualized using diagrams.

In future work, we would like to extend the study of the programming model, investigate a selection of basic FJ-QUAs, and ways to combine them. Furthermore, we would like to understand whether stronger consistency guarantees are possible for subclasses of eventually consistent transactions, and whether such classes can be automatically recognized or synthesized.

Acknowledgments. We thank Marc Shapiro for introducing us to a principled world of eventual consistency, and for general guidance. We also thank Tom Ball, Sean McDirmid and Benjamin Wood for inspired discussions, helpful examples, and constructive comments.

References

1. Abadi, M., Birrell, A., Harris, T., Isard, M.: Semantics of transactional memory and automatic mutual exclusion. In: Principles of Programming Languages, POPL (2008)
2. Burckhardt, S., Baldassin, A., Leijen, D.: Concurrent programming with revisions and isolation types. In: Object-Oriented Programming, Systems, Languages, and Applications, OOPSLA (2010)
3. Burckhardt, S., Leijen, D., Fähndrich, M.: Roll forward, not back: A case for deterministic conflict resolution. In: Workshop on Determinism and Correctness in Parallel Progr. (2011)
4. Burckhardt, S., Leijen, D., Fähndrich, M., Sagiv, M.: Eventually consistent transactions (full version). Technical Report MSR-TR-2011-117, Microsoft (2011)
5. Burckhardt, S., Leijen, D., Yi, J., Sadowski, C., Ball, T.: Two for the price of one: A model for parallel and incremental computation (distinguished paper award). In: Object-Oriented Programming, Systems, Languages, and Applications, OOPSLA (2011)
6. Burckhardt, S., Leijen, D.: Semantics of Concurrent Revisions. In: Barthe, G. (ed.) ESOP 2011. LNCS, vol. 6602, pp. 116–135. Springer, Heidelberg (2011); Full version as Microsoft Technical Report MSR-TR-2010-94
7. Decandia, G., Hastorun, D., Jampani, M., Kakulapati, G., Lakshman, A., Pilchin, A., Sivasubramanian, S., Vosshall, P., Vogels, W.: Dynamo: amazon's highly available key-value store. In: Symposium on Operating Systems Principles, pp. 205–220 (2007)
8. Fekete, A., Liarokapis, D., O'Neil, E., O'Neil, P., Shasha, D.: Making snapshot isolation serializable. ACM Trans. Database Syst. 30(2), 492–528 (2005)
9. Gilbert, S., Lynch, N.: Brewer's conjecture and the feasibility of consistent, available, partition-tolerant web services. SIGACT News 33, 51–59 (2002)
10. Gray, J., Helland, P., O'Neil, P., Shasha, D.: The dangers of replication and a solution. Sigmod Record 25, 173–182 (1996)
11. Herlihy, M., Koskinen, E.: Transactional boosting: a methodology for highly-concurrent transactional objects. In: Principles and Practice of Parallel Programming, PPoPP (2008)
12. Imine, A., Rusinowitch, M., Oster, G., Molli, P.: Formal design and verification of operational transformation algorithms for copies convergence. Theoretical Computer Science 351, 167–183 (2006)
13. Kaplan, H.: Persistent data structures. In: Handbook on Data Structures and Applications, pp. 241–246. CRC Press (1995)
14. Koskinen, E., Parkinson, M., Herlihy, M.: Coarse-grained transactions. In: Principles of Programming Languages, POPL (2010)
15. Petersen, K., Spreitzer, M., Terry, D., Theimer, M., Demers, A.: Flexible update propagation for weakly consistent replication. Operating Systems Review 31, 288–301 (1997)
16. Saito, Y., Shapiro, M.: Optimistic replication. ACM Computing Surveys 37, 42–81 (2005)
17. Shapiro, M., Kemme, B.: Eventual consistency. In: Encyclopedia of Database Systems, pp. 1071–1072 (2009)
18. Shapiro, M., Preguia, N., Baquero, C., Zawirski, M.: Conflict-free replicated data types (2011)
19. Sun, C., Ellis, C.: Operational transformation in real-time group editors: issues, algorithms, and achievements. In: Conference on Computer Supported Cooperative Work, pp. 59–68 (1998)
20. Terry, D., Theimer, M., Petersen, K., Demers, A., Spreitzer, M., Hauser, C.: Managing update conflicts in bayou, a weakly connected replicated storage system. SIGOPS Oper. Syst. Rev. 29, 172–182 (1995)
21. Valdes, J., Tarjan, R., Lawler, E.: The recognition of series parallel digraphs. In: ACM Symposium on Theory of Computing, pp. 1–12 (1979)

Concurrent Library Correctness on the TSO Memory Model

Sebastian Burckhardt[1], Alexey Gotsman[2], Madanlal Musuvathi[1], and Hongseok Yang[3]

[1] Microsoft Research
[2] IMDEA Software Institute
[3] University of Oxford

Abstract. Linearizability is a commonly accepted notion of correctness for libraries of concurrent algorithms. Unfortunately, it is only appropriate for sequentially consistent memory models, while the hardware and software platforms that algorithms run on provide weaker consistency guarantees. In this paper, we present the first definition of linearizability on a weak memory model, Total Store Order (TSO), implemented by x86 processors. We establish that our definition is a correct one in the following sense: while proving a property of a client of a concurrent library, we can soundly replace the library by its abstract implementation related to the original one by our generalisation of linearizability. This allows abstracting from the details of the library implementation while reasoning about the client. We have developed a tool for systematically testing concurrent libraries against our definition and applied it to several challenging algorithms.

1 Introduction

Concurrent software developers nowadays rely heavily on libraries of concurrency patterns and high-performance concurrent data structures, such as java.util.concurrent for Java and Intel's Threading Building Blocks for C++. The algorithms implemented by these libraries are very efficient, with the downside being that they are notoriously difficult to design and implement. More surprisingly, it is often difficult to understand even what it means for them to be correct! Correctness of concurrent libraries is commonly formalised by the notion of *linearizability* [11], which fixes a certain correspondence between the library and its abstract specification, the latter usually sequential, with methods implemented atomically. Unfortunately, the classical definition of linearizability is only appropriate for sequentially consistent (SC) memory models, in which accesses to shared memory occur in a global-time linear order. At the same time, most multiprocessors (x86 [15], Power [17], ARM [1]) and programming languages (Java [12], C++ [2]) provide weaker memory models that allow more efficient implementations at the expense of exhibiting counterintuitive behaviours in some cases.

In this paper, we present the first definition of linearizability on a weak memory model, Total Store Order (TSO), implemented by x86 processors [15] (Section 4). We show that our definition is a correct one in the sense that it validates what we call the Abstraction Theorem: while proving a property of a client of a concurrent library, we can soundly replace the library by its abstract implementation related to the original one by

H. Seidl (Ed.): ESOP 2012, LNCS 7211, pp. 87–107, 2012.

our generalisation of linearizability (Theorem 4, Section 5). The abstract implementation is usually simpler than the original one, with commands executing at a coarser grain of atomicity. The Abstraction Theorem thus formalises the intuitive requirement for a good definition of linearizability, which is that the library should provide an illusion of such a simpler atomic implementation. It also has a practical value as a compositional verification technique: it allows abstracting from the details of the library implementation while reasoning about its client, despite subtle interactions between the two caused by the weak memory model. As a corollary of the Abstraction Theorem, we establish that the proposed notion of linearizability is compositional (Corollary 5, Section 5).

To demonstrate that our notion of linearizability is appropriate for practical concurrent algorithms, we have developed a tool for systematically testing such algorithms against the definition and applied it to several examples (Section 6). We have also proved the linearizability of one of the algorithms formally (Theorem 3, Section 4). The algorithms considered are challenging to reason about and to specify, as they sometimes exhibit behaviours not reproducible on a sequentially consistent memory model.

The TSO Memory Model. The most intuitive way to explain the TSO memory model is operationally (Section 2), using an abstract multiprocessor machine in which every CPU has a *store buffer*. The buffer holds write requests that were issued by the CPU, but have not yet been *flushed* into the shared memory. A command that would like to write to a location in memory stores the corresponding write request in the store buffer of the CPU executing it, thus avoiding the need to block the CPU while the write completes.The CPU may decide to flush a store buffer entry into the main memory at any time, subject to maintaining the FIFO ordering of the buffer: the oldest write will be flushed first. A command that would like to read from a location in memory returns the value stored in the newest entry for this location in the store buffer of the CPU executing it; if such an entry does not exist, it accesses the memory directly.

The behaviour of programs running on TSO can sometimes be counterintuitive. For example, consider two memory locations x and y initially holding 0. On standard x86 processors, if two CPUs respectively write 1 to x and y and then read from y and x, as in the following program, it is possible for both to read 0 in the same execution:

$$\texttt{x = y = 0;}$$
$$\texttt{x = 1; b = y;} \quad \| \quad \texttt{y = 1; a = x;}$$
$$\{\mathtt{a} = \mathtt{b} = 0\}$$

This outcome cannot happen on a sequentially consistent machine, where both reads and writes access the memory directly. On TSO, it happens when the reads from y and x occur before the writes to them have propagated from the store buffers of the corresponding CPUs to the main memory. To exclude such behaviours, TSO processors provide special instructions, called *memory barriers*, that force the store buffer of the corresponding CPU to be flushed completely before executing the next instruction. Adding memory barriers after the writes to x and y in the above program would make it produce only SC behaviours. However, barriers incur a performance penalty.

Technical Challenges. The presence of store buffers leads to subtle interactions between a library and its client that make it challenging to define linearizability. Showing linearizability requires us to provide, for every execution of the concrete library implementation, an execution of the abstract library interacting with the client in a similar way (in a certain technical sense). Interactions between the library and the client are usually defined in terms of *histories*, which, in the classical definition, are sequences of calls to and returns from the library, along with the values passed. In the case of TSO, however, this would not describe all interactions between the two components, since one of them can exhibit a side effect on the other via a store buffer. For example, a memory barrier inside a library method will flush entries written there by client as well as library code. More subtly, write commands in a library method can insert entries into the store buffer without ensuring that they get flushed by the time the method returns. For this reason, on TSO, the method return point does not characterise the time by which the effects of these writes will be visible to the client (see the seqlock example in Section 4). To define the notion of linearizability on TSO that validates the Abstraction Theorem and is compositional, we thus need histories to describe the information relevant to the client about how the library uses store buffers. The classical notion of linearizability [11], which is not aware of store buffers, cannot specify this.

Main Ideas. Our main insight lies in identifying the additional information that we need to record in histories to get a definition of linearizability on TSO validating the Abstraction Theorem. Namely, the contents of a store buffer can be viewed as a sandwich consisting of blocks of entries inserted there by an invocation of a library method or a fragment of the client code between two such invocations. We show that the behaviour of the library with regards to the store buffer that can affect the client is completely described by the moments of time at which the first and the last elements of any given library layer in the sandwich get flushed. Roughly speaking, the time when a library layer starts to get flushed defines an assumption the library makes about the client: since store buffers are FIFO, the library requires the previous client layer in the buffer to be flushed completely before this. The time by which a library layer is flushed completely represents a guarantee the library provides to the client: this action enables the next client layer to be flushed starting from this point of time.

To specify this, we enrich histories with additional actions denoting the times when a layer of entries inserted by every library method invocation starts to get flushed and is flushed completely. Linearizability then requires preserving the order between some of these actions in a history of the concrete library implementation when providing a matching history of the abstract library implementation. As we show, this is sufficient to establish the Abstraction Theorem.

The proposed definition of linearizability on TSO requires a novel way of specifying libraries. In the classical definition, the specification of a library method often consists of one atomic action. Since on TSO writes can be delayed in the store buffer, such a specification according to our notion of linearizability is often given by two atomic actions: one that atomically writes entries into the store buffer, and one that flushes them into the memory, possibly after the method returns. The resulting specification captures the effects of using the store buffer visible to the client, yet is simpler than the implementation: it ensures that all the locations written to by a library method will be written to the memory atomically, albeit at some later time. We provide examples of such specifications in Section 4 and [5, Appendix B].

2 TSO semantics

In this section, we present the operational semantics of the TSO memory model, following [15], along with our modifications to it needed to define linearizability.

Notation. We write A^+ and A^* for the sets of all nonempty, respectively, possibly empty finite sequences of elements of a set A. We denote the empty sequence with ε and the concatenation of sequences α_1 and α_2 with $\alpha_1\alpha_2$. When we deal with sequences of sequences, for clarity we sometimes put an element of a sequence that is itself a sequence into brackets $\langle\cdot\rangle$. For example, $\alpha_1 \langle\beta\rangle \alpha_2$ denotes a sequence containing another sequence β as one of its elements. We write $g[x : y]$ for the function that has the same value as g everywhere, except for x, where it has the value y. We write _ for an expression whose value is irrelevant and implicitly existentially quantified. We denote the powerset of a set X with $\mathcal{P}(X)$, and the disjoint union of sets with $\uplus$.

Programming Language. We consider a machine with n CPUs, indexed by $\mathsf{CPUid} = \{1, \ldots, n\}$ and a shared memory. The machine executes programs of the following form:

$$L ::= \{m = C_m \mid m \in M\} \qquad\qquad C(L) ::= \mathsf{let}\ L\ \mathsf{in}\ C_1 \parallel \ldots \parallel C_n$$

A program consists of a declaration of a library L, implementing a set of methods $M \subseteq \mathsf{Method}$, and its client, specifying a command C_t to be run by the (hardware) thread in each CPU t. For the above program we let $\mathsf{sig}(L) = M$. To simplify presentation, we assume that the program is stored separately from the memory.

It is technically convenient for us to abstract from a particular syntax of thread and method bodies C_t and C_m and represent them using *control-flow graphs*. Namely, assume a set of primitive commands PComm (defined below). A control-flow graph (CFG) over the set PComm is a tuple $(N, T, \mathsf{start}, \mathsf{end})$, consisting of the set of program positions N, the control-flow relation $T \subseteq N \times \mathsf{PComm} \times N$, and the initial and final positions $\mathsf{start}, \mathsf{end} \in N$. The edges of the CFG are annotated with primitive commands from PComm.

We represent a program $C(L)$ by a collection of CFGs: the client command C_t for a CPU t is represented by $(N_t, T_t, \mathsf{start}_t, \mathsf{end}_t)$, and the body C_m of a method m by $(N_m, T_m, \mathsf{start}_m, \mathsf{end}_m)$. We often view this collection of CFGs for $C(L)$ as a single graph consisting of the node set $N = \biguplus_{t=1}^{n} N_t \uplus \biguplus_{m\in\mathsf{sig}(L)} N_m$ and the edge set $T = \biguplus_{t=1}^{n} T_t \uplus \biguplus_{m\in\mathsf{sig}(L)} T_m$.

Machine Configurations. The set of possible configurations Config of our machine is defined in Figure 1. The special configuration $\top$ results from the machine executing an illegal instruction, such as dereferencing a non-existent memory location. An ordinary configuration $(\mathsf{pc}, \theta, b, h, K) \in \mathsf{Config}$ consists of several components. The first one $\mathsf{pc} \in \mathsf{CPUid} \to \mathsf{Pos}$ gives the current instruction pointer of every CPU. When a CPU executes client code, its instruction pointer defines the program position of the client command being executed. Otherwise, it is given by a pair whose first component is the program position of the current library command, and the second one is the client position to return to when the library method finishes executing (one return position is sufficient, since, as explained below, we disallow nested method calls).

$$\begin{array}{lll}
\mathsf{Loc} = \mathbb{N} & \mathsf{Val} = \mathbb{Z} & \mathsf{Heap} = \mathsf{Loc} \rightharpoonup_{fin} \mathsf{Val} \\
\mathsf{Pos} = N \uplus (N \times N) & \mathsf{Reg} = \{\mathtt{r}_1, \dots, \mathtt{r}_m\} & \mathsf{RegBank} = \mathsf{Reg} \to \mathsf{Val} \\
\mathsf{Buff} = ((\mathsf{Loc} \times \mathsf{Val})^+ \cup \{\mathsf{lock}, \mathsf{call}, \mathsf{ret}\})^* & & \\
\mathsf{Config} = \{\top\} \cup ((\mathsf{CPUid} \to \mathsf{Pos}) \times (\mathsf{CPUid} \to \mathsf{RegBank}) \times & & \\
\qquad (\mathsf{CPUid} \to \mathsf{Buff}) \times \mathsf{Heap} \times \mathcal{P}(\mathsf{CPUid})) & &
\end{array}$$

Fig. 1. The set of machine configurations

Each CPU in the machine has a set of registers Reg, whose values are defined by $\theta \in \mathsf{CPUid} \to \mathsf{RegBank}$. The machine memory $h \in \mathsf{Heap}$ is represented as a finite partial function from existing memory locations to the values they store. The component $K \in \mathcal{P}(\mathsf{CPUid})$ defines the set of *active* CPUs that can currently execute a command and is used to implement atomic execution of certain commands.

The component $b \in \mathsf{CPUid} \to \mathsf{Buff}$ describes the state of all store buffers in the machine, each represented by a sequence of write requests with newest coming first. The contents of store buffers in our configurations differ from those prescribed by the TSO memory model [15] in two ways.

First, in TSO every entry in a store buffer is represented by a single location-value pair, whereas we use a sequence of those. In our semantics, all the locations in such a sequence are written to the memory atomically. This functionality is not provided by the hardware; we use it for expressing the semantics of library specifications, which might include atomic blocks performing several writes (see the seqlock example in Section 4).

Second, to formulate linearizability, we need to maintain some auxiliary information about executions, recorded by call, ret and lock entries in a store buffer. The marker lock is used to implement atomic commands performing several writes to different locations in memory. The markers call and ret get added to the buffer upon a call to or a return from the library, respectively, and thus delimit entries added by library method invocations and client code. They are used to generate additional actions in histories of interactions between the client and the library needed to define linearizability on TSO. We note that, despite store buffers in our configurations including call and ret markers, the semantics we define below corresponds to the standard TSO one, in the sense that erasing the markers from store buffers in all configurations of a given execution yields a valid execution in the standard TSO semantics.

Primitive Commands. The set of primitive commands is defined as follows:

$$\mathsf{PComm} = \mathsf{Local} \uplus \mathsf{Read} \uplus \mathsf{Write} \uplus \{m \mid m \in \mathsf{Method}\} \uplus \{\mathsf{lock}, \mathsf{unlock}, \mathsf{xlock}, \mathsf{xunlock}\}.$$

Here Local, Read and Write are unspecified sets of commands such that:

- commands in Local access only CPU registers;
- commands in Read read a single location in memory and write its contents into the register $\mathtt{r}_1$;
- commands in Write write to a single location in memory.

We also have library method calls and the commands lock and unlock that lock the machine, allowing several commands to be executed atomically, and unlock it. We assume that parameters and return values of methods are passed via CPU registers. If a client needs to preserve register values when calling a library method, it can save them in memory before the call and restore them when the method returns. The xlock and xunlock commands act as lock and unlock, except they have a built-in memory barrier, flushing the store buffer of the CPU executing the command. We call a sequence of commands bracketed by lock and unlock, or xlock and xunlock, an *atomic block*.

For every command $c \in \mathsf{Local} \uplus \mathsf{Read} \uplus \mathsf{Write}$, we assume a transformer:

- $f_c : \mathsf{RegBank} \to \mathcal{P}(\mathsf{RegBank})$ for $c \in \mathsf{Local}$ defining how the command changes the registers of the CPU executing it;
- $f_c : \mathsf{RegBank} \to \mathcal{P}(\mathsf{Loc})$ for $c \in \mathsf{Read}$ defining the location read;
- $f_c : \mathsf{RegBank} \to \mathcal{P}(\mathsf{Loc} \times \mathsf{Val})$ for $c \in \mathsf{Write}$ defining the location and the value written.

Note that we allow the execution of primitive commands to be non-deterministic. As in this paper we are dealing with low-level programs, we do not assume a built-in allocator, and thus do not consider commands for memory (de)allocation as primitive.

We place certain restrictions on CFGs over the above set PComm. Namely, we assume that on any path in a CFG, (x)lock and (x)unlock commands alternate correctly. In particular, we disallow nested (x)lock instructions. We assume that every method called in the program is defined, and we disallow nested method calls as well as method calls inside atomic blocks.

Let E, F denote expressions over the set of registers Reg, and $[\![E]\!]r$ the result of evaluating the expression E in the register bank r. Then we can define sample primitive commands

$$\mathsf{havoc} \in \mathsf{Local}, \quad \mathsf{assume}(E) \in \mathsf{Local}, \quad \mathsf{read}(E) \in \mathsf{Read}, \quad \mathsf{write}(E, F) \in \mathsf{Write}$$

with the following semantics:

$$f_{\mathsf{havoc}}(r) = \mathsf{RegBank}; \qquad f_{\mathsf{assume}(E)}(r) = \{r\}, \text{ if } [\![E]\!]r \neq 0;$$
$$f_{\mathsf{read}(E)}(r) = \{[\![E]\!]r\}; \qquad f_{\mathsf{assume}(E)}(r) = \emptyset, \text{ if } [\![E]\!]r = 0;$$
$$f_{\mathsf{write}(E,F)}(r) = \{([\![E]\!]r, [\![F]\!]r)\}.$$

The read and write commands have the expected meaning. The havoc command assigns arbitrary values to all registers. The assume(E) command acts as a filter on states, choosing only those where E evaluates to non-zero values. Using assume(E), a conditional branch on the value of E can be implemented with the CFG edges $(v, \mathsf{assume}(E), v_1)$ and $(v, \mathsf{assume}(!E), v_2)$, where $!E$ denotes the C-style negation.

Given the above commands, a memory barrier can be implemented as "xlock; xunlock". We can also implement the well-known atomic compare-and-swap (CAS) operation. A CAS takes three arguments: a memory address `addr`, an expected value `v1` and a new value `v2`. It atomically reads the memory address and updates it with the new value when the address contains the expected value; otherwise, it does nothing. In our language, we define `CAS(addr, v1, v2)` as syntactic sugar for the control-flow graph representation of:

```
xlock;
if (*addr == v1) { *addr = v2; xunlock; return 1; }
else { xunlock; return 0; }
```

Actions and Traces. Transitions in our operational semantics are labelled using *actions* of the form

$$\varphi \in \mathsf{Act} ::= (t, \mathsf{read}(x, u)) \mid (t, \mathsf{write}(x, u)) \mid (t, \mathsf{flush}(x, u)) \mid (t, \mathsf{flush}(\mathsf{call})) \mid (t, \mathsf{flush}(\mathsf{ret})) \mid (t, \mathsf{lock}) \mid (t, \mathsf{unlock}) \mid (t, \mathsf{xlock}) \mid (t, \mathsf{xunlock}) \mid (t, \mathsf{call}\ m(r)) \mid (t, \mathsf{ret}\ m(r))$$

where $t \in \mathsf{CPUid}$, $x \in \mathsf{Loc}$, $u \in \mathsf{Val}$, $m \in \mathsf{Method}$ and $r \in \mathsf{RegBank}$. Here $(t, \mathsf{write}(x, u))$ corresponds to enqueuing a pending write of u to the location x into the store buffer of CPU t, $(t, \mathsf{flush}(x, u))$ to flushing a pending write of u to the location x from the store buffer of t into the shared memory, $(t, \mathsf{flush}(\mathsf{call}))$ or $(t, \mathsf{flush}(\mathsf{ret}))$ to discarding a call or ret marker from the head of a store buffer. The last two actions record moments of time when entries in a store buffer written by a given library method invocation start to get flushed and are flushed completely, which are needed in the formulation of linearizability as we explained in Section 1. The rest of the actions have the expected meaning. Since parameters and return values of library methods are passed via CPU registers, we record their values in call and return actions.

We call a (finite or infinite) sequence of actions a *trace* and adopt the standard notation: $\lambda(i)$ is the i-th action in the trace λ, $|\lambda|$ is the length of the trace λ ($|\lambda| = \omega$ if λ is infinite), and $\lambda|_t$ is the projection of λ to actions by CPU t.

Program Semantics. The operational semantics of a program $C(L)$ is defined by the transition relation $\longrightarrow_{C(L)}$: $\mathsf{Config} \times \mathsf{Act}^* \times \mathsf{Config}$ in Figure 2. We remind the reader that T in the figure is the control-flow relation of $C(L)$. To handle transitions inside the library code, we lift it to program positions $N \uplus (N \times N)$ as follows:

$$\hat{T} = T \cup \{((v, v_0), c, (v', v_0)) \mid (v, c, v') \in T \wedge v_0 \in N\}.$$

The LOCAL rule handles the execution of commands that access registers only. These and other commands can only be executed by a CPU t if it is included into the set of active CPUs, represented by the last component of a configuration.

A write by a CPU to a location in memory does not happen immediately; instead, a pair of the location and the value to be written is added to the tail of the corresponding store buffer (WRITE). Recall that the newest entry comes first in the store buffer. When the location being written does not exist, the write command faults (WRITE-$\top$).

The READ rule uses $\mathsf{lookup}(\alpha, h, x)$ to find the value stored for the address x in the store buffer α of the CPU executing the command or the memory h:

$$\mathsf{lookup}(\alpha, h, x) = \begin{cases} u, & \text{if } \alpha = \alpha_1 \langle \beta_1 \, (x, u) \, \beta_2 \rangle \, \alpha_2 \text{ and} \\ & \alpha_1, \beta_1 \text{ do not contain entries for } x; \\ h(x), & \text{if } x \in \mathsf{dom}(h) \text{ and } \alpha \text{ does not contain entries for } x; \\ \top, & \text{otherwise.} \end{cases}$$

If there are entries for x in the store buffer, the read takes the value in the newest one; otherwise, it looks up the value in memory. If the location being read does not exist, lookup returns $\top$. According to READ, the value read is stored in the register $\mathtt{r}_1$.

$$\frac{t \in K \quad (\rho, c, \rho') \in \hat{T} \quad c \in \mathsf{Local} \quad r' \in f_c(r)}{\mathsf{pc}[t:\rho], \theta[t:r], b, h, K \xrightarrow{\varepsilon}_{C(L)} \mathsf{pc}[t:\rho'], \theta[t:r'], b, h, K} \ \text{LOCAL}$$

$$\frac{(\rho, c, \rho') \in \hat{T} \quad c \in \mathsf{Write} \quad (x,u) \in f_c(r) \quad x \in \mathsf{dom}(h)}{\mathsf{pc}[t:\rho], \theta[t:r], b[t:\alpha], h, K \xrightarrow{(t,\mathsf{write}(x,u))}_{C(L)} \mathsf{pc}[t:\rho'], \theta[t:r], b[t:(x,u)\,\alpha], h, K} \ \text{WRITE}$$

$$\frac{t \in K \quad (\rho, c, \rho') \in \hat{T} \quad c \in \mathsf{Write} \quad (x,u) \in f_c(r) \quad x \notin \mathsf{dom}(h)}{\mathsf{pc}[t:\rho], \theta[t:r], b, h, K \xrightarrow{\varepsilon}_{C(L)} \top} \ \text{WRITE-}\top$$

$$\frac{t \in K \quad (\rho, c, \rho') \in \hat{T} \quad c \in \mathsf{Read} \quad x \in f_c(r) \quad u = \mathsf{lookup}(\alpha, h, x) \neq \top}{\mathsf{pc}[t:\rho], \theta[t:r], b[t:\alpha], h, K \xrightarrow{(t,\mathsf{read}(x,u))}_{C(L)} \mathsf{pc}[t:\rho'], \theta[t:r[\mathtt{r}_1:u]], b[t:\alpha], h, K} \ \text{READ}$$

$$\frac{t \in K \quad (\rho, c, \rho') \in \hat{T} \quad c \in \mathsf{Read} \quad x \in f_c(r) \quad \mathsf{lookup}(\alpha, h, x) = \top}{\mathsf{pc}[t:\rho], \theta[t:r], b[t:\alpha], h, K \xrightarrow{\varepsilon}_{C(L)} \top} \ \text{READ-}\top$$

$$\frac{(\rho, \mathsf{lock}, \rho') \in \hat{T}}{\mathsf{pc}[t:\rho], \theta, b[t:\alpha], h, \mathsf{CPUid} \xrightarrow{(t,\mathsf{lock})}_{C(L)} \mathsf{pc}[t:\rho'], \theta, b[t:\mathsf{lock}\,\alpha], h, \{t\}} \ \text{LOCK}$$

$$\frac{(\rho, \mathsf{unlock}, \rho') \in \hat{T}}{\begin{array}{l}\mathsf{pc}[t:\rho], \theta, b[t:(x_1,u_1)\dots(x_l,u_l)\,\mathsf{lock}\,\alpha], h, \{t\} \xrightarrow{(t,\mathsf{unlock})}_{C(L)} \\ \qquad \mathsf{pc}[t:\rho'], \theta, b[t:\langle (x_1,u_1)\dots(x_l,u_l)\rangle\,\alpha], h, \mathsf{CPUid}\end{array}} \ \text{UNLOCK}$$

$$\frac{}{\begin{array}{l}\mathsf{pc}, \theta, b[t:\alpha\,\langle (x_1,u_1)\dots(x_l,u_l)\rangle], h, \mathsf{CPUid} \xrightarrow{(t,\mathsf{flush}(x_l,u_l))\dots(t,\mathsf{flush}(x_1,u_1))}_{C(L)} \\ \qquad \mathsf{pc}, \theta, b[t:\alpha], h[x_l:u_l]\dots[x_1:u_1], \mathsf{CPUid}\end{array}} \ \text{FLUSH}$$

$$\frac{\beta \in \{\mathsf{call}, \mathsf{ret}\}}{\mathsf{pc}, \theta, b[t:\alpha\beta], h, \mathsf{CPUid} \xrightarrow{(t,\mathsf{flush}(\beta))}_{C(L)} \mathsf{pc}, \theta, b[t:\alpha], h, \mathsf{CPUid}} \ \text{FLUSH-MARKER}$$

$$\frac{(\rho, \mathsf{xlock}, \rho') \in \hat{T}}{\mathsf{pc}[t:\rho], \theta, b[t:\varepsilon], h, \mathsf{CPUid} \xrightarrow{(t,\mathsf{xlock})}_{C(L)} \mathsf{pc}[t:\rho'], \theta, b[t:\varepsilon], h, \{t\}} \ \text{XLOCK}$$

$$\frac{(\rho, \mathsf{xunlock}, \rho') \in \hat{T}}{\begin{array}{l}\mathsf{pc}[t:\rho], \theta, b[t:(x_1,u_1)\dots(x_l,u_l)], h, \{t\} \xrightarrow{(t,\mathsf{flush}(x_l,u_l))\dots(t,\mathsf{flush}(x_1,u_1))(t,\mathsf{xunlock})}_{C(L)} \\ \qquad \mathsf{pc}[t:\rho'], \theta, b[t:\varepsilon], h[x_l:u_l]\dots[x_1:u_1], \mathsf{CPUid}\end{array}} \ \text{XUNLOCK}$$

$$\frac{(v, m, v') \in T}{\begin{array}{l}\mathsf{pc}[t:v], \theta[t:r], b[t:\alpha], h, \mathsf{CPUid} \xrightarrow{(t,\mathsf{call}\ m(r))}_{C(L)} \\ \qquad \mathsf{pc}[t:(\mathsf{start}_m, v')], \theta[t:r], b[t:\mathsf{call}\,\alpha], h, \mathsf{CPUid}\end{array}} \ \text{CALL}$$

$$\frac{}{\begin{array}{l}\mathsf{pc}[t:(\mathsf{end}_m, v')], \theta[t:r], b[t:\alpha], h, \mathsf{CPUid} \xrightarrow{(t,\mathsf{ret}\ m(r))}_{C(L)} \\ \qquad \mathsf{pc}[t:v'], \theta[t:r], b[t:\mathsf{ret}\,\alpha], h, \mathsf{CPUid}\end{array}} \ \text{RET}$$

Fig. 2. Operational TSO semantics

A CPU executing lock makes itself the only active CPU, preventing the others from executing commands[1] (LOCK). The commands executed within the corresponding atomic block, i.e., until the CPU calls unlock (UNLOCK) are thus not interleaved with commands of other CPUs. A lock command also adds a lock marker to the tail of the store buffer, thus delimiting the write requests issued within the atomic block. The corresponding unlock command then uses the lock marker to gather these write requests into a single buffer entry. Since we prohibit method calls inside atomic blocks, this entry does not contain call or ret markers.

A CPU may at any point decide to flush the entry at the head of the store buffer into memory (FLUSH). All the writes in the entry are flushed at the same time, thus ensuring that writes made in an atomic block take effect atomically. A CPU can also discard the marker at the head of the store buffer (FLUSH-MARKER). Although this does not modify the memory, we use the corresponding action, recorded in the transition relation, to formulate linearizability (Section 4). For technical reasons, it is convenient for us to prohibit flushes inside an atomic block delimited by lock and unlock. Thus, the FLUSH and FLUSH-MARKER require the set of active CPUs to be CPUid.

The xlock command (XLOCK) can only be executed when the store buffer is empty and thus forces the CPU to flush its store buffer beforehand using FLUSH and FLUSH-MARKER. For this reason, it does not need to insert a lock marker into the buffer: by the end of the atomic block the buffer will only contain writes issued inside it. The xunlock command flushes all these entries into the memory (XUNLOCK).

The rules CALL and RET handle calls to and returns from methods. Upon a method call, the return point is saved as a component in the new thread position, a call marker is added to the tail of the store buffer, and the method starts executing from the corresponding starting node of its CFG. Upon a return, the return point is read from the current program position, and a ret marker is added to the tail of the store buffer. Note that configurations in CALL and RET rules have CPUid as the set of active CPUs, since we prohibit method calls inside atomic blocks.

We note that the store buffers arising in executions of $C(L)$ as defined in Figure 2 are not arbitrary elements of Buff, but satisfy certain properties: e.g., call and ret markers in them alternate correctly, and they contain at most one lock marker. We formalise such properties in [5, Appendix A].

Implementations of the TSO memory model usually guarantee that store buffers are fair, in the sense that, eventually, every write request in a buffer will be flushed into the memory. Our results can be extended to accommodate this constraint; however, we do not handle it in this paper so as not to obfuscate presentation.

A *computation* of $C(L)$ is a sequence of transitions using $\longrightarrow_{C(L)}$. For a computation τ, we let trace(τ) be the trace obtained by concatenating all the annotations of transitions in τ. In the following, we assume that program properties of interest are linear-time properties over sets of program traces. We denote with $\xrightarrow{\lambda}^*_{C(L)}$ the reflexive and transitive closure of $\longrightarrow_{C(L)}$, where λ is obtained by concatenating the transition annotations.

[1] The semantics of TSO [15] locks only the memory bus in this case, which allows other CPUs to execute local commands affecting only their registers. For simplicity, we chose to disallow all commands.

Let $I \subseteq \mathsf{Heap}$ be the set of initial heaps that the program $C(L)$ expects to execute from. We define the set of its initial configurations as

$$\Sigma_0(I) = \{(\mathsf{pc}_0, \theta_0, b_0, h_0, \mathsf{CPUid}) \mid \forall t \in \mathsf{CPUid}.\, \mathsf{pc}_0(t) = \mathsf{start}_t \wedge b_0(t) = \varepsilon \wedge h_0 \in I\}.$$

We define the semantics $[\![C(L)]\!]I$ of $C(L)$ executing from I as the set of computations with initial configurations from $\Sigma_0(I)$. We say that the program $C(L)$ is *safe* for I, if it is not the case that $\sigma_0 \xrightarrow{\lambda}{}^*_{C(L)} \top$ for some λ and $\sigma_0 \in \Sigma_0(I)$. Informally, a program is safe when it accesses only allocated memory. Safety can be established using existing logics for reasoning about programs running on TSO [16,20].

3 Library-Local and Client-Local Semantics

Consider a library L and a program $C(L)$ using this library:

$$L = \{m = C_m \mid m \in M\}, \qquad C(L) = \mathsf{let}\ L\ \mathsf{in}\ C_1 \parallel \ldots \parallel C_n.$$

To formulate the definition of linearizability and the Abstraction Theorem, we need to give a semantics to parts of $C(L)$: the library L considered in isolation from its client and the client C considered in isolation from the implementation of the library it uses. In this section, we specialise the semantics of programs in Section 2 to such *library-local* and *client-local* semantics describing all possible behaviours of the corresponding components.

Let us lift the operation of the disjoint union of heaps to sets of heaps pointwise:

$$\forall I_1, I_2 \subseteq \mathsf{Heap}.\, I_1 \circ I_2 = \{h_1 \uplus h_2 \mid h_1 \in I_1 \wedge h_2 \in I_2\}.$$

We assume that the set I of initial heaps of $C(L)$ satisfies $I = I_c \circ I_l$ for some $I_c, I_l \subseteq \mathsf{Heap}$ such that for any $h_c \in I_c$ and $h_l \in I_l$, $h_c \uplus h_l$ is defined. Here I_c and I_l are meant to represent parts of initial heaps used by the client C and the library L, respectively; the initial heaps of $C(L)$ are obtained as the $\circ$-combination of these.

Recall that n is the number of CPUs in our machine. To give a library-local semantics to L, we consider the program $\mathsf{MGC}(L) = \mathsf{let}\ L\ \mathsf{in}\ C_1^{\mathsf{mgc}} \parallel \ldots \parallel C_n^{\mathsf{mgc}}$, where C_t^{mgc} has the CFG

$$(\{v^t_{\mathsf{mgc}}\}, \{(v^t_{\mathsf{mgc}}, \mathsf{havoc}, v^t_{\mathsf{mgc}}), (v^t_{\mathsf{mgc}}, m, v^t_{\mathsf{mgc}}) \mid m \in \mathsf{sig}(L)\}, v^t_{\mathsf{mgc}}, v^t_{\mathsf{mgc}}).$$

The program $\mathsf{MGC}(L)$ is the *most general client* of the library L, whose hardware threads on every CPU repeatedly invoke library methods in any order and with any parameters possible. The latter are passed via registers, set arbitrarily by the havoc command. The set of computations $[\![\mathsf{MGC}(L)]\!]I_l$ thus includes all library behaviours under any possible client (this fact is formalised in Lemma 6, Section 5).

In practice, a library often tolerates only calls from clients adhering to a certain policy. For example, a spinlock implementation might expect client calls to `acquire` and `release` methods to alternate. We can take this into account by restricting the most general client appropriately. While libraries in our examples do rely on the client satisfying such constraints, to simplify presentation we do not formalise them here.

To define the client-local semantics of the client C, we consider the program

$$C_M(\cdot) = \mathsf{let}\ \{m = C_m^{\mathsf{stub}} \mid m \in M\}\ \mathsf{in}\ C_1 \parallel \ldots \parallel C_n$$

where the body C_m^{stub} of every method m has the CFG $(\{v_{\mathsf{start}}^m\}, \{(v_{\mathsf{start}}^m, \mathsf{havoc}, v_{\mathsf{end}}^m)\}, v_{\mathsf{start}}^m, v_{\mathsf{end}}^m)$. That is, every method in $C_M(\cdot)$ is implemented by a stub that returns immediately after having been called, scrambling all the registers. Since return values of library methods are stored in registers, the set of computations $[\![C_M(\cdot)]\!]I_c$ generates all executions of the client assuming any behaviour of the library it uses.

Note that both library-local and client-local semantics allow store buffer entries of the corresponding component to be flushed non-deterministically while the other component is running, since this is possible in the semantics of the whole program. Similarly, we add call and ret markers to the store buffer when calling a method stub in the client-local and library-local semantics.

We say that a client C, respectively, a library L is safe for I_c, respectively, I_l, if so is $C_M(\cdot)$, respectively, $\mathsf{MGC}(L)$ (see Section 2). As we have noted before, the safety of a library or a client can be established using logics for TSO [16,20]. Note that in the client-local or the library-local semantics, the program runs on the state owned by the corresponding component and faults when accessing memory locations not belonging to it. Thus, the safety of the client and the library ensures that they cannot corrupt each other's state. We rely crucially on this in establishing the Abstraction Theorem for the notion of linearizability we propose. It can also be shown that, when the client C and the library L are safe, so is the complete program $C(L)$ (Lemma 6, Section 5).

4 Linearizability on TSO

When defining linearizability, we are not interested in internal steps recorded in library computations, but only in the interactions of the library with its client. We record such interactions using *histories*, which are traces including only actions from the following subset of Act:

$$\mathsf{HAct} ::= (t, \mathsf{call}\ m(r)) \mid (t, \mathsf{ret}\ m(r)) \mid (t, \mathsf{flush(call)}) \mid (t, \mathsf{flush(ret)})$$

where $t \in \mathsf{CPUid}$, $m \in \mathsf{Method}$, $r \in \mathsf{RegBank}$. Recall that here r records the values of registers of the CPU that calls a library method or returns from it, which serve as parameters or return values. We define the history $\mathsf{history}(\tau)$ corresponding to a computation τ of the program $C(L)$ by projecting $\mathsf{trace}(\tau)$ to actions from HAct.

In contrast to histories used in the classical definition of linearizability [11], ours include two new types of actions needed for defining linearizability on TSO: $(t, \mathsf{flush(call)})$ and $(t, \mathsf{flush(ret)})$, denoting times when the CPU t flushes a call or a ret marker from its store buffer. We first formulate our definition, and then explain the motivation behind it.

Definition 1. *The **linearizability relation** is a binary relation $\sqsubseteq$ on histories defined as follows: $H \sqsubseteq H'$ if $\forall t \in \mathsf{CPUid}.\, H|_t = H'|_t$ and there is a bijection $\pi\colon \{1, \ldots, |H|\} \to \{1, \ldots, |H'|\}$ such that $\forall i.\, H(i) = H'(\pi(i))$ and*

$$(i < j \wedge (H(i) = (\_, \mathsf{ret}\ \_) \vee H(i) = (\_, \mathsf{flush(ret)})) \\ \wedge (H'(j) = (\_, \mathsf{call}\ \_) \vee H'(j) = (\_, \mathsf{flush(call)}))) \Rightarrow \pi(i) < \pi(j).$$

That is, a history H' linearizes a history H when it is a permutation of the latter preserving the order of certain types of actions. We lift the notion of linearizability to libraries using the library-local semantics of Section 3.

Definition 2. *For libraries L_1 and L_2 safe for I_l and such that* $\mathsf{sig}(L_1) = \mathsf{sig}(L_2)$, *we say that L_2* ***linearizes*** *L_1, written $L_1 \sqsubseteq L_2$, if*

$$\forall H_1 \in \mathsf{history}([\![\mathsf{MGC}(L_1)]\!] I_l).\, \exists H_2 \in \mathsf{history}([\![\mathsf{MGC}(L_2)]\!] I_l).\, H_1 \sqsubseteq H_2.$$

Thus, L_2 linearizes L_1 if every behaviour of the latter under the most general client may be reproduced in a linearized form by the former.

Discussion. A good definition of linearizability has to allow replacing a library implementation with its specification while keeping client behaviours reproducible (as formalised by the Abstraction Theorem in Section 5). However, linearizability itself is defined between libraries considered in isolation from their clients. In Definition 2, this is achieved by considering executions of libraries under their most general clients (Section 3), which can only refer to store buffer entries inserted by write commands in library code. When a library is used by a client, the store buffer mixes entries inserted by the two components. As we noted in Section 1, in this case the library can affect the client via the store buffer, e.g., by executing a memory barrier or leaving an unflushed entry blocking newer client entries from being flushed. The $(\_, \mathsf{flush}(\mathsf{call}))$ and $(\_, \mathsf{flush}(\mathsf{ret}))$ actions in histories record the necessary information about library behaviour of this kind, as we now explain.

Recall the analogy from Section 1, where we viewed the contents of a store buffer as a sandwich consisting of blocks of entries inserted there by an invocation of a library method or a fragment of client computation between two such invocations. The call and ret markers delimit the layers in this sandwich. For example, at some point in an execution of $C(L)$, the store buffer of some CPU might have the following contents:

$$\mathsf{ret}\,(x_5, u_5)\,\mathsf{call}\,(x_4, u_4)\,\mathsf{ret}\,(x_3, u_3)\,(x_2, u_2)\,\mathsf{call}\,(x_1, u_1), \qquad (1)$$

where the leftmost end contains the newest entry. From the call and ret markers, we can immediately conclude that the write to x_1 was inserted by the client before calling a library method, the writes to x_2 and x_3 were by the library method invocation, the write to x_4 was again by the client, and the write to x_5 was by the next method invocation on this CPU.

The most general client exercises the library methods under all possible input parameters, but does not perform writes by itself. For this reason, a store buffer in the most general client of a library never has entries between a call marker and an older ret marker (we formalise this in [5, Appendix A]). For example, a computation of the most general client of the library with the same library method invocations as in the one producing (1) might have the store buffer

$$\mathsf{ret}\,(x_5, u_5)\,\mathsf{call}\,\mathsf{ret}\,(x_3, u_3)\,(x_2, u_2)\,\mathsf{call}, \qquad (2)$$

which contains only library entries from (1). Thus, when considering a library in isolation from its client in defining linearizability, the call and ret markers let us determine the places in the store buffer where client entries might be located in a corresponding execution of a complete program.

Consider an execution of the most general client of a library in which the CPU flushes a library entry (e.g., (x_3, u_3) in (2)). Since store buffers are FIFO, in the corresponding execution of a particular client with the same library behaviour, this will *assume* that the client entries in the store buffer older than it have been flushed (e.g., (x_1, u_1) in (1)). Conversely, flushing a library entry (e.g., (x_3, u_3) in (1)) preceding a client one (e.g., (x_4, u_4) in (1)) will *guarantee* that the client entry can now be flushed. For the Abstraction Theorem to hold, in Definition 2 we need to make sure that the executions of the most general clients producing histories H_1 and H_2 make the same assumptions and give the same guarantees concerning times when client entries are flushed. This is the reason for including flushes of call and ret markers into histories. The position of a $(t, \mathsf{flush}(\mathsf{call}))$ action in a history produced by the most general client defines a moment of time by which, in a complete program, all older client writes in the store buffer of t *must* be flushed for the library to be able to flush the entries from the layer following the call marker. The position of a $(t, \mathsf{flush}(\mathsf{ret}))$ action defines a moment starting from which the client entries from the layer following the ret marker *may* be flushed. In our definition of linearizability, we require that the two histories considered have the same history actions describing how store buffers are modified during the execution. Hence, in two executions corresponding to the histories, libraries make the same assumptions and give the same guarantees concerning the use of store buffers.

Like the classical definition of linearizability, ours requires preserving the order between non-overlapping library method invocations; two invocations do not overlap in a history if the return of one precedes the call of the other. This is needed for the Abstraction Theorem to hold, since the client code executed in between two non-overlapping method invocations can notice their order. To handle TSO correctly, our definition also takes into account intervals during which all the writes of a library method invocation were being flushed: it requires preserving the order between two such non-overlapping intervals or non-overlapping interval of this kind and a library method invocation. This is expressed by preserving the order of $(\_, \mathsf{flush}(\mathsf{ret}))$ preceding $(\_, \mathsf{flush}(\mathsf{call}))$, $(\_, \mathsf{flush}(\mathsf{ret}))$ preceding $(\_, \mathsf{call}\_)$, and $(\_, \mathsf{ret}\_)$ preceding $(\_, \mathsf{flush}(\mathsf{call}))$. The requirement is again needed to validate the Abstraction Theorem.

We note that our definition of linearizability is flexible in the following sense: it puts restrictions on times when call and ret markers are flushed, but not on how many ordinary entries a given method invocation inserts into the store buffer. For example, this allows us to relate a library implementation writing to some part of the memory accessed only by a given CPU to its specification that does not write to any local state.

Example. Even though we formalise our results for programs represented by their CFGs, for readability in our examples we use a C-like language. Its programs can be translated to CFGs in the standard way. We assume that global variables are allocated at fixed addresses in memory, and local variables are stored in CPU registers.

Figure 3 presents a simplified version of a seqlock [3]—an efficient implementation of a readers-writer protocol based on version counters used in the Linux kernel. Two memory addresses `x1` and `x2` make up a conceptual register that a single hardware thread can write to, and any number of other threads can attempt to read from. A version

```
word x1 = 0, x2 = 0;
word c = 0;

write(in word d1, in word d2) {
  c++;
  x1 = d1; x2 = d2;
  c++;
}
```

```
read(out word d1, out word d2) {
  word c0;
  do {
    do { c0 = c; } while (c0 % 2);
    d1 = x1; d2 = x2;
  } while (c != c0);
}
```

Fig. 3. Seqlock implementation L_{seqlock}

```
word x1 = 0, x2 = 0;

write(in word d1, in word d2) { lock; x1 = d1; x2 = d2; unlock; }

read(out word d1, out word d2) { lock; d1 = x1; d2 = x2; unlock; }
```

Fig. 4. Seqlock specification $L^{\sharp}_{\mathsf{seqlock}}$. Here `nondet()` represents a non-deterministic choice.

number is stored at c. The writing thread maintains the invariant that the version number is odd during writing by incrementing it before the start of and after the finish of writing. A reader checks that the version number is even before attempting to read (otherwise it could see an inconsistent result by reading while x1 and x2 are being written). After reading, the reader checks that the version has not changed, thereby ensuring that no write has overlapped the read. Note that neither the `write` nor the `read` operation includes a memory barrier, which means that writes to x1, x2 and c may not be visible to readers immediately.

We give a specification to seqlock using the abstract implementation in Figure 4. Instead of using a version counter, this implementation just locks the machine while reading from or writing to x1 and x2. According to the semantics of Section 2, the writes to x1 and x2 performed by `write` are stored in a single entry of the corresponding store buffer and are written to the shared memory atomically. This specifies that the implementation of a seqlock indeed ensures the illusion of atomicity. However, we also need our specification to capture the effect of the library executing on a weak memory model—the fact that the writes to x1 and x2, although executed atomically, may still be delayed due to the presence of store buffers. This is because the delay can be noticed by certain clients and can result in a non-SC behaviour. For example, using a seqlock, we can reproduce the example from Section 1 yielding non-SC behaviour as shown in Figure 4. To capture this, the specification of `write` ensures atomicity by a pair of lock and unlock commands, which do not flush the writes to the memory immediately.

Thus, we have two atomic actions associated with the abstract `write` method: one that writes to the store buffer and the other that flushes the writes to the memory, possibly after the method returns. This is different from the classical definition of linearizability on a sequentially consistent memory model [11], which requires methods in the specification to be implemented by one atomic action.

```
             x1 = x2 = y = 0;
write(1, 1);    ||  y = 1;
b = y;          ||  read(&a1, &a2);
             {a1 = b2 = b = 0}
```

Fig. 5. A client of L_{seqlock} producing a non-SC behaviour

As the following theorem shows, the abstract implementation $L^{\sharp}_{\mathsf{seqlock}}$ in Figure 4 indeed linearizes the concrete one L_{seqlock} in Figure 3.

Theorem 3. $L_{\mathsf{seqlock}} \sqsubseteq L^{\sharp}_{\mathsf{seqlock}}$.

The proof is given in [5, Appendix A]; here we discuss it informally. The proof is similar to proofs of classical linearizability using linearization points [11], although here methods of the abstract implementation contain more than one atomic action. We consider the most general clients of the concrete and the abstract implementations of the library running alongside each other. For every execution of the client of the concrete library, we construct the corresponding execution of the client of the abstract one by firing transitions of the latter at certain times during the execution of the former.

For example, the abstract `read` method is executed when the corresponding concrete one reads `x2` for the last time. The code of the abstract `write` method is executed when the concrete one writes to `x2`. Finally, a store buffer entry containing writes to `x1` and `x2` by the abstract `write` method is flushed together with the second write to `c` by the corresponding concrete method invocation. To prove that this flush in the abstract implementation does not contradict the FIFO ordering of store buffers, we maintain an invariant relating the contents of the store buffers in the concrete and the abstract seqlock implementations.

Programs Producing Only SC Behaviours. By this time, the reader may wonder whether it is always necessary to expose the behaviour of a library with respect to store buffers in its specification. After all, many programs running on TSO only produce SC behaviours, and there are ways of effectively checking this [14,6,7]. Therefore, a valid question is whether we can use the usual definition of linearizability for libraries producing only SC behaviours when they are used by clients also behaving SC. Unfortunately, in general the answer is no. This is because, even if the most general client of a library $\mathsf{MGC}(L)$ and its client $C_{\mathsf{sig}(L)}(\cdot)$ only produce SC behaviours when considered in isolation, this may not be the case for the complete program $C(L)$ due to interactions of the two components via the store buffer. For example, the most general client of a single seqlock produces only SC behaviours, as it satisfies the triangular race freedom criterion of [14]. However, Figure 4 shows that if we use a seqlock *together with* a client that also happens to be SC by itself, we can get non-SC behaviours. This is not surprising: a seqlock is meant to ensure the atomicity of writes to and reads from a pair of locations, but it is not meant to make these reads and writes strongly consistent. Thus, the classical definition of linearizability is not sufficient to specify libraries even when constraining separate components of a program to behave SC.

5 Abstraction Theorem

We now justify that the notion of linearizability proposed in Section 4 is a correct one by establishing the Abstraction Theorem that allows abstracting an implementation of a library with its specification while reasoning about its client.

For a computation τ of $C(L)$ obtained from the semantics of Section 2, we denote with $\mathsf{client}(\tau)$ the projection of its trace $\lambda = \mathsf{trace}(\tau)$ to actions relevant to the client, i.e., executed by the client code or corresponding to flushes of client entries in store buffers. Formally, we include an action φ such that $\lambda = \lambda' \varphi \lambda''$ into the projection if:

- φ is included into $\mathsf{history}(\tau)$; or
- φ is not a flush action and is outside an invocation of a library method, i.e., it is not the case that $\lambda|_t = \lambda_1\,(t, \mathsf{call}\ \_)\,\lambda_2 \varphi \lambda_3$, where λ_2 does not contain a $(t, \mathsf{ret}\ \_)$ action; or
- φ corresponds to a flush of a client entry in a store buffer, i.e., it is not the case that $\lambda|_t = \lambda_1\,(t, \mathsf{flush}(\mathsf{call}))\,\lambda_2 \varphi \lambda_3$, where λ_2 does not contain a $(t, \mathsf{flush}(\mathsf{ret}))$ action.

We lift client to sets of computations pointwise.

The Abstraction Theorem states that the behaviour of a client of a concurrent library will stay reproducible on TSO if we replace the library by its abstract implementation related to the original one by our definition of linearizability.

Theorem 4 (Abstraction). *Consider $C(L_1)$ and $C(L_2)$ such that C is safe for I_c, L_1 and L_2 are safe for I_l and $L_1 \sqsubseteq L_2$. Then $C(L_1)$ and $C(L_2)$ are safe for $I = I_c \circ I_l$ and* $\mathsf{client}([\![C(L_1)]\!]I) \subseteq \mathsf{client}([\![C(L_2)]\!]I)$.

We provide a proof outline below and give the complete proof in [5, Appendix A]. The requirement that the client C be safe in the theorem is required to replace one library implementation with another: it ensures that C cannot access the internals of the library implementation.

From Theorem 4 it follows that, while reasoning about a client $C(L_1)$ of a library L_1, we can soundly replace L_1 with a simpler library L_2 linearizing L_1: if a linear-time property over client actions holds over $C(L_2)$, it will also hold over $C(L_1)$. Note that the abstract implementation is usually simpler than the original one (in most cases implemented using atomic blocks, like the one in Figure 4), which eases the proof of the resulting program. Thus, the proposed notion of linearizability and Theorem 4 enable compositional reasoning about programs running on TSO: they allow decomposing the verification of a whole program into the verification of its constituent components. We give an example of using this technique in Section 6.

The following corollary of Theorem 4, proved in [5, Appendix A], states that, like the classical notion of linearizability [11], ours is compositional: if several non-interacting libraries are linearizable, then so is their composition. Formally, consider libraries $L_1, \ldots, L_k$ with disjoint sets of declared methods and sets of initial heaps $I_1, \ldots, I_k$ such that

$$\forall \{i_1, \ldots, i_l\} \subseteq \{1, \ldots, k\}.\, \forall h_1 \in I_{i_1}, \ldots, h_l \in I_{i_l}.\, h_1 \uplus \ldots \uplus h_l \text{ is defined.}$$

We let the *composition* L of $L_1, \ldots, L_k$ be the library implementing all of their methods and having the set of initial heaps $I_1 \circ \ldots \circ I_k$.

Corollary 5 (Compositionality). *Consider libraries $L_1, \ldots, L_k$ and $L_1^\sharp, \ldots, L_k^\sharp$ such that L_j and $L_j^\sharp$ are safe for I_j, $j = 1..k$. Let L and $L^\sharp$ be the compositions of the respective sets of libraries. If $L_j \sqsubseteq L_j^\sharp$ for $j = 1..k$, then $L \sqsubseteq L^\sharp$.*

Proof Outline for Theorem 4. The proof of Theorem 4 relies on the following lemmas, proved in [5, Appendix A]. The first lemma shows that a computation of $C(L)$ generates two computations in the client-local and library-local semantics with the same history.

Lemma 6 (Decomposition). *If $C_{\mathsf{sig}(L)}(\cdot)$ and $\mathsf{MGC}(L)$ are safe for I_c and I_l, respectively, then $C(L)$ is safe for $I_c \circ I_l$ and*

$$\forall \tau \in [\![C(L)]\!](I_c \circ I_l).\, \exists \eta \in [\![C_{\mathsf{sig}(L)}(\cdot)]\!]I_c.\, \exists \xi \in [\![\mathsf{MGC}(L)]\!]I_l.\\ \mathsf{history}(\eta) = \mathsf{history}(\xi) \wedge \mathsf{client}(\tau) = \mathsf{client}(\eta).$$

The following lemma presents the core of the transformation used to convert a computation of $C(L_1)$ into one of $C(L_2)$ in Theorem 4: it shows that a computation of a most general client can be transformed into another of its computations with a given history linearized by the history of the original one.

Lemma 7 (Rearrangement). *Consider a library L safe for I_l and histories H, H' such that $H \sqsubseteq H'$. Then*

$$\forall \tau' \in [\![\mathsf{MGC}(L)]\!]I_l.\, \mathsf{history}(\tau') = H' \Rightarrow \exists \tau \in [\![\mathsf{MGC}(L)]\!]I_l.\, \mathsf{history}(\tau) = H.$$

Finally, the following lemma states that any pair of client-local and library-local computations agreeing on the history can be combined into a valid computation of $C(L)$.

Lemma 8 (Composition). *If $C_{\mathsf{sig}(L)}(\cdot)$ and $\mathsf{MGC}(L)$ are safe for I_c and I_l, respectively, then*

$$\forall \eta \in [\![C_{\mathsf{sig}(L)}(\cdot)]\!]I_c.\, \forall \xi \in [\![\mathsf{MGC}(L)]\!]I_l.\, \mathsf{history}(\eta) = \mathsf{history}(\xi) \Rightarrow\\ \exists \tau \in [\![C(L)]\!](I_c \circ I_l).\, \mathsf{client}(\tau) = \mathsf{client}(\eta).$$

Most of the proof of the Decomposition Lemma (Lemma 6) deals with maintaining a splitting of the state of $C(L)$ into the parts owned by the client and the library, including store buffer entries. The resulting partial states then define the computations of $C_{\mathsf{sig}(L)}(\cdot)$ and $\mathsf{MGC}(L)$. Conversely, the Composition Lemma (Lemma 8) composes the states of $C_{\mathsf{sig}(L)}(\cdot)$ and $\mathsf{MGC}(L)$ into states of $C(L)$ to construct an execution of the latter. The proof of the Rearrangement Lemma (Lemma 7) transforms τ' into τ by repeatedly permuting transitions in the computation according to a certain strategy to make its history equal to H.

Proof of Theorem 4. Lemma 6 implies that $C(L)$ is safe. We now need to transform a computation $\tau_1 \in [\![C(L_1)]\!]I$ of $C(L_1)$ into a computation $\tau_2 \in [\![C(L_2)]\!]I$ with the same client trace projection: $\mathsf{client}(\tau_1) = \mathsf{client}(\tau_2)$. To this end, we use the semantics of Section 3, which defines the interpretation of L_1, L_2, $C_{\mathsf{sig}(L_1)}(\cdot)$ and their compositions. Namely, to transform τ_1 into τ_2, we first apply Lemma 6 to generate two computations from τ_1—a library-local computation $\xi_1 \in [\![\mathsf{MGC}(L_1)]\!]I_l$ and a client-local one $\eta \in [\![C_{\mathsf{sig}(L_1)}(\cdot)]\!]I_c$—such that $\mathsf{client}(\tau_1) = \mathsf{client}(\eta)$ and $\mathsf{history}(\tau_1) = \mathsf{history}(\eta) = \mathsf{history}(\xi_1)$. Note that the computation η of C thus constructed excludes the internal library actions. Since $L_1 \sqsubseteq L_2$, for some computation $\xi_2 \in [\![\mathsf{MGC}(L_2)]\!]I_l$, we have $\mathsf{history}(\xi_1) \sqsubseteq \mathsf{history}(\xi_2)$. By Lemma 7, ξ_2 can be transformed into a computation $\xi_2' \in [\![\mathsf{MGC}(L_2)]\!]I_l$ such that $\mathsf{history}(\xi_2') = \mathsf{history}(\xi_1) = \mathsf{history}(\eta)$. We then use Lemma 8 to compose the library-local computation ξ_2' with the client-local one η into a computation $\tau_2 \in [\![C(L_2)]\!]I$ such that $\mathsf{client}(\tau_2) = \mathsf{client}(\eta) = \mathsf{client}(\tau_1)$. □

6 Checking Linearizability on TSO

We have implemented a tool called LINTSO for systematically testing concurrent libraries for our notion of linearizability. Our intention in implementing the tool is twofold. First, the tool allows developers of concurrent libraries to find violations of linearizability quickly. The second (and more important) goal is to use the tool to perform a sanity check of our definition of linearizability by making sure that real-world algorithms that are commonly accepted as correct are linearizable with respect to it.

LINTSO is similar in spirit to the LINE-UP tool for checking linearizability on a sequentially consistent memory model [4]. It takes as input a concrete and an abstract implementation of a library (such as the ones in Figures 3 and 4) along with a (bounded) test harness that calls into the library. LINTSO then composes the input with an operational model of TSO such that sequentially consistent behaviors of the resulting program emulate TSO behaviors of the input. This allows LINTSO to use existing model checkers, such as CHESS [13], to systematically enumerate the behaviors of the harness and the library on TSO.

In a first phase, LINTSO exhaustively generates all histories of the input harness calling into the abstract version of the library. In a subsequent phase, LINTSO systematically enumerates the TSO behaviors of the harness and the concrete version of the library. For every such behavior, LINTSO uses the linearizability condition to check if the behavior is consistent with respect to some history observed in the first phase. Any violation is reported as an error.

If the enumeration in the second phase completes, then LINTSO guarantees that the abstract implementation linearizes the concrete one for the given harness. If the number of possible computations in this phase is too large, a subset of them can be considered by bounding the number of context switches [13]. Obviously, this does not provide a complete guarantee of linearizability, as only (possibly a subset of computations of) one of the infinitely many harnesses is considered.

In our experiments we considered the following concurrent algorithms that were identified as challenges in [14]:

- seqlock, the readers-writer lock we discussed in Section 4;
- simple spinlock, which does not provide fairness guarantees;
- ticketed spinlock, ensuring fairness using a variant of the Bakery algorithm;
- initialisation using double-checked locking.

We provide their code and specifications in [5, Appendix B]. The seqlock and the spinlock implementations are used in various versions of the Linux kernel [3]. The above algorithms are optimised for the TSO memory model and, when used in certain ways, can exhibit behaviours that cannot be reproduced on a sequentially consistent memory model. In fact, the correctness of the spinlock implementations was a subject of debate among Linux developers [14].

In more detail, the simple and ticketed spinlocks do not execute a memory barrier after writing a value into the lock data structure saying that the lock is free. According to the semantics of TSO, this does not violate mutual exclusion: delaying the write in the store buffer can only lead to CPUs that want to acquire the lock waiting longer. As in the case of a seqlock (Figure 4), the specification of a spinlock captures the fact that the lock release can be delayed.

The initialisation using double-checked locking first checks if an object is initialised by reading a corresponding flag without acquiring the lock for the object. Since the read is not preceded by a memory barrier, on TSO this can cause it to return 'uninitialised' even after the object has been in fact initialised. This does not violate the correctness of the algorithm, since the flag is then re-checked with the lock held.

For simple harnesses of the above examples, consisting of up to 3 threads, each performing up to 3 operations, LINTSO performed the check in a matter of minutes. The specification histories were generated exhaustively, and the implementation histories for computations up to a maximum of two preemptions (the CHESS default). In all cases, the tool did not detect any errors. As a further sanity check, we introduced simple errors in the examples, e.g., by replacing xunlock with an unlock in the concrete version. LINTSO was able to find all of them.

We used Theorem 4 to modularise checking the linearizability of the intialisation using double-checked locking. Namely, Theorem 4 allowed us to consider the specification of the spinlock used in this example, instead of a particular implementation. This cut down the number of interleavings to be analysed and made the analysis more efficient. Additionally, it allowed us to prove the linearizability of the algorithm regardless of the particular spinlock implementation used (e.g., the simple or ticketed spinlock). This is just one example of using the Abstraction Theorem to verify concurrent programs compositionally.

7 Related Work and Conclusion

All the definitions of linearizability proposed for various settings so far [11,8,10,9] have assumed a sequentially consistent memory model. This paper is the first to define a notion of linearizability on a weak memory model and show that it validates the Abstraction Theorem (Theorem 4). Our result is based on a novel insight about what information should be kept in histories to specify interactions between the library and the client due to the weak memory model. Even though in this paper we considered only one weak memory model—TSO, implemented by x86 processors [15]—our insights form a starting point for investigating weaker memory models, such as those of Power [17] and ARM [1] processors, and the C++ language [2].

Our work lays the foundation for future correctness proofs for implementations of concurrent algorithms in operating system kernels [3] and language run-times [2]. In particular, we hope that it should be possible to develop a logic for establishing the proposed notion of linearizability formally, based on existing logics for proving safety properties on TSO [20,16] and linearizability on sequentially consistent memory models [18,19]. This should make proofs such as that of Theorem 3 easier to carry out.

We also intend to investigate definitions of linearizability on weak memory models in cases when the library and the client interact in more complicated ways. For example, in this paper we did not consider the transfer of data structure ownership between the library and the client, assuming that they communicate only by passing values of a primitive type. We believe that our approach to handling weak memory can be married with a previous generalisation of linearizability for ownership transfer on a sequentially consistent memory model [9].

Acknowledgements. We thank Scott Owens, Ian Wehrman and the anonymous reviewers for comments that helped to improve the paper. Yang was supported by EPSRC.

References

1. Alglave, J., Fox, A., Ishtiaq, S., Myreen, M.O., Sarkar, S., Sewell, P., Zappa Nardelli, F.: The semantics of Power and ARM multiprocessor machine code. In: DAMP (2009)
2. Batty, M., Owens, S., Sarkar, S., Sewell, P., Weber, T.: Mathematizing C++ concurrency. In: POPL (2011)
3. Bovet, D., Cesati, M.: Understanding the Linux Kernel, 3rd edn. O'Reilly (2005)
4. Burckhardt, S., Dern, C., Musuvathi, M., Tan, R.: Line-up: A complete and automatic linearizability checker. In: PLDI (2010)
5. Burckhardt, S., Gotsman, A., Musuvathi, M., Yang, H.: Concurrent library correctness on the TSO memory model, extended version (2012), `http://www.software.imdea.org/~gotsman`
6. Burckhardt, S., Musuvathi, M.: Effective Program Verification for Relaxed Memory Models. In: Gupta, A., Malik, S. (eds.) CAV 2008. LNCS, vol. 5123, pp. 107–120. Springer, Heidelberg (2008)
7. Cohen, E., Schirmer, B.: From Total Store Order to Sequential Consistency: A Practical Reduction Theorem. In: Kaufmann, M., Paulson, L.C. (eds.) ITP 2010. LNCS, vol. 6172, pp. 403–418. Springer, Heidelberg (2010)
8. Filipović, I., O'Hearn, P., Rinetzky, N., Yang, H.: Abstraction for Concurrent Objects. In: Castagna, G. (ed.) ESOP 2009. LNCS, vol. 5502, pp. 252–266. Springer, Heidelberg (2009)
9. Gotsman, A., Yang, H.: Linearizability with ownership transfer. Draft (2011), `http://www.software.imdea.org/~gotsman`
10. Gotsman, A., Yang, H.: Liveness-Preserving Atomicity Abstraction. In: Aceto, L., Henzinger, M., Sgall, J. (eds.) ICALP 2011, Part II. LNCS, vol. 6756, pp. 453–465. Springer, Heidelberg (2011)
11. Herlihy, M.P., Wing, J.M.: Linearizability: a correctness condition for concurrent objects. TOPLAS 12 (1990)
12. Manson, J., Pugh, W., Adve, S.V.: The Java memory model. In: POPL (2005)
13. Musuvathi, M., Qadeer, S., Ball, T., Basler, G., Nainar, P.A., Neamtiu, I.: Finding and reproducing heisenbugs in concurrent programs. In: OSDI (2008)
14. Owens, S.: Reasoning about the Implementation of Concurrency Abstractions on x86-TSO. In: D'Hondt, T. (ed.) ECOOP 2010. LNCS, vol. 6183, pp. 478–503. Springer, Heidelberg (2010)

15. Owens, S., Sarkar, S., Sewell, P.: A Better x86 Memory Model: x86-TSO. In: Berghofer, S., Nipkow, T., Urban, C., Wenzel, M. (eds.) TPHOLs 2009. LNCS, vol. 5674, pp. 391–407. Springer, Heidelberg (2009)
16. Ridge, T.: A Rely-Guarantee Proof System for x86-TSO. In: Leavens, G.T., O'Hearn, P., Rajamani, S.K. (eds.) VSTTE 2010. LNCS, vol. 6217, pp. 55–70. Springer, Heidelberg (2010)
17. Sarkar, S., Sewell, P., Alglave, J., Maranget, L., Williams, D.: Understanding POWER multiprocessors. In: PLDI (2011)
18. Vafeiadis, V.: Modular fine-grained concurrency verification. PhD Thesis. Technical Report UCAM-CL-TR-726, University of Cambridge (2008)
19. Vafeiadis, V.: Automatically Proving Linearizability. In: Touili, T., Cook, B., Jackson, P. (eds.) CAV 2010. LNCS, vol. 6174, pp. 450–464. Springer, Heidelberg (2010)
20. Wehrman, I., Berdine, J.: A proposal for weak-memory local reasoning. In: LOLA (2011)

Automated Verification of Equivalence Properties of Cryptographic Protocols*

Rohit Chadha[1], Ştefan Ciobâcă[1], and Steve Kremer[1,2]

[1] LSV, ENS Cachan & CNRS & INRIA
[2] INRIA Nancy - Grand-Est

Abstract. Indistinguishability properties are essential in formal verification of cryptographic protocols. They are needed to model anonymity properties, strong versions of confidentiality and resistance to offline guessing attacks, and can be conveniently modeled using process equivalences. We present a novel procedure to verify equivalence properties for bounded number of sessions. Our procedure is able to verify trace equivalence for determinate cryptographic protocols. On determinate protocols, trace equivalence coincides with observational equivalence which can therefore be automatically verified for such processes. When protocols are not determinate our procedure can be used for both under- and over-approximations of trace equivalence, which proved successful on examples. The procedure can handle a large set of cryptographic primitives, namely those which can be modeled by an optimally reducing convergent rewrite system. Although, we were unable to prove its termination, it has been implemented in a prototype tool and has been effectively tested on examples, some of which were outside the scope of existing tools.

1 Introduction

Cryptographic protocols are distributed programs which rely on the use of cryptography to secure electronic transactions such as those that arise in electronic commerce and wireless communication. They are also being applied in new domains such as in Internet voting—legally binding political elections in Estonia, Norway and Switzerland offer the possibility for Internet voting in 2011. This has led to increasing demands on the complexity of desired security properties, leading to more complex cryptographic protocols. Given the socio-economic-political consequences and the history of incorrect design of cryptographic protocols, the need for formal proofs of correctness of protocols has been widely recognized. Formal reasoning about cryptographic protocols is challenging as one has to reason against all potentially malicious behavior—all communication between protocol participants is assumed to be under the control of an adversary.

In order to make the task of formal analysis amenable to automation, usually the assumption of black-box cryptography and unbounded computational power

* This work was partially supported by ANR projects ARA SESUR AVOTÉ and JCJC VIP no 11 JS02 006 01 and the ERC grant agreement n° 258865, project ProSecure.

H. Seidl (Ed.): ESOP 2012, LNCS 7211, pp. 108–127, 2012.

of the adversary is made. This adversarial model is often called the Dolev-Yao model and is derived from Dolev and Yao's seminal paper [29]. It has proved extremely successful, and there are several automated tools [10,6,31] that can automatically check trace-properties such as (weak forms of) confidentiality and authentication. While trace-based properties are certainly important, many crucial security properties can only be expressed in terms of *indistinguishability* (or equivalence). They include strong flavors of confidentiality [11]; resistance to guessing attacks in password based protocols [8]; and anonymity properties in private authentication [3], electronic voting [26,7], vehicular networks [24] and RFID protools [5,15]. More generally, indistinguishability allows to model security by the means of ideal systems, which are correct by construction [4,25]. Indistinguishability properties of cryptographic protocols are naturally modeled by the means of *observational* and *testing equivalences* in cryptographic extensions of process calculi, e.g., the spi [4] and the applied-pi calculus [2]. While we have good tools for automated verification of trace properties, the situation is different for indistinguishability properties.

State-of-the-Art. Hüttel [34] showed undecidability of observational equivalence in the spi calculus, even for the finite control fragment, as well as decidability for the finite, i.e., replication-free, fragment of the spi calculus. The decidability result however only holds for a fixed set of cryptographic primitives and does not yield a practical algorithm. Current results [12] allow to approximate observational equivalence for an unbounded number of sessions. However, this approximation does not suffice to conclude for many applications, *e.g.*, [26,5]. Our approach overcomes these limitations for some applications in [26]. We still cannot conclude for the e-passport example in [5], albeit for a different reason: our procedure does not currently handle else branches in protocols.

Symbolic bisimulations have also been devised for the spi [14,13,39] and applied pi calculus [27,35] to avoid unbounded branching due to adversary inputs. However, only [27,39] and [14] yield a decision procedure, again only approximating observational equivalence. The results of [27] have been further refined to show a decision procedure on a restricted class of *simple* processes [23]. They rely on a procedure deciding the equivalence of constraint systems, introduced by Baudet [8], for the special case of verifying the existence of guessing attacks. Baudet's procedure allows arbitrary cryptographic primitives that can be modeled as a subterm convergent rewrite systems [1]. An alternate procedure achieving the same goal was proposed by Chevalier and Rusinowitch [19]. However, both procedures are highly non-deterministic and do not yield a reasonable algorithm that could be implemented. Therefore, Cheval *et al.* [17] have designed a new procedure and a prototype tool to decide the equivalence of constraint systems, but only for a fixed set of primitives. Tools have also been implemented for checking testing equivalence [30], open bisimulation [39] and trace equivalence [18] for a bounded number of sessions but again only for a limited set of primitives. One may note that [18] is the only decision procedure to consider negative tests (else branches), crucial in several case studies [5,3].

Our Contribution. We introduce a new procedure for verifying equivalence properties for processes specified in a cryptographic process calculus (without replication). Our main contributions are as follows.

- Our procedure checks for two equivalences which over- and under-approximate the standard notion of trace equivalence $\approx_t$ for cryptographic protocols: the under-approximation can be used to prove protocols correct while the over-approximation can be used to rule out incorrect protocols.
- Cortier and Delaune [23] have shown that observational equivalence coincides with $\approx_t$ for the class of *determinate* processes. They also give a decision procedure for a strict sub-class of determinate processes, namely, *simple* processes. We show that for determinate processes the coarser relation coincides with $\approx_t$, and our procedure can be used to verify observational equivalence for the whole class of determinate processes.
- A novelty of our procedure is that it is based on a *fully abstract* modeling of symbolic traces in *first-order Horn clauses*. This is in contrast to the constraint-solving techniques employed in [39,17,18,8,19] for verifying under-approximations of observational equivalence. Techniques based on Horn clauses have been extensively used, e.g., in [10,40,33], for an unbounded number of sessions. Of these tools, only ProVerif [10,12] can verify an equivalence property, which is an under-approximation of observational equivalence. Horn clause modeling of an unbounded number of sessions of security protocols may allow false attacks. In contrast, we show our modeling of a bounded number of sessions for determinate protocols to be precise.
- Our modeling is fully abstract for arbitrary cryptographic primitives that can be modeled as a convergent rewrite system which has the *finite variant property*. Not only this strictly includes the class of primitives that can be modeled as subterm convergent rewrite systems, but this also allows us to handle a larger class of cryptographic primitives than [39,17,18,8,19,10]. For example, this allows us to handle trapdoor commitment as used by Okamoto for electronic voting in [38]. Although we were unable to prove termination of our procedure, we conjecture it to terminate for the class of cryptographic primitives that can be modeled as subterm convergent rewrite systems. Our conjecture is supported by experimental evidence.
- Our procedure is implemented in the AKiSs (Active Knowledge in Security protocols) prototype tool and used among others to give the first automated proof of anonymity for the electronic voting protocol presented in [32].

Technical proofs are given in an accompanying technical report [16].

2 Preliminaries

Terms. Let $\mathcal{F}$ be a signature, i.e., a finite set of function symbols and *ar* a function that assigns to each function symbol a natural number, its arity. A function symbol of arity 0 is called a *constant*. Given a set of *atoms* $\mathcal{A}$ and a signature $\mathcal{F}$, we denote by $\mathcal{T}_{\mathcal{F},\mathcal{A}}$ the set of terms built inductively from $\mathcal{A}$ by applying functions symbols in $\mathcal{F}$. Given sets of atoms $\mathcal{A}_1, \mathcal{A}_2, \ldots, \mathcal{A}_n$, we denote the set $\mathcal{T}_{\mathcal{F},\cup_{1\leq i\leq n}\mathcal{A}_i}$ by $\mathcal{T}_{\mathcal{F},\mathcal{A}_1,\mathcal{A}_2,\ldots\mathcal{A}_n}$. We assume that we have the following countably infinite pairwise disjoint sets: a set $\mathcal{N}$ of *private names*, $\mathcal{M}$ of *public names*, a set $\mathcal{C}$ of *public channel names*, a set $\mathcal{W}$ of *parameters*, and a set $\mathcal{X}$ of *message variables*. Intuitively, elements of the set $\mathcal{N}$ represent nonces generated by honest principals of a protocol, elements of $\mathcal{M}$ represent nonces available both to the adversary and to the honest participants and elements of $\mathcal{C}$ represent names of public channels (e.g. the name of a public network). Elements of $\mathcal{W}$ are pointers used by the adversary to refer to messages output by the honest participants in a protocol. We fix an enumeration $w_1, w_2, \ldots$ of the elements of $\mathcal{W}$. We let x, y, z range over $\mathcal{X}$. We also define the following set of terms:

- Terms denotes the set of all terms $\mathcal{T}_{\mathcal{F},\mathcal{N},\mathcal{M},\mathcal{W},\mathcal{X}}$.
- $\mathsf{Messages}$ denotes the set of *messages* $\mathcal{T}_{\mathcal{F},\mathcal{N},\mathcal{M}}$.
- $\mathsf{SMessages}$ denotes the set of *symbolic messages* $\mathcal{T}_{\mathcal{F},\mathcal{N},\mathcal{M},\mathcal{X}}$.

If t is a term, we denote by $vars(t)$ the set of variables appearing in t, by $names(t)$ the set of names (public or private) appearing in t. The functions $vars$, $names$ are extended to sequences and sets of terms as expected.

Example 1. Consider the signature $\mathcal{F} = \{\mathsf{enc}, \mathsf{dec}, \mathsf{pair}, \mathsf{fst}, \mathsf{snd}\}$. The term $t = \mathsf{pair}(\mathsf{enc}(a, k_1, r_1), \mathsf{enc}(b, k_2, r_2))$ models the pair of the asymmetric encryptions of public names a and b with keys k_1, resp. k_2 and randomness r_1, resp. r_2.

A substitution is a partial function $\sigma : \mathcal{W} \cup \mathcal{X} \to \mathsf{Terms}$. We restrict substitutions to map elements of $\mathcal{W}$ to elements of $\mathsf{Messages}$ and elements of $\mathcal{X}$ to elements of $\mathsf{SMessages}$. The domain of σ shall be denoted by $dom(\sigma)$. We denote by $\sigma[X]$ the substitution whose domain is restricted to X. We only consider substitutions with finite domains. As usual, a substitution extends homomorphically to terms and we write $t\sigma$ for the term obtained by applying σ to t.

Rewriting and Unification. Two terms s and t are (syntactically) *unifiable* if there exists a substitution σ such that $s\sigma = t\sigma$. We denote by $\mathrm{mgu}(s,t)$ their most general unifier. We assume that the reader is familiar with basic notions of rewriting and only briefly introduce our notations. A rewrite system R is a set of rewrite rules of the form $\ell \to r$ where $\ell, r \in \mathsf{Terms}$, $names(l, r) = \emptyset$ and $vars(r) \subseteq (\ell)$. We write $t \to_{\mathsf{R}} u$ when a term t can be rewritten in one step to u. $\to_{\mathsf{R}}^*$ denotes the transitive and reflexive closure of $\to_{\mathsf{R}}$. We only consider convergent rewrite systems and denote by $t{\downarrow_{\mathsf{R}}}$ the normal form of a term t. Two terms s and t are said to be equal modulo R, written $s =_{\mathsf{R}} t$, if $s{\downarrow_{\mathsf{R}}} = t{\downarrow_{\mathsf{R}}}$. Given a substitution σ, $\sigma{\downarrow_R}$ is the substitution such that $dom(\sigma{\downarrow_{\mathsf{R}}}) = dom(\sigma)$ and for all $u \in dom(\sigma)$, $\sigma{\downarrow_R}(u) = \sigma(u){\downarrow_{\mathsf{R}}}$. We shall omit R when clear from the context.

Example 2. Let $\mathcal{F}$ be the signature in Example 1. Consider the rewrite system $\mathsf{R} = \{\mathsf{dec}(\mathsf{enc}(x, y, z), y) \to x, \mathsf{fst}(\mathsf{pair}(x, y)) \to x, \mathsf{snd}(\mathsf{pair}(x, y)) \to y\}$. The first rule models that a message can be decrypted, provided decryption uses the same key (represented by variable y) as encryption. The last two rules model projection of the first and second component of a pair. We have that $t = \mathsf{fst}(\mathsf{pair}(\mathsf{dec}(\mathsf{enc}(a, k, r), k), b)) \to_{\mathsf{R}} \mathsf{fst}(\mathsf{pair}(a, b)) \to_{\mathsf{R}} a = t{\downarrow_{\mathsf{R}}}$.

We recall the notion of complete set of variants for a convergent rewrite system [22]:

Definition 1. *A set of substitutions* variants$(t_1, \ldots, t_k)$ *is called a* complete set of variants *of terms* $t_1, \ldots, t_k$ *if for any substitution* ω *there exist* $\sigma \in$ variants$(t_1, \ldots, t_k)$ *and a substitution* τ *such that for all* $1 \leq j \leq k$ *we have that* $\omega[vars(t_j)]\downarrow = (\sigma\downarrow\tau)[vars(t_j)]$ *and* $(t_j\omega)\downarrow = (t_j\sigma)\downarrow\tau$.

Intuitively, the set of variants of t represents a pre-computation such that any instance of t in normal form is *syntactically* equal to an instance of $t\sigma_i\downarrow$ for some i, without the need to apply further rewrite steps. A rewrite system has the *finite variant property* if for any finite sequence of terms a finite, complete set of variants exists. An algorithm for computing complete sets of variants which is correct whenever the rewrite system is *optimally reducing* [37] is presented in [21]. Optimally reducing rewrite systems include subterm convergent systems [1] (and hence the classical Dolev Yao theories for encryption, signatures and hash functions), as well as a theory for modeling blind signatures. Complete sets of variants can be used to compute finite complete sets of unifiers modulo R [21], which are formally defined in [16] and denoted by $\mathrm{mgu}_{\mathsf{R}}$. We assume, henceforth, that rewrite systems in this paper have the finite variant property.

Frames, Deducibility and Static Equivalence. We will use the notion of a *frame* [2] to represent messages which have been recorded by an attacker.

Definition 2. *A* frame φ *is a substitution* $\{w_1 \mapsto t_1, \ldots, w_n \mapsto t_n\}$ *where* $t_i \in$ Messages *$(1 \leq i \leq n)$.*

Please note, in our definition, every frame φ with $|dom(\varphi)| = n$ has $dom(\varphi) = \{w_1, \ldots, w_n\}$. The set of all frames is denoted as Frames. The adversary can use the messages learnt from the run of a protocol to construct new messages. This is modeled as the deducibility relation.

Definition 3. *Any term in* $\mathcal{T}_{\mathcal{F},\mathcal{M},\mathcal{W}}$ *is said to be a recipe. We say that* a message t is deducible from φ with a recipe r *(written as* $\varphi \vdash^r t$*) if* $t \in$ Messages *and* $r\varphi =_{\mathsf{R}} t$. *We write* Recipes *for the set* $\mathcal{T}_{\mathcal{F},\mathcal{M},\mathcal{W}}$.

Example 3. Consider the signature $\mathcal{F}$ and the rewrite system R in Example 2. Let $\varphi = \{w_1 \mapsto \mathsf{enc}(s,k,r), w_2 \mapsto k\}$ where $s, k, r \in \mathcal{N}$ are private names. We have that $\varphi \vdash^{\mathsf{dec}(w_1,w_2)} s$. Note that $\mathsf{dec}(w_1, k) \notin$ Recipes as $k \in \mathcal{N}$. If s were public instead of being private (ie, $s \in \mathcal{M}$ instead of $s \in \mathcal{N}$) then we also have that $\varphi \vdash^s s$; as public names are always deducible.

Static equivalence captures indistinguishability of sequences of messages:

Definition 4. *Let* $r_1, r_2 \in$ Recipes. *A* test $r_1 \stackrel{?}{=} r_2$ holds *in a frame* φ *(written* $(r_1 = r_2)\varphi$*) if* $\varphi \vdash^{r_1} t$ *and* $\varphi \vdash^{r_2} t$ *for some* t, i.e., r_1 *and* r_2 *are recipes for the same term in* φ.

A frame φ_1 *is* statically included *in* φ_2 *(written* $\varphi_1 \sqsubseteq_s \varphi_2$*) iff for all* $r_1, r_2 \in$ Recipes *we have that* $(r_1 = r_2)\varphi_1$ *implies* $(r_1 = r_2)\varphi_2$. *Two frames* φ_1 *and* φ_2 *are* statically equivalent *(written* $\varphi_1 \approx_s \varphi_2$*) iff* $\varphi_1 \sqsubseteq_s \varphi_2$ *and* $\varphi_2 \sqsubseteq_s \varphi_1$.

Example 4. Let $a, b \in \mathcal{M}$ and $r, k, k' \in \mathcal{N}$. We have that $\{w_1 \mapsto \mathsf{enc}(a,k,r), w_2 \mapsto k\} \not\approx_s \{w_1 \mapsto \mathsf{enc}(b,k,r), w_2 \mapsto k\}$ because the test $(dec(w_1, w_2) = a)$ distinguishes the two frames. However, $\{w_1 \mapsto \mathsf{enc}(a,k,r), w_2 \mapsto k'\} \approx_s \{w_1 \mapsto \mathsf{enc}(b,k,r), w_2 \mapsto k'\}$. Moreover, we have that $\{w_1 \mapsto a, w_2 \mapsto b\} \sqsubseteq_s \{w_1 \mapsto a, w_2 \mapsto a\}$ while $\{w_1 \mapsto a, w_2 \mapsto a\} \not\sqsubseteq_s \{w_1 \mapsto a, w_2 \mapsto b\}$.

3 A Cryptographic Process Calculus

We model cryptographic protocols using a simple process calculus which has similarities with the applied pi-calculus [2].

Syntax. We model a bounded number of instances of a cryptographic protocol as a *finite* set of traces. Traces are defined using sequences of *actions* generated by the following grammar:

$$a ::= \mathbf{in}(c, x) \mid \mathbf{out}(c, t) \mid [s \stackrel{?}{=} t]$$

where $x \in \mathcal{X}, s, t \in \mathsf{SMessages}, c \in \mathcal{C}$. A *trace* T is a sequence of actions $T = a_1.a_2.\dots.a_n$. As usual, a receive action $\mathbf{in}(c, x)$ acts as a binding construct for x. We assume the usual definitions of free and bound variables for traces. We also assume that each variable is bound at most once. A trace is *ground* if it does not contain any free variables. The set of ground traces shall be represented as $\mathsf{GndTraces}$. A set of traces $P = \{T_1, \dots, T_n\}$ is said to be a *process*. A process is ground if all of its traces are ground. We identify traces with singleton processes.

Remark 1. We do not have an ν operator: the binding happens implicitly by the use of private names in $\mathcal{N}$. We have also not explicitly included the parallel operator $\mid$ and the choice operator $+$. One could include these and generate the corresponding set of traces. Thus, there is no loss in expressivity. However, an explicit enumeration of the traces can result in an exponential number of traces.

Semantics. The semantics of a process is defined using the semantics of its traces. The semantics of a trace is given in terms of a labeled transition system T. We assume that all interactions between protocol participants are mediated by the adversary. The labeled transition system records the interaction of the protocol participants with the adversary. The set of labels of T is defined using the set $\mathsf{Recipes}$. Recall that the set $\mathsf{Recipes}$ is the set $\mathcal{T}_{\mathcal{F},\mathcal{M},\mathcal{W}}$ (see Section 2). The set of labels, Labels, is $\{\, \mathbf{in}(c, r), \mathbf{out}(c), \mathbf{test} \mid r \in \mathsf{Recipes}, c \in \mathcal{C}\,\}$.

The labeled transition system T is a subset of $(\mathsf{GndTraces} \times \mathsf{Frames}) \times \mathsf{Labels} \times (\mathsf{GndTraces} \times \mathsf{Frames})$. We write $(T, \varphi) \xrightarrow{\ell} (T', \varphi')$ whenever $((T, \varphi), \ell, (T', \varphi')) \in \mathsf{T}$. The frame in the transition system is used to record the messages that the protocol participants have sent in the past. The relation $\xrightarrow{\ell}$ is defined as follows:

$$\textsc{Receive}\ \frac{\varphi \vdash^r t}{(\mathbf{in}(c, x).T, \varphi) \xrightarrow{\mathbf{in}(c,r)} (T\{x \mapsto t\}, \varphi)} \qquad \textsc{Test}\ \frac{s =_{\mathsf{R}} t}{([s \stackrel{?}{=} t].T, \varphi) \xrightarrow{\mathbf{test}} (T, \varphi)}$$

$$\textsc{Send}\ \frac{}{(\mathbf{out}(c, t).T, \varphi) \xrightarrow{\mathbf{out}(c)} (T, \varphi \cup \{w_{|dom(\varphi)|+1} \mapsto t\})}$$

The label $\mathbf{in}(c, r)$ indicates a message sent by the adversary over the channel c and r is the recipe that adversary uses to create this message. The label $\mathbf{out}(c)$ indicates a message sent over the public channel c and transition rule SEND records the message sent in the frame. Finally, the rule Test is an internal action.

We write $(T, \varphi) \overset{\ell}{\Rightarrow} (T', \varphi')$ when either $(T, \varphi) \xrightarrow{\mathbf{test}^*, \ell, \mathbf{test}^*} (T', \varphi')$ and $\ell \neq \mathbf{test}$ or $(T, \varphi) \xrightarrow{\mathbf{test}^*} (T', \varphi')$ and $\ell = \mathbf{test}$, where $\mathbf{test}^*$ denotes an arbitrary number of **test** actions. We also write $(T_0, \varphi_0) \xrightarrow{\ell_1, \ldots, \ell_n} (T_n, \varphi_n)$ when $(T_0, \varphi_0) \xrightarrow{\ell_1} (T_1, \varphi_1) \ldots \xrightarrow{\ell_n} (T_n, \varphi_n)$ (and similarly for the $\Rightarrow$ relation) and say that $\ell_1 \ldots \ell_n$ is a *run* of (T_0, φ_0). If P is a process, we write $(P, \varphi) \xrightarrow{\ell_1, \ldots, \ell_n} (T', \varphi')$ (resp. $\xRightarrow{\ell_1, \ldots, \ell_n} (T', \varphi')$) if there exists a trace $T \in P$ such that $(T, \varphi) \xrightarrow{\ell_1, \ldots, \ell_n} (T', \varphi')$ (resp. $(T, \varphi) \xRightarrow{\ell_1, \ldots, \ell_n} (T', \varphi')$).

Process Equivalences. We will now define different flavors of trace equivalence which will be useful in this paper. We first recall the standard definition of trace equivalence in cryptographic process algebras.

Definition 5. ***(Trace equivalence)*** *A ground process P is said to be* trace-included *in a ground process Q (written $P \sqsubseteq_t Q$) if whenever $(P, \emptyset) \xRightarrow{\ell_1, \ldots, \ell_n} (T, \varphi)$ then there exist T', φ' such that $(Q, \emptyset) \xRightarrow{\ell_1, \ldots, \ell_n} (T', \varphi')$ and $\varphi \approx_s \varphi'$. Two processes P and Q are* trace-equivalent *(written $P \approx_t Q$) if $P \sqsubseteq_t Q$ and $Q \sqsubseteq_t P$.*

We will also define two other notions of trace equivalence, one coarser and one more fine-grained. We start by describing the coarser trace equivalence.

Definition 6. *Given ground processes P and Q, we say that $P \sqsubseteq_{ct} Q$ if whenever $(P, \emptyset) \xRightarrow{\ell_1, \ldots, \ell_n} (T, \varphi)$ then there exist T', φ' such that $(Q, \emptyset) \xRightarrow{\ell_1, \ldots, \ell_n} (T', \varphi')$ and $\phi \sqsubseteq_s \phi'$. We say that $P \approx_{ct} Q$ if $P \sqsubseteq_{ct} Q$ and $Q \sqsubseteq_{ct} P$.*

The following example illustrates the difference between $\approx_t$ and $\approx_{ct}$.

Example 5. Let P and Q be the ground processes defined as follows: $P = \{\, \mathbf{out}(c, a).\mathbf{out}(c, a) \,\}$ and $Q = \{\, \mathbf{out}(c, a).\mathbf{out}(c, a), \mathbf{out}(c, a).\mathbf{out}(c, b) \,\}$. Clearly $P \sqsubseteq_{ct} Q$. Observe also that $Q \sqsubseteq_{ct} P$. This is because $\{w_1 \mapsto a, w_2 \mapsto b\} \sqsubseteq_s \{w_1 \mapsto a, w_2 \mapsto a\}$. Thus, $P \approx_{ct} Q$. But $P \not\approx_t Q$.

We show, however, that these two notions coincide for the class of *determinate processes.* In the context of the applied pi calculus determinate processes were previously studied by Cortier and Delaune in [23].

Definition 7. ***(Determinate process)*** *A ground process P is determinate if whenever $(P, \emptyset) \xRightarrow{\ell_1, \ldots, \ell_n} (T, \varphi)$ and $(P, \emptyset) \xRightarrow{\ell_1, \ldots, \ell_n} (T', \varphi')$ then $\varphi \approx_s \varphi'$.*

Intuitively, determinate processes are processes in which the adversary's static knowledge at any instance is completely determined by its past interaction with the protocol participants. Note that any ground trace is determinate.

As already mentioned above, it was demonstrated in [23] that trace equivalence coincides with observational equivalence for determinate processes. We show that $\approx_t$ and $\approx_{ct}$ also coincide for this class of processes.

Theorem 1. *If P and Q are ground processes then $P \approx_t Q$ implies $P \approx_{ct} Q$. Furthermore, if P and Q are determinate, then $P \approx_{ct} Q$ implies $P \approx_t Q$.*

We introduce a more fine-grained notion of trace equivalence, denoted $\approx_{ft}$.

Definition 8. *Given ground processes P and Q, we say that $P \sqsubseteq_{ft} Q$ whenever for all trace $T \in P$ there exists a trace $T' \in Q$ such that $T \approx_t T'$. We say that $P \approx_{ft} Q$ if $P \sqsubseteq_{ft} Q$ and $Q \sqsubseteq_{ft} P$.*

It follows directly form the definition that $\approx_{ft} \subset \approx_t$. The difference between these two relations is illustrated by the following example.

Example 6. Let P and Q be ground processes defined as follows:

$$\begin{aligned} P = \{\ & \mathbf{out}(c, enc(a,k)).\mathbf{out}(c, enc(b,k)).\mathbf{in}(c,x).[x = enc(a,k)].\mathbf{out}(c,k), \\ & \mathbf{out}(c, enc(a,k)).\mathbf{out}(c, enc(b,k)).\mathbf{in}(c,x).[x = enc(b,k)].\mathbf{out}(c,k)\} \\ Q = \{\ & \mathbf{out}(c, enc(a,k)).\mathbf{out}(c, enc(b,k)).\mathbf{in}(c,x).[x = enc(dec(x,k),k)].\mathbf{out}(c,k)\} \end{aligned}$$

where $k \in \mathcal{N}$ is a private name and a, b are constants. The test $x = enc(dec(x,k),k)$ simply checks whether x is an encryption with key k. It is not difficult to see that $P \approx_t Q$ but $P \not\approx_{ft} Q$.

Our procedure is able to check $\approx_{ct}$ (and hence $\approx_t$) for determinate processes. For non-determinate processes, we can check $\approx_{ft}$ and an over-approximation of $\approx_{ct}$ (see [16] for details) in order to under- and over-approximate $\approx_t$: as traces are determinate a procedure for checking $\approx_{ct}$ can be used to verify $\approx_{ft}$.

4 Modeling Traces as Horn Clauses

Our procedure is based on a fully abstract modeling of a trace into first-order Horn clauses. We give the details of this modeling; we start by giving some definitions that we need for defining the predicates used in the logic.

Symbolic Labels and Symbolic Runs. We define the set of *symbolic labels* as

$$\mathsf{SLabels} = \{\mathbf{in}(c,t), \mathbf{out}(c), \mathbf{test} \mid t \in \mathsf{SMessages}, c \in \mathcal{C}\}$$

and the set of *symbolic runs* as the set of finite sequences of symbolic labels (see Figure 1). The empty sequence is denoted by ϵ. We will often be lazy and write (empty space) for ϵ. Intuitively, a symbolic label stands for a set of possible labels, and a symbolic run stands for a set of possible runs of the protocol.

Symbolic Recipes. We assume a set $\mathcal{Y}$ of *recipe variables* disjoint from $\mathcal{X}$. The set of terms $\mathcal{T}_{\mathcal{F},\mathcal{M},\mathcal{W},\mathcal{Y}}$ shall be called *symbolic recipes* and denoted by $\mathsf{SRecipes}$. We use capital letters X, Y, Z to range over $\mathcal{Y}$. Intuitively, a symbolic recipe stands for a set of recipes. We can extend the definition of substitutions to include variables from $\mathcal{Y}$ in its domain: we only consider substitutions that map variables in $\mathcal{Y}$ to $\mathsf{SRecipes}$. A ground substitution must map variables in $\mathcal{Y}$ to $\mathsf{Recipes}$. The notions of mgu and $\mathrm{mgu}_{\mathsf{R}}$ is extended to symbolic recipes as expected.

Predicates. The predicates used in our modeling and the semantics of the predicates are given in Figure 1. The predicates are interpreted over a triple– a trace T, a frame φ and a substitution σ. We have four kinds of predicates, all of which have a symbolic run as an argument. Intuitively, the *reachability predicate* r_w says that each run represented by w is possible. The intruder knowledge predicate $\mathsf{k}_w(R,t)$ says that whenever a run represented by w happens, the (symbolic) message t can be constructed by the intruder using the (symbolic) recipe R. The identity predicate $\mathsf{i}_w(R,R')$ says that whenever the (symbolic) run SR happens, the (symbolic) recipes R and R' are recipes for the same (symbolic) term. The reachable identity predicate $\mathsf{ri}_w(R,R')$ is a short form for the conjunction of the predicates r_w and $\mathsf{i}_w(R,R')$.

Formulas and Statements. We consider first-order formulas built using the above predicates and the usual connectives (conjunction, disjunction, negation, implication, existential and universal quantification). As in the case of predicates, a formula is interpreted over a triple consisting of a trace T, a frame φ and a substitution σ; and the semantics is defined as expected. For ground formulas we do not need the substitution σ and when a formula f is ground we simply write $(T,\varphi) \models f$ to denote that this formula holds for (T,φ). If moreover, $dom(\varphi) = \emptyset$, we simply write $T \models f$ for $(T,\emptyset) \models f$.

Symbolic Runs ($\ell \in \mathsf{SLabels}$):
$u, v, w := \epsilon \mid \ell, w$

Predicates ($w \in \mathsf{SRuns}, R \in \mathsf{SRecipes}, t \in \mathsf{SMessages}$):
r_w (Reachability predicate)
$\mathsf{k}_w(R,t)$ (Intruder knowledge predicate)
$\mathsf{i}_w(R,R')$ (Identity predicate)
$\mathsf{ri}_w(R,R')$ (Reachable identity predicate)

Semantics ($\ell_i \in \mathsf{SLabels}, R \in \mathsf{SRecipes}, t \in \mathsf{SMessages}, T \in \mathsf{GndTraces}, \varphi \in \mathsf{Frames}$, σ a ground substitution):

$(T,\varphi_0,\sigma) \models \mathsf{r}_{\ell_1,\ldots,\ell_i}$ if $(T,\varphi_0) \xrightarrow{L_1} (T_1,\varphi_1) \xrightarrow{L_2} \ldots \xrightarrow{L_n} (T_n,\varphi_n)$ such that $\ell_i\sigma =_{\mathsf{R}} L_i\varphi_{i-1}$ for all $1 \le i \le n$

$(T,\varphi_0,\sigma) \models \mathsf{k}_{\ell_1,\ldots,\ell_i}(R,t)$ if when $(T,\varphi_0) \xrightarrow{L_1} (T_1,\varphi_1) \xrightarrow{L_2} \ldots \xrightarrow{L_n} (T_n,\varphi_n)$ such that $\ell_i\sigma =_{\mathsf{R}} L_i\varphi_{i-1}$ for all $1 \le i \le n$ then $\varphi_n \vdash^{R\sigma} t\sigma$

$(T,\varphi_0,\sigma) \models \mathsf{i}_{\ell_1,\ldots,\ell_i}(R,R')$ if there exists t s.t. $(T,\varphi_0,\sigma) \models \mathsf{k}_{\ell_1,\ldots,\ell_i}(R,t)$ and $(T,\varphi_0,\sigma) \models \mathsf{k}_{\ell_1,\ldots,\ell_i}(R',t)$

$(T,\varphi_0,\sigma) \models \mathsf{ri}_{\ell_1,\ldots,\ell_i}(R,R')$ if $(T,\varphi_0,\sigma) \models \mathsf{r}_{\ell_1,\ldots,\ell_i}$ and $(T,\varphi_0,\sigma) \models \mathsf{i}_{\ell_1,\ldots,\ell_i}(R,R')$

Fig. 1. Predicates

We now identify a subset of the formulas, which we shall call statements. Statements shall take the form of Horn clauses.

Definition 9. *A* statement *is a Horn clause of the form* $H \Leftarrow B_1, \ldots, B_n$ *where:*

1. $H \in \{\mathsf{r}_{\ell_1,\ldots,\ell_k}, \mathsf{k}_{\ell_1,\ldots,\ell_k}(R,t), \mathsf{i}_{\ell_1,\ldots,\ell_k}(R,R'), \mathsf{ri}_{\ell_1,\ldots,\ell_k}(R,R')\}$
2. *For each* $1 \le i \le n$, $B_i = \mathsf{k}_{\ell_1,\ldots,\ell_{j_i}}(X_i, t_i)$

for some $\ell_1, \ldots, \ell_k \in \mathsf{SLabels}$, $t \in \mathsf{SMessages}$, $R, R' \in \mathsf{SRecipes}$, $j_i \le k$, $t_1, \ldots, t_n \in \mathsf{SMessages}$ *and* $X_1, \ldots, X_n \in \mathcal{Y}$. *Furthermore* $X_1, \ldots, X_n$ *are distinct variables and if* $H = \mathsf{k}_{\ell_1,\ldots,\ell_k}(R,t)$ *then* $vars(t) \subseteq vars(t_1, \ldots, t_n)$.

As usual, we implicitly assume that in a Horn clause all variables are universally quantified. Hence, all statements are closed formulas.

The Set of Seed Statements. Our procedure is based on a fully abstract modeling of a trace in first-order Horn clauses. In this section, given a trace T we define a set of statements $\mathsf{seed}(T)$ that serve as a starting point for the modeling. We also establish that $\mathsf{seed}(T)$ is a sound and (partially) complete abstraction of the trace T. In order to formally define $\mathsf{seed}(T)$, we start by fixing some conventions.

Let $T = a_1.a_2.\ldots.a_n$ be a ground trace. We assume the following naming conventions: *(i)* if a_i is a receive action then $a_i = \mathbf{in}(c_i, x_i)$; *(ii)* $x_i \neq x_j$ for any $i \neq j$; *(iii)* if a_i is a send action then $a_i = \mathbf{out}(c_i, t_i)$; *(iv)* if a_i is a test action then $a_i = [s_i \stackrel{?}{=} t_i]$. Moreover, for each $1 \le i \le n$, let $\ell_i \in \mathsf{SLabels}$ be as follows:

$$\ell_i = \begin{cases} \mathbf{in}(c_i, x_i) & \text{if } a_i = \mathbf{in}(c_i, x_i) \\ \mathbf{out}(c_i) & \text{if } a_i = \mathbf{out}(c_i, t_i) \\ \mathbf{test} & \text{if } a_i = [s_i \stackrel{?}{=} t_i] \end{cases}.$$

For each $0 \le m \le n$, let the sets $R(m)$, $S(m)$ and $T(m)$ respectively denote the indices of the receive actions, send actions and test actions amongst $a_1, \ldots, a_m$. Formally, $R(m) = \{i \mid 1 \le i \le m, a_i = \mathbf{in}(c_i, x_i)\}$, $S(m) = \{i \mid 1 \le i \le m, a_i = \mathbf{out}(c_i, t_i)\}$ and $T(m) = \{i \mid 1 \le i \le m, a_i = [s_i \stackrel{?}{=} t_i]\}$ Given a set of public names $\mathcal{M}_0 \subseteq \mathcal{M}$, *set of seed statements* associated to T and $\mathcal{M}_0$, denoted $\mathsf{seed}(T, \mathcal{M}_0)$, is defined to be the set of statements given in Figure 2. If $\mathcal{M}_0 = \mathcal{M}$, then $\mathsf{seed}(T, \mathcal{M})$ is said to be the set of seed statements associated to T and in this case we write $\mathsf{seed}(T)$ as a shortcut for $\mathsf{seed}(T, \mathcal{M})$. While constructing $\mathsf{seed}(T, \mathcal{M})$, we apply $\mathrm{mgu}_{\mathsf{R}}$ to all tests. In addition, we also apply finite variants. This allows us to *get rid* of rewriting in our procedure.

For a set of statements K, we denote by $\mathcal{H}(K)$ the least Herbrand model of $K \cup \{\mathsf{k}_{\ell_1,\ldots,\ell_{n+1}}(X,x) \Leftarrow \mathsf{k}_{\ell_1,\ldots,\ell_n}(X,x)\}_{n\in\mathbb{N}} \cup \{\mathsf{i}_{\ell_1,\ldots,\ell_{n+1}}(X_1,X_2) \Leftarrow \mathsf{i}_{\ell_1,\ldots,\ell_n}(X_1,X_2)\}_{n\in\mathbb{N}}$. We show that as far as reachability predicates and intruder knowledge predicates are concerned, the set $\mathsf{seed}(T)$ is a complete abstraction T.

Theorem 2. *Let* T *be a ground trace.*

- *(Soundness.) For any* $f \in \mathsf{seed}(T) \cup \mathcal{H}(\mathsf{seed}(T))$ *we have that* $T \models f$.
- *(Completeness.) If* $(T, \emptyset) \xrightarrow{L_1,\ldots,L_m} (S, \varphi)$ *then (i)* $\mathsf{r}_{L_1\varphi\downarrow,\ldots,L_m\varphi\downarrow} \in \mathcal{H}(\mathsf{seed}(T))$, *and (ii) if* $\varphi \vdash^R t$ *then* $\mathsf{k}_{L_1\varphi\downarrow,\ldots,L_m\varphi\downarrow}(R, t\downarrow) \in \mathcal{H}(\mathsf{seed}(T))$.

$$\mathsf{r}_{\ell_1\sigma\tau\downarrow,\ldots,\ell_m\sigma\tau\downarrow} \Leftarrow \{\mathsf{k}_{\ell_1\sigma\tau\downarrow,\ldots,\ell_{j-1}\sigma\tau\downarrow}(X_j, x_j\sigma\tau\downarrow)\}_{j\in R(m)}$$
for all $0 \leq m \leq n$
for all $\sigma \in \mathrm{mgu}_{\mathsf{R}}(\{s_k = t_k\}_{k\in T(m)})$
for all $\tau \in \mathrm{variants}(\ell_1\sigma, \ldots, \ell_m\sigma)$

$$\mathsf{k}_{\ell_1\tau\downarrow,\ldots,\ell_m\tau\downarrow}(w_{|S(m)|}, t_m\tau\downarrow) \Leftarrow \{\mathsf{k}_{\ell_1\tau\downarrow,\ldots,\ell_{j-1}\tau\downarrow}(X_j, x_j\tau\downarrow)\}_{j\in R(m)}$$
for all $m \in S(n)$
for all $\tau \in \mathrm{variants}(\ell_1, \ldots, \ell_m, t_m)$

$$\mathsf{k}(c, c) \Leftarrow$$
for all public names $c \in \mathcal{M}_0$

$$\mathsf{k}_{\ell_1,\ldots,\ell_m}(f(Y_1, \ldots, Y_k), f(y_1, \ldots, y_k)\tau\downarrow) \Leftarrow \{\mathsf{k}_{\ell_1,\ldots,\ell_m}(Y_j, y_j\tau\downarrow)\}_{j\in\{1,\ldots,k\}}$$
for all $0 \leq m \leq n$
for all function symbols f of arity k
for all $\tau \in \mathrm{variants}(f(y_1, \ldots, y_k))$.

Fig. 2. Seed statements

Remark 2. Note that the set $\mathsf{seed}(T)$ is only partially complete as we have not shown above that if $\varphi \vdash^R t$ and $\varphi \vdash^{R'} t$ then $\mathsf{i}_{L_1\varphi\downarrow,\ldots,L_m\varphi\downarrow} \in \mathcal{H}(\mathsf{seed}(T))$. We will shortly show how the completeness of $\mathsf{seed}(T)$ can be built upon to achieve a) full abstraction of T and b) procedures for checking equivalences $\approx_{ct}$ and $\sqsubseteq_{ft}$.

5 Procedure for Deciding Trace Equivalence

We now present a procedure for verifying trace equivalence. At a high level, this consists of the following two steps that we will detail later.

1. A saturation procedure which constructs a set of *simple* statements from the set $\mathsf{seed}(T)$ which we will call *solved* statements. The saturation procedure ensures that the set of solved statements is a complete abstraction of T.
2. Given two ground processes P and Q, we saturate the set of seed statements for traces of P and Q and then use the solved statements to decide whether P and Q are trace equivalent.

5.1 Knowledge Bases and Saturation

The saturation procedure manipulates a set of statements called a knowledge base.

Definition 10. *Given a statement $f = H \Leftarrow B_1, \ldots, B_n$,*

- *f is said to be* solved *if for all $1 \leq i \leq n$, $B_i = \mathsf{k}_{\ell_1,\ldots,\ell_{j_i}}(X_i, x_i)$ for some variables $x_i \in \mathcal{X}, X_i \in \mathcal{Y}$.*
- *f is said to be* well-formed *if whenever it is solved and $H = \mathsf{k}_{\ell_1,\ldots,\ell_k}(R, t)$, we have that $t \notin \mathcal{X}$.*

$$\textsc{Resolution}\ \frac{\begin{array}{c} f \in K, g \in K_{\mathsf{solved}}, \\ f = \Big(H \Leftarrow \mathsf{k}_{uv}(X,t), B_1, \ldots, B_n\Big) \quad g = \Big(\mathsf{k}_w(R,t') \Leftarrow B_{n+1}, \ldots, B_m\Big) \\ \sigma = \mathrm{mgu}(\mathsf{k}_u(X,t), \mathsf{k}_w(R,t')) \quad t \notin \mathcal{X} \end{array}}{K = K \oplus h \text{ where } h = \Big((H \Leftarrow B_1, \ldots, B_m)\sigma\Big)}$$

$$\textsc{Equation}\ \frac{\begin{array}{c} f, g \in K_{\mathsf{solved}}, \quad f = \Big(\mathsf{k}_u(R,t) \Leftarrow B_1, \ldots, B_n\Big) \\ g = \Big(\mathsf{k}_{u'v'}(R',t') \Leftarrow B_{n+1}, \ldots, B_m\Big) \quad \sigma = \mathrm{mgu}(\mathsf{k}_u(\_,t), \mathsf{k}_{u'}(\_,t')) \end{array}}{K = K \oplus h \text{ where } h = \Big((\mathsf{i}_{u'v'}(R,R') \Leftarrow B_1, \ldots, B_m)\sigma\Big)}$$

$$\textsc{Test}\ \frac{\begin{array}{c} f, g \in K_{\mathsf{solved}}, \quad f = \Big(\mathsf{i}_u(R,R') \Leftarrow B_1, \ldots, B_n\Big) \\ g = \Big(\mathsf{r}_{u'v'} \Leftarrow B_{n+1}, \ldots, B_m\Big) \quad \sigma = \mathrm{mgu}(u,u') \end{array}}{K = K \oplus h \text{ where } h = \Big((\mathsf{ri}_{u'v'}(R,R') \Leftarrow B_1, \ldots, B_m)\sigma\Big)}$$

Fig. 3. Saturation rules

A set of well-formed *statements is called a* knowledge base. *If K is a knowledge base, we define $K_{\mathsf{solved}} = \{f \in K \mid f \text{ is solved}\}$ to be the knowledge base restricted to the solved statements.*

Given an initial knowledge base K, the saturation procedure produces another knowledge base $\mathsf{sat}(K)$ as follows. First, new statements are *generated.* Then the knowledge base is *updated* with the new statements. This two-step process continues until a fixed-point is achieved. We describe the two steps in the procedure.

Generating New Statements. Given a knowledge base K, new statements f are generated by applying the rules in Figure 3.

Update. The first step while updating the knowledge base by f is to convert f into a canonical form.

Definition 11. *Given a solved deduction statement f, we define its* canonical form *to be the statement $f\Downarrow$ obtained by first applying Rule* Rename *as many times as possible and then applying Rule* Remove *as many times as possible:*

$$\textsc{Rename}\ \frac{H \Leftarrow \mathsf{k}_u(X,x), \mathsf{k}_{uv}(Y,x), B_1, \ldots, B_n}{(H \Leftarrow \mathsf{k}_u(X,x), B_1, \ldots, B_n)\{Y \mapsto X\}}$$

$$\textsc{Remove}\ \frac{H \Leftarrow \mathsf{k}_u(X,x), B_1, \ldots, B_n \qquad x \notin vars(H)}{H \Leftarrow B_1, \ldots, B_n}$$

For any other type of statement, the canonical form $f\Downarrow$ is defined to be f.

It is easy to see that any fact f can be converted into a canonical form. After a canonical form has been obtained, we perform another check before $f\Downarrow$ can be added to the knowledge base. Intuitively, this check ensures that we add enough identity predicates in the knowledge base. We need the following definition for the update rule.

Definition 12. *The set of* consequences *of a knowledge base K, denoted* $\mathbf{cons}(K)$*, is the smallest set such that:*

$$\text{AXIOM}\ \frac{}{\mathsf{k}_{uv}(R,t) \Leftarrow \mathsf{k}_u(R,t), B_1, \ldots, B_m \in \mathbf{cons}(K)}$$

$$\text{RES}\ \frac{H \Leftarrow B_1, \ldots, B_n \in K \qquad \sigma \text{ a substitution} \quad B_1\sigma \Leftarrow C_1, \ldots, C_m \in \mathbf{cons}(K), \ldots, B_n\sigma \Leftarrow C_1, \ldots, C_m \in \mathbf{cons}(K)}{H\sigma \Leftarrow C_1, \ldots, C_m \in \mathbf{cons}(K)}$$

Given a knowledge base K and a statement f, the *update of K by f*, denoted $K \oplus f$, is defined to be $K \cup \{f\Downarrow\}$ if the head of f is not of the form $\mathsf{k}_{\ell_1,\ldots,\ell_k}(R,t)$. Otherwise, let

$$f\Downarrow = \mathsf{k}_{\ell_1,\ldots,\ell_k}(R,t) \Leftarrow \mathsf{k}_{\ell_1,\ldots,\ell_{i_1}}(X_1,t_1), \ldots, \mathsf{k}_{\ell_1,\ldots,\ell_{i_n}}(X_n,t_n)$$

and $K \oplus f =$

- $K \cup \{f\Downarrow\}$ if f is solved and for any R' we have that $\mathsf{k}_{\ell_1,\ldots,\ell_k}(R',t) \Leftarrow \mathsf{k}_{\ell_1,\ldots,\ell_{i_1}}(X_1,t_1), \ldots, \mathsf{k}_{\ell_1,\ldots,\ell_{i_n}}(X_n,t_n) \notin \mathbf{cons}(K_{\mathsf{solved}})$.
- $K \cup \{\mathsf{i}_{\ell_1,\ldots,\ell_k}(R,R') \Leftarrow \{\mathsf{k}_{\ell_1,\ldots,\ell_{i_j}}(X_j,t_j)\}_{j\in\{1,\ldots,n\}}\}$ if f is solved and R' is such that $\mathsf{k}_{\ell_1,\ldots,\ell_k}(R',t) \Leftarrow \mathsf{k}_{\ell_1,\ldots,\ell_{i_1}}(X_1,t_1), \ldots, \mathsf{k}_{\ell_1,\ldots,\ell_{i_n}}(X_n,t_n) \in \mathbf{cons}(K_{\mathsf{solved}})$.
- $K \cup \{f\Downarrow\}$ if f is not solved.

Note that update is not a function, namely that there may be several $R', i_1, \ldots, i_n$ such that $\mathsf{k}_{\ell_1,\ldots,\ell_k}(R',t) \Leftarrow \mathsf{k}_{\ell_1,\ldots,\ell_{i_1}}(X_1,t_1), \ldots, \mathsf{k}_{\ell_1,\ldots,\ell_{i_n}}(X_n,t_n) \in \mathbf{cons}(K_{\mathsf{solved}})$. However, we need to compute only one such R'.

Initial Knowledge Base. One question that naturally arises is what is the initial knowledge base for the saturation procedure. Given a ground trace T, the initial knowledge base for the saturation procedure is defined as follows.

Definition 13. *Given a set of statements S, the* initial knowledge base *associated to S, denoted $K_i(S)$, is defined to be the empty knowledge base updated by the set S, i.e., $K_i(S) = \emptyset \oplus_{f\in S} f$. If T is a ground trace, we write $K_i(T)$ for $K_i(\mathsf{seed}(T))$.*

Observe that $K_i(T)$ depends on the order in which statements in $\mathsf{seed}(T)$ are updated. The exact order, however, is not important and our results hold regardless of the order chosen. The saturation procedure takes $K_i(T)$ as an input and produces a knowledge base $\mathsf{sat}(K_i(T))$. The reason for choosing $K_i(T)$ instead of $\mathsf{seed}(T)$ as the starting point of the saturation procedure is that $\mathsf{seed}(T)$ may not be a knowledge base, i.e., may contain non well-formed statements. The set $K_i(T)$ is, however, a knowledge base.

Proposition 1. *Given a ground trace T, the set $K_i(T)$ is a knowledge base.*

Soundness and Completeness of the Saturation Procedure. We shall now show that the set of solved statements in $\mathsf{sat}(K_i(T))$ is a sound and complete abstraction of a ground trace T. Given a set of statements K we denote by $\mathcal{H}_{\mathsf{e}}(K)$ the smallest set of ground terms such that

- $\mathcal{H}(K) \subseteq \mathcal{H}_{\mathsf{e}}(K)$,
- $\mathcal{H}_{\mathsf{e}}(K)$ is closed under congruence rules for each $\mathsf{i}_w(R, R') \in \mathcal{H}_{\mathsf{e}}(K)$, and
- i_w is monotonic in w, i.e., $\mathsf{i}_u(R, R') \in \mathcal{H}_{\mathsf{e}}(K)$ implies $\mathsf{i}_{uv}(R, R') \in \mathcal{H}_{\mathsf{e}}(K)$.

A formal definition is given in [16].

Theorem 3. *Let T be a ground trace and let $K = \mathsf{sat}(K_i(T))$.*

- *(Soundness.) For any $f \in K \cup \mathcal{H}_{\mathsf{e}}(K)$ we have $T \models f$.*
- *(Completeness.) If $(T, \emptyset) \xrightarrow{L_1,\ldots,L_n} (S, \varphi)$ then (i) $\mathsf{r}_{L_1\varphi\downarrow,\ldots,L_n\varphi\downarrow} \in \mathcal{H}_{\mathsf{e}}(K_{\mathsf{solved}})$, (ii) if $\varphi \vdash^R t$ then $\mathsf{k}_{L_1\varphi\downarrow,\ldots,L_n\varphi\downarrow}(R, t\downarrow) \in \mathcal{H}_{\mathsf{e}}(K_{\mathsf{solved}})$, and (iii) if $\varphi \vdash^R t$ and $\varphi \vdash^{R'} t$, then $\mathsf{i}_{L_1\varphi\downarrow,\ldots,L_n\varphi\downarrow}(R, R') \in \mathcal{H}_{\mathsf{e}}(K_{\mathsf{solved}})$.*

Effectiveness of the Saturation Procedure. We have shown that the set of solved statements in $\mathsf{sat}(K_i(T))$ form a sound and complete abstraction for the trace T. However this set is infinite and may not be effectively computable. This may be because of following reasons.

- The set $\mathsf{seed}(T)$ for a ground trace T is infinite. Hence the saturation procedure may continue forever. We will, however, shortly show that for the saturation procedure we only need to consider the saturation of the set $K_i(\mathsf{seed}(T, \mathcal{M}_0))$ where $\mathcal{M}_0$ is the set of public names occurring in T (see Lemma 1). The set $\mathsf{sat}(K_i(T))$ can then be computed from this set. Since the set $K_i(\mathsf{seed}(T, \mathcal{M}_0))$ is finite, this means that all intermediate knowledge bases in the saturation procedure are finite.
- For the update rule, we have to check that given a knowledge base K, term t, labels $\ell_1, \ldots, \ell_k$, indices $1 \leq i_1, \ldots i_n \leq k$, variables $x_1, \ldots, x_n \in \mathcal{X}$ and recipe variables $X_1, \ldots, X_n \in \mathcal{Y}$, whether

  $$\exists R.\ \mathsf{k}_{\ell_1,\ldots,\ell_k}(R, t) \Leftarrow \mathsf{k}_{\ell_1,\ldots,\ell_{i_1}}(X_1, x_1), \ldots, \mathsf{k}_{\ell_1,\ldots,\ell_{i_n}}(X_n, x_n) \in \mathbf{cons}(K_{\mathsf{solved}}).$$

  Furthermore, if the check succeeds then we have to compute one such R. We will show that can be achieved if K is finite (see Lemma 2).
- The saturation procedure may itself not terminate even if the initial knowledge base is finite. As pointed out in the Introduction, we conjecture that the saturation procedure terminates for subterm convergent rewrite systems, but were unable to show the termination.

The following lemma allows us to compute the $\mathsf{sat}(K_i(T))$ from the set $\mathsf{sat}(K_i(\mathit{seed}(M_0, T)))$ where M_0 is the set of public names occurring in T.

Lemma 1. *Let T be a ground trace and $M_T \subseteq \mathcal{M}$ be the public names occurring in T. Let $K_{\mathcal{M}} = \{\{\mathsf{k}(m, m) \Leftarrow\}_{m \in \mathcal{M}} \cup \{\mathsf{i}(m, m) \Leftarrow\}_{m \in \mathcal{M}} \cup \{\mathsf{ri}(m, m) \Leftarrow\}_{m \in \mathcal{M}}\}$. Then $\mathsf{sat}(K_i(T)) = \mathsf{sat}(K_i(\mathit{seed}(M_T, T))) \cup K_{\mathcal{M}}$.*

The following lemma implies that the update step terminates if we only have a finite number of solved statements in the knowledge base.

Lemma 2. *Given a finite set of statements K, term t, labels $\ell_1, \ldots, \ell_k$, indices $1 \leq i_1, \ldots i_n \leq k$, variables $x_1, \ldots, x_n \in \mathcal{X}$ and recipe variables $X_1, \ldots, X_n \in \mathcal{Y}$, it is decidable if there is an R such that $\mathsf{k}_{\ell_1,\ldots,\ell_k}(R, t) \Leftarrow \mathsf{k}_{\ell_1,\ldots,\ell_{i_1}}(X_1, x_1), \ldots, \mathsf{k}_{\ell_1,\ldots,\ell_{i_n}}(X_n, x_n) \in \mathbf{cons}(K_{\mathsf{solved}})$. If the answer to the decision procedure is "Yes", then we can compute one such R.*

5.2 Algorithm for Checking Equivalence

Once we constructed saturated knowledge bases for the seed statements for ground determinate processes P_0 and P_1, we can check trace equivalence $\approx_{ct}$. The algorithm for checking $\approx_{ct}$ for determinate processes, automatically gives an algorithm for checking $\approx_{ft}$ for non-determinate processes. It suffices to check for $T \sqsubseteq_{ct} P$ for a ground trace T and ground determinate process P. This basically involves checking two tests which are summarized in Figure 4. We briefly describe them below.

- REACH checks whether all sequence of actions executable by T are also executable by P. To do this, we carry out the following operations for *each* statement $\mathsf{r}_{l_1,\ldots,l_n} \Leftarrow \{\mathsf{k}_{w_i}(X_i, x_i)\}_{i \in \{1,\ldots,m\}}\big) \in \{\mathsf{sat}(\mathsf{seed}(T))\}_{\mathsf{solved}}$. *(a)* First we pick fresh constants $c_1, \ldots, c_k$ for each of the variables occurring in $l_1, \ldots, l_n$ and fix a bijection σ between them. *(b)* Next for each $1 \leq i \leq n$ s.t. l_i is $\mathbf{in}(d_i, t_i)$, we construct *one* recipe R_i such that $\mathsf{k}_{l_1\sigma,\ldots,l_{i-1}\sigma}(R_i, t_i\sigma) \in \mathcal{H}(\{\mathsf{sat}(\mathsf{seed}(T))\}_{\mathsf{solved}})$. Such an R_i exists thanks to the completeness of the saturation procedure. We let $M_i = \mathbf{in}(d_i, R_i)$. *(c)* For each $1 \leq i \leq n$ s.t. $l_i = \mathbf{test}$ or $\mathbf{out}(d_i)$ we let $M_i = l_i$. *(d)* We check if $(P, \emptyset) \xRightarrow{M_1,\ldots,M_n} (T', \varphi)$. If all the REACH tests pass then we go to test IDENTITY. Otherwise we declare T to be not trace-contained in P.
- The test IDENTITY checks that all the equality tests that hold after an execution of T hold after a similar execution in P. In order to do this, we carry out the following operations for *each* statement $\mathsf{ri}_{l_1,\ldots,l_n}(R, R') \Leftarrow \{\mathsf{k}_{w_i}(X_i, x_i)\}_{i \in \{1,\ldots,m\}}\big) \in \{\mathsf{sat}(\mathsf{seed}(T))\}_{\mathsf{solved}}$. We construct $M_1, \ldots, M_n$ as in the REACH test and check if there is a T' such that $(P, \emptyset) \xRightarrow{M_1,\ldots,M_n} (T', \varphi)$ and the recipes $R\{\, X_i \mapsto x_i\sigma \,\}$ and $R'\{\, X_i \mapsto x_i\sigma \,\}$ are equal in frame φ.

Note that performing the tests requires deciding if, given t, and w, $\mathsf{k}_w(R, t) \in \mathcal{H}(K)$ for some recipe R for a knowledge base K containing only solved statements. This is similar to checking if $\big(\mathsf{k}_w(R, t) \Leftarrow\big) \in \mathbf{cons}(K)$.

Theorem 4. *Let T be a ground trace and let P be a ground determinate process. Let K be the set of solved statements from a saturated knowledge base associated to T. Then $T \sqsubseteq_{ct} P$ iff all the tests in Figure 4 hold.*

$$\text{REACH}\ \frac{\begin{array}{c}\left(\mathsf{r}_{l_1,\ldots,l_n} \Leftarrow \{\mathsf{k}_{w_i}(X_i,x_i)\}_{i\in\{1,\ldots,m\}}\right) \in \{\mathsf{sat}(\mathsf{seed}(T))\}_{\mathsf{solved}} \\ c_1,\ldots,c_k \text{ fresh constants} \\ \sigma : vars(l_1,\ldots,l_n) \to \{c_1,\ldots,c_k\} \text{ is a bijection} \\ \mathsf{k}_{l_1\sigma,\ldots,l_{i-1}\sigma}(R_i,t_i\sigma) \in \mathcal{H}(\{\mathsf{sat}(\mathsf{seed}(T))\}_{\mathsf{solved}}) \text{ for all } i \text{ s.t. } l_i = \mathbf{in}(d_i,t_i) \\ M_i = l_i \text{ if } l_i \in \{\mathbf{test},\mathbf{out}(\_)\} \qquad M_i = \mathbf{in}(d_i,R_i) \text{ if } l_i = \mathbf{in}(d_i,t_i)\end{array}}{(P,\emptyset) \xRightarrow{M_1,\ldots,M_n} (T',\varphi)}$$

$$\text{IDENTITY}\ \frac{\begin{array}{c}\left(\mathsf{ri}_{l_1,\ldots,l_n}(R,R') \Leftarrow \{\mathsf{k}_{w_i}(X_i,x_i)\}_{i\in\{1,\ldots,m\}}\right) \in \{\mathsf{sat}(\mathsf{seed}(T))\}_{\mathsf{solved}} \\ c_1,\ldots,c_k \text{ fresh constants} \\ \sigma : vars(l_1,\ldots,l_n) \to \{c_1,\ldots,c_k\} \text{ is a bijection} \\ \mathsf{k}_{l_1\sigma,\ldots,l_{i-1}\sigma}(R_i,t_i\sigma) \in \mathcal{H}(\{\mathsf{sat}(\mathsf{seed}(T))\}_{\mathsf{solved}}) \text{ for all } i \text{ s.t. } l_i = \mathbf{in}(t_i) \\ M_i = l_i \text{ if } l_i \in \{\mathbf{test},\mathbf{out}(\_)\} \qquad M_i = \mathbf{in}(d_i,R_i) \text{ if } l_i = \mathbf{in}(d_i,t_i)\end{array}}{(P,\emptyset) \xRightarrow{M_1,\ldots,M_n} (T',\varphi) \text{ such that } (R\omega = R'\omega)\varphi \text{ where } \omega = \{X_i \mapsto x_i\sigma\}}$$

Fig. 4. Tests for checking trace inclusion

6 Prototype and Case Studies

We implemented the procedure for checking equivalence in a prototype, AKISS (Active Knowledge In Security protocolS). AKISS is written in OCaml and has about 2000 lines of source code, including code for computing complete sets of finite variants and complete sets of equational unifiers. For protocol specification, we allow for an operator *interleave* which models parallel composition of processes and an operator *sequence* for modeling protocols structured in phases.

We used AKISS to verify the equivalences in Examples 5 and 6. Using AKISS we were able to verify strong secrecy for Denning-Sacco-Blanchet [11] and Needham-Schroeder-Lowe (NSL) [36], resistance to guessing attacks in the EKE protocol [9], and, more interestingly, anonymity of the FOO [32] and Okamoto [38] electronic voting protocols.[1] To our knowledge, AKISS is the only tool that can verify FOO and Okamoto automatically. We briefly discuss the salient points of these examples below. AKISS along with all the discussed examples is available on: `http://www.lsv.ens-cachan.fr/~ciobaca/akiss/`. Details of the modeling can also be found in [16].

Strong Flavors of Confidentiality. The *strong secrecy* property was introduced by Blanchet in [11] and we rephrase it here in our setting. Let P be a protocol with x as the only free variable of P. Then x is said to be *strongly secret* if

$$\mathbf{in}(c,x_1).\mathbf{in}(c,x_2).(P\{x \mapsto x_1\}) \approx_t \mathbf{in}(c,x_1).\mathbf{in}(c,x_2).(P\{x \mapsto x_2\}).$$

[1] Please note that as defined in [38], modeling of Okamoto's protocol requires private channels. As we do not have private channels in our calculus, we transform the protocol so that every message sent by honest participants on a private channel is sent encrypted under a key not known to the adversary

Intuitively, the attacker cannot distinguish the processes using variables x_1 and x_2 even though it can choose arbitrary (public) values for these variables. The definition generalizes to multiple variables in the expected way. We illustrate this property on a Denning-Sacco-Blanchet protocol. Informally, the protocol can be described as follows.

$$\mathsf{A} \to \mathsf{B} : \mathsf{aenc}(\mathsf{sign}(\mathsf{pair}(\mathsf{pk}(ska), \mathsf{pair}(\mathsf{pk}(skb, k))), ska), \mathsf{pk}(skb))$$
$$\mathsf{B} \to \mathsf{A} : \mathsf{enc}(x, k)$$

A sends to B a fresh symmetric session key k together with A's and B's public keys. This is signed with A's secret key and (asymmetrically) encrypted with B's public key. Upon receiving this message, B decrypts it, checks the signature and uses the fresh session key to symmetrically encrypt a secret x. We used AKiSs to verify this protocol for strong secrecy of x (with one session of A and B). This protocol is determinate, and hence we used $\approx_{ct}$ to verify the protocol. The verification succeeds as expected.

A variant of the protocol [11] consists in letting A also send out a secret y encrypted with k changing the first message to

$$\mathsf{A} \to \mathsf{B} : \mathsf{pair}(\mathsf{aenc}(\mathsf{sign}(\mathsf{pair}(\mathsf{pk}(ska), \mathsf{pair}(\mathsf{pk}(skb, k))), ska), \mathsf{pk}(skb)), \mathsf{enc}(y, k))$$

In this case the protocol does not respect strong secrecy of x, y as, by choosing $x_1 = y_1$ and $x_2 \neq y_2$, the attacker can distinguish the two situations by testing the equality of the encryptions of x and y. This attack is again found by AKiSs. AKiSs also verifies strong secrecy of the nonce generated by the responder in the Needham-Schroeder-Lowe (NSL) [36] protocol. Once again, the modeling of NSL leads to determinate processes, and we used $\approx_{ct}$ for our verification.

We also used AKiSs to verify the above protocols for *real-or-random* secrecy. This property is useful to model resistance to offline guessing attacks in password protocols [8]. We show that the EKE protocol [9] is resistant to offline guessing attacks. As EKE also leads to determinate processes, we used the $\approx_{ct}$ relation.

Anonymity for Electronic Voting Protocol. A voting protocol must respect voter privacy: the adversary should not be able to learn how each voter voted. AKiSs can automatically verify voter privacy in the FOO electronic voting protocol [32] and the Okamoto protocol [38]. Voter privacy is naturally modeled as an equivalence property [26,7]: it is not possible to distinguish the situation where honest voter A votes 'yes' and honest B votes 'no' from the situation that A votes 'no' and B votes 'yes'. Note that our modeling of the protocols is exactly the same as in [26]. We assume that *only* voters A and B are honest while all other entities are dishonest. An arbitrary number of dishonest voters are however subsumed by the attacker and need not be modeled directly. Both the protocols do not lead to determinate processes. Therefore, we proved the relation $\approx_{ft}$. To our knowledge, no other tool can handle this automatically. We are aware of two other attempts for verifying the FOO protocol. Using ProVerif [11], Delaune *et al.* [28], verify a transformation of the protocol. However, the soundness of this transformation has never been proven. Chothia *et al.* [20] verify a different notion of anonymity (also based on process equivalence) using the μCRL tool. However, the attacker they consider is only an observer that cannot interact with the protocol participants, yielding a finite state system.

Efficiency. On a standard modern laptop, AKiSs takes a few minutes (e.g. 3 mins for FOO) to carry out the above verification. The use of a multi-core server already reduces these timings by about 40%. We expect that some optimizations of the saturation procedure and the use of more efficient data structures will diminish these times significantly. Most of the computational effort goes into the saturation of the traces. Interleaving individual roles of a protocol introduces an exponential blowup on the number of traces and saturations to perform. However, it would be straightforward to scale to larger protocols and more sessions by parallelizing the saturation of these traces (e.g. on clusters of machines).

7 Conclusion and Future Work

We present a novel Horn-clause resolution based procedure for verifying equivalence properties for a bounded number of sessions of cryptographic protocols. This approach is validated by implementing it in the tool AKiSs, and we are able to handle examples which are out of the scope of existing tools.

There are several directions for future work. The implementation of the tool should be optimized and more examples from electronic voting, RFID protocols and auction protocols which all have requirements stated in terms of equivalences should be analyzed. We would also like to take disequalities into account. It will allow to verify processes with else branches, important in a number of practical examples, e.g., passport protocols discussed in [5]. Another direction would be to extend the procedure to allow AC (Associative/Commutative) operators in order to treat protocols based on exclusive-or or Diffie-Hellman exponentiations.

References

1. Abadi, M., Cortier, V.: Deciding knowledge in security protocols under equational theories. Theoretical Computer Science 387(1-2), 2–32 (2006)
2. Abadi, M., Fournet, C.: Mobile values, new names, and secure communication. In: 28th Symposium on Principles of Programming Languages (POPL 2001), pp. 104–115. ACM Press (2001)
3. Abadi, M., Fournet, C.: Private authentication. Theoretical Computer Science 322(3), 427–476 (2004)
4. Abadi, M., Gordon, A.D.: A calculus for cryptographic protocols: The spi calculus. Inf. Comput. 148(1), 1–70 (1999)
5. Arapinis, M., Chothia, T., Ritter, E., Ryan, M.D.: Analysing unlinkability and anonymity using the applied pi calculus. In: 23rd Computer Security Foundations Symposium (CSF 2010), pp. 107–121. IEEE Comp. Soc. Press (2010)

6. Armando, A., Basin, D., Boichut, Y., Chevalier, Y., Compagna, L., Cuellar, J., Drielsma, P.H., Heám, P.C., Kouchnarenko, O., Mantovani, J., Mödersheim, S., von Oheimb, D., Rusinowitch, M., Santiago, J., Turuani, M., Viganò, L., Vigneron, L.: The AVISPA Tool for the Automated Validation of Internet Security Protocols and Applications. In: Etessami, K., Rajamani, S.K. (eds.) CAV 2005. LNCS, vol. 3576, pp. 281–285. Springer, Heidelberg (2005)
7. Backes, M., Hritcu, C., Maffei, M.: Automated verification of remote electronic voting protocols in the applied pi-calculus. In: 21st Computer Security Foundations Symposium (CSF 2008). IEEE Comp. Soc. Press (2008)
8. Baudet, M.: Deciding security of protocols against off-line guessing attacks. In: 12th Conference on Computer and Communications Security (CCS 2005), pp. 16–25. ACM Press (2005)
9. Bellovin, S.M., Merritt, M.: Encrypted key exchange: Password-based protocols secure against dictionary attacks. In: Symposium on Security and Privacy (S&P 1992), pp. 72–84. IEEE Comp. Soc. Press (1992)
10. Blanchet, B.: An Efficient Cryptographic Protocol Verifier Based on Prolog Rules. In: 14th Computer Security Foundations Workshop (CSFW 2001), pp. 82–96. IEEE Comp. Soc. Press (2001)
11. Blanchet, B.: Automatic proof of strong secrecy for security protocols. In: Symposium on Security and Privacy (S&P 2004), pp. 86–100 (2004)
12. Blanchet, B., Abadi, M., Fournet, C.: Automated Verification of Selected Equivalences for Security Protocols. In: Symposium on Logic in Computer Science, pp. 331–340. IEEE Comp. Soc. Press (2005)
13. Borgström, J.: Equivalences and Calculi for Formal Verifiation of Cryptographic Protocols. Phd thesis, EPFL, Switzerland (2008)
14. Borgström, J., Briais, S., Nestmann, U.: Symbolic Bisimulation in the Spi Calculus. In: Gardner, P., Yoshida, N. (eds.) CONCUR 2004. LNCS, vol. 3170, pp. 161–176. Springer, Heidelberg (2004)
15. Bruso, M., Chatzikokolakis, K., den Hartog, J.: Analysing unlinkability and anonymity using the applied pi calculus. In: 23rd Computer Security Foundations Symposium (CSF 2010), pp. 107–121. IEEE Comp. Soc. Press (2010)
16. Chadha, R., Ciobâcă, Ş., Kremer, S.: Automated verification of equivalence properties of cryptographic protocols. Technical report (October 2011), `http://hal.inria.fr/inria-00632564/en/`
17. Cheval, V., Comon-Lundh, H., Delaune, S.: Automating Security Analysis: Symbolic Equivalence of Constraint Systems. In: Giesl, J., Hähnle, R. (eds.) IJCAR 2010. LNCS (LNAI), vol. 6173, pp. 412–426. Springer, Heidelberg (2010)
18. Cheval, V., Comon-Lundh, H., Delaune, S.: Trace equivalence decision: Negative tests and non-determinism. In: 18th Conference on Computer and Communications Security (CCS 2011), pp. 321–330. ACM Press (2011)
19. Chevalier, Y., Rusinowitch, M.: Decidability of equivalence of symbolic derivations. Journal of Automated Reasoning (2010)
20. Chothia, T., Orzan, S., Pang, J., Torabi Dashti, M.: A Framework for Automatically Checking Anonymity with μCRL. In: Montanari, U., Sannella, D., Bruni, R. (eds.) TGC 2006. LNCS, vol. 4661, pp. 301–318. Springer, Heidelberg (2007)
21. Ciobâcă, Ş.: Computing finite variants for subterm convergent rewrite systems. Research Report LSV-11-06, LSV, ENS Cachan, France (2011)
22. Comon-Lundh, H., Delaune, S.: The Finite Variant Property: How to Get Rid of Some Algebraic Properties. In: Giesl, J. (ed.) RTA 2005. LNCS, vol. 3467, pp. 294–307. Springer, Heidelberg (2005)

23. Cortier, V., Delaune, S.: A method for proving observational equivalence. In: 22nd Computer Security Foundations Symposium (CSF 2009), pp. 266–276. IEEE Comp. Soc. Press (2009)
24. Dahl, M., Delaune, S., Steel, G.: Formal Analysis of Privacy for Vehicular Mix-Zones. In: Gritzalis, D., Preneel, B., Theoharidou, M. (eds.) ESORICS 2010. LNCS, vol. 6345, pp. 55–70. Springer, Heidelberg (2010)
25. Delaune, S., Kremer, S., Pereira, O.: Simulation based security in the applied pi calculus. In: 29th Conference on Foundations of Software Technology and Theoretical Computer Science (FSTTCS 2009). Leibniz International Proceedings in Informatics, vol. 4, pp. 169–180. Leibniz-Zentrum für Informatik (2009)
26. Delaune, S., Kremer, S., Ryan, M.D.: Verifying privacy-type properties of electronic voting protocols. Journal of Computer Security 17(4), 435–487 (2009)
27. Delaune, S., Kremer, S., Ryan, M.D.: Symbolic bisimulation for the applied pi calculus. Journal of Computer Security 18(2), 317–377 (2010)
28. Delaune, S., Ryan, M.D., Smyth, B.: Automatic verification of privacy properties in the applied pi-calculus. In: 2nd Joint iTrust and PST Conferences on Privacy, Trust Management and Security (IFIPTM 2008). IFIP Conference Proceedings, vol. 263, pp. 263–278. Springer, Heidelberg (2008)
29. Dolev, D., Yao, A.: On the security of public key protocols. In: 22nd Symposium on Foundations of Computer Science (FOCS 1981), pp. 350–357. IEEE Comp. Soc. Press (1981)
30. Durante, L., Sisto, R., Valenzano, A.: Automatic testing equivalence verification of spi calculus specifications. ACM Transactions on Software Engineering and Methodology 12(2), 222–284 (2003)
31. Escobar, S., Meadows, C., Meseguer, J.: Maude-NPA: Cryptographic Protocol Analysis Modulo Equational Properties. In: Aldini, A., Barthe, G., Gorrieri, R. (eds.) FOSAD 2007/2008/2009. LNCS, vol. 5705, pp. 1–50. Springer, Heidelberg (2009)
32. Fujioka, A., Okamoto, T., Ohta, K.: A Practical Secret Voting Scheme for Large Scale Elections. In: Zheng, Y., Seberry, J. (eds.) AUSCRYPT 1992. LNCS, vol. 718, pp. 244–251. Springer, Heidelberg (1993)
33. Goubault-Larrecq, J.: Deciding $\mathcal{H}_1$ by resolution. Information Processing Letters 95(3), 401–408 (2005)
34. Hüttel, H.: Deciding framed bisimilarity. In: 4th International Workshop on Verification of Infinite-State Systems (INFINITY 2002), pp. 1–20 (2002)
35. Liu, J., Lin, H.: A Complete Symbolic Bisimulation for Full Applied Pi Calculus. In: van Leeuwen, J., Muscholl, A., Peleg, D., Pokorný, J., Rumpe, B. (eds.) SOFSEM 2010. LNCS, vol. 5901, pp. 552–563. Springer, Heidelberg (2010)
36. Lowe, G.: Breaking and Fixing the Needham-Schroeder Public-Key Protocol Using FDR. In: Margaria, T., Steffen, B. (eds.) TACAS 1996. LNCS, vol. 1055, pp. 147–166. Springer, Heidelberg (1996)
37. Narendran, P., Pfenning, F., Statman, R.: On the unification problem for cartesian closed categories. J. Symb. Log. 62(2), 636–647 (1997)
38. Okamoto, T.: Receipt-Free Electronic Voting Schemes for Large Scale Elections. In: Christianson, B., Lomas, M. (eds.) Security Protocols 1997. LNCS, vol. 1361, pp. 25–35. Springer, Heidelberg (1998)
39. Tiu, A., Dawson, J.: Automating open bisimulation checking for the spi-calculus. In: 23rd Computer Security Foundations Symposium (CSF 2010), pp. 307–321. IEEE Comp. Soc. Press (2010)
40. Weidenbach, C.: Towards an Automatic Analysis of Security Protocols in First-Order Logic. In: Ganzinger, H. (ed.) CADE 1999. LNCS (LNAI), vol. 1632, pp. 314–328. Springer, Heidelberg (1999)

The Call-by-Need Lambda Calculus, Revisited

Stephen Chang and Matthias Felleisen

College of Computer Science
Northeastern University
Boston, Massachusetts, USA
{stchang,matthias}@ccs.neu.edu

Abstract. The existing call-by-need λ calculi describe lazy evaluation via equational logics. A programmer can use these logics to safely ascertain whether one term is behaviorally equivalent to another or to determine the value of a lazy program. However, neither of the existing calculi models evaluation in a way that matches lazy implementations.

Both calculi suffer from the same two problems. First, the calculi never discard function calls, even after they are completely resolved. Second, the calculi include re-association axioms even though these axioms are merely administrative steps with no counterpart in any implementation.

In this paper, we present an alternative axiomatization of lazy evaluation using a single axiom. It eliminates both the function call retention problem and the extraneous re-association axioms. Our axiom uses a grammar of contexts to describe the exact notion of a *needed computation*. Like its predecessors, our new calculus satisfies consistency and standardization properties and is thus suitable for reasoning about behavioral equivalence. In addition, we establish a correspondence between our semantics and Launchbury's natural semantics.

Keywords: call-by-need, laziness, lambda calculus.

1 A Short History of the λ Calculus

Starting in the late 1950s, programming language researchers began to look to Church's λ calculus [6] for inspiration. Some used it as an analytic tool to understand the syntax and semantics of programming languages, while others exploited it as the basis for new languages. By 1970, however, a disconnect had emerged in the form of call-by-value programming, distinct from the notion of β and normalization in Church's original calculus. Plotkin [25] reconciled the λ calculus and Landin's SECD machine for the ISWIM language [16] with the introduction of a notion of correspondence and with a proof that two distinct variants of the λ calculus corresponded to two distinct variants of the ISWIM programming language: one for call-by-value and one for call-by-name.

In the early 1970s, researchers proposed call-by-need [12, 14, 28], a third kind of parameter passing mechanism that could be viewed as yet another variant of the ISWIM language. Call-by-need is supposed to represent the best of both worlds. While call-by-value ISWIM always evaluates the argument of a function,

H. Seidl (Ed.): ESOP 2012, LNCS 7211, pp. 128–147, 2012.

the call-by-name variant evaluates the argument every time it is needed. Hence, if an argument (or some portion) is never needed, call-by-name wins; otherwise call-by-value is superior because it avoids re-evaluation of arguments. Call-by-need initially proceeds like call-by-name, evaluating a function's body before the argument—until the value of the argument is needed; at that point, the argument is evaluated and the resulting value is used from then onward. In short, call-by-need evaluates an argument at most once, and only if needed.

Since then, researchers have explored a number of characterizations of call-by-need [8, 11, 13, 15, 23, 24, 26]. Concerning this paper, three stand out. Launchbury's semantics [17] specifies the meaning of complete programs with a Kahn-style natural semantics. The call-by-need λ calculi of Ariola and Felleisen [2–4], and of Maraist, Odersky, and Wadler [4, 20, 21] are equational logics in the spirit of the λ calculus.

The appeal of the λ calculus has several reasons. First, a calculus is sound with respect to the observational (behavioral) equivalence relation [22]. It can therefore serve as the starting point for other, more powerful logics. Second, its axioms are rich enough to mimic machine evaluation, meaning programmers can reduce programs to values without thinking about implementation details. Finally, the λ calculus gives rise to a substantial meta-theory [5, 7] from which researchers have generated useful and practical results for its cousins.

Unfortunately, neither of the existing by-need calculi model lazy evaluation in a way that matches lazy language implementations. Both calculi suffer from the same two problems. First, unlike the by-name and by-value calculi, the by-need calculi never discard function calls, even after the call is resolved and the argument is no longer needed. Lazy evaluation does require some accumulation of function calls due to the delayed evaluation of arguments but the existing calculi adopt the extreme solution of retaining every call. Indeed, the creators of the existing calculi acknowledge that a solution to this problem would strengthen their work but they could not figure out a proper solution.

Second, the calculi include re-association axioms even though these axioms have no counterpart in any implementation. The axioms are mere administrative steps, needed to construct β-like redexes. Hence, they should not be considered computationally on par with other axioms.

In this paper, we overcome these problems with an alternative axiomatization. Based on a single axiom, it avoids the retention of function calls and eliminates the extraneous re-association axioms. The single axiom uses a grammar of contexts to describe the exact notion of a *needed computation*. Like its predecessors, our new calculus satisfies consistency and standardization properties and is thus suitable for reasoning about behavioral equivalence. In addition, we establish an intensional correspondence with Launchbury's semantics.

The second section of this paper recalls the two existing by-need calculi in some detail. The third section presents our new calculus, as well as a way to derive it from Ariola and Felleisen's calculus. Sections 4 and 5 show that our calculus satisfies the usual meta-theorems and that it is correct with respect to Launchbury's semantics. Finally, we discuss some possible extensions.

2 The Original Call-by-Need λ Calculi

The original call-by-need λ calculi are independently due to two groups: Ariola and Felleisen [2, 3] and Maraist, et al. [20, 21]. They were jointly presented at POPL in 1995 [4]. Both calculi use the standard set of terms as syntax:

$$e = x \mid \lambda x.e \mid e\,e \qquad \text{(Terms)}$$

Our treatment of syntax employs the usual conventions, including Barendregt's standard hygiene condition for variable bindings [5]. Figure 1 specifies the calculus of Maraist et al., λ_{mow}, and λ_{af}, Ariola and Felleisen's variant. Nonterminals in some grammar productions have subscript tags to differentiate them from similar sets elsewhere in the paper. Unsubscripted definitions have the same denotation in all systems.

$v_m = x \mid \lambda x.e$	$v = \lambda x.e$
	$a_{af} = v \mid (\lambda x.a_{af})\,e$
$C = [\,] \mid \lambda x.C \mid C\,e \mid e\,C$	$E_{af} = [\,] \mid E_{af}\,e \mid (\lambda x.E_{af})\,e \mid (\lambda x.E_{af}[x])\,E_{af}$
$(\lambda x.C[x])\,v_m = (\lambda x.C[v_m])\,v_m \quad (\mathcal{V})$	$(\lambda x.E_{af}[x])\,v = (\lambda x.E_{af}[v])\,v \quad (\mathit{deref})$
$(\lambda x.e_1)\,e_2\,e_3 = (\lambda x.e_1\,e_3)\,e_2 \quad (\mathcal{C})$	$(\lambda x.a_{af})\,e_1\,e_2 = (\lambda x.a_{af}\,e_2)\,e_1 \quad (\mathit{lift})$
$(\lambda x.e_1)((\lambda y.e_2)\,e_3) = (\lambda y.(\lambda x.e_1)\,e_2)\,e_3 \quad (\mathcal{A})$	$(\lambda x.E_{af}[x])\,((\lambda y.a_{af})\,e) = (\lambda y.(\lambda x.E_{af}[x])\,a_{af})\,e \quad (\mathit{assoc})$
$(\lambda x.e_1)\,e_2 = e_1, x \notin fv(e_1) \quad (\mathcal{G})$	

Fig. 1. Existing call-by-need λ calculi (left: λ_{mow}, right: λ_{af})

In both calculi, the analog to the β axiom—also called a *basic notion of reduction* [5]—replaces variable occurrences, one at a time, with the value of the function's argument. Value substitution means that there is no duplication of work as far as argument evaluation is concerned. The function call is retained because additional variable occurrences in the function body may need the argument. Since function calls may accumulate, the calculi come with axioms that re-associate bindings to pair up functions with their arguments. For example, re-associating $(\lambda x.(\lambda y.\lambda z.z)\,v_y)\,v_x\,v_z$ in λ_{af} exposes a *deref* redex:

$$(\lambda x.(\lambda y.\underline{\lambda z.z})\,v_y)\,v_x\,\underline{v_z} \overset{lift}{\rightarrow} (\lambda x.(\lambda y.\underline{\lambda z.z})\,v_y\,\underline{v_z})\,v_x \overset{lift}{\rightarrow} (\lambda x.(\lambda y.\underline{(\lambda z.z)\,v_z})\,v_y)\,v_x$$

The two calculi differ from each other in their timing of variable replacements. The λ_{mow} calculus allows the replacement of a variable with its value anywhere in the body of its binding λ. The λ_{af} calculus replaces a variable with its argument only if evaluation of the function body needs it, where "need" is formalized via so-called evaluation contexts (E_{af}). Thus evaluation contexts in λ_{af} serve the double purpose of specifying demand for arguments and the standard reduction strategy. The term $(\lambda x.\lambda y.x)\, v$ illustrates this difference between the two calculi. According to λ_{mow}, the term is a $\mathcal{V}$ redex and reduces to $(\lambda x.\lambda y.v)\, v$, whereas in λ_{af}, the term is irreducible because the x occurs in an inner, unapplied λ, and is thus not "needed."

Also, λ_{mow} is more lenient than λ_{af} when it comes to re-associations. The λ_{af} calculus re-associates the left or right hand side of an application only if it has been completely reduced to an answer, but λ_{mow} permits re-association as soon as one nested function layer is revealed. In short, λ_{mow} proves more equations than λ_{af}, i.e., $\boldsymbol{\lambda_{af}} \subset \boldsymbol{\lambda_{mow}}$.

In λ_{af}, programs reduce to answers:

$$\texttt{eval}_{af}(e) = \texttt{done} \text{ iff there exists an answer } a_{af} \text{ such that } \boldsymbol{\lambda_{af}} \vdash e = a_{af}$$

In contrast, Maraist et al. introduce a "garbage collection" axiom into λ_{mow} to avoid answers and to use values instead. This suggests the following definition:

$$\texttt{eval}_{mow}(e) = \texttt{done} \text{ iff there exists a value } v_m \text{ such that } \boldsymbol{\lambda_{mow}} \vdash e = v_m$$

This turns out to be incorrect, however. Specifically, let $\texttt{eval}_{name}$ be the analogous call-by-name evaluator. Then $\texttt{eval}_{af} = \texttt{eval}_{name}$ but $\texttt{eval}_{mow} \neq \texttt{eval}_{name}$. Examples such as $(\lambda x.\lambda y.x)\, \Omega$ confirm the difference.

In recognition of this problem, Maraist et al. use Ariola and Felleisen's axioms and evaluation contexts to create their Curry-Feys-style standard reduction sequences. Doing so reveals the inconsistency of λ_{mow} with respect to Plotkin's *correspondence criteria* [25]. According to Plotkin, a useful calculus *corresponds to* a programming language, meaning its axioms (1) satisfy the Church-Rosser and Curry-Feys Standardization properties, and (2) define a standard reduction function that is equal to the evaluation function of the programming language. Both the call-by-name and the call-by-value λ calculi satisfy these criteria with respect to call-by-name and call-by-value SECD machines for ISWIM, respectively. So does λ_{af} with respect to a call-by-need SECD machine, but some of λ_{mow}'s axioms cannot be used as standard reduction relations.

Finally, the inclusion of $\mathcal{G}$ is a brute-force attempt to address the function call retention problem. Because $\mathcal{G}$ may discard arguments even before the function is called, both sets of authors consider it too coarse and acknowledge that a tighter solution to the function call retention issue would "strengthen the calculus and its utility for reasoning about the implementations of lazy languages" [4].

3 A New Call-by-Need λ Calculus

Our new calculus, λ_{need}, uses a single axiom, β_{need}. The new axiom evaluates the argument when it is first demanded, replaces all variable occurrences with that result, and then discards the argument and thus the function call. In addition, the axiom performs the required administrative scope adjustments as part of the same step, rendering explicit re-association axioms unnecessary. In short, every reduction step in our calculus represents computational progress.

Informally, to perform a reduction, three components must be identified:

1. the next demanded variable,
2. the function that binds that demanded variable,
3. and the argument to that function.

In previous by-need calculi the re-association axioms rewrite a term so that the binding function and its argument are adjacent.

Without the re-association axioms, finding the function that binds the demanded variable and its argument requires a different kind of work. The following terms show how the demanded variable, its binding function, and its argument can appear at seemingly arbitrary locations in a program:

- $(\underline{\lambda x}.(\lambda y.\lambda z.\underline{x})\, e_y)\, \underline{e_x}\, e_z$
- $(\lambda x.(\underline{\lambda y}.\lambda z.\underline{y})\, \underline{e_y})\, e_x\, e_z$
- $(\lambda x.(\lambda y.\underline{\lambda z}.\underline{z})\, e_y)\, e_x\, \underline{e_z}$

Our β_{need} axiom employs a grammar of contexts to describe the path from a demanded variable to its binding function and from there to its argument.

The first subsection explains the syntax and the contexts of λ_{need} in a gradual fashion. The second subsection presents the β_{need} axiom and also shows how to derive it from Ariola and Felleisen's λ_{af} calculus.

3.1 Contexts

Like the existing by-need calculi, the syntax of our calculus is that of Church's original calculus. In λ_{need}, calculations evaluate terms e to answers $A[v]$, which generalize answers from Ariola and Felleisen's calculus:

$$
\begin{aligned}
e &= x \mid \lambda x.e \mid e\, e && \text{(Terms)}\\
v &= \lambda x.e && \text{(Values)}\\
a &= A[v] && \text{(Answers)}\\
A &= [\ ] \mid A[\lambda x.A]\, e && \text{(Answer Contexts)}
\end{aligned}
$$

Following Ariola and Felleisen, the basic axiom uses evaluation contexts to specify the notion of demand for variables:

$$E = [\ ] \mid E\, e \mid \ldots \qquad \text{(Evaluation Contexts)}$$

The first two kinds, taken from λ_{af}, specify that a variable is demanded, and that a variable in the operator position of an application is demanded, respectively.

Since the calculus is to model program evaluation, we are primarily interested in demanded variables under a λ-abstraction. This kind of evaluation context is defined using an answer context A:

$$E = \ldots \mid A[E] \mid \ldots \qquad \text{(Another Evaluation Context)}$$

Using answer contexts, this third evaluation context dictates that demand exists under a λ if a corresponding argument exists for that λ. Note how *an answer context descends under the same number of λs as arguments for those λs.* In particular, for any term $A[\lambda x.e_1]\,e_2$, e_2 is always the argument of $\lambda x.e_1$. The third evaluation context thus generalizes the function-is-next-to-argument requirement found in both call-by-name and call-by-value. The generalization is needed due to the retention of function calls in λ_{need}.

Here are some example answer contexts that might be used:

$$A_0 = \underbrace{(\lambda x.[\;])\,e_x}$$

$$A_1 = \underbrace{(\lambda x.\,\underbrace{(\lambda y.[\;])\,e_y})\,e_x}$$

$$A_2 = \underbrace{(\lambda x.\,\underbrace{(\lambda y.\,\underbrace{(\lambda z.[\;])\,e_z})\,e_y})\,e_x}$$

An underbrace matches each function to its argument. The examples all juxtapose functions and their arguments. In contrast, the next two separate functions from their arguments:

$$A_3 = (\lambda x.\lambda y.\lambda z.[\;])\,e_x\,e_y\,e_z$$

$$A_4 = (\lambda x.\underbrace{(\lambda y.\lambda z.[\;])\,e_y})\,e_x\,e_z$$

To summarize thus far, when a demanded variable is discovered under a λ, the surrounding context looks like this:

$$A[E[x]]$$

where both the function binding x and its argument are in A. The decomposition of the surrounding context into A and E assumes that A encompasses as many function-argument pairs as possible; in other words, it is impossible to merge the outer part of E with A to form a larger answer context.

To know which argument corresponds to the demanded variable, we must find the λ that binds x in A. To this end, we split answer contexts so that we can "highlight" a function-argument pair within the context:

$$\hat{A} = [\;] \mid A[\hat{A}]\,e \qquad \text{(Partial Answer Contexts–Outer)}$$

$$\check{A} = [\;] \mid A[\lambda x.\check{A}] \qquad \text{(Partial Answer Contexts–Inner)}$$

Using these additional contexts, any answer context can be decomposed into

$$\hat{A}[A[\lambda x.\check{A}[\;]]\,e]$$

where e is the argument of $\lambda x.\check{A}[\;]$. For a fixed function-argument pair in an answer context, this partitioning into $\hat{A}$, A, and $\check{A}$ is unique. The $\hat{A}$ subcontext represents the part of the answer context around the chosen function-argument pair; the $\check{A}$ subcontext represents the part of the answer context in its body; and A here is the subcontext between the function and its argument. Naturally we must demand that $\hat{A}$ composed with $\check{A}$ is an answer context as well so that the overall context remains an answer context. The following table lists the various subcontexts for the example A_4 for various function-argument pairs:

	$A_4 = (\lambda x.(\lambda y.\lambda z.[\;])\, e_y)\, e_x\, e_z$		
$\hat{A} =$	$[\;]\, e_z$	$(\lambda x.[\;])\, e_x\, e_z$	$[\;]$
$A =$	$[\;]$	$[\;]$	$(\lambda x.(\lambda y.[\;])\, e_y)\, e_x$
$\check{A} =$	$(\lambda y.\lambda z.[\;])\, e_y$	$\lambda z.[\;]$	$[\;]$
$A_4 =$	$\hat{A}[A[\lambda x.\check{A}]\, e_x]$	$\hat{A}[A[\lambda y.\check{A}]\, e_y]$	$\hat{A}[A[\lambda z.\check{A}]\, e_z]$

Now we can define the fourth kind of evaluation context:

$$E = \ldots \mid \hat{A}[A[\lambda x.\check{A}[E[x]]]\, E], \quad \text{where } \hat{A}[\check{A}] \in A \qquad \text{(Final Eval. Context)}$$

This final evaluation context shows how demand shifts to an argument when a function parameter is in demand within the function body.

3.2 The β_{need} Axiom and a Derivation

Figure 2 summarizes the syntax of λ_{need} as developed in the preceding section.[1] In this section we use these definitions to formulate the β axiom for our calculus.

$$
\begin{aligned}
e &= x \mid \lambda x.e \mid e\, e && \text{(Terms)}\\
v &= \lambda x.e && \text{(Values)}\\
a &= A[v] && \text{(Answers)}\\
A &= [\;] \mid A[\lambda x.A]\, e && \text{(Answer Contexts)}\\
\hat{A} &= [\;] \mid A[\hat{A}]\, e && \text{(Partial Answer Contexts–Outer)}\\
\check{A} &= [\;] \mid A[\lambda x.\check{A}] && \text{(Partial Answer Contexts–Inner)}\\
E &= [\;] \mid E\, e \mid A[E] \mid \hat{A}[A[\lambda x.\check{A}[E[x]]]\, E], && \text{(Evaluation Contexts)}\\
&\qquad \text{where } \hat{A}[\check{A}] \in A
\end{aligned}
$$

Fig. 2. The syntax and contexts of the new call-by-need λ calculus, λ_{need}

Here is the single axiom of λ_{need}:

$$\hat{A}[A_1[\lambda x.\check{A}[E[x]]]\, A_2[v]] = \hat{A}[A_1[A_2[\check{A}[E[x]]\{x{:=}v\}]]], \qquad (\beta_{need})$$
$$\text{where } \hat{A}[\check{A}] \in A$$

[1] We gratefully acknowledge Casey Klein's help with the A production.

A β_{need} redex determines which parameter x of some function is "in demand" and how to locate the corresponding argument $A_2[v]$, which might be an answer not necessarily a value. The contexts from the previous section specify the path from the binding position (λ) to the variable occurrence and the argument. A β_{need} reduction substitutes the value in $A_2[v]$ for all free occurrences of the function parameter—just like in other λ calculi. In the process, the function call is discarded. Since the argument has been reduced to a value, there is no duplication of work, meaning our calculus satisfies the requirements of lazy evaluation. Lifting A_2 to the top of the evaluation context ensures that its bindings remain intact and visible for v.

Here is a sample reduction in λ_{need}, where $\longrightarrow$ is the one-step reduction:

$$((\lambda x.(\underline{\lambda y.\lambda z.\mathbf{z}\ y\ x})\ \lambda y.y)\ \lambda x.x)\ \underline{\lambda z.z} \quad (1)$$

$$\longrightarrow (\lambda x.(\underline{\lambda y.(\lambda z.\underline{\underline{z}})\ \mathbf{y}\ x})\ \underline{\lambda y.y})\ \lambda x.x \quad (2)$$

$$\longrightarrow (\lambda x.((\underline{\lambda z.\mathbf{z}})\ \underline{\lambda y.y})\ x)\ \lambda x.x \quad (3)$$

$$\longrightarrow (\underline{\lambda x.(\lambda y.\underline{\underline{y}})\ \mathbf{x}})\ \underline{\lambda x.x} \quad (4)$$

The "in demand" variable is in bold; its binding λ and argument are underlined. Line 1 is an example of a reduction that involves a non-adjoined function and argument pair. In line 2, the demand for the value of z (twice underlined) triggers a demand for the value of y; line 4 contains a similar demand chain.

$$
\begin{aligned}
v &= \lambda x.e && \text{(Values)}\\
a_{af} &= A_{af}[v] && \text{(Answers)}\\
A_{af} &= [\,]\mid (\lambda x.A_{af})\,e && \text{(Answer Contexts)}\\
E_{af} &= [\,]\mid E_{af}\,e \mid A_{af}[E_{af}] \mid (\lambda x.E_{af}[x])\,E_{af} && \text{(Evaluation Contexts)}
\end{aligned}
$$

$$
\begin{aligned}
(\lambda x.E_{af}[x])\,v &= E_{af}[x]\{x:=v\} && (\beta'_{need})\\
(\lambda x.A_{af}[v])\,e_1\,e_2 &= (\lambda x.A_{af}[v\,e_2])\,e_1 && (\mathit{lift}')\\
(\lambda x.E_{af}[x])\,((\lambda y.A_{af}[v])\,e) &= (\lambda y.A_{af}[(\lambda x.E_{af}[x])\,v])\,e && (\mathit{assoc}')
\end{aligned}
$$

Fig. 3. A modified calculus, $\lambda_{af\text{-}mod}$

To furnish additional intuition into β_{need}, we use the rest of the section to derive it from the axioms of λ_{af}. The $\lambda_{af\text{-}mod}$ calculus in figure 3 combines λ_{af} with two insights. First, Garcia et al. [13] observed that when the answers in λ_{af}'s *lift* and *assoc* redexes are nested deeply, multiple re-associations are performed consecutively. Thus we modify *lift* and *assoc* to perform all these re-associations in one step.[2] The modified calculus defines answers via answer contexts, A_{af}, and the modified *lift′* and *assoc′* axioms utilize these answer contexts to do the multi-step re-associations. Thus programs in this modified calculus reduce to answers

[2] The same modifications cannot be applied to $\mathcal{C}$ and $\mathcal{A}$ in λ_{mow} because they allow earlier re-association and thus not all the re-associations are performed consecutively.

$A_{af}[v]$. Also, the A_{af} answer contexts are identical to the third kind of evaluation context in $\lambda_{af\text{-}mod}$ and the new definition of E_{af} reflects this relationship.

Second, Maraist et al. [19] observed that once an argument is reduced to a value, all substitutions can be performed at once. The β'_{need} axiom exploits this idea and performs a full substitution. Obviously β'_{need} occasionally performs more substitutions than *deref*. Nevertheless, any term with an answer in λ_{af} likewise has an answer when reducing with β'_{need}.

Next an inspection of the axioms shows that the contractum of a *assoc*′ redex contains a β'_{need} redex. Thus the *assoc*′ re-associations and β'_{need} substitutions can be performed with one merged axiom:[3]

$$(\lambda x.E_{af}[x])\, A_{af}[v] = A_{af}[E_{af}[x]\{x{:=}v\}] \qquad (\beta''_{need})$$

The final step is to merge *lift*′ with β''_{need}, which requires our generalized answer and evaluation contexts. A naïve attempt may look like this:

$$A_1[\lambda x.E[x]]\, A_2[v] = A_1[A_2[E[x]\{x{:=}v\}]] \qquad (\beta'''_{need})$$

As the examples in the preceding subsection show, however, the binding occurrence for the "in demand" parameter x may not be the inner-most binding λ once the re-association axioms are eliminated. That is, in comparison with β_{need}, β'''_{need} incorrectly assumes E is always next to the binder. We solve this final problem with the introduction of partial answer contexts.

4 Consistency, Determinism, and Soundness

If a calculus is to model a programming language, it must satisfy some essential properties, most importantly a Church-Rosser theorem and a Curry-Feys standardization theorem [25]. The former guarantees consistency of evaluation; that is, we can define an evaluator *function* with the calculus. The latter implies that the calculus comes with a *deterministic* evaluation strategy. Jointly these properties imply the calculus is *sound* with respect to observational equivalence.

4.1 Consistency: Church-Rosser

The λ_{need} calculus defines an evaluator for a by-need language:

$$\texttt{eval}_{need}(e) = \texttt{done} \text{ iff there exists an answer } a \text{ such that } \boldsymbol{\lambda_{need}} \vdash e = a$$

To prove that the evaluator is indeed a (partial) function, we prove that the notion of reduction satisfies the Church-Rosser property.

Theorem 1. $eval_{need}$ *is a partial function.*

Proof. The theorem is a direct consequence of lemma 1 (Church-Rosser).

[3] Danvy et al. [8] dub a β''_{need} redex a "potential redex" in unrelated work.

Our strategy is to define a parallel reduction relation for λ_{need} [5]. Define $\rightarrow$ to be the compatible closure of a β_{need} reduction, and $\twoheadrightarrow$ to be the reflexive, transitive closure of $\rightarrow$. Additionally, define $\Rightarrow$ to be the relation that reduces β_{need} redexes in parallel.

Definition 1 ($\Rightarrow$).

$$\begin{aligned}
e &\Rightarrow e\\
\hat{A}[A_1[\lambda x.\check{A}[E[x]]]\,A_2[v]] &\Rightarrow \hat{A}'[A_1'[A_2'[\check{A}'[E'[x]]\{x:=v'\}]]],\\
&\quad \textit{if } \hat{A}[\check{A}] \in A,\ \hat{A}'[\check{A}'] \in A,\ \hat{A} \Rightarrow \hat{A}', A_1 \Rightarrow A_1',\\
&\quad A_2 \Rightarrow A_2', \check{A} \Rightarrow \check{A}',\ E \Rightarrow E',\ v \Rightarrow v'\\
e_1\,e_2 &\Rightarrow e_1'\,e_2',\ \textit{if } e_1 \Rightarrow e_1',\ e_2 \Rightarrow e_2'\\
\lambda x.e &\Rightarrow \lambda x.e',\ \textit{if } e \Rightarrow e'
\end{aligned}$$

The parallel reduction relation $\Rightarrow$ relies on notion of parallel reduction for contexts; for simplicity, we overload the relation symbol to denote both relations.

Definition 2 ($\Rightarrow$ for Contexts).

$$\begin{aligned}
[\;] &\Rightarrow [\;]\\
A_1[\lambda x.A_2]\,e &\Rightarrow A_1'[\lambda x.A_2']\,e',\ \textit{if } A_1 \Rightarrow A_1',\ A_2 \Rightarrow A_2',\ e \Rightarrow e'\\
A[\hat{A}]\,e &\Rightarrow A'[\hat{A}']\,e',\ \textit{if } A \Rightarrow A',\ \hat{A} \Rightarrow \hat{A}',\ e \Rightarrow e'\\
A[\lambda x.\check{A}] &\Rightarrow A'[\lambda x.\check{A}'],\ \textit{if } A \Rightarrow A',\ \check{A} \Rightarrow \check{A}'\\
E\,e &\Rightarrow E'\,e',\ \textit{if } E \Rightarrow E',\ e \Rightarrow e'\\
A[E] &\Rightarrow A'[E'],\ \textit{if } A \Rightarrow A',\ E \Rightarrow E'\\
\hat{A}[A[\lambda x.\check{A}[E_1[x]]]\,E_2] &\Rightarrow \hat{A}'[A'[\lambda x.\check{A}'[E_1'[x]]]\,E_2'],\\
&\quad \textit{if } \hat{A}[\check{A}] \in A,\ \hat{A} \Rightarrow \hat{A}',\ A \Rightarrow A',\\
&\quad \check{A} \Rightarrow \check{A}',\ E_1 \Rightarrow E_1',\ E_2 \Rightarrow E_2'
\end{aligned}$$

Lemma 1 (Church-Rosser). *If $e \twoheadrightarrow e_1$ and $e \twoheadrightarrow e_2$, then there exists a term e' such that $e_1 \twoheadrightarrow e'$ and $e_2 \twoheadrightarrow e'$.*

Proof. By lemma 2, $\Rightarrow$ satisfies a diamond property. Since $\Rightarrow$ extends $\rightarrow$, $\twoheadrightarrow$ is also the transitive-reflexive closure of $\Rightarrow$, so $\twoheadrightarrow$ also satisfies a diamond property.

Lemma 2 (Diamond Property of $\Rightarrow$). *If $e \Rightarrow e_1$ and $e \Rightarrow e_2$, there exists e' such that $e_1 \Rightarrow e'$ and $e_2 \Rightarrow e'$.*

Proof. The proof proceeds by structural induction on the derivation of $e \Rightarrow e_1$.

4.2 Deterministic Behavior: Standard Reduction

A language calculus should also come with a deterministic algorithm for applying the reductions to evaluate a program. Here is our *standard reduction*:

$$E[e] \longmapsto E[e'], \text{ where } e\ \beta_{need}\ e'$$

Our standard reduction strategy picks exactly one redex in a term.

Proposition 1 (Unique Decomposition). *For all closed terms e, e either is an answer or $e = E[e']$ for a unique evaluation context E and β_{need} redex e'.*

Proof. The proof proceeds by structural induction on e.

Since our calculus satisfies the unique decomposition property, we can use the standard reduction relation to define a (partial) evaluator function:

$$\texttt{eval}^{\text{sr}}_{need}(e) = \texttt{done} \text{ iff there exists an answer } a \text{ such that } e \longmapsto\!\!\!\!\rightarrow a$$

where $\longmapsto\!\!\!\!\rightarrow$ is the reflexive, transitive closure of $\longmapsto$. Proposition 1 shows $\texttt{eval}^{\text{sr}}_{need}$ is a function. The following theorem confirms that it equals $\texttt{eval}_{need}$.

Theorem 2. $\textit{eval}_{need} = \textit{eval}^{sr}_{need}$

Proof. The theorem follows from lemma 3, which shows how to obtain a standard reduction sequence for any arbitrary reduction sequence. The front-end of the former is a series of standard reduction steps.

Definition 3 (Standard Reduction Sequences $\mathcal{R}$).

- $x \subset \mathcal{R}$
- $\lambda x.e_1 \diamond \cdots \diamond \lambda x.e_m \in \mathcal{R}$, *if* $e_1 \diamond \cdots \diamond e_m \in \mathcal{R}$
- $e_0 \diamond e_1 \diamond \cdots \diamond e_m \in \mathcal{R}$, *if* $e_0 \longmapsto e_1$ *and* $e_1 \diamond \cdots \diamond e_m \in \mathcal{R}$
- $(e_1\, e_1')\diamond\cdots\diamond(e_m\, e_1')\diamond(e_m\, e_2')\diamond\cdots\diamond(e_m\, e_n') \in \mathcal{R}$, *if* $e_1\diamond\cdots\diamond e_m, e_1'\diamond\cdots\diamond e_n' \in \mathcal{R}$.

Lemma 3 (Curry-Feys Standardization). $e \twoheadrightarrow e'$ *iff there exists* $e_1 \diamond \cdots \diamond e_n \in \mathcal{R}$ *such that* $e = e_1$ *and* $e' = e_n$.

Proof. Replace $\twoheadrightarrow$ with $\Rightarrow$s, and the lemma immediately follows from lemma 4.

The key to the remaining proofs is a size metric for parallel reductions.

Definition 4 (Size of $\Rightarrow$ Reduction).

$$\begin{array}{ll}
\left|e \Rightarrow e\right| & = 0 \\
\left|(e_1\, e_2) \Rightarrow (e_1'\, e_2')\right| & = \left|e_1 \Rightarrow e_1'\right| + \left|e_2 \Rightarrow e_2'\right| \\
\left|\lambda x.e \Rightarrow \lambda x.e'\right| & = \left|e \Rightarrow e'\right| \\
\left|r\right| & = 1 + \left|\hat{A} \Rightarrow \hat{A}'\right| + \left|A_1 \Rightarrow A_1'\right| + \left|\check{A}[E[x]] \Rightarrow \check{A}'[E'[x]]\right| + \\
& \qquad \left|A_2 \Rightarrow A_2'\right| + \#(x, \check{A}'[E'[x]]) \times \left|v \Rightarrow v'\right| \\
\multicolumn{2}{l}{\quad \textit{where } r = \hat{A}[A_1[\lambda x.\check{A}[E[x]]]\, A_2[v]] \Rightarrow \hat{A}'[A_1'[A_2'[\check{A}'[E'[x]]\{x{:=}v'\}]]]} \\
\#(x, e) & = \textit{the number of free occurrences of } x \textit{ in } e
\end{array}$$

The size of a parallel reduction of a context equals the sum of the sizes of the parallel reductions of the subcontexts and subterms that comprise the context.

Lemma 4. *If* $e_0 \Rightarrow e_1$ *and* $e_1\diamond\cdots\diamond e_n \in \mathcal{R}$, *there exists* $e_0\diamond e_1'\diamond\cdots\diamond e_p'\diamond e_n \in \mathcal{R}$.

Proof. By triple lexicographic induction on (1) length n of the given standard reduction sequence, (2) $\left|e_0 \Rightarrow e_1\right|$, and (3) structure of e_0.[4]

[4] We conjecture that the use of Ralph Loader's technique [18] may simplify our proof.

4.3 Observational Equivalence

Following Morris [22] two expressions e_1 and e_2 are observationally equivalent, $e_1 \simeq e_2$, if they are indistinguishable in all contexts. Formally, $e_1 \simeq e_2$ if and only if $\mathtt{eval}_{need}(C[e_1]) = \mathtt{eval}_{need}(C[e_2])$ for all contexts C, where

$$C = [\ ] \mid \lambda x.C \mid C\,e \mid e\,C \qquad \text{(Contexts)}$$

An alternative definition of the behavioral equivalence relation uses co-induction. In either case, λ_{need} is sound with respect to observational equivalence.

Theorem 3 (Soundness). *If* $\boldsymbol{\lambda_{need}} \vdash e_1 = e_2$*, then* $e_1 \simeq e_2$.

Proof. Following Plotkin, a calculus is sound if it satisfies Church-Rosser and Curry-Feys theorems.

5 Correctness

Ariola and Felleisen [3] prove that λ_{af} defines the same evaluation function as the call-by-name λ calculus. Nakata and Hasegawa [23] additionally demonstrate extensional correctness of the same calculus with respect to Launchbury's natural semantics [17]. In this section, we show that λ_{need} defines the same evaluation function as Launchbury's semantics. While our theorem statement is extensional, the proof illuminates the tight intensional relationship between the two systems.

5.1 Overview

The gap between the λ_{need} standard reduction "machine" and Launchbury's natural semantics is huge. While the latter's store-based natural semantics uses the equivalent of assignment statements to implement the "evaluate once, only when needed" policy, the λ_{need} calculus exclusively relies on term substitutions. To close the gap, we systematically construct a series of intermediate systems that makes comparisons easy, all while ensuring correctness at each step. A first step is to convert the natural semantics into a store-based machine [27].

To further bridge the gap we note that a single-use assignment statement is equivalent to a program-wide substitution of shared expressions [10]. A closely related idea is to reduce shared expressions simultaneously. This leads to a parallel program rewriting system, dubbed $\lambda_{\parallel}$. Equipped with $\lambda_{\parallel}$ we get closer to λ_{need} but not all the way there because reductions in λ_{need} and $\lambda_{\parallel}$ are too coarse-grained for direct comparison. Fortunately, it is easy to construct an intermediate transition system that eliminates the remainder of the gap. We convert λ_{need} to an equivalent CK transition system [9], where the program is partitioned into a control string (C) and an explicit context (K) and we show that there is a correspondence between this transition system and $\lambda_{\parallel}$.

Figure 4 outlines our proof strategy pictorially. The four horizontal layers correspond to the four rewriting systems. While λ_{need} and $\lambda_{\parallel}$ use large steps to

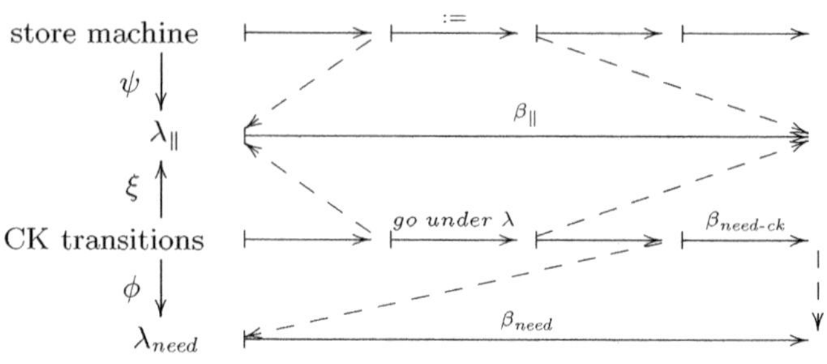

Fig. 4. Summary of correctness proof technique

progress from term to term, the machine-like systems take several small steps. The solid vertical arrows between the layers figure indicate how mapping functions relate the rewriting sequences and the dashed arrows show how the smaller machine steps correspond to the larger steps of λ_{need} and $\lambda_{\parallel}$:

- The ψ function maps states from the store-based machine to terms in the $\lambda_{\parallel}$ world. For every step in the natural-semantics machine, the resulting operation in $\lambda_{\parallel}$ is either a no-op or a $\beta_{\parallel}$ reduction, with assignment in the store-machine being equivalent to program-wide substitution in $\lambda_{\parallel}$.
- Similarly, the ξ function maps states of the CK transition system to the $\lambda_{\parallel}$ space and for every CK transition, the resulting $\lambda_{\parallel}$ operation is also either a no-op or a $\beta_{\parallel}$ reduction, with the transition that descends under a λ-abstraction being equivalent to substitution in $\lambda_{\parallel}$.
- Finally, the ϕ function maps states of the CK transition system to λ_{need} terms and is used to show that the CK system and λ_{need} are equivalent. For every CK transition, the equivalent λ_{need} operation is either a no-op or a β_{need} reduction.

Syntax

$$\begin{aligned} S_L &= \langle e, F_L s, \Gamma\rangle && \text{(States)}\\ F_L s &= F_L, \ldots && \text{(List of Frames)}\\ F_L &= (\mathtt{arg}\, e) \mid (\mathtt{var}\ x) && \text{(Frames)}\\ \Gamma &= (x{\mapsto}e, \ldots) && \text{(Heaps)} \end{aligned}$$

Transitions

$$\begin{aligned} \langle e_1\, e_2, F_L s, \Gamma\rangle &\overset{ckh}{\longmapsto} \langle e_1, ((\mathtt{arg}\, e_2), F_L s), \Gamma\rangle && (\textit{push-arg-ckh})\\ \langle \lambda x.e_1, ((\mathtt{arg}\, e_2), F_L s), \Gamma\rangle &\overset{ckh}{\longmapsto} \langle e_1\{x{:=}y\}, F_L s, (\Gamma, y{\mapsto}e_2)\rangle,\ y \text{ fresh} && (\textit{descend-lam-ckh})\\ \langle x, F_L s, (\Gamma, x \mapsto e)\rangle &\overset{ckh}{\longmapsto} \langle e, ((\mathtt{var}\ x), F_L s), \Gamma\rangle && (\textit{lookup-var-ckh})\\ \langle v, ((\mathtt{var}\ x), F_L s), \Gamma\rangle &\overset{ckh}{\longmapsto} \langle v, F_L s, (\Gamma, x \mapsto v)\rangle && (\textit{update-heap-ckh}) \end{aligned}$$

Fig. 5. The natural semantics as an abstract machine

Subsections 5.2 and 5.3 present the store-based machine and the parallel rewriting semantics, respectively, including a proof of equivalence. Subsection 5.4 presents the CK system and subsection 5.5 explains the rest of the proof.

5.2 Adapting Launchbury's Natural Semantics

Figure 5 describes the syntax and transitions of the store machine.[5] It is dubbed CKH because it resembles a three-register machine [9]: a machine state S_L is comprised of a control string (C), a list of frames (K) that represents the control context in an inside-out manner, and a heap (H). The ... notation means "zero of more of the preceding kind of element." An $(\texttt{arg}\, e)$ frame represents the argument in an application and the $(\texttt{var}\ x)$ frame indicates that a heap expression is the current control string. Parentheses are used to group a list of frames when necessary. The initial machine state for a program e is $\langle e, (), () \rangle$. Computation terminates when the control string is a value and the list of frames is empty.

The *push-arg-ckh* transition moves the argument in an application to a new arg frame in the frame list and makes the operator the next control string. When that operator is a λ-abstraction, the *descend-lam-ckh* transition adds its argument to the heap,[6] mapped to a fresh variable name, and makes the body of the operator the new control string. The *lookup-var-ckh* transition evaluates an argument from the heap when the control string is a variable. The mapping is removed from the heap and a new $(\texttt{var}\ x)$ frame remembers the variable whose corresponding expression is under evaluation. Finally, when the heap expression is reduced to a value, the *update-heap-ckh* transition extends the heap again.

5.3 Parallel Rewriting

The syntax of the parallel λ-rewriting semantics is as follows:

$$\begin{aligned} e_{\parallel} &= e \mid e_{\parallel}{}^{x} && \text{(Terms)} \\ v_{\parallel} &= v \mid v_{\parallel}{}^{x} && \text{(Values)} \\ E_{\parallel} &= [\ ] \mid E_{\parallel}\, e_{\parallel} \mid E_{\parallel}{}^{x} && \text{(Evaluation Contexts)} \end{aligned}$$

This system expresses computation with a selective parallel reduction strategy. When a function application is in demand, the system substitutes the argument for all free occurrences of the bound variable, regardless of the status of the argument. When an instance of a substituted argument is reduced, however, all instances of the argument are reduced in parallel. Here is a sample reduction:

$$(\lambda x.x\,x)\,(I\,I) \overset{\parallel}{\longmapsto} (I\,I)^x\,(I\,I)^x \overset{\parallel}{\longmapsto} I^x\,I^x \overset{\parallel}{\longmapsto} I$$

[5] To aid comparisons, we slightly alter Launchbury's rules (and the resulting machine) to use pure λ terms. Thus we avoid Launchbury's preprocessing and special syntax.

[6] The notation $(\varGamma, x{\mapsto}e)$ is a heap $\varGamma$, extended with the variable-term mapping $x{\mapsto}e$.

The $\lambda_\parallel$ semantics keeps track of arguments via labeled terms $e_\parallel{}^x$, where labels are variables. Values in $\lambda_\parallel$ also include labeled λ-abstractions. Reducing a labeled term triggers the simultaneous reduction of all other terms with the same label. Otherwise, labels do not affect program evaluation.

We require that all expressions with the same label must be identical.

Definition 5. *A program* $e_\parallel$ *is* consistently labeled (CL) *when for any two subterms* $e_{\parallel 1}^{x_1}$ *and* $e_{\parallel 2}^{x_2}$ *of* $e_\parallel$, $x_1 = x_2$ *implies* $e_{\parallel 1} = e_{\parallel 2}$.

In the reduction of $\lambda_\parallel$ programs, evaluation contexts $E_\parallel$ determine which part of the program to reduce next. The $\lambda_\parallel$ evaluation contexts are the call-by-name evaluation contexts with the addition of the labeled $E_\parallel{}^x$ context, which dictates that a redex search goes under labeled terms. Essentially, when searching for a redex, terms tagged with a label are treated as if they were unlabeled.

The parallel semantics can exploit simpler evaluation contexts than λ_{need} because substitution occurs as soon as an application is encountered:

$$E_\parallel[((\lambda x.e_{\parallel 1})^{\vec{y}})\, e_{\parallel 2}] \overset{\parallel}{\longmapsto} \begin{cases} E_\parallel[e_\parallel], & \text{if } [\ ] \text{ is not under a label in } E_\parallel \\ E_\parallel[e_\parallel]\{\!\{z \Leftarrow E_{\parallel 2}[e_\parallel]\}\!\}, & \text{if } E_\parallel[\ ] = E_{\parallel 1}[(E_{\parallel 2}[\ ])^z] \\ & \text{and } [\ ] \text{ is not under a label in } E_{\parallel 2} \end{cases} \qquad (\beta_\parallel)$$
$$\text{where } e_\parallel = e_{\parallel 1}\{x := e_{\parallel 2}^{w}\}, w \text{ fresh}$$

On the left-hand side of $\beta_\parallel$, the program is partitioned into a context and a β-like redex. A term $e^{\vec{y}}$ may have any number of labels and possibly none. On the right-hand side, the redex is contracted to a term $e_{\parallel 1}\{x := e_{\parallel 2}^{w}\}$ such that the argument is tagged with an unique label w. Obsolete labels $\vec{y}$ are discarded.

There are two distinct ways to contract a redex: when the redex is not under any labels and when the redex occurs under at least one label. For the former, the redex is the only contracted part of the program. For the latter, all other instances of that labeled term are similarly contracted. In this second case, the evaluation context is further subdivided as $E_\parallel[\ ] = E_{\parallel 1}[(E_{\parallel 2}[\ ])^z]$, where z is the label nearest the redex, i.e., $E_{\parallel 2}$ contains no additional labels. A whole-program substitution function is used to perform the parallel reduction:

$$\begin{aligned} e_{\parallel 1}^{x}\{\!\{x \Leftarrow e_\parallel\}\!\} &= e_\parallel{}^x \\ e_{\parallel 1}^{x}\{\!\{y \Leftarrow e_\parallel\}\!\} &= (e_{\parallel 1}\{\!\{y \Leftarrow e_\parallel\}\!\})^x,\ x \neq y \\ (\lambda x.e_{\parallel 1})\{\!\{x \Leftarrow e_\parallel\}\!\} &= \lambda x.(e_{\parallel 1}\{\!\{x \Leftarrow e_\parallel\}\!\}) \\ (e_{\parallel 1}\, e_{\parallel 2})\{\!\{x \Leftarrow e_\parallel\}\!\} &= (e_{\parallel 1}\{\!\{x \Leftarrow e_\parallel\}\!\}\, e_{\parallel 2}\{\!\{x \Leftarrow e_\parallel\}\!\}) \\ \text{otherwise, } e_{\parallel 1}\{\!\{x \Leftarrow e_\parallel\}\!\} &= e_{\parallel 1} \end{aligned}$$

Rewriting terms with $\beta_\parallel$ preserves the consistent labeling property.

Proposition 2. *If* $e_\parallel$ *is CL and* $e_\parallel \overset{\parallel}{\longmapsto} e_\parallel{}'$, *then* $e_\parallel{}'$ *is CL.*

The ψ function reconstructs a $\lambda_{\parallel}$ term from a CKH machine configuration:

$$\boxed{\psi : S_L \to e_{\parallel}}$$

$$\begin{aligned}\psi(\langle e, ((\mathtt{var}\ x), F_{L}s), \Gamma\rangle) &= \psi(\langle x, F_{L}s, (x \mapsto e, \Gamma)\rangle)\\ \psi(\langle e_1, ((\mathtt{arg}\, e_2), F_{L}s), \Gamma\rangle) &= \psi(\langle e_1\, e_2, F_{L}s, \Gamma\rangle)\\ \psi(\langle e, (), \Gamma\rangle) &= e\{\!\{\Gamma\}\!\}\end{aligned}$$

The operation $e\{\!\{\Gamma\}\!\}$, using overloaded notation, replaces all free variables in e with their corresponding terms in Γ and tags them with appropriate labels.

Lemma 5 demonstrates the bulk of the equivalence of the store machine and $\lambda_{\parallel}$.[7] The rest of the equivalence proof is straightforward [9].

Lemma 5. *If* $\langle e, F_{L}s, \Gamma\rangle \overset{ckh}{\longmapsto} \langle e', F_{L}s', \Gamma'\rangle$, *then either:*

1. $\psi(\langle e, F_{L}s, \Gamma\rangle) = \psi(\langle e', F_{L}s', \Gamma'\rangle)$
2. $\psi(\langle e, F_{L}s, \Gamma\rangle) \overset{\parallel}{\longmapsto} \psi(\langle e', F_{L}s', \Gamma'\rangle)$

5.4 A Transition System for Comparing λ_{need} and $\lambda_{\parallel}$

The CK layer in figure 4 mediates between $\lambda_{\parallel}$ and λ_{need}. The corresponding transition system resembles a two-register CK machine [9]. Figure 6 describes the syntax and the transitions of the system.[8]

Syntax

$$\begin{aligned} S &= \langle e, Fs\rangle && \text{(States)}\\ Fs &= F, \ldots && \text{(List of Frames)}\\ F &= (\mathtt{arg}\, e) \mid (\mathtt{lam}\, x) \mid (\mathsf{bod}\, x\, Fs\, Fs) && \text{(Frames)}\end{aligned}$$

Transitions

$$\langle e_1\, e_2, Fs\rangle \overset{ck}{\longmapsto} \langle e_1, ((\mathtt{arg}\, e_2), Fs)\rangle \qquad (\mathit{push\text{-}arg\text{-}ck})$$

$$\langle \lambda x.e, Fs\rangle \overset{ck}{\longmapsto} \langle e, ((\mathtt{lam}\, x), Fs)\rangle \quad \text{if } \mathtt{balance}(Fs) > 0 \qquad (\mathit{descend\text{-}lam\text{-}ck})$$

$$\langle x, (Fs_1, (\mathtt{lam}\, x), Fs_2, (\mathtt{arg}\, e), Fs)\rangle \overset{ck}{\longmapsto} \langle e, ((\mathsf{bod}\, x\, Fs_1\, Fs_2), Fs)\rangle \qquad (\mathit{lookup\text{-}var\text{-}ck})$$
$$\text{if } \phi_F(Fs_1) \in \check{A}[E], \phi_F(Fs_2) \in A, \phi_F(Fs) \in E[\hat{A}], \hat{A}[\check{A}] \in A$$

$$\langle v, (Fs_3, (\mathsf{bod}\, x\, Fs_1\, Fs_2), Fs)\rangle \overset{ck}{\longmapsto} \langle v, (Fs_1\{x := v\}, Fs_3, Fs_2, Fs)\rangle \quad \text{if } \phi_F(Fs_3) \in A \qquad (\beta_{need\text{-}ck})$$

Fig. 6. A transition system for comparing λ_{need} and $\lambda_{\parallel}$

States consist of a subterm and a list of frames representing the context. The first kind of frame represents the argument in an application and the second

[7] The lemma relies on an extension of the typical α-equivalence classes of terms to include variables in labels as well.

[8] The CK transition system is a proof-technical device. Unlike the original CK machine, ours is ill-suited for an implementation.

frame represents a λ-abstraction with a hole in the body. The last kind of frame has two frame list components, the first representing a context in the body of the λ, and the second representing the context between the λ and its argument. The variable in this last frame is the variable bound by the λ expression under evaluation. The initial state for a program e is $\langle e, ()\rangle$, where $()$ is an empty list of frames, and evaluation terminates when the control string is a value and the list of frames is equivalent to an answer context.

The *push-arg-ck* transition makes the operator in an application the new control string and adds a new `arg` frame to the frame list containing the argument. The *descend-lam-ck* transition goes under a λ, making the body the control string, but only if that λ has a corresponding argument in the frame list, as determined by the `balance` function, defined as follows:

$$\boxed{\texttt{balance} : \mathit{Fs} \rightarrow \mathbb{Z}}$$

$$\begin{aligned}\texttt{balance}(\mathit{Fs}_3, (\texttt{bod}\, x\; \mathit{Fs}_1\; \mathit{Fs}_2), \mathit{Fs}) &= \texttt{balance}(\mathit{Fs}_3)\\ \texttt{balance}(\mathit{Fs}) &= \texttt{\#arg-frames}(\mathit{Fs}) - \texttt{\#lam-frames}(\mathit{Fs})\\ &\qquad \mathit{Fs} \text{ contains no } \texttt{bod} \text{ frames}\end{aligned}$$

The `balance` side condition for *descend-lam-ck* dictates that evaluation goes under a λ only if there is a matching argument for it, thus complying with the analogous evaluation context. The `balance` function employs `#arg-frames` and `#lam-frames` to count the number of `arg` or `lam` frames, respectively, in a list of frames. Their definitions are elementary and therefore omitted.

The *lookup-var-ck* transition is invoked if the control string is a variable, somewhere in a λ body, and the rest of the frames have a certain shape consistent with the corresponding parts of a β_{need} redex. With this transition, the argument associated with the variable becomes the next control string and the context around the variable in the λ body and the context between the λ and argument are saved in a new `bod` frame. Finally, when an argument is an answer, indicated by a value control string and a `bod` frame in the frame list—with the equivalent of an answer context in between—the value gets substituted into the body of the λ according to the $\beta_{need\text{-}ck}$ transition. The $\beta_{need\text{-}ck}$ transition uses a substitution function on frame lists, $\mathit{Fs}\{x{:=}e\}$, which overloads the notation for regular term substitution and has the expected definition.

Figure 7 defines metafunctions for the CK transition system. The ϕ function converts a CK state to the equivalent λ_{need} term, and uses ϕ_F to convert a list of frames to an evaluation context.

Now we can show that an evaluator defined with $\overset{ck}{\longmapsto}$ is equivalent to $\texttt{eval}^{\mathrm{sr}}_{need}$. The essence of the proof is a lemma that relates the shape of CK transition sequences to the shape of λ_{need} standard reduction sequences. The rest of the equivalence proof is straightforward [9].

Lemma 6. *If* $\langle e, \mathit{Fs}\rangle \overset{ck}{\longmapsto} \langle e', \mathit{Fs}'\rangle$, *then either:*

1. $\phi(\langle e, \mathit{Fs}\rangle) = \phi(\langle e', \mathit{Fs}'\rangle)$
2. $\phi(\langle e, \mathit{Fs}\rangle) \longmapsto \phi(\langle e', \mathit{Fs}'\rangle)$

$$\boxed{\phi : S \to e}$$

$$\phi(\langle e, Fs \rangle) = \phi_F(Fs)[e]$$

$$\boxed{\phi_F : Fs \to E}$$

$$\begin{aligned}
\phi_F(()) &= [\ ] \\
\phi_F((\mathtt{lam}\, x), Fs) &= \phi_F(Fs)[\lambda x.[\ ]] \\
\phi_F((\mathtt{arg}\, e), Fs) &= \phi_F(Fs)[[\ ]\, e] \\
\phi_F((\mathtt{bod}\, x\, Fs_1\, Fs_2), Fs) &= \\
&\phi_F(Fs)[\phi_F(Fs_2)[\lambda x.\phi_F(Fs_1)[x]]\,[\ ]]
\end{aligned}$$

$$\boxed{\xi : S \to e_{\parallel}}$$

$$\xi(\langle e, Fs \rangle) = \xi_F(Fs, e)$$

$$\boxed{\xi_F : Fs \times e_{\parallel} \to e_{\parallel}}$$

$$\begin{aligned}
\xi_F((), e_{\parallel}) &= e_{\parallel} \\
\xi_F(((\mathtt{arg}\, e_{\parallel 1}), Fs), e_{\parallel}) &= \xi_F(Fs, e_{\parallel}\, e_{\parallel 1}) \\
\xi_F(((\mathtt{bod}\, x\, Fs_1\, Fs_2), Fs), e_{\parallel}) &= \\
&\xi_F((Fs_1, (\mathtt{lam}\, x), Fs_2, (\mathtt{arg}\, e_{\parallel}), Fs), x) \\
\xi_F(((\mathtt{lam}\, x), Fs_1, (\mathtt{arg}\, e_{\parallel 1}), Fs_2), e_{\parallel}) &= \\
&\xi_F((Fs_1, Fs_2), e_{\parallel}\{x := e_{\parallel}{}^{y}_{1}\}) \\
&\phi_F(Fs_1) \in A,\ y \text{ fresh}
\end{aligned}$$

Fig. 7. Functions to map CK states to λ_{need} (ϕ) and $\lambda_{\parallel}$ (ξ)

Finally, we show how the CK system corresponds to $\lambda_{\parallel}$. The ξ function defined in figure 7 constructs a $\lambda_{\parallel}$ term from a CK configuration.

Lemma 7. *If* $\langle e, Fs \rangle \overset{ck}{\longmapsto} \langle e', Fs' \rangle$, *then either:*

1. $\xi(\langle e, Fs \rangle) = \xi(\langle e', Fs' \rangle)$
2. $\xi(\langle e, Fs \rangle) \overset{\parallel}{\longmapsto} \xi(\langle e', Fs' \rangle)$

5.5 Relating All Layers

In the previous subsections, we have demonstrated the correspondence between $\lambda_{\parallel}$, the natural semantics, and the λ_{need} standard reduction sequences via lemmas 5 through 7. We conclude this section with the statement of an extensional correctness theorem, where $\mathtt{eval}_{natural}$ is an evaluator defined with the store machine transitions. The theorem follows from the composition of the equivalences of our specified rewriting systems.

Theorem 4. $eval_{need} = eval_{natural}$

6 Extensions and Variants

Data Constructors Real-world lazy languages come with data structure construction and extraction operators. Like function arguments, the arguments to a data constructor should not be evaluated until there is demand for their values [12, 14]. The standard λ calculus encoding of such operators [5] works well:

$$\mathtt{cons} = \lambda x.\lambda y.\lambda s.s\, x\, y, \quad \mathtt{car} = \lambda p.p\, \lambda x.\lambda y.x, \quad \mathtt{cdr} = \lambda p.p\, \lambda x.\lambda y.y$$

Adding true algebraic systems should also be straightforward.

Recursion Our λ_{need} calculus represents just a core λ calculus and does not include an explicit `letrec` constructor for cyclic terms. Since cyclic programming is an important idiom in lazy programming languages, others have extensively explored cyclic by-need calculi, e.g., Ariola and Blum [1], and applying their solutions to our calculus should pose no problems.

7 Conclusion

Following Plotkin's work on call-by-name and call-by-value, we present a call-by-need λ calculus that expresses computation via a single axiom in the spirit of β. Our calculus is close to implementations of lazy languages because it captures the idea of by-need computation without retaining every function call and without need for re-associating terms. We show that our calculus satisfies Plotkin's criteria, including an intensional correspondence between our calculus and a Launchbury-style natural semantics. Our future work will leverage our λ_{need} calculus to derive a new abstract machine for lazy languages.

Acknowledgments. We thank J. Ian Johnson, Casey Klein, Vincent St-Amour, Asumu Takikawa, Aaron Turon, Mitchell Wand, and the ESOP 2012 reviewers for their feedback on early drafts. This work was supported in part by NSF Infrastructure grant CNS-0855140 and AFOSR grant FA9550-09-1-0110.

References

1. Ariola, Z., Blom, S.: Cyclic Lambda Calculi. In: Ito, T., Abadi, M. (eds.) TACS 1997. LNCS, vol. 1281, pp. 77–106. Springer, Heidelberg (1997)
2. Ariola, Z.M., Felleisen, M.: The call-by-need lambda-calculus. Tech. Rep. CIS-TR-94-23, University of Oregon (1994)
3. Ariola, Z.M., Felleisen, M.: The call-by-need lambda calculus. J. Funct. Program. 7, 265–301 (1997)
4. Ariola, Z.M., Maraist, J., Odersky, M., Felleisen, M., Wadler, P.: A call-by-need lambda calculus. In: Proc. 22nd Symp. on Principles of Programming Languages, pp. 233–246 (1995)
5. Barendregt, H.P.: Lambda Calculus, Syntax and Semantics. North-Holland (1985)
6. Church, A.: The Calculi of Lambda Conversion. Princeton University Press (1941)
7. Curry, H.B., Feys, R.: Combinatory Logic, vol. I. North-Holland (1958)
8. Danvy, O., Millikin, K., Munk, J., Zerny, I.: Defunctionalized Interpreters for Call-by-Need Evaluation. In: Blume, M., Kobayashi, N., Vidal, G. (eds.) FLOPS 2010. LNCS, vol. 6009, pp. 240–256. Springer, Heidelberg (2010)
9. Felleisen, M., Findler, R.B., Flatt, M.: Semantics Engineering with PLT Redex. MIT Press (2009)
10. Felleisen, M., Friedman, D.P.: A syntactic theory of sequential state. Theor. Comput. Sci. 69(3), 243–287 (1989)
11. Friedman, D.P., Ghuloum, A., Siek, J.G., Winebarger, O.L.: Improving the lazy Krivine machine. Higher Order Symbolic Computation 20, 271–293 (2007)

12. Friedman, D.P., Wise, D.S.: Cons should not evaluate its arguments. In: Proc. 3rd Intl. Colloq. on Automata, Languages and Programming. pp. 256–284 (1976)
13. Garcia, R., Lumsdaine, A., Sabry, A.: Lazy evaluation and delimited control. In: Proc. 36th Symp. on Principles of Programming Languages, pp. 153–164 (2009)
14. Henderson, P., Morris Jr., J.H.: A lazy evaluator. In: Proc. 3rd Symp. on Principles of Programming Languages, pp. 95–103 (1976)
15. Josephs, M.B.: The semantics of lazy functional languages. Theor. Comput. Sci. 68(1) (1989)
16. Landin, P.J.: The next 700 programming languages. Comm. ACM 9, 157–166 (1966)
17. Launchbury, J.: A natural semantics for lazy evaluation. In: Proc. 20th Symp. on Principles of Programming Languages, pp. 144–154 (1993)
18. Loader, R.: Notes on simply typed lambda calculus. Tech. Rep. ECS-LFCS-98-381, Department of Computer Science, University of Edinburgh (1998)
19. Maraist, J., Odersky, M., Turner, D.N., Wadler, P.: Call-by-name call-by-value, call-by-need, and the linear lambda calculus. In: Proc. 11th Conference on Mathematical Foundations of Programminng Semantics, pp. 370–392 (1995)
20. Maraist, J., Odersky, M., Wadler, P.: The call-by-need lambda calculus (unabridged). Tech. Rep. 28/94, Universität Karlsruhe (1994)
21. Maraist, J., Odersky, M., Wadler, P.: The call-by-need lambda calculus. J. Funct. Program. 8, 275–317 (1998)
22. Morris, J.H.: Lambda Calculus Models of Programming Languages. Ph.D. thesis, MIT (1968)
23. Nakata, K., Hasegawa, M.: Small-step and big-step semantics for call-by-need. J. Funct. Program. 19(6), 699–722 (2009)
24. Peyton Jones, S.L., Salkild, J.: The spineless tagless g-machine. In: Proc. 4th Conf. on Functional Programming Lang. and Computer Architecture, pp. 184–201 (1989)
25. Plotkin, G.D.: Call-by-name, call-by-value and the lambda-calculus. Theor. Comput. Sci. 1, 125–159 (1975)
26. Purushothaman, S., Seaman, J.: An adequate operational semantics for sharing in lazy evaluation. In: Proc. 4th European Symp. on Program, pp. 435–450 (1992)
27. Sestoft, P.: Deriving a lazy abstract machine. J. Func. Program. 7(3), 231–264 (1997)
28. Wadsworth, C.P.: Semantics and Pragmatics of the Lambda Calculus. Ph.D. thesis, Oxford University (1971)

A Compositional Specification Theory for Component Behaviours

Taolue Chen[1], Chris Chilton[1], Bengt Jonsson[2], and Marta Kwiatkowska[1]

[1] Department of Computer Science, University of Oxford, UK
[2] Department of Information Technology, Uppsala University, Sweden

Abstract. We propose a compositional specification theory for reasoning about components that interact by synchronisation of input and output (I/O) actions, in which the specification of a component constrains the temporal ordering of interactions with the environment. Such a theory is motivated by the need to support composability of components, in addition to modelling environmental assumptions, and reasoning about run-time behaviour. Models can be specified operationally by means of I/O labelled transition systems augmented by an inconsistency predicate on states, or in a purely declarative manner by means of traces. We introduce a refinement preorder that supports safe-substitutivity of components. Our specification theory includes the operations of parallel composition for composing components at run-time, logical conjunction for independent development, and quotient for incremental development. We prove congruence properties of the operations and show correspondence between the operational and declarative frameworks.

Keywords: specification theory, compositionality, components, I/O automata, interface automata, logic LTS, refinement, conjunction, quotient.

1 Introduction

An important paradigm for developing complex reactive systems is component-based design, where systems are composed from components, which themselves can be realised by smaller components. Component-based design can be supported by a specification theory, which allows the mixing of specifications and implementations, admits refinement, and provides composition operators. A specification theory suitable for components should be equipped with a *refinement* preorder which is substitutive, to facilitate component reuse. As a minimum, the composition operators should include structural *parallel composition*, for inferring component interactions at run-time; *conjunction*, to facilitate independent development constrained by several specifications; and *quotienting*, which supports incremental development in the following sense: given a specification of the full system, together with components implementing part of that system, quotienting allows one to find the coarsest specification of the remaining portion of the system to be implemented. Further useful operators include: *disjunction*, which finds a common specification that a collection of components implement; and *hiding*, which supports abstraction of components.

H. Seidl (Ed.): ESOP 2012, LNCS 7211, pp. 148–168, 2012.

In this paper, we consider systems of components that interact by synchronisation of input and output actions, in which outputs are non-blocking. A specification should describe properties on the ordering of a component's interactions with its environment; it should also describe the assumptions on the environment under which these properties are guaranteed, thereby supporting assume-guarantee reasoning. A number of proposals for such specification theories have been put forward. As detailed in the survey of related work below, we find that they suffer from limitations or unnecessary complications.

The main contribution of our paper is a comprehensive, compositional specification theory for components that generalises existing frameworks by supporting all the above-mentioned operators, while retaining conceptual simplicity and strong algebraic properties of the operations. The framework permits the mixing of abstract component specifications and I/O labelled transition systems (called Logic IOLTSs), without restricting to determinism as in [1]. Our refinement is based on traces, hence admitting a simpler formulation than similar notions based on e.g. alternating simulation [2] or modalities [3,4], so is more amenable to language-theoretic constructs. From this formulation, we demonstrate that the induced mutual refinement is a congruence for the operators.

In contrast to existing I/O automata [5] and interface automata [2], we are able to express: (1) *assumptions* on the input provided by the environment; (2) *underspecification*, meaning that it is uncertain what the allowable interactions are; and (3) various (run-time) *errors*, including communication mismatch, bad behaviour, or divergence (an infinite amount of internal computation without any visible interaction). We show that all these features can be expressed using only the single concept of *inconsistency*, which we have adapted from the Logic LTSs of Lüttgen and Vogler [6,7], where input and output actions are not distinguished. Inconsistency is a property of states or interaction traces, which represents the possibility of some abnormal condition. Once an inconsistency has occurred, there is no escaping from it. Following the lead of CSP [8], we thus allow for chaotic behaviour to ensue once an inconsistency has arisen.

Related Work. Our specification theory, in particular Logic IOLTSs, is inspired by the Logic LTS framework due to Lüttgen and Vogler [6], a compositional theory that admits as specifications LTSs without I/O distinctions. Their inconsistency predicate is induced from inequality of ready-sets, rather than communication mismatches as in our case. Refinement is based on ready-simulation; alphabetised parallel and conjunction are considered, but not quotient.

The operational component model in our framework has been greatly influenced by I/O automata [5] and interface automata [2]: both are based on I/O LTSs, with the proviso that I/O automata must be input-enabled, meaning that each state of the automaton is willing to accept any input. We differ from I/O automata by not imposing input-enabledness and from interface automata by working with an explicit representation of inconsistencies. Another difference is refinement, which for interface automata is defined in terms of alternating simulation, rather than traces; the original definition in [2] is simplified in [9], but works only for input-deterministic interface automata. It should be noted that, unlike [2,9], we use an associative variant of parallel composition, which combines an input and output into an output (as in [10]). Furthermore, we provide a definition of conjunction corresponding to shared refinement of interface automata, which substantially generalises that of [11] for synchronous components. Moreover, our quotienting operator on Logic IOLTSs generalises that in [12] defined only for deterministic components.

There are a number of process-algebraic frameworks that deal with asynchronous I/O interaction. We mention a characterisation of I/O automata by De Nicola and Segala [13], which is actually a generalisation (and also applicable to interface automata), since the inconsistent process Ω allows to distinguish between good and bad inputs. Similarly to our approach, refinement in [13] is given by trace containment, but does not extend to inconsistent trace containment. This is because we allow a Logic IOLTS to become inconsistent after emitting an output, whereas a process can only become inconsistent through receiving a bad input. Finally, we remark that [13] supports a number of operators of a specification theory, but does not deal with conjunction or quotient.

Our work is also related to the ioco theory in model based testing [14]. The ioco relation is similar to our refinement, but lacks compositionality of operators, so is not well-suited to a specification theory for components.

There have been several CSP-based frameworks that deal with asynchronous communication; of these, the receptive process theory (RPT) [15] utilises a model of concurrency similar to ours in that outputs are non-blocking. RPT also considers quotient (referred to as factorisation), but for the restricted class of delay-insensitive networks [16] that differ from our setting.

A further class of component-based modelling formalisms is based on may/must modalities. A specification theory for components has been devised in [17] based on modalities [3,4], but the definition of quotient is more restrictive than ours. Larsen *et al.* have made an effort in relating modal transition systems with interface automata [1]. The approach of modal I/O automata is based on a game-like definition of refinement, which we claim to be more complex than ours, see, e.g., the discussion of parallel composition in [4]. The framework in [4] can support reasoning about liveness properties which our framework does not (although they both support reasoning of safety properties). However, our framework can be easily extended by introducing quiescent states, and additionally considering containment of quiescent traces to reason about liveness.

Outline. The paper begins by introducing declarative specifications in Section 2, before considering operational specifications in Section 3. We focus on three composition operators: parallel, conjunction and quotient; omitting disjunction and hiding for reasons of space. The paper ends with a statement of full-abstraction results in Section 4. Proofs can be found in the accompanying technical report [18].

2 A Declarative Theory of Components

In this section, we model components abstractly by means of declarative specifications. We introduce a substitutive refinement preorder together with three compositional operators on declarative specifications.

A declarative specification comes equipped with an interface, together with a set of behaviours over the interface. The interface is represented by a set of input actions and a set of output actions, which are necessarily disjoint, while the behaviour is characterised by traces.

Definition 1 (Declarative specification). *A declarative specification $\mathcal{P}$ is a tuple $\langle \mathcal{A}^I_\mathcal{P}, \mathcal{A}^O_\mathcal{P}, T_\mathcal{P}, F_\mathcal{P} \rangle$ in which $\mathcal{A}^I_\mathcal{P}$ and $\mathcal{A}^O_\mathcal{P}$ are disjoint sets referred to as inputs and outputs respectively (the union of which is denoted by $\mathcal{A}_\mathcal{P}$), $T_\mathcal{P} \subseteq \mathcal{A}^*_\mathcal{P}$ is a non-empty set of permissible traces, and $F_\mathcal{P} \subseteq \mathcal{A}^*_\mathcal{P}$ is a set of inconsistent traces. The trace sets must satisfy the constraints:*

1. *$F_\mathcal{P} \subseteq T_\mathcal{P}$*
2. *If $t \in T_\mathcal{P}$ and $i \in \mathcal{A}^I_\mathcal{P}$, then $ti \in T_\mathcal{P}$*
3. *$T_\mathcal{P}$ is prefix closed*
4. *If $t \in F_\mathcal{P}$ and $t' \in \mathcal{A}^*_\mathcal{P}$, then $tt' \in F_\mathcal{P}$.*

Outputs are under the control of the component, whereas inputs are issued by the environment. This means that, after any successful interaction between the component and the environment, the environment can issue any input i, even if it will be refused by the component. Naturally, if i is refused by the component after the trace t, we deem ti to be an inconsistent trace, since a communication mismatch has occurred. Given this treatment of inputs, we say that our theory is *not* input-enabled, even though $T_\mathcal{P}$ is closed under input-extensions.

Example 1. A drinks machine dispenses either a tea or a coffee after a coin has been inserted. The drinks machine has sufficient water to produce only 2 drinks, after which a further coin insertion renders the machine inoperable. This behaviour can be encoded by the declarative specification $DM = \langle \{\pounds\}, \{t, c\}, T, F_1 \cup F_2 \rangle$, where:

- $T = \{\epsilon, \pounds, \pounds(c+t), \pounds(c+t)\pounds, \pounds(c+t)\pounds(c+t)\} \cup F_1 \cup F_2$
- $F_1 = \pounds(c+t)\pounds(c+t)\pounds(\pounds+c+t)^*$ insertion of third coin after two dispensations
- $F_2 = (\epsilon+\pounds(c+t))\pounds\pounds(\pounds+c+t)^*$ insertion of second coin before dispensation.

From hereon let $\mathcal{P}$, $\mathcal{Q}$ and $\mathcal{R}$ be declarative specifications with signatures $\langle \mathcal{A}^I_\mathcal{P}, \mathcal{A}^O_\mathcal{P}, T_\mathcal{P}, F_\mathcal{P} \rangle$, $\langle \mathcal{A}^I_\mathcal{Q}, \mathcal{A}^O_\mathcal{Q}, T_\mathcal{Q}, F_\mathcal{Q} \rangle$ and $\langle \mathcal{A}^I_\mathcal{R}, \mathcal{A}^O_\mathcal{R}, T_\mathcal{R}, F_\mathcal{R} \rangle$ respectively.

2.1 Refinement

As refinement corresponds to safe substitutivity, for $\mathcal{Q}$ to be used in place of $\mathcal{P}$ we require that $\mathcal{Q}$ must exist safely in *any* environment that $\mathcal{P}$ can exist in safely.

Whether an environment is safe for a specification depends on the sequences of message exchanges afforded by the component. If an environment can prevent a component from performing an inconsistent trace, then the environment is said to be safe.

We do not insist that a component $\mathcal{Q}$ must have the same interface as the component $\mathcal{P}$ to be refined. Instead $\mathcal{Q}$ must be accepting of at least all of $\mathcal{P}$'s inputs, while restricting to a subset of $\mathcal{P}$'s outputs. This can be formalised by the covariant relationship $\mathcal{A}^I_{\mathcal{P}} \subseteq \mathcal{A}^I_{\mathcal{Q}}$ on inputs and the contravariant constraint $\mathcal{A}^O_{\mathcal{Q}} \subseteq \mathcal{A}^O_{\mathcal{P}}$ on outputs.

In order to establish that refinement holds, we perform a weak form of alphabet equalisation on the inputs of the component to be refined. We refer to this operation as lifting. Informally, lifting extends the trace sets of $\mathcal{P}$ by explicitly refusing any input in $\mathcal{A}^I_{\mathcal{Q}} \setminus \mathcal{A}^I_{\mathcal{P}}$, after which it allows for arbitrary behaviour.

Definition 2 (Lifting). *Let $\mathcal{P}$ be a declarative specification, and let $\mathcal{A}^I_{\mathcal{Q}}$ be a set of input actions. The lifting of trace sets $T_{\mathcal{P}}$ and $F_{\mathcal{P}}$ to $\mathcal{A}^I_{\mathcal{Q}}$, written as $T_{\mathcal{P}} \uparrow \mathcal{A}^I_{\mathcal{Q}}$ and $F_{\mathcal{P}} \uparrow \mathcal{A}^I_{\mathcal{Q}}$ respectively, is defined as:*

- $T_{\mathcal{P}} \uparrow \mathcal{A}^I_{\mathcal{Q}} = T_{\mathcal{P}} \cup \{tit' : t \in T_{\mathcal{P}},\ i \in \mathcal{A}^I_{\mathcal{Q}} \setminus \mathcal{A}^I_{\mathcal{P}} \text{ and } t' \in (\mathcal{A}^I_{\mathcal{Q}} \cup \mathcal{A}_{\mathcal{P}})^*\}$
- $F_{\mathcal{P}} \uparrow \mathcal{A}^I_{\mathcal{Q}} = F_{\mathcal{P}} \cup \{tit' : t \in T_{\mathcal{P}},\ i \in \mathcal{A}^I_{\mathcal{Q}} \setminus \mathcal{A}^I_{\mathcal{P}} \text{ and } t' \in (\mathcal{A}^I_{\mathcal{Q}} \cup \mathcal{A}_{\mathcal{P}})^*\}$.

Recall that an environment is safe for a component if the environment can prevent the component from performing an inconsistent trace. As outputs are under the control of the component itself, a safe environment must refuse to issue an input on any trace from which there is a sequence of output actions after the input that allows the trace to become inconsistent.

Under such an arrangement, for each declarative specification $\mathcal{P}$ we can define the safe declarative specification $\mathcal{E}(\mathcal{P})$ containing all of $\mathcal{P}$'s permissible and inconsistent traces, but also satisfying the additional property: if $t \in T_{\mathcal{P}}$ and there exists $t' \in (\mathcal{A}^O_{\mathcal{P}})^*$ such that $tt' \in F_{\mathcal{P}}$, then $t \in F_{\mathcal{E}(\mathcal{P})}$. This has the effect of forcing all inconsistent traces to become inconsistent on the environment's issue of a bad input. If the environment respects this safe specification, by not issuing any input that results in an inconsistent trace, then the component can never encounter an inconsistent trace. Note that if $\epsilon \in F_{\mathcal{E}(\mathcal{P})}$ then there is no environment that can prevent $\mathcal{P}$ from performing an inconsistent trace. However, for uniformity we still refer to $\mathcal{E}(\mathcal{P})$ as the safe specification of $\mathcal{P}$.

Definition 3 (Safe specification). *Let $\mathcal{P}$ be a declarative specification. The most general safe specification for $\mathcal{P}$ is a declarative specification $\mathcal{E}(\mathcal{P}) = \langle \mathcal{A}^I_{\mathcal{P}}, \mathcal{A}^O_{\mathcal{P}}, T_{\mathcal{E}(\mathcal{P})}, F_{\mathcal{E}(\mathcal{P})} \rangle$, where $T_{\mathcal{E}(\mathcal{P})} = T_{\mathcal{P}} \cup F_{\mathcal{E}(\mathcal{P})}$ and $F_{\mathcal{E}(\mathcal{P})} = \{tt' \in \mathcal{A}^*_{\mathcal{P}} : t \in T_{\mathcal{P}} \text{ and } \exists t'' \in (\mathcal{A}^O_{\mathcal{P}})^* \cdot tt'' \in F_{\mathcal{P}}\}$.*

We can now define our substitutive refinement preorder. From the safe specification associated with an arbitrary declarative specification, it is easy to see whether a declarative specification can be substituted safely in place of another. Note that $F_{\mathcal{Q}} \subseteq F_{\mathcal{P}} \uparrow \mathcal{A}^I_{\mathcal{Q}}$ would be too strong to use for the last clause, as we are only interested in trace containment up to the point where an environment can issue a bad input.

Definition 4 (Refinement). *For declarative specifications $\mathcal{P}$ and $\mathcal{Q}$, $\mathcal{Q}$ is said to be a refinement of $\mathcal{P}$, written $\mathcal{Q} \sqsubseteq_{dec} \mathcal{P}$, iff:*

1. $\mathcal{A}^I_\mathcal{P} \subseteq \mathcal{A}^I_\mathcal{Q}$
2. $\mathcal{A}^O_\mathcal{Q} \subseteq \mathcal{A}^O_\mathcal{P}$
3. $T_{\mathcal{E}(\mathcal{Q})} \subseteq T_{\mathcal{E}(\mathcal{P})} \uparrow \mathcal{A}^I_\mathcal{Q}$
4. $F_{\mathcal{E}(\mathcal{Q})} \subseteq F_{\mathcal{E}(\mathcal{P})} \uparrow \mathcal{A}^I_\mathcal{Q}$.

As refinement is based on an extension of language inclusion, its complexity is in P, assuming regularity of the trace sets. Note that lifting maintains regularity.

Equivalence of declarative specifications in our framework is defined in terms of mutual refinement.

Definition 5 (Equivalence). *Let $\mathcal{P}$ and $\mathcal{Q}$ be declarative specifications. Then $\mathcal{P}$ and $\mathcal{Q}$ are said to be equivalent, written $\mathcal{P} \equiv_{dec} \mathcal{Q}$, iff $\mathcal{P} \sqsubseteq_{dec} \mathcal{Q}$ and $\mathcal{Q} \sqsubseteq_{dec} \mathcal{P}$.*

Lemma 1 (Preorder). *Refinement is both reflexive and transitive.*

2.2 Parallel Composition

The parallel composition operator on declarative specifications yields a declarative specification representing the combined effect of its operands running asynchronously. We do not consider synchronous parallel composition, as this does not make sense when dealing with non-blocking output actions. To preserve the effect that a single output from a component can be received by multiple components in the environment, we must define the parallel composition to repeatedly broadcast an output: this means that an input $a?$ and output $a!$ combine to form an output $a!$ (as in certain variants of I/O automata), rather than a hidden action τ as is the case in Milner's CCS.

Not all declarative specifications can be composed with one another; we restrict to those that are said to be *composable*. $\mathcal{P}$ and $\mathcal{Q}$ are composable for parallel composition only if $\mathcal{A}^O_\mathcal{P} \cap \mathcal{A}^O_\mathcal{Q} = \emptyset$. This restriction is meaningful if we consider inputs on an interface as buttons and outputs as lights. Given two distinct components, it is not possible for them to share a common light, whereas it is possible to push their buttons at the same time. In practice, issues of composability can be avoided by employing renaming, if this is considered to be appropriate.

Definition 6 (Parallel composition). *Let $\mathcal{P}$ and $\mathcal{Q}$ be declarative specifications such that $\mathcal{A}^O_\mathcal{P}$ and $\mathcal{A}^O_\mathcal{Q}$ are disjoint. Then $\mathcal{P} \parallel \mathcal{Q}$ is the declarative specification $\langle \mathcal{A}^I_{\mathcal{P}||\mathcal{Q}}, \mathcal{A}^O_{\mathcal{P}||\mathcal{Q}}, T_{\mathcal{P}||\mathcal{Q}}, F_{\mathcal{P}||\mathcal{Q}} \rangle$, where:*

- $\mathcal{A}^I_{\mathcal{P}||\mathcal{Q}} = (\mathcal{A}^I_\mathcal{P} \cup \mathcal{A}^I_\mathcal{Q}) \setminus (\mathcal{A}^O_\mathcal{P} \cup \mathcal{A}^O_\mathcal{Q})$
- $\mathcal{A}^O_{\mathcal{P}||\mathcal{Q}} = \mathcal{A}^O_\mathcal{P} \cup \mathcal{A}^O_\mathcal{Q}$
- $T_{\mathcal{P}||\mathcal{Q}} = \{t \in \mathcal{A}^*_{\mathcal{P}||\mathcal{Q}} : t \upharpoonright \mathcal{A}_\mathcal{P} \in T_\mathcal{P} \text{ and } t \upharpoonright \mathcal{A}_\mathcal{Q} \in T_\mathcal{Q}\} \cup F_{\mathcal{P}||\mathcal{Q}}$
- $F_{\mathcal{P}||\mathcal{Q}} = \{tt' \in \mathcal{A}^*_{\mathcal{P}||\mathcal{Q}} : t \upharpoonright \mathcal{A}_\mathcal{P} \in F_\mathcal{P} \text{ and } t \upharpoonright \mathcal{A}_\mathcal{Q} \in T_\mathcal{Q}, \text{ or } t \upharpoonright \mathcal{A}_\mathcal{P} \in T_\mathcal{P} \text{ and } t \upharpoonright \mathcal{A}_\mathcal{Q} \in F_\mathcal{Q}\}$.

Informally, a trace is permissible in $\mathcal{P} \parallel \mathcal{Q}$ if its projection onto $\mathcal{A}_{\mathcal{P}}$ is a trace of $\mathcal{P}$ and its projection onto $\mathcal{A}_{\mathcal{Q}}$ is a trace of $\mathcal{Q}$. A trace is inconsistent if it has a prefix whose projection onto the alphabet of one of the components is inconsistent and the projection onto the alphabet of the other component is a permissible trace of that component.

We demonstrate the following result, a corollary of which is that mutual refinement is a congruence for parallel, subject to composability.

Theorem 1 (Compositionality of parallel). *Let $\mathcal{P}$, $\mathcal{Q}$ and $\mathcal{R}$ be declarative specifications such that $\mathcal{P}$ and $\mathcal{R}$ are composable for parallel composition, and $\mathcal{A}^I_{\mathcal{Q}} \cap \mathcal{A}^O_{\mathcal{R}} \subseteq \mathcal{A}^I_{\mathcal{P}} \cap \mathcal{A}^O_{\mathcal{R}}$. If $\mathcal{Q} \sqsubseteq_{dec} \mathcal{P}$, then $\mathcal{Q} \parallel \mathcal{R} \sqsubseteq_{dec} \mathcal{P} \parallel \mathcal{R}$.*

2.3 Conjunction

The conjunction operator on declarative specifications can be thought of as finding a common implementation for a number of properties, each of which are represented by declarative specifications. Naturally, any implementation of these properties should be a refinement of each of the properties to be implemented. The conjunction (or shared refinement) of two declarative specifications $\mathcal{P}$ and $\mathcal{Q}$ is the *coarsest* declarative specification that refines both $\mathcal{P}$ and $\mathcal{Q}$. Thus conjunction is the meet operator on the refinement preorder.

As for parallel composition, conjunction can only be performed on composable components. $\mathcal{P}$ and $\mathcal{Q}$ are composable for conjunction only if the sets $\mathcal{A}^I_{\mathcal{P}} \cup \mathcal{A}^I_{\mathcal{Q}}$ and $\mathcal{A}^O_{\mathcal{P}} \cup \mathcal{A}^O_{\mathcal{Q}}$ are disjoint.

Definition 7 (Conjunction). *Let $\mathcal{P}$ and $\mathcal{Q}$ be declarative specifications such that $\mathcal{A}^I_{\mathcal{P}} \cup \mathcal{A}^I_{\mathcal{Q}}$ and $\mathcal{A}^O_{\mathcal{P}} \cup \mathcal{A}^O_{\mathcal{Q}}$ are disjoint. Then $\mathcal{P} \wedge \mathcal{Q}$ is the declarative specification $\langle \mathcal{A}^I_{\mathcal{P}\wedge\mathcal{Q}}, \mathcal{A}^O_{\mathcal{P}\wedge\mathcal{Q}}, T_{\mathcal{P}\wedge\mathcal{Q}}, F_{\mathcal{P}\wedge\mathcal{Q}} \rangle$, where:*

- $\mathcal{A}^I_{\mathcal{P}\wedge\mathcal{Q}} = \mathcal{A}^I_{\mathcal{P}} \cup \mathcal{A}^I_{\mathcal{Q}}$
- $\mathcal{A}^O_{\mathcal{P}\wedge\mathcal{Q}} = \mathcal{A}^O_{\mathcal{P}} \cap \mathcal{A}^O_{\mathcal{Q}}$
- $T_{\mathcal{P}\wedge\mathcal{Q}} = T_{\mathcal{P}} \uparrow \mathcal{A}^I_{\mathcal{Q}} \cap T_{\mathcal{Q}} \uparrow \mathcal{A}^I_{\mathcal{P}}$
- $F_{\mathcal{P}\wedge\mathcal{Q}} = F_{\mathcal{P}} \uparrow \mathcal{A}^I_{\mathcal{Q}} \cap F_{\mathcal{Q}} \uparrow \mathcal{A}^I_{\mathcal{P}}$.

Conjunction has strong connections with the logical 'and' operator in Boolean algebra, as shown below. Mutual refinement is a congruence for conjunction, subject to composability.

Theorem 2 (Properties of conjunction).

- *Conjunction is the greatest lower bound operator for $\sqsubseteq_{dec}$*
- *$\mathcal{R} \sqsubseteq_{dec} \mathcal{P}$ and $\mathcal{R} \sqsubseteq_{dec} \mathcal{Q}$ iff $\mathcal{R} \sqsubseteq_{dec} \mathcal{P} \wedge \mathcal{Q}$*
- *$\mathcal{P} \wedge \mathcal{Q} \equiv_{dec} \mathcal{Q}$ iff $\mathcal{Q} \sqsubseteq_{dec} \mathcal{P}$.*

Theorem 3 (Compositionality of conjunction). *Let $\mathcal{P}$, $\mathcal{Q}$ and $\mathcal{R}$ be declarative specifications such that $\mathcal{P}$ is composable with $\mathcal{R}$ for conjunction. If $\mathcal{Q} \sqsubseteq_{dec} \mathcal{P}$, then $\mathcal{Q} \wedge \mathcal{R} \sqsubseteq_{dec} \mathcal{P} \wedge \mathcal{R}$.*

2.4 Quotient

The final operation that we consider on the specification theory is that of quotienting, which has strong connections to synthesis. Given a specification for a system $\mathcal{R}$, together with a component $\mathcal{P}$ implementing part of $\mathcal{R}$, the quotient yields the *coarsest* specification for the remaining part of $\mathcal{R}$ to be implemented. Thus, the parallel composition of the quotient with $\mathcal{P}$ should be a refinement of the system-wide specification $\mathcal{R}$. Therefore, quotient can be thought of as the adjoint of parallel composition.

As $\mathcal{P}$ is a sub-component of $\mathcal{R}$, we make the reasonable assumption that $\mathcal{A}_\mathcal{P} \subseteq \mathcal{A}_\mathcal{R}$. Moreover, a necessary condition for the existence of the quotient is that $\mathcal{A}^O_\mathcal{P} \subseteq \mathcal{A}^O_\mathcal{R}$, otherwise refinement will fail on the alphabet containment checks.

Definition 8 (Quotient). *Let $\mathcal{P}$ and $\mathcal{R}$ be declarative specifications such that $\mathcal{A}^O_\mathcal{P} \subseteq \mathcal{A}^O_\mathcal{R}$ and $\mathcal{A}_\mathcal{P} \subseteq \mathcal{A}_\mathcal{R}$. The quotient of $\mathcal{P}$ from $\mathcal{R}$ is the specification $\mathcal{R}/\mathcal{P}$ with signature $\langle \mathcal{A}^I_{\mathcal{R}/\mathcal{P}}, \mathcal{A}^O_{\mathcal{R}/\mathcal{P}}, T_{\mathcal{R}/\mathcal{P}}, F_{\mathcal{R}/\mathcal{P}} \rangle$, where:*

- $\mathcal{A}^I_{\mathcal{R}/\mathcal{P}} = \mathcal{A}^O_\mathcal{P} \cup \mathcal{A}^I_\mathcal{R}$
- $\mathcal{A}^O_{\mathcal{R}/\mathcal{P}} = \mathcal{A}^O_\mathcal{R} \setminus \mathcal{A}^O_\mathcal{P}$
- $T_{\mathcal{R}/\mathcal{P}} = \{t \in \mathcal{A}^*_\mathcal{R} : \forall t' \text{ a prefix of } t \cdot L(t') \text{ and } \forall t'' \in {\mathcal{A}^I_{\mathcal{R}/\mathcal{P}}}^* \cdot L(tt'')\}$
- $F_{\mathcal{R}/\mathcal{P}} = \{t \in \mathcal{A}^*_\mathcal{R} : (t \restriction \mathcal{A}_\mathcal{P} \in T_\mathcal{P} \implies t \in F_{\mathcal{E}(\mathcal{R})}) \text{ and } \forall t' \text{ a prefix of } t \cdot L(t')\}$
- $L(t) = (t \restriction \mathcal{A}_\mathcal{P} \in F_\mathcal{P} \implies t \in F_{\mathcal{E}(\mathcal{R})}) \text{ and } (t \restriction \mathcal{A}_\mathcal{P} \in T_\mathcal{P} \implies t \in T_\mathcal{R})$.

The alphabet of the quotient contains all of the actions from $\mathcal{A}_\mathcal{R}$ and $\mathcal{A}_\mathcal{P}$ so that $\mathcal{R}/\mathcal{P}$ can fully control $\mathcal{P}$ and emulate the behaviour of $\mathcal{R}$. Yet still, simple examples reveal that there may not exist a component $\mathcal{Q}$ over an interface consisting of inputs $\mathcal{A}^I_{\mathcal{R}/\mathcal{P}}$ and outputs $\mathcal{A}^O_{\mathcal{R}/\mathcal{P}}$ such that $\mathcal{P} \,||\, \mathcal{Q} \sqsubseteq_{dec} \mathcal{R}$. Unfortunately, the existence of the quotient cannot be ascertained by a syntactic check on the alphabets of $\mathcal{P}$ and $\mathcal{R}$.

In Definition 8 we referred to $\mathcal{R}/\mathcal{P}$ as a specification, but not a declarative specification. As the following theorem shows, if $T_{\mathcal{R}/\mathcal{P}}$ is non-empty (a condition of being a declarative specification), then the quotient exists.

Theorem 4 (Existence of quotient). *Let $\mathcal{P}$ and $\mathcal{R}$ be declarative specifications such that $\mathcal{A}^O_\mathcal{P} \subseteq \mathcal{A}^O_\mathcal{R}$ and $\mathcal{A}_\mathcal{P} \subseteq \mathcal{A}_\mathcal{R}$. Then there exists a declarative specification $\mathcal{Q}$ with input actions $\mathcal{A}^I_{\mathcal{R}/\mathcal{P}}$ and output actions $\mathcal{A}^O_{\mathcal{R}/\mathcal{P}}$ such that $\mathcal{P} \,||\, \mathcal{Q} \sqsubseteq_{dec} \mathcal{R}$ iff $T_{\mathcal{R}/\mathcal{P}} \neq \emptyset$.*

The next two theorems show that $\mathcal{R}/\mathcal{P}$ satisfies the required properties of quotient when $T_{\mathcal{R}/\mathcal{P}}$ is non-empty, and that quotient is well-behaved with respect to refinement.

Theorem 5 (Properties of quotient). *Let $\mathcal{P}$ and $\mathcal{R}$ be declarative specifications such that $\mathcal{A}^O_\mathcal{P} \subseteq \mathcal{A}^O_\mathcal{R}$ and $\mathcal{A}_\mathcal{P} \subseteq \mathcal{A}_\mathcal{R}$. If $T_{\mathcal{R}/\mathcal{P}} \neq \emptyset$, then $\mathcal{P} \,||\, (\mathcal{R}/\mathcal{P}) \sqsubseteq_{dec} \mathcal{R}$ and for any declarative specification $\mathcal{Q}$ over inputs $\mathcal{A}^I_{\mathcal{R}/\mathcal{P}}$ and outputs $\mathcal{A}^O_{\mathcal{R}/\mathcal{P}}$ such that $\mathcal{P} \,||\, \mathcal{Q} \sqsubseteq_{dec} \mathcal{R}$ it holds that $\mathcal{Q} \sqsubseteq_{dec} \mathcal{R}/\mathcal{P}$.*

Theorem 6 (Compositionality of quotient). *Let $\mathcal{P}$, $\mathcal{Q}$ and $\mathcal{R}$ be declarative specifications such that $\mathcal{Q} \sqsubseteq_{dec} \mathcal{P}$.*

- *If $\mathcal{Q}/\mathcal{R}$ and $\mathcal{P}/\mathcal{R}$ are defined, then $\mathcal{Q}/\mathcal{R} \sqsubseteq_{dec} \mathcal{P}/\mathcal{R}$.*
- *If $\mathcal{R}/\mathcal{Q}$ and $\mathcal{R}/\mathcal{P}$ are defined, and $(\mathcal{A}^I_{\mathcal{Q}} \cap \mathcal{A}^O_{\mathcal{R}}) \setminus \mathcal{A}_{\mathcal{P}} = \emptyset$, then $\mathcal{R}/\mathcal{Q} \sqsupseteq_{dec} \mathcal{R}/\mathcal{P}$.*

3 An Operational Theory of Components

In this section we take an operational view of components, by specifying their allowable interactions in terms of Logic IOLTSs, an I/O version of labelled transition systems augmented by an inconsistency predicate on states. We remain faithful to the trace-based substitutive preorder, and cast refinement at the operational level in terms of declarative refinement. For any operational model, we can derive an equivalent declarative specification, meaning that the observable safe interactions between the models and an arbitrary environment are indistinguishable.

To support a compositional theory of components, we define the operations of parallel composition, conjunction and quotient directly on our operational models. We further show that compositionality results for the operators on the declarative framework carry over to the operational framework as well.

An explicit definition of implementation is not provided for our models, although there are a number of candidates. One such suggestion for the characterisation of implementations would be the set of specifications in which no inconsistent states are reachable. We leave this for the user to decide.

We can now define the operational models formally. For a set $\mathcal{A}$, write $\mathcal{A}^\tau$ as shorthand for $\mathcal{A} \cup \{\tau\}$, where it is assumed that $\tau \notin \mathcal{A}$.

Definition 9 (IOLTS). *An* I/O labelled transition system (IOLTS) P *is a tuple* $\langle S_{\mathsf{P}}, \mathcal{A}^I_{\mathsf{P}}, \mathcal{A}^O_{\mathsf{P}}, \longrightarrow_{\mathsf{P}} \rangle$, *where* S_{P} *is a (possibly infinite) collection of processes (states),* $\mathcal{A}^I_{\mathsf{P}}$ *and* $\mathcal{A}^O_{\mathsf{P}}$ *are disjoint sets referred to as the inputs and outputs (the union of which we denote by* $\mathcal{A}_{\mathsf{P}}$*), and* $\longrightarrow_{\mathsf{P}} \subseteq S_{\mathsf{P}} \times \mathcal{A}^\tau_{\mathsf{P}} \times S_{\mathsf{P}}$ *is the transition relation.*

Note that since we do not insist on our components being fully input-enabled (unlike I/O automata [5]), meaning that at any stage a component can refuse to accept an input issued by the environment or another component, we must extend IOLTSs to reason about potential communication mismatches that occur during interactions. We accomplish this by augmenting IOLTSs with an inconsistency predicate for tracking mismatches. The resulting model, called a Logic IOLTS, takes its inspiration from the Logic LTSs of Lüttgen and Vogler [6,7], although we have a different interpretation of inconsistency.

Definition 10 (Logic IOLTS). *A* Logic IOLTS P *is a tuple* $\langle S_{\mathsf{P}}, \mathcal{A}^I_{\mathsf{P}}, \mathcal{A}^O_{\mathsf{P}}, \longrightarrow_{\mathsf{P}}, F_{\mathsf{P}} \rangle$ *in which* $\langle S_{\mathsf{P}}, \mathcal{A}^I_{\mathsf{P}}, \mathcal{A}^O_{\mathsf{P}}, \longrightarrow_{\mathsf{P}} \rangle$ *is an IOLTS, and* $F_{\mathsf{P}} \subseteq S_{\mathsf{P}}$ *is an inconsistency predicate on states satisfying the property: if* $p \in S_{\mathsf{P}}$ *can diverge (meaning there is an infinite sequence of* τ*-transitions emanating from* p*), then* $p \in F_{\mathsf{P}}$.

The inconsistency predicate annotates states that correspond to run-time errors such as communication mismatches, underspecification, or divergent behaviour. Regardless of why a state is inconsistent, we assume that on encountering an inconsistency, unspecified behaviour can ensue. Consequently, inconsistent states are resemblant of the process CHAOS from CSP [8].

Figure 1 shows a number of Logic IOLTSs represented pictorially. We adopt the convention of enclosing the transition system within a box corresponding to the interface of the component. Labelled arrows pointing at the interface correspond to inputs, whereas arrows emanating from the interface correspond to outputs. As a matter of clarity, we only represent the states that are reachable by a sequence of transitions from the process we are interested in. States annotated with an F are deemed to be inconsistent.

We introduce nomenclature for handling stability and hidden τ-transitions. A relation $\stackrel{\epsilon}{\Longrightarrow}_{\mathsf{P}} \subseteq S_{\mathsf{P}} \times S_{\mathsf{P}}$ is defined by $p \stackrel{\epsilon}{\Longrightarrow}_{\mathsf{P}} p'$ iff $p(\stackrel{\tau}{\longrightarrow}_{\mathsf{P}})^* p'$. Generalising $\stackrel{\epsilon}{\Longrightarrow}_{\mathsf{P}}$ for visible actions $a \in \mathcal{A}$, we obtain $p \stackrel{a}{\Longrightarrow}_{\mathsf{P}} p'$ iff there exist p_a and p'_a such that $p \stackrel{\epsilon}{\Longrightarrow}_{\mathsf{P}} p_a \stackrel{a}{\longrightarrow}_{\mathsf{P}} p'_a \stackrel{\epsilon}{\Longrightarrow}_{\mathsf{P}} p'$, and $p \stackrel{\dashv a}{\Longrightarrow}_{\mathsf{P}} p'$ iff there exists p_a such that $p \stackrel{a}{\longrightarrow}_{\mathsf{P}} p_a \stackrel{\epsilon}{\Longrightarrow}_{\mathsf{P}} p'$. The extension to words $w = a_1 \ldots a_n$ is defined in the natural way by $p \stackrel{w}{\Longrightarrow}_{\mathsf{P}} p'$ iff $p \stackrel{a_1}{\Longrightarrow}_{\mathsf{P}} \ldots \stackrel{a_n}{\Longrightarrow}_{\mathsf{P}} p'$.

Furthermore, for a compositional operator $\oplus$, and sets A and B, we write $A \oplus B$ for the set $\{a \oplus b : a \in A \text{ and } b \in B\}$. This allows us to use a process-algebraic notation for states.

From hereon, let $\mathsf{P} = \langle S_{\mathsf{P}}, \mathcal{A}^I_{\mathsf{P}}, \mathcal{A}^O_{\mathsf{P}}, \longrightarrow_{\mathsf{P}}, F_{\mathsf{P}} \rangle$, $\mathsf{Q} = \langle S_{\mathsf{Q}}, \mathcal{A}^I_{\mathsf{Q}}, \mathcal{A}^O_{\mathsf{Q}}, \longrightarrow_{\mathsf{Q}}, F_{\mathsf{Q}} \rangle$ and $\mathsf{R} = \langle S_{\mathsf{R}}, \mathcal{A}^I_{\mathsf{R}}, \mathcal{A}^O_{\mathsf{R}}, \longrightarrow_{\mathsf{R}}, F_{\mathsf{R}} \rangle$ be three Logic IOLTSs, and let p_{P}, q_{Q} and r_{R} be processes in the Logic IOLTSs P, Q and R respectively.

3.1 Refinement

In keeping with the declarative framework, we wish refinement to correspond to safe-substitutivity. Hence, we cast refinement at the operational level in terms of refinement at the declarative level. To do this, we define a mapping $[\![\cdot]\!]^*$ from operational models to declarative models (Definition 13) that preserves the environments that the models can interact harmoniously with.

An essential feature of operational refinement is that the mapping from operational to declarative models preserves the safe traces of the component. For a declarative specification $\mathcal{P}$, a trace t is said to be immediately-safe iff t is permissible, but not inconsistent (i.e., t lies within $T_{\mathcal{P}} \setminus F_{\mathcal{P}}$). If t is contained within $T_{\mathcal{P}} \setminus F_{\mathcal{E}(\mathcal{P})}$, we say that t is safe. The calculation of the safe traces for a Logic IOLTS is slightly more involved, because it is necessary to deal with non-determinism and τ-transitions.

Definition 11 (Immediately-safe states). *The set of immediately-safe states that a process p_{P} can be in after following the trace t is given by $h_{p_{\mathsf{P}}}(t)$, where $h_{p_{\mathsf{P}}} : \mathcal{A}^*_{\mathsf{P}} \longrightarrow 2^{S_{\mathsf{P}}}$ is defined as:*

– $$h_{p_{\mathsf{P}}}(\epsilon) = \begin{cases} \emptyset & \textit{if } p_{\mathsf{P}} \stackrel{\epsilon}{\Longrightarrow}_{\mathsf{P}} p' \textit{ with } p' \in F_{\mathsf{P}} \\ \{p' \in S_{\mathsf{P}} : p \stackrel{\epsilon}{\Longrightarrow}_{\mathsf{P}} p'\} & \textit{otherwise} \end{cases}$$

– $h_{p_P}(to) = \begin{cases} \emptyset & \textit{if } \exists p' \in h_{p_P}(t) \textit{ such that } p' \stackrel{\dashv o}{\Longrightarrow}_P p'' \textit{ with } p'' \in F_P \\ \{p'' \in S_P : \exists p' \in h_{p_P}(t) \cdot p' \stackrel{\dashv o}{\Longrightarrow}_P p''\} & \textit{otherwise} \end{cases}$
when $o \in \mathcal{A}^O_P$

– $h_{p_P}(ti) = \begin{cases} \emptyset & \textit{if } \exists p' \in h_{p_P}(t) \textit{ such that } p' \stackrel{\dashv i}{\Longrightarrow}_P p'' \textit{ with } p'' \in F_P, \textit{ or } p' \stackrel{i}{\not\longrightarrow}_P \\ \{p'' \in S_P : \exists p' \in h_{p_P}(t) \cdot p' \stackrel{\dashv i}{\Longrightarrow}_P p''\} & \textit{otherwise} \end{cases}$
when $i \in \mathcal{A}^I_P$.

Definition 12 (Safe traces). *A trace t of p_P is immediately-safe iff $h_{p_P}(t) \neq \emptyset$ and is safe iff $h_{p_{\mathcal{E}(P)}}(t) \neq \emptyset$, where $\mathcal{E}$ propagates inconsistencies backwards over output and τ transitions. The set of immediately-safe traces of p_P is denoted $IST(p_P)$, while the set of safe traces is denoted $ST(p_P)$.*

An immediately-safe trace t of a process p characterises a permissible exchange between p and an arbitrary environment, such that t will never encounter an inconsistent state under any resolution of p's non-determinism. Relating this intuition to Definitions 11 and 12, suppose p and the environment can safely communicate on the trace t. If from some state that p is in after following t it can perform an output o, and every o it can output will never make the system inconsistent, then the environment must be willing to accept that output. Conversely, the environment can only safely issue an input i after t if i can be accepted from every state the process is in after following t, without making the system inconsistent. We must impose these restrictions to account for the fact that the process cannot be expected to know how to resolve its non-determinism prior to its communication with the environment.

Definition 13 (Model mapping). *The* model mapping *function* $[\![\cdot]\!]^*$ *from Logic IOLTSs to declarative specifications is defined by* $[\![p_P]\!]^* = \langle \mathcal{A}^I_P, \mathcal{A}^O_P, T_{[\![p_P]\!]^*}, F_{[\![p_P]\!]^*}\rangle$*, where:*

– $T_{[\![p_P]\!]^*} = \{t : p_P \stackrel{t}{\Longrightarrow}_P\} \cup F \cup FI$
– $F_{[\![p_P]\!]^*} = F \cup FI$
– $F = \{tt' : p_P \stackrel{t}{\Longrightarrow}_P p',\ p' \in F_P \textit{ and } t' \in \mathcal{A}^*_P\}$
– $FI = \{tit' : p_P \stackrel{t}{\Longrightarrow}_P p',\ i \in \mathcal{A}^I_P,\ p' \stackrel{i}{\not\longrightarrow}_P \textit{ and } t' \in \mathcal{A}^*_P\}$.

Theorem 7 (Model mapping preserves safe traces). *For an arbitrary process p_P, $IST(p_P) = T_{[\![p_P]\!]^*} \setminus F_{[\![p_P]\!]^*}$ and $ST(p_P) = T_{[\![p_P]\!]^*} \setminus F_{\mathcal{E}([\![p_P]\!]^*)}$.*

Having defined a mapping from operational to declarative models, we can now define operational refinement in the obvious way.

Definition 14 (Operational refinement). *Process q_Q is said to be a refinement of process p_P, written $q_Q \sqsubseteq_{op} p_P$, iff $[\![q_Q]\!]^* \sqsubseteq_{dec} [\![p_P]\!]^*$.*

Lemma 2 (Operational preorder). *Refinement is reflexive and transitive.*

Under the assumption of finiteness, we note that refinement checking is PSPACE-complete. This is similar to traces refinement in CSP, where the worst-case is rarely observed in practice.

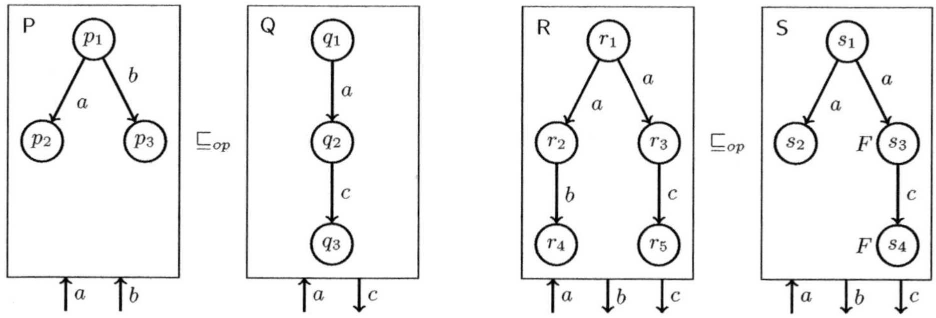

Fig. 1. Refinement of Logic IOLTSs

Definition 15 (Operational equivalence). *Processes* p_P *and* q_Q *are said to be equivalent, written* $p_P \equiv_{op} q_Q$*, iff* $q_Q \sqsubseteq_{op} p_P$ *and* $p_P \sqsubseteq_{op} q_Q$.

Looking at the refinements in Figure 1, from q_1 the environment can safely issue a, after which it must be willing to accept c. Clearly a can be safely accepted by p_1, and as p_2 does not issue a c output the environment will be perfectly happy. Moreover, as the environment is not permitted to issue a b in q_1 there is no harm in p_1 being able to handle this behaviour. Hence $p_1 \sqsubseteq_{op} q_1$. Now, $r_1 \sqsubseteq_{op} s_1$ as r_1 is willing to accept the input a from the environment, which is not the case in s_1. This is because we cannot trust s_1 to resolve its non-determinism on a in an optimistic way by always moving to s_2.

Example 2. To formally check $p_1 \sqsubseteq_{op} q_1$, it is necessary to resort to the definition of refinement on declarative specifications (Definition 4). It can easily be checked that all of the conditions of that definition hold by considering the sets below, obtained by computing the model mapping of the processes p_1 and q_1.

- $F_{[\![p_1]\!]^*} = F_{\mathcal{E}([\![p_1]\!]^*)} = (a+b)(a+b)^+$
- $F_{[\![q_1]\!]^*} = F_{\mathcal{E}([\![q_1]\!]^*)} = (a+ac)a(a+c)^*$
- $T_{[\![p_1]\!]^*} = (a+b)^*$
- $T_{[\![q_1]\!]^*} = \{\epsilon, a, ac\} \cup (a+ac)a(a+c)^*$
- $X \uparrow \mathcal{A}^I_{\mathcal{P}} = X \cup (\epsilon + a + ac + (aa+aca)(a+c)^*)b(a+b+c)^*$ for $X \in \{F_{[\![q_1]\!]^*}, T_{[\![q_1]\!]^*}\}$.

3.2 Error-Completion

In order to simplify the definitions of the operators in our specification theory for the operational framework, we introduce the error-completion of a Logic IOLTS. This is a transformation that leaves the mapping from a Logic IOLTS to a declarative specification unchanged.

The error-completion of a Logic IOLTS provides an explicit operational representation for the inconsistent traces that would arise in mapping the Logic IOLTS to its corresponding declarative specification. Consequently, an error-completed Logic IOLTS is closed under input extensions. It is this property that simplifies the definitions of the operators in our framework. We do not say that an error-completed Logic IOLTS is input-enabled, however, as we can distinguish good inputs from bad inputs.

Definition 16 (Error-completion). *Let* P *be a Logic IOLTS, and assume* $f_{\mathsf{P}} \notin S_{\mathsf{P}}$. *The* error-completion *of* P *is a Logic IOLTS* $\mathsf{P}_\bot = \langle S_{\mathsf{P}_\bot}, \mathcal{A}^I_{\mathsf{P}}, \mathcal{A}^O_{\mathsf{P}}, \longrightarrow_{\mathsf{P}_\bot}, F_{\mathsf{P}_\bot} \rangle$, *where:*

- $S_{\mathsf{P}_\bot} = S_{\mathsf{P}} \cup \{f_{\mathsf{P}}\}$
- $\longrightarrow_{\mathsf{P}_\bot} = \longrightarrow_{\mathsf{P}} \cup \{(f, a, f) : f \in F_{\mathsf{P}_\bot}$ *and* $a \in \mathcal{A}_{\mathsf{P}}\} \cup \{(s, a, f_{\mathsf{P}}) : a \in \mathcal{A}^I_{\mathsf{P}}$ *and* $\nexists s' \cdot s \xrightarrow{a}_{\mathsf{P}} s'\}$
- $F_{\mathsf{P}_\bot} = F_{\mathsf{P}} \cup \{f_{\mathsf{P}}\}$.

As remarked, the error-completion of a Logic IOLTS preserves the mapping from Logic IOLTSs to declarative specifications, as the next lemma shows. Note that the corresponding declarative specifications are equal, rather than declaratively equivalent.

Lemma 3 (Error-completion respects mappings). *For any process* p_{P}, $[\![p_{\mathsf{P}}]\!]^* = [\![p_{\mathsf{P}_\bot}]\!]^*$.

Besides simplifying the definition of the compositional operators in our specification theory, error-completion of a Logic IOLTS also simplifies the definition of the model mapping function.

Lemma 4 (Simplified model mapping). *Let* p *be a process in Logic IOLTS* $\mathsf{P}_\bot$. *Then* $[\![p]\!]^* = \langle \mathcal{A}^I_{\mathsf{P}}, \mathcal{A}^O_{\mathsf{P}}, T_{[\![p]\!]^*}, F_{[\![p]\!]^*} \rangle$, *where:*

- $T_{[\![p]\!]^*} = \{t : p \xRightarrow{t}_{\mathsf{P}_\bot}\}$
- $F_{[\![p]\!]^*} = \{tt' : p \xRightarrow{t}_{\mathsf{P}_\bot} p' \xRightarrow{t'}_{\mathsf{P}_\bot}$ *and* $p' \in F_{\mathsf{P}_\bot}\}$.

3.3 Parallel Composition

As for declarative specifications, the parallel composition of Logic IOLTSs yields a Logic IOLTS representing the combined effect of its operands running asynchronously. We insist that any given output should be under the control of one component only. Therefore Logic IOLTSs P and Q are composable for parallel composition only if $\mathcal{A}^O_{\mathsf{P}} \cap \mathcal{A}^O_{\mathsf{Q}} = \emptyset$.

Definition 17 (Parallel composition). *Let* P *and* Q *be Logic IOLTSs composable for parallel composition. Then the parallel composition of* P *and* Q *is a Logic IOLTS* $\mathsf{P} \,||\, \mathsf{Q} = \langle S, \mathcal{A}^I, \mathcal{A}^O, \longrightarrow, F \rangle$, *where:*

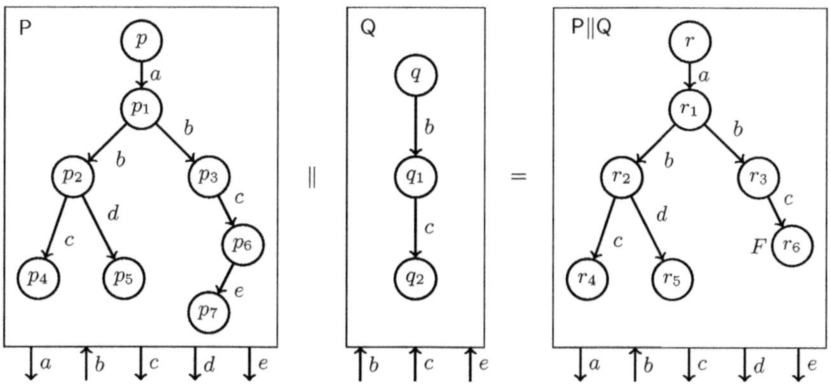

Fig. 2. Example of parallel composition on Logic IOLTSs

- $S = S_{\mathsf{P}_\perp} \mid\mid S_{\mathsf{Q}_\perp}$
- $\mathcal{A}^I = (\mathcal{A}^I_{\mathsf{P}} \cup \mathcal{A}^I_{\mathsf{Q}}) \setminus (\mathcal{A}^O_{\mathsf{P}} \cup \mathcal{A}^O_{\mathsf{Q}})$
- $\mathcal{A}^O = \mathcal{A}^O_{\mathsf{P}} \cup \mathcal{A}^O_{\mathsf{Q}}$
- $\longrightarrow$ *is the smallest relation satisfying the following rules:*
  P1. If $p \xrightarrow{a}_{\mathsf{P}_\perp} p'$ *with* $a \in \mathcal{A}^\tau_{\mathsf{P}} \setminus \mathcal{A}_{\mathsf{Q}}$*, then* $p \mid\mid q \xrightarrow{a} p' \mid\mid q$
  P2. If $q \xrightarrow{a}_{\mathsf{Q}_\perp} q'$ *with* $a \in \mathcal{A}^\tau_{\mathsf{Q}} \setminus \mathcal{A}_{\mathsf{P}}$*, then* $p \mid\mid q \xrightarrow{a} p \mid\mid q'$
  P3. If $p \xrightarrow{a}_{\mathsf{P}_\perp} p'$ *and* $q \xrightarrow{a}_{\mathsf{Q}_\perp} q'$ *with* $a \in \mathcal{A}_{\mathsf{P}} \cap \mathcal{A}_{\mathsf{Q}}$*, then* $p \mid\mid q \xrightarrow{a} p' \mid\mid q'$.
- $F = (S_{\mathsf{P}_\perp} \mid\mid F_{\mathsf{Q}_\perp}) \cup (F_{\mathsf{P}_\perp} \mid\mid S_{\mathsf{Q}_\perp})$.

Conditions P1 to P3 ensure that the parallel composition of Logic IOLTSs interleave on independent actions and synchronise on common actions. For P3, given the parallel composability constraint, synchronisation can take place between an output and an input, or two inputs. Figure 2 shows how the parallel composition operator works in practice, although we omit non-enabled input transitions to inconsistent states. In particular, the example demonstrates how inconsistencies can be introduced through non-input enabledness, as in state r_6 corresponding to $p_6 \mid\mid q_2$.

Reassuringly, parallel composition of Logic IOLTSs yields a Logic IOLTS. The following theorem shows the relationship between parallel composition on Logic IOLTSs and parallel composition on declarative specifications.

Theorem 8 (Parallel correspondences). *Let* P *and* Q *be Logic IOLTSs composable for parallel composition. For processes* p_{P} *and* q_{Q}*, it holds that* $[\![p_{\mathsf{P}} \mid\mid q_{\mathsf{Q}}]\!]^* = [\![p_{\mathsf{P}}]\!]^* \mid\mid [\![q_{\mathsf{Q}}]\!]^*$.

3.4 Conjunction

In keeping with conjunction of declarative specifications, Logic IOLTSs P and Q are composable for conjunction only if the sets $\mathcal{A}^I_{\mathsf{P}} \cup \mathcal{A}^I_{\mathsf{Q}}$ and $\mathcal{A}^O_{\mathsf{P}} \cup \mathcal{A}^O_{\mathsf{Q}}$ are disjoint.

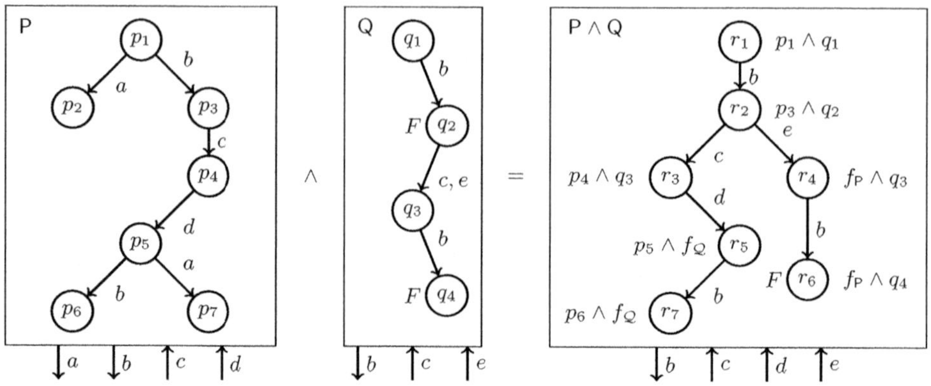

Fig. 3. Example of conjunction on Logic IOLTSs

Definition 18 (Conjunction). *Let* P *and* Q *be Logic IOLTSs composable for conjunction. Then the conjunction of* P *and* Q *is a Logic IOLTS* $\mathsf{P} \wedge \mathsf{Q} = \langle S, \mathcal{A}^I_\mathsf{P} \cup \mathcal{A}^I_\mathsf{Q}, \mathcal{A}^O_\mathsf{P} \cap \mathcal{A}^O_\mathsf{Q}, \longrightarrow, F \rangle$*, where:*

- $S = S_{\mathsf{P}_\perp} \wedge S_{\mathsf{Q}_\perp}$
- $\longrightarrow$ *is the smallest relation satisfying the following rules:*
  C1. If $a \in \mathcal{A}^O_\mathsf{P} \cap \mathcal{A}^O_\mathsf{Q}$, $p \xrightarrow{a}_{\mathsf{P}_\perp} p'$ *and* $q \xrightarrow{a}_{\mathsf{Q}_\perp} q'$, *then* $p \wedge q \xrightarrow{a} p' \wedge q'$
  C2. If $a \in \mathcal{A}^I_\mathsf{P} \cap \mathcal{A}^I_\mathsf{Q}$, $p \xrightarrow{a}_{\mathsf{P}_\perp} p'$ *and* $q \xrightarrow{a}_{\mathsf{Q}_\perp} q'$, *then* $p \wedge q \xrightarrow{a} p' \wedge q'$
  C3. If $a \in \mathcal{A}^I_\mathsf{P} \setminus \mathcal{A}^I_\mathsf{Q}$ *and* $p \xrightarrow{a}_{\mathsf{P}_\perp} p'$, *then* $p \wedge q \xrightarrow{a} p' \wedge f_\mathsf{Q}$
  C4. If $a \in \mathcal{A}^I_\mathsf{Q} \setminus \mathcal{A}^I_\mathsf{P}$ *and* $q \xrightarrow{a}_{\mathsf{Q}_\perp} q'$, *then* $p \wedge q \xrightarrow{a} f_\mathsf{P} \wedge q'$
  C5. If $p \xrightarrow{\tau}_{\mathsf{P}_\perp} p'$, *then* $p \wedge q \xrightarrow{\tau} p' \wedge q$
  C6. If $q \xrightarrow{\tau}_{\mathsf{Q}_\perp} q'$, *then* $p \wedge q \xrightarrow{\tau} p \wedge q'$
- $F = F_{\mathsf{P}_\perp} \wedge F_{\mathsf{Q}_\perp}$.

The idea behind the definition of conjunction for $p \wedge q$ is that p and q must synchronise on common actions, interleave on τ-transitions, and on encountering independent input actions behave like the respective component to which the action belongs. On encountering a state $p \wedge q$ in which one of $p \in F_\mathsf{P}$ or $q \in F_\mathsf{Q}$ holds, let it be p, we know that whatever the behaviour of $p \wedge q$ it will always be a refinement of p. So the most general refinement of $p \wedge q$ will actually be q. This is supported by the fact that inconsistent states in the error-completed Logic IOLTS admit arbitrary behaviour.

Figure 3 shows the conjunction of processes p_1 and q_1 in the Logic IOLTSs P and Q (although for clarity we omit inputs leading to inconsistent states). In state r_1 corresponding to $p_1 \wedge q_1$, the b-output transitions of p_1 and q_1 synchronise. Independent output actions such as the a-transition in p_1 are not permitted to proceed, because it would not be the case that r_1 could be used safely in place of q_1 if this transition were to be permitted. State r_2 can evolve into r_3 by synchronising the c-inputs of p_3 and q_2, while it can also evolve into r_4 by proceeding on the independent input e of q_2. From this point, r_4 behaves like q_3, because e is an input-violation of p_3. Similar reasoning applies to r_3's evolution into r_5 by receiving the d-input.

As for parallel composition, there is a correspondence between conjunction at the operational and declarative levels.

Theorem 9 (Conjunction correspondences). *Let* P *and* Q *be Logic IOLTSs composable for conjunction. For processes* p_{P} *and* q_{Q}*, it holds that* $[\![p_{\mathsf{P}} \wedge q_{\mathsf{Q}}]\!]^* = [\![p_{\mathsf{P}}]\!]^* \wedge [\![q_{\mathsf{Q}}]\!]^*$.

3.5 Quotient

Non-determinism and τ-transitions arising in Logic IOLTSs make the definition of quotient more involved than the other operators we have considered on operational models. To ensure that the quotient is the coarsest specification, it is necessary to track the non-determinism of the system-wide specification and its partial implementation. This is because the non-determinism can affect the safe traces of a Logic IOLTS.

As for declarative specifications, we only compute the quotient of process p_{P} from r_{R} when $\mathcal{A}^O_{\mathsf{P}} \subseteq \mathcal{A}^O_{\mathsf{R}}$ and $\mathcal{A}_{\mathsf{P}} \subseteq \mathcal{A}_{\mathsf{R}}$. The quotient is the coarsest specification q over an interface consisting of inputs $\mathcal{A}^O_{\mathsf{P}} \cup \mathcal{A}^I_{\mathsf{R}}$ and outputs $\mathcal{A}^O_{\mathsf{R}} \setminus \mathcal{A}^O_{\mathsf{P}}$ such that $p_{\mathsf{P}} \mid\mid q \sqsubseteq_{op} r_{\mathsf{R}}$. If such a q exists, we denote it by $r_{\mathsf{R}}/p_{\mathsf{P}}$.

Before defining the quotient-construction, we introduce some functions and predicates that simplify the presentation.

Definition 19. *For Logic IOLTS* P*, set of states* $S \subseteq S_{\mathsf{P}_\perp}$ *and action* $a \in \mathcal{A}_{\mathsf{P}}$*, define:*

- $\mathsf{succ}^{\epsilon}_{\mathsf{P}}(S) = \{s' : s \stackrel{\epsilon}{\Longrightarrow}_{\mathsf{P}_\perp} s' \textit{ with } s \in S\}$
- $\mathsf{succ}^{a}_{\mathsf{P}}(S) = \{s' : s \stackrel{\dashv a}{\Longrightarrow}_{\mathsf{P}_\perp} s' \textit{ with } s \in S\}$.

Definition 20 (Quotient Logic IOLTS). *Let* P *and* R *be Logic IOLTSs such that* $\mathcal{A}^O_{\mathsf{P}} \subseteq \mathcal{A}^O_{\mathsf{R}}$ *and* $\mathcal{A}_{\mathsf{P}} \subseteq \mathcal{A}_{\mathsf{R}}$*. The quotient of* P *from* R *is the Logic IOLTS* $\mathsf{R}/\mathsf{P} = \langle S_{\mathsf{R}/\mathsf{P}}, \mathcal{A}^I_{\mathsf{R}/\mathsf{P}}, \mathcal{A}^O_{\mathsf{R}/\mathsf{P}}, \longrightarrow, F_{\mathsf{R}/\mathsf{P}}\rangle$*, where:*

- $S_{\mathsf{R}/\mathsf{P}} = \{R/P : R \subseteq S_{\mathsf{R}_\perp} \textit{ and } P \subseteq S_{\mathsf{P}_\perp}\}$
- $\mathcal{A}^I_{\mathsf{R}/\mathsf{P}} = \mathcal{A}^O_{\mathsf{P}} \cup \mathcal{A}^I_{\mathsf{R}}$
- $\mathcal{A}^O_{\mathsf{R}/\mathsf{P}} = \mathcal{A}^O_{\mathsf{R}} \setminus \mathcal{A}^O_{\mathsf{P}}$
- $\longrightarrow$ *is the smallest relation satisfying the following rules:*
  - *Q1.* $R'/P' \stackrel{a}{\longrightarrow} \mathsf{succ}^a_{\mathsf{R}}(R')/\mathsf{succ}^a_{\mathsf{P}}(P')$ *providing:*
    - *(a)* $a \in \mathcal{A}^I_{\mathsf{P}} \cap \mathcal{A}^I_{\mathsf{R}}$ *implies* $\mathsf{succ}^a_{\mathsf{R}}(R') \cap F_{\mathcal{E}(\mathsf{R})} = \emptyset$
    - *(b)* $a \in \mathcal{A}^O_{\mathsf{P}} \cap \mathcal{A}^O_{\mathsf{R}}$ *implies* $\mathsf{succ}^a_{\mathsf{R}}(R') \cap F_{\mathcal{E}(\mathsf{R})} = \emptyset$ *and* $\mathsf{succ}^a_{\mathsf{P}}(P') \neq \emptyset$
    - *(c)* $a \in \mathcal{A}^I_{\mathsf{P}} \cap \mathcal{A}^O_{\mathsf{R}}$ *implies* $\mathsf{succ}^a_{\mathsf{P}}(P') \cap F_{\mathsf{P}} = \emptyset$ *and* $\mathsf{succ}^a_{\mathsf{R}}(R') \neq \emptyset$
  - *Q2.* $R'/P' \stackrel{a}{\longrightarrow} \mathsf{succ}^a_{\mathsf{R}}(R')/P'$ *providing:*
    - *(a)* $a \in \mathcal{A}^I_{\mathsf{R}} \setminus \mathcal{A}_{\mathsf{P}}$ *implies* $\mathsf{succ}^a_{\mathsf{R}}(R') \cap F_{\mathcal{E}(\mathsf{R})} = \emptyset$
    - *(b)* $a \in \mathcal{A}^O_{\mathsf{R}} \setminus \mathcal{A}_{\mathsf{P}}$ *implies* $\mathsf{succ}^a_{\mathsf{R}}(R') \neq \emptyset$.

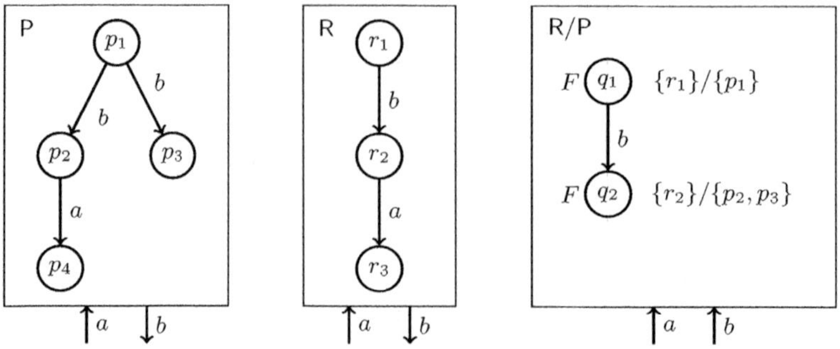

Fig. 4. Example showing non-existence of quotient on Logic IOLTSs

- *$R'/P' \in F_{\mathsf{R}/\mathsf{P}}$ iff at least one of the following rules holds:*
  F1. $R' = \emptyset$ or $P' = \emptyset$
  F2. $F_{\mathcal{E}(\mathsf{R}_\bot)} \cap R' \neq \emptyset$ or $F_{\mathsf{P}_\bot} \cap P' \neq \emptyset$
  F3. $R'/P' \xrightarrow{a} R''/P''$ with $a \in \mathcal{A}^I_{\mathsf{R}/\mathsf{P}}$ and $R''/P'' \in F_{\mathsf{R}/\mathsf{P}}$.

Definition 21 (Quotient). *Let* P *and* R *be Logic IOLTSs such that $\mathcal{A}^O_\mathsf{P} \subseteq \mathcal{A}^O_\mathsf{R}$ and $\mathcal{A}_\mathsf{P} \subseteq \mathcal{A}_\mathsf{R}$. The* quotient *of process p_P from process r_R, written $r_\mathsf{R}/p_\mathsf{P}$, is the process $\mathsf{succ}^\epsilon_\mathsf{R}(r_\mathsf{R})/\mathsf{succ}^\epsilon_\mathsf{P}(p_\mathsf{P})$ in the Logic IOLTS* R//P *obtained from* R/P *by removing all transitions immediately leading to a state in $F_{\mathsf{R}/\mathsf{P}}$, and removing all states R/P such that $R/P \in F_{\mathsf{R}/\mathsf{P}}$ and $R \notin F_{\mathcal{E}(\mathsf{R})}$. If $\mathsf{succ}^\epsilon_\mathsf{R}(r_\mathsf{R})/\mathsf{succ}^\epsilon_\mathsf{P}(p_\mathsf{P})$ is not contained in* R//P*, then the quotient is not defined.*

As for declarative specifications, the quotient of p_P from r_R may not exist. The following theorem shows that definedness of the quotient according to the previous definition coincides precisely with the existence of such a quotient.

Theorem 10 (Existence of quotient). *Let* P *and* R *be Logic IOLTSs such that $\mathcal{A}^O_\mathsf{P} \subseteq \mathcal{A}^O_\mathsf{R}$ and $\mathcal{A}_\mathsf{P} \subseteq \mathcal{A}_\mathsf{R}$. Then $r_\mathsf{R}/p_\mathsf{P}$ is defined (i.e. $r_\mathsf{R} \in F_{\mathcal{E}(\mathsf{R})}$ or $r_\mathsf{R}/p_\mathsf{P} \notin F_{\mathsf{R}/\mathsf{P}}$) iff there exists a process q in a Logic IOLTS with inputs $\mathcal{A}^I_{\mathsf{R}/\mathsf{P}}$ and outputs $\mathcal{A}^O_{\mathsf{R}/\mathsf{P}}$ such that $p_\mathsf{P} \mid\mid q \sqsubseteq_{op} r_\mathsf{R}$.*

Consequently, the constraint $r_\mathsf{R} \notin F_{\mathcal{E}(\mathsf{R})}$ and $r_\mathsf{R}/p_\mathsf{P} \in F_{\mathsf{R}/\mathsf{P}}$ gives a precise characterisation of whether the quotient exists or not. When the quotient does exist, it behaves in exactly the same way as for declarative specifications.

Theorem 11 (Quotient correspondences). *Let* P *and* R *be Logic IOLTSs such that $\mathcal{A}^O_\mathsf{P} \subseteq \mathcal{A}^O_\mathsf{R}$ and $\mathcal{A}_\mathsf{P} \subseteq \mathcal{A}_\mathsf{R}$. If $r_\mathsf{R}/p_\mathsf{P} \notin F_{\mathsf{R}/\mathsf{P}}$ or $r_\mathsf{R} \in F_{\mathcal{E}(\mathsf{R})}$, then $[\![r_\mathsf{R}/p_\mathsf{P}]\!]^* = [\![r_\mathsf{R}]\!]^*/[\![p_\mathsf{P}]\!]^*$.*

Figure 4 provides an example in which processes p_1 and r_1 have no quotient. This tallies with Theorem 10, as we have $\{r_1\}/\{p_1\} \in F_{\mathsf{R}/\mathsf{P}}$ when $r_1 \notin F_{\mathcal{E}(\mathsf{R})}$. On the other hand, quotients exist for the processes p_1 and r_1 of Figures 5 and 6. This is also supported by Theorem 10, as $\{r_1\}/\{p_1\} \notin F_{\mathsf{R}/\mathsf{P}}$ for the processes in both figures.

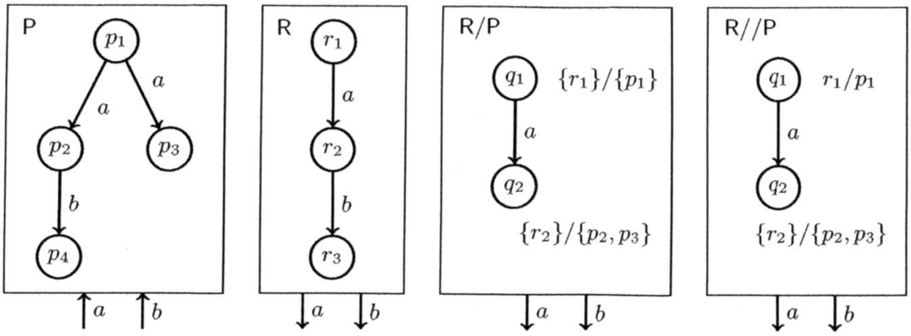

Fig. 5. Example of quotient on Logic IOLTSs with no inconsistencies

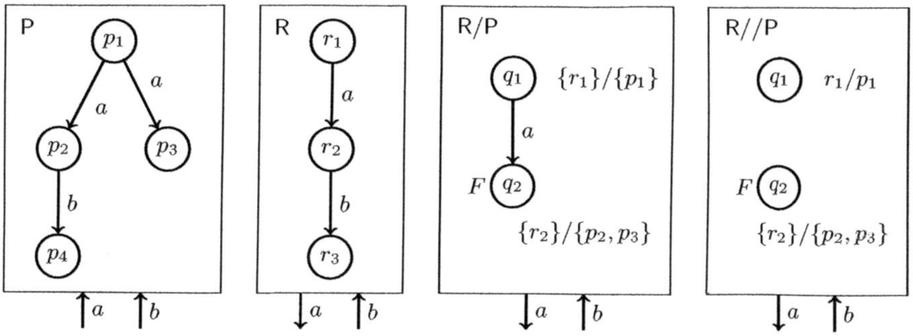

Fig. 6. Example of quotient on Logic IOLTSs with inconsistencies

For Figure 6, the quotient is the single consistent state $\{r_1\}/\{p_1\}$. This is because in going from R/P to R//P we remove the transition labelled by the output a between the processes $\{r_1\}/\{p_1\}$ and $\{r_2\}/\{p_2, p_3\}$, as the latter state is inconsistent. Maintaining this transition would yield an invalid quotient as $p_1 \parallel (r_1/p_1)$ would be inconsistent when r_1 is consistent. It is safe to discard this transition only because it is an output. Recalling the definition of $\sqsubseteq_{op}$, for safe-substitutivity it is perfectly safe to suppress outputs on the left that would have occurred on the right.

4 Full-Abstraction Results

In this section we present full-abstraction results that relate our declarative and operational equivalences based on trace containment to a simple equivalence, which ensures that an inconsistent process must have an inconsistent specification. The result is shown by employing a testing scenario where processes are placed in parallel with an arbitrary composable process in order to establish their equivalence with regard to the observation of consistency.

Definition 22 (Declarative inconsistency equivalence). *Let $\mathcal{P}$ and $\mathcal{Q}$ be declarative specifications.* Declarative inconsistency equivalence, *denoted by* $\equiv^F_{dec}$, *is given by* $\mathcal{P} \equiv^F_{dec} \mathcal{Q}$ *iff* $\mathcal{A}^I_{\mathcal{P}} = \mathcal{A}^I_{\mathcal{Q}}$, $\mathcal{A}^O_{\mathcal{P}} = \mathcal{A}^O_{\mathcal{Q}}$ *and* $\epsilon \in F_{\mathcal{P}} \iff \epsilon \in F_{\mathcal{Q}}$.

Declarative equivalence can be established by placing each process in parallel with arbitrary composable tester processes and observing whether the simple inconsistency equivalence is maintained.

Theorem 12. *Let $\mathcal{P}$ and $\mathcal{Q}$ be declarative specifications. Then:*

$$\mathcal{P} \equiv_{dec} \mathcal{Q} \textit{ iff } \forall \mathcal{R} \cdot \mathcal{A}^O_{\mathcal{R}} \cap (\mathcal{A}^O_{\mathcal{P}} \cup \mathcal{A}^O_{\mathcal{Q}}) = \emptyset \implies \mathcal{E}(\mathcal{P} \mid\mid \mathcal{R}) \equiv^F_{dec} \mathcal{E}(\mathcal{Q} \mid\mid \mathcal{R}).$$

From this characterisation of $\equiv_{dec}$, we obtain a full-abstraction result with respect to parallel composition and $\equiv^F_{dec}$. Our definition of full-abstraction is taken from [19] (Definition 16), which means that $\equiv_{dec}$ is the coarsest congruence with respect to the operators of our specification theory and $\equiv^F_{dec}$.

Corollary 1 (Declarative full-abstraction). *Declarative equivalence $\equiv_{dec}$ is fully-abstract with respect to parallel, conjunction, quotient and $\equiv^F_{dec}$.*

We can now present analogous results for our operational models.

Definition 23 (Operational inconsistency equivalence). *Let p_{P} and q_{Q} be processes of Logic IOLTSs* P *and* Q. Operational inconsistency equivalence, *denoted by* $\equiv^F_{op}$, *is given by* $p_{\mathsf{P}} \equiv^F_{op} q_{\mathsf{Q}}$ *iff* $\mathcal{A}^I_{\mathsf{P}} = \mathcal{A}^I_{\mathsf{Q}}$, $\mathcal{A}^O_{\mathsf{P}} = \mathcal{A}^O_{\mathsf{Q}}$ *and* $p_{\mathsf{P}} \in F_{\mathsf{P}} \iff q_{\mathsf{Q}} \in F_{\mathsf{Q}}$.

Theorem 13. *Let p_{P} and q_{Q} be processes of Logic IOLTSs* P *and* Q. *Then:*

$$p_{\mathsf{P}} \equiv_{op} q_{\mathsf{Q}} \textit{ iff } \forall r_{\mathsf{R}} \cdot \mathcal{A}^O_{\mathsf{R}} \cap (\mathcal{A}^O_{\mathsf{P}} \cup \mathcal{A}^O_{\mathsf{Q}}) = \emptyset \implies \mathcal{E}(p_{\mathsf{P}} \mid\mid r_{\mathsf{R}}) \equiv^F_{op} \mathcal{E}(q_{\mathsf{Q}} \mid\mid r_{\mathsf{R}}),$$

where $\mathcal{E}$ applied to processes in Logic IOLTSs propagates the inconsistency predicate backwards over all output and τ labelled transitions.

Corollary 2 (Operational full-abstraction). *Operational equivalence $\equiv_{op}$ is fully-abstract with respect to parallel, conjunction, quotient and $\equiv^F_{op}$.*

5 Conclusion and Future Work

We have developed a compositional specification theory for components that may be modelled operationally, closely mirroring actual implementations, or in an abstract manner by means of declarative specifications. Both frameworks admit a simple refinement relation, defined in terms of traces, which corresponds to safe-substitutivity. We define asynchronous parallel composition, conjunction and quotient, and prove that the induced equivalence is a congruence for these operations. It is straightforward to extend our framework with disjunction and hiding. The simplicity of our formalism facilitates reasoning about the temporal ordering of interactions needed for assume-guarantee inference. Although not considered in this paper, our framework supports reasoning about safety properties in the context of assume-guarantee. Liveness properties may also be considered, but this requires the introduction of quiescence or infinite behaviours, the latter being achieved with the help of ω-automata techniques.

Acknowledgments. The authors are supported by EU FP7 project CONNECT and ERC Advanced Grant VERIWARE. We would also like to thank the anonymous reviewers for their insightful comments.

References

1. Larsen, K.G., Nyman, U., Wasowski, A.: Modal I/O Automata for Interface and Product Line Theories. In: De Nicola, R. (ed.) ESOP 2007. LNCS, vol. 4421, pp. 64–79. Springer, Heidelberg (2007)
2. de Alfaro, L., Henzinger, T.A.: Interface automata. SIGSOFT Softw. Eng. Notes 26, 109–120 (2001)
3. Raclet, J.B., Badouel, E., Benveniste, A., Caillaud, B., Passerone, R.: Why are modalities good for Interface Theories? In: Proc. 9th International Conference on Application of Concurrency to System Design, ACSD 2009, pp. 119–127. IEEE Computer Society (2009)
4. Raclet, J.B., Badouel, E., Benveniste, A., Caillaud, B., Legay, A., Passerone, R.: Modal Interfaces: Unifying Interface Automata and Modal Specifications. In: Proc. 7th International Conference on Embedded Software, EMSOFT 2009, pp. 87–96. ACM (2009)
5. Lynch, N.A., Tuttle, M.R.: An introduction to input/output automata. CWI Quarterly 2, 219–246 (1989)
6. Lüttgen, G., Vogler, W.: Conjunction on processes: Full abstraction via ready-tree semantics. Theor. Comput. Sci. 373, 19–40 (2007)
7. Lüttgen, G., Vogler, W.: Ready simulation for concurrency: It's logical! Inf. Comput. 208, 845–867 (2010)
8. Brookes, S.D., Hoare, C.A.R., Roscoe, A.W.: A theory of communicating sequential processes. J. ACM 31, 560–599 (1984)
9. de Alfaro, L., Henzinger, T.A.: Interface-based design. In: Broy, M., Grünbauer, J., Harel, D., Hoare, T. (eds.) Engineering Theories of Software Intensive Systems. NATO Science Series II: Mathematics, Physics and Chemistry, vol. 195, pp. 83–104. Springer, Heidelberg (2005)
10. de Alfaro, L.: Game Models for Open Systems. In: Dershowitz, N. (ed.) Verification (Manna Festschrift). LNCS, vol. 2772, pp. 269–289. Springer, Heidelberg (2004)
11. Doyen, L., Henzinger, T.A., Jobstmann, B., Petrov, T.: Interface theories with component reuse. In: Proc. 8th ACM International Conference on Embedded Software, EMSOFT 2008, pp. 79–88. ACM (2008)
12. Bhaduri, P., Ramesh, S.: Interface synthesis and protocol conversion. Form. Asp. Comput. 20, 205–224 (2008)
13. Nicola, R.D., Segala, R.: A process algebraic view of input/output automata. Theor. Comput. Sci. 138, 391–423 (1995)
14. Tretmans, J.: Model-Based Testing and Some Steps towards Test-Based Modelling. In: Bernardo, M., Issarny, V. (eds.) SFM 2011. LNCS, vol. 6659, pp. 297–326. Springer, Heidelberg (2011)
15. Josephs, M.B.: Receptive process theory. Acta Inf. 29, 17–31 (1992)
16. Josephs, M.B., Kapoor, H.K.: Controllable delay-insensitive processes. Fundam. Inf. 78, 101–130 (2007)

17. Raclet, J.B.: Residual for component specifications. Electr. Notes Theor. Comput. Sci. 215, 93–110 (2008)
18. Chen, T., Chilton, C., Jonsson, B., Kwiatkowska, M.: A Compositional Specification Theory for Component Behaviours. Technical Report RR-12-01, Department of Computer Science, University of Oxford (2012)
19. van Glabbeek, R.J.: Full abstraction in structural operational semantics (extended abstract). In: Proceedings of the Third International Conference on Methodology and Software Technology: Algebraic Methodology and Software Technology, pp. 75–82. Springer, Heidelberg (1994)

Probabilistic Abstract Interpretation

Patrick Cousot and Michael Monerau

Courant Institute, NYU and École Normale Supérieure, France

Abstract. Abstract interpretation has been widely used for verifying properties of computer systems. Here, we present a way to extend this framework to the case of probabilistic systems.

The probabilistic abstraction framework that we propose allows us to systematically lift any classical analysis or verification method to the probabilistic setting by separating in the program semantics the probabilistic behavior from the (non-)deterministic behavior. This separation provides new insights for designing novel probabilistic static analyses and verification methods.

We define the concrete probabilistic semantics and propose different ways to abstract them. We provide examples illustrating the expressiveness and effectiveness of our approach.

1 Introduction

As programs get larger and larger, it has become untractable to verify their properties and/or correctness by hand or testing. Formal methods have thus been developed in order to be able to verify program properties automatically, at least in part. One of them is abstract interpretation which has proved successful both in solving hard problems and scaling up nicely.

When probabilities come into play, the verification of program properties is even more difficult. Our work precisely tackles this issue, that is *verifying properties of probabilistic programs*. We propose a formal, general and modular framework, extending the classical abstract interpretation framework to take probabilities into account, allowing for crafting of new analyses, as well as lifting of existing non-probabilistic analyses to the probabilistic setting.

Probabilities come into play because of *program randomness* (such as calls to a random number generator `rand()`) and *input randomness* (for which a distribution may be known). Usually, all this randomness is forgotten for non-determinism. It is sound but loses a lot of information. So our goal here is to *use* hypotheses on randomness to be able to infer more precise probabilistic program properties.

The goals of having probabilistic static analyses are various, let alone the fact that we can actually verify some probabilistic properties on the program. A couple of more original examples of interesting applications are to enable compilers to gain access to more useful information to decide register allocations or cache/scratchpad allocations, or to provide useful information about branching for Just In Time compilers without having to do any profiling or execution, among many other applications.

There is a lot of work on probabilistic program construction and verification methods [13, 15, 19, 23], probabilistic model-checking [11], probabilistic abstract model-checking [2, 27, 29], probabilistic abstract interpretation [21, 25, 28], with, in the case of

H. Seidl (Ed.): ESOP 2012, LNCS 7211, pp. 169–193, 2012.

model-checking and abstract interpretation, existing applications to biological pathways [1, 3, 18]. One of our objectives is to unify and generalize these frameworks.

2 The Abstract Interpretation Framework

Abstract interpretation is a theory of approximation. Applied to semantics of computer programs, it allows oneself for generic design of static analyses [5].

The *concrete semantics* $S[\![\mathrm{P}]\!]$ of a program P is, by hypothesis, an element $S[\![\mathrm{P}]\!] \in \mathcal{D}$, where $\mathcal{D}$ is a fixed *semantics domain*. It is often expressed as a least fixpoint $S[\![\mathrm{P}]\!] = \mathrm{lfp}^{\leq} F_{\mathrm{P}}$ where the *concrete transformer* is $F_{\mathrm{P}} : \mathcal{D} \longrightarrow \mathcal{D}$ and $\leq$ is the *concrete semantic partial order* on $\mathcal{D}$.

Semantic properties of programs are elements of the *concrete domain* $\langle \wp(\mathcal{D}), \subseteq\rangle$ where $\subseteq$ is logical implication. A program P is said to *verify a property* $\Gamma \in \wp(\mathcal{D})$ iff $S[\![\mathrm{P}]\!] \in \Gamma \iff \{S[\![\mathrm{P}]\!]\} \subseteq \Gamma$, which is often undecidable or intractable so that approximations are necessary for total automation.

A partially ordered *abstract domain* $\langle \mathcal{A}, \sqsubseteq\rangle$ is considered and linked to the concrete domain by means of a *Galois connection* $\langle \wp(\mathcal{D}), \subseteq\rangle \underset{\alpha}{\overset{\gamma}{\leftrightarrows}} \langle \mathcal{A}, \sqsubseteq\rangle$ defined such that $\forall P \in \wp(\mathcal{D}) : \forall Q \in \mathcal{A} : \alpha(P) \sqsubseteq Q \iff P \subseteq \gamma(Q)$. For example the interval abstraction is $\langle \wp(\mathbb{Z}), \subseteq\rangle \underset{\alpha}{\overset{\gamma}{\leftrightarrows}} \langle \mathcal{I}(\mathbb{Z}), \sqsubseteq_I\rangle$ with $I(\mathbb{Z}) \triangleq \{\bot\} \cup \{[a, b] \mid a \leqslant b\}$, $\alpha(\emptyset) \triangleq \bot$, and $\alpha(S) = [\min S, \max S]$ when $S \neq \emptyset$ where $\min \mathbb{Z} \triangleq -\infty$, $\max \mathbb{Z} \triangleq +\infty$, and $\sqsubseteq_I$ is interval inclusion. In a Galois connection one adjoint uniquely determines the other (which we often leave implicit). Galois connections are used for the sake of simplicity although not necessary (a concretization function γ may be sufficient [7]). The only way to know what is the meaning of *verifying an abstract property* $Q \in \mathcal{A}$ is to evaluate the concretization function γ. Indeed, by definition it means that $S[\![\mathrm{P}]\!] \subseteq \gamma(Q)$, i.e. P verifies the property $\gamma(Q)$.

Static analysis consists in computing an *abstract semantics* $S[\![\mathrm{P}]\!]^\sharp$ of the program that is less precise but still *sound* $S[\![\mathrm{P}]\!] \subseteq \gamma(S[\![\mathrm{P}]\!]^\sharp)$ (and sometimes even *complete* for a given class of properties when it loses no essential information for proofs). Thus the program P is said to satisfy an abstract property $Q \in \mathcal{A}$ iff $S[\![\mathrm{P}]\!]^\sharp \sqsubseteq Q$ (which implies $S[\![\mathrm{P}]\!] \subseteq \gamma(S[\![\mathrm{P}]\!]^\sharp)$ since γ is increasing and $\subseteq$ transitive). An adequate cost/precision ratio consists in choosing $\langle \mathcal{A}, \sqsubseteq\rangle$ and $S[\![\mathrm{P}]\!]^\sharp$ to be algorithmically tractable hence imprecise so incomplete but nevertheless precise enough so that $S[\![\mathrm{P}]\!]^\sharp \sqsubseteq Q$ implies $S[\![\mathrm{P}]\!] \subseteq \gamma(Q)$. Soundness is always guaranteed along the way by the framework.

3 Probabilistic Concrete Semantics

Our approach relies on basic concepts of classical abstract interpretation that we recalled in Sect. 2 and probability theory [16].

In this section, we introduce how we describe the semantics of probabilistic programs (or systems). It is a very general way of associating a semantics with any probabilistic system. That is, it is not tied to a particular description of probabilities nor to a specific programming language but rather allows for a precise construction of semantics for any probabilistic situation.

3.1 Definition

We look at probabilistic systems as a superposition of (non)-deterministic systems. That is, when a probabilistic program is run we consider that it can be any element of a specific set of (non)-deterministic programs chosen by a random experience. It is as if *all* the random choices that will be made in the subsequent execution are decided by an oracle at startup (although a program knows only during the course of its execution about which random choices have been made up to the current execution point and ignores the later ones[1]).

Definition 1 (Probabilistic semantics). A *probabilistic semantics* $S_p[\![P]\!] \in \mathcal{D}_p \triangleq \Omega \rightarrowtail \mathcal{D}$ of a program P is a measurable function of a probability space $\langle \Omega, \mathcal{E}, \mu \rangle$ into a semantics domain $\mathcal{D}$ (considered as a measurable space $\langle \mathcal{D}, O \rangle$ with observable semantic properties in $O \subseteq \wp(\mathcal{D})$). □

By *observable*, we mean that semantic properties in O will be the ones we eventually have probabilistic information upon.

The meaning of the probabilistic semantics $S_p[\![P]\!]$ is that when a scenario $\omega \in \Omega$ is picked (randomly according to μ), then the execution of the program P yields the (non)-deterministic semantics $S_p[\![P]\!](\omega) \in \mathcal{D}$. That is, ω embodies all the possible random choices that the program will have to make during its execution. $\mathcal{D}$ can be any non-probabilistic semantics domain (e.g. the powerset of maximal execution traces as in Ex. 4 below or any of its abstractions [4] such as the prefix trace semantics in Ex. 1). This definition covers most probabilistic models of computation found in the literature such as program semantics [17], Markov decision processes [2, 3, 10, 11, 22, 29], etc.

Example 1. Suppose the program P starts by tossing a coin `x = random(1,2)`, and then executes other statements. The prefix trace semantics of P would be described by $\Omega = \{\omega_1, \omega_2\}$ and $S_p[\![P]\!] \in \mathcal{D}_p = \Omega \rightarrowtail \mathcal{D}$, where $\mathcal{D} = \wp(\mathcal{S}^+)$ is the set of finite sequences of states and the observable properties are simply $\wp(\mathcal{D})$, defined as $S_p[\![P]\!](\omega_1) = \{$ prefix traces of P starting with `x = 1` $\}$ and $S_p[\![P]\!](\omega_2) = \{$prefix traces of P starting with `x = 2`$\}$. Then the definition of μ would tell what is the probability of scenarios ω_1 and ω_2. For a non-biased coin, μ would be defined by $\mu(\{\omega_1\}) = 1/2, \mu(\{\omega_2\}) = 1/2, \mu(\emptyset) = 0, \mu(\Omega) = 1$. □

Example 2 (Markov chains). Markov chains can be formalized in our framework by taking $\Omega = [0, 1]^{\mathbb{N}}$ (sequences of elements in [0,1]) with the uniform Lebesgue measure. For a specific sequence $u_n \in \Omega$, the execution of the Markov chain is as follows.

From a state s_0, at step $i \geq 0$, where multiple states $s_1, \ldots, s_k$ of the Markov chain can be chosen for the next step and where the probability of going to state s_a is $p_a \in [0, 1]$. By definition, $\sum_{1 \leq a \leq k} p_a = 1$, so $[0, 1]$ can be divided in k segments S_a each of length p_a. Now, choose $s_{i+1} = s_a$ such that $u_i \in S_a$. □

Definition 2 (Probability of a program property). The probability that a program P has property $\Phi \in O$ is $\mathbf{Pr}(S_p[\![P]\!] \in \Phi) = S_p[\![P]\!](\mu)(\Phi)$. □

Example 3. The semantics $S_p[\![P]\!] \in \mathcal{D}_p = \Omega_P \rightarrowtail \mathcal{D}_P$ of P as shown in Fig. 1 can be defined with $\mathcal{D}_P \triangleq \mathbb{Z}^3$ denoting the final value of the variables `x`, `y` and `z` and

[1] This is usually formalized by a filtration in measure theory/probabilities.

$$\begin{array}{l}
\texttt{x = 1}\ {}_{\frac{1}{2}}\!\oplus\ \texttt{x = 2;}\\
\texttt{y = 0}\ {}_{\frac{\texttt{x}}{3}}\!\oplus\ \texttt{y = 1;}\\
\texttt{if (y = 0) then}\\
\quad \texttt{z = 2}\ {}_{\frac{1}{4}}\!\oplus\ \texttt{z = 4}\\
\texttt{else}\\
\quad \texttt{z = 1}\ {}_{\frac{1}{5}}\!\oplus\ \texttt{z = 3}
\end{array}$$

ω	$S_p[\![\mathrm{P}]\!](\omega)$	$\mu(\{\omega\})$
$\overleftarrow{x}\,\overleftarrow{y}\,\overleftarrow{z}$	$\langle 1, 0, 2\rangle$	$\frac{1}{2}\cdot\frac{1}{3}\cdot\frac{1}{4}=\frac{1}{24}$
$\overleftarrow{x}\,\overleftarrow{y}\,\overrightarrow{z}$	$\langle 1, 0, 4\rangle$	$\frac{1}{2}\cdot\frac{1}{3}\cdot\frac{3}{4}=\frac{1}{8}$
$\overleftarrow{x}\,\overrightarrow{y}\,\overleftarrow{\overline{z}}$	$\langle 1, 1, 1\rangle$	$\frac{1}{2}\cdot\frac{1}{3}\cdot\frac{1}{5}=\frac{1}{30}$
$\overleftarrow{x}\,\overrightarrow{y}\,\overrightarrow{\overline{z}}$	$\langle 1, 1, 3\rangle$	$\frac{1}{2}\cdot\frac{1}{3}\cdot\frac{4}{5}=\frac{2}{15}$
$\overrightarrow{x}\,\overleftarrow{y}\,\overleftarrow{z}$	$\langle 2, 0, 2\rangle$	$\frac{1}{2}\cdot\frac{2}{3}\cdot\frac{1}{4}=\frac{1}{12}$
$\overrightarrow{x}\,\overleftarrow{y}\,\overrightarrow{z}$	$\langle 2, 0, 4\rangle$	$\frac{1}{2}\cdot\frac{2}{3}\cdot\frac{3}{4}=\frac{1}{4}$
$\overrightarrow{x}\,\overrightarrow{y}\,\overleftarrow{\overline{z}}$	$\langle 2, 1, 1\rangle$	$\frac{1}{2}\cdot\frac{2}{3}\cdot\frac{1}{5}=\frac{1}{15}$
$\overrightarrow{x}\,\overrightarrow{y}\,\overrightarrow{\overline{z}}$	$\langle 2, 1, 3\rangle$	$\frac{1}{2}\cdot\frac{2}{3}\cdot\frac{4}{5}=\frac{4}{15}$

Fig. 1. Program P and its probabilistic concrete semantics

$\Omega_{\mathrm{P}} \triangleq \left\{\omega \in \{\overleftarrow{x}, \overrightarrow{x}\}\cdot\{\overleftarrow{y}, \overrightarrow{y}\}\cdot\{\overleftarrow{z}, \overrightarrow{z}, \epsilon\}\cdot\{\overleftarrow{\overline{z}}, \overrightarrow{\overline{z}}, \epsilon\} \mid |\omega| = 3\right\}$ where $\overleftarrow{x}$ (resp. $\overrightarrow{x}$) denotes the left (resp. right) branch of the first probabilistic choice on x, $\overleftarrow{y}$ (resp. $\overrightarrow{y}$) denotes the left (resp. right) branch of the second probabilistic choice on y, and $\overleftarrow{z}$ and $\overrightarrow{z}$ (resp. $\overleftarrow{\overline{z}}$ and $\overrightarrow{\overline{z}}$) denotes the left or right branch of the third (resp. fourth) probabilistic choice on z. Note that the second probabilistic choice depends on the *value* of x.

We suppose that any scenario is observable, so observable properties are simply $\wp(\Omega_{\mathrm{P}})$, and $\sum_{\omega\in\Omega_{\mathrm{P}}}\mu(\{\omega\}) = 1$. The probability that z = 3 is $\frac{2}{5}$ since $\Phi = \{\langle x, y, z\rangle \in \mathbb{Z}^3 \mid z = 3\}$ and $\mathbf{Pr}(S_p[\![\mathrm{P}]\!] \in \Phi) = \frac{2}{15} + \frac{4}{15} = \frac{2}{5}$. □

3.2 Fixpoint Semantics

This formalization allows us to give an easy definition of probabilistic semantics as fixpoints. Indeed, let $F_\omega : \mathcal{D} \longrightarrow \mathcal{D}$ denote the fixpoint semantic transformer for the (non)-deterministic program P(ω) such that $S_p[\![\mathrm{P}]\!](\omega) = \mathrm{lfp}^{\preceq} F_\omega$. Now define the lifted operator $F_p : (\Omega \to \mathcal{D}) \longrightarrow (\Omega \to \mathcal{D})$ as $F_p(\lambda\,\omega\bullet X_\omega) \triangleq \lambda\,\omega\bullet F_\omega(X_\omega)$. It easily follows from the definition that $S_p[\![\mathrm{P}]\!] = \mathrm{lfp}^{\dot{\preceq}} F_p$. Thus, we can use the usual abstract interpretation framework since semantics are still fixpoints.

Definition 3 (Probabilistic fixpoint semantics). Let $\langle\mathcal{D}, \preceq\rangle$ be a cpo, $\langle\Omega, \mathcal{E}, \mu\rangle$ where $\mathcal{E} \subseteq \wp(\Omega)$ is a probabilistic space, $F[\![\mathrm{P}]\!] : \Omega \longrightarrow \mathcal{D} \longrightarrow \mathcal{D}$ be a pointwise continuous transformer for program P. The probabilistic fixpoint semantics of P is $S_p[\![\mathrm{P}]\!] \triangleq \mathrm{lfp}^{\dot{\preceq}} F_p[\![\mathrm{P}]\!]$ where $\dot{\preceq}$ is the pointwise extension of $\preceq$ and the probabilistic transformer is $F_p[\![\mathrm{P}]\!](s_{\mathcal{P}})\omega \triangleq F[\![\mathrm{P}]\!](\omega)(s_{\mathcal{P}}(\omega))$ such that $F_p[\![\mathrm{P}]\!] : \mathcal{D}_p \longrightarrow \mathcal{D}_p$. □

Lemma 1. Under the conditions of Def. 1 and 3, $S_p[\![\mathrm{P}]\!] \triangleq \mathrm{lfp}^{\dot{\preceq}} F_p[\![\mathrm{P}]\!] = \lambda\,\omega\bullet\,\mathrm{lfp}^{\preceq} F[\![\mathrm{P}]\!](\omega)$ is a probabilistic semantics. □

Example 4 (Probabilistic maximal trace semantics). Let $\langle\Omega, \mathcal{E}, \mu\rangle$ be a probability space, Σ be a set of states, Σ^+ be the non-empty finite sequences of states, $\Sigma^* \triangleq \Sigma^+ \cup \{\epsilon\}$ where ϵ is the *empty trace*, Σ^∞ be infinite sequences of states, $\Sigma^{+\infty} \triangleq \Sigma^+ \cup \Sigma^\infty$, and

$\Sigma^{*\infty} \triangleq \Sigma^* \cup \Sigma^\infty$. The *probabilistic maximal trace semantics* is $S_p^{+\infty}[\![\mathrm{P}]\!] \in \Omega \rightarrowtail \wp(\Sigma^{+\infty})$. For each scenario ω, $S_p^{+\infty}[\![\mathrm{P}]\!]\omega$ describes a finite maximal or infinite execution of program P and, following [4], can be defined in fixpoint form.

Define *sequencing* as $X \mathbin{;} Y \triangleq X^\infty \cup \{\sigma s \sigma' \mid \sigma s \in X^+ \wedge s\sigma' \in Y\}$ where $X^\infty \triangleq X \cap \Sigma^\infty$ and $X^+ \triangleq X \cap \Sigma^+$ and the *restriction* $Y\rceil_X \triangleq \{s\sigma' \in Y \mid \exists \sigma : \sigma s \in X^+\}$ so that $X \mathbin{;} Y = X \mathbin{;} (Y\rceil_X)$. This is extended pointwise to $(X \mathbin{;} Y)\omega \triangleq X(\omega) \mathbin{;} Y(\omega)$. For a while language, we would have ($\mathbb{B} \triangleq \{\mathrm{tt}, \mathrm{ff}\}$, $\mathrm{ff} \Rightarrow \mathrm{tt}$)

$$
\begin{aligned}
&S_p^{+\infty}[\![\texttt{skip}]\!]\omega \triangleq \{ss \mid s \in \Sigma\}\\
&S_p^{+\infty}[\![\texttt{x} := e]\!]\omega \triangleq \left\{ss[\texttt{x} := \mathcal{E}[\![e]\!](\omega)s] \mid s \in \Sigma\right\}^2, \qquad \mathcal{E}[\![e]\!] : \Omega \rightarrowtail (\Sigma \longrightarrow \Sigma)\\
&S_p^{+\infty}[\![C_1 ; C_2]\!] \triangleq S_p^{+\infty}[\![C_1]\!] \mathbin{;} S_p^{+\infty}[\![C_2]\!]\\
&S_p^{+\infty}[\![b]\!]\omega \triangleq \left\{s \mid \mathcal{E}[\![b]\!](\omega)s\right\}^3, \qquad \mathcal{E}[\![b]\!] : \Omega \rightarrowtail (\Sigma \longrightarrow \mathbb{B})\\
&S_p^{+\infty}[\![\texttt{if } b \texttt{ then } C_1 \texttt{ else } C_2]\!] \triangleq S_p^{+\infty}[\![b]\!] \mathbin{;} S_p^{+\infty}[\![C_1]\!] \mathbin{\dot\cup} S_p^{+\infty}[\![\neg b]\!] \mathbin{;} S_p^{+\infty}[\![C_2]\!]\\
&S_p^{+\infty}[\![\texttt{while } b \texttt{ do } C]\!] \triangleq \mathrm{lfp}^{\dot\sqsubseteq} \lambda X \bullet S_p^{+\infty}[\![b]\!] \mathbin{\dot\cup} S_p^{+\infty}[\![\neg b]\!] \mathbin{;} S_p^{+\infty}[\![C]\!] \mathbin{;} X
\end{aligned}
$$

where $\sqsubseteq$ is the *computational ordering* on infinite traces of [4] (such that $(X \sqsubseteq Y) \triangleq (X^+ \subseteq Y^+ \wedge X^\infty \supseteq Y^\infty)$ and $\dot\sqsubseteq$ is the pointwise extension of $\sqsubseteq$. We do not specify the dependence on ω which would also be possible as e.g. in the *Semantics 2* of [17]. □

3.3 Probabilistic Concrete Transformers

Observe that in Def. 3, probabilistic transformers are defined pointwise. A transformer $F : \mathcal{D}_p \longrightarrow \mathcal{D}_p$ is the lifting of the non-deterministic transformer for each scenario: for all $s_\mathcal{P} \in \mathcal{D}_p$, $F(s_\mathcal{P})(\omega) = F_\omega(s_\mathcal{P}(\omega))$.

It follows that the different probabilistic transformers F_ω do not need to share any common properties. But if they do (e.g. they describe two slightly different paths in the control flow graph of the probabilistic program), it can be exploited by the analysis.

In particular, this framework implies the very important fact that transformers that do not correspond to probabilistic statements have a particular form: all the F_ω are the same. Indeed, this can be understood by the fact that the evolution of the program after a particular non-probabilistic statement does not depend on what scenario has been chosen at the beginning of the execution.

Example 5. If the statement after `x = random(1,2)` is `x = x+1` and has G as its transformer, then for any ω_i, G_{ω_i} has just the effect of incrementing the value of `x` by one, regardless of the fact that `x` took the value 1 or 2. □

However, the F_ω are distinct in full generality (e.g. it is the case for `x = random(1,2)`).

3.4 Examples of Probabilistic Semantics

Since each possible (non)-deterministic semantics of the probabilistic program is an outcome of a scenario, the framework totally separates the probabilistic behavior (on

[2] The valuation $\mathcal{E}[\![e]\!]s$ of a pure expression e in state s does not depend on ω when the expression e is not random (i.e. does not use any random variable and/or statement).

[3] The valuation $\mathcal{E}[\![b]\!]s$ of a pure condition b in state s does not depend on ω when the condition b is not random.

the Ω and μ side) from the (non)-deterministic semantic one (located in the $\mathcal{D}$ part). As we will see later, it allows for independent and fruitful abstractions.

Example 6 (Trace to transition system abstraction and profiling). For all $s, s' \in \Sigma$, consider the abstractions $\langle \Omega \rightarrowtail \wp(\Sigma^{+\infty}), \dot{\subseteq} \rangle \xleftarrow[\alpha_s]{\gamma_s} \langle \mathbb{B}, \Leftarrow \rangle$ where $\overrightarrow{\mathsf{reach}}(s) \triangleq \{\sigma s \sigma' \mid \sigma \in \Sigma^* \wedge \sigma' \in \Sigma^{*\infty}\}$ and $\alpha_s(s_{\mathcal{P}}) \triangleq (\exists \omega \in \Omega : s_{\mathcal{P}}(\omega) \in \overrightarrow{\mathsf{reach}}(s))$ as well as $\langle \Omega \rightarrowtail \wp(\Sigma^{+\infty}), \dot{\subseteq} \rangle \xleftarrow[\alpha_{\langle s, s' \rangle}]{\gamma_{\langle s, s' \rangle}} \langle \mathbb{B}, \Leftarrow \rangle$ where $\overrightarrow{\mathsf{succ}}(s, s') \triangleq \{\sigma s s' \sigma' \mid \sigma \in \Sigma^* \wedge \sigma' \in \Sigma^{*\infty}\}$ and $\alpha_{\langle s, s' \rangle}(s_{\mathcal{P}}) \triangleq (\exists \omega \in \Omega : s_{\mathcal{P}}(\omega) \in \overrightarrow{\mathsf{succ}}(s, s'))$. The property that a state $s \in \Sigma$ is definitely reached is $\mathsf{reach}(s) \triangleq \alpha_s(S_p^{+\infty}[\![\mathrm{P}]\!])$ which has probability $\mathbf{Pr}_s \triangleq \mathbf{Pr}(\mathsf{reach}(s))$. The property that a transition $\langle s, s' \rangle \in \Sigma^2$ is definitely chosen is $\mathsf{succ}(s, s') \triangleq \alpha_{\langle s, s' \rangle}(S_p^{+\infty}[\![\mathrm{P}]\!])$ which has probability $\mathbf{Pr}_{\langle s, s' \rangle} \triangleq \mathbf{Pr}(\mathsf{succ}(s, s'))$. We have $\mathbf{Pr}_s = \sum_{s' \in \Sigma} \mathbf{Pr}_{\langle s, s' \rangle}$. The probability attached to a transition $\langle s, s' \rangle \in \Sigma^2$ is the probability of choosing this transition knowing that execution has reached state s which is the conditional probability $\mathbf{Pr}_{\langle s, s' \rangle | s} \triangleq \mathbf{Pr}(\mathsf{succ}(s, s') \mid \mathsf{reach}(s)) = \frac{\mathbf{Pr}_{\langle s, s' \rangle}}{\mathbf{Pr}_s}$ when state s is reachable. In practice, this conditional probability can often be estimated by statistical profiling. This probabilistic transition system is the abstract probabilistic semantics of probabilistic programs that exhibit discrete probabilistic choices considered in many papers such as [11, 13, 15, 23]. □

Example 7 (Trace to control flow graph abstraction). Continuing Ex. 4 and 6, consider the case of states which are pairs $\langle c, m \rangle$ of a control state $c \in \Gamma$ and a memory state $m \in M$ where Γ is finite. Consider the abstraction $\langle \wp(\Sigma \times \Sigma), \subseteq \rangle \xleftarrow[\alpha_G]{\gamma_G} \langle \wp(\Gamma \times \Gamma), \subseteq \rangle$ of states $\langle c, m \rangle$ by their control state c, $\alpha_G(S) \triangleq \{\langle c, c' \rangle \mid \exists m, m' \in M : \langle \langle c, m \rangle, \langle c', m' \rangle \rangle \in S\}$. The control flow graph (CFG) abstraction $\alpha_G \circ \alpha_\tau$ collects control transitions along traces of T. Similar to Ex. 6, the probability attached to an arc $\langle c, c' \rangle \in \Gamma^2$ is the probability of choosing this arc knowing that control has reached c which is the conditional probability $\mathbf{Pr}_{\langle c, c' \rangle | c} \triangleq \mathbf{Pr}(\mathsf{succ}(c, c') \mid \mathsf{reach}(c))$ when c is reachable. Compilers construct over-approximations of this CFG syntactically (not taking e.g. conditionals hence code unreachability into account) and often unsoundly (e.g. considering equiprobability of branches or using profiling). □

Ex. 8 below shows that instead of the trace semantics of Ex. 4 we could have considered as well any denotational, predicate transformer, or axiomatic semantics in the abstract interpretation hierarchy of semantics [4].

Example 8 (Probabilistic abstract semantics). Let $\langle \Omega, \mathcal{E}, \mu \rangle$ be a probability space and $\mathrm{lfp}^{\dot{\preceq}} F_p[\![\mathrm{P}]\!]$ where $F_p : C_p \longrightarrow C_p$ be the probabilistic concrete fixpoint semantics based on the classical concrete semantics $\mathrm{lfp}^{\preceq} F_\omega$ where $\langle C, \preceq \rangle$ is a cpo and $F_\omega : C \longrightarrow C$ for all $\omega \in \Omega$. Consider the classical abstraction $\langle C, \preceq \rangle \xleftarrow[\alpha]{\gamma} \langle \mathcal{A}, \sqsubseteq \rangle$. Let $\mathrm{lfp}^{\dot{\sqsubseteq}} F_p^\sharp$ where $F_p^\sharp : \mathcal{A}_p \longrightarrow \mathcal{A}_p$ be the probabilistic abstract fixpoint semantics based on the classical sound abstract semantics $\mathrm{lfp}^{\preceq} F_\omega \preceq \gamma(\mathrm{lfp}^{\sqsubseteq} F_\omega^\sharp)$ where $\langle \mathcal{A}, \sqsubseteq \rangle$ is a cpo and $F_\omega^\sharp : \mathcal{A} \longrightarrow \mathcal{A}$. Then $\mathrm{lfp}^{\dot{\preceq}} F_p \mathrel{\dot{\preceq}} \gamma_{\mathcal{P}}(\mathrm{lfp}^{\dot{\sqsubseteq}} F_p^\sharp)$ so that the probabilistic lifting of a sound classical abstraction is sound in the sense that in scenario ω, the abstract semantics is $(\mathrm{lfp}^{\dot{\sqsubseteq}} F_p^\sharp)(\omega) = \mathrm{lfp}^{\sqsubseteq} F_\omega^\sharp$. □

$\mathcal{D}$			semantics domain
$\wp(\mathcal{D})$			semantic property domain
$\mathcal{D}_p$	$\triangleq$	$\Omega \rightarrowtail \mathcal{D}$	probabilistic semantics domain
$\mathcal{D}_p^V$	$\subseteq$	$\mathcal{D}_p$	downsized probabilistic semantic domain
$\wp\left(\mathcal{D}_p\right)$	$=$	$\wp(\Omega \rightarrowtail \mathcal{D})$	probabilistic property domain
$\wp\left(\mathcal{D}_p^V\right)$	$\subseteq$	$\wp\left(\mathcal{D}_p\right)$	downsized probabilistic property domain
$\wp(\mathcal{D})_p$	$\triangleq$	$\Omega \rightarrowtail \wp(\mathcal{D})$	collecting semantics domain
$\wp(\mathcal{D})_p^V$	$\subseteq$	$\wp(\mathcal{D})_p$	downsized collecting semantic domain
$\wp\left(\wp(\mathcal{D})_p^V\right)$			properties of collecting semantics domain
$\mathcal{I}_{\dot\subseteq}(\wp(\mathcal{D})_p^V)$			downset properties of collecting semantics domain
$\wp\left(\wp(\mathcal{D})_p^V\right)/_{\doteq}$			probabilistic concrete collecting semantics domain

Fig. 2. Concrete and abstract semantics domains

In practice, the simple abstractions considered in Ex. 8 are not powerful enough, in particular because Ω is in general infinite and needs further abstractions and we want to consider more general probabilistic properties as defined in next Sect. 4.

4 Probabilistic Concrete Collecting Semantics

The concrete/abstract semantics domains introduced here are summarized in Fig. 2.

4.1 Definition

Concrete properties of programs are elements of the usual concrete domain: the powerset of the program semantics domain, denoted by $\wp\left(\mathcal{D}_p\right) = \wp(\Omega \rightarrowtail \mathcal{D})$. The logical implication order is $\subseteq$.

Definition 4 (Probabilistic concrete collecting semantics). Under the conditions of Def. 1, the *probabilistic concrete property domain* is the complete lattice $\langle \wp\left(\mathcal{D}_p\right), \subseteq, \emptyset, \mathcal{D}_p, \cup, \cap\rangle$. The *probabilistic collecting semantics* of a program P is its strongest probabilistic property $\{S_p[\![\mathrm{P}]\!]\}$ [6]. □

The probabilistic concrete property domain $\wp\left(\mathcal{D}_p\right)$ allows us to express any particular probabilistic property.

Example 9 (Probability of a program property). The probabilistic property of verifying a non-probabilistic property $\Gamma \in \wp(\mathcal{D})$ with probability at least 0.7 is:

$$\Phi = \left\{s_{\mathcal{P}} \in \mathcal{D}_p \mid \mathbf{Pr}(s_{\mathcal{P}} \in \Gamma) \geq 0.7\right\} = \left\{s_{\mathcal{P}} \in \mathcal{D}_p \;\middle|\; \int_{\Omega} \chi_\Gamma(s_{\mathcal{P}}(\omega))d\mu(\omega) \geq 0.7\right\}. \square$$

The probabilistic concrete property domain $\wp\left(\mathcal{D}_p\right)$ also makes it possible to express program properties that are specifically probabilistic, as illustrated by the following examples 10 and 11.

Example 10 (Game gain expectation). Assume a gambling program P allows the owner to win or lose some money at the end of its execution. The win or loss amount for a specific program semantics is given by a measurable function $\kappa : \mathcal{D} \rightarrowtail \mathbb{Z}$, $\mathbb{Z}$ having the σ-algebra $\wp(\mathbb{Z})$. Then it is straightforward to define the property that a probabilistic program is on expectation a winning strategy:

$$\Phi' = \left\{ s_{\mathcal{P}} \in \mathcal{D}_p \mid \mathbb{E}(\kappa \circ s_{\mathcal{P}}) > 0 \right\} = \left\{ s_{\mathcal{P}} \in \mathcal{D}_p \,\middle|\, \int_{\Omega} \kappa(s_{\mathcal{P}}(\omega)) d\mu(\omega) > 0 \right\} . \quad \square$$

Example 11 (Probabilistic temporal logics). The probabilistic μ-calculus of [22] or the linear-time probabilistic temporal logic of [12] describe probabilistic properties of execution traces. So their semantics can be described by (abstractions of) elements of $\wp(\Omega \rightarrowtail \Sigma^{\infty})$. □

Of course, we basically have no effective way to automatically compute an integral on an arbitrary space Ω. This is not a problem since Def. 4 is a concrete semantics which is not required to be computable nor decidable in any way. This undecidability problem will be tackled by considering abstract semantics.

4.2 Downsizing the Concrete Collecting Domain

Allowing semantics to be any measurable function ensures a good expressivity but may be *too precise*. It is often preferable not to distinguish between similar situations. Indeed, making concrete semantics too verbose makes abstractions less precise, because abstract transformers take meaningless concrete semantics into account. It will become clearer when we design abstract transformers in Sect. 5.3.

Example 12. In the case of Ex. 1 of the non-biased coin above, swapping the values of $S_p[\![\mathrm{P}]\!](\omega_1)$ and $S_p[\![\mathrm{P}]\!](\omega_2)$ is impactless: both objects have exactly the same behavior. What changes is that the scenarios do not have the same *meaning* in both cases: in the first case ω_i stands for the *situation when* $x = i$ whereas it stands for the *situation when* $x = 3 - i$ in the other one. □

To overcome this issue, we simply abstract away similar situations by restricting the concrete domain to the *relevant* semantics. It is not possible to define *relevant* formally as it depends on the specific instance of the framework. Therefore, we assume that there exists a *sanity checker*: it is a characteristic function $V : \mathcal{D}_p \longrightarrow \{0, 1\}$ that decides whether a semantics in $\mathcal{D}_p$ is valid, i.e. is actually of interest. The sanity checker V defines the corresponding set $\mathcal{D}_p^V \triangleq \{s_{\mathcal{P}} \in \mathcal{D}_p \mid V(s_{\mathcal{P}}) = 1\}$.

Thus, the *valid/real* concrete semantics domain is $\wp\left(\mathcal{D}_p^V\right)$ instead of $\wp\left(\mathcal{D}_p\right)$. Actually, $\mathcal{D}_p$ is a particular $\mathcal{D}_p^V$ with V accepting everything.

This process of downsizing a domain $\wp\left(\mathcal{D}_p^{V'}\right)$ to a domain $\wp\left(\mathcal{D}_p^V\right)$ when $\mathcal{D}_p^V \subseteq \mathcal{D}_p^{V'}$ (i.e. V is more restrictive than V') is a simple abstraction where the abstraction $\alpha_{V,V'}(S) \triangleq \{s_{\mathcal{P}} \in S \mid V(s_{\mathcal{P}}) = 1\}$ for $S \subseteq \mathcal{D}_p^{V'}$ simply *forgets* every semantics that is not in $\mathcal{D}_p^V$. It is a Galois connection:

$$\langle \wp\left(\mathcal{D}_p^{V'}\right), \subseteq \rangle \xleftarrow[\alpha_{V,V'}]{\gamma_{V,V'}} \langle \wp\left(\mathcal{D}_p^V\right), \subseteq \rangle .$$

Thus, for any sanity checker V, $\wp\left(\mathcal{D}_p^V\right)$ is an abstraction of $\wp\left(\mathcal{D}_p\right)$. The more restrictive is the sanity checker, the more precise the subsequent abstractions will be (see the abstraction of transformers in Sect. 5.3).

5 Probabilistic Abstract Semantics

We explore here three directions to abstract the probabilistic concrete collecting semantics of Sect. 4. The first one (I) in Sect. 5.1 is to abstract on the semantics side, i.e. abstract $\mathcal{D}$ (this is where it is possible to plug existing non-probabilistic analyses). The second (II) in Sect. 5.2 is to abstract the scenario space Ω by losing some precision on the probabilistic part of the semantics. Finally, the third axis (III) in Sect. 5.3 is to abstract the measurable functions representing the semantics by their distributions.

It is a comprehensive description of the way to *lift* any non-probabilistic analysis to the probabilistic setting. For instance, we can then obtain information such as "$x \in [1,4]$ with probability 0.7" instead of "x is always in $[1,4]$" which may not be provable without probabilistic hypotheses.

5.1 (I) Abstracting the Semantics

Given a classical abstract interpretation $\langle \wp(\mathcal{D}), \subseteq \rangle \underset{\alpha}{\overset{\gamma}{\leftrightarrows}} \langle \mathcal{A}, \sqsubseteq \rangle$ such as the interval abstraction, we now describe a way to *lift* any such non-probabilistic analysis to the probabilistic setting. The probabilistic properties considered in Sect. 4 belong to $\wp\left(\mathcal{D}_p^V\right) \subseteq \wp(\Omega \rightarrowtail \mathcal{D})$ where classical properties $\wp(\mathcal{D})$ on which to apply classical abstractions do not appear explicitly. So we have to abstract $\wp\left(\mathcal{D}_p^V\right)$ into a probabilistic collecting semantics domain in which classical properties $\wp(\mathcal{D})$ appear explicitly.

An Inadequate Solution. An immediate solution is to take the classical collecting semantics on each scenario, leading to measurable functions in the set $\wp(\mathcal{D})_p \triangleq \Omega \rightarrowtail \wp(\mathcal{D})$ where the σ-algebra taken on $\wp(\mathcal{D})$ is the powerset of the one on $\mathcal{D}$. The natural logical order between these objects is the pointwise order

$$\forall s, s' \in \wp(\mathcal{D})_p^V, s \leq s' \text{ iff } s \mathrel{\dot{\subseteq}} s' .$$

Indeed, $\leq$ means that a probabilistic semantic property is more precise than another one if it is the case on every scenario.

However, the problem is now that we cannot reason on $\wp(\mathcal{D})_p \triangleq \Omega \rightarrowtail \wp(\mathcal{D})$ in classical logical terms with the logical implication $\subseteq$ because elements are not sets but functions. And there is no simple order that works with further abstractions.

Probabilistic Collecting Semantics. So, to express properties of these objects, as above, we turn to the powerset $\wp\left(\wp(\mathcal{D})_p\right) = \wp(\Omega \rightarrowtail \wp(\mathcal{D}))$, where the implication order is the inclusion order $\subseteq$ on the sets. This leads to the consideration of properties of the pointwise collecting semantics so that we can manipulate properties of semantic properties. For example, the strongest property of a program semantics $S_p[\![\mathrm{P}]\!] \in \mathcal{D}_p = \Omega \rightarrowtail \mathcal{D}$ is $\{\lambda\,\omega \bullet \{S_p[\![\mathrm{P}]\!]\omega\}\}$. It is interesting to note that while this step is implicit in the non-probabilistic case[4] (see Sect. 5.2), it is essential in the probabilistic setting.

The concrete collecting domain may have to be downsized as in Sect. 4.2 by considering $\wp(\mathcal{D})_p^V$ which is the restriction of $\wp(\mathcal{D})_p$ to functions that are coherent with V in the straightforward sense, i.e. any concretization verifies V.

The correspondence between the downsized probabilistic property domain and the properties of the collecting semantics domain is given by the easily proven Galois connection

$$\langle \wp\left(\mathcal{D}_p^V\right),\ \subseteq\rangle \xrightleftharpoons[\alpha_{\mathcal{D}}]{\gamma_{\mathcal{D}}} \langle \wp\left(\wp(\mathcal{D})_p^V\right),\ \subseteq\rangle$$

where $\alpha_{\mathcal{D}}$ and $\gamma_{\mathcal{D}}$ are defined for all $S \in \wp\left(\mathcal{D}_p^V\right)$ and $T \in \wp\left(\wp(\mathcal{D})_p^V\right)$ as:

$$\alpha_{\mathcal{D}}(S) \triangleq \left\{t_{\mathcal{P}} \in \wp(\mathcal{D})_p^V \;\middle|\; \exists s_{\mathcal{P}} \in S : \forall \omega \in \Omega : t_{\mathcal{P}}(\omega) = \{s_{\mathcal{P}}(\omega)\}\right\} = \left\{\lambda\,\omega \in \Omega \bullet \{s_{\mathcal{P}}(\omega)\} \;\middle|\; s_{\mathcal{P}} \in S\right\}$$
$$\gamma_{\mathcal{D}}(T) \triangleq \left\{s_{\mathcal{P}} \in \mathcal{D}_p^V \;\middle|\; \exists t_{\mathcal{P}} \in T : \forall \omega \in \Omega : s_{\mathcal{P}}(\omega) \in t_{\mathcal{P}}(\omega)\right\} .$$

And actually, the only question we are interested in is to know whether a collecting semantics $C \in \wp(\mathcal{D})_p^V$ satisfies a property $S \in \wp\left(\wp(\mathcal{D})_p^V\right)$ or any more precise property, that is $C \in \downarrow S$ where $\downarrow S \triangleq \left\{s' \in \wp(\mathcal{D})_p^V \;\middle|\; \exists s \in S, s' \mathrel{\dot{\subseteq}} s\right\}$ is the downward closed set of S (or *downset*) for $\dot{\subseteq}$. It shows that the properties of interest are downward closed sets $\mathcal{I}_{\dot{\subseteq}}\left(\wp(\mathcal{D})_p^V\right)$ in $\wp\left(\wp(\mathcal{D})_p^V\right)$ themselves ordered by $\subseteq$.

The correspondence between $\langle \wp\left(\wp(\mathcal{D})_p^V\right),\ \subseteq\rangle$ and $\langle \mathcal{I}_{\dot{\subseteq}}\left(\wp(\mathcal{D})_p^V\right),\ \subseteq\rangle$ is a straightforward Galois connection $\langle \wp\left(\wp(\mathcal{D})_p^V\right),\ \subseteq\rangle \xrightleftharpoons[\alpha_{\downarrow}]{\gamma_{\downarrow}} \langle \mathcal{I}_{\dot{\subseteq}}\left(\wp(\mathcal{D})_p^V\right),\ \subseteq\rangle$ defined by $\alpha_{\downarrow}(S) \triangleq \downarrow S = \{s' \in \wp(\mathcal{D})_p^V \mid \exists s \in S, s' \mathrel{\dot{\subseteq}} s\}$, and accordingly $\gamma_{\downarrow}(I) \triangleq \{s \mid \forall s' \in \wp(\mathcal{D})_p^V : (s' \mathrel{\dot{\subseteq}} s) \implies s' \in I\}$. The proof is left to the reader.

$C \in \downarrow S$ can also be expressed as $\forall s \in C : \exists s' \in S : s \mathrel{\dot{\subseteq}} s'$. This leads to define a pre-order $\ddot{\subseteq}$ where the Hoare preorder $\ddot{\sqsubseteq}$ is defined for any $\dot{\sqsubseteq}$ as follows

$$\forall S, S' \in \wp\left(\wp(\mathcal{D})_p^V\right), S \mathrel{\ddot{\sqsubseteq}} S' \text{ iff } \forall s \in S : \exists s' \in S' : s \mathrel{\dot{\sqsubseteq}} s' .$$

To get a partial order, it is necessary to quotient by the associated equivalence relation $S \mathrel{\ddot{\equiv}} S' \triangleq S \mathrel{\ddot{\sqsubseteq}} S' \wedge S' \mathrel{\ddot{\sqsubseteq}} S$. In the rest of the paper, we denote by $[S]_{\equiv} \triangleq \{S' \mid S' \equiv S\}$ the equivalence class of the element S for the equivalence relation $\equiv$, or simply $[S]$ when the relation $\equiv$ is obvious from the context.

We have $\langle \mathcal{I}_{\dot{\subseteq}}(\wp(\mathcal{D})_p^V),\ \subseteq\rangle \xrightleftharpoons[\ddot{\alpha}_{\mathcal{I}}]{\ddot{\gamma}_{\mathcal{I}}} \langle \wp\left(\wp(\mathcal{D})_p^V\right)/_{\ddot{\equiv}_{\subseteq}},\ \ddot{\subseteq}\rangle$ meaning that the complete downset lattice of initial segments $\langle \mathcal{I}_{\dot{\subseteq}}(\wp(\mathcal{D})_p^V),\ \subseteq\rangle$ is Galois-isomorphic to the complete lattice $\langle \wp\left(\wp(\mathcal{D})_p^V\right)/_{\ddot{\equiv}_{\subseteq}},\ \ddot{\subseteq}\rangle$ where $\ddot{\alpha}_{\mathcal{I}}(I) \triangleq [I]_{\ddot{\equiv}_{\subseteq}}$ and $\ddot{\gamma}_{\mathcal{I}}([S]_{\ddot{\equiv}_{\subseteq}}) \triangleq \{s \mid \exists s' \in S : s \mathrel{\dot{\subseteq}} s'\}$. The proof is left to the reader.

[4] When $\Omega = \{\bullet\}$, $\wp(\Omega \rightarrowtail \mathcal{D})$ is isomorphic to $\wp(\mathcal{D})$, so we essentially get $\wp(\wp(\mathcal{D}))$ which, in the classical case, is often abstracted into $\wp(\mathcal{D})$ by $\langle \wp(\wp(\mathcal{D})),\ \subseteq\rangle \xrightleftharpoons[\alpha_{\cup}]{\gamma_{\cup}} \langle \wp(\mathcal{D}),\ \subseteq\rangle$ where $\alpha_{\cup}(P) \triangleq \bigcup P$ and $\gamma_{\cup}(Q) \triangleq \wp(Q)$, which amounts to taking initial segments for the order $\subseteq$. See Sect. 5.2 for more details.

The two visions $\langle \mathcal{I}_{\dot{\sqsubseteq}}(\wp(\mathcal{D})_p^V), \subseteq\rangle \xleftrightarrow[\ddot{\alpha}_I]{\ddot{\gamma}_I} \langle \wp\left(\wp(\mathcal{D})_p^V\right)/_{\doteqdot}, \ddot{\sqsubseteq}\rangle$ are equivalent, but we find the "$\ddot{\sqsubseteq}$-approach" much more intuitive for the rest of this paper. It accounts to looking at sets of properties simply as "what may happen is over-approximated by these elements" instead of "everything that can happen is to be found in this set".

Example 13. Consider Ω and the interval property $\Gamma = \{\lambda\omega \bullet x \in [1, 10]\}$ (i.e. the set of mesurable functions where for each scenario ω, x is in $[1, 10]$) where $\sqsubseteq$ is interval inclusion. Let the program semantics be $S_p[\![\mathrm{P}]\!] = \{\lambda\omega \bullet x \in [3, 3], \lambda\omega \bullet x \in [7, 7]\}$. The fact that program "P satisfies property Γ" is $\left[S_p[\![\mathrm{P}]\!]\right] \ddot{\sqsubseteq} [\Gamma]$, i.e. $S_p[\![\mathrm{P}]\!] \ddot{\sqsubseteq} \Gamma$ or equivalently $\forall s \in S_p[\![\mathrm{P}]\!] : \exists s' \in \Gamma : s \dot{\sqsubseteq} s'$ that is $\forall s \in S_p[\![\mathrm{P}]\!] : \exists s' \in \Gamma : \forall\omega \in \Omega : s(\omega) \sqsubseteq s'(\omega)$ which holds since $[3, 3] \sqsubseteq [1, 10]$ and $[7, 7] \sqsubseteq [1, 10]$. Note that we do *not* have the inclusion $\{S_p[\![\mathrm{P}]\!]\} \subseteq \Gamma$, so the Hoare order is really what is meaningful for us. □

In particular, a set with only $\top$ is larger than any other one. The above explanations justify the following definition.

Definition 5 (Probabilistic concrete collecting semantics domain). The *probabilistic concrete collecting semantics domain* is

$$\langle \wp\left(\wp(\mathcal{D})_p^V\right)/_{\doteqdot}, \ddot{\sqsubseteq}\rangle\,. \qquad \square$$

This will be the base domain for the abstractions we describe below, coming from the Galois connection

$$\langle \wp\left(\mathcal{D}_p^V\right), \subseteq\rangle \xleftrightarrow[\alpha_{\mathcal{D}}]{\gamma_{\mathcal{D}}} \langle \wp\left(\wp(\mathcal{D})_p^V\right), \subseteq\rangle \xleftrightarrow[\ddot{\alpha}_I \circ \alpha_{\downarrow}]{\gamma_{\downarrow} \circ \ddot{\gamma}_I} \langle \wp\left(\wp(\mathcal{D})_p^V\right)/_{\doteqdot_{\subseteq}}, \ddot{\subseteq}\rangle$$

such that lem. 2 below is satisfied.

Lemma 2. Given a probabilistic property $\Phi \in \wp(\mathcal{D})_p^V$, we have

$$\ddot{\alpha}_I \circ \alpha_{\downarrow} \circ \alpha_{\mathcal{D}}(\Phi) = \left[\left\{\lambda\omega \bullet \{s_{\mathcal{P}}(\omega)\} \mid s_{\mathcal{P}} \in \Phi\right\}\right]_{\doteqdot_{\subseteq}}. \qquad \square$$

Proof. $\ddot{\alpha}_I \circ \alpha_{\downarrow} \circ \alpha_{\mathcal{D}}(\Phi)$

$= \ddot{\alpha}_I \circ \alpha_{\downarrow}\left(\left\{t_{\mathcal{P}} \in \wp(\mathcal{D})_p^V \mid \exists s'_{\mathcal{P}} \in \Phi : \forall\omega \in \Omega : t_{\mathcal{P}}(\omega) = \{s'_{\mathcal{P}}(\omega)\}\right\}\right)$ ⟅def. $\alpha_{\mathcal{D}}$ and $\wp(\mathcal{D})_p^V$⟆

$= \ddot{\alpha}_I\left(\left\{s_{\mathcal{P}} \in \wp(\mathcal{D})_p^V \mid \exists t_{\mathcal{P}} \in \wp(\mathcal{D})_p^V : \exists s'_{\mathcal{P}} \in \Phi : \forall\omega \in \Omega : t_{\mathcal{P}}(\omega) = \{s'_{\mathcal{P}}(\omega)\} \wedge \forall\omega \in \Omega : s_{\mathcal{P}}(\omega) \subseteq t_{\mathcal{P}}(\omega)\right\}\right)$ ⟅def. $\alpha_{\downarrow}$, $\wp(\mathcal{D})_p^V$ and $\dot{\subseteq}$⟆

$= \left[\left\{s_{\mathcal{P}} \in \wp(\mathcal{D})_p^V \mid \exists s'_{\mathcal{P}} \in \Phi : \forall\omega \in \Omega : s_{\mathcal{P}}(\omega) \subseteq \{s'_{\mathcal{P}}(\omega)\}\right\}\right]_{\doteqdot_{\subseteq}}$ ⟅set theory and def. $\ddot{\alpha}_I$⟆

$= \left[\left\{\lambda\omega \bullet \emptyset\right\} \cup \left\{\lambda\omega \bullet \{s'_{\mathcal{P}}(\omega)\} \mid s'_{\mathcal{P}} \in \Phi\right\}\right]_{\doteqdot_{\subseteq}}$

⟅since $s_{\mathcal{P}}(\omega) \subseteq \{s'_{\mathcal{P}}(\omega)\}$ implies $s_{\mathcal{P}}(\omega) = \emptyset$ or $s_{\mathcal{P}}(\omega) = \{s'_{\mathcal{P}}(\omega)\}$⟆

$= \left[\left\{\lambda\omega \bullet \{s'_{\mathcal{P}}(\omega)\} \mid s'_{\mathcal{P}} \in \Phi\right\}\right]_{\doteqdot_{\subseteq}}$ ⟅def. $\doteqdot_{\subseteq}$.⟆ □

Example 14 (Probabilistic maximal trace collecting semantics). Continuing Ex. 4, the probabilistic maximal trace semantics is $S_p^{+\infty}[\![\mathrm{P}]\!] \in \Omega \rightarrowtail \mathcal{D}$ where $\mathcal{D} \triangleq \wp(\Sigma^{+\infty})$ so that the *probabilistic maximal powertraces collecting semantics* is $S_p^{\{\{+\infty\}\}}[\![\mathrm{P}]\!] \triangleq \ddot{\alpha}_I \circ \alpha_{\downarrow} \circ \alpha_{\mathcal{D}}(\{S_p^{+\infty}[\![\mathrm{P}]\!]\})$ proving, by Lem. 2, that

$$S_p^{\{\{+\infty\}\}}[\![\mathrm{P}]\!] = \left[\left\{\lambda\omega \bullet \{S_p^{+\infty}[\![\mathrm{P}]\!](\omega)\}\right\}\right]_{\doteqdot_{\sqsubseteq}} \in \wp(\Omega \rightarrowtail \wp(\wp(\Sigma^{+\infty})))/_{\doteqdot}. \qquad \square$$

Lemma 3. A probabilistic semantics $s_{\mathcal{P}} \in \mathcal{D}_p$ satisfies a probabilistic property $\Phi \in \wp(\mathcal{D})^V_p$ if and only if $s_{\mathcal{P}} \in \gamma_{\mathcal{D}}(\Phi)$ if and only if $\ddot{\alpha}_{\mathcal{I}} \circ \alpha_{\downarrow} \circ \alpha_{\mathcal{D}}(\{s_{\mathcal{P}}\}) \ddot{\subseteq} \left[\{\Phi\}\right]_{\doteqdot_{\subseteq}}$. □

The proof is straightforward from the definitions and is left to the reader.

Example 15 (Probability of trace properties). Continuing Ex. 4, the probability that the trace semantics $S_p^{+\infty}[\![\mathrm{P}]\!]$ satisfies an observable property $\Phi \in \mathcal{F} \subseteq \wp(\wp(\Sigma^{+\infty}))$ (such as determinism $\Phi = \{\{\sigma\} \mid \sigma \in \Sigma^{+\infty}\}$) is given by the distribution $S_p^{+\infty}[\![\mathrm{P}]\!](\mu) : \mathcal{F} \longrightarrow [0, 1]$ such that $S_p^{+\infty}[\![\mathrm{P}]\!](\mu)\Phi = \mathbf{Pr}\left(S_p^{+\infty}[\![\mathrm{P}]\!] \in \Phi\right) = \mathbf{Pr}\left(\forall\omega : S_p^{+\infty}[\![\mathrm{P}]\!](\omega) \in \Phi\right) = \mathbf{Pr}\left(S_p^{+\infty}[\![\mathrm{P}]\!](\omega) \in \{\lambda\,\omega \bullet \Phi' \mid \Phi' \subseteq \Phi\}\right) = \mathbf{Pr}\left(S_p^{+\infty}[\![\mathrm{P}]\!](\omega) \in \downarrow\{\lambda\,\omega \bullet \Phi\}\right)$ which, by Lem. 3, is

$$\mathbf{Pr}\left(\ddot{\alpha}_{\mathcal{I}} \circ \alpha_{\downarrow} \circ \alpha_{\mathcal{D}}(\{s_{\mathcal{P}}\}) \ddot{\subseteq} \left[\{\downarrow\{\lambda\,\omega \bullet \Phi\}\}\right]_{\doteqdot_{\sqsubseteq}}\right) = \mathbf{Pr}\left(\ddot{\alpha}_{\mathcal{I}} \circ \alpha_{\downarrow} \circ \alpha_{\mathcal{D}}(\{s_{\mathcal{P}}\}) \ddot{\subseteq} \left[\{\lambda\,\omega \bullet \Phi\}\right]_{\doteqdot_{\sqsubseteq}}\right)$$

$$= \int_{\Omega} \chi_{\left[\{\lambda_{\omega} \bullet \Phi\}\right]_{\doteqdot_{\sqsubseteq}}} (\ddot{\alpha}_{\mathcal{I}} \circ \alpha_{\downarrow} \circ \alpha_{\mathcal{D}} \circ S_p^{+\infty}[\![\mathrm{P}]\!](\omega))\mathrm{d}\mu(\omega).$$ □

Semantics Abstraction. Now that we gained access to semantic properties, we can generalize $\langle\wp(\mathcal{D}), \subseteq\rangle$ to any concrete domain $\langle C, \leq\rangle$. We assume that we have a Galois connection with an abstract domain $\mathcal{A}$: $\langle C, \leq\rangle \underset{\alpha}{\overset{\gamma}{\leftrightarrows}} \langle\mathcal{A}, \sqsubseteq\rangle$ as mentioned above. However, it is required that C and $\mathcal{A}$ are measurable spaces (as before, their σ-algebra express observable behaviors), and that α and γ are measurable functions.

The semantics abstraction is now by composition. Thus, noting $C_p = \Omega \rightarrowtail C$ and $\mathcal{A}_p = \Omega \rightarrowtail \mathcal{A}$, the concrete and abstract semantics domains are $\langle\wp\left(C_p\right)/_{\equiv_{\leq}}, \ddot{\leq}\rangle$ and $\langle\wp\left(\mathcal{A}_p\right)/_{\equiv_{\sqsubseteq}}, \ddot{\sqsubseteq}\rangle$.

The abstraction is defined by composition in terms of elements of C_p and $\mathcal{A}_p$, and it is then lifted to powersets and equivalence classes to be coherent with the domains just mentioned. So, for $s_{\mathcal{P}} \in C_p$, $\alpha \circ s_{\mathcal{P}} \in \mathcal{A}_p$ and conversely, if $t_{\mathcal{P}} \in \mathcal{A}_p$, then $\gamma \circ t_{\mathcal{P}} \in C_p$. It defines the Galois connection

$$\langle\wp\left(C_p\right)/_{\doteqdot_{\leq}}, \ddot{\leq}\rangle \underset{\ddot{\alpha}_{\alpha}}{\overset{\ddot{\gamma}_{\alpha}}{\leftrightarrows}} \langle\wp\left(\mathcal{A}_p\right)/\doteqdot_{\sqsubseteq}, \ddot{\sqsubseteq}\rangle$$

pointwise where

$$\ddot{\alpha}_{\alpha} \triangleq \lambda[S] \bullet \left[\left\{\lambda\,\omega \bullet \alpha \circ s_{\mathcal{P}}(\omega) \;\middle|\; s_{\mathcal{P}} \in S\right\}\right]_{\doteqdot_{\sqsubseteq}} \qquad \ddot{\gamma}_{\alpha} \triangleq \lambda[T] \bullet \left[\left\{s_{\mathcal{P}} \in C_p \;\middle|\; \exists t \in T,\, s_{\mathcal{P}} \dot{\leq} \gamma \circ t\right\}\right]_{\doteqdot_{\leq}}$$

(it is easy to verify that these functions are well-defined, i.e. they do not depend on the representent picked for $[S]$ and $[T]$, and that they are properly measurable).

Example 16 (Set of traces to traces abstraction). Continuing Ex. 4 and 14, consider the abstraction of sets of traces into traces $\langle\wp(\wp(\Sigma^{+\infty})), \subseteq\rangle \underset{\alpha_{\cup}}{\overset{\gamma_{\cup}}{\leftrightarrows}} \langle\wp(\Sigma^{+\infty}), \subseteq\rangle$ with $\alpha_{\cup}(S) \triangleq \bigcup S$ and $\gamma_{\cup}(T) = \wp(T)$ as first performed in most classical static analyses. The *probabilistic trace collecting semantics* is

$$S_p^{\{+\infty\}}[\![\mathrm{P}]\!] \triangleq \ddot{\alpha}_{\alpha_\cup}(S_p^{\{\{+\infty\}\}}[\![\mathrm{P}]\!]) \in \wp(\Omega \rightarrowtail \wp(\Sigma^{+\infty}))/_{\ddot{\equiv}_\subseteq}$$

$$= \ddot{\alpha}_{\alpha_\cup}\Big(\big[\{\lambda\,\omega\bullet\{S_p^{+\infty}[\![\mathrm{P}]\!](\omega)\}\}\big]_{\ddot{\equiv}_\subseteq}\Big) \qquad \text{(def. } S_p^{\{\{+\infty\}\}}[\![\mathrm{P}]\!] \text{ in Ex. 14)}$$

$$= \Big[\big\{\lambda\,\omega\bullet\alpha_\cup(s_{\mathcal{P}}(\omega)) \;\big|\; s_{\mathcal{P}} \in \big[\{\lambda\,\omega\bullet\{S_p^{+\infty}[\![\mathrm{P}]\!](\omega)\}\}\big]_{\ddot{\equiv}_\subseteq}\big\}\Big]_{\ddot{\equiv}_\subseteq} \qquad \text{(def. } \ddot{\alpha}_{\alpha_\cup}\text{)}$$

$$= \Big[\big\{\lambda\,\omega\bullet\alpha_\cup\big(\{S_p^{+\infty}[\![\mathrm{P}]\!](\omega)\}\big)\big\}\Big]_{\ddot{\equiv}_\subseteq} \qquad \text{(def. } \ddot{\equiv}_\subseteq\text{)}$$

$$= \Big[\big\{\lambda\,\omega\bullet S_p^{+\infty}[\![\mathrm{P}]\!](\omega)\big\}\Big]_{\ddot{\equiv}_\subseteq} \qquad \text{(def. } \alpha_\cup\text{)} \qquad \square$$

Example 17 (Traces to reachability abstraction). Continuing Ex. 4, 14, and 16, consider the reachability abstraction $\langle\wp(\Sigma^{+\infty}),\ \subseteq\rangle \xrightleftharpoons[\alpha_r]{\gamma_r} \langle\wp(\Sigma),\ \subseteq\rangle$ such that $\alpha_r(T) \triangleq \{s \in \Sigma \mid \exists\sigma,\sigma' : \sigma s \sigma' \in T\}$ collecting states along traces of T. Applying the above semantics abstraction, the *probabilistic reachability semantics* is

$$S_p^r[\![\mathrm{P}]\!] \triangleq \ddot{\alpha}_{\alpha_r}(S_p^{\{+\infty\}}[\![\mathrm{P}]\!]) \in \wp(\Omega \rightarrowtail \wp(\Sigma^{+\infty}))/_{\ddot{\equiv}}$$

$$= \ddot{\alpha}_{\alpha_r}\Big(\big[\{\lambda\,\omega\bullet S_p^{+\infty}[\![\mathrm{P}]\!](\omega)\}\big]_{\ddot{\equiv}_\subseteq}\Big) \qquad \text{(def. } S_p^{\{+\infty\}}[\![\mathrm{P}]\!] \text{ in Ex. 16)}$$

$$= \Big[\big\{\lambda\,\omega\bullet\alpha_r(s_{\mathcal{P}}(\omega)) \;\big|\; s_{\mathcal{P}} \in \big[\{\lambda\,\omega\bullet S_p^{+\infty}[\![\mathrm{P}]\!](\omega)\}\big]_{\ddot{\equiv}_\subseteq}\big\}\Big]_{\ddot{\equiv}_\subseteq} \qquad \text{(def. } \ddot{\alpha}_{\alpha_r}\text{)}$$

$$= \Big[\big\{\lambda\,\omega\bullet\alpha_r\big(S_p^{+\infty}[\![\mathrm{P}]\!](\omega)\big)\big\}\Big]_{\ddot{\equiv}_\subseteq} \qquad \text{(def. } \ddot{\equiv}_\subseteq\text{)}$$

$$= \Big[\big\{\lambda\,\omega\bullet\{s\in\Sigma \mid \exists\sigma,\sigma' : \sigma s\sigma' \in S_p^{+\infty}[\![\mathrm{P}]\!](\omega)\}\big\}\Big]_{\ddot{\equiv}_\subseteq} \qquad \text{(def. } \alpha_r\text{)}$$

The probabilistic reachability semantics is therefore the downward closed set of the function taking each scenario to the minimal reachability abstraction of its behavior. $\square$

Example 18 (Probability of invariance properties). Continuing the trace to reachability abstraction example 17, the probability that a program invariant $I \in \wp(\Sigma)$ holds during execution (assuming that the abstract property I is properly measurable) is

$$S_p^{+\infty}[\![\mathrm{P}]\!](\mu)(\gamma_r(I))$$

$$\triangleq \mathbf{Pr}(S_p^{+\infty}[\![\mathrm{P}]\!] \in \gamma_r(I)) \qquad \text{(def. 2 of property probability)}$$

$$= \mathbf{Pr}(\ddot{\alpha}_{\mathcal{I}} \circ \alpha_\downarrow \circ \alpha_{\mathcal{D}}(S_p^{+\infty}[\![\mathrm{P}]\!]) \mathrel{\ddot{\subseteq}} [\{\gamma_r(I)\}]_{\ddot{\equiv}_\subseteq}) \qquad \text{(Lem. 3)}$$

$$= \mathbf{Pr}(\ddot{\alpha}_{\alpha_r} \circ \ddot{\alpha}_{\mathcal{I}} \circ \alpha_\downarrow \circ \alpha_{\mathcal{D}}(S_p^{+\infty}[\![\mathrm{P}]\!]) \mathrel{\ddot{\subseteq}} [\{\lambda\,\omega\bullet I\}]_{\ddot{\equiv}_\subseteq}) \qquad \text{(Galois connexion } \alpha_r, \gamma_r\text{)}$$

$$= \mathbf{Pr}(S_p^r[\![\mathrm{P}]\!] \mathrel{\ddot{\subseteq}} [\{\lambda\,\omega\bullet I\}]_{\ddot{\equiv}_\subseteq}) \qquad \text{(def. } S_p^r[\![\mathrm{P}]\!] \text{ in Ex. 17.)}$$

Therefore we can define the *invariant probability semantics* $S_i[\![\mathrm{P}]\!] \triangleq \lambda I \bullet \mathbf{Pr}(S_p^{+\infty}[\![\mathrm{P}]\!] \in \gamma_r(I)) = \mathbf{Pr}(S_p^r[\![\mathrm{P}]\!] \mathrel{\ddot{\subseteq}} [\{\lambda\,\omega\bullet I\}])$. An axiomatic definition of the abstract semantics $S_i[\![\mathrm{P}]\!]$ can be calculated from the definition of $S_p^{+\infty}[\![\mathrm{P}]\!]$ in Ex. 4 using standard abstract interpretation techniques. For example

- $S_i[\![\mathtt{skip}]\!]I \triangleq \mathbf{Pr}(S_p^{+\infty}[\![\mathtt{skip}]\!] \in \gamma_r(I))$ (def. $S_i[\![\mathtt{skip}]\!]$)

$$= \mathbf{Pr}(\{ss \mid s \in \Sigma\} \in \gamma_r(I)) \qquad \text{(def. } S_p^{+\infty}[\![\mathtt{skip}]\!]\text{)}$$

$$= \mathbf{Pr}(s \in I) = \int_\Omega \chi_I\,\mathrm{d}\mu \qquad \text{(def. } \gamma_r \text{ and distributions)}$$

- $S_i[\![C_1\,;C_2]\!]I \triangleq \mathbf{Pr}(S_p^{+\infty}[\![C_1\,;C_2]\!] \in \gamma_r(I))$ (def. $S_i[\![C_1\,;C_2]\!]$)

$$= \mathbf{Pr}(S_p^{+\infty}[\![C_1]\!] \,;\, S_p^{+\infty}[\![C_2]\!] \in \gamma_r(I)) \qquad \text{(def. } S_p^{+\infty}[\![C_1\,;C_2]\!]\text{)}$$

$= \mathbf{Pr}(S_p^{+\infty}[\![C_1]\!] \in \gamma_r(I) \wedge S_p^{+\infty}[\![C_2]\!] \in \gamma_r(I))$ ⟨def. ⨾ and γ_r⟩

$= \mathbf{Pr}(S_p^{+\infty}[\![C_1]\!] \in \gamma_r(I)) \times \mathbf{Pr}(S_p^{+\infty}[\![C_2]\!] \in \gamma_r(I))$ ⟨Probability theory⟩

$= S_i[\![C_1]\!]I \times S_i[\![C_2]\!]I$ ⟨def. $S_i[\![C]\!]$⟩

and similarly for other commands using fixpoint abstraction [6, Th. 7.1.0.4-(3)] for loops. □

The series of examples 4, 14, 16, 17, and 18 shows that the probabilistic abstract interpretation framework is compositional in that the abstraction of an abstraction is an abstraction. Sec. 5.2 below makes the link with classical static analysis approaches.

5.2 (II) Abstracting the Scenario Space Ω

Definition. The scenario space Ω is chosen arbitrarily among all the measured spaces that could describe the random behavior at hand. Several Ω spaces could describe the same probabilistic system, or we might want to "group" several scenarios together because they look the same from the level of details we need.

Satisfyingly enough, it is possible to change the Ω space by a simple abstraction. Let Ω be a measurable space with a distribution μ, and Ω' be a set. Suppose there exists a surjective mapping $q : \Omega \twoheadrightarrow \Omega'$, then it is possible to abstract a probabilistic semantics expressed over Ω by one over Ω'.

First, we define the observable events on Ω' as the smallest set making q measurable. We note $\mathcal{A}_p(\Omega) \triangleq \Omega \rightarrowtail \mathcal{A}$ for the probabilistic semantics domain over Ω and $\langle \mathcal{A}, \sqsubseteq, \sqcup \rangle$. Then

$$\langle \wp\left(\mathcal{A}_p(\Omega)\right)/_{\ddot{\equiv}}, \ddot{\sqsubseteq} \rangle \xleftarrow[\alpha_{\Omega,\Omega'}]{\gamma_{\Omega,\Omega'}} \langle \wp\left(\mathcal{A}_p(\Omega')\right)/_{\ddot{\equiv}}, \ddot{\sqsubseteq} \rangle$$

where

$$\gamma_{\Omega,\Omega'} \triangleq \left[\lambda [S']\cdot\left\{s_{\mathcal{P}} \in \mathcal{A}_p \;\middle|\; \exists s'_{\mathcal{P}} \in S' : \forall \omega \in \Omega : s_{\mathcal{P}}(\omega) \sqsubseteq s'_{\mathcal{P}}(q(\omega))\right\}\right]_{\ddot{\equiv}_{\sqsubseteq}}$$

$$\alpha_{\Omega,\Omega'} \triangleq \left[\lambda [S]\cdot\left\{\lambda \omega' \in \Omega' \cdot \bigsqcup_{\omega \in q^{-1}(\{\omega'\})} s(\omega) \;\middle|\; s \in S\right\}\right]_{\ddot{\equiv}_{\sqsubseteq}}$$

and it can be verified that these definitions do not depend on the chosen representants S and S'.

The law μ' on Ω' is the image of the law μ by q, i.e. for all measurable sets $X' \subseteq \Omega', \mu'(X') = \mu(q^{-1}(X'))$.

Non-Determinism as an Abstraction. Merging scenarios by using a surjective q that identifies their image amounts to forgetting the probabilistic information on them, and seeing them just as a "new scenario". It means that when in the new compound scenario, the program can actually *non-deterministically* be in either one of the initial scenarios. That is why all their semantics are joined in the $\alpha_{\Omega,\Omega'}$ definition, and the probability of the new scenario is the sum of the probabilities of the source ones.

Thus, non-determinism is simply expressible in our framework by the Ω-abstraction. And while non-determinism is expressible between some scenarios, all the other probabilistic informations about the other scenarios are kept unchanged and used. Moreover, the non-determinism impacts as little as possible because the new compound scenario still behaves well with respect to the rest of the semantics.

Classical Abstract Interpretation as an Abstraction. Along those lines, it is natural to find classical abstract interpretation as a limit Ω-abstraction: forgetting all probabilistic information in the semantics should give back the classical abstract interpretation framework.

It is exactly what happens if Ω' is taken as a singleton $\Omega_\bullet = \{\bullet\}$ with the trivial probability measure on it (in this case, the semantics describes *anything* that can happen as the join of all possible outcomes, without knowing what is the probability for each actual behavior). We call this abstraction the "safe abstraction".

$$\langle \wp\left(\mathcal{A}_p(\Omega)\right)/_{\doteqdot_\sqsubseteq}, \ddot{\sqsubseteq}\rangle \underset{\alpha_{\Omega,\{\bullet\}}}{\overset{\gamma_{\Omega,\{\bullet\}}}{\leftrightarrows}} \langle \wp\left(\mathcal{A}_p(\Omega_\bullet)\right)/_{\doteqdot_\sqsubseteq}, \ddot{\sqsubseteq}\rangle$$

where $\mathcal{A}_p(\Omega_\bullet) \triangleq \{\bullet\} \rightarrowtail \mathcal{A}$ is isomorphic to $\mathcal{A}$, and so $\langle \wp\left(\mathcal{A}_p(\Omega_\bullet)\right)/_{\doteqdot_\sqsubseteq}, \ddot{\sqsubseteq}\rangle$ is order-isomorphic to $\langle \wp(\mathcal{A})/_{\doteqdot_\sqsubseteq}, \ddot{\sqsubseteq}\rangle$.

In classical abstract interpretation, we are usually just interested in properties such as $S[\![\mathrm{P}]\!]^\sharp \sqsubseteq Q$. It means that when we have a semantics that can be any element of $Q_{\mathcal{P}} \in \wp(\mathcal{A})$, we say that the most precise abstract state describing it is $\sqcup Q_{\mathcal{P}}$. It amounts to applying the following *join-abstraction*

$$\langle \wp(\mathcal{A})/_{\doteqdot}, \ddot{\sqsubseteq}\rangle \underset{\alpha_\sqcup}{\overset{\gamma_\sqcup}{\leftrightarrows}} \langle \mathcal{A}, \sqsubseteq\rangle$$

where

$$\alpha_\sqcup \triangleq \lambda[S]\bullet \bigsqcup_{Q\in S} Q \quad \text{and} \quad \gamma_\sqcup \triangleq \lambda Q \bullet [\downarrow Q]_{\doteqdot} \ .$$

This Galois connection abstracts the probabilistic abstract interpretation framework back to the classical abstract interpretation framework, an abstraction which is not always expressible in other more specific frameworks e.g. [24, 26, 25].

5.3 (III) Abstracting Probabilistic Semantics by Distributions

Law-Abstraction. Starting from the *abstract probabilistic semantics* of Sect. 5.1

$$S_p[\![\mathrm{P}]\!]^\sharp \in \mathcal{A}_p \triangleq \Omega \rightarrowtail \mathcal{A}, \quad \text{where} \quad \langle \mathcal{A}, \sqsubseteq\rangle \text{ is a cpo,}$$

we have the semantic properties in the domain

$$\left[\downarrow\{S_p[\![\mathrm{P}]\!]^\sharp\}\right]_{\doteqdot_\sqsubseteq} \in \wp\left(\mathcal{A}_p\right)/_{\doteqdot_\sqsubseteq} \ .$$

In this semantics, the dependencies between scenarios and the associated abstract semantics have been preserved. But this is something that we may not desire for static analysis because it would lead to combinatorial explosion. One solution considered in Sect. 5.2 is to abstract the scenario space Ω. Another abstraction is to consider the distribution of the abstract semantics, that is, the function giving the probability of any observable abstract property. Remembering only the distribution from a measurable function is actually an abstraction. Note that usual probabilistic analysis tools start actually from (abstractions of) this level of abstraction to build their analysis e.g.

[1, 3, 13, 15, 21, 28, 29], lacking the insight and soundness justifications that we developed above.

The order between the laws should reflect the intuition we have on lattices and logical implication. The information that we need from the distribution is actually restricted to downward closed sets because we want to answer questions like "What is $\mathbf{Pr}(S_p[\![\mathrm{P}]\!]^\sharp \sqsubseteq Q)$?", which is given by the function $\lambda Q \bullet S_p[\![\mathrm{P}]\!]^\sharp(\mu)(\downarrow Q)$ (where $\downarrow$ is this time the classical downward operator in the lattice $\mathcal{A}$).

Thus, we say that a law $\nu \in \mathcal{L}_{\mathcal{A}}$ ($\mathcal{L}_{\mathcal{A}}$ denotes the set of probability laws on $\mathcal{A}$, $\mathcal{L}_{\mathcal{A}} \subseteq \wp(\mathcal{A}) \longrightarrow [0,1]$) is more precise than another one ν' if it puts more weight on the bottom of the abstract lattice $\mathcal{A}$. That is, the logical order between laws on $\mathcal{A}$ is

$$\nu \leq \nu' \iff \forall Q \in \mathcal{A} \ : \ \nu(\downarrow Q) \geq \nu'(\downarrow Q)$$

The idea behind this logical order is essential to the understanding of the whole approach. As usual, logical orders should reflect that smaller abstract properties imply greater ones. Here, the intuition on the order $\nu \leq \nu'$ is that ν assigns a higher probability than ν' to more precise properties in $\langle \mathcal{A}, \sqsubseteq \rangle$, so more precise properties have better chances to hold.

Classically, it is safe to approximate $x \in [1, 10]$ by $x \in [1, 20]$. It is just less precise, because $[1, 10] \subseteq [1, 20]$. In the probabilistic case, the analogous situation would be "$x \in [1, 10]$ is true with probability one", approximated by "$x \in [1, 10]$ with probability $1/2$ and $x \in [1, 20]$ with probability $1/2$". Of course, the former situation is more precise than the second one, and this is reflected by the $\leq$ order.

Formally, the $\leq$ order checks that anywhere in the lattice, the most precise law is at least as precise as the other one, with at least as much probability.

It is interesting to note that as we mentioned before, if Ω is shrunk to a singleton $\Omega_\bullet$, the only valid probabilities for properties are 0 and 1, and the $\leq$ order boils down to $\sqsubseteq$ between abstract states and gives back the classical abstract interpretation framework.

The order $\leq$ is then lifted to the powersets by using the Hoare order once again, with $N, N' \subseteq \mathcal{L}_{\mathcal{A}}$

$$N \mathrel{\ddot{\preceq}} N' \iff \forall \nu \in N \ : \ \exists \nu' \in N' \ : \ \nu \leq \nu' \ .$$

In fact, we take for $\mathcal{L}_{\mathcal{A}}$ a subset of the laws on $\mathcal{A}$ because some laws do not have a meaning for the semantics at hand. If a non-biased coin is tossed, it makes no sense to speak of having tails with probability $1/3$. It is not a proper abstract semantics. To circumvent this issue, we restrict from now on $\mathcal{L}_{\mathcal{A}}$ to the elements l that have at least one corresponding function, i.e. a function in $\mathcal{A}_p$ such that $f(\mu) = l$.

We are now ready to define the Galois connection that unifies all of this

$$\langle \wp\left(\mathcal{A}_p\right)/_{\doteqdot_{\sqsubseteq}}, \ddot{\sqsubseteq} \rangle \xleftarrow[\alpha_{\mathcal{L}}]{\gamma_{\mathcal{L}}} \langle \wp(\mathcal{L}_{\mathcal{A}})/_{\doteqdot_{\leq}}, \ddot{\preceq} \rangle$$

where $\alpha_{\mathcal{L}} \triangleq \lambda [S]_{\doteqdot_{\sqsubseteq}} \bullet [\{s(\mu) \mid s \in S\}]_{\doteqdot_{\leq}}$ and $\gamma_{\mathcal{L}} \triangleq \lambda [N]_{\doteqdot_{\leq}} \bullet \left[\{s \in \mathcal{A}_p \mid s(\mu) \in N\}\right]_{\doteqdot_{\sqsubseteq}}$. As usual, it is easily shown that these functions are well-defined regardless of the chosen representant of the equivalence classes.

Example 19 (Probabilistic constant propagation). Consider the very simple probabilistic program P : `x = 0` $_{\frac{2}{3}}\oplus$ `x = 1` whose abstract probabilistic semantics is defined by $\Omega = \{\omega_0, \omega_1\}$ and the constant propagation lattice $\mathcal{A} \triangleq \{\bot, \top\} \cup \mathbb{Z}$ ordered by $\forall z \in \mathbb{Z} : \bot \sqsubset z \sqsubset \top$ as

$$S_p[\![\mathrm{P}]\!]^\sharp(\omega_0) = 0, \quad \mu(\{\omega_0\}) = \tfrac{2}{3}, \quad S_p[\![\mathrm{P}]\!]^\sharp(\omega_1) = 1, \quad \mu(\{\omega_1\}) = \tfrac{1}{3}.$$

The strongest probabilistic program property is

$$\left[\downarrow S_p[\![\mathrm{P}]\!]^\sharp\right]_{\ddot{\equiv}} = \left[\left\{\lambda\,\omega \bullet \left(\!\left|\ \omega = \omega_0 \ \text{?}\ \{\bot, 0\} \ \text{:}\ \{\bot\} \ \middle\|\ \omega = \omega_1 \ \text{?}\ \{\bot, 1\} \ \text{:}\ \{\bot\}\ \right|\!\right)\right\}\right]_{\ddot{\equiv}}$$

The order $\ddot{\sqsubseteq}$ is such that e.g. $[\lambda\,\omega \bullet \{\bot, 0\}]_{\ddot{\equiv}} \ \ddot{\sqsubseteq}\ [\lambda\,\omega \bullet \{\bot, 0, \top\}]_{\ddot{\equiv}}$ since $0 \sqsubseteq \top$. We have $[\{\nu\}]_{\ddot{\equiv}_{\preceq}} = \alpha_{\mathcal{L}}\left(\left[\downarrow\{S_p[\![\mathrm{P}]\!]^\sharp\}\right]_{\ddot{\equiv}}\right)$ and $\nu \prec \nu'$ as follows (assuming $Z \subseteq (\mathbb{Z} \setminus \{0, 1\}) \cup \{\top\}$)

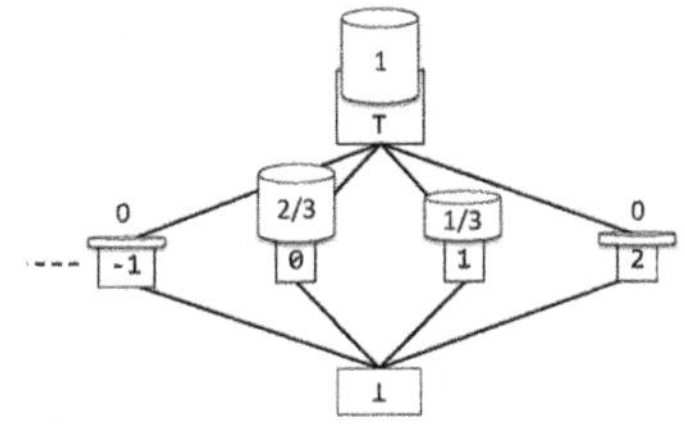

P	$\{\bot, Z\}$	$\{\bot, 0, Z\}$	$\{\bot, 1, Z\}$	$\{\bot, 0, 1, Z\}$
$\nu(\downarrow P)$	0	$\frac{2}{3}$	$\frac{1}{3}$	1
$\nu'(\downarrow P)$	0	0.5	0.2	1

□

Example 20. The final distribution of the constant and parity analysis of a simplified version P' of the probabilistic program P of Ex. 3 is provided below

```
x = 0 2/3⊕ x = 1;
if (x = 0) then
   y = 2 1/4⊕ y = 4
else
   y = 1 1/5⊕ y = 3
```

Program P'

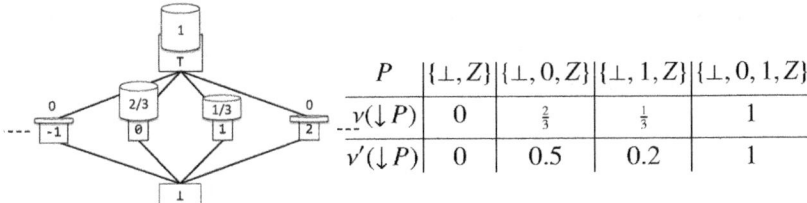

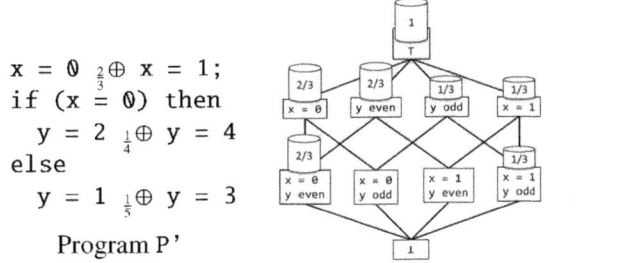

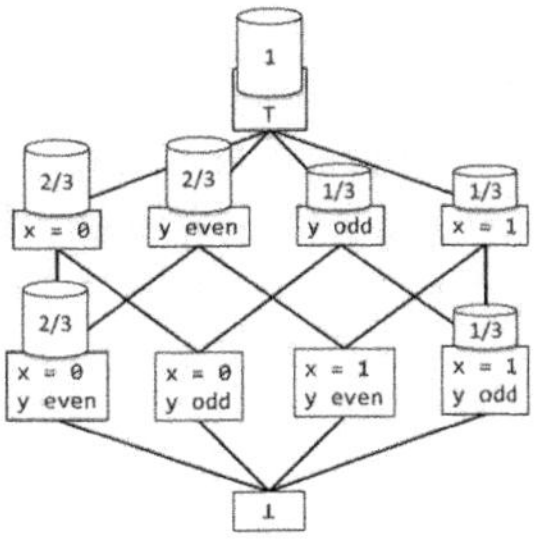

□

Example 21. Note that it is not a paradox to have in the abstract, for example :

$$\mathbf{Pr}\,(x \in [0, 10]) > \mathbf{Pr}\,(x \in [0, 5]) + \mathbf{Pr}\,(x \in [5, 10])$$

Indeed the analysis may not have managed to infer the exact value of $\mathbf{Pr}\,(x \in [0, 5])$ by lack of completeness, but only an under-estimation. □

In practice, distributions need only to be considered for atoms of atomic lattices (`x = 0, y even` $_{\frac{2}{3}}\oplus$ `x = 1, y odd` in Ex. 20) and more generally only for the join-irreducible elements. Further examples based on sets of probability distributions are given in [21].

Law-Abstraction Transformers. Along with the abstract domain that we just described, it is essential to construct the corresponding abstract transformers.

They are operators that take as input a (set of) semantic properties distribution and transform it according to their corresponding statement, over-approximating the concrete semantics of the statement.

Let us say that a statement S has a corresponding concrete transformer $F^{\mathsf{S}} : \mathcal{D}_p \longrightarrow \mathcal{D}_p$ defined as $F^{\mathsf{S}}_p(\lambda\,\omega \bullet X_\omega) \triangleq \lambda\,\omega \bullet F^{\mathsf{S}}_\omega(X_\omega)$, following Sec. 3.2.

It follows from this definition that for any $s \in \mathcal{D}^V_p$, the distribution of s is transformed by F^{S} in the following way, where $\Phi \subseteq \mathcal{D}$

$$\mathbf{Pr}\left(F^{\mathsf{S}}(s) \in \Phi\right) = \int_\Omega \chi_\Phi\left(F^{\mathsf{S}}_\omega(s(\omega))\right)\mathrm{d}\mu(\omega) = \int_\Omega \chi_{(F^{\mathsf{S}}_\omega)^{-1}(\Phi)}(s(\omega))\mathrm{d}\mu(\omega) \tag{1}$$

i.e. to know the probability that a semantic property is verified after applying a transformer, we measure the probability of the scenarios leading to that property after the transformation.

In the general case, this integral cannot be simplified. In particular, it cannot be expressed generally as a function of the input distribution s only. As a consequence, there is no straightforward way to go from a concrete transformer to an abstract one that transforms elements of $\langle \wp(\mathcal{L}_{\mathcal{A}})/_{\ddot{\equiv}_{\leq}}, \ddot{\preceq}\rangle$, other than by using the classical formula: $(F^{\mathsf{S}})^\sharp = \alpha \circ F^{\mathsf{S}} \circ \gamma$ where α and γ are the appropriate abstraction and concretization functions that link the abstract domain to the most concrete one.

In practice, one has to design the transformers by hand, making sure that they are over-approximations of the above mentioned optimal abstract transformers. Note that this is a process that was made silently in the related works, but taking them as axioms without proving their soundness in respect to the concrete semantics (see e.g. Sect. 7.4 and 7.5).

We see here that the precision of the sanity checker V (see Sect. 4.2) is crucial to the precision of the abstract transformers. Indeed, the smaller the set $F^{\mathsf{S}} \circ \gamma$, the more precise $(F^{\mathsf{S}})^\sharp$ is. It makes sense: if $(F^{\mathsf{S}})^\sharp$ has to be sound with respect to the "right" concrete semantics *and* some "useless" ones, it is less precise than if it just has to account for the right ones. That is why defining precise sanity checkers is so important to easily craft sound and precise abstract transformers.

But the issue is not as problematic as it may seem. Indeed, in the vast majority of cases, equation (1) can be further simplified to only depend upon the distribution of s.

When the transformer corresponds to a *non-random* statement, then by definition the operators F_ω are all equal as seen in Ex. 5, and the equation boils down to

$$\mathbf{Pr}\left(F^{\mathsf{S}}(s) \in \Phi\right) = \int_\Omega \chi_\Phi\left(F^{\mathsf{S}}(s(\omega))\right)\mathrm{d}\mu(\omega) = \int_\Omega \chi_\Phi(F^{\mathsf{S}}(\omega))\mathrm{d}s(\mu)(\omega)$$

where "$\mathrm{d}s(\mu)(\omega)$" denotes that the integral is taken according to the probability measure of s. Thus the new distribution is now computed as a simple function of the distribution of s, an information that is kept in the abstract state in the $\langle \wp(\mathcal{L}_{\mathcal{A}})/_{\ddot{\equiv}_{\leq}}, \ddot{\preceq}\rangle$ domain.

Of course, to apply to the $\langle \wp(\mathcal{L}_{\mathcal{A}})/_{\ddot{\equiv}_{\leq}}, \ddot{\preceq}\rangle$ domain, this process has to be lifted pointwise to sets (and thus equivalence classes) — it is straighforward.

Example 22. Suppose that x is a random integer variable in a fixed program, the statement `x++` would have such an abstract transformer. Indeed, the action of the statement does not depend on the actual value of x. In any scenario, it increments the value of x by one. Evaluating the above integral, we see that, for instance, the probability of x being 4 after the transformer is the probability of x being 3 before, which is exactly what we expect. □

As we just saw, it is far easier to define abstract transformers for non-random statements than for random ones. So how should we craft transformers for random statements?

First, let us note it is a good thing that non-random transformers are seamlessly lifted to the probabilistic case. It is certainly desirable. On the other hand, building the abstract transformers for random statements requires more knowledge because we have to create a function as precise as possible verifying the soundness equation, without formal indication on how to do it. It looks pretty normal after all, because handling probabilistic behaviors must necessarily imply more work at some point.

That being said, our experience is that in most practical instantiations of the framework, there will not be that many probabilistic constructs to find transformers for (typically, just calls to `rand()`-like functions). For these statements, the probabilistic behavior is well-known, and sound abstract transformers are pretty straightforward to build.

6 Iterating in the Abstract and Branch Prediction

The goal of this section is to show how to instrumentalize all the theory that has been developed so far to build a probabilistic static analyzer. Essentially, it boils down to building as precise abstract transformers as possible for classic programming languages constructs such as conditional and loops. Once this is done, it just remains to use classical abstract interpretation based fixpoint approximation through custom iteration schemes, e.g. [9].

6.1 Conditionals

Knowing the semantic properties distribution after a conditional requires to know as precisely as possible the probability that the condition is actually true or false. It is intuitively clear: the more a branch is likely to be executed, the more it will have an impact on the final outcome.

Formally, assume that $Q \in \mathcal{A}$, $l_s \in \mathcal{L}_{\mathcal{A}}$ is the law of a semantics $s \in \mathcal{D}_p^V$, S is the statement "`if` b `then` C_1 `else` C_2", and assume that the probability that the condition b is true when evaluated is fixed and equal to p_b, then for any $\Phi \in \wp(\mathcal{A})$

$$
\begin{aligned}
& [\![\mathrm{S}]\!](l_s)(\Phi) = \mathbf{Pr}([\![\mathrm{S}]\!](s) \in \Phi) && \wr \text{def. distribution} \wr \\
= \ & \mathbf{Pr}\big([\![C_1]\!](s) \in \Phi \wedge [\![\mathrm{b}]\!](s)\big) \vee ([\![C_2]\!](s) \in \Phi \wedge [\![\neg b]\!](s)) \\
= \ & \mathbf{Pr}\big([\![C_1]\!](s) \in \Phi \wedge [\![\mathrm{b}]\!](s)\big) + \mathbf{Pr}\big([\![C_2]\!](s) \in \Phi \wedge [\![\neg b]\!](s)\big) && \wr \text{probability theory} \wr \\
= \ & p_b \times \mathbf{Pr}\big([\![C_1]\!](s) \in \Phi \mid [\![\mathrm{b}]\!](s)\big) + (1 - p_b) \times \mathbf{Pr}\big([\![C_2]\!](s) \in \Phi \mid [\![\neg \mathrm{b}]\!](s)\big) && \wr \text{cond. prob.} \wr
\end{aligned}
$$

The abstract transformer of statement S depends heavily on p_b. Unfortunately, it may be the case that the analysis cannot determine the exact value of p_b. There can be two main reasons for that

– *Lack of precision*: the evaluation of the condition may involve variables that we do not have precise enough information about. Moreover, as we do not have always the optimal abstract transfer functions, we are likely to lose precision along the way: the probability that we know for a condition to be true is unfortunately just a minoration (because, for example, the analyzer could show that the condition is met with probability only 0.5 instead of 0.7 by lack of completeness).
– *Measurability*: the condition is not probabilistic, or we do not have the necessary probabilistic setting to determine it (it may have been abstracted away by an Ω-abstraction from Sect. 5.2). Indeed, the previous calculus is valid only if the events $[\![\mathrm{b}]\!](s)$ (b is true) and $[\![\neg\mathrm{b}]\!](s)$ (b is false) are observable. Otherwise, the value of p_b is not even defined.

Whatever the cause of the uncertainty may be, we end up with p_b being unknown in a set $p_b \in P_b \subseteq [0,1]$. At this point, the best is to separately analyze the branches of the conditional and compute $P_1(\Phi) = \mathbf{Pr}\,([\![C_1]\!](s) \in \Phi \mid [\![\mathrm{b}]\!](s))$ and $P_2(\Phi) = \mathbf{Pr}\,([\![C_2]\!](s) \in \Phi \mid [\![\neg\mathrm{b}]\!](s))$. Then the set of possible outcome distributions is $\{l \in \mathcal{L}_A \mid \exists p \in P_b : \forall \Phi \in \wp(\mathcal{A}) : l(\Phi) = pP_1(\Phi) + (1-p)P_2(\Phi)\}$.

In the same spirit, if P_1 and/or P_2 cannot be accurately determined, then their values belong to some subsets of [0, 1] that we try to compute as precisely as possible.

This process must then be lifted to sets (and then easily to equivalence classes) to accomodate the abstract domain $\langle \wp(\mathcal{L}_{\mathcal{A}}) /_{\ddot{\equiv}_{\leq}}, \ddot{\preceq} \rangle$.

6.2 Loops

As usual, loops are even more difficult to analyze. It combines the issues of evaluating conditional probabilities with the need to evaluate the number and effects of iterating through the loop.

We describe here a few strategies to design abstract transformers for `while` loops. There are many others that could apply to more specific cases, but we will remain as general as possible to give a good overview. We assume we have the statement S: "`while` b `do` C".

The General Case. In the favorable case, the probability of entering the loop after $i \geq 0$ iterations is known, and we denote it by $p_{\mathtt{loop}}(i)$. Following the same idea than in the case of the conditional, we have

$$\begin{aligned}
& [\![\mathrm{S}]\!](l_s)(\Phi) = \mathbf{Pr}([\![\mathrm{S}]\!](s) \in \Phi) && \text{(def. distribution)} \\
= \;& \mathbf{Pr}([\![\mathrm{S}]\!](s) \in \Phi \wedge 0 \text{ iteration}) + \mathbf{Pr}([\![\mathrm{S}]\!](s) \in \Phi \wedge \geq 1 \text{ iterations}) && \text{(dichotomy)} \\
= \;& \mathbf{Pr}([\![\mathrm{S}]\!](s) \in \Phi \wedge 0 \text{ iteration}) + \mathbf{Pr}([\![\mathrm{S}]\!](s) \in \Phi \wedge 1 \text{ iterations}) + \mathbf{Pr}([\![\mathrm{S}]\!](s) \in \Phi \wedge \geq 2 \text{ iterations}) && \\
= \;& \ldots && \text{(dichotomy)} \\
= \;& \sum_{i \geq 0} \mathbf{Pr}([\![\mathrm{S}]\!](s) \in \Phi \wedge i \text{ iterations}) && \text{(converges because positive terms and sum} \leq 1\text{)} \\
= \;& \sum_{i \geq 0} p_{\mathtt{loop}}(i) \times \mathbf{Pr}([\![\mathrm{S}]\!](s) \in \Phi \mid i \text{ iterations}) && \text{(cond. prob.)}
\end{aligned}$$

The nice thing here is that the computation of the iterations is separate for each number of iterations. For $i \geq 0$ iterations, the transformer of the loop is simply the composition of the conditional evaluation and the body execution i times. The second term that accounts for the probability that the loop actually does not terminate cannot be *a priori* eliminated, although it can sometimes be ruled out if the analysis does have more information on the context.

As in the conditional case, the crux of the matter is to obtain as good evaluations as possible for $p_{\text{loop}}(i)$ and the body transformer.

Non-Probabilistic Loops. If the truth of the condition b of the loop is not a measurable semantic property, then the analysis cannot determine what is the probability to enter the loop. Thus $p_{\text{loop}}(i)$ is only known to be anything in $[0, 1]$, and the analysis has to contain the set of all corresponding possible probabilistic measures.

As usual, custom widening operators may have to be used to guarantee termination depending on the underlying abstract domain.

An Example of an Ad-Hoc Loop Transfer Function. We now present a particular case of a loop transformer that may apply in a variety of cases, as an example to show how to craft specific loop abstract transformers for specific situations.

Suppose that the analyzer knows that the loop always terminates and that $p_{\text{loop}}(i)$ decreases as i increases, but that it cannot deduce from the body of the loop how it does so. In that case, the above equation is of no practical use. One way would be to go with the transfer function from 6.2 as it is sound, but it can be quite imprecise.

The approach we choose here is to unroll the loop for $N > 0$ iterations and over-approximate anything that can happen after. Reusing the above calculus, we have

$$
\begin{aligned}
& [\![\mathrm{S}]\!](l_s)(\Phi) = \mathbf{Pr}([\![\mathrm{S}]\!](s) \in \Phi) && \wr \text{def. distribution} \int \\
= & \sum_{i \geq 0} p_{\text{loop}}(i) \times \mathbf{Pr}([\![\mathrm{S}]\!](s) \in \Phi \mid i \text{ iterations}) && \wr \text{conditional probability} \int \\
= & \sum_{i=0}^{N} p_{\text{loop}}(i) \times \mathbf{Pr}([\![\mathrm{S}]\!](s) \in \Phi \mid i \text{ iterations}) + \sum_{i>N} p_{\text{loop}}(i) \times \mathbf{Pr}([\![\mathrm{S}]\!](s) \in \Phi \mid i \text{ iterations})
\end{aligned}
$$

By hypothesis, for all $i > N$, $p_{\text{loop}}(i) \leq p_{\text{loop}}(N)$. So we deduce that

$$\sum_{i>N} p_{\text{loop}}(i) \times \mathbf{Pr}([\![\mathrm{S}]\!](s) \in \Phi \mid i \text{ iterations}) \leq p_{\text{loop}}(N)$$

In that case, the transfer function for the first iterations is thus calculated by simply composing the body transfer function and the conditional N times, we note it l_N. Then to take the second term into account, the set of resulting distributions is $\{l \in \mathcal{L}_{\mathcal{A}} \mid \forall \Phi \in \wp(\mathcal{A}) : |l(\Phi) - l_N(\Phi)| \leq p_{\text{loop}}(N)\}$. The soundness is guaranteed by the above calculus.

Note that the transformer could be made more precise because the uncertainty applies only to properties that are impacted by the execution of the body, we do not take that into account in the above definition.

This approach can be made even more precise as N need not be fixed in advance: the loop can be iterated until the probability of going through it again is less than a specified cutoff $\varepsilon > 0$ (so that the source of imprecision $p_{\mathtt{loop}}(N)$ is tightly bounded) ; and if it is not witnessed after a specified number of iterations $N_{\max}$, then the above mechanism is used.

7 Related Work: Some Well-Known Techniques as Probabilistic Abstractions

7.1 Markov Chains/Decision Processes

Markov chains are random discrete transitions systems with a finite or countable number of possible states such that the next state depends only on the current state and not on the past or the future. Assuming in Ex. 4 that $S_p^{+\infty}[\![\mathtt{P}]\!]$ is a stationary stochastic process (all executions do terminate) on a countable state space Σ (for simplicity on the non-negative integers), the Markov chain with the transition matrix $[\mathsf{succ}(s, s')]_{s,s'\in\Sigma}$ has the same steady-state behavior, and similar short-term statistics [20, Proposition A.1.1]. In case of non-stationarity (non-termination), alternatives are to add history (considering states in $\Sigma' \triangleq \Sigma^+$) or to define $\mathbf{Pr}_{\langle s,\, s'\rangle} \triangleq \lim_{n\to\infty} \frac{1}{n}\mathbf{Pr}(S_p^{+\infty}[\![\mathtt{P}]\!] \in \{\sigma s s'\sigma' \mid \sigma s \in \Sigma^+ \wedge s'\sigma' \in \Sigma^{+\infty}\})$. So every process is (almost) Markov, which justifies this standard abstraction of probabilistic program semantics [22].

7.2 Probabilistic Model Checking

Probabilistic model checking [11] is often based on the Markov chain abstraction of Sect. 7.1. The fundamental notion of *probabilistic reachability* for Markov decision processes can be generalized to programs by considering the abstraction $\alpha(X) \triangleq \lambda s \bullet \mathbf{Pr}(S_p^{+\infty}[\![\mathtt{P}]\!]1_{\{s\}} \cap \gamma_r(X) \neq \emptyset)$ of the maximal trace semantics similar to Ex. 17. It is further abstracted by the *probability interval abstraction* $\alpha_m(X) \triangleq \min\{\alpha(X)s \mid s \in \Sigma\}$ and $\alpha_M(X) \triangleq \max\{\alpha(X)s \mid s \in \Sigma\}$ which is computable for finite systems [3, Sect. 6], [10, Sect. 3], [11, Sect. 4], or their reduced product [29, Sect. 3], etc. However programs generally have an unbounded concrete semantics so a (traditional) finite abstraction is often too imprecise [8]. This is the main reason for considering infinitary abstractions in this paper.

7.3 Quantitative Abstraction

[24, 26] propose a formulation of abstract interpretation on Hilbert spaces for real or complex quantitative abstractions of distribution-based semantics which can be reformulated using abstraction (2) of traces (e.g. where states are sets of λ-terms and transitions are reductions of these λ-terms). However, they do not stick to the usual soundness notion [26, Sect.5.2]: they are interested in behaviors on expectations and the "strict" soundness that we enforced from the beginning has to be relaxed using more permissive concretization functions.

7.4 Probabilistic Strongest Postcondition Semantics

Following Ex. 4, we let $\langle \Omega, \mathcal{E}, \mu \rangle$ be a probability space. The probabilistic semantics postulated in [14] is a distribution transformer abstracting the probabilistic maximal trace semantics $S_p^{+\infty}[\![\mathtt{P}]\!] : \Omega \rightarrowtail \Sigma^{+\infty}$.

Given a distribution $\delta \in \mathcal{L}_\Sigma$ of the initial states, the abstraction $\alpha_s : (\Omega \rightarrowtail \wp(\Sigma^{+\infty})) \longrightarrow (\mathcal{L}_\Sigma \longrightarrow \mathcal{L}_\Sigma)$ of $X \in \wp(\Sigma^{+\infty})$ is the distribution of the final states, if any, so that

$$\alpha_s(\lambda\,\omega \bullet X(\omega))\delta s' \triangleq \sum_{s\in\Sigma} \delta(s) \times \mathbf{Pr}(\exists \sigma : s\sigma s' \in X^+) \tag{2}$$

The abstract semantics is $S_s[\![\mathtt{P}]\!] \triangleq \alpha_s(S_p^{+\infty}[\![\mathtt{P}]\!])$. For example

$$\begin{aligned}
&- \alpha_s(S_p^{+\infty}[\![\mathtt{skip}]\!])\delta s' = \alpha_s(\{ss \mid s \in \Sigma\})\delta s' && \text{(def. } S_p^{+\infty}[\![\mathtt{skip}]\!]\text{)}\\
&= \sum_{s\in\Sigma} \delta(s) \times \mathbf{Pr}(s = s') = \delta(s') && \text{(def. } \alpha_s \text{ so that } S_s[\![\mathtt{skip}]\!]\delta = \delta\text{)}
\end{aligned}$$

$$\begin{aligned}
&- \alpha_s(S_p^{+\infty}[\![\mathtt{if}\ c\ \mathtt{then}\ A\ \mathtt{else}\ B]\!])\delta s'\\
&= \sum_{s\in\Sigma} \delta(s) \times \mathbf{Pr}(\exists \sigma : s\sigma s' \in \{s\sigma' \mid \mathcal{E}[\![c]\!]s \wedge s\sigma' \in S_p^{+\infty}[\![A]\!]^+\} \cup \{s\sigma' \mid \mathcal{E}[\![\neg c]\!]s \wedge s\sigma' \in S_p^{+\infty}[\![B]\!]^+\})\\
&\qquad \text{(def. } \alpha_s \text{ and } S_p^{+\infty}[\![\mathtt{if}\ c\ \mathtt{then}\ A\ \mathtt{else}\ B]\!]\text{)}\\
&= \sum_{s\in\Sigma} \delta(s)\times(\mathbf{Pr}(\mathcal{E}[\![c]\!]s)\times\mathbf{Pr}(\exists\sigma : s\sigma s' \in S_p^{+\infty}[\![A]\!]^+) + (1-\mathbf{Pr}(\mathcal{E}[\![c]\!]s))\times\mathbf{Pr}(\exists\sigma : s\sigma s' \in S_p^{+\infty}[\![B]\!]^+\})) && \text{(probability law)}\\
&= \sum_{s\in\Sigma} \delta(s) \times (c \times \mathbf{Pr}(\exists \sigma : s\sigma s' \in S_p^{+\infty}[\![A]\!]^+) + (1-c) \times \mathbf{Pr}(\exists \sigma : s\sigma s' \in S_p^{+\infty}[\![B]\!]^+))\\
&\qquad \text{(by [14] implicitly assuming that } \mathbf{Pr}(\mathcal{E}[\![c]\!]s) = c \text{ where } c \in \mathbb{R}^*\text{)}\\
&= c \times \alpha_s(S_p^{+\infty}[\![A]\!])\delta s' + (1-c) \times \alpha_s(S_p^{+\infty}[\![B]\!])\delta s' && \text{(def. } \alpha_s\text{)}
\end{aligned}$$

proving that $S_s[\![\mathtt{if}\ c\ \mathtt{then}\ A\ \mathtt{else}\ B]\!] = c \times S_s[\![A]\!] + (1-c) \times S_s[\![B]\!]$ pointwise and similarly for other commands using fixpoint abstraction [6, Th. 7.1.0.4-(3)] for loops.

These theorems are, up to logical notations, the axioms postulated in [14]. The probabilistic strongest postcondition abstraction in equation (2) is frequently used as collecting semantics for forward static analysis e.g. [21] for Markov decision processes.

7.5 Probabilistic Weakest Precondition Semantics

Whereas [14] is a forward abstraction as explained in Sect. 7.4, [15, 23] is the corresponding backward abstraction providing probabilistic weakest preconditions

$$\alpha_w(X)\delta s \triangleq \sum_{s'\in\Sigma} \mathbf{Pr}(\exists \sigma : s\sigma s' \in X^+) \times \delta(s') \tag{3}$$

The abstract semantics is $S_w[\![\mathtt{P}]\!] \triangleq \alpha_w(S_p^{+\infty}[\![\mathtt{P}]\!])$. For example

$$\begin{aligned}
&S_w[\![C_1\,;C_2]\!]\delta = \alpha_w(S_p^{+\infty}[\![C_1\,;C_2]\!])\delta && \text{(def. } S_w[\![\mathtt{P}]\!]\text{)}\\
&= \lambda\,s \bullet \sum_{s'\in\Sigma} \mathbf{Pr}(\exists \sigma : s\sigma s' \in S_p^{+\infty}[\![C_1]\!]^+ \,\mathbin{;}\, S_p^{+\infty}[\![C_2]\!]^+) \times \delta(s') && \text{(def. } \alpha_w \text{ and } S_p^{+\infty}[\![C_1\,;C_2]\!]\text{)}
\end{aligned}$$

$$= \lambda s \bullet \sum_{s' \in \Sigma} \mathbf{Pr}(\exists \sigma', s'', \sigma'' : s\sigma' s'' \in S_p^{+\infty}[\![C_1]\!]^+ \wedge s''\sigma s' \in S_p^{+\infty}[\![C_2]\!]^+) \times \delta(s')$$

$$\text{(def. } \mathbin{⨾} \text{ with } s\sigma s' = s\sigma' s'' \sigma s' \text{)}$$

$$= \lambda s \bullet \sum_{s' \in \Sigma} \mathbf{Pr}(\exists \sigma : s\sigma s' \in S_p^{+\infty}[\![C_1]\!]^+) \times \left(\sum_{s'' \in \Sigma} \mathbf{Pr}(\exists \sigma'' : s'\sigma'' s'' \in S_p^{+\infty}[\![C_2]\!]^+) \times \delta(s'') \right)$$

$$\text{(conditional probabability)}$$

$$= \lambda s \bullet \alpha_w(S_p^{+\infty}[\![C_1]\!])(\lambda s' \bullet \sum_{s'' \in \Sigma} \mathbf{Pr}(\exists \sigma'' : s'\sigma'' s'' \in S_p^{+\infty}[\![C_2]\!]^+) \times \delta(s''))(s) \quad \text{(def. } \alpha_w \text{)}$$

$$= \lambda s \bullet \alpha_w(S_p^{+\infty}[\![C_1]\!])(\alpha_w(S_p^{+\infty}[\![C_2]\!])(\delta))(s) \qquad \text{(def. } \alpha_w \text{)}$$

$$= \lambda s \bullet S_w[\![C_1]\!](S_w[\![C_2]\!](\delta))(s) \qquad \text{(def. } S_w[\![C]\!] \text{)}$$

$$= S_w[\![C_1]\!] \circ S_w[\![C_2]\!](\delta) \qquad \text{(def. } \circ \text{)}$$

which is the definition of $S_w[\![C_1\,;C_2]\!]$ postulated in [15, Sect. 4]. The probabilistic choice $C_1\ {}_p\!\oplus C_2$ requires additional hypotheses as in Sect. 7.1 while iteration is handled by fixpoint abstraction [6, Th. 7.1.0.4-(3)]. The probabilistic weakest precondition abstraction (3), or at least its discrete equivalent, is frequently used as collecting semantics for backward static analysis e.g. [22, 29] for Markov decision processes and further abstracted by the probabilistic intervals of Sect. 7.2.

8 Future Work and Conclusion

We have introduced new principles of probabilistic abstract interpretation for designing probabilistic semantics and static analysis methods. The framework is very general, highly expressive so as to set forth any probabilistic and computational situation. The framework separates probabilities (μ) from semantics ($S_p[\![\mathrm{P}]\!]$) so the probabilistic and semantics abstractions are self-reliant. Their abstractions can each be fine-tuned independently by easy adaptation of standard proof and static analysis methods.

Future work includes the case of absence of a best abstraction, the study of relational law-abstractions, improvement of branch prediction, implementation and experiments. It will also be essential to develop precise widening operators and abstract transformers to keep enough precision during the fixpoint calculation.

Work supported in part by the CMACS NSF Expeditions in Computing award 0926166.

References

[1] Camporesi, F., Feret, J., Koeppl, H., Petrov, T.: Automatic reduction of stochastic rules-based models in a nutshell. Amer. Inst. of Physics, AIP 1281(2) (2010)

[2] Chadha, R., Viswanathan, M., Viswanathan, R.: Least Upper Bounds for Probability Measures and Their Applications to Abstractions. In: van Breugel, F., Chechik, M. (eds.) CONCUR 2008. LNCS, vol. 5201, pp. 264–278. Springer, Heidelberg (2008)

[3] Coletta, A., Gori, R., Levi, F.: Approximating probabilistic behaviors of biological systems using abstract interpretation 229(1), 165–182 (2009)

[4] Cousot, P.: Constructive design of a hierarchy of semantics of a transition system by abstract interpretation. TCS 277(1-2), 47–103 (2002)

[5] Cousot, P., Cousot, R.: Abstract interpretation: a unified lattice model for static analysis of programs by construction or approximation of fixpoints. In: POPL, pp. 238–252 (1977)
[6] Cousot, P., Cousot, R.: Systematic design of program analysis frameworks. In: POPL, pp. 269–282 (1979)
[7] Cousot, P., Cousot, R.: Abstract interpretation frameworks. J. Logic and Comp. 2(4), 511–547 (1992)
[8] Cousot, P., Cousot, R.: Comparing the Galois Connection and Widening/Narrowing Approaches to Abstract Interpretation. In: Bruynooghe, M., Wirsing, M. (eds.) PLILP 1992. LNCS, vol. 631, pp. 269–295. Springer, Heidelberg (1992)
[9] Cousot, P., Cousot, R., Feret, J., Mauborgne, L., Miné, A., Rival, X.: Why does Astrée scale up? FMSD 35(3), 229–264 (2009)
[10] D'Argenio, P.R., Jeannet, B., Jensen, H.E., Larsen, K.G.: Reduction and Refinement Strategies for Probabilistic Analysis. In: Hermanns, H., Segala, R. (eds.) PAPM-PROBMIV 2002. LNCS, vol. 2399, pp. 57–76. Springer, Heidelberg (2002)
[11] Forejt, V., Kwiatkowska, M., Norman, G., Parker, D.: Automated Verification Techniques for Probabilistic Systems. In: Bernardo, M., Issarny, V. (eds.) SFM 2011. LNCS, vol. 6659, pp. 53–113. Springer, Heidelberg (2011)
[12] Hansson, H., Jonsson, B.: A logic for reasoning about time and reliability. FAC 6(5), 512–535 (1994)
[13] Hehner, E.: Probabilistic Predicative Programming. In: Kozen, D. (ed.) MPC 2004. LNCS, vol. 3125, pp. 169–185. Springer, Heidelberg (2004)
[14] Hehner, E.: A probability perspective. FAC 23(4), 391–419 (2011)
[15] Katoen, J.-P., McIver, A.K., Meinicke, L.A., Morgan, C.C.: Linear-Invariant Generation for Probabilistic Programs: Automated Support for Proof-Based Methods. In: Cousot, R., Martel, M. (eds.) SAS 2010. LNCS, vol. 6337, pp. 390–406. Springer, Heidelberg (2010)
[16] Klenke, A.: Probability Theory: A Comprehensive Course. Springer, Heidelberg (2007)
[17] Kozen, D.: Semantics of probabilistic programs. JCSS 22, 328–350 (1981)
[18] Kwiatkowska, M., Norman, G., Parker, D.: Using probabilistic model checking in systems biology. PER 35(4), 14–21 (2008)
[19] McIver, A., Morgan, C.: Abstraction, Refinement and Proof for Probabilistic Systems. Springer, Heidelberg (2005)
[20] Meyn, S.: Control Techniques for Complex Networks. CUP (2007)
[21] Monniaux, D.: Abstract Interpretation of Probabilistic Semantics. In: SAS 2000. LNCS, vol. 1824, pp. 322–340. Springer, Heidelberg (2000)
[22] Monniaux, D.: Abstract interpretation of programs as Markov decision processes. SCP 58(1–2), 179–205 (2005)
[23] Morgan, C., McIver, A., Seidel, K., Sanders, J.: Probabilistic predicate transformers. TOPLAS 18(3), 325–353 (1996)
[24] Di Pierro, A., Hankin, C., Wiklicky, H.: Probabilistic lambda-calculus and quantitative program analysis. JLC 15(2), 159–179 (2005)
[25] Di Pierro, A., Wiklicky, H.: Concurrent constraint programming: towards probabilistic abstract interpretation. In: PPDP, pp. 127–138. ACM (2000)
[26] Di Pierro, A., Wiklicky, H.: Probabilistic Abstract Interpretation and Statistical Testing (Extended Abstract). In: Hermanns, H., Segala, R. (eds.) PAPM-PROBMIV 2002. LNCS, vol. 2399, pp. 211–212. Springer, Heidelberg (2002)
[27] Roy, P., Parker, D., Norman, G., de Alfaro, L.: Symbolic magnifying lens abstraction in Markov decision processes. In: QEST 2008, pp. 103–112. IEEE (2008)
[28] Smith, M.: Probabilistic abstract interpretation of imperative programs using truncated normal distributions 220(3), 43–59 (2008)
[29] Wachter, B., Zhang, L.: Best Probabilistic Transformers. In: Barthe, G., Hermenegildo, M. (eds.) VMCAI 2010. LNCS, vol. 5944, pp. 362–379. Springer, Heidelberg (2010)

Multiparty Session Types Meet Communicating Automata

Pierre-Malo Deniélou and Nobuko Yoshida

Department of Computing, Imperial College London

Abstract. Communicating finite state machines (CFSMs) represent processes which communicate by asynchronous exchanges of messages via FIFO channels. Their major impact has been in characterising essential properties of communications such as freedom from deadlock and communication error, and buffer boundedness. CFSMs are known to be computationally hard: most of these properties are undecidable even in restricted cases. At the same time, multiparty session types are a recent typed framework whose main feature is its ability to efficiently enforce these properties for mobile processes and programming languages. This paper ties the links between the two frameworks to achieve a two-fold goal. On one hand, we present a generalised variant of multiparty session types that have a direct semantical correspondence to CFSMs. Our calculus can treat expressive forking, merging and joining protocols that are absent from existing session frameworks, and our typing system can ensure properties such as safety, boundedness and liveness on distributed processes by a polynomial time type checking. On the other hand, multiparty session types allow us to identify a new class of CFSMs that automatically enjoy the aforementioned properties, generalising Gouda et al's work [12] (for two machines) to an arbitrary number of machines.

1 Introduction

Multiparty Session Types The importance that distributed systems are taking today underlines the necessity for precise specifications and full correctness guarantees for interactions (protocols) between distributed components. To that effect, multiparty session types [3, 14] are a type discipline that can enforce strong communication safety for distributed processes [3, 14], via a choreographic specification (called *global type*) of the interaction between several peers. Global types are then projected to end-point types (called *local types*), against which processes can be statically type-checked. Well-typed processes are guaranteed to interact correctly, following the global protocol. The tool chain (projection and type-checking) is decidable in polynomial time and automatically guarantees properties such as type safety, deadlock freedom, and progress. Multiparty session types are thus directly applicable to the design and implementation of real distributed programming languages. They are used for structured protocol programming in contexts such as security [8, 22], protocol optimisations for distributed objects [21] and parallel algorithms [17], and have recently lead to industrial projects [19, 20].

Communicating Automata. or Communicating Finite State Machines (CFSMs) [5], are a classical model for protocol specification and verification. Before being used in many industrial contexts, CFSMs have been a pioneer theoretical formalism in which

H. Seidl (Ed.): ESOP 2012, LNCS 7211, pp. 194–213, 2012.

distributed safety properties could be formalised and studied. Building a connection between communicating automata and session types allows to answer some open questions in session types which have been asked since [13]. The first question is about expressiveness: to which class of CFSMs do session types correspond? The second question concerns the semantical correspondence between session types and CFSMs: how do the safety properties that session types guarantee relate to those of CFSMs? The third question is about efficiency: why do session types provide polynomial algorithms while general CFSMs are undecidable?

A First Answer. to these questions has been recently given in the *binary* case: a two-machine subclass (which had been studied by Gouda et al. in 1984 [12] and later by Villard [23]) of half-duplex systems [7] (defined as systems where at least one of the two communication buffers between two parties is always empty) has been found to correspond to *binary* session types [13]. This subclass, compatible deterministic two-machine without mixed states [12] (see § 3 and § 6), automatically satisfies the safety properties that binary session types can guarantee. It also explains why binary session types offer a tractable framework since, in two-machine half-duplex systems, safety properties and buffer boundedness are decidable in polynomial time [7]. However, in half-duplex systems with three machines or more, these problems are undecidable (Theorem 36 [7]). This shows that an extension to multiparty is very challenging, leading to two further questions. Can we use a multiparty session framework [14] to define a new class of deadlock-free CFSMs with more than two machines? How far can we extend global session type languages to capture a wider class of well-behaved CFSMs, still preserving expected properties and enabling type-checking processes and languages?

Our Answer. is a *theory of generalised multiparty session types*, which can automatically generate, through projection and translation, a new class of safe CFSMs, which we call *multiparty session automata* (MSA). We use MSA as a semantical interpretation of types to prove the safety and liveness of expressive multiparty session mobile processes, allowing complexly structured protocols, including the Alternating Bit Protocol, to be simply represented. Our generalised multiparty session type framework can be summarised by the following diagram:

Generalised Global Type	—Projection→	Local Types $\approx$ CFSMs (MSA)	—Type checking→	General Multiparty Processes

Generalised Global Types. This paper proposes a new global type syntax which encompasses previous systems [3, 14] with extended constructs (join and merge) and generalised graph syntax. Its main feature is to explicitly distinguish the branching points (where choices are made) from the forking points (where concurrent, interleaved interaction can take place). Such a distinction is critical to avoid the state explosion and to directly and efficiently type session-based languages and processes.

Fig. 1 illustrates our new syntax on a running example, named Trade. For the intuition, Trade is also represented as a BPMN-like [4] activity diagram, where '+' is for exclusive gateways and '|' for parallel ones, following session type conventions.

This scenario (from [6, § 7.3]) comprehensively combines recursion, fork, join, choice and merge. It models a protocol where a seller S relies on a broker B to negotiate and sell an item to a client C. The seller sends a message *Item* to the broker, the

$$
\begin{array}{rl}
\mathbf{G}_{\text{Trade}} & = \mathsf{def} \\
\mathbf{x}_0 & = \mathtt{S} \to \mathtt{B} : \mathit{Item}\langle\mathsf{string}\rangle; \mathbf{x}_1 \\
\mathbf{x}_5 + \mathbf{x}_1 & = \mathbf{x}_2 \\
\mathbf{x}_2 & = \mathbf{x}_3 + \mathbf{x}_6 \\
\mathbf{x}_3 & = \mathtt{B} \to \mathtt{C} : \mathit{Offer}\langle\mathsf{nat}\rangle; \mathbf{x}_4 \\
\mathbf{x}_4 & = \mathtt{C} \to \mathtt{B} : \mathit{Counter}\langle\mathsf{nat}\rangle; \mathbf{x}_5 \\
\mathbf{x}_6 & = \mathbf{x}_7 \mid \mathbf{x}_8 \\
\mathbf{x}_7 & = \mathtt{B} \to \mathtt{S} : \mathit{Final}\langle\mathsf{nat}\rangle; \mathbf{x}_9 \\
\mathbf{x}_8 & = \mathtt{B} \to \mathtt{C} : \mathit{Result}\langle\mathsf{nat}\rangle; \mathbf{x}_{10} \\
\mathbf{x}_9 \mid \mathbf{x}_{10} & = \mathbf{x}_{11} \\
\mathbf{x}_{11} & = \mathsf{end} \quad \mathsf{in}\ \mathbf{x}_0
\end{array}
$$

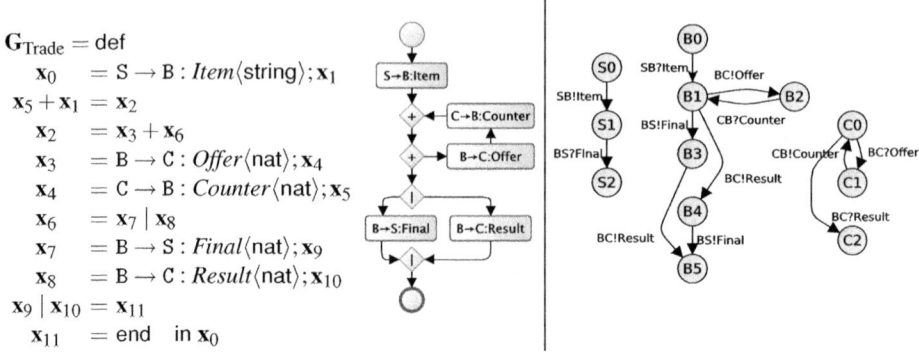

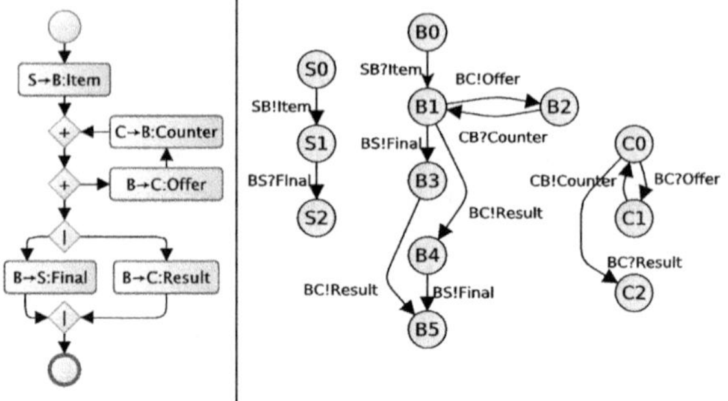

Fig. 1. Trade Example: Global Type and CFSM

broker then has a choice between entering the negotiation loop *Offer-Counter* with the client as many times as he chooses, or finishing the protocol by concurrently sending *both* messages *Final* and *Result* to the seller and the client respectively.

$\mathbf{G}_{\text{Trade}}$ is called a *global type* as it represents the choreography of the interactions and not just a collection of local behaviours. It is of the form $\mathsf{def}\ \widetilde{G}\ \mathsf{in}\ \mathbf{x}_0$ where $\widetilde{G}$ represents the transitions between states, and where $\mathbf{x}_0$ is the initial state of all the participants. A transition of the form $\mathbf{x}_0 = \mathtt{S} \to \mathtt{B} : \mathit{Item}\langle\mathsf{string}\rangle; \mathbf{x}_1$ corresponds to the emission of a message *Item* carrying a value of type string from S to B, followed by the interactions that happen in $\mathbf{x}_1$. A transition $\mathbf{x}_2 = \mathbf{x}_3 + \mathbf{x}_6$ denotes a choice (done by one of the participants, here B) between following with $\mathbf{x}_3$ or $\mathbf{x}_6$. A transition $\mathbf{x}_6 = \mathbf{x}_7 \mid \mathbf{x}_8$ describes that the interaction should continue concurrently with the actions of $\mathbf{x}_7$ and of $\mathbf{x}_8$. In a symmetric way, a transition $\mathbf{x}_5 + \mathbf{x}_1 = \mathbf{x}_2$ merges two branches that are mutually exclusive, while a transition $\mathbf{x}_9 \mid \mathbf{x}_{10} = \mathbf{x}_{11}$ joins two concurrent interaction threads reaching points $\mathbf{x}_9$ and $\mathbf{x}_{10}$ into a single thread starting from $\mathbf{x}_{11}$.

Local Types and CFSMs. We build the formal connection between multiparty session types, CFSMs and processes by first projecting a global type to the local type of each end-point. We then show that the local types are *implementable* as CFSMs. This defines a new subclass of CFSMs, named Multiparty Session Automata, or MSA, that are not limited to two machines or to half-duplex communications, and that automatically satisfy distributed safety and progress.

To illustrate this relationship between local types and MSA, we give in Fig. 1 the CFSM representation of Trade: on the left is the seller S, at the centre the broker B, on the right the client C. These communicating automata correspond to the collection of local behaviours represented by the local types (shown later in Ex. 3.1). Each automaton starts from an initial state $\mathtt{S}_0$, $\mathtt{B}_0$ or $\mathtt{C}_0$ and allows some transitions to be activated. Transitions can either be outputs of the form SB!*Item* where SB indicates the channel between the seller S and the broker B and where *Item* is the message label; or inputs of the symmetric form SB?*Item*. When a sending action happens, the message label is appended to the channel's FIFO queue. Activating an input action requires the expected label to appear on top of the specified queue.

Our Contributions. are listed below, with the corresponding section number:

- We introduce new generalised multiparty (global and local) session types that solve open problems of expressiveness and algorithmic projection posed in [6] (§ 2).
- We give a CFSM interpretation of local types that defines a formal semantics for global types and allows the standardisation of distributed safety properties between session type systems and communicating automata (§ 3).
- We define multiparty session automata, a new communicating automata subclass that automatically satisfy strong distributed safety properties, solving open questions from [7, 23] (§ 3).
- We develop a new typing system for multiparty session mobile processes generalised with choice, fork, merge and join constructs (§ 4, § 5.1), and prove that typed processes conform the safety and liveness properties defined in CFSMs (§ 5.2).
- We compare our framework with existing session type theories and CFSMs results (§ 6). Our framework (global type well-formedness checking, projection, type-checking) is notably polynomial in the size of the global type or mobile processes.

The long version [18] provides proofs, auxiliary definitions and examples.

2 Generalised Multiparty Sessions

2.1 Global Types for Generalised Multiparty Sessions

This subsection introduces new *generalised global types*, whose expressiveness encompasses previous session frameworks. [1]The new features are flexible fork, choice, merge and join operations for precise thread management.

$\mathbf{G}$ ::=	$\mathsf{def}\ \widetilde{G}\ \mathsf{in}\ \mathbf{x}$	Global type	U ::=	$\langle \mathbf{G} \rangle \mid \mathsf{bool} \mid \mathsf{nat} \mid \cdots$	Sorts	
G ::=	$\mathbf{x} = \mathsf{p} \to \mathsf{p}' : l\langle U \rangle ; \mathbf{x}'$	Labelled messages		$\mathbf{x} \mid \mathbf{x}' = \mathbf{x}''$	Join	
|	$\mathbf{x} = \mathbf{x}' \mid \mathbf{x}''$	Fork		$\mathbf{x} + \mathbf{x}' = \mathbf{x}''$	Merge	
|	$\mathbf{x} = \mathbf{x}' + \mathbf{x}''$	Choice		$\mathbf{x} = \mathsf{end}$	End	

A global type $\mathbf{G} = \mathsf{def}\ \widetilde{G}\ \mathsf{in}\ \mathbf{x}_0$ describes an interaction between a fixed number of participants. The prescribed interaction starts from $\mathbf{x}_0$, which we call the *initial state*, and proceeds according to the transitions specified in $\widetilde{G}$. The *state variables* $\mathbf{x}$ in $\widetilde{G}$ represent the successive distributed states of the interaction. Transitions can be *labelled message exchanges* $\mathbf{x} = \mathsf{p} \to \mathsf{p}' : l\langle U \rangle ; \mathbf{x}'$ where p and p' denote the sending and receiving *participants* (process identities), U is the payload type of the message and l its label. This transition specifies that p can go from $\mathbf{x}$ to the continuation $\mathbf{x}'$ by sending message l, while p' goes from $\mathbf{x}$ to $\mathbf{x}'$ by receiving it. All other participants can go from $\mathbf{x}$ to $\mathbf{x}'$ for free. Sort types U include shared channel types $\langle \mathbf{G} \rangle$ or base types.$\mathbf{x} = \mathbf{x}' + \mathbf{x}''$ represents the choice (made by exactly one participant) between continuing with $\mathbf{x}'$ or $\mathbf{x}''$ and $\mathbf{x} = \mathbf{x}' \mid \mathbf{x}''$ represents forking the interactions, allowing the interleaving of actions at $\mathbf{x}'$ and $\mathbf{x}''$. These forking threads are eventually collected by joining construct $\mathbf{x}' \mid \mathbf{x}'' = \mathbf{x}$. Similarly choices are closed by merging construct $\mathbf{x}' + \mathbf{x}'' = \mathbf{x}$, where two mutually exclusive paths share a continuation. $\mathbf{x} = \mathsf{end}$ denotes session termination.

[1] We omit the delegation for space reason. Its inclusion is straightforward, see [18].

The motivation behind this choice of graph syntax is to support general graphs. A traditional global type syntax tree, with operators fork | and choice +, even with recursion [3, 6, 10, 14], is limited to series-parallel graphs.

Example 2.1 (Generalised Global Types)). We now give several example, with their graph representation. We keep this representation informal throughout this paper (although there is an exact match with the syntax: variables are edges and transitions are nodes). The examples are numbered 1–7, with increasing complexity.

1.
$$\begin{aligned} \mathbf{G}_1 = \mathsf{def}\ \mathbf{x}_0 &= \mathtt{Alice} \to \mathtt{Bob} : \mathit{Msg}\langle\mathsf{nat}\rangle; \mathbf{x}_1 \\ \mathbf{x}_1 &= \mathsf{end}\ \mathsf{in}\ \mathbf{x}_0 \end{aligned}$$

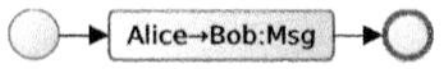

2.
$$\begin{aligned} \mathbf{G}_2 = \mathsf{def}\ \mathbf{x}_0 &= \mathbf{x}_1 + \mathbf{x}_2 \\ \mathbf{x}_1 &= \mathtt{Alice} \to \mathtt{Bob} : \mathit{Book}\langle\mathsf{string}\rangle; \mathbf{x}_3 \\ \mathbf{x}_2 &= \mathtt{Alice} \to \mathtt{Bob} : \mathit{Film}\langle\mathsf{string}\rangle; \mathbf{x}_4 \\ \mathbf{x}_3 + \mathbf{x}_4 &= \mathbf{x}_5 \\ \mathbf{x}_5 &= \mathsf{end}\ \mathsf{in}\ \mathbf{x}_0 \end{aligned}$$

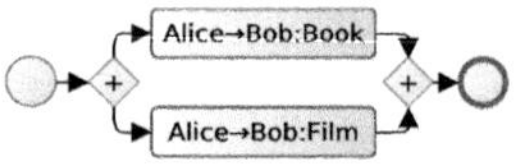

3.
$$\begin{aligned} \mathbf{G}_3 = \mathsf{def}\ \mathbf{x}_0 &= \mathbf{x}_1 \mid \mathbf{x}_2 \\ \mathbf{x}_1 &= \mathtt{Alice} \to \mathtt{Bob} : \mathit{Book}\langle\mathsf{string}\rangle; \mathbf{x}_3 \\ \mathbf{x}_2 &= \mathtt{Bob} \to \mathtt{Alice} : \mathit{Film}\langle\mathsf{string}\rangle; \mathbf{x}_4 \\ \mathbf{x}_3 \mid \mathbf{x}_4 &= \mathbf{x}_5 \\ \mathbf{x}_5 &= \mathsf{end}\ \mathsf{in}\ \mathbf{x}_0 \end{aligned}$$

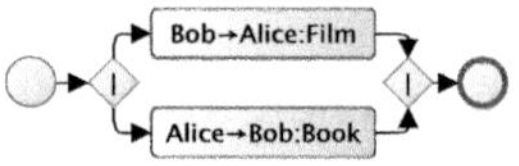

4.
$$\begin{aligned} \mathbf{G}_4 = \mathsf{def}\ \mathbf{x}_0 + \mathbf{x}_2 &= \mathbf{x}_1 \\ \mathbf{x}_1 &= \mathtt{Alice} \to \mathtt{Bob} : \mathit{Msg}\langle\mathsf{string}\rangle; \mathbf{x}_2\ \mathsf{in}\ \mathbf{x}_0 \end{aligned}$$

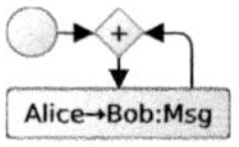

6.
$$\begin{aligned} \mathbf{G}_6 = \mathsf{def}\ \mathbf{x}_0 &= \mathbf{x}_1 + \mathbf{x}_3 \\ \mathbf{x}_1 &= \mathtt{Alice} \to \mathtt{Bob} : \mathit{Book}\langle\mathsf{string}\rangle; \mathbf{x}_2 \\ \mathbf{x}_2 &= \mathtt{Bob} \to \mathtt{Carol} : \mathit{Item}\langle\mathsf{nat}\rangle; \mathbf{x}_4 \\ \mathbf{x}_3 &= \mathtt{Alice} \to \mathtt{Carol} : \mathit{Film}\langle\mathsf{string}\rangle; \mathbf{x}_5 \\ \mathbf{x}_4 + \mathbf{x}_5 &= \mathbf{x}_6 \\ \mathbf{x}_6 &= \mathtt{Carol} \to \mathtt{Bob} : \mathit{Order}\langle\mathsf{string}\rangle; \mathbf{x}_7 \\ \mathbf{x}_7 &= \mathsf{end}\ \mathsf{in}\ \mathbf{x}_0 \end{aligned}$$

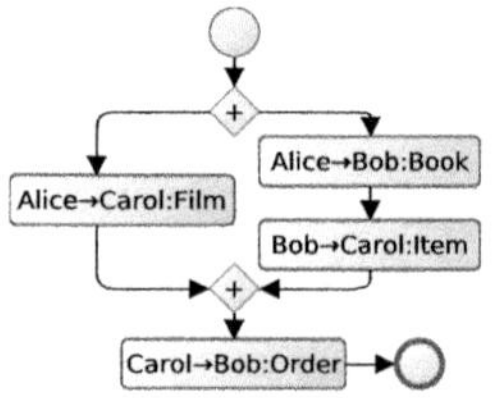

7.
$$\begin{aligned} \mathbf{G}_{AB} = \mathsf{def}\ \mathbf{x}_0 &= \mathbf{x}_1 \mid \mathbf{x}_2 \\ \mathbf{x}_1 + \mathbf{x}_3 &= \mathbf{x}_4 \\ \mathbf{x}_2 + \mathbf{x}_5 &= \mathbf{x}_6 \\ \mathbf{x}_4 &= \mathtt{Alice} \to \mathtt{Bob} : \mathit{Msg}_1\langle\mathsf{string}\rangle; \mathbf{x}_7 \\ \mathbf{x}_7 &= \mathbf{x}_8 \mid \mathbf{x}_9 \\ \mathbf{x}_8 &= \mathtt{Bob} \to \mathtt{Alice} : \mathit{Ack}_1\langle\mathsf{unit}\rangle; \mathbf{x}_{10} \\ \mathbf{x}_6 \mid \mathbf{x}_9 &= \mathbf{x}_{11} \\ \mathbf{x}_{11} &= \mathtt{Alice} \to \mathtt{Bob} : \mathit{Msg}_2\langle\mathsf{string}\rangle; \mathbf{x}_{12} \\ \mathbf{x}_{12} &= \mathbf{x}_{13} \mid \mathbf{x}_{14} \\ \mathbf{x}_{13} &= \mathtt{Bob} \to \mathtt{Alice} : \mathit{Ack}_2\langle\mathsf{unit}\rangle; \mathbf{x}_5 \\ \mathbf{x}_{10} \mid \mathbf{x}_{14} &= \mathbf{x}_3\ \mathsf{in}\ \mathbf{x}_0 \end{aligned}$$

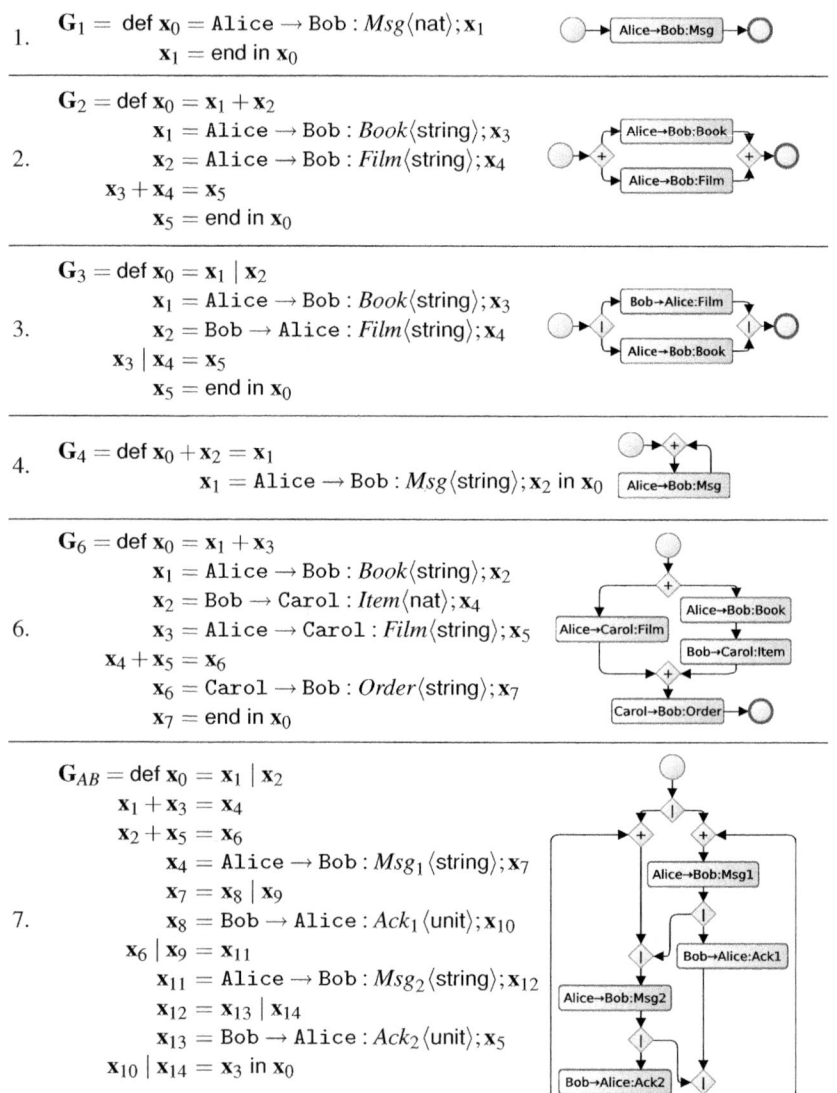

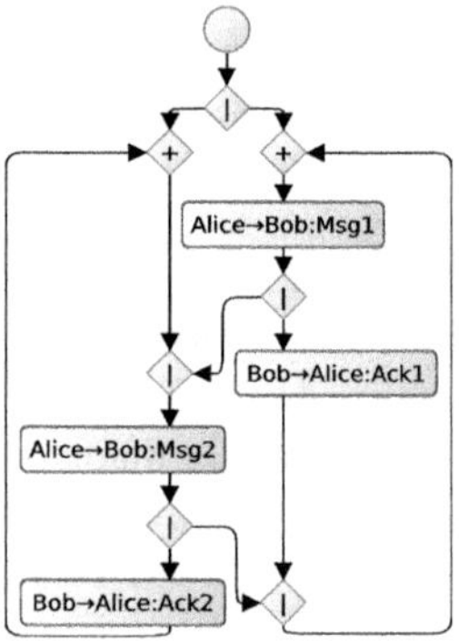

1. A simple one-message (*Msg* of type nat) is exchanged between `Alice` and `Bob`.
2. A protocol with a simple choice between messages *Book* and *Film*.

3. Alice and Bob concurrently exchange the messages *Book* and *Film*.
4. A protocol where Alice keeps sending successive messages to Bob (recursion is written using merging).
5. The Trade example from § 1 (Fig. 1) shows how choice, recursion and parallelism can be integrated to model a three party protocol.
6. $\mathbf{G}_6$ features an initial choice between directly contacting Carol or to do it through Bob. Note that without the last interaction from Carol to Bob (in $\mathbf{x}_6$), if the chosen path leads to $\mathbf{x}_3$, Bob enters a deadlock, waiting forever for a message from Alice.
7. $\mathbf{G}_{AB}$ gives a representation of ***the Alternating Bit Protocol***. Alice repeatedly sends to Bob alternating messages Msg_1 and Msg_2 but will always concurrently wait for the acknowledgement Ack_i to send Msg_i. This interaction structure requires a general graph syntax and is thus not representable in any existing session type framework, and is difficult in other formalisms (see § 6). We emphasise the fact that, not only it is representable in our syntax, but our framework is able to demonstrate its progress and safety and enforce it on realistic processes.

2.2 Well-formed Global Types

This subsection defines three well-formedness conditions for global types.

Sanity Conditions. within global types prevent possible syntactic confusions about which continuations to follow at any given point. A global type $\mathbf{G} = \mathsf{def}\ \widetilde{G}\ \mathsf{in}\ \mathbf{x}_0$ satisfies the *sanity* conditions if it satisfies the following conditions.

1. (**Unambiguity**) Every state variable $\mathbf{x}$ except $\mathbf{x}_0$ should appear exactly once on the left-hand side and once on the right-hand side of the transitions in $\widetilde{G}$.
2. (**Unique start**) $\mathbf{x}_0$ appears exactly once, on the left-hand side.
3. (**Unique end**) end appears at most once.
4. (**Thread correctness**) The transitions $\widetilde{G}$ define a connected graph where threads are always collected by joins.

$$
\begin{aligned}
\mathbf{G}_{\neg\mathsf{thr}} = \mathsf{def}\ & \mathbf{x}_0 = \mathbf{x}_1 + \mathbf{x}_2 \\
& \mathbf{x}_1 = \mathtt{Alice} \to \mathtt{Bob}: \mathit{Book}\langle\mathsf{string}\rangle; \mathbf{x}_3 \\
& \mathbf{x}_2 = \mathtt{Alice} \to \mathtt{Bob}: \mathit{Film}\langle\mathsf{string}\rangle; \mathbf{x}_4 \\
& \mathbf{x}_3 \mid \mathbf{x}_4 = \mathbf{x}_5 \\
& \mathbf{x}_5 = \mathtt{Bob} \to \mathtt{Alice}: \mathit{Price}\langle\mathsf{nat}\rangle; \mathbf{x}_6 \\
& \mathbf{x}_6 = \mathsf{end}\ \mathsf{in}\ \mathbf{x}_0
\end{aligned}
$$

The conditions (1–3) are self-explanatory. (Thread correctness) aims at verifying connexity, the ability to reach end (liveness) and that global types should always join states that occur concurrently and only them: this prevents both deadlocks and state explosion (see [18] for the polynomial verification algorithm). In $\mathbf{G}_{\neg\mathsf{thr}}$ (written above), an illegal join waits for two mutually exclusive messages: as a consequence, Bob is in a deadlock, waiting for both *Book* and *Film* to arrive from Alice.

Local Choice is essential for the consistency of a global type with respect to choice (branching). For $\mathbf{G} = \mathsf{def}\ \widetilde{G}\ \mathsf{in}\ \mathbf{x}_0$, we need to check that each choice is clearly labelled, local to a participant (the choice of which branch to follow should be made by a unique participant) and propagated to the others. To this effect, we define a function $Rcv(\widetilde{G})(\mathbf{x})$ below, which computes the set of all the participants that will be expecting at least one message starting from state $\mathbf{x}$. Additionally, $Rcv(\widetilde{G})(\mathbf{x})$ returns the label l of the received message and the merging points $\tilde{\mathbf{x}}$ encountered. We say that the equality $Rcv(\widetilde{G})(\mathbf{x}_1) = Rcv(\widetilde{G})(\mathbf{x}_2)$ holds if $\forall(\mathtt{p} : l_1 : \tilde{\mathbf{x}}_1) \in Rcv(\widetilde{G})(\mathbf{x}_1), \forall(\mathtt{p} : l_2 : \tilde{\mathbf{x}}_2) \in Rcv(\widetilde{G})(\mathbf{x}_2), l_1 \neq l_2 \vee \tilde{\mathbf{x}}_1, \tilde{\mathbf{x}}_2$ share a non-null suffix (i.e. the two branches have merged). Note that $\mathbf{G}_6$ in Ex. 2.1 satisfies this condition (the *Rcv* sets of both branches contain `Bob` and `Carol`).

$$
\begin{array}{ll}
Rcv(\widetilde{G})(\mathbf{x}) = Rcv(\widetilde{G},\emptyset,\emptyset)(\mathbf{x}) & \text{(remembers recursive calls and receivers)}\\
Rcv(\widetilde{G},\tilde{\mathbf{x}},\tilde{\mathtt{p}})(\mathbf{x}) = Rcv(\widetilde{G},\tilde{\mathbf{x}},\tilde{\mathtt{p}})(\mathbf{x}') & \text{if } \mathbf{x} = \mathtt{p} \to \mathtt{p}' : l\langle U\rangle; \mathbf{x}' \in \widetilde{G} \wedge \mathtt{p}' \in \tilde{\mathtt{p}} \text{ or if } \mathbf{x} \mid \mathbf{x}'' = \mathbf{x}' \in \widetilde{G}\\
Rcv(\widetilde{G},\tilde{\mathbf{x}},\tilde{\mathtt{p}})(\mathbf{x}) = \{\mathtt{p}' : l : \tilde{\mathbf{x}}\} \cup Rcv(\widetilde{G},\tilde{\mathbf{x}},\mathtt{p}'\tilde{\mathtt{p}})(\mathbf{x}') & \text{if } \mathbf{x} = \mathtt{p} \to \mathtt{p}' : l\langle U\rangle; \mathbf{x}' \in \widetilde{G} \wedge \mathtt{p}' \notin \tilde{\mathtt{p}}\\
Rcv(\widetilde{G},\tilde{\mathbf{x}},\tilde{\mathtt{p}})(\mathbf{x}) = Rcv(\widetilde{G},\tilde{\mathbf{x}},\tilde{\mathtt{p}})(\mathbf{x}') \cup Rcv(\widetilde{G},\tilde{\mathbf{x}},\tilde{\mathtt{p}})(\mathbf{x}'') & \text{if } \mathbf{x} = \mathbf{x}' + \mathbf{x}'' \in \widetilde{G} \text{ or } \mathbf{x} = \mathbf{x}' \mid \mathbf{x}'' \in \widetilde{G}\\
Rcv(\widetilde{G},\tilde{\mathbf{x}},\tilde{\mathtt{p}})(\mathbf{x}) = \emptyset & \text{if } \mathbf{x} + \mathbf{x}' = \mathbf{x}'' \in \widetilde{G} \wedge \mathbf{x}'' \in \tilde{\mathbf{x}} \text{ or if } \mathbf{x} = \mathsf{end} \in \widetilde{G}\\
Rcv(\widetilde{G},\tilde{\mathbf{x}},\tilde{\mathtt{p}})(\mathbf{x}) = Rcv(\widetilde{G},\tilde{\mathbf{x}}\mathbf{x}'',\tilde{\mathtt{p}})(\mathbf{x}'') & \text{if } \mathbf{x}' + \mathbf{x} = \mathbf{x}'' \in \widetilde{G} \wedge \mathbf{x}'' \notin \tilde{\mathbf{x}}
\end{array}
$$

$$
\begin{array}{l}
\mathbf{G}_{\neg\mathrm{loc}} = \mathsf{def}\ \mathbf{x}_0 = \mathbf{x}_1 + \mathbf{x}_2\\
\quad \mathbf{x}_1 = \mathtt{Alice} \to \mathtt{Bob} : \mathit{Book}\langle \mathsf{string}\rangle; \mathbf{x}_3\\
\quad \mathbf{x}_2 = \mathtt{Bob} \to \mathtt{Alice} : \mathit{Film}\langle \mathsf{string}\rangle; \mathbf{x}_4\\
\mathbf{x}_3 + \mathbf{x}_4 = \mathbf{x}_5\\
\quad \mathbf{x}_5 = \mathsf{end}\ \mathsf{in}\ \mathbf{x}_0
\end{array}
$$

To guarantee that choices are local to a participant, we also define a function that asserts that, for a choice $\mathbf{x} = \mathbf{x}_1 + \mathbf{x}_2 \in \widetilde{G}$, a unique sender $\mathtt{p}$ is active in each branch $\mathbf{x}_1$ and $\mathbf{x}_2$. This is written $ASend(\widetilde{G})(\mathbf{x}) = \mathtt{p}$ and is undefined if there is more than one active sender (i.e. if the choice is not localised at a unique participant $\mathtt{p}$) (the definition is in [18]). As an example, we give above an illegal global type $\mathbf{G}_{\neg\mathrm{loc}}$ where `Alice` and `Bob` are respectively the active sender of branches $\mathbf{x}_1$ and $\mathbf{x}_2$: as both branches do not agree, the mutual exclusion of *Book* and *Film* can be violated.

Definition 2.1 (Local Choice). A global type $\mathbf{G} = \mathsf{def}\ \widetilde{G}\ \mathsf{in}\ \mathbf{x}_0$ satisfies the local choice conditions if for every transition $\mathbf{x} = \mathbf{x}' + \mathbf{x}'' \in \widetilde{G}$, we have **(1) (Choice awareness)** $Rcv(\widetilde{G})(\mathbf{x}') = Rcv(\widetilde{G})(\mathbf{x}'')$; and **(2) (Unique sender)** $\exists \mathtt{p}, ASend(\widetilde{G})(\mathbf{x}) = \mathtt{p}$.

Linearity. In order to avoid processes with race-conditions, we impose that no participant can be faced with two concurrent receptions where messages can have the same label. This condition, *linearity*, is enforced by comparing the results of $Lin(\widetilde{G})(\mathbf{x}_1)$ and $Lin(\widetilde{G})(\mathbf{x}_2)$ whenever a forking transition $\mathbf{x} = \mathbf{x}_1 \mid \mathbf{x}_2$ is in $\widetilde{G}$. The *Lin* function works in a similar way on message labels as the *Rcv* function on message receivers (linearity is to forks what choice awareness is to choice) and it thus omitted here. As an example, linearity would prevent the labels *Msg*1 and *Msg*2 from both being renamed *Msg*0 in $\mathbf{G}_{AB}$ (since they can be received concurrently and thus confused), but would allow the two labels of $\mathbf{G}_3$ to be identical (they are received by two different parties). Note that the linearity condition incidentally prevents the unbounded creation of threads.

Definition 2.2 (Linearity). *A global type* $\mathbf{G} = \mathsf{def}\ \widetilde{G}\ \mathsf{in}\ \mathbf{x}_0$ *satisfies the linearity condition if, for every transition* $\mathbf{x} = \mathbf{x}' \mid \mathbf{x}'' \in \widetilde{G}$*, we have* $Lin(\widetilde{G})(\mathbf{x}') = Lin(\widetilde{G})(\mathbf{x}'')$.

Well-formedness. We say that a global type $\mathbf{G} = \mathsf{def}\ \widetilde{G}\ \mathsf{in}\ \mathbf{x}_0$ is *well-formed*, if it satisfies the *sanity*, *local choice* and *linearity* conditions. These conditions are related to similar CFSM properties, as discussed in § 3.2. We can easily check that global types from Ex. 2.1 are well-formed. Since *Rcv*, *ASend* and *Lin* can be computed in polynomial time in the size of $\mathbf{G}$ by a simple syntax graph traversal, we have:

Proposition 2.1 (Well-formedness Verification). *Given* $\mathbf{G}$*, we can determine whether* $\mathbf{G}$ *is well-formed or not in polynomial time.*

3 Multiparty Session Automata (MSA) and their Properties

This section starts by defining local types, details the translation from local types into CFSMs, and shows that these CFSMs guarantee the properties given in § 3.3. We call this class of communicating systems *multiparty session automata* (MSA).

3.1 Local Types and the Projection Algorithm

Local types represent the actions of session end-points that each process implementation must follow. As for global types, a local type $\mathbf{T}$ follows the shape of a state machine definition: local types are of the form $\mathsf{def}\ \widetilde{T}\ \mathsf{in}\ \mathbf{x}_0$.

$$
\begin{array}{lll|ll|ll}
\mathbf{T} ::= & \mathsf{def}\ \widetilde{T}\ \mathsf{in}\ \mathbf{x} & \text{local type} & & & & \\
T ::= & \mathbf{x} = !\langle \mathrm{p}, l\langle U\rangle\rangle.\mathbf{x}' & \text{send} & \mathbf{x} = \mathbf{x}' \oplus \mathbf{x}'' & \text{internal choice} & \mathbf{x} = \mathbf{x}' \mid \mathbf{x}'' & \text{fork} \\
\mid & \mathbf{x} = ?\langle \mathrm{p}, l\langle U\rangle\rangle.\mathbf{x}' & \text{receive} & \mathbf{x} = \mathbf{x}' \,\&\, \mathbf{x}'' & \text{external choice} & \mathbf{x} \mid \mathbf{x}' = \mathbf{x}'' & \text{join} \\
\mid & \mathbf{x} = \mathbf{x}' & \text{indirection} & \mathbf{x} + \mathbf{x}' = \mathbf{x}'' & \text{merge} & \mathbf{x} = \mathsf{end} & \text{end}
\end{array}
$$

The local type for send ($!\langle \mathrm{p}, l\langle U\rangle\rangle$) corresponds to the action of sending to p a message with label l and type U, while receive ($?\langle \mathrm{p}, l\langle U\rangle\rangle$) is the action of receiving from p a message with label l and type U. Other behaviours are the indirection (nop), internal choice, external choice, merge, fork, join and end. Note that merge is used for both internal and external choices.

We define the projection of a well-formed global type $\mathbf{G}$ to the local type of participant p (written $\mathbf{G} \upharpoonright \mathrm{p}$) below. The projection is straightforward: $\mathbf{x} = \mathrm{p} \to \mathrm{q} : l\langle U\rangle;\mathbf{x}'$ is an output from p's viewpoint and an input from q's viewpoint; otherwise it creates an indirection link from $\mathbf{x}$ to $\mathbf{x}'$ (i.e. this message exchange is invisible). Choice $\mathbf{x} = \mathbf{x}' + \mathbf{x}''$ is projected to the internal choice if p is the unique (thanks to the local choice well-formedness condition of definition 2.1) participant deciding on which branch to choose; otherwise the projection gives an external choice. For local types, we also define a congruence relation $\equiv$ over $\widetilde{T}$ which eliminates the indirections ($\widetilde{T}, \mathbf{x} = \mathbf{x}' \equiv \widetilde{T}[\mathbf{x}/\mathbf{x}']$) and locally irrelevant choices, and removes the unused local threads. See [18].

$$
\begin{array}{rcl|rcl}
\mathsf{def}\ \widetilde{G}\ \mathsf{in}\ \mathbf{x} \upharpoonright \mathrm{p} & = & \mathsf{def}\ \widetilde{G} \upharpoonright_{\widetilde{G}} \mathrm{p}\ \mathsf{in}\ \mathbf{x} & \mathbf{x} = \mathbf{x}' + \mathbf{x}'' \upharpoonright_{\widetilde{G}} \mathrm{p} & = & \mathbf{x} = \mathbf{x}' \oplus \mathbf{x}'' \\
\mathbf{x} = \mathrm{p} \to \mathrm{p}' : l\langle U\rangle;\mathbf{x}' \upharpoonright_{\widetilde{G}} \mathrm{p} & = & \mathbf{x} = !\langle \mathrm{p}', l\langle U\rangle\rangle.\mathbf{x}' & & & (\text{if } \mathrm{p} = \mathit{ASend}(\widetilde{G})(\mathbf{x})) \\
\mathbf{x} = \mathrm{p} \to \mathrm{p}' : l\langle U\rangle;\mathbf{x}' \upharpoonright_{\widetilde{G}} \mathrm{p}' & = & \mathbf{x} = ?\langle \mathrm{p}, l\langle U\rangle\rangle.\mathbf{x}' & \mathbf{x} = \mathbf{x}' + \mathbf{x}'' \upharpoonright_{\widetilde{G}} \mathrm{p} & = & \mathbf{x} = \mathbf{x}' \,\&\, \mathbf{x}'' \\
\mathbf{x} = \mathrm{p} \to \mathrm{p}' : l\langle U\rangle;\mathbf{x}' \upharpoonright_{\widetilde{G}} \mathrm{p}'' & = & \mathbf{x} = \mathbf{x}'\ (\mathrm{p} \notin \{\mathrm{p}, \mathrm{p}'\}) & & & (\text{otherwise}) \\
\mathbf{x} \mid \mathbf{x}' = \mathbf{x}'' \upharpoonright_{\widetilde{G}} \mathrm{p} & = & \mathbf{x} \mid \mathbf{x}' = \mathbf{x}'' & \mathbf{x} + \mathbf{x}' = \mathbf{x}'' \upharpoonright_{\widetilde{G}} \mathrm{p} & = & \mathbf{x} + \mathbf{x}' = \mathbf{x}'' \\
\mathbf{x} = \mathbf{x}' \mid \mathbf{x}'' \upharpoonright_{\widetilde{G}} \mathrm{p} & = & \mathbf{x} = \mathbf{x}' \mid \mathbf{x}'' & \mathbf{x} = \mathsf{end} \upharpoonright_{\widetilde{G}} \mathrm{p} & = & \mathbf{x} = \mathsf{end}
\end{array}
$$

Proposition 3.1 (Projection). *Given a well-formed* $\mathbf{G}$*, the computation of* $\mathbf{G} \upharpoonright \mathrm{p}$ *is linear in the size of* $\mathbf{G}$.

Example 3.1 (Trade Example). We illustrate our projection algorithm by showing the result of the projection of the global type $\mathbf{G}_{\mathrm{Trade}}$ from § 1 to the three local types of the seller $\mathbf{T}_{\mathrm{TradeS}}$, the broker $\mathbf{T}_{\mathrm{TradeB}}$ and the client $\mathbf{T}_{\mathrm{TradeC}}$. Local type congruence rules are used to simplify the result. When comparing with the CFSMs of Fig. 1, one can observe the similarities but also that local types make the interaction structure clearer and more compact thanks to more precise type constructs ($\oplus$, & and $|$).

$$\begin{array}{ll}
\mathbf{T}_{\mathsf{TradeS}} = & \mathsf{def}\ \mathbf{x}_0 = !\langle \mathtt{SB}, \mathit{Item}\langle\mathsf{string}\rangle\rangle.\mathbf{x}_1 \\
& \mathbf{x}_1 = ?\langle \mathtt{BS}, \mathit{Final}\langle\mathsf{nat}\rangle\rangle.\mathbf{x}_{10} \\
& \mathbf{x}_{10} = \mathsf{end}\quad \mathsf{in}\ \mathbf{x}_0
\end{array}$$

$$\begin{array}{ll}
\mathbf{T}_{\mathsf{TradeC}} = & \mathsf{def}\ \mathbf{x}_5 + \mathbf{x}_0 = \mathbf{x}_2 \\
& \mathbf{x}_2 = \mathbf{x}_3\ \&\ \mathbf{x}_6 \\
& \mathbf{x}_3 = ?\langle \mathtt{BC}, \mathit{Offer}\langle\mathit{nat}\rangle\rangle.\mathbf{x}_4 \\
& \mathbf{x}_4 = !\langle \mathtt{CB}, \mathit{Counter}\langle\mathsf{nat}\rangle\rangle.\mathbf{x}_5 \\
& \mathbf{x}_6 = ?\langle \mathtt{BC}, \mathit{Result}\langle\mathsf{nat}\rangle\rangle.\mathbf{x}_{10} \\
& \mathbf{x}_{10} = \mathsf{end}\quad \mathsf{in}\ \mathbf{x}_0
\end{array}$$

$$\begin{array}{ll}
\mathbf{T}_{\mathsf{TradeB}} = & \mathsf{def}\ \mathbf{x}_0 = ?\langle \mathtt{SB}, \mathit{Item}\langle\mathsf{string}\rangle\rangle.\mathbf{x}_1 \\
& \mathbf{x}_5 + \mathbf{x}_1 = \mathbf{x}_2 \\
& \mathbf{x}_2 = \mathbf{x}_3 \oplus \mathbf{x}_6 \\
& \mathbf{x}_3 = !\langle \mathtt{BC}, \mathit{Offer}\langle\mathsf{nat}\rangle\rangle.\mathbf{x}_4 \\
& \mathbf{x}_4 = ?\langle \mathtt{CB}, \mathit{Counter}\langle\mathsf{nat}\rangle\rangle.\mathbf{x}_5 \\
& \mathbf{x}_6 = \mathbf{x}_7 \mid \mathbf{x}_8 \\
& \mathbf{x}_7 = !\langle \mathtt{BS}, \mathit{Final}\langle\mathsf{nat}\rangle\rangle.\mathbf{x}_9 \\
& \mathbf{x}_8 = !\langle \mathtt{CB}, \mathit{Result}\langle\mathsf{nat}\rangle\rangle.\mathbf{x}_{10} \\
& \mathbf{x}_9 \mid \mathbf{x}_{10} = \mathbf{x}_{11} \\
& \mathbf{x}_{11} = \mathsf{end}\quad \mathsf{in}\ \mathbf{x}_0
\end{array}$$

3.2 Communicating Finite State Machines

In this subsection, we give some preliminary notations (following [7]) and definitions that are relevant to establishing the CFSM connection to local types.

Definitions. ε is the empty word. $\mathbb{A}$ is a finite alphabet and $\mathbb{A}^*$ is the set of all finite words over $\mathbb{A}$. $|x|$ is the length of a word x and $x.y$ or xy the concatenation of two words x and y. Let $\mathcal{P}$ be a set of process identities fixed throughout the paper: $\mathcal{P} \subseteq \{\mathtt{Alice}, \mathtt{Bob}, \mathtt{Carol}, \ldots, \mathtt{A}, \mathtt{B}, \mathtt{C}, \ldots, \mathtt{S}, \ldots\}$.

Definition 3.1 (CFSM). A communicating finite state machine is a finite transition system given by a 5-tuple $M = (Q, C, q_0, \mathbb{A}, \delta)$ where (1) Q is a finite set of *states*; (2) $C = \{\mathtt{pq} \in \mathcal{P}^2 \mid \mathtt{p} \neq \mathtt{q}\}$ is a set of channels; (3) $q_0 \in Q$ is an initial state; (4) $\mathbb{A}$ is a finite *alphabet* of messages, and (5) $\delta \subseteq Q \times (C \times \{!, ?\} \times \mathbb{A}) \times Q$ is a finite set of *transitions*.

In transitions, $\mathtt{pq}!a$ denotes the *sending* action of a from process $\mathtt{p}$ to process $\mathtt{q}$, and $\mathtt{pq}?a$ denotes the *receiving* action of a from $\mathtt{p}$ by $\mathtt{q}$. $\pi, \pi', \ldots$ range over actions. A state $q \in Q$ whose outgoing transitions are all labelled with sending (resp. receiving) actions is called a *sending* (resp. *receiving*) state. A state $q \in Q$ which does not have any outgoing transition is called a *final* state. If q has both sending and receiving outgoing transitions, then q is called *mixed*.

A *path* in M is a finite sequence of $q_0, \ldots, q_n$ ($n \geq 1$) such that $(q_i, \pi, q_{i+1}) \in \delta$ ($0 \leq i \leq n-1$), and we write $q \xrightarrow{\pi} q'$ if $(q, \pi, q') \in \delta$. M is *connected* if for every state $q \neq q_0$, there is a path from q_0 to q. Hereafter we assume each CFSM is connected.

A CFSM $M = (Q, C, q_0, \mathbb{A}, \delta)$ is *deterministic* if for all states $q \in Q$ and all actions π, $(q, \pi, q'), (q, \pi, q'') \in \delta$ imply $q' = q''$.[2]

Definition 3.2 (CS). A (communicating) system S is a tuple $S = (M_\mathtt{p})_{\mathtt{p} \in \mathcal{P}}$ of CFSMs such that $M_\mathtt{p} = (Q_\mathtt{p}, C, q_{0\mathtt{p}}, \mathbb{A}, \delta_\mathtt{p})$.

[2] "Deterministic" often means the same channel should carry a unique value, i.e. if $(q, c!a, q') \in \delta$ and $(q, c!a', q'') \in \delta$ then $a = a'$ and $q' = q''$. Here we follow a different definition [7] in order to represent branching type constructs.

Let $S = (M_p)_{p\in\mathcal{P}}$ such that $M_p = (Q_p, C, q_{0p}, \mathbb{A}, \delta_p)$ and $\delta = \uplus_{p\in\mathcal{P}} \delta_p$. A configuration of S is a tuple such that $s = (\vec{q}; \vec{w})$ with $\vec{q} = (q_p)_{p\in\mathcal{P}}$ with $q_p \in Q_p$ and $\vec{w} = (w_{pq})_{p\neq q\in\mathcal{P}}$ with $w_{pq} \in \mathbb{A}^*$. A configuration $s' = (\vec{q}'; \vec{w}')$ is *reachable* from another configuration $s = (\vec{q}; \vec{w})$ by the *firing of the transition* t, written $s \to s'$ or $s \xrightarrow{t} s'$, if there exists $a \in \mathbb{A}$ such that either:

1. $t = (q_p, pq!a, q'_p) \in \delta_p$ and (a) $q'_{p'} = q_{p'}$ for all $p' \neq p$; and (b) $w'_{pq} = w_{pq}.a$ and $w'_{p'q'} = w_{p'q'}$ for all $p'q' \neq pq$; or
2. $t = (q_q, pq?a, q'_q) \in \delta_q$ and (a) $q'_{p'} = q_{p'}$ for all $p' \neq q$; and (b) $w_{pq} = a.w'_{pq}$ and $w'_{p'q'} = w_{p'q'}$ for all $p'q' \neq pq$.

The condition (1-b) puts the content a to a channel pq, while (2-b) gets the content a from a channel pq. The reflexive and transitive closure of $\to$ is $\to^*$. For a transition $t = (s, \pi, s')$, we write $\ell(t) = \pi$. We write $s_1 \xrightarrow{t_1\cdots t_m} s_{m+1}$ for $s_1 \xrightarrow{t_1} s_2 \cdots \xrightarrow{t_m} s_{m+1}$. We use the metavariable φ to designate sequences of transitions of the form $t_1 \cdots t_m$. The *initial configuration* of the system is $s_0 = (\vec{q}_0; \vec{\varepsilon})$ with $\vec{q}_0 = (q_{0p})_{p\in\mathcal{P}}$. A *final configuration* of the system is $s_f = (\vec{q}; \vec{\varepsilon})$ with all $q_p \in \vec{q}$ final. A configuration s is *reachable* if $s_0 \to^* s$ and we define the *reachable set* of S as $RS(S) = \{s \mid s_0 \to^* s\}$.

Properties Let S be a communicating system, t one of its transitions and $s = (\vec{q}; \vec{w})$ one of its configurations. The following definitions follow [7, Definition 12].

1. s is *stable* if all its buffers are empty, i.e., $\vec{w} = \vec{\varepsilon}$.
2. s is a *deadlock configuration* if $\vec{w} = \vec{\varepsilon}$ and each q_p is a receiving state, i.e. all machines are blocked, waiting for messages.
3. s is an *orphan message configuration* if all $q_p \in \vec{q}$ are final but $\vec{w} \neq \emptyset$, i.e. there is at least an orphan message in a buffer.
4. s is an *unspecified reception configuration* if there exists $q \in \mathcal{P}$ such that q_q is a receiving state and $(q_q, pq?a, q'_q) \in \delta$ implies that $|w_{pq}| > 0$ and $w_{pq} \notin a\mathbb{A}^*$, i.e q_q is prevented from receiving any message from buffer pq.

The set of *receivers* of transitions $s_1 \xrightarrow{t_1\cdots t_m} s_{m+1}$ is defined as $Rcv(t_1 \cdots t_m) = \{q \mid \exists i \leq m, t_i = (s_i, pq?a, s_{i+1})\}$. The set of *active senders* are defined as $ASend(t_1 \cdots t_m) = \{p \mid \exists i \leq m, t_i = (s_i, pq!a, s_{i+1}) \wedge \forall k < i.\ t_k \neq (s_k, p'p?b, s_{k+1})\}$ and represent the participants who could immediately send from state s_1. These definitions match the global types ones. A sequence of transitions (an execution) $s_1 \xrightarrow{t_1} s_2 \cdots s_m \xrightarrow{t_m} s_{m+1}$ is said to be *k-bounded* if all channels of all intermediate configurations s_i do not contain more than k messages.

Definition 3.3 (Properties). Let S be a communicating system.

1. S satisfies the *local choice* property if, for all $s \in RS(S)$ and $s \xrightarrow{\varphi_1} s_1$ and $s \xrightarrow{\varphi_2} s_2$, there exists $\varphi'_1, \varphi'_2, s'_1, s'_2$ such that $s_1 \xrightarrow{\varphi'_1} s'_1$ and $s_2 \xrightarrow{\varphi'_2} s'_2$ with $Rcv(\varphi_1\varphi'_1) = Rcv(\varphi_2\varphi'_2)$ and $ASend(\varphi_1\varphi'_1) = ASend(\varphi_2\varphi'_2)$.
2. S is *deadlock-free* (resp. *orphan message-free*, *reception error-free*) if $s \in RS(S)$, s is not a deadlock (resp. orphan message, unspecified reception) configuration.
3. S is *strongly bounded* if the contents of buffers of all reachable configurations form a finite set.
4. S satisfies the *progress property* if for all $s \in RS(S)$, $s \longrightarrow^* s'$ implies s' is either final or $s' \longrightarrow s''$; and S satisfies the *liveness property*[3] if for all $s \in RS(S)$, there exists $s \longrightarrow^* s'$ such that s' is final.

[3] The terminology follows [6].

3.3 Multiparty Session Automata (MSA)

We now give a translation from local types to CFSMs, specifying the sequences of actions in a local type as transitions of a CFSM. We use the following notation to keep track of local states:

$$\mathtt{X} ::= \mathbf{x} \quad | \quad \mathtt{X} \,|\, \mathtt{X} \qquad \mathtt{X}[\_] ::= \_ \quad | \quad \mathtt{X}[\_] \,|\, \mathtt{X} \quad | \quad \mathtt{X} \,|\, \mathtt{X}[\_]$$

We also define an equivalence relation $\equiv_{\widetilde{T}}$ that identifies two states if one of them allows the actions of the other:

$$\mathtt{X} \,|\, \mathtt{X}' \equiv_{\widetilde{T}} \mathtt{X}' \,|\, \mathtt{X} \qquad \mathtt{X} \,|\, (\mathtt{X}' \,|\, \mathtt{X}'') \equiv_{\widetilde{T}} (\mathtt{X} \,|\, \mathtt{X}') \,|\, \mathtt{X}''$$

$$\frac{\mathbf{x} = \mathbf{x}' \in \widetilde{T}}{\mathtt{X}[\mathbf{x}] \equiv_{\widetilde{T}} \mathtt{X}[\mathbf{x}']} \quad \frac{\mathbf{x} = \mathbf{x}' \,|\, \mathbf{x}'' \in \widetilde{T}}{\mathtt{X}[\mathbf{x}] \equiv_{\widetilde{T}} \mathtt{X}[\mathbf{x}' \,|\, \mathbf{x}'']} \quad \frac{\mathbf{x} \,|\, \mathbf{x}' = \mathbf{x}'' \in \widetilde{T}}{\mathtt{X}[\mathbf{x} \,|\, \mathbf{x}'] \equiv_{\widetilde{T}} \mathtt{X}[\mathbf{x}'']} \quad \frac{\mathbf{x} = \mathbf{x}' \,\&\, \mathbf{x}'' \in \widetilde{T}}{\mathtt{X}[\mathbf{x}] \equiv_{\widetilde{T}} \mathtt{X}[\mathbf{x}']} \quad \frac{\mathbf{x} = \mathbf{x}' \,\&\, \mathbf{x}'' \in \widetilde{T}}{\mathtt{X}[\mathbf{x}] \equiv_{\widetilde{T}} \mathtt{X}[\mathbf{x}'']}$$

$$\frac{\mathbf{x} = \mathbf{x}' \oplus \mathbf{x}'' \in \widetilde{T}}{\mathtt{X}[\mathbf{x}] \equiv_{\widetilde{T}} \mathtt{X}[\mathbf{x}']} \quad \frac{\mathbf{x} = \mathbf{x}' \oplus \mathbf{x}'' \in \widetilde{T}}{\mathtt{X}[\mathbf{x}] \equiv_{\widetilde{T}} \mathtt{X}[\mathbf{x}'']} \quad \frac{\mathbf{x} + \mathbf{x}' = \mathbf{x}'' \in \widetilde{T}}{\mathtt{X}[\mathbf{x}] \equiv_{\widetilde{T}} \mathtt{X}[\mathbf{x}'']} \quad \frac{\mathbf{x} + \mathbf{x}' = \mathbf{x}'' \in \widetilde{T}}{\mathtt{X}[\mathbf{x}'] \equiv_{\widetilde{T}} \mathtt{X}[\mathbf{x}'']}$$

Definition 3.4 (Translation from Local Types to MSA). Let $\mathbf{T} = \mathsf{def}\ \widetilde{T}\ \mathsf{in}\ \mathbf{x}_0$ be the local type of participant p projected from $\mathbf{G}$. The automaton corresponding to $\mathbf{T}$ is $\mathcal{A}(\mathbf{T}) = (Q, C, q_0, \mathbb{A}, \delta)$ where:

- Q is defined as the set of states $\mathtt{X}$ built from the recursion variables $\{\mathbf{x}_i\}$ of $\mathbf{T}$. Q is defined up to the equivalence relation $\equiv_{\widetilde{T}}$.
- $C = \{\mathrm{pq} \mid \mathrm{p}, \mathrm{q} \in \mathbf{G}\}$; $q_0 = \mathbf{x}_0$; and $\mathbb{A}$ is the set of $\{l \in \mathbf{G}\}$
- δ is defined by: $\begin{array}{l}(\mathtt{X}[\mathbf{x}], (\mathrm{pp}'!l), \mathtt{X}[\mathbf{x}']) \in \delta \text{ if } \mathbf{x} = !\langle \mathrm{p}', l\langle U \rangle\rangle.\mathbf{x}' \in \widetilde{T} \\ (\mathtt{X}[\mathbf{x}], (\mathrm{p}'\mathrm{p}?l), \mathtt{X}[\mathbf{x}']) \in \delta \text{ if } \mathbf{x} = ?\langle \mathrm{p}', l\langle U \rangle\rangle.\mathbf{x}' \in \widetilde{T}\end{array}$

We call ***Multiparty Session Automata (MSA)***, communicating systems S of the form $(\mathcal{A}(\mathbf{G} \upharpoonright \mathrm{p}))_{\mathrm{p} \in \mathbf{G}}$ when $\mathbf{G}$ is a well-formed global type.

The generation of an MSA from a global type $\mathbf{G}$ is exponential in the size of $\mathbf{G}$. It is however polynomial in the absence of parallel composition. Note that neither well-formedness nor type-checking requires the explicit generation of MSAs.

MSA Examples. The following shows local types (projections from Ex. 2.1) and their corresponding automata. The Trade example from Fig. 1 and Ex. 3.1 is another complete example of MSA.

1. $\mathbf{G}_1 \upharpoonright \mathtt{Alice} = \mathsf{def}\ \mathbf{x}_0 = !\langle \mathtt{Bob}, \mathit{Msg}\langle \mathsf{nat} \rangle\rangle.\mathbf{x}_1$
   $\mathbf{x}_1 = \mathsf{end}\ \mathsf{in}\ \mathbf{x}_0$

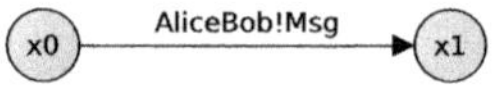

2. $\mathbf{G}_2 \upharpoonright \mathtt{Bob} = \mathsf{def}\ \mathbf{x}_0 = \mathbf{x}_1 \& \mathbf{x}_2$
   $\mathbf{x}_1 = ?\langle \mathtt{Alice}, \mathit{Book}\langle \mathsf{string} \rangle\rangle.\mathbf{x}_3$
   $\mathbf{x}_2 = ?\langle \mathtt{Alice}, \mathit{Film}\langle \mathsf{string} \rangle\rangle.\mathbf{x}_4$
   $\mathbf{x}_3 + \mathbf{x}_4 = \mathbf{x}_5$
   $\mathbf{x}_5 = \mathsf{end}\ \mathsf{in}\ \mathbf{x}_0$

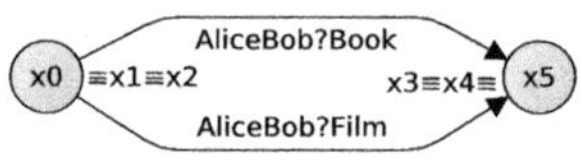

3. $\mathbf{G}_3 \upharpoonright \mathtt{Alice} = \mathsf{def}\ \mathbf{x}_0 = \mathbf{x}_1 \mid \mathbf{x}_2$
   $\mathbf{x}_1 = !\langle \mathtt{Bob}, \mathit{Book}\langle \mathsf{string} \rangle\rangle.\mathbf{x}_3$
   $\mathbf{x}_2 = ?\langle \mathtt{Bob}, \mathit{Film}\langle \mathsf{string} \rangle\rangle.\mathbf{x}_4$
   $\mathbf{x}_3 \mid \mathbf{x}_4 = \mathbf{x}_5$
   $\mathbf{x}_5 = \mathsf{end}\ \mathsf{in}\ \mathbf{x}_0$

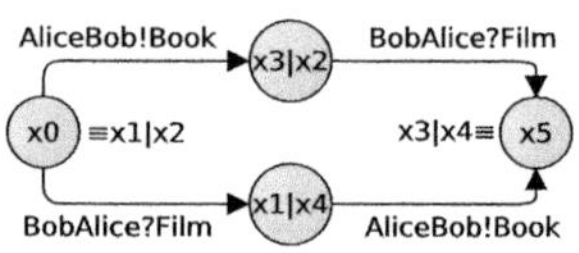

1. The MSA of the projection of $\mathbf{G}_1$ to `Alice` has two states and one transition.
2. Since `Bob` is receiving `Alice`'s messages, the projection of $\mathbf{G}_2$ to `Bob` gives an external choice. The automaton has two nodes $\mathbf{x}_0$ (equivalent to $\mathbf{x}_1$ and $\mathbf{x}_2$) and $\mathbf{x}_5$ (equivalent to $\mathbf{x}_3$ and $\mathbf{x}_4$), and two transitions between these nodes.
3. $\mathbf{G}_3$ has two concurrent communications. It results in an automaton for `Alice` with four nodes, reflecting the interleavings of the concurrent interactions.

3.4 Properties of MSAs

This subsection proves that MSA satisfy the properties defined in definition 3.3. We qualify executions of the form $s \xrightarrow{\varphi_1} s_1 \xrightarrow{\varphi_2} s_2$ with $s \in RS(S)$ such that φ_1 is an alternation of sending and corresponding receive actions (i.e. the action $\mathsf{pq}!a$ is immediately followed by $\mathsf{pq}?a$) and φ_2 is only sending actions as being *stable-outputs*. The key property is Lemma 3.1(3), whose proof is non-trivial and relies on Lemma 3.1(2) and well-formed conditions of global types (except choice awareness in definition 2.1). Then Lemma 3.1(4) (the existence of *stable executions* [7]) directly leads to unspecified reception error-freedom and orphan message freedom. For the deadlock-freedom, we require choice awareness of Lemma 3.1(1), ensured by the same condition in definition 2.1. Theorem 3.2 uses the results from [9, § 3]; in Theorem 3.3, progress is proved from Theorem 3.1, while liveness directly uses the thread correctness condition.

Lemma 3.1 (Properties of MSAs). *Suppose S is a MSA.*

1. (local choice) *S satisfies a local choice condition.*
2. (diamond property) *Suppose* $s \in RS(S)$ *and* $s \xrightarrow{t_1} s_1$ *and* $s \xrightarrow{t_2} s_2$ *where (1)* t_1 *and* t_2 *are both inputs; or (2)* t_1 *is an output and* t_2 *is an input, then there exists* s' *such that* $s_1 \xrightarrow{t_1'} s'$ *and* $s_2 \xrightarrow{t_2'} s'$ *where* $\ell(t_1) = \ell(t_2')$ *and* $\ell(t_2) = \ell(t_1')$.
3. (stable-outputs decomposition) *Suppose* $s \in RS(S)$. *Then there exists* $s_0 \xrightarrow{\varphi_1} \cdots \xrightarrow{\varphi_n} s$ *where each* φ_i *is stable-outputs.*
4. (stable) *Suppose* $s_0 \xrightarrow{\varphi_1} \cdots \xrightarrow{\varphi_n} s$ *with* φ_i *stable-outputs. Then there exists an execution* $\xrightarrow{\varphi'}$ *such that* $s \xrightarrow{\varphi'} s_3$ *and* s_3 *is stable, and there is a 1-buffer execution* $s_0 \xrightarrow{\varphi''} s_3$.

Theorem 3.1 (Safety Properties). *A MSA S is free from unspecified reception errors, orphan messages and deadlock.*

Theorem 3.2 (Strong Boundedness). *Consider a MSA S, generated from the local types of* $\mathbf{G}$. *If all actions that are within a cycle in* $\mathbf{G}$ *are also part of causal input-output cycle (IO-causality) [9, 14],*[4] *then S is strongly bounded.*

Theorem 3.3 (Progress and Liveness). *A MSA S satisfies the progress property. If a MSA S is generated from the local types of* $\mathbf{G}$ *and* $\mathbf{G}$ *contains* end, *then S satisfies the liveness property.*

4 General Multiparty Session Processes

This section introduces *general multiparty session processes* . Our new system handles (1) new external and internal choice operators that allow branching with different receivers and merging with different senders; and (2) forking and joining threads which are not verifiable by standard session type systems [3, 6, 14].

[4] It is formally defined in [9, 14] and [18].

Syntax. The syntax of processes is defined below.

$v ::= a \mid \texttt{true} \mid \texttt{false} \mid \ldots$	values		$e ::= v \mid x \mid e \wedge e \mid \ldots$	expression
$\mathbf{P} ::= \mathsf{def}\ \widetilde{P}\ \mathsf{in}\ \mathbf{X}$	definition		$h ::= \emptyset \mid h \cdot (\mathtt{p}, \mathtt{q}, l\langle v \rangle)$	messages
$P ::=$	process transition		$\mathbf{X} ::=$	state
$\mid \mathbf{x}(\tilde{x}) = x\langle \mathbf{G} \rangle.\mathbf{x}'(\tilde{e})$	init		$\mid \mathbf{x}(\tilde{v})$	thread
$\mid \mathbf{x}(\tilde{x}) = x[\mathtt{p}](y).\mathbf{x}'(\tilde{e})$	request		$\mid \mathbf{X} \mid \mathbf{X}$	parallel
$\mid \mathbf{x}(\tilde{x}) = x!\langle \mathtt{p}, l\langle e \rangle \rangle.\mathbf{x}'(\tilde{e})$	send		$\mid (\nu a)\mathbf{X}$	restriction
$\mid \mathbf{x}(\tilde{x}) = x?\langle \mathtt{p}, l(y) \rangle.\mathbf{x}'(\tilde{e})$	receive		$\mid \mathbf{0}$	null
$\mid \mathbf{x}(\tilde{x}) = \mathbf{x}'(\tilde{y}) \mid \mathbf{x}''(\tilde{z})$	parallel		$\mathbf{N} ::=$	network
$\mid \mathbf{x}(\tilde{x}) = \texttt{if}\ e\ \texttt{then}\ \mathbf{x}'(\tilde{e}')\ \texttt{else}\ \mathbf{x}''(\tilde{e}'')$	conditional		$\mid \mathbf{P}$	def
$\mid \mathbf{x}(\tilde{x}) = \mathbf{x}'(\tilde{x})\ \&\ \mathbf{x}''(\tilde{x})$	external choice		$\mid \mathbf{N} \parallel \mathbf{N}$	parallel
$\mid \mathbf{x}(\tilde{y}) \mid \mathbf{x}'(\tilde{z}) = \mathbf{x}''(\tilde{x})$	join		$\mid (\nu a)\mathbf{N}$	new name
$\mid \mathbf{x}(\tilde{x}) + \mathbf{x}'(\tilde{x}) = \mathbf{x}''(\tilde{x})$	merge		$\mid \mathbf{0}$	null
$\mid \mathbf{x}(\tilde{x}) = (\nu a)\ \mathbf{x}'(a\tilde{x})$	new name		$\mid (\nu s)\mathbf{N}$	new session
$\mid \mathbf{x}(\tilde{x}) = \mathbf{0}$	null		$\mid s : h$	queue
			$\mid a\langle s \rangle[\mathtt{p}]$	invitation

A process always starts from a definition $\mathbf{P} = \mathsf{def}\ \widetilde{P}\ \mathsf{in}\ \mathbf{x}(\tilde{v})$, where the parameters of $\mathbf{x}$ in $\widetilde{P}$ are to be instantiated by $\tilde{v}$. The form of process actions $\widetilde{P}$ follows global and local types and rely on a functional style to pass values around continuations. Variables $\tilde{x}$ in $\mathbf{x}(\tilde{x})$ occurring on the left-hand side of a process action are binding variables on the right-hand side. Variables y in request and receive are also binding (e.g. in $\mathbf{x}(x,z) = z?\langle \mathtt{p}, l(y) \rangle.\mathbf{x}'(x,y,z)$, the final z is bound by z in $\mathbf{x}(x,z)$, while y is bound by the input).

A session is initialised by a transition of the form $\mathbf{x}(\tilde{x}) = x\langle \mathbf{G} \rangle.\mathbf{x}'(\tilde{e})$ where $\mathbf{G}$ is a global type. It attributes a global interaction pattern defined in $\mathbf{G}$ to the shared channel a that x gets substituted to. The variables in $\tilde{e}$ are all bound by $\tilde{x}$. After a session initialisation, participants can accept the session with $\mathbf{x}(\tilde{x}) = x[\mathtt{p}](y).\mathbf{x}'(\tilde{e})$ (as long as x is substituted by the same share channel a as the initialisation), starting the interaction: the variables in $\tilde{e}$ are bound by $\tilde{x}$ and by y, which, at run-time, receives the session channel.

The sending action $x!\langle \mathtt{p}, l\langle e \rangle \rangle$ allows in session x to send to p a value e labelled by a constant l. The reception $x?\langle \mathtt{p}, l(y) \rangle.\mathbf{x}'(\tilde{e})$ expects from p a message with a label l. The message payload is then received in variable y, which binds in $\mathbf{x}'(\tilde{e})$.

$\mathbf{x}(\tilde{x}) = \mathbf{x}'(\tilde{y}) \mid \mathbf{x}''(\tilde{z})$ represent forking threads (i.e. $P \mid Q$): $\tilde{y}$ and $\tilde{z}$ are subsets of $\tilde{x}$. The conditional ($\texttt{if}\ e\ \texttt{then}\ \mathbf{x}'(\tilde{e}')\ \texttt{else}\ \mathbf{x}''(\tilde{e}'')$) and the external choices ($\mathbf{x}'(\tilde{x})\ \&\ \mathbf{x}''(\tilde{x})$) are extensions of the traditional selection and branching actions of session types. The join action collects parallel threads, while the merge action collects internal and external choices. Note that external choice, fork, join and merge only allow a restricted use of bound variables for continuations. $\mathbf{x}(\tilde{x}) = (\nu a)\mathbf{x}'(a\tilde{x})$ creates a new shared name a. $\mathbf{0}$ is an inactive agent. For simplicity, we omit the action of leaving a session.

The process states $\mathbf{X}$ are defined from the state variables present in $\widetilde{P}$. The network $\mathbf{N}$ is a parallel composition of definition agents, with restrictions of the form $(\nu a)\mathbf{N}$.

Once a session is running, our operational semantics uses run-time syntax not directly accessible to the programmer. $\mathbf{X} \mid \mathbf{X}'$ and $(\nu a)\mathbf{X}$ are for example only accessible at run-time. Session instances are represented by session restriction $(\nu s)P$. The message buffer $s : h$ stores the messages in transit for the session instance s. A session invitation $a[\mathrm{p}]\langle s\rangle$ invites participant p to start the session s announced on channel a.

A network which only consists of shared name restrictions and parallel compositions of $\mathsf{def}\ \widetilde{P}\ \mathsf{in}\ \mathbf{x}(\vec{v})$ is called *initial*.

Operational Semantics. We define the operational semantics for processes and networks below. We use the following labels to organise the reduction of processes.

$$\alpha,\beta \ ::= \ \tau \mid s[\mathrm{p},\mathrm{q}]!l\langle v\rangle \mid s[\mathrm{p},\mathrm{q}]?l\langle v\rangle \mid a\langle \mathbf{G}\rangle \mid a\langle \mathrm{p}\rangle[s]$$

The rules are divided into two parts. The first part corresponds to a transition relation of the form $\widetilde{P} \vdash \mathbf{X} \xrightarrow{\alpha} \mathbf{X}'$ representing that a process in a state $\mathbf{X}$ can move to state $\mathbf{X}'$ with action α. The second part defines reductions within networks (with unlabelled transitions $\mathbf{N} \to \mathbf{N}'$). $e \downarrow v$ denotes the evaluation of expression e to v.

$$\frac{x[\tilde{v}/\tilde{x}] = a \qquad \tilde{e}[\tilde{v}/\tilde{x}] \downarrow \vec{v}'}{\mathbf{x}(\tilde{x}) = x\langle \mathbf{G}\rangle.\mathbf{x}'(\tilde{e}) \vdash \mathbf{x}(\tilde{v}) \xrightarrow{a\langle \mathbf{G}\rangle} \mathbf{x}'(\vec{v}')}\,[\text{INIT}] \qquad \frac{x[\tilde{v}/\tilde{x}] = a \qquad \tilde{e}[\tilde{v}/\tilde{x}][s/y] \downarrow \vec{v}'}{\mathbf{x}(\tilde{x}) = x[\mathrm{p}](y).\mathbf{x}'(\tilde{e}) \vdash \mathbf{x}(\tilde{v}) \xrightarrow{a\langle s\rangle[\mathrm{p}]} \mathbf{x}'(\vec{v}')}\,[\text{ACC}]$$

$$\frac{x[\tilde{v}/\tilde{x}] = s[\mathrm{q}] \qquad e[\tilde{v}/\tilde{x}] \downarrow v \qquad \tilde{e}[\tilde{v}/\tilde{x}] \downarrow \vec{v}'}{\mathbf{x}(\tilde{x}) = x!\langle \mathrm{p}, l\langle e\rangle\rangle.\mathbf{x}'(\tilde{e}) \vdash \mathbf{x}(\tilde{v}) \xrightarrow{s[\mathrm{q},\mathrm{p}]!l\langle v\rangle} \mathbf{x}'(\vec{v}')}\,[\text{SEND}]$$

$$\frac{x[\tilde{v}/\tilde{x}] = s[\mathrm{q}] \qquad \tilde{e}[\tilde{v}/\tilde{x}][v/y] \downarrow \vec{v}'}{\mathbf{x}(\tilde{x}) = x?\langle \mathrm{p}, l(y)\rangle.\mathbf{x}'(\tilde{e}) \vdash \mathbf{x}(\tilde{v}) \xrightarrow{s[\mathrm{p},\mathrm{q}]?l\langle v'\rangle} \mathbf{x}'(\vec{v}')}\,[\text{RCV}] \qquad \frac{a \notin \tilde{v}}{\mathbf{x}(\tilde{x}) = (\nu a)\mathbf{x}'(a\tilde{x}) \vdash \mathbf{x}(\tilde{v}) \xrightarrow{\tau} (\nu a)\mathbf{x}'(a\tilde{v})}\,[\text{NEW}]$$

$$\frac{e[\tilde{v}/\tilde{x}] \downarrow \mathsf{true} \qquad \tilde{e}'[\tilde{v}/\tilde{x}] \downarrow \vec{v}'}{\mathbf{x}(\tilde{x}) = \texttt{if}\ e\ \texttt{then}\ \mathbf{x}'(\tilde{e}')\ \texttt{else}\ \mathbf{x}''(\tilde{e}'') \vdash \mathbf{x}(\tilde{v}) \xrightarrow{\tau} \mathbf{x}'(\vec{v}')}\,[\text{IFT}]$$

$$\frac{\widetilde{P}, \mathbf{x}(\tilde{x}) = \mathbf{x}'(\tilde{x})\ \&\ \mathbf{x}''(\tilde{x}) \vdash \mathbf{x}'(\tilde{v}) \xrightarrow{\alpha} \mathbf{X}}{\widetilde{P}, \mathbf{x}(\tilde{x}) = \mathbf{x}'(\tilde{x})\ \&\ \mathbf{x}''(\tilde{x}) \vdash \mathbf{x}(\tilde{v}) \xrightarrow{\alpha} \mathbf{X}}\,[\text{EXT}] \qquad \frac{\widetilde{P} \vdash \mathbf{X} \xrightarrow{\alpha} \mathbf{X}'}{\mathsf{def}\ \widetilde{P}\ \mathsf{in}\ \mathbf{X} \xrightarrow{\alpha} \mathsf{def}\ \widetilde{P}\ \mathsf{in}\ \mathbf{X}'}\,[\text{DEF}] \qquad \frac{\mathbf{P} \xrightarrow{\tau} \mathbf{P}'}{\mathbf{P} \to \mathbf{P}'}\,[\text{TAU}]$$

$$\frac{\mathbf{P} \xrightarrow{s[\mathrm{p},\mathrm{q}]!l\langle v\rangle} \mathbf{P}'}{\mathbf{P} \mid\mid s : h \to \mathbf{P}' \mid\mid s : h \cdot (\mathrm{p},\mathrm{q},l\langle v\rangle)}\,[\text{PUT}] \qquad \frac{\mathbf{P} \xrightarrow{s[\mathrm{p},\mathrm{q}]?l\langle v\rangle} \mathbf{P}'}{\mathbf{P} \mid\mid s : (\mathrm{p},\mathrm{q},l\langle v\rangle) \cdot h \to \mathbf{P}' \mid\mid s : h}\,[\text{GET}]$$

$$\frac{\mathbf{P} \xrightarrow{a\langle \mathbf{G}\rangle} \mathbf{P}' \qquad \mathrm{p}_0,\ldots,\mathrm{p}_k \in \mathbf{G} \qquad s \notin \mathsf{fn}(\mathbf{P}')}{\mathbf{P} \to (\nu s)(\mathbf{P}' \mid\mid s : \varepsilon \mid\mid a\langle s\rangle[\mathrm{p}_0] \mid\mid \ldots \mid\mid a\langle s\rangle[\mathrm{p}_k])}\,[\text{INIT}_N] \qquad \frac{\mathbf{P} \xrightarrow{a\langle s\rangle[\mathrm{p}]} \mathbf{P}'}{\mathbf{P} \mid\mid a\langle s\rangle[\mathrm{p}] \to \mathbf{P}'}\,[\text{ACC}_N]$$

Rule [SEND] emits a message from p to q, substituting variables $\tilde{x}$ by $\tilde{v}$ and evaluating e to v. Rule [RCV] inputs a message and instantiates y to the received value v. Rule [INIT] initiates a session, while rule [ACC] emits a signal which signifies the process's readiness to participate in a session. Rule [IFT] internally selects the first branch with respect to the value of e ([IFF] is similarly defined). Rule [NEW] creates a new shared name. Rule [EXT] is the external choice, which invokes either the left or right state variable, depending on which label α is received.

Rules [DEF] and [TAU] promote processes to the network level. [INIT$_N$] is used in combination with [INIT]. It creates an empty queue $s : \varepsilon$ together with invitations for each participant. Rule [ACC$_N$] consumes an invitation to participate to the session if someone has been signalled ready (via [ACC]). Other contextual rules are standard (we omit the structure rules, $\equiv$). We write $\longrightarrow^*$ for the multi-step reduction.

Example 4.1 (Trade Example). We write here an implementation of the Trade example from § 1. The reader can refer to Fig. 1 and Ex. 3.1 for the global and local types.

$$\begin{array}{rl} \mathbf{P}_{\mathsf{S}} = \mathsf{def} & \mathbf{x}(x,y) = x\langle \mathbf{G}_{\mathrm{Trade}}\rangle.\mathbf{x}'(x,y) \\ & \mathbf{x}'(x,y) = x[\mathtt{S}](z).\mathbf{x}_0(y,z) \\ & \mathbf{x}_0(y,z) = z\,!\,\langle \mathtt{B}, \mathit{Item}\langle y\rangle\rangle.\mathbf{x}_1(z) \\ & \mathbf{x}_1(z) = z\,?\,\langle \mathtt{B}, \mathit{Final}(y)\rangle.\mathbf{x}_{10}(z,y) \\ & \mathbf{x}_{10}(z,y) = \mathbf{0} \qquad \mathsf{in}\ \mathbf{x}(a, \text{``HGG''}) \end{array}$$

$$\begin{array}{rl} \mathbf{P}_{\mathsf{C}} = \mathsf{def} & \mathbf{x}(x,i) = x[\mathtt{C}](z).\mathbf{x}_0(i,z) \\ & \mathbf{x}_5(i,z) + \mathbf{x}_0(i,z) = \mathbf{x}_2(i,z) \\ & \mathbf{x}_2(i,z) = \mathbf{x}_3(i,z)\ \&\ \mathbf{x}_6(i,z) \\ & \mathbf{x}_3(i,z) = z\,?\,\langle \mathtt{B}, \mathit{Offer}(y)\rangle.\mathbf{x}_4(i,z,y) \\ & \mathbf{x}_4(i,z,y) = z\,!\,\langle \mathtt{B}, \mathit{Counter}\langle i\rangle\rangle.\mathbf{x}_5(i+5,z) \\ & \mathbf{x}_6(i,z) = z\,?\,\langle \mathtt{B}, \mathit{Result}(y)\rangle.\mathbf{x}_{10}(y,z) \\ & \mathbf{x}_{10}(y,z) = \mathbf{0} \qquad \mathsf{in}\ \mathbf{x}(a,50) \end{array}$$

$\mathbf{P}_{\mathsf{S}}$ and $\mathbf{P}_{\mathsf{C}}$, respectively correspond to the seller S and client C. $\mathbf{P}_{\mathsf{S}}$ initiates the session by announcing $\mathbf{G}_{\mathrm{Trade}}$ on shared name a. According to rule [INIT$_N$], it creates a session name s, a message buffer and invitations for S, B and C. $\mathbf{P}_{\mathsf{S}}$ then joins the session as the seller S, the variable z being used to contain the session name. $\mathbf{P}_{\mathsf{S}}$ proceeds with $\mathbf{x}_0(y,z)$ where y is the string "HGG" and z the session name. The execution of $\mathbf{x}_0(y,z)$ sends a message *Item* with payload "HGG" in the message buffer. $\mathbf{P}_{\mathsf{C}}$ starts in $\mathbf{x}(a,50)$ where a is the shared name and 50 the price it is ready to offer initially. It joins the session as the client C, gets in variable z the session name s and continues with $\mathbf{x}_0(i,z)$. The message *Offer* is then countered as many times needed with a slowly increased proposed price.

5 Properties of Generalised Multiparty Session Processes

5.1 Typing Generalised Multiparty Session Processes

Environments. We use u to denote a shared channel a and its variable x and c to denote a session channel $s[\mathrm{p}]$ or its variable. The grammar of environments are defined as:

$$\Gamma ::= \emptyset \mid \Gamma, u : U \qquad \Delta ::= \emptyset \mid \Delta, c : \mathbf{T} \qquad \Sigma ::= \emptyset \mid \Sigma, \mathbf{x} : \tilde{U}$$

Γ is the *standard environment* which associates variables to sort types and shared names to global types. Δ is the *session environment* which associates channels to session types. Σ keeps tracking state variable associations. We write $\Gamma, u : U$ only if $u \notin \mathsf{dom}(\Gamma)$. Similarly for other variables.

Judgements. The different judgements that are used are:

$\Gamma \vdash e : U$	Expression e has type U under Γ
$\Gamma \vdash P \triangleright \Sigma \parallel \Sigma'$	Left/right variables in P have types Σ/Σ' under Γ
$\Gamma \vdash \mathbf{P} \triangleright \Delta$	Process $\mathbf{P}$ has type Δ under Γ
$\Gamma, \widetilde{P} \vdash \mathbf{X} \triangleright \Delta$	State variable $\mathbf{X}$ has type Δ under Γ and $\widetilde{P}$
$\Gamma \vdash \mathbf{N} \triangleright \Delta$	Network $\mathbf{N}$ has type Δ under Γ

Typing Rules. We only list two typing rules. There is one main difference with existing multiparty typing system: to type a process $\mathbf{P}$, we need to gather for every session the typing constraints of the transitions $\widetilde{P}$ in $\mathbf{P}$, keeping track of associations such as $\mathbf{x}_1 = !\langle \mathrm{p}, l\langle U\rangle\rangle.\mathbf{x}_2$. We rely on an effective use of "matching" between local types and inferred transitions to keep the typing system for initial processes simple.

$$\frac{\tilde{y} : \tilde{U} \vdash \tilde{e} : \tilde{U}' \quad \tilde{y} : \tilde{U} \vdash x : \langle \mathbf{G}\rangle \quad \forall i, \mathbf{T}_i = \mathbf{T}'_i \uplus \mathbf{x} = \mathbf{x}'}{\vdash \mathbf{x}(\tilde{y}\tilde{z}) = x\langle \mathbf{G}\rangle.\mathbf{x}'(\tilde{e}\tilde{z}) \triangleright \mathbf{x} : \tilde{U}\tilde{\mathbf{T}} \parallel \mathbf{x}' : \tilde{U}'\tilde{\mathbf{T}}'}\,[\textsc{Init}]$$

$$\frac{\tilde{y} : \tilde{U} \vdash \tilde{e} : \tilde{U}' \quad \tilde{y} : \tilde{U} \vdash x : \langle \mathbf{G}\rangle \quad \forall i, \mathbf{T}_i = \mathbf{T}'_i \uplus \mathbf{x} = \mathbf{x}' \quad \mathbf{T} = \mathbf{G} \upharpoonright \mathrm{p}}{\vdash \mathbf{x}(\tilde{y}\tilde{z}) = x[\mathrm{p}](y).\mathbf{x}'(\tilde{e}\tilde{z}y) \triangleright \mathbf{x} : \tilde{U}\tilde{\mathbf{T}} \parallel \mathbf{x}' : \tilde{U}'\tilde{\mathbf{T}}'\mathbf{T}}\,[\textsc{Req}]$$

In the rules, $\tilde{y}$ and $\tilde{z}$ correspond to sorts and session types, respectively. Rule [INIT] types the initialisation. $\tilde{y}$ should cover x and variables in $\tilde{e}$ appearing in the right hand side. The type system records that every z_i should have type $\mathbf{T} \uplus \mathbf{x} = \mathbf{x}'$, which means that we record $\mathbf{x} = \mathbf{x}'$ at the head of $\mathbf{T}$ (formally defined as: $\mathsf{def}\ \mathbf{x} = \mathbf{x}', \widetilde{T}\ \mathsf{in}\ \mathbf{x}$ if $\mathbf{T} = \mathsf{def}\ \widetilde{T}\ \mathsf{in}\ \mathbf{x}'$). Rule [REQ] is similar except we record the introduced projected session type $\mathbf{T} = \mathbf{G} \upharpoonright \mathtt{p}$.

Proposition 5.1 (Decidability). *Assuming the new and bound names and variables in* $\mathbf{N}$ *are annotated by types, type checking of* $\Gamma \vdash \mathbf{N}$ *terminates in polynomial time.*

5.2 Properties of Typed Multiparty Session Processes

This subsection shows that typed processes enjoy the same properties as MSAs defined in definition 3.3. The correspondence with CFSMs makes the statements of the properties of processes formally rigorous and eases the proofs.

Let ℓ range over transition labels for types: $\ell ::= \tau \mid !\langle \mathtt{p}, l\langle U \rangle\rangle \mid ?\langle \mathtt{p}, l\langle U \rangle\rangle$. We define below a labelled transition relation between types $\mathbf{T} \xrightarrow{\ell} \mathbf{T}'$, defined modulo structure rules (for join and merge) and type equality.

$$
\begin{array}{rcll}
\mathsf{def}\ \widetilde{T}\ \mathsf{in}\ \mathbf{x} & \equiv & \mathsf{def}\ \widetilde{T}'\ \mathsf{in}\ \mathbf{x} \quad (\widetilde{T} = \widetilde{T}') & \lfloor\text{EQ}\rfloor \\
\mathsf{def}\ \mathbf{x}_1 + \mathbf{x}_2 = \mathbf{x}, \widetilde{T}\ \mathsf{in}\ \mathbf{x}_i & \equiv & \mathsf{def}\ \mathbf{x}_1 + \mathbf{x}_2 = \mathbf{x}, \widetilde{T}\ \mathsf{in}\ \mathbf{x} \quad (i = 1 \text{ or } i = 2) & \lfloor\text{MERGE}\rfloor \\
\mathsf{def}\ \mathbf{x}_1 \mid \mathbf{x}_2 = \mathbf{x}, \widetilde{T}\ \mathsf{in}\ \mathbf{x}_1 \mid \mathbf{x}_2 & \equiv & \mathsf{def}\ \mathbf{x}_1 \mid \mathbf{x}_2 = \mathbf{x}, \widetilde{T}\ \mathsf{in}\ \mathbf{x} & \lfloor\text{JOIN}\rfloor \\
\mathsf{def}\ \mathbf{x} = !\langle \mathtt{p}, l\langle U \rangle\rangle.\mathbf{x}', \widetilde{T}\ \mathsf{in}\ \mathbf{x} & \xrightarrow{!\langle \mathtt{p}, l\langle U \rangle\rangle} & \mathsf{def}\ \mathbf{x} = !\langle \mathtt{p}, l\langle U \rangle\rangle.\mathbf{x}', \widetilde{T}\ \mathsf{in}\ \mathbf{x}' & \lfloor\text{SEND}_\ell\rfloor \\
\mathsf{def}\ \mathbf{x} = ?\langle \mathtt{p}, l\langle U \rangle\rangle.\mathbf{x}', \widetilde{T}\ \mathsf{in}\ \mathbf{x} & \xrightarrow{?\langle \mathtt{p}, l\langle U \rangle\rangle} & \mathsf{def}\ \mathbf{x} = ?\langle \mathtt{p}, l\langle U \rangle\rangle.\mathbf{x}', \widetilde{T}\ \mathsf{in}\ \mathbf{x}' & \lfloor\text{RECV}_\ell\rfloor \\
\mathsf{def}\ \mathbf{x} = \mathbf{x}_1 \oplus \mathbf{x}_2, \widetilde{T}\ \mathsf{in}\ \mathbf{x} & \xrightarrow{\tau} & \mathsf{def}\ \mathbf{x} = \mathbf{x}_1 \oplus \mathbf{x}_2, \widetilde{T}\ \mathsf{in}\ \mathbf{x}_i \quad (i = 1 \text{ or } i = 2) & \lfloor\text{COND}\rfloor
\end{array}
$$

$$
\frac{\mathsf{def}\ \widetilde{T}\ \mathsf{in}\ \mathbf{x}_1 \xrightarrow{\ell} \mathsf{def}\ \widetilde{T}\ \mathsf{in}\ \mathbf{x}_1'}{\mathsf{def}\ \mathbf{x} = \mathbf{x}_1\ \&\ \mathbf{x}_2, \widetilde{T}\ \mathsf{in}\ \mathbf{x}_1 \xrightarrow{\ell} \mathsf{def}\ \mathbf{x} = \mathbf{x}_1\ \&\ \mathbf{x}_2, \widetilde{T}\ \mathsf{in}\ \mathbf{x}_1'}\ \lfloor\text{CHOICE}\rfloor
$$

$$
\frac{\mathsf{def}\ \widetilde{T}\ \mathsf{in}\ \mathbf{x}_1 \xrightarrow{\ell} \mathsf{def}\ \widetilde{T}\ \mathsf{in}\ \mathbf{x}_1'}{\mathsf{def}\ \widetilde{T}\ \mathsf{in}\ \mathbf{x}_1 \mid \mathbf{X}_2 \xrightarrow{\ell} \mathsf{def}\ \widetilde{T}\ \mathsf{in}\ \mathbf{x}_1' \mid \mathbf{X}_2}\ \lfloor\text{PAR}\rfloor
\qquad
\frac{\mathbf{T}_1 \xrightarrow{!\langle \mathtt{q}, l\langle U \rangle\rangle} \mathbf{T}_1' \quad \mathbf{T}_2 \xrightarrow{?\langle \mathtt{p}, l\langle U \rangle\rangle} \mathbf{T}_2'}{(s[\mathtt{p}] : \mathbf{T}_1, s[\mathtt{q}] : \mathbf{T}_2, \Delta) \to (s[\mathtt{p}] : \mathbf{T}_1', s[\mathtt{q}] : \mathbf{T}_2', \Delta)}\ [\text{COM}]
$$

The sending and receiving actions occur when the state variable $\mathbf{x}$ points to sending and receiving types (Rules $\lfloor\text{SEND}_l\rfloor$ and $\lfloor\text{RECV}_l\rfloor$). Others are contextual rules. We also use the labelled transition relation between environments, denoted by $(\Gamma, \Delta) \xrightarrow{\alpha} (\Gamma', \Delta')$ where the main rule is $\lfloor\text{COM}\rfloor$ which represents the reduction between a message queue and a process at the network level. Other omitted rules are straightforward.

The following theorem, which is often called *type soundness*, states that if a process (resp. network) emits a label (resp. performs a reduction), then the environment can do the corresponding action, and the resulting process and the environment match.

Theorem 5.1 (Subject Congruence, Transition and Reduction).
1. *Suppose* $\Gamma, \widetilde{P} \vdash \mathbf{X} \rhd \Delta$ *and* $\widetilde{P} \vdash \mathbf{X} \equiv \mathbf{X}'$. *Then* $\Gamma, \widetilde{P} \vdash \mathbf{X}' \rhd \Delta$. *Similarly for* $\mathbf{P}$ *and* $\mathbf{N}$.
2. $\Gamma, \widetilde{P} \vdash \mathbf{X} \rhd \Delta$ *and* $\widetilde{P} \vdash \mathbf{X} \xrightarrow{\alpha} \mathbf{X}'$ *imply* $\Gamma', \widetilde{P} \vdash \mathbf{X}' \rhd \Delta'$ *with* $(\Gamma, \Delta) \xrightarrow{\alpha} (\Gamma', \Delta')$.
3. $\Gamma \vdash \mathbf{P} \rhd \Delta$ *and* $\mathbf{P} \xrightarrow{\alpha} \mathbf{P}'$ *imply* $\Gamma' \vdash \mathbf{P}' \rhd \Delta'$ *with* $(\Gamma, \Delta) \xrightarrow{\alpha} (\Gamma', \Delta')$.
4. $\Gamma \vdash \mathbf{N} \rhd \Delta$ *and* $\mathbf{N} \longrightarrow \mathbf{N}'$ *imply* $\Gamma \vdash \mathbf{N}' \rhd \Delta'$ *with* $\Delta \longrightarrow^* \Delta'$.

We also use the following one-to-one correspondence between local state automata and local types. We write $\xrightarrow{\tilde{\ell}}$ for $\xrightarrow{\ell_1} \cdots \xrightarrow{\ell_n}$. We use the notation $\xRightarrow{\ell}$ for $(\xrightarrow{\tau})^* \xrightarrow{\ell} (\xrightarrow{\tau})^*$ and similarly for $\xRightarrow{\tilde{\ell}}$. The proof is straightforward by the definition in § 3.3.

Theorem 5.2 (CFSMs and Local Types). $(\mathbf{G} \upharpoonright \mathtt{p}) \xRightarrow{\tilde{\ell}}$ *iff* $\mathcal{A}(\mathbf{G} \upharpoonright \mathtt{p}) \xrightarrow{\tilde{\ell}}$.

We say P has ***a type error*** if expressions in P contain either a type error for a value or constant in the standard sense (e.g. $(\mathsf{true}+7)$) or ***a reception error*** (e.g. the sender sends a value with label l_0 while the receiver does not expect label l_0). The following theorem is derived by Theorems 5.1 and 5.2.

Theorem 5.3 (Type Safety). *Suppose* $\Gamma \vdash \mathbf{N}$. *For any* $\mathbf{N}'$ *such that* $\mathbf{N} \longrightarrow^* \mathbf{N}'$, $\mathbf{N}'$ *has no type error.*

Using Theorem 3.2, boundedness is derived as Theorem 5.4.

Theorem 5.4 (Boundedness). *Suppose for all* $\mathbf{G}$ *in* Γ, $\mathcal{A}(\{\mathbf{G} \upharpoonright \mathsf{p}_i\}_{1\leq i\leq n})$ *with* $\mathsf{p}_1,...,\mathsf{p}_n \in \mathbf{G}$ *is strongly bounded. Then for all* $\mathbf{N}'$ *such that* $\Gamma \vdash \mathbf{N}$ *and* $\mathbf{N} \longrightarrow^* \mathbf{N}'$, *the reachable contents of a given channel buffer is finite.*

This result can be extended to other variants such as existential boundedness or K-boundedness [12] by applying the global buffer analysis on $\langle \mathbf{G} \rangle$ from [9].

5.3 Advanced Properties in a Single Multiparty Session

We now focus on advanced properties guaranteed when only a single multiparty session executes. We say $\mathbf{N}$ is *simple* [14, 24] if $\mathbf{N}_0 \longrightarrow^* \mathbf{N}$ such that $\mathbf{N}_0 \equiv \mathbf{P}_1 \mid\mid \cdots \mid\mid \mathbf{P}_n$ and $\Gamma \vdash \mathbf{N}_0$ where each $\mathbf{P}_i$ is either an initiator $\mathsf{def}\, \mathbf{x}_0(x) = x\langle \mathbf{G} \rangle.\mathbf{x}_1, \mathbf{x}_1 = \mathbf{0}\ \mathsf{in}\ \mathbf{x}_0(a)$ or an acceptor $\mathsf{def}\, \mathbf{x}_0(x) = x[\mathsf{p}](y).\mathbf{x}_1, \widetilde{P}\ \mathsf{in}\ \mathbf{x}_0(a)$ where $\widetilde{P}$ does not contain any initiator, acceptor or name creator. This means that, once the session is started, all processes continue within that session without any interference by other sessions. In a simple network, we can guarantee the following completeness result (the reverse direction of Theorem 5.1).

Theorem 5.5 (Completeness). *Below we assume* $\mathbf{X}$, $\mathbf{P}$ *and* $\mathbf{N}$ *are sub-terms of derivations from a simple network. Then:* $\Gamma, \widetilde{P} \vdash \mathbf{X} \triangleright \Delta$ *and* $(\Gamma, \Delta) \xrightarrow{\alpha} (\Gamma', \Delta')$ *imply* $\widetilde{P} \vdash \mathbf{X} \xrightarrow{\alpha} \mathbf{X}'$ *with* $\Gamma', \widetilde{P} \vdash \mathbf{X}' \triangleright \Delta'$. *Similarly* $\mathbf{P}$ *and* $\mathbf{N}$ *satisfy the reversed direction of Theorem 5.1.*

We say $\mathbf{N}$ is a ***deadlock*** if all processes are blocked, waiting for messages. Formally $\mathbf{N}$ is a *deadlock* if there exists $\mathbf{N}'$ such that $\mathbf{N} \longrightarrow^* \mathbf{N}' = (\nu s)(s : \emptyset \mid\mid \mathbf{P}'_1 \mid\mid \cdots \mid\mid \mathbf{P}'_n) \mid\mid \mathbf{N}''$ and for all $1 \leq j \leq n$, if $\mathbf{P}'_j \xrightarrow{\alpha_j} \mathbf{P}''_j$ then $\alpha_j = s[\mathsf{p}, \mathsf{q}]?l\langle v \rangle$ (i.e., $\mathbf{P}'_j$ is an input process). The following theorem can be proved by the deadlock-freedom of MSA (Theorem 3.1) and Completeness (Theorem 5.5) with Theorem 5.2.

Theorem 5.6 (Deadlock Freedom). *Suppose* $\Gamma \vdash \mathbf{N}$ *is simple. Then there is no reduction such that* $\mathbf{N} \longrightarrow^* \mathbf{N}'$ *and* $\mathbf{N}'$ *is a deadlock.*

Below (1), is by Theorem 5.5 and (2) is by Theorems 5.2 and 5.5 with (1).

Theorem 5.7. (1) **(Progress)** *Suppose* $\Gamma \vdash \mathbf{N}$ *is simple. Then for all* $\mathbf{N} \longrightarrow^* \mathbf{N}'$, *either* $\mathbf{N}' \equiv \mathbf{0}$ *or* $\mathbf{N}' \longrightarrow \mathbf{N}''$. (2) **(Liveness)** *Suppose* $a : \langle \mathbf{G} \rangle \vdash \mathbf{N}$ *and* $\mathcal{A}(\{\mathbf{G} \upharpoonright \mathsf{p}_i\}_{1\leq i\leq n})$ *satisfies liveness with* $\mathsf{p}_1,...,\mathsf{p}_n \in \mathbf{G}$. *Assume* $\mathbf{N} \longrightarrow^* (\nu s)(s : h \mid\mid \mathbf{P}_1 \mid\mid \mathbf{P}_2 \mid\mid \cdots \mid\mid \mathbf{P}_n)$ *such that* $a : \langle \mathbf{G} \rangle \vdash \mathbf{P}_j \triangleright s[\mathsf{p}_j] : \mathbf{T}_j$. *Then there exits a reduction such that* $\mathbf{N} \longrightarrow^* \mathbf{0}$.

Thanks to the strong correspondence that typing enforces between processes behaviours and automata, we have proved that all the good properties enjoyed by MSA generated by a global type $\mathbf{G}$ also hold in the processes typed by the same $\mathbf{G}$.

6 Related Work

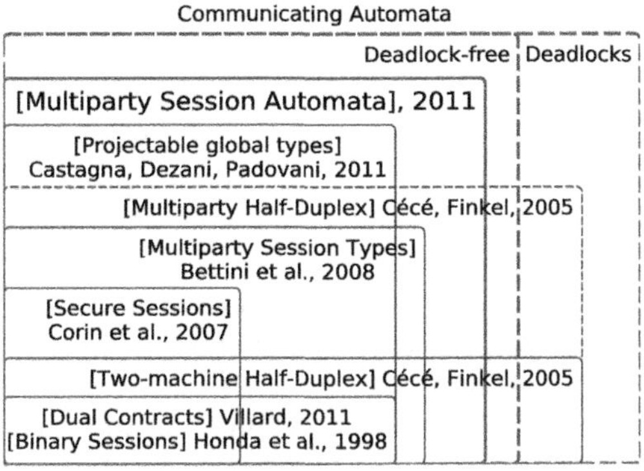

The relationship with other session types and CFSMs is summarised in the diagram. The outside box represents communicating automata, with the undecidable separation between deadlock-free and deadlocking machines. Within it, we represent the known inclusions between session and CFSMs systems. First, *binary* (two party) session types [13] correspond to the set of compatible half-duplex deterministic two-machine systems without mixed states [12, 23] (compatible means that each send is matched by a receive, and vice-versa). This is not the case for the MSA generated from secure session specifications [8], which satisfy strong sequentiality properties and are multiparty. They can however be shown to be *restricted half-duplex* in [7, § 4.1.2] (i.e. at most one queue is non-empty). The original multiparty session types [3, 14], which correspond to our system when parallel composition is disallowed, are a subset of the *natural multiparty extension of half-duplex system* [7, § 4.1.2] where each pair of machines is linked by two buffered channels, one in each direction, such that at most one is non-empty. Our MSA can have mixed states and are not half-duplex, as shown in $\mathbf{G}_3$ (Ex. 2.1 (3), both `Alice` and `Bob` can fill both buffers concurrently). From this picture are omitted Gouda et al.'s pioneering work [12] and Villard's extension [16] of [23] to unreliable systems, which proves that safety properties and boundedness are still decidable. These works [12, 16, 23] only treat the two-machine case.

Finally, we mention two related works by Castagna et al. [6] and Bultan et al. [1, 2]. The first two papers [1, 6] focus on proving the semantical correspondence between global and local descriptions. In Castagna et al. [6], global choreographies are described by a language of types with general fork ($\wedge$), choice ($\vee$) and repetition $(G)^*$ (which represents a finite loop of zero or more interactions of G). Note that these global types of [6] use series-parallel syntax trees and are thus limited by the lack of support for general joins and merges. This prevents many examples, such as the Alternating Bit Protocol $\mathbf{G}_{AB}$ in Ex. 2.1 (7), the Trade example from § 1 and $\mathbf{G}_6$ in Ex. 2.1 (6), from being algorithmically projectable (i.e. implementable). In [1], on the other hand, global specifications are given by a finite state machine with no special support for parallel composition. In both cases, their systems do not treat the extended causality between sends and receives (the OO-causality and II-causality at different channels [14]). They also do not give a practical (language-based) framework, from types to processes to tackle real programs. In terms of results, [6] proposes well-formedness conditions under which local types correspond to global types, while [1] describes a sound and complete decision algorithm for realising (i.e. projecting) a choreography specification. Our work avoid this theoretical completeness question by using sufficient well-formedness conditions and by directly giving a global type semantics in terms of local automata. Recently, [2] extends [1] to tackle the synchronisability problem (equivalent to our Lemma 3.1 (3)). They however do not go as far as deadlock-freedom, progress and liveness.

When comparing these works with ours, the main differences are: (1) unlike [23] and ours, [1, 6] only investigate the relationship between global and local specifications, not from types (contracts) to programs or processes to ensure safety properties; (2) while the semantical tools are close (formal languages, finite state machines), there are subtle differences concerning buffer-boundedness [1, 2], finite recursion [6] and causality [1, 2, 6]; (3) Bultan et al. [1, 2] do not propose any global description language, while Castagna et al.'s language [6] is not rich enough compared to ours; and (4) the algorithmic projectability in [6] is more limited than ours, and [1, 2] only propose exponential decision results, limiting their applicability.

Message Sequence Graphs (MSGs). In terms of expressiveness, a very comparable system is the extension of Message sequence charts (MSCs) to *Message Sequence Graphs* (MSGs). MSGs are finite transition systems where each state embeds a single MSC. Many variants of MSGs are investigated in the literature [11] in order to provide efficient conditions for verification and implementability, i.e. projectability to CFSMs. Some of these conditions in MSGs are similar to ours: for example, our local choice condition corresponds to the local choice condition with additional data of [11, Def. 2]. A detailed comparison between MSGs and global types is given in [6, § 7.1].

In general MSGs are however incomparable with our framework because MSGs' transition system is global and non-deterministic. We aim our global type language to be more compact, precise and suitable for programming. For example, extending the Alternating Bit Protocol $\mathbf{G}_{AB}$ to three parties can be easily done in our system (see [18]), while it can only be written in a complex extension of MSGs, called Compositional MSGs (CMSGs). The main benefit of our type-based approach is that there is no gap between specifications and programs: we can instantly check the properties of programs by static type-checking. More investigation on global types and MSGs properties would however bring mutual benefits by identifying the expressiveness differences.

7 Conclusion and Future Work

We have introduced a new framework of multiparty session types which is tightly linked to CFSMs, and showed that a new class of CFSMs, that we called multiparty session automata (MSA), generated from global types, automatically satisfy safety and liveness properties, extending the results in [12] to multiple machines. We use MSA to define and prove precise safety and liveness properties for well-typed mobile processes. The syntax of our session types and processes brings expressiveness to new levels (general fork, choice, merging and joining) that have not been reached by existing systems [3, 6, 14], while keeping a polynomial tool chain. Our general choice is already included into Scribble 1.0 [20], an industrial language to describe application-level protocols among communicating systems based on the multiparty session type theory.

Future work include finding a characterisation of MSA that is independent of session types, investigating model checking for MSA to justify typed bisimulations [15], relating MSA with models of true concurrency, including Mazurkiewicz traces, extending MSA to parameterisation [24], multiroles [10] and multiparty contracts [16, 23].

Acknowledgments. We are grateful to the anonymous reviewers, Kohei Honda, Raymond Hu, Étienne Lozes, Rumyana Neykova and Jules Villard for their helpful comments. This work was supported by EPSRC EP/F003757/01 and G015635/01.

References

1. Basu, S., Bultan, T., Ouederni, M.: Deciding choreography realizability. In: POPL 2012. ACM (to appear, 2012)
2. Basu, S., Bultan, T., Ouederni, M.: Synchronizability for Verification of Asynchronously Communicating Systems. In: Kuncak, V., Rybalchenko, A. (eds.) VMCAI 2012. LNCS, vol. 7148, pp. 56–71. Springer, Heidelberg (2012)
3. Bettini, L., Coppo, M., D'Antoni, L., De Luca, M., Dezani-Ciancaglini, M., Yoshida, N.: Global Progress in Dynamically Interleaved Multiparty Sessions. In: van Breugel, F., Chechik, M. (eds.) CONCUR 2008. LNCS, vol. 5201, pp. 418–433. Springer, Heidelberg (2008)
4. Business Process Model and Notation, `http://www.bpmn.org`
5. Brand, D., Zafiropulo, P.: On communicating finite-state machines. J. ACM 30, 323–342 (1983)
6. Castagna, G., Dezani-Ciancaglini, M., Padovani, L.: On Global Types and Multi-party Sessions. In: Bruni, R., Dingel, J. (eds.) FORTE 2011 and FMOODS 2011. LNCS, vol. 6722, pp. 1–28. Springer, Heidelberg (2011)
7. Cécé, G., Finkel, A.: Verification of programs with half-duplex communication. Inf. Comput. 202(2), 166–190 (2005)
8. Corin, R., Deniélou, P.M., Fournet, C., Bhargavan, K., Leifer, J.: Secure implementations for typed session abstractions. In: CSF, pp. 170–186 (2007)
9. Deniélou, P.M., Yoshida, N.: Buffered Communication Analysis in Distributed Multiparty Sessions. In: Gastin, P., Laroussinie, F. (eds.) CONCUR 2010. LNCS, vol. 6269, pp. 343–357. Springer, Heidelberg (2010)
10. Deniélou, P.M., Yoshida, N.: Dynamic multirole session types. In: POPL, pp. 435–446. ACM (2011), full version, Prototype at, `http://www.doc.ic.ac.uk/~pmalo/dynamic`
11. Genest, B., Muscholl, A., Peled, D.: Message Sequence Charts. In: Desel, J., Reisig, W., Rozenberg, G. (eds.) ACPN 2003. LNCS, vol. 3098, pp. 537–558. Springer, Heidelberg (2004)
12. Gouda, M., Manning, E., Yu, Y.: On the progress of communication between two finite state machines. Information and Control 63, 200–216 (1984)
13. Honda, K., Vasconcelos, V.T., Kubo, M.: Language Primitives and Type Discipline for Structured Communication-Based Programming. In: Hankin, C. (ed.) ESOP 1998. LNCS, vol. 1381, pp. 122–138. Springer, Heidelberg (1998)
14. Honda, K., Yoshida, N., Carbone, M.: Multiparty Asynchronous Session Types. In: POPL 2008, pp. 273–284. ACM (2008)
15. Kouzapas, D., Yoshida, N., Honda, K.: On Asynchronous Session Semantics. In: Bruni, R., Dingel, J. (eds.) FORTE 2011 and FMOODS 2011. LNCS, vol. 6722, pp. 228–243. Springer, Heidelberg (2011)
16. Lozes, E., Villard, J.: Reliable contracts for unreliable half-duplex communications. In: WS-FM. Springer, Heidelberg (2011) (to appear)
17. Ng, N., Yoshida, N., Pernet, O., Hu, R., Kryftis, Y.: Safe Parallel Programming with Session Java. In: De Meuter, W., Roman, G.-C. (eds.) COORDINATION 2011. LNCS, vol. 6721, pp. 110–126. Springer, Heidelberg (2011)
18. Online Appendix, `http://www.doc.ic.ac.uk/~malo/msa/`
19. Savara JBoss Project, `http://www.jboss.org/savara`
20. Scribble JBoss Project, `http://www.jboss.org/scribble`
21. Sivaramakrishnan, K.C., Nagaraj, K., Ziarek, L., Eugster, P.: Efficient Session Type Guided Distributed Interaction. In: Clarke, D., Agha, G. (eds.) COORDINATION 2010. LNCS, vol. 6116, pp. 152–167. Springer, Heidelberg (2010)
22. Swamy, N., Chen, J., Fournet, C., Strub, P.Y., Bharagavan, K., Yang, J.: Secure distributed programming with value-dependent types. In: ICFP, pp. 266–278. ACM (2011)
23. Villard, J.: Heaps and Hops. Ph.D. thesis, ENS Cachan (2011)
24. Yoshida, N., Deniélou, P.M., Bejleri, A., Hu, R.: Parameterised Multiparty Session Types. In: Ong, L. (ed.) FOSSACS 2010. LNCS, vol. 6014, pp. 128–145. Springer, Heidelberg (2010)

Complete Monitors for Behavioral Contracts*

Christos Dimoulas, Sam Tobin-Hochstadt, and Matthias Felleisen

Northeastern University, Boston, Massachusetts, USA
{chrdimo,samth,matthias}@ccs.neu.edu

Abstract. A behavioral contract in a higher-order language may invoke methods of unknown objects. Although this expressive power allows programmers to formulate sophisticated contracts, it also poses a problem for language designers. Indeed, two distinct semantics have emerged for such method calls, dubbed *lax* and *picky*. While *lax* fails to protect components in certain scenarios, *picky* may blame an uninvolved party for a contract violation.

In this paper, we present *complete monitoring* as the fundamental correctness criterion for contract systems. It demands correct blame assignment as well as complete monitoring of all channels of communication between components. According to this criterion, *lax* and *picky* are indeed incorrect ways to monitor contracts. A third semantics, dubbed *indy*, emerges as the only correct variant.

Keywords: higher-order programming, behavioral contracts, contract checking.

1 Blame Correctness Is Not Enough

Programmers embrace Eiffel-style contracts [7] because they can write them in the language itself and they understand them as executable boolean expressions. Conventionally, programmers use contracts to supplement method signatures with relatively simple conditions: a *non-empty* list expected here; a *positive* number promised there; a field whose value is always a string *of a specific length*. They also understand that the contract system checks these conditions when a method is called and/or when a call returns. If the condition evaluates to false, it is either the method's or the caller's fault.

In a higher-order contract system [4], such as the one for Racket [5], programmers can also specify conditions on functions and objects. Here is an example:

```
;; contract for the derivative function
;; for some natural number n and reals δ, ε:
(->d ([f (0<real<1? . -> . 0<real<1?)])
     (fp (0<real<1? . -> . real?))
     #:post-cond
     (for/and ([i (in-range 0 n)])
       (define x (random-number))
       (define slope (/ (- (f (- x ε)) (f (+ x ε))) (* 2 ε)))
       (<= (abs (- slope (fp x))) δ)))
```

* Supported in part by AFOSR grant FA9550-09-1-0110 and the DARPA CRASH program.

H. Seidl (Ed.): ESOP 2012, LNCS 7211, pp. 214–233, 2012.

It specifies a computational differentiation operator `d/dx` for functions on the unit interval. The specification promises to map a function `f` to a function `fp` that computes a number close to the slope of `f` at `x`.

Due to Rice's theorem, it is impossible to check such contracts directly. Instead contracted functions are wrapped in a monitor that checks the promised property every time it is used during the remainder of the computation. Since such a use may take place after the function returns in a third-party component, the naive understanding of first-order contracts and blame assignment does not apply here.

Thus higher-order values inject several new elements into the realm of contracts. First, it is now important to explicitly think of components as contract parties. These parties agree on monitoring properties for values that flow back and forth across component boundaries. Second, blame assignment requires tracking of contracts and parties because the producer is not necessarily the last function called. In the above example, `d/dx` returns a higher-order value with the requirement to call it on reals between 0 and 1, but a call involving some negative real may take place much later. Third, contracts are no longer predicates on flat values but may involve calls to unknown functions. For instance, the post-condition for `d/dx` tests whether the result `fp` satisfies the desired "slope property" for `f` on some randomly chosen numbers.

Calls to unknown functions pose a challenge for contract designers. To this day it is unclear how a correct contract system should deal with such calls. Take a second look at the above example. Its contract uses `random-number`, which, as it turns out, may produce complex numbers in Racket. Depending on the semantics of contracts, the example behaves in one of three ways:

1. Findler and Felleisen [4] consider contracts a part of the specification and thus "correct by definition." According to their *lax* semantics, the post condition passes the random number to `f` and `fp`. If these functions handle complex numbers, fine; otherwise, execution fails in an unpredictable manner.
2. Blume and McAllester [1] propose an alternative *picky* semantics. According to their proposal, the contracts for `f` and `fp` prohibits their application to complex numbers, and their reuse catches contract-internal problems [6].
3. In prior work [3], we show, however, that *picky* may blame the wrong party for a contract violations and may thus point programmers in the wrong direction in their search for bugs. A variant of *picky*, dubbed *indy*, is shown to be *blame correct*.

Sadly, blame correctness cannot differentiate between *lax* and *indy*. Since *lax* may trigger crashes in the presence of precise specifications, it is clearly not correct. Worse, blame correctness admits contract systems that ignore contracts completely.

We conjecture that a programmer would like the guarantee that the values produced by their components are never used in violation to the interface specifications and, conversely, that their components are not handed values that do not live up to the promises of the specifications. In response, we present a generalization of blame correctness, called *complete monitoring*. We take the ownership-and-obligation framework of blame correctness and extend it so that a component may not manipulate values that it does not create or that have not been transferred from other components via a—possibly vacuous—contract. In short, a complete contract system monitors *all* value flows across component boundaries.

The next section introduces our technical framework, which we exploit to to present informally *complete monitors* in section 3 and subsequently define them formally in section 4. This latter section also presents our main result, the complete monitoring theorem. Sections 5 and 6 illustrate the additional benefits of complete monitors with two examples. Finally, the last section discusses related work.

2 Beyond Blame Correctness

CPCF [2,3] extends a conventional, typed and higher-order functional language, with contracts for base values and first-class functions:

Types	$\tau = o \mid \tau{\to}\tau \mid \mathsf{con}(\tau)$
	$o = \mathsf{I} \mid \mathsf{B}$
Contracts	$\kappa = \mathtt{flat}(e) \mid \kappa \mapsto \kappa \mid \kappa \overset{d}{\mapsto} (\lambda x.\kappa)$
Terms	$e = v \mid x \mid e\,e \mid \mu x{:}\tau.e \mid e+e \mid e-e \mid e \wedge e \mid e \vee e$
	$\mid \mathtt{zero?}(e) \mid \mathtt{if}\;e\;e\;e \mid \mathtt{mon}_l^{l,l}(\kappa, e)$
Values	$v = \mathsf{c} \mid \lambda x{:}\tau.e$
Base Values	$\mathsf{c} = 0 \mid 1 \mid -1 \mid \ldots \mid \mathtt{tt} \mid \mathtt{ff}$

Contracts for flat values, $\mathtt{flat}(e)$, employ predicates that may use the full expressive power of CPCF. Contracts for functions, $\kappa_1 \mapsto \kappa_2$, consist of a pre-condition contract κ_1 for the argument to the function and a post-condition contract κ_2 for its result. Dependent function contracts, $\kappa_1 \overset{d}{\mapsto} (\lambda x.\kappa_2)$, bind the argument to the function to x and make it visible in κ_2. They thus express how the result may depend on the argument.

A contract κ can be attached to a term e using the monitor construct $\mathtt{mon}_j^{k,l}(\kappa, e)$. Monitors carry three labels: k, l and j.[1] Labels are identifiers for the high-level components that make up a program. A monitor splits a program into three components, dubbed the *contract parties*: a server named k, a client named l, and a contract named j, which may coincide with k or l in a programming language. Intuitively a monitor makes sure that any interaction between the server module and the client module is in accordance with the contract. In CPCF, e plays the role of the server module and the context of $\mathtt{mon}_j^{k,l}(\kappa, e)$ the role of the client. The contract κ is what they agree on concerning the exchange of values.

Component labels play an important role in case a contract failure is detected during contract checking. They are used to pinpoint the contract violator. CPCF syntax is extended with intermediate terms for contract checking:

$$e = \ldots \mid \mathtt{error}_l^l \mid \mathtt{check}_l^l(e, v)$$

Findler and Felleisen [4] show that the above constructs are sufficient to build a semantics for checking higher-order contracts. However, since the goal of our investigation is to verify that the contract system obliges values to meet their specifications as they flow from one component into another, we add the idea of *ownership* for terms and values to the semantics. We use it to keep track of value migration. Ownership of a term e

[1] The labels correspond to source locations or component names in an implementation.

by a component l is expressed with the ownership annotation $|e|^l$. Ownership captures formally that a component owns a value (term) if it can affect or manipulate its flow. In a reduction semantics, the flow of values is modeled via substitution (β_v). Hence, our semantics must attach a new ownership annotation to every value that is substituted for a variable. In CPCF, this means we must treat every function application as a potential boundary crossing. Thus when an annotated value occurs in a function body, its occurrence signals the presence of a *foreign* value and marks a boundary. In sum, the initial owner of a value is its creator but as the value flows through function application, it accumulates more owners, one for each boundary it crosses with the top-most to be the most recent owner.

In addition to ownership, we ensure correct blame assignment by keeping track not only of the owner of each value but also the responsible party for the specifications that are checked against a value upon a component boundary crossing. The *obligations* of a contract party l are the set of ground-type sub-contracts of a contract κ for which l is responsible. Intuitively, the contract system should not blame a party if the party's obligations are satisfied. For a function contract we know that the client is responsible for the pre-condition and the server responsible for the post-condition. For any flat contract, the server is responsible. Generalizing this approach gives us a way to determine the responsible parties for each flat sub-contract of a given contract using type theory terminology: the server is responsible for all flat contracts in positive positions and the client is responsible for all flat contracts in negative positions. CPCF turns obligations into explicit annotations on flat contracts. Thus $\lfloor \texttt{flat}(e) \rfloor^{\bar{l}}$ denotes that the set of parties $\bar{l}$ is responsible for the given flat contract.

Here is CPCF with the annotations for ownership and obligations:

$$
\begin{array}{lll}
\textbf{Contracts} & \kappa = & \lfloor \texttt{flat}(e) \rfloor^{\bar{l}} \mid \kappa \mapsto \kappa \mid \kappa \overset{d}{\mapsto} (\lambda x.\kappa) \\
\textbf{Terms} & e = & \ldots \mid |e|^l \\
\textbf{Values} & v = & \ldots \mid |v|^l
\end{array}
$$

With obligations and ownership we reify dynamic boundary crossings via syntactic annotations and the specifications that need to be checked. If this *independent* instrumentation coincides in the source code with the monitors and blame labels that the contract system utilizes and the reductions preserve this property, we know that the contract system monitors all communication between components.

Synchronization of ownership and monitors means that the owner of the context of a monitor is the same as the label at the client position of the monitor and the owner of the guarded term is the same as the label in the server position of the monitor. Due to the presence of run-time terms, there is one more case where the labels of the contract system have to agree with ownership. CPCF uses $\texttt{check}_j^k(e, v)$ to check flat contracts. This implies that the checking code e is owned by the contract party j. We consider this construct as another point where values change components and the owner of e must be the contract party.

Synchronization of obligations and blame labels means that the label at the server position of a monitor is a member of the obligations annotations on positive ground-type subcontracts of the monitor's contract and similarly for the client label and negative ground-type subcontracts.

In principle, ownership and obligations could be just observers of the reduction sequence that do not affect evaluation. However, to prove that the contract system allows values to migrate from one component to another only when they are under its control, we use ownership to impose restrictions on value flows between components. We enforce a *single owner* policy that disallows mixing terms with different owners. Instead our reduction relation ensures that foreign values within a component are wrapped in contract checks or that the contract system has completely verified all (flat) specifications during the absorption of a foreign value into a component.

Reduction Rules	$E^l[\cdots]$		$\xrightarrow{m} E^l[\cdots]$	
	$\|\|\mathtt{n}_1\|\|^l + \|\|\mathtt{n}_2\|\|^l$	.	$\mathtt{n}$	where $n_1 + n_2 = n$
	$\|\|\mathtt{n}_1\|\|^l - \|\|\mathtt{n}_2\|\|^l$	.	$\mathtt{n}$	where $n_1 - n_2 = n$
	$\mathtt{zero?}(\|\|0\|\|^l)$	.	$\mathtt{tt}$	
	$\mathtt{zero?}(\|\|\mathtt{n}\|\|^l)$	.	$\mathtt{ff}$	if $n \neq 0$
	$\|\|v_1\|\|^l \wedge \|\|v_2\|\|^l$	.	v	where $v_1 \wedge v_2 = v$
	$\|\|v_1\|\|^l \vee \|\|v_2\|\|^l$	.	v	where $v_1 \vee v_2 = v$
	$\mathtt{if}\ \|\|\mathtt{tt}\|\|^l\ e_1\ e_2$	.	e_1	
	$\mathtt{if}\ \|\|\mathtt{ff}\|\|^l\ e_1\ e_2$	.	e_2	
	$\|\|\lambda x.e\|\|^l\ \|\|v\|\|^l$	.	$\|\{\|v\|^l/x\}e\|^l$	
	$\mu x.e$	.	$\{\|\mu x.e\|^l/x\}e$	
	$\mathtt{mon}_j^{k,l}(\kappa_1 \mapsto \kappa_2, v)$	.	$\lambda x.\mathtt{mon}_j^{k,l}(\kappa_2, v\ \mathtt{mon}_j^{l,k}(\kappa_1, x))$	
	$\mathtt{mon}_j^{k,l}(\lfloor \mathtt{flat}(e) \rfloor^{\bar{l}'}, \|\|\mathtt{c}\|\|^{l'})$	.	$\mathtt{check}_j^k(e\ \mathtt{c}, \mathtt{c})$	
	$\mathtt{check}_j^k(\|\|\mathtt{tt}\|\|^j, v)$	.	v	
	$\mathtt{check}_j^k(\|\|\mathtt{ff}\|\|^j, v)$	.	$\mathtt{error}_j^k$	
	$E^l[\mathtt{error}_j^k]$		$\xrightarrow{m} \mathtt{error}_j^k$	

Eval. Contexts

$$
\begin{aligned}
E^l \ = \ & E^l\,e \mid v\,E^l \mid E^l + e \mid v + E^l \mid E^l - e \mid v - E^l \mid E^l \wedge e \\
\mid \ & v \wedge E^l \mid E^l \vee e \mid v \vee E^l \mid \mathtt{zero?}(E^l) \mid \mathtt{if}\ E^l\ e\ e \\
\mid \ & \mathtt{mon}_j^{l,k}(\kappa, E^{l_o}) \mid \mathtt{mon}_j^{l',k}(\kappa, E^l) \mid |E^{l_o}|^l \mid |E^l|^{l'} \\
\mid \ & \mathtt{check}_l^k(E^{l_o}, v) \mid \mathtt{check}_{l'}^k(E^l, v) \\
E^{l_o} \ = \ & [\,] \mid E^{l_o}\,e \mid v\,E^{l_o} \mid E^{l_o} + e \mid v + E^{l_o} \mid E^{l_o} - e \\
\mid \ & v - E^{l_o} \mid E^{l_o} \wedge e \mid v \wedge E^{l_o} \mid E^{l_o} \vee e \mid v \vee E^{l_o} \\
\mid \ & \mathtt{zero?}(E^{l_o}) \mid \mathtt{if}\ E^{l_o}\ e\ e
\end{aligned}
$$

Fig. 1. CPCF semantics enforces the single-owner policy

To implement this policy, we require all terms in a *redex* to have a single owner. Put differently, our semantics does not perform operations on values that have ownership annotations with different owners. We use $||e||^l$ to denote that e may have no ownership annotations but if it has one then the owner label is l for all such annotations:

$$||e||^l = |...|e|^l...|^l \qquad \text{where for all labels } k \text{ and terms } e',\ e \neq |e'|^k.$$

The *single owner* policy becomes critical for defining the reduction semantics for CPCF. A component should be able to perform an operation if and only if it is the owner of all the arguments of the redex. This implies that either the arguments inherit their implicit ownership annotation from the context or that they come with an explicit ownership annotation that matches with the owner of the context. We model implicit ownership with *labeled evaluation contexts*; see figure 1.

The reduction relation of figure 1 implements the single owner policy by reducing redexes only if the label of the hole matches the owner of the pieces of the redex. For instance the rule for function application is more restrictive than the original rule for CPCF [3]. The latter allows the function and the argument to have different and multiple owners. In contrast, the new rule fires only if l, the owner of the component, is also the only owner of the function and the argument. The argument is substituted in the body of the function, annotated with the common owner so that it keeps its ownership annotation no matter where it lands in the function body. The context absorbs the body of the function, which thus obtains the context's ownership annotation. Since the function and the context have the same owner, however, the body of the function retains its original owner. This rationale explains all the rules, including the rules for monitors where the client label must be the same as the label of the context. When the reduction rules create new values, as in the case of primitives operators, the context becomes directly responsible for the new value and thus no additional ownership annotation is necessary. Finally, the $\mathtt{check}^k_j(e,v)$ rules enable executing checking code e that originates from j inside l, the owner of the hole. Doing so ensures that the `check` term is treated as a component boundary and the result of e must be owned by j in order for `check` to reduce. If the check fails, and an error is raised and blames the initial owner k of v.

Values retain their owner as long as they move inside the same component. They change owner only when flat contract checking succeeds. When the check succeeds, the contract system gives permission to the surrounding component l to absorb `c`, and `c` changes hands between k and l.

The reduction rules concerning monitors for dependent function contracts come in three flavors: $l(ax)$, $p(icky)$ and $i(indy)$. Here are their formal definitions:

$$E^l[\mathtt{mon}^{k,l}_j(\kappa_1 \overset{d}{\mapsto} (\lambda x.\kappa_2), v)] \overset{l}{\rightarrow} E^l[\lambda x.\mathtt{mon}^{k,l}_j(\{x/^c x\}\kappa_2, v\,\mathtt{mon}^{l,k}_j(\kappa_1, x))]$$

$$E^l[\mathtt{mon}^{k,l}_j(\kappa_1 \overset{d}{\mapsto} (\lambda x.\kappa_2), v)] \overset{p}{\rightarrow} E^l[\lambda x.\mathtt{mon}^{k,l}_j(\underline{\{\mathtt{mon}^{l,k}_j(\kappa_1, x)/^c x\}\kappa_2}, v\,\mathtt{mon}^{l,k}_j(\kappa_1, x))]$$

$$E^l[\mathtt{mon}^{k,l}_j(\kappa_1 \overset{d}{\mapsto} (\lambda x.\kappa_2), v)] \overset{i}{\rightarrow} E^l[\lambda x.\mathtt{mon}^{k,l}_j(\underline{\{\mathtt{mon}^{l,j}_j(\kappa_1, x)/^c x\}\kappa_2}, v\,\mathtt{mon}^{l,k}_j(\kappa_1, x))]$$

The intuition behind these rules is explained at the end of the section.

The reductions employ a special function $\{e/^c x\}\kappa_2$ for substituting a term e for x in a post-condition κ_2 of a dependent contract:

$$\begin{aligned}
\{e/^c x\}\lfloor \mathtt{flat}(|e'|^{l'})\rfloor^{\bar{l}} &= \lfloor \mathtt{flat}(\{|e|^{l'}/x\}|e'|^{l'})\rfloor^{\bar{l}} \\
\{e/^c x\}(\kappa_1 \mapsto \kappa_2) &= \{e/^c x\}\kappa_1 \mapsto \{e/^c x\}\kappa_2 \\
\{e/^c x\}(\kappa_1 \overset{d}{\mapsto} (\lambda x.\kappa_2)) &= \{e/^c x\}\kappa_1 \overset{d}{\mapsto} (\lambda x.\kappa_2) \\
\{e/^c x\}(\kappa_1 \overset{d}{\mapsto} (\lambda y.\kappa_2)) &= \{e/^c x\}\kappa_1 \overset{d}{\mapsto} (\lambda y.\{e/^c x\}\kappa_2) \text{ where } x \neq y
\end{aligned}$$

The substitution in the post-condition implements a hidden application of $\lambda x.\kappa_2$ to v. The special substitution function makes sure that the argument is wrapped with an ownership annotation for the owner of $\lambda x.\kappa_2$, which is also the owner of the contract [3].

$$\boxed{\Gamma; l \Vdash e}$$

$$\frac{}{\Gamma; l \Vdash \mathtt{c}} \qquad \frac{\Gamma; l \Vdash e_1 \quad \Gamma; l \Vdash e_2}{\Gamma; l \Vdash e_1\ e_2} \qquad \frac{\Gamma; l \Vdash e_1 \quad \Gamma; l \Vdash e_2 \quad \Gamma; l \Vdash e_3}{\Gamma; l \Vdash \mathtt{if}\ e_1\ e_2\ e_3}$$

$$\frac{\Gamma; l \Vdash e_1}{\Gamma; l \Vdash \mathtt{zero?}(e_1)} \qquad \frac{\Gamma; l \Vdash e_1 \quad \Gamma; l \Vdash e_2}{\Gamma; l \Vdash e_1 + e_2} \qquad \frac{\Gamma; l \Vdash e_1 \quad \Gamma; l \Vdash e_2}{\Gamma; l \Vdash e_1 - e_2}$$

$$\frac{\Gamma; l \Vdash e_1 \quad \Gamma; l \Vdash e_2}{\Gamma; l \Vdash e_1 \wedge e_2} \qquad \frac{\Gamma; l \Vdash e_1 \quad \Gamma; l \Vdash e_2}{\Gamma; l \Vdash e_1 \vee e_2} \qquad \frac{\Gamma \uplus \{x : l\}; l \Vdash e}{\Gamma; l \Vdash \lambda x.e}$$

$$\frac{\Gamma \uplus \{x : l\}; l \Vdash e}{\Gamma; l \Vdash \mu x.e} \qquad \frac{\Gamma; l \Vdash e}{\Gamma; l \Vdash |e|^l} \qquad \frac{\Gamma(x) = l}{\Gamma; l \Vdash x} \qquad \frac{\Gamma; k \Vdash e \quad k \neq l \quad \Gamma; \{k\}; \{l\}; j \rhd \kappa}{\Gamma; l \Vdash \mathtt{mon}_j^{k,l}(\kappa, |e|^k)}$$

Fig. 2. Well-formed source programs

As mentioned, ownership annotations and obligations may not appear at arbitrary places in a program. To ensure the correctness of these annotations, we use a static well-formedness judgment, $\Gamma; l \Vdash e$, for source programs e. The interesting cases in source syntax are the ones concerning variables, variable bindings, ownership annotations and contract monitors, and they appear at the bottom of figure 2. The occurrence of a free variable in a term is one of the ways foreign values can flow into a component. The environment Γ keeps track of the origin of values bound to variables. It records the owner of the spot where a binder for a variable is introduced. To ensure that components are free of foreign terms we force the single owner policy, i.e., ownership annotations inside a component must carry the same owner label as the component. We can embed foreign code in a component under the protection of the contract system, that is, a component can contain foreign terms as long as they are wrapped in a monitor annotation and they are explicitly marked as foreign terms with an appropriate ownership annotation. In such cases the client label on the monitor must match the owner of the surrounding component and the server label must coincide with the explicit ownership annotation on the guarded term. Note that this also allows the embedding of free variables as long as they are monitored. Furthermore, the rule forces the client and blame labels on monitors in the source code to be different to emphasize that monitors are used on the boundaries between different components in the source code.

The rule for well-formed monitors requires that the contract is well-formed, i.e., that obligations inside of a contract are properly attributed. Figure 3 shows the rules for well-formed contracts. The judgment $\Gamma; \bar{k}; \bar{l}; j \rhd \kappa$ has three label-related parts. The first, $\bar{k}$, includes the set of parties responsible for the flat contracts on positive positions in κ. The second, $\bar{l}$, corresponds to the parties responsible for the negative positions. Finally, j is the owner of the contract code. The initial values of these labels are drawn

$\boxed{\Gamma; \bar{k}; \bar{l}; j \rhd \kappa}$

$$\frac{\Gamma; j \Vdash e}{\Gamma; \bar{k}; \bar{l}; j \rhd \lfloor \texttt{flat}(|e|^{j}) \rfloor^{\bar{k}}} \qquad \frac{\Gamma; \bar{l}; \bar{k}; j \rhd \kappa_1 \quad \Gamma; \bar{k}; \bar{l}; j \rhd \kappa_2}{\Gamma; \bar{k}; \bar{l}; j \rhd \kappa_1 \mapsto \kappa_2} \qquad \frac{\Gamma; \bar{l}; \bar{k} \cup \{j\}; j \rhd \kappa_1 \quad \Gamma \uplus \{x : j\}; \bar{k}; \bar{l}; j \rhd \kappa_2}{\Gamma; \bar{k}; \bar{l}; j \rhd \kappa_1 \overset{d}{\mapsto} (\lambda x.\kappa_2)}$$

Fig. 3. Well-formed contracts

from the monitor expression, and they are propagated by a structural traversal of κ to its pieces. The server label is initially the only member of the labels responsible for the positive pieces of the contracts while the client label is the only member of the parties responsible for the negative pieces. Also the contract label of the monitor is appointed as owner party of the contract's code. In the case of function contracts, the set of responsible parties are reversed in the pre-condition [4] and for dependent function contracts the contract party j is added to the set of labels responsible for the pre-condition. In the latter case, we record in the environment the variable x that binds the argument in the post-condition with the contract party as its owner. After all, x is a binder that belongs to the contract's code. Finally, for flat contracts the rules require that the obligation annotations on the contract coincide with the set of parties responsible for the positive pieces of the contract and that the party j is explicitly marked as the owner of the contract code.

Note: This semantics of CPCF differs from the semantics of our previous work. The main deviation is the introduction of the single owner policy. It helps us prove complete monitoring, a deep notion of correctness for a contract system that subsumes blame correctness.

In our previous result, ownership and obligations are used to verify that whenever a contract error is raised, its witness value is owned by the party that is blamed and that the party failed to satisfy one of its obligations. The *picky* semantics fails to live up to this standard [3]. The problem with *picky* is due to the way the semantics decorates the monitor that protects the argument in the post-condition of a dependent contract on a function f. More specifically, the monitor holds the server of f responsible for invalid uses of the argument inside the contract despite the fact that the server does not have control over the flow of values in the contract.

The *indy* semantics eliminates this shortcoming of *picky*. It treats the contract as a separate party that is responsible for the use of values that flow in the contract. Thus the semantics injects monitors that protect the argument and hold the contract itself responsible for any use of the argument in the post-condition of a dependent contract. The obligations of the contract party are the flat contracts in negative position of the pre-conditions of dependent contracts, which also explains why we use sets of labels for the obligation annotations. A flat contract can be part of the obligations of the contract party and, also, of the client or the server.

Our blame correctness criterion, though, is not strong enough to decide whether *lax* is preferable to *indy*, or vice versa, as both of them are blame correct. In fact it admits contract systems that permit uncontrolled flow of values between components. The problem lies with the way the original semantics of CPCF treats ownership. It allows for components to mix freely and for values to acquire multiple owners as they cross boundaries. For instance a term $|e|^l$ can show up without any restrictions as a sub-term of a term $|e'|^k$. Similarly a value $|...|v|^{l_1}...|^{l_n}$ comes with multiple owners as the annotations keep track of the whole history of migrations from one module to another. These annotations do not affect evaluation, however, because it ignores them and proceeds as if they are not there.

Our new semantics turn ownership into a computational device that is exploited to enforce the single owner policy. This change enables us to state when a contract system is a *complete monitor* for all specified properties. **End note**

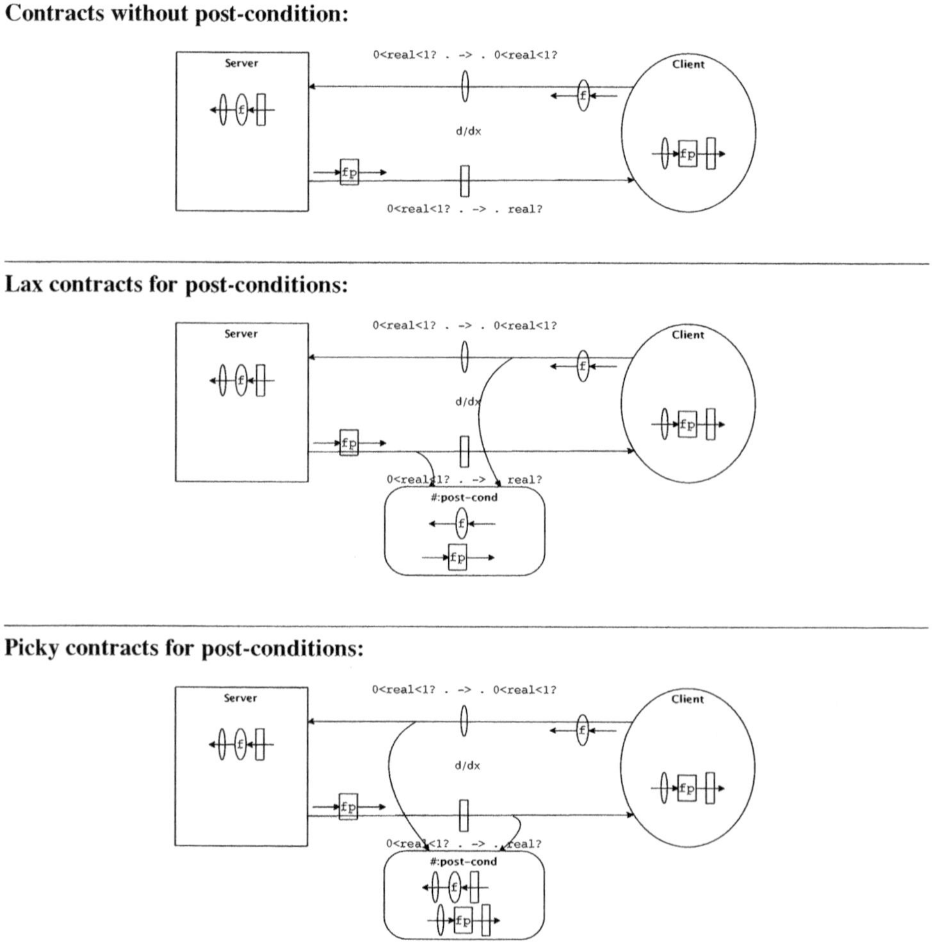

Fig. 4. Monitoring in pictures

3 Complete Monitors with Pictures

While we can use the CPCF model to articulate a formal criterion of monitoring completeness, it can also provide an intuitive understanding of the idea. In this section, we present three pictures of contract monitoring that employ some of the elements of the CPCF model and introduce complete monitors on this basis.

The first picture in figure 4 illustrates how the contract system monitors the contract of `d/dx` without its **`#:post-cond`** clause. The client owns `f` and applies `d/dx` to it. Pictorially, it ships `f` to the server over the `d/dx` channel. The contract system monitors the channel and attaches the appropriate pieces of the contract to `f`. Thus the server component receives a wrapped version of `f`. The wrapper checks that the argument and the result of any application to `f` are real numbers between 0 and 1. The result of the application, `fp`, returns to the client component via a similar channel.

Our pictures use shapes to express *ownership* of values. Thus `f` comes in an *ellipsis* to match the shape of the client and `fp` is in a *rectangle*, like the server component that creates the function. If the client were to pass `fp` back to the server to create the second derivative of `f`, the value would come in an ellipsis around the rectangle and the contract wrapper. In other words, wrapping shapes within shapes illustrates how the semantics uses ownership to keep track of a value's provenance.

Similarly, shapes on the input-output arrows mark *obligations*. In particular, the flat contracts that guard channels have the same shape as the component responsible for satisfying them. The characterization holds for both components and higher-order values that flow back and forth and receive wrappers.

In a graphical form, our picture suggests that if the initial program is *well-formed*, meaning it separates the client and the server component with a properly formed contract boundary, a complete contract system preserves a two-part invariant. The first part dictates that each value has the same shape as its origin and, if the origin differs from the current host component, then the contract system guards the value with contracts. The second part adds that the host component is responsible for meeting the pre-condition for the uses of the foreign value and the origin component is responsible for the post-condition.

Even though the invariant seems easy to maintain, adding back the **`#:post-cond`** clause shows that doing so poses subtle challenges. Concretely, a post condition clause consists of a piece of code and thus introduces a new component. In a real-world language such as Racket, this new component could exist within the server module, the client module, or as a third-party component all by itself [3, §2.3]. No matter where it exists, it hosts both `f` and `fp`, and this co-habitation is the source of all subtleties.

The new component connects to the `d/dx` channels with its own branch channels and can thus absorb the values from these channels. As the second picture of figure 4 shows, the *lax* semantics allows `f` and `fp` to enter the new component before they flow through the monitors—meaning no guards are attached to these new channels. Since `f` and `fp` have different owners, at least one of the values must be considered a foreign value and, as such, inhabits the component without the necessary guard.

In contrast to *lax*, *picky* protects these additional channels of communication, too. Figure 4 explains this idea with forks in the channels *behind* the monitors that protect the channels. Unfortunately, the obligations for the flat contracts in the **`#:post-cond`** component do not agree with the second part of the completeness invariant. That is, at least one of the two values inhabits the new component as a foreign value but is protected by misshaped contracts.

As the next section shows, the third contract monitoring system, dubbed *indy*, addresses both parts of the invariant across the entire computation. Technically, our framework serves as an independent specification of the contract system and excludes scenarios such as the two above by halting computation when the single-owner policy breaks.

4 Complete Monitors Formally

The CPCF semantics enforces the single owner policy. If a redex does not respect it, the evaluation gets stuck. Since embeddings of foreign terms in a component are wrapped with contract monitors, such stuck states are evidence that a value has leaked from one component to another without the contract system's approval. If a contract system can eliminate all such stuck states and force programs to reduce to a value or to diverge or to raise a contract error, then the contract system insulates the components of the program and regulates exchanges of values between them. We call such a contract system a *complete monitor*.

Definition 1 (Complete Monitors for CPCF). *A contract semantics m specifies a* complete monitor *if for all well typed terms e_0 such that $\varnothing; l_o \Vdash e_0$,*

- $e_0 \overset{m}{\rightarrow}_* v$ *or,*
- *for all e_1 such that $e_0 \overset{m}{\rightarrow}_* e_1$ there exists e_2 such that $e_1 \overset{m}{\rightarrow} e_2$ or,*
- $e_0 \overset{m}{\rightarrow}_* e_1 \overset{m}{\rightarrow}_* \mathtt{error}^k_j$ *and there is at least an e_1 of the form $E^l[\mathtt{mon}^{k,l}_j(\lfloor \mathtt{flat}(e) \rfloor^{\bar{l}}, v)]$ and for all such terms e_1, $v = |v_1|^k$ and $k \in \bar{l}$.*

Complete monitoring takes advantage of the ownership and obligation annotations to verify that well-formed programs do not get stuck. In addition if a contract error is raised indicating contract j failed, then for all checks of flat contracts from j, the owner k of the guarded value is identical to the server label on the contract monitor and the flat contract is part of the obligations of k. Clearly, this gives more guarantees than *blame correctness*.

At first glance *complete monitoring* appears too weak to establish the correctness of a contract system; it simply guarantees that when a value crosses a boundary, the contract system attaches *some* contract to it and that if a contract violation is detected, blame is assigned to the party that contributed the witness value. What complete monitoring does *not* require is that the contract system (1) attaches the *proper* contracts to migrating values and (2) checks flat contracts. Point 1 concerns the decomposition of compound contracts, i.e., a contract system must check the pieces of a compound value (for example, functions) with the proper pieces of their contracts (for example, domain and range). In CPCF, this property comes for free with type soundness which forces the proper distribution of compound contracts over their pieces to retain type safety. As for point 2, it is necessary to ensure that a contract system actually executes the application of the predicate to the witness value. Again, this is obvious in the case of CPCF and it is easy to check in general. In short, complete monitoring is the main ingredient language designers must check if they wish to implement a correct contract system; the remaining properties can be validated by inspection.

We show now that *indy* is a *complete monitor* while *lax* is not. The proof of complete monitoring follows a subject reduction technique similar to those of type soundness [10]. The first subsection presents the construction of the subject, progress and preservation, and how these results imply completeness for *indy*. The second subsection presents how we construct a counter-example showing the incompleteness of *lax* and *picky*.

4.1 Indy Is a Complete Monitor

The judgments for well-formed terms and well-formed contracts imply both the single owner policy for components and the agreement between monitor labels, ownership and obligation annotations for monitors. They are too weak, however, for the proof because they do not cover all intermediate terms. The semantics of CPCF uses a superset of the source language of CPCF to deal with errors and contract checks. Moreover, evaluation constructs monitor terms that are not well-formed according to our rules. Fortunately this is only temporary; after some reduction steps, the terms become well-formed again.

In order to account for the extra intermediate terms, we generalize well-formedness for terms and contracts. The generalized judgment for well-formed terms in most cases is almost the same as the corresponding source code judgment. Figure 5 shows only the extra/modified rules.

$$\boxed{\Gamma; l \Vdash e}$$

$$\frac{}{\Gamma; l \Vdash \texttt{error}^k_j} \qquad \frac{\Gamma; j \models e \qquad \Gamma; l \Vdash v}{\Gamma; l \Vdash \texttt{check}^k_j(e, v)} \qquad \frac{\Gamma; k \models e \qquad \Gamma; \{k\}; \{l\}; j \rhd \kappa}{\Gamma; l \Vdash \texttt{mon}^{k,l}_j(\kappa, e)}$$

Fig. 5. Well-formed intermediate terms

According to section 2 a monitor in the source code is well-formed if its negative label matches the owner of the monitor, its contract is well-formed and the guarded term is explicitly annotated as property of the server. For intermediate terms this last condition is too strict. The reduction rules for monitors of function contracts and dependent function contracts result in monitors where the protected term is a variable or an application. Because this happens in a restricted way a fixed number of steps yield monitors where the guarded term comes with the correct ownership annotation.

We capture these cases with the judgment of loosely well-formed terms $\Gamma; l \models e$; see figure 6 for the definition. A term with an ownership annotation with label l is both well-formed and loosely well-formed if the owner of the term is l. A variable is loosely well-formed if the environment verifies that the variable shows up in the same component l as its owner. After all, the variable is going to be substituted with a value of shape $|v|^l$. An application is loosely well formed if the operator has form $|e_1|^l$, the operand is well-formed under l, and l is also the owner of the application. After the application is performed the resulting term is owned by l.

As for $\Gamma; l \Vdash \mathtt{check}^k_j(e,v)$, well-formedness requires that e is loosely well-formed under j and v well-formed under l, the owner of the check. The second part is necessary because v is going to be embedded in the component l as is if the check succeeds. The first is required because the contract check e establishes a component boundary separating l from j. Our approach demands that all such boundaries are indicated explicitly with ownership annotations. However, when the check is first created, e is an application with shape $|e_1|^j\ v$. Again, after, the application the ownership annotations appear at the right place and until then loose well-formedness suffices to admit the term.

$\boxed{\Gamma; l \vDash e}$

$$\frac{\Gamma; l \Vdash e}{\Gamma; l \vDash |e|^l} \qquad \frac{\Gamma(x) = l}{\Gamma; l \vDash x} \qquad \frac{\Gamma; l \Vdash e_1 \qquad \Gamma; l \Vdash e_2}{\Gamma; l \vDash |e_1|^l\ e_2}$$

Fig. 6. Loosely well-formed terms

The judgment for well-formed contracts requires a minor change:

$$\frac{\Gamma; j \Vdash e \qquad \bar{k} \subseteq \bar{k'}}{\Gamma; \bar{k}; \bar{l}; j \rhd \lfloor \mathtt{flat}(|e|^j) \rfloor^{\bar{k'}}}$$

The rule for flat contracts is weakened so that it requires the parties responsible for the positive pieces of the contract to be a subset of the obligations of the flat contract rather than the same set.

Now we are ready to prove *indy* correct.

Theorem 1. $\xrightarrow{i}$ *is a complete monitor.*

The proof is direct consequence of two major lemmas: progress and preservation. A well-formed typed, term reduces to another term unless is a value or a contract error.

Lemma 1. *(Progress) For all e such that* $\varnothing; l \Vdash e$, $e = v$ *or* $e = \mathtt{error}^k_j$ *or* $e \xrightarrow{i} e_0$.

If a well-formed term reduces according to *indy*, it reduces to a well-formed term.

Lemma 2. *(Preservation) For all e and* e_0 *such that* $\varnothing; l_o \Vdash e$ *and* $e \xrightarrow{i} e_0$, $\varnothing; l_o \Vdash e_0$.

4.2 Neither Lax Nor Picky Is a Complete Monitor

In contrast to *indy*, *lax* is not a complete monitor.

As an example where *lax* does not manage to live up to complete monitoring, consider the following program.

$$\Pi^0_l = \mathtt{mon}^{k,l_o}_l(\kappa_l, |\lambda h_1.h_1\ \lambda x.5\ (\lambda g.g\ 1)|^k)\ (\lambda f.\lambda h_2.h_2\ \lambda x.6)$$

where

$$\begin{aligned}
\kappa_l &= ((\lfloor \mathtt{P?}_l \rfloor^{l_o} \mapsto \lfloor \mathtt{P?}_l \rfloor^{k}) \overset{d}{\mapsto} (\lambda f.\kappa_l^1)) \mapsto \lfloor \mathtt{P?}_l \rfloor^{k} \\
\kappa_l^1 &= ((\lfloor \mathtt{P?}_l \rfloor^{k} \mapsto \lfloor \mathtt{P?}_l \rfloor^{l_o}) \overset{d}{\mapsto} (\lambda g.\kappa_l^2)) \mapsto \lfloor \mathtt{P?}_l \rfloor^{k} \\
\kappa_l^2 &= \lfloor \mathtt{flat}(|\lambda x.\mathtt{zero?}(f\ 1 - g\ 0)|^{l}) \rfloor^{k} \\
\mathtt{P?}_l &= \mathtt{flat}(|\lambda x.x > 0|^{l}).
\end{aligned}$$

For all $l \in \mathbb{L}$ if $k \neq l_o$, then $\varnothing; l_o \Vdash \Pi_l^0$. The constraint on k and l_o comes from the rules for well-formed source terms and captures the intuition that contracts are used as the interface between different components.

Π_l^0 is a not a unique program but rather a schema of programs. Label l can be any label including k and l_o. Also Π_l^0 is not interesting in terms of computation. What makes it an example worth considering is its contract κ_l and more specifically its flat sub-contract κ_l^2. Note that κ_l^2 invokes f on a positive number and g on 0. In addition the value bound to f, $f_v = \lambda x.5$, comes from the client l_o while the value bound to g, $g_v = \lambda x.6$, originates from the server k. We start by showing that l must equal l_o in order to satisfy complete monitoring. The reduction of Π_l^0 eventually applies f_v to 1. After the substitution of f_v for f in κ_l^2 we get

$$\kappa_l^{\dagger} = \lfloor \mathtt{flat}(|\lambda x.\mathtt{zero?}(||f_v|^{l_o}|^{l}\ 1 - g\ 0)|^{l}) \rfloor^{k}.$$

In order for the *lax* system to satisfy the complete monitoring condition, $\kappa_l^{\dagger}$ must remain well formed:

$$\{f : l, g : l\}; \{k\}; \{\}; l \rhd \kappa_l^{\dagger}.$$

This judgment, however, demands that $\{f : l, g : l\}; l \Vdash ||f_v|^{l_o}|^{l}$, which in turn requires that l must be equal to l_o. If so, the contract looks like this:

$$\kappa_{l_o}^{\dagger} = \lfloor \mathtt{flat}(|\lambda x.\mathtt{zero?}(||f_v|^{l_o}|^{l_o}\ 1 - g\ 0)|^{l_o}) \rfloor^{k}.$$

The next few steps of the reduction process produce a state that is inconsistent with complete monitoring. Specifically, κ_l^2 also applies g_v to 0:

$$\kappa_{l_o}^{\dagger\dagger} = \lfloor \mathtt{flat}(|\lambda x.\mathtt{zero?}(||f_v|^{l_o}|^{l_o}\ 1 - ||g_v|^{k}|^{l_o}\ 0)|^{l_o}) \rfloor^{k}.$$

And this last contract disagrees with the subject because k cannot equal l_o. More specifically

$$\{f : l_o, g : l_o\}; \{k\}; \{\}; l_o \not\rhd \kappa_{l_o}^{\dagger\dagger}$$

since $\{f : l_o, g : l_o\}; l_o \nVdash ||g_v|^{k}|^{l_o}$.

Our example shows that independently of the choice of l, Π_l^0 does not respect preservation under the *lax* semantics. As a consequence *lax* can violate the single owner policy. Indeed $\Pi_{l_o}^0 \xrightarrow{l}_* E^{l_o}[||g_v|^{k}|^{l_o}\ 0]$. This last state is a stuck state as it involves the application of a function that has multiple owner tags, i.e., it has crossed contract-free boundaries between distinct components.

Theorem 2. *$\xrightarrow{l}$ is not a complete monitor.*

The same example shows that *picky* CPCF is not a complete monitor.

Theorem 3. *$\xrightarrow{p}$ is not a complete monitor.*

5 Mutation Needs Complete Monitors

The principle of complete monitoring provides guidance for the addition of linguistic features to CPCF. Concretely, consider the addition of reference cells, i.e., sharable, mutable data. Doing so requires both a notation for contracts on cells and also a mechanism that monitors all channels of communication between components that exchange cells.

We investigate this setting via CPCF!, an imperative variant of CPCF. The source syntax of CPCF!, figure 7, extends the source syntax of CPCF with the standard operators of a language with mutable cells. CPCF! also comes with contracts for mutable cells, $\mathtt{ref/c}(\kappa)$. Intuitively the contract specifies that the protected cell should conform at any point with κ. CPCF!, just like CPCF, is typed. The type system and its soundness impose no challenges, and are omitted.

Types	$\tau = \ldots \mid \mathsf{ref}(\tau)$	**Values**	$v = \ldots \mid loc \mid \gamma$
Contracts	$\kappa = \ldots \mid \mathtt{ref/c}(\kappa)$	**Guards**	$\gamma = \mathtt{G}\{v\ (\kappa\ l\ l\ l)\}$
Terms	$e = \ldots \mid \mathtt{ref}(e) \mid \mathtt{get}(e) \mid \mathtt{set}(e,e)$		

Fig. 7. CPCF! syntax (left) and intermediate syntax (right)

The additions to the source syntax demand additions to the definitions of well-formed terms and contracts. The first are straightforward requiring that the arguments of the operators related to store are well-formed under the same owner as the operator:

$$\frac{\Gamma;l \Vdash e}{\Gamma;l \Vdash \mathtt{ref}(e)} \qquad \frac{\Gamma;l \Vdash e}{\Gamma;l \Vdash \mathtt{get}(e)} \qquad \frac{\Gamma;l \Vdash e_1 \qquad \Gamma;l \Vdash e_2}{\Gamma;l \Vdash \mathtt{set}(e_1,e_2)}$$

The second addition poses a small challenge. The same component can read from, and write to, a mutable cell. Thus the distinction between clients and servers of the contents of the cells collapses. To reflect this insight, the rule for well-formed contracts on cells merges the parties responsible for the negative and positive pieces of the contract when assigning obligations for the contract that protects the contents of a cell. All parties $\bar{l}$ and $\bar{k}$ have the obligation to treat the contents according to the contract both as clients and servers:

$$\frac{\Gamma;\bar{l}\bar{k};\bar{l}\bar{k};j \rhd \kappa}{\Gamma;\bar{k};\bar{l};j \rhd \mathtt{ref/c}(\kappa)}$$

Mutable cells are represented at run-time as memory locations loc. To enforce contract checks on the contents of memory locations we have to delay checking until a component tries to read the location. For that reason we introduce guards $\mathtt{G}\{v\ (\kappa\ k\ l\ j)\}$ as intermediate terms. They are contract monitors similar to $\mathtt{mon}_j^{k,l}(\kappa,e)$. The difference is that in contrast with monitors, guards are values, and thus they attach themselves permanently around locations when the locations cross component boundaries. Figure 7 shows the intermediate syntax for CPCF! that extends the intermediate syntax of CPCF.

The definition of the reduction relation for CPCF! demands some preparation. Locations require the presence of the addition of a store, which changes the shape of states. They now have two parts: e and σ. The reduction relation describes now transitions between such states: $E^l[e], \sigma \overset{m}{\rightarrow} E^l[e'], \sigma'$. Moreover we derive additional evaluation contexts from the new operators just like for the primitive operators in CPCF.

Now we are ready for the reduction relation of CPCF!. The reduction rules for CPCF become also reduction rules for CPCF! after adding the same store on both sides of each rule. The additional operations on mutable data, figure 8, are straightforward when they are performed directly on store locations. They only fire when the context owns the location in order to guarantee that a component can read or write to properly acquired cells. Things become interesting when a component other than the creator and owner of the location tries to access or modify the location's contents. Doing so requires a guard $\mathtt{G}\{v\ (\kappa\ k\ l\ j)\}$. Guards are the result of a monitor of a contract $\mathtt{ref/c}(\kappa)$ on a value v. They contain the guarded value, the contract κ and the labels that decorate the monitor. A $\mathtt{get}(||\gamma||^l)$ opens the guard γ and delegates the $\mathtt{get}$ operation to the value that resides in γ. Moreover it wraps the result with a monitor built out of the contract and the labels from γ. This ensures that the contract is checked when the host component tries to use the value obtained from the location.

Writing a value v' to a mutable cell via a guard γ is also delegated to the value that resides in γ; v' is wrapped with the appropriate contract monitor. However, in this case the semantics must take into account two other factors. First, a $\mathtt{set}$ operation creates a flow of values in the opposite direction than a $\mathtt{get}$ operation. Thus the server for the new content of the location should be the client for the old one and vice versa. Second, the result of $\mathtt{set}$ should be the same guard γ as the one applied on the operation. This ensures that the location remains protected. To achieve this, the reduction rule reverses the labels on the monitor of the term that is written in the location and wraps the whole operation with a monitor that is going to reproduce γ. Finally the rule expands the operation into a function application so that v' becomes explicitly decorated with the label of the host component before written to the location.

$$\begin{array}{ll}
E^l[\mathtt{ref}(v)], \sigma & \overset{m}{\rightarrow} E^l[loc], \sigma' \\
\quad \text{where } loc \notin dom(\sigma) \text{ and } \sigma' = \sigma \uplus \{loc \mapsto v\} & \\
E^l[\mathtt{get}(||loc||^l)], \sigma & \overset{m}{\rightarrow} E^l[|v|^l], \sigma \\
\quad \text{where } \sigma = \sigma' \uplus \{loc \mapsto v\} & \\
E^l[\mathtt{set}(||loc||^l, v')], \sigma & \overset{m}{\rightarrow} E^l[|loc|^l], \sigma' \\
\quad \text{where } \sigma = \sigma'' \uplus \{loc \mapsto v\} \text{ and } \sigma' = \sigma'' \uplus \{loc \mapsto v'\} & \\
E^l[\mathtt{mon}_j^{k,l}(\mathtt{ref/c}(\kappa), v)], \sigma & \overset{m}{\rightarrow} E^l[\mathtt{G}\{v\ (\kappa\ k\ l\ \ j)\}], \sigma \\
E^l[\mathtt{get}(||\gamma||^l)], \sigma & \overset{m}{\rightarrow} E^l[|\mathtt{mon}_j^{k,l}(\kappa, \mathtt{get}(v))|^l], \sigma \\
\quad \text{where } \gamma = \mathtt{G}\{v\ (\kappa\ k\ l\ \ j)\} & \\
E^l[\mathtt{set}(||\gamma||^l, ||v'||^l)], \sigma & \overset{m}{\rightarrow} E^l[|(\lambda x.\mathtt{mon}_j^{k,l}(\mathtt{ref/c}(\kappa), \mathtt{set}(v, \mathtt{mon}_j^{l,k}(\kappa, x))))\ v''|^l], \sigma \\
\quad \text{where } \gamma = \mathtt{G}\{v\ (\kappa\ k\ l\ \ j)\} \text{ and } v'' = |v'|^l &
\end{array}$$

Fig. 8. Operations on mutable data

Proving that CPCF! is a complete monitor follows the same pattern as for CPCF. We first adapt the definition of complete monitoring to a store semantics.

Definition 2 (Complete Monitors for CPCF!). *A contract semantics m specifies a* complete monitor *if for all well typed terms e_0 such that $\varnothing; l_o \Vdash e_0$,*

- $e_0, \varnothing \xrightarrow{m}_* v, \sigma_1$ *or,*
- *for all terms e_1 and stores σ_1 such that $e_0, \varnothing \xrightarrow{m}_* e_1, \sigma_1$ there exists term e_2 and store σ_2 such that $e_1, \sigma_1 \xrightarrow{m} e_2, \sigma_2$ or,*
- $e_0, \varnothing \xrightarrow{m}_* e_1, \sigma_1 \xrightarrow{m}_* \texttt{error}^k_j, \sigma_2$ *and there is at least an e_1 such that e_1 is of the form $E^l[\texttt{mon}^{k,l}_j(\lfloor \texttt{flat}(e) \rfloor^{\bar{l}}, v)]$ and for all such terms e_1, $v = |v_1|^k$ and $k \in \bar{l}$.*

Then we generalize well-formedness for source code and contracts to intermediate terms and prove preservation and progress main lemmas. The subject consists of two new judgments, $\Sigma;\Gamma;l \Vdash e$ and $\Sigma;\Gamma;\bar{k};\bar{l};j \rhd \kappa$.

The most important modification to the corresponding subject in CPCF is the introduction of store ownership, which establishes that the store is well-formed. The store ownership relates locations and owners. A store is well-formed if its contents are well-formed under the owner store ownership points to.

$$\frac{\text{for all } loc \in dom(\sigma),\ \Sigma;\varnothing;\Sigma(loc) \Vdash \sigma(loc)}{\Sigma \sim \sigma}$$

This is necessary for the same reason that store typing is necessary to prove type soundness for languages with mutable data: it admits circularity in the store.

The generalized judgment for well-formed terms and contracts is almost the same as the corresponding well-formed judgments in CPCF. The differences are the additional rules for store operations and that together with the environment, it propagates the ownership typing. There are also rules for guards and locations:

$$\frac{\Sigma(loc) = l}{\Sigma;\Gamma;l \Vdash loc} \qquad \frac{\Sigma;\Gamma;k \Vdash v \quad \Sigma;\Gamma;\{k,l\};\{k,l\};j \rhd \kappa}{\Sigma;\Gamma;l \Vdash \texttt{G}\{|v|^k\ (\kappa\ k\ l\ j)\}}$$

A location is well-formed only under the owner that is associated with in the store ownership. Well-formed guards are only those where the guarded value is explicitly annotated as owned by the component with the positive label (k) in the guard. Furthermore, the contract κ must be also well-formed. The last label (j) serves as the owner of the contract's code. Since guards are used to protect locations and locations can be used by components both for writing and reading both the negative label l and positive label k must be responsible for the positive and negative pieces of κ.

Furthermore we need to extend the CPCF rules for loosely well-formed terms with store ownership. We also add two rules due to store related operations:

$$\frac{\Sigma;\Gamma;l \Vdash e}{\Sigma;\Gamma;l \vDash \texttt{get}(|e|^l)} \qquad \frac{\Sigma;\Gamma;l \Vdash e_1 \quad \Sigma;\Gamma;l \Vdash e_2}{\Sigma;\Gamma;l \vDash \texttt{set}(|e_1|^l, e_2)}$$

The `get` and `set` operators are loosely well-formed if the term in the position of the mutable cell is tagged with the owner of the operation. The reduction semantics guarantees that reducing the operation produces a term explicitly owned by l.

We can now show that the *indy* semantics is a complete monitor for CPCF!.

Theorem 4. $\xrightarrow{i}$ *is a complete monitor.*

6 Complete Monitors Enable Typed-Untyped Interaction

Typed Racket [8] enables mixing typed modules with untyped Racket modules. Type-like contracts prevent untyped code from violating the type discipline when interacting with typed code. Tobin-Hochstadt and Felleisen [8] define and prove the soundness of this approach in a multi-lingual setting via a so-called Blame Theorem, a name due to Wadler and Findler [9], which establishes that a program execution can only raise contract violations due to the untyped part.

To prove type soundness for an imperative version of this system we create an untyped sister language of CPCF!, UCPCF!, with a shared term syntax, and prove the corresponding blame theorem exploiting complete monitoring for CPCF!. As CPCF! has only base types, function types, and reference types, it suffices to consider only the corresponding contracts:

$$\kappa = \lfloor \mathtt{I} \rfloor^{\bar{l}} \mid \lfloor \mathtt{B} \rfloor^{\bar{l}} \mid \kappa \mapsto \kappa \mid \mathtt{ref/c}(\kappa)$$

This restriction enables a series of additional simplifications in our framework. First, flat contracts contain only built-in predicates and not arbitrary code. Thus their code is not the property of any specific party. This decision is reflected in simpler rules for well-formed flat contracts:

$$\frac{}{\Gamma;\bar{k};\bar{l};j \rhd \lfloor \mathtt{I} \rfloor^{\bar{k}}} \qquad \frac{}{\Gamma;\bar{k};\bar{l};j \rhd \lfloor \mathtt{B} \rfloor^{\bar{k}}}$$

Second, the omission of dependent function contracts makes the distinction between *lax*, *picky* and *indy* irrelevant. We use $\rightarrow$ without any subscript to denote the reduction relation for UCPCF!.

Third, checking of flat contracts does not require the special check construct:

$$\begin{array}{ll} E^l[\mathtt{mon}_j^{k,l}(\lfloor \mathtt{I} \rfloor^{\bar{l}'}, ||\mathtt{n}||^{l'})], \sigma \rightarrow E^l[\mathtt{n}], \sigma & \\ E^l[\mathtt{mon}_j^{k,l}(\lfloor \mathtt{I} \rfloor^{\bar{l}'}, ||\mathtt{c}||^{l'})], \sigma \rightarrow E^l[\mathtt{error}_j^k], \sigma & \text{if } \mathtt{c} \neq \mathtt{n} \\ E^l[\mathtt{mon}_j^{k,l}(\lfloor \mathtt{B} \rfloor^{\bar{l}'}, ||\mathtt{c}||^{l'})], \sigma \rightarrow E^l[\mathtt{c}], \sigma & \text{if } \mathtt{c} \in \{\mathtt{tt}, \mathtt{ff}\} \\ E^l[\mathtt{mon}_j^{k,l}(\lfloor \mathtt{B} \rfloor^{\bar{l}'}, ||\mathtt{c}||^{l'})], \sigma \rightarrow E^l[\mathtt{error}_j^k], \sigma & \text{if } \mathtt{c} \notin \{\mathtt{tt}, \mathtt{ff}\} \end{array}$$

The untyped nature of UCPCF! obliges us to extend the reduction relation of the language. Type soundness for CPCF! allowed us to ignore redexes like $||v_1||^l \; ||v_2||^l$ where v_1 is not a function. In UCPCF! such states *can* occur. We deal with them by introducing dynamic type errors $\mathtt{error}_{\mathcal{T}}^l$ where l is the owner of the hole in which the ill-formed redex occurs.

This change must be propagated to our definition of complete monitoring. The definition of the property includes an extra case for run-time type errors.

Definition 3 (Complete Monitors for UCPCF!). *A contract semantics m specifies a* complete monitor *if for all terms e_0 such that $\varnothing; l_o \Vdash e_0$,*

- $e_0, \varnothing \xrightarrow{m}_* v, \sigma$ *or,*
- $e_0, \varnothing \xrightarrow{m}_* \mathtt{error}_{\mathcal{T}}^l, \sigma$ *or*

- *for all terms* e_1 *and stores* σ_1 *such that* $e_0, \varnothing \xrightarrow{m}_* e_1, \sigma_1$ *there exists term* e_2 *and store* σ_2 *such that* $e_1, \sigma_1 \xrightarrow{m} e_2, \sigma_2$ *or,*
- $e_0, \varnothing \xrightarrow{m}_* e_1, \sigma_1 \xrightarrow{m}_* \mathtt{error}^k_j, \sigma_2$ *where* $j \neq \mathcal{T}$, *and there is at least an* e_1 *such that* e_1 *is of the form* $E^l[\mathtt{mon}^{k,l}_j(\lfloor \mathtt{I} \rfloor^{\bar{l}'}, v)]$ *or* e_1 *is of the form* $E^l[\mathtt{mon}^{k,l}_j(\lfloor \mathtt{B} \rfloor^{\bar{l}'}, v)]$ *and for all such* e_1, $v = |v_1|^k$ *and* $k \in \bar{l}$.

The addition of run-time type errors does not eliminate all stuck states. The single owner policy still must hold for a redex to reduce. We can show, though, that these stuck states are not reachable and establish that $\rightarrow$ *is* a complete monitor for UCPCF!.

Since CPCF! and UCPCF! share the same source code syntax, there is a subset of UCPCF! programs that are well-typed under CPCF!'s sound type system. We use $\mathcal{S}, \mathcal{G} \vdash e : \tau$ to express that a term e has type τ given type environment $\mathcal{G}$ and store typing $\mathcal{S}$. For simplicity we assume that there are only two component labels, u for untyped code and t for typed code. We can extend CPCF!'s type system to allow for embedding of untyped UCPCF! code:

$$\frac{\mathcal{S}, \mathcal{G} \vdash e}{\mathcal{S}, \mathcal{G} \vdash \mathtt{mon}^{u,t}_j(\kappa, e) : \mathcal{T}[[\kappa]]} \qquad \frac{\mathcal{S}, \mathcal{G} \vdash v}{\mathcal{S}, \mathcal{G} \vdash \mathtt{G}\{v\ (\kappa\ u\ t\ j)\} : \mathcal{T}[[\kappa]]}$$

The meta-function $\mathcal{T}$ maps a contract to the corresponding type. For flat contracts, $\mathcal{T}[[\lfloor \mathtt{I} \rfloor^{\bar{k}}]] = \mathsf{I}$ and $\mathcal{T}[[\lfloor \mathtt{B} \rfloor^{\bar{k}}]] = \mathsf{B}$.

The judgment $\mathcal{S}, \mathcal{G} \vdash e$ denotes that any typed code embedded in untyped code is well-typed. The judgment structurally decomposes e. Things become more interesting when a sub-term is typed:

$$\frac{\mathcal{S}, \mathcal{G} \vdash e : \mathcal{T}[[\kappa]]}{\mathcal{S}, \mathcal{G} \vdash \mathtt{mon}^{t,u}_j(\kappa, e)} \qquad \frac{\mathcal{S}, \mathcal{G} \vdash v : \mathcal{T}[[\mathtt{ref/c}(\kappa)]]}{\mathcal{S}, \mathcal{G} \vdash \mathtt{G}\{v\ (\kappa\ t\ u\ j)\}}$$

Free variables and locations in typed code can only originate from typed code. This goes hand in hand with the idea that a well-formed term can only refer to variables and locations of the same owner as the term and writing and reading foreign mutable cells can be done only through guards.

We can now state and prove the Blame Theorem.

Theorem 5. *(Blame Theorem) For all UCPCF! terms* e_0 *such that* $\varnothing, \varnothing \vdash e_0$ *and* $\varnothing; u \Vdash e_0$, $e_0 \not\rightarrow_* \mathtt{error}^t_j$.

In our setting the proof of the theorem benefits greatly from complete monitoring as it allows us to reduce the space of the proof cases. For instance when typed code retrieves values from the store, complete monitoring guarantees that those are either the property of typed code and thus, from type soundness for CPCF!, they are well-typed, or they come from the untyped code and thus they are wrapped in a contract monitor. This observation reduces the proof cases essentially to only those that create new contract monitors. There we utilize the subject introduced in this section to make sure that the new monitors that contain terms from the typed party are protecting the code with contracts that correspond to their type.

In essence the proof of the Blame Theorem says that typed terms e can only show up inside monitors of the form $\mathtt{mon}^{t,u}_j(\kappa, e)$ and that for some $\mathcal{S}$ and $\mathcal{G}$, $\mathcal{S}, \mathcal{G} \vdash e : \mathcal{T}[[\kappa]]$.

Since type safety guarantees that type errors $\texttt{error}^t_{\mathcal{T}}$ do not emerge in any case, we must only rule out contract errors blaming the typed code. From complete monitoring, this requires a failure of a contract check of the form $\texttt{mon}^{t,u}_j(\kappa, ||\texttt{c}||^t)$ where κ is a flat contract. However, this is impossible since $\varnothing, \varnothing \vdash \texttt{c} : \mathcal{T}[[\kappa]]$ and by the semantics for flat contract monitors and the translation of contracts to types no such check can fail. Thus no error blaming the typed code ever occurs.

7 Related Work

Our results are based on decades-long research in behavioral contract systems and tracking of provenance. A review of and comparison with results in these fields can be found in the related work section of Dimoulas et al. [3].

Here we focus on the critically important work of Zdancewic et al. [11]. They use the idea of principals for proving type abstraction. In their semantics, each component is a different principal that allows other principals to access its data only through abstract operators. If a principal tries to manipulate directly data that it does not own, the evaluation gets stuck. In the type system foreign data is given an abstract type. Thus if the type system is sound all stuck states are unreachable.

While Zdancewic et al. directly inspire our single owner policy, our semantics is unrelated to theirs and we apply the idea to define and prove a novel property of contract systems instead of type systems.

References

1. Blume, M., McAllester, D.: Sound and complete models of contracts. Journal of Functional Programming 16(4-5), 375–414 (2006)
2. Dimoulas, C., Felleisen, M.: On contract satisfaction in a higher-order world. ACM Transactions on Programming Languages and Systems (TOPLAS) 33(5), 16:1 – 16:29 (2011)
3. Dimoulas, C., Findler, R.B., Flanagan, C., Felleisen, M.: Correct blame for contracts: No more scapegoating. In: POPL, pp. 215 – 226 (2011)
4. Findler, R.B., Felleisen, M.: Contracts for higher-order functions. In: ICFP, pp. 48–59 (2002)
5. Flatt, M.: PLT: Reference: Racket. Tech. Rep. PLT-TR-2010-1, PLT Inc. (2010), `http://racket-lang.org/tr1/`
6. Greenberg, M., Pierce, B.C., Weirich, S.: Contracts made manifest. In: POPL, pp. 353–364 (2010)
7. Meyer, B.: Eiffel: The Language. Prentice Hall (1992)
8. Tobin-Hochstadt, S., Felleisen, M.: Interlanguage migration: from scripts to programs. In: DLS, pp. 964–974 (2006)
9. Wadler, P., Findler, R.B.: Well-Typed Programs Can't Be Blamed. In: Castagna, G. (ed.) ESOP 2009. LNCS, vol. 5502, pp. 1–16. Springer, Heidelberg (2009)
10. Wright, A.K., Felleisen, M.: A syntactic approach to type soundness. Information and Computation 115(1), 38–94 (1994)
11. Zdancewic, S., Grossman, D., Morrisett, G.: Principals in programming languages: A syntactic proof technique. In: ICFP, pp. 197–207 (1999)

A Systematic Approach to Delimited Control with Multiple Prompts

Paul Downen and Zena M. Ariola

University of Oregon
{pdownen,ariola}@cs.uoregon.edu

Abstract. We formalize delimited control with multiple prompts, in the style of Parigot's $\lambda\mu$-calculus, through a series of incremental extensions by starting with the pure λ-calculus. Each language inherits the semantics and reduction theory of its parent, giving a systematic way to describe each level of control.

Keywords: Delimited control, dynamic variables, shift, reset, multiple prompts.

1 Introduction

Control operators have become an integral part of modern programming languages. In particular, the flexible abstraction of continuation-based control is becoming more mainstream in high-level languages. The classic control operator is call-with-current-continuation, or call/cc, which has appeared in languages such as Scheme and Ruby. call/cc allows the programmer to capture the surrounding context of an expression, creating a continuation that serves as a return point to "the rest of the program" from where call/cc was called. This style of control abstraction is called *abortive*, since invoking a continuation captured by call/cc aborts the computation currently in progress, and immediately returns to the context stored in the continuation. Even though call/cc is a very flexible control operator, it has limits. For example, call/cc alone is not enough to simulate mutable state in an otherwise state-free language.

Compared to abortive control, delimited control provides a more powerful abstraction. The difference of delimited control is that the continuation behaves like a normal function, so that multiple continuations may be composed together. In addition, the scope of the control operator can be managed by setting a *prompt*, limiting the context that can be captured. The shift and reset operators, as presented by Danvy and Filinski [5], are expressive enough to simulate mutable state. In fact, Filinski [11,12] showed that the combination of shift and reset is enough to give a direct style encoding for any effect written in monadic style, as well as several layered effects.

An interesting extension of delimited control is the addition of multiple prompts that can each delimit a different portion of the context. Dybvig, Peyton Jones, and Sabry [8] define a general framework for delimited control in the presence of multiple prompts, in which higher-level control operators may be defined. They

H. Seidl (Ed.): ESOP 2012, LNCS 7211, pp. 234–253, 2012.

provide an operational semantics and a monadic translation into a pure λ-calculus extended with stacks, as well as an implementation of the monadic effect in Haskell. A direct implementation of delimited control with multiple prompts in OCaml is given by Kiselyov [14]. In addition, Kiselyov, Shan, and Sabry [15] give a language that combines both delimited control and dynamic variables, showing that the two effects interact in subtle ways. Garcia *et al.* [13] showed that delimited control with multiple prompts can represent call-by-need evaluation.

The goal of this paper is to provide a reduction theory for delimited control with multiple prompts. Ariola *et al.* have formalized abortive and delimited control [2] in the style of Parigot's call-by-value $\lambda\mu$, leading to a calculus called $\lambda\mu\widehat{\mathsf{tp}}$. We use $\lambda\mu\widehat{\mathsf{tp}}$ as a reference point since it has a well-understood reduction theory that directly expresses the operational semantics. By extending $\lambda\mu\widehat{\mathsf{tp}}$ with multiple prompts, we clearly delineate the reduction of delimited control with multiple prompts in a way that is not apparent in the usual presentations based on operational semantics. Our approach is to build up to the expressive power of shift and shift_0 with multiple prompts in incremental steps, while using intermediate languages as stepping stones. We start with the pure λ-calculus and make small extensions to each language that are compatible with the previous semantics. Separate concerns, such as binding and capture, are explicitly apparent in the syntax of the language. The end result is a calculus that expresses delimited control with multiple prompts, which arises naturally from the representation of the semantics. Our contributions are:

- A better understanding of the dynamic nature of the prompt, in the context of delimited control with a single prompt. We express this in terms of an intermediate language with one dynamic variable that avoids recursive bindings.
- A set of small, incremental extensions of $\lambda\mu\widehat{\mathsf{tp}}$, providing more expressive languages that are compatible with the existing semantics. Each extension enables direct encodings of additional, useful language constructs, and arises as a natural extension of a less expressive language or intermediate language.
- A reduction theory for control with multiple prompts that is sound with respect to the *continuation passing style* (CPS) semantics and expressive enough to lead to the final answer. This reduction theory is compatible with the one of $\lambda\mu\widehat{\mathsf{tp}}$.

The overall strategy of the paper is as follows. In Sections 2, 3, 4, 6, 7, and 9, we define our languages of interest. We start with the λ-calculus (in 2), and extend it with control ($\lambda\mu$ in 3) and then with delimited control ($\lambda\mu\widehat{\mathsf{tp}}$ in 4). Then, we branch out in two separate directions, extending $\lambda\mu\widehat{\mathsf{tp}}$ with multiple prompts ($\lambda\widehat{\mu}$ in 6) and also transparent prompts ($\lambda\mu\widehat{\mathsf{tp}}^{\uparrow}$ in 7). Finally, we bring $\lambda\widehat{\mu}$ and $\lambda\mu\widehat{\mathsf{tp}}^{\uparrow}$ together, giving us a language of delimited control and multiple prompts ($\lambda\widehat{\mu}^{\uparrow}$ in 9). We present the semantics of the new languages in three different ways: first as a *CPS transformation* from the source language to the pure λ-calculus, then as a set of *reduction rules*, and finally as an *operational semantics*. The CPS transformation implements a big-step evaluator for the language written in the λ-calculus, and is used as our primary reference point for the definition of the semantics. The reduction rules are a set of local program transformations in the source language that correspond to reductions performed in the CPS transformed program. The operational semantics arise as both a restriction on the reduction rules and as the equivalent small-step evaluator for the CPS transformation, and is derived by defunctionalizing the continuation of the CPS [19,4]. We wrap up these sections with a discussion on expressiveness by encoding control operators in the language. In Sections 5 and 8 we present two intermediate languages which are used as stepping stones for defining the CPS transformations of our primary languages, and provide a good framework for designing extensions.

2 Lambda Calculus: λ

The syntax of λ-calculus includes variables, function abstraction, and function application. Unless otherwise specified, we let the set of *Values* be $V ::= x \mid \lambda x.t$.

$$t \in Term ::= V \mid t_1\ t_2 \qquad\qquad V \in Value ::= x \mid \lambda x.t$$

In this paper we are going to focus on the call-by-value setting, which restricts substitution to values, as described by the β_v reduction rule: $(\lambda x.t)\ V \to t\{V/x\}$. An alternative way of presenting the semantics is to perform a translation which hard-wires the evaluation strategy into the term itself. The transformation is called *continuation passing style* (CPS); it splits a program into the current work to be done and the rest of the computation, which is called a *continuation*. The call-by-value CPS transform of the λ-calculus is defined as follows:

$$\mathcal{C}_\lambda[\![x]\!]k = k\ x \quad \mathcal{C}_\lambda[\![\lambda x.t]\!]k = k\ \lambda x.\mathcal{C}_\lambda[\![t]\!] \quad \mathcal{C}_\lambda[\![t_1\ t_2]\!]k = \mathcal{C}_\lambda[\![t_1]\!]\lambda f.\mathcal{C}_\lambda[\![t_2]\!]\lambda s.f\ s\ k$$

Variables and functions are both values, so during evaluation they are just passed to the current continuation. The only non-value case, where actual computation occurs, is in the function application step. First, the function is evaluated, and its value is bound to f in the top continuation. Second, the argument is evaluated and its value is bound to s in the next continuation. Finally, with values for both terms, the function value is applied to the argument value, and the computation continues with the original continuation k.

In the output of this transformation, terms are maps from continuations, k, to final answers. Continuations, then, are maps from values to final answers. This means that the CPS translation of a term does not execute by itself, it must be given some initial continuation in order to begin the process of evaluation. Following the sequent calculus tradition, we add the counterpart of this initial continuation to the syntax, which explicitly marks the *top-level*, or final return point of the whole program. We name this continuation $*$ and specify that running a term consists of coupling that term with $*$, written as $[*]t$, which we call a command. Operationally, the command $[*]t$ is interpreted as evaluating the term t in the empty context. We extend the syntax of our call-by-value calculus with two new syntactic categories:

$$c \in Command ::= [q]t \qquad q \in CoTerm ::= * \qquad t \in Term ::= V \mid t_1\ t_2$$

We also extend our previous CPS transform $\mathcal{C}_\lambda$ with clauses for commands and the constant $*$.

$$\mathcal{C}_\lambda[\![[q]t]\!] = \mathcal{C}_\lambda[\![t]\!]\ \mathcal{C}_\lambda[\![q]\!] \qquad\qquad \mathcal{C}_\lambda[\![*]\!] = \lambda x.x$$

The interpretation of the command $[q]t$ is to evaluate the term t in the context q, which means to pass the continuation represented by q to the term. The initial continuation $*$ just returns the value it is given without modifying it.

3 Lambda Calculus with Control: Parigot's $\lambda\mu$

Felleisen [9] extended the call-by-value lambda calculus with continuation abstraction. This allows a term to store its evaluation context as a special function and to reinstall this context by invoking that function. The function representing a continuation never returns to the call site. Here, we instead follow Parigot's approach [18] because it provides a reduction theory which more accurately simulates the operational semantics [1]. In Parigot's $\lambda\mu$, continuations are not functions. Similarly to the the top-level, continuations belong to a separate syntactic category of co-terms. Intuitively, terms are producers of values, whereas continuations are consumers of values. The invocation of a continuation is a command. The syntax of $\lambda\mu$ extends the class of terms and co-terms as follows:

$$c \in Command ::= [q]t \quad t \in Term ::= V \mid t_1\ t_2 \mid \mu\alpha.c \quad q \in CoTerm ::= \alpha \mid *$$

We define the CPS semantics of $\lambda\mu$ by extending $\mathcal{C}_\lambda$ for the new syntax:

$$\mathcal{C}_{\lambda\mu}[\![\mu\alpha.c]\!]k = (\lambda\alpha.\mathcal{C}_{\lambda\mu}[\![c]\!])\ k \qquad\qquad \mathcal{C}_{\lambda\mu}[\![\alpha]\!] = \alpha$$

The reduction semantics is then given by the following reduction rules:

$$(\lambda x.t)\ V \to t\{V/x\} \qquad E_1[\mu\alpha.c] \to c\{[\alpha](E_1[t])/[\alpha]t\} \qquad [q]\mu\alpha.c \to c\{q/\alpha\}$$

Where the one-step evaluation context E_1 is defined as: $E_1 ::= \Box\ t \mid V\ \Box$. The term $\mu\alpha.c$ propagates its evaluation context piece-by-piece to each invocation of α in c, until it reaches the top of its surrounding command. The rule makes use of a new notion of substitution, called *structural substitution*; $c\{[\alpha](E_1[t])/[\alpha]t\}$ should be read as: substitute each occurrence of $[\alpha]t$ in command c with $[\alpha](E_1[t])$. When iterated, these two rules perform the big-step capturing reduction that substitutes the entire evaluation context up to the top of the command. The operational semantics of $\lambda\mu$ is:

$$[*]E[(\lambda x.t)\ V] \mapsto [*]E[t\{V/x\}] \qquad\qquad [*]E[\mu\alpha.c] \mapsto c\{[*]E[t]/[\alpha]t\}$$

Where the evaluation context is: $E ::= \Box \mid E\ t \mid V\ E$. The operational semantics is sound and complete with respect to the CPS transform: $\mathcal{C}_{\lambda\mu}[\![[*]t]\!] \mapsto\!\!\!\!\!\rightarrow V$ iff $[*]t \mapsto\!\!\!\!\!\rightarrow [*]V$.

Expressiveness. Parigot's $\lambda\mu$ equipped with the top-level constant $*$ gives us the ability to express the call/cc ($\mathcal{K}$) and the abort ($\mathcal{A}$) control operators. One can also express Felleisen's $\mathcal{C}$ operator, which is definable in terms of call/cc and abort.

$$\begin{array}{ll} \mathcal{K} = \lambda h.\mu\alpha.[\alpha]h\ (\lambda x.\mu\_.[\alpha]x) & \mathcal{A}\ t = \mu\_.[*]t \\ \mathcal{C} = \lambda h.\mathcal{K}\ (\lambda k.\mathcal{A}\ (h\ k)) = \lambda h.\mu\alpha.[*]h\ (\lambda x.\mu\_.[\alpha]x) & \end{array} \tag{1}$$

4 Delimited Control: $\lambda\mu\widehat{\mathsf{tp}}$

Delimiting control means temporarily re-defining the top-level in a program, limiting the extent to which the evaluation context may be captured. Examples of delimited control are the shift ($\mathcal{S}$) and reset ($\#$) operators given in the seminal paper of Danvy and Filinski [5]. Felleisen [10,9] also extended his control theory with a reset operator which he calls prompt. The prompt operator is shown to be necessary in providing a fully abstract model of λ-calculus [20].

In [2], it is shown that delimited control can be explained by replacing the top-level constant $*$ with the rebindable dynamic continuation variable $\widehat{\mathsf{tp}}$. The syntax of $\lambda\mu\widehat{\mathsf{tp}}$ is:

$$c \in Comm. ::= [q]t \quad t \in Term ::= V \mid t_1\ t_2 \mid \mu q.c \quad q \in CoTerm ::= \alpha \mid \widehat{\mathsf{tp}} \tag{2}$$

The dynamic nature of $\widehat{\mathsf{tp}}$ is due to the fact that in a function like $\lambda x.\mu\_.[\widehat{\mathsf{tp}}]x$, the binding of $\widehat{\mathsf{tp}}$ is taken from the environment active at the call site and not in the environment active when the function is defined. This dynamic nature is captured by adding the following reduction rule to the reduction theory of $\lambda\mu$:

$$\mu\widehat{\mathsf{tp}}.[\widehat{\mathsf{tp}}]V \to V$$

4.1 Continuation Passing Style ($\mathcal{C}^2_{\lambda\mu\widehat{\mathsf{tp}}}$)

We extend the $\mathcal{C}_{\lambda\mu}$ transform to give $\mathcal{C}_{\lambda\mu\widehat{\mathsf{tp}}}$, the CPS transform for $\lambda\mu\widehat{\mathsf{tp}}$.

$$\mathcal{C}_{\lambda\mu\widehat{\mathsf{tp}}}[\![\mu\widehat{\mathsf{tp}}.c]\!]k = k\ (\mathcal{C}_{\lambda\mu\widehat{\mathsf{tp}}}[\![c]\!]) \qquad \mathcal{C}_{\lambda\mu\widehat{\mathsf{tp}}}[\![\widehat{\mathsf{tp}}]\!] = \lambda x.x$$

Here, $\widehat{\mathsf{tp}}$ takes the place of the old constant $*$. However, now we also have a binding form for $\widehat{\mathsf{tp}}$. When $\widehat{\mathsf{tp}}$ is bound over a command, the current continuation is set aside and that command is run to completion. Then, when the command has produced an answer value, that value is fed to the original continuation and that context is restored. Unfortunately, the above translation of $\mu\widehat{\mathsf{tp}}.c$ is not in CPS form, since the term $\mathcal{C}_{\lambda\mu\widehat{\mathsf{tp}}}[\![c]\!]$ is an application instead of a value. One can remedy the situation by taking the output from $\mathcal{C}_{\lambda\mu\widehat{\mathsf{tp}}}$ and running it through the CPS transform $\mathcal{C}_{\lambda}$ [5]. The composition of the two CPS transforms gives us $\mathcal{C}^2_{\lambda\mu\widehat{\mathsf{tp}}}$, a double CPS transform. There is no change to the clauses inherited from $\mathcal{C}_{\lambda\mu}$ since they were already in full CPS form. The only difference is in the translation of $\widehat{\mathsf{tp}}$:

$$\mathcal{C}^2_{\lambda\mu\widehat{\mathsf{tp}}}[\![\mu\widehat{\mathsf{tp}}.c]\!]k = \lambda\gamma.\mathcal{C}^2_{\lambda\mu\widehat{\mathsf{tp}}}[\![c]\!]\lambda x.k\ x\ \gamma \qquad \mathcal{C}^2_{\lambda\mu\widehat{\mathsf{tp}}}[\![\widehat{\mathsf{tp}}]\!] = \lambda x.\lambda\gamma.\gamma\ x$$

The CPS transform of a term is now a function requiring both a continuation k and a meta-continuation γ. In addition, continuations now take both a value and a meta-continuation as parameters. Here, the initial value for the meta-continuation is γ_ι which is initialized to $\lambda x.x$.

Notice that we are now in the same situation as we were with the pure λ-calculus. The CPS translation of both terms and commands take an extra argument, but this fact is not reflected in the syntax of $\lambda\mu\widehat{\mathsf{tp}}$. To reconcile the difference between the CPS transform and the source language, we extend the syntax of $\lambda\mu\widehat{\mathsf{tp}}$ in the same way we extended the pure λ-calculus. We add a second-order command, or meta-command, which explicitly names the meta-continuation of the underlying first-order command. Since we can only mark the initial meta-continuation of a command, we add the constant $\circledast$, which is the meta-top-level of the program. Thus, we extend the syntax of $\lambda\mu\widehat{\mathsf{tp}}$ given in (2) with meta-commands:

$$q^2 \in \mathit{CoTerm}^2 ::= \circledast \qquad\qquad c^2 \in \mathit{Command}^2 ::= [q^2]c$$

The double CPS translation of meta-commands and the meta-top-level $\circledast$ follow the same pattern as commands and the top-level in the pure λ-calculus:

$$\mathcal{C}^2_{\lambda\mu\widehat{\mathsf{tp}}}[\![[q^2]c]\!] = \mathcal{C}^2_{\lambda\mu\widehat{\mathsf{tp}}}[\![c]\!]\ \mathcal{C}^2_{\lambda\mu\widehat{\mathsf{tp}}}[\![q^2]\!] \qquad \mathcal{C}^2_{\lambda\mu\widehat{\mathsf{tp}}}[\![\circledast]\!] = \lambda x.x$$

The standard way to evaluate the CPS form of term t in this system is to provide the initial continuation $\lambda x.\lambda\gamma.\gamma\ x$ and the initial meta-continuation $\lambda x.x$, which translates to evaluating the meta-command $[\circledast][\widehat{\mathsf{tp}}]t$. If the meta-command is reduced to $[\circledast][\widehat{\mathsf{tp}}]V$, then the value V is the final answer.

Expressiveness. The rebindable top-level is the additional power that allows us to encode shift ($\mathcal{S}$) and reset ($\#$) in $\lambda\mu\widehat{\mathsf{tp}}$:

$$\#t = \mu\widehat{\mathsf{tp}}.[\widehat{\mathsf{tp}}]t \qquad\qquad \mathcal{S} = \lambda h.\mu\alpha.[\widehat{\mathsf{tp}}]h\ (\lambda x.\mu\widehat{\mathsf{tp}}.[\alpha]x)$$

The above encoding resembles Filinski's encoding [11] of $\mathcal{S}$ and $\#$ in terms of Felleisen's $\mathcal{C}$ and $\#$ operators. One can also encode a slightly different abort operator, $\mathcal{A}^{\widehat{\mathsf{tp}}}$, which aborts up to the nearest binding of $\widehat{\mathsf{tp}}$. This operator is expressible in terms of shift alone.

$$\mathcal{A}^{\widehat{\mathsf{tp}}}\ t = \mathcal{S}\ \lambda\_.t = \mu\_.[\widehat{\mathsf{tp}}]t \tag{3}$$

The behavior of this operator is different from the original abort, in that it does not exit the program completely, but only removes the context up to the nearest binding of $\widehat{\mathsf{tp}}$.

Unbound $\widehat{\mathsf{tp}}$. It is important to note that in the above definition of $\lambda\mu\widehat{\mathsf{tp}}$, the $\widehat{\mathsf{tp}}$ variable is always bound throughout the entire execution of the program. In a sense, the meta-continuation, which is responsible for giving the current binding for $\widehat{\mathsf{tp}}$, already comes with $\widehat{\mathsf{tp}}$ bound to the *true* top-level of the program. Next, we analyze the impact of this choice.

Example 1. The following example shows the successful evaluation of a meta-command with an unbound use of $\widehat{\mathsf{tp}}$, which is equivalent to the shift expression $\mathcal{S}\lambda\_.9 = \mu\alpha.[\widehat{\mathsf{tp}}](\lambda\_.9)\ (\lambda x.\mu\widehat{\mathsf{tp}}.[\alpha]x)$.

$$[\circledast][\widehat{\mathsf{tp}}]\mu\alpha.[\widehat{\mathsf{tp}}]((\lambda\_.9)\ (\lambda x.\mu\widehat{\mathsf{tp}}.[\alpha]x)) \twoheadrightarrow [\circledast][\widehat{\mathsf{tp}}]9$$

$$\mathcal{C}^2_{\lambda\mu\widehat{\mathsf{tp}}}[\![[\circledast][\widehat{\mathsf{tp}}]9]\!] = \mathcal{C}^2_{\lambda\mu\widehat{\mathsf{tp}}}[\![\widehat{\mathsf{tp}}]\!]\ 9\ \mathcal{C}^2_{\lambda\mu\widehat{\mathsf{tp}}}[\![\circledast]\!] = \mathcal{C}^2_{\lambda\mu\widehat{\mathsf{tp}}}[\![\circledast]\!]\ 9 = 9$$

Alternative Initial Conditions. But what if we want to begin evaluation with $\widehat{\mathsf{tp}}$ initially unbound? To do this, we will need to add the true top-level of the program, $*$, back to our grammar along with a different meta-top-level in which $\widehat{\mathsf{tp}}$ is considered unbound. Our syntax of $\lambda\mu\widehat{\mathsf{tp}}$ becomes:

$$\begin{aligned} c^2 \in \mathit{Command}^2 &::= [q^2]c & t \in \mathit{Term} &::= V \mid t_1\ t_2 \mid \mu\widetilde{\alpha}.c \\ c \in \mathit{Command} &::= [q]t & q \in \mathit{CoTerm} &::= \widetilde{\alpha} \mid * \\ q^2 \in \mathit{CoTerm}^2 &::= \bullet & \widetilde{\alpha} \in \mathit{CoVar} &::= \alpha \mid \widehat{\mathsf{tp}} \end{aligned}$$

Note that we now have both notions of abort as defined in (1) and (3). $\mathcal{A}^{\widehat{\mathsf{tp}}}$ removes the context up to the nearest binding of $\widehat{\mathsf{tp}}$, whereas $\mathcal{A}$ removes the context of the entire rest of the program.

The $\mathcal{C}^2_{\lambda\mu\widehat{\mathsf{tp}}}$ transform is extended with clauses for the new top-level and meta-top-level. The meaning of the constant $*$ is easy to define, but $\bullet$ is more tricky.

$$\mathcal{C}^2_{\lambda\mu\widehat{\mathsf{tp}}}[\![*]\!] = \lambda x.\lambda\gamma.x \qquad\qquad \mathcal{C}^2_{\lambda\mu\widehat{\mathsf{tp}}}[\![\bullet]\!] = \gamma_0\ \textbf{where}\ \gamma_0\ \text{free}$$

When $*$ is invoked with a value, the program immediately exits with that value as a final answer. The meta-continuation is thrown away because the current binding of $\widehat{\mathsf{tp}}$ is not needed. If the $\widehat{\mathsf{tp}}$ continuation is given a value without being bound, then the program gets stuck; since $\widehat{\mathsf{tp}}$ was not defined there is not enough information to continue. We need to map this stuck state down to the target language of $\mathcal{C}^2_{\lambda\mu\widehat{\mathsf{tp}}}$: the pure λ-calculus. A natural way to do this is to make $\bullet$, the meta-top-level in which $\widehat{\mathsf{tp}}$ is unbound, a free variable. Then, invoking an unbound $\widehat{\mathsf{tp}}$ with a value is translated to a stuck term.

The reduction semantics of $\lambda\mu\widehat{\mathsf{tp}}$ is extended with one more rule to reduce an invocation of $*$ under a binding for $\widehat{\mathsf{tp}}$.

$$\mu\widehat{\mathsf{tp}}.[*]V \to \mu\_.[*]V$$

The meaning of $[*]V$ is to throw away the bindings of $\widehat{\mathsf{tp}}$ in γ and return with the value V as the final answer. Therefore, we can throw away an adjacent binding of $\widehat{\mathsf{tp}}$ by turning it into an abort.

Example 2. Let's revisit the previous example using $*$ and $\bullet$ to initialize execution instead of $\widehat{\mathsf{tp}}$ and $\circledast$.

$$[\bullet][*]\mu\alpha.[\widehat{\mathsf{tp}}]((\lambda\_.9)\ (\lambda x.\mu\widehat{\mathsf{tp}}.[\alpha]x)) \twoheadrightarrow [\bullet][\widehat{\mathsf{tp}}]9$$
$$\mathcal{C}^2_{\lambda\mu\widehat{\mathsf{tp}}}[\![[\bullet][\widehat{\mathsf{tp}}]9]\!] = \mathcal{C}^2_{\lambda\mu\widehat{\mathsf{tp}}}[\![\widehat{\mathsf{tp}}]\!]\ 9\ \mathcal{C}^2_{\lambda\mu\widehat{\mathsf{tp}}}[\![\bullet]\!] = \mathcal{C}^2_{\lambda\mu\widehat{\mathsf{tp}}}[\![\bullet]\!]\ 9 = \gamma_0\ 9$$

Since $\widehat{\mathsf{tp}}$ was not initialized we get an error, represented by the stuck term $\gamma_0\ 9$.

The reduction rules of $\lambda\mu\widehat{\mathsf{tp}}$ are sound and complete with respect to $\mathcal{C}_{\lambda\mu\widehat{\mathsf{tp}}}$.

Theorem 1. *If* $\mathcal{C}^2_{\lambda\mu\widehat{\mathsf{tp}}}[\![[\bullet][*]t]\!] \twoheadrightarrow V$ *then* $[\bullet][*]t \twoheadrightarrow [\bullet][*]V$.
If $M \to M'$ *then* $\mathcal{C}^2_{\lambda\mu\widehat{\mathsf{tp}}}[\![M]\!] = \mathcal{C}^2_{\lambda\mu\widehat{\mathsf{tp}}}[\![M']\!]$.

Where the meta-syntactic variable M ranges over terms, commands, and meta-commands. Here and throughout the paper, equality between terms in the λ-calculus are up to $\beta\eta$ reduction.

Even though we replaced $\circledast$ with $\bullet$ in our language, we haven't actually lost anything. We can regain the original initial conditions by providing a binding for $\widehat{\mathsf{tp}}$ at the top of the program.

Theorem 2. $\mathcal{C}^2_{\lambda\mu\widehat{\mathsf{tp}}}[\![[\bullet][*]\mu\widehat{\mathsf{tp}}.c]\!] = \mathcal{C}^2_{\lambda\mu\widehat{\mathsf{tp}}}[\![[\circledast]c]\!]$

5 Intermediate Languages of Dynamic Binding: $\lambda\widehat{\mathsf{tp}}$, $\lambda\widehat{\mathsf{tp}}^b$

Ariola *et al.* [2] showed how the CPS of $\lambda\mu\widehat{\mathsf{tp}}$ can be factored into a state-passing transformation to $\lambda\mu$ extended with subtraction combined with a translation to λ-calculus with pairs. In order to better understand the dynamic nature of the prompt binding, we investigate an alternative decomposition. We start by translating away the control effects from $\lambda\mu\widehat{\mathsf{tp}}$ ($\mathcal{C}_{\lambda\mu\widehat{\mathsf{tp}}}$), leaving behind the dynamic binding of $\widehat{\mathsf{tp}}$. We then translate away the dynamic binding by first adopting a typical environment passing translation ($\mathcal{D}_{\lambda\widehat{\mathsf{tp}}}$). This however leads to an incorrect interpretation of the dynamic nature of $\widehat{\mathsf{tp}}$. We thus propose another way of translating the dynamic binding that models the behavior of the prompt ($\mathcal{D}_{\lambda\widehat{\mathsf{tp}}^b}$).

5.1 Translating Control ($\mathcal{C}_{\lambda\mu\widehat{\mathsf{tp}}}$)

We start with a CPS transform from $\lambda\mu\widehat{\mathsf{tp}}$ to an intermediate language with one dynamic variable, $\lambda\widehat{\mathsf{tp}}$, with the following syntax:

$$c \in Closure ::= [e]t \qquad\qquad t \in Term ::= V \mid t_1\ t_2 \mid \widehat{\mathsf{tp}}$$
$$\widetilde{x} \in Var ::= x \mid \widehat{\mathsf{tp}} \qquad\qquad V \in Value ::= x \mid \lambda\widetilde{x}.t$$

Where e is the empty *Environment* $\bullet$. The $\mathcal{C}_{\lambda\mu\widehat{\mathsf{tp}}}$ transform defines the call-by-value application and the context capturing behavior of $\mu\widetilde{\alpha}.c$ while using the dynamic variable in $\lambda\widehat{\mathsf{tp}}$ to manage the binding of $\widehat{\mathsf{tp}}$.

$$\mathcal{C}_{\lambda\mu\widehat{\mathsf{tp}}}[\![[q^2]c]\!] = [\mathcal{C}_{\lambda\mu\widehat{\mathsf{tp}}}[\![q^2]\!]]\mathcal{C}_{\lambda\mu\widehat{\mathsf{tp}}}[\![c]\!] \qquad \mathcal{C}_{\lambda\mu\widehat{\mathsf{tp}}}[\![x]\!]k = k\ x$$
$$\mathcal{C}_{\lambda\mu\widehat{\mathsf{tp}}}[\![[q]t]\!] = \mathcal{C}_{\lambda\mu\widehat{\mathsf{tp}}}[\![t]\!]\ \mathcal{C}_{\lambda\mu\widehat{\mathsf{tp}}}[\![q]\!] \qquad \mathcal{C}_{\lambda\mu\widehat{\mathsf{tp}}}[\![\lambda x.t]\!]k = k\ \lambda x.\mathcal{C}_{\lambda\mu\widehat{\mathsf{tp}}}[\![t]\!]$$
$$\mathcal{C}_{\lambda\mu\widehat{\mathsf{tp}}}[\![\alpha]\!] = \alpha \qquad \mathcal{C}_{\lambda\mu\widehat{\mathsf{tp}}}[\![t_1\ t_2]\!]k = \mathcal{C}_{\lambda\mu\widehat{\mathsf{tp}}}[\![t_1]\!]\lambda f.\mathcal{C}_{\lambda\mu\widehat{\mathsf{tp}}}[\![t_2]\!]\lambda s.f\ s\ k$$
$$\mathcal{C}_{\lambda\mu\widehat{\mathsf{tp}}}[\![\widehat{\mathsf{tp}}]\!] = \lambda x.\widehat{\mathsf{tp}}\ x \qquad \mathcal{C}_{\lambda\mu\widehat{\mathsf{tp}}}[\![\mu\tilde{\alpha}.c]\!]k = (\lambda\tilde{\alpha}.\mathcal{C}_{\lambda\mu\widehat{\mathsf{tp}}}[\![c]\!])\ k$$
$$\mathcal{C}_{\lambda\mu\widehat{\mathsf{tp}}}[\![*]\!] = \lambda x.x \qquad \mathcal{C}_{\lambda\mu\widehat{\mathsf{tp}}}[\![\bullet]\!] = \bullet$$

Note that $\mathcal{C}_{\lambda\mu\widehat{\mathsf{tp}}}[\![\widehat{\mathsf{tp}}]\!]$ is η-expanded. Otherwise, in the translation of $[\widehat{\mathsf{tp}}]\mu\alpha.c$ one would obtain $(\lambda\alpha.\mathcal{C}_{\lambda\mu\widehat{\mathsf{tp}}}[\![c]\!])\ \widehat{\mathsf{tp}}$. Since $\widehat{\mathsf{tp}}$ is not a value, the dynamic binding would be looked up when α is defined, instead of when it is called. To better understand the reason consider the following example.

Example 3. In $[*]\mu\widehat{\mathsf{tp}}.[\widehat{\mathsf{tp}}]\mu\alpha.[\alpha]((\mu\widehat{\mathsf{tp}}.[\alpha]I)\ x)$, notice that α is invoked with a value under a rebinding of $\widehat{\mathsf{tp}}$. The renaming of $\widehat{\mathsf{tp}}$ for α is captured by the more recent binding, as shown by the reduction:

$$[*]\mu\widehat{\mathsf{tp}}.[\widehat{\mathsf{tp}}]\mu\alpha.[\alpha]((\mu\widehat{\mathsf{tp}}.[\alpha]I)\ x) \to [*]\mu\widehat{\mathsf{tp}}.[\widehat{\mathsf{tp}}]((\mu\widehat{\mathsf{tp}}.[\widehat{\mathsf{tp}}]I)\ V)$$

If we instead adopt the transform $\mathcal{C}_{\lambda\mu\widehat{\mathsf{tp}}}[\![\widehat{\mathsf{tp}}]\!] = \widehat{\mathsf{tp}}$ then we would have to bind α to the current value of $\widehat{\mathsf{tp}}$, which is $*$.

5.2 Translating Dynamic Binding ($\mathcal{D}_{\lambda\widehat{\mathsf{tp}}}$)

For a first attempt at defining the dynamic binding of $\widehat{\mathsf{tp}}$, we try a simple environment-passing style transform, $\mathcal{D}_{\lambda\widehat{\mathsf{tp}}}$, where the environment is just the value currently bound to $\widehat{\mathsf{tp}}$. In the case that $\widehat{\mathsf{tp}}$ isn't bound, as in the initial environment $\bullet$, we use the free variable γ_0. That is, we have $\mathcal{D}_{\lambda\widehat{\mathsf{tp}}}[\![\bullet]\!] = \gamma_0$. The rest of the transform is:

$$\mathcal{D}_{\lambda\widehat{\mathsf{tp}}}[\![[e]t]\!] = \mathcal{D}_{\lambda\widehat{\mathsf{tp}}}[\![t]\!]\ \mathcal{D}_{\lambda\widehat{\mathsf{tp}}}[\![e]\!] \qquad \mathcal{D}_{\lambda\widehat{\mathsf{tp}}}[\![\lambda x.t]\!]\gamma = \lambda x.\lambda\gamma'.\mathcal{D}_{\lambda\widehat{\mathsf{tp}}}[\![t]\!]\gamma'$$
$$\mathcal{D}_{\lambda\widehat{\mathsf{tp}}}[\![x]\!]\gamma = x \qquad \mathcal{D}_{\lambda\widehat{\mathsf{tp}}}[\![\lambda\widehat{\mathsf{tp}}.t]\!]\gamma = \lambda v.\lambda\gamma'.\mathcal{D}_{\lambda\widehat{\mathsf{tp}}}[\![t]\!]v$$
$$\mathcal{D}_{\lambda\widehat{\mathsf{tp}}}[\![\widehat{\mathsf{tp}}]\!]\gamma = \gamma \qquad \mathcal{D}_{\lambda\widehat{\mathsf{tp}}}[\![t_1\ t_2]\!]\gamma = (\mathcal{D}_{\lambda\widehat{\mathsf{tp}}}[\![t_1]\!]\gamma)\ (\mathcal{D}_{\lambda\widehat{\mathsf{tp}}}[\![t_2]\!]\gamma)\ \gamma$$

This transform is equivalent to a simplified version of Moreau's calculus of dynamic binding [17] with only one dynamic variable.

Unfortunately, this definition of dynamic binding does not properly capture the meaning of the rebindable top-level since it creates vicious cycles, as shown in the reduction of $\mathcal{D}_{\lambda\widehat{\mathsf{tp}}} \circ \mathcal{C}_{\lambda\mu\widehat{\mathsf{tp}}}[\![[\widehat{\mathsf{tp}}]\mu\widehat{\mathsf{tp}}.[\widehat{\mathsf{tp}}]x]\!]\gamma$:

$$(\lambda v.\lambda\gamma'.v\ x\ v)\ (\lambda y.\lambda\gamma'.\gamma'\ y\ \gamma')\ \gamma \to (\lambda y.\lambda\gamma'.\gamma'\ y\ \gamma')\ x\ (\lambda y.\lambda\gamma'.\gamma'\ y\ \gamma') \to \dots$$

This does not match the reductions of $\lambda\mu\widehat{\mathsf{tp}}$, since one has: $[\widehat{\mathsf{tp}}]\mu\widehat{\mathsf{tp}}.[\widehat{\mathsf{tp}}]x \to [\widehat{\mathsf{tp}}]x$. In Moreau's [17] framework, this corresponds to the reduction:

$$\mathbf{dlet}\,\widehat{\mathsf{tp}} = (\lambda y.\widehat{\mathsf{tp}}\ y)\,\mathbf{in}\,\widehat{\mathsf{tp}}\ x \twoheadrightarrow \mathbf{dlet}\,\widehat{\mathsf{tp}} = (\lambda y.\widehat{\mathsf{tp}}\ y)\,\mathbf{in}(\lambda y.\widehat{\mathsf{tp}}\ y)\ x \twoheadrightarrow \dots$$

Remark 1. One can understand the dynamic abstraction $\lambda\widehat{\mathsf{tp}}.t$ in terms of a static abstraction and dynamic let, as $\lambda v.\,\mathbf{dlet}\,\widehat{\mathsf{tp}} = v\,\mathbf{in}\,t$, where the transform of **dlet** is $\mathcal{D}_{\lambda\widehat{\mathsf{tp}}}[\![\mathbf{dlet}\,\widehat{\mathsf{tp}} = v\,\mathbf{in}\,t]\!]\gamma = \mathcal{D}_{\lambda\widehat{\mathsf{tp}}}[\![t]\!]v$.

5.3 Backtracking the Environment ($\mathcal{D}_{\lambda\widehat{\mathsf{tp}}^b}$)

We see vicious cycles arise because dynamic binding allows for self-reference. In order to evaluate the application $\widehat{\mathsf{tp}}\ V$, we (1) lookup the value f most recently bound to $\widehat{\mathsf{tp}}$, and (2) evaluate $f\ V$ in the current environment where f is still bound. The root of our problem is in step (2). Instead, we want to evaluate $f\ V$ in a different environment where that same f isn't bound. In particular, we want to backtrack to the environment that was active just before f was bound to $\widehat{\mathsf{tp}}$. To do this, we restrict the grammar of $\lambda\widehat{\mathsf{tp}}$ so that $\widehat{\mathsf{tp}}$ can only be used as an immediate application, giving us $\lambda\widehat{\mathsf{tp}}^b$.

$$t \in Term ::= V \mid t_1\ t_2 \mid \widehat{\mathsf{tp}}\ t$$

We then modify $\mathcal{D}_{\lambda\widehat{\mathsf{tp}}}$ to match the restricted grammar. In particular, we change dynamic binding and application of $\widehat{\mathsf{tp}}$ to backtrack to a previous environment.

$$\mathcal{D}_{\lambda\widehat{\mathsf{tp}}^b}[\![\lambda\widehat{\mathsf{tp}}.t]\!]\gamma = \lambda v.\lambda\gamma'.\mathcal{D}_{\lambda\widehat{\mathsf{tp}}^b}[\![t]\!]\gamma'[\widehat{\mathsf{tp}} \mapsto v] \qquad \gamma[\widehat{\mathsf{tp}} \mapsto v] = \lambda x.v\ x\ \gamma$$
$$\mathcal{D}_{\lambda\widehat{\mathsf{tp}}^b}[\![\widehat{\mathsf{tp}}\ t]\!]\gamma = \gamma(\widehat{\mathsf{tp}})\ (\mathcal{D}_{\lambda\widehat{\mathsf{tp}}^b}[\![t]\!]\gamma) \qquad \gamma(\widehat{\mathsf{tp}}) = \gamma$$

When we bind a value v to $\widehat{\mathsf{tp}}$, we wrap v in a function that will return to the previous dynamic environment when applied. Since values bound to $\widehat{\mathsf{tp}}$ are equipped with their own environment, we do not need to pass the current dynamic environment to the application $\widehat{\mathsf{tp}}\ V$. Compare the new translation of $\widehat{\mathsf{tp}}\ V$ with the original one: $\mathcal{D}_{\lambda\widehat{\mathsf{tp}}}[\![\widehat{\mathsf{tp}}\ V]\!]\gamma = \gamma\ V\ \gamma$. Notice that the restriction on how $\widehat{\mathsf{tp}}$ is used allows us to eliminate the self-application of the environment γ. With the new backtracking definition of dynamic binding, we no longer create the same cycle as before in the reduction of $\mathcal{D}_{\lambda\widehat{\mathsf{tp}}^b} \circ \mathcal{C}_{\lambda\mu\widehat{\mathsf{tp}}}[\![[\widehat{\mathsf{tp}}]\mu\widehat{\mathsf{tp}}.[\widehat{\mathsf{tp}}]x]\!]\gamma$:

$$(\lambda v.\lambda\gamma'.v\ x\ \gamma')\ (\lambda y.\lambda\gamma'.\gamma'\ y)\ \gamma \to (\lambda y.\lambda\gamma'.\gamma'\ y)\ x\ \gamma \to \gamma\ x = [\![\widehat{\mathsf{tp}}\ x]\!]\gamma$$

When we compose the two phases together, we get the derived translation $\mathcal{D}_{\lambda\widehat{\mathsf{tp}}^b} \circ \mathcal{C}_{\lambda\mu\widehat{\mathsf{tp}}}$, which is exactly the same as our original translation $\mathcal{C}^2_{\lambda\mu\widehat{\mathsf{tp}}}$.

Theorem 3. $\mathcal{D}_{\lambda\widehat{\mathsf{tp}}^b} \circ \mathcal{C}_{\lambda\mu\widehat{\mathsf{tp}}} = \mathcal{C}^2_{\lambda\mu\widehat{\mathsf{tp}}}$

Remark 2. Note that the definition of $*$ in $\mathcal{C}^2_{\lambda\mu\widehat{\mathsf{tp}}}$ is exactly the environment-passing style translation of the initial continuation $\lambda x.x$. The backtracking behavior we present here is also necessary to express exceptions with dynamic variables. A similar encoding was given by Moreau[17] using an abort operator to reinstall the right environment.

6 Control with Multiple Prompts: $\lambda\widehat{\mu}$ via $\widehat{\lambda}^b$

We want to extend $\lambda\mu\widehat{\text{tp}}$ with a multiple prompts so that binding prompt $\widehat{\alpha}$ does not interfere with prompt $\widehat{\beta}$ and vice versa. This is different from the nested definition of resets in the CPS hierarchy [7]. Unfortunately, this means that we cannot use the iterated layered CPS approach to define our prompts. However, now that we have factored the transform for $\lambda\mu\widehat{\text{tp}}$ into two passes that flow through an intermediate language with dynamic binding, it is easy to extend the calculus to have multiple prompts by simply using an intermediate language with multiple dynamic variables, $\widehat{\lambda}^b$, whose syntax is:

$$c \in Closure ::= [e]t \qquad t \in Term ::= V \mid t_1\ t_2 \mid \widehat{x}\ t$$
$$\widetilde{x} \in Var ::= x \mid \widehat{x} \qquad V \in Value ::= x \mid \lambda\widetilde{x}.t$$

Where e is the empty environment $\bullet$. The definition of $\widehat{\lambda}^b$ uses the same environment-passing style translation as $\lambda\widehat{\text{tp}}^b$. The only thing that needs to change from $\lambda\widehat{\text{tp}}^b$ to $\widehat{\lambda}^b$ is dynamic binding and lookup. Now that there is more than one variable, we may have to search through the environment for the variable that we want.

$$\gamma(\widehat{x}) = \gamma\ \ulcorner\widehat{x}\urcorner \qquad \gamma[\widehat{x} \mapsto v] = \lambda p.\ \textbf{if}\ p \equiv \ulcorner\widehat{x}\urcorner\ \textbf{then}\ \lambda x.v\ x\ \gamma\ \textbf{else}\ \gamma\ p$$

Here the quotation brackets, $\ulcorner\cdot\urcorner$, reify the dynamic variables into terms in the target language. These terms must all be distinct and have decidable equality.

The language of control with multiple prompts, $\lambda\widehat{\mu}$, is a simple extension of $\lambda\mu\widehat{\text{tp}}$ with multiple dynamic top-level binders.

$$c^2 \in Command^2 ::= [q^2]c \qquad t \in Term ::= V \mid t_1\ t_2 \mid \mu\widetilde{\alpha}.c$$
$$c \in Command ::= [q]t \qquad q \in CoTerm ::= \widetilde{\alpha} \mid *$$
$$q^2 \in CoTerm^2 ::= \bullet \qquad \widetilde{\alpha} \in CoVar ::= \alpha \mid \widehat{\alpha}$$

The semantics of $\lambda\widehat{\mu}$ is just the composed transform $\mathcal{D}_{\widehat{\lambda}^b} \circ \mathcal{C}_{\lambda\widehat{\mu}}$, exactly as in Section 5.3 except that multiple dynamic variables are used by $\mathcal{C}_{\lambda\widehat{\mu}}$, with one unique variable for each different prompt. The reduction rules for multiple prompts are a generalization of the reduction rules for single prompt $\widehat{\text{tp}}$.

$$\mu\widehat{\alpha}.[\widehat{\alpha}]V \to V \qquad \mu\widehat{\alpha}.[\widehat{\beta}]V \to \mu\_.[\widehat{\beta}]V \qquad \mu\widehat{\alpha}.[*]V \to \mu\_.[*]V$$

Where $\widehat{\alpha} \neq \widehat{\beta}$. Just like how invocation of $*$ throws away the dynamic environment, invocation of the prompt $\widehat{\beta}$ will throw away portions of its dynamic environment until the correct binding is found. Then the usual η-reduction of prompts is available to resolve the invocation of the prompt.

To define the operational semantics for $\lambda\widehat{\mu}$, we first give the evaluation contexts for $\lambda\widehat{\mu}$, which can be derived from a defunctionalization [19,4] of the continuation and environment used in the $\mathcal{D}_{\widehat{\lambda}^b} \circ \mathcal{C}_{\lambda\widehat{\mu}}$ transform.

$$E ::= \square \mid E\ t \mid V\ E \qquad F ::= [q]E \qquad E^2 ::= \square \mid F[\mu\widehat{\alpha}.E^2] \qquad F^2 ::= [q^2]E^2$$

The context E is just the standard call-by-value evaluation context for the pure λ-calculus. The meta-context E^2 drills down through any number of dynamic bindings for continuation variables. Both F and F^2 are convenient shorthand for a (meta-)context embedded in a (meta-)command, and correspond exactly with the continuation and meta-continuation in the CPS transform for $\lambda\widehat{\mu}$.

The operational rules are derived from the fine-grained reduction rules using the call-by-value contexts for $\lambda\widehat{\mu}$ to restrict where they may apply.

$$F^2[F[(\lambda x.t)\ V]] \mapsto F^2[F[t\{V/x\}]] \qquad F^2[F[\mu\alpha.c]] \mapsto F^2[c\{F[t]/[\alpha]t\}]$$
$$F^2[F[\mu\widehat{\alpha}.E^2_{\widehat{\alpha}}[[\widehat{\alpha}]V]]] \mapsto F^2[F[V]] \qquad [q^2]E^2[[*]V] \mapsto [q^2][*]V$$

Where $E^2_{\widehat{\alpha}}$ does not contain a binding for $\widehat{\alpha}$. The reduction rules for $\lambda\widehat{\mu}$ are sound with respect to the transform $\mathcal{D}_{\widehat{\lambda}^b} \circ \mathcal{C}_{\lambda\widehat{\mu}}$, and the operational semantics is complete with respect to the transform. Also, since the operational semantics are just a coarse, limited form of the reduction rules, it follows that the reductions are complete with respect to the operational semantics and that the operational semantics is sound with respect to the transform.

Theorem 4. *If $M \to M'$ then $\mathcal{D}_{\widehat{\lambda}^b} \circ \mathcal{C}_{\lambda\widehat{\mu}}[\![M]\!] = \mathcal{D}_{\widehat{\lambda}^b} \circ \mathcal{C}_{\lambda\widehat{\mu}}[\![M']\!]$. If $\mathcal{D}_{\widehat{\lambda}^b} \circ \mathcal{C}_{\lambda\widehat{\mu}}[\![[\bullet][*]t]\!] \mapsto\!\!\!\!\!\rightarrow V$ then $[\bullet][*]t \mapsto\!\!\!\!\!\rightarrow [\bullet][*]V$. If $c^2 \mapsto c'^2$ then $c^2 \twoheadrightarrow c'^2$.*

Expressiveness. With multiple prompts, we get the ability to set multiple points in the program that we can abort to at will, giving us the multi-prompt reset ($\#^{\widehat{\alpha}}$) and abort ($\mathcal{A}^{\widehat{\alpha}}$) operators.

$$\#^{\widehat{\alpha}}t = \mu\widehat{\alpha}.[\widehat{\alpha}]t \qquad \mathcal{A}^{\widehat{\alpha}}t = \mu\_.[\widehat{\alpha}]t$$

We can also encode exception handling with multiple independent exceptions.

$$\textbf{raise}\ e\ t = (\lambda x.\mathcal{A}^{\widehat{e}}\,\mathsf{Exn}\,x)\ t$$
$$t\,\textbf{handle}\,e\ x \Rightarrow u = \textbf{case}\,\#^{\widehat{e}}\,\mathsf{OK}\,t\,\textbf{of}\,\mathsf{OK}\,x \Rightarrow x \mid \mathsf{Exn}\,x \Rightarrow u$$

The expression **raise** $e\ t$ evaluates t and then aborts to the dynamically nearest handler for e with an exception. The handling expression $t\,$**handle**$\,e\ x \Rightarrow u$ attempts to evaluate t. If t successfully results in a value (represented as $\mathsf{OK}\,v$), then value v is returned. Otherwise, if an exception for e is raised (represented as $\mathsf{Exn}\,v$), then u is evaluated with the raised value v bound to x.

7 Delimited Control with Transparent Prompts: $\boldsymbol{\lambda\mu\widehat{\mathsf{tp}}^{\uparrow}}$

We now take a break from $\lambda\widehat{\mu}$ and multiple prompts, and return to $\lambda\mu\widehat{\mathsf{tp}}$ in order to examine an alternate extension. Another important delimited control operator to consider is shift_0 ($\mathcal{S}_0$) [16]. The difference between shift and shift_0 is that when shift captures its immediate context, it leaves the nearest delimiting reset in place, whereas shift_0 removes the nearest reset after capturing its context. As discussed previously in Section 4, shift and reset have encodings in $\lambda\mu\widehat{\mathsf{tp}}$. However, to capture the additional behavior of shift_0 we need to extend $\lambda\mu\widehat{\mathsf{tp}}$ with the ability to render the binding of a prompt transparent, making it immediately disappear and letting underlying terms see through to their surrounding context. The new command $\uparrow^{\widehat{\mathsf{tp}}} t$ represents lifting the unevaluated term t through the most recent binding of $\widehat{\mathsf{tp}}$ and embedding the term in that context. The syntax of $\lambda\mu\widehat{\mathsf{tp}}^{\uparrow}$ is:

$$c^2 \in Command^2 ::= [q^2]c \qquad t \in Term ::= V \mid t_1\ t_2 \mid \mu\widetilde{\alpha}.c$$
$$c \in Command ::= [q]t \mid \uparrow^{\widehat{\mathsf{tp}}} t \qquad q \in CoTerm ::= \widetilde{\alpha} \mid *$$
$$q^2 \in CoTerm^2 ::= \bullet \qquad \widetilde{\alpha} \in CoVar ::= \alpha \mid \widehat{\mathsf{tp}}$$

We define a CPS for $\lambda\mu\widehat{\mathsf{tp}}^{\uparrow}$ in the style of Materzok and Biernacki's [16] definition of shift_0. This is an extension of the basic $\mathcal{C}_{\lambda\mu}$ transform.

$$\mathcal{C}_{\lambda\mu\widehat{\mathsf{tp}}^{\uparrow}}[\![\mu\widehat{\mathsf{tp}}.c]\!]k = \mathcal{C}_{\lambda\mu\widehat{\mathsf{tp}}^{\uparrow}}[\![c]\!]\ k \quad \mathcal{C}_{\lambda\mu\widehat{\mathsf{tp}}^{\uparrow}}[\![\uparrow^{\widehat{\mathsf{tp}}} t]\!] = \mathcal{C}_{\lambda\mu\widehat{\mathsf{tp}}^{\uparrow}}[\![t]\!] \quad \mathcal{C}_{\lambda\mu\widehat{\mathsf{tp}}^{\uparrow}}[\![\widehat{\mathsf{tp}}]\!] = \lambda x.\lambda k.k\ x$$

Note that the translation of $\mu\widehat{\mathsf{tp}}.c$ in $\mathcal{C}_{\lambda\mu\widehat{\mathsf{tp}}^{\uparrow}}$ is different from the one in $\mathcal{C}_{\lambda\mu\widehat{\mathsf{tp}}}$. Rather than always running the command to completion, and then passing the result to the bound continuation k, we pass k as an extra argument to the command. A continuation bound to $\widehat{\mathsf{tp}}$ is set aside and carried along in the command as an extra argument. Then, in the case of $[\widehat{\mathsf{tp}}]V$, the list of extra arguments is accessed and V is returned to the most recent one. On the other hand, in the case of $\uparrow^{\widehat{\mathsf{tp}}} t$, the continuation most recently bound to $\widehat{\mathsf{tp}}$ is accessed and used to evaluate t.

For the purpose of comparison with $\mathcal{C}^2_{\lambda\mu\widehat{\mathsf{tp}}}$, we run the output of $\mathcal{C}_{\lambda\mu\widehat{\mathsf{tp}}^{\uparrow}}$ through the CPS transform $\mathcal{C}_{\lambda}$, which gives us the double CPS transform $\mathcal{C}^2_{\lambda\mu\widehat{\mathsf{tp}}^{\uparrow}}$.

$$\mathcal{C}^2_{\lambda\mu\widehat{\mathsf{tp}}^{\uparrow}}[\![\mu\widehat{\mathsf{tp}}.c]\!]k = \lambda\gamma.\mathcal{C}^2_{\lambda\mu\widehat{\mathsf{tp}}^{\uparrow}}[\![c]\!]\lambda t.t\ k\ \gamma$$
$$\mathcal{C}^2_{\lambda\mu\widehat{\mathsf{tp}}^{\uparrow}}[\![\uparrow^{\widehat{\mathsf{tp}}} t]\!]\gamma = \gamma\ \mathcal{C}^2_{\lambda\mu\widehat{\mathsf{tp}}^{\uparrow}}[\![t]\!] \qquad \mathcal{C}^2_{\lambda\mu\widehat{\mathsf{tp}}^{\uparrow}}[\![\widehat{\mathsf{tp}}]\!] = \lambda x.\lambda\gamma.\gamma\ \lambda k.k\ x$$

The small difference in the binding of $\widehat{\mathsf{tp}}$ becomes immediately apparent in the type of the meta-continuation. In $\lambda\mu\widehat{\mathsf{tp}}$, the meta-continuation takes values to final answers. In $\lambda\mu\widehat{\mathsf{tp}}^{\uparrow}$, on the other hand, the meta-continuation takes *terms* to final answers. The more general type allows the translation of $\uparrow^{\widehat{\mathsf{tp}}} t$ to pass t unevaluated to the meta-continuation. The translation of $[\widehat{\mathsf{tp}}]V$ now has to compensate for this extra generality. When the $\widehat{\mathsf{tp}}$ continuation is given a value x and meta-continuation γ, it wraps that value up in the trivial term that immediately returns x, and passes the new term to γ.

We can also define the transformation in terms of $\lambda\widehat{\mathsf{tp}}^{b}$, as in Section 5. Extending the meta-continuation becomes a binding to the dynamic variable $\widehat{\mathsf{tp}}$, and application of the meta-continuation becomes application of $\widehat{\mathsf{tp}}$.

$$\mathcal{C}_{\lambda\mu\widehat{\mathsf{tp}}^{\uparrow}}[\![\mu\widehat{\mathsf{tp}}.c]\!]k = (\lambda\widehat{\mathsf{tp}}.\mathcal{C}_{\lambda\mu\widehat{\mathsf{tp}}^{\uparrow}}[\![c]\!])\ (\lambda t.t\ k)$$
$$\mathcal{C}_{\lambda\mu\widehat{\mathsf{tp}}^{\uparrow}}[\![\uparrow^{\widehat{\mathsf{tp}}} t]\!] = \widehat{\mathsf{tp}}\ \mathcal{C}_{\lambda\mu\widehat{\mathsf{tp}}^{\uparrow}}[\![t]\!] \qquad \mathcal{C}_{\lambda\mu\widehat{\mathsf{tp}}^{\uparrow}}[\![\widehat{\mathsf{tp}}]\!] = \lambda x.\widehat{\mathsf{tp}}\ \lambda k.k\ x$$

Notice the difference between the two uses of $\widehat{\mathsf{tp}}$. In $[\widehat{\mathsf{tp}}]t$, resolution of the $\widehat{\mathsf{tp}}$ variable is delayed in a function that is passed to the term t, which may be captured by the time the continuation is used. In contrast, $\uparrow^{\widehat{\mathsf{tp}}} t$, directly applies $\widehat{\mathsf{tp}}$ to a term, immediately resolving the dynamic binding in the current environment.

Reduction of the new command is similar to $[\widehat{\mathsf{tp}}]t$, but with different priorities between the continuation and the term. In $\mu\widehat{\mathsf{tp}}.[\widehat{\mathsf{tp}}]t$, $\widehat{\mathsf{tp}}$ is η-reduced only when t is a value. The opposite occurs with $\mu\widehat{\mathsf{tp}}.\uparrow^{\widehat{\mathsf{tp}}} t$, where $\widehat{\mathsf{tp}}$ is η-reduced immediately, before t can be fully reduced to a value.

$$\mu\widehat{\mathsf{tp}}.[\widehat{\mathsf{tp}}]V \to V \qquad\qquad \mu\widehat{\mathsf{tp}}.\uparrow^{\widehat{\mathsf{tp}}} t \to t$$

As before, operational rules are given by deriving the evaluation context from the continuation and meta-continuation used in $\mathcal{C}_{\lambda\mu\widehat{\mathsf{tp}}^{\uparrow}}$, restricting where reduction may apply.

$$E ::= \square \mid E\ t \mid T\ E \qquad F ::= [q]E \qquad E^2 ::= \square \mid F[\mu\widehat{\mathsf{tp}}.E^2] \qquad F^2 ::= [q^2]E^2$$

With the evaluation contexts, the operational rules are just a coarse-grained representation of the fine-grained reduction rules.

$$F^2[F[(\lambda x.t)\ V]] \mapsto F^2[F[t\{V/x\}]] \qquad F^2[F[\mu\alpha.c]] \mapsto F^2[c\{F[t]/[\alpha]t\}]$$
$$F^2[F[\mu\widehat{\mathsf{tp}}.[\widehat{\mathsf{tp}}]V]] \mapsto F^2[F[V]] \qquad F^2[F[\mu\widehat{\mathsf{tp}}.\uparrow^{\widehat{\mathsf{tp}}} t]] \mapsto F^2[F[t]]$$
$$[q^2]E^2[[*]V] \mapsto [q^2][*]V$$

The reduction rules and operational semantics are sound and complete with respect to the transform $\mathcal{C}^2_{\lambda\mu\widehat{\mathsf{tp}}^{\uparrow}}$ as in Section 6.

Theorem 5. *If $M \to M'$ then $\mathcal{C}^2_{\lambda\mu\widehat{\mathsf{tp}}^{\uparrow}}[\![M]\!] = \mathcal{C}^2_{\lambda\mu\widehat{\mathsf{tp}}^{\uparrow}}[\![M']\!]$. If $\mathcal{C}^2_{\lambda\mu\widehat{\mathsf{tp}}^{\uparrow}}[\![[\bullet][*]t]\!] \mapsto\!\!\!\!\!\rightarrow V$ then $[\bullet][*]t \mapsto\!\!\!\!\!\rightarrow [\bullet][*]V$. If $c^2 \mapsto c'^2$ then $c^2 \twoheadrightarrow c'^2$.*

Expressiveness. To encode shift_0 ($\mathcal{S}_0$) in $\lambda\mu\widehat{\mathsf{tp}}^{\uparrow}$, we need to use $\uparrow^{\widehat{\mathsf{tp}}}$ to make the nearest binding of $\widehat{\mathsf{tp}}$ transparent to its body. For comparison, we repeat shift's encoding:

$$\#t = \mu\widehat{\mathsf{tp}}.[\widehat{\mathsf{tp}}]t \quad \mathcal{S} = \lambda h.\mu\alpha.[\widehat{\mathsf{tp}}]h\ (\lambda x.\mu\widehat{\mathsf{tp}}.[\alpha]x) \quad \mathcal{S}_0 = \lambda h.\mu\alpha.\uparrow^{\widehat{\mathsf{tp}}} h\ (\lambda x.\mu\widehat{\mathsf{tp}}.[\alpha]x)$$

We can derive the operational rules for the three control operators from the operational semantics of $\lambda\mu\widehat{\mathsf{tp}}^{\uparrow}$. The two-part definition of evaluation contexts mirrors Materzok and Biernacki's[16] presentation of $\mathcal{S}_0$ using contexts and trails. The derived rules show that the only difference between shift and shift_0 is the presence or absence of the reset after capture.

$$E ::= \square \mid E\ t \mid V\ E \qquad D ::= \square \mid D[E[\#\square]]$$
$$D[E[(\lambda x.t)\ V]] \mapsto D[E[t\{V/x\}]] \qquad D[E[\#V]] \mapsto D[E[V]]$$
$$D[E'[\#E[\mathcal{S}_0\ V]]] \mapsto D[E'[V\ (\lambda x.\#E[x])]] \quad D[E[\mathcal{S}\ V]] \mapsto D[V\ (\lambda x.\#E[x])]$$

8 Intermediate Language of Dynamic Unbinding: $\lambda\widehat{\mathsf{tp}}^{\Leftarrow}$

Recall that in Section 5, we had to ensure that the dynamic binding was non-cyclic in order to properly model prompts. We accomplished this by backtracking to a previous version of the dynamic environment whenever $\widehat{\mathsf{tp}}$ was applied to a value. While the backtracking semantics of $\lambda\widehat{\mathsf{tp}}^{b}$ and $\widehat{\lambda}^{b}$ can also be used to encode shift_0 and multiple prompt abort, it does not scale well beyond that. The only time we can backtrack the environment is when we have a value to pass to a dynamic variable. Instead, we can generalize the effect by allowing a form of dynamic backtracking over a term. We modify $\lambda\widehat{\mathsf{tp}}^{b}$ with the ability to undo a binding over an unevaluated term t, giving us $\lambda\widehat{\mathsf{tp}}^{\Leftarrow}$.

$$c \in Closure ::= [e]t \qquad\qquad t \in Term ::= V \mid x \Leftarrow \widehat{\mathsf{tp}}\,\mathbf{in}\,t \mid t_1\ t_2$$
$$\widetilde{x} \in Var ::= x \mid \widehat{\mathsf{tp}} \qquad\qquad V \in Value ::= x \mid \lambda\widetilde{x}.t$$

Where e is the empty environment $\bullet$. The new term, $x \Leftarrow \widehat{\mathsf{tp}}\,\mathbf{in}\,t$, has the effect of undoing the most recent binding of $\widehat{\mathsf{tp}}$ in the current environment, exposing the previous dynamic environment to the term t while rebinding the value to x. In essence, $x \Leftarrow \widehat{\mathsf{tp}}\,\mathbf{in}\,t$ is the reverse effect of a dynamic binding. The direct application $\widehat{\mathsf{tp}}\ V$ can be expressed notationally by the new term: $f \Leftarrow \widehat{\mathsf{tp}}\,\mathbf{in}\,f\ V$.

The translation of $\lambda\widehat{\mathsf{tp}}^{\Leftarrow}$ is a modification of the basic environment-passing style transform $\mathcal{D}_{\lambda\widehat{\mathsf{tp}}^{b}}$. We must change how the environment is represented in order to express the additional effect on the dynamic environment. We could implement $\mathcal{D}_{\lambda\widehat{\mathsf{tp}}^{\Leftarrow}}$ in a concrete way, representing the environment as a list structure to store a history of dynamic bindings.

$$\mathcal{D}_{\lambda\widehat{\mathsf{tp}}^{\Leftarrow}}[\![\lambda\widehat{\mathsf{tp}}.t]\!]\gamma = \lambda v.\lambda\gamma'.\mathcal{D}_{\lambda\widehat{\mathsf{tp}}^{\Leftarrow}}[\![t]\!]\gamma[\widehat{\mathsf{tp}} \mapsto v] \qquad \gamma[\widehat{\mathsf{tp}} \mapsto v](\widehat{\mathsf{tp}}) = \langle v, \gamma\rangle$$
$$\mathcal{D}_{\lambda\widehat{\mathsf{tp}}^{\Leftarrow}}[\![x \Leftarrow \widehat{\mathsf{tp}}\,\mathbf{in}\,t]\!]\gamma = \mathbf{let}\,\langle x, \gamma'\rangle = \gamma(\widehat{\mathsf{tp}})\,\mathbf{in}\,\mathcal{D}^{u}[\![t]\!]\gamma'$$

Here, binding $\widehat{\mathsf{tp}}$ to a new value v in an environment γ just stores that binding as the most recent one in γ, while looking up the binding of $\widehat{\mathsf{tp}}$ returns both the value as well as the dynamic environment that was previously active before $\widehat{\mathsf{tp}}$ was bound. The term $x \Leftarrow \widehat{\mathsf{tp}}\,\mathbf{in}\,t$ uses the extra information returned by lookup to evaluate t using the previous environment.

By refunctionalizing [6] the concrete list structure of the environment, we get a translation from $\lambda\widehat{\mathsf{tp}}^{\Leftarrow}$ to the pure λ-calculus.

$$\mathcal{D}_{\lambda\widehat{\mathsf{tp}}^{\Leftarrow}}[\![\lambda\widehat{\mathsf{tp}}.t]\!]\gamma = \lambda v.\lambda\gamma'.\mathcal{D}_{\lambda\widehat{\mathsf{tp}}^{\Leftarrow}}[\![t]\!]\gamma[\widehat{\mathsf{tp}} \mapsto v] \qquad \gamma(\widehat{\mathsf{tp}}) = \gamma$$
$$\mathcal{D}_{\lambda\widehat{\mathsf{tp}}^{\Leftarrow}}[\![x \Leftarrow \widehat{\mathsf{tp}}\,\mathbf{in}\,t]\!]\gamma = \gamma(\widehat{\mathsf{tp}})\ \lambda x.\mathcal{D}^{u}[\![t]\!] \qquad \gamma[\widehat{\mathsf{tp}} \mapsto v] = \lambda q.q\ v\ \gamma$$

Looking up the current binding of $\widehat{\mathsf{tp}}$ is just an application of the current environment. The two return values are implemented by having lookup take a continuation which accepts both the value bound to $\widehat{\mathsf{tp}}$ as well as the previous environment. With the new syntax for rolling back the dynamic environment, we can translate $\lambda\mu\widehat{\mathsf{tp}}^{\uparrow}$ into $\lambda\widehat{\mathsf{tp}}^{\Leftarrow}$ in a more concise way, where k is bound directly to $\widehat{\mathsf{tp}}$.

$$\mathcal{C}^u_{\lambda\mu\widehat{\mathsf{tp}}^\uparrow}[\![\mu\widehat{\mathsf{tp}}.c]\!]k = (\lambda\widehat{\mathsf{tp}}.\mathcal{C}_{\lambda\mu\widehat{\mathsf{tp}}^\uparrow}[\![c]\!])\ k$$

$$\mathcal{C}^u_{\lambda\mu\widehat{\mathsf{tp}}^\uparrow}[\![\uparrow^{\widehat{\mathsf{tp}}}\ t]\!] = k \Leftarrow \widehat{\mathsf{tp}}\,\mathbf{in}\,\mathcal{C}_{\lambda\mu\widehat{\mathsf{tp}}^\uparrow}[\![t]\!]k \qquad \mathcal{C}^u_{\lambda\mu\widehat{\mathsf{tp}}^\uparrow}[\![\widehat{\mathsf{tp}}]\!] = \lambda x.k \Leftarrow \widehat{\mathsf{tp}}\,\mathbf{in}\,k\ x$$

9 Delimited Control with Multiple Prompts: $\boldsymbol{\lambda\widehat{\mu}^\uparrow}$ via $\boldsymbol{\widehat{\lambda}^\Leftarrow}$

With just the simple addition of multiple prompts, we still don't have enough expressive power in $\lambda\widehat{\mu}$ to encode shift and reset with multiple prompts. The dilemma is that in the presence of multiple prompts, a shift up to prompt $\widehat{\alpha}$ not only captures its immediate context up to the nearest reset, but also captures all contexts bound behind non-matching resets until it finds a reset for $\widehat{\alpha}$. The continuation that shift captures will then restore the captured context as well as seamlessly inserting a partial meta-context in place. In order to express the full power of shift with multiple prompts, we will need some way of directly manipulating the meta-context. This is reminiscent of the way shift_0 removes the most recent binding of $\widehat{\mathsf{tp}}$ and exposes that context to an underlying term. So in order to fully express shift with multiple prompts, we need to incorporate both multiple prompt binding from Section 6 as well as transparent prompts from Section 7. In other words we need to merge multiple dynamic variables from $\widehat{\lambda}^b$ in Section 6 with the ability to roll back the dynamic environment from $\lambda\widehat{\mathsf{tp}}^\Leftarrow$ in Section 8.

9.1 Dynamic Unbinding with Multiple Variables: $\boldsymbol{\widehat{\lambda}^\Leftarrow}$

The shift operator with multiple prompts only captures a prefix of the meta-context, up to the binding of a specific prompt. What we need is a way to roll back the dynamic environment up to a given binding, while also remembering all the information that would otherwise be discarded. That is, we need to extend the dynamic unbinding effect from $x \Leftarrow \widehat{x}\,\mathbf{in}\,t$ to give us both the value that was stored in $\widehat{x}$ as well as a trace of all the changes to the environment after $\widehat{x}$ was bound. This trace is just a prefix of the current environment, and can be used later to replay the changes over a future state of the environment, extending it with all the dynamic bindings that were removed.

We merge both $\widehat{\lambda}$ and $\lambda\widehat{\mathsf{tp}}^\Leftarrow$, by combining both multiple dynamic variables and reversal of dynamic binding, giving us $\widehat{\lambda}^\Leftarrow$.

$$c \in \mathit{Closure} ::= [e]t \qquad\qquad e \in \mathit{Environment} ::= \bullet$$

$$t \in \mathit{Term} ::= V \mid t_1\ t_2 \mid \langle \Delta, x\rangle \Leftarrow \widehat{x}\,\mathbf{in}\,t \mid [\Delta]t \qquad\qquad \widetilde{x} \in \mathit{Var} ::= x \mid \widehat{x}$$

The new class of variables, Δ, ranges over environment prefixes. Intuitively, the term $\langle \Delta, x\rangle \Leftarrow \widehat{x}\,\mathbf{in}\,t$ undoes the most recent binding of $\widehat{x}$, binding the value stored in $\widehat{x}$ to x while also capturing the prefix of the environment more recent than $\widehat{x}$ into Δ. Then, the term t is evaluated in the dynamic environment that was in place immediately before $\widehat{x}$ was bound. Closure under the prefix, $[\Delta]t$, extends the surrounding environment with all the dynamic bindings stored in Δ.

Like before, the direct application $\widehat{x}\ V$ can be notationally defined with the more general prefix-capturing form: $\langle \_, f\rangle \Leftarrow \widehat{x}\,\mathbf{in}\, f\ V$.

The semantics of $\widehat{\lambda}^{\Leftarrow}$, like $\lambda\widehat{\mathsf{tp}}^{\Leftarrow}$, requires a redefinition of the dynamic environment. When we query the environment, we now must remember the previously active environment as well as the prefix of bindings that were skipped over in order to find the requested variable. Like in Section 8, we first define the new environment in a concretely, using lists to implement environments and prefixes and tuples to return multiple values.

$$\mathcal{D}_{\widehat{\lambda}^{\Leftarrow}}[\![\langle\Delta, x\rangle \Leftarrow \widehat{x}\,\mathbf{in}\,t]\!]\gamma = \mathbf{let}\,\langle\Delta, x, \gamma'\rangle = \gamma(\widehat{x})\,\mathbf{in}\,\mathcal{D}_{\widehat{\lambda}^{\Leftarrow}}[\![t]\!]\gamma'$$

$$\mathcal{D}_{\widehat{\lambda}^{\Leftarrow}}[\![[\Delta]t]\!]\gamma = (\Delta @ \mathcal{D}_{\widehat{\lambda}^{\Leftarrow}}[\![t]\!])\ \gamma$$

$$\begin{aligned} \gamma[\widehat{x} \mapsto v](\widehat{x}) &= \langle [], v, \gamma\rangle \\ \gamma[\widehat{y} \mapsto v](\widehat{x}) &= \mathbf{let}\,\langle\Delta, u, \gamma'\rangle = \gamma(\widehat{x}) \\ &\quad\ \mathbf{in}\,\langle\Delta[\widehat{y} \mapsto v], u, \gamma'\rangle \end{aligned} \qquad \begin{aligned} []@t &= t \\ \Delta[\widehat{x} \mapsto v]@t &= \Delta@(\lambda\gamma.t\ \gamma[\widehat{x} \mapsto v]) \end{aligned}$$

Dynamic variable lookup now builds up the prefix of bindings that are skipped over in order to find the correct variable. This prefix of bindings can then be used elsewhere to extend a term's dynamic environment. Note that when a prefix extends a term, the bindings in that prefix are more recent than the surrounding dynamic environment and are bound in exactly the same order in which they originally occurred.

Taking the concrete implementation, we can derive the pure λ-calculus encoding by refunctionalizing the data structures. The environment prefix is now a function mapping terms to terms which implements the extension operation from before. Multiple return values are emulated by taking a continuation that accepts each of the three return values separately.

$$\mathcal{D}_{\widehat{\lambda}^{\Leftarrow}}[\![\langle\Delta, x\rangle \Leftarrow \widehat{x}\,\mathbf{in}\,t]\!]\gamma = \gamma(\widehat{x})\ \lambda\Delta.\lambda x.\mathcal{D}_{\widehat{\lambda}^{\Leftarrow}}[\![t]\!] \qquad \mathcal{D}_{\widehat{\lambda}^{\Leftarrow}}[\![[\Delta]t]\!]\gamma = \Delta\ \mathcal{D}_{\widehat{\lambda}^{\Leftarrow}}[\![t]\!]\ \gamma$$

$$\gamma(\widehat{x}) = \gamma\ \ulcorner\widehat{x}\urcorner \qquad \gamma[\widehat{x} \mapsto v] = \lambda p.\,\mathbf{if}\,p \equiv \ulcorner\widehat{x}\urcorner\,\mathbf{then}\,\lambda q.q\ (\lambda t.t)\ v\ \gamma$$
$$\mathbf{else}\,\lambda q.\gamma\ p\ \lambda\delta.q\ (\lambda t.\delta\ \lambda\gamma'.t\ \gamma'[\widehat{x} \mapsto v])$$

9.2 Capture Up to a Prompt: $\lambda\widehat{\mu}^{\uparrow}$

We are now finally ready to define the full calculus with capture up to an arbitrary prompt. $\lambda\widehat{\mu}^{\uparrow}$ extends $\lambda\widehat{\mu}$ with the ability to capture a prefix of the meta-context up to a prompt, and then later extend the current meta-context with that prefix.

$$\begin{aligned} c^2 \in \mathit{Command}^2 &::= [q^2]c \\ c \in \mathit{Command} &::= [q]t \mid \mu^2\Delta\uparrow^{\widehat{\alpha}}.t \mid [\Delta]c \\ q^2 \in \mathit{CoTerm}^2 &::= \bullet \end{aligned} \qquad \begin{aligned} t \in \mathit{Term} &::= V \mid t_1\ t_2 \mid \mu\widetilde{\alpha}.c \\ q \in \mathit{CoTerm} &::= \widetilde{\alpha} \mid * \\ \widetilde{\alpha} \in \mathit{CoVar} &::= \alpha \mid \widehat{\alpha} \end{aligned}$$

The command $\mu^2\Delta\uparrow^{\widehat{\alpha}}.t$ captures a portion of its meta-context as Δ, up to the nearest binding of the prompt $\widehat{\alpha}$. Then, that portion of the meta-context is removed and the most recent binding of $\widehat{\alpha}$ becomes unbound. t is then evaluated in the context formerly bound to $\widehat{\alpha}$ and the remaining meta-context.

The CPS translation from $\lambda\widehat{\mu}^{\uparrow}$ to $\widehat{\lambda}^{\Leftarrow}$ is a merging of $\mathcal{C}_{\lambda\widehat{\mu}}$ and $\mathcal{C}^{u}_{\lambda\mu\widehat{\mathsf{tp}}^{\uparrow}}$. The new syntactic forms in $\lambda\widehat{\mu}^{\uparrow}$ can be defined in terms of the intermediate language $\widehat{\lambda}^{\Leftarrow}$. Capturing a portion of the meta-context up to $\widehat{\alpha}$ translates to capturing a prefix of the dynamic environment while unbinding $\widehat{\alpha}$, and extending the meta-context becomes extending the dynamic environment. Like in $\mathcal{C}^{u}_{\lambda\mu\widehat{\mathsf{tp}}^{\uparrow}}$, the invocation of a prompt is changed due to the change in the way dynamic variable lookup is performed. The CPS transform for $\lambda\widehat{\mu}^{\uparrow}$ is an extension of the basic $\mathcal{C}_{\lambda\mu}$ transform.

$$\mathcal{C}_{\lambda\widehat{\mu}^{\uparrow}}[\![\mu^2\Delta\uparrow^{\widehat{\alpha}}.t]\!] = \langle\Delta,\alpha\rangle \Leftarrow \widehat{\alpha}\,\mathbf{in}\,\mathcal{C}_{\lambda\widehat{\mu}^{\uparrow}}[\![t]\!]\alpha$$

$$\mathcal{C}_{\lambda\widehat{\mu}^{\uparrow}}[\![[\Delta]c]\!] = [\Delta]\mathcal{C}_{\lambda\widehat{\mu}^{\uparrow}}[\![c]\!] \qquad \mathcal{C}_{\lambda\widehat{\mu}^{\uparrow}}[\![\widehat{\alpha}]\!] = \lambda x.\langle\_,\alpha\rangle \Leftarrow \widehat{\alpha}\,\mathbf{in}\,\alpha\ x$$

The final derived transform shares a resemblance with the one given by Dybvig *et al.* [8]. However, since we only treat shift/shift$_0$-like operators, the environment is an ordered list of bindings, rather than an arbitrary marked stack.

The reduction rules for capture up to a prompt must incrementally move a prefix of the meta-context into the underlying term. Rather than move the complete context bound to a prompt all at once, we can use the ordinary μ-abstraction to capture that context and move it inward to where it is needed. By using an ordinary μ-abstraction, we can capture the context formerly bound to $\widehat{\beta}$ one step at a time.

$$\mu\widehat{\alpha}.\mu^2\Delta\uparrow^{\widehat{\alpha}}.t \to t\{c/[\Delta]c\} \qquad \mu\widehat{\beta}.\mu^2\Delta\uparrow^{\widehat{\alpha}}.t \to \mu\beta.\mu^2\Delta\uparrow^{\widehat{\alpha}}.t\{[\Delta][\beta]\mu\widehat{\beta}.c/[\Delta]c\}$$

When under a non-matching prompt $\widehat{\beta}$, $\mu^2\Delta\uparrow^{\widehat{\alpha}}.t$ must take the context currently bound to $\widehat{\beta}$ and rebind it to $\widehat{\beta}$ wherever Δ is invoked in t. This can be done by giving the context a fresh static name with a static μ-abstraction, and binding $\widehat{\beta}$ to that continuation variable inside of Δ. The static μ-abstraction is then able to reduce further, incrementally absorbing its context and filling in the renewed bindings for $\widehat{\beta}$ inside Δ. If instead $\mu^2\Delta\uparrow^{\widehat{\alpha}}.t$ is under a binding of the prompt $\widehat{\alpha}$, then t is placed in the context bound to $\widehat{\alpha}$ and Δ is eliminated in t, since there is no more prefix for it to capture.

The operational semantics for $\lambda\widehat{\mu}^{\uparrow}$ is an extension of the semantics for $\lambda\widehat{\mu}$. The evaluation contexts and operational rules for $\lambda\widehat{\mu}$ hold for $\lambda\widehat{\mu}^{\uparrow}$. We only need to include the additional rule for the command $\mu^2\Delta\uparrow^{\widehat{\alpha}}.t$.

$$E ::= \Box \mid E\ t \mid V\ E \qquad F ::= [q]E \qquad E^2 ::= \Box \mid F[\mu\widehat{\alpha}.E^2] \qquad F^2 ::= [q^2]E^2$$

$$F^2[F[\mu\widehat{\alpha}.E^2_{\widehat{\alpha}}[\mu^2\Delta\uparrow^{\widehat{\alpha}}.t]]] \mapsto F^2[F[t\{E^2_{\widehat{\alpha}}[c]/[\Delta]c\}]]$$

Where $E^2_{\widehat{\alpha}}$ does not contain a binding for $\widehat{\alpha}$. Like with $\lambda\widehat{\mu}$ the reduction rules and operational semantics are sound and complete with respect to the transform $\mathcal{D}_{\widehat{\lambda}^{\Leftarrow}} \circ \mathcal{C}_{\lambda\widehat{\mu}^{\uparrow}}$.

Theorem 6. *If* $M \to M'$ *then* $\mathcal{D}_{\widehat{\lambda}^{\Leftarrow}} \circ \mathcal{C}_{\lambda\widehat{\mu}^{\uparrow}}[\![M]\!] = \mathcal{D}_{\widehat{\lambda}^{\Leftarrow}} \circ \mathcal{C}_{\lambda\widehat{\mu}^{\uparrow}}[\![M']\!]$.
If $\mathcal{D}_{\widehat{\lambda}^{\Leftarrow}} \circ \mathcal{C}_{\lambda\widehat{\mu}^{\uparrow}}[\![[\bullet][*]t]\!] \mapsto\!\!\!\rightarrow V$ *then* $[\bullet][*]t \mapsto\!\!\!\rightarrow [\bullet][*]V$. *If* $c^2 \mapsto c'^2$ *then* $c^2 \twoheadrightarrow c'^2$.

Expressiveness. With capture of the dynamic environment up to a given prompt, we can encode the full behavior of both shift and shift_0 with multiple prompts:

$$\mathcal{S}_0^{\widehat{\alpha}} = \lambda h.\mu\beta.\mu^2\varDelta \uparrow^{\widehat{\alpha}}.h\ (\lambda x.\mu\widehat{\alpha}.[\varDelta][\beta]x) \qquad \#^{\widehat{\alpha}}t = \mu\widehat{\alpha}.[\widehat{\alpha}]t$$
$$\mathcal{S}^{\widehat{\alpha}} = \lambda h.\mu\beta.\mu^2\varDelta \uparrow^{\widehat{\alpha}}.\mu\widehat{\alpha}.[\widehat{\alpha}]h\ (\lambda x.\mu\widehat{\alpha}.[\varDelta][\beta]x)$$

$\mathcal{S}^{\widehat{\alpha}}\ h$ captures the current context as well as the dynamic prefix up to the most recent binding of the prompt $\widehat{\alpha}$, which is kept in place. Then, h is given a function which, when applied, will evaluate its argument in the captured context and dynamic prefix under a new binding of $\widehat{\alpha}$. $\mathcal{S}_0^{\widehat{\alpha}}$ is like $\mathcal{S}^{\widehat{\alpha}}$ except that after capturing the dynamic prefix, the prompt $\widehat{\alpha}$ is unbound and the context bound to $\widehat{\alpha}$ is exposed to the given function. The only difference in their encodings is that $\mathcal{S}^{\widehat{\alpha}}$ replaces the reset of $\widehat{\alpha}$ after capturing the meta-context, while $\mathcal{S}_0^{\widehat{\alpha}}$ does not.

Using the operational semantics from Section 9.2, we can derive the operational semantics for our encoding of the $\#^{\widehat{\alpha}}$, $\mathcal{S}^{\widehat{\alpha}}$, and $\mathcal{S}_0^{\widehat{\alpha}}$ control operators.

$$E ::= \Box \mid E\ t \mid V\ E \qquad D ::= \Box \mid D[E[\#^{\widehat{\alpha}}\Box]]$$
$$D[E[(\lambda x.t)\ V]] \mapsto D[E[t\{V/x\}]] \qquad D[E[\#^{\widehat{\alpha}}V]] \mapsto D[E[V]]$$
$$D[E[\#^{\widehat{\alpha}}D'[E'[\mathcal{S}^{\widehat{\alpha}}\ V]]]] \mapsto D[E[\#^{\widehat{\alpha}}V\ (\lambda x.\#^{\widehat{\alpha}}D'[E'[x]])]] \quad \textbf{where}\ \#^{\widehat{\alpha}} \notin D'$$
$$D[E[\#^{]}D'[E'[\mathcal{S}_0^{\widehat{\alpha}}\ V]\widehat{\alpha}]] \mapsto D[E[V\ (\lambda x.\#^{\widehat{\alpha}}D'[E'[x]])]] \quad \textbf{where}\ \#^{\widehat{\alpha}} \notin D'$$

10 Conclusion

We have provided a calculus which allows us to study delimited control with multiple prompts. To do this, we used an intermediate language of dynamic binding in order to define the semantics of multiple prompts. Kiselyov *et al.* [15] have also investigated the relationship between dynamic binding and delimited control by giving a language that gives the programmer access to both. Interestingly, their approach is the opposite of ours. They directly define the dynamic binding in terms of delimited control with multiple prompts. On the other hand, we use the conceptually simpler notion of dynamic binding as a stepping stone for understanding delimited control with multiple prompts.

Our interest in delimited control with multiple prompts came from the desire of formalizing a call-by-need abstract machine. Both call-by-value and call-by-name λ-calculi can be presented in the sequent calculus style as abstract machines, where the active redex is always at the top of the term [3]. With call-by-need, however, the active redex can become buried under bindings of delayed terms during evaluation. As discussed by Garcia *et al.* [13], call-by-need can be represented in terms of delimited control with multiple prompts. In that spirit, we want to achieve a deeper understanding of the equational theory of delimited control in the presence of more than one prompt, aiming at formalizing classical lazy evaluation in the sequent setting. As future work, we plan to tackle completeness of the equational theory with respect to the CPS semantics. We are also interested in understanding the type theory that arises from the CPS semantics.

Acknowledgments. We would like to thank Olivier Danvy, Hugo Herbelin, Alexis Saurin, Ian Zerny, and the anonymous referees for their valuable comments and suggestions. Paul Downen and Zena M. Ariola have been supported by NSF grant CCF-0917329. This research has been developed under INRIA Équipe Associée SEMACODE.

References

1. Ariola, Z.M., Herbelin, H.: Control reduction theories: The benefit of structural substitution. J. Funct. Program. 18, 373–419 (2008)
2. Ariola, Z.M., Herbelin, H., Sabry, A.: A type-theoretic foundation of delimited continuations. HOSC 22(3), 233–273 (2009)
3. Curien, P.L., Herbelin, H.: The duality of computation. In: ICFP 2000, pp. 233–243 (2000)
4. Danvy, O.: On evaluation contexts, continuations, and the rest of the computation. In: ACM SIGPLAN Workshop on Continuations, pp. 13–23 (2004)
5. Danvy, O., Filinski, A.: A functional abstraction of typed contexts. Tech. Rep. 89/12, DIKU, University of Copenhagen, Copenhagen, Denmark (1989)
6. Danvy, O., Millikin, K.: Refunctionalization at work. Science of Computer Programming 74(8), 534–549 (2009)
7. Danvy, O., Filinski, A.: Abstracting control. In: Proceedings of the 1990 ACM Conference on LISP and Functional Programming, pp. 151–160. ACM Press (1990)
8. Dybvig, R., Jones, S.P., Sabry, A.: A monadic framework for delimited continuations. Journal of Functional Programming 17(06), 687–730 (2007)
9. Felleisen, M.: The theory and practice of first-class prompts. In: POPL 1988 (1988)
10. Felleisen, M., Friedman, D., Kohlbecker, E.: A syntactic theory of sequential control. Theoretical Computer Science 52(3), 205–237 (1987)
11. Filinski, A.: Representing monads. In: POPL 1994, pp. 446–457 (1994)
12. Filinski, A.: Representing layered monads. In: POPL 1999, pp. 175–188 (1999)
13. Garcia, R., Lumsdaine, A., Sabry, A.: Lazy evaluation and delimited control. In: Proceedings of POPL 2009, pp. 153–164. ACM, New York (2009)
14. Kiselyov, O.: Delimited control in OCaml, abstractly and concretely: System description. Functional and Logic Programming, 304–320 (2010)
15. Kiselyov, O., Shan, C.-c., Sabry, A.: Delimited dynamic binding. In: Proceedings of the Eleventh ACM SIGPLAN International Conference on Functional Programming, ICFP 2006, pp. 26–37. ACM, New York (2006)
16. Materzok, M., Biernacki, D.: Subtyping delimited continuations. In: Proceeding of the 16th ACM SIGPLAN International Conference on Functional Programming, ICFP 2011, pp. 81–93. ACM, New York (2011)
17. Moreau, L.: A syntactic theory of dynamic binding. HOSC 11(3), 233–279 (1998)
18. Parigot, M.: $\lambda\mu$-Calculus: An Algorithmic Interpretation of Classical Natural Deduction. In: Voronkov, A. (ed.) LPAR 1992. LNCS, vol. 624, pp. 190–201. Springer, Heidelberg (1992)
19. Reynolds, J.C.: Definitional interpreters for higher-order programming languages. In: Proceedings of the 25th ACM National Conference, pp. 717–740 (1972)
20. Sitaram, D., Felleisen, M.: Reasoning with continuations II: Full abstraction for models of control. In: Conference on Lisp and Functional Programming (1990)

Generate, Test, and Aggregate

A Calculation-based Framework for Systematic Parallel Programming with MapReduce*

Kento Emoto[1], Sebastian Fischer**, and Zhenjiang Hu[2]

[1] The University of Tokyo
[2] National Institute of Informatics, Tokyo

Abstract. MapReduce, being inspired by the map and reduce primitives available in many functional languages, is the de facto standard for large scale data-intensive parallel programming. Although it has succeeded in popularizing the use of the two primitives for hiding the details of parallel computation, little effort has been made to emphasize the programming methodology behind, which has been intensively studied in the functional programming and program calculation fields. We show that MapReduce can be equipped with a programming theory in calculational form. By integrating the generate-and-test programing paradigm and semirings for aggregation of results, we propose a novel parallel programming framework for MapReduce. The framework consists of two important calculation theorems: the shortcut fusion theorem of semiring homomorphisms bridges the gap between specifications and efficient implementations, and the filter-embedding theorem helps to develop parallel programs in a systematic and incremental way. We give nontrivial examples that demonstrate how to apply our framework.

1 Introduction

MapReduce [6], the de facto standard for large scale data-intensive applications, is a remarkable parallel programming model, allowing for easy parallelization of data intensive computations over many machines in a cloud. It is used routinely at companies such as Yahoo!, Google, Amazon, and Facebook. Despite its abstract interface that effectively hides the details of parallelization, data distribution, load balancing, and fault tolerance, developing efficient MapReduce parallel programs remains as a challenge in practice.

As a concrete example, consider the known statistics problem of inferring a sequence of hidden states of a probabilistic model that most likely causes a sequence of observations [13] (see details in Section 6). This problem is important

* An extended version of this paper including more explanations and an additional section on generalizing our approach to arbitrary algebraic data types is available as Technical Report METR2011-34, University of Tokyo, `http://www.keisu.t.u-tokyo.ac.jp/research/techrep/`

** supported by the German Academic Exchange Service (DAAD)

H. Seidl (Ed.): ESOP 2012, LNCS 7211, pp. 254–273, 2012.

in natural language processing and error code correction, but it is far from easy for one to come up with an efficient MapReduce program to solve it. The problem becomes more difficult, if we would like to find the most likely sequence with additional requirements such that the sequence should contain a specific state exactly five times, or that the sequence should not contain a specific state anywhere after another. The main difficulty in programming with MapReduce is that nontrivial problems are usually not in a simple divide-and-conquer form that can be easily mapped to MapReduce without producing an exponential number of intermediate candidates. Moreover, the inputs may not just form a simple set of elements as in MapReduce; rather they are often structured as lists.

The MapReduce framework was inspired by the map and reduce (fold) primitives available in many functional languages. Although it has successfully popularized the use of these two primitives for hiding the details of parallel computation, little effort has been made to emphasize the programming methodology behind, which has been intensively studied in functional programming and program calculation [1, 3, 8, 14, 22]. This lack of programming methodology for MapReduce has led to publication of too many papers about MapReduce applications [18], each addressing a solution to one specific problem, even if quite a lot of problems follow a common pattern and can be solved generally.

To remedy this situation, we will show that MapReduce can be equipped with a programming theory in calculational form [3, 15, 24], which can be applied to give efficient solutions to a wide class of problems. For illustration, we consider a general class of problems which can be specified in the following generate-test-and-aggregate (GTA for short) form (here, $\circ$ denotes function composition):

$$aggregate \circ test \circ generate$$

Problems that match this specification can be solved by first generating possible solution candidates, then keeping those candidates that pass a test of a certain condition, and finally selecting a valid solution or making a summary of valid solutions with an aggregating computation. For example, the above statistics problem may be informally specified by generating all possible sequences of state transitions, keeping those that satisfy a certain condition, and selecting one that maximizes the products of probabilities (see Section 6).

Like other programming theories in calculational form [15, 24], the big challenges in the development of our calculation theory are to decide a structured form such that any program in this form is guaranteed to be efficiently parallelized, and to show how a specification can be systematically mapped to the structured form. To this end, we refine the specification with constraints on each of its components.

- The generator should be parallelizable in a divide-and-conquer manner and polymorphic over semiring structures, guaranteeing that the final program can be coded with MapReduce efficiently.
- The condition for the test should be defined structurally in terms of a list homomorphism.

– The aggregator should be a semiring computation (semiring homomorphism), guaranteeing that the aggregating computation is structured in a way that matches with the generator.

These constraints, as will be seen later, can be satisfied for practical problems such as the statistics problem mentioned above. An interesting result of this paper is that any specification that satisfies these constraints can be automatically mapped to an efficient parallel program in, but not limited to, MapReduce.

In this paper, by integrating the generate-and-test programing paradigm and semirings for result aggregation, we propose a novel parallel programming framework that is centered on two calculation theorems, the *semiring fusion theorem* and the *filter embedding theorem.* These two calculation theorems play an important role for the systematic development of efficient parallel programs in MapReduce for a problem that is specified by a semiring-polymorphic generator, a test with a homomorphic predicate, and a semiring homomorphism as aggregator. Our main technical contributions can be summarized as follows.

– We propose a new formalization of GTA problems in the context of parallel computation based on the *semiring fusion theorem.* We show how a generator can be specified as a list homomorphism polymorphic over semirings, an aggregator can be specified as a semiring homomorphism, and fusion of their composition can be done for free and results in an efficient homomorphism parallelizable by MapReduce.
– We propose a new systematic and incremental development of parallel programs for more complicated GTA problems based on the *filter embedding theorem.* The filter-embedding theorem allows a semiring homomorphism to absorb preceding tests yielding a new semiring homomorphism. We give nontrivial examples that demonstrate how to apply our framework.

The rest of the paper is organized as follows. We start with background on lists, monoids, homomorphisms, and MapReduce in Section 2. Then, after exemplifying our approach to specify parallel programs by means of the knapsack problem in Section 3, we focus on two important calculation theorems, the shortcut fusion theorem for semiring homomorphisms in Section 4, and the filter embedding theorem in Section 5. We discuss a more complex application in Section 6. Finally, we discuss related work in Section 7 and conclude in Section 8.

2 Background: Lists, Monoids and MapReduce

The notation in this paper is reminiscent of Haskell [2]. Function application is denoted by a space and the argument may be written without brackets, so that $(f\ a)$ means $f(a)$ in ordinary notation. Functions are curried: they always take one argument and return a function or a value, and the function application associates to the left and binds more strongly than any other operator, so that $f\ a\ b$ means $(f\ a)\ b$ and $f\ a \otimes b$ means $(f\ a) \otimes b$. Function composition is denoted by $\circ$, and $(f \circ g)\ x = f\ (g\ x)$ according to its definition. Binary operators can be used as functions by sectioning as follows: $a \oplus b = (a\oplus)\ b = (\oplus b)\ a = (\oplus)\ a\ b$.

2.1 Lists, Monoids, and Homomorphisms

Lists are finite sequences of values of the same type. A list is either empty, a singleton, or the concatenation of two other lists. We write $[\,]$ for the empty list, $[x]$ for the singleton list with element x, and $xs \mathbin{+\!\!+} ys$ for the concatenation of two lists xs and ys. For example, the term $[1] \mathbin{+\!\!+} [2] \mathbin{+\!\!+} [3]$ denotes a list with three elements, often abbreviated as $[1,2,3]$. We write $[A]$ for the type of lists with elements of type A.

Definition 1 (Monoid). *Given a set M and a binary operator $\odot$ on M, the pair $(M,\odot)$ is called a* monoid *if and only if $\odot$ is associative and has an identity $\imath_\odot \in M$:*

$$(a \odot b) \odot c = a \odot (b \odot c)$$
$$\imath_\odot \odot a = a = a \odot \imath_\odot$$

For example, $([A], \mathbin{+\!\!+})$ is a monoid: $\mathbin{+\!\!+}$ is associative and $[\,]$ is its identity.

Homomorphisms are structure preserving mappings. In the case of monoids they respect the binary operation and its identity.

Definition 2 (Monoid Homomorphism). *Given two monoids $(M,\odot)$ and $(M',\odot')$, a function $hom{:}M \to M'$ is called* monoid homomorphism from $(M,\odot)$ to $(M',\odot')$ *if and only if:*

$$hom\ \imath_\odot = \imath_{\odot'}$$
$$hom\ (x \odot y) = hom\ x \odot' hom\ y$$

For example, the function sum for summing up all elements in a list is a monoid homomorphism from $([\mathbb{Z}], \mathbin{+\!\!+})$ to $(\mathbb{Z}, +)$:

$$sum\ [\,] = 0$$
$$sum\ [x] = x$$
$$sum\ (xs \mathbin{+\!\!+} ys) = sum\ xs + sum\ ys$$

There is more than one monoid homomorphism from $([\mathbb{Z}], \mathbin{+\!\!+})$ to $(\mathbb{Z}, +)$ but the property $sum\ [x] = x$ characterizes sum uniquely, because $[A]$ is the free monoid over A: for every result monoid, a list homomorphism (monoid homomorphism from lists) is characterized uniquely by its result on singleton lists.

List homomorphisms are relevant to parallel programming because associativity allows to distribute the computation evenly among different processors or even machines by the well-known divide-and-conquer parallel paradigm [5, 22].

2.2 MapReduce

MapReduce [6] is a parallel programming technique, made popular by Google, used for processing large amounts of data. Such processing can be completed in a reasonable amount of time only by distributing the work to multiple machines in parallel. Each machine processes a small subset of the data. We will not discuss the details of MapReduce in this paper.

List homomorphisms fit well with MapReduce, because their input list can be freely divided and distributed among machines. In fact, it has been shown recently that list homomorphisms can be efficiently implemented using MapReduce [19]. Our approach builds on such an implementation which is orthogonal to our work. Therefore, if we can derive an efficient list homomorphism to solve a problem, we can solve the problem efficiently with MapReduce, enjoying its advantages such as automatic load-balancing, fault-tolerance, and scalability.

Some readers might feel that there is a mismatch between a typical MapReduce computation and computations in GTA style, because the size of the results generated by map in the former is often proportional to the size of the input data while the latter appears to have much larger intermediate results. This mismatch is a strength of our approach: based on a *naively-designed GTA specification* our calculation theorems can provide an *efficient MapReduce implementation with intermediate results proportional to the size of the input,* i.e., efficient list homomorphisms. Our approach makes MapReduce applicable to applications appearing not to match the MapReduce pattern. As a consequence, it allows programmers to implement MapReduce algorithms by providing an often simpler specification in GTA form.

3 Running Example: The Knapsack Problem

In this section we give a simple example of how to specify parallel algorithms in GTA form. We give a clear but inefficient specification of the knapsack problem following this structure and use it throughout Sections 4 and 5 to show how to transform such specifications into efficient parallel programs.

The knapsack problem is to fill a knapsack with items, each of certain value and weight, such that the total value of packed items is maximal while adhering to a weight restriction of the knapsack. For example, if the maximum total weight of our knapsack is 5kg and there are three items (¥2000, 1kg), (¥3000, 3kg), and (¥4000, 3kg) then the best we can do is pick the selection (¥2000, 1kg), (¥4000, 3kg) with total value ¥6000 and weight 4kg because all selections with larger value exceed the weight restriction.

The function *knapsack*, which takes as input a list of value-weight pairs (both positive integers) and computes the maximum total value of a selection of items not heavier than a total weight w, can be written as a composition of three functions:

$$knapsack = maxvalue \circ filter\ ((\leqslant w) \circ weight) \circ sublists$$

- The function *sublists* is the generator. From the given list of pairs it computes all possible selections of items, that is, all 2^n sublists if the input list has length n.
- The function *filter* $((\leqslant w) \circ weight)$ is the test. It discards all generated sublists whose total weight exceeds w and keeps the rest.
- The function *maxvalue* is the aggregator. From the remaining sublists adhering to the weight restriction it computes the maximum of all total values.

The function *sublists* can be defined as follows:

$$\begin{aligned} sublists\ [\,] &= \wr[\,]\wr \\ sublists\ [x] &= \wr[\,]\wr \uplus \wr[x]\wr \\ sublists\ (xs +\!\!+\ ys) &= sublists\ xs \times_{+\!\!+} sublists\ ys \end{aligned}$$

The result of *sublists* is a bag of lists which we denote using $\wr$ and $\wr$. The symbol $\uplus$ denotes bag union and $\times_{+\!\!+}$ the lifting of list concatenation to bags, concatenating every list in one bag with every list in the other. The function *sublists* is a monoid homomorphism: $\times_{+\!\!+}$ is associative and $\wr[\,]\wr$ is its identity.

The function *filter* filters a bag according to the given predicate. We pass as predicate the composition of the function *weight* that adds all weights in a list and the function $(\leqslant w)$ that checks the weight restriction. Like *sublists*, *weight* is a monoid homomorphism:

$$\begin{aligned} weight\ [\,] &= 0 \\ weight\ [(v, w)] &= w \\ weight\ (xs +\!\!+\ ys) &= weight\ xs + weight\ ys \end{aligned}$$

Finally, *maxvalue* computes the maximum of summing up the values of each list in a bag using the maximum operator $\uparrow$.

$$\begin{aligned} maxvalue\ \wr\wr &= -\infty \\ maxvalue\ \wr[\,]\wr &= 0 \\ maxvalue\ \wr[(v, w)]\wr &= v \\ maxvalue\ (b \uplus b') &= maxvalue\ b \uparrow maxvalue\ b' \\ maxvalue\ (b \times_{+\!\!+} b') &= maxvalue\ b + maxvalue\ b' \end{aligned}$$

Regarding the last equation, remember that the lifted list concatenation $\times_{+\!\!+}$ appends each list in one bag with each in the other, and, therefore, the maximum total value of the concatenated lists is the sum of the maximum total values of the lists in each bag. This observation relies on distributivity of $+$ over $\uparrow$, a property that we will revisit in the next section.

4 Semiring Fusion

In this section we show how to derive efficient parallel programs from specifications in generate-and-aggregate form:

$$aggregate \circ generate$$

This form is a simplified version of GTA form, missing the test. We define specific kinds of generators and aggregators that allow such specifications to be implemented efficiently and provide a theorem that shows how to calculate efficient parallel implementations. Such a calculation can turn an exponential-time specification into a linear-time implementation.

4.1 Semirings and Their Homomorphisms

The specification for the function *maxvalue* in Section 3 shows that it is a monoid homomorphism with respect to two different monoids over the same set (bags of lists). We now consider an algebraic structure that relates two such monoids.

Definition 3 (Semiring). *A triple* $(S, \oplus, \otimes)$ *is called a* semiring *if and only if* $(S, \oplus)$ *and* $(S, \otimes)$ *are monoids, and additionally* $\oplus$ *is commutative,* $\otimes$ *distributes over* $\oplus$*, and* $\imath_\oplus$ *is a zero of* $\otimes$*:*

$$a \oplus b = b \oplus a$$
$$a \otimes (b \oplus c) \ = (a \otimes b) \oplus (a \otimes c)$$
$$(a \oplus b) \otimes c \ = (a \otimes c) \oplus (b \otimes c)$$
$$\imath_\oplus \otimes a = \imath_\oplus = a \otimes \imath_\oplus$$

We have already seen two semirings in Section 3:

- $(\mathbb{Z}_{-\infty}, \uparrow, +)$ is a semiring because both $\uparrow$ and $+$ are associative, commutative and have identities $-\infty$ and 0, respectively, where $\mathbb{Z}_{-\infty} = \mathbb{Z} \cup \{-\infty\}$. Moreover, $+$ distributes over $\uparrow$ and $-\infty$ is a zero of $+$.
- $(\wr[A]\wr, \uplus, \times_{++})$ is a semiring for every set A because $\uplus$ is associative and commutative and $\times_{++}$ is associative. Moreover, $\wr\wr$ and $\wr[\,]\wr$ are the identities of $\uplus$ and $\times_{++}$, respectively. Interestingly, $\times_{++}$ distributes over $\uplus$ and, clearly, $\wr\wr$ is a zero of $\times_{++}$. Readers who verify distributivity of $\times_{++}$ will make crucial use of the ability to reorder bag elements.

Definition 4 (Semiring Homomorphism). *Given two semirings* $(S, \oplus, \otimes)$ *and* $(S', \oplus', \otimes')$*, a function* $hom : S \to S'$ *is a* semiring homomorphism *from* $(S, \oplus, \otimes)$ *to* $(S', \oplus', \otimes')$ *if and only if it is a monoid homomorphism from* $(S, \oplus)$ *to* $(S', \oplus')$ *and a monoid homomorphism from* $(S, \otimes)$ *to* $(S', \otimes')$*.*

The *maxvalue* function presented in Section 3 is a semiring homomorphism from $(\wr[\mathbb{Z}_{-\infty} \times \mathbb{Z}_{-\infty}]\wr, \uplus, \times_{++})$ to $(\mathbb{Z}_{-\infty}, \uparrow, +)$. It additionally satisfies the property $maxvalue\ \wr[(v, w)]\wr = v$ which characterizes it uniquely because bags of lists over a set A form the free semiring.

Lemma 1 (Free Semiring). *Given a set* A*, a semiring* $(S, \oplus, \otimes)$*, and a function* $f : A \to S$ *there is exactly one semiring homomorphism* $h : \wr[A]\wr \to S$ *from* $(\wr[A]\wr, \uplus, \times_{++})$ *to* $(S, \oplus, \otimes)$ *that satisfies* $h\ \wr[x]\wr = f\ x$*.* □

The unique homomorphism can be thought of as applying f to each list element, then accumulating the results in each list using the operator $\otimes$, and finally accumulating those results using the operator $\oplus$.

4.2 Polymorphic Generators

We now return to the generator *sublists* defined in Section 3. This function almost exclusively uses the semiring operations of the semiring $\wr[A]\wr$ and their identities. The only exception is $\wr[x]\wr$ constructed from an element $x \in A$.

We can generalize *sublists* by parameterizing it with operations $\oplus$ and $\otimes$ of an arbitrary semiring (and their identities) as well as an *embedding function* that constructs semiring elements from elements of a (potentially) different type:

$$\begin{aligned}
sublists_{\oplus,\otimes}\ f\ [\,] &= \imath_{\otimes} \\
sublists_{\oplus,\otimes}\ f\ [x] &= \imath_{\otimes} \oplus f\ x \\
sublists_{\oplus,\otimes}\ f\ (xs +\!\!+\ ys) &= sublists_{\oplus,\otimes}\ f\ xs \otimes sublists_{\oplus,\otimes}\ f\ ys
\end{aligned}$$

This function is called *polymorphic over semirings* because it can construct a result in an arbitrary semiring determined by the passed semiring operators and embedding function. It is a generalization of *sublists* because

$$sublists = sublists_{\uplus,\times_{+\!\!+}}\ (\lambda x \to \wr[x]\wr)$$

The anonymous function passed as argument constructs a singleton bag containing a singleton list with the argument x.

Definition 5 (Polymorphic Semiring Generator). *A function*

$$generate_{\oplus,\otimes} : (A \to S) \to [A] \to S$$

that is polymorphic over an arbitrary semiring $(S, \oplus, \otimes)$ *is called a* polymorphic semiring generator.

The function $sublists_{\oplus,\otimes}$ is a *polymorphic semiring generator* and, being a monoid homomorphism for any semiring, it can be executed in parallel. We could also pass the operations of the semiring $\mathbb{Z}_{-\infty}$ to compute a result in $\mathbb{Z}_{-\infty}$.

$$sublists_{\uparrow,+}\ (\lambda(v,w) \to v) : \wr[\mathbb{Z}_{-\infty} \times \mathbb{Z}_{-\infty}]\wr \to \mathbb{Z}_{-\infty}$$

What does this function compute? Theorem 1, which is a variant of short-cut fusion for semiring homomorphisms, casts light on this question.

Theorem 1 (Semiring Fusion). *Given a set* A*, a semiring* $(S, \oplus, \otimes)$*, a semiring homomorphism aggregate from* $(\wr[A]\wr, \uplus, \times_{+\!\!+})$ *to* $(S, \oplus, \otimes)$*, and a polymorphic semiring generator generate, the following equation holds:*

$$aggregate \circ generate_{\uplus,\times_{+\!\!+}}\ (\lambda x \to \wr[x]\wr) = generate_{\oplus,\otimes}\ (\lambda x \to aggregate\ \wr[x]\wr)$$

Proof. *Free Theorem*[1] *[26].*

We can use Theorem 1 to see what $sublists_{\uparrow,+}\ (\lambda(v,w) \to v)$ computes.

$$\begin{aligned}
& maxvalue \circ sublists \\
=\ & maxvalue \circ sublists_{\uplus,\times_{+\!\!+}}\ (\lambda(v,w) \to \wr[(v,w)]\wr) \\
=\ & sublists_{\uparrow,+}\ (\lambda(v,w) \to maxvalue\ \wr[(v,w)]\wr) \\
=\ & sublists_{\uparrow,+}\ (\lambda(v,w) \to v)
\end{aligned}$$

---

[1] The proof can be automated using an online tool: `http://www-ps.iai.uni-bonn.de/cgi-bin/free-theorems-webui.cgi`

This derivation shows that $sublists_{\uparrow,+}$ $(\lambda(v,w) \to v)$ computes the maximum of all total values of sublists of the input list, but—unlike the intuitive formulation at the beginning of the equation chain—efficiently. While the run time of *maxvalue* ∘ *sublists* is exponential in the length of the input list (because the result of *sublists* has exponential size), the run time of the derived version $sublists_{\uparrow,+}$ $(\lambda(v,w) \to v)$ is linear in the length of the input list (it adds up all positive values in the input).

Of course, this is of little use for solving the knapsack problem posed in Section 3 because the input list in this problem contains only positive values and *maxvalue* ∘ *sublists*, thus, computes the total value of all available items.

For solving the knapsack problem, it is crucial to compute the maximum value only of those sublists of the input list which adhere to the weight restriction. We need to account for the test that implements this restriction which is the topic of the next section.

5 Filter Embedding

We cannot apply Theorem 1 to transform specifications of the form

$$aggregate \circ test \circ generate$$

because the intermediate test goes in the way of fusing the aggregator with the generator. We now show how specific instantiations of *test* allow to rewrite specifications like above into the form

$$postprocess \circ aggregate' \circ generate$$

where *aggregate′* is a semiring homomorphism derived from *aggregate* and *test*, and *postprocess* maps the result type of *aggregate′* to the result type of *aggregate*. This form then allows to fuse *aggregate′* with *generate* to derive an efficient implementation.

This transformation is possible if

$$test = filter\ (ok \circ hom)$$

is a filter where the predicate is a composition of a monoid homomorphism $hom : [A] \to M$ into a finite monoid M and a function $ok : M \to Bool$ that maps elements of M to Booleans.

Before we describe the general theorem in Section 5.2, we develop the underlying ideas by deriving an efficient implementation from the *knapsack* specification. This development may seem to require some clever insights but users of our approach do *not* need to follow the same path when transforming their own specifications. We chose to present the ideas using a concrete example first, to make them seem less clever in the subsequent generalization. Others can simply *apply* our general theorem to their specifications rather than repeating our development for each specification on their own. We can even provide an API that supports specifications in GTA form and implements them as efficient parallel programs automatically.

5.1 Developing Intuitions by Example

In Section 3 we have specified the *knapsack* function as follows:

$$knapsack = maxvalue \circ filter\ ((\leqslant w) \circ weight) \circ sublists$$

This specification is almost of the form we require:

- *maxvalue*, the aggregator, is a semiring homomorphism and
- the predicate used for filtering is a composition of the monoid homomorphism *weight* and the function $(\leqslant w)$ that maps the result of *weight* into the Booleans.

However, the result type of *weight* is $\mathbb{N}$ which is an infinite monoid, not a finite one. We can remedy the situation by defining $M_w = \{0, \ldots, w+1\}$ and

$$\begin{aligned} weight_w\ [\,] &= 0 \\ weight_w\ [n] &= (w+1) \downarrow n \\ weight_w\ (ms +\!\!+ ns) &= weight_w\ ms +_w weight_w\ ns \\ \textbf{where}\ m +_w n &= (w+1) \downarrow (m+n) \end{aligned}$$

The operator $+_w$ implements addition but limits the result by computing the minimum with $w+1$ by using the minimum operator $\downarrow$. For non-negative arguments it is associative and 0 is its identity. Consequently, $weight_w$ is a monoid homomorphism into the finite monoid $(M_w, +_w)$ for all weight restrictions w.

To transform the function $maxvalue \circ filter\ ((\leqslant w) \circ weight_w)$ into the form $postprocess_w \circ maxvalue_w$ we need to invent a semiring to use as result type of $maxvalue_w$. The idea is to compute simultaneously for all weights in M_w the maximum value of lists with exactly that weight. The function $postprocess_w$ then computes the maximum over all values associated to weights $\leqslant w$.

We use $w = 5$ as an example, so semiring elements can be represented as 7-tuples over $\mathbb{Z}_{-\infty}$. The function $postprocess_5$ is defined as follows:

$$postprocess_5\ (v_0, v_1, v_2, v_3, v_4, v_5, v_6) = v_0 \uparrow v_1 \uparrow v_2 \uparrow v_3 \uparrow v_4 \uparrow v_5$$

It computes the maximum of all values v_i associated with weights $i \leqslant 5$. The entry v_6 for the weight 6 accumulates the maximum value corresponding to all weights $\geqslant 6$ because $+_w$ cuts off greater sums.

We now turn $\mathbb{Z}^7_{-\infty}$ into a semiring $(\mathbb{Z}^7_{-\infty}, \uparrow^7, +^7)$. To compute the maximum value associated to each weight of two 7-tuples, we use the underlying maximum operation on values.

$$\begin{aligned} &(v_0, v_1, v_2, v_3, v_4, v_5, v_6) \uparrow^7 (v'_0, v'_1, v'_2, v'_3, v'_4, v'_5, v'_6) = \\ &\quad (v_0 \uparrow v'_0, v_1 \uparrow v'_1, v_2 \uparrow v'_2, v_3 \uparrow v'_3, v_4 \uparrow v'_4, v_5 \uparrow v'_5, v_6 \uparrow v'_6) \end{aligned}$$

This operator clearly inherits associativity and commutativity from the underlying maximum operator and its identity is

$$(-\infty, -\infty, -\infty, -\infty, -\infty, -\infty, -\infty)$$

The operator $+^7$ is more interesting. From two 7-tuples that associate maximum values to each weight in M_5 it computes another 7-tuple that associates maximum values to the combined weights. For example, to find the maximum value associated to the weight 3, it computes the maximum of all sums of values associated to weights that sum up to 3 (we omit the part for larger weights):

$$\begin{aligned}
&(v_0, v_1, v_2, v_3, v_4, v_5, v_6) +^7 (v_0', v_1', v_2', v_3', v_4', v_5', v_6') = \\
&\quad (v_0 + v_0' \\
&\quad , (v_0 + v_1') \uparrow (v_1 + v_0') \\
&\quad , (v_0 + v_2') \uparrow (v_1 + v_1') \uparrow (v_2 + v_0') \\
&\quad , (v_0 + v_3') \uparrow (v_1 + v_2') \uparrow (v_2 + v_1') \uparrow (v_3 + v_0') \\
&\quad , \ldots)
\end{aligned}$$

This operator is associative and its identity is

$$(0, -\infty, -\infty, -\infty, -\infty, -\infty, -\infty)$$

We now define $maxvalue_5$ as *the* (cf. Lemma 1) semiring homomorphism that satisfies the following equation:

$$\begin{aligned}
&maxvalue_5 \wr[(v, w)]\int = (val\ 0, val\ 1, val\ 2, val\ 3, val\ 4, val\ 5, val\ 6) \\
&\quad \textbf{where}\ val\ i = \textbf{if}\ i \equiv (w \downarrow 6)\ \textbf{then}\ v\ \textbf{else}\ -\infty
\end{aligned}$$

When applied to a singleton bag that contains a list with exactly one item, $maxvalue_5$ associates to almost all weights the value $-\infty$ with one exception: the value of the given item is associated to its weight (or to the weight 6 if it is heavier).

Our Main Theorem 3 below, now implies that for $w = 5$

$$knapsack = postprocess_5 \circ sublists_{\uparrow^7, +^7} (\lambda(v, w) \rightarrow maxvalue_5 \wr[(v, w)]\int)$$

The run time of the transformed version of *knapsack* is $O(nw^2)$ if there are n items and the weight restriction is w. As $sublists_{\uparrow^7, +^7}$ is a monoid homomorphism we can execute it in parallel, say using p processors, which leads to the run time $O((\log p + \frac{n}{p})w^2)$. This complexity resembles the run time of other parallel algorithms to solve the knapsack problem. The standard sequential algorithm has run time $O(nw)$.

Unlike existing algorithms to solve the knapsack problem, our approach can be generalized to other specifications in GTA form. The *knapsack* function is a special case well suited to highlight the ideas behind our approach, which we now generalize.

5.2 The Generalized Theorem

We now generalize the ideas of Section 5.1 to support

- arbitrary polymorphic semiring generators,
- arbitrary filters with homomorphic predicates, and
- arbitrary semiring homomorphisms as aggregators.

In Section 5.1 we have used a semiring of 7-tuples storing maximum values corresponding to each weight in M_5. In general, if we have a finite monoid M and a semiring S, then the set

$$S^M = \{\{f_m\}_{m \in M} | f_m \in S\}$$

of families of elements in S indexed by M is a semiring too. Indexed families are a generalization of tuples and we write f_m for the element in S indexed by the value $m \in M$ if $f \in S^M$ is an indexed family. We give definitions of indexed families by defining their value in S for each $m \in M$.

Lemma 2 (Lifted Semiring). *Given a finite monoid $(M, \odot)$ and a semiring $(S, \oplus, \otimes)$ the triple $(S^M, \oplus_M, \otimes_M)$ where*

$$\begin{aligned}(f \oplus_M f')_m &= f_m \oplus f'_m \\ (f \otimes_M f')_m &= \bigoplus_{\substack{k,l \in M \\ k \odot l = m}} (f_k \otimes f'_l)\end{aligned}$$

is a semiring and

$$\begin{aligned}(\imath_{\oplus_M})_m &= \imath_{\oplus} \\ (\imath_{\otimes_M})_m &= \textbf{if } m \equiv \imath_{\odot} \textbf{ then } \imath_{\otimes} \textbf{ else } \imath_{\oplus}\end{aligned}$$

Proof. *The monoid laws for $\oplus_M$ follow directly from those of $\oplus$. We leave the proof of the laws for $\otimes_M$ to interested readers.*

The definition of $\oplus_M$ uses the underlying $\oplus$ operator just like the definition of $\uparrow^7$ in Section 5.1 uses $\uparrow$. The operator $\otimes_M$, like $+^7$, computes for each m the maximum of all sums of values associated to weights that add up to m if we instantiate $\odot$ and $\otimes$ with $+$ and $\oplus$ with $\uparrow$. The identities also reflect their specific counterparts from Section 5.1.

Intuitively, given a monoid homomorphism $hom : [A] \to M$, a semiring homomorphism $aggregate : \wr[A]\wr \to S$, and a bag of lists ls, we can associate to ls an indexed family $f^{ls} \in S^M$ that describes for each $m \in M$ the result of applying *aggregate* to a bag of exactly those lists $l \in ls$ that satisfy $hom\ l = m$:

$$f^{ls}_m = aggregate\ (filter\ ((m \equiv) \circ hom)\ ls)$$

Considering different instantiations for ls, we can observe the following identities:

$$\begin{aligned}f^{\wr\wr}_m &= \imath_{\oplus} \\ f^{\wr[]\wr}_m &= \textbf{if } m \equiv \imath_{\odot} \textbf{ then } \imath_{\otimes} \textbf{ else } \imath_{\oplus} \\ f^{ls \uplus ls'}_m &= f^{ls}_m \oplus f^{ls'}_m \\ f^{ls \times_{++} ls'}_m &= \bigoplus_{\substack{k,l \in M \\ k \odot l = m}} (f^{ls}_k \otimes f^{ls'}_l)\end{aligned}$$

They reflect the definitions of the semiring operations for S^M and their identities. Because of these *homomorphic equations for f^{ls}*, we can compute f^{ls} using a semiring homomorphism $aggregate_M$ that satisfies

$$\begin{aligned}&(aggregate_M \wr[x]\int)_m\\&= f_m^{\wr[x]\int}\\&= aggregate\ (filter\ ((m \equiv) \circ hom)\ \wr[x]\int)\\&= \mathbf{if}\ hom\ [x] \equiv m\ \mathbf{then}\ aggregate\ \wr[x]\int\ \mathbf{else}\ \imath_\oplus\end{aligned}$$

According to Lemma 1 this semiring homomorphism is unique.

Definition 6 (Lifted Homomorphism). *Given a set A, a finite monoid $(M, \odot)$, a monoid homomorphism hom from $([A], +\!\!+)$ to $(M, \odot)$, a semiring $(S, \oplus, \otimes)$, and a semiring homomorphism aggregate from $(\wr[A]\int, \uplus, \times_{+\!\!+})$ to $(S, \oplus, \otimes)$, the function*

$$aggregate_M : \wr[A]\int \to S^M$$

is the unique semiring homomorphism from $(\wr[A]\int, \uplus, \times_{+\!\!+})$ to $(S^M, \oplus_M, \otimes_M)$ that satisfies

$$(aggregate_M \wr[x]\int)_m = \mathbf{if}\ hom\ [x] \equiv m\ \mathbf{then}\ aggregate\ \wr[x]\int\ \mathbf{else}\ \imath_\oplus$$

The function $aggregate_M$ generalizes the function $maxvalue_5$ by using *aggregate* and $\imath_\oplus$ instead of *maxvalue* and $-\infty$.

Once we have computed f^{ls}, we can use a function $ok : M \to Bool$ to combine all results f_m^{ls} for $m \in M$ with $ok\ m = True$ to get the result of

$$aggregate\ (filter\ (ok \circ hom)\ ls) = \bigoplus_{\substack{m \in M\\ ok\ m = True}} (aggregate\ (filter\ ((m \equiv) \circ hom)\ ls))$$

According to this equation, we can *partition* the bag of accepted lists according to elements of M and *aggregate them individually* because *aggregate* is a semiring homomorphism. The postprocessor defined next combines such individual aggregations.

Definition 7 (Postprocessor). *Given sets M (finite) and S and a function $ok : M \to Bool$ the function $postprocess_M\ ok : S^M \to S$ is defined as follows:*

$$postprocess_M\ ok\ f = \bigoplus_{\substack{m \in M\\ ok\ m = True}} f_m$$

It is clearly a generalization of $postprocess_5$ which computes the maximum of all values associated to weights $\leqslant 5$.

We can now prove the theorem which constitutes the second half of our approach. It clarifies how to embed an arbitrary filter with a homomorphic predicate into an arbitrary semiring homomorphism.

Theorem 2 (Filter Embedding). *Given a set A, a finite monoid $(M, \odot)$, a monoid homomorphism hom from $([A], +\!\!+)$ to $(M, \odot)$, a semiring $(S, \oplus, \otimes)$, a semiring homomorphism aggregate from $(\wr[A]\int, \uplus, \times_{+\!\!+})$ to $(S, \oplus, \otimes)$, and a function $ok : M \to Bool$ the following equation holds:*

$$aggregate \circ filter\ (ok \circ hom) = postprocess_M\ ok \circ aggregate_M$$

Proof. The following calculation combines previous observations and definitions to show the claimed identity.

$$
\begin{aligned}
& \quad aggregate\ (filter\ (ok \circ hom)\ ls) \\
= & \quad \{\ \textit{Partition, individual aggregation}\ \} \\
& \quad \bigoplus_{\substack{m \in M \\ ok\ m = True}} (aggregate\ (filter\ ((m \equiv) \circ hom)\ ls)) \\
= & \quad \{\ \textit{Definition of } f^{ls}, \textit{ and Definition 7}\ \} \\
& \quad postprocess_M\ ok\ f^{ls} \\
= & \quad \{\ \textit{Definition 6, homomorphic equations for } f^{ls}\ \} \\
& \quad postprocess_M\ ok\ (aggregate_M\ ls)
\end{aligned}
$$

Our main result combines the theorems from Sections 4 and 5. It allows, under certain conditions, to transform specifications in GTA form into efficient parallel algorithms.

Main Theorem 3 (Filter-embedding Semiring Fusion). *Given a set A, a finite monoid $(M, \odot)$, a monoid homomorphism hom from $([A], +\!\!+)$ to $(M, \odot)$, a semiring $(S, \oplus, \otimes)$, a semiring homomorphism aggregate from $(\wr[A]\int, \uplus, \times_{+\!\!+})$ to $(S, \oplus, \otimes)$, a function $ok : M \to Bool$, and a polymorphic semiring generator generate, the following equation holds:*

$$
\begin{aligned}
& aggregate \circ filter\ (ok \circ hom) \circ generate_{\uplus, \times_{+\!\!+}}\ (\lambda x \to \wr[x]\int) \\
& \quad = postprocess_M\ ok \circ generate_{\oplus_M, \otimes_M}\ (\lambda x \to aggregate_M\ \wr[x]\int)
\end{aligned}
$$

Proof. Combining Theorems 1 and 2.

Filter-embedding Semiring Fusion is not restricted to parallel algorithms. It can be used to calculate efficient programs from specifications that use arbitrary polymorphic semiring generators.

It is worth noting that it is possible to remove the finiteness requirement for monoids and define a lifted semiring of finite mappings of unbounded and unknown size. We require the finiteness only in order to be able to describe the complexity of the resulting parallel algorithms more accurately.

If the generator happens to be a list homomorphism, like *sublists*, then associativity of list concatenation allows the resulting program to be executed in parallel by distributing the input list evenly among available processors. The complexity of a derived program using *sublists* as generator is linear in the size of the input list and quadratic in the size of the range M of the homomorphic predicate because the semiring multiplication of the lifted semiring S^M, which is used to combine all list elements, can be implemented by ranging over $M \times M$.

6 A More Complex Application

In this section we describe how to use our framework to derive an efficient parallel implementation for a practical problem in statistics. We further demonstrate how to extend the derived basic program incrementally.

6.1 Finding a Most Likely Sequence of Hidden States

We now revisit the statistics problem mentioned in Section 1 which is to find a sequence of hidden states of a probabilistic model that most likely causes a sequence of observed events. For example, for speech recognition, the acoustic signal could be the sequence of observed events, and a string of text the sequence of hidden states.

Given a sequence $x = (x_1, \ldots, x_n)$ of observed events, a set S of states in a hidden Markov model, probabilities $P_{\text{yield}}(x_i \mid z_j)$ of events x_i being caused by states $z_j \in S$, and probabilities $P_{\text{trans}}(z_i \mid z_j)$ of states z_i appearing immediately after states z_j, the objective is to find a sequence $z = (z_0, \ldots, z_n)$ of hidden states that is most likely to cause the sequence x of events such that every z_i causes x_i for $i > 0$ and z_0 is an initial state. This problem can be formalized by the following expression.

$$\underset{z \in S^{n+1}}{\mathbf{arg\,max}} \left(\prod_{i=1}^{n} P_{\text{yield}}(x_i \mid z_i) P_{\text{trans}}(z_i \mid z_{i-1}) \right)$$

To derive an efficient parallel algorithm to solve this problem, we transform this expression to fit in our framework.

To eliminate the index $i - 1$, we let the expression range over pairs of hidden states in $S \times S$ and introduce a predicate *trans* to restrict the considered lists of state pairs. Intuitively, *trans* y is *True* if and only if the given sequence y of state pairs describes consecutive transitions

$$((z_0, z_1), (z_1, z_2), \ldots, (z_{n-2}, z_{n-1}), (z_{n-1}, z_n))$$

and *False* otherwise. Introducing the function

$$\mathit{prob}\ (x, (s, t)) = P_{\text{yield}}(x \mid t) P_{\text{trans}}(t \mid s)$$

the expression above can be transformed into the following equivalent expression.

$$\underset{\substack{y \in (S \times S)^n \\ \mathit{trans}\ y = \mathit{True}}}{\mathbf{arg\,max}} \left(\prod_{i=1}^{n} \mathit{prob}\ (x_i, y_i) \right)$$

In a first step, we specify only the maximum probability in GTA form. We show how to compute a state sequence corresponding to this probability by using a different aggregator later.

Representing sequences of states and events as lists, we can write the transformed specification as follows.

$$\begin{aligned} \mathit{maxLikeliness} = {} & \mathit{maxprob} \circ \\ & \mathit{filter}\ (\mathit{trans} \circ \mathit{map}\ (\lambda(x, (s, t)) \to (s, t))) \circ \\ & \mathit{assignTrans}_{\uplus, \times_{+\!\!+}}\ (\lambda x \to \wr[x]\wr) \end{aligned}$$

The polymorphic semiring generator $\mathit{assignTrans}_{\oplus,\otimes}$ is defined as the unique monoid homomorphism from $([X], +\!\!+)$ to the multiplicative monoid $(T, \otimes)$ of an arbitrary semiring $(T, \oplus, \otimes)$ that satisfies

$$assignTrans_{\oplus,\otimes}\ f\ [x] = reduce_{\oplus}\ [f\ (x,(s,t)) \mid s \leftarrow S, t \leftarrow S]$$

Here, $reduce_{\oplus}$ is a monoid homomorphism from $([T], +\!\!+)$ to $(T, \oplus)$ that satisfies $reduce_{\oplus}\ [x] = x$. Intuitively, $assignTrans_{\uplus,\times_{+\!\!+}}\ (\lambda x \rightarrow \wr[x]\wr)$ produces a bag of event sequences where all possible combinations of state transitions are attached.

The predicate *trans* is defined as $not \circ (\Box\ \equiv) \circ reduce_{\diamond}$ where $reduce_{\diamond}$ is a monoid homomorphism from $([S \times S], +\!\!+)$ to the finite monoid $((S \times S)_{\Box}, \diamond)$ and $(S \times S)_{\Box}$ is $(S \times S) \cup \{\imath_{\diamond}, \Box\}$. Here, $\Box$ is a zero of $\diamond$ and

$$(s,t) \diamond (u,v) = \mathbf{if}\ t \equiv u\ \mathbf{then}\ (s,v)\ \mathbf{else}\ \Box$$

Intuitively, $reduce_{\diamond}$ returns the boundaries of a given sequence of state transitions if they are consecutive ($\imath_{\diamond}$ if the sequence is empty) and $\Box$ otherwise.

The aggregator *maxprob* is the unique semiring homomorphism from $(\wr[X \times (S \times S)]\wr, \uplus, \times_{+\!\!+})$ to $([0,1], \uparrow, *)$[2] that satisfies

$$maxprob\ \wr[(x,(s,t))]\wr = prob\ (x,(s,t))$$

Intuitively, it computes all total probabilities of state sequences causing the observed event sequence by multiplying the individual probabilities given by *prob* and then computes the maximum of all total probabilities.

The range of $reduce_{\diamond}$ has size $|S|^2 + 2$, thus, applying Theorem 3 to the specification of *maxLikeliness* yields an implementation with the total cost $O(n|S|^4)$ if n denotes the length of an input event sequence. As *assignTrans* is a monoid homomorphism we can execute it in parallel, say using p processors, which leads to the run time $O((\log p + \frac{n}{p})|S|^4)$. For a given probabilistic model, where S is fixed, the result is a linear-time parallel algorithm. This is in contrast to the specification which would generate an intermediate result of size $|S|^{2n}$. Interestingly, the derived program is equivalent to a program obtained by parallelizing the Viterbi algorithm [12, 13] using matrix multiplication over a semiring [21].

Computing Sequences of States. We can compute both the maximum probability and the corresponding state sequences using an alternative aggregator *maxprobSeq* which can replace *maxprob* above and is characterized by

$$maxprobSeq\ \wr[(x,(s,t))]\wr = (prob\ (x,(s,t)), \wr[t]\wr)$$

The result is an element in the semiring $([0,1] \times \wr[S]\wr, \uparrow', *')$ where the identities of $\uparrow'$ and $*'$ are $(0, \wr\wr)$ and $(1, \wr[\,]\wr)$, respectively, and the semiring operations are defined as follows:

$$\begin{aligned}(a,x) \uparrow' (b,y) &= \mathbf{if}\ a > b\ \mathbf{then}\ (a,x)\ \mathbf{else\ if}\ a < b\ \mathbf{then}\ (b,y)\ \mathbf{else}\ (a, x \uplus y)\\ (a,x) *' (b,y) &= (a * b, x \times_{+\!\!+} y)\end{aligned}$$

The bag in the second component of the result contains all most likely sequences. In practice, we may use non-deterministic choice to compute one of them, though operators with non-deterministic choice do not satisfy the semiring laws, so the specification and the implementation might pick different results.

---

[2] To avoid confusion, note that $[0, 1]$ is the unit interval, that is, the set of all real numbers x such that $0 \le x \le 1$, not the list of the two elements.

6.2 Incremental Refinement

By using Theorem 2 multiple times, it is possible to implement specifications with multiple filters, not only one.

For example, we can compute the most likely sequence of hidden states satisfying certain conditions, such as "state s is used exactly five times," or "state t does not appear anywhere after state s." Our framework guarantees an efficient implementation also for these restricted problems if the conditions can be defined by a homomorphic predicate.

For the first condition we use the monoid homomorphism $count_w\ p$ into $(M_w, +_w)$ characterized by $count_w\ p\ [x] = \mathbf{if}\ p\ x\ \mathbf{then}\ 1\ \mathbf{else}\ 0$. It computes the number of list elements that satisfy the given predicate p. Based on $count_w$ we can define the predicate *fixedTimes* which only allows sequences of states that contain a given state s exactly w times:

$$fixedTimes\ s\ w = (w \equiv) \circ count_w\ (\lambda(x,(t,u)) \to s \equiv u)$$

To check the second condition whether a state t occurs anywhere after a state s we can define a monoid homomorphism $after\ s\ t$ into $((Bool \times Bool)_{\Box}, \star)$ that returns a pair of Booleans that indicate whether the argument list contains the states s and t, or $\Box$ if t occurs anywhere after s.[3] Here, *after* is characterized by

$$after\ s\ t\ [(x,(u,v))] = (s \equiv v, t \equiv v),$$

$\Box$ is a zero of $\star$ and $(s_1,t_1) \star (s_2,t_2) = \mathbf{if}\ s_1 \wedge t_2\ \mathbf{then}\ \Box\ \mathbf{else}\ (s_1 \mid s_2, t_1 \mid t_2)$. Based on *after* we can express a test which only allows sequences of states that do not contain a given state t after s as $not \circ (\Box \equiv) \circ after\ s\ t$.

Since both homomorphisms have finite ranges, we can get linear-time parallel algorithms for the restricted problems. We can even combine both predicates or add similar conditions such as "state s is used more than k times," or "state s is used at most k times" and still get an efficient parallel implementation.

In general, the most difficult task for programmers specifying GTA algorithms is the design of predicates for filtering, while basic generators and aggregators can be reused for many problems. To guarantee the efficiency of programs derived by our calculation theorems, a user has to design a predicate based on a finite monoid. One approach to design such a predicate is to use a regular expression or monadic second order logic expression [25], relying on the fact that a finite monoid can be derived from a finite automaton. For example, an additional condition "we cannot choose items K and J at the same time" to the knapsack problem can be specified by a regular expression `(.*K.*J.*|.*J.*K.*)` composed with the negation function *not*.

7 Related Work

The research on parallelization via derivation of list homomorphisms has gained great interest [5,11,22]. The main approaches include the third homomorphism

[3] $(Bool \times Bool)_{\Box} = (Bool \times Bool) \cup \{\Box\}$ and $\imath_\star = (False, False)$.

theorem based method [10, 20], function composition based method [4, 7, 14], and matrix multiplication based method [21]. Our work is a continued effort in this direction, giving a new approach based on semiring homomorphisms, which is in sharp contrast to the existing work based on monoid homomorphisms. By introducing bags of lists as well as semirings and the GTA form, our method eases defining effectively-parallelizable specifications for practical problems such as the knapsack problem, the discussed statistical problems, and querying problems, because the GTA form with bag of lists is a natural form of specifications for these combinatorial problems. Basically, specifications of these problems are too complex to be handled by the mentioned previous approaches. The previous work cannot directly help users to solve these problems, because it requires users to make parallelizable sequential specifications that are almost equivalent to the efficient programs our proposed method derives. However, previous approaches are still useful to build a parallelizable GTA specification which requires its components (generators and predicates) to be parallel programs.

There has been a lot of work about using MapReduce to parallelize various kinds of problems [17]. Some formal work has been devoted to the study of a computation model of MapReduce (compared to the PRAM model of computation) [16]. However, little work has been done on systematic construction of MapReduce programs. We tackle this problem via semiring homomorphisms.

Our shortcut fusion theorem for semiring fusion is much related to the known shortcut deforestation [8, 23] which is based on a free theorem [26] and is practically useful for optimization of sequential programs. Different from the traditional shortcut deforestation focusing on the data constructors of the intermediate data structure that are passed from one function to another, our shortcut fusion focuses on the semiring operations in the intermediate data structure. It is this semiring structure that allows for flexible rearrangement of computation for efficient parallel execution.

Goodman [9] extended the CYK parsing algorithm by substituting various semirings for the Boolean semiring, so that one can reuse the algorithm for various computations such as counting the number of parsings, computing the probability of generating the given string, and finding the best k-parsing. We can reuse his semirings in our GTA form for computing similar variations.

8 Conclusion

We propose a calculation-based framework for the systematic development of efficient MapReduce programs in the form of GTA algorithms. The core of the framework consists of two calculation theorems for semiring fusion and filter embedding. Semiring fusion connects a specification in GTA form and an efficient implementation by a free theorem, while filter embedding transforms the composition of a semiring homomorphism and a test into another semiring homomorphism which enables incremental development of parallel algorithms. Our approach allows to develop efficient parallel algorithms by combining simpler homomorphisms (for generation, testing, and aggregation) into more complex ones, which is easier than defining the efficient parallel algorithms directly. In contrast to existing approaches, our theorems allow to modify an efficient algorithm by adding homomorphic filters in the "naive world" which is easier than modifying it in the "efficient world". Our new framework is not only theoretically interesting, but also practically significant in solving nontrivial problems.

For example, we have shown how to derive an efficient parallel implementation of a known statistics problem and found that it is equivalent to an existing algorithm for the same problem. This result shows that our approach generalizes existing techniques and provides a common framework to express them. We expect that our approach can be applied to typical "big-data" problems, like finding patterns in historical financial data, and plan to investigate such applications as future work.

Moreover, we plan to implement the developed programming theory as a domain specific language or a library, for example upon Hadoop [27], so that typical MapReduce problems can be tackled using our GTA approach. Our theorems can be easily mechanized because of their simple calculational form.

References

1. Bird, R.: An introduction to the theory of lists. In: Broy, M. (ed.) Logic of Programming and Calculi of Discrete Design, pp. 5–42. Springer, Heidelberg (1987)
2. Bird, R.: Introduction to Functional Programming using Haskell. Prentice Hall (1998)
3. Bird, R., de Moor, O.: Algebras of Programming. Prentice Hall (1996)
4. Chin, W.N., Khoo, S.C., Hu, Z., Takeichi, M.: Deriving Parallel Codes via Invariants. In: SAS 2000. LNCS, vol. 1824, pp. 75–94. Springer, Heidelberg (2000)
5. Cole, M.: Parallel programming with list homomorphisms. Parallel Processing Letters 5(2), 191–203 (1995)
6. Dean, J., Ghemawat, S.: Mapreduce: simplified data processing on large clusters. Communications of the ACM 51, 107–113 (2008)
7. Fisher, A.L., Ghuloum, A.M.: Parallelizing complex scans and reductions. In: Proceedings of the ACM SIGPLAN 1994 Conference on Programming Language Design and Implementation (PLDI 1994), pp. 135–146. ACM (1994)
8. Gill, A., Launchbury, J., Peyton Jones, S.L.: A short cut to deforestation. In: Conference on Functional Programming Languages and Computer Architecture, pp. 223–232 (1993)
9. Goodman, J.: Semiring parsing. Computational Linguistics 25, 573–605 (1999)
10. Gorlatch, S.: Systematic Efficient Parallelization of Scan and Other List Homomorphisms. In: Fraigniaud, P., Mignotte, A., Robert, Y., Bougé, L. (eds.) Euro-Par 1996. LNCS, vol. 1124, pp. 401–408. Springer, Heidelberg (1996)
11. Grant-Duff, Z., Harrison, P.: Parallelism via homomorphism. Parallel Processing Letters 6(2), 279–295 (1996)
12. He, Y.: Extended viterbi algorithm for second order hidden markov process. In: 9th International Conference on Pattern Recognition, vol. 2, pp. 718–720. IEEE Press (1988)
13. Ho, T.J., Chen, B.S.: Novel extended viterbi-based multiple-model algorithms for state estimation of discrete-time systems with markov jump parameters. IEEE Transactions on Signal Processing 54(2), 393–404 (2006)

14. Hu, Z., Takeichi, M., Chin, W.N.: Parallelization in calculational forms. In: 25th ACM Symposium on Principles of Programming Languages (POPL 1998), pp. 316–328. ACM Press, San Diego (1998)
15. Hu, Z., Yokoyama, T., Takeichi, M.: Program Optimizations and Transformations in Calculation Form. In: Lämmel, R., Saraiva, J., Visser, J. (eds.) GTTSE 2005. LNCS, vol. 4143, pp. 144–168. Springer, Heidelberg (2006)
16. Karloff, H., Suri, S., Vassilvitskii, S.: A model of computation for mapreduce. In: Proceedings of the Twenty-First Annual ACM-SIAM Symposium on Discrete Algorithms, SODA 2010, pp. 938–948. SIAM (2010)
17. Lin, J., Dyer, C.: Data-Intensive Text Processing with MapReduce. Morgan and Claypool Publishers (2010)
18. List, M.A.P. (2011), `http://www.mendeley.com/groups/1058401/mapreduce-applications/papers/`
19. Liu, Y., Hu, Z., Matsuzaki, K.: Towards Systematic Parallel Programming over MapReduce. In: Jeannot, E., Namyst, R., Roman, J. (eds.) Euro-Par 2011, Part II. LNCS, vol. 6853, pp. 39–50. Springer, Heidelberg (2011)
20. Morita, K., Morihata, A., Matsuzaki, K., Hu, Z., Takeichi, M.: Automatic inversion generates divide-and-conquer parallel programs. In: ACM SIGPLAN 2007 Conference on Programming Language Design and Implementation (PLDI 2007), pp. 146–155. ACM Press (2007)
21. Sato, S., Iwasaki, H.: Automatic parallelization via matrix multiplication. In: Proceedings of the 32nd ACM SIGPLAN Conference on Programming Language Design and Implementation (PLDI 2011), pp. 470–479. ACM (2011)
22. Skillicorn, D.B.: The Bird-Meertens Formalism as a Parallel Model. In: NATO ARW "Software for Parallel Computation" (1992)
23. Takano, A., Meijer, E.: Shortcut deforestation in calculational form. In: Proc. Conference on Functional Programming Languages and Computer Architecture, pp. 306–313. La Jolla, California (1995)
24. Takano, A., Hu, Z., Takeichi, M.: Program transformation in calculational form. ACM Computing Surveys 30(3) (1998)
25. Thomas, W.: Automata on infinite objects. In: Handbook of Theoretical Computer Science, Formal Models and Sematics, vol. B, pp. 133–192. Elsevier and MIT Press (1990)
26. Wadler, P.: Theorems for free! In: Proceedings of the Fourth International Conference on Functional Programming Languages and Computer Architecture, FPCA 1989, pp. 347–359. ACM (1989)
27. White, T.: Hadoop: The Definitive Guide. O'Reilly Media (2009)

Trace Spaces: An Efficient New Technique for State-Space Reduction

Lisbeth Fajstrup[1], Éric Goubault[2], Emmanuel Haucourt[2], Samuel Mimram[2], and Martin Raussen[1]

[1] Department of Mathematical Sciences, Aalborg University
[2] CEA, LIST*

Abstract. State-space reduction techniques, used primarily in model-checkers, all rely on the idea that some actions are independent, hence could be taken in any (respective) order while put in parallel, without changing the semantics. It is thus not necessary to consider all execution paths in the interleaving semantics of a concurrent program, but rather some equivalence classes. The purpose of this paper is to describe a new algorithm to compute such equivalence classes, and a representative per class, which is based on ideas originating in algebraic topology. We introduce a geometric semantics of concurrent languages, where programs are interpreted as directed topological spaces, and study its properties in order to devise an algorithm for computing dihomotopy classes of execution paths. In particular, our algorithm is able to compute a control-flow graph for concurrent programs, possibly containing loops, which is "as reduced as possible" in the sense that it generates traces modulo equivalence. A preliminary implementation was achieved, showing promising results towards efficient methods to analyze concurrent programs, with very promising results compared to partial-order reduction techniques.

Introduction

Formal verification of concurrent programs is traditionally considered as a difficult problem because it might involve checking all their possible schedulings, in order to verify all the behaviors the programs may exhibit. This is particularly the case for checking for liveness or reachability properties, or in the case of verification methods that imply traversal of some important parts of the graph of execution, such as model-checking [4] and abstract testing [6]. Fortunately, many of the possible executions are equivalent (we say *dihomotopic*) in the sense that one can be obtained from the other by permuting independent instructions, therefore giving rise to the same results. In order to analyze a program, it is thus enough (and much faster) to analyze one representative in each dihomotopy class of execution traces.

We introduce in this paper a new algorithm to reduce the state-space explosion during the analysis of concurrent systems. It is based on former work of some of the authors, most notably [24] where the notion of trace space is introduced and studied, and also builds up considerably on the geometric semantics approach to concurrent systems,

* This work has been supported by the PANDA ("Parallel and Distributed Analysis", ANR-09-BLAN-0169) French ANR project and by ESF project ACAT.

H. Seidl (Ed.): ESOP 2012, LNCS 7211, pp. 274–294, 2012.

as developed in [13]. Some fundamentals of the mathematics involved can be found in [19]. The main contributions of this article are the following: we develop and improve the algorithms for computing trace spaces of [24] by reformulating them in order to devise an efficient implementation for them, we generalize this algorithm to programs which may contain loops and thus exhibit an infinite number of behaviors, we apply these algorithms to a toy shared-memory language whose semantics is given in the style of [12], but in this paper, formulated in terms of d-spaces [19], and we report on the implementation and experimentation of our algorithms on trace spaces – an industrial case-study using those methods is also detailed in [3].

Stubborn sets [25], sleep sets and persistent sets [15] are among the most popular methods used for diminishing the complexity of model-checking using transition systems; they are in particular used in SPIN [1], with which we compare our work experimentally in Section 2.5. They are based on semantic observations using Petri nets in the first case and Mazurkiewicz trace theory in the other one. We believe that these are special forms of dihomotopy-based reduction as developed in this paper when cast in our geometric framework, using the adjunctions of [18]. Of course, the trace spaces we are computing have some acquaintance with traces as found in trace theory [7]: basically, traces in trace theory are points of trace spaces, and composition of traces modulo dihomotopy is concatenation in trace theory. Trace spaces are more general in that they consider general directed topological spaces and not just partially commutative monoids; they also include all information related to higher-dimensional (di-)homotopy categories, and not just the fundamental category, as in trace theory. Trace spaces are also linked with component categories, introduced by some of the authors [14,17], and connected components of trace spaces can also be computed using the algorithm introduced in [16].

Contents of the paper. We first define formally the programming language we are considering (Section 1.1) as well as an associated geometric semantics, (Section 1.2). We then introduce an algorithm for computing an effective combinatorial representation of trace spaces as well as an efficient implementation of it (Section 2), and extend this algorithm in order to handle program containing loops (Section 3). Finally, we discuss various applications, in particular to static analysis (Section 3.5) and possible extensions of the algorithm and conclude.

1 Geometric Semantics of Concurrent Processes

1.1 A Toy Shared-Memory Concurrent Language

In this paper, we consider a toy imperative shared-memory concurrent language as grounds for experimentation. In this formalism, a program can be constituted of multiple subprograms which are run in parallel. The environment provides a set of resources $\mathcal{R}$, where each resource $a \in \mathcal{R}$ can be used by at most κ_a subprograms at the same time, the integer $\kappa_a \in \mathbb{N}$ being called the *capacity* of the resource a. In particular, a *mutex* is a resource of capacity 1.

Whenever a program wants to access a resource a, it should acquire a lock by performing the action P_a which allows access to a, if the lock is granted. Once it does not need the resource anymore, the program can release the lock by performing the action V_a, following again the notation set up by Dijkstra [8]. If a subprogram tries to acquire a lock on a resource a when the resource has already been locked κ_a times, the subprogram is stuck until the resource is released by an other subprogram. In order to be realistic even though simple, the language considered here also comprises a sequential composition operator ., a non-deterministic choice operator $+$ and a loop construct $(-)^*$, with similar semantics as in regular languages (it should be thought as a `while` construct), as well as a parallel composition operator $|$ to launch two subprograms in parallel.

Programs p are defined by the following grammar:

$$p \quad ::= \quad \mathbf{1} \quad | \quad P_a \quad | \quad V_a \quad | \quad p.p \quad | \quad p|p \quad | \quad p+p \quad | \quad p^*$$

Programs are considered modulo a *structural congruence* $\equiv$ which imposes that operators ., $+$ and $|$ are associative and admit $\mathbf{1}$ as neutral element. A *thread* is a program which does not contain the parallel composition operator $|$.

1.2 Geometric Semantics

We introduce here a semantics based on (directed) topological spaces. The geometric semantics will allow a different representation of n pairwise independent actions (as the surface of an n-cube) and n truly concurrent actions as the full n-cube.

We denote by $I = [0,1] \subseteq \mathbb{R}$ the standard euclidean interval. A *path* p in a topological space X is a continuous map $p : I \to X$, and the points $p(0)$ and $p(1)$ are respectively called the *source* and *target* of the path. Given two paths p and q such that $p(1) = q(0)$, we define their *concatenation* as the path $p \cdot q$ defined by

$$(p \cdot q)(t) = \begin{cases} p(2t) & \text{if } 0 \leqslant t \leqslant 1/2 \\ q(2t-1) & \text{if } 1/2 \leqslant t \leqslant 1 \end{cases}$$

A topological space can be equipped with a notion of "direction" as follows [19]:

Definition 1. *A* directed topological space *(or* d-space *for short)* $X = (X, dX)$ *consists of a topological space* X *together with a set* dX *of paths in* X *(the* directed paths*) such that*

1. constant paths*: every constant path is directed,*
2. reparametrization*:* dX *is closed under precomposition with (non necessarily surjective) increasing maps* $I \to I$*, which are called* reparametrizations*,*
3. concatenation*:* dX *is closed under concatenation.*

A morphism of d-spaces $f : X \to Y$*, a* directed map*, is a continuous function* $f : X \to Y$ *which preserves directed paths, in the sense that* $f(dX) \subseteq dY$*.*

The category of d-spaces is complete and cocomplete [19]. This allows us to abstractly define some constructions on d-spaces, which extend usual constructions on topological spaces, that we detail here explicitly by describing the associated directed paths.

- The *terminal d-space* $\star$ is the space reduced to one point.
- The *cartesian product* $X \times Y$ of two d-spaces X and Y has $d(X \times Y) = dX \times dY$.
- The *disjoint union* $X \uplus Y$ of two d-spaces X and Y is such that $d(X \uplus Y) = dX \uplus dY$.

- The *amalgamation* $X[x = y]$ of two points x and y in a d-space X is the d-space X where x and y have been identified, together with the expected set of directed paths.
- Given a d-space X and a topological space $Y \subseteq X$, the *subspace* Y can be canonically equipped with a structure of d-space by $dY = \{p \in dX \ / \ p(I) \subseteq Y\}$.

The geometric semantics of a program is defined using those constructions as follows:

Definition 2. *To every program p, we associate a d-space G_p together with a pair of points $b_p, e_p \in G_p$, respectively called* beginning *and* end, *and a* resource function *$r_p : \mathcal{R} \times G_p \to \mathbb{Z}$ which indicates the number of locks the program holds at a given point. The definition of these is done by induction on the structure of p as follows:*

$G_1 = \star, \quad b_1 = *, \quad e_1 = *, \quad r_1(a,x) = 0$	
$G_{P_a} = \vec{I}, \quad b_{P_a} = 0, \quad e_{V_a} = 1,$ $r_{P_a}(b,x) = \begin{cases} -1 & \text{if } b = a \text{ and } x > 0 \\ 0 & \text{if } b \neq a \text{ or } x = 0 \end{cases}$	$G_{V_a} = \vec{I}, \quad b_{V_a} = 0, \quad e_{V_a} = 1,$ $r_{V_a}(b,x) = \begin{cases} 1 & \text{if } b = a \text{ and } x = 1 \\ 0 & \text{if } b \neq a \text{ or } x < 1 \end{cases}$
$G_{p.q} = (G_p \uplus \vec{I} \uplus G_q)[e_p = 0, 1 = b_q],$ $b_{p.q} = b_p, \quad e_{p.q} = e_q,$ $r_{p.q}(a,x) = \begin{cases} r_p(a,x) & \text{if } x \in G_p \\ r_p(a,e_p) + r_q(a,x) & \text{if } x \in G_q \end{cases}$	$G_{p+q} = (G_p \uplus G_q)[b_p = b_q, e_p = e_q],$ $b_{p+q} = b_p, \quad e_{p+q} = e_q,$ $r_{p+q}(a,x) = \begin{cases} r_p(a,x) & \text{if } x \in G_p \\ r_q(a,x) & \text{if } x \in G_q \end{cases}$
$G_{p\|q} = G_p \times G_q,$ $b_{p\|q} = (b_p, b_q), \quad e_{p\|q} = (e_p, e_q),$ $r_{p\|q}(a,(x,y)) = r_p(a,x) + r_q(a,y)$	$G_{p^*} = G_p[b_p = e_p],$ $b_{p^*} = b_p, \quad e_{p^*} = b_p,$ $r_{p^*}(a,x) = r_p(a,x)$

Given a program p, the forbidden region *is the d-space $F_p \subseteq G_p$ defined by*

$$F_p = \{x \in G_p \ / \ \exists a \in \mathcal{R}, \ \kappa_a + r_p(a,x) < 0 \ \text{ or } \ r_p(a,x) > 0\}$$

The geometric realization *of a process p, is defined as the d-space $H_p = G_p \setminus F_p$.*

We sometimes write 0 and ∞ for the beginning and the end points respectively of a geometric realization, and say that a path $p : \vec{I} \to G_p$ is *total* when it has 0 as source and ∞ as target. It is easy to show that the geometric semantics of a program is well-defined in the sense that two structurally congruent programs give rise to isomorphic geometric realizations.

Example 1. The processes

$$P_a.V_a | P_a.V_a \qquad\qquad P_a.P_b.V_b.V_a | P_b.P_a.V_a.V_b \qquad\qquad P_a.(V_a.P_a)^* | P_a.V_a$$

respectively have the following geometric realizations, which all consist of a space with some "holes", drawn in gray, induced by the forbidden region:

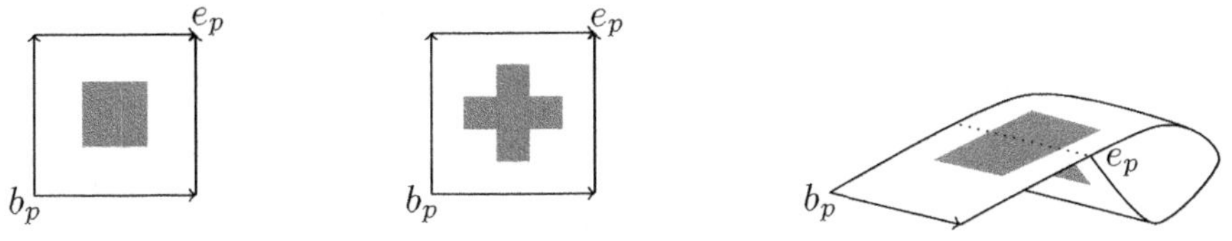

The space in the middle is sometimes called the "Swiss flag" because of its form and is interesting because it exhibits both a deadlock and an unreachable region [13].

2 Computing Trace Spaces

2.1 Trace Spaces

In topology, two paths p and q are often considered as equivalent when q can be obtained by deforming continuously p (or vice versa), this equivalence relation being called *homotopy*. The corresponding variant of this relation in the case of directed topological spaces is called *dihomotopy* and is formally defined as follows. In the category of d-spaces, the object $\vec{I}$ is *exponentiable*, which means that for every d-space Y, one can associate a d-space $Y^{\vec{I}}$ such that there is a natural bijection between morphisms $X \times \vec{I} \to Y$ and morphisms $X \to Y^{\vec{I}}$. The underlying space of $Y^{\vec{I}}$ is the set of functions $\vec{I} \to Y$ with the compact-open topology (also called uniform convergence topology), and the directed paths $h : \vec{I} \to Y^{\vec{I}}$ are the functions such that $t \mapsto h(t)(u)$ is increasing for every $u \in \vec{I}$. Finally, two paths are said to be dihomotopic when one can be continuously deformed into the other:

Definition 3. *The* dihomotopy *is defined as the smallest equivalence relation on paths such that two directed paths $p, q : \vec{I} \to X$ are dihomotopic when there exists a directed path $h : \vec{I} \to X^{\vec{I}}$ with p as source and q as target.*

Example 2. In the geometric semantics of the program $P_b.V_b.P_a.V_a \mid P_a.V_a$, the two paths above the hole are dihomotopic, whereas the path below is not dihomotopic to the two others:

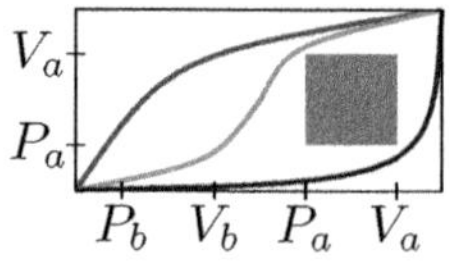

The intuition underlying the geometric semantics is that two dihomotopic paths correspond to execution traces differing by inessential commutations of instructions, thus giving rise to the same result.

Given two points x and y of a d-space X, we write $X(x, y)$ for the subset of $X^{\vec{I}}$ consisting of dipaths from x to y. A *trace* is the equivalence class of a path modulo surjective reparametrization, and a *scheduling* is the equivalence class of a trace modulo dihomotopy. We write $\vec{T}(X)(x, y)$ for the *trace space* obtained from $X(x, y)$ by identifying paths equivalent up to reparametrization, and simply $\vec{T}(X)$ for $\vec{T}(X)(0, \infty)$. In particular, we have $\vec{T}(X)(x, y) \neq \emptyset$ if and only if there exists a directed path in X going from x to y.

In this section, we reformulate the algorithm for computing the trace space $\vec{T}(X)$ up to dihomotopy equivalence, originally introduced in [24], in order to achieve an efficient implementation of it. For simplicity, we restrict here to spaces which are geometric realizations of programs of the form

$$p \quad = \quad p_0 \mid p_1 \mid \cdots \mid p_{n-1} \tag{1}$$

where the p_i are built up only from $\mathbf{1}$, concatenation, resource locking and resource unlocking (extending the algorithm to programs which may contain loops requires significant generalizations which are described in Section 3). In this case, the geometric realization is of the form

$$G_p = \vec{I^n} \setminus \bigcup_{i=0}^{l-1} R^i$$

where $\vec{I^n}$ denotes the cartesian product of n copies of $\vec{I}$, and each $R^i = \prod_{j=0}^{n-1} \vec{I_j^i}$ is a rectangle. We suppose here that each R^i is homothetic to the n-dimensional open rectangle, i.e. each directed interval $\vec{I_j^i}$ is of the form $\vec{I_j^i} =]x_j^i, y_j^i[$, and generalize this at the end of the section. The restrictions on the form of the programs are introduced here only to simplify our exposition: programs with choice can be handled by computing the trace spaces on each branch and program with loops can be handled by suitably unfolding the loops so that all the possible behaviors are exhibited (a detailed presentation of this is given in Section 3, which will enable to handle the full language). We suppose fixed a program with n threads and l forbidden open rectangles, and consistently use the notations above.

Example 3. The geometric realization of the programs

$$P_a.V_a.P_b.V_b|P_a.V_a.P_b.V_b \qquad \text{and} \qquad P_a.V_a.P_b.V_b|P_b.V_b.P_a.V_a$$

are respectively

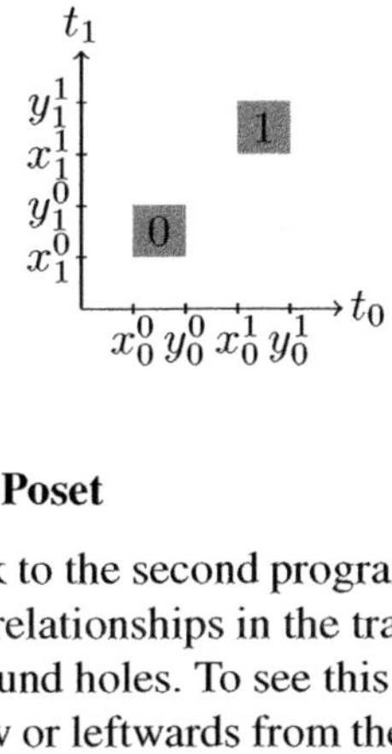

and

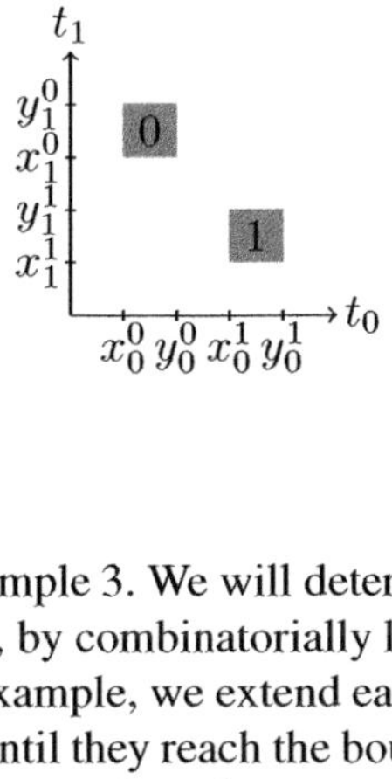

2.2 The Index Poset

Let us come back to the second program of Example 3. We will determine the different traces, and their relationships in the trace space, by combinatorially looking at the way they can turn around holes. To see this in that example, we extend each hole in parallel to the axes, below or leftwards from the holes, until they reach the boundary of the state space. These new obstructions impose traces to go the other way around each hole: the existence of deadlocks, given these new constraints in the trace space allows us to determine whether traces going one way or the other around each hole exist. In fact, this combinatorial information precisely computes all of the trace space [24].

In the second program of Example 3, there are four possibilities to extend once each of the two holes:

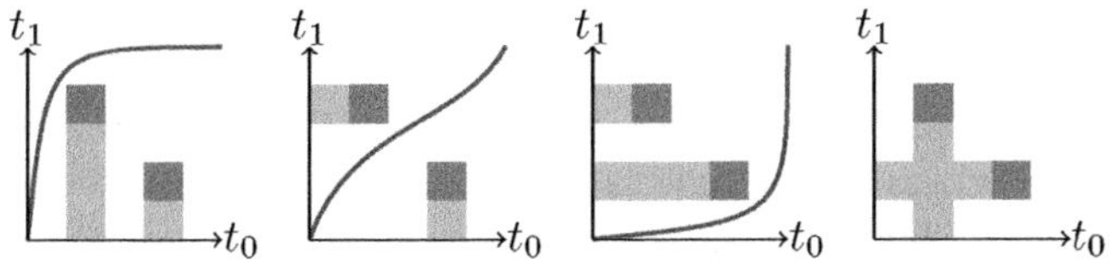

(2)

Notice that there exists a total path in the first three spaces (as depicted above), whereas there is none in the last one.

A simple way to encode the combinatorial information about the extension of holes is through boolean matrices. We write $\mathcal{M}_{l,n}$ for the poset of $l \times n$ matrices, with l rows (the number of holes R^i) and n columns (the dimension of the space, i.e. the number of threads in the program), with coefficients in $\mathbb{Z}/2\mathbb{Z}$, with the pointwise ordering such that $0 \leqslant 1$: we have $M \leqslant N$ whenever

$$\forall (i,j) \in [0:l[\times[0:n[, \qquad M(i,j) \leqslant N(i,j) \tag{3}$$

where $[m : n[$ denotes the set $\{m, \ldots, n-1\}$ of integers and $M(i,j)$ denotes the (i,j)-th coefficient of M. We also write $\mathcal{M}^R_{l,n}$ for the subposet of $\mathcal{M}_{l,n}$ consisting of matrices whose row vectors are all different from the zero vector, and $\mathcal{M}^C_{l,n}$ for the subposet of $\mathcal{M}_{l,n}$ consisting of matrices whose column vectors are all unit vectors (containing exactly one coefficient 1).

Given a matrix $M \in \mathcal{M}_{l,n}$, we define X_M as the subspace of X obtained by extending downwards each forbidden rectangle R^i in every direction j' different from j for every j such that $M(i,j) = 1$. Formally,

$$X_M = \vec{I}^n \setminus \bigcup_{M(i,j)=1} \tilde{R}^i_j$$

where $\tilde{R}^i_j = \prod_{j'=0}^{j-1}[0, y^i_{j'}[\times]x^i_j, y^i_j[\times\prod_{j'=j+1}^{n-1}[0, y^i_{j'}[$, see (2) and Example 4 below.

In order to study whether there is a total path in the space associated to a matrix, we define a map $\Psi : \mathcal{M}_{l,n} \to \mathbb{Z}/2\mathbb{Z}$ by $\Psi(M) = 1$ iff $\vec{T}(X_M) = \emptyset$, i.e. there is no total path in X_M. A matrix M is *dead* when $\Psi(M) = 1$ and *alive* otherwise. The map Ψ can easily be shown to be order preserving.

Definition 4. *We write*

$$\mathcal{D}(X) = \{M \in \mathcal{M}^C_{l,n} \;/\; \Psi(M) = 1\}$$

for the set of (column) dead matrices and

$$\mathcal{C}(X) = \{M \in \mathcal{M}^R_{l,n} \;/\; \Psi(M) = 0\}$$

for the set of alive matrices (with non-empty rows), which is called the index poset *– it is implicitly ordered by the relation* (3).

Example 4. In the example above, the three extensions of holes (2) are respectively encoded by the following matrices:

$$\begin{pmatrix}1&0\\1&0\end{pmatrix} \quad \begin{pmatrix}0&1\\1&0\end{pmatrix} \quad \begin{pmatrix}0&1\\0&1\end{pmatrix} \quad \begin{pmatrix}1&0\\0&1\end{pmatrix}$$

The last matrix is dead and the three others are alive. The last matrix being dead indicates that there is no way a trace can pass left of the upper left hole and carry on passing below the lower right hole.

A reason why the matrices in the index poset are convenient objects to study the schedulings is that they are topologically very simple [24]:

Proposition 1. *For any matrix $M \in \mathcal{M}^R_{l,n}$, the space $X_M(x,y)$ is either empty or contractible: any two paths with the same source x and target y are dihomotopic. In particular, for any matrix $M \in \mathcal{C}(X)$, the space $X_M(0,\infty)$ is always contractible.*

Our main interest in the index poset is that it enables us to compute the schedulings (i.e. maximal paths modulo dihomotopy) of the space: these schedulings are in bijection with alive matrices in $\mathcal{C}(X)$ modulo an equivalence relation called *connexity*, which is defined as follows. Given two matrices $M, N \in \mathcal{M}_{l,n}$, their *intersection* $M \wedge N$ is defined as the matrix $M \wedge N$ such that $(M \wedge N)(i,j) = \min(M(i,j), N(i,j))$.

Definition 5. *Two matrices M and N are* connected *when their intersection does not contain any row filled with* 0.

The dihomotopy classes of total paths in X can finally be computed thanks to the following property:

Proposition 2. *The connected components of $\mathcal{C}(X)$ are in bijection with schedulings in X.*

Example 5. Consider the program $p = q|q|q$ where $q = P_a.V_a$. The associated trace space X_p is a cube minus a cube (as shown in Example 8). The matrices in $\mathcal{C}(X_p)$ are

$$\begin{pmatrix}1&0&0\end{pmatrix} \quad \begin{pmatrix}0&1&0\end{pmatrix} \quad \begin{pmatrix}0&0&1\end{pmatrix} \quad \begin{pmatrix}0&1&1\end{pmatrix} \quad \begin{pmatrix}1&0&1\end{pmatrix} \quad \begin{pmatrix}1&1&0\end{pmatrix}$$

and they are all (transitively) connected. For instance, $\begin{pmatrix}0&1&1\end{pmatrix} \wedge \begin{pmatrix}1&0&1\end{pmatrix} = \begin{pmatrix}0&0&1\end{pmatrix}$. The program p thus has exactly one total scheduling, as expected.

Intuitively, alive matrices describe sets of dihomotopic total paths (Proposition 1) and the fact that two matrices have non-zero rows in their intersection means that there are paths which satisfy the constraints imposed by both matrices, i.e. the two matrices describe the same dihomotopy class of total paths.

2.3 Computing Dihomotopy Classes

The computation of the dihomotopy classes of total paths in the geometric semantics X of a given program will be performed in three steps:

1. we compute the set $\mathcal{D}(X)$ of dead matrices,
2. we use $\mathcal{D}(X)$ to compute the index poset $\mathcal{C}(X)$,
3. we deduce the homotopy classes of total paths by quotienting $\mathcal{C}(X)$ by the connexity relation.

These steps are detailed below.

Given a subset I of $[0:l[$ and an index $j \in [0:n[$, we write $y^I_j = \min\{y^i_j \mid i \in I\}$ (by convention $y^{\emptyset}_j = \infty$). Given a matrix $M \in \mathcal{M}_{l,n}$, we define the set of *non-zero rows* of M by $R(M) = \{i \in [0:l[\;/\; \exists j \in [0:n[,\ M(i,j) \neq 0\}$. It can be shown that a matrix M is dead if and only if the space X_M contains a deadlock. From the characterization of deadlocks in geometric semantics given in [11], the following characterization of dead matrices can therefore be deduced:

Proposition 3. *A matrix $M \in \mathcal{M}^C_{l,n}$ is in $\mathcal{D}(X)$ iff it satisfies*

$$\forall (i,j) \in [0:l[\times[0:n[, \quad M(i,j) = 1 \Rightarrow x^i_j < y^{R(M)}_j \tag{4}$$

Example 6. In the example below with $l = 2$ and $n = 2$, the matrix $M = \begin{pmatrix} 0 & 1 \\ 1 & 0 \end{pmatrix}$ is dead (we suppose that $x^i_j = 1 + i(j+1)$ and $y^i_j = 3 + i(j+1) - j$):

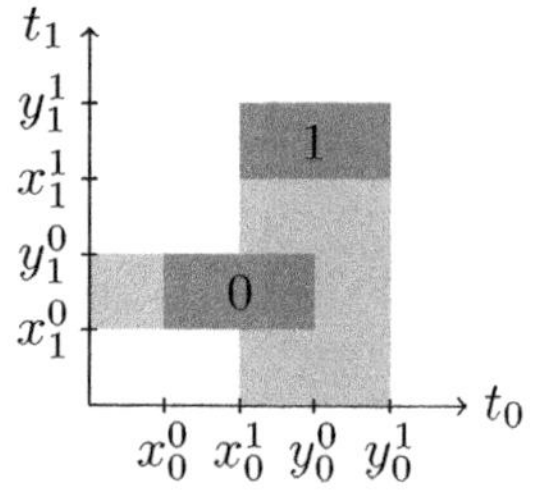

$$x^0_1 = 1 < 2 = y^{\{0,1\}}_1$$
$$x^1_0 = 2 < 3 = y^{\{0,1\}}_0$$

The above proposition enables us to compute the set of dead matrices, for instance by enumerating all matrices and checking whether they satisfy condition 4 (a more efficient method is described in Section 2.4). From this set, the index poset $\mathcal{C}(X)$ can be determined using the following property:

Proposition 4. *A matrix $M \in \mathcal{M}_{l,n}$ is not in $\mathcal{C}(X)$ iff there exists a matrix $N \in \mathcal{D}(X)$ such that $N \leqslant M$. In other words, $M \in \mathcal{C}(X)$ iff for every matrix $N \in \mathcal{D}(X)$ there exists indexes $i \in [0:l[$ and $j \in [0:n[$ such that $M(i,j) = 0$ and $N(i,j) = 1$.*

Notice that the poset $\mathcal{C}(X)$ is downward closed (because Ψ is order preserving) and one is naturally interested in the subset $\mathcal{C}_{\max}(X)$ of *maximal* matrices in order to describe it. Proposition 4 provides a simple-minded algorithm for computing (maximal) matrices in $\mathcal{C}(X)$. We write $\mathcal{D}(X) = \{D_0, \ldots, D_{p-1}\}$. We then compute the sets C_k of maximal matrices M such that for every $i \in [0:k[$ we have $D_i \nleqslant M$. We start from the set $C_0 = \{\mathbf{1}\}$ where $\mathbf{1}$ is the matrix containing only 1 as coefficients. Given a matrix M, we write $M^{\neg(i,j)}$ for the matrix obtained from M by replacing the (i,j)-th coefficient by $1 - M(i,j)$. The set C_{k+1} is then computed from C_k by doing the following for all matrices $M \in C_k$ such that $D_k \leqslant M$:

1. remove M from C_k,
2. for every (i,j) such that $D_k(i,j) = 1$,
   - remove every matrix $N \in C_k$ such that $N \leqslant M^{\neg(i,j)}$,
   - if there exists no matrix $N \in C_k$ such that $M^{\neg(i,j)} \leqslant N$, add $M^{\neg(i,j)}$ to C_k.

The set $\mathcal{C}_{\max}(X)$ is obtained as C_p. If we remove the second point and replace it by

2'. for every (i,j) such that $D_k(i,j) = 1$ and $M^{\neg(i,j)} \in \mathcal{M}^R_{l,n}$, add $M^{\neg(i,j)}$ to C_k.

we compute a set C_p such that $\mathcal{C}_{\max}(X) \subseteq C_p \subseteq \mathcal{C}(X)$, which is enough to compute connected components and has proved faster to compute in practice.

Example 7. Consider again Example 3. The algorithm starts with

$$C_0 = \left\{ M_0 = \begin{pmatrix} 1\,1 \\ 1\,1 \end{pmatrix} \right\}$$

For C_1, we must have $D_0 \nleqslant M_0$ so we swap any of the two ones in the first row:

$$C_1 = \left\{ M_1 = \begin{pmatrix} 0\,1 \\ 1\,1 \end{pmatrix}, M_2 = \begin{pmatrix} 1\,0 \\ 1\,1 \end{pmatrix} \right\}$$

Similarly for C_2, we have to swap the bits on the second row so that $D_1 \nleqslant M_i$:

$$C_2 = \left\{ M_3 = \begin{pmatrix} 0\,1 \\ 0\,1 \end{pmatrix}, M_4 = \begin{pmatrix} 0\,1 \\ 1\,0 \end{pmatrix}, M_5 = \begin{pmatrix} 1\,0 \\ 0\,1 \end{pmatrix}, M_6 = \begin{pmatrix} 1\,0 \\ 1\,0 \end{pmatrix} \right\}$$

Finally, we have $D_2 \nleqslant M_i$, excepting $D_2 \leqslant M_5$, so we swap the bits in position $(1,1)$ and in position $(2,2)$:

$$M_5' = \begin{pmatrix} 0\,0 \\ 0\,1 \end{pmatrix} \leqslant M_3 \qquad M_5'' = \begin{pmatrix} 1\,0 \\ 0\,0 \end{pmatrix} \leqslant M_6$$

Since we are only interested in maximal matrices, we end up with $C_3 = \{M_6, M_4, M_3\}$. The trace spaces corresponding to those matrices are the three first depicted in (2). None of those matrices being connected, the trace space up to dihomotopy consists of exactly 3 distinct points.

Other implementations of the algorithm can be obtained by reformulating the computation of $\mathcal{C}_{\max}(X)$ as finding a minimal transversal in a hypergraph, for which efficient algorithms have been proposed [21].

We have supposed up to now that the forbidden region was a union of rectangles R^i, each such rectangle being a product of open intervals $\vec{I}_j^i =]x_j^i, y_j^i[$. The algorithm given above can easily be generalized to the case where the rectangles R^i can "touch the boundary" in some dimensions, i.e. the intervals $\vec{I}_j^i$ are either of the form $]x_j^i, y_j^i[$ or $[0, y_j^i[$ or $]x_j^i, \infty]$ or $[0, \infty]$. For example, the process $P_a.V_a|P_a.V_a|P_a.V_a$, with $\kappa_a = 1$, generates such a forbidden region. We write $B \in \mathcal{M}_{l,n}$ for the *boundary matrix*, which is the matrix such that $B(i,j) = 0$ whenever $x_j^i = 0$ (i.e. the i-th interval touches the lowest boundary in dimension j) and $B(i,j) = 1$ otherwise. The matrices of $\mathcal{D}(X)$ are the matrices $M \in \mathcal{M}_{n,l}$ of the form $M = N \wedge B$, for some matrix $N \in M_{n,l}^C$, which satisfy (4) and such that

$$\forall j \in C(M), \qquad y_j^{R(M)} = \infty \tag{5}$$

where $C(M)$ is the set of indexes of null columns of M.

2.4 An Efficient Implementation

In order to compute the set $\mathcal{D}(X)$ of dead matrices, the general idea is to enumerate all the matrices $M \in \mathcal{M}_{l,n}^C$ and check whether they satisfy the condition (4). Of course, a direct implementation of this idea would be highly inefficient since there are l^n matrices in $\mathcal{M}_{l,n}^C$. In order to improve this, we try to detect "as soon as possible" when a matrix

```
let rec compute_dead j m rows yrows =
  if j = n then dead := m :: !dead else
    for i = 0 to l − 1 do
      try
        let changed_rows = not (Set.mem i rows) in
        let rows = Set.add i rows in
        let m = Array.copy m in
        if bounds(i,j) = 1 then m.(j) ←None else m.(j) ←Some i;
        (match m.(j) with
            | Some i →if x_j^i ⩾ yrows.(j) then raise Exit
            | None → if yrows.(j) ≠∞ then raise Exit);
        let yrows =
          let j' = j in
          if not changed_rows then yrows else
            Array.mapi (fun j yrj →
                if yrj ⩽ y_j^i then yrj else
                  match m.(j) with
                    | None →
                        if j ⩽ j' && y_j^i≠∞ then raise Exit; y_j^i
                    | Some i →
                        if x_j^i ⩾ y_j^i then raise Exit; y_j^i
                        ) yrows
        in
        compute_dead (j+1) m rows yrows
      with Exit → ()
    done
```

Fig. 1. Algorithm for computing dead matrices

does not satisfy the condition: we first fix the coefficient in the first column of M and check whether it is possible for a matrix with this first column to be dead, then we fix the second column and so on. In fact, we have to check that every coefficient (i, j) such that $M(i, j) = 1$ satisfies $x^i_j < y^{R(M)}_j$. Now, suppose that we know some of the coefficients (i, j) for which $M(i, j) = 1$. We therefore know a subset $I \subseteq R(M)$ of the non-zero rows. If for one of these coefficients we have $x^i_j \geqslant y^I_j$, we know that the matrix cannot satisfy the condition (4) because $x^i_j \geqslant y^I_j \geqslant y^{R(M)}_j$. A similar reasoning can be held for condition (5).

The actual function computing the dead matrices is presented in Figure 1, in pseudo-OCaml code. This recursive function fills j-th column of the matrix M (whose columns with index below j are supposed to be already fixed) and performs the check: it tries to set the i-th coefficient to 1 (and all the others to 0) for every $i \in [0 : l[$. If a matrix beginning as M (up to the j-th column) cannot be dead, the computation is aborted by raising the Exit exception. When all the columns have been computed the matrix is added to the list *dead* of dead matrices. Since a matrix $M \in \mathcal{M}^C_{l,n}$ has at most one non-null coefficient in a given column, it will be coded as an array of length n whose j-th element is either None when all the elements of the j-th column are null, or Some i

when the i-th coefficient of the j-th column is 1 and the others are 0. The argument $rows$ is the set of indexes of known non-null rows of M and $yrows$ is an array of length n such that $yrows.(j)= y_j^{rows}$. The matrix $bounds$ is the matrix previously noted B used to perform the check (5). Notice that the algorithm takes advantage of the fact that when the coefficient i chosen for the j-th column is already in $rows$ (i.e. when the variable $changed\_rows$ is false) then many computations can be spared because the coefficients y_j^{rows} are not changed.

Once the set of dead matrices computed, the set $\mathcal{C}(X)$ of alive matrices is then computed using the naive algorithm of Section 2.3, exemplified in Example 7. We have also implemented a simple hypergraph transversal algorithm [2] but it did not bring significant improvements, more elaborate algorithms might give better results though. Finally, the representatives of traces are computed as the connected components (in the sense of Proposition 2) of $\mathcal{C}(X)$, in a straightforward way. An explicit sequence of instructions corresponding to every representative M can easily be computed: it corresponds to the sequence of instructions crossed by any increasing total path in the d-space X_M.

2.5 An Example: The n Dining Philosophers

In order to illustrate the performances of our algorithm, we present below the computation times for the well-known n dining philosophers program [9] whose schedulings are in $O(2^n)$, hence is pushing any algorithm that would determine the essential schedules to its (exponential) limits. It is constituted of n processes p_k in parallel, using n mutexes a_i, defined by $p_k = P_{a_k}.P_{a_{k+1}}.V_{a_k}.V_{a_{k+1}}$, where the indexes on mutexes a_i are taken modulo n. Such a program generates $2^n - 2$ distinct schedulings, which our program finds correctly. The table below summarizes the execution time and memory consumption for our tool ALCOOL (programmed in OCaml), as well as for the model checker SPIN [1] implementing partial order reduction techniques. Whereas SPIN is not significantly slower, it consumes much more memory and starts to use swap from $n = 12$ (thus failing to give an answer in a reasonable time for $n > 12$). Notice that the implementation of SPIN is finely tuned and also benefits from `gcc` optimizations, whereas there is room for many improvements in ALCOOL. In particular, most of the time is spent in computing dead matrices and the algorithm of Section 2.4 could be improved by finding a heuristic to suitably sort holes so that failures to satisfy condition (4) are detected earlier. The present algorithm is also significantly faster than some of the author's previous contribution [16]: for instance, it was unable to generate these maximal dipaths because of memory requirements, for n philosophers with $n > 8$ (in the benchmarks of [16], it was taking already 13739s, on a 1GHz laptop computer though, to generate just the component category for 9 philosophers).

n	sched.	ALC. (s)	ALC. (MB)	SP. (s)	SP. (MB)
10	1022	5	4	8	179
11	2046	32	9	42	816
12	4094	227	26	313	3508
13	8190	1681	58	∞	∞
14	16382	13105	143	∞	∞

Since the size of the output is generally exponential in the size of the input, there is no hope to find an algorithm which has less than an exponential worst-case complexity (which our algorithm clearly has). However, since our goal is to program actual tools to very concurrent programs, practical improvements in the execution time or memory consumption are really interesting from this point of view. We have of course tried our tool on many more examples, which confirm the improvement trend, and shall be presented in a longer version of the article.

3 Programs with Loops

3.1 Paths in Deloopings

One of the most challenging part of verifying concurrent programs consists in verifying programs with loops since those contain a priori an infinite number of possible execution traces. We extend here the previous methodology and, given a program containing loops, we compute a (finite!) automaton whose accepted paths describe the schedulings of the program: this automaton, can thus be considered as a control flow graph of the concurrent program. Of course, we are then able to use the traditional methods in static analysis, such as abstract interpretation, to study the program (this is briefly presented in Section 3.5). This section builds on some ideas being currently developed by Fajstrup [10], however most of the properties presented in this section are entirely new. To the best of our knowledge, this is the first works in which geometric methods are used in order devise a practical algorithm to handle programs containing loops. A particularly interesting feature of our method lies in the fact that it consider the broad "geometry of holes" and can thus associate a small control flow graph to a given program, see Section 3.4.

In the following, we suppose fixed a program of the form $p = p_0|p_1|\ldots|p_{n-1}$ as in (1), with n threads. We write

$$p^* \quad = \quad p_0^* \mid p_1^* \mid \ldots \mid p_{n-1}^*$$

for the associated "looping program". Our goal in this section is to describe the schedulings of such a program p^* (the restriction on the form of the programs considered here was only done to simplify our presentation and the methodology can be extended to handle all well-bracketed programs generated by the grammar, without any essential technical difficulty added). Following Section 1.2, its geometrical semantics consists of an n-dimensional torus with rectangular holes. As previously, for simplicity, we suppose that these holes do not intersect the boundaries, i.e. that p satisfies the hypothesis of Section 2.1. Given an n-dimensional vector $v = (v_0, \ldots, v_{n-1})$ with coefficients in $\mathbb{N}$, the *v-delooping* of p, written p^v, is the program $p_0^{v_0}|p_1^{v_1}|\ldots|p_{n-1}^{v_{n-1}}$, where $p_j^{v_j}$ denotes the concatenation of v_j copies of p_j. A *scheduling* in p is a scheduling in the previous sense (i.e. a total path modulo homotopy) in p^v for some vector v.

Example 8. Consider the program $p = q|q|q$ of Example 5, where $q = P_a.V_a$. Its geometric realization X_p is pictured on the left, and its $(3, 2, 2)$-delooping $X_{p^{(3,2,2)}}$ is pictured on the right.

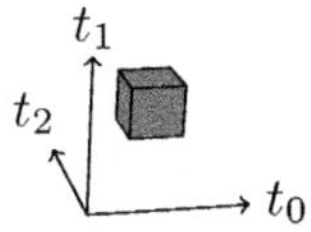

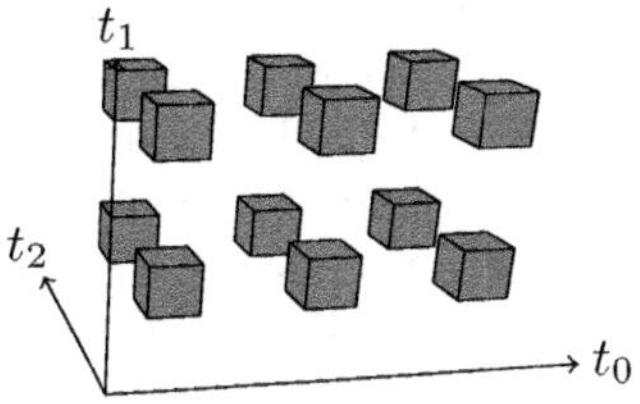

Given two spaces X and Y which are hypercubes with holes (which is the case for the geometric realizations of the programs we are considering here), we write $X \oplus_j Y$ for the space obtained by identifying the j-th target face of the hypercube X with the j-th source face of the hypercube Y, and call it the *j-gluing* of X and Y. Formally, this can be defined as in Section 1.2 as $X \oplus_j Y = X \uplus Y / \sim$, where the relation $\sim$ identifies points $x \in X$ and $y \in Y$ such that $x_j = \infty$, $y_j = 0$ and $x_{j'} = y_{j'}$ for every dimension $j' \neq j$, and directed paths are defined in a similar fashion. Notice that, by definition, there is a canonical embedding of X (resp. Y) into $X \oplus_j Y$, which will allow us to implicitly consider X (resp. Y) as a subspace of $X \oplus_j Y$ in the following.

Example 9. The $(3, 2, 2)$-delooping of Example 8 is

$$X_{p^{(3,2,2)}} \quad = \quad (Y \oplus_1 Y) \oplus_2 (Y \oplus_1 Y) \qquad \text{with} \qquad Y = X_p \oplus_0 X_p \oplus_0 X_p$$

More generally, any v-delooping p^v of a program p of the form (1) can be obtained by gluing copies X_p^w of X_p, indexed by a vector w such that for every dimension i with $0 \leqslant i < n$, we have $0 \leqslant w_i < v_i$ (what we will simply write $0 \leqslant w < v$).

Given two scheduling matrices M and N encoding extensions of holes of such a program p (cf. Section 2.2), we reuse the notation and write $M \oplus_j N$ for the obvious matrix coding extension of holes in the space $X_p \oplus_j X_p$. At this point, it is crucial to notice that the holes described by N in the second copy of X_p can have an effect on the first copy of X_p (when they are extended to 0 in the direction j), what we call the *j-shadow of N*, and write $X_{N|_j}$.

Example 10. With the program p of Example 8, consider the matrices $M = (1\ 0\ 0)$ and $N = (0\ 0\ 1)$. We have $M \oplus_0 N = \begin{pmatrix} 1\ 0\ 0 \\ 0\ 0\ 1 \end{pmatrix}$, the space $X_{M \oplus_0 N}$ is pictured on the left, and the 0-shadow $X_{N|_0}$ of N is pictured on the right:

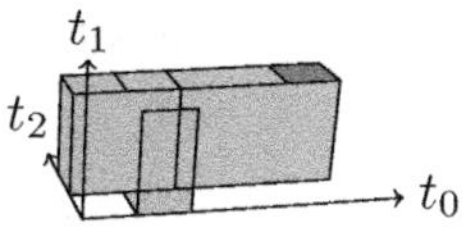

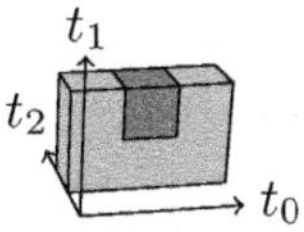

The above example makes clear that the space corresponding to a scheduling $M \oplus_j N$ is of the form $X_{M \oplus_j N} = (X_M \cap X_{N|_j}) \otimes_j X_N$, i.e. the holes in the first copy come either from M or from shadows of N. Moreover, the holes in the space $X_{N|_j}$ are hypercubes which are products of intervals of the form $\prod_{0 \leqslant j < n} \vec{I}_j$, where each interval $\vec{I}_j$ is of the form $]x_j^i, y_j^i[$ or $[0, y_j^i[$ or $[0, \infty]$, with $0 \leqslant i < l$. The shadows can therefore be coded as matrices (using a slightly different coding from the one used up to now, the precise way they are coded being quite irrelevant) and we write $N|_j$ for the matrix coding the j-shadow of n, which can easily be computed from N and j. A scheduling matrix M can obviously be seen as a particular "shadow", enabling us to use the same notation for both, and we write $M \cup N$ for the union of two shadows M and N, so that $X_{M \cup N} = X_M \cap X_N$. Finally, given a shadow M, the algorithm described in Section 2.3 can easily be adapted to the new coding in order to determine whether the space X_M is alive.

3.2 The Shadow Automaton

The trace space of a program p^* is not finite in the general case. We show here that it can however be described as the set of paths of an automaton that we call the *shadow automaton*: this automaton provides us with a *finite presentation* of the set of schedulings.

Consider the v-delooping p^v of a program p. The space X_{p^v} consists of the gluing of copies of X_p indexed by vectors w such that $0 \leqslant w < v$ and similarly, a scheduling M of X_{p^v} consists of the gluing of matrices M^w. Clearly, if some submatrix M^w is dead then the whole matrix M is dead:

Lemma 1. *If a matrix M is alive then all its submatrices M^w are alive.*

However, the converse is not true because a scheduling M^w might create a deadlock with the shadows coming from matrices above it. For instance in Example 8, the matrix $M = (1\ 0\ 0) \oplus_0 (0\ 1\ 1)$ is not alive because the space $X_{M^{(0,0,0)}}$ induced by the submatrix $M^{(0,0,0)}$ is contained in the space X_N, where $N = (1\ 1\ 1)$ is a dead matrix:

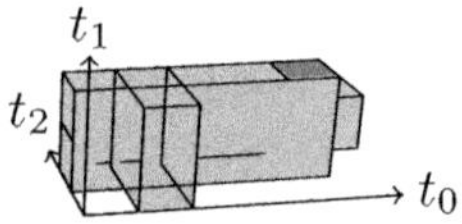

In order to generate all the possible schedulings M^w visited by a total path in X_{p^v}, we therefore have to take in account the shadows dropped by scheduling of copies of X_p in its future. We will construct an automaton which will consider the visited schedulings of the path, starting from the end, and maintains the shadow they produce on the next state in a given direction j, so that we can compute the possible previous matrices in direction j such that the whole matrix is not dead. Formally,

Definition 6. *The* shadow automaton *of a program p is a non-deterministic automaton whose*

- *states are shadows*
- *transitions $N \xrightarrow{j,M} N'$ are labeled by a direction j (with $0 \leqslant j < n$) and a scheduling M*

defined as the smallest automaton

- *containing the empty scheduling* $\emptyset$
- *and such that for every state* N'*, for every direction* j *and for every scheduling* M *such that the scheduling* $M \cup N'$ *is alive, and* M *is maximal with this property, there is a transition* $N \xrightarrow{j,M} N'$ *with* $N = (M \cup N')|_j$.

All the states of the automaton are both initial and final.

Example 11. Consider the program $p = q|q$ with $q = P_a.V_a$ whose geometric semantics is a square with a square hole. The associated shadow automaton is

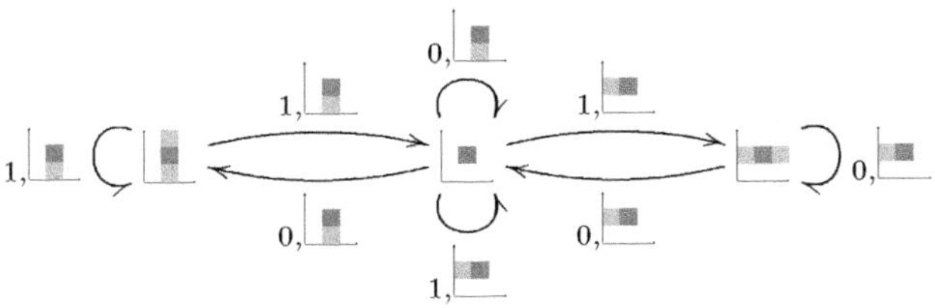

For instance the transition 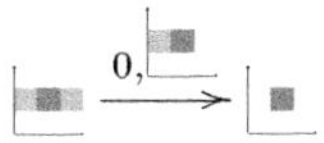 is computed as follows: we take the shadow $M =$ 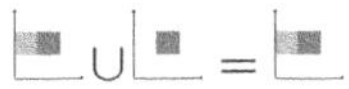 and compute its shadow in direction 0, i.e. on the left, to compute the source of the transition. This shadow is , namely: .

The interest of the automaton lies in the fact that fully describes the possible schedulings crossed by a total path in a scheduling of a delooping X_{p^v}:

Theorem 1. *Suppose that* M *is a scheduling of* X_{p^v}*, obtained by gluing schedulings* M^w *of* X_p*. Then there exists a total path in* X_M *going through the subspaces* $X_{M^{w_0}}, X_{M^{w_1}}, \ldots, X_{M^{w_m}}$ *in this order, such that* w_k *and* w_{k+1} *only differ by one coordinate* j_k *(i.e. the path exits from* $X_{M^{w_k}}$ *through its* j_k*-th face), if and only if there exists a path labeled as follows in the shadow automaton:*

$$N_0 \xrightarrow{j,M^{w_0}} N_1 \xrightarrow{j_0,M^{w_1}} N_2 \quad \cdots \quad N_m \xrightarrow{j_{m-1},M^{w_m}} N_{m+1}$$

for some states N_i *and dimension* j.

Example 12. With the program p of Example 11, the following paths in the $(2,2)$-delooping

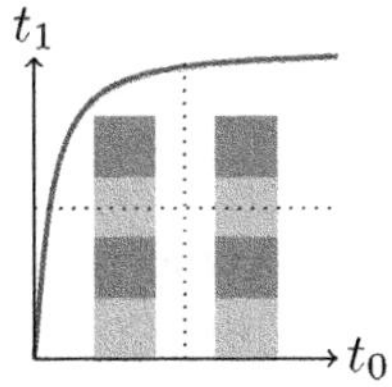

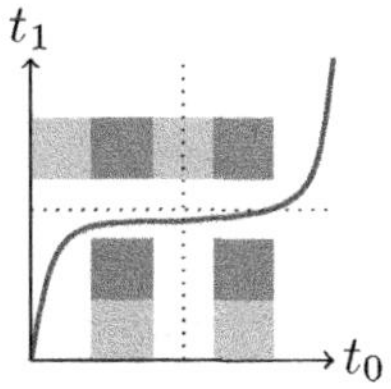

are respectively witnessed by the following paths of the shadow automaton:

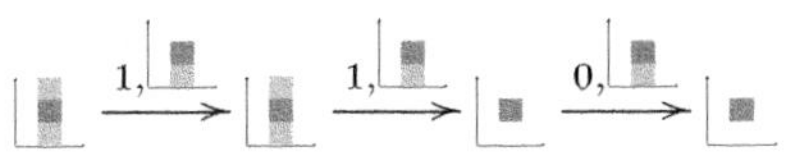

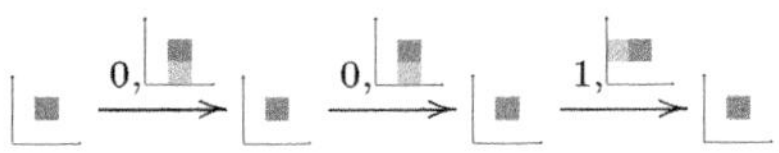

3.3 Reducing the Size of the Shadow Automaton

The size of the shadow automaton grows very quickly when the complexity of the trace space grows. For instance, for the program p of Example 8, the shadow automaton has already 19 states and 80 transitions. We describe here some ways to reduce the automaton while preserving Theorem 1. Namely, we should remark that the automaton is not minimal in the following sense. By Proposition 1, given a scheduling M two total paths X_M are necessarily homotopic: an alive scheduling thus describes an homotopy class of total paths. By Theorem 1, the schedulings "visited" by a total path in X_{p^v} are described by a path in the shadow automaton, therefore every homotopy class of total paths in X_{p^v} is described by at least one path in the scheduling automaton. The shadow automaton is not minimal in the sense that generally, an homotopy class is described by more than one path in the scheduling automaton.

Determinization. First, our non-deterministic automaton can be determinized using classical algorithms of automata theory, which in practice greatly reduce their size: the determinized automaton for the program of Example 8 has only 4 states and 24 transitions.

Example 13. The determinized automata for Examples 11 and 8 are respectively:

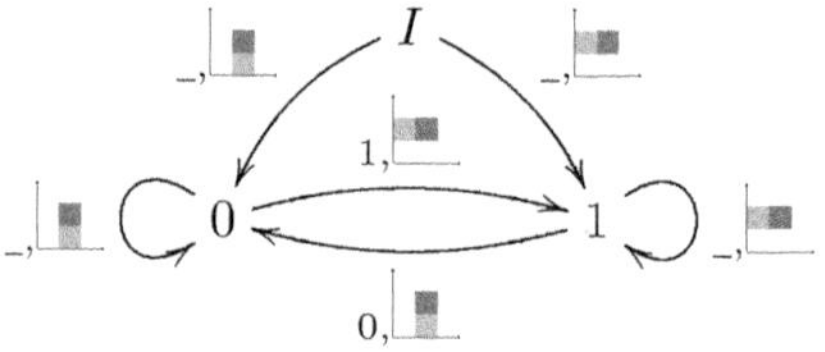

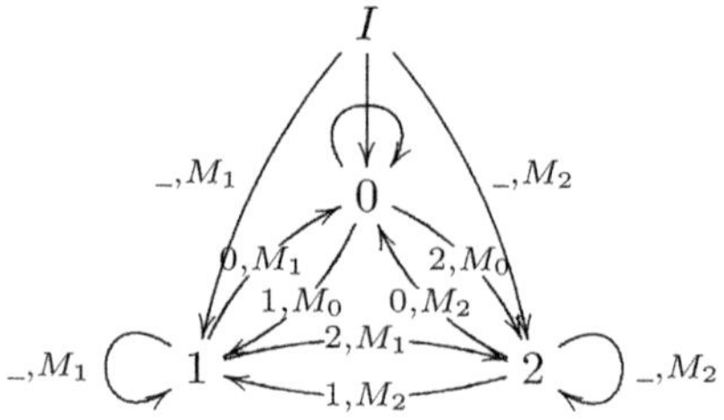

with

$M_0 =$ 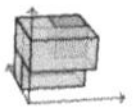 $M_1 =$ 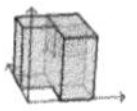 $M_2 =$ 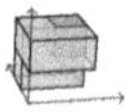

where "_" means any direction j. The state I is initial and all the states are final.

Quotient under connexity. A way to further reduce the automaton consists in quotienting the scheduling matrices labeling the arrows of the automaton under the connexity relation of Definition 5 before determinizing the automaton, which is formally justified by Proposition 2.

Example 14. The shadow automaton corresponding to the program Example 8 quotiented under connexity, determinized and minimized is simply the automaton I ⟳ $_,M$ where $M = M_1 = M_2 = M_3$ up to connexity (the matrices M_i are those defined in Example 13).

We are currently investigating further conditions in order to construct the minimal automaton describing the trace space associated to a looping program, but the conditions mentioned above are already providing us with promisingly small automata.

3.4 Preliminary Implementation and Benchmark

A preliminary implementation of the computation of the shadow automaton was done. The algorithm implemented is currently quite simple, but we plan to generalize the algorithm of Section 2.4 soon, which is not complicated from a theoretical point of view but much more involved technically, in order to achieve better performances. Most experiments lead so far are already promising and make it clear that taking in account the geometry of the state-space enables us to reduce, sometimes drastically, the size of the control flow graph corresponding to the program to be analyzed.

Example 15. The *two-phase locking protocol* is a simple discipline for distributed databases, in which the processes first lock all the mutexes for the resources they are going to use and free all of them in the end [20]. This can be modeled as a program $q_{n,l}$ consisting of n copies of the process $p = P_{a_1} \ldots . P_{a_l} .V_{a_1} \ldots . V_{a_l}$ in parallel (each of these process is using l resources). For instance, the geometric semantics of $q_{2,2} = p|p$ is shown below. Notice that this state space is equivalent to a space with only one hole up to dihomotopy. More generally, given $l \geqslant 1$, it can be shown that the geometric semantics of $q_{n,l}$ is equivalent to $q_{n,1}$, which our algorithm is able to take into account! Namely, the size of the shadow automaton associated to $q^*_{n,l}$ only depends on n whereas the number of states of the automaton produced by SPIN is exponential in l (with n fixed). Below are presented the size (states, transitions) of the non-deterministic automaton (s, t), determinized automaton (s',t') and SPIN's automaton (s_{SPIN}, t_{SPIN}) for the two-phase locking process described in Example 15, for some values of n and l.

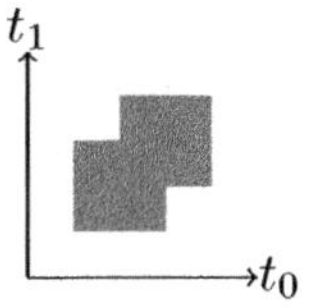

n	l	s	t	s'	t'	s_{SPIN}	t_{SPIN}
2	1	3	8	3	10	58	65
2	2	3	8	3	10	112	129
2	3	3	8	3	10	180	209
3	1	19	90	4	24	171	218
3	2	19	90	4	24	441	602
3	3	19	90	4	24	817	1128

3.5 An Application to Static Analysis

Now that we have the reduced shadow automaton, we can explain how one can perform static analysis by *abstract interpretation* [5] on concurrent systems, in an economic way. The systematic design and proof of correctness of such abstract analysis is left for a future article, the aim of this section is to give an intuition why the computations of Section 3 are relevant to static analysis by abstract interpretation. The idea is to associate, to each node n of the shadow automaton, a set of values A_n that program variables can take if computation follows a transition path whose last vertex is n. Among the actions the program can take along this scheduling, we consider only the *greedy* ones, that is the ones which execute all possible actions permitted by the dihomotopy class of schedulings ending by n.

Suppose that we want to analyze the program

$$p^* \quad = \quad \left(P_a.\,(a := a-1)\,.V_a\right)^*\left|\left(P_a.\left(a := \frac{a}{2}\right).V_a\right)^*\right. \tag{6}$$

What are the possible sets of values reached, for a, starting with $a \in [0, 1]$? The associated shadow automaton S_p has been determined in Example 13 (this automaton is reduced) together with relations, that we will not be using in this article, yet. In many ways, this reduced shadow automaton plays the role of a compact *control flow graph* for the program we are analyzing. Calling $M_0 =$  and $M_1 =$ , X_{M_0} has the effect on environment: $a := a/2$ and X_{M_1} has as effect: $a := a - 1$.

We are now in a position to interpret the arrows of the shadow automaton as simple *abstract transfer functions* and produce a system of equations for which we want to determine a least-fixed point, to get the invariant of the program at the (multi-)control point which is the pair of the heads of the loops of each process. The interpretation on the shadow automaton now gives (ignoring the initial state I in that picture, for simplicity's sake) can be graphically pictured as:

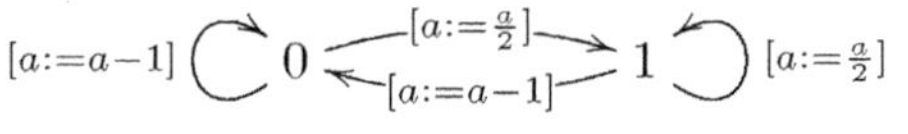

Given the abstract transfer functions on each edge of the shadow automaton, we produce as customary the abstract semantic equations, one per node, by joining all transfer functions correspond to ingoing edges to that node:

$$\begin{pmatrix} A_0 \\ A_1 \end{pmatrix} = F \begin{pmatrix} A_0 \\ A_1 \end{pmatrix} = \begin{pmatrix} I \cup (A_0 - 1) \cup (A_1 - 1) \\ I \cup \frac{A_1}{2} \cup \frac{A_0}{2} \end{pmatrix} \tag{7}$$

This set of semantic equations can be seen as a least-fixed point equation, that we can solve using any of our favorite tool, for instance Kleene iteration and widening/narrowing, on any abstract domain, such as the domain of intervals as in the example below. The least-fixed point formulation that we are looking for is thus $A^\infty = \bigvee_{[0,1]} F$, where F is the function defined in (7) and $I = [0, 1]$. A Kleene iteration on this monotonic function F on the lattice of intervals over $\mathbb{R}$ reveals that $A_0^\infty = A_1^\infty =]-\infty, 1]$.

We have presented this example in order to show how the reduced shadow automaton can be used in order to use usual static analysis methods on concurrent programs, avoiding state-space explosion as much as possible. It has the advantage of being short, however it does not really show the main interest of our technique: the scheduling automaton allows us to take in account properties which tightly depend on the way the synchronizations constraint the executions of the programs.

4 Conclusion and Future Work

We have presented an algorithm in order to compute a finite presentation of the trace space of concurrent programs, which may contain loops. An application to abstract interpretation has also described but remains to be implemented. In order to give a simple presentation of the algorithm, we have restricted ourselves here to programs of a simple form (in particular, we have omitted non-determinism). We shall extend our algorithm to more realistic programming languages in a subsequent article. Our approach can also be applied to languages with other synchronization primitives (monitors, send/recv, etc.), for which there are simple geometric semantics available. There are also many possible general improvements of the algorithm; the most appealing one would perhaps be to find a way to have a more modular way of computing the total schedulings by combining locally computed schedulings in $\vec{T}(X)(x, y)$ with varying endpoints x and y. In a near future, the schedulings provided by the algorithm will be used by our tool ALCOOL to analyze concurrent programs using abstract interpretation, thus providing one of the first tools able to do such a static analysis on concurrent programs without forgetting most of the possible synchronizations during their execution.

On the theoretical side, we envisage to study in details and use the structure of the index poset $\mathcal{C}(X)$ which contains much more information than only the schedulings of the program. Namely, it can be equipped with a structure of *prodsimplicial set* [22] (a structure similar to simplicial sets but whose elements are products of simplexes), whose geometric realization provides a topological space which is homotopy equivalent to the trace space $\vec{T}(X)$ [24]. This essentially means that $\mathcal{C}(X)$ contains all the geometry of the trace space and we plan to try to benefit from all the information it provides about the possible computations of a program. Our ALCOOL prototype actually implements this computation – using a combinatorial presentation of the prodsimplicial sets known as *simploidal sets* [23] – which will be reported elsewhere.

References

1. The SPIN Model-Checker, `http://spinroot.com/`
2. Berge, C.: Hypergraphs, vol. 445. North Holland Mathematical Library (1989)
3. Bonichon, R., Canet, G., Correnson, L., Goubault, E., Haucourt, E., Hirschowitz, M., Labbé, S., Mimram, S.: Rigorous Evidence of Freedom from Concurrency Faults in Industrial Control Software. In: Flammini, F., Bologna, S., Vittorini, V. (eds.) SAFECOMP 2011. LNCS, vol. 6894, pp. 85–98. Springer, Heidelberg (2011)
4. Clarke Jr., E.M., Grumberg, O., Peled, D.A.: Model Checking. MIT Press (1999)
5. Cousot, P., Cousot, R.: Systematic design of program analysis frameworks. In: Proceedings of Principles Of Programming Languages, pp. 269–282. ACM Press (1979)
6. Cousot, P., Cousot, R.: Abstract interpretation based program testing. In: Proc. of the SSGRR 2000 Computer & eBusiness International Conference (2000)
7. Diekert, V., Rozenberg, G.: The Book of Traces. World Scientific (1995)
8. Dijkstra, E.: The Structure of the THE Operating System. Com. of the ACM 11(15) (1968)
9. Dijkstra, E.W.: Hierarchical ordering of sequential processes. Acta Informatica 1(2) (1971)
10. Fajstrup, L.: Trace spaces of directed tori with rectangular holes. Technical Report R-2011-08, Aalborg Univ. (2001)
11. Fajstrup, L., Goubault, É., Raußen, M.: Detecting Deadlocks in Concurrent Systems. In: Sangiorgi, D., de Simone, R. (eds.) CONCUR 1998. LNCS, vol. 1466, pp. 332–347. Springer, Heidelberg (1998)
12. Fajstrup, L., Sokolowski, S.: Infinitely running concurrent processes with loops from a geometric viewpoint. ENTCS 39(2) (2000)
13. Fajstrup, L., Raußen, M., Goubault, E.: Algebraic topology and concurrency. Theor. Comput. Sci. 357(1-3), 241–278 (2006)
14. Fajstrup, L., Raußen, M., Goubault, E., Haucourt, E.: Components of the fundamental category. Appl. Cat. Struct. 12(1), 81–108 (2004)
15. Godefroid, P., Wolper, P.: Using Partial Orders for the Efficient Verification of Deadlock Freedom and Safety Properties. In: Larsen, K.G., Skou, A. (eds.) CAV 1991. LNCS, vol. 575, pp. 332–342. Springer, Heidelberg (1992)

16. Goubault, É., Haucourt, E.: A Practical Application of Geometric Semantics to Static Analysis of Concurrent Programs. In: Abadi, M., de Alfaro, L. (eds.) CONCUR 2005. LNCS, vol. 3653, pp. 503–517. Springer, Heidelberg (2005)
17. Goubault, E., Haucourt, E.: Components of the fundamental category II. Applied Categorical Structures 15(4), 387–414 (2007)
18. Goubault, E., Mimram, S.: Formal relationships between geometrical and classical models for concurrency. CoRR, abs/1004.2818 (2010)
19. Grandis, M.: Directed Algebraic Topology, Models of Non-Reversible Worlds. New Mathematical Monographs, vol. 13. Cambridge University Press (2009)
20. Gunawardena, J.: Homotopy and concurrency. Bulletin of the EATCS 54, 184–193 (1994)
21. Kavvadias, D.J., Stavropoulos, E.C.: Evaluation of an Algorithm for the Transversal Hypergraph Problem. In: Vitter, J.S., Zaroliagis, C.D. (eds.) WAE 1999. LNCS, vol. 1668, pp. 72–84. Springer, Heidelberg (1999)
22. Kozlov, D.: Combinatorial Algebraic Topology. Springer, Heidelberg (2007)
23. Peltier, S., Fuchs, L., Lienhardt, P.: Simploidals sets: Definitions, Operations and Comparison with Simplicial Sets. Discrete Applied Math. 157, 542–557 (2009)
24. Raussen, M.: Simplicial models of trace spaces. Alg. & Geom. Top. 10, 1683–1714 (2010)
25. Valmari, A.: A Stubborn Attack on State Explosion. In: Clarke, E., Kurshan, R.P. (eds.) CAV 1990. LNCS, vol. 531, pp. 156–165. Springer, Heidelberg (1991)

A Process Algebra for Wireless Mesh Networks

Ansgar Fehnker[1,4], Rob van Glabbeek[1,4], Peter Höfner[1,4], Annabelle McIver[2,1], Marius Portmann[1,3], and Wee Lum Tan[1,3]

[1] NICTA
[2] Department of Computing, Macquarie University
[3] School of ITEE, The University of Queensland
[4] Computer Science and Engineering, University of New South Wales

Abstract. We propose a process algebra for wireless mesh networks that combines novel treatments of local broadcast, conditional unicast and data structures. In this framework, we model the Ad-hoc On-Demand Distance Vector (AODV) routing protocol and (dis)prove crucial properties such as loop freedom and packet delivery.

1 Introduction

Wireless Mesh Networks (WMNs) have recently gained considerable popularity and are increasingly deployed in a wide range of application scenarios, including emergency response communication, intelligent transportation systems, mining, video surveillance, etc. WMNs are essentially self-organising wireless ad-hoc networks that can provide broadband communication without relying on a wired backhaul infrastructure. This has the benefit of rapid and low-cost network deployment. WMNs can be considered a superset of Mobile Ad-hoc Networks (MANETs), where a network consists exclusively of mobile end user devices such as laptops or smartphones. In contrast to MANETs, WMNs typically also contain stationary infrastructure devices called mesh routers. However, this distinction is not relevant for the purpose of this paper; what matters is that both MANETs and WMNs share the characteristic of highly dynamic network topologies, due to node mobility and the variable nature of wireless links.

In WMNs, a routing protocol is used to establish and maintain network connectivity through paths between source and destination node pairs. As a consequence, the routing protocol is one of the key factors determining the performance and reliability of WMNs. Traditionally, the main tools for evaluating and validating network protocols are simulation and test-bed experiments. The key limitations of these approaches are that they are very expensive, time consuming and non-exhaustive, i.e., they only cover a very limited set of network scenarios. As a result, protocol errors and limitations are still found many years after the definition and standardisation; for example, see [14].

Formal methods have a great potential in helping to address this problem, and can provide valuable tools for design, evaluation and verification of WMN routing protocols. The overall goal is to reduce the "time-to-market" for better (new or modified) WMN protocols, and to increase the reliability and performance of the corresponding networks.

H. Seidl (Ed.): ESOP 2012, LNCS 7211, pp. 295–315, 2012.

In this paper, we propose a process algebra that provides a step towards this goal. It combines novel treatments of data structures, conditional unicast and local broadcast, and allows formalisation of all important aspects of a routing protocol. All these features are necessary to model "real life" WMNs. Data structures are used to store and maintain information, e.g. routing tables. The conditional unicast construct allows us to model that a node in a network sends a message to a particular neighbour, and if this fails, for example because the receiver has moved out of transmission range, error handling is initiated. Finally, the local broadcast primitive, which allows a node to send messages to all its immediate neighbours, models the wireless broadcast mechanism implemented by the physical and data link layer of wireless standards relevant for WMNs. Our formalisation assumes that any broadcast message *is* received by all nodes within transmission range.[1] This abstraction enables us to interpret a failure of guaranteed message delivery as an imperfection in the protocol, rather than as a result of a chosen formalism not allowing guaranteed delivery.

To demonstrate the use of our algebra, in [6] we use it to formally model and reason about the Ad-Hoc On-Demand Distance Vector (AODV) routing protocol [16]—we outline this work here. AODV is one of the most relevant and widely used routing protocols in WMNs. Our model covers the complete core functionality of AODV and abstracts from timing and optional features only. The process algebra proposed in this paper allows us to prove critical protocol properties of AODV, such as loop freedom. We also use our model to show limitations of AODV, e.g. that AODV does not guarantee that messages are always delivered to their destinations, even if a stable route exists (cf. Section 3.4).

2 A Process Algebra for Wireless Routing Protocols

In this section we propose AWN, a process algebra for the specification of WMN routing protocols such as AODV. It models a WMN as an encapsulated parallel composition of network nodes. On each node several sequential processes may be running in parallel. Network nodes communicate with their direct neighbours—those nodes that are in transmission range—using either broadcast or unicast. Due to mobility of nodes and variability of wireless links, nodes can move in or out of transmission range. The encapsulation of the entire network inhibits communications between network nodes and the outside world, with the exception of the receipt and delivery of data packets from or to clients [2] of the modelled protocol that may be hooked up to various nodes.

[1] In reality, communication is only half-duplex: a network node cannot receive messages while sending and hence messages can be lost. However, the CSMA protocol used at the link layer—not modelled here—keeps the probability of packet loss due to two nodes (within range) sending at the same time rather low. Since we are examining imperfect protocols, we first of all want to establish how they behave under optimal conditions. For this reason we abstract from probabilistic reasoning by assuming no message loss at all, rather than working with a lossy broadcast formalism that offers no guarantees that any message will ever arrive.

[2] The application layer that initiates packet sending and awaits receipt of a packet.

2.1 A Language for Sequential Processes

The internal state of a process is determined, in part, by the values of certain data variables that are maintained by that process. To this end, we assume a data structure with several types, variables ranging over these types, operators and predicates. First order predicate logic yields terms (or *data expressions*) and formulas to denote data values and statements about them. Our data structure always contains the types $\mathtt{DATA}$, $\mathtt{MSG}$, $\mathtt{IP}$ and $\mathcal{P}(\mathtt{IP})$ of *application layer data*, *messages*, *IP addresses*—or any other node identifiers—and *sets of IP addresses*.

In addition, we assume a set of *process names*. Each process name X comes with a *defining equation*

$$X(\mathtt{var}_1, \ldots, \mathtt{var}_n) \stackrel{def}{=} p\ ,$$

in which $n \in \mathbb{N}$, the $\mathtt{var}_i$ are variables and p is a *sequential process expression* defined by the grammar below. It may contain the variables $\mathtt{var}_i$ as well as X. However, all occurrences of data variables in p have to be *bound*.[3] The choice of the underlying data structure and the process names with their defining equations can be tailored to any particular application of our language.

The *sequential process expressions* are given by the following grammar:

$$\begin{aligned} SP &::= X(\mathit{exp}_1, \ldots, \mathit{exp}_n) \mid [\varphi]SP \mid [\![\mathtt{var} := \mathit{exp}]\!]SP \mid SP + SP \mid \\ &\quad\ \alpha.SP \mid \textbf{unicast}(\mathit{dest}, \mathit{ms}).SP \blacktriangleright SP \\ \alpha &::= \textbf{broadcast}(\mathit{ms}) \mid \textbf{groupcast}(\mathit{dests}, \mathit{ms}) \mid \textbf{send}(\mathit{ms}) \mid \\ &\quad\ \textbf{deliver}(\mathit{data}) \mid \textbf{receive}(\mathtt{msg}) \end{aligned}$$

Here X is a process name, exp_i a data expression of the same type as $\mathtt{var}_i$, φ a data formula, $\mathtt{var} := \mathit{exp}$ an assignment of a data expression exp to a variable $\mathtt{var}$ of the same type, dest, dests, data and ms data expressions of types $\mathtt{IP}$, $\mathcal{P}(\mathtt{IP})$, $\mathtt{DATA}$ and $\mathtt{MSG}$, respectively, and $\mathtt{msg}$ a data variable of type $\mathtt{MSG}$.

Given a valuation of the data variables by concrete data values, the sequential process $[\varphi]p$ acts as p if φ evaluates to $\mathtt{true}$, and deadlocks if φ evaluates to $\mathtt{false}$. In case φ contains free variables that are not yet interpreted as data values, values are assigned to these variables in any way that satisfies φ, if possible. The sequential process $[\![\mathtt{var} := \mathit{exp}]\!]p$ acts as p, but under an updated valuation of the data variable $\mathtt{var}$. The sequential process $p + q$ may act either as p or as q, depending on which of the two processes is able to act at all. In a context where both are able to act, it is not specified how the choice is made. The sequential process $\alpha.p$ first performs the action α and subsequently acts as p. The action $\textbf{broadcast}(\mathit{ms})$ broadcasts (the data value bound to the expression) ms to the other network nodes within transmission range, whereas $\textbf{unicast}(\mathit{dest}, \mathit{ms}).p \blacktriangleright q$ is a process that tries to unicast the message ms to

---

[3] An occurrence of a data variable in p is *bound* if it is one of the variables $\mathtt{var}_i$, a variable $\mathtt{msg}$ occurring in a subexpression $\textbf{receive}(\mathtt{msg}).q$, a variable $\mathtt{var}$ occurring in a subexpression $[\![\mathtt{var} := \mathit{exp}]\!]q$, or an occurrence in a subexpression $[\varphi]q$ of a variable occurring free in φ. Here q is an arbitrary sequential process expression.

Table 1. Structural operational semantics for sequential process expressions

$$\xi, \textbf{broadcast}(ms).p \xrightarrow{\textbf{broadcast}(\xi(ms))} \xi, p$$

$$\xi, \textbf{groupcast}(dests, ms).p \xrightarrow{\textbf{groupcast}(\xi(dests),\xi(ms))} \xi, p$$

$$\xi, \textbf{unicast}(dest, ms).p \blacktriangleright q \xrightarrow{\textbf{unicast}(\xi(dest),\xi(ms))} \xi, p$$

$$\xi, \textbf{unicast}(dest, ms).p \blacktriangleright q \xrightarrow{\neg\textbf{unicast}(\xi(dest))} \xi, q$$

$$\xi, \textbf{send}(ms).p \xrightarrow{\textbf{send}(\xi(ms))} \xi, p$$

$$\xi, \textbf{deliver}(data).p \xrightarrow{\textbf{deliver}(\xi(data))} \xi, p$$

$$\xi, \textbf{receive}(\texttt{msg}).p \xrightarrow{\textbf{receive}(m)} \xi[\texttt{msg} := m], p \qquad (\forall m \in \texttt{MSG})$$

$$\xi, [\![\texttt{var} := exp]\!]p \xrightarrow{\tau} \xi[\texttt{var} := \xi(exp)], p$$

$$\frac{\emptyset[\texttt{var}_i := \xi(exp_i)]_{i=1}^{n}, p \xrightarrow{a} \zeta, p'}{\xi, X(exp_1, \ldots, exp_n) \xrightarrow{a} \zeta, p'} \quad (X(\texttt{var}_1, \ldots, \texttt{var}_n) \stackrel{def}{=} p) \qquad (\forall a \in \text{Act})$$

$$\frac{\xi, p \xrightarrow{a} \zeta, p'}{\xi, p + q \xrightarrow{a} \zeta, p'} \quad \frac{\xi, q \xrightarrow{a} \zeta, q'}{\xi, p + q \xrightarrow{a} \zeta, q'} \quad \frac{\xi \xrightarrow{\varphi} \zeta}{\xi, [\varphi]p \xrightarrow{\tau} \zeta, p} \qquad (\forall a \in \text{Act})$$

the destination *dest*; if successful it continues to act as p and otherwise as q. In other words, **unicast**(*dest*, *ms*).p is prioritised over q; only if the action **unicast**(*dest*, *ms*) is not possible, the alternative q will happen. It models an abstraction of an acknowledgment-of-receipt mechanism that is typical for unicast communication but absent in broadcast communication, as implemented by the link layer of relevant wireless standards such as IEEE 802.11. The process **groupcast**(*dests*, *ms*).p tries to transmit *ms* to all destinations *dests*, and proceeds as p regardless of whether any of the transmissions is successful. Unlike **unicast** and **broadcast**, the expression **groupcast** does not have a unique counterpart in networking. Depending on the protocol and the implementation it can be an iterative unicast, a broadcast, or a multicast; thus **groupcast** abstracts from implementation details. The action **send**(*ms*) synchronously transmits a message to another process running on the same node; this action can occur only when this other sequential process is able to receive the message. The sequential process **receive**(`msg`).p receives any message m (a data value of type `MSG`) either from another node, from another sequential process running on the same node or from the client hooked up to the local node. It then proceeds as p, but with the data variable `msg` bound to the value m. The submission of data from a client is modelled by the receipt of a message `newpkt`(d, *dip*), where the function `newpkt` generates a message containing the data d and the intended destination *dip*. Data is delivered to the client by **deliver**(*data*).

The internal state of a sequential process described by an expression p is determined by p, together with a *valuation* ξ associating values $\xi(\texttt{var})$ to variables `var` maintained by this process. Valuations naturally extend to ξ-*closed* expressions—those in which all variables are either bound or in the domain of ξ. The structural operational semantics of Table 1 is in the style of Plotkin [17] and describes how one internal state can evolve into another by performing

Table 2. Structural operational semantics for parallel process expressions

$$\frac{P \xrightarrow{a} P'}{P \langle\!\langle Q \xrightarrow{a} P' \langle\!\langle Q} \ (\forall a \neq \mathbf{receive}(m)) \qquad \frac{Q \xrightarrow{a} Q'}{P \langle\!\langle Q \xrightarrow{a} P \langle\!\langle Q'} \ (\forall a \neq \mathbf{send}(m))$$

$$\frac{P \xrightarrow{\mathbf{receive}(m)} P' \qquad Q \xrightarrow{\mathbf{send}(m)} Q'}{P \langle\!\langle Q \xrightarrow{\tau} P' \langle\!\langle Q'} \ (\forall m \in \mathtt{MSG})$$

an *action*. The set Act of actions consists of $\mathbf{broadcast}(m)$, $\mathbf{groupcast}(D,m)$, $\mathbf{unicast}(\mathit{dip},m)$, $\neg\mathbf{unicast}(\mathit{dip})$, $\mathbf{send}(m)$, $\mathbf{deliver}(d)$, $\mathbf{receive}(m)$ and internal actions τ, for each choice of $m \in \mathtt{MSG}$, $\mathit{dip} \in \mathtt{IP}$, $D \in \mathcal{P}(\mathtt{IP})$ and $d \in \mathtt{DATA}$. Here, $\neg\mathbf{unicast}(\mathit{dip})$ denotes a failed unicast. Moreover $\xi[\mathtt{var} := v]$ denotes the valuation that assigns the value v to the variable $\mathtt{var}$, and agrees with ξ on all other variables. The empty valuation $\emptyset$ assigns values to no variables. Hence $\emptyset[\mathtt{var}_i := v_i]_{i=1}^{n}$ is the valuation that *only* assigns the values v_i to the variables $\mathtt{var}_i$ for $i = 1, \ldots, n$. The rule for process names in Table 1 (Line 9) says that a process, named X, has the same transitions as the body p of its defining equation. (See [6] for details.) Finally, $\xi \xrightarrow{\varphi} \zeta$ says that ζ is an extension of ξ, i.e., a valuation that agrees with ξ on all variables on which ξ is defined, and evaluates other variables occurring free in φ, such that the formula φ holds under ζ. All variables not free in φ and not evaluated by ξ are also not evaluated by ζ.

2.2 A Language for Parallel Processes

Parallel process expressions are given by the grammar

$$PP ::= \xi, SP \mid PP \langle\!\langle PP ,$$

where SP is a sequential process expression and ξ a valuation. An expression ξ, p denotes a sequential process expression equipped with a valuation of the variables it maintains. The process $P \langle\!\langle Q$ is a parallel composition of P and Q, running on the same network node. As formalised in Table 2, an action $\mathbf{receive}(m)$ of P synchronises with an action $\mathbf{send}(m)$ of Q into an internal action τ. These receive actions of P and send actions of Q cannot happen separately. All other actions of P and Q occur interleaved in $P \langle\!\langle Q$. The variables of sequential processes running on the same node are maintained separately, and thus cannot be shared.

Though $\langle\!\langle$ is a restricted version of synchronisation, which only allows information flow "in one direction", it reflects reality of WMNs. Usually two sequential processes run on the same node: $P \langle\!\langle Q$. The main process P deals with all protocol details of the node, e.g., message handling and maintaining the data such as routing tables. The process Q manages the queueing of messages as they arrive; it is always able to receive a message even if P is busy. The use of message queueing in combination with $\langle\!\langle$ is crucial, since otherwise incoming messages would be lost when the process is busy dealing with other messages[4], which would not be an accurate model of what happens in real implementations.

[4] Assuming that one employs the optional augmentation of Section 2.5.

Table 3. Structural operational semantics for node expressions

$$\frac{P \xrightarrow{\textbf{broadcast}(m)} P'}{ip\!:\!P\!:\!R \xrightarrow{R\,:\,\textbf{*cast}(m)} ip\!:\!P'\!:\!R} \qquad \frac{P \xrightarrow{\textbf{groupcast}(D,m)} P'}{ip\!:\!P\!:\!R \xrightarrow{R\cap D\,:\,\textbf{*cast}(m)} ip\!:\!P'\!:\!R}$$

$$\frac{P \xrightarrow{\textbf{unicast}(dip,m)} P' \quad dip \in R}{ip\!:\!P\!:\!R \xrightarrow{\{dip\}\,:\,\textbf{*cast}(m)} ip\!:\!P'\!:\!R} \qquad \frac{P \xrightarrow{\neg\textbf{unicast}(dip)} P' \quad dip \notin R}{ip\!:\!P\!:\!R \xrightarrow{\tau} ip\!:\!P'\!:\!R}$$

$$\frac{P \xrightarrow{\textbf{deliver}(d)} P'}{ip\!:\!P\!:\!R \xrightarrow{ip\,:\,\textbf{deliver}(d)} ip\!:\!P'\!:\!R} \qquad \frac{P \xrightarrow{\textbf{receive}(m)} P'}{ip\!:\!P\!:\!R \xrightarrow{\{ip\}\neg\emptyset\,:\,\textbf{arrive}(m)} ip\!:\!P'\!:\!R}$$

$$\frac{P \xrightarrow{\tau} P'}{ip\!:\!P\!:\!R \xrightarrow{\tau} ip\!:\!P'\!:\!R} \qquad ip\!:\!P\!:\!R \xrightarrow{\emptyset\neg\{ip\}\,:\,\textbf{arrive}(m)} ip\!:\!P\!:\!R$$

$$ip\!:\!P\!:\!R \xrightarrow{\textbf{connect}(ip,ip')} ip\!:\!P\!:\!R \cup \{ip'\} \qquad ip\!:\!P\!:\!R \xrightarrow{\textbf{disconnect}(ip,ip')} ip\!:\!P\!:\!R - \{ip'\}$$

2.3 A Language for Networks

We model network nodes in the context of a WMN by *node expressions* of the form $ip\!:PP\!:R$. Here $ip \in \texttt{IP}$ is the *address* of the node, PP is a parallel process expression, and $R \in \mathcal{P}(\texttt{IP})$ is the *range* of the node—the set of nodes that are currently within transmission range of ip.

A *partial network* is then modelled by a *parallel composition* $\|$ of node expressions, one for every node in the network, and a *complete network* is a partial network within an *encapsulation operator* $[\_]$ that limits the communication of network nodes and the outside world to the receipt and the delivery of data packets to and from the application layer attached to the modelled protocol in the network nodes. This yields a grammar for network expressions:

$$N ::= [M] \qquad\qquad M ::= \;\; ip : PP : R \;\;|\;\; M\|M\;.$$

The operational semantics of node and network expressions of Tables 3 and 4 uses transition labels $R\!:\!\textbf{*cast}(m)$, $H\neg K\!:\!\textbf{arrive}(m)$, $\textbf{connect}(ip, ip')$, $\textbf{disconnect}(ip, ip')$, $ip\!:\!\textbf{newpkt}(d, dip)$, $ip\!:\!\textbf{deliver}(d)$ and τ. Again, $m \in \texttt{MSG}$, $d \in \texttt{DATA}$, $R \in \mathcal{P}(\texttt{IP})$, and $ip, ip' \in \texttt{IP}$. Moreover, $H, K \in \mathcal{P}(\texttt{IP})$ are sets of IP addresses. The action $R\!:\!\textbf{*cast}(m)$ casts a message m that can be received by the set R of network nodes. We do not distinguish whether this message has been broadcast, groupcast or unicast—the differences show up merely in the value of R. Recall that $D \in \mathcal{P}(\texttt{IP})$ denotes a set of intended destinations, and $dip \in \texttt{IP}$ a single destination. A failed unicast attempt on the part of its process is modelled as an internal action τ on the part of a node expression. The action $\textbf{send}(m)$ of a process does not give rise to any action of the corresponding node—this action of a sequential process cannot occur without communicating with a receive action of another sequential process running on the same node.

The action $H\neg K\!:\!\textbf{arrive}(m)$ states that the message m simultaneously arrives at all addresses $ip \in H$, and fails to arrive at all addresses $ip \in K$. The rules of

Table 4. Structural operational semantics for network expressions

$$\frac{M \xrightarrow{R:\mathbf{*cast}(m)} M' \quad N \xrightarrow{H\neg K:\mathbf{arrive}(m)} N'}{M\|N \xrightarrow{R:\mathbf{*cast}(m)} M'\|N' \qquad N\|M \xrightarrow{R:\mathbf{*cast}(m)} N'\|M'} \quad \left(\begin{array}{c} H \subseteq R \\ K \cap R = \emptyset \end{array}\right)$$

$$\frac{M \xrightarrow{H\neg K:\mathbf{arrive}(m)} M' \quad N \xrightarrow{H'\neg K':\mathbf{arrive}(m)} N'}{M\|N \xrightarrow{(H\cup H')\neg(K\cup K'):\mathbf{arrive}(m)} M'\|N'}$$

$$\frac{M \xrightarrow{R:\mathbf{*cast}(m)} M'}{[M] \xrightarrow{\tau} [M']} \qquad \frac{M \xrightarrow{\{ip\}\neg K:\mathbf{arrive}(\mathtt{newpkt}(d,dip))} M'}{[M] \xrightarrow{ip:\mathbf{newpkt}(d,dip)} [M']}$$

$$\frac{M \xrightarrow{a} M'}{M\|N \xrightarrow{a} M'\|N} \quad \frac{N \xrightarrow{a} N'}{M\|N \xrightarrow{a} M\|N'} \quad \frac{M \xrightarrow{a} M'}{[M] \xrightarrow{a} [M']} \quad \left(\forall a \in \left\{\begin{array}{c} ip\!:\!\mathbf{deliver}(d), \tau \\ \mathbf{connect}(ip, ip') \\ \mathbf{disconnect}(ip, ip') \end{array}\right\}\right).$$

Table 4 let an $R\!:\!\mathbf{*cast}(m)$-action of one node synchronise with an $\mathbf{arrive}(m)$ of all other nodes, where this $\mathbf{arrive}(m)$ amalgamates the arrival of message m at the nodes in the transmission range R, and the non-arrival at the other nodes. The rules for $\mathbf{arrive}(m)$ in Table 3 state that arrival of a message at a node happens if and only if the node receives it, whereas non-arrival can happen at any time. This embodies our assumption that, at any time, any message that is transmitted to a node within range of the sender is actually received by that node. (The eighth rule in Table 3, having no premises, may appear to say that any node ip has the option to disregard any message at any time. However, the encapsulation operator (below) prunes away all such disregard-transitions that do not synchronise with a cast action for which ip is out of range.)

Internal actions τ and the action $ip\!:\!\mathbf{deliver}(d)$ are simply inherited by node expressions from the processes that run on these nodes, and are interleaved in the parallel composition of nodes that makes up a network. Finally, we allow actions $\mathbf{connect}(ip, ip')$ and $\mathbf{disconnect}(ip, ip')$ for $ip, ip' \in \mathtt{IP}$ modelling a change in network topology. These actions can be thought of as occurring nondeterministically, or as actions instigated by the environment of the modelled network protocol. In this formalisation node ip' may be in the range of node ip, meaning that ip can send to ip', even when the reverse does not hold. For some applications, in particular the one to AODV in [6], it is useful to assume that ip' is in the range of ip if and only if ip is in the range of ip'. This symmetry can be enforced by adding the following rules to Table 3

$$ip\!:\!P\!:\!R \xrightarrow{\mathbf{connect}(ip',ip)} ip\!:\!P\!:\!R \cup \{ip'\} \qquad ip\!:\!P\!:\!R \xrightarrow{\mathbf{disconnect}(ip',ip)} ip\!:\!P\!:\!R - \{ip'\}$$

$$\frac{ip \notin \{ip', ip''\}}{ip\!:\!P\!:\!R \xrightarrow{\mathbf{connect}(ip',ip'')} ip\!:\!P\!:\!R} \qquad \frac{ip \notin \{ip', ip''\}}{ip\!:\!P\!:\!R \xrightarrow{\mathbf{disconnect}(ip',ip'')} ip\!:\!P\!:\!R}$$

and replacing the last three rules for (dis)connect actions by

$$\frac{M \xrightarrow{a} M' \quad N \xrightarrow{a} N'}{M\|N \xrightarrow{a} M'\|N'} \qquad \frac{M \xrightarrow{a} M'}{[M] \xrightarrow{a} [M']} \qquad \left(\forall a \in \left\{\begin{array}{c} \mathbf{connect}(ip, ip') \\ \mathbf{disconnect}(ip, ip') \end{array}\right\}\right).$$

The main purpose of the encapsulation operator is to ensure that no messages will be received that have never been sent. In a parallel composition of network nodes, any action **receive**(m) of one of the nodes *ip* manifests itself as an action $H\neg K$: **arrive**(m) of the parallel composition, with $ip \in H$. Such actions can happen (even) if within the parallel composition they do not communicate with an action ***cast**(m) of another component, because they might communicate with a ***cast**(m) of a node that is yet to be added to the parallel composition. However, once all nodes of the network are accounted for, we need to inhibit unmatched arrive actions, as otherwise our formalism would allow any node at any time to receive any message. One exception are those arrive actions that stem from an action **receive**(`newpkt(data, dip)`) of a sequential process running on a node, as those actions represent communication with the environment.

The encapsulation operator passes through internal actions, as well as delivery of data packets at destination nodes, this being an interaction with the outside world. ***cast**(m)-actions are declared internal actions at this level; they cannot be steered by the outside world. The connect and disconnect actions are passed through in Table 4, thereby placing them under control of the environment; to make them nondeterministic, their rules should have a τ-label in the conclusion, or alternatively the actions **connect**(ip, ip') and **disconnect**(ip, ip') should be thought of as internal. Finally, actions **arrive**(m) are simply blocked by the encapsulation—they cannot occur without synchronising with a ***cast**(m) — except for $\{ip\}\neg K$: **arrive**(`newpkt`(d, dip)) with $d \in$ `DATA` and $dip \in$ `IP`. This action represents a new data packet d that is submitted by a client of the modelled protocol to node *ip*, for delivery at destination *dip*.

2.4 Results on the Process Algebra

Our process algebra admits translation into one without data structures (although we cannot describe the target algebra without using data structures): the idea is to replace processes ξ, p by $\mathcal{T}_\xi(p)$, where $\mathcal{T}_\xi$ is defined inductively by

$$\mathcal{T}_\xi(\textbf{broadcast}(ms).p) = \textbf{broadcast}(\xi(ms)).\mathcal{T}_\xi(p),$$
$$\mathcal{T}_\xi(\textbf{receive}(\texttt{msg}).p) = \textstyle\sum_{m\in\texttt{MSG}} \textbf{receive}(m).\mathcal{T}_{\xi[\texttt{msg}:=m]}(p),$$
$$\mathcal{T}_\xi(X(exp_1,\ldots,exp_n)) = X_{\xi(exp_1),\ldots,\xi(exp_n)}, \text{ etc.}$$

This requires the introduction of a process name $X_{\vec{v}}$ for every substitution instance $\vec{v}$ of the arguments of X. The resulting process algebra has a structural operational semantics in the *de Simone* format, generating the same transition system—up to strong bisimilarity, $\leftrightarrow$ —as the original. It follows that $\leftrightarrow$, and many other semantic equivalences, are congruences on our language [19].

Theorem 2.1. *Strong bisimilarity is a congruence for all operators of our language.*

This is a deep result that usually takes many pages to establish (e.g., [20]). Here we get it directly from the existing theory on structural operational semantics, as a result of carefully designing our language within the disciplined framework described by de Simone [19]. □

Theorem 2.2. *$\langle\!\langle$ is associative, and $\|$ is associative and commutative, up to $\underline{\leftrightarrow}$.*

Proof. The operational rules for these operators fit a format presented in [5], guaranteeing associativity up to $\underline{\leftrightarrow}$. The *ASSOC*-de Simone format of [5] applies to all transition system specifications (TSSs) in de Simone format, and allows 7 different types of rules (named 1–7) for the operators in question. Our TSS is in De Simone format; the three rules for $\langle\!\langle$ of Table 2 are of types 1, 2 and 7, respectively. To be precise, it has rules 1_a for $a \in \text{Act} \setminus \{\textbf{receive}(m) \mid m \in \texttt{MSG}\}$, rules 2_a for $a \in \text{Act} \setminus \{\textbf{send}(m) \mid m \in \texttt{MSG}\}$, and rules $7_{(a,b)}$ for $(a,b) \in \{(\textbf{receive}(m), \textbf{send}(m)) \mid m \in \texttt{MSG}\}$. Moreover, the partial *communication function* $\gamma : \text{Act} \times \text{Act} \rightharpoonup \text{Act}$ is given by $\gamma(\textbf{receive}(m), \textbf{send}(m)) = \tau$. The main result of [5] is that an operator is guaranteed to be associative, provided that γ is associative and six conditions are fulfilled. In the absence of rules of types 3, 4, 5 and 6, five of these conditions are trivially fulfilled, and the remaining one reduces to

$$7_{(a,b)} \;\Rightarrow\; (1_a \Leftrightarrow 2_b) \;\wedge\; (2_a \Leftrightarrow 2_{\gamma(a,b)}) \;\wedge\; (1_b \Leftrightarrow 1_{\gamma(a,b)})\ .$$

Here 1_a says that rule 1_a is present, etc. This condition is met for $\langle\!\langle$ because the antecedent holds only when taking $(a,b) = (\textbf{receive}(m), \textbf{send}(m))$ for some $m \in \texttt{MSG}$. In that case 1_a is false, 2_b is false, and 2_a, 2_τ, 1_b and 1_τ are true. Moreover, $\gamma(\gamma(a,b),c)$ and $\gamma(a,\gamma(b,c))$ are never defined, thus making γ trivially associative. The argument for $\|$ being associative proceeds likewise. Here the only nontrivial condition is the associativity of γ, given by

$$\begin{aligned}\gamma(R\!:\!{*}\textbf{cast}(m), H\neg K\!:\!\textbf{arrive}(m)) &= \gamma(H\neg K\!:\!\textbf{arrive}(m), R\!:\!{*}\textbf{cast}(m))\\ &= R\!:\!{*}\textbf{cast}(m)\ ,\end{aligned}$$

provided $H \subseteq R$ and $K \cap R = \emptyset$, and

$$\gamma(H\neg K\!:\!\textbf{arrive}(m), H'\neg K'\!:\!\textbf{arrive}(m)) = (H \cup H')\neg(K \cup K')\!:\!\textbf{arrive}(m)\ .$$

Commutativity of $\|$ follows by symmetry. □

2.5 Optional Augmentation to Ensure Non-blocking Broadcast

Our process algebra, as presented above, is intended for networks in which each node is *input enabled* [11], meaning that it is always ready to receive any message, i.e., able to engage in the transition $\textbf{receive}(m)$ for any $m \in \texttt{MSG}$. In our model of AODV [6] we ensure this by equipping each node with a message queue that is always able to accept messages for later handling—even when the main sequential process is currently busy. This makes our model *non-blocking*, meaning that no sender can be delayed in transmitting a message simply because one of the potential recipients is not ready to receive it.

However, the operational semantics does allow blocking if one would (mis)use the process algebra to model nodes that are not input enabled. This is a logical consequence of insisting that any broadcast message *is* received by all nodes within transmission range.

Since the possibility of blocking can be regarded as a bad property of broadcast formalisms, one may wish to take away the expressiveness of the language that allows modelling a blocking broadcast. This is the purpose of the following optional augmentations of our operational semantics.

The first possibility is the addition of the rule $\dfrac{P \xrightarrow{\textbf{receive}(m)}\!\!\!\!\!/\;\;}{ip{:}P{:}R \xrightarrow{\{ip\}\neg\emptyset\,:\,\textbf{arrive}(m)} ip{:}P{:}R}$. It states that a message may arrive at a node *ip* regardless whether the node is ready to receive it; if it is not ready, the message is simply ignored, and the process running remains in the same state.

A variation on the same idea, elaborated in [6, Sect. 4.5], stems from the *Calculus of Broadcasting Systems* [18]. It consists in eliminating the negative premise in the above rule in favour of *discard* actions, thereby remaining within the de Simone format of structural operational semantics. Either of these two optional augmentations of our semantics gives rise to the same transition system. Moreover, when modelling networks in which all nodes are input enabled—as we do in [6]—the added rule for node expressions will never be used, and the resulting transition system is the same whether we use augmentation or not.

2.6 Illustrative Example

To illustrate the use of our process algebra AWN, we consider a network of two nodes a and b ($a, b \in \mathtt{IP}$) on which the same process is running, although starting in different states. The process describes a simple (toy-)protocol: whenever a new data packet for destination *dip* "appears",[5] the data is broadcast through the network until it finally reaches *dip*. A node alternates between broadcasting, and receiving and handling a message. The *data* stemming from a message received by node *ip* will be delivered to the application layer if the message is destined for *ip* itself. Otherwise the node forwards the message. Every message travelling through the network and handled by the protocol has the form $\mathtt{mg}(\mathit{data}, \mathit{dip})$, where $\mathit{data} \in \mathtt{DATA}$ is the data to be sent and $\mathit{dip} \in \mathtt{IP}$ is its destination. The behaviour of each node can be modelled by:

$$\begin{aligned}
&\mathtt{X}(\mathtt{ip};\mathtt{data},\mathtt{dip}) \stackrel{def}{=} \textbf{broadcast}(\mathtt{mg}(\mathtt{data},\mathtt{dip})).\mathtt{Y}(\mathtt{ip})\\
&\mathtt{Y}(\mathtt{ip}) \stackrel{def}{=} \textbf{receive}(\mathtt{m}).([\mathtt{m}{=}\mathtt{mg}(\mathtt{data},\mathtt{dip}) \wedge \mathtt{dip}{=}\mathtt{ip}]\ \textbf{deliver}(\mathtt{data}).\mathtt{Y}(\mathtt{ip})\\
&\qquad\qquad + [\mathtt{m}{=}\mathtt{mg}(\mathtt{data},\mathtt{dip}) \wedge \mathtt{dip}{\neq}\mathtt{ip}]\ \mathtt{X}(\mathtt{ip};\mathtt{data},\mathtt{dip}))\ .
\end{aligned}$$

If a node is in a state $\mathtt{X}(\mathit{ip}; \mathit{data}, \mathit{dip})$, where $\mathit{ip} \in \mathtt{IP}$ is the node's stored value of its own IP address, it will broadcast $\mathtt{mg}(\mathit{data}, \mathit{dip})$ and continue in state $\mathtt{Y}(\mathit{ip})$, meaning that all information about the message is dropped. If a node in state $\mathtt{Y}(\mathit{ip})$ receives a message m—a value that will be assigned to the variable m—it has two ways to continue: process $[\mathtt{m}{=}\mathtt{mg}(\mathtt{data},\mathtt{dip}) \wedge \mathtt{dip}{=}\mathtt{ip}]\ \textbf{deliver}(\mathtt{data}).\mathtt{Y}(\mathtt{ip})$ is enabled if the incoming message has the form $\mathtt{mg}(\mathit{data}, \mathit{dip})$ and the node itself is the destination of the message ($\mathtt{dip}{=}\mathtt{ip}$). In that case the data distilled from m will be delivered to the application layer, and the process returns to $\mathtt{Y}(\mathit{ip})$. Alternatively, if $[\mathtt{m}{=}\mathtt{mg}(\mathtt{data},\mathtt{dip}) \wedge \mathtt{dip}{\neq}\mathtt{ip}]$, the process continues as

[5] In this small example, we assume that new data packets just appear "magically"; of course one could use the message newpkt(data,dip) instead.

$\mathtt{X}(ip; data, dip)$, which will then broadcast another message with contents *data* and *dip*. Note that calls to processes use expressions as parameters.

Let us have a look at three scenarios. First, assume that the nodes a and b are within transmission range of each other; node a in state $\mathtt{X}(a; d, b)$, and node b in $\mathtt{Y}(b)$. This is formally expressed as $[a : \mathtt{X}(a; d, b) : \{b\} \parallel b : \mathtt{Y}(b) : \{a\}]$, although for compactness of presentation, below we just write $[\mathtt{X}(a; d, b) \parallel \mathtt{Y}(b)]$. In this case, node a broadcasts the message $\mathtt{mg}(d, b)$ and continues as $\mathtt{Y}(a)$. Node b receives the message, **delivers** d (after evaluation of the message) and continues as $\mathtt{Y}(a)$. Formally, we get transitions from one state to the other:

$$[\mathtt{X}(a; d, b) \parallel \mathtt{Y}(b)] \xrightarrow{a:\mathbf{*cast}(\mathtt{mg}(d,b))} \xrightarrow{\tau} \xrightarrow{b:\mathbf{deliver}(d)} [\mathtt{Y}(a) \parallel \mathtt{Y}(b)].$$

Here, the τ-transition is the action of evaluating the first of the two guards of a process $\mathtt{Y}$, and we left out the two intermediate expressions.

Second, assume that the nodes are not within transmission range, with the initial process of a and b the same as above; formally $[a : \mathtt{X}(a; d, b) : \emptyset \parallel b : \mathtt{Y}(b) : \emptyset]$. As before, node a broadcasts $\mathtt{mg}(d, b)$ and continues in $\mathtt{Y}(a)$; but this time the message is not received by any node; hence no message is forwarded or delivered and both nodes end up running process $\mathtt{Y}$.

For the last scenario, we assume that a and b are within transmission range and that they have the initial states $\mathtt{X}(a; d, b)$ and $\mathtt{X}(b; e, a)$. Without the augmentation of Section 2.5, the network expression $[\mathtt{X}(a; d, b) \parallel \mathtt{X}(b; e, a)]$ admits no transitions at all; neither node can broadcast its message, because the other node is not listening. With the optional augmentation, assuming that node a sends first:

$$\begin{aligned}[\mathtt{X}(a; d, b) \parallel \mathtt{X}(b; e, a)] &\xrightarrow{a:\mathbf{*cast}((\mathtt{mg}(d,b))} [\mathtt{Y}(a) \parallel \mathtt{X}(b; e, a)] \\ &\xrightarrow{b:\mathbf{*cast}(\mathtt{mg}(e,a))} \xrightarrow{\tau} \xrightarrow{a:\mathbf{deliver}(e)} [\mathtt{Y}(a) \parallel \mathtt{Y}(b)].\end{aligned}$$

Unfortunately, node b is initially in a state where it cannot receive a message, so a's message "remains unheard" and b will never deliver that message. To avoid this behaviour, and ensure that both messages get delivered, as happens in real WMNs, a message queue can be introduced (see Section 3.2). Using a message queue, the optional augmentation is not needed, since any node is always in a state where it can receive a message.

3 Routing Protocols

The features of our process algebra were largely determined by what we needed to enable a complete and accurate formalisation of wireless network protocols and their properties.

We use the proposed algebra to formally model and reason about the Ad hoc On-demand Distance Vector (AODV) routing protocol [16]. Due to lack of space, we can only briefly report on our formalisation and the properties proved. All details can be found in [6].

Since routing protocols for WMNs are based on common concepts in wireless networks in general, such as local broadcast, we do expect that our process algebra can easily be used to model other wireless network protocols.

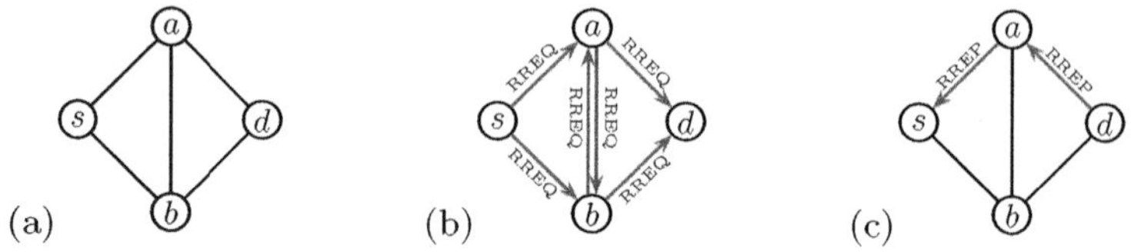

Fig. 1. Example network topology

3.1 Ad-Hoc On-Demand Distance Vector Routing Protocol

AODV [16] is a widely-used routing protocol designed for MANETs, and is one of the four protocols currently standardised by the IETF MANET working group[6]. It also forms the basis of new WMN routing protocols, including the upcoming IEEE 802.11s wireless mesh network standard [10].

AODV is a reactive protocol: routes are established only on demand. A route from a source node s to a destination node d is a sequence of nodes $[s, n_1, \ldots, n_k, d]$, where n_1, ..., n_k are intermediate nodes located on the path from s to d. Its basic operation can best be explained using a simple example topology shown in Fig. 1(a), where edges connect nodes within transmission range. We assume node s wants to send a data packet to node d, but s does not have a valid routing table entry for d. Node s initiates a route discovery mechanism by broadcasting a route request (RREQ) message, which is received by s's immediate neighbours a and b. We assume that neither a nor b knows a route to the destination node d.[7] Therefore, they simply re-broadcast the message, as shown in Fig. 1(b). Each RREQ message has a unique identifier which allows nodes to ignore duplicate RREQ messages that they have handled before.

When forwarding the RREQ message, each intermediate node updates its routing table and adds a "reverse route" entry to s, indicating via which next hop the node s can be reached, and the distance in number of hops. Once the first RREQ message is received by the destination node d (we assume via a), d also adds a reverse route entry in its routing table, saying that node s can be reached via node a, at a distance of 2 hops.

Node d then responds by sending a route reply (RREP) message back to node s, as shown in Fig. 1(c). In contrast to the RREQ message, the RREP is unicast, i.e., it is sent to an individual next hop node only. The RREP is sent from d to a, and then to s, using the reverse routing table entries created during the forwarding of the RREQ message. When processing the RREP message, a node creates a "forward route" entry into its routing table. For example, upon receiving the RREP via a, node s creates an entry saying that d can be reached via a, at a distance of 2 hops. At the completion of the route discovery process, a route has been established from s to d, and data packets can start to flow.

In the event of link and route breaks, AODV uses route error (RERR) messages to inform affected nodes. Sequence numbers are another important aspect

[6] `http://datatracker.ietf.org/wg/manet/charter/`

[7] In case an intermediate node knows a route to d, it directly sends a route reply back.

Table 5. Data structure

Type	Variables	Description
IP	ip, dip, oip, rip, sip, nhip	node identifiers
SQN	sn, dsn, rsn	sequence numbers
K	dsk	sequence-number-status flag
F	flag	route validity
$\mathbb{N}$	hops	hop counts
R	r	routing table entries
RT	rt	routing tables
RREQID	rreqid	request identifiers
P		pending-request flag
STORE	store	store of queued data packets
MSG	msg	messages
[MSG]	msgs	message queues
$\mathcal{P}$(IP)	pre	sets of identifiers (precursors, destinations, ...)
IP $\rightharpoonup$ SQN	dests	sets of destinations with sequence numbers
$\mathcal{P}$(IP $\times$ RREQID)	rreqs	sets of request identifiers with originator IP

Constant/Predicate	Description
0 : SQN, 1 : SQN	unknown, smallest sequence number
$<\ \subseteq$ SQN $\times$ SQN	strict order on sequence numbers
kno, unk : K	constants to distinguish known and unknown sqns
val, inv : F	constants to distinguish valid and invalid routes
pen, non-pen : P	constants to distinguish (non-)pending RREQs
[] : [MSG]	empty queue

Operator	Description
setP : STORE $\times$ IP $\times$ P $\rightarrow$ STORE	set the pending-request flag
$(\_,\_,\_,\_,\_,\_,\_)$: IP$\times$SQN$\times$K$\times$F$\times$ $\mathbb{N}$ $\times$IP$\times\mathcal{P}$(IP) $\rightarrow$ R	generates a routing table entry
inc : SQN $\rightarrow$ SQN	increments the sequence number
sqn : RT $\times$ IP $\rightarrow$ SQN	returns the sequence number of a particular route
flag : RT $\times$ IP $\rightharpoonup$ F	returns the validity of a particular route
dhops : RT $\times$ IP $\rightharpoonup$ $\mathbb{N}$	returns the hop count of a particular route
nhop : RT $\times$ IP $\rightharpoonup$ IP	returns the next hop of a particular route
precs : RT $\times$ IP $\rightharpoonup$ $\mathcal{P}$(IP)	returns the set of precursors of a particular route
vD, kD : RT $\rightarrow$ $\mathcal{P}$(IP)	returns the set of valid, known destinations
addpreRT : RT $\times$ IP $\times$ $\mathcal{P}$(IP) $\rightharpoonup$ RT	adds a set of precursors to an entry inside a table
update : RT $\times$ R $\rightharpoonup$ RT	updates a routing table with a route (if fresh enough)
invalidate : RT $\times$ (IP $\rightharpoonup$ SQN) $\rightarrow$ RT	invalidates a set of routes within a routing table
rrep : $\mathbb{N}$ $\times$IP $\times$ SQN $\times$ IP $\times$ IP $\rightarrow$ MSG	generates a route reply
rerr : (IP $\rightharpoonup$ SQN) $\times$ IP $\rightarrow$ MSG	generates a route error message

of AODV, and are used to indicate the freshness of routing table entries for the purpose of preventing routing loops.

3.2 A Formal Model of AODV

Our formalisation of AODV is a faithful rendering of the IETF's specification [16] with the exception of time and any optional features. Additionally, we model the submission, forwarding and delivery of data packets—this is not part of the AODV standard, but crucial to trigger the route discovery process of AODV.

In this section we give an overview of the formal model, setting out the details only for the RREP message handling. Full details are available in [6, Sect. 6].

Table 5 lists the types and operators needed for the formalisation presented in this section. For example, RT is the type of routing tables—modelled as set of entries (*dip*, *dsn*, *dsk*, *flag*, *hops*, *nhip*, *pre*), each providing information on a route of length *hops* with ultimate destination *dip*. The next hop address on that route is *nhip*. The value *dsn* is a *sequence number*, intended to describe the "freshness" of this entry, with *dsk* a Boolean indicating whether or not that number is known to be an up-to-date indicator of the freshness of the entry. The values *flag* and *pre*, respectively, describe the validity of the entry, and its *precursors*—a set of nodes that "rely" on it to ensure the validity of their own entries. In a routing table *rt* there is at most one entry for each destination *dip*; $\texttt{sqn}(rt, dip)$ denotes the sequence number of that entry and likewise for the operators `flag` and `dhops`. Another example is $\texttt{update}(rt, r)$, which updates a routing table *rt* with an entry *r*. This is one of the major activities of AODV. It adds $r := (dip, dsn, dsk, flag, hops, nhip, pre)$ to the routing table *rt* if no entry for *dip* is present. The existing entry is overwritten by *r* if the latter's sequence number is larger ($dsn > \texttt{sqn}(rt, dip)$) or, in case of equal sequence numbers, the existing entry is invalid, or the new hop count smaller ($dsn = \texttt{sqn}(rt, dip) \wedge (\texttt{flag}(rt, dip) = \texttt{inv} \vee hops < \texttt{dhops}(rt, dip))$).

A network is modelled as a parallel composition of its constituent nodes.[8] For all nodes of a network—characterised by a set $\mathbf{IP} \subseteq \texttt{IP}$ of unique identifiers $ip \in \mathbf{IP}$—the node expression $ip : P : R$ is initialised with the parallel process

$$P \quad := \quad \xi, \texttt{AODV(ip,rt,sn,rreqs,store)} \ \langle\!\langle \ \zeta, \texttt{QMSG(msgs)} \ .$$

The sequential process `AODV(ip,rt,sn,rreqs,store)` deals with the detailed message handling of the node, manages its routing table `rt`, stores its own sequence number in `sn`, records all route requests seen so far in `rreqs` and maintains in `store` packets to be sent. The process `QMSG(msgs)` manages the queueing of messages as they arrive; it is always able to receive a message even if `AODV` is busy updating `rt`, forwarding requests etc. Whenever a message arrives `QMSG(msgs)` appends it to the queue `msgs`, passing it on to `AODV` whenever it can. The composition $\langle\!\langle$ is crucial here to express this "buffering mechanism" occurring in actual implementations of AODV.

Any node is initialised with its own identifier stored in the variable `ip`, an empty routing table, the sequence number 1, and empty sets of seen route requests and stored data packets. Also the queue of received messages is empty.

The process `AODV` receives messages from `QMSG` and then, depending on their types, delegates the response to the appropriate process : `PKT` (for data), `RREQ` (for requests), `RREP` (for replies) and `RERR` (for errors). In this paper we give only the specification of `RREP` (cf. Process 1); the specifications of the other processes can be found in [6, Sect. 6].

Usually, `RREP` updates the routing table with information from the route reply message `rrep(hops,dip,dsn,oip,sip)`, meaning that it is a reply to a former request initiated by `oip` for destination `dip`, that it was sent by (1-hop neighbour) `sip`, and that it takes `hops` hops from `sip` to `dip`. The sequence number `dsn` measures the "freshness" of this information. In case the current node is `oip`, receipt of this message establishes a route from `oip` to `dip`. Only when the new information leads to an actual update of the routing table (Line 2), and the

[8] Here, associativity and commutativity of $\|$ (Theorem 2.2) is essential.

Process 1. RREP handling

```
RREP(hops , dip , dsn , oip , sip ; ip , rt , sn , rreqs , store) ≝
1.  /*routing that describes the handling of a received route reply*/
2.  [ rt ≠ update(rt, (dip, dsn, kno, val, hops+1, sip, ∅)) ]    /*the routing table has to be updated*/
3.    (
4.      ⟦rt := update(rt, (dip, dsn, kno, val, hops + 1, sip, ∅))⟧
5.      [ oip = ip ]    /*this node is the originator of the corresponding RREQ*/
6.        ⟦store := setP(store, dip, non-pen)⟧    /*set queue-flag to non-pending*/
7.        /*a packet may now be sent; this is done in the process AODV*/
8.        AODV(ip,sn,rt,rreqs,store)
9.      + [ oip ≠ ip ]    /*this node is not the originator; forward RREP*/
10.       (
11.         [ oip ∈ vD(rt) ]    /*valid route to oip*/
12.           /*add next hop towards oip as precursor and forward the route reply*/
13.           ⟦rt := addpreRT(rt, dip, {nhop(rt, oip)})⟧
14.           ⟦rt := addpreRT(rt, nhop(rt, dip), {nhop(rt, oip)})⟧
15.           unicast(nhop(rt,oip),rrep(hops + 1,dip,dsn,oip,ip)) .
16.             AODV(ip,sn,rt,rreqs,store)
17.           ▶ /*If the packet transmission is unsuccessful, a RERR message is generated*/
18.             ⟦dests := {(rip, inc(sqn(rt, rip))) | rip ∈ vD(rt) ∧ nhop(rt, rip) = nhop(rt, oip)}⟧
19.             ⟦rt := invalidate(rt, dests)⟧
20.             ⟦pre := ⋃{precs(rt, rip) | (rip, ∗) ∈ dests}⟧
21.             ⟦dests := {(rip, rsn) | (rip, rsn) ∈ dests  ∧  precs(rt, rip) ≠ ∅⟧
22.             groupcast(pre,rerr(dests,ip)) . AODV(ip,sn,rt,rreqs,store)
23.         + [ oip ∉ vD(rt) ]    /*no valid route to oip*/
24.           AODV(ip,sn,rt,rreqs,store)
25.       )
26.   )
27. + [ rt = update(rt, (dip, dsn, kno, val, hops + 1, sip, ∅)) ]    /*the routing table is not updated*/
28.   (
29.     [ oip = ip ]    /*this node is the originator of the corresponding RREQ*/
30.       ⟦store := setP(store, dip, non-pen)⟧    /*set queue-flag to non-pending*/
31.       AODV(ip,sn,rt,rreqs,store)
32.     + [ oip ≠ ip ]    /*this node is not the originator; drop RREP*/
33.       AODV(ip,sn,rt,rreqs,store)
34.   )
```

current node is not the final destination `oip` of the route reply (Line 9), the RREP message will be forwarded (Line 15). In case the unicast is unsuccessful (Line 17), the link connecting the current node to `nhop(rt, oip)` must be broken and the process initiates the procedure for error reporting (Lines 18–22). This involves determining which other nodes are "interested" in that link, because it contributes to their routes. Those interested nodes are stored in the precursor lists inside `rt` and an error message is sent to the nodes it finds there via the action **groupcast**. Before that, the node marks as invalid all routes in its routing table which use the failed link, and increments their sequence numbers (Lines 18–19).

3.3 Invariants

All processes except `QMSG` maintain the five data variables `ip`, `sn`, `rt`, `rreqs` and `store`. Next to that `QMSG` maintains the variable `msgs`. Hence, these 6 variables can be evaluated at any time. Moreover, every node expression in the transition system looks like

$$ip : (\xi, P \;\langle\!\langle\; \zeta, \texttt{QMSG}(\texttt{msgs})) : R \;,$$

where P is a state either in the process AODV, PKT, RREQ, RREP or RERR. Hence the state of the transition system for a node ip is determined by the process P, the range R, and the two valuations ξ and ζ. If a network consists of a (finite) set $\mathbf{IP} \subseteq \mathtt{IP}$ of nodes, a reachable network expression N is an encapsulated parallel composition of node expressions—one for each $ip \in \mathbf{IP}$. To distil current information about a node from N, we define the following projections for valuation ξ and range R:

$$R_N^{ip} := R, \text{ where } ip : (*, * \langle\!\langle *, *) : R \text{ is a node expression of } N \ ,$$
$$\xi_N^{ip} := \xi, \text{ where } ip : (\xi, * \langle\!\langle *, *) : * \text{ is a node expression of } N \ .$$

For example, $\xi_N^{ip}(\mathtt{rt})$ evaluates the current routing table maintained by node ip in the network expression N.

Proposition 3.1. If a route reply is sent by a node ip_c, different from the destination of the route, then the content of ip_c's routing table must be consistent with the information inside the message, i.e., if

$$N \xrightarrow{R:*\mathbf{cast}(\mathtt{rrep}(hops_c, dip_c, dsn_c, *, ip_c))} N'$$

then $dip_c \in \mathtt{kD}(\xi_N^{ip_c}(\mathtt{rt}))$, $\mathtt{sqn}(\xi_N^{ip_c}(\mathtt{rt}), dip_c) = dsn_c$, $\mathtt{dhops}(\xi_N^{ip_c}(\mathtt{rt}), dip_c) = hops_c$, and $\mathtt{flag}(\xi_N^{ip_c}(\mathtt{rt}), ip_c) = \mathtt{val}$.

Proof. We have to check all cases where a route reply is sent. Here we restrict ourselves to RREP; the entire proof can be found in [6, Prop. 7.10(b)]. A route reply occurs only in Line 15, where a message $\xi(\mathtt{rrep}(\mathtt{hops}+1, \mathtt{dip}, \mathtt{dsn}, \mathtt{oip}, \mathtt{ip}))$ is unicast. Here ξ is the current valuation ξ_N^{ip}.

Hence $hops_c := \xi(\mathtt{hops})+1$, $dip_c := \xi(\mathtt{dip})$, $dsn_c := \xi(\mathtt{dsn})$, $ip_c := \xi(\mathtt{ip}) = ip$ and $\xi_N^{ip_c} = \xi$. Using $(\xi(\mathtt{dip}), \xi(\mathtt{dsn}), \mathtt{kno}, \mathtt{val}, \xi(\mathtt{hops})+1, \xi(\mathtt{sip}), \emptyset)$ as new entry, the routing table is updated at Line 4. With exception of its precursors, which are irrelevant here, the routing table does not change between Lines 4 and 15; nor do the values of the variables hops, dip and dsn. Line 2 guarantees that during the update in Line 4, the new entry is inserted into the routing table, so

$$\begin{array}{lcl cl}
\mathtt{sqn}(\xi(\mathtt{rt}), \xi(\mathtt{dip})) & = & \xi(\mathtt{dsn}) & = & dsn_c \\
\mathtt{dhops}(\xi(\mathtt{rt}), \xi(\mathtt{dip})) & = & \xi(\mathtt{hops}) + 1 & = & hops_c \\
\mathtt{flag}(\xi(\mathtt{rt}), \xi(\mathtt{dip})) & = & \xi(\mathtt{val}) & = & \mathtt{val}\ .
\end{array}$$

□

The classical notion of loop freedom is a term that informally means that "a packet never goes round in cycles without (at some point) being delivered". This dynamic definition is not only hard to formalise, it is also too restrictive a requirement for AODV. There are situations where packets are sent in cycles, but which are not considered "bad". This can happen when the destination is highly mobile and the packet "follows" the destination and keeps travelling through the network. Therefore, the sense of loop freedom is much better captured by a static invariant, saying that at any given time the collective routing tables of the nodes do not admit a loop.

To this end we define the *routing graph* of network expression N with respect to destination *dip* by $\mathcal{R}_N(dip) := (\mathbf{IP}, E)$, where all nodes of the network form the set of vertices and there is an arc $(ip, ip') \in E$ iff $ip \neq dip$ and $(dip, *, *, \mathtt{val}, *, ip', *) \in \xi_N^{ip}(\mathtt{rt})$.

An arc in a routing graph states that ip' is the next hop on a valid route to *dip* known by *ip*; a path in a routing graph describes a route towards *dip* discovered by AODV. We say that a network expression N is *loop free* if the corresponding routing graphs $\mathcal{R}_N(dip)$ are loop free, for all $dip \in \mathbf{IP}$. A routing protocol, such as AODV, is *loop free* iff all reachable network expressions are loop free.

To prove loop freedom of AODV, we first establish a useful invariant.

Theorem 3.2. Along a path towards a destination *dip* in the routing graph of a reachable network expression N, until it reaches either *dip* or a node without a valid routing table entry to dip, either the sequence number strictly increases, or this number stays the same and the hop count strictly decreases.

$$\begin{aligned}
&dip \in \mathtt{vD}(\xi_N^{ip}(\mathtt{rt})) \cap \mathtt{vD}(\xi_N^{nhip}(\mathtt{rt})) \ \wedge\ nhip \neq dip \\
&\Rightarrow \mathtt{sqn}(\xi_N^{ip}(\mathtt{rt}), dip) < \mathtt{sqn}(\xi_N^{nhip}(\mathtt{rt}), dip) \ \vee\ \big(\mathtt{sqn}(\xi_N^{ip}(\mathtt{rt}), dip) = \mathtt{sqn}(\xi_N^{nhip}(\mathtt{rt}), dip) \\
&\quad \wedge\ \mathtt{dhops}(\xi_N^{ip}(\mathtt{rt}), dip) > \mathtt{dhops}(\xi_N^{nhip}(\mathtt{rt}), dip)\big)\ ,
\end{aligned}$$

where N is a reachable network expression and $nhip := \mathtt{nhop}_N^{ip}(dip)$ is the IP address of the next hop.

The proof uses Proposition 3.1; it can be found in [6].

From this, we immediately conclude that AODV is loop free.

More precisely, *our* AWN-specification of AODV is loop free. It is our belief that, up to the abstraction of time and any optional features presented in [16], it reflects precisely the intention and the meaning of the RFC. However, when formalising AODV, we came across ambiguities, which yield different possible interpretations. Such interpretations can be seen as variants of AODV and, as we discovered, only a few of them are loop free. Since loop freedom is a sine qua non for routing protocols like AODV, we endeavour to resolve the ambiguities as much as possible by discarding the interpretations that lead to loops.

We briefly explain one of the problems found. A crucial requirement in the proof of Theorem 3.2 is that sequence numbers in routing table entries are never decreased, and increased upon invalidating the entry. Following the RFC literally, a "node initiates processing for a RERR message"[9], "if it receives a RERR from a neighbor"[9]. For every destination to be invalidated the "destination sequence number"[9] is "copied from the incoming RERR"[9]. We have shown that this copying in combination with *self-entries* (entries for *ip* in *ip*'s own routing table)[10] violate the above requirement and yield loops; a detailed example is given in [6]. In our specification this behaviour does not occur since we slightly modified the invalidation procedure [6, Sect. 5] to ensure an increase of sequence number for an invalidated entry, in the spirit of Section 6.2 of the RFC.

[9] Section 6.11 of the RFC [16].

[10] In our model we allow self-entries, since they are not explicitly forbidden; they also occur in real implementations, e.g., Kernel AODV [1]; they are forbidden by others such as AODV-UU [2].

3.4 Formalising Temporal Properties

Our formalism enables verification of correctness properties. While some properties, such as loop freedom, are invariants on the routing tables, others require reasoning about the temporal order of transitions. We use Computation Tree Logic (CTL) to specify and discuss one such property, namely *packet delivery.*

CTL uses the path quantifiers **A** and **E**, and the temporal operators $\mathbf{G}, \mathbf{F}, \mathbf{X}$, and **U**. The (state) formula $\mathbf{A}\phi$ is satisfied in a state if all paths starting in that state satisfy ϕ, while $\mathbf{E}\phi$ is satisfied if some path satisfies ϕ. The (path) formulas $\mathbf{G}\phi, \mathbf{F}\phi$ and $\mathbf{X}\phi$ mean that ϕ holds globally in all states, in some state, and in the next state of a path, respectively. The *until* $\phi\mathbf{U}\psi$ means that, until a state occurs along the path that satisfies ψ, property ϕ has to hold. In CTL a temporal operator is always immediately preceded by a path quantifier. Here CTL is interpreted on the unfolding into a tree of the transition system generated by our operational semantics.

The property of *packet delivery* says that if a client submits a packet, it will eventually be delivered to the destination. However, in a WMN it is not guaranteed that this property holds, since nodes can get disconnected, e.g. due to node mobility. A useful formulation has to be weaker. AODV should guarantee *packet delivery* only if an end-to-end route exists long enough. More precisely, AODV should guarantee delivery of a packet submitted by a client at node *oip* with destination *dip*, when *oip* is connected to *dip* and afterwards no link in the network gets disconnected. This means that for any pair *oip* and *dip*, and any data *d*, the following should hold:

$$\begin{aligned}&\mathbf{AG}(\mathit{oip} : \mathbf{newpkt}(d, \mathit{dip}) \wedge \mathbf{connected}^*(\mathit{oip}, \mathit{dip}))\\ &\quad\Rightarrow \mathbf{AF}(\mathbf{disconnect}(*, *) \vee (\mathit{dip} : \mathbf{deliver}(d))) \ .\end{aligned}$$

$\mathit{oip}\!:\!\mathbf{newpkt}(d, \mathit{dip})$ models submission of a new packet at *oip*, $\mathit{dip}\!:\!\mathbf{deliver}(d)$ that the destination receives it, and $\mathbf{disconnect}(*, *)$ the action of disconnecting. We treat these transitions as predicates, with the understanding that along a path the state immediately succeeding such a transition satisfies it. The predicate $\mathbf{connected}^*(\mathit{oip}, \mathit{dip})$ is true if there are exist nodes $\mathit{ip}_0, \ldots, \mathit{ip}_n$ such that $\mathit{ip}_0 = \mathit{oip}$, $\mathit{ip}_n = \mathit{dip}$ and $\mathit{ip}_i \in R_N^{\mathit{ip}_{i-1}}$. for $i = 1, \ldots, n$.

Surprisingly, AODV does not satisfy this property. One cause is that AODV nodes do not forward route replies from which they do not learn anything new. However, the information may be vital for the potential recipients of the forwarding. See [6, Sect. 8] for further discussion of a counterexample.

4 Related Work

Several process algebras for MANETs have been proposed: CBS# [15], CWS [13], CMAN [8], CMN [12], the ω-calculus [20] and RBPT [7]. All these languages, as well as ours, feature a form of local broadcast, in which a single message, sent by one node, can be received by other nodes within transmission range, given an arbitrary topology. In CWS the topology is fixed, whereas the other formalisms deal with arbitrary changes in topology.

The latter four formalisms model a *lossy* broadcast, in which a potential receiver may lose a message; in CBS# and CWS, any node within range must receive a message m sent to it, provided the node is *ready* to receive it, i.e., in a state that admits a transition **receive**(m). This proviso makes all these calculi *non-blocking*, meaning that no sender can be delayed in sending a message simply because one of the potential recipients is not ready to receive it.

The syntax of CBS# and CWS does not permit the construction of meaningful nodes that are always ready to receive a message. Hence our model is the first that assumes that any message is received by a potential recipient within range. It is this feature that allows us to evaluate whether a protocol satisfies the *packet delivery* property. *Any* routing protocol formalised in any of the other formalisms would automatically fail to satisfy such a property.

Besides this ensured broadcast, the novel *conditional unicast* operator chooses a continuation process dependent on whether the message can be delivered. This operator is essential for the correct formalisation of AODV. In practice such an operator may be implemented by means of an acknowledgement mechanism; however, this is done at the link layer, from which the AODV specification [16], and hence our formalism, abstracts. One could formalise a conditional unicast as a standard unicast in the scope of a priority operator [4]; however, our operator prioritises, while allowing an operational semantics within the de Simone format.

Although our treatment of data structures follows the classical approach of universal algebra, and is in the spirit of formalisms like μCRL [9], we have not seen a process algebra that freely mixes in imperative programming constructs like variable assignment. Yet this helps to properly capture AODV and other routing protocols.

Our formalisation of AODV [6], which is partly shown here, has grown from elaborating a partial formalisation of AODV in [20]. The features of our process algebra were largely determined by what we needed to enable a complete and accurate formalisation of this protocol. We conjecture that the same formalism is also applicable to a wide range of other wireless protocols.

Loop freedom is a crucial property of network protocols, commonly claimed to hold for AODV [16]. In [6] we show that several *interpretations* of AODV—consistent ways to revolve the ambiguities in the RFC—fail to be loop free, while proving loop freedom of others. A preliminary draft of AODV has been shown to be not loop free (for other reasons) in [3]. In [21] a proof sketch of loop freedom for a restricted version of AODV is given, using an interactive theorem prover.

5 Conclusion and Outlook

We have proposed a novel algebra covering major aspects of WMN routing protocols. We have accurately modelled the core of AODV, a widely used protocol of practical relevance. In contrast to other works, our model covers the crucial aspect of data handling, such as maintaining routing table information. We have formalised and proven some of AODV's general properties. Our model provides, in combination with abstraction from lower network layers, a practical and powerful tool for WMN protocol specification, evaluation and verification.

Our analysis of AODV uncovered several ambiguities in the RFC [16]. Finding ambiguities and unexpected behaviour is not uncommon for RFCs in general. This shows that the specification of a reasonably rich protocol such as AODV cannot be described precisely and unambiguously by simple (English) text only; formal methods are indispensable for this purpose.

More detailed analysis requires the addition of time and probability: the former to cover aspects such as AODV's handling (deletion) of stale routing table entries and the latter to model the probability associated with lossy links.

References

1. Kernel AODV (v. 2.2.2), NIST, http://www.antd.nist.gov/wctg/aodv_kernel/ (accessed January 6, 2012)
2. AODV-UU: An implementation of the AODV routing protocol (IETF RFC 3561), http://sourceforge.net/projects/aodvuu/ (accessed January 6, 2012)
3. Bhargavan, K., Obradovic, D., Gunter, C.A.: Formal verification of standards for distance vector routing protocols. J. ACM 49(4), 538–576 (2002), http://dx.doi.org/10.1145/581771.581775
4. Cleaveland, R., Lüttgen, G., Natarajan, V.: Priority in process alegbra. In: Handbook of Process Algebra, ch.12, pp. 711–765. Elsevier (2001)
5. Cranen, S., Mousavi, M.R., Reniers, M.A.: A Rule Format for Associativity. In: van Breugel, F., Chechik, M. (eds.) CONCUR 2008. LNCS, vol. 5201, pp. 447–461. Springer, Heidelberg (2008)
6. Fehnker, A., van Glabbeek, R.J., Höfner, P., McIver, A., Portmann, M., Tan, W.L.: A process algebra for wireless mesh networks used for modelling, verifying and analysing AODV. Tech. Rep. 5513, NICTA (2012), http://www.nicta.com.au/pub?id=5513
7. Ghassemi, F., Fokkink, W.J., Movaghar, A.: Restricted broadcast process theory. In: Proc. IEEE SEFM 2008 (2008)
8. Godskesen, J.C.: A Calculus for Mobile Ad Hoc Networks. In: Murphy, A.L., Ryan, M. (eds.) COORDINATION 2007. LNCS, vol. 4467, pp. 132–150. Springer, Heidelberg (2007)
9. Groote, J.F., Ponse, A.: The syntax and semantics of μCRL. In: Algebra of Communicating Processes 1994. Workshops in Computing, pp. 26–62. Springer, Heidelberg (1995)
10. Hiertz, G.R., Denteneer, D., Max, S., Taori, R., Cardona, J., Berlemann, L., Walke, B.: IEEE 802.11s: the WLAN mesh standard. IEEE Wireless Communications 17(1), 104–111 (2010), http://dx.doi.org/10.1109/MWC.2010.5416357
11. Lynch, N., Tuttle, M.: An introduction to input/output automata. CWI-Quarterly 2(3), 219–246 (1989); centrum voor Wiskunde en Informatica, Amsterdam, The Netherlands
12. Merro, M.: An observational theory for mobile ad hoc networks. Inf. Comput. 207(2), 194–208 (2009)
13. Mezzetti, N., Sangiorgi, D.: Towards a calculus for wireless systems. Electr. Notes Theor. Comput. Sci. 158, 331–353 (2006)
14. Miskovic, S., Knightly, E.W.: Routing primitives for wireless mesh networks: Design, analysis and experiments. In: IEEE INFOCOM, pp. 2793–2801 (2010), http://dx.doi.org/10.1109/INFCOM.2010.5462111

15. Nanz, S., Hankin, C.: A framework for security analysis of mobile wireless networks. Theor. Comput. Sci. 367, 203–227 (2006)
16. Perkins, C., Belding-Royer, E., Das, S.: Ad hoc on-demand distance vector (AODV) routing. RFC 3561 (2003), `http://www.ietf.org/rfc/rfc3561.txt`
17. Plotkin, G.: A structural approach to operational semantics. The Journal of Logic and Algebraic Programming 60- 61, 17–139 (2004) (originally appeared in 1981)
18. Prasad, K.V.S.: A calculus of broadcasting systems. Sci. Comput. Program. 25(2-3), 285–327 (1995)
19. de Simone, R.: Higher-level synchronising devices in MEIJE-SCCS. Theor. Comput. Sci. 37, 245–267 (1985)
20. Singh, A., Ramakrishnan, C.R., Smolka, S.A.: A process calculus for mobile ad hoc networks. Science of Computer Programming 75, 440–469 (2010)
21. Zhou, M., Yang, H., Zhang, X., Wang, J.: The proof of AODV loop freedom. In: Proc. IEEE WCSP (2009)

On the Correctness of the SIMT Execution Model of GPUs

Axel Habermaier and Alexander Knapp

Institute for Software and Systems Engineering, University of Augsburg
{habermaier, knapp}@informatik.uni-augsburg.de

Abstract. GPUs are becoming a primary resource of computing power. They use a single instruction, multiple threads (SIMT) execution model that executes batches of threads in lockstep. If the control flow of threads within the same batch diverges, the different execution paths are scheduled sequentially; once the control flows reconverge, all threads are executed in lockstep again. Several thread batching mechanisms have been proposed, albeit without establishing their semantic validity or their scheduling properties. To increase the level of confidence in the correctness of GPU-accelerated programs, we formalize the SIMT execution model for a stack-based reconvergence mechanism in an operational semantics and prove its correctness by constructing a simulation between the SIMT semantics and a standard interleaved multi-thread semantics. We also demonstrate that the SIMT execution model produces unfair schedules in some cases. We discuss the problem of unfairness for different batching mechanisms like dynamic warp formation and a stack-less reconvergence strategy.

1 Introduction

Since the introduction of general purpose programming frameworks for *graphics processing units* (GPUs) a few years ago, GPUs are capable of accelerating many other kinds of data-parallel algorithms aside from graphics computations. Speedups of one or two orders of magnitude compared to CPU-based implementations have been achieved for applications in the fields of molecular dynamics, medical imaging, seismic imaging, fluid dynamics, and many others [8, 21]. GPUs are well suited for such massively parallel problems because of their high computational power and memory bandwidth. CPUs, on the other hand, are more optimized for sequential code containing many data-dependent branch instructions. The model of computation of GPUs is therefore unlike the traditional one of CPUs, even though they are converging [17].

GPUs typically launch thousands of threads to execute a data-parallel program. Each thread executes the program on different input data akin to the *single program, multiple data* (SPMD) principle. NVIDIA GPUs based on the FERMI architecture process up to 512 threads in parallel, with thousands more being idle and waiting to be scheduled later on [21]. Instead of executing each thread individually, however, the hardware transparently batches several threads together for improved efficiency. The threads of a batch always execute the same instruction in *lockstep* on a *single instruction, multiple data* (SIMD) unit, i.e., in parallel on different operands [24]. As threads are batched dynamically at runtime, GPUs based on NVIDIA's FERMI architecture or

H. Seidl (Ed.): ESOP 2012, LNCS 7211, pp. 316–335, 2012.

on AMD's GRAPHICS CORE NEXT design have no explicit support for SIMD vectors in their instruction sets [16, 23], which distinguishes them from classical SIMD architectures [14]. NVIDIA uses the term *single instruction, multiple threads* (SIMT) to describe the SPMD- and SIMD-like execution model of their hardware [24].

A batch of threads that is executed in lockstep is called a *warp* or *wavefront* by NVIDIA and AMD, respectively. Current NVIDIA hardware always uses a warp size of 32 threads, whereas AMD's GRAPHICS CORE NEXT architecture has a wavefront size of 64 [16, 24]. The SIMT design promises significant performance benefits especially for graphics applications [14], but is in general not well-suited for code that heavily relies on data-dependent control flow instructions: If the control flow of threads of the same warp diverges, execution of the warp is serialized for each unique path, disabling the threads that did not take the path. The hardware must therefore track the threads' activation states and schedule all paths for execution one after another. Once all paths complete, the threads reconverge and proceed in lockstep again. It is desirable to reconverge threads as soon as possible for performance reasons, as otherwise many hardware units remain unused [24]. There are several different mechanisms to handle divergent control flow on a SIMT architecture [4], which differ in thread scheduling and performance; in particular, FERMI uses a *stack-based reconvergence mechanism* based on *immediate post-dominators*, enabling full C++ support on the GPU [5, 20].

The growing complexity of GPU-based software potentially increases the number of software errors, while at the same time the more wide-spread adoption requires a higher level of confidence in program correctness. For formal proofs of correctness, however, not only a precise understanding but also a formal foundation of the underlying SIMT execution model is required. We therefore provide a formal semantics for NVIDIA's stack-based reconvergence mechanism. To keep the formalization concise, it is based on a high-level programming language, disregarding much of NVIDIA's technical environment (a full discussion based on the assembly-level language PTX including the memory model can be found in [9]). We analyze the semantic validity of this execution model by comparing it to a standard interleaved multi-thread semantics: We construct and prove a simulation that demonstrates that each warp execution including serializations on control-flow divergences corresponds to an interleaved multi-thread execution. In this sense, the SIMT execution model is *correct* with respect to the interleaving semantics. However, there is a difference between the two models regarding fairness of execution. In the interleaving model, generally weak fairness is assumed such that every enabled thread will eventually take a step. In contrast, FERMI's stack-based reconvergence mechanism does not guarantee such a fairness condition, rather its *unfair scheduling* of divergent threads prevents some otherwise valid programs from terminating in certain corner cases. We discuss the issue of unfairness for both NVIDIA's mechanism and for alternative SIMT implementations and provide a sufficient criterion for detecting such situations.

Overview. Section 2 gives a brief overview of the hardware architecture and introduces NVIDIA's SIMT execution model with the help of an example. Section 3 presents the formalization of this execution model. The interleaved multi-thread semantics and their simulation of the SIMT behavior are given in Sect. 4. Section 5 then discusses the issue of unfairness and Sect. 6 summarizes our findings and gives an outlook to future work.

2 SIMT Hardware Model

To set the context for the remainder of the paper, we give an overview of the FERMI architecture and its programming model, omitting all graphics-related details. We focus on NVIDIA's *Compute Unified Device Architecture* (CUDA – particularly, batches of threads are referred to as *warps*), as it is representative for other GPU programming frameworks and hardware designs: The underlying principles also apply to *DirectCompute*, the *Open Computing Language* (OPENCL), and AMD's GPUs [1, 13, 16, 22, 24]. Hennessy and Patterson [11] provide a more detailed introduction to CUDA and FERMI and contrast FERMI's design with traditional vector and SIMD architectures.

2.1 Hardware Architecture and Programming Model

CUDA programs launch parallel *compute kernels* on the GPU. Kernels are typically executed by thousands of threads in parallel, organized into a hierarchy: A *grid* represents a set of threads executing the same kernel in a data-parallel fashion similar to the SPMD principle. Grids are divided into *thread blocks*, each of which is assigned to a particular *SIMT core* by the hardware. Threads belonging to the same block communicate via a special on-chip memory on the SIMT core. Threads of different thread blocks share data using the GPU's global memory, which is not guaranteed to be consistent. The SIMT core splits thread blocks into *warps*, which comprise a fixed number of *scalar threads* that are executed in lockstep by an array of *scalar processors* on the SIMT core.

GPUs have multiple SIMT cores that execute warps as SIMD groups on the scalar processors. Typically, there are more warps allocated on a SIMT core than can be executed in parallel. This enables the GPU to hide high-latency memory operations: Instead of using advanced hardware mechanism such as prediction and out-of-order execution, GPUs exploit the massive parallelism of the thread hierarchy by interleaving the execution of different warps; switching between warps incurs no overhead. Different warps are executed independently, hence there is no performance gain or penalty when they are executing common or disjoint code paths.

The focus of this paper is divergence and reconvergence within a warp, so we mainly consider one single warp only; Sect. 5.2 discusses alternative SIMT implementations, some of which take multiple warps into consideration to improve efficiency.

2.2 SIMT Control Flow

SIMT cores execute warps in lockstep, that is, each thread of a warp executes the same instruction in parallel on different operands. In this way, instruction fetch and decoding costs are amortized over all threads of a warp and memory operations performed by threads of the same warp can often be coalesced into fewer memory accesses, which is likely to result in significant performance benefits [14, 24]. To support a wide variety of programs, however, the SIMT cores must be able to deal with diverging control flow that occurs when at least two threads of the same warp take different paths due to a data-dependent control flow instruction. Earlier GPU designs serialized the execution of the remainder of the program once the control flow diverges. Serialization without a reconvergence mechanism results in a low utilization of processing resources for branch-heavy programs and performance drops by a factor proportional to the warp size in the worst case [19]. Consequently, today's GPU architectures implement mechanisms for reconverging threads once their control flows return to a common path. Our focus in this paper is the formalization of an operational semantics for NVIDIA's stack-based reconvergence mechanism as outlined by Hennessy and Patterson [11] and explained in detail in one of NVIDIA's US patent applications [5]. Neither AMD nor NVIDIA provide any official information on their SIMT implementations.

2.3 Stack-Based SIMT Reconvergence

The main idea of a stack-based reconvergence mechanism is to store information about control flow divergence and reconvergence in a *reconvergence stack*. Possible causes for divergence are branches and loops with conditions depending on thread-specific data as well as loops and function calls with bodies containing data-dependent `break` or `return` statements. Whenever the control flow might diverge, a *token* is pushed onto the reconvergence stack. Tokens store both the *continuation* of a potentially divergent instruction and the threads participating in its execution. Once the control flows reconverge (or the execution of the branch, loop, or function call completes without causing any divergence at all), the topmost token is popped off the stack and the SIMT core uses the information contained in the token to continue the execution of the program.

The reconvergence stack belongs to the *execution state* of a warp, also comprising a *program counter* (PC), an *active mask*, and a *disable mask*. The active mask indicates which threads are active and participate in the execution of the instruction referred to by the warp's PC. Inactive threads do not execute the instruction and their respective scalar processors remain idle. The disable mask records the *disable state* of each thread: b or r indicate that the thread executed a `break` or `return` instruction, respectively, whereas 0 means that the thread is not disabled. Only threads with a disable state of 0 can be reactivated when a token is popped off the stack, thereby guaranteeing the correct handling of nested control flow instructions within a compute kernel.

Each token on the reconvergence stack is of a specific type and comprises an active mask and a program counter. Once a token is popped off the stack, the token's PC indicates the next instruction to be executed by the warp, the active mask determines which threads are activated or deactivated, and the token type affects the update operations performed on the warp's current active and disable masks. The type of a token is either div or sync for branches, brk for loops, or call for function calls. A div token stores all the information required for the execution of the second path of a branch after the first path terminates, while sync and brk tokens mark the *reconvergence points* of branches and `while` loops (i.e., their continuations), respectively. It seems that the reconvergence point of a control flow statement always corresponds to the statement's *immediate post-dominator* [5, 20], which denotes the first instruction that must be executed by all divergent (and still active) threads before they return from the current function. The return address of a function call is stored in the corresponding call token on the reconvergence stack, hence no function call stack is required to store return addresses (such a stack would only be necessary to push and pop function arguments). Tokens of types brk and call are also used to determine all instructions a thread must skip after executing a `break` or `return`.

The execution state of a warp is stored directly on the SIMT core, but older entries of the stack may be spilled to global memory if necessary, making operations on the stack potentially time-consuming. In fact, the disable mask is merely an optimization that eliminates the need to modify the stack when threads are deactivated [5].

Example 1. We demonstrate how NVIDIA's SIMT implementation handles nested control flow instructions by means of Prog. 1's compute kernel `main`; the kernel serves no real purpose other than an illustrative one. Note that when Prog. 1 is run on a GPU, the actual execution is likely to differ from what is described below, as the compiler performs (semantics preserving) control flow optimizations to minimize the overhead incurred by operations on the reconvergence stack; particularly, the compiler will most certainly inline the call to `func`.

Table 1 depicts the evolution of the warp's execution state as the kernel is being executed. The active mask is shown as a bit field with a value of 1 at position n indicating that the thread with id n is active; the disable mask is also given in a similar bit field like fashion. The rightmost column represents the reconvergence stack with the topmost token on the left. Each consecutive pair of rows shows how the instruction pointed to by the PC in between them manipulates the warp's execution state. Figure 1 shows the control flow graph of the `while` loop in function `func` of Prog. 1, highlighting the immediate post-dominators of the loop at line 4 and the branch at line 5.

We assume a warp size of four for illustration purposes, with all four threads being active initially (in situations where the number of threads executing a kernel is not a multiple of the warp size, there are underpopulated warps with idle scalar processors). The global pointer variables `a` and `b` are assumed to be shared arrays of length four, acting as the kernel's input and output parameters; we avoid function parameters and return values to simplify matters, even though they are supported by CUDA, OPENCL, and DirectCompute. We assume that the values of the arrays `a` and `b` are $0, 1, 1, 1$ and $0, 1, 1, 3$ for indices 0 to 3, respectively. For each thread executing the kernel, the thread-local variable `tid` contains the unique id of the thread (0 for the first thread, 1 for the second one, and so on), which is used to index into the arrays.

Execution of the compute kernel begins at line 14 where all threads of the warp call `func` in lockstep. A call token is pushed onto the stack, with its program counter set to the return address of the call, i.e., 15. The token's active mask marks all four threads as active, meaning that all four threads should eventually execute the `return` at line 15.

Execution continues at line 3 where all threads initialize their local variables `i` and `j`. Subsequently, the `while` loop is encountered and a brk token is pushed onto the stack. The loop condition evaluates to false for thread 0, hence the corresponding bit in the active mask is set to 0 and the thread does not participate in the execution of the loop. Next, the remaining threads push a sync token onto the stack because of the `if` instruction at line 5. The token's PC is set to the instruction at line 9, which is the reconvergence point where all threads taking one of the two paths of the branch should be executed in lockstep again. As thread 0 is not active when the `if` instruction is encountered, its bit in the sync token's active mask is not set. The branch statement also causes a div token to be pushed onto the stack, as threads 1 and 2 take the else-path and thread 3 takes the then-path; if no divergence had occurred, the stack would remain unchanged. Execution of both paths is serialized, with current NVIDIA hardware

```
1  __shared int *a, *b;
2  void func() {
3       int i = a[tid], j = b[tid];
4       while (i > 0) {
5           if (j > 2 * i)
6               b[tid] += i;
7           else
8               break;
9           --i;
10      }
11      return;
12 }
13 void main() {
14      func();
15      return;
16 }
```

Program 1. A compute kernel with nested control flow instructions

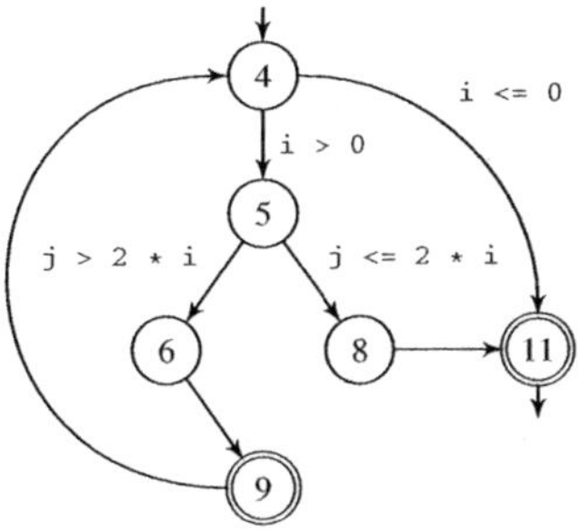

Fig. 1. Control flow graph of the `while` statement in Prog. 1; immediate post-dominators are highlighted

Table 1. Evolution of the warp's execution state during the execution of Prog. 1

PC	Active Mask	Disabled Mask	Top of Stack		
	1111	0000	–	–	
14					
	1111	0000	(call, 1111, 15)	–	
3					
	1111	0000	(call, 1111, 15)	–	
4					
	0111	0000	(brk, 1111, 11)	(call, 1111, 15)	
5					
	0110	0000	(div, 0001, 6)	(sync, 0111, 9)	...
8					
	0001	0bb0	(sync, 0111, 9)	(brk, 1111, 11)	...
6					
	0001	0bb0	(brk, 1111, 11)	(call, 1111, 15)	
9					
	0001	0bb0	(brk, 1111, 11)	(call, 1111, 15)	
4					
	1111	0000	(call, 1111, 15)	–	
11					
	1111	0000	–	–	
15					
	1111	0000	–	–	

executing the else-path first. Thus, thread 3 is disabled and threads 1 and 2 continue execution at line 8. The div token stores the information required to execute the then-path once the else-path is completed. For this reason, the token's PC is set to point to the instruction of the then-path at line 6 and its active mask has only thread 3 activated.

Threads 1 and 2 execute the `break` statement at line 8. Their bits in the active mask are cleared and their disable states are set to b. Consequently, there no longer are any active threads, so the warp pops the div token off the stack that causes thread 3 to execute the then-path of the branch at line 6. After the execution of the assignment, the end of the then-path is reached, causing the sync token to be popped off the stack. Execution now resumes at line 9; however, the warp cannot just use the token's active mask, as threads 1 and 2 executed a `break` and should therefore not participate in the execution of the loop anymore. To support such arbitrary nested control flow instructions within a compute kernel, the token's active mask is combined with the warp's disable mask, resulting in threads 1 and 2 to remain disabled in this case because their disable states have not yet been reset to 0.

Thread 3 returns to the beginning of the loop at line 4. As the condition evaluates to false, there no longer are any active threads and the warp subsequently pops the brk token off the stack. A token of type brk resets a disable state of b of all threads that are active in the token's active mask. Hence, all four threads execute the `return` instruction at line 11 that causes the threads to jump to the function's return address by popping the call token off the stack. They execute the next `return` statement at line 15, which completes the execution of the compute kernel. □

During the compilation of a compute kernel written in a structured programming language like CUDA-C, branches and loops are replaced by unstructured conditional jumps. The compiler preserves the structural information by adding special flags and instructions into the assembly-level code, allowing the hardware to efficiently determine the immediate post-dominators [5, 23]. Our formalization of the SIMT execution model disregards these low-level implementation details and focuses on a structured programming language instead. A formal semantics of the SIMT behavior based on NVIDIA's assembly-level language PTX can be found in [9].

3 Formalization of the SIMT Execution Model

We formalize the SIMT behavior as discussed in the preceding section in an operational semantics for a C-like high-level language. We focus on the main ideas of the mechanism and omit other hardware supported features such as indirect branches and function calls, as these can be reduced to sequences of their direct counterparts [5]. Due to the stack-based reconvergence mechanism, we base our formalization of the SIMT semantics on an instruction stack that unifies the treatment of statements from the structured programming language and the warp management tokens.

3.1 Basic Domains and Language Grammar

We assume a syntactic category *Var* of *variable identifiers* with typical element x (all metavariables may occur in an arbitrarily adorned form) and a syntactic category *Func* of *function identifiers*, of which f will be a typical element. We also assume a syntactic category *Expr* of (side effect-free arithmetical) *expressions* over *Var*, ranged over by e, which we do not specify more precisely.

Our programming language is a simple while-language with function calls; we distinguish between *statements*, *statement lists*, and *programs*. The grammar of (C-like) statements and statement lists is as follows:

$$\begin{aligned}
\mathit{Stm} \ni s ::= {} & \texttt{;} \mid x \texttt{ = } e\texttt{;} \\
& \mid \texttt{if (}e\texttt{) } S_1 \texttt{ else } S_2 \\
& \mid \texttt{while (}e\texttt{) } S \mid \underline{\texttt{while}} \texttt{ (}e\texttt{) } S \mid \texttt{break;} \\
& \mid f\texttt{();} \mid \texttt{return;} \\
\mathit{Stms} \ni S ::= {} & s \mid s\ S
\end{aligned}$$

Stm does not include a separate sequential composition but relies on statement lists instead. The statements `while` and $\underline{\texttt{while}}$ are required to distinguish between the first iteration of a loop and subsequent iterations, which do not generate further brk tokens. The domain $\mathit{Prog} \subseteq \mathit{Stms}$ of programs, ranged over by P, singles out those statement lists that do not contain $\underline{\texttt{while}}$ and have `break;` only within `while` loops. A *function environment* $\varphi \in \mathit{FuncEnv} = \mathit{Func} \rightarrow \mathit{Prog}$ maps each function identifier to a program.

Statement lists are executed by threads θ taken from a domain of *thread identifiers* Thread; the domain of all subsets of Thread is ranged over by Θ. Threads can share variables or have their own local copies depending on the initialization of the threads' *variable environments*. A variable environment $\nu \in \mathit{VarEnv} = \mathit{Var} \rightarrow \mathit{Addr}$ of a thread assigns an *address* from the domain Addr to each variable in a program. A *thread environment* $\eta \in \mathit{ThreadEnv} = \mathit{Thread} \rightarrow \mathit{VarEnv}$ maps a thread to its variable environment. We assume a *memory* type $\mathit{Mem} = \mathit{Addr} \rightarrow \mathit{Val}$, ranged over by μ, holding integer values $\mathit{Val} = \mathbb{Z}$ that is accessible by all threads (we disregard caching).

3.2 Warp Configurations and Transitions

The execution state of a warp consists of an *instruction stack* comprising statements and *tokens*, an *active mask*, and a *disable mask*. In contrast to the informal description in Sect. 2.3, our formal model does not maintain a separate reconvergence stack.

A thread is considered active if it is contained in the warp's active mask $\Theta \subseteq \mathit{Thread}$; we write Θ^+ for an active mask with at least one active thread, i.e., $\Theta^+ \neq \emptyset$. A disable mask Δ is defined as a function in $\mathit{DisableMask} = \mathit{Thread} \rightarrow \mathit{DisableState}$, which maps a thread to its disable state δ that is either 0, b, or r. *Token types* are denoted by t and have a value of either div, sync, brk, or call. A token $\tau = t_\Theta$ comprises a token type t and an active mask Θ. Warp instruction stacks are given by

$$\mathit{WStack} \ni W ::= \varepsilon \mid s\, W \mid \tau\, W ,$$

combining tokens and statements. In contrast to Sect. 2.3, a token's continuation is not given by a program counter but rather as the remainder of the instruction stack.

A *warp configuration* $\varphi, \eta \rhd W, \Theta, \Delta, \mu$ consists of a static and a dynamic part, separated by $\rhd$. The former comprises a function environment φ and a thread environment η, whereas the latter contains a warp instruction stack W, an active mask Θ, a disable mask Δ, and a memory μ. An *initial* warp configuration is of the form $\varphi, \eta \rhd P\ \mathsf{call}_\Theta, \Theta, \{\Theta \mapsto 0\}, \mu$ where P is a program, Θ is an arbitrary subset of threads and μ is an arbitrary memory. For reasons of uniformity, we assume that there always is a call token at the bottom of the stack which corresponds to the invocation of the compute kernel. A *warp transition* $\varphi, \eta \rhd W, \Theta, \Delta, \mu \Rightarrow^{\mathrm{w}} W', \Theta', \Delta', \mu'$ describes a step transforming a warp configuration into another warp configuration, not repeating the static parts of the configurations.

3.3 Warp Operational Semantics

The *warp operational semantics* is the smallest binary relation $\Rightarrow^{\mathrm{w}}$ on warp configurations which is closed under the rules in Table 2. These are, in fact, rule schemes where

Table 2. Operational semantics of a warp

(skip^{w})	$\texttt{;}, \Theta^+ \Rightarrow^{\text{w}} \varepsilon, \Theta^+$
(assign^{w})	$\eta \rhd x\ \texttt{=}\ e\texttt{;}, \Theta^+, \mu \Rightarrow^{\text{w}} \varepsilon, \Theta^+, \mu\{\eta(\Theta^+)(x) \mapsto \mathcal{E}[\![e]\!]\, \eta(\Theta^+)\, \mu\}$
(if^{w})	$\eta \rhd \texttt{if (}e\texttt{)}\ S_1\ \texttt{else}\ S_2, \Theta^+, \mu \Rightarrow^{\text{w}}$ $S_2\ \mathsf{div}_{act(\Theta^+, e, \eta, \mu)}\ S_1\ \mathsf{sync}_{\Theta^+}, \Theta^+ \setminus act(\Theta^+, e, \eta, \mu), \mu$
(while^{w})	$\eta \rhd \texttt{while (}e\texttt{)}\ S, \Theta^+, \mu \Rightarrow^{\text{w}} S\ \underline{\texttt{while}}\ \texttt{(}e\texttt{)}\ S\ \mathsf{brk}_{\Theta^+}, act(\Theta^+, e, \eta, \mu), \mu$
($\underline{\text{while}}^{\text{w}}$)	$\eta \rhd \underline{\texttt{while}}\ \texttt{(}e\texttt{)}\ S, \Theta^+, \mu \Rightarrow^{\text{w}} S\ \underline{\texttt{while}}\ \texttt{(}e\texttt{)}\ S, act(\Theta^+, e, \eta, \mu), \mu$
(break^{w})	$\texttt{break;}\ [S]\ \tau, \Theta^+, \Delta \Rightarrow^{\text{w}} \tau, \emptyset, \Delta\{\Theta^+ \mapsto \mathsf{b}\}$
(call^{w})	$\varphi \rhd f\texttt{();}, \Theta^+ \Rightarrow^{\text{w}} \varphi(f)\ \mathsf{call}_{\Theta^+}, \Theta^+$
(return^{w})	$\texttt{return;}\ [S]\ \tau, \Theta^+, \Delta \Rightarrow^{\text{w}} \tau, \emptyset, \Delta\{\Theta^+ \mapsto \mathsf{r}\}$
(token^{w})	$\tau, \Theta_1, \Delta_1 \Rightarrow^{\text{w}} \varepsilon, \Theta_2, \Delta_2$ where $(\Theta_2, \Delta_2) = enable(\Delta_1, \tau)$
(inact^{w})	$S\ \tau, \emptyset \Rightarrow^{\text{w}} \tau, \emptyset$

warp transitions are obtained by replacing the metavariables with suitable instances. We use the following notational conventions: We only give the initial segment of the instruction stack W that is of relevance for the given rule; the remainder of W is omitted and remains unchanged. Similarly, we drop all other irrelevant parts of an operational judgement that remain unchanged. For example, the rule

$$\varphi, \eta \rhd f\texttt{();}\ W, \Theta^+, \Delta, \mu \Rightarrow^{\text{w}} \varphi(f)\ \mathsf{call}_{\Theta^+}\ W, \Theta^+, \Delta, \mu$$

is abbreviated as follows, where Θ^+ is not omitted (even though it remains unchanged) as it has to be stored in the call token and the rule may only be applied to warp configurations with a non-empty set of active threads:

$$\varphi \rhd f\texttt{();}, \Theta^+ \Rightarrow^{\text{w}} \varphi(f)\ \mathsf{call}_{\Theta^+}, \Theta^+ .$$

The operational rules in Table 2 process the instruction stack of a warp configuration disregarding all possible compiler or hardware optimizations. The skip operation `;` is simply popped off the instruction stack; like all other rules except for (token^{w}) and (inact^{w}), it can only be applied to warp configurations with at least one active thread.

To execute an assignment $x\ \texttt{=}\ e\texttt{;}$, all active threads use the function $\mathcal{E}[\![-]\!] : \mathit{Expr} \to \mathit{VarEnv} \times \mathit{Mem} \to \mathit{Val}$ to evaluate e before any of them write to x, thereby avoiding potential nondeterminism. However, the order of conflicting writes (that is, $\eta(\theta_1)(x) = \eta(\theta_2)(x)$ but $\mathcal{E}[\![e]\!]\, \eta(\theta_1)\, \mu \neq \mathcal{E}[\![e]\!]\, \eta(\theta_2)\, \mu$ for two active threads $\theta_1, \theta_2 \in \Theta$) is undefined [24]; this is modeled by the nondeterminism in the instantiation of the rule (assign^{w}): $\mu\{\eta(\Theta^+)(x) \mapsto \mathcal{E}[\![e]\!]\, \eta(\Theta^+)\, \mu\}$ abbreviates the memory update

$$\mu\{\eta(\theta_1)(x) \ldots \eta(\theta_n)(x) \mapsto \mathcal{E}[\![e]\!]\, \eta(\theta_1)\, \mu \ldots \mathcal{E}[\![e]\!]\, \eta(\theta_n)\, \mu\}$$

for some arbitrary order of threads $\theta_i \in \Theta^+$.

An `if` statement pushes two tokens onto the stack: The sync token marks the re-convergence point where all active threads Θ^+ are reactivated again; provided that they do not execute a `break` or `return` instruction in the meantime. The div token stores the information needed to execute the then-path of the branch once the execution of the else-path is completed. The rule (if^{w}) uses the function

$$act(\Theta, e, \eta, \mu) = \{\theta \in \Theta \mid \mathcal{E}[\![e]\!]\, \eta(\theta)\, \mu \neq 0\}$$

to determine the set of threads for which expression e evaluates to true (i.e. non-zero).

A `while` statement at the top of the instruction stack is replaced by a sequence of instructions: First, a brk token storing the continuation for all threads exiting the loop is pushed onto the stack. Second, a corresponding <u>`while`</u> statement is created, which does not generate another brk token once it is encountered. Finally, the statement list forming the `while` statement's body is pushed onto the stack. Whether there are any threads for which the loop condition holds is again determined by the function act.

A `break` or `return` statement deactivates all active threads and sets their disable state to b or r, respectively. $[S]$ denotes a possibly empty statement list, so either `break` and `return` are directly followed by a token τ or all statements up to the next token on the stack are skipped.

A call to a function f places the program $\varphi(f)$ on the top of the stack. The call token that is pushed onto the stack beforehand stores the currently active threads Θ^+, all of which are reactivated once the warp begins to execute the continuation of the call token.

When a token is popped off the instruction stack, the warp's active and disable masks are updated. The reactivation of an inactive thread depends on the type of the token and the thread's disable state. For instance, a thread with a disable state of r may only be reactivated if the token is of type call. The predicate

$$awaits(\delta, t) \leftrightarrow (\delta = \mathsf{b} \rightarrow t = \mathsf{brk}) \wedge (\delta = \mathsf{r} \rightarrow t = \mathsf{call})$$

establishes this relationship between disable states and token types. The function $enable$ clears the disable states of all threads for which $awaits$ holds. Furthermore, it replaces the warp's active mask with the one of the token, removing all threads with a disable state other than 0. Formally, we define $enable$ as

$$\begin{aligned} enable(\Delta_1, t_\Theta) &= (\{\theta \in \Theta \mid \Delta_2(\theta) = 0\}, \Delta_2) \\ \text{where } \Delta_2 &= \Delta_1\{\{\theta \in \Theta \mid awaits(\Delta_1(\theta), t)\} \mapsto 0\}\,. \end{aligned}$$

Particularly, $enable$ only changes the disable states of threads that are contained in the token's active mask, otherwise threads would be reactivated too soon; this has already been illustrated in Ex. 1. For another example, consider a thread θ that executes a `return` statement in the else-path of a branch, while the other threads Θ of the warp call another function f' when they later execute the if-path of the branch. Once the control flow returns from f', θ's disable state remains unchanged because θ is not active in the call token corresponding to the invocation of f'. Hence, when the sync token of the branch is subsequently popped, θ is removed from the token's active mask before it is copied into the warp's execution state because its disable state is still set to r.

The rule (inact^{w}) is used to skip all statements up to the topmost token on the stack if the warp's active mask is empty. Such a situation typically arises when the condition of a `while` statement evaluates to false for all active threads or when a token does not activate any threads at all. The latter occurs when all threads return from a function call within an `if`-statement, for example. In that case, the rule $(\text{inact}^{\text{w}})$ skips all statements up to the next token, which is then dealt with by the rule $(\text{token}^{\text{w}})$. Once the last token is popped of the stack, the compute kernel terminates, as the last token on the instruction stack is the call token corresponding to the invocation of the compute kernel.

Example 2. We apply our formal semantics of the SIMT execution model to the compute kernel `main` of Prog. 1. As in Ex. 1, we illustrate active and disable masks as bit fields and omit the memory as well as the function and thread environments for reasons of brevity (observe that our formal model treats indexed array accesses such as `b[tid]` as regular variables; we assume that the thread environment is initialized such that no variables are shared). The following shows the derivation sequence of Prog. 1 beginning with the `while` statement at line 4 and ending just before the execution of the `return` statement at line 11. Again considering only four threads as in Ex. 1, the first warp configuration is given as `while (i > 0) ... return;` $W, 1111, 0000$ with $W = \mathsf{call}_{1111}$ `return;` call_{1111} denoting the remainder of the instruction stack; W contains two call tokens that correspond to the invocations of `func` and `main`. Recall that the values of the shared arrays `a` and `b` are $0, 1, 1, 1$ and $0, 1, 1, 3$ for indices 0 to 3, respectively.

	$\texttt{while (i > 0)} \ldots \texttt{return;}\ W,$	1111, 0000
$\xRightarrow{\text{while}}_{\text{w}}$	$\texttt{if (j > 2 * i) b[tid] += i; else break; --i;}$ $\underline{\texttt{while}}\ \texttt{(i > 0)} \ldots \mathsf{brk}_{1111}\ \texttt{return;}\ W,$	0111, 0000
$\xRightarrow{\text{if}}_{\text{w}}$	$\texttt{break;}\ \mathsf{div}_{0001}\ \texttt{b[tid] += i;}\ \mathsf{sync}_{0111}\ \texttt{--i;}$ $\underline{\texttt{while}}\ \texttt{(i > 0)} \ldots \mathsf{brk}_{1111}\ \texttt{return;}\ W,$	0110, 0000
$\xRightarrow{\text{break}}_{\text{w}}$	$\mathsf{div}_{0001}\ \texttt{b[tid] += i;}\ \mathsf{sync}_{0111}\ \texttt{--i;}$ $\underline{\texttt{while}}\ \texttt{(i > 0)} \ldots \mathsf{brk}_{1111}\ \texttt{return;}\ W,$	0000, 0bb0
$\xRightarrow{\text{token}}_{\text{w}}$	$\texttt{b[tid] += i;}\ \mathsf{sync}_{0111}\ \texttt{--i;}$ $\underline{\texttt{while}}\ \texttt{(i > 0)} \ldots \mathsf{brk}_{1111}\ \texttt{return;}\ W,$	0001, 0bb0
$\xRightarrow{\text{assign}}_{\text{w}}$	$\mathsf{sync}_{0111}\ \texttt{--i;}\ \underline{\texttt{while}}\ \texttt{(i > 0)} \ldots \mathsf{brk}_{1111}\ \texttt{return;}\ W,$	0001, 0bb0
$\xRightarrow{\text{token}}_{\text{w}}$	$\texttt{--i;}\ \underline{\texttt{while}}\ \texttt{(i > 0)} \ldots \mathsf{brk}_{1111}\ \texttt{return;}\ W,$	0001, 0bb0
$\xRightarrow{\text{assign}}_{\text{w}}$	$\underline{\texttt{while}}\ \texttt{(i > 0)} \ldots \mathsf{brk}_{1111}\ \texttt{return;}\ W,$	0001, 0bb0
$\xRightarrow{\underline{\text{while}}}_{\text{w}}$	$\texttt{if (j > 2 * i) b[tid] += i; else break; --i;}$ $\underline{\texttt{while}}\ \texttt{(i > 0)} \ldots \mathsf{brk}_{1111}\ \texttt{return;}\ W,$	0000, 0bb0
$\xRightarrow{\text{inact}}_{\text{w}}$	$\mathsf{brk}_{1111}\ \texttt{return;}\ W,$	0000, 0bb0
$\xRightarrow{\text{token}}_{\text{w}}$	$\texttt{return;}\ W,$	1111, 0000

The application of the rule $(\underline{\text{while}}^{\text{w}})$ pushes the entire body of the `while` statement onto the instruction stack again, even though there no longer are any active threads. However, the body of a `while` statement consists of statements only, hence no new tokens are pushed onto the stack. The rule $(\text{inact}^{\text{w}})$ is therefore able to skip all statements on the stack up to the brk token. When the rule $(\text{token}^{\text{w}})$ pops the brk token off the stack, the function *enable* reactivates all threads with a disable state of b. In contrast, the threads remain disabled when the div and sync tokens are encountered. □

The following lemma summarizes a few invariants of *reachable* warp configurations. A warp configuration w is reachable if a finite sequence of warp transitions transforms some initial warp configuration into w; a warp transition is reachable if the warp configuration on its left hand side is reachable.

As can be seen by inspecting the operational rules for warps in Table 2, no token intervenes a div token and a sync token and the active mask of a sync token comprises both the currently active threads and the active mask of the previous div token. Similarly, each `while` statement is directly followed by a brk token and the currently active threads are contained in the brk token's active mask. By induction and observing that no warp rule alters previously pushed tokens, the active mask of a token τ_1 is a subset of the active mask of another token τ_2 lower on the stack, if neither token is of type div. Analogously, the warp's current active mask always is a subset of the active masks of all tokens on the stack; except for div tokens, which always disable all active threads. A full proof of this lemma can be found in the accompanying technical report [10].

Lemma 1. *Let $\varphi, \eta \rhd W, \Theta, \Delta, \mu$ be a reachable warp configuration.*
1. *If $W = \mathsf{div}_{\Theta'}\ W_0$, then $W_0 = S\ \mathsf{sync}_{\Theta''}\ W_1$ and $\Theta \cup \Theta' \subseteq \Theta''$.*
2. *If $W =$ `while` $(e)\ S\ W_0$, then $W_0 = \mathsf{brk}_{\Theta'}\ W_1$ and $\Theta \subseteq \Theta'$.*
3. *If $W = W_1\ t_{1,\Theta_1}\ W_2\ t_{2,\Theta_2}\ W_3$ and $t_1 \neq \mathsf{div} \neq t_2$, then $\Theta_1 \subseteq \Theta_2$.*
4. *If $W = W_1\ t_{\Theta'}\ W_2$, then $\Theta \cap \Theta' = \emptyset$ if $t = \mathsf{div}$ or $\Theta \subseteq \Theta'$ otherwise.*

4 Simulating SIMT Execution by Interleaved Multi-Threading

The formalization of the SIMT execution model in the preceding section allows us to formally establish its semantic validity by constructing a simulation relation between the warp semantics and a standard interleaved multi-thread semantics. The simulation shows that the SIMT execution model is *correct* in the sense that warps execute control flow instructions in a way that can be reproduced by a certain schedule of the interleaved thread semantics.

4.1 Interleaved Multi-Thread Semantics

The concepts of active masks, disable masks, and divergence do not apply to individual threads. However, threads still depend on an instruction stack that comprises statements and *contexts* c. Similar to the tokens in a warp's instruction stack, contexts denote the thread's continuations once a loop is exited or a `break` or `return` statement is executed. Thread instruction stacks are defined as follows, with contexts c being either brk or call:

$$\mathit{TStack} \ni T ::= \varepsilon \mid s\,T \mid c\,T\,.$$

A *thread configuration* $\varphi, \nu \rhd T, \mu$ consists of a function environment φ, a variable environment ν, a thread instruction stack T, and a memory μ. A *thread transition* $\varphi, \nu \rhd T, \mu \Rightarrow^{\mathsf{t}} T', \mu'$ transforms a thread configuration into another thread configuration.

The rules of our *thread operational semantics* $\Rightarrow^{\mathsf{t}}$ are given in Table 4, where we reuse our notational conventions for warps. It is a fairly standard small-step semantics (see e.g. [26]), so we only remark the following: Contexts that reach the top of the

Table 4. Operational semantics of a single thread

$$(\mathrm{skip}^{\mathrm{t}}) \quad \texttt{;} \Rightarrow^{\mathrm{t}} \varepsilon$$

$$(\mathrm{assign}^{\mathrm{t}}_{\mathrm{rd}}) \quad \nu \rhd x \texttt{ = } e\texttt{;}, \mu \Rightarrow^{\mathrm{t}} x \texttt{ = } v\texttt{;}, \mu \quad \text{where } \mathcal{E}[\![e]\!]\, \nu\, \mu = v$$

$$(\mathrm{assign}^{\mathrm{t}}_{\mathrm{wr}}) \quad \nu \rhd x \texttt{ = } v\texttt{;}, \mu \Rightarrow^{\mathrm{t}} \varepsilon, \mu\{\nu(x) \mapsto v\}$$

$$(\mathrm{if}^{\mathrm{t}}_{\mathrm{tt}}) \quad \nu \rhd \texttt{if (}e\texttt{) } S_1 \texttt{ else } S_2, \mu \Rightarrow^{\mathrm{t}} S_1, \mu \quad \text{if } \mathcal{E}[\![e]\!]\, \nu\, \mu \neq 0$$

$$(\mathrm{if}^{\mathrm{t}}_{\mathrm{ff}}) \quad \nu \rhd \texttt{if (}e\texttt{) } S_1 \texttt{ else } S_2, \mu \Rightarrow^{\mathrm{t}} S_2, \mu \quad \text{if } \mathcal{E}[\![e]\!]\, \nu\, \mu = 0$$

$$(\mathrm{while}^{\mathrm{t}}_{\mathrm{tt}}) \quad \nu \rhd \texttt{while (}e\texttt{) } S, \mu \Rightarrow^{\mathrm{t}} S\ \underline{\texttt{while}}\ \texttt{(}e\texttt{) } S\ \mathsf{brk}, \mu \quad \text{if } \mathcal{E}[\![e]\!]\, \nu\, \mu \neq 0$$

$$(\mathrm{while}^{\mathrm{t}}_{\mathrm{ff}}) \quad \nu \rhd \texttt{while (}e\texttt{) } S, \mu \Rightarrow^{\mathrm{t}} \varepsilon, \mu \quad \text{if } \mathcal{E}[\![e]\!]\, \nu\, \mu = 0$$

$$(\underline{\mathrm{while}}^{\mathrm{t}}_{\mathrm{tt}}) \quad \nu \rhd \underline{\texttt{while}}\ \texttt{(}e\texttt{) } S, \mu \Rightarrow^{\mathrm{t}} S\ \underline{\texttt{while}}\ \texttt{(}e\texttt{) } S, \mu \quad \text{if } \mathcal{E}[\![e]\!]\, \nu\, \mu \neq 0$$

$$(\underline{\mathrm{while}}^{\mathrm{t}}_{\mathrm{ff}}) \quad \nu \rhd \underline{\texttt{while}}\ \texttt{(}e\texttt{) } S, \mu \Rightarrow^{\mathrm{t}} \varepsilon, \mu \quad \text{if } \mathcal{E}[\![e]\!]\, \nu\, \mu = 0$$

$$(\mathrm{break}^{\mathrm{t}}) \quad \texttt{break;}\ [S]\ \mathsf{brk} \Rightarrow^{\mathrm{t}} \varepsilon$$

$$(\mathrm{call}^{\mathrm{t}}) \quad \varphi \rhd f\texttt{();} \Rightarrow^{\mathrm{t}} \varphi(f)\ \mathsf{call}$$

$$(\mathrm{return}^{\mathrm{t}}) \quad \texttt{return;}\ T_{\neg\mathsf{call}}\ \mathsf{call} \Rightarrow^{\mathrm{t}} \varepsilon$$

$$(\mathrm{context}^{\mathrm{t}}) \quad c \Rightarrow^{\mathrm{t}} \varepsilon$$

instruction stack are simply discarded by the rule $(\mathrm{context}^{\mathrm{t}})$. When a thread encounters a `break` or `return` statement, it skips all statements up to the next brk or call context on the stack, respectively. $T_{\neg\mathsf{call}}$ denotes a possibly empty list of instructions that does not contain any call contexts.

Multiple threads interleave execution. An *interleaved thread configuration* $\varphi, \eta \rhd \varsigma, \mu$ uses a *thread stack function* $\varsigma : \mathit{Thread} \to \mathit{TStack}$ to determine the instruction stack of each thread participating in the execution. An *interleaved thread transition* $\varphi, \eta \rhd \varsigma, \mu \Rightarrow^{\mathrm{i}} \varsigma', \mu'$ describes a step transforming an interleaved thread configuration into another interleaved thread configuration by selecting an arbitrary thread and executing a thread transition. With the help of our notational conventions for warps, the rule for our interleaved thread semantics $\Rightarrow^{\mathrm{i}}$ is given as:

$$\frac{\varphi, \eta(\theta) \rhd \varsigma(\theta), \mu \Rightarrow^{\mathrm{t}} T, \mu'}{\varphi, \eta \rhd \varsigma, \mu \Rightarrow^{\mathrm{i}} \varsigma\{\theta \mapsto T\}, \mu'} \,.$$

The thread semantics handles assignments in two steps: The rule $(\mathrm{assign}^{\mathrm{t}}_{\mathrm{rd}})$ evaluates the expression before the rule $(\mathrm{assign}^{\mathrm{t}}_{\mathrm{wr}})$ performs the actual memory update; if there was only one rule for assignments, the interleaved thread semantics would be unable to simulate the SIMT execution model. For instance, consider a statement `x = x + 1` for some shared variable `x`. As a warp executes all of its n active threads in lockstep, the value of `x` is incremented by 1 in total. With only one assignment rule for threads, the interleaved thread semantics would always increment `x` by n. With the two rules for assignment, however, the interleaved semantics nondeterministically increments `x` by l with $1 \leq l \leq n$, depending on the order in which the threads apply the rules $(\mathrm{assign}^{\mathrm{t}}_{\mathrm{rd}})$ and $(\mathrm{assign}^{\mathrm{t}}_{\mathrm{wr}})$. The simulation of the SIMT behavior therefore applies the rule $(\text{assign}^{\text{t}}_{\text{rd}})$ to all active threads before any of them applies the rule $(\text{assign}^{\text{t}}_{\text{wr}})$; in the example, this guarantees that x is incremented by 1.

4.2 Simulation Relation

Figure 2 shows the intended simulation relation between the warp semantics and the interleaved thread semantics: Any reachable warp transition shall be matched by a finite sequence of zero, one, or more interleaved thread transitions (written as $\Rightarrow^{\text{i},*}$). Based on the simulation of one single warp transition, we extend the simulation to sequences of reachable warp transitions, meaning that all warp executions are correct with regard to the interleaved thread semantics.

$$\begin{array}{ccc} \varphi, \eta \rhd \pi_\Theta(W, \Delta), \mu & \overset{\text{i},*}{=\!=\!=\!=\!\Rightarrow} & \pi_{\Theta'}(W', \Delta'), \mu' \\ \uparrow \gamma & & \gamma \uparrow \\ \varphi, \eta \rhd W, \Theta, \Delta, \mu & \overset{\text{w}}{\Longrightarrow} & W', \Theta', \Delta', \mu' \end{array}$$

Fig. 2. Simulation of a reachable warp transition by a sequence of interleaved thread transitions

The simulation depends on the mutually recursive *projection* functions $\pi_\theta, \pi_{\neg\theta} : \mathit{WStack} \times \mathit{DisableState} \to \mathit{TStack}$ defined in Table 5 for each $\theta \in \mathit{Thread}$ that transform a warp instruction stack into a thread instruction stack. π_θ projects active threads, whereas $\pi_{\neg\theta}$ is used for inactive ones. The former simply outputs all statements it encounters, replaces all brk and call tokens by brk and call contexts, removes all sync and div tokens as they have no meaning for an individual thread, and deactivates the thread whenever a div token is encountered by calling $\pi_{\neg\theta}$. In the definition of π_θ, the active masks of the tokens on the stack do not have to be considered because of Lem. 1(4). For an inactive thread, $\pi_{\neg\theta}$ skips all instructions until it encounters an *activation token*, i.e., a token that reactivates the thread. The function $\mathit{actToken}$ determines whether a given token is a thread's activation token:

$$\mathit{actToken}_\theta(t_\Theta, \delta) \leftrightarrow \theta \in \Theta \wedge \mathit{awaits}(\delta, t) \ .$$

The projection functions π_θ and $\pi_{\neg\theta}$ are combined into the curried thread stack function $\pi_\Theta : (\mathit{WStack} \times \mathit{DisableMask}) \to \mathit{Thread} \to \mathit{TStack}$ with

$$\pi_\Theta(W, \Delta)(\theta) = \begin{cases} \pi_\theta(W, \Delta(\theta)) & \text{if } \theta \in \Theta \\ \pi_{\neg\theta}(W, \Delta(\theta)) & \text{otherwise} \ , \end{cases}$$

parameterized by Θ, which is used by the conversion function γ of Fig. 2 to turn warp configurations into interleaved thread configurations.

The existence proof for the simulation relation relies on a series of lemmata that relate warp configurations to interleaved thread configurations. The full proofs of the lemmata can be found in the accompanying technical report [10].

The first lemma establishes a relationship between the functions $\mathit{actToken}$ and enable, ensuring that a warp correctly activates inactive threads: It only activates inactive threads when it reaches their activation token and conversely, inactive threads are reactivated once their activation token is encountered.

Table 5. Definitions of the projection functions

$$\pi_\theta(\varepsilon, \delta) = \varepsilon$$
$$\pi_\theta(s\ W, \delta) = s\ \pi_\theta(W, \delta)$$
$$\pi_\theta(\mathsf{call}_\Theta\ W, \delta) = \mathsf{call}\ \pi_\theta(W, \delta)$$
$$\pi_\theta(\mathsf{brk}_\Theta\ W, \delta) = \mathsf{brk}\ \pi_\theta(W, \delta)$$
$$\pi_\theta(\mathsf{sync}_\Theta\ W, \delta) = \pi_\theta(W, \delta)$$
$$\pi_\theta(\mathsf{div}_\Theta\ W, \delta) = \pi_{\neg\theta}(W, \delta)$$

$$\pi_{\neg\theta}(\varepsilon, \delta) = \varepsilon$$
$$\pi_{\neg\theta}(s\ W, \delta) = \pi_{\neg\theta}(W, \delta)$$
$$\pi_{\neg\theta}(\tau\ W, \delta) = \begin{cases} \pi_\theta(W, 0) & \text{if } \mathit{actToken}_\theta(\tau, \delta) \\ \pi_{\neg\theta}(W, \delta) & \text{otherwise} \end{cases}$$

Lemma 2. *Let $\varphi, \eta \rhd W, \Theta, \Delta, \mu$ be a reachable warp configuration, $\theta \notin \Theta$, and τ a token in W. Then $\mathit{actToken}_\theta(\tau, \Delta(\theta))$ is true if and only if $\mathit{enable}(\Delta, \tau) = (\Theta', \Delta')$ with $\theta \in \Theta'$.*

Using Lem. 2, we can show that all inactive threads of a reachable warp configuration simulate an arbitrary operational warp transition by simply remaining idle. This is because the instruction stacks of inactive threads remain unchanged.

Lemma 3. *Let $\varphi, \eta \rhd W, \Theta, \Delta, \mu \Rightarrow^{\mathrm{w}} W', \Theta', \Delta', \mu'$ be a reachable warp transition and let $\theta \notin \Theta$. Then $\pi_\Theta(W, \Delta)(\theta) = \pi_{\Theta'}(W', \Delta')(\theta)$.*

For the active threads in a reachable warp configuration, we would also like to proceed by focusing on a single thread, showing that each single active thread can simulate a warp transition. Assignments, however, are a special case that requires all active threads to be considered, as the order of conflicting writes to the same memory address is undefined. Lemma 4 therefore covers the simulation of assignments separately where $\Rightarrow^{\mathrm{i},+}$ denotes a finite sequence of one or more interleaved thread transitions. Lemma 5 covers the remaining cases focusing solely on one active thread; $\Rightarrow^{\mathrm{t},=}$ denotes zero or one thread transitions.

Lemma 4. *Let $\varphi, \eta \rhd W, \Theta, \Delta, \mu \Rightarrow^{\mathrm{w}} W', \Theta', \Delta', \mu'$ be a reachable warp transition using the rule* (assign^{w})*. Then $\varphi, \eta \rhd \pi_\Theta(W, \Delta), \mu \Rightarrow^{\mathrm{i},+} \pi_{\Theta'}(W', \Delta'), \mu'$.*

Lemma 5. *Let $\varphi, \eta \rhd W, \Theta, \Delta, \mu \Rightarrow^{\mathrm{w}} W', \Theta', \Delta', \mu'$ be a reachable warp transition not using the rule* (assign^{w}) *and let $\theta \in \Theta$. Then $\varphi, \eta(\theta) \rhd \pi_\Theta(W, \Delta)(\theta), \mu \Rightarrow^{\mathrm{t},=} \pi_{\Theta'}(W', \Delta')(\theta), \mu'$.*

The combination of Lemmata 3, 4, and 5 proves that there always exists a sequence of interleaved thread transitions to simulate some arbitrary reachable warp transition. This result is summarized in the following proposition, completing the proof of the simulation relation shown in Fig. 2.

Proposition 1. *Let $\varphi, \eta \rhd W, \Theta, \Delta, \mu \Rightarrow^{\mathrm{w}} W', \Theta', \Delta', \mu'$ be a reachable warp transition. Then $\varphi, \eta \rhd \pi_\Theta(W, \Delta), \mu \Rightarrow^{\mathrm{i},*} \pi_{\Theta'}(W', \Delta'), \mu'$.*

The full simulation result follows from Prop. 1 by induction: All sequences of reachable warp transitions can be simulated by sequences of interleaved thread transitions.

Theorem 1 (Simulation of the SIMT Execution Model). *Let* $\varphi, \eta \rhd W, \Theta, \Delta, \mu \Rightarrow^{\mathrm{w},*} W', \Theta', \Delta', \mu'$ *be a sequence of reachable warp transitions. Then* $\varphi, \eta \rhd \pi_{\Theta}(W, \Delta), \mu \Rightarrow^{\mathrm{i},*} \pi_{\Theta'}(W', \Delta'), \mu'$.

From Thm. 1 it follows directly that all threads simulating the execution of a warp terminate once the warp terminates, that is, they have fully executed the program. Lemma 3 shows that the instruction stacks of inactive threads do not change, hence ensuring that inactive threads do not skip any instructions. Additionally, Lemmata 2 and 3 guarantee that inactive threads are not left behind if the warp pops their activation token off the stack. However, the SIMT execution model cannot ensure that all inactive threads will eventually be reactivated, even though the call token at the bottom of the stack is an activation token for all threads: In some cases, there are tokens on the instruction stack that are never reached again; the instruction stack is continuously modified without shrinking below a certain threshold. Theorem 1 holds even for non-terminating programs, hence the interleaved thread semantics is still able to simulate the warp execution. Obvious reasons for non-termination are bugs causing non-terminating loops or infinite recursion; there is, however, a more fundamental problem with the SIMT execution model: unfairness.

5 Unfairness of the SIMT Execution Model

Divergent threads within a warp must be scheduled and executed one after another. Today's GPUs use an *unfair* scheduling strategy in the sense that one of the divergent paths is fully executed before execution of the second path begins; if the first one does not terminate, the second one is not executed at all. For some programs, this unfair scheduling strategy makes it impossible for the warp to eventually terminate, even though in the interleaved semantics all weakly fair schedules terminate (where weak fairness means that no thread is left behind indefinitely).

The SIMT execution model is not part of CUDA's or OPENCL's specification [13, 24]; instead, it is considered an implementation detail that programmers can "essentially ignore" for "the purposes of correctness" according to NVIDIA [24, p. 62]. Our findings in the preceding section support this statement insofar as they formally show that warps execute control flow instructions as if each thread executed them individually in some schedule. The correctness of the SIMT execution model (in the sense of simulatability) is therefore unaffected by fairness considerations. On the other hand, unfairness potentially affects program termination and thus *program correctness*, which may be the reason for the qualifying "essentially" in NVIDIA's statement.

5.1 Programs Affected by the Unfairness Problem

We first illustrate the problem of unfairness with two example programs before discussing it more generally: Suppose that in Prog. 2, the variable `lock` is shared among all threads of the warp with an initial value of 0, whereas `tid` stores the id of each thread. Execution of the program terminates if the interleaved thread semantics chooses a fair schedule; namely, it eventually executes the thread with id 0, causing the condition of the loop to evaluate to false for all other threads, which then terminate. A warp, on the other hand, schedules the else-path before allowing thread 0 to set `lock` to `1`.

The loop therefore never terminates, thereby preventing the program from terminating. If the hardware were to execute the if-path first or if the conditional statement were reversed, the program would successfully terminate.

Program 3 (with `lock` and `tid` as above) also does not terminate when executed by a warp, although the unfairness has a different cause in this case. As the warp first encounters the loop, the condition evaluates to true for all threads except for thread 0. As the warp chooses the immediate post-dominator of the loop as the reconvergence point, thread 0 is not allowed to continue execution. Instead, the warp continuously executes the remaining threads, which never leave the loop as thread 0 never increments the value of `lock`. Again, a fair interleaved schedule would eventually allow each thread to increment `lock`, resulting in a successful termination of the program.

Programs affected by the unfairness problem are uncommon in practice. Particularly, Prog. 2 uses shared variables without any means of synchronization in both paths of an `if` statement, which is generally considered bad programming practice. Even if the code was not affected by the unfairness problem, it exploits the implicit knowledge about the sequential execution of the paths and might therefore break on future hardware if this assumption is no longer valid. Busy-loops like the one in Prog. 3 are often used in an attempt to implement global synchronization mechanisms that all NVIDIA GPUs are currently lacking [24]. Global synchronization is in fact impossible to implement, though not because of unfairness issues: A compute kernel might be executed by more threads than the hardware is capable of allocating concurrently, hence threads at the synchronization point might be waiting for threads that do not even exist yet and cannot be allocated, resulting in a deadlock.

The following lemma provides a sufficient criterion for programs that are unaffected by the unfairness problem. It is based on a new kind of thread transition $\rightsquigarrow^{\mathsf{t}}_{\eta}$ defined as

$$\frac{\varphi, \eta(\theta) \rhd T, \mu \Rightarrow^{\mathsf{t}} T', \mu'}{\varphi, \eta(\theta) \rhd T, \mu \rightsquigarrow^{\mathsf{t}}_{\eta} T', \mu''} \quad \text{where } \forall a \in \mathit{Addr} \,.\, a \notin \mathit{saddr}(\eta) \rightarrow \mu''(a) = \mu'(a)$$

with $\mathit{saddr}(\eta)$ denoting the set of addresses shared among the threads of thread environment η. Such a thread transition makes arbitrary changes to the contents of all shared addresses. If all possible sequences of $\rightsquigarrow^{\mathsf{t}}_{\eta}$ transitions terminate for all threads, the warp execution is guaranteed to terminate as well. Assume for a contradiction that the warp execution does not terminate. Then by Thm. 1 there is an infinite sequence of $\Rightarrow^{\mathsf{t}}$ transitions with a corresponding infinite sequence of $\rightsquigarrow^{\mathsf{t}}_{\eta}$ for at least one thread.

Lemma 6. *Let* $\varphi, \eta \rhd P\ \mathsf{call}_{\Theta}, \Theta, \{\Theta \mapsto 0\}, \mu_0$ *be an initial warp configuration. If there is no infinite sequence* $\varphi, \eta(\theta) \rhd P\ \mathsf{call}, \mu_0 \rightsquigarrow^{\mathsf{t}}_{\eta} T_1, \mu_1 \rightsquigarrow^{\mathsf{t}}_{\eta} T_2, \mu_2 \rightsquigarrow^{\mathsf{t}}_{\eta} \ldots$ *for all* $\theta \in \Theta$*, then* $\varphi, \eta \rhd P\ \mathsf{call}_{\Theta}, \Theta, \{\Theta \mapsto 0\}, \mu_0 \Rightarrow^{\mathsf{w},*} \varepsilon, \Theta', \Delta', \mu'$.

Lemma 6 is only a sufficient condition for warp termination, but not a necessary one as exemplified by Prog. 4. Assuming that the shared variable `next` is initialized to 0, `tid` stores each thread's id, and the warp size is 32, the warp execution terminates: The condition of the `if` statement eventually evaluates to true for all threads, so `next` is equal to 32 at some point and the loop terminates. By contrast, a sequence of $\rightsquigarrow^{\mathsf{t}}_{\eta}$ transitions that always resets `next` to 0 obviously never terminates.

```
if (tid == 0)
  lock = 1;
else
  while (lock != 1) {}
```

Program 2. Unfair scheduling of divergent branches

```
while (lock != tid) {}
// ...
++lock;
```

Program 3. Reconverging at the immediate post-dominator results in unfair schedules

```
while (next != 32) {
  if (tid == next)
    ++next;
}
```

Program 4. Lem. 6 is not a necessary condition for warp termination

In practice, however, infinite sequences of $\rightsquigarrow^{\mathrm{t}}_{\eta}$ transitions are rarely caused by shared variables: Most compute kernels do not use shared variables in a way that affects loops or recursion and graphics APIs have only recently introduced shared variables or atomic operations for some shader types [12, 22].

5.2 Unfairness of Alternative SIMT Execution Models

Several alternative implementations of the SIMT execution model have been proposed, be it for performance reasons or generality [4, 6, 7, 18]. A stack-less approach, for instance, replaces the warp's reconvergence stack by a set of program counters, one for each thread and updated appropriately, that the warp uses to handle reconvergence. We formalize this stack-less warp semantics $\rightrightarrows^{\mathrm{w}}$ as follows, where the abstract function $\mathit{schedule} : (\mathit{Thread} \to \mathit{TStack}) \to 2^{\mathit{Thread}}$ selects a set of threads with the same PC, that is, a set of threads for which $\forall \theta, \theta' \in \mathit{schedule}(\varsigma) \,.\, \varsigma(\theta) = \varsigma(\theta')$ holds:

$$\frac{(\varphi, \eta(\theta) \rhd \varsigma(\theta), \mu \Rightarrow^{\mathrm{t}} T'_\theta, \mu'_\theta)_{\theta \in \Theta}}{\varphi, \eta \rhd \varsigma, \mu \rightrightarrows^{\mathrm{w}} \varsigma\{(\theta \mapsto T'_\theta)_{\theta\in\Theta}\}, \mu\{(a \mapsto \mu'_\theta(a))_{\theta\in\Theta, a\in \mathit{Addr}}\}}$$

where $\mathit{schedule}(\varsigma) = \Theta$

Collange [4] suggests a similar stack-less approach. By contrast, however, our stack-less semantics $\rightrightarrows^{\mathrm{w}}$ does not consider (function call) stack pointers when selecting the next PC to execute, as that only affects performance but does not influence correctness or fairness. As reconvergence is based on equality of program counters, the fairness of $\rightrightarrows^{\mathrm{w}}$ and Collange's approach depends on the fairness of the choice function *schedule*. Particularly, Collange's lowest program counter scheduling policy makes the overall mechanism unfair.

Fung et al. propose a stack-less technique for more than one warp: *dynamic warp formation* [7]. The SIMT core dynamically regroups all of its threads with the same PC into one or more warps. Fairness depends on the warp scheduling policy; of the five suggested policies, only DTime selecting the oldest warp is generally fair. *Thread block compaction* [6] is another approach proposed by Fung et al. It reintroduces the reconvergence stack, albeit at the thread block level. The stack is used for block-wide synchronization at divergent branches and reconvergence points; divergent warps are regrouped into non-divergent ones, restoring the original warp groupings upon encountering the reconvergence point. Due to the synchronization, thread block compaction suffers from the unfairness problem.

Meng et al. [18] propose *dynamic warp subdivision* where warps are dynamically subdivided on branch (or memory) divergence. Each so-called *warp-split* is individually scheduled, therefore execution of divergent paths is interleaved. Additionally, threads might reconverge at some point past the immediate post-dominator, reuniting the warp-splits. Their approach consequently has the potential of solving the unfairness problem; in practice, however, unfairness is still an issue as warp subdivision is only allowed on statically determined "appropriate" branches in order to avoid undesirable *over-subdivision*.

6 Conclusions and Future Work

The single instruction, multiple threads execution model used by today's GPUs groups threads into batches that execute a compute kernel in lockstep, requiring a special mechanism to efficiently and correctly handle divergent control flow. Our formalization of the SIMT execution model allows us to prove its correctness in the sense that each SIMT execution corresponds to a standard interleaved multi-thread execution for some schedule. SIMT execution potentially affects program termination, however, as divergent threads are scheduled in an unfair way. Some alternative implementations of the SIMT execution model also exhibit this unwanted behavior.

As more and more GPU-accelerated algorithms are used in safety- or security-critical applications such as medical imaging [8, 21], the importance of formally verified program correctness increases. In particular, GPUs are capable of accelerating model checking algorithms that in turn are used in formal analyses of various problems in a wide range of application domains [2, 3]. Our work establishes the semantic validity of the underlying SIMT execution model, contributing to the development of formal verification tools and mechanisms for GPU-based applications. We plan to use a theorem prover to verify correctness and other properties of GPU-based programs.

Several research papers propose changes to the SIMT execution model in order to improve efficiency and performance. While the main point of interest is performance for the time being, new mechanisms should also explore the possibilities of solving the unfairness problem to avoid unexpected non-termination, especially since the current trend is the unification of the CPU and GPU programming models: For example, the CUDA 4.1 compiler is based on the LLVM compiler infrastructure [15] with the intention of allowing CUDA programs to run on either the GPU or the CPU [25]. In order to make the verification of program correctness independent of the execution model, we plan to study stronger criteria for the preservation of termination and other liveness properties when the underlying hardware uses the SIMT execution model instead of a weakly fair multi-thread semantics. Furthermore, it might be worthwhile to check whether our findings can be generalized to the SIMD execution models found in some contemporary CPU architectures.

References

1. AMD. Evergreen Family Instruction Set Architecture, Reference Guide (2011)
2. Barnat, J., Brim, L., Ceska, M., Lamr, T.: CUDA Accelerated LTL Model Checking. In: Proc. 15th Int. Conf. Parallel and Distributed Systems (ICPADS 2009), pp. 34–41 (2009)

3. Bošnački, D., Edelkamp, S., Sulewski, D., Wijs, A.: GPU-PRISM: An Extension of PRISM for General Purpose Graphics Processing Units. In: Proc. 9th Int. Wsh. Parallel and Distributed Methods in Verification (PDMV 2010), pp. 17–19 (2010)
4. Collange, S.: Stack-less SIMT Reconvergence at Low Cost. Technical Report HAL-00622654, INRIA (2011)
5. Coon, B.W., Nickolls, J.R., Nyland, L., Mills, P.C., Lindholm, J.E.: Indirect Function Call Instructions in a Synchronous Parallel Thread Processor, United States Patent Application #2009/0240931 (2009)
6. Fung, W.W.L., Aamodt, T.M.: Thread Block Compaction for Efficient SIMT Control Flow. In: Proc. 17th IEEE Int. Symp. High Performance Computer Architecture (HPCA 2011), pp. 25–36 (2011)
7. Fung, W.W.L., Sham, I., Yuan, G., Aamodt, T.M.: Dynamic Warp Formation and Scheduling for Efficient GPU Control Flow. In: Proc. 40th Ann. IEEE/ACM Int. Symp. Microarchitecture (MICRO 2007), pp. 407–420 (2007)
8. Garland, M., Le Grand, S., Nickolls, J., Anderson, J., Hardwick, J., Morton, S., Phillips, E., Zhang, Y., Volkov, V.: Parallel Computing Experiences with CUDA. IEEE Micro 28(4), 13–27 (2008)
9. Habermaier, A.: The Model of Computation of CUDA and its Formal Semantics. Technical Report 2011-14, University of Augsburg (2011)
10. Habermaier, A., Knapp, A.: On the Correctness of the SIMT Execution Model of GPUs. Technical Report 2012-1, University of Augsburg (2012)
11. Hennessy, J.L., Patterson, D.A.: Computer Architecture: A Quantitative Approach, 5th edn. Elsevier Science & Technology (2011)
12. Khronos Group Inc. The OpenGL Shading Language 4.20, Revision 6 (2011)
13. Khronos OpenCL Working Group. The OpenCL Specification 1.2, Revision 15 (2011)
14. Levinthal, A., Porter, T.: Chap – A SIMD Graphics Processor. SIGGRAPH Comput. Graph. 18, 77–82 (1984)
15. The LLVM Compiler Infrastructure, `http://www.llvm.org/` (01/04/2012)
16. Mantor, M., Houston, M.: AMD Graphic Core Next: Low Power High Performance Graphics & Parallel Compute. Presentation at the AMD Fusion Developer Summit (2011)
17. Mark, W.: Future Graphics Architectures. ACM Queue 6, 54–64 (2008)
18. Meng, J., Tarjan, D., Skadron, K.: Dynamic Warp Subdivision for Integrated Branch and Memory Divergence Tolerance. In: Proc. 37th Ann. Int. Symp. Computer Architecture (ISCA 2010), pp. 235–246 (2010)
19. Moy, S., Lindholm, J.E.: Method and System for Programmable Pipelined Graphics Processing with Branching Instructions, United States Patent #6,947,047 (2005)
20. Muchnick, S.S.: Advanced Compiler Design and Implementation. Morgan Kaufmann Publishers Inc. (1997)
21. Nickolls, J.R., Dally, W.: The GPU Computing Era. IEEE Micro 30(2), 56–69 (2010)
22. NVIDIA. DirectCompute Programming Guide 3.2 (2010)
23. NVIDIA. cuobjdump. CUDA Toolkit 4.1 (2011)
24. NVIDIA. NVIDIA CUDA C Programming Guide 4.1 (2011)
25. NVIDIA. NVIDIA Opens Up CUDA Platform by Releasing Compiler Source Code (2011), `http://tiny.cc/NvidiaLLVM` (01/04/2012)
26. Reynolds, J.C.: Theories of Programming Languages. Cambridge University Press (1998)

Reasoning about Lock Placements

Peter Hawkins, Alex Aiken*, Kathleen Fisher**,
Martin Rinard, and Mooly Sagiv

Stanford University, Tufts University, MIT, Tel Aviv University

Abstract. A *lock placement* describes, for each heap location, which lock guards the location, and under what circumstances. We formalize methods for reasoning about lock placements, making precise the interactions between the program, the heap structure, and the lock placement.

1 Introduction

Most concurrent software uses *locks* as a primitive for ensuring mutual exclusion between threads. While it is correct to say that the key characteristic of a lock is that it may be held by only one thread at a time, such a description fails to capture the higher-level purposes for which programmers use locks. Universally, locks are used to protect data, guaranteeing that only one thread operates on particular parts of the store at a time. The association between locks and the data they protect is, however, implicit, and in the presence of mutable data structures it is not even clear how to describe the relationship between a possibly changing set of locks and the changing heap the locks protect.

This paper investigates what it means for locks to protect data. So far as we are aware, there are no proposals in the literature for even stating the relationship between locks and the data they protect that capture the range of ways in which locks are used in practice. In particular, we are interested in explaining *speculative locks* and the common case in which updates to the heap change which data locks protect. We believe ours is the first proposal to address these issues.

To explain our results, we begin with a slightly informal, simple, obviously correct, but impractical locking protocol. We assume the heap consists of a graph of *objects* (nodes), each of which has a set of *fields* (edges) that point to other objects. We also assume that concurrent operations are expressed as transactions that execute atomically (e.g., atomic blocks). Every heap edge has a *logical lock*. Each transaction t must obey a standard two-phase locking protocol:

- Acquire all logical locks of every edge read or written by t.
- Perform the reads and writes of t.
- Release all of t's logical locks.

* This work was supported by NSF grants CCF-0702681 and CNS-050955.

** The views expressed are those of the author and do not reflect the official policy or position of the Department of Defense or U.S. Government. Distribution Statement A (Approved for Public Release, Distribution Unlimited).

H. Seidl (Ed.): ESOP 2012, LNCS 7211, pp. 336–356, 2012.

It is a classic result [8] that any interleaving of such transactions is *serializable* (equivalent to some sequential schedule of the transactions). However in practice acquiring a separate lock for every field of every object touched by a transaction is exorbitantly expensive. Thus, practical locking protocols use fewer locks. For example, a tree data structure might have a single lock at the root, or a hash table may have one lock per hash bucket, with no locks on the bucket contents.

The key insight is that the programmer has made an optimization: many logical locks are represented by a single *physical lock*. We can still think of a transaction as acquiring all of the logical locks required, but now instead of acquiring the lock on the actual edge e it must instead acquire the physical lock $\psi(e)$ assigned to the edge by a *lock placement* ψ, which is a mapping from logical locks to the physical locks that implement them. For example, in the tree case $\psi(e) = \rho$ for every edge in the tree, where ρ is the tree's root. For the hash table, $\psi(e) = l_i$, where the i-th bucket has an associated physical lock l_i for every field e in the i-th bucket. If the same physical locks represents multiple logical locks then transactions need only acquire the single physical lock to obtain access to multiple heap locations.

Lock placements capture common idioms for programming with locks:

- Locking at different granularities corresponds to different lock placements. For example, each element of a tree may have its own lock, or there may be a single coarse-grained lock. Lock placements make explicit which locations are guarded by the same lock, and where that lock is placed.
- It is sometimes beneficial to place the lock guarding an object o in a field of o itself, which means that o cannot be locked without first accessing o in an unlocked state. Lock placements can describe such *speculative* locking, allowing us to reason about transactions that make use of it.
- Which locks guard which fields often changes over time. As a simple example, consider a heap in which all `nil` fields are guarded by a global lock, and all non-`nil` fields are guarded by a speculative lock in the object the field points to. When a `nil` field is assigned an object the global lock is *split* and no longer guards the field, and when a pointer field is assigned `nil` that field is *merged* into the global lock. Lock placements can depend on the state of the heap and so naturally capture lock splitting and merging.

We develop our results incrementally, beginning with flat "heaps" that are just a set of global variables with no pointers (Section 2). In this simple setting we formalize the key notions of lock placements and *stability*, we give a proof system for showing that transaction traces are *well-locked*, and we prove that well-locked transactions are serializable. We then consider heaps that are mutable trees (Section 3), where the main complication is that logical locks are now named by heap paths, which may be updated concurrently. Finally, we consider a class of mutable DAG heaps (Section 4) based on *decompositions* [13]; sharing complicates lock placements as there may be multiple access paths to an object.

For space reasons, all proofs are in the technical report [12]. Because our focus is on formalizing lock placements, we do not consider liveness properties, such as

$m \in \mathcal{M}$	memory locations		$l \in \mathcal{L},\ L \subseteq \mathcal{L}$	locks, lock sets
$b ::= \mathsf{F} \mid \mathsf{T}$	booleans		$\omega ::= m \mapsto b$	heap assertions
$\psi \subseteq \mathcal{M} \to 2^{L \times \Phi}$	lock placements		$\Phi \ni \phi ::= b \mid \omega \mid \phi \vee \phi \mid \phi \wedge \phi$	guards
$t ::= \mathsf{wr}(m, b) \mid \mathsf{obs}(m) = b \mid \mathsf{rd}(m) = b \mid \mathsf{lock}\ l \mid \mathsf{unlock}\ l$				transaction ops.

Fig. 1. Locations, Lock Placements, Transaction Operations

deadlock, or optimizations, such as early release, since these issues are orthogonal to the ones we explore. The standard techniques for ensuring deadlock-freedom apply, including both static techniques (imposing a total ordering on locks) and dynamic techniques (using a contention manager to resolve deadlocks at run-time).

2 Flat Maps

We first consider a simple class of heaps defined over a fixed set of *memory locations* $\mathcal{M}$. A *flat map heap* is a set of mappings $\{m \mapsto b\}_{m \in \mathcal{M}}$ from each location $m \in \mathcal{M}$ to a boolean value b. Let $\mathcal{L}$ be a fixed set of *physical locks*; in this section we assume that memory locations and locks are disjoint. For ease of exposition we consider only exclusive locks — that is, if a transaction holds a lock then no other transaction may acquire concurrent access to the same lock.

A common correctness criterion for concurrent transactions is *serializability*. Informally a concurrent execution of a set of transactions is serializable if the reads and writes transactions make to the heap are equivalent to the reads and writes in some serial schedule of the same transactions. Serializability ensures we can reason about programs as if only one transaction executes at a time.

A *transaction* $\mathbf{T}$ is a sequence $t^1 t^2 \ldots$ of the atomic *transaction operations* given in Figure 1: a possibly unstable read of location m yielding b ($\mathsf{rd}(m) = b$), a logical observation of location m yielding b ($\mathsf{obs}(m) = b$), a write of b to location m ($\mathsf{wr}(m, b)$), a lock of a physical lock l ($\mathsf{lock}\ l$), or an unlock of physical lock l ($\mathsf{unlock}\ l$). With the exception of the rd and obs operations the concrete semantics of transaction operations are standard; the details are in the technical report [12]. We assume the execution of operations is sequentially consistent.

The transaction language distinguishes between between high-level obs operations, which are observations of the state of memory that affect the outcome of a transaction and for which the locking protocol must ensure serializability, and low-level rd operations, which do not directly affect the outcome of a transaction and need not be serializable. A transaction may freely perform a rd operation on any location at any time, regardless of the locks that it holds, however there is no guarantee that the value read will remain *stable*; a read is *stable* only if no concurrent transaction may write to the same location and invalidate the value that was read. If a transaction holds locks that ensure that the value returned by a rd operation is stable and cannot be altered by concurrent transactions, then a transaction may logically obs the result of the read operation and use that value to perform computation. The distinction between stable and unstable reads is key to reasoning about *speculative locking* (Section 2.1).

(a)	(b)		(c)	
1: lock l	1: lock l_1	9: unlock l_1	1: lock l_1	9: obs$(m_4) = \mathsf{F}$
2: rd$(m_1) = \mathsf{T}$	2: rd$(m_1) = \mathsf{T}$	10: unlock l_0	2: rd$(m_1) = \mathsf{T}$	10: unlock l_4
3: obs$(m_1) = \mathsf{T}$	3: obs$(m_1) = \mathsf{T}$		3: obs$(m_1) = \mathsf{T}$	11: unlock l_3
4: rd$(m_3) = \mathsf{F}$	4: rd$(m_3) = \mathsf{F}$		4: lock l_3	12: unlock l_1
5: obs$(m_3) = \mathsf{F}$	5: obs$(m_3) = \mathsf{F}$		5: rd$(m_3) = \mathsf{F}$	
6: rd$(m_4) = \mathsf{F}$	6: lock l_0		6: obs$(m_3) = \mathsf{F}$	
7: obs$(m_4) = \mathsf{F}$	7: rd$(m_4) = \mathsf{F}$		7: lock l_4	
8: unlock l	8: obs$(m_4) = \mathsf{F}$		8: rd$(m_4) = \mathsf{F}$	

Fig. 2. Transaction traces that observe the values of locations m_1, m_3, and m_4 under (a) coarse, (b) intermediate, and (c) fine-grained lock placements

2.1 Lock Placements

We associate a *logical lock* with every heap location $m \in \mathcal{M}$. Whenever a transaction observes or changes the value of a memory location it must hold the associated logical lock. It is inefficient to attach a distinct lock to every memory location; instead we use a smaller set of *physical locks* (or simply *locks*) $\mathcal{L}$ to implement logical locks; a *lock placement* maps logical locks to physical locks. Different placement functions describe different granularities of locking.

Formally, a *lock placement* ψ for a boolean heap is a mapping from each location $m \in \mathcal{M}$ to a guarded set of locks that protect it. Each entry in $\psi(m)$ is a pair of a lock $l \in \mathcal{L}$ and a *guard* ϕ, which is a condition under which l protects m. A guard is a boolean combination of heap assertions $m \mapsto b$; for a given memory location each lock may only appear at most once on the left hand side of a guarded lock pair, and the set of guards must be mutually exclusive, and total, that is, exactly one guard is true for any given heap state.

For example, suppose $\mathcal{M} = \{m_0, \ldots, m_{k-1}\}$. Different placements allow us to describe a range of different locking granularities:

- A coarse-grain locking strategy protects every memory location with the same lock, that is, set $L = \{l\}$ and set $\psi(m_i) = \{(l, \mathsf{T})\}$ for all i. To observe or write to any memory location a transaction must hold lock l.
- An medium-grain locking strategy stripes memory locations across a small set of locks. Set $L = \{l_0, \ldots, l_{p-1}\}$, and then set $\psi(m_i) = \{(l_{(i \bmod p)}, \mathsf{T})\}$ for all i. To observe or write to memory location m_i, we must hold lock $l_{(i \bmod p)}$.
- A fine-grain strategy associates a distinct lock with every memory location. Set $L = \{l_0, \ldots, l_{k-1}\}$ and set $\psi(m_i) = \{(l_i, \mathsf{T})\}$ for all i. To observe or write to memory location m_i we must hold lock l_i.

Figure 2 shows three variants of a transaction that reads memory locations m_1, m_3 and m_4 (chosen arbitrarily for the example), observing values T, F, and F respectively. The figure shows a variant of the transaction for each locking granularity, using $p = 2$ physical locks in the medium-grain case.

A *speculative lock placement* is a placement in which the identity of a lock that protects a memory location depends on the memory location itself. For example a simple speculative placement ψ_s is as follows. Let $L = \{l_f, l_t\}$ and $\mathcal{M} = \{m\}$.

(a)	(b)		(c)
1: $\mathsf{rd}(m) = \mathsf{T}$	1: $\mathsf{rd}(m) = \mathsf{T}$	7: $\mathsf{obs}(m) = \mathsf{F}$	1: $\mathsf{lock}\ l_f$
2: $\mathsf{lock}\ l_t$	2: $\mathsf{lock}\ l_t$	8: $\mathsf{unlock}\ l_f$	2: $\mathsf{lock}\ l_t$
3: $\mathsf{rd}(m) = \mathsf{T}$	3: $\mathsf{rd}(m) = \mathsf{F}$		3: $\mathsf{rd}(m) = \mathsf{T}$
4: $\mathsf{obs}(m) = \mathsf{T}$	4: $\mathsf{unlock}\ l_t$		4: $\mathsf{wr}(m, \mathsf{F})$
5: $\mathsf{unlock}\ l_t$	5: $\mathsf{lock}\ l_f$		5: $\mathsf{unlock}\ l_t$
	6: $\mathsf{rd}(m) = \mathsf{F}$		6: $\mathsf{unlock}\ l_f$

Fig. 3. Traces that read and write location m under the speculative lock placement ψ_s

Set $\psi_s(m) = l_f$ if $m \mapsto \mathsf{F}$, or l_t if $m \mapsto \mathsf{T}$ Under this placement, lock l_f protects memory location m if m contains the value F, whereas lock l_t protects memory location m if m contains the value T.

A more realistic example of speculative lock placement is motivated by transactional predication [2] which uses a speculative placement of STM metadata. We use a collection $\mathcal{M} = \{m_1, \ldots, m_k\}$ of memory locations to model a concurrent set. Location m_i has value T if value i is present in the set. We use $L = \{l_\perp, l_1, \ldots, l_k\}$ and the placement $\psi(m_i) = l_\perp$ if $m_i \mapsto \mathsf{F}$, or l_i if $m_i \mapsto \mathsf{T}$. The speculative placement allows us to attach a distinct lock to every entry present in the set, without also requiring that we keep around a distinct lock for every entry that is absent from the set. Two transactions that operate on keys present in the set only contend on the same lock if they are accessing the same key. Transactions that operate on keys that are absent will however contend on $l_\perp$; this strategy is effective if we expect sets to have at most a small fraction of all possible elements at any one time. If necessary, we can reduce contention on absent entries to arbitrarily low levels by striping the logical locks protecting absent entries across a set of physical locks $l_\perp^1, l_\perp^2, \ldots$ as discussed earlier.

It may not be immediately obvious how to acquire a lock on a memory location when we do not know which lock to take without knowing the value of the memory location. The key to this apparent circularity is that a transaction can use unstable reads to guess the identity of the correct lock; once the transaction has acquired the lock it can redo the read to verify that its guess was correct. If the transaction guesses correctly, then the second read is stable. If the transaction guesses incorrectly it can release the lock and repeat the process. Figure 3(a) shows a transaction that observes the state of m under the speculative lock placement ψ_s. If another transaction had raced, we might have had to retry the read, as shown in Figure 3(b). Finally, to perform an update, we must hold both locks, as shown in Figure 3(c); otherwise by changing m we might implicitly release a lock that another transaction holds on the state of m.

2.2 Well-Locked Transactions

We represent the state of a transaction as two sets: the *observation set* Ω and a *lock set* L. The observation set Ω is a set of heap assertions $m \mapsto b$ that represent a transaction's local view of the heap. The lock set L is a set of *physical locks* held by the transaction. Every heap assertion in the observation set must be *stable*;

$$\boxed{\text{FLock}}\ \frac{l \notin L}{\Omega, L \vdash_\psi \mathsf{lock}\ l; \Omega, L \cup \{l\}} \qquad \boxed{\text{FUnlock}}\ \frac{l \in L \quad L' = L \setminus \{l\} \quad \Omega' = \lceil \Omega \mid L'; \psi \rceil}{\Omega, L \vdash_\psi \mathsf{unlock}\ l; \Omega', L'}$$

$$\boxed{\text{FRdUnstable}}\ \frac{\Omega' = \Omega \cup \{m \mapsto b\} \qquad \neg\mathsf{locked}_\psi(m, \Omega', L)}{\Omega, L \vdash_\psi \mathsf{rd}(m) = b; \Omega, L} \qquad \boxed{\text{FRdStable}}\ \frac{\Omega' = \Omega \cup \{m \mapsto b\} \qquad \mathsf{locked}_\psi(m, \Omega', L)}{\Omega, L \vdash_\psi \mathsf{rd}(m) = b; \Omega', L}$$

$$\boxed{\text{FObserve}}\ \frac{(m \mapsto b) \in \Omega}{\Omega, L \vdash_\psi \mathsf{obs}(m) = b; \Omega, L} \qquad \boxed{\text{FWrite}}\ \frac{m \in \mathrm{dom}\,\Omega \qquad \Omega' = \Omega[m \mapsto b] \qquad (\forall m', l, \phi.\ (l, \phi) \in \psi(m') \land m \in \mathrm{dom}\,\phi \implies l \in L)}{\Omega, L \vdash_\psi \mathsf{wr}(m, b); \Omega', L}$$

Fig. 4. Well-locked transaction operations: $\Omega, L \vdash_\psi t; \Omega', L'$

informally, the facts in the observation set are logically locked and cannot be invalidated by a concurrent interfering transaction. We write $\Omega[m \mapsto b]$ to denote the result of adding or updating the heap observation $m \mapsto b$ to Ω, replacing any existing observations about m. The predicate $\mathsf{locked}_\psi(m, \Omega, L)$ holds for heap location m if a transaction with heap observations Ω and locks L has logically locked location m under lock placement ψ, where $\Omega \vdash \phi$ denotes entailment:

$$\mathsf{locked}_\psi(m, \Omega, L) = \exists (l, \phi) \in \psi(m).\ \ l \in L \land \Omega \vdash \phi$$

The judgement $\Omega, L \vdash_\psi t; \Omega', L'$ defined in Figure 4 characterizes *well-locked operations*. The judgment holds if whenever a transaction with observations Ω and holding locks L executes operation t, then on completion of the operation the transaction has new observations Ω' and locks L'. Given the set of physical operations that a transaction performs, the well-lockedness judgement computes the set of stable observations of the transaction, and ensures that a transaction only logically observes and writes locations on which it holds logical locks.

The (FLock) rule allows a transaction to acquire a lock l if the transaction does not already have l in its set of locks L; acquiring a lock has no affect on the observation set Ω. The (FUnlock) rule allows a transaction to release any lock l in its lock set L; any facts in Ω that were protected by l are no longer stable, so the rule uses the *stabilization operator* to compute a new stable set of observations Ω'. The *stabilization* of a set of observations Ω_0 under locks L and placement ψ, written $\lceil \Omega_0 \mid L; \psi \rceil$, is the limit of the monotonic sequence:

$$\Omega_{i+1} = \{m \mapsto b \in \Omega_i \mid \mathsf{locked}_\psi(m, \Omega_i, L)\}$$

Note that the limit always exists, because Ω_0 is finite (since it is constructed by a finite transaction execution) and the empty set is always a fixed point of the equation if no larger set is. A set of observations Ω is *stable* under locks L and placement ψ if Ω is its own stabilization, that is, $\Omega = \lceil \Omega \mid L; \psi \rceil$.

Rule (FObserve) states that a transaction may logically observe any stable fact from its stable observation set Ω. The (FRdUnstable) rule allows a transaction to perform a speculative read on a memory location on which the transaction does not hold a lock; however since the result may not be stable the rule does not update the set Ω. To enable reasoning about speculation, the determination whether the read is stable or not occurs in a context that includes the read of m; since we assume that reads are atomic, there is an instant in time at which both the old stable facts in Ω and the newly read value of m hold, and it is in that context that we determine stability. The (FRDSTABLE) rule allows a transaction to read memory locations on which it holds a lock; since such a read is stable the rule updates the set of observations Ω with the newly read information about the heap. Finally the (FWRITE) rule requires that a transaction can only update a location m if it holds the lock on m; furthermore the lock for any location m' for which m appears in a guard must also be held by the transaction—hence no transaction can destabilize the observations of another transaction. The last condition together with $\mathsf{locked}_\psi(m, \Omega, L)$ imply that $\mathsf{locked}_\psi(m, \Omega', L)$ holds, which is why the latter is not listed as a precondition of the rule.

A transaction $\mathbf{T} = t^1 \ldots t^k$ is *well-locked* if there exists a sequence of lock sets L^i and observation sets Ω^i such that

$$L^0 = L^k = \emptyset, \quad \Omega^0 = \Omega^k = \emptyset, \qquad \text{and } \Omega^{i-1}, L^{i-1} \vdash_\psi t^i; \Omega^i, L^i \text{ for } 1 \leq i \leq k.$$

As an example of applying the rules, consider again the speculative read transaction shown in Figure 3(b). Let Ω^i and L^i denote the lock sets of the transaction after line i. Initially we have $\Omega^0 = \emptyset$ and $L^0 = \emptyset$. The read on line 1 is unstable, so $\Omega^1 = \emptyset$ and $L^1 = \emptyset$. The lock on line 2 adds an entry to the lock set l_t, so $\Omega^2 = \emptyset$ and $L^2 = \{l_t\}$. The read on line 3 yields $m \mapsto \mathsf{F}$, however the read would only be stable if $\mathsf{locked}_\psi(m, \{m \mapsto \mathsf{F}\}, \{l_t\})$ holds, which it does not; once again we have $\Omega^3 = \emptyset$ and $L^3 = \{l_t\}$. Lines 4 and 5 update the lock set; we have $\Omega^4 = \Omega^5 = \emptyset$, $L^4 = \emptyset$, and $L^5 = \{l_f\}$. The read on line 6 once again yields $m \mapsto \mathsf{F}$, but this time the predicate $\mathsf{locked}_\psi(m, \{m \mapsto \mathsf{F}\}, \{l_f\})$ holds and the read is stable, yielding $\Omega^6 = \{m \mapsto \mathsf{F}\}$ and $L^6 = \{l_f\}$. The logical observation of $m \mapsto \mathsf{F}$ on line 7 is permitted by the judgement since we know $m \mapsto \mathsf{F}$ is part of the stable heap; the observation and lock sets are unchanged ($\Omega^7 = \Omega^6$, $L^7 = L^6$). Finally, line 8 releases lock l_f, so we have $L^8 = \emptyset$. The assertion about m in Ω^7 is no longer stable, so the stabilization operator removes it from the observation set, finally yielding $\Omega^8 = \emptyset$.

2.3 Serializability of Well-Locked Transactions

A *schedule* s for a set of transactions $\mathbf{T}_1, \ldots, \mathbf{T}_k$ is a permutation of the concatenation of all transactions in the set, such that each transaction $\mathbf{T}_i$ is a subsequence of s. Formally, a schedule is *valid* if it corresponds to an execution of the concrete semantics (see the technical report [12] for details). Informally, validity requires the execution respect the mutual exclusion property of locks, and memory accesses must accurately reflect the state of the global heap. A schedule is *serial* if operations of different transactions are not interleaved.

Lemma 1. *Let s be a valid schedule of well-locked transactions $\{\mathbf{T}_1, \ldots, \mathbf{T}_k\}$. Let Ω_i^j and L_i^j be the set of observations and locks of transaction i after schedule step j. Let h^j be the heap after schedule step j. Then for all time steps j the lock sets $\{L_i^j\}_{i=1}^k$ are disjoint, and the observation sets $\{\Omega_i^j\}_{i=1}^k$ are stable, have disjoint domains, and heap h^j is an extension of each $\{\Omega_i^j\}_{i=1}^k$.*

The disjointness of observation sets in Lemma 1 follows from the exclusivity of physical locks. If we allowed shared/exclusive locks, then we would also need to allow observation sets to overlap on values protected by shared locks.

A well-locked transaction $\mathbf{T} = (t^i)_{i=1}^k$ is *logically two-phase* if the domains of the observation sets of the transaction have a growing phase and a shrinking phase, that is, there exists some j such that for all i where $1 \leq i \leq j$, we have $\operatorname{dom} \Omega^{i-1} \subseteq \operatorname{dom} \Omega^i$ and for all i where $j < i \leq k$ we have $\operatorname{dom} \Omega^{i-1} \supseteq \operatorname{dom} \Omega^i$.

A *logical schedule* $\hat{\mathbf{s}}$ is the subsequence of a schedule $\mathbf{s}$ consisting of all the obs and wr operations. Two operations *conflict* if they access the same memory location m. Two schedules $\mathbf{s}_1$ and $\mathbf{s}_2$ are *conflict-equivalent* if the logical schedule $\hat{\mathbf{s}}_1$ can be turned into the logical schedule $\hat{\mathbf{s}}_2$ by a sequence of swaps of adjacent non-conflicting operations.

Lemma 2. *Any valid schedule of a set of well-locked, logically two-phase transactions $\{\mathbf{T}_1, \ldots, \mathbf{T}_k\}$ is conflict-equivalent to a serial logical schedule.*

2.4 Shared/Exclusive Logical Locks

A limitation of the protocol just presented is that locks are exclusive — holding a lock gives a transaction sole access to an edge, even if the transaction only wants to read the edge. Lock placement is a separate issue from whether non-exclusive locks exist for reading. Exclusive locks are sufficient to illustrate all of the important features of our techniques and have the advantage of not introducing the extra and extraneous complications of supporting non-exclusive access. However, non-exclusive locks are important, and so we briefly illustrate how to extend our approach to locks providing shared read access.

To allow shared access to fields we relax the requirement that guards must be mutually exclusive, thereby allowing each logical lock to map to many physical locks at the same time. Under the relaxed definition of placement, a transaction has shared access to a memory location m if it holds at least one of the locks that protect m, whereas a transaction has exclusive access to m if it holds all of the locks that protect m. Formally, a transaction has shared access to a memory location m if $\mathsf{locked}_\psi(m, \Omega, L)$ holds. We also define a new predicate

$$\mathsf{exclusive}_\psi(m, \Omega, L) = \forall (l, \phi) \in \psi(m).\ \ l \in L \vee \Omega \vdash \neg\phi$$

which holds for heap location m if a transaction with heap observations Ω and locks L has an exclusive logical lock on location m under lock placement ψ.

To show serializability, we need to add an additional precondition to the (FWRITE) rule requiring that a transaction have exclusive access to any memory location it writes. The statement of the proof of Lemma 1 must be altered since different observation sets may share fields on which they hold a shared lock— only the exclusively held fields must be disjoint between transactions. Finally we must update the definition of a two-phase transaction to ensure that transactions only release exclusive access to a field in the shrinking phase of a transaction.

$f, \mathbf{f}, \mathcal{F}$	fields	x, y, ρ	object names	$e ::= \mathsf{nil} \mid x$	expressions
$\omega ::= x.f \mapsto e$	heap assertions			$\psi \subseteq 2^{\mathbf{f}} \rightarrow 2^{\mathbf{f}}$	placements

$t ::= \mathsf{wr}(x.f, e) \mid \mathsf{obs}(x.f) = e \mid \mathsf{rd}(x.f) = e \mid x = \mathsf{new}() \mid \mathsf{lock}\ x \mid \mathsf{unlock}\ x$ trans. ops.

Fig. 5. Tree transactions

3 Mutable Tree-Structured Heaps

In Section 2 we described a locking protocol for flat heaps with a fixed set of memory locations and locks. In this section we extend our results to dynamically allocated, mutable tree-shaped heaps with a placement function based on paths.

A *tree heap* h consists of a set of objects, each with a unique name, usually denoted x or y. Every object has a fixed set of fields $\mathcal{F}$. Each object field $x.f$ contains a pointer either to some object y or nil. The heap contains a distinguished *root object*, named ρ. In a quiescent state, that is, in the absence of running transactions, we require that the heap be a forest.

We associate a logical lock with every field of every object in the heap. Unlike the flat heaps of Section 2 we do not assume that we have a separate set of physical locks distinct from the set of memory locations; instead, following the practice of languages such as Java, we require that every heap object can function as a physical lock, and we use a lock placement function to describe a policy for mapping the logical locks attached to fields onto the physical locks (the objects). To define the lock placement, we use access paths from the root ρ to name both the fields we want to protect and the objects whose physical locks protect them.

We extend the set of transaction operations of Section 2 to read from and write to fields of objects, to handle dynamic allocation of new objects, and to apply lock and unlock operations to objects rather than a separate set of locks. The transaction operations, shown in Figure 5, are: write an expression e (either an object y or nil) to field f of object x ($\mathsf{wr}(x.f, e)$)), a possibly unstable read of field f of object x yielding result e ($\mathsf{rd}(x.f) = e$), a stable observation of field f of object x yielding e ($\mathsf{obs}(x.f) = e$), allocation of a fresh object ($x = \mathsf{new}()$), locking an object ($\mathsf{lock}\ x$), and unlocking an object ($\mathsf{unlock}\ x$).

3.1 Lock Placements

We name edges in the heap as a non-empty field path (a sequence of field names) $\mathbf{f} = f_1 f_2 \ldots$ from the root, ending in the edge in question. Since the path names a field in the heap, the path must be non-empty. We also name objects using fields, except that the path ends at the object the field points to; note that in the case of objects the empty path names the root of the heap. A *lock placement* ψ is a function from non-empty paths to paths, which maps every edge in a heap to an object whose attached physical lock protects it.

Consider heaps with fields drawn from the set $\mathcal{F} = \{a, b\}$. We can protect every edge of the heap with a single coarse-grain lock by setting $\psi_1(\mathbf{f}) = \epsilon$ for all $\mathbf{f}$. If we want different locks for the a and b subtrees, we can use the lock placement

$$\psi_2(\mathbf{f}) = a \text{ if } a \prec \mathbf{f},\ b \text{ if } b \prec \mathbf{f},\ \text{and } \epsilon \text{ if } \mathbf{f} = a \text{ or } \mathbf{f} = b \quad (1)$$

where $\mathbf{g} \prec \mathbf{f}$ denotes that $\mathbf{g}$ is a prefix of $\mathbf{f}$. For example, in Figure 6(a), under placement ψ_2 the lock at ρ protects the edges ρx and ρy, the lock at x protects the edges xz and xu, and the lock at y protects the edge yv.

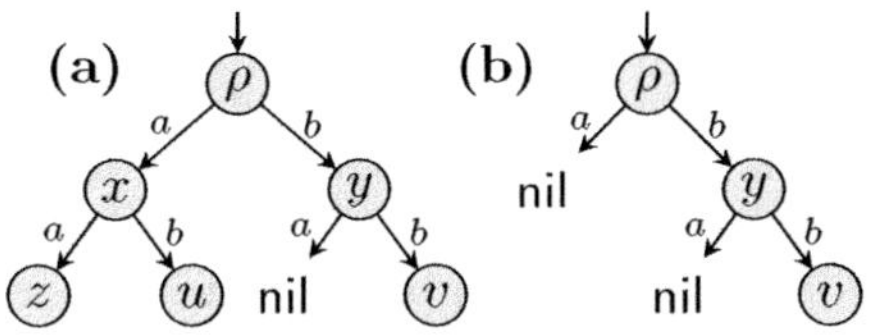

Fig. 6. Examples of tree heaps. Nodes represent objects, whereas edges represent fields. Node ρ is the root object

If for an edge $\mathbf{f}$ the placement path $\psi(\mathbf{f})$ leads to nil in the heap, we use the lock on the object preceding the edge to nil in the placement path. For example, consider Figure 6(b) under the placement ψ_2. According to the placement, the lock that protects the edge named by path ab is $\psi_2(ab) = a$, however edge a from the root ρ points to nil. Instead, we use the lock on the longest non-nil prefix of $\psi_2(ab)$, namely ρ itself.

(a)	(b)		(c)	
lock ρ	lock ρ	unlock w	rd$(\rho.b) = y$	unlock w
rd$(\rho.b) = y$	rd$(\rho.b) = y$	unlock y	lock y	unlock y
obs$(\rho.b) = y$	obs$(\rho.b) = y$	unlock ρ	rd$(\rho.b) = y$	
lock y	lock y		obs$(\rho.b) = y$	
$w =$ new ()	rd$(y.a) =$ nil		rd$(y.a) =$ nil	
wr$(y.a, w)$	$w =$ new ()		$w =$ new ()	
unlock y	lock w		lock w	
unlock ρ	wr$(y.a, w)$		wr$(y.a, w)$	

Fig. 7. Three transaction traces that add a new outgoing edge labelled a from node y to the tree of Figure 6(b) under the lock placements (a) ψ_2, (b) ψ_3, and (c) ψ_4

Modifications to the heap may implicitly alter the mapping from logical locks to physical locks. If a transaction updates an edge, then the transaction must hold all logical locks whose mapping to physical locks may change both before and after the update. For example consider again the lock placement ψ_2 in the context of the tree heap shown in Figure 6(b). According to the placement the lock on ρ protects the edge a from the root; however since edge a points to nil, edges on any path that begins with a are also protected by the lock at a. If a transaction were to set $\rho.a$ to point to a fresh vertex w, the lock at w would now protect the edges on paths that begin with a; the transaction has *split* the logical roles of the lock at ρ before the write between the lock at ρ and the lock on new node w. Whenever a transaction splits or merges locks (e.g., by setting the field $\rho.a$ to nil again), it must hold every lock involved.

Figure 7(a) shows a trace of a transaction that adds a new edge labeled a from object y to a fresh object w to the heap of Figure 6(b) under placement ψ_2. The transaction acquires two locks, namely the lock at ρ that protects the edge from ρ to y, and the lock at y that protects the entire subtree rooted at y. We need not hold a lock on w when adding w into the tree since no path in the range of the placement function is a suffix of the path to the updated edge ba.

If we desire finer-grained locking, we can use a lock attached to every object to protect the fields of that object by using the placement function $\psi_3(\mathbf{g}f) = \mathbf{g}$ for any $\mathbf{g}, f$. The lock placement ψ_3 places the lock that protects each edge f on the object at the head of the edge. Figure 7(b) shows a trace of a transaction that again adds the edge labeled a from node y to a fresh node w to the heap of Figure 6(b), this time under lock placement ψ_3. Unlike the transaction of Figure 7(a), we need to ensure that by adding the new edge the write does not implicitly change the mapping from edges to locks. The well-lockedness conditions, which we introduce shortly, require that a transaction hold all physical locks which may map to different logical locks before and after a write. The operation $\mathsf{rd}(y.a) = \mathsf{nil}$ verifies that there is no existing subtree of y reachable via edge a. Before the update the lock at y protects every possible edge reachable from $y.a$, however after the write the lock y only protects the edge $y.a$ itself, whereas the lock at w protects everything reachable from node w. Hence we must hold lock w when performing the write, since adding the edge splits the lock at y. (In general one must hold locks when connecting objects into the heap, however in this specific case, since the write which links w to the heap is the last write in the transaction it would be possible to optimize away the lock and unlock.)

Finally, if we set $\psi_4(\mathbf{f}) = \mathbf{f}$ we obtain a speculative placement where each edge is protected by a lock at its target. Figure 7(c) once again shows a transaction that adds a fresh edge labeled a to node w, this time using placement ψ_4. The transaction begins with a speculative read to guess that the identity of the object whose lock protects $\rho.b$ is y. After locking y, the transaction performs the read again; since the read still returns y, the read is stable since the transaction already holds lock y. The transaction then performs a read of $y.a$ which returns nil. The value of the placement function for edge $y.a$ is $\psi(ba) = ba$, however since edge ba points to nil, the lock on the longest non-nil prefix of ba protects ba, in this case path b (node y). Since we hold the lock on y already, we know that the read of $y.a$ is also stable. Finally, the transaction must hold the lock on w when adding it to the heap to maintain the invariant that a transaction must hold all physical locks whose logical/physical mapping changes as a consequence of a write.

3.2 Well-Locked Transactions

We represent a transaction's state by three sets. As before, L is the set of locks that transaction holds, and Ω is a set of stable heap observations of the form $x.f \mapsto e$. We do not require Ω be a forest; a transaction may create any heap shapes it desires within its local heap. However, the forest invariant must be restored when the transaction releases objects in its local heap back into the global heap. Enforcing this condition is the purpose of the set Γ. An object x is a member of Γ if the transaction has shown that there is no globally visible path from the root to x (i.e., the transaction has locked the edge to x). The well-lockedness rules for tree heaps ensure that there is at most one globally-visible edge to any node and hence the globally-visible part of the heap is a forest. At

$$\boxed{\text{TLock}}\quad \frac{x \notin L}{\Omega, \Gamma, L \vdash_\psi \mathsf{lock}\ x; \Omega, \Gamma, L \cup \{x\}} \qquad \boxed{\text{TUnlock}}\quad \frac{x \in L \quad L' = L \setminus \{x\} \quad (\Omega', \Gamma') = \lceil \Omega; \Gamma \mid L'; \psi \rceil \quad \mathsf{forest}(\Omega, \Omega', \Gamma, \Gamma')}{\Omega, \Gamma, L \vdash_\psi \mathsf{unlock}\ x; \Omega', \Gamma', L'}$$

$$\boxed{\text{TNew}}\quad \frac{\Omega' = \Omega \cup \{x.f \mapsto \mathsf{nil} \mid f \in \mathcal{F}\} \quad x \notin \operatorname{dom} \Omega \quad x \notin \Gamma \quad \Gamma' = \Gamma \cup \{x\}}{\Omega, \Gamma, L \vdash_\psi x = \mathsf{new}(); \Omega', \Gamma', L} \qquad \boxed{\text{TObserve}}\quad \frac{(x.f \mapsto e) \in \Omega}{\Omega, \Gamma, L \vdash_\psi \mathsf{obs}(x.f) = e; \Omega, \Gamma, L}$$

$$\boxed{\text{TRdUnstable}}\quad \frac{x.f \notin \operatorname{dom} \Omega \quad \Omega' = \Omega \cup \{x.f \mapsto e\} \quad \neg\mathsf{locked}_\psi(x.f, \Omega', \Gamma, L)}{\Omega, \Gamma, L \vdash_\psi \mathsf{rd}(x.f) = e; \Omega, \Gamma, L}$$

$$\boxed{\text{TRdStable}}\quad \frac{x.f \notin \operatorname{dom} \Omega \quad \Omega' = \Omega \cup \{x.f \mapsto e\} \quad \mathsf{locked}_\psi(x.f, \Omega', \Gamma, L) \quad \Gamma' = \begin{cases} \Gamma & \text{if } e = \mathsf{nil} \\ \Gamma \cup \{y\} & \text{if } e = y \end{cases}}{\Omega, \Gamma, L \vdash_\psi \mathsf{rd}(x.f) = e; \Omega', \Gamma', L}$$

$$\boxed{\text{TWrite}}\quad \frac{x.f \in \operatorname{dom} \Omega \quad \Omega' = \Omega[x.f \mapsto e] \quad (\forall \mathbf{g}, \mathbf{h}.\ (\Omega \vdash \mathbf{g} \sim x) \wedge \mathbf{g}f \preceq \psi(\mathbf{h}) \implies \mathsf{pathlocked}_\psi(\mathbf{h}, \Omega, L) \wedge \mathsf{pathlocked}_\psi(\mathbf{h}, \Omega', L))}{\Omega, \Gamma, L \vdash_\psi \mathsf{wr}(x.f, e); \Omega', \Gamma, L}$$

Fig. 8. Well-locked tree operations: $\Omega, \Gamma, L \vdash_\psi t; \Omega', \Gamma', L'$

the start of every transaction Γ is the empty set. Transactions add entries to Γ by discovering global edges to nodes and transferring them into their local heap Ω; entries are removed from Γ when pointers to objects are released from the stable heap Ω back into the global heap.

The *path alias* judgement $\Omega \vdash \mathbf{f} \sim x$ holds if $\mathbf{f}$ is a path in Ω from the root to location x; that is, if $|\mathbf{f}| = k$, then there is a sequence of vertices $\mathbf{v} = v_0 v_1 \cdots$ such that $(\rho.f_0 \mapsto v_0) \in \Omega$, $(v_{i-1}.f_{i-1} \mapsto v_i) \in \Omega$ for all $1 < i < k-1$, and $v_{k-1}.f_{k-1} \mapsto x$. We write $\mathbf{f} \in \Omega$ if the path $\mathbf{f}$ from the root vertex exists in Ω, that is, $\Omega \vdash \mathbf{f} \sim x$ holds for some object x.

The *restriction of a path* $\mathbf{f}$ to a local heap Ω, written $\mathbf{f}|_\Omega$, is defined as

$$\mathbf{f}|_\Omega = \mathbf{f} \text{ if } \mathbf{f} \in \Omega, \text{ or } \mathbf{g} \text{ if } \exists \mathbf{g}, h.\ \mathbf{g}h \preceq \mathbf{f} \wedge \Omega \vdash \mathsf{nil} \sim \mathbf{g}h.$$

The restriction of path $\mathbf{f}$ is either $\mathbf{f}$ itself if present in the heap, or the longest prefix of the path present in the heap where no edge points to nil. The restriction of a path is undefined if the path $\mathbf{f}$ leaves the stable local heap Ω.

We hold the lock on an edge reached via a path if we hold the corresponding lock placement, restricted to the heap:

$$\mathsf{pathlocked}_\psi(\mathbf{f}, \Omega, L) ::= \exists x \in L.\ \Omega \vdash \psi(\mathbf{f})|_\Omega \sim x$$

We hold the lock on a field f of an object x under observations Ω, objects Γ and locks L, written $\mathsf{locked}_\psi(x.f, \Omega, \Gamma, L)$, if we hold a lock on field f on every path in the local heap, and furthermore there are no paths to x outside the local heap. Formally,

$$\mathsf{locked}_\psi(x.f, \Omega, \Gamma, L) ::= x \in \Gamma \wedge \forall \mathbf{g}.\ (\Omega \vdash x \sim \mathbf{g} \implies \mathsf{pathlocked}_\psi(\mathbf{g}f, \Omega, L))$$

If the local heap Ω contains cycles, observe that there may be infinitely many paths $\mathbf{g}$ and the predicate is well-defined in this case. To verify the absence of paths to x from outside the local heap, it is sufficient to check that $x \in \Gamma$, because any object $y \notin \Gamma$ is outside the local heap and thus has no stable fields and cannot form part of a path to x. Further, the definition of the locked predicate implies that if there is no path from the root ρ to node x, then the fields of x are locked for any transaction with $x \in \Gamma$; thus newly allocated objects can be added to Γ without taking a lock since they are disconnected from the global heap.

The judgement $\Omega, \Gamma, L \vdash_\psi t; \Omega', \Gamma', L'$ defined in Figure 8 captures the class of *well-locked tree operations*. If the judgement holds, then a transaction that executes operation t under stable observation set Ω, objects Γ, and lock set L yields a new stable observation set Ω', objects Γ' and lock set L'. The (TNew) rule states that all of the fields of a newly allocated object x point to nil, and since there can be no path to x in the heap all of x's fields are stable and $x \in \Gamma$. As before, the (TLock) rule allows a transaction to acquire a lock it does not yet hold and has no affect on either Ω or Γ.

In the (TUnlock) rule, the stabilization operator is slightly more involved than in the case of flat heaps, because we must compute not just the stable set of heap facts, but also the set of objects for which the transaction has locked the incoming path: if an edge $x.f \mapsto y$ drops out of the stable observation set because a lock is released, the transaction can no longer assume it holds locks on all of the paths to object y. The stabilization (Ω', Γ') of a local heap Ω_0 and global heap Γ_0 under locks L and placement ψ, written $(\Omega', \Gamma') = \lceil \Omega_0; \Gamma_0 \mid L; \psi \rceil$, is the limit of the monotonically decreasing sequence:

$$\Omega_{i+1} = \{x.f \mapsto e \in \Omega_i \mid \mathsf{locked}_\psi(x.f, \Omega_i, \Gamma_i, L)\} \quad \Gamma_{i+1} = \Gamma_i \setminus \{y \mid x.f \mapsto y \in \Omega_i \setminus \Omega_{i+1}\}$$

Rule (TUnlock) requires that transactions maintain the *forest condition*

$$\mathsf{forest}(\Omega, \Omega', \Gamma, \Gamma') ::= \forall y. \left(|\{x.f \mid (x.f \mapsto y) \in \Omega \setminus \Omega'\}| = \begin{cases} 1 & \text{if } y \in \Gamma \setminus \Gamma' \\ 0 & \text{otherwise} \end{cases} \right).$$

The forest condition ensures that a transaction may only release a pointer to a node y into the global heap if there are no other references to y in the global heap ($y \in \Gamma$). Furthermore, the condition also ensures that a transaction cannot release two or more pointers to the same location y into the global heap.

The rules (TObserve), (TRdUnstable), and (TRdStable) are similar to the rules in Section 2, updated to reflect that the heap now involves objects and fields. Note that (TRdStable) adds the object that is the target of the read to Γ in the case that the field is not nil.

The most interesting rule is (TWrite). Writing a field $x.f \mapsto y$ not only changes the paths to y, it changes the paths to every object reachable from y. Thus, as a result of a single field update, the placements may change for y and edges reachable from y. Furthermore, fields no longer reachable from $x.f$ after the update also may have altered lock placements. For this reason a transaction must hold locks on every edge reachable from $x.f$ both before and after the update. These conditions are necessary for safety, but need not be burdensome if the lock placement has a suitable granularity. For example, if the subtrees rooted at x and y are locked by the locks at x and y respectively, the update requires two locks.

A transaction $\mathbf{T} = t^1 \dots t^k$ is *well-locked* if there exists a sequence of lock sets L^i, observation sets Ω^i, and object sets Γ^i such that $L^0 = L^k = \emptyset$, $\Omega^0 = \emptyset$, $\Gamma^0 = \emptyset$, and $\Omega^{i-1}, \Gamma^{i-1}, L^{i-1} \vdash_\psi t^i; \Omega^i, \Gamma^i, L^i$ for $1 \leq i \leq k$. A well-locked transaction must begin with all three sets Ω, Γ, L empty. Furthermore at the end of the transaction the set of locks L must be empty again, and hence a transaction must release all of its locks. We do not require that Ω or Γ be empty at the conclusion of a transaction; however since the transaction may not hold any locks on termination, any part of the heap that is stable and in Ω with an empty lock set cannot be reachable from the global heap and is garbage.

Lemma 3. *Let* $\mathbf{s}$ *be a valid schedule of a set of well-locked transactions* $\{\mathbf{T}_1, \ldots, \mathbf{T}_k\}$. *Let* Ω_i^j, Γ_i^j, *and* L_i^j *be the set of observations, objects, and locks of each transaction after schedule step* j. *Let* h^j *be the heap after schedule step* j, *and suppose* h^0 *is a forest. Then for all time steps* j:

- *the lock sets* $\{L_i^j\}_{i=1}^k$ *are disjoint, the sets* $\{\Gamma_i^j\}_{i=1}^k$ *are disjoint,*
- *the observation sets* $\{\Omega_i^j\}_{i=1}^k$ *are stable, have disjoint domains, and heap* h^j *is an extension of each* $\{\Omega_i^j\}_{i=1}^k$, *and*
- *the global heap* h^j *less edges present in the local heaps* $\{\Omega_i^j\}_{i=1}^k$ *is a forest. Further if* $x \in \Gamma_i^j$ *then all pointers to* x *are in some local heap* $\Omega_{i'}^j$.

Finally, we have a logical serializability lemma analogous to Lemma 2, which can be extended to shared/exclusive locks as for flat heaps:

Lemma 4. *Any valid schedule of a set of well-locked, logically two-phase tree transactions* $\{\mathbf{T}_1, \ldots, \mathbf{T}_k\}$ *is conflict-equivalent to a serial logical schedule.*

4 Transactions on DAGs of Bounded Degree

At the core of the locking protocol of Section 3 is the invariant that the global heap is a forest. Since lock placements are defined using access paths, for soundness the locking protocol must show that a transaction holds locks that protect an edge on every possible path. In a forest there is at most one path between nodes.

In this section we show how to relax the forest restriction and apply lock placements to a class of directed acyclic graph heaps with a bounded number of paths to each node. The technical machinery developed so far remains almost unchanged, with the exception that the forest condition is replaced by a condition that allows for more paths to an object. One hurdle, however, is that we need some way to describe the aliasing patterns in the heap, for otherwise it is not possible to define what it means to be sound for any locking protocol. We use a recent proposal for describing a large class of heaps with sharing [13], which describe *decomposition heaps* whose shape matches a static description given by a *decomposition heap shape.* We stress that our results are not limited to the class of heaps described in [13]; our techniques could be applied analogously to any number of other methods for describing the possible shapes of the heap. The point is that we need some description of the sharing patterns in the heap, and one good choice is to use decomposition heaps.

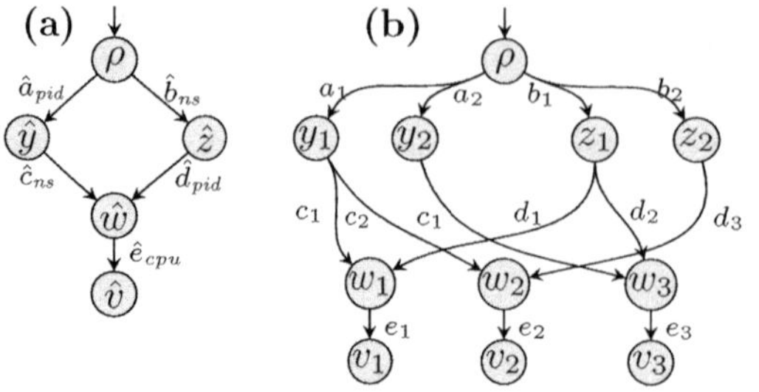

Fig. 9. (a): A decomposition heap shape, and **(b)**: a decomposition heap that is an instance of decomposition heap shape (a)

A *decomposition heap shape* $\hat{h}$ is a rooted, connected, directed acyclic graph $(\hat{V}, \hat{E})$ consisting of a set of vertices $\hat{V} = \{\hat{u}, \hat{v}, \dots\}$ and a set of edges $\hat{E} \subseteq \hat{V} \times \hat{F} \times \hat{V}$ labeled with field names drawn from a set $\hat{F}$. We require that every edge in a decomposition shape have a unique field label. Figure 9(a) gives a decomposition heap shape describing the data structures of a simple process scheduler. Every process has associated fields *pid* (process id), *ns* (name space), and the process' assigned *cpu*; a pair of a *pid* and a *ns* uniquely identify a process. To find the cpu of a particular process, we can first look up the the process id by following edge $\hat{a}_{pid}$ and then the process' name space by following edge $\hat{c}_{ns}$, or we can first look up the name space by following edge $\hat{b}_{ns}$ and then the process id by following edge $\hat{d}_{pid}$. For a given pair of process id and name space, the shared node $\hat{w}$ in the decomposition shape assures us we will get the same result regardless of which path we take.

A decomposition shape is a static description of a class of heaps. Let $\mathsf{in}(\hat{v})$ be the set of field names incoming to $\hat{v}$ in a decomposition and let $\mathsf{out}(\hat{v})$ be the set of outgoing field names. A heap (V, E) is an *instance* of a decomposition $\hat{d}$ if

- every vertex in V is an instance v_i of some vertex $\hat{v} \in \hat{V}$,
- every edge $(u_i, f_j, v_k) \in E$ is an instance of some $(\hat{u}, \hat{f}, \hat{v}) \in \hat{E}$, and
- every vertex v_i has exactly one instance f_i of every incoming edge $\hat{f} \in \mathsf{in}(\hat{v})$.

These conditions are a relaxation of usual definition of a valid instance [13], but suffice for our purposes. The last condition provides a bound on the in-degree of a vertex, which is the key to applying path-based lock placements to decomposition heaps. Figure 9(b) shows a heap that is an instance of the process scheduler decomposition shape of Figure 9(a). The nodes are objects in memory. Every edge $\hat{f}$ from a vertex $\hat{u}$ to a vertex $\hat{v}$ of the decomposition shape has a corresponding set of edges $\{f_1, f_2, \cdots\}$ outgoing from any instance u_i of $\hat{u}$ in a decomposition heap. Intuitively, each vertex (object) u has a container data structure called f that contains references to a set of instances of $\hat{v}$. For example in Figure 9(b), the root object ρ has a set of process id's (the a_i) and a set of name spaces (the b_i). Note how the decomposition shape in Figure 9(a) is replicated across a number of different instances in Figure 9(b) with the stated sharing properties.

The well-lockedness rules defined below quantify over all suffixes of a path $\mathbf{f}$. To keep our transaction-language small, we require that the set of possible instances f_i of each abstract edge $\hat{f}$ be drawn from a bounded set; that is $i \in \{1, \dots, k\}$ for some k. The bounded set restriction can be lifted by extending the transaction language with an iteration operation that allows a transaction to iterate over all

(a)		(b)	
1: lock ρ	9: $\mathsf{wr}(y_2.c_7, w_4)$	1: $\mathsf{rd}(\rho.a_2) = y_2$	9: $\mathsf{rd}(y_2.c_7) = \mathsf{nil}$
2: $\mathsf{rd}(\rho.a_2) = y_2$	10: $\mathsf{wr}(z_2.d_5, w_4)$	2: lock y_2	10: $\mathsf{rd}(z_2.c_5) = \mathsf{nil}$
3: $\mathsf{rd}(\rho.b_2) = z_2$	11: unlock ρ	3: $\mathsf{rd}(\rho.a_2) = y_2$	11: $w_4 = \mathsf{new}\ \hat{w}$
4: $\mathsf{obs}(\rho.a_2) = y_2$		4: $\mathsf{obs}(\rho.a_2) = y_2$	12: $\mathsf{wr}(y_2.c_7, w_4)$
5: $\mathsf{obs}(\rho.b_2) = z_2$		5: $\mathsf{rd}(\rho.b_2) = z_2$	13: $\mathsf{wr}(z_2.d_5, w_4)$
6: $\mathsf{rd}(y_2.c_7) = \mathsf{nil}$		6: lock z_2	14: unlock z_2
7: $\mathsf{rd}(z_2.d_5) = \mathsf{nil}$		7: $\mathsf{rd}(\rho.b_2) = z_2$	15: unlock y_2
8: $w_4 = \mathsf{new}\ \hat{w}$		8: $\mathsf{obs}(\rho.b_2) = z_2$	

Fig. 10. Example transactions that add a new node w_4 with access paths a_2c_7 and b_2d_5 to the decomposition heap instance shown in Figure 9(b), under (a) lock placement $\psi_1(\mathbf{f}) = \epsilon$, and (b) lock placement $\psi_3(\mathbf{f}) = a_i$ if $a_i \preceq \mathbf{f}$, and b_j if $b_j \preceq \mathbf{f}$.

instances of an edge from a vertex; the addition of iteration allows the rules to conclude the a fact holds for all instances of an abstract edge $\hat{f}$.

The transaction operations on DAGs are similar to those on trees (Section 3). The operations (Figure 11), are: write an expression e (either nil or some v_k to field f_j of object u_i ($\mathsf{wr}(u_i.f_j, e)$)), a possibly unstable read of field f_j of object u_i yielding result e ($\mathsf{rd}(u_i.f_j) = e$), a logical observation of field f_j of object u_i yielding e ($\mathsf{obs}(u_i.f_j) = e$), allocation of a fresh object of type $\hat{v}$ ($v_i = \mathsf{new}\ \hat{v}$), locking an object (lock v_i), and unlocking an object (unlock v_i).

4.1 Lock Placements

Lock placements are defined exactly as in the tree case: ψ is a function from non-empty heap paths to paths, which maps every edge in a heap to an object whose lock protects it. Because edges may now have multiple paths that reach them, a transaction must hold locks on all paths to an edge to perform a stable read or to write the edge.

We now illustrate some of the possibilities for lock placements on decomposition heaps. For our standard first example, by setting $\psi_1(\mathbf{f}) = \epsilon$ for all $\mathbf{f}$ we can use a single lock at the root of the heap to protect every edge in a decomposition instance. Figure 10(a) shows a well-locked transaction that adds a fresh instance of $\hat{w}$, namely w_4, to the heap of Figure 9(b) under lock placement ψ_1. Acquiring the lock on ρ protects the entire heap graph; the transaction then adds w_4 under both the access path a_2c_7 and b_2d_5.

Another possibility is to use the placement $\psi_2(\mathbf{f}) = \epsilon$ if $\mathbf{f} \in \{a_i, b_i, a_ic_j, a_id_j\}$, a_ic_j if $\mathbf{f} = a_ic_je_k$, and b_id_j if $\mathbf{f} = b_id_je_k$ which uses a lock at the root to protect instances of edges $\hat{a}$, $\hat{b}$, $\hat{c}$, and $\hat{d}$, and locks at instances of node $\hat{w}$ to protect instances of edge $\hat{e}$. Instances of edge $\hat{e}$ can be reached by two different paths, and thus to observe $\hat{e}$ a transaction must acquire locks on both paths.

Finally, we can use a speculative lock placement. We could protect instances of edges $\hat{a}$ and $\hat{b}$ using speculative locks placed at their targets, and use locks at y and z to protect edges $\hat{c}$, $\hat{d}$, and $\hat{e}$, via the lock placement $\psi_3(\mathbf{f}) = a_i$ if $a_i \preceq \mathbf{f}$, and b_j if $b_j \preceq \mathbf{f}$. Figure 10(b) again shows a transaction that adds a fresh instance w_4 of node $\hat{w}$, this time under the speculative lock placement ψ_3.

$\psi \subseteq 2^{\hat{\mathbf{f}}} \to 2^{\hat{\mathbf{f}}}$	placements	$u_i, v_j, \mathcal{V}$	object names	$\hat{u}, \hat{v}$	vertices
$e ::= \mathsf{nil} \mid v_i$	expressions	$\omega ::= u_i.f \mapsto e$	heap assertions	$\hat{f}, \hat{\mathbf{f}}, f_i, \mathbf{f}$	fields

$t ::= \mathsf{wr}(u_i.f, e) \mid \mathsf{obs}(u_i.f) = e \mid \mathsf{rd}(u_i.f) = e \mid v_i = \mathsf{new}\ \hat{v} \mid \mathsf{lock}\ v_i \mid \mathsf{unlock}\ v_i$ ops.

Fig. 11. Decomposition transactions

4.2 Well-Locked Transactions

As in the case of tree heaps we represent the state of a transaction using three sets: Ω (the local stable heap), L (the held set of locks), and Γ. Sets Ω and L are defined as for trees, but we extend the definition of Γ to DAGs with sharing.

The purpose of Γ is to track objects for which the transaction holds locks on incoming edges. In particular, if a transaction does not hold locks on some incoming edges to an object o, then there may be a path from the global heap to o and the transaction cannot rely on the stability of o's fields. Thus Γ is the transaction's view of the global heap and what other transactions might be able to do to objects of interest to the transaction. The global heap view Γ is a mapping from each vertex v_i in the heap to the subset of the incoming edge labels of the decomposition $\mathsf{in}(\hat{v})$ known to be absent from the global heap (i.e., either non-existent or locked by the transaction). We maintain the invariant that in the global heap there is at most one edge to any instance of a decomposition vertex $\hat{v}$ labeled with an instance of each $\hat{f} \in \mathsf{in}(\hat{v})$. If $\Gamma(v_i) = \emptyset$, then v_i may have an instance of each incoming edge in $\mathsf{in}(\hat{f})$ in the global heap. If $\Gamma(v_i) = \{\hat{f}\}$ then v has no incoming edge in the global heap labeled with an instance of $\hat{f}$. If $\Gamma(v) = \mathsf{in}(\hat{v})$ then v has no incoming edges from the global heap.

As before, we hold the lock on an edge reached via a path if we hold the path's corresponding lock placement, restricted to the heap:

$$\mathsf{pathlocked}_\psi(\mathbf{f}, \Omega, L) ::= \exists v_i \in L.\ \Omega \vdash \mathbf{g} \sim v_i \wedge \psi(\mathbf{f})|_\Omega = \mathbf{g},$$

where $\mathbf{f}_\Omega$ is the restriction of path $\mathbf{f}$ to heap Ω, defined in Section 3.

The judgement $\Omega, \Gamma \vdash \mathsf{exposed}(x)$ holds if there may be a path to vertex x in the heap that does not lie entirely in the stable observation set Ω; the judgement is defined by the inference rules:

$$\frac{\Gamma(v_k) \neq \mathsf{in}(\hat{v})}{\Omega, \Gamma \vdash \mathsf{exposed}(v_k)} \qquad \frac{\Omega, \Gamma \vdash \mathsf{exposed}(u_i) \wedge (u_i.f_j \mapsto v_k) \in \Omega}{\Omega, \Gamma \vdash \mathsf{exposed}(v_k)}$$

We hold the lock on a field $x.f$ if we hold a lock on that field on every path in the local heap, and there are no paths to x outside the local heap:

$$\mathsf{locked}_\psi(v_i.f_j, \Omega, \Gamma, L) ::= \neg\mathsf{exposed}(v_i)\ \wedge\ \forall \mathbf{g}.\ (\Omega \vdash \mathbf{g} \sim v_i \implies \mathsf{pathlocked}_\psi(\mathbf{g}f_j, \Omega, L))$$

The judgement $\Omega, \Gamma, L \vdash_\psi t; \Omega', \Gamma', L'$ defined by the rules in Figure 12 describes the class of *well-locked decomposition operations*, analogous to the class of well-locked tree operations of Section 3. The judgement holds if a transaction executing operation t under local heap Ω, global heap approximation Γ, and locks L yields an updated local heap Ω', global heap approximation Γ', and lock set L'. The (DNEW) rule states that the fields of a newly allocated object v_i point to nil; furthermore there can be no heap paths to a freshly allocated object so

$$\textsc{(DNew)}\ \frac{\Omega' = \Omega \cup \{v_i.f_j \mapsto \mathsf{nil} \mid \hat{f} \in \mathsf{out}(\hat{v})\} \quad v_i \notin \mathrm{dom}\,\Omega \quad \Gamma' = \Gamma[v_i \mapsto \mathsf{in}(\hat{v})] \quad v_i \notin \mathrm{dom}\,\Gamma}{\Omega, \Gamma, L \vdash_\psi v_i = \mathsf{new}\ \hat{v}; \Omega', \Gamma', L}$$

$$\textsc{(DLock)}\ \frac{v_i \notin L}{\Omega, \Gamma, L \vdash_\psi \mathsf{lock}\ v_i; \Omega, \Gamma, L \cup \{v_i\}}$$

$$\textsc{(DUnlock)}\ \frac{v_i \in L \quad L' = L \setminus \{v_i\} \quad (\Omega', \Gamma') = \lceil \Omega; \Gamma \mid L'; \psi \rceil \quad \mathsf{balias}(\Omega, \Omega', \Gamma, \Gamma')}{\Omega, \Gamma, L \vdash_\psi \mathsf{unlock}\ v_i; \Omega', \Gamma', L'}$$

$$\textsc{(DObserve)}\ \frac{(u_i.f_j \mapsto e) \in \Omega}{\Omega, \Gamma, L \vdash_\psi \mathsf{obs}(u_i.f_j) = e; \Omega, \Gamma, L}$$

$$\textsc{(DRdUnstable)}\ \frac{u_i.f_j \notin \mathrm{dom}\,\Omega \quad \Omega' = \Omega \cup \{u_i.f_j \mapsto e\} \quad \neg\mathsf{locked}_\psi(u_i.f_j, \Omega', \Gamma, L)}{\Omega, \Gamma, L \vdash_\psi \mathsf{rd}(u_i.f_j) = e; \Omega, \Gamma, L}$$

$$\textsc{(DRdStable)}\ \frac{u_i.f_j \notin \mathrm{dom}\,\Omega \quad \Omega' = \Omega \cup \{u_i.f_j \mapsto e\} \quad \mathsf{locked}_\psi(u_i.f_j, \Omega', \Gamma, L) \quad \Gamma' = \begin{cases} \Gamma & \text{if } e = \mathsf{nil} \\ \Gamma[v_i \mapsto \Gamma(v_i) \cup \{\hat{f}\}] & \text{if } e = v_i \end{cases}}{\Omega, \Gamma, L \vdash_\psi \mathsf{rd}(u_i.f_j) = e; \Omega', \Gamma', L}$$

$$\textsc{(DWrite)}\ \frac{u_i.f_j \in \mathrm{dom}\,\Omega \quad \Omega' = \Omega[u_i.f_j \mapsto e] \quad (\forall \mathbf{g}, \mathbf{h}.\ (\Omega \vdash \mathbf{g} \sim u_i) \wedge \mathbf{g}f \preceq \psi(\mathbf{h}) \implies \mathsf{pathlocked}_\psi(\mathbf{h}, \Omega, L) \wedge \mathsf{pathlocked}_\psi(\mathbf{h}, \Omega', L))}{\Omega, \Gamma, L \vdash_\psi \mathsf{wr}(u_i.f_j, e); \Omega', \Gamma, L}$$

Fig. 12. Well-locked decomposition operations: judgement $\Omega, \Gamma, L \vdash_\psi t; \Omega', \Gamma', L'$

assertions about the fields of v_i are stable and $\Gamma(v_i) = \mathsf{in}(\hat{v})$. The (DLock) rule allows a transaction to acquire a lock that it does not hold at any time.

The (DUnlock) rule allows a transaction to release any lock that it holds; the rule applies the stabilization operation to remove any newly unstable facts from Ω. Similar to the tree case, the *stabilization* (Ω', Γ') of a local heap Ω_0 and global heap Γ_0 under locks L and placement ψ, written $(\Omega', \Gamma') = \lceil \Omega_0; \Gamma_0 \mid L; \psi \rceil$, is the limit of the monotonically decreasing sequence:

$$\Omega_{i+1} = \{u_j.f_k \mapsto e \in \Omega_i \mid \mathsf{locked}_\psi(u_j.f_k, \Omega_i, \Gamma_i, L)\}$$
$$\Gamma_{i+1} = \Gamma_i \setminus \{v_k \mapsto \hat{f} \mid u_i.f_j \mapsto v_k \in \Omega_i \setminus \Omega_{i+1}\}$$

To ensure there is at most instance of any edge $\hat{f} \in \mathsf{in}(\hat{v})$ in the global heap, the rule requires the *bounded alias* condition $\mathsf{balias}(\Omega, \Omega', \Gamma, \Gamma')$, defined as

$$\forall v_k.\ |\{u_i.f_j \mid (u_i.f_j \mapsto v_k) \in \Omega \setminus \Omega'\}| = 1, \text{ if } \hat{f} \in \Gamma(v_k) \setminus \Gamma'(v_k) \text{ or } 0, \text{ otherwise.}$$

The bounded alias condition ensures that a transaction may only release an edge with abstract label $\hat{f}$ to a node v_k into the global heap if there are no other edges to v_k labeled $\hat{f}$ in the global heap ($\hat{f} \in \Gamma(v_k)$). The condition also forbids releasing two pointers with the same label $\hat{f}$ to the same node v_k into the heap.

Rule (DObserve) states that a transaction may logically observe stable heap facts. The (DRdUnstable) rule allows a transaction to read a value speculatively at any time, however unstable reads do not update Ω or Γ. A transaction may perform a stable read of a pointer if it holds the appropriate lock, transferring the pointer from the global heap into Ω and updating Γ accordingly. Finally, a transaction may write to a field if it holds the associated lock and holds locks on any edges whose logical/physical mapping may change due to the update.

A transaction $\mathbf{T} = t^1 \ldots t^k$ is *well-locked* if there exists a sequence of lock sets L^i, observation sets Ω^i, and global heap sets Γ^i such that $L^0 = L^k = \emptyset$, $\Omega^0 = \emptyset$, $\Gamma^0 = \emptyset$, and $\Omega^{i-1}, \Gamma^{i-1}, L^{i-1} \vdash_\psi t^i; \Omega^i, \Gamma^i, L^i$ for $1 \leq i \leq k$.

Lemma 5. *Let* s *be a valid schedule of well-locked transactions* $\{\mathbf{T}_1, \ldots, \mathbf{T}_k\}$. *Let* Ω_i^j, Γ_i^j, *and* L_i^j *be the set of observations, global heaps, and locks of each transaction after schedule step* j. *Let* h^j *be the heap after schedule step* j, *and suppose the part of* h^0 *reachable from the root is a tree. Then for all time steps* j:

- *the lock sets* $\{L_i^j\}_{i=1}^k$ *are disjoint, and the non-alias sets* $\{\Gamma_i\}_{i=1}^k$ *are disjoint,*
- *the observation sets* $\{\Omega_i^j\}_{i=1}^k$ *are stable, disjoint, and heap* h^j *is an extension of each* $\{\Omega_i^j\}_{i=1}^k$, *and*
- *Let heap* h *be the heap* h^j *less edges present in the local heaps* $\{\Omega_i^j\}_{i=1}^k$. *Then for every vertex* $v \in h$ *and edge label* $\hat{f} \in \mathsf{in}(\hat{v})$ *either there is exactly one edge labeled with an instance of* $\hat{f}$ *pointing to* v *in* h, *or* $\hat{f} \in \Gamma_i^j$ *for some* i *and there are no edges labeled with an instance of* $\hat{f}$ *pointing to* v *in* h.

Finally, we have a logical serializability lemma similar to Lemma 2 and Lemma 4, which can be extended to shared/exclusive locks using the approach in Section 2.4.

Lemma 6. *Any valid schedule of well-locked, logically two-phase decomposition transactions* $\{\mathbf{T}_1, \ldots, \mathbf{T}_k\}$ *is conflict-equivalent to a serial logical schedule.*

5 Related Work

Two-phase locking was originally introduced in the context of transactions operating over abstract entities, each with its own associated lock [8]. The core technical idea of this paper is that we can use two-phase locking to show serializability of a wide class of locking strategies by adding a layer of indirection between logical locks, which are the entities that are the subject of the original two-phase locking protocol, and the physical locks that implement them. Other authors have also advocated more logical notions of locking [5].

Various authors have investigated techniques for inferring locks to implement atomic sections [16,14,7,11,3,4,20]. A related problem is automatically optimizing programs with explicit locking by combining multiple locks into one [6]. A key part of this class of work is constructing a mapping from program objects to the locks that protect them, similar to our lock placement language. The lock placements we propose are much more flexible; in particular existing formalisms cannot handle the class of path placements we propose in this paper, such as speculative locks, or lock placements that vary with heap updates. A possible future application of our methods is extending lock inference techniques to take advantage of the additional expressive power of our techniques.

A novel feature of our proposal is that we can reason about speculative lock placements. Speculative locking is used in practice in highly concurrent libraries and has appeared in the literature in the context of software transactional memory [2]. Although we present our ideas in the context of pessimistic locks, the same idea can also be used to reason about speculative placements of STM metadata.

A variety of locking protocols have been proposed in the literature that extend two-phase locking to handle dynamically changing heaps and to allow early release. Examples include the dynamic tree and DAG locking protocols [1] and domination locking [9]. Existing protocols use the lock on each object to protect that object's fields, whereas our work investigates a more flexible space of mappings. We do not address early release as it is orthogonal to the issues of lock placement.

The concept of a stable set and stabilization is related to rely-guarantee logic [15] and its developments [19]. Concurrent extensions of separation logic, such as Concurrent Separation Logic [17], RGSep [18] and work on storable locks [10] allow local reasoning about programs with shared mutable state that is accessed concurrently. Our work complements work on direct reasoning about concurrent code; we propose a locking protocol, parameterized by a lock placement, by which we can show conflict-serializability for code that obeys the protocol.

6 Conclusion

We have formalized lock placements, showing that such diverse concepts as lock granularity, speculative locks, lock splitting and merging, and dynamically changing lock assignments can all be expressed using a lock placement that maps each heap field to a lock that guards it. We described a series of proof systems for showing that transaction traces are well-locked and therefore serializable, applied to flat heaps, tree-structured heaps, and to DAG heaps with bounded degree.

References

1. Attiya, H., Ramalingam, G., Rinetzky, N.: Sequential verification of serializability. In: POPL, pp. 31–42. ACM, New York (2010)
2. Bronson, N.G., Casper, J., Chafi, H., Olukotun, K.: Transactional predication: high-performance concurrent sets and maps for STM. In: PODC, pp. 6–15. ACM, New York (2010)
3. Cherem, S., Chilimbi, T., Gulwani, S.: Inferring locks for atomic sections. In: PLDI, pp. 304–315. ACM, New York (2008)
4. Cunningham, D., Gudka, K., Eisenbach, S.: Keep Off the Grass: Locking the Right Path for Atomicity. In: Hendren, L. (ed.) CC 2008. LNCS, vol. 4959, pp. 276–290. Springer, Heidelberg (2008)
5. Deshmukh, J., Ramalingam, G., Ranganath, V.-P., Vaswani, K.: Logical Concurrency Control from Sequential Proofs. In: Gordon, A.D. (ed.) ESOP 2010. LNCS, vol. 6012, pp. 226–245. Springer, Heidelberg (2010)
6. Diniz, P.C., Rinard, M.C.: Lock coarsening: Eliminating lock overhead in automatically parallelized object-based programs. JPDC 49(2), 218–244 (1998)
7. Emmi, M., Fischer, J.S., Jhala, R., Majumdar, R.: Lock allocation. In: POPL, pp. 291–296. ACM, New York (2007)
8. Eswaran, K.P., Gray, J.N., Lorie, R.A., Traiger, I.L.: The notions of consistency and predicate locks in a database system. Commun. ACM 19, 624–633 (1976)
9. Golan-Gueta, G., Bronson, N., Aiken, A., Ramalingam, G., Sagiv, M., Yahav, E.: Automatic fine-grained locking using shape properties. In: OOPSLA (2011)

10. Gotsman, A., Berdine, J., Cook, B., Rinetzky, N., Sagiv, M.: Local Reasoning for Storable Locks and Threads. In: Shao, Z. (ed.) APLAS 2007. LNCS, vol. 4807, pp. 19–37. Springer, Heidelberg (2007)
11. Halpert, R.L., Pickett, C.J.F., Verbrugge, C.: Component-based lock allocation. In: PACT, pp. 353–364. IEEE Computer Society, Washington, DC (2007)
12. Hawkins, P., Aiken, A., Fisher, K., Rinard, M., Sagiv, M.: Reasoning about lock placements (extended version). Tech. rep., Stanford University (2011), http://theory.stanford.edu/~hawkinsp/papers/tr/lockplacements.pdf
13. Hawkins, P., Aiken, A., Fisher, K., Rinard, M., Sagiv, M.: Data representation synthesis. In: PLDI, pp. 38–49. ACM, New York (2011)
14. Hicks, M., Foster, J.S., Pratikakis, P.: Lock inference for atomic sections. In: TRANSACT (2006)
15. Jones, C.: Development methods for computer programs including a notion of interference. Ph.D. thesis, Oxford University (1981)
16. McCloskey, B., Zhou, F., Gay, D., Brewer, E.: Autolocker: Synchronization inference for atomic sections. In: POPL, pp. 346–358. ACM, New York (2006)
17. O'Hearn, P.W.: Resources, concurrency, and local reasoning. Theoretical Computer Science 375(1-3), 271–307 (2007)
18. Vafeiadis, V., Parkinson, M.: A Marriage of Rely/Guarantee and Separation Logic. In: Caires, L., Vasconcelos, V.T. (eds.) CONCUR 2007. LNCS, vol. 4703, pp. 256–271. Springer, Heidelberg (2007)
19. Wickerson, J., Dodds, M., Parkinson, M.: Explicit Stabilisation for Modular Rely-Guarantee Reasoning. In: Gordon, A.D. (ed.) ESOP 2010. LNCS, vol. 6012, pp. 610–629. Springer, Heidelberg (2010)
20. Zhang, Y., Sreedhar, V., Zhu, W., Sarkar, V., Gao, G.: Minimum Lock Assignment: A Method for Exploiting Concurrency among Critical Sections. In: Amaral, J.N. (ed.) LCPC 2008. LNCS, vol. 5335, pp. 141–155. Springer, Heidelberg (2008)

Reasoning about Multi-stage Programs*

Jun Inoue[2] and Walid Taha[1,2]

[1] Halmstad University, SE-301 18 Halmstad, Sweden
[2] Rice University, Houston TX 77005, USA
ji2@rice.edu, walid.taha@hh.se

Abstract. We settle three basic questions that naturally arise when verifying multi-stage functional programs. Firstly, does adding staging to a language compromise any equalities that hold in the base language? Unfortunately it does, and more care is needed to reason about terms with free variables. Secondly, staging annotations, as the name "annotations" suggests, are often thought to be orthogonal to the behavior of a program, but when is this formally guaranteed to be true? We give termination conditions that characterize when this guarantee holds. Finally, do multi-stage languages satisfy useful, standard extensional facts—for example, that functions agreeing on all arguments are equivalent? We provide a sound and complete notion of applicative bisimulation, which establishes such facts or, in principle, any valid program equivalence. These results greatly improve our understanding of staging, and allow us to prove the correctness of quite complicated multi-stage programs.

1 Introduction

Multi-stage programming (MSP) allows programmers to write generic code without sacrificing performance; programmers can write code generators that are themselves generic but are staged to generate specialized, efficient code. Generic codes are excellent targets for verification because they are verified only once and used many times, improving modularity of the correctness proof. However, few formal studies have considered verifying generators written with MSP, and MSP research has predominantly focused on applications that confirm performance benefits [5,4,12,8,6] and on type systems [28,17,32,16,29,30].

A key assumption behind the use of MSP is that it enhances performance while preserving the structure of the code, and that it therefore does not interfere much with reasoning [18,4]. The power function is a good example of MSP preserving structure, presented here in MetaOCaml syntax.

```
let rec power  n x = if n = 1 then x else x * power (n-1) x
let rec genpow n x = if n = 1 then x else .<.~x * .~(genpow (n-1) x)>.
let stpow n = .!.<fun z → .~(genpow n .<z>.)>.
```

* Supported in part by NSF grant CCF-0747431; NSF Award # 0747431, "Multi-stage programming for object-oriented languages"; and NSF Award # 0720857, "Building physically safe embedded systems".

H. Seidl (Ed.): ESOP 2012, LNCS 7211, pp. 357–376, 2012.

The `power` function subsumes all functions of the form `fun x` $\rightarrow$ `x*x*...*x` but incurs recursive calls each time it is called. Staging annotations can eliminate this overhead by unrolling the recursion in `genpow`. Brackets `.<`e`>.` delay an expression e. An escape `.~`e must occur within brackets and causes e to be evaluated without delay. The e should return a code value `.<`e'`>.`, and e' replaces `.~`e. For example if `n` $= 2$, the `genpow n .<z>.` in `stpow` returns a delayed multiplication `.<z*z>.`. This is an open term, but MetaOCaml allows manipulation of open terms under escapes. Run `.!`e compiles and runs the code generated by e, so `stpow 2` evaluates to the closure `fun z` $\rightarrow$ `z*z`, which has no recursion. These annotations in MetaOCaml are hygienic (i.e., preserve static scoping [9]), but are otherwise like LISP's quasiquote, unquote, and eval [20].

This example is typical of MSP usage, where a staged program `stpow` is meant as a drop-in replacement for the unstaged program `power`. Note that if we are given only `stpow`, we can reconstruct the unstaged program `power` by erasing the staging annotations from `stpow`—we say that `power` is the *erasure* of `stpow`. Given the similarity of these programs, if we are to verify `stpow`, we naturally expect `stpow` $\approx$ `power` to hold for a suitable equivalence ($\approx$) and hope to get away with proving that `power` satisfies whatever specifications it has, in lieu of `stpow`. We expect `power` to be easier to tackle, since it has no staging annotations and should therefore be amenable to conventional reasoning techniques designed for single-stage programs. But three key questions must be addressed before we can apply this strategy confidently:

Conservativity. Do all reasoning principles valid in a single-stage language carry over to its multi-stage extension?

Conditions for Sound Erasure. In the power example, staging seems to preserve semantics, but clearly this is not always the case: if Ω is non-terminating, then `.<`Ω`>.` $\not\approx \Omega$ for any sensible ($\approx$). When do we know that erasing annotations preserves semantics?

Extensional Reasoning. How, in general, do we prove equivalences of the form $e \approx t$? It is known that hygienic, purely functional MSP satisfies intensional equalities like β [27], but are too weak to prove such properties as extensionality (i.e., functions agreeing on all inputs are equivalent). Extensional facts like this are indispensable for reasoning about functions, like `stpow` and `power`.

This paper settles these questions, focusing on the untyped, purely functional case with hygiene. We work without types to avoid committing to the particulars of any specific type system, since there are multiple useful type systems for MSP [28,29,30]. It also ensures that our results apply to dynamically typed languages [9]. Hygiene is widely accepted as a safety feature, and it ensures many of the nice theoretical properties of MSP, which makes it easy to reason about programs, and which we exploit in this study. We believe imperative MSP is not yet ready for an investigation like this. Types are essential for having sane operational semantics without scope extrusion [16], but there is no decisive solution to this problem, and the jury is still out on many of the trade-offs. The foundations for imperative hygienic MSP does not seem to have matured to the level of the functional theory that we build upon here.

1.1 Contributions

We extend previous work on the call-by-name (CBN) multi-stage λ calculus, λ^U [27], to cover call-by-value (CBV) as well (Section 2). In this calculus, we show the following results.

Unsoundness of Reasoning Under Substitutions. Unfortunately, the answer to the conservativity question is "no." Because λ^U can express open-term manipulation (see `genpow` above), equivalences proved under closing substitutions are not always valid without substitution, for such a proof implicitly assumes that only closed terms are interesting. We illustrate clearly how this pathology occurs using the surprising fact $(\lambda\_.0)\ x \not\approx 0$, and explain what can be done about it (Section 3). The rest of the paper will show that a lot can be achieved despite this drawback.

Conditions for Sound Erasure. We show that reductions of a staged term are simulated by equational rewrites of the term's erasure. This gives simple termination conditions that guarantee erasure to be semantics-preserving (Section 4). Considering CBV in isolation turns out to be unsatisfactory, and borrowing CBN facts is essential in establishing the termination conditions for CBV. Intuitively, this happens because annotations change the evaluation strategy, and the CBN equational theory subsumes reductions in all other strategies whereas the CBV theory does not.

Soundness of Extensional Properties. We give a sound and complete notion of applicative bisimulation [1,10] for λ^U. Bisimulation gives a general extensional proof principle that, in particular, proves extensionality of λ abstractions. It also justifies reasoning under substitutions in some cases, limiting the impact of the non-conservativity result (Section 5).

Throughout the paper, we emphasize the general insights about MSP that we can gain from our results. The ability to verify staged programs fall out from general principles, which we will demonstrate using the power function as a running example. A technical report [14] gives proof details and discussions that we cut out due to space limitations. This paper is intelligible by itself, but we note throughout the paper what additional information to expect in the report.

The most substantial additional material in the report is a correctness proof of the longest common subsequence (LCS) algorithm, meant for readers who wish to see how the erasure idea fares on more complex programs than `power`. LCS uses a sophisticated code-generation scheme that requires `let`-insertion coupled with continuation-passing style (CPS) and monadic memoization [26]. These features make an exact description of the generated code hard to pin down; nonetheless, a proof similar to that of `power` can be adapted fairly straightforwardly.

2 The λ^U Calculus: Syntax, Semantics, and Equational Theory

This section presents the multi-stage λ calculus λ^U. This is a simple but expressive calculus that models all possible uses of brackets, escape, and run in

Levels $\ell, m \in \mathbb{N}$ *Variables* $x, y \in Var$ *Constants* $c, d \in Const$

Expressions $e, t \in E ::= c \mid x \mid \lambda x.e \mid e\ e \mid \langle e \rangle \mid \tilde{}e \mid !e$

Exact Level $\mathrm{lv} : E \to \mathbb{N}$ where

$$\mathrm{lv}\, x \stackrel{\text{def}}{=} 0 \quad \mathrm{lv}\, c \stackrel{\text{def}}{=} 0 \quad \mathrm{lv}(e_1\ e_2) \stackrel{\text{def}}{=} \max(\mathrm{lv}\, e_1, \mathrm{lv}\, e_2) \quad \mathrm{lv}(\tilde{}e) \stackrel{\text{def}}{=} \mathrm{lv}\, e + 1$$

$$\mathrm{lv}(\lambda x.e) \stackrel{\text{def}}{=} \mathrm{lv}\, e \quad \mathrm{lv}\langle e \rangle \stackrel{\text{def}}{=} \max(\mathrm{lv}\, e - 1, 0) \quad \mathrm{lv}(!e) \stackrel{\text{def}}{=} \mathrm{lv}\, e$$

Stratification $e^\ell, t^\ell \in E^\ell \stackrel{\text{def}}{=} \{e : \mathrm{lv}\, e \le \ell\}$

Values $u^0, v^0 \in V^0 ::= c \mid \lambda x.e^0 \mid \langle e^0 \rangle$

$u^{\ell+1}, v^{\ell+1} \in V^{\ell+1} ::= e^\ell$

Programs $p \in Prog \stackrel{\text{def}}{=} \{e^0 : \mathrm{FV}(e^0) = \varnothing\}$

Contexts $C \in Ctx ::= \bullet \mid \lambda x.C \mid C\ e \mid e\ C \mid \langle C \rangle \mid \tilde{}C \mid !C$

Fig. 1. Syntax of λ^U, parametrized in a set of constants *Const*

MetaOCaml's purely functional core, sans types. The syntax and operational semantics of λ^U for both CBN and CBV are minor extensions of previous work [27] to allow arbitrary constants. The CBN equational theory is more or less as in [27], but the CBV equational theory is new.

Notation. A set S may be marked as CBV ($S_{\mathbf{v}}$) or CBN ($S_{\mathbf{n}}$) if its definition varies by evaluation strategy. The subscript is dropped in assertions and definitions that apply to both evaluation strategies. Syntactic equality (α equivalence) is written ($\equiv$). The set of free variables in e is written $\mathrm{FV}(e)$. For a set S, we write S_{cl} to mean $\{e \in S : \mathrm{FV}(e) = \varnothing\}$.

2.1 Syntax and Operational Semantics

The syntax of λ^U is shown in Figure 1. A term is delayed when more brackets enclose it than do escapes, and a program must not have an escape in any non-delayed region. We track *levels* to model this behavior. A term's exact level $\mathrm{lv}\, e$ is its nesting depth of escapes minus brackets, and a program is a closed, exactly level-0 term. A level-0 value (i.e., a value in a non-delayed region) is a constant, an abstraction, or a code value with no un-delayed region. At level $\ell > 0$ (i.e., inside ℓ pairs of brackets), a value is any lower-level term. Throughout the article, "the set of terms with exact level at most ℓ", written E^ℓ, is a much more useful concept than "the set of terms with exact level exactly ℓ". When we say "e has level ℓ" we mean $e \in E^\ell$, whereas "e has exact level ℓ" means $\mathrm{lv}\, e = \ell$. A context C is a term with exactly one subterm replaced by a hole $\bullet$, and $C[e]$ is the term obtained by replacing the hole with e, with variable capture. Staging annotations use the same nesting rules as LISP's quasiquote and unquote [9], but we stress that they preserve scoping: e.g., $\langle \lambda x.\tilde{}(\lambda x.\langle x \rangle)\rangle \equiv \langle \lambda x.\tilde{}(\lambda y.\langle y \rangle)\rangle \not\equiv \langle \lambda y.\tilde{}(\lambda x.\langle y \rangle)\rangle$.

A term is unstaged if its annotations are erased in the following sense; it is staged otherwise. The `power` function is the erasure of `stpow` modulo η reduction.

Evaluation Contexts (Productions marked $[\phi]$ apply only if the guard ϕ is true.)

$$\text{(CBN) } \mathcal{E}^{\ell,m} \in ECtx_{\mathbf{n}}^{\ell,m} ::= \bullet[m=\ell] \mid \lambda x.\mathcal{E}^{\ell,m}[\ell>0] \mid \langle \mathcal{E}^{\ell+1,m}\rangle \mid \tilde{}\mathcal{E}^{\ell-1,m}[\ell>0] \mid\, !\,\mathcal{E}^{\ell,m} \mid \mathcal{E}^{\ell,m}\, e^{\ell} \mid v^{\ell}\, \mathcal{E}^{\ell,m}[\ell>0] \mid c\, \mathcal{E}^{\ell,m}[\ell=0]$$

$$\text{(CBV) } \mathcal{E}^{\ell,m} \in ECtx_{\mathbf{v}}^{\ell,m} ::= \bullet[m=\ell] \mid \lambda x.\mathcal{E}^{\ell,m}[\ell>0] \mid \langle \mathcal{E}^{\ell+1,m}\rangle \mid \tilde{}\mathcal{E}^{\ell-1,m}[\ell>0] \mid\, !\,\mathcal{E}^{\ell,m} \mid \mathcal{E}^{\ell,m}\, e^{\ell} \mid v^{\ell}\, \mathcal{E}^{\ell,m}$$

Substitutable Arguments $a, b \in Arg ::= v^0$ (CBV) $\quad a, b \in Arg ::= e^0$ (CBN)

Small-steps $e^{\ell} \underset{\ell}{\leadsto} t^{\ell}$ where:

$$\text{SS-}\beta\ \frac{\text{(CBN)}}{(\lambda x.e^0)\, t^0 \underset{0}{\leadsto} [t^0/x]e^0} \qquad \text{SS-}\beta_{\mathbf{v}}\ \frac{\text{(CBV)}}{(\lambda x.e^0)\, v^0 \underset{0}{\leadsto} [v^0/x]e^0} \qquad \text{SS-}\delta\ \frac{(c,d) \in \operatorname{dom}\delta}{c\, d \underset{0}{\leadsto} \delta(c,d)}$$

$$\text{SS-}E\ \frac{}{\tilde{}\langle e^0\rangle \underset{1}{\leadsto} e^0} \qquad \text{SS-}R\ \frac{}{!\,\langle e^0\rangle \underset{0}{\leadsto} e^0} \qquad \text{SS-C}\text{TX}\ \frac{e^m \underset{m}{\leadsto} t^m}{\mathcal{E}^{\ell,m}[e^m] \underset{\ell}{\leadsto} \mathcal{E}^{\ell,m}[t^m]}$$

Fig. 2. Operational semantics of λ^U, parametrized in an interpretation (partial) map $\delta : Const \times Const \rightharpoonup \{v \in V_{\text{cl}}^0 : v \equiv \|v\|\}$

Definition 1 (Erasure). Define the erasure $\|e\|$ by

$$\|x\| \stackrel{\text{def}}{\equiv} x \qquad \|c\| \stackrel{\text{def}}{\equiv} c \qquad \|\lambda x.e\| \stackrel{\text{def}}{\equiv} \lambda x.\|e\| \qquad \|\tilde{}e\| \stackrel{\text{def}}{\equiv} \|e\|$$

$$\|e_1\ e_2\| \stackrel{\text{def}}{\equiv} \|e_1\|\ \|e_2\| \qquad \|\langle e\rangle\| \stackrel{\text{def}}{\equiv} \|e\| \qquad \|!\,e\| \stackrel{\text{def}}{\equiv} \|e\|$$

The operational semantics is given in Figure 2; examples are provided below. Square brackets denote guards on grammatical production rules; for instance, $ECtx_{\mathbf{n}}^{\ell,m} ::= \bullet[m=\ell] \mid \ldots$ means $\bullet \in ECtx_{\mathbf{n}}^{\ell,m}$ iff $m = \ell$. An ℓ, m-evaluation context $\mathcal{E}^{\ell,m}$ takes a level-m redex and yields a level-ℓ term. Redex contractions are: β reduction at level 0, δ reduction at level 0, run-bracket elimination at level 0, and escape-bracket elimination at level 1. CBN uses SS-β and CBV uses SS-$\beta_{\mathbf{v}}$. All other rules are common to both evaluation strategies.

Small-steps specify the behavior of deterministic evaluators. Every term decomposes in at most one way as $\mathcal{E}^{\ell,m}[t]$ where t is a level-m redex, and the small-step reduct is unique if it exists. The δ reductions are given by a partial map $\delta : Const \times Const \rightharpoonup \{v \in V_{\text{cl}}^0 : v \equiv \|v\|\}$, which is undefined for ill-formed pairs like $\delta(\texttt{not}, 5)$. We assume constant applications do not return staged terms.

The difference between CBV and CBN evaluation contexts is that CBV can place the hole inside the argument of a level-0 application, but CBN can do so only if the operator is a constant. This difference accounts for the fact that CBV application is always strict at level 0, while CBN application is lazy if the operator is a λ but strict if it is a constant. At level > 0, both evaluation strategies simply walk over the syntax tree of the delayed term to look for escapes, including ones that occur inside the arguments of applications.

Notation. We write $\lambda_{\mathbf{n}}^U \vdash e \underset{\ell}{\leadsto} t$ for a CBN small-step judgment and $\lambda_{\mathbf{v}}^U \vdash e \underset{\ell}{\leadsto} t$ for CBV. We use similar notation for $(\Downarrow)$, $(\Uparrow)$, and $(\approx)$ defined below. For any relation R, let R^* be its reflexive-transitive closure. The metavariables $a, b \in Arg$ will range over substitutable arguments, i.e., e^0 for CBN and v^0 for CBV.

For example, $p_1 \equiv (\lambda y.\langle 40 + y\rangle)\ (1 + 1)$ is a program. Its value is determined by $(\underset{0}{\rightsquigarrow})$, which works like in conventional calculi. In CBN, $\lambda^U_{\mathbf{n}} \vdash p_1 \underset{0}{\rightsquigarrow} \langle 40 + (1 + 1)\rangle$. The redex $(1+1)$ is not selected for contraction because $(\lambda y.\langle 40+y\rangle) \bullet \notin ECtx^{0,0}_{\mathbf{n}}$. In CBV, $(\lambda y.\langle 40 + y\rangle) \bullet \in ECtx^{0,0}$, so $(1 + 1)$ is selected for contraction: $\lambda^U_{\mathbf{v}} \vdash p_1 \underset{0}{\rightsquigarrow} (\lambda y.\langle 40 + y\rangle)\ 2 \underset{0}{\rightsquigarrow} \langle 40 + 2\rangle$.

Let $p_2 \equiv \langle \lambda z.z\ (\tilde{}[(\lambda\_.\langle z\rangle)\ 1])\rangle$, where we used square brackets [ ] as parentheses to improve readability. Let e^0 be the subterm inside square brackets. In both CBN and CBV, p_2 decomposes as $\mathcal{E}[e^0]$, where $\mathcal{E} \equiv \langle \lambda z.z\ (\tilde{}\bullet)\rangle \in ECtx^{0,0}$, and e^0 is a level-0 redex. Note the hole of $\mathcal{E}$ is under a binder and the redex e^0 is open, though p_2 is closed. The hole is also in argument position in the application $z\ (\tilde{}\bullet)$ even for CBN. This application is delayed by brackets, so the CBN/CBV distinction is irrelevant until the delay is canceled by !. Hence, $p_2 \underset{0}{\rightsquigarrow} \langle \lambda z.z\ (\tilde{}\langle z\rangle)\rangle \underset{0}{\rightsquigarrow} \langle \lambda z.z\ z\rangle$.

As usual, this "untyped" formalism can be seen as dynamically typed. In this view, ˜ and ! take code-type arguments, where code is a distinct type from functions and base types. Thus $\langle \lambda x.x\rangle\ 1$, $\langle \tilde{}0\rangle$, and $!5$ are all stuck. Stuckness on variables like $x\ 5$ does not arise in programs for conventional languages because programs are closed, but in λ^U evaluation contexts can pick redexes under binders so this type of stuckness does become a concern; see Section 3.

Remark. Binary operations on constants are modeled by including their partially applied variants. To model addition we take $Const \supseteq \mathbb{Z} \cup \{+\} \cup \{+_k : k \in \mathbb{Z}\}$ and set $\delta(+, k) = +_k$, $\delta(+_k, k') =$ (the sum of k and k'). For example, in prefix notation, $(+\ 3\ 5) \underset{0}{\rightsquigarrow} (+_3\ 5) \underset{0}{\rightsquigarrow} 8$. Conditionals are modeled by taking $Const \supseteq \{(), \mathtt{true}, \mathtt{false}, \mathtt{if}\}$ and setting $\delta(\mathtt{if}, \mathtt{true}) = \lambda a.\lambda b.a\ ()$ and $\delta(\mathtt{if}, \mathtt{false}) = \lambda a.\lambda b.b\ ()$. Then, e.g., $\mathtt{if\ true}\ (\lambda\_.1)\ (\lambda\_.0) \underset{0}{\rightsquigarrow} (\lambda a.\lambda b.a\ ())\ (\lambda\_.1)\ (\lambda\_.0) \underset{0}{\rightsquigarrow}^* 1$.

Definition 2 (Termination and Divergence). An $e \in E^\ell$ *terminates* to $v \in V^\ell$ at level ℓ iff $e \underset{\ell}{\rightsquigarrow}^* v$, written $e \Downarrow^\ell v$. We write $e \Downarrow^\ell$ to mean $\exists v.\ e \Downarrow^\ell v$. If no such v exists, then e *diverges* ($e \Uparrow^\ell$). Note that divergence includes stuckness.

The operational semantics induces the usual notion of observational equivalence, which relate terms that are interchangeable under all program contexts.

Definition 3 (Observational Equivalence). $e \approx t$ iff for every C such that $C[e], C[t] \in Prog$, $C[e] \Downarrow^0 \Longleftrightarrow C[t] \Downarrow^0$ holds and whenever one of them terminates to a constant, the other also terminates to the same constant.

2.2 Equational Theory

The equational theory of λ^U is a proof system containing four inference rules: compatible extension ($e = t \Longrightarrow C[e] = C[t]$), reflexivity, symmetry, and transitivity. The CBN axioms are $\lambda^U_{\mathbf{n}} \stackrel{\text{def}}{=} \{\beta, E_U, R_U, \delta\}$, while CBV axioms are

$\lambda_{\mathbf{v}}^U \stackrel{\text{def}}{=} \{\beta_{\mathbf{v}}, E_U, R_U, \delta\}$. Each axiom is shown below. If $e = t$ can be proved from a set of axioms Φ, then we write $\Phi \vdash e = t$, though we often omit the $\Phi \vdash$ in definitions and assertions that apply uniformly to both CBV and CBN. Reduction is a term rewrite induced by the axioms: $\Phi \vdash e \longrightarrow t$ iff $e = t$ is derivable from the axioms by compatible extension alone.

Name	Axiom	Side Condition
β	$(\lambda x.e^0)\ t^0 = [t^0/x]e^0$	
$\beta_{\mathbf{v}}$	$(\lambda x.e^0)\ v^0 = [v^0/x]e^0$	
E_U	$\tilde{}\langle e\rangle = e$	
R_U	$!\,\langle e^0\rangle = e^0$	
δ	$c\ d = \delta(c,d)$	$(c,d) \in \operatorname{dom}\delta$

For example, axiom $\beta_{\mathbf{v}}$ gives $\lambda_{\mathbf{v}}^U \vdash (\lambda\_.0)\ 1 = 0$. By compatible extension under $\langle\bullet\rangle$, we have $\langle(\lambda\_.0)\ 1\rangle = \langle 0\rangle$, in fact $\langle(\lambda\_.0)\ 1\rangle \longrightarrow \langle 0\rangle$. Note $\langle(\lambda\_.0)\ 1\rangle \not\rightsquigarrow_0 \langle 0\rangle$ because brackets delay the application, but reduction allows all left-to-right rewrites by the axioms, so $\langle(\lambda\_.0)\ 1\rangle \longrightarrow \langle 0\rangle$ nonetheless. Intuitively, $\langle(\lambda\_.0)\ 1\rangle \not\rightsquigarrow_0 \langle 0\rangle$ because an evaluator does not perform this rewrite, but $\langle(\lambda\_.0)\ 1\rangle \longrightarrow \langle 0\rangle$ because this rewrite is semantics-preserving and a static analyzer or optimizer is allowed to perform it.

Just like the plain λ calculus, λ^U satisfies the Church-Rosser property, so every term has at most one normal form (irreducible reduct). Church-Rosser also ensures that reduction and provable equality are more or less interchangeable, and when we investigate the properties of provable equality, we usually do not lose generality by restricting our attention to the simpler notion of reduction.

Theorem 4 (Church-Rosser Property). $e = e' \iff \exists t.\ e \longrightarrow^* t \longleftarrow^* e'$.

Provable equality is an approximation of observational equivalence. The containment $(=) \subset (\approx)$ is proper because $(\approx)$ is not semi-decidable (since λ^U is Turing-complete) whereas $(=)$ clearly is. There are several useful equivalences in $(\approx) \setminus (=)$, which we will prove by applicative bisimulation. Provable equality is nonetheless strong enough to discover the value of any term that has one, so the assertion "e terminates (at level ℓ)" is interchangeable with "e reduces to a (level-ℓ) value".

Theorem 5 (Soundness). $(=) \subset (\approx)$.

Theorem 6. If $e \in E^\ell, v \in V^\ell$, then $e \Downarrow^\ell v \implies (e \longrightarrow^* v \wedge e = v)$ and $e = v \in V^\ell \implies (\exists u \in V^\ell . u = v \wedge e \longrightarrow^* u \wedge e \Downarrow^\ell u)$.

The CBN version of the equational theory given here is not identical to [27], but generalizes the E_U rule from $\tilde{}\langle e^0\rangle = e^0$ to $\tilde{}\langle e\rangle = e$. This minor generalization comes in handy for eliminating redundant escapes and brackets. An example is found in the proof that substitution preserves $(\approx)$:

Proposition 7. $e \approx t \implies [a/x]e \approx [a/x]t$.

Proof. The idea is to plug e, t into the context $(\lambda x.\bullet)\ a$ and to apply $\beta/\beta_{\mathbf{v}}$ to get $[a/x]e = (\lambda x.e)\ a \approx (\lambda x.t)\ a = [a/x]t$. However, $\beta/\beta_{\mathbf{v}}$ does not apply if e, t are not level 0, so we have to make them level 0. Take $\ell = \max(\mathrm{lv}\, e, \mathrm{lv}\, t)$. Then

$$(\lambda x.\langle\langle\cdots\langle e\rangle\cdots\rangle\rangle)\ a \approx (\lambda x.\langle\langle\cdots\langle t\rangle\cdots\rangle\rangle)\ a\ , \tag{1}$$

where e and t are each enclosed in ℓ pairs of brackets. Now $\beta/\beta_{\mathbf{v}}$ applies, and we get $\langle\langle\cdots\langle[a/x]e\rangle\cdots\rangle\rangle \approx \langle\langle\cdots\langle[a/x]t\rangle\cdots\rangle\rangle$. Escaping both sides ℓ times gives

$$\tilde{}\,\tilde{}\cdots\tilde{}\langle\langle\cdots\langle[a/x]e\rangle\cdots\rangle\rangle \approx \tilde{}\,\tilde{}\cdots\tilde{}\langle\langle\cdots\langle[a/x]t\rangle\cdots\rangle\rangle\ . \tag{2}$$

Then applying the E_U rule ℓ times gives $[a/x]e \approx [a/x]t$. The old E_U rule $\tilde{}\langle e^0\rangle = e^0$ would apply only once here because the level of the $\langle\langle\cdots\langle[a/x]e\rangle\cdots\rangle\rangle$ part increases—so the generalization is strictly necessary. □

Theorem 7 shows that applying substitutions to an equivalence does not compromise its validity. This fact plays a role in the completeness proof of applicative bisimulation (to be introduced in Section 5), but we will leave those details to the technical report. The more interesting, and surprising, fact is that the converse fails in $\lambda^U_{\mathbf{v}}$—we cannot in general conclude $e \approx t$ from $\forall a.\ [a/x]e \approx [a/x]t$. We will discuss this issue in Section 3.

Remark. R_U and $\beta/\beta_{\mathbf{v}}$ cannot be generalized in a similar fashion as they involve demotion—moving a term from one level to another. If we generalized R_U to $!\,\langle e\rangle = e$, the e on the left appears in more brackets than on the right, so on the left we need more escapes than on the right to un-delay a subterm of e. For instance, if t is some divergent level-0 term, $\langle !\,\langle\tilde{}t\rangle\rangle = \langle\tilde{}t\rangle$ is an instance of the generalized R_U rule, but $\langle !\,\langle\tilde{}t\rangle\rangle \Downarrow^0$ while $\langle\tilde{}t\rangle \Uparrow^0$. The correct R_U rule avoids this problem by restricting e to level 0, thus $!\,\langle e^0\rangle = e^0$. The technical report proves that equational rules entailing unrestricted demotion are always unsound.

3 Closing Substitutions Compromise Validity

Here is a striking example of how reasoning in λ^U differs from reasoning in single-stage calculi. Traditionally, CBV calculi admit the equational rule

$$(\beta_x)\ \ (\lambda y.e^0)\ x = [x/y]e^0\ .$$

Plotkin's seminal λ_V [22], for example, does so implicitly by taking variables to be values, defining $x \in V$ where V is the set of values for λ_V. But β_x is *not* admissible in $\lambda^U_{\mathbf{v}}$. For example, the terms $(\lambda\_.0)\ x$ and 0 may seem interchangeable, but in $\lambda^U_{\mathbf{v}}$ they are distinguished by the program context $\mathcal{E} \stackrel{\text{def}}{\equiv} \langle\lambda x.\tilde{}[(\lambda\_.\langle 1\rangle)\ \bullet]\rangle$:

$$\langle\lambda x.\tilde{}[(\lambda\_.\langle 1\rangle)\ ((\lambda\_.0)\ x)]\rangle \Uparrow^0 \ \text{ but } \langle\lambda x.\tilde{}[(\lambda\_.\langle 1\rangle)\ 0]\rangle \Downarrow^0 \langle\lambda x.1\rangle\ . \tag{3}$$

(Once again, we are using [ ] as parentheses to enhance readability.) The term on the left is stuck because $x \notin V^0$ and $x \not\xrightarrow{0}$. Intuitively, the value of x is demanded before anything is substituted for it. If we apply a substitution σ that replaces x by a value, then $\sigma((\lambda\_.0)\ x) = \sigma 0$, so the standard technique of reasoning under closing substitutions is unsound. Note the β_x redex itself need not contain staging annotations; thus, adding staging to a language can compromise some existing equivalences, i.e., staging is a non-conservative language extension.

The problem here is that λ^U_{v} can evaluate open terms. Some readers may recall that λ_V *reduces* open terms just fine while admitting β_x, but the crucial difference is that λ^U *evaluates* (small-steps) open terms under program contexts whereas λ_V never does. Small-steps are the specification for implementations, so if they can rewrite an open subterm of a program, implementations must be able to perform that rewrite as well. By contrast, reduction is just a semantics-preserving rewrite, so implementations may or may not be able to perform it.

Implementations of λ^U_{v} including MetaOCaml have no runtime values, or data structures, representing the variable x—they implement $x \notin V^0$. They never perform $(\lambda\_.0)\ x \underset{0}{\rightsquigarrow} 0$, for if they were forced to evaluate $(\lambda\_.0)\ x$, then they would try to evaluate the x as required for CBV and throw an error. Some program contexts in λ^U do force the evaluation of open terms, e.g., the $\mathcal{E}$ given above. We must then define a small-step semantics with $(\lambda\_.0)\ x \underset{0}{\not\rightsquigarrow} 0$, or else we would not model actual implementations, and we must reject β_x, for it is unsound for $(\approx)$ in such a small-step semantics. In other words, lack of β_x is an inevitable consequence of the way practical implementations behave.

Even in λ_V, setting $x \in V$ is technically a mistake because λ_V implementations typically do not have runtime representations for variables either. But in λ_V, whether a given evaluator implements $x \in V$ or $x \notin V$ is unobservable. Small-steps on a λ_V program (which is closed by definition) never contract open redexes because evaluation contexts cannot contain binders. Submitting programs to an evaluator will never tell if it implements $x \in V$ or $x \notin V$. Therefore, in λ_V, there is always no harm in pretending $x \in V$. A small-step semantics with $x \in V$ gives the same $(\approx)$ as one with $x \notin V$, and β_x is sound for this $(\approx)$.

Now, the general, more important, problem is that reasoning under substitutions is unsound, i.e., $\forall \sigma.\ \sigma e \approx \sigma t \not\Longrightarrow e \approx t$. The lack of β_x is just an example of how this problem shows up in reasoning. We stress that the real challenge is this more general problem with substitutions because, unfortunately, β_x is not only an illustrative example but also a tempting straw man. Seeing β_x alone, one may think that its unsoundness is some idiosyncrasy that can be fixed by modifying the calculus. For example, type systems can easily recover β_x by banishing all stuck terms including β_x redexes. But this little victory over β_x does not justify reasoning under substitutions, and how or whether we can achieve the latter is a much more difficult question. It is unclear if any type systems justify reasoning under substitutions in general, and it is even less clear how to prove that.

Surveying which refinements (including, but not limited to the addition of type systems) for λ^U let us reason under substitutions and why is an important topic for future study, but it is beyond the scope of this paper. In this paper, we focus instead on showing that we can achieve a lot without committing to anything more complicated than λ^U. In particular, we will show with applicative bisimulation (Section 5) that the lack of β_x is not a large drawback after all, as a refined form of β_x can be used instead:

$$(C\beta_x)\quad \lambda x.C[(\lambda y.e^0)\ x] = \lambda x.C[[x/y]e^0]\ ,$$

with the side conditions that $C[(\lambda y.e^0)\ x], C[[x/y]e^0] \in E^0$ and that C does not shadow the binding of x. Intuitively, given just the term $(\lambda y.e^0)\ x$, we cannot tell if x is well-leveled, i.e., bound at a lower level than its use, so that a value is substituted for x before evaluation can reach it. $C\beta_x$ remedies this problem by demanding a well-leveled binder. As a special case, β_x is sound for any subterm in the erasure of a closed term—that is, the erasure of any self-contained generator.

4 The Erasure Theorem

In this section we present the Erasure Theorem for λ^U and derive simple termination conditions that guarantee $e \approx \|e\|$.

4.1 Theorem Statement

The theorem statement differs for CBN and CBV. Let us see CBN first. The intuition behind the theorem is that all that staging annotations do is to describe and enforce an evaluation strategy. They may force CBV, CBN, or some other strategy that the programmer wants, but CBN reduction can simulate any strategy because the redex can be chosen from anywhere.[1] Thus, erasure commutes with CBN reductions (Figure 3(a)). The same holds for provable equalities.

Theorem 8 (CBN Erasure). If $\lambda^U_{\mathbf{n}} \vdash e \longrightarrow^* t$ then $\lambda^U_{\mathbf{n}} \vdash \|e\| \longrightarrow^* \|t\|$. Also, if $\lambda^U_{\mathbf{n}} \vdash e = t$ then $\lambda^U_{\mathbf{n}} \vdash \|e\| = \|t\|$.

How does this Theorem help prove equivalences of the form $e \approx \|e\|$? The theorem gives a simulation of reductions from e by reductions from $\|e\|$. If e reduces to an unstaged term $\|t\|$, then simulating that reduction from $\|e\|$ gets us to $\|\|t\|\|$, which is just $\|t\|$; thus $e \longrightarrow^* \|t\| \longleftarrow^* \|e\|$ and $e = \|e\|$. Amazingly, this witness $\|t\|$ can be *any* reduct of e, as long as it is unstaged! In fact, by Church-Rosser, any t with $e = \|t\|$ will do. So staging is correct (i.e., semantics-preserving, or $e \approx \|e\|$) if we can find this $\|t\|$. As we will show in Section 4.2, this search boils down to a termination check on the generator.

Lemma 9 (CBN Correctness). $(\exists t.\ \lambda^U_{\mathbf{n}} \vdash e = \|t\|) \Longrightarrow \lambda^U_{\mathbf{n}} \vdash e = \|e\|$.

CBV satisfies a property similar to Theorem 8, but the situation is more subtle. Staging modifies the evaluation strategy in CBV as well, but not all of them can be simulated in the erasure by CBV reductions, for $\beta_{\mathbf{v}}$ reduces only a subset

---

[1] This only means that reductions under exotic evaluation strategies are semantics-preserving rewrites under CBN semantics. CBN evaluators may not actually perform such reductions unless forced by staging annotations.

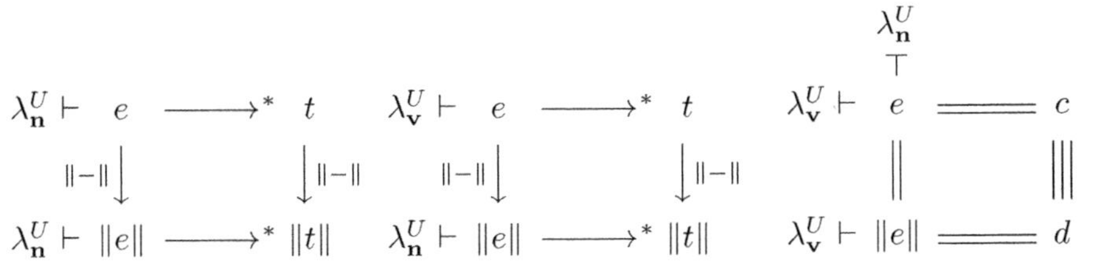

(a) CBN erasure. (b) CBV erasure. (c) CBV correctness lemma.

Fig. 3. Visualizations of the Erasure Theorem and the derived correctness lemma

of β redexes. For example, if $\Omega \in E^0$ is divergent, then $(\lambda\_.0)\ \langle\Omega\rangle \longrightarrow 0$ in CBV, but the erasure $(\lambda\_.0)\ \Omega$ does not CBV-reduce to 0 since Ω is not a value. However, it is the case that $\lambda^U_{\mathbf{n}} \vdash (\lambda\_.0)\ \Omega \longrightarrow 0$ in CBN. In general, erasing CBV reductions gives CBN reductions (Figure 3(b)).

Theorem 10 (CBV Erasure). If $\lambda^U_{\mathbf{v}} \vdash e \longrightarrow^* t$ then $\lambda^U_{\mathbf{n}} \vdash \|e\| \longrightarrow^* \|t\|$. Also, if $\lambda^U_{\mathbf{v}} \vdash e = t$ then $\lambda^U_{\mathbf{n}} \vdash \|e\| = \|t\|$.

This theorem has similar ramifications as the CBN Erasure Theorem, but with the caveat that they conclude in CBN despite having premises in CBV. In particular, if e is CBV-equal to an erased term, then $e = \|e\|$ in CBN.

Corollary 11. $(\exists t.\ \lambda^U_{\mathbf{v}} \vdash e = \|t\|) \Longrightarrow \lambda^U_{\mathbf{n}} \vdash e = \|e\|$.

CBN equalities given by this corollary may at first seem irrelevant to CBV programs, but in fact if we show that e and $\|e\|$ CBV-reduce to constants, then the CBN equality can be safely cast to CBV equality. Figure 3(c) summarizes this reasoning. Given e, suppose we found some c, d that satisfy the two horizontal CBV equalities. Then from the top equality, Theorem 11 gives the left vertical one in CBN. As CBN equality subsumes CBV equality, tracing the diagram counterclockwise from the top right corner gives $\lambda^U_{\mathbf{n}} \vdash c = d$ in CBN. Then the right vertical equality $c \equiv d$ follows by the Church-Rosser property in CBN. Tracing the diagram clockwise from the top left corner gives $\lambda^U_{\mathbf{v}} \vdash e = \|e\|$.

Lemma 12 (CBV Correctness). If $\lambda^U_{\mathbf{v}} \vdash e = c$ and $\lambda^U_{\mathbf{v}} \vdash \|e\| = d$, then $\lambda^U_{\mathbf{v}} \vdash e = \|e\|$.

Thus, we can prove $e = \|e\|$ in CBV by showing that each side terminates to some constant, *in CBV*. Though we borrowed CBN facts to derive this lemma, the lemma itself leaves no trace of CBN reasoning.

4.2 Example: Erasing Staged Power

Let us show how the Erasure Theorem applies to `stpow`. First, some technicalities: MetaOCaml's constructs are interpreted in λ^U in the obvious manner, e.g., `let x = ` e ` in ` t stands for $(\lambda x.t)\ e$ and `let rec f x = ` e stands for `let f = ` $\Theta(\lambda f.\lambda x.e)$ where Θ is some fixed-point combinator. We assume λ^U has integers and booleans. For conciseness, we treat top-level bindings `genpow` and `stpow` like macros, so $\|$`stpow`$\|$ is the erasure of the recursive function to which `stpow` is bound with `genpow` inlined, not the erasure of a variable named `stpow`.

As a caveat, we might want to prove `stpow` $\approx$ `power` but this goal is not quite right. The whole point of `stpow` is to process the first argument without waiting for the second, so it can disagree with `power` when partially applied, e.g., `stpow 0` $\Uparrow^0$ but `power 0` $\Downarrow^0$. We sidestep this issue for now by concentrating on positive arguments, and discuss divergent cases in Section 5.2.

To prove $k > 0 \Longrightarrow$ `stpow` k = `power` k for CBN, we only need to check that the code generator `genpow` k terminates to some `.<`$\|e\|$`>.`; then the `.!` in `stpow` will take out the brackets and we have the witness required for Theorem 9. To say that something terminates to `.<`$\|e\|$`>.` roughly means that it is a two-stage program, which is true for almost all uses of MSP that we are aware of. This use of the Erasure Theorem is augmented by the observation $\|$`stpow`$\|$ = `power`—these functions are not syntactically equal, the former containing an η redex.

Lemma 13. $\lambda^U_{\mathbf{n}} \vdash \|$`stpow`$\|$ = `power`

Proof. Contract the η expansion by (CBN) β. □

Proposition 14 (Erasing CBN Power). $\forall k \in \mathbb{Z}^+.\ \lambda^U_{\mathbf{n}} \vdash$ `stpow` k = `power` k.

Proof. Induction on k gives some e s.t. `genpow` k `.<x>.` = `.<`$\|e\|$`>.`, so

$$\texttt{stpow}\ k = \texttt{.!.<fun x} \rightarrow \texttt{.\~{}(genpow}\ k\ \texttt{.<x>.)>.}$$
$$= \texttt{.!.<fun x} \rightarrow \texttt{.\~{}.<}\|e\|\texttt{>.>.} = \texttt{fun x} \rightarrow \ \|e\|$$

hence `stpow` k = $\|$`stpow`$\|$ k = `power` k by Lemmas 9 and 13. □

The proof for CBV is similar, but we need to fully apply both `stpow` and its erasure to confirm that they both reach some constant. The beauty of Theorem 12 is that we do not have to know what those constants are. Just as in CBN, the erasure $\|$`stpow`$\|$ is equivalent to `power`, but note this part of the proof uses $C\beta_x$.

Lemma 15. $\lambda^U_{\mathbf{n}} \vdash \|$`stpow`$\| \approx$ `power`

Proof. Contract the η expansion by $C\beta_x$. □

Proposition 16 (Erasing CBV Power). For $k \in \mathbb{Z}^+$ and $m \in \mathbb{Z}$, $\lambda^U_{\mathbf{v}} \vdash$ `stpow` $k\ m \approx$ `power` $k\ m$.

Proof. We stress that this proof works entirely with CBV equalities; we have no need to deal with CBN once Theorem 12 is established. By induction on k, we prove that $\exists e.$ `genpow` k `.<x>.` = `.<`$\|e\|$`>.` and $[m/\mathtt{x}]\|e\| \Downarrow^0 m'$ for some $m' \in \mathbb{Z}$. We can do so without explicitly figuring out what $\|e\|$ looks like. The case $k = 1$ is easy; for $k > 1$, the returned code is `.<x *` $\|e'\|$`>.`where $[m/\mathtt{x}]\|e'\|$ terminates to an integer by inductive hypothesis, so this property is preserved. Then

$$\texttt{stpow}\ k\ m = \texttt{.!.<fun x} \rightarrow \texttt{.\~{}(genpow}\ k\ \texttt{.<x>.)>.}\ m$$
$$= \texttt{.!.<fun x} \rightarrow \ \|e\|\texttt{>.}\ m = [m/x]\|e\| = m' \in \mathit{Const}.$$

Clearly `power` $k\ m$ terminates to a constant. By Theorem 15, $\|$`stpow`$\|$ $k\ m$ also yields a constant, so by Theorem 12, `stpow` $k\ m$ = $\|$`stpow`$\|$ $k\ m \approx$ `power` $k\ m$. □

These proofs illustrate our answer to the erasure question in the introduction. Erasure is semantics-preserving if the generator terminates to $\langle \|e\| \rangle$ in CBN, or if the staged and unstaged terms terminate to constants in CBV. Showing the latter requires propagating type information and a termination assertion for the generated code. Type information would come for free in a typed system, but it can be easily emulated in an untyped setting. Hence we see that correctness of staging generally reduces to termination not just in CBN but also in CBV—in fact, the correctness proof is essentially a modification of the termination proof.

4.3 Why CBN Facts Are Necessary for CBV Reasoning

So far, we have let erasure map CBV equalities to the superset of CBN equalities and performed extra work to show that the particular CBN equalities we derived hold in CBV as well. A natural, alternative idea is to find a subset of CBV reductions that erase to CBV reductions. This alternative approach does work [31,14], but we show here that it only works in simple cases.

The problem with erasing CBV reductions is that the argument in a $\beta_{\mathbf{v}}$ redex may have a divergent erasure. If we restrict $\beta_{\mathbf{v}}$ to

$$(\beta_{\mathbf{v}\Downarrow}) \quad (\lambda x.e^0)\ v^0 = [v^0/x]e^0 \text{ provided } \lambda^U_{\mathbf{v}} \vdash \|v^0\| \Downarrow^0 ,$$

which checks that the argument's erasure terminates, then reductions under the axiom set $\lambda^U_{\mathbf{v}\Downarrow} \stackrel{\text{def}}{=} \{\beta_{\mathbf{v}\Downarrow}, E_U, R_U, \delta\}$ erase to CBV reductions. But $\beta_{\mathbf{v}\Downarrow}$ is much too crude, for it cannot reduce $(\lambda y.e^0)\ \langle x \rangle$ (note $x \Uparrow^0$) and fails to handle programs as simple as `stpow`. A natural solution is to check carefulness under substitutions:

$$(\beta_{\mathbf{v}\Downarrow}/\sigma) \quad (\lambda x.e^0)\ v^0 = [v^0/x]e^0 \text{ provided } \lambda^U_{\mathbf{v}} \vdash \sigma\|v^0\| \Downarrow^0 .$$

Ignoring some technical details, if we let $\lambda^U_{\mathbf{v}\Downarrow}/\sigma \stackrel{\text{def}}{=} \{\beta_{\mathbf{v}\Downarrow}/\sigma, E_U, R_U, \delta\}$ for any substitution $\sigma : Var \underset{\text{fin}}{\rightharpoonup} V^0$, then $\lambda^U_{\mathbf{v}\Downarrow}/\sigma \vdash e = t$ implies $\lambda^U_{\mathbf{v}} \vdash \sigma e = \sigma t$. This observation suffices to verify `stpow` (see the technical report for a demonstration).

However, careful reductions quickly become unwieldy in the face of binders. For instance, if we write `let` x `=` e `in` t as a shorthand for $(\lambda x.t)\ e$, clearly

```
.!.<let y = 0 in let x = y in .~((λz.z) .<x+y>.)>.
```

is equivalent to its erasure. To prove this, we might observe that $\beta_{\mathbf{v}\Downarrow}/[0,0/x,y] \vdash$ $(\lambda z.z)$ `.<x+y>.` $=$ `.<x+y>.`; however, the "compatible extension",

$$\lambda^U_{\mathbf{v}\Downarrow}/[0,0/x,y] \vdash \texttt{let } x \texttt{ = } y \texttt{ in .\~{}((}\lambda z.z\texttt{) .<}x\texttt{+}y\texttt{>.)} = \dots ,$$

does not hold because the x in $\lambda^U_{\mathbf{v}\Downarrow}/[0,0/x,y]$ cannot refer to the x bound in the object term (else we would have to give up hygiene).

In general, we must reason under different substitutions in different scopes, and it is tricky to propagate the results obtained under $\lambda^U_{\mathbf{v}\Downarrow}/\sigma$ to an outer context where some variables in σ may have gone out of scope. While it may not be possible to pull off the bookkeeping, we find ourselves fighting against hygiene rather than exploiting it. In this sense, restricting CBV reductions gives a less useful approach than appealing to CBN reasoning results, especially for programs that generate nested binders. The longest common subsequence found in the technical report is an example of such a generator.

5 Applicative Bisimulation

This section presents applicative bisimulation [1,10], a well-established tool for analyzing higher-order functional programs. Bisimulation is sound and complete for $(\approx)$, and justifies $C\beta_x$ (Section 3) and extensionality, allowing us to handle the divergence issues ignored in Section 4.2.

5.1 Proof by Bisimulation

Intuitively, for a pair of terms to applicatively bisimulate, they must both terminate or both diverge, and if they terminate, their values must bisimulate again under experiments that examine their behavior. In an experiment, functions are called, code values are run, and constants are left untouched. Effectively, this is a bisimulation under the transition system consisting of evaluation $(\Downarrow)$ and experiments. If eRt implies that either $e \approx t$ or e,t bisimulate, then $R \subseteq (\approx)$.

Definition 17 (Relation Under Experiment). Given a relation $R \subseteq E \times E$, let $\widetilde{R} \stackrel{\text{def}}{=} R \cup (\approx)$. For $\ell > 0$ set $u\ R_\dagger^\ell\ v$ iff $u\widetilde{R}v$. For $\ell = 0$ set $u\ R_\dagger^0\ v$ iff either:

- $u \equiv v \in \mathit{Const}$,
- $u \equiv \lambda x.e$ and $v \equiv \lambda x.t$ for some e, t s.t. $\forall a.([a/x]e)\widetilde{R}([a/x]t)$, or
- $u \equiv \langle e \rangle$ and $v \equiv \langle t \rangle$ for some e, t s.t. $e\widetilde{R}t$.

Definition 18 (Applicative Bisimulation). An $R \subseteq E \times E$ is an *applicative bisimulation* iff every pair $(e, t) \in R$ satisfies the following: let $\ell = \max(\mathrm{lv}\, e, \mathrm{lv}\, t)$; then for any finite substitution $\sigma : \mathit{Var} \xrightharpoonup[\text{fin}]{} \mathit{Arg}$ we have $\sigma e \Downarrow^\ell \Longleftrightarrow \sigma t \Downarrow^\ell$, and if $\sigma e \Downarrow^\ell u \wedge \sigma t \Downarrow^\ell v$ then $u\ R_\dagger^\ell\ v$.

Theorem 19. Given $R \subset E \times E$, define $R^\bullet \stackrel{\text{def}}{=} \{(\sigma e, \sigma t) : eRt, (\sigma : \mathit{Var} \xrightharpoonup[\text{fin}]{} \mathit{Arg})\}$. Then $R \subseteq (\approx)$ iff $R^\bullet$ is an applicative bisimulation.

This is our answer to the extensional reasoning question in the introduction: this theorem shows that bisimulation can in principle derive *all* valid equivalences, including all extensional facts. Unlike in single-stage languages [1,13,10], σ ranges over non-closing substitutions, which may not substitute for all variables or may substitute open terms. Closing substitutions are unsafe since λ^U has open-term evaluation. But for CBV, bisimulation gives a condition under which substitution is safe, i.e., when the binder is at level 0 (in the definition of $\lambda x.e\ R_\dagger^0\ \lambda x.t$). In CBN this is not an advantage as $\forall a.[a/x]e\widetilde{R}[a/x]t$ entails $[x/x]e\widetilde{R}[x/x]t$, but bisimulation is still a more approachable alternative to $(\approx)$.

The importance of the substitution in $\lambda x.e\ R_\dagger^0\ \lambda x.t$ for CBV is best illustrated by the proof of extensionality, from which we get $C\beta_x$ introduced in Section 3.

Proposition 20. If $e, t \in E^0$ and $\forall a.\ (\lambda x.e)\ a \approx (\lambda x.t)\ a$, then $\lambda x.e \approx \lambda x.t$.

Proof. Take $R \stackrel{\text{def}}{=} \{(\lambda x.e, \lambda x.t)\}^\bullet$. To see that R is a bisimulation, fix σ, and note that $\sigma\lambda x.e$, $\sigma\lambda x.t$ terminate to themselves at level 0. By Barendregt's variable convention [2], x is fresh for σ, thus $\sigma\lambda x.e \equiv \lambda x.\sigma e$ and $\sigma\lambda x.t \equiv \lambda x.\sigma t$. We must check $[a/x]\sigma e \approx [a/x]\sigma t$: by assumption $\sigma[a/x]e \approx \sigma[a/x]t$, and one can show that σ and $[a/x]$ commute modulo $(\approx)$. Hence by Theorem 19, $\lambda x.e \approx \lambda x.t$. □

Corollary 21 (Soundness of $C\beta_x$). If $C[(\lambda y.e^0)\ x], C[[x/y]e^0] \in E^0$ and C does not bind x, then $\lambda x.C[(\lambda y.e^0)\ x] \approx \lambda x.C[[x/y]e^0]$.

Proof. Apply both sides to an arbitrary a and use Theorem 20 with $\beta/\beta_{\mathbf{v}}$. □

The proof of Theorem 20 would have failed in CBV had we defined $\lambda x.e\ R^0_\dagger\ \lambda x.t \iff e\widetilde{R}t$, without the substitution. For when $e \equiv (\lambda\_.0)\ x$ and $t \equiv 0$, the premise $\forall a.[a/x]e \approx [a/x]t$ is satisfied but $e \not\approx t$, so $\lambda x.e$ and $\lambda x.t$ do not bisimulate with this weaker definition. The binding in $\lambda x.e \in E^0$ is guaranteed to be well-leveled, and exploiting it by inserting $[a/x]$ in the comparison is strictly necessary to get a complete (as in "sound and complete") notion of bisimulation.

Howe's method [13] is used to prove Theorem 19, but adapting this method to λ^U is surprisingly tricky because λ^U's bisimulation must handle substitutions inconsistently: in Theorem 18 we cannot restrict our attention to σ's that substitute away any particular variable, but in Theorem 17, for $\lambda x.e\ R^0_\dagger\ \lambda x.t$, we must restrict our attention to the case where substitution eliminates x. Proving Theorem 19 entails coinduction on a self-referential definition of bisimulation; however, Theorem 17 refers not to the bisimulation whose definition it is a part of, but to a different bisimulation that holds only under substitutions that eliminate x. To solve this problem, we recast bisimulation to a family of relations indexed by a set of variables to be eliminated, so that the analogue of Theorem 17 can refer to a different member of the family. Theorem 19 is then proved by mutual coinduction. See the technical report for more details.

Remark. Extensionality is a common addition to the equational theory for the plain λ calculus, usually called the ω rule [21,15]. But unlike ω in the plain λ calculus, λ^U functions must agree on open-term arguments as well. This is no surprise since λ^U functions do receive open arguments during program execution. However, we know of no specific functions that fail to be equivalent because of open arguments. Whether extensionality can be strengthened to require equivalence only under closed arguments is an interesting open question.

Remark. The only difference between Theorem 18 and applicative bisimulation in the plain λ calculus is that Theorem 18 avoids applying closing substitutions. Given that completeness can be proved for this bisimulation, it seems plausible that the problem with reasoning under substitutions is the only thing that makes conservativity fail. Hence it seems that for *closed* unstaged terms, λ^U's $(\approx)$ could actually coincide with that of the plain λ calculus. Such a result would make a perfect complement to the Erasure Theorem, for it lets us completely forget about staging when reasoning about an erased program. We do not have a proof of this conjecture, however. Conservativity is usually proved through a denotational semantics, which is notoriously difficult to devise for hygienic MSP. It will at least deserve separate treatment from this paper.

5.2 Example: Tying Loose Ends on Staged Power

In Section 4.2, we sidestepped issues arising from the fact that `stpow 0` $\Uparrow^0$ whereas `power 0` $\Downarrow^0$. If we are allowed to modify the code, this problem is usually easy to avoid, for example by making `power` and `genpow` terminate on non-positive arguments. If not, we can still persevere by finessing the statement of correctness. The problem is partial application, so we can force `stpow` to be fully applied before it executes by stating $\texttt{power} \approx \lambda n.\lambda x.\texttt{stpow}\ n\ x$.

Lemma 22. Let $e' \approx_{\Uparrow} t'$ mean $e' \approx t' \vee (\sigma e' \Uparrow^{\ell} \wedge \sigma t' \Uparrow^{\ell})$ where $\ell = \max(\text{lv}\, e', \text{lv}\, t')$. For a fixed e, t, if for every $\sigma : \mathit{Var} \underset{\text{fin}}{\rightharpoonup} \mathit{Arg}$ we have $\sigma e \approx_{\Uparrow} \sigma t$, then $e \approx t$.

Proof. Notice that $\{(e,t)\}^{\bullet}$ is an applicative bisimulation. □

Proposition 23 (CBN `stpow` is Correct). $\lambda_{\mathrm{n}}^{U} \vdash \texttt{power} \approx \lambda n.\lambda x.\texttt{stpow}\ n\ x$.

Proof. We just need to show $\forall e,t \in E^0.\ \texttt{power}\ e\ t \approx_{\Uparrow} \texttt{stpow}\ e\ t$, because then $\forall e,t \in E^0.\ \forall \sigma : \mathit{Var} \underset{\text{fin}}{\rightharpoonup} \mathit{Arg}.\ \sigma(\texttt{power}\ e\ t) \approx_{\Uparrow} \sigma(\texttt{stpow}\ e\ t)$, whence $\texttt{power} \approx \lambda n.\lambda x.\texttt{stpow}\ n\ x$ by Theorem 22 and extensionality. So fix arbitrary, potentially open, $e,t \in E^0$, and split cases on the behavior of e. As evident from the following argument, the possibility that e,t contain free variables is not a problem here.
[If $e \Uparrow^0$ or $e \Downarrow^0 u \notin \mathbb{Z}^+$] Both $\texttt{power}\ e\ t$ and $\texttt{stpow}\ e\ t$ diverge.
[If $e \Downarrow^0 m \in \mathbb{Z}^+$] Using Theorem 14, $\texttt{power}\ e = \texttt{power}\ m \approx \texttt{stpow}\ m = \texttt{stpow}\ e$, so $\texttt{power}\ e\ t \approx \texttt{stpow}\ e\ t$. □

Proposition 24 (CBV `stpow` is Correct). $\lambda_{\mathrm{v}}^{U} \vdash \texttt{power} \approx \lambda n.\lambda x.\texttt{stpow}\ n\ x$.

Proof. By the same argument as in CBN, we just need to show $\texttt{power}\ u\ v \approx_{\Uparrow} \texttt{stpow}\ u\ v$ for arbitrary $u, v \in V^0$.
[If $u \notin \mathbb{Z}^+$] Both $\texttt{power}\ u\ v$ and $\texttt{stpow}\ u\ v$ get stuck at `if n = 0`.
[If $u \in \mathbb{Z}^+$] If $u \equiv 1$, then $\texttt{power}\ 1\ v = v = \texttt{stpow}\ 1\ v$. If $u > 1$, we show that the generated code is strict in a subexpression that requires $v \in \mathbb{Z}$. Observe that $\texttt{genpow}\ u\ \texttt{.<x>.} \Downarrow^0 \texttt{.<}e\texttt{>.}$ where e has the form $\texttt{.<x * }t\texttt{>.}$. For $[v/x]e \Downarrow^0$ it is necessary that $v \in \mathbb{Z}$. It is clear that $\texttt{power}\ u\ v \Downarrow^0$ requires $v \in \mathbb{Z}$. So either $v \notin \mathbb{Z}$ and $\texttt{power}\ u\ v \Uparrow^0$ and $\texttt{stpow}\ u\ v \Uparrow^0$, in which case we are done, or $v \in \mathbb{Z}$ in which case Theorem 16 applies. □

Remark. Real code should not use $\lambda n.\lambda x.\texttt{stpow}\ n\ x$, as it re-generates and recompiles code upon every invocation. Application programs should always use `stpow`, and one must check (outside of the scope of verifying the function itself) that `stpow` is always eventually fully applied so that the η expansion is benign.

6 Related Works

Taha [27] first discovered λ^U, which showed that functional hygienic MSP admits intensional equalities like β, even under brackets. However, [27] showed the mere existence of the theory and did not explore how to use it for verification, or how to prove extensional equivalences. Moreover, though [27] laid down the operational semantics of both CBV and CBN, it gave an equational theory for only CBN and left the trickier CBV unaddressed.

Yang pioneered the use of an "annotation erasure theorem", which stated $e \Downarrow^0 \langle\|t\|\rangle \implies \|t\| \approx \|e\|$ [31]. But there was a catch: the assertion $\|t\| \approx \|e\|$ was asserted in the unstaged base language, instead of the staged language—translated to our setting, the conclusion of the theorem was $\lambda \vdash \|t\| \approx \|e\|$ and not $\lambda^U \vdash \|t\| \approx \|e\|$. In practical terms, this meant that the context of deployment of the staged code could contain no further staging. Code generation must be done offline, and application programs using the generated $\|t\|$ must be written in a single-stage language, or else no guarantee was made. This interferes with combining analyses of multiple generators and precludes dynamic code generation by run (.!). Yang also worked with operational semantics, and did not explore in depth how equational reasoning interacts with erasure.

This paper can be seen as a confluence of these two lines of research: we complete λ^U by giving a CBV theory with a comprehensive study of its peculiarities, and adapt erasure to produce an equality in the staged language λ^U.

Berger and Tratt [3] devised a Hoare-style program logic for the typed language Mini-$\mathrm{ML}_e^\Box$. They develop a promising foundation and prove strong properties about it such as relative completeness, but concrete verification tasks considered concern relatively simplistic programs. Mini-$\mathrm{ML}_e^\Box$ also prohibits manipulating open terms, so it does not capture the challenges of reasoning about free variables, which was one of the main challenges to which we faced up. Insights gained from λ^U should help extend such logics to more expressive languages, and our proof techniques will be a good toolbox to lay on top of them.

For MSP with variable capture, Choi et al. [7] recently proposed an alternative approach with different trade-offs than ours. They provide an "unstaging" translation of staging annotations into environment-passing code. Their translation is semantics preserving with no proof obligations but leaves an unstaged program that is complicated by environment-passing, whereas our erasure approach leaves a simpler unstaged program at the expense of additional proof obligations. It will be interesting to see how these approaches compare in practice or if they can be usefully combined, but for the moment they seem to fill different niches.

7 Conclusion and Future Work

We addressed three basic concerns for verifying staged programs. We showed that staging is a non-conservative extension because reasoning under substitutions is unsound in a MSP language, even if we are dealing with unstaged terms. Despite this drawback, untyped functional MSP has a rich set of useful properties.

We proved that simple termination conditions guarantee that erasure preserves semantics, which reduces the task of proving the irrelevance of annotations on a program's semantics to the better studied problem of proving termination. We showed a sound and complete notion of applicative bisimulation for this setting, which allows us to reason under substitution in some cases. In particular, the shocking lack of β_x in λ^U_v is of limited practical relevance as we have $C\beta_x$ instead.

These results improve our general understanding of hygienic MSP. We better know the multi-stage λ calculus' similarities with the plain λ calculus (e.g., completeness of bisimulation), as well as its pathologies and the extent to which they are a problem. The Erasure Theorem gives intuitions on what staging annotations can or cannot do, with which we may educate the novice multi-stage programmer. This understanding has brought us to a level where the proof of a sophisticated generator like LCS is easily within reach.

This work may be extended in several interesting directions. We have specifically identified some open questions about λ^U: which type systems allow reasoning under substitutions, whether it is conservative over the plain λ calculus for closed terms, and whether the extensionality principle can be strengthened to require equivalence for only closed-term arguments.

Devising a mechanized program logic would also be an excellent goal. Berger and Tratt's system [3] may be a good starting point, although whether to go with Hoare logic or to recast it in equational style is an interesting design question. A mechanized program logic may let us automate the particularly MSP-specific proof step of showing that erasure preserves semantics. The Erasure Theorem reduces this problem to essentially termination checks, and we can probably capitalize on recent advances in automated termination analysis [11].

Bisimulation is known to work for single-stage imperative languages, though in quite different flavors from applicative bisimulation [19]. Adapting them to MSP would make the emerging imperative hygienic MSP languages [16,24,30] susceptible to analysis. The Erasure Theorem does not apply as-is to imperative languages since modifying evaluation strategies can commute the order of effects. Two mechanisms will be key in studying erasure for imperative languages—one for tracking which effects are commuted with which, and one for tracking mutual (in)dependence of effects, perhaps separation logic [23] for the latter. In any case, investigation of imperative hygienic MSP may have to wait until the foundation matures, as noted in the introduction.

Finally, this work focused on functional (input-output) correctness of staged code, but quantifying performance benefits is also an important concern for a staged program. It will be interesting to see how we can quantify the performance of a staged program through formalisms like improvement theory [25].

Acknowledgments. We would like to thank Gregory Malecha, Edwin Westbrook, and Mathias Ricken for their input on the technical content of this paper. We are grateful to Veronica Gaspez and Bertil Svensson for their feedback. We thank Halmstad University for their support in completing this work. The first author has received significant guidance and supervision from Robert

Cartwright, Vivek Sarkar, and Marcia O'Malley, who, together with the second author, constitute the first author's doctoral thesis committee. We thank Carol Sonenklar and Ray Hardesty for their input on the writing.

References

1. Abramsky, S.: The Lazy Lambda Calculus, pp. 65–116. Addison-Wesley, Boston (1990)
2. Barendregt, H.P.: The Lambda Calculus: Its Syntax and Semantics. Studies in Logic and The Foundations of Mathematics. North-Holland (1984)
3. Berger, M., Tratt, L.: Program Logics for Homogeneous Meta-programming. In: Clarke, E.M., Voronkov, A. (eds.) LPAR-16 2010. LNCS, vol. 6355, pp. 64–81. Springer, Heidelberg (2010)
4. Brady, E., Hammond, K.: A verified staged interpreter is a verified compiler. In: 5th International Conference on Generative Programming and Component Engineering, pp. 111–120. ACM (2006)
5. Carette, J., Kiselyov, O.: Multi-stage Programming with Functors and Monads: Eliminating Abstraction Overhead from Generic Code. In: Glück, R., Lowry, M. (eds.) GPCE 2005. LNCS, vol. 3676, pp. 256–274. Springer, Heidelberg (2005)
6. Carette, J., Kiselyov, O., Shan, C.-C.: Finally Tagless, Partially Evaluated: Tagless Staged Interpreters for Simpler Typed Languages. In: Shao, Z. (ed.) APLAS 2007. LNCS, vol. 4807, pp. 222–238. Springer, Heidelberg (2007)
7. Choi, W., Aktemur, B., Yi, K., Tatsuta, M.: Static analysis of multi-staged programs via unstaging translation. In: 38th Annual ACM SIGPLAN-SIGACT Symposium on Principles of Programming Languages, pp. 81–92. ACM, New York (2011)
8. Cohen, A., Donadio, S., Garzaran, M.J., Herrmann, C., Kiselyov, O., Padua, D.: In search of a program generator to implement generic transformations for high-performance computing. Sci. Comput. Program. 62(1), 25–46 (2006)
9. Dybvig, R.K.: Writing hygienic macros in scheme with syntax-case. Tech. Rep. TR356, Indiana University Computer Science Department (1992)
10. Gordon, A.D.: Bisimilarity as a theory of functional programming. Theoretical Computer Science 228(1-2), 5–47 (1999)
11. Heizmann, M., Jones, N., Podelski, A.: Size-Change Termination and Transition Invariants. In: Cousot, R., Martel, M. (eds.) SAS 2010. LNCS, vol. 6337, pp. 22–50. Springer, Heidelberg (2010)
12. Herrmann, C.A., Langhammer, T.: Combining partial evaluation and staged interpretation in the implementation of domain-specific languages. Sci. Comput. Program. 62(1), 47–65 (2006)
13. Howe, D.J.: Proving congruence of bisimulation in functional programming languages. Inf. Comput. 124(2), 103–112 (1996)
14. Inoue, J., Taha, W.: Reasoning about multi-stage programs. Tech. rep., Rice University Computer Science Department (October 2011)
15. Intrigila, B., Statman, R.: The Omega Rule is $\mathbf{\Pi}_1^1$-Complete in the $\lambda\beta$-Calculus. In: Ronchi Della Rocca, S. (ed.) TLCA 2007. LNCS, vol. 4583, pp. 178–193. Springer, Heidelberg (2007)
16. Kameyama, Y., Kiselyov, O., Shan, C.-C.: Shifting the stage: Staging with delimited control. In: 2009 ACM SIGPLAN Workshop on Partial Evaluation and Program Manipulation, pp. 111–120. ACM, New York (2009)

17. Kim, I.S., Yi, K., Calcagno, C.: A polymorphic modal type system for LISP-like multi-staged languages. In: 33rd ACM SIGPLAN-SIGACT Symposium on Principles of Programming Languages, pp. 257–268. ACM, New York (2006)
18. Kiselyov, O., Swadi, K.N., Taha, W.: A methodology for generating verified combinatorial circuits. In: Proc. of EMSOFT, pp. 249–258. ACM (2004)
19. Koutavas, V., Wand, M.: Small bisimulations for reasoning about higher-order imperative programs. In: 2006 ACM SIGPLAN Symposium on Partial Evaluation and Semantics-based Program Manipulation, pp. 141–152. ACM, New York (2006)
20. Muller, R.: M-LISP: A representation-independent dialect of LISP with reduction semantics. ACM Trans. Program. Lang. Syst., 589–616 (1992)
21. Plotkin, G.D.: The λ-calculus is ω-incomplete. J. Symb. Logic, 313–317 (June 1974)
22. Plotkin, G.D.: Call-by-name, call-by-value and the λ-calculus. Theor. Comput. Sci. 1(2), 125–159 (1975)
23. Reynolds, J.C.: Separation logic: A logic for shared mutable data structures. In: 17th Annual IEEE Symposium on Logic in Computer Science, pp. 55–74 (2002)
24. Rompf, T., Odersky, M.: Lightweight modular staging: A pragmatic approach to runtime code generation and compiled DSLs. In: 9th International Conference on Generative Programming and Component Engineering (2010)
25. Sands, D.: Improvement Theory and its Applications, pp. 275–306. Cambridge University Press, New York (1998)
26. Swadi, K., Taha, W., Kiselyov, O., Pašalić, E.: A monadic approach for avoiding code duplication when staging memoized functions. In: 2006 ACM SIGPLAN Symposium on Partial Evaluation and Semantics-based Program Manipulation, pp. 160–169. ACM, New York (2006)
27. Taha, W.: Multistage Programming: Its Theory and Applications. Ph.D. thesis, Oregon Graduate Institute (1999)
28. Taha, W., Nielsen, M.F.: Environment classifiers. In: 30th ACM SIGPLAN-SIGACT Symposium on Principles of Programming Languages, pp. 26–37. ACM, New York (2003)
29. Tsukada, T., Igarashi, A.: A Logical Foundation for Environment Classifiers. In: Curien, P.-L. (ed.) TLCA 2009. LNCS, vol. 5608, pp. 341–355. Springer, Heidelberg (2009)
30. Westbrook, E., Ricken, M., Inoue, J., Yao, Y., Abdelatif, T., Taha, W.: Mint: Java multi-stage programming using weak separability. In: 2010 Conference on Programming Language Design and Implementation (2010)
31. Yang, Z.: Reasoning about code-generation in two-level languages. Tech. Rep. RS-00-46, BRICS (2000)
32. Yuse, Y., Igarashi, A.: A modal type system for multi-level generating extensions with persistent code. In: 8th ACM SIGPLAN International Conference on Principles and Practice of Declarative Programming, pp. 201–212. ACM, New York (2006)

Fictional Separation Logic

Jonas Braband Jensen and Lars Birkedal

IT University of Copenhagen

Abstract. Separation logic formalizes the idea of local reasoning for heap-manipulating programs via the frame rule and the separating conjunction $P * Q$, which describes states that can be split into *separate* parts, with one satisfying P and the other satisfying Q. In standard separation logic, separation means physical separation. In this paper, we introduce *fictional separation logic*, which includes more general forms of fictional separating conjunctions $P * Q$, where $*$ does not require physical separation, but may also be used in situations where the memory resources described by P and Q overlap. We demonstrate, via a range of examples, how fictional separation logic can be used to reason locally and modularly about mutable abstract data types, possibly implemented using sophisticated sharing. Fictional separation logic is defined on top of standard separation logic, and both the meta-theory and the application of the logic is much simpler than earlier related approaches.

Keywords: Separation Logic, Local Reasoning, Modularity.

1 Introduction

Separation logic is a kind of Hoare logic for *local* reasoning about programs with shared mutable state. Locality is achieved by use of the $*$ connective and the frame rule:

$$\frac{\{P\}\ C\ \{Q\}}{\{P * R\}\ C\ \{Q * R\}}$$

Recall that in standard separation logic, $P * R$ is satisfied by a heap if it can be split into two *separate* (disjoint) parts satisfying P and R respectively. The frame rule expresses that if command C is well-specified with precondition P and postcondition Q, then C will preserve any disjoint invariant R, intuitively (and formally in standard models) because of physical heap *separation.*

In many situations, however, physical separation is too strong a requirement – we would like to be able to reason locally using $*$-connectives and frame rules in situations where we do not have physical separation, but where we do have some form of logical or *fictional separation*[1]. The key idea is that fictional separation should allow us to reason separately about updates to shared resources, as long as the updates follow some kind of discipline to guarantee that updates to one

[1] The term "fictional separation" is derived from the phrase "fiction of disjointness", which, to the best of our knowledge, was introduced by Philippa Gardner [8].

H. Seidl (Ed.): ESOP 2012, LNCS 7211, pp. 377–396, 2012.

side of the $*$ do not affect the truth of the other side. Permission accounting models [5,4,10] provide a familiar simple instance of this idea: they allow us to reason separately about shared heaps as long as we do not update but only read those heaps. In recent work on separation logic for concurrency [7,11] and for abstraction [8,9], it is possible to describe more elaborate patterns of sharing. We return to this when we discuss related work in Section 7.

In this paper we introduce *fictional separation logic* and demonstrate, via examples, how the logic can be used to reason locally and modularly about mutable abstract data types, possibly implemented using sophisticated sharing.

Before turning to the technical presentation, we consider a simple example.

Example: Bit Pair. Consider a small library for manipulating pointers to bit pairs. It has a constructor, destructor and some accessors that conform to the following specification in standard higher-order separation logic [2]:

$$
\begin{aligned}
&\exists B_1, B_2 : loc \times bool \to \mathcal{P}(heap).\\
&\quad \{emp\}\ \mathsf{bp\_new}()\ \{B_1(\mathsf{ret}, \mathit{false}) * B_2(\mathsf{ret}, \mathit{false})\} \wedge\\
&\quad \{B_1(\mathsf{p}, \_) * B_2(\mathsf{p}, \_)\}\ \mathsf{bp\_free}(\mathsf{p})\ \{emp\} \wedge\\
&\quad \forall i \in \{1,2\}.\ (\forall b.\ \{B_i(\mathsf{p}, b)\}\ \mathsf{bp\_get}i(\mathsf{p})\ \{B_i(\mathsf{p}, b) \wedge \mathsf{ret} = b\}) \wedge\\
&\qquad\qquad\qquad \{B_i(\mathsf{p}, \_)\}\ \mathsf{bp\_set}i(\mathsf{p}, \mathsf{b})\ \{B_i(\mathsf{p}, \mathsf{b})\}.
\end{aligned}
$$

Note the use of existential quantification over representation predicates B_1 and B_2; they correspond to what Parkinson and Bierman call *abstract predicates* [18]. The special variable ret in postconditions denotes the return value. As usual, the underscore is used for an existentially-quantified variable.

Implementing this naïvely and verifying the implementation is straightforward in standard separation logic. Simply let the constructor allocate two consecutive heap cells and let the accessors dereference either their p parameter or p + 1. For the verification, instantiate $B_i(p, b)$ to $(p + (i - 1)) \mapsto b$.

But this implementation uses at least twice as much heap space as necessary. The least we could do is to allocate only one (integer) heap cell and store the pair of bits in its least significant bits. A possible implementation is the following, where / denotes integer division, and % denotes modulo:

```
bp_new() { p := alloc 1; [p] := 0; return p }
bp_free(p) { free p }
bp_get1(p) { x := [p]; return x % 2 }
bp_get2(p) { x := [p]; return x / 2 }
bp_set1(p,b) { x := [p]; [p] := b + x/2*2 }
bp_set2(p,b) { x := [p]; [p] := 2*b + x%2 }
```

The original specification is unfortunately unprovable for this implementation, even though the two implementations have completely identical behaviour when observed by a client that cannot inspect their internal memory.

The problem is that the abstract module specification is not sufficiently abstract since it requires that the constructor creates two heap chunks that are physically disjoint. In other words, the abstract module specification reveals patterns of sharing or, as is the case here, lack of sharing, that really ought to be internal to the module implementation. Moving to a heap model with bit-level separation will not solve the essence of this problem. Indeed, a third implementation could store the two bits in an integer that is divisible by 3 when B_1 is true and divisible by 5 when B_2 is true. In this case, the fictional separation comes from arithmetic properties of the integers.

In fictional separation logic, we existentially quantify not only over representation predicates B_1 and B_2, but also over the choice of separation algebra, Σ, and an interpretation map I (explained below). The abstract module specification then looks like this:

$$\begin{aligned} &\exists \Sigma : \mathit{sepalg}.\ \exists I : \Sigma \searrow \mathit{heap}.\ \exists B_1, B_2 : \mathit{loc} \times \mathit{bool} \rightarrow \mathcal{P}(\Sigma). \\ &\quad I.\ \{\mathit{emp}\}\ \mathsf{bp\_new}()\ \{B_1(\mathsf{ret}, \mathit{false}) * B_2(\mathsf{ret}, \mathit{false})\} \wedge \\ &\quad I.\ \{B_1(\mathsf{p}, \_) * B_2(\mathsf{p}, \_)\}\ \mathsf{bp\_free}(\mathsf{p})\ \{\mathit{emp}\} \wedge \\ &\quad \forall i \in \{1,2\}.\ (\forall b.\ I.\ \{B_i(\mathsf{p}, b)\}\ \mathsf{bp\_get}i(\mathsf{p})\ \{B_i(\mathsf{p}, b) \wedge \mathsf{ret} = b\}) \wedge \\ &\quad\quad\quad\quad I.\ \{B_i(\mathsf{p}, \_)\}\ \mathsf{bp\_set}i(\mathsf{p}, \mathsf{b})\ \{B_i(\mathsf{p}, \mathsf{b})\}. \end{aligned}$$

The intention is that the interpretation map I should explain how elements of the separation algebra Σ are represented by predicates on physical heaps.

Note that the Hoare triples are now prefixed by I – we refer to such a predicate $I.\ \{P\}\ C\ \{Q\}$ as an *indirect Hoare triple.* The intention is that I records (1) which separation algebra P and Q should be interpreted over, and (2) how P and Q are translated into physical heap predicates, such that the triple meaningfully corresponds to a suitably translated triple in standard separation logic.

This module specification does not reveal information about sharing or lack of sharing, because Σ and I are abstract, i.e., existentially quantified. Client code can now be verified relative to this abstract module specification and since, as we will show, fictional separation logic supports the standard proof rules (and some additional rules), the verification of client code is as easy as it is in standard separation logic. We return to this example in Section 3.2 and show how both implementations of bit pairs satisfy the above abstract specification. We will consider an example of client code verification in Section 4.1.

Outline. The remainder of this paper is organized as follows. We first present some formal preliminaries in Section 2 and then go on to present four sections on fictional separation logic. In each of these sections, we first describe some theory and then present examples that demonstrate how to use the theory in program verification. Basic fictional separation logic and the indirect triple are defined in Section 3. In Section 4 we define separating products of interpretations, which allow clients to use several modules at the same time, and in Section 5 we define a notion of indirect entailment and show how to use it to define fractional permissions within fictional separation logic. We discuss how to stack several levels of abstraction in Section 6, and we conclude and discuss related work in Section 7. To focus on the core ideas, we present fictional separation logic for a simple sequential imperative programming language with procedures, but it should be clear that the ideas are applicable to richer programming languages.

Proofs and further examples can be found in the online appendix [14].

2 Formal Preliminaries

2.1 Abstract Assertion Logic

The meaning of separation logic assertions is often parametrized on a *separation algebra* (SA) [6], which is an abstraction of the heap model. There are several competing definitions of separation algebra in the literature [6,10,12]; we use the one from [12]:[2]

Definition 1. *A* separation algebra *is a partial commutative monoid* $(\Sigma, \circ, 0)$. *We write* $\sigma \doteq \sigma_1 \circ \sigma_2$ *when the* $\sigma_1 \circ \sigma_2$ *is defined and has value* σ.

Given a separation algebra $(\Sigma, \circ, 0)$, the powerset $\mathcal{P}(\Sigma)$ forms a complete boolean BI algebra, i.e., a model of the assertion language of classical separation logic, where the connectives are defined in the standard way [6]:

$$\top \triangleq \Sigma \qquad \bot \triangleq \emptyset$$
$$P \wedge Q \triangleq P \cap Q \qquad P \vee Q \triangleq P \cup Q$$
$$\forall x : A.\ P(x) \triangleq \bigcap_{x:A} P(x) \qquad \exists x : A.\ P(x) \triangleq \bigcup_{x:A} P(x)$$
$$P \Rightarrow Q \triangleq \{\sigma \mid \sigma \in P \Rightarrow \sigma \in Q\} \qquad emp \triangleq \{0\}$$
$$P * Q \triangleq \{\sigma \mid \exists \sigma_1, \sigma_2.\ \sigma \doteq \sigma_1 \circ \sigma_2 \wedge \sigma_1 \in P \wedge \sigma_2 \in Q\}$$
$$P \mathrel{-\!\!*} Q \triangleq \{\sigma_2 \mid \forall \sigma_1.\ \forall \sigma \doteq \sigma_1 \circ \sigma_2.\ \sigma_1 \in P \Rightarrow \sigma \in Q\}$$

As usual, entailment is defined as $P \vdash Q \triangleq P \subseteq Q$. We refer to the elements of $\mathcal{P}(\Sigma)$ as (semantic) assertions.

2.2 Programming Language

The logic we will introduce in the next section is mostly independent of the underlying programming language, but we will fix a particular language here for clarity. It is a simple imperative language in the style of [20], extended with simple procedures:

$$C ::= x := e \mid [e] := e \mid x := [e] \mid x := \mathsf{alloc}\ e \mid \mathsf{free}\ e$$
$$\mid C; C \mid \mathsf{if}\ e\ \mathsf{then}\ C\ \mathsf{else}\ C \mid \mathsf{while}\ e\ \mathsf{do}\ C \mid \mathsf{call}\ x := f(\bar{e})$$

---

[2] The original definition of SA [6] also required *cancellativity*: that if $\sigma' \doteq \sigma \circ \sigma_1$ and $\sigma' \doteq \sigma \circ \sigma_2$ then $\sigma_1 = \sigma_2$. This is too restrictive for our purposes, so we do not include it in the general definition of a SA.

The commands are, respectively, assignment, heap write, heap read, allocation, deallocation, sequencing, conditional, loop and function call. The argument to alloc specifies how many consecutive heap locations should be allocated.

There is no module system at the language level. When we talk about a module in this paper, it simply refers to a collection of functions.

The operational semantics of the language is defined in a standard way, using the following memory model:

$$\begin{array}{rlrl} C : \mathit{cmd} & \text{(see above)} & v : \mathit{val} & \triangleq \mathit{loc} \uplus \{\mathsf{null}\} \uplus \mathbb{Z} \uplus \{\mathsf{true}, \mathsf{false}\} \\ x, y : \mathit{var} & \triangleq \mathit{string} & s : \mathit{stack} & \triangleq \mathit{var} \to \mathit{val} \\ f : \mathit{func\_name} & \triangleq \mathit{string} & e : \mathit{expr} & \triangleq \mathit{stack} \to \mathit{val} \\ l : \mathit{loc} & \triangleq \mathbb{N} & h : \mathit{heap} & \triangleq \mathit{loc} \rightharpoonup_{\mathsf{fin}} \mathit{val} \end{array}$$

$$\mathit{program} \triangleq \mathit{func\_name} \rightharpoonup_{\mathsf{fin}} \mathit{var}^* \times \mathit{cmd} \times \mathit{expr}$$

Verification always takes place in an implicit global context of type *program* that maps each function name to a parameter list, function body and return expression. The only type of syntactic entities in this paper is *cmd*. Assertions, specifications, inference rules, and even programming language expressions, are semantic. If desired, a syntactic system could be built on top of this, but it would serve no purpose in this paper.

As usual, *heap* is a separation algebra with composition being the union of disjoint maps and the identity being the empty map. In addition to the connectives from Section 2.1, the separation algebra of heaps also has the *points-to* assertion: $l \mapsto v \triangleq \{[l \mapsto v]\}$. We make this more precise in Section 2.4.

2.3 Specification Logic

A specification $S : \mathit{spec}$ is a logical proposition about the program under consideration. The specification logic has the connectives $(\top, \bot, \wedge, \vee, \forall, \exists, \Rightarrow)$ as operators on *spec* and entailment $(\vdash)$ as a relation on *spec*. These interact according to the standard rules of intuitionistic logic.

We assume that there is a definition of the Hoare triple $\{P\}\ C\ \{Q\} : \mathit{spec}$. Intuitively, if $S \vdash \{P\}\ C\ \{Q\}$, then under the assumptions of S, if the command C runs in a state satisfying P, it will not fault, and if it terminates, the resulting state satisfies Q. The Hoare triple is assumed to satisfy the standard structural and command-specific rules of separation logic [20].

The definition of *spec* and the Hoare triple, as well as the proofs that they satisfy the rules of separation logic, are standard and not important here. See, e.g., [1] for a definition of *spec* that allows for (mutually) recursive procedures and is formalized in Coq.

The assertions P, Q used in the Hoare triple are of type $\mathit{asn}(\mathit{heap})$, where $\mathit{asn}(\Sigma) \triangleq \mathit{stack} \to \mathcal{P}(\Sigma)$. Connectives and rules for $\mathcal{P}(\Sigma)$ can be lifted pointwise to $\mathit{asn}(\Sigma)$, so we will conflate the two in the following.

2.4 Constructing Separation Algebras

In this subsection we record some simple ways of constructing separation algebras, which will be useful in the following.

Given a set A and a SA $(\Sigma, \circ, 0)$, we write $A \overset{\text{fin}}{\rightharpoonup} \Sigma$ for the set of total maps $f : A \to \Sigma$ for which only a finite number of values $a : A$ have $f(a) \neq 0$. That is, f has finite support. The set $A \overset{\text{fin}}{\rightharpoonup} \Sigma$ is itself a SA with composition being pointwise and only defined when the composition in Σ is defined at every point.

We let $[a \mapsto \sigma]$ be the map in $A \overset{\text{fin}}{\rightharpoonup} \Sigma$ which maps a to σ and every other element to 0. Observe that $[a \mapsto 0]$ is the constant 0 map.

For $f : A \overset{\text{fin}}{\rightharpoonup} \Sigma$, define $supp(f) = \{a \mid f(a) \neq 0\}$.

A *permission algebra* (PA) [6] is a partial commutative semigroup; i.e., it is like a SA but may not have a unit element. The product of two PAs (SAs) is also a PA (SA); composition is pointwise, and it is defined only when defined on both components. Any set A can be seen as the *empty PA* ($A_\emptyset$) by letting the composition be undefined for all operands. Moreover, any set A can be seen as the *equality PA* ($A_=$) by letting the composition have $x \circ x \doteq x$ for all x and making it undefined for non-equal operands. Finally, any PA Π can be made into a SA $\Pi_\perp$ by adding a unit element.

In this terminology, the SA of heaps is $heap = loc \overset{\text{fin}}{\rightharpoonup} val_{\emptyset\perp}$.

3 Fictional Separation Logic

The basic idea of fictional separation logic is that assertions are not just expressed in a single separation algebra, chosen in advance to match the programming language, but instead each module may define its own domain-specific SA. Each such SA is interpreted into another SA and eventually to the SA of heaps. Given separation algebras $(\Sigma, \circ_\Sigma, 0_\Sigma)$ and $(\Sigma', \circ_{\Sigma'}, 0_{\Sigma'})$, an *interpretation* I is of type

$$\Sigma \searrow \Sigma' \triangleq \{I : \Sigma \to \mathcal{P}(\Sigma') \mid I(0_\Sigma) = \{0_{\Sigma'}\}\}.$$

The side condition is not strictly necessary but will ease presentation later.[3]

The logic revolves around the *indirect triple*, defined as

$$I.\ \{P\}\ C\ \{Q\} \triangleq \forall \phi.\ \{\exists \sigma \in P.\ I(\sigma \circ \phi)\}\ C\ \{\exists \sigma \in Q.\ I(\sigma \circ \phi)\}.$$

Here I is an interpretation map of type $\Sigma \searrow heap$, and $P, Q : asn(\Sigma)$, for the same SA Σ. The triple and the all-quantifier on the right-hand side are the ones from the standard specification logic (Section 2.3).

As mentioned in Section 2.3, we implicitly lift operators and constants from $\mathcal{P}(\Sigma)$ into $asn(\Sigma)$. In the definition above, the $(\in)$ operator has been lifted in this way for brevity. Following usual practice, there is also an implicit assumption that the partial composition is well-defined. Written out in full detail, the precondition on the right hand side above is the following element of $asn(heap)$:

$$\lambda s : stack.\ \{h \mid \exists \sigma \in P(s).\ \exists \sigma' \doteq \sigma \circ \phi.\ h \in I(\sigma')\}.$$

[3] It simplifies the rule CreateL from Figure 1.

The postcondition is similar, only with Q instead of P.

The quantification over all possible abstract frames ϕ bakes the frame rule into the indirect triple definition, much as in [3], except that here the frame is in a more abstract SA.

The standard specification logic structural rules of CONSEQUENCE, EXISTS and FRAME hold for the indirect triple. For brevity we just show the frame rule:

$$\frac{\mathit{modifies}(C) \cap \mathit{fv}(R) = \emptyset \qquad S \vdash I.\ \{P\}\ C\ \{Q\}}{S \vdash I.\ \{P * R\}\ C\ \{Q * R\}}\ \text{FRAME}$$

Here, $\mathit{modifies}(C)$ is the set of program variables possibly assigned to by C [20]. The usual rules for control flow commands (if, while, call and (;)) also hold. Proofs and a discussion of the conjunction rule are in the online appendix [14].

The unit interpretation on Σ is simply $1_\Sigma \triangleq \lambda\sigma : \Sigma.\ \{\sigma\}$; it is used to relate the standard separation logic triple to the indirect triple, as expressed by the following rule:[4]

$$\frac{S \vdash 1_{heap}.\ \{P\}\ C\ \{Q\}}{S \vdash \{P\}\ C\ \{Q\}}\ \text{BASIC}$$

We typically drop the subscript on 1_Σ since it can be inferred from the context.

3.1 Proof Patterns

In this subsection we include a couple of rules and lemmas that are often useful for reasoning about examples in fictional separation logic.

In practice, pre- and postconditions are often singletons, possibly conjoined with a *pure assertion*, i.e., one that either contains every σ or no σ. The following rule relates that special case to standard separation logic. The validity of this rule follows easily from the definition of the indirect triple.

$$\frac{p, q \text{ pure} \qquad S \vdash \forall\phi.\ \{I(\sigma \circ \phi) \wedge p\}\ C\ \{I(\sigma' \circ \phi) \wedge q\}}{S \vdash I.\ \{\{\sigma\} \wedge p\}\ C\ \{\{\sigma'\} \wedge q\}}\ \text{ENTER1}$$

The name of this rule, like all other rules in this paper, suggests reading it from the bottom up; i.e., given a proof obligation matching its conclusion, "enter" the abstract scope by exchanging the conclusion for its premise.

We will see in examples that interpretation functions often follow a particular pattern. The following lemma records useful facts about this pattern. It uses the iterated separating conjunction [20] operator ($\forall_*$), defined as

$$\forall_* a \in \{a_1, \ldots, a_n\}.\ P(a) \triangleq P(a_1) * \ldots * P(a_n).$$

Lemma 1. *If $I : (A \overset{\text{fin}}{\rightharpoonup} \Sigma) \searrow heap$ with $I(f) = \forall_* a \in supp(f).\ P(a, f(a))$, then*

a. $I(f) * I(g) \dashv\vdash I(f \circ g)$ if $supp(f) \cap supp(g) = \emptyset$.
b. $I(f) * I(g) \vdash I(f \circ g)$ if $\forall a.\ (P(a, \_) * P(a, \_) \vdash \bot)$.
c. If p, q are pure, then the following rule is valid.

$$\frac{S \vdash \forall\phi.\ \{I([a \mapsto \sigma\circ\phi]) \wedge p\}\ C\ \{I([a \mapsto \sigma'\circ\phi]) \wedge q\}}{S \vdash I.\ \{\{[a \mapsto \sigma]\} \wedge p\}\ C\ \{\{[a \mapsto \sigma']\} \wedge q\}}$$

[4] Double lines mean that the rule can be used both from top to bottom and vice-versa.

3.2 Example: Bit Pair

We now return to the example of bit pairs from Section 1 and explain how to prove that the implementation with sharing meets the abstract module specification. (It is obvious how the naïve implementation meets the specification: choose I to be 1_{heap} and apply BASIC.)

Choose the witnesses of the existentials as follows (we convert freely between *bool* and $\{0,1\}$).

$$\begin{aligned} \Sigma &= loc \overset{\text{fin}}{\rightharpoonup} (\{1,2\} \overset{\text{fin}}{\rightharpoonup} bool_{\emptyset\bot}) \\ I(f) &= \forall_{*} p \in supp(f).\ supp(f(p)) = \{1,2\} \wedge p \mapsto (f(p)(1) + 2 \cdot f(p)(2)) \\ B_i(p,b) &= \{[p \mapsto [i \mapsto b]]\} \end{aligned}$$

Composition and unit in Σ follows from the constructions in Section 2.4. This resembles the SA used for object-oriented languages, where each object may have several fields.

The intuition behind the choice of I is that by requiring the support at each point to be the full set, i.e., $\{1,2\}$, we can control what we expect to find in the frame ϕ. For a function such as bp_get1, this means that since $B_1(\mathsf{p}, b)$ is assumed in the precondition, we are sure to find $B_2(\mathsf{p}, b')$ in the frame, for some b'. Showing that the frame is preserved then amounts to showing that the frame also contains $B_2(\mathsf{p}, b')$ after executing the function body – and showing that any other $p' \neq \mathsf{p}$ mentioned in the frame is unaffected, but we will see below that Lemma 1 on pointwise interpretation functions makes that easy.

We now have to show that the implementation of each function matches its specification with this choice of witnesses for the existentials. This is straightforward, because every function in this example has a specification that matches a combination of ENTER1 and Lemma 1. These rules reduce the proof obligations to statements in standard separation logic.

First note that the following *saturation lemma* holds for the interpretation map for bit pairs:

$$I([\_ \mapsto [i \mapsto b] \circ \phi]) \vdash \exists b'.\ \phi = [3-i \mapsto b'].$$

We present here the proof of bp_get1. Let $C = (\mathsf{x} := [\mathsf{p}])$, i.e., the body of bp_get1.

$$\dfrac{\dfrac{\dfrac{\dfrac{\dfrac{}{\forall b_2.\ \{\mathsf{p} \mapsto (b + 2 \cdot b_2)\}\ C\ \{\mathsf{p} \mapsto (b + 2 \cdot b_2) \wedge \mathsf{x}\%2 = b\}}\ \text{(trivial)}}{\forall b_2.\ \{I([\mathsf{p} \mapsto [1 \mapsto b, 2 \mapsto b_2]])\}\ C\ \{I([\mathsf{p} \mapsto [1 \mapsto b, 2 \mapsto b_2]]) \wedge \mathsf{x}\%2 = b\}}\ \text{(definition)}}{\forall \phi.\ \{I([\mathsf{p} \mapsto [1 \mapsto b] \circ \phi])\}\ C\ \{I([\mathsf{p} \mapsto [1 \mapsto b] \circ \phi]) \wedge \mathsf{x}\%2 = b\}}\ \text{Saturation}}{I.\ \{\{[\mathsf{p} \mapsto [1 \mapsto b]]\}\}\ C\ \{\{[\mathsf{p} \mapsto [1 \mapsto b]]\} \wedge \mathsf{x}\%2 = b\}}\ \text{Lemma 1c}}{I.\ \{B_1(\mathsf{p}, b)\}\ C\ \{B_1(\mathsf{p}, b) \wedge \mathsf{x}\%2 = b\}}\ \text{(definition)}$$

Notice that the overhead of showing that the abstract specification is met is fairly small and straightforward.

3.3 Example: Monotonic Counter

A monotonic counter is an integer stored in the heap with operations for reading it and incrementing it but not for decrementing it. The implementation could look like this:

```
mc_new() { c := alloc 1; [c] := 0; return c }
mc_read(c) { x := [c]; return x }
mc_inc(c) { x := [c]; [c] := x+1 }
```

Reasoning about monotonic counters was posed as a verification challenge by Pilkiewicz and Pottier [19]. They discussed the challenge in a type-and-capability system, so the presentation is somewhat different than for separation logic, but the idea is the same. The counter should have a representation predicate $MC(c, i)$ that can be freely duplicated; i.e., $MC(c, i) \vdash MC(c, i) * MC(c, i)$. It should be possible to frame out one of the copies while the other copy is used to call the increment function; when the first copy is later framed back in, it can soundly be used to call the read function since its postcondition only guarantees that the returned value is *at least* the value from the representation predicate.

The specification in fictional separation logic looks like this:

$$\begin{aligned}
&\exists \Sigma : sepalg.\ \exists I : \Sigma \searrow heap.\ \exists MC : loc \times \mathbb{Z} \to \mathcal{P}(\Sigma). \\
&\quad (\forall c, j.\ \forall i \leq j.\ (MC(c, j) \dashv\vdash MC(c, j) * MC(c, i))) \wedge \\
&\quad I.\ \{emp\}\ \mathsf{mc_new()}\ \{MC(\mathsf{ret}, 0)\} \wedge \\
&\quad (\forall i.\ I.\ \{MC(\mathsf{c}, i)\}\ \mathsf{mc_read(c)}\ \{MC(\mathsf{c}, i) \wedge \mathsf{ret} \geq i\}) \wedge \\
&\quad (\forall i.\ I.\ \{MC(\mathsf{c}, i)\}\ \mathsf{mc_inc(c)}\ \{MC(\mathsf{c}, i+1)\}).
\end{aligned}$$

The fact about MC has several corollaries that are useful for clients:

$$\begin{aligned}
MC(c, i) &\dashv\vdash MC(c, i) * MC(c, i) \\
i \leq j \wedge MC(c, j) &\vdash MC(c, i) * \top \\
MC(c, i) * MC(c, j) &\vdash MC(c, max(i, j))
\end{aligned}$$

Compared to the solution by Pilkiewicz and Pottier, this solution has several advantages. Our solution can be specified and verified without changing the implementation to account for limitations in the verification system [19, end of Sect. 4]. Moreover, it can be verified in the simple system of fictional separation logic, whereas there exists no soundness proof yet for the very complicated type system used by Pilkiewicz and Pottier.

To verify our specification against the implementation shown above, choose the existentials as follows:

$$\begin{aligned}
\Sigma &= loc \overset{\text{fin}}{\rightharpoonup} \mathbb{Z}_\perp \text{ where composition in } \mathbb{Z} \text{ is } max \\
I(f) &= \forall_* c \in supp(f).\ \exists j \geq f(c).\ c \mapsto j \\
MC(c, i) &= \{[c \mapsto i]\}
\end{aligned}$$

The property about MC is straightforward to verify in the assertion logic. Verification of the three functions is shown in the online appendix [14].

$$\frac{S \vdash I * J.\ \{P^{\mathsf{L}}\}\ C\ \{Q^{\mathsf{L}}\}}{S \vdash I.\ \{P\}\ C\ \{Q\}}\ \textsc{CreateL} \qquad \frac{S \vdash I.\ \{P\}\ C\ \{Q\}}{S \vdash I * J.\ \{P^{\mathsf{L}}\}\ C\ \{Q^{\mathsf{L}}\}}\ \textsc{ForgetL}$$

$$\frac{S \vdash I * J.\ \{P^{\mathsf{L}}\}\ C\ \{Q \times \top\}}{S \vdash I * 1.\ \{P^{\mathsf{L}}\}\ C\ \{Q \times \top\}}\ \textsc{LeakL} \qquad \frac{p \text{ pure}}{(p \wedge P) \times Q \dashv\vdash p \wedge (P \times Q)}\ \textsc{Prod-Pure}$$

Fig. 1. Selected inference rules for separating products, using notation $P^{\mathsf{L}} \triangleq P \times emp$

There are some limitations in the specification. There can be no function to deallocate a counter because its representation predicate can be freely shared. The absence of deallocation means that this specification is more suited for a garbage-collected language. Also, the specification does not guarantee that consecutive calls to mc_read will return the same value; it would be valid to implement mc_read such that it has the side effect of incrementing the counter. These limitations are also present in the specification by Pilkiewicz and Pottier.

4 Clients and Separating Products

To allow clients of multiple libraries to know about more than one separation algebra and interpretation function, we introduce *separating products* of interpretations.

Given interpretations $I_1 : \Sigma_1 \searrow \Sigma$ and $I_2 : \Sigma_2 \searrow \Sigma$, their separating product $I_1 * I_2$ has type $\Sigma_1 \times \Sigma_2 \searrow \Sigma$ and is defined as

$$I_1 * I_2 \triangleq \lambda(\sigma_1, \sigma_2).\ I_1(\sigma_1) * I_2(\sigma_2).$$

Figure 1 shows a collection of inference rules about separating products. At the bottom of a proof tree, just above application of Basic, a client should use CreateL for each module that will be used. In that rule, $P^{\mathsf{L}} \triangleq P \times emp$, where $(\times)$ is simply the Cartesian product lifted into *asn*. To write that out, $P_1 \times P_2 \triangleq \lambda s.\ \{(\sigma_1, \sigma_2) \mid \sigma_1 \in P_1(s) \wedge \sigma_2 \in P_2(s)\}$.

The CreateL rule requires the command C to clean up the state abstracted by J completely; i.e., that state must satisfy *emp* in the postcondition. When this is not possible, for example in the Monotonic Counters example, we can instead use the LeakL rule.

Before calling a library function, a client will, as usual, have to frame out irrelevant facts. There, it can be useful to know that $(P * Q)^{\mathsf{L}} \dashv\vdash P^{\mathsf{L}} * Q^{\mathsf{L}}$ and that $P \times Q \dashv\vdash P^{\mathsf{L}} * Q^{\mathsf{R}}$, where $P^{\mathsf{R}} \triangleq emp \times P$. After applying the frame rule, the client can then ignore the irrelevant separation algebras using the ForgetL rule, which is just the CreateL rule inverted.

Pure assertions can move in and out of products as described by the Prod-Pure rule. There are of course rules CreateR, ForgetR and LeakR symmetric to the ones in Figure 1, and further structural rules can be defined to handle commutativity and associativity with separating products.

4.1 Example: Client of Two Modules

Assume we have a client program C that uses both the bit pair and the monotonic counter modules, and we want to show that it has precondition *emp* and postcondition $\top$. We suggest $\top$ in the postcondition because there is no deallocation function for monotonic counters as mentioned earlier.

The standard pattern for this is to assume the module specifications at the bottom of the tree and then move from the standard triple to the appropriate indirect triple by applying BASIC once and then CREATE or LEAK for each module, reading from the bottom up. Abbreviate the bit pair and monotonic counter specifications, minus the existentials, as S_{bp} and S_{mc} respectively. The bottom of the proof for C then looks like this.

$$\dfrac{\dfrac{\dfrac{\dfrac{S_{\text{bp}} \wedge S_{\text{mc}} \vdash I_{\text{bp}} * I_{\text{mc}}.\ \{emp \times emp\}\ C\ \{emp \times \top\}}{S_{\text{bp}} \wedge S_{\text{mc}} \vdash I_{\text{bp}} * 1.\ \{emp \times emp\}\ C\ \{emp \times \top\}}\ \text{LEAKL}}{S_{\text{bp}} \wedge S_{\text{mc}} \vdash 1.\ \{emp\}\ C\ \{\top\}}\ \text{CREATER}}{S_{\text{bp}} \wedge S_{\text{mc}} \vdash \{emp\}\ C\ \{\top\}}\ \text{BASIC}}{(\exists \Sigma, I_{\text{bp}}, B_1, B_2.\ S_{\text{bp}}) \wedge (\exists \Sigma, I_{\text{mc}}, MC.\ S_{\text{mc}}) \vdash \{emp\}\ C\ \{\top\}}\ \exists\text{L}$$

The bottom proof step applies the standard existential-left rule from sequent calculus twice.

If C uses the heap directly, not just through the two modules, it should apply CREATE once more to get the interpretation $I_{\text{bp}} * I_{\text{mc}} * 1$ on the indirect triple.

Further up in the proof tree, there will eventually be a point where it is necessary to call a function belonging to one of the modules, e.g., the bit pairs. The following pattern is used to ignore irrelevant modules during the call.

$$\dfrac{\dfrac{\dfrac{S \vdash I_{\text{bp}}.\ \{P\}\ \mathsf{call}\ f\ \{Q\}}{S \vdash I_{\text{bp}} * I_{\text{mc}}.\ \{P^{\mathsf{L}}\}\ \mathsf{call}\ f\ \{Q^{\mathsf{L}}\}}\ \text{FORGETL}}{S \vdash I_{\text{bp}} * I_{\text{mc}}.\ \{P^{\mathsf{L}} * {R_1}^{\mathsf{L}} * {R_2}^{\mathsf{R}}\}\ \mathsf{call}\ f\ \{Q^{\mathsf{L}} * {R_1}^{\mathsf{L}} * {R_2}^{\mathsf{R}}\}}\ \text{FRAME}}{S \vdash I_{\text{bp}} * I_{\text{mc}}.\ \{(P * R_1) \times R_2\}\ \mathsf{call}\ f\ \{(Q * R_1) \times R_2\}}\ \text{CONSEQUENCE}$$

Note that this kind of reasoning will not be so explicit in practice; a simple tool can easily elide these steps.

In this section we considered a generic client; see the online appendix [14] for a concrete example client using bit pairs and monotonic counters.

4.2 Example: Wrapper

This example demonstrates how a module can extend the abstraction of another module by using a separating product. We will see that this example gives a compelling argument against solving the fiction-of-disjointness problem by letting the client carry around an explicit but opaque frame as done in [16, Chapter 5].

Consider first the following specification of a collection data structure.

$$
\begin{aligned}
S_{\mathrm{Coll}}(\Sigma : \mathit{sepalg}, I : \Sigma \searrow \mathit{heap}, \mathit{Coll} : \mathit{loc} \times \mathcal{P}_{\mathsf{fin}}(\mathit{val}) \to \mathcal{P}(\Sigma)) \triangleq \forall c, V.& \\
(\mathit{Coll}(c, \_) * \mathit{Coll}(c, \_) \vdash \bot) \wedge& \\
I.\ \{\mathit{emp}\}\ \mathsf{coll\_new}()\ \{\mathit{Coll}(\mathsf{ret}, \emptyset)\} \wedge& \\
I.\ \{\mathit{Coll}(\mathsf{c}, V)\}\ \mathsf{coll\_free}(\mathsf{c})\ \{\mathit{emp}\} \wedge& \\
I.\ \{\mathit{Coll}(\mathsf{c}, V)\}\ \mathsf{coll\_clone}(\mathsf{c})\ \{\mathit{Coll}(\mathsf{c}, V) * \mathit{Coll}(\mathsf{ret}, V)\} \wedge& \\
I.\ \{\mathit{Coll}(\mathsf{c}, V)\}\ \mathsf{coll\_contains}(\mathsf{c}, \mathsf{v})\ \{\mathit{Coll}(\mathsf{c}, V) \wedge \mathsf{ret} = (\mathsf{v} \in V)\} \wedge& \\
I.\ \{\mathit{Coll}(\mathsf{c}, V)\}\ \mathsf{coll\_add}(\mathsf{c}, \mathsf{v})\ \{\mathit{Coll}(\mathsf{c}, V \cup \{\mathsf{v}\})\} \wedge& \\
I.\ \{\mathit{Coll}(\mathsf{c}, V)\}\ \mathsf{coll\_remove}(\mathsf{c}, \mathsf{v})\ \{\mathit{Coll}(\mathsf{c}, V \setminus \{\mathsf{v}\})\}.&
\end{aligned}
$$

This is a standard specification of a finite collection, except for the coll_clone function. This function could be implemented by simply copying the contents of the collection to a new data structure; in standard separation logic, that would be the only possible implementation because of the ($*$) in the postcondition.

In fictional separation logic, it might also be implemented by using *copy on write* – the reference-counting technique in which the contents are initially shared between two collections and only copied when the need arises because one of them is modified [17]. The purpose of including coll_clone here is to have a reason why this library should be specified with fictional separation logic.

Consider now a wrapper module of indirect references to collections. The implementation could be this:

```
wcoll_new(c) { w := alloc 1; [w] := c; return w }
wcoll_contains(w,v) { c := [w]; return coll_contains(c,v) } ...
```

Functions wcoll_add, wcoll_remove and wcoll_free would be implemented analogously to wcoll_contains, forwarding the call. A more useful wrapper module would, of course, add some functionality, such as caching the last query to wcoll_contains or counting the number of calls to wcoll_add, but the essence remains the same.

We can give the following specification to this code.

$$
\begin{aligned}
&\forall \Sigma, I, \mathit{Coll}.\ S_{\mathrm{Coll}}(\Sigma, I, \mathit{Coll}) \Rightarrow \\
&\quad \exists \mathit{WColl} : \mathit{loc} \times \mathcal{P}_{\mathsf{fin}}(\mathit{val}) \to \mathcal{P}(\mathit{heap} \times \Sigma).\ \forall V. \\
&\quad 1 * I.\ \{\mathit{Coll}(\mathsf{c}, V)^{\mathsf{R}}\}\ \mathsf{wcoll\_new}(\mathsf{c})\ \{\mathit{WColl}(\mathsf{ret}, V)\} \wedge \\
&\quad 1 * I.\ \{\mathit{WColl}(\mathsf{w}, V)\}\ \mathsf{wcoll\_contains}(\mathsf{w}, \mathsf{v})\ \{\mathit{WColl}(\mathsf{w}, V) \wedge \mathsf{ret} = (\mathsf{v} \in V)\} \wedge ...
\end{aligned}
$$

Observe that this is an example of one specification depending on another, by being universal in the parameters of the S_{Coll} specification from above. (See [1] for more general cases of this design pattern, in standard higher-order separation logic.) For the example implementation above, the proof of the specification should instantiate the existential as $\mathit{WColl}(w, V) = \exists c.\ w \mapsto c \times \mathit{Coll}(c, V)$. As a side remark, this specification could be made more abstract, so that it would reveal less implementation detail, by hiding the use of the 1-interpretation behind an existential.

The specification of the constructor, wcoll_new, is an example of ownership transfer: ownership of memory described by an abstract predicate ($Coll(\mathsf{c}, V)$) is transferred from the caller to the module. The specification intentionally does not reveal whether the transfer happened simply by storing a pointer, as in our example implementation, or whether the constructor allocated a new collection (or another container data structure), manually copied the contents of the given collection to that, and then freed the given collection.

For comparison, to mimic this in standard separation logic, one could take inspiration from Krishnaswami's design pattern [16, Chapter 5] and let the representation predicate of the collection module describe all the collections that may share data; i.e., $H : \mathcal{P}_{\mathsf{fin}}(loc \times \mathcal{P}_{\mathsf{fin}}(val)) \to \mathcal{P}(heap)$. The constructor specification would then be along the lines of the following, where $\uplus$ denotes union of sets of tuples with disjoint first components, and $Coll'(c, V) \triangleq \{(c, V)\}$.

$$\{H(Coll'(\mathsf{c}, V) \uplus \phi)\}\ \mathsf{wcoll\_new(c)}\ \{\exists \sigma.\ H(\sigma \uplus \phi) * WColl'(\mathsf{ret}, \sigma, V)\}.$$

This specification allows the same implementation freedom as the fictional separation logic version does, and the caller is guaranteed that the abstract frame ϕ is preserved. But it is a completely undesirable specification in practice because the $WColl'$ predicate can never be detached from the H predicate that it may share data with. This means that all the accessor functions must have both $WColl'$ and H in their pre- and postconditions. Even worse, clients need to keep track of the opaque σ that links the two together.

5 Indirect Entailment

There is no restriction that a physical heap can only be in the image of a single abstract σ. Therefore we can sometimes change abstract pre- and postconditions in a more powerful way than what the rule of consequence allows; we present an application of this idea in the next subsection. First, we define *indirect entailment*:

$$P \models_I Q \triangleq \forall \phi.\ \big((\exists \sigma \in P.\ I(\sigma \circ \phi)) \vdash (\exists \sigma \in Q.\ I(\sigma \circ \phi))\big).$$

We can now state the *indirect rule of consequence*:

$$\frac{P \models_I P' \qquad S \vdash I.\ \{P'\}\ C\ \{Q'\} \qquad Q' \models_I Q}{S \vdash I.\ \{P\}\ C\ \{Q\}}\ \text{ROC-INDIRECT}$$

Its correctness is immediate from the definitions.

The definition of indirect entailment is quite similar to the indirect triple. In fact, if $I : \Sigma \searrow heap$ for some Σ, then $P \models_I Q$ if and only if $\vdash I.\ \{P\}\ skip\ \{Q\}$.

For any I, the relation ($\models_I$) is reflexive and transitive and is a superrelation of ($\vdash$). Judgements $P \models_I Q$ can also be studied as a kind of degenerate assertion logic; in that case, the standard natural-deduction introduction and elimination rules for ($\top, \bot, \vee, \exists$) hold, and so do ($\Rightarrow$)-introduction and ($\wedge, \forall$)-elimination. It is also possible to reason locally on both sides of a separating conjunction, and the existential-left rule holds; i.e.,

$$\frac{P \models_I P' \qquad Q \models_I Q'}{P * Q \models_I P' * Q'} \qquad\qquad \frac{\forall x.\ (P(x) \models_I Q)}{\exists x.\ P(x) \models_I Q}$$

We discuss more rules for ($\models_I$) in the online appendix [14].

5.1 Example: Fractional Permissions

Permission accounting [5,4,10] is a solution to simple sharing problems where just read-only data is shared. The points-to predicate is generalized to carry a permission, so $l \overset{z}{\mapsto} v$ denotes a z-permission to access heap location l. If z is a read-only permission, then there are no write permissions to l available to others, and therefore its value stays v. If z is a write permission, then there are no other read or write permissions for l available to others.

A write permission can be split across the $*$ into several read-only permissions. If it is known that all read-only permissions have been accounted for, then they can be re-assembled into a write permission. Permissions are clearly useful for sharing data read-only between threads in concurrent programs, but it also has uses in a sequential setting [13,15].

We will now show how fractional permissions, a particular permission accounting scheme, can be encoded in fictional separation logic. This allows us to use fractional permissions where we need it, without having fractional permissions in the base logic! A permission z is a rational number satisfying $0 < z \leq 1$. The write permission is 1, and all smaller numbers are read-only permissions. We will define the assertion $l \overset{z}{\mapsto} v$ such that the splitting and joining of permissions can be described by the following inference rule.

$$\frac{}{l \overset{z_1}{\mapsto} v_1 * l \overset{z_2}{\mapsto} v_2 \dashv\vdash v_1 = v_2 \wedge z_1 + z_2 \leq 1 \wedge l \overset{z_1+z_2}{\longmapsto} v_1} \ \textsc{Fractions}$$

We first define the SA of heaps with fractional permissions as usual [4]:

$$\begin{aligned} \Sigma_{\text{fp}} &\triangleq \mathit{Ptr} \overset{\text{fin}}{\rightharpoonup} (\mathit{Val}_= \times \mathit{Perm})_\perp, \text{ where} \\ \mathit{Perm} &\triangleq \{z : \mathbb{Q} \mid 0 < z \leq 1\} \\ z_1 \dotplus z_2 &\triangleq \begin{cases} z_1 + z_2 & \text{if } z_1 + z_2 \leq 1 \\ \text{undefined} & \text{otherwise} \end{cases} \end{aligned}$$

Since $(\mathit{Perm}, \dotplus)$ is a permission algebra, Σ_{fp} is a separation algebra (see Section 2.4). We define the fractional points-to predicate by $l \overset{z}{\mapsto} v \triangleq \{[l \mapsto (v, z)]\}$ and can then easily verify the Fractions rule.

To make use of all this, we define an interpretation $I_{\text{fp}} : \Sigma_{\text{fp}} \searrow \mathit{heap}$. The idea is the same as for the interpretation function in the bit pair example (Section 3.2): assume we have the full knowledge (permission) for each described heap location.

$$I_{\text{fp}}(f) \triangleq \forall_* l \in \mathit{supp}(f).\ \exists v.\ f(l) = (v, 1) \wedge l \mapsto v.$$

We can now prove a specification of the heap read command for fractional permissions. For clarity, let us just consider the case where the variable name being assigned to is fresh (formally we treat free variables as in [1]):

$$\frac{x \notin fv(e, e')}{\vdash I_{\text{fp}}.\ \{e \overset{z}{\mapsto} e'\}\ x := [e]\ \{e \overset{z}{\mapsto} e' \wedge x = e'\}}$$

Let us sketch the proof of this rule. We first expand the definition of the fractional points-to predicate in the conclusion:

$$\vdash I_{\text{fp}}.\ \{\{[e \mapsto (e', z)]\}\}\ x := [e]\ \{\{[e \mapsto (e', z)]\} \wedge x = e'\}.$$

By applying Lemma 1c, we can reduce this to the proof obligation

$$\vdash \forall\phi.\ \{I_{\text{fp}}([e \mapsto (e', z) \circ \phi])\}\ x := [e]\ \{I_{\text{fp}}([e \mapsto (e', z) \circ \phi]) \wedge x = e'\},$$

which is now a statement in standard separation logic that can be discharged using a saturation lemma like in Section 3.2. Intuitively, I_{fp} in the precondition gives us the points-to predicate needed for applying the standard read rule. The postcondition requires us to prove that I_{fp} holds for the same parameter, which is easy since the heap did not change.

We can also prove the write and allocation rules using the above approach, but we will instead show how to use indirect entailment to get even simpler proofs. The following indirect bi-entailment expresses that having the full permission to a location ($z = 1$) is the same as having a standard points-to predicate for it:

$$\frac{}{(l \overset{1}{\mapsto} v)^{\mathsf{L}} \;=\!\!|\!\!\models_{I_{\text{fp}} * 1} (l \mapsto v)^{\mathsf{R}}}$$

With this lemma, proved in the online appendix [14], the write and allocation rules follow almost immediately from their standard separation logic versions. For instance, the fractional write rule is derived as follows.

$$\dfrac{\dfrac{\dfrac{\dfrac{}{\vdash 1.\ \{e \mapsto \_\}\ [e] := e'\ \{e \mapsto e'\}}\ \textsc{Basic, Write-std}}{\vdash I_{\text{fp}} * 1.\ \{(e \mapsto \_)^{\mathsf{R}}\}\ [e] := e'\ \{(e \mapsto e')^{\mathsf{R}}\}}\ \textsc{ForgetR}}{\vdash I_{\text{fp}} * 1.\ \{(e \overset{1}{\mapsto} \_)^{\mathsf{L}}\}\ [e] := e'\ \{(e \overset{1}{\mapsto} e')^{\mathsf{L}}\}}\ \textsc{ROC-Indirect}}{\vdash I_{\text{fp}}.\ \{e \overset{1}{\mapsto} \_\}\ [e] := e'\ \{e \overset{1}{\mapsto} e'\}}\ \textsc{CreateL}$$

6 Stacking

Intuitively, fictional separation logic allows us to pretend we are working in a high-level memory model Σ if we show how to interpret that high-level memory model down to *heap*. It is then natural to investigate whether we can stack an even higher-level memory model Σ' on top of that construction and interpret Σ' down to Σ. Of course, this should generalize to arbitrary levels of stacking.

In this section, we present a theory of stacking that allows this while interacting well with the features introduced in previous sections and not being a burden on the logic when not in use. It is important to stress that it is in many cases possible for one module to depend on and extend the abstraction of another module *without* using stacking; c.f. the wrapper example in Section 4.2.

The most basic way to combine two interpretations is to compose them as relations. Given interpretations $I : \Sigma_1 \searrow \Sigma_2$ and $J : \Sigma_2 \searrow \Sigma_3$, their relational composition $(I\,;J)$ has type $\Sigma_1 \searrow \Sigma_3$ and is defined as

$$I\,; J \triangleq \lambda\sigma_1.\ \exists\sigma_2' \in I(\sigma_1).\ J(\sigma_2').$$

That is, $\sigma_3 \in (I\,;J)(\sigma_1)$ if and only if $\exists\sigma_2' \in I(\sigma_1).\ \sigma_3 \in J(\sigma_2')$.

We can show the following rule for working with relational composition:

$$\frac{S \vdash \forall\phi.\ J.\ \{\exists\sigma \in P.\ I(\sigma \circ \phi)\}\ C\ \{\exists\sigma \in Q.\ I(\sigma \circ \phi)\}}{S \vdash (I\,;J).\ \{P\}\ C\ \{Q\}}\ \textsc{RelComp}$$

Reading the rule from the bottom up, RelComp allows peeling off the top layer of a multi-layered interpretation, making its frame explicit. This is desirable when verifying an implementation that extends upon the J-interpretation using I. Perhaps J is opaque at the point where this rule is applied.

Relational composition masks the J-interpretation to the outside; in particular, it masks the frame in Σ_2 that goes into J, which means that the converse of RelComp does not hold. In many situations, including the next example, we want to give specifications that expose both the Σ_1-algebra and the Σ_2-algebra in order to be useful to clients that do not have their data exclusively in Σ_1. This discussion motivates our definition of the *stacking* composition. Given interpretations $I : \Sigma_1 \searrow \Sigma_2$ and $J : \Sigma_2 \searrow \Sigma_3$, their stacking $I \succ J$ has type $\Sigma_1 \times \Sigma_2 \searrow \Sigma_3$ and is defined as

$$I \succ J \triangleq (I * 1)\,;J.$$

With this definition, we now get a generalization of RelComp in the form of the following rule, which holds in both directions:

$$\frac{S \vdash \forall\phi.\ J.\ \{\exists\sigma \in P_1.\ I(\sigma \circ \phi) * P_2\}\ C\ \{\exists\sigma \in Q_1.\ I(\sigma \circ \phi) * Q_2\}}{S \vdash I \succ J.\ \{P_1 \times P_2\}\ C\ \{Q_1 \times Q_2\}}\ \textsc{StackComp}$$

The special case of this rule where $P_2 = Q_2 = emp$ is similar to RelComp. The special case where $P_1 = Q_1 = emp$ leads to a rule that is more like a stacking version of Forget and Create (Section 4).

There is a generalization of the Enter1 rule to stacking:

$$\frac{S \vdash \forall\phi.\ J.\ \{I(\sigma \circ \phi) * P\}\ C\ \{I(\sigma' \circ \phi) * Q\}}{S \vdash I \succ J.\ \{\{\sigma\} \times P\}\ C\ \{\{\sigma'\} \times Q\}}\ \textsc{Enter1Stack}$$

This rule is simply a special case of StackComp. Notice that $(I \succ 1) = (I * 1)$, so these inference rules can also be applied to separating products in some cases.

A module may use stacking internally but hide that fact if the stacking does not need to be visible to its clients. This can be achieved by collapsing the stacking composition to a relational composition by the following rule:

$$\frac{S \vdash I \succ J.\ \{P^{\mathsf{L}}\}\ C\ \{Q^{\mathsf{L}}\}}{S \vdash (I\,;J).\ \{P\}\ C\ \{Q\}}\ \textsc{StackRel}$$

6.1 Example: Abstract Fractional Permissions

We saw the example of fractional permissions in Section 5.1, where the points-to predicate was extended to carry a permission. With stacking, we can use essentially the same construction to extend the *Coll* predicate from Section 4.2 to carry a permission. Just like the heap-read command could execute with any partial permission, while heap write required full permission, we can prove that coll_clone and coll_contains can execute with any partial permission, while the other functions require full permission.

Formally, we can prove the validity of the following specification.

$$
\begin{aligned}
&\forall \Sigma, I, \mathit{Coll}.\ S_{\mathrm{Coll}}(\Sigma, I, \mathit{Coll}) \Rightarrow \\
&\quad \exists \Sigma' : \mathit{sepalg}.\ \exists I' : \Sigma' \searrow \Sigma. \\
&\quad \exists \mathit{FColl} : \mathit{Perm} \times \mathit{loc} \times \mathcal{P}_{\mathsf{fin}}(\mathit{val}) \to \mathcal{P}(\Sigma').\ \forall V, V', c, z, z'. \\
&\qquad (\mathit{FColl}^{z}(c, V) * \mathit{FColl}^{z'}(c, V') \dashv\vdash V = V' \wedge z + z' \leq 1 \wedge \mathit{FColl}^{z+z'}(c, V)) \wedge \\
&\qquad (\mathit{FColl}^{1}(c, V)^{\mathsf{L}} \dashv\models_{I' \succ I} \mathit{Coll}(c, V)^{\mathsf{R}}) \wedge \\
&\qquad I' \succ I.\ \{\mathit{FColl}^{z}(\mathsf{c}, V)^{\mathsf{L}}\}\ \mathsf{coll\_contains(c, v)}\ \{\mathit{FColl}^{z}(\mathsf{c}, V)^{\mathsf{L}} \wedge \mathsf{ret} = (\mathsf{v} \in V)\} \wedge \\
&\qquad I' \succ I.\ \{\mathit{FColl}^{z}(\mathsf{c}, V)^{\mathsf{L}}\}\ \mathsf{coll\_clone(c)}\ \{\mathit{FColl}^{z}(\mathsf{c}, V)^{\mathsf{L}} * \mathit{FColl}^{1}(\mathsf{ret}, V)^{\mathsf{L}}\}.
\end{aligned}
$$

The elements of the specification are all the same as for the standard fractional permissions in Section 5.1. It is written such that the stacking is revealed to clients, allowing them to use the fractional and non-fractional collections together and convert between them using the indirect bi-entailment in the specification. There is thus no need for specifying fractional versions of the remaining functions since the indirect bi-entailment allows reusing the original specifications.

Notice that we can define *FColl* and prove fractional versions of all the functions without knowing their implementation or how *Coll*, I or Σ are defined. In particular, the implementations of coll_clone and coll_contains are allowed to modify the underlying heap, but they still appear read-only through the indirect specification.

If it is not necessary for fractional and non-fractional collections to coexist and share footprints from the perspective of clients, the StackRel rule could be used to hide the stacking in this specification. Then the specification can be made to look as simple as the original specification in Section 4.2 by hiding $(I' \,;\, I)$ behind an existential.

We can verify the specification by choosing the existentials as follows:

$$
\begin{aligned}
\Sigma' &= \mathit{loc} \overset{\mathsf{fin}}{\rightharpoonup} (\mathcal{P}_{\mathsf{fin}}(\mathit{val})_{=} \times \mathit{Perm})_{\bot} \\
I'(f) &= \forall_{*} c \in \mathit{supp}(f).\ \exists V.\ f(c) = (V, 1) \wedge \mathit{Coll}(c, V) \\
\mathit{FColl}^{z}(c, V) &= \{[c \mapsto (V, z)]\}
\end{aligned}
$$

This is very similar to the original fractional permissions example, and the proofs are also similar.

7 Discussion and Related Work

Simplicity has been a major goal for this theory, particularly in three places: (1) clients of a module that uses fictional separation internally should be able to reason with the same ease as in standard separation logic; (2) the overhead in verifying an implementation with fictional separation should be minimal; and (3) correctness of the meta-theory should be easy to prove. The three goals are listed in order of importance since they represent tasks to be carried out by a decreasing number of people.

We believe that the first simplicity goal has been achieved in most situations, though clients of multiple modules with complex stacking patterns may benefit from tool support for composing the interpretations. The second goal has been achieved in the sense that it is easy to verify examples like those presented in this paper and, moreover, the separation algebras needed can be assembled from standard constructions. The third goal has been reached through judicious choice of definitions, especially by defining the indirect triple in terms of the standard triple – it has been possible to conduct all meta-theoretical proofs without unfolding the definition of the standard triple [14]. Because we work directly in the semantics of the logic, it should be natural to encode this theory in the Coq proof assistant, extending our existing Coq formalization of separation logic [1].

A major inspiration for fictional separation logic has been the design pattern used by Krishnaswami [16, Chapter 5] for specifying data structures with fictional disjointness in standard separation logic. The technique is to define a per-module custom separation logic (not separation *algebra*) and let the client manage the abstract frame, which is explicitly present in every function specification. Fictional separation logic makes the essential part of this design pattern formal, allowing the abstract frame to be managed implicitly by the indirect triple and enabling a general and comprehensive theory on these custom separation logics, instead of scattering the theory across modules on an ad-hoc basis. See also the discussion in Section 4.2. We ignore Krishnaswami's concept of a *ramification operator* since it would make the resulting logic too different from separation logic.

The work on *locality-breaking transformations* (LBT) for context logic, a kind of non-commutative separation logic, by Dinsdale-Young, Gardner and Wheelhouse [8,9] can also be seen as a formalization of Krishnaswami's design pattern, though they were developed independently. LBT is in the field of program refinement, which means that not only are pre- and postconditions of a triple transformed across abstraction layers, like in fictional separation logic, but the command is also transformed. Despite that difference, the intuition and proof obligations are similar to fictional separation logic: verifying a module implementation involves showing that all atomic operations preserve an abstract frame from a per-module context algebra. Reasoning in LBT is fundamentally in two stages, though: a client program and proof are always created at the high level and are subsequently transformed to the low level outside the logic. In fictional separation logic, moving between the levels is done within the logic itself, and the separation algebras are first-class entities in the logic. Hence, as we have seen, we can take advantage of all the features in the specification logic, e.g., to hide the definition of a separation algebra behind an existential quantifier. The soundness proofs of the meta-theory in [9] are much more complicated than ours, despite their much less expressive specification logic; it appears to be caused by their proof-theoretic approach to soundness as opposed to our semantic approach.

In terms of what examples can be encoded, fictional separation logic is quite close to the *concurrent abstract predicates* (CAP) framework [7,11] restricted to sequential programs. CAP has been developed for reasoning about concurrent programs in which several threads may work on the same shared memory; when restricting attention to sequential programs, CAP thus allows to specify and reason about modules that are implemented using sharing. The CAP approach, seen from our perspective, is to fix one particular separation algebra for all modules, which is sufficiently powerful to handle most cases of sharing. The algebra is specialized to each module by giving a per-module protocol definition, with access to the various stages in the protocol controlled by permission accounting. These explicit protocols, describing what atomic modifications may be performed on shared memory regions, give verification tasks a completely different flavour and intuition compared to fictional separation logic. In a sequential setting, the two systems are therefore very different solutions to the same problem. Concurrent abstract predicates is fundamentally rooted in a concurrent setting, though, which complicates the proof system. In particular, program verification requires showing *stability* of all intermediate pre- and postconditions in a proof.

Future work includes extending fictional separation logic to richer programming languages. Our preliminary investigations suggest that it is straightforward to extend the logic to a language with function pointers, by using the idea of nested triples [21] to specify such pointers. In fictional separation logic we will, of course, use *indirect* nested triples. To make it possible to call a function f with a function argument that uses an interpretation stacked on top of f's own interpretation, one can specify both f and its argument through a stacking of interpretations.

We are also interested in extending fictional separation logic to a concurrent language in order to find out whether it can retain its simplicity.

Acknowledgements. We would like to thank Jesper Bengtson, Thomas Dinsdale-Young, Filip Sieczkowski, Kasper Svendsen, Peter Sestoft and Jacob Thamsborg for helpful feedback and discussions.

References

1. Bengtson, J., Jensen, J.B., Sieczkowski, F., Birkedal, L.: Verifying Object-Oriented Programs with Higher-Order Separation Logic in Coq. In: van Eekelen, M., Geuvers, H., Schmaltz, J., Wiedijk, F. (eds.) ITP 2011. LNCS, vol. 6898, pp. 22–38. Springer, Heidelberg (2011)
2. Biering, B., Birkedal, L., Torp-Smith, N.: BI-hyperdoctrines, higher-order separation logic, and abstraction. ACM Transactions on Programming Languages and Systems 29(5) (2007)

3. Birkedal, L., Torp-Smith, N., Yang, H.: Semantics of separation-logic typing and higher-order frame rules for algol-like languages. Logical Methods in Computer Science 2(5:1) (August 2006)
4. Bornat, R., Calcagno, C., O'Hearn, P.W., Parkinson, M.J.: Permission accounting in separation logic. In: Proceedings of POPL, pp. 259–270 (2005)
5. Boyland, J.: Checking Interference with Fractional Permissions. In: Cousot, R. (ed.) SAS 2003. LNCS, vol. 2694, pp. 55–72. Springer, Heidelberg (2003)
6. Calcagno, C., O'Hearn, P.W., Yang, H.: Local action and abstract separation logic. In: Proceedings of LICS (2007)
7. Dinsdale-Young, T., Dodds, M., Gardner, P., Parkinson, M.J., Vafeiadis, V.: Concurrent Abstract Predicates. In: D'Hondt, T. (ed.) ECOOP 2010. LNCS, vol. 6183, pp. 504–528. Springer, Heidelberg (2010)
8. Dinsdale-Young, T., Gardner, P., Wheelhouse, M.: Abstraction and Refinement for Local Reasoning. In: Leavens, G.T., O'Hearn, P., Rajamani, S.K. (eds.) VSTTE 2010. LNCS, vol. 6217, pp. 199–215. Springer, Heidelberg (2010)
9. Dinsdale-Young, T., Gardner, P., Wheelhouse, M.: Abstraction and refinement for local reasoning (February 2011); journal submission
10. Dockins, R., Hobor, A., Appel, A.W.: A Fresh Look at Separation Algebras and Share Accounting. In: Hu, Z. (ed.) APLAS 2009. LNCS, vol. 5904, pp. 161–177. Springer, Heidelberg (2009)
11. Dodds, M., Jagannathan, S., Parkinson, M.J.: Modular reasoning for deterministic parallelism. In: Proceedings of POPL (2011)
12. Gotsman, A., Berdine, J., Cook, B.: Precision and the conjunction rule in concurrent separation logic. In: Proceedings of MFPS (2011)
13. Haack, C., Hurlin, C.: Resource usage protocols for iterators. In: Proceedings of IWACO (2008)
14. Jensen, J.B., Birkedal, L.: Fictional separation logic: Appendix (2011), `http://itu.dk/~jobr/research/fsl-appendix.pdf`
15. Jensen, J.B., Birkedal, L., Sestoft, P.: Modular verification of linked lists with views via separation logic. Journal of Object Technology 10, 2:1–2:20 (2011)
16. Krishnaswami, N.R.: Verifying Higher-Order Imperative Programs with Higher-Order Separation Logic. Ph.D. thesis, Carnegie Mellon University (2011)
17. Meyers, S.: More Effective C++: 35 New Ways to Improve Your Programs and Designs, 1st edn. Addison-Wesley Professional (1996)
18. Parkinson, M.J., Bierman, G.M.: Separation logic and abstraction. In: Proceedings of POPL, pp. 247–258 (2005)
19. Pilkiewicz, A., Pottier, F.: The essence of monotonic state. In: Proceedings of TLDI (2011)
20. Reynolds, J.C.: Separation logic: A logic for shared mutable data structures. In: Proceedings of LICS, pp. 55–74 (2002)
21. Schwinghammer, J., Birkedal, L., Reus, B., Yang, H.: Nested Hoare Triples and Frame Rules for Higher-Order Store. In: Grädel, E., Kahle, R. (eds.) CSL 2009. LNCS, vol. 5771, pp. 440–454. Springer, Heidelberg (2009)

Validating $LR(1)$ Parsers

Jacques-Henri Jourdan[1,2], François Pottier[2], and Xavier Leroy[2]

[1] École Normale Supérieure
[2] INRIA Paris-Rocquencourt

Abstract. An $LR(1)$ parser is a finite-state automaton, equipped with a stack, which uses a combination of its current state and one lookahead symbol in order to determine which action to perform next. We present a validator which, when applied to a context-free grammar $\mathcal{G}$ and an automaton $\mathcal{A}$, checks that $\mathcal{A}$ and $\mathcal{G}$ agree. Validating the parser provides the correctness guarantees required by verified compilers and other high-assurance software that involves parsing. The validation process is independent of which technique was used to construct $\mathcal{A}$. The validator is implemented and proved correct using the Coq proof assistant. As an application, we build a formally-verified parser for the C99 language.

1 Introduction

Parsing remains an essential component of compilers and other programs that input textual representations of structured data. Its theoretical foundations are well understood today, and mature technology, ranging from parser combinator libraries to sophisticated parser generators, is readily available to help implementing parsers.

The issue we focus on in this paper is that of *parser correctness*: how to obtain formal evidence that a parser is correct with respect to its specification? Here, following established practice, we choose to specify parsers via context-free grammars enriched with semantic actions.

One application area where the parser correctness issue naturally arises is formally-verified compilers such as the CompCert verified C compiler [1]. Indeed, in the current state of CompCert, the passes that have been formally verified start at abstract syntax trees (AST) for the CompCert C subset of C and extend to ASTs for three assembly languages. Upstream of these verified passes are lexing, parsing, type-checking and elaboration passes that are still in need of formal verification in order to attain end-to-end verification. The present paper addresses this need for the parsing pass. However, its results are more generally applicable to all high-assurance software systems where parsing is an issue.

There are many ways to build confidence in a parser. Perhaps the simplest way is to instrument an unverified parser so that it produces full parse trees, and, at every run of the compiler, check that the resulting parse tree conforms to the grammar. This approach is easy to implement but does not establish completeness (all valid inputs are accepted) or unambiguity (for each input, there is at most one parse tree). Another approach is to apply program proof

H. Seidl (Ed.): ESOP 2012, LNCS 7211, pp. 397–416, 2012.

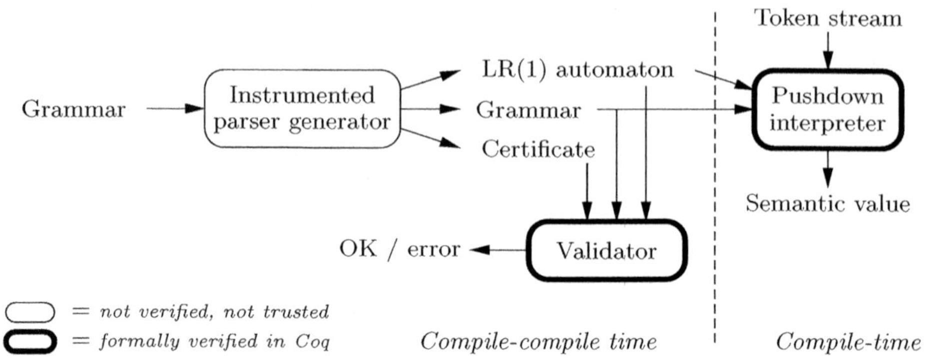

Fig. 1. General architecture

directly to a hand-written or generated parser. However, such a proof is tedious, especially if the parser was automatically generated, and must be re-done every time the the parser is modified. Yet another approach, developed by Barthwal and Norrish [2,3], is to formally verify, once and for all, a parser generator, guaranteeing that whenever the verified generator succeeds, the parser that it produces is correct with respect to the input grammar. However, Barthwal and Norrish's proof is specific to a particular parser generator that only accepts *SLR* grammars. It so happens that the ISO C99 grammar we are interested in is not *SLR*. Before being applicable to CompCert, Barthwal and Norrish's work would, therefore, have to be extended in nontrivial ways to a richer class of grammars such as *LALR*.

In this paper, we develop a fourth approach: *a posteriori* verified validation of an $LR(1)$ automaton produced by an untrusted parser generator, as depicted in Fig. 1. After every run of the parser generator (that is, at *compile-compile time*), the source grammar $\mathcal{G}$, the generated automaton $\mathcal{A}$, and auxiliary information acting as a certificate are fed in a *validator*, which checks whether $\mathcal{A}$ recognizes the same language as $\mathcal{G}$. If so, the build of the compiler proceeds; if not, it is aborted with an error.

The first contribution of this paper is the algorithm that performs this validation. It is relatively simple, and, to the best of our knowledge, original. It applies indifferently to many flavors of $LR(1)$ automata, including $LR(0)$ (a degenerate case), *SLR* [4], *LALR* [5], Pager's method [6], and canonical $LR(1)$ [7]. The second contribution is a soundness proof for this algorithm, mechanized using the Coq proof assistant, guaranteeing with the highest confidence that if the validation of an automaton $\mathcal{A}$ against a grammar $\mathcal{G}$ succeeds, then the automaton $\mathcal{A}$ and the interpreter that executes it form a correct parser for $\mathcal{G}$. The last contribution is an experimental assessment of our approach over the ISO C99 grammar, demonstrating applicability to realistic parsers of respectable size.

In summary, the approach to high-confidence parsing developed in this paper is attractive for several reasons: (1) it provides correctness guarantees about an $LR(1)$ parser as strong as those obtained by verifying a $LR(1)$ parser generator;

(2) only the validator needs to be formally verified, but not the parser generator itself, reducing the overall proof effort; (3) the validator and its soundness proof are reusable with different parser generators and different flavors of $LR(1)$ parsing; (4) existing, mature parser generators such as Menhir [8] can be used with minimal instrumentation, giving users the benefits of the extensive diagnostics produced by these generators.

This paper is organized as follows. In §2, we review context-free grammars, $LR(1)$ automata, and their meaning. In §3, we establish three properties of automata, namely soundness (§3.1), safety (§3.2) and completeness (§3.3). Safety and completeness are true only of some automata: we present a set of conditions that are sufficient for these properties to hold and that can be automatically checked by a validator. After presenting some facts about our Coq implementation (§4), we discuss its application to a C99 parser in the setting of CompCert (§5). We conclude with discussions of related work (§6) and directions for future work (§7).

Our modifications to Menhir are available as part of the standard release [8]. Our Coq code is not yet part of the CompCert release, but is available online [9].

2 Grammars and Automata

2.1 Symbols

We fix an alphabet of *terminal symbols* a and an alphabet of *non-terminal symbols* A, where an *alphabet* is a finite set. A *symbol* X is either a terminal symbol or a non-terminal symbol. We write α for a *sentential form*, that is, a finite sequence of symbols.

2.2 Grammars

We fix a grammar $\mathcal{G}$, where a *grammar* consists of:

1. a *start symbol* S;
2. an alphabet of *productions* p;
3. for every symbol X, a type $[\![X]\!]$.

The first two components are standard. (The syntax of productions will be presented shortly.) The third component, which is not usually found in textbooks, arises because we are interested not in recognition, but in parsing: that is, we would like not only to decide whether the input is valid, but also to construct a *semantic value*. In other words, we would like to consider that a grammar defines not just a *language* (a set of words) but a *relation* between words and semantic values. However, before we do so, we must answer the question: what is the type of semantic values? It should be decided by the user, that is, it should be part of the grammar. Furthermore, one should allow distinct symbols to carry different types of semantic values. For instance, a terminal symbol that stands for an identifier might carry a string, while a non-terminal symbol that stands for an arithmetic expression might carry an abstract syntax tree, that is, a value of a user-defined inductive type. If we were to force the user to adopt a single universal type of semantic values, the user's code would become polluted with tags and dynamic tests, and it would not be possible for the user to argue that these tests cannot fail. For this reason, for every symbol X, we allow the user to choose the type $[\![X]\!]$ of the semantic values carried by X. (In Coq, $[\![X]\!]$ has type `Type`.) By abuse of notation, if α is a (possibly empty) sequence of symbols $X_1 \ldots X_n$, we write $[\![\alpha]\!]$ for the tuple type $[\![X_1]\!] \times \ldots \times [\![X_n]\!]$.

How are semantic values constructed? The answer is two-fold. The semantic values carried by terminal symbols are constructed by the lexer: in other words, they are part of the input that is submitted to the parser. The semantic values carried by non-terminal symbols are constructed by the parser: when a production is reduced, a semantic action is executed. Let us now examine each of these two aspects in greater detail.

The input of the parser is a stream of tokens, where a *token* is a dependent pair (a, v) of a terminal symbol a and a semantic value v of type $[\![a]\!]$. We assume that this stream is infinite. There is no loss of generality in this assumption: if one wishes to work with a finite input stream, one can complete it with an infinite number of copies of a new "end-of-stream" token. In the following, we write w for a finite sequence of tokens and ω for an infinite stream of tokens.

A *production* p is a triple of the form $A \longrightarrow \alpha \; \{f\}$. (Above, we have written that productions form an alphabet, that is, they are numbered. We abuse notation and elide the details of the mapping from productions-as-numbers to productions-as-triples.) The left-hand side of a production is a non-terminal symbol A. The right-hand side consists of a sentential form α and a *semantic action* f of type $[\![\alpha]\!] \rightarrow [\![A]\!]$. The semantic action, which is provided by the user, indicates how a tuple of semantic values for the right-hand side α can be transformed into a semantic value for the left-hand side A. In our approach, the semantic action plays a dual role: on the one hand, it is part of the grammar, and plays a role in the definition of the semantics of the grammar; on the other hand, it is used, at runtime, by the parser. The semantic action is a Coq function and is supplied by the user as part of the grammar. (The parser generator Menhir views semantic actions as pieces of text, so no modification is needed for it to support Coq semantic actions instead of Objective Caml semantic actions.)

2.3 Semantics of Grammars

The semantics of grammars is usually defined in terms of a relation between symbols X and words w, written $X \longrightarrow w$, pronounced: "X derives w". As announced earlier, we extend this relation with a third parameter, a semantic value v of type $[\![X]\!]$. Thus, we write $X \xrightarrow{v} w$, pronounced: "X derives w producing v". The inductive definition of this relation is as follows:

$$a \xrightarrow{v} (a, v) \qquad\qquad \frac{A \longrightarrow X_1 \ldots X_n \; \{f\} \text{ is a production} \qquad \forall i \in \{1, \ldots, n\} \quad X_i \xrightarrow{v_i} w_i}{A \xrightarrow{f(v_1, \ldots, v_n)} w_1 \ldots w_n}$$

This semantics is used when we state that the parser is sound and complete with respect to the grammar (Theorems 1 and 3).

2.4 Automata

We fix an automaton $\mathcal{A}$, where an *automaton* consists of:

1. an alphabet of *states* σ, with a distinguished *initial state*, written *init*;
2. an action table;
3. a goto table;
4. for every non-initial state σ, an incoming symbol, written *incoming*(σ).

A *non-initial state* is a state other than *init*.

An *action table* is a total mapping of pairs (σ, a) to actions. The idea is, if σ is the current state of the automaton and a is the terminal symbol currently found at the head of the input stream, then the corresponding action instructs the automaton what to do next. An *action* is one of *shift* σ' (where σ' is non-initial), *reduce* p (where p is a production), *accept*, and *reject*. In particular, the situation where the action table maps (σ, a) to *shift* σ' can be thought of graphically as an edge, labeled a, from σ to σ'.

Remark 1. Our description of the action table as a mapping of pairs (σ, a) to actions appears to imply that the parser *must* peek at the next input token a *before* it can decide upon the next action. This might seem perfectly acceptable: because we have assumed that the input stream is infinite, there always is one more input token. In practice, however, more care is required. There are situations where the input stream is effectively infinite and nevertheless one must not allow the parser to systematically peek at the next token. For instance, the input stream might be connected to a keyboard, where a user is entering commands. If the parser has been asked to recognize one command, then, upon finding the end of a command, it should terminate and report success *without* attempting to read one more token: otherwise, it runs the risk of blocking until further keyboard input is available!

In order to address this problem, we allow our automata to sometimes take a *default action* without peeking at the next input token. We adopt the following convention: if, for a certain state σ and for all terminal symbols a, the entries found at (σ, a) in the action table are identical, then the automaton, when in state σ, determines which action should be taken *without* consulting the input stream[1].

[1] Of course, it would be inefficient to naïvely test whether one entire column of the action table contains identical entries. In reality, Menhir produces (and our Coq code uses) a two-level action table, where the first level is indexed only by a state σ and indicates whether there exists a default action, and the second level (which is consulted only if there is no default action) is indexed by a state σ and a terminal symbol a.

A *goto table* is a partial mapping of pairs (σ, A) to non-initial states. If the goto table maps (σ, A) to σ', then the automaton can take a transition from σ to σ' after recognizing a word that derives from A. This can be thought of graphically as an edge, labeled A, from σ to σ'. This table is a partial mapping: a state σ may have no outgoing edge labeled A.

A well-formed *LR* automaton has the property that, for every non-initial state σ, all of the edges that enter σ carry a common label. (The initial state *init* has no incoming edges.) We refer to this label as the *incoming symbol* of σ. Although we could have our validator reconstruct this information, we ask the user to supply it as part of the description of the automaton. We require that this information be consistent with the action and goto tables, as follows. If the action table maps (σ, a) to *shift* σ', then we require $\mathit{incoming}(\sigma') = a$. Similarly, if the goto table maps (σ, A) to σ', then we require $\mathit{incoming}(\sigma') = A$. We encode these requirements directly in the types of the action and goto tables, using dependent types, so we do not need to write validation code for them.

2.5 Semantics of Automata

We give semantics to automata by defining an interpreter for automata. The interpreter is a function named $\mathit{parse}(\cdot,\cdot)$. Its first (and main) argument is a token stream ω. We need an auxiliary argument, the "fuel", which is discussed further on.

The interpreter maintains a *stack* s, which is a list of dependent pairs of a non-initial state σ and a semantic value v of type $[\![\mathit{incoming}(\sigma)]\!]$. Indeed, $\mathit{incoming}(\sigma)$ is the (terminal or non-terminal) symbol that was recognized prior to entering state σ, and v is a semantic value associated with this symbol. We write $s(\sigma, v)$ for a stack whose top cell is the pair (σ, v) and whose tail is the stack s. At the beginning of a run, the stack is empty. At every moment, the *current state* of the automaton is the state found in the top stack cell if the stack is non-empty; it is the initial state *init* if the stack is empty[2].

In several places, the interpreter can generate an internal error, revealing a flaw in the automaton. Indeed, it is sometimes much easier to write an interpreter that can encounter an internal error, and prove *a posteriori* that this situation never arises if the automaton satisfies certain properties, than to define *a priori* an interpreter than never encounters an internal error. In other words, instead of hardwiring *safety* (that is, the absence of internal errors) into the definition of the interpreter, we make it a separate theorem (Theorem 2).

We use an error monad to deal with internal errors. In this paper, we use $\lightning$ to denote an internal error. By abuse of notation, we elide the "return" operation of the error monad. Thus, the interpreter produces either $\lightning$ or a parse result (defined below).

We also need a way of dealing with the possibility of non-termination. Again, it is not possible to prove *a priori* that the interpreter terminates. When an

[2] In many textbooks, one does not consider semantic values, so the stack is a list of states; at the beginning of a run, the stack is a singleton list of the state *init*; the stack is never empty, so the current state is always the one found on top of the stack.

LR automaton reduces a unit production (of the form $A \longrightarrow A'$) or an epsilon production (of the form $A \longrightarrow \varepsilon$), the size of the stack does not decrease. There do exist automata, as per the definition of §2.4, whose interpretation does not terminate. It is not clear, at present, what property one could or should require of the automaton in order to ensure termination. (We discuss this issue in §7.)

We adopt a simple and pragmatic approach to this problem: in addition to the token stream, the interpreter requires an integer argument n, which we refer to as the *fuel*. In the main loop of the interpreter, each iteration consumes one unit of fuel. If the interpreter runs out of fuel, it stops and reports that it was not able to terminate normally. We write *out-of-fuel* for this outcome.

Thus, a *parse result* is one of: *out-of-fuel*, which was explained above; *reject*, which means that the input is invalid; and *parsed* v ω, which means that the input is valid, that the semantic value associated with the prefix of the input that was recognized is v, and that the remainder of the input is ω. (The value v has type $[\![S]\!]$, where S is the start symbol of the grammar. The value ω is a token stream.)

In summary, the interpreter accepts a token stream and a certain amount of fuel and produces either $\lightning$ or a parse result, as defined above.

The interpreter works in a standard manner. At each step, it looks up the action table at (σ, a), where σ is the current state of the automaton and (a, v) is the next input token. Then,

1. if the action is *shift* σ', the input token (a, v) is consumed, and the new cell (σ', v) is pushed onto the stack. Because *incoming*$(\sigma') = a$ holds, it is possible to *cast* the value v from the type $[\![a]\!]$ to the type $[\![\mathit{incoming}(\sigma')]\!]$: this is required for this new stack cell to be well-typed.
2. if the action is *reduce* $A \longrightarrow X_1 \dots X_n$ $\{f\}$, the interpreter *attempts* to pop n cells off the stack, say $(\sigma_1, v_1) \dots (\sigma_n, v_n)$, and *dynamically checks* that *incoming*$(\sigma_i) = X_i$ holds for every $i \in \{1, \dots, n\}$. If the stack does not have at least n cells, or if this check fails, then an internal error occurs. Otherwise, thanks to the success of these dynamic checks, each of the semantic values v_i can be cast from the type $[\![\mathit{incoming}(\sigma_i)]\!]$ to the type $[\![X_i]\!]$. Thus, the tuple $(v_1, \dots, v_n)$ admits the type $[\![X_1 \dots X_n]\!]$, and is a suitable argument for the semantic action f. The application of f to this tuple yields a new semantic value v of type $[\![A]\!]$. There remains for the interpreter to consult the goto table at the current state and at the non-terminal symbol A. If this entry in the goto table is undefined, an internal error occurs. Otherwise, this entry contains a state σ', and (after another cast) the new cell (σ', v) is pushed onto the stack.
3. if the action is *accept*, the interpreter attempts to pop one cell off the stack, say (σ, v), and checks that *incoming*$(\sigma) = S$ holds, where S is the start symbol of the grammar. Thus, the value v can be cast to the type $[\![S]\!]$. (This can be thought of as reducing a special production $S' \longrightarrow S$.) The interpreter then checks that the stack is now empty and terminates with the parse result *parsed* v ω, where ω is what remains of the input stream.
4. if the action is *reject*, the interpreter stops with the parse result *reject*.

In summary, there are four possible causes for an internal error: a dynamic check of the form $incoming(\sigma) = X$ may fail; an attempt to pop a cell off the stack fails if the stack is empty; an attempt to consult the goto table fails if the desired entry is undefined; an attempt to accept fails if the stack is nonempty.

3 Correctness Properties and Validation

We now show how to establish three properties of the automaton $\mathcal{A}$ with respect to the grammar $\mathcal{G}$. These properties are *soundness* (the parser accepts only valid inputs), *safety* (no internal error occurs), and *completeness* (the parser accepts all valid inputs). By design of our interpreter, the first property is true of all automata, whereas the latter two are true only of some automata. For safety and for completeness, we present a set of conditions that are sufficient for the desired property to hold and that can be automatically checked by a validator.

3.1 Soundness

The soundness theorem states that if the parser accepts a finite prefix w of the input stream ω, then (according to the grammar) the start symbol S derives w. More precisely, if the parser accepts w and produces a semantic value v, then v is the value associated with this particular derivation of w from S, that is, the relation $S \xrightarrow{v} w$ holds.

Theorem 1 (Soundness). *If* $parse(\omega, n) = parsed\ v\ \omega'$ *holds, then there exists a word* w *such that* $\omega = w\omega'$ *and* $S \xrightarrow{v} w$.

No hypotheses about the automaton are required, because the situations where "something is wrong" and soundness might be endangered are detected at run-time by the interpreter and lead to internal errors. In other words, we have shifted most of the burden of the proof from the soundness theorem to the safety theorem.

In order to prove this theorem, it is necessary to establish an invariant stating that the symbols associated with the states found in the stack derive the input word that has been consumed. For this purpose, we introduce a new predicate, written $s \Longrightarrow w$, which relates a stack s with a token word w. It is inductively defined as follows:

$$\varepsilon \Longrightarrow \varepsilon \qquad \frac{s \Longrightarrow w_1 \qquad incoming(\sigma) \xrightarrow{v} w_2}{s(\sigma, v) \Longrightarrow w_1 w_2}$$

Then, the main soundness invariant can be stated as follows: if the parser has consumed the input word w and if the current stack is s, then $s \Longrightarrow w$ holds.

3.2 Safety

The safety theorem states that if the automaton passes the *safety validator* (which we describe further on) then the interpreter never encounters an internal error. A *validator* is a Coq term of type `bool`, which has access to the grammar, to the automaton, and to certain additional annotations that serve as hints (and which we describe below as well). Thus, the safety theorem takes the following form:

Theorem 2 (Safety). *If the criteria enforced by the safety validator are satisfied, then* $parse(\omega, n) \neq \lightning$ *for every input stream* ω *and for every integer "fuel"* n.

All of the causes of internal errors that were previously listed (§2.5) have to do with a stack that does not have the expected shape (e.g., it has too few cells) or contents (e.g. some cell contains a semantic value of inappropriate type, or contains a state for which no entry exists in the goto table). Thus, in order to ensure safety, we must have precise control of the shape and contents of the stack.

Recall that a stack s is a sequence of pairs $(\sigma_1, v_1) \ldots (\sigma_n, v_n)$. In what follows, it is convenient to abstractly describe the structure of such a stack in two ways. First, we are interested in the underlying sequence of symbols: we write $symbols(s)$ for the sequence of symbols $incoming(\sigma_1) \ldots incoming(\sigma_n)$. Second, we are interested in the underlying sequence of states: we write $states(s)$ for the sequence of singleton sets $\{init\}\{\sigma_1\} \ldots \{\sigma_n\}$. (We use singleton sets here because we will shortly be interested in approximating these singleton sets with larger sets of states Σ.)

A key remark is the following: the sequences $symbols(s)$ and $states(s)$ are not arbitrary. They follow certain patterns, or, in other words, they respect a certain invariant. This invariant will be sufficient to guarantee safety.

How do we find out what this invariant is? Two approaches come to mind: either the safety validator could reconstruct this invariant by performing a static analysis of the automaton (this would require a least fixed point computation), or the parser generator could produce a description of this invariant, which the safety validator would verify (this would require checking that a candidate fixed point is indeed a fixed point). We somewhat arbitrarily adopt the latter approach. The former approach appears viable as well, especially if one exploits a pre-existing verified library for computing least fixed points.

Thus, the annotations that the safety validator requires (and that the parser generator must produce) form a description of the safety invariant. For each non-initial state σ, these annotations are:

1. a sequence of symbols, written $pastSymbols(\sigma)$;
2. a sequence of sets of states, written $pastStates(\sigma)$.

(There is a redundancy, which we discuss in §7.) These annotations are meant to represent approximate (conservative) information about the shape and contents of the stack. In order to explain their meaning, let us now define the safety invariant in terms of these annotations.

We begin by defining the relations that exist between abstract descriptions of the stack and concrete stacks. We need two such relations. The *suffix ordering* between two *sequences of symbols* is defined in the usual way: that is, $X_m \ldots X_1$ is a suffix of $X'_n \ldots X'_1$ if and only if $m \leq n$ holds and $X_i = X'_i$ holds for every

$i \in \{1, \ldots, m\}$. The *suffix ordering* between two *sequences of sets of states* is defined in the same manner, up to pointwise superset ordering: that is, $\Sigma_m \ldots \Sigma_1$ is a suffix of $\Sigma'_n \ldots \Sigma'_1$ if and only if $m \leq n$ and $\Sigma_i \supseteq \Sigma'_i$ holds for every $i \in \{1, \ldots, m\}$.

Equipped with these suffix orderings, which serve as abstraction relations, we can define the safety invariant. This is a predicate over a stack, written *safe s*. It is inductively defined as follows:

$$\mathit{safe}\ \varepsilon \qquad\qquad \frac{\begin{array}{c}\mathit{pastSymbols}(\sigma) \text{ is a suffix of } \mathit{symbols}(s)\\ \mathit{pastStates}(\sigma) \text{ is a suffix of } \mathit{states}(s)\\ \mathit{safe}\ s\end{array}}{\mathit{safe}\ s(\sigma, v)}$$

A stack $s(\sigma, v)$ is safe if (a) the annotations *pastSymbols*(σ) and *pastStates*(σ) associated with the current state σ are correct approximate descriptions of the tail s of the stack and (b) the tail s is itself safe. Less formally, *pastSymbols*(σ) and *pastStates*(σ) are static descriptions of a suffix of the stack (i.e., the part of the stack that is closest to the top). The rest of the stack, beyond this statically known suffix, is unknown. Nevertheless, this information is sufficient (if validation succeeds) to show that internal errors cannot occur: for instance, it guarantees that, whenever we attempt to pop k cells off the stack, at least k cells are present.

Now, in order to ensure that *safe s* is indeed an invariant of the interpreter, the validator must check that the annotations *pastSymbols*(σ) and *pastStates*(σ) are consistent. Furthermore, the validator must verify a few extra conditions which, together with the invariant, ensure safety. The safety validator checks that the following properties are satisfied:

1. For every transition, labeled X, of a state σ to a new state σ',
   - *pastSymbols*(σ') is a suffix of *pastSymbols*(σ)*incoming*(σ),
   - *pastStates*(σ') is a suffix of *pastStates*$(\sigma)\{\sigma\}$.
2. For every state σ that has an action of the form *reduce* $A \longrightarrow \alpha\ \{f\}$,
   - α is a suffix of *pastSymbols*(σ)*incoming*(σ),
   - If *pastStates*$(\sigma)\{\sigma\}$ is $\Sigma_n \ldots \Sigma_0$ and if the length of α is k, then for every state $\sigma' \in \Sigma_k$, the goto table is defined at (σ', A). (If k is greater than n, take Σ_k to be the set of all states.)
3. For every state σ that has an *accept* action,
   - $\sigma \neq \mathit{init}$,
   - $\mathit{incoming}(\sigma) = S$,
   - $\mathit{pastStates}(\sigma) = \{\mathit{init}\}$.

Thanks to the finiteness of the alphabets, these conditions are clearly and efficiently decidable.

These conditions do not depend in any way on the manner in which lookahead is exploited to determine the next action. In other words, an $LR(1)$ automaton is safe if and only if the underlying non-deterministic $LR(0)$ automaton is safe. Thus, the safety validator is insensitive to which method was used to construct the $LR(1)$ automaton.

3.3 Completeness

The completeness theorem states that if the automaton passes the *completeness validator* (which we describe further on), if a prefix w of the input is valid, and if enough fuel is supplied, then the parser accepts w and constructs a correct semantic value. (The theorem also allows for the possibility that the parser might encounter an internal error. This concern was dealt with in §3.2, so we need not worry about it here.)

Theorem 3 (Completeness). *If the criteria enforced by the completeness validator are satisfied and if $S \xrightarrow{v} w$ holds, then there exists n_0 such that for all ω and for all $n \geq n_0$, either $parse(w\omega, n) = \lightning$ or $parse(w\omega, n) = parsed\ v\ \omega$.*

The Coq version of this result is in fact more precise. We prove that a suitable value of n_0 is the size of the derivation tree for the hypothesis $S \xrightarrow{v} w$, and we prove that this is the least suitable value, that is, $n < n_0$ implies $parse(w\omega, n) =$ *out-of-fuel*.

In order to guarantee that the automaton is complete, the validator must check that each state has "enough" permitted actions for every valid input to be eventually accepted. But how do we know, in a state σ, which actions should be permitted? We can answer this question if we know which set of $LR(1)$ items is associated with σ. Recall that an *item* is a quadruple $A \longrightarrow \alpha_1 \bullet \alpha_2\ [a]$, where $A \longrightarrow \alpha_1\alpha_2\ \{f\}$ is a production and a is a terminal symbol. The intuitive meaning of an item is: "we have recognized α_1; we now hope to recognize α_2 and find that it is followed with a; if this happens, then we will be able to reduce the production $A \longrightarrow \alpha_1\alpha_2\ \{f\}$".

Our items are relative to an *augmented* grammar, where a virtual production $S' \longrightarrow S$ has been added. This means that we can have items of the form $S' \longrightarrow \bullet\ S\ [a]$ (these appear in the initial state of the automaton) and items of the form $S' \longrightarrow S \bullet\ [a]$ (these appear in the final, accepting state).

The parser generator knows which set of items is associated with each state of the automaton. We require that this information be transmitted to the completeness validator. (One could instead reconstruct this information, and one would not even need to prove the correctness of the algorithm that reconstructs it; but it is not clear what one would gain by doing so.)

With this information, the validator carries out two kinds of checks. First, it checks that each state σ has "enough" actions: that is, the presence of certain items in *items*(σ) implies that certain actions must be permitted. Second, it checks that the sets *items*(σ) are *closed* and *consistent*: that is, the presence of certain items in *items*(σ) implies that certain items must be present in *items*(σ) (this is *closure*) and in *items*(σ'), where σ' ranges over the successor states of σ (this is *consistency*).

The definition of the closure property, which appears below, relies on the knowledge of the "*first*" sets, which in turn requires the knowledge of which non-terminal symbols are "*nullable*". It is well-known that "*first*" and "*nullable*" form the least fixed point of a certain system of positive equations. Again, we could have the validator compute this least fixed point; instead, we require that it be transmitted from the parser generator to the validator, and the validator just checks that it is a fixed point.

In summary, the annotations that the completeness validator requires (and that the parser generator must produce) are:

1. for each state σ, a set of items, written $items(\sigma)$.
2. for each non-terminal symbol A, a set of terminal symbols $first(A)$;
3. for each non-terminal symbol A, a Boolean value $nullable(A)$.

The properties that the completeness validator enforces are:

1. "*first*" and "*nullable*" are fixed points of the standard defining equations.
2. For every state σ, the set $items(\sigma)$ is closed, that is, the following implication holds:

$$\frac{\begin{array}{c} A \longrightarrow \alpha_1 \bullet A'\alpha_2\ [a] \in items(\sigma) \\ A' \longrightarrow \alpha'\ \{f'\} \text{ is a production} \\ a' \in first(\alpha_2 a) \end{array}}{A' \longrightarrow \bullet\, \alpha'\ [a'] \in items(\sigma)}$$

3. For every state σ, if $A \longrightarrow \alpha \bullet\ [a] \in items(\sigma)$, where $A \neq S'$, then the action table maps (σ, a) to *reduce* $A \longrightarrow \alpha\ \{f\}$.
4. For every state σ, if $A \longrightarrow \alpha_1 \bullet a\alpha_2\ [a'] \in items(\sigma)$, then the action table maps (σ, a) to *shift* σ', for some state σ' such that:

$$A \longrightarrow \alpha_1 a \bullet \alpha_2\ [a'] \in items(\sigma')$$

5. For every state σ, if $A \longrightarrow \alpha_1 \bullet A'\alpha_2\ [a'] \in items(\sigma)$, then the goto table either is undefined at (σ, A') or maps (σ, A') to some state σ' such that:

$$A \longrightarrow \alpha_1 A' \bullet \alpha_2\ [a'] \in items(\sigma')$$

6. For every terminal symbol a, we have $S' \longrightarrow \bullet\, S\ [a] \in items(init)$.
7. For every state σ, if $S' \longrightarrow S \bullet\ [a] \in items(\sigma)$, then σ has a default *accept* action.

These conditions are clearly decidable. In order to achieve reasonable efficiency, we represent items in a compact way: first, we group items that have a common $LR(0)$ core; second, we use a natural number to indicate the position of the "bullet". Thus, in the end, we manipulate triples of a production identifier p, an integer index into the right-hand side of p, and a set of terminal symbols. Furthermore, we use the standard library `FSets` [10], which implements finite sets in terms of balanced binary search trees, in order to represent sets of items.

The various known methods for constructing $LR(1)$ automata differ only in how they decide to merge, or not to merge, certain states that have a common $LR(0)$ core. The completeness validator is insensitive to this aspect: as long as no conflict arises due to excessive merging, an arbitrary merging strategy can be employed.

There is a relatively simple intuition behind the proof of Theorem 3. Suppose an oracle gives us a proof of $S \xrightarrow{v} w$, that is, a parse tree. Then, the parser, confronted with the input w, behaves in a very predictable way: it effectively performs a depth-first traversal of this parse tree. When the parser performs a *shift* action, it visits a (terminal) leaf of the parse tree; when it performs a reduce action, it visits a (non-terminal) node of the parse tree. At any time, the parser's stack encodes the path that leads from the root of the tree down to the current node of the traversal, and holds the semantic values associated with parse tree nodes that have been fully processed, but whose parent has not been fully processed yet. At any time, the unconsumed input corresponds to the fringe of the part of the parse tree that has not been traversed yet.

This invariant allows us to prove that the parser cannot reject the input $w\omega$. Instead, it keeps shifting and reducing until it has traversed the entire parse tree. At this point, it has consumed exactly w, and it must accept and produce exactly v. Note that there is no need to implement an "oracle". We simply prove that if *there exists* a parse tree, then the parser behaves *as if* it were traversing this parse tree, and accepts at the end.

In order to make this intuition precise, we define an invariant that relates the stack, the unconsumed input, and a path in the parse tree provided by the "oracle". The definition of this invariant is quite technical, but can be summed up as follows. There exists a path in the "oracle" parse tree such that:

1. The path begins at the root of the parse tree.
2. For each node in this path, the children of this node can be divided in three consecutive segments (or, at the last node in the path, in two segments):
   - children that have already been visited: the semantic value associated with each of these children is stored in a stack cell;
   - the child that is being visited (absent if we are at the bottom of the path): this child is the next node in the path;
   - children that will be visited in the future: their fringes correspond to segments of the unconsumed input stream.
3. The unconsumed input begins with the concatenation of the fringes of the "unvisited children" of all nodes in the path.
4. The sequence of all stack cells is in one-to-one correspondence with the concatenation of the sequences of "visited children" of all nodes in the path.
5. As per the previous item, each stack cell (σ, v) is associated with a certain child y of a certain node x in the path. Then, the semantic value carried by the node y must be precisely v. Furthermore, if the node x is labeled with the production $A \longrightarrow \alpha_1 X \alpha_2$ and if the child y corresponds to the symbol X, then the item $A \longrightarrow \alpha_1 X \bullet \alpha_2\ [a]$ appears in $items(\sigma)$, where a is the first symbol in the partial fringe that begins "after" the node x.

During parsing, this path evolves in the following ways:

1. Between two actions: if the first unvisited child of the last node of the path exists and is not a terminal leaf, then the next action of the automaton will take place under this child. It is then necessary to extend the path: this

child becomes the last node of the path. This extension process is repeated as many times as possible.
2. When shifting: if the first unvisited child of the last node exists and is a terminal leaf, then the next action must be a *shift* action. This child is considered visited and transferred to the first segment of children of the last node. The path itself is unchanged.
3. When reducing: if the last node of the path has no unvisited child, then the next action must be a *reduce* action for the production that corresponds to this node. Then, the path is shortened by one node: that is, if x and y are the last two nodes in the path, then x becomes the last node in the path, and y becomes the last visited child of x.

3.4 Unambiguity

It is easy to prove the following result.

Theorem 4. *Suppose there exists a token. If the criteria enforced by the safety and completeness validators are satisfied, then the grammar is unambiguous.*

The proof goes as follows. Suppose that the automaton is safe and complete. Suppose further that, for some word w, both $S \xrightarrow{v_1} w$ and $S \xrightarrow{v_2} w$ hold. By the safety hypothesis, the parser never encounters an internal error $\lightning$. Thus, by the completeness hypothesis, given a sufficiently large amount of fuel, the parser, applied to $w\omega$ (where ω is arbitrary), must produce v_1, and by a similar argument, must produce v_2. However, our automata are deterministic by definition: *parse* is a function. Thus, v_1 and v_2 must coincide.

4 Coq Formalization

All of the results presented in this paper were mechanized using the Coq 8.3pl1 proof assistant. The Coq formalization is fairly close to the definitions, theorems and proofs outlined in this paper.

We use of dependent types to support semantic values and semantic actions whose types are functions of the corresponding symbols and productions. This enables us to support user-supplied semantic actions with essentially no proof overhead compared with a "pure" parser that only produces a parse tree.

We make good use of Coq's module system: the validator and the interpreter are functors parameterized over abstract types for terminal and non-terminal symbols. The only constraints over these two types of symbols are that they must be finite (so that it is possible to decide universal quantifications over symbols) and they must come with a decidable total order (so that they can be used in conjunction with the `FSets` library).

The Coq formalization is pleasantly small: about 2500 lines, excluding comments. The executable specifications of the safety validator and the completeness validator are about 200 lines each. The proofs of soundness, safety, and completeness account for 200, 500, and 700 lines, respectively.

5 Experimentation on a C99 Parser

The grammar. Our starting point is the context-free grammar given in Annex A of the ISO C99 standard [11]. We omit the productions that support unprototyped "K&R-style" function definitions, since such old-style definitions are considered "an obsolescent feature" [11, section 6.11.7] and are not supported by subsequent passes of the CompCert compiler.

Both this slightly simplified C grammar and the original ISO C99 grammar are ambiguous. There are three distinct sources of ambiguity.

The first source of ambiguity is the classic "dangling-else" problem, which introduces a shift-reduce conflict in the $LR(1)$ automaton. We eliminated this conflict by a slight modification to the grammar, distinguishing two non-terminal symbols for statements: one that prohibits `if` statements without an `else` part, and the other that permits them.

The second source of ambiguity is the well-known problem with typedef names (identifiers bound to a type by a `typedef` declaration), which must be distinguished from other identifiers. For example, "`a * b;`" is to be parsed as a declaration of a variable `b` of type "pointer to `a`" if `a` is a typedef name, but stands for the multiplication of `a` by `b` otherwise. To avoid major ambiguities in the grammar, it is mandatory to use two distinct terminal symbols, *typedef-name* and *variable-name*, and rely on the lexer to classify identifiers into one of these two terminal symbols. The traditional way of doing so, affectionately referred to as "the lexer hack", is to have the semantic actions of the parser maintain a table of typedef names currently in scope, and to have the lexer consult this table to classify identifiers. We were reluctant to perform such side effects within the semantic actions of our verified parser. Instead, like Padioleau [12], we interpose a "pre-parser" between the lexer and the verified parser, whose sole purpose is to keep track of typedef names currently in scope and classify identifiers as either *typedef-name* or *variable-name* in the token stream that feeds the verified parser. For simplicity of implementation, the pre-parser is actually a full-fledged but unverified C99 parser that implements the standard "lexer hack" scheme.

The third and last source of ambiguity is also related to typedef names, but more subtle. Consider the declaration "`int f(int (a));`" where `a` is a typedef name. It can be read as "a function `f` with one parameter named `a` of type `int`", but also as "a function `f` with one anonymous parameter of function type `a` $\rightarrow$ `int`". The original ISO C99 standard leaves this ambiguity open, but Technical Corrigendum 2 specifies that the second interpretation is the correct one [11, clause 6.7.5.3(11)]. Again, we rely on our pre-parser to correctly resolve this ambiguity (via well-chosen precedence annotations) and to ensure that identifiers in binding positions are correctly classified as typedef names (if previously bound by `typedef` and not to be redeclared, as in the example above) or as variable names (in all other cases, even if previously bound by `typedef`).

Generating the parser. We use the Menhir parser generator [8] modified to produce not only an $LR(1)$ automaton but also a representation of the source grammar as well as the various annotations needed by the validator. All outputs are produced as Coq terms and definitions that can be directly read into Coq. The modifications to Menhir are small (less than 500 lines of Caml code) and reside in just one new module.

Our modified C99 grammar comprises 87 terminal symbols, 72 non-terminal symbols, and 263 productions. The $LR(1)$ automaton generated by Menhir using Pager's method contains 505 states. (The grammar is in fact $LALR$, and the automaton produced by Menhir is indeed identical to the $LALR$ automaton that would be produced by an $LALR$ parser generator.) The generated Coq file is approximately 4.5 Mbytes long, of which 6% correspond to the automaton, 2% to the description of the grammar, and the remaining 92% are annotations (item sets, mostly).

Validating the parser. Running the validator on this output, using Coq's built-in virtual machine execution engine (the `Eval vm_compute` tactic), takes 19 seconds: 4s to validate safety and 15s to validate completeness[3]. Coq takes an additional 32s to read and type-check the file generated by Menhir, for a total processing time of 51s. While not negligible, these validation times are acceptable in practice. In order to further reduce the validation time, one could probably use improved data structures or extract the validator to natively-compiled OCaml code; but there is no pressing need.

Running the parser. With some elbow grease, we were able to replace CompCert 1.9's unverified parser (an $LALR$ automaton produced by OCamlYacc) with our new verified parser. The verified parser runs about 5 times slower than the old one, increasing overall compilation times by about 20%. There are two major reasons for this slowdown. One is that we effectively parse the input twice: once in the pre-parser, to track typedef names, and once "for good" in the verified parser. Another reason is that the interpreter that executes the verified parser is written in Coq, then extracted to Caml, and performs redundant runtime checks compared with OCamlYacc's execution engine, which is coded in C and performs no runtime checks whatsoever. (We discuss the issue of redundant checks in §7.)

6 Related Work

Although parsing is a classic and extremely well-studied topic, the construction of verified parsers seems to have received relatively little interest.

Pottier and Régis-Gianas [13] show that, for a fixed $LR(1)$ automaton, the inductive invariant that describes the stack and guarantees safety (§3.2) can be expressed as a generalized algebraic data type (GADT). They show that if one constructs a parser by *specializing* the interpreter for this automaton, then a type-checker equipped with GADTs can verify the safety of this parser. In addition to a safety guarantee, this approach yields a performance gain with respect to an ML implementation, because the weaker type system of ML imposes the use of redundant tags and dynamic checks (e.g. stack cells must be redundantly tagged

[3] All timings were measured on a Core i7 3.4GHz processor, using a single core.

with *nil* or *cons*). Here, the interpreter is *generic*, and, even though it is provably safe, it does perform redundant dynamic checks. (We discuss this issue in §7.)

Barthwal and Norrish [2] and Barthwal [3] use the HOL4 proof assistant to formalize *SLR* [4] parsing. For a context-free grammar, they construct an *SLR* parser, and are able to prove it sound and complete: the guarantees that they obtain are analogous to our Theorems 1 and 3. Like us, they omit a proof that the parser terminates when presented with an illegal input. (We discuss this issue in §7.) Although their parsers are executable, they are probably not efficient, because the parser construction and parser execution phases are not distinguished in the usual manner: in particular, while the parser is running, states are still represented as sets of $LR(1)$ items. Because Barthwal and Norrish formalize the parser construction process, their formalization is relatively heavyweight and represents over 20 000 lines of definitions and proofs. In contrast, because we rely on a validator, our approach is more lightweight (2500 lines). It is also more versatile: we can validate $LR(1)$ automata constructed by any means, including $LR(0)$, *SLR*, *LALR*, Pager's method, and Knuth's canonical $LR(1)$ construction. We believe that this versatility is important in practice: for instance, we have verified that the C99 grammar is *LALR* but not *SLR*. One disadvantage of our approach is that we cannot exclude the possibility that the parser generator (which is not verified) fails or produces an incorrect automaton. Fortunately, this problem is detected at validation time. In our application to CompCert, it is detected when CompCert itself is built, that is, before CompCert is distributed to its users.

Parsing Expression Grammars (PEGs) are a declarative formalism for specifying recursive descent parsers. Ford [14,15] and other authors [16] have investigated their use as an alternative to the more traditional and better established context-free grammars. Koprowski and Binsztok [17] formalize the semantics of PEGs, extended with semantic actions, in Coq. They implement a well-formedness check, which ensures that the grammar is not left-recursive. Under this assumption, they are able to prove that a straightforward (non-memoizing) PEG interpreter is terminating. The soundness and completeness of the interpreter are immediate, because the interpreter is just a functional version of the semantics of PEGs, which is originally presented under a relational form. Wisnesky *et al.* [18] implement a verified packrat parser (that is, a PEG parser that achieves linear time and space complexity via memoization) using the experimental programming language Ynot, which is itself embedded within Coq. Because Ynot is a Hoare logic for partial correctness, the parser is not proved to terminate.

We are definitely not the first to embrace *a posteriori* validation as an effective way to obtain correctness guarantees for compilers and program generators. This idea goes back at least to Samet's 1975 Ph.D. thesis [19] and was further developed under the name *translation validation* by Pnueli *et al.* [20] and by Necula [21]. Tristan and Leroy exploit the idea that formally-verified validators for advanced compiler optimizations provide soundness guarantees as strong as direct compiler verification [22]. Another example of a formally-verified validator is the JVM bytecode verifier of Klein and Nipkow [23].

7 Conclusions and Future Work

The approach to high-assurance parsing that we have developed, based on *a posteriori* validation of an untrusted parser generator, appears effective so far. The validation algorithms are simple enough that they could be integrated into production parser generators and used as sanity checkers and debugging aids, even in contexts where strong assurance is not required.

This work can be extended in several directions, including proving additional properties of our $LR(1)$ parser, improving its efficiency, and extending our work to more expressive parsing formalisms. We now review some of these directions.

We have not proved that our parser terminates. Completeness (Theorem 3) implies that it terminates when supplied with a valid input. However, there remains a possibility that it might diverge when faced with an invalid input. In fact, we have proof that the properties enforced by the safety and completeness validators are not sufficient to ensure termination. So, more requirements must be enforced, but we are not sure, at present, what these requirements should be. Aho and Ullman prove that *canonical* $LR(1)$ parsers terminate [24, Theorem 5.13]. Their argument exploits the following property of canonical $LR(1)$ parsers: "as soon as [the consumed input and] the first input symbol of the remaining input are such that no possible suffix could yield a sentence in $\mathcal{L}(\mathcal{G})$, the parser will report error". This property, however, is *not* true of non-canonical $LR(1)$ parsers. By merging several states of the canonical automaton that have a common $LR(0)$ core, the non-canonical construction methods introduce spurious reductions: a non-canonical automaton can perform a few extra reductions before it detects an error. Thus, Aho and Ullman's proof does not seem to apply to non-canonical $LR(1)$ parsers.

We have not proved that our parser does not peek one token past the end of the desired input. We claim that this property holds: the automata produced by Menhir use default actions for this purpose (see Remark 1 in §2.4). However, at present, we cannot even *state* this property, because it is an intensional property of the function *parse*: "if $parse(\omega, n) = parsed\ v\ \omega'$, then ω' has not been forced". In order to allow this property to be stated, one approach would be to reformulate the parser so that it no longer has access to the token stream, but must instead interact explicitly with the producer of the token stream, by producing "peek" or "discard" requests together with a continuation.

We have defined a "cautious" interpreter, which can in principle encounter an internal error, and we have proved, after the fact, that (if the safety validator is satisfied, then) this situation never arises. This allows us to separate the definition of the interpreter and the safety argument. A potentially significant drawback of this approach is that it entails a performance penalty at runtime: even though we have a proof that the dynamic checks performed by the cautious interpreter are redundant, these checks are still present in the code, and slow down the parser. An anonymous reviewer pointed out that, without modifying any of our existing code, it should be possible to define an "optimistic" interpreter, which performs no runtime checks, and is subject to the precondition that the cautious interpreter does not fail. Sozeau's "`Program`" extensions [25] could be used to facilitate the construction of this optimistic interpreter. In the end, only the optimistic interpreter would be executed, and the cautious interpreter would serve only as part of the proof. We would like to thank this reviewer for this attractive idea, which we have not investigated yet.

Some of the hints that we require are redundant. In particular, *pastSymbols* (§3.2) is entirely redundant, since it can in fact be deduced from *pastStates* and *incoming*. This redundancy is due to historical reasons, and could be eliminated. This might help speed up the type-checking and validation of the annotations.

Beyond $LR(1)$ parsing, we believe that validation techniques can apply to other parsing formalisms. It would be particularly interesting to study GLR, for which we hope that our validators could be re-used with minimal changes.

Our experience with the C99 grammar agrees with common wisdom on the importance of supporting precedence and associativity declarations in order to keep parser specifications concise and readable. It is well-known how to take these declarations into account when generating $LR(1)$ automata, but the resulting automata are no longer complete with respect to the grammar. How could we modify our definition of the meaning of a grammar so as to take precedence declarations into account? How could we then extend our validation algorithms?

References

1. Leroy, X.: Formal verification of a realistic compiler. Communications of the ACM 52, 107–115 (2009)
2. Barthwal, A., Norrish, M.: Verified, Executable Parsing. In: Castagna, G. (ed.) ESOP 2009. LNCS, vol. 5502, pp. 160–174. Springer, Heidelberg (2009)
3. Barthwal, A.: A formalisation of the theory of context-free languages in higher order logic. PhD thesis, Australian National University (December 2010)
4. DeRemer, F.L.: Simple $LR(k)$ grammars. Communications of the ACM 14(7), 453–460 (1971)
5. Anderson, T., Eve, J., Horning, J.J.: Efficient $LR(1)$ parsers. Acta Informatica 2, 12–39 (1973)
6. Pager, D.: A practical general method for constructing $LR(k)$ parsers. Acta Informatica 7, 249–268 (1977)
7. Knuth, D.E.: On the translation of languages from left to right. Information & Control 8, 607–639 (1965)
8. Pottier, F., Régis-Gianas, Y.: The Menhir parser generator, `http://gallium.inria.fr/~fpottier/menhir/`
9. Jourdan, J.H., Pottier, F., Leroy, X.: Coq code for validating $LR(1)$ parsers, `http://www.eleves.ens.fr/home/jjourdan/parserValidator.tgz`
10. Filliâtre, J.-C., Letouzey, P.: Functors for Proofs and Programs. In: Schmidt, D. (ed.) ESOP 2004. LNCS, vol. 2986, pp. 370–384. Springer, Heidelberg (2004)
11. ISO/IEC: Programming languages — C (2007) International standard ISO/IEC 9899:TC3
12. Padioleau, Y.: Parsing C/C++ Code without Pre-processing. In: de Moor, O., Schwartzbach, M.I. (eds.) CC 2009. LNCS, vol. 5501, pp. 109–125. Springer, Heidelberg (2009)
13. Pottier, F., Régis-Gianas, Y.: Towards efficient, typed LR parsers. Electronic Notes in Theoretical Computer Science 148(2), 155–180 (2006)

14. Ford, B.: Packrat parsing: simple, powerful, lazy, linear time. In: ACM International Conference on Functional Programming (ICFP), pp. 36–47 (October 2002)
15. Ford, B.: Parsing expression grammars: a recognition-based syntactic foundation. In: ACM Symposium on Principles of Programming Languages (POPL), pp. 111–122 (January 2004)
16. Warth, A., Douglass, J.R., Millstein, T.D.: Packrat parsers can support left recursion. In: ACM Workshop on Evaluation and Semantics-Based Program Manipulation (PEPM), pp. 103–110 (January 2008)
17. Koprowski, A., Binsztok, H.: TRX: A formally verified parser interpreter. Logical Methods in Computer Science 7 (2011)
18. Wisnesky, R., Malecha, G., Morrisett, G.: Certified web services in Ynot. In: Workshop on Automated Specification and Verification of Web Systems (July 2009)
19. Samet, H.: Automatically Proving the Correctness of Translations Involving Optimized Code. PhD thesis, Stanford University (1975)
20. Pnueli, A., Siegel, M., Singerman, E.: Translation Validation. In: Steffen, B. (ed.) TACAS 1998. LNCS, vol. 1384, pp. 151–166. Springer, Heidelberg (1998)
21. Necula, G.C.: Translation validation for an optimizing compiler. In: ACM Conference on Programming Language Design and Implementation (PLDI), pp. 83–95. ACM Press (2000)
22. Tristan, J.B., Leroy, X.: A simple, verified validator for software pipelining. In: ACM Symposium on Principles of Programming Languages (POPL), pp. 83–92. ACM Press (2010)
23. Klein, G., Nipkow, T.: A machine-checked model for a Java-like language, virtual machine and compiler. ACM Transactions on Programming Languages and Systems 28, 619–695 (2006)
24. Aho, A.V., Ullman, J.D.: The theory of parsing, translation, and compiling. Prentice-Hall (1972)
25. Sozeau, M.: Program-ing finger trees in Coq. In: ACM International Conference on Functional Programming (ICFP), pp. 13–24 (September 2007)

Adding Equations to System F Types

Neelakantan R. Krishnaswami[1] and Nick Benton[2]

[1] Max Planck Institute for Software Systems
neelk@mpi-sws.org
[2] Microsoft Research
nick@microsoft.com

Abstract. We present an extension of System F with types for term-level equations. This internalization of the rich equational theory of the polymorphic lambda calculus yields an expressive core language, suitable for formalizing features such as Haskell's rewriting rules mechanism or Extended ML signatures.

1 Introduction

Abstraction, modularity and information hiding are fundamental principles of software engineering and language design. Yet programming against an interface is often difficult, as conventional type systems can express only the most basic of the many assumptions and guarantees made by a module. The problem is that *too much* information is hidden, or only present in informal, ambiguous documentation. Dependent types allow much richer interfaces but come with their own costs, including a significant increase in the complexity of the language. Hoare-style program logics also allow much more expressive interfaces, but as well as being highly complex are arguably too decoupled from the underlying programming language; logics have their own syntax and typing cannot exploit logical specifications.

Compilers face problems similar to those of developers. If an optimizing compiler respects the modular structure of a program, it loses vital information that it could use to generate better code. But looking through abstractions to implementations is expensive and non-modular. Some compilers produce enriched interfaces for compiled modules that summarize the results of static analyses but the connection between this metadata and the program is often somewhat ad hoc, making it hard to soundly exploit the extra information in non-trivial transformations of client code.

In this paper, we address the question of how to incorporate more precise module specifications into a language via an extension of System F, the paradigmatic calculus for studying data abstraction. We restrict attention to specifications of a particular form, viz. equations between terms, understood as contextual equivalences. Equations are made part of the type system, making precise how they may be scoped, passed around and exploited. In this regard, our system resembles a restricted form of dependent types. However, equations are not actually proved within the language. A denotational model makes precise what semantic

H. Seidl (Ed.): ESOP 2012, LNCS 7211, pp. 417–435, 2012.

conditions must be verified in order to establish equalities; various techniques, from automatic analyses to interactive manual proofs, could be soundly used to check the conditions. This aspect resembles the treatment of entailment checking as a delegated semantic side-condition in Hoare-style program logics. The contributions of the paper may be summarized as follows:

- We extend the type system of F with a type of term-level equations.
- We illustrate how expressive this language is by encoding some of patterns of programming with dependent types and GADTs.
- We give a very simple parametric [20,22] relational semantics to our extended language.
- We prove that our extended language is type-safe and terminating.
- We illustrate how the addition of equations enables useful new reasoning patterns in parametricity proofs, such as proofs of the equivalence of existential ML-style module interfaces with Church-style datatype encodings.

2 Informal Overview

This section describes our language, $F_=$, semi-formally, and gives examples of its use. The grammar is shown in Figure 1. The types of $F_=$ are the usual ones of System F, extended with a new type former $e \equiv_A e'$, which asserts the equality of e and e' at type A. Since types now contain terms, and in particular term-level variables, we change the syntax of the function type from $A \to B$ to $(x : A) \to B$, so that function arguments of type A can be referenced within B. This resembles the dependent product of dependent type theory, and ensures that the argument of a function can be mentioned in any returned equality types.

The terms of the language include those of System F, including variables x; type abstractions $\Lambda\alpha.\ e$ and type applications $e\ [A]$; and term abstractions $\lambda x.\ e$ and term application $e\ e'$. We defer giving the precise typing rules until Section 3, but they very closely resemble their counterparts in System F.

There are also two new term-level constants: $\bullet$ and abort. The term $\bullet$ is the sole inhabitant of the equality type $e \equiv_A e'$ when the equation holds (the type is uninhabited otherwise). We remark that $\bullet$ does not provide any intrinsic evidence of the equality — the right to introduce a $\bullet$ arises as a semantic side-condition. The absence of evidence keeps the term language very simple, since the $\bullet$ is merely a placeholder for the reflection of a fact in the semantic model back into the language's type system. The abort constant allows equational information to influence typing: it has arbitrary type, but only if the context is (semantically) inconsistent. One can thus do deep semantic proofs to justify complicated equations, inject those into the types, and then use simple syntactic means to handle the plumbing which pushes facts around to other parts of the program.

Figure 2 presents the notational abbreviations that we use in the remainder of the paper. These are mostly well-known Church encodings, but note particularly the weak sum type $\exists x : A.\ B$. We'll also assume standard syntactic sugar (e.g. projections, case analysis) associated with these abbreviations in examples. (The model we present in Section 3 can be used to show that these suggestive abbreviations actually have the intended semantics.)

Types	$A ::= \alpha \mid \forall\alpha.\ A \mid (x : A) \to B \mid e \equiv_A e'$
Terms	$e ::= \Lambda\alpha.\ e \mid e\,[A] \mid \lambda x.\ e \mid e\,e' \mid \bullet \mid \mathsf{abort} \mid x$
Values	$v ::= \Lambda\alpha.\ e \mid \lambda x.\ e \mid \bullet$
Contexts	$\Gamma ::= \cdot \mid \Gamma, \alpha \mid \Gamma, x : A$

Fig. 1. Syntax

$$
\begin{aligned}
A \to B &= (x : A) \to B, \text{ when } x \notin \mathrm{FV}(B)\\
\forall x : A.\ B &= (x : A) \to B\\
\forall x_1 : A_1, \ldots, x_n : A_n.\ B &= \forall x_1 : A_1.\ \ldots \forall x_n : A_n.\ B\\
A \times B &= \forall\alpha.\ (A \to B \to \alpha) \to \alpha\\
1 &= \forall\alpha.\ \alpha \to \alpha\\
\exists x : A.\ B &= \forall\alpha.\ ((x : A) \to B \to \alpha) \to \alpha\\
\exists x_1 : A_1, \ldots, x_n : A_n.\ B &= \exists x_1 : A_1.\ \ldots \exists x_n : A_n.\ B\\
\exists\alpha.\ A &= \forall\beta.\ (\forall\alpha.\ A \to \beta) \to \beta\\
A + B &= \forall\alpha.\ (A \to \alpha) \to (B \to \alpha) \to \alpha\\
\bot &= \forall\alpha.\ \alpha\\
\neg A &= A \to \bot
\end{aligned}
$$

Fig. 2. Type Abbreviations

2.1 Examples

Refined Typings. Equations allow extra constraints to be imposed on arguments and extra guarantees to be given for results. For example, a function that should only be called with commutative binary operations on a type A might be given a type like

$$(f : A \to A \to A) \to (\forall a : A, a' : A. f\,a\,a' \equiv_A f\,a'\,a) \to A$$

For producing values together with assertions of their equational properties, one makes use of existential packages. For example, a function yielding idempotent unary operations on A from arguments of type B could be typed as

$$B \to (\exists f : A \to A. \forall a : A. f\,(f\,a) \equiv_A f\,a)$$

Clients can project both the underlying value and the equational information from such packages and use them to justify their own equations.

Datatype Encodings. More useful examples of $F_=$ involve enriching the signatures of modules, encoded using second-order existential types in the standard way [17,21]. We now give a few examples of how one can type abstract datatypes in $F_=$, encapsulating types, operations on those types and algebraic properties satisfied by those operations.

Booleans We begin by giving an $F_=$ encoding of an interface to the Booleans.

$$
\begin{array}{l}
\exists \mathsf{bool}, \\
\quad \mathit{true} : \mathsf{bool}, \\
\quad \mathit{false} : \mathsf{bool}, \\
\quad \mathit{if} : \forall \alpha.\ \mathsf{bool} \to \alpha \to \alpha \to \alpha. \\
\quad \forall \alpha, a : \alpha, a' : \alpha.\ \mathit{if}\ [\alpha]\ \mathit{true}\ a\ a' \equiv_\alpha a\ \times \\
\quad \forall \alpha, a : \alpha, a' : \alpha.\ \mathit{if}\ [\alpha]\ \mathit{false}\ a\ a' \equiv_\alpha a'
\end{array}
$$

The signature exposes constructors and eliminators for the boolean type, together with their β-theory as equational properties. A natural question is how this module type relates to the traditional Church encoding of booleans. One can certainly give an implementation of the abstract datatype in terms of that encoding, in which bool is instantiated with $\forall \alpha.\ \alpha \to \alpha \to \alpha$. More surpisingly perhaps, as we will show more formally in Section 4, the extended module type uniquely characterizes the booleans, and $F_=$ allows clients to exploit the consequences of this semantic fact. Note that the interface does not explicitly state any of the properties which ordinarily characterize datatypes, such as the disjointness of *true* and *false*, or that they are the only constructors for the boolean type. However, the presence of the eliminator and its equational theory, plus parametricity, are sufficient to derive these properties: parametricity ensures that *true* and *false* are the only way to construct the booleans, and furthermore, they must be disjoint, or else we could use the equational theory of *if* to derive a contradiction.

Natural Numbers As an example of a non-finite type, we can give an interface for the type of natural numbers:

$$
\begin{array}{l}
\exists \mathsf{nat}, \\
\quad z : \mathsf{nat}, \\
\quad s : \mathsf{nat} \to \mathsf{nat}, \\
\quad \mathit{iter} : \forall \alpha.\ \alpha \to (\alpha \to \alpha) \to \mathsf{nat} \to \alpha. \\
\quad \forall \alpha, i, f.\ \mathit{iter}\ [\alpha]\ i\ f\ z \equiv_\alpha i\ \times \\
\quad \forall \alpha, i, f, x.\ \mathit{iter}\ [\alpha]\ i\ f\ (s\ x) \equiv_\alpha f(\mathit{iter}\ [\alpha]\ i\ f\ x)
\end{array}
$$

This interface says that we have an abstract type nat, with constructors z and s. We have an eliminator *iter*, and two equations explaining how to eliminate zero and successor.

This signature does *not* expose the representation of nat, nor does it specify the implementation of *iter*. We are free to implement the natural numbers in any way we like – for example, with a binary (rather than unary) representation. Furthermore, in Section 4 we will prove that this signature is isomorphic to the Church encoding of the natural numbers, which means that any implementation of this type actually is an implementation of the natural numbers.

Lists Here is a possible interface for the type of lists of booleans.

$$
\begin{array}{l}
\exists \mathsf{List}_{\mathsf{bool}}, \\
\quad \mathit{nil} : \mathsf{List}_{\mathsf{bool}},
\end{array}
$$

$$
\begin{aligned}
& cons : \mathsf{bool} \to \mathsf{List}_{\mathsf{bool}} \to \mathsf{List}_{\mathsf{bool}}, \\
& map : (\mathsf{bool} \to \mathsf{bool}) \to \mathsf{List}_{\mathsf{bool}} \to \mathsf{List}_{\mathsf{bool}}, \\
& fold : \forall \alpha.\ \alpha \to (\mathsf{bool} \to \alpha \to \alpha) \to \mathsf{List}_{\mathsf{bool}} \to \alpha, \\
& map\ id_{\mathsf{bool}} \equiv_{\mathsf{List}_{\mathsf{bool}}} id_{\mathsf{List}_{\mathsf{bool}}} \times \\
& \forall f.\ map\ f\ nil \equiv_{\mathsf{List}_{\mathsf{bool}}} nil \times \\
& \forall f, b, bs.\ map\ f\ (cons\ b\ bs) \equiv_{\mathsf{List}_{\mathsf{bool}}} cons\ (f\ b)\ (map\ f\ bs) \times \\
& \forall f, g : \mathsf{bool} \to \mathsf{bool}.\ (map\ f) \circ (map\ g) \equiv_{\mathsf{List}_{\mathsf{bool}}} map\ (f \circ g) \times \\
& \forall \alpha, a, f.\ fold\ [\alpha]\ a\ f\ nil \equiv_{\alpha} a \times \\
& \forall \alpha, a, f, b, bs.\ fold\ [\alpha]\ a\ f\ (cons\ b\ bs) \equiv_{\alpha} f\ b\ (fold\ [\alpha]\ a\ f\ bs)
\end{aligned}
$$

This example illustrates that the interface does not have to precisely match the constructors of the Church encoding for lists — in this interface, we include the *map* operation. However, since the interface tells us what the behavior of *map* is, we can still prove that all values of list type can be built up just from *nil* and *cons*.

This lets us greatly extend the interface to a module, without having to give up natural reasoning principles for it. For example, suppose we extend lists with a left fold operator, characterized by the following signature:

$$
\begin{aligned}
& foldl : \forall \alpha.\ \alpha \to (\mathsf{bool} \to \alpha \to \alpha) \to \mathsf{List}_{\mathsf{bool}} \to \alpha \\
& \forall \alpha, i, f.\ foldl\ [\alpha]\ i\ f\ nil \equiv_{\alpha} i \\
& \forall \alpha, i, f, b, bs.\ foldl\ [\alpha]\ i\ f\ (cons\ b\ bs) \equiv_{\alpha} foldl\ [\alpha]\ (f\ b\ i)\ f\ bs
\end{aligned}
$$

With this definition in hand, clients can establish things like the fact that if a function is associative and commutative, then the left and right folds coincide — a fact which we can encode in types:

$$
\begin{aligned}
& assoc_A(f) \triangleq \forall a_1, a_2, a_3.\ f\ (f\ a_1\ a_2)\ a_3 \equiv_A f\ a_1 (f\ a_2\ a_3) \\
& comm_A(f) \triangleq \forall a_1, a_2.\ f\ a_1\ a_2 \equiv_A f\ a_2\ a_1
\end{aligned}
$$

$$
\forall \alpha, f, i, bs.\ assoc_{\alpha}(f) \to comm_{\alpha}(i) \to fold\ f\ i\ bs \equiv_{\alpha} foldl\ f\ i\ bs
$$

Here we exploit the usual Curry-Howard pun, using the function type to do the duty of a logical implication. The proof of the equation above goes by induction on the nil/cons structure of lists, which is only possible because we can prove that this structure exists via parametricity.

2.2 Applications

Deforestation of Higher-Order Programs. Consider the following sequence of equational rewrites.

$$
\begin{aligned}
(map\ not) \circ (map\ not) &= map\ (not \circ not) \\
&= map\ id_{\mathsf{bool}} \\
&= id_{\mathsf{List}_{\mathsf{bool}}}
\end{aligned}
$$

This is a standard example of deforestation [15], in which two intermediate data structures (a negated list and a double-negated list) are not generated, in order to save memory usage. Deforestation offers many interesting examples, since it appeals to equational properties which go well beyond simple inlining and other forms of compile-time β-reduction.

However, now consider the following expression h:

$$h \triangleq \lambda map.\ (map\ not) \circ (map\ not)$$

The question is, can the body of h be simplified? In general, the answer will be no — unless we can prove that only *map* functionals satisfying the right equational properties flow into the lambda, we are not justified in rewriting this expression. Hence we are in the somewhat ironic position that deforestation — an optimization invented to make higher-order programming more efficient — is often inapplicable in client programs which make use of higher-order functions.

One way around this difficulty would be if we could prove the soundness of these transformations in *open* contexts, where we don't know exactly which lambda-terms might flow into a higher-order program. By adding the necessary information as type data to the programming language, we can rely on the necessary equational properties to hold without having to make the concrete bindings of terms like *map* and *not* visible.

So by rewriting h to pass in the desired properties, we can ensure that a rewriting is performable *in an open context*:

$$\begin{aligned} h\ :\ & ((map : \mathsf{bool} \to \mathsf{bool}) \to \mathsf{List}_{\mathsf{bool}} \to \mathsf{List}_{\mathsf{bool}}) \\ & \to map\ id_{\mathsf{bool}} \equiv_{\mathsf{List}_{\mathsf{bool}} \to \mathsf{List}_{\mathsf{bool}}} id_{\mathsf{List}_{\mathsf{bool}}} \\ & \to \forall f, g : \mathsf{bool} \to \mathsf{bool}.\ (map\ f) \circ (map\ g) \equiv_{\mathsf{List}_{\mathsf{bool}} \to \mathsf{List}_{\mathsf{bool}}} map\ (f \circ g) \\ & \to \mathsf{List}_{\mathsf{bool}} \to \mathsf{List}_{\mathsf{bool}} \end{aligned}$$

$$h \triangleq \lambda map.\ \lambda pf.\ \lambda pf'.\ (map\ not) \circ (map\ not)$$

Here, we do not need to know what the actual implementation of *map* is, since we have stipulated that the function h must be called only with functions which have the equational properties we need them to satisfy, and hence we can conclude that h is equivalent to *id*.

GADT-style Encodings and Making Unsafe Operations Safe. Generalized algebraic data types [11] extend ordinary algebraic datatypes with index information permitting static types to contain information about the specific data constructors used to build them. This lets programmers use dynamic runtime tests to gain additional information about the static type of terms. Since our type system lets us directly place information about terms into types, many of these encodings can be fit into our framework.

Concretely, consider the following specification of an option type.

$$\begin{aligned} & \exists \mathsf{option}_A, \\ & \quad none : \mathsf{option}_A, \\ & \quad some : A \to \mathsf{option}_A, \\ & \quad case : \forall \alpha.\ \mathsf{option}_A \to \alpha \to (A \to \alpha) \to \alpha. \end{aligned}$$

$$\forall \alpha.\ (v : \alpha) \to (f : A \to \alpha) \to \mathit{case}\ [\alpha]\ \mathit{none}\ v\ f \equiv_{\alpha} v \ \times$$
$$\forall \alpha.\ (a : A) \to (v : \alpha) \to (f : A \to \alpha) \to \mathit{case}\ [\alpha]\ (\mathit{some}\ a)\ v\ f \equiv_{\alpha} f\ a$$

This specification follows the pattern of the boolean and list types earlier, containing the *none* and *some* constructors as well as the *case* eliminator for them, plus equations describing the β-theory of *case*.

We can use this specification to write refined case programs which return type-level evidence of equalities. First, we define a variant case function that returns not only a value, but also a proof that the returned value is equal to the input.

$$\begin{array}{l} \mathit{case}' \ : \ (x : \mathsf{option}_A) \to (x \equiv_{\mathsf{option}_A} \mathit{none}) + (\exists a : A.\ x \equiv_{\mathsf{option}_A} \mathit{some}\ a) \\ \mathit{case}' \triangleq \lambda x.\ \mathit{case}\ [\ldots]\ (\mathit{inl}\ \bullet)\ (\lambda a.\ \mathit{inr}\ (a, \bullet)) \end{array}$$

As can be seen from the type, case' takes an option and returns a sum type. If the argument is *none*, it returns the left branch containing the static fact that the argument is *none*, and if the argument is a *some*, then it returns a value a such that *some* a is equal to the argument of *case*. All of the equality type terms are witnessed by $\bullet$ terms.

$$\begin{array}{l} \mathit{valOf} \ : \ (x : \mathsf{option}_A) \to \neg(x \equiv_{\mathsf{option}_A} \mathit{none}) \to A \\ \mathit{valOf} \triangleq \lambda x.\ \lambda pf.\ \mathit{case}\ [A]\ \mathsf{abort}\ (\lambda a.\ a) \end{array}$$

This operator takes an option and a proof that it is not equal to *none*. This lets us pass abort as an argument in the untaken branch, since we know the *case* can only be reduced when it has a proof that its argument is not *none*.

As before, these operations are provably correct only when injectivity and disjointness hold, and again, these properties are provable from the interface specification. As a result, we can define these apparently-unsafe operators *outside* the body of the module, since our program *valOf* only relies on the equational properties specified in the interface, and not on the specifics of the implementation.

3 Syntax and Semantics

Before proceeding to the metatheory, we give a high-level overview of the structure of this section.

1. We give the syntax of terms and types, and an *untyped* operational semantics for our programming language. This language contains an abort construct which can get stuck.
2. We define a "pre-typing" relation, which judges whether terms and types are syntactically well-formed. Unlike a true type system, our pretyping system is (by design) unsound: there are no restrictions on the use of the abort connective.
3. However, the pretyping relation offers enough structure that we can define a binary logical relation giving semantics to each of the type constructors, by structural induction on the pretyping relation.

$$\frac{}{v \Downarrow v} \qquad \frac{e_0 \Downarrow \lambda x.\, e_0' \qquad [e_1/x]e_0' \Downarrow v}{e_0\; e_1 \Downarrow v} \qquad \frac{e_0 \Downarrow \Lambda\alpha.\, e_0' \qquad [A/\alpha]e_0 \Downarrow v}{e_0\; [A] \Downarrow v}$$

Fig. 3. Operational Semantics

$$\boxed{\Gamma \rhd \mathsf{ok}} \qquad \boxed{\Gamma \rhd A} \qquad \boxed{\Gamma \rhd e : A}$$

$$\frac{}{\cdot \rhd \mathsf{ok}} \qquad \frac{\Gamma \rhd \mathsf{ok}}{\Gamma, \alpha \rhd \mathsf{ok}} \qquad \frac{\Gamma \rhd \mathsf{ok} \qquad \Gamma \rhd A}{\Gamma, x : A \rhd \mathsf{ok}}$$

$$\frac{\Gamma \rhd \mathsf{ok} \qquad \alpha \in \Gamma}{\Gamma \rhd \alpha} \qquad \frac{\Gamma, \alpha \rhd A}{\Gamma \rhd \forall\alpha.\, A} \qquad \frac{\Gamma \rhd A \qquad \Gamma, x : A \rhd B}{\Gamma \rhd (x : A) \to B}$$

$$\frac{\Gamma \rhd A \qquad \Gamma \rhd e : A \qquad \Gamma \rhd e' : A}{\Gamma \rhd e \equiv_A e'}$$

$$\frac{\Gamma, x : A \rhd e : B}{\Gamma \rhd \lambda x.\, e : (x : A) \to B} \qquad \frac{\Gamma \rhd e : (x : A) \to B \qquad \Gamma \rhd e' : A}{\Gamma \rhd e\; e' : [e/x]B}$$

$$\frac{\Gamma, \alpha \rhd e : A}{\Gamma \rhd \Lambda\alpha.\, e : \forall\alpha.\, A} \qquad \frac{\Gamma \rhd e : \forall\alpha.\, B \qquad \Gamma \rhd A}{\Gamma \rhd e\; [A] : [A/\alpha]B} \qquad \frac{\Gamma \rhd \mathsf{ok} \qquad x : A \in \Gamma}{\Gamma \rhd x : A}$$

$$\frac{\Gamma \rhd e \equiv_A e'}{\Gamma \rhd \bullet : e \equiv_A e'}\;(\textsc{Danger1}) \qquad \frac{\Gamma \rhd A}{\Gamma \rhd \mathsf{abort} : A}\;(\textsc{Danger2})$$

Fig. 4. Pretyping Relation

4. Then, we give the true typing relation, which refines the pretyping relation to include semantic side-conditions on equality formation and the use of abort.
5. Finally, we prove the identity extension lemma for the true typing relation.

Readers familiar with PER models for System F (e.g., [6]) will find this proof structure quite familiar. We begin with an untyped model of computation as a universe, and then define a semantics of types as relations on the universe by induction on the derivation of the pretyping relation. The main technical novelty in our approach is that our types may contain terms, and we thus need to interpret types in a context containing interpretations of the terms.

The operational semantics for our programming language is given in Figure 3, and is a standard call-by-name semantics. There is no evaluation rule for the constant $\bullet$, since it has no explicit elimination form. There is no reduction rule for abort — this term creates a stuck computation, since it indicates unreachable code.

In Figure 4, we give the pretyping rules. We have three judgements:

- The $\Gamma \rhd$ ok judgement judges whether a context is well-formed, and
- the $\Gamma \rhd A$ judgement judges whether a type A is well-formed in context Γ, and
- the $\Gamma \rhd e : A$ judgement judges whether a term e is well-formed with respect to pretype A in context Γ.

All three of these judgements are mutually-recursive, since the equality type $e \equiv_A e'$ contains terms, and its well-formedness rule asserts that e and e' must have pretype A. The rules mostly resemble F's rules, with the variation that both term and type applications need to perform a substitution (rather than solely type application, as in ordinary System F).

The two surprising rules of the system are DANGER1 and DANGER2, which are the rules for introducing the equality type and the abort keyword. As a result, the pretype system is obviously unsound, since we can freely introduce the stuck term abort wherever we like.

Of course, we will eventually refine these two rules so that equalities can only be used to introduce true equalities, and abort can only be used in contexts under which we can prove that evaluation can never reach that point. Do note, however, that in this setting, it is the existence of abort which gives the equality type its force. There are no elimination rules for equality types, and so the only way that programs can make use of equalities is to exploit the equations in context to write abort at certain places.

Now, we state the basic syntactic substitution properties of the calculus.

Theorem 1. *(Syntactic Substitution) Suppose* $\Gamma \rhd A$ *and* $\Gamma \rhd e : B$. *Then*

- *If* $\Gamma, \alpha, \Gamma' \rhd ok$ *then* $\Gamma, [A/\alpha]\Gamma' \rhd ok$.
- *If* $\Gamma, \alpha, \Gamma' \rhd B$ *then* $\Gamma, [A/\alpha]\Gamma' \rhd [A/\alpha]B$.
- *If* $\Gamma, \alpha, \Gamma' \rhd e' : C$ *then* $\Gamma, [A/\alpha]\Gamma' \rhd [A/\alpha]e' : [A/\alpha]C$.
- *If* $\Gamma, x : A, \Gamma' \rhd ok$ *then* $\Gamma, [e/x]\Gamma' \rhd ok$.
- *If* $\Gamma, x : A, \Gamma' \rhd B$ *then* $\Gamma, [e/x]\Gamma' \rhd [e/x]B$.
- *If* $\Gamma, x : A, \Gamma' \rhd e' : C$ *then* $\Gamma, [e/x]\Gamma' \rhd [e/x]e' : [e/x]C$.

The proofs of these theorems are a routine structural induction.

To add semantic side-conditions to the DANGER1 and DANGER2 rules, we need to give a relational semantics of types, since we need to be able to compare terms for equality. In Figure 6, we give the logical relation defining the relational interpretation of types, as a structural recursion over the pretyping derivations $\Gamma \rhd A$. For each type constructor, we give the relation defining equality at that type. Furthermore, since we are defining our relations by induction on the structure of the pretyping derivation $\Gamma \rhd A$, we also parameterize this relation by a grounding substitution γ.

The two key judgements in this relation begin with $Env(\Gamma \rhd \text{ok})$, which defines the set of well-formed grounding substitutions for the environment Γ. As a context consists of a sequence of type variables α and term variables $x : A$, the grounding substitutions consist of sequences of triples (A, A', R) of closed types and the relations between the terms of those types, which ground the type

$$
\begin{aligned}
(\cdot)_0 &= \cdot \\
(\gamma, (e, e')/x)_0 &= \gamma_0, (e/x) \\
(\gamma, (A, A', R)/\alpha)_0 &= \gamma_0, (A/\alpha) \\
\\
(\cdot)_1 &= \cdot \\
(\gamma, (e, e')/x)_1 &= \gamma_1, (e'/x) \\
(\gamma, (A, A', R)/\alpha)_1 &= \gamma_1, (A'/\alpha) \\
\\
\gamma(e) &= (\gamma_0(e), \gamma_1(e)) \\
\gamma(A) &= (\gamma_0(e), \gamma_1(A))
\end{aligned}
$$

Fig. 5. Operations on Relational Substitutions

variables α, and pairs of expressions (e, e') which lie in the relation for A to ground each term variable.

As γ is a relational substitution, we also need operations to extract ordinary substitutions from it. These operations are defined in Figure 5. Given γ, the substitution γ_0 takes the left components of the relational substitution, and γ_1 takes the right components. We write $\gamma(e)$ as shorthand for the pair $(\gamma_0(e), \gamma_1(e))$, and similarly we write $\gamma(A)$ for $(\gamma_0(A), \gamma_1(A))$.

The environment relation is used mutually-recursively to define the relation $Val(\Gamma \rhd A)(\gamma)$, which relates pairs of closed values of type A in the context Γ closed by the substitution γ. This definition follows the usual pattern of logical relations: type variables α look up the appropriate relation in the context γ, and the value relation for function space $(x : A) \to B$ relates two functions f and g if they take related arguments to related results.

The interpretation of the universal quantifier $\forall\alpha.\ B$ says that two terms are related if for all value relations between pretypes A and A' the type application preserves the relation. By quantifying over relations between arbitrary values, we avoid recursively mentioning the definition of the logical relation, and thereby avoid circularity. This is a syntactic version of the techniques used in PER models of polymorphism: fixing a universe ahead of time lets us consider the intersection of all relations on that universe, without running afoul of the apparent circularity of impredicative quantification.

Finally, we define the value relation for equality types $Val(\Gamma \rhd e \equiv_A e')(\gamma)$ as the pair $(\bullet, \bullet)$, but *only if* the pair $(\gamma_0(e), \gamma_1(e'))$ is in the relation for A. Otherwise the relation is empty. This gives the semantic sense in which the equality type is an equality type: it is a type containing a single unit value when the equality is true, and is the empty type when it is not.

We also include the definition $Exp(\Gamma \rhd A)(\gamma)$, which are pairs of expressions reducing to values related by $Val(\Gamma \rhd A)(\gamma)$. This is an auxiliary definition simplifying the definitions of values and environments.

Having fixed the semantics of types, we give the true typing rules in Figure 7. As before, we have three mutually-recursive judgements, $\Gamma \vdash \text{ok}$, for well-formed contexts, $\Gamma \vdash A$, for well-formed types, and $\Gamma \vdash e : A$ for well-typing. All of the typing rules precisely mirror the pretyping rules, with the exception of the equality and abort rules.

$$
\begin{aligned}
&\mathit{Val}(\Gamma \rhd \alpha)(\gamma) = \text{let } (A, B, R) \;=\; \gamma(\alpha) \text{ in } R \\
&\mathit{Val}(\Gamma \rhd (x : A) \to B)(\gamma) = \\
&\quad \left\{ \langle \lambda x.\, e, \lambda x.\, e' \rangle \;\middle|\; \begin{array}{l} \cdot \rhd \lambda x.\, e : \gamma_0((x : A) \to B) \text{ and} \\ \cdot \rhd \lambda x.\, e' : \gamma_1((x : A) \to B) \text{ and} \\ \forall e_0, e_0' \in \mathit{Exp}(\Gamma \rhd A)(\gamma). \\ \quad \langle [e_0/x]e, [e_0'/x]e' \rangle \in \mathit{Exp}(\Gamma, x : A \rhd B)(\gamma, \langle e_0, e_0' \rangle /x) \end{array} \right\} \\
&\mathit{Val}(\Gamma \rhd \forall \alpha.\, B)(\gamma) = \\
&\quad \left\{ \langle \Lambda \alpha.\, e, \Lambda \alpha'.\, e' \rangle \;\middle|\; \begin{array}{l} \cdot \rhd \Lambda \alpha.\, e : \gamma_0(\forall \alpha.\, B) \text{ and} \\ \cdot \rhd \Lambda \alpha.\, e' : \gamma_1(\forall \alpha.\, B) \text{ and} \\ \forall A, A', R. \\ \quad \cdot \rhd A \text{ and } \cdot \rhd A' \text{ and} \\ \quad R \subseteq \{\langle v, v' \rangle \mid \cdot \rhd v : A \text{ and } \cdot \rhd v' : A'\} \text{ and} \\ \quad \langle [A/\alpha]e, [A'/\alpha']e' \rangle \in \mathit{Exp}(\Gamma, \alpha \rhd B)(\gamma, (A, A', R)/\alpha) \end{array} \right\} \\
&\mathit{Val}(\Gamma \rhd e_0 \equiv_A e_1)(\gamma) = \{\langle \bullet, \bullet \rangle \mid \langle \gamma_0(e_0), \gamma_1(e_1) \rangle \in \mathit{Exp}(\Gamma \rhd A)(\gamma)\}
\end{aligned}
$$

$$
\begin{aligned}
&\mathit{Exp}(\Gamma \rhd A)(\gamma) = \\
&\quad \left\{ \langle e_0, e_1 \rangle \;\middle|\; \begin{array}{l} \cdot \rhd e_0 : \gamma_0(A) \text{ and } \cdot \rhd e_1 : \gamma_1(A) \text{ and} \\ \exists v_0, v_1. \begin{array}{l} \gamma_0(e_0) \Downarrow v_0 \text{ and } \gamma_1(e_1) \Downarrow v_1 \text{ and} \\ \langle v_0, v_1 \rangle \in \mathit{Val}(\Gamma \rhd A)(\gamma) \end{array} \end{array} \right\}
\end{aligned}
$$

$$
\begin{aligned}
&\mathit{Env}(\cdot \rhd \text{ok}) = \{\langle\rangle\} \\
&\mathit{Env}(\Gamma, x : A \rhd \text{ok}) = \{(\gamma, \langle e, e' \rangle /x) \mid \gamma \in \mathit{Env}(\Gamma \rhd \text{ok}) \text{ and } (e, e') \in \mathit{Exp}(\Gamma \rhd A)(\gamma)\} \\
&\mathit{Env}(\Gamma, \alpha \rhd \text{ok}) = \\
&\quad \left\{ (\gamma, (A, A', R)/\alpha) \;\middle|\; \begin{array}{l} \gamma \in \mathit{Env}(\Gamma \rhd \text{ok}) \text{ and } \cdot \rhd A \text{ and } \cdot \rhd A' \text{ and} \\ R \subseteq \{\langle v, v' \rangle \mid \cdot \rhd v : A \text{ and } \cdot \rhd v' : A'\} \end{array} \right\}
\end{aligned}
$$

Fig. 6. Relational Semantics

Each of these has a semantic side-condition controlling when they can be used. These side-conditions mean that the type-checking problem is not decidable, since potentially arbitrary mathematical reasoning may be needed to show that the rule applies. However, the soundness theorem for the language ensures that once the side-conditions are discharged, then evaluation cannot alter the typability of of the program under reduction.

The premise of the equality rule contains the non-syntactic premise that $\Gamma \models e = e' : A$. This means that in all semantic environments $\gamma \in \mathit{Env}(\Gamma \rhd \text{ok})$, the pair $(\gamma_0(e), \gamma_1(e'))$ must lie in the expression relation for the type A. This means that the two expressions must be equivalent to introduce an equality type.

Similarly, the premise of the abort rule is that $\Gamma \models \bot$ must hold, which means that there are *no* environments in $\mathit{Env}(\Gamma \rhd \text{ok})$. This means that the context Γ is a contradictory one, with no environments that can satisfy it.

Now, we can prove a semantic version of the substitution theorem.

Theorem 2. *(Semantic Substitution)*

- *Suppose* $\Gamma \rhd A$ *and* $(\gamma, \gamma(A)/\alpha, \gamma') \in \mathit{Env}(\Gamma, \alpha, \Gamma' \rhd ok)$. *Then*
  - $(\gamma, \gamma') \in \mathit{Env}(\Gamma, [A/\alpha]\Gamma' \rhd ok)$
  - *If* $(v, v') \in \mathit{Val}(\Gamma, \alpha, \Gamma' \rhd e)(B)(\gamma, \gamma(A)/\alpha, \gamma')$, *then* $(v, v') \in \mathit{Val}(\Gamma, [A/\alpha]\Gamma' \rhd [A/\alpha]B)(\gamma, \gamma')$.
  - *If* $(e, e') \in \mathit{Exp}(\Gamma, \alpha, \Gamma' \rhd e)(B)(\gamma, \gamma(A)/\alpha, \gamma')$, *then* $(e, e') \in \mathit{Exp}(\Gamma, [A/\alpha]\Gamma' \rhd [A/\alpha]B)(\gamma, \gamma')$.
- *Suppose* $\Gamma \rhd e : A$ *and* $(\gamma, \gamma(e)/x, \gamma') \in \mathit{Env}(\Gamma, x : A, \Gamma' \rhd ok)$. *Then*
  - $(\gamma, \gamma) \in \mathit{Env}(\Gamma, [e/x]\Gamma' \rhd ok)$.
  - *If* $(v, v') \in \mathit{Val}(\Gamma, x : A, \Gamma' \rhd e)(A)(\gamma, \gamma(e)/x, \gamma')$, *then* $(v, v') \in \mathit{Val}(\Gamma, [e/x]\Gamma' \rhd [e/x]A)(\gamma, \gamma')$.
  - *If* $(e, e') \in \mathit{Exp}(\Gamma, x : A, \Gamma' \rhd e)(A)(\gamma, \gamma(e)/x, \gamma')$, *then* $(e, e') \in \mathit{Exp}(\Gamma, [e/x]\Gamma' \rhd [e/x]A)(\gamma, \gamma')$.

These theorems follow from induction on the context and type pre-well-formedness judgements. We can use these theorems to prove Reynolds' abstraction theorem for our language.

Theorem 3. *(Abstraction Theorem) If* $\Gamma \vdash e : A$, *then* $\Gamma \models e = e : A$.

This theorem follows from a structural induction on the typing derivation, making use of the semantic substitution principles. Normalization and type-preservation follow immediately.

Corollary 1. *(Normalization) If* $\cdot \vdash e : A$, *then* $\exists v$ *such that* $e \Downarrow v$.

Corollary 2. *(Type Preservation) If* $\cdot \vdash e : A$ *and* $e \Downarrow v$, *then* $\cdot \vdash v : A$.

It is worth noting that the type preservation lemma is *exact* — the type of the result is exactly the same as the type of the original. We do not need any notion of type equality beyond the same syntactic equality (modulo α) that System F needed.

4 Existential Representations of Inductive Datatypes

A surprising feature of the examples in Section 2 is that we gave an apparently *existential* encoding of inductive datatypes such as the booleans. This is a little surprising, since the Church encodings of these types in System F are *universal*.

As a concrete example, recall the Church encoding of the boolean type.

- The type of Church booleans $\mathsf{cbool} = \forall\alpha.\ \alpha \to \alpha \to \alpha$.
- Truth is defined as $\Lambda\alpha.\ \lambda a.\ \lambda a'.\ a$.
- Falsity is defined as $\Lambda\alpha.\ \lambda a.\ \lambda a'.\ a'$.
- The conditional is $\mathit{if} : \mathsf{cbool} \to \forall\alpha.\ \alpha \to \alpha \to \alpha \triangleq \lambda b.\ b$.

Contrast this with the interface we gave for the boolean type:

$$\boxed{\Gamma \models e = e' : A} \qquad \boxed{\Gamma \models \bot}$$

$$\begin{array}{lcl} \Gamma \models e_0 = e_1 : A & \iff & \forall \gamma \in \mathit{Env}(\Gamma \rhd \mathrm{ok}).\ (\gamma_0(e_0), \gamma_1(e_1)) \in \mathit{Exp}(\Gamma \rhd A)(\gamma) \\ \Gamma \models \bot & \iff & \mathit{Env}(\Gamma \rhd \mathrm{ok}) = \emptyset \end{array}$$

$$\boxed{\Gamma \vdash \mathrm{ok}} \qquad \boxed{\Gamma \vdash A} \qquad \boxed{\Gamma \vdash e : A}$$

$$\frac{}{\cdot \vdash \mathrm{ok}} \qquad \frac{\Gamma \vdash \mathrm{ok}}{\Gamma, \alpha \vdash \mathrm{ok}} \qquad \frac{\Gamma \vdash \mathrm{ok} \quad \Gamma \vdash A}{\Gamma, x : A \vdash \mathrm{ok}}$$

$$\frac{\Gamma \vdash \mathrm{ok} \quad \alpha \in \Gamma}{\Gamma \vdash \alpha} \qquad \frac{\Gamma, \alpha \vdash A}{\Gamma \vdash \forall \alpha.\ A} \qquad \frac{\Gamma \vdash A \quad \Gamma, x : A \vdash B}{\Gamma \vdash (x : A) \to B}$$

$$\frac{\Gamma \vdash A \quad \Gamma \vdash e : A \quad \Gamma \vdash e' : A}{\Gamma \vdash e \equiv_A e'}$$

$$\frac{\Gamma, x : A \vdash e : B}{\Gamma \vdash \lambda x.\ e : (x : A) \to B} \qquad \frac{\Gamma \vdash e : (x : A) \to B \quad \Gamma \vdash e' : A}{\Gamma \vdash e\ e' : [e/x]B} \qquad \frac{\Gamma, \alpha \vdash e : A}{\Gamma \vdash \Lambda \alpha.\ e : \forall \alpha.\ A}$$

$$\frac{\Gamma \vdash e : \forall \alpha.\ B \quad \Gamma \vdash A}{\Gamma \vdash e\,[A] : [A/\alpha]B} \qquad \frac{\Gamma \vdash e \equiv_A e' \quad \Gamma \models e = e' : A}{\Gamma \vdash \bullet : e \equiv_A e'} \qquad \frac{\Gamma \vdash A \quad \Gamma \models \bot}{\Gamma \vdash \mathsf{abort} : A}$$

$$\frac{\Gamma \vdash \mathrm{ok} \quad x : A \in \Gamma}{\Gamma \vdash x : A}$$

Fig. 7. Typing

$$\begin{array}{l} B \equiv \\ \quad \exists \mathsf{bool} \\ \quad\ \ \mathit{true} : \mathsf{bool}, \\ \quad\ \ \mathit{false} : \mathsf{bool}, \\ \quad\ \ \mathit{if} : \forall \alpha.\ \mathsf{bool} \to \alpha \to \alpha \to \alpha. \\ \quad\ \ \forall \alpha, a : \alpha, a' : \alpha.\ \mathit{if}\ [\alpha]\ \mathit{true}\ a\ a' \equiv_\alpha a\ \times \\ \quad\ \ \forall \alpha, a : \alpha, a' : \alpha.\ \mathit{if}\ [\alpha]\ \mathit{false}\ a\ a' \equiv_\alpha a' \end{array}$$

Unlike the Church encoding, the interface completely conceals the representation type of the booleans, as well as the implementations of truth, falsity and if-then-else. The only constraint we place in the interface is to require the β-theory of the booleans to hold.

Now we will show that these two implementations of the booleans are actually the same. To do this, first note that we somehow need to compare an *arbitrary* element of the existential type to a particular set of elements of the Church type. Luckily, we have precisely the tools we need with the equality types of our calculus. The Church booleans can be represented as elements of the type

$$
\begin{array}{l}
B' \equiv \\
\quad \exists\ \mathit{true} : \mathsf{cbool}, \\
\quad\quad \mathit{false} : \mathsf{cbool}, \\
\quad\quad \mathit{true} \equiv_{\mathsf{cbool}} \Lambda\alpha.\ \lambda a.\ \lambda a'.\ a\ \times \\
\quad\quad \mathit{false} \equiv_{\mathsf{cbool}} \Lambda\alpha.\ \lambda a.\ \lambda a'.\ a'
\end{array}
$$

By using equality types, we ensure that we have a tuple whose first element is Church truth and whose second element is Church falsity.

This gives us the material we need to prove the following theorem:

Theorem 4. *(Equivalence of Boolean Types) We have an isomorphism between the types B and B'.*

Proof. To show this holds, we wil give explicit maps $i : B \to B'$ and $j : B' \to B$. Then we will show that $\cdot \models i \circ j = id : B'$ and that $\cdot \models j \circ i = id : B$. We give the definitions below, using the syntax for tuples and existentials for clarity.

$$i : B \to B' \triangleq \lambda b.\ \langle \Lambda\alpha.\ \lambda a.\ \lambda a'.\ a, \Lambda\alpha.\ \lambda a.\ \lambda a'.\ a', \bullet, \bullet\rangle$$

$$j : B' \to B \triangleq \lambda b'.\ \begin{array}{lcl} \mathrm{let}\ t & = & \Lambda\alpha.\ \lambda a.\ \lambda a'.\ a\ \mathrm{in} \\ \mathrm{let}\ f & = & \Lambda\alpha.\ \lambda a.\ \lambda a'.\ a'\ \mathrm{in} \\ \mathrm{let}\ \mathit{if} & = & \Lambda\alpha.\ \lambda x.\ \lambda y.\ \lambda b.\ b\ [\alpha]\ x\ y\ \mathrm{in} \\ \multicolumn{3}{l}{\mathit{pack}\ \langle \mathsf{cbool}, t, f, \mathit{if}, \bullet, \bullet\rangle} \end{array}$$

The $B \to B'$ direction ignores its argument, and simply returns the obvious tuple inhabiting B'. The $B' \to B$ direction also ignores its argument, and returns an instance of the existential representation which uses the Church booleans as the representation type.

Therefore, each composition is a constant function, and so showing that it is equivalent to the identity function means showing that all elements of B are equivalent, and similarly for B'. The case for B' is easy, and the interesting case fo B reduces to the problem of showing that any element of the existential boolean type is equivalent to element using the Church booleans as its representation type.

This follows from unwinding the definitions. To do this, we introduce a relation that (unsurprisingly) relates Church truth to the true value of the hidden existential type, and Church falsity to the false value of the hidden existential type. Then, the equations for the hidden existential implementation of B can be used to show that the hidden implementation of *if* is equivalent to the Church implementation.

Similarly, we can relate (an extended version of) the existential natural number interface given in Section 2 with the Church encoding $\mathsf{churchnat} = \forall\alpha.\ \alpha \to (\alpha \to \alpha) \to \alpha$.

$$
\begin{array}{l}
N \equiv \\
\quad \exists \mathsf{nat} \\
\quad\quad z : \mathsf{nat},
\end{array}
$$

$$
\begin{array}{l}
\quad s : \mathsf{nat} \to \mathsf{nat}, \\
\quad \mathit{pred} : \mathsf{nat} \to \mathsf{option}_{\mathsf{nat}}, \\
\quad \mathit{iter} : \forall \alpha.\ \mathsf{nat} \to \alpha \to (\alpha \to \alpha) \to \alpha. \\
\quad \mathit{pred}\ z \equiv_{\mathsf{option}_{\mathsf{nat}}} \mathit{none}\ \times \\
\quad \forall n.\ \mathit{pred}\ (s\ n) \equiv_{\mathsf{option}_{\mathsf{nat}}} \mathit{some}\ n\ \times \\
\quad \forall \alpha, i, f.\ \mathit{iter}\ [\alpha]\ z\ i\ f \equiv_{\alpha} i\ \times \\
\quad \forall n, \alpha, i, f.\ \mathit{iter}\ [\alpha]\ (s\ n)\ i\ f \equiv_{\alpha} f\ (\mathit{iter}\ [\alpha]\ n\ i\ f)
\end{array}
$$

$$
\begin{array}{l}
N' \equiv \\
\quad \exists z : \mathsf{churchnat}, \\
\quad\quad s : \mathsf{churchnat} \to \mathsf{churchnat}, \\
\quad\quad - : z \equiv_{,} \Lambda\alpha.\ \lambda i.\ \lambda f.\ i \\
\quad\quad - : s \equiv_{\mathsf{churchnat} \to \mathsf{churchnat}} \lambda n.\ \Lambda\alpha.\ \lambda i.\ \lambda f.\ f\ (n\ \alpha\ i\ f)
\end{array}
$$

We can then prove the equivalence of these two types.

Theorem 5. *(Equivalence of Natural Number Types) There exists an isomorphism between N and N'.*

Proof. The proof of this theorem follows exactly the same pattern as for the booleans. Ultimately we will end up showing that arbitrary elements of N are equivalent to the representation using the Church natural numbers. To do this, we will also need to define the predecessor function *pred* on the Church naturals, which is a linear time operation.

The most interesting thing about this theorem is not the proof, which is standard, but rather the fact that we extended the natural number interface with the predecessor *pred*. The fact that the representation of natural numbers is completely hidden in the existential style means that we can (for example) use a representation of the natural numbers in which the predecessor is cheap to compute. This contrasts with the explicit unary representation of the Church encoding, in which the predecessor is necessarily linear time. As a result, we can relate this slow implementation to fast ones without any difficulties.

This all relies critically on the equations. In the absence of equations specifying the behavior of the predecessor, there is no way to have this constructor while ensuring that the type really does represent the natural numbers object, since there could be many implementations which are type-correct (in F) but lack the necessary equational properties. However, with equations we can add operations for efficiency without ruining the reasoning properties of the datatype, by cutting down the set of reasonable implementations until only ones equivalent to the intended datatype are possible. (We made extensive use of this in our list example in Section 2.)

This is why we have not proven a general representation theorem for all polynomial datatypes. While a representation theorem does not seem hard to come by in the case where the constructors and fold-style eliminators constitute the interface, it seems that we should consider a representation theorems in the more interesting case in which the interfaces are augmented with extra operations that improve the computational efficiency of implementation. However, it remains unclear to us what such interfaces should be, in general.

5 Related Work

5.1 System R and Plotkin-Abadi Logic

The two most prominent systems for reasoning about parametricity are System R [1,4] and Plotkin-Abadi logic [19]. These logics can be viewed as program logics a la Hoare logic, in that they fix a programming logic (System F), and then give a logical system for reasoning about terms in that language.

Our language can be understood as an attempt to take a small fragment of these logics, and then reflect them back into the types of F. This naturally suggests two directions. First, might it be worthwhile to add more of these logics to the type system of $F_=$? In this first paper, we wished to illustrate just how much is achievable with a very modest addition to the type theory of System F, but the extension is a very natural question.

In particular, all of the semantic side-conditions have been discharged by working directly with the relational semantics. By building a logic for parametricity, we could potentially use it to give a proof system for equalities and aborts. However, the presence of abort in our language means that such a logic could not be a simple replay of the developments of [1] or [19], though.

5.2 Dependent Types

The appearance of terms in types in our calculus is rather reminiscent of systems of dependent types, such as Martin-Löf type theory [16] or the calculus of constructions [10]. Indeed, the realizability semantics we use for $F_=$ is quite similar to the semantics of extensional type theories such as Nuprl [9]. Furthermore, we share with extensional type theory the property that typechecking is not syntax-directed: our proof term for equality, $\bullet$, does not contain the evidence of equality. This is similar to the equality reflection property of extensional type theory, in which proof terms for introducing equalities may depend on propositional equality proofs not evident in the proof term.

However, the semantics of our equality type is a bit different from the equality of dependent type theory. In type theory the elimination form for the equality type $e \equiv_A e'$ is used to cast terms of type $B[e]$ into ones of type $B[e']$. As a result, actually deriving a contradiction (i.e., a terms of type $\bot$) from an impossible equality (e.g., a proof of $0 \equiv_{\mathbb{N}} 1$) requires using a large elimination to turn contradictions into proofs of falsity.

In our setting, we instead admit the use of the abort keyword in any inconsistent context, which allows us to make use of contradictions without having to explicitly support large eliminations.

5.3 The Haskell Rules Mechanism

The Glasgow Haskell compiler contains a mechanism called *rules* [12], which allow programmers to specify equational rewrite rules (such as $(map\ f) \circ (map\ g) \mapsto map\ (f \circ g)$) as part of library interfaces. However, these rewrite rules are restricted to referring to top-level module identifiers, and rewriting cannot be applied to an expression unless the term in question refers to *exactly* the same variables as the rules definition referred to. This restriction means that rules — which were a feature whose purpose is to lower the cost of good higher-order style — are much less effective when applied to higher-order code (where operators such as *map* may flow in as arguments to functions).

Our type theory illustrates that it is possible to integrate Haskell-style rules into a simple type theory treating rewrite rules as first-class types. One particularly interesting direction to investigate is adding rules to type classes, which would permit stating the equational assumptions about polymorphic terms. E.g., Haskell's Functor typeclass has a method with type

$$\mathit{fmap} : \mathsf{Functor}\ F \Rightarrow (\alpha \to \beta) \to F\ \alpha \to F\ \beta$$

It is intended that *fmap* is functorial — that is, that $\mathit{fmap}\ \mathit{id} = \mathit{id}$, and that $(\mathit{fmap}\ f) \circ (\mathit{fmap}\ g) = \mathit{fmap}\ (f \circ g)$. By placing these equations into the Functor interface and verifying the typeclass instances, they could even be used to drive optimizations of client code.

5.4 Extended ML

One of the earliest serious attempts to extend a functional language with equational specifications was the Extended ML [13] project. In this work, SML module signatures were extended with algebraic signatures stating the intended equational properties of the abstract datatypes.

This work was quite ambitious, and it involved a rather large fragment of ML including features such as exceptions and non-termination. Furthermore, the concept of algebraic signature was generalized well beyond equational properties to include full logical predicates. However, the technical ambition of this approach meant that its semantics were never fully settled (the question of polymorphism was especially vexing, as was the specification of imperative ML code).

In this paper, we have avoided effects to maximize the force of parametricity. This lets us specify quite sophisticated properties (e.g., initiality) with a bare minimum of additional syntactic and semantic machinery. One especially nice feature of our work is that the presence of equation makes it very natural to connect Church-style datatype encodings with the existential style of data abstraction more common in ML (and exploited by EML).

These days, there are quite well-developed semantic frameworks in place to model polymorphic languages with features like nontermination, recursive types, and higher order state [18,7]. However, in spite of this machinery, it is simply an unavoidable fact that fewer equations hold when effects are present. To what extent the reduced of validity equational reasoning limits the use of equality types is unclear. One approach to this problem may be to encapsulate effects in a monadic type, and then use other techniques (such as Hoare logic [14]) to reason about the monadic code.

6 Future Work

There are two strands of future work. First, there is the theoretical strand. The first question is whether our termination result can be strengthened into a strong normalization result, which would require a more sophisticated logical relation [2].

Second, it may be possible to give a logic for this calculus along the lines of Plotkin-Abadi logic, and then use the rules of that calculus to give proof terms for the equality type. This would make typechecking decidable, and might make an interesting basis for a dependent type theory with parametricity, along the lines of [5]. While this is a challenging problem, the extreme simplicity of our semantics offers reasonable grounds for hope.

ML-style modules support the "strong" dot-notation elimination form [8], whereas our existential encoding uses F-style existentials with a"weak" let-binding eliminator. Recently, Rossberg, Russo and Dreyer have shown [21] how to translate ML-style modules into System F, and it would be interesting to study if a similar translation could take ML signatures extended with equations and translate into $F_=$.

On a practical note, how can equation types be profitably employed in optimizations? Connecting equations to optimizations is an intriguing problem.

Finally, our type system emits proof obligations at each introduction of an equality or use of an abort. It would be useful to ship these proof obligations off to a theorem prover such as Coq. Doing so will require a certain amount of care, since parametricity is essential to the arguments we make, and we will need to make use of recent work [3] on representing the semantics of polymorphism in type theory.

References

1. Abadi, M., Cardelli, L., Curien, P.-L.: Formal parametric polymorphism. In: Principles of Programming Languages, pp. 157–170 (1993)
2. Abel, A.: Weak $\beta\eta$-Normalization and Normalization by Evaluation for System F. In: Cervesato, I., Veith, H., Voronkov, A. (eds.) LPAR 2008. LNCS (LNAI), vol. 5330, pp. 497–511. Springer, Heidelberg (2008)
3. Atkey, R.: Syntax for Free: Representing Syntax with Binding Using Parametricity. In: Curien, P.-L. (ed.) TLCA 2009. LNCS, vol. 5608, pp. 35–49. Springer, Heidelberg (2009)
4. Bellucci, R., Abadi, M., Curien, P.-L.: A Model for Formal Parametric Polymorphism: A PER Interpretation for System R. In: Dezani-Ciancaglini, M., Plotkin, G. (eds.) TLCA 1995. LNCS, vol. 902, pp. 32–46. Springer, Heidelberg (1995)
5. Bernardy, J.-P., Jansson, P., Paterson, R.: Parametricity and dependent types. In: Hudak, P., Weirich, S. (eds.) Proceeding of the 15th ACM SIGPLAN International Conference on Functional Programming, ICFP 2010, pp. 345–356. ACM (2010)
6. Birkedal, L., Møgelberg, R.E., Petersen, R.L.: Domain-theoretical models of parametric polymorphism. Theoretical Computer Science 388(1-3), 152–172 (2007)
7. Birkedal, L., Støvring, K., Thamsborg, J.: Realisability semantics of parametric polymorphism, general references and recursive types. Mathematical Structures in Computer Science 20(4), 655–703 (2010)

8. Cardelli, L., Leroy, X.: Abstract types and the dot notation. In: Broy, M., Jones, C.B. (eds.) Proceedings IFIP TC2 Working Conference on Programming Concepts and Methods, pp. 479–504. North-Holland (1990)
9. Constable, R.L., Allen, S.F., Bromley, M., Cleaveland, R., Cremer, J.F., Harper, R.W., Howe, D.J., Knoblock, T.B., Mendler, N.P., Panangaden, P., Sasaki, J.T., Smith, S.F.: Implementing mathematics with the Nuprl proof development system. Prentice Hall (1986)
10. Coquand, T., Huet, G.P.: The calculus of constructions. Inf. Comput. 76(2/3), 95–120 (1988)
11. Jones, S.P., Vytiniotis, D., Weirich, S., Washburn, G.: Simple unification-based type inference for GADTs. In: Reppy, J.H., Lawall, J.L. (eds.) Proceedings of the 11th ACM SIGPLAN International Conference on Functional Programming, ICFP 2006, Portland, Oregon, USA, September 16-21, pp. 50–61. ACM (2006)
12. Jones, S.P., Tolmach, A., Hoare, T.: Playing by the rules: rewriting as a practical optimisation technique in GHC. In: Haskell Workshop (2001)
13. Kahrs, S., Sannella, D., Tarlecki, A.: The definition of Extended ML: A gentle introduction. Theoretical Computer Science 173(2), 445–484 (1997)
14. Krishnaswami, N.R.: Verifying Higher-Order Imperative Programs with Higher-Order Separation Logic. PhD thesis, Carnegie Mellon University (2011)
15. Marlow, S., Wadler, P.: Deforestation for higher-order functions. In: Launchbury, J., Sansom, P.M. (eds.) Functional Programming, Workshops in Computing, pp. 154–165. Springer, Heidelberg (1992)
16. Martin-Löf, P.: Intuitionistic Type Theory. Bibliopolis (1984)
17. Mitchell, J.C., Plotkin, G.D.: Abstract types have existential type. ACM Trans. Program. Lang. Syst. 10, 470–502 (1988)
18. Neis, G., Dreyer, D., Rossberg, A.: Non-parametric parametricity. In: Hutton, G., Tolmach, A.P. (eds.) Proceeding of the 14th ACM SIGPLAN International Conference on Functional Programming, pp. 135–148. ACM (2009)
19. Plotkin, G.D., Abadi, M.: A Logic for Parametric Polymorphism. In: Bezem, M., Groote, J.F. (eds.) TLCA 1993. LNCS, vol. 664, pp. 361–375. Springer, Heidelberg (1993)
20. Reynolds, J.C.: Types, abstraction and parametric polymorphism. In: IFIP Congress, pp. 513–523 (1983)
21. Rossberg, A., Russo, C.V., Dreyer, D.: F-ing modules. In: Proceedings of the 5th ACM SIGPLAN Workshop on Types in Language Design and Implementation, TLDI 2010, ACM (2010)
22. Wadler, P.: The Girard-Reynolds isomorphism (second edition). Theoretical Computer Science 375(1-3), 201–226 (2007)

GMETA: A Generic Formal Metatheory Framework for First-Order Representations*

Gyesik Lee[1], Bruno C.D.S. Oliveira[2], Sungkeun Cho[2], and Kwangkeun Yi[2]

[1] Hankyong National University, Korea
gslee@hknu.ac.kr
[2] ROSAEC Center, Seoul National University, Korea
{bruno,skcho,kwang}@ropas.snu.ac.kr

Abstract. This paper presents GMETA: a generic framework for *first-order representations* of variable binding that provides *once and for all* many of the so-called infrastructure lemmas and definitions required in mechanizations of formal metatheory. The key idea is to employ *datatype-generic programming* (DGP) and *modular programming* techniques to deal with the infrastructure overhead. Using a generic *universe* for representing a large family of object languages we define datatype-generic libraries of infrastructure for first-order representations such as *locally nameless* or *de Bruijn* indices. Modules are used to provide *templates*: a convenient interface between the datatype-generic libraries and the end-users of GMETA. We conducted case studies based on the POPLmark challenge, and showed that dealing with challenging binding constructs, like the ones found in System $F_{<:}$, is possible with GMETA. All of GMETA's generic infrastructure is implemented in the Coq theorem prover. Furthermore, due to GMETA's modular design, the libraries can be easily used, extended, and customized by users.

Keywords: Mechanization, variable binding, first-order representations, POPLmark challenge, datatype-generic programming, Coq.

1 Introduction

A key issue in mechanical developments of formal metatheory for programming languages concerns the representation and manipulation of terms with variable binding. There are two main approaches to address this issue: *first-order* and *higher-order* approaches. In first-order approaches variables are typically encoded using names or natural numbers, whereas higher-order approaches such as higher-order abstract syntax (HOAS) use the function space in the meta-language to encode binding of the object language.

Higher-order approaches are appealing because issues like capture-avoidance and alpha-equivalence can be handled once and for all. This is why such approaches are used in logical frameworks such as Hybrid (Momigliano et al. 2008),

* This work was supported by the Engineering Research Center of Excellence Program of Korea Ministry of Education, Science and Technology(MEST)/National Research Foundation of Korea(NRF) (Grants R11-2008-007-01002-0 and 2010-0001717).

H. Seidl (Ed.): ESOP 2012, LNCS 7211, pp. 436–455, 2012.

		term	type
term	Variables	$bsubst_{\mathsf{term} \times \mathsf{term}}$	$bsubst_{\mathsf{term} \times \mathsf{type}}$
	Parameters	$fsubst_{\mathsf{term} \times \mathsf{term}}$	$fsubst_{\mathsf{term} \times \mathsf{type}}$
type	Variables	$bsubst_{\mathsf{type} \times \mathsf{term}}$	$bsubst_{\mathsf{type} \times \mathsf{type}}$
	Parameters	$fsubst_{\mathsf{type} \times \mathsf{term}}$	$fsubst_{\mathsf{type} \times \mathsf{type}}$

Fig. 1. Possible variations of substitutions for parameters and variables for a language with two syntactic sorts (term and type) in the locally nameless style

Abella (Gacek 2008), or Twelf (Pfenning and Schürmann 1999); and have also been advocated (Despeyroux et al. 1995; Chlipala 2008) in general-purpose theorem provers like Coq (Coq Development Team 2009).

The main advantage of first-order approaches, and the reason why they are so popular in theorem provers like Coq, is that they are close to pen-and-paper developments and they do not require special support from the theorem prover.

However, the main drawback of first-order approaches is that the tedious infrastructure required for handling variable binding has to be repeated each time for a new object language. For each binding construct in the language, there is a set of *infrastructure operations* and associated *lemmas* that should be implemented. In the locally nameless style (Aydemir et al. 2008) and locally named (McKinna and Pollack 1993) styles we usually need operations like substitution for parameters (free variables) and for (bound) variables as well some associated lemmas. For de Bruijn indices (de Bruijn 1972) we need similar infrastructure, but for operations such as substitution and shifting instead.

Often, the majority of the total number of lemmas and definitions in a formalization consists of basic infrastructure. Figure 1 illustrates the issue using a simple language with two syntactic sorts (types and terms) supporting binding constructs for both type and term variables and assuming a locally nameless style. In the worst case scenario, 8 different types of substitution are needed. We need substitutions for parameters and variables, and for each of these we need to consider all four combinations of substitutions using types and terms. While not all operations are necessary in formalizations, many of them are. For example, System $F_{<:}$, which is the language described in the POPLMark challenge (Aydemir et al. 2005), requires 6 out of the 8 substitutions. Because for each operation we need to also prove a number of associated lemmas, solutions to the POPLMark challenge typically have a large percentage of lemmas and definitions just for infrastructure. In the solution by Aydemir et al. (2008), infrastructure amounts to 65% of the total number of definitions and lemmas (see also Figure 10). In realistic formalizations the situation is often not better: Rossberg et al. (2010) report a combinatorial explosion of infrastructure lemmas and operations as the number of syntactic sorts and binding constructs increases.

Importantly, considering only *homogeneous* operations (like $bsubst_{\mathsf{term} \times \mathsf{term}}$), which perform substitutions of variables on terms of the same sort (term), is insufficient. Generally we must also consider *heterogeneous* operations, like $bsubst_{\mathsf{type} \times \mathsf{term}}$, where the sort of variables being substituted (type) is not of

```
(*@Iso type_iso {
  Parameter type_fvar,
  Variable  type_bvar,
  Binder    type_all _
}*)
Inductive type :=
 | type_fvar  : ℕ → type
 | type_bvar  : ℕ → type
 | type_top   : type
 | type_arrow : type → type → type
 | type_all   : type → type → type.
```

```
(*@Iso term_iso {
  Parameter term_fvar,
  Variable  term_bvar,
  Binder    term_abs _,
  Binder    term_tabs _ binds type
}*)
Inductive term :=
 | term_fvar : ℕ → term
 | term_bvar : ℕ → term
 | term_app  : term → term → term
 | term_abs  : type → term → term
 | term_tapp : term → type → term
 | term_tabs : type → term → term.
```

Fig. 2. Syntax definitions and GMeta isomorphism annotations for a locally nameless style version of System $F_{<:}$ in Coq

the same as the terms which are being substituted into (term). Languages like System F have type abstractions in terms ($\Lambda X.e$) and require operations like $bsubst_{\mathsf{type}\times\mathsf{term}}$ and $fsubst_{\mathsf{type}\times\mathsf{term}}$ for substituting type variables in terms.

1.1 Our Solution

To deal with the combinatorial explosion of infrastructure operations and lemmas, we propose the use of *datatype-generic programming* (DGP) and *modular programming* techniques. The key idea is that, with DGP, we can define once and for all the tedious infrastructure lemmas and operations in a generic way and, with modules, we can provide a convenient interface for users to instantiate such generic infrastructure to their object languages.

This idea is realized in GMeta: a generic framework for first-order representations of variable binding implemented in Coq[1]. In GMeta, a DGP *universe* (Martin-Löf 1984) is used to represent a large family of object languages and includes constructs for representing the binding structure of those languages. The universe is independent of the particular choice of first-order representations: it can be instantiated, for example, to *locally nameless* or *de Bruijn* representations. GMeta uses that universe to provide libraries with the infrastructure for various first-order representations.

The infrastructure is reused by users through so-called *templates*. Templates are functors parameterized by isomorphisms between the object language and the corresponding representation of that language in the universe. By instantiating templates with isomorphisms, users get access to a module that provides infrastructure tailored for a particular binding construct in their own object language. For example, for System $F_{<:}$, the required infrastructure is provided by 3 modules which instantiate GMeta's locally nameless template:

[1] We also have an experimental Agda implementation.

Module $M_{\mathsf{term}\times\mathsf{term}} := \mathit{LNTemplate\ term\_iso\ term\_iso}$.
Module $M_{\mathsf{type}\times\mathsf{type}} := \mathit{LNTemplate\ type\_iso\ type\_iso}$.
Module $M_{\mathsf{type}\times\mathsf{term}} := \mathit{LNTemplate\ type\_iso\ term\_iso}$.

Each module corresponds to one of the 3 combinations needed in System $F_{<:}$, and contains the relevant lemmas and operations. By using this scheme we can deal with the general case of object languages with N syntactic sorts, just by expressing the combinations needed in that language. Moreover GMETA can also provide some more specialized templates for additional reuse and it is easy for users to define their own types of infrastructure and customized templates.

Since isomorphisms can be mechanically generated from the inductive definition of the object language, provided a few annotations, GMETA also includes optional tool support for generating such isomorphisms automatically. Figure 2 illustrates these annotations for System $F_{<:}$. Essentially, the keyword Iso introduces an isomorphism annotation, while the keywords Parameter, Variable and Binder provide the generator with information about which constructors correspond, respectively, to the parameters, variables or binders. Therefore, at the cost of just a few annotations or explicitly creating an isomorphism by hand, GMETA provides much of the tedious infrastructure boilerplate that would constitute a large part of the whole development otherwise.

1.2 Contributions

Our main contribution is to investigate how DGP techniques can deal with the infrastructure overhead required by formalizations using first-order representations. More concretely, the contributions of this paper are:

- *Sound, generic, reusable and extensible infrastructure for first-order representations*: The main advantages of using DGP are that it allows a library-based approach in which 1) the infrastructure can be defined and verified once and for all *within* the meta-logic itself; and 2) extending the infrastructure is easy since it just amounts to extending the library.
- *Heterogeneous generic operations and lemmas*: Of particular interest is the ability of GMETA to deal with binding constructs involving multiple syntactic sorts, such as binders found in the System F family of languages, using heterogeneous generic operations and lemmas.
- *Case studies using the POPLmark challenge*: To validate our approach in practice, we conducted case studies using the POPLmark challenge. Compared to other solutions, our approach shows significant savings in the number of definitions and lemmas required by formalizations.
- *Coq implementation and other resources*: The GMETA framework Coq implementation is available online[2] along with other resources such as tutorials and more case studies.

[2] `http://ropas.snu.ac.kr/gmeta/`
The implementation is based on Coq Version 8.2pl2.

		style	savings
STLC	GMeta vs Aydemir et al.	LN	52%
$F_{<:}$	GMeta vs Aydemir et al.	LN	38%
	GMeta vs Vouillon	dB	35%

Fig. 3. Savings in various formalizations in terms of numbers of definitions and lemmas

2 Case Studies

In order to verify the effectiveness of GMeta in reducing the infrastructure overhead, we conducted case studies using locally nameless and de Bruijn representations. Since the results in terms of savings were similar, and due to space limitations, we mainly discuss the locally nameless case studies in this paper. The details of the de Bruijn case studies can be found on GMeta's online webpage. Our two case studies are a solution to the POPLmark challenge parts 1A+2A, and a formalization of the STLC.

GMeta can reduce the infrastructure overhead because it provides reuse of boilerplate definitions and lemmas. By boilerplate we mean the following:

- *Common operations:* operations such as sets of parameters and (bound) variables, term size or different forms of substitution-like operations (such as substitutions for parameters and variables in the locally nameless style; or shifting in the de Bruijn style).
- *Lemmas about common operations:* lemmas about properties of the common operations, such as several forms of permutation lemmas about substitutions.
- *Lemmas involving well-formedness:* many lemmas about common operations only hold when a term is well-formed under a certain environment. Since well-formedness is a notion that appears in many systems and it is often mechanical, we consider such lemmas boilerplate.

The biggest benefit of GMeta is that it significantly lowers the overheads required in mechanical formalizations by providing reuse of the basic infrastructure. Figure 3 shows the savings that GMeta achieved relative to the reference solutions by Aydemir et al. (2008) and Vouillon (2007). Note that in GMeta only user-defined code is counted. In all case studies more than 35% of the total numbers of definitions were saved. We conducted case studies in both System $F_{<:}$ and STLC. A more detailed discussion and evaluation is given in Section 6.

3 GMeta Design

This section gives a general overview of GMeta's design and discusses the techniques used by us to make GMeta convenient to use.

As depicted in Figure 4, the GMeta framework is structured into 5 layers of modules. The structure is hierarchical, with the more general modules at the top and the more specific modules at the bottom.

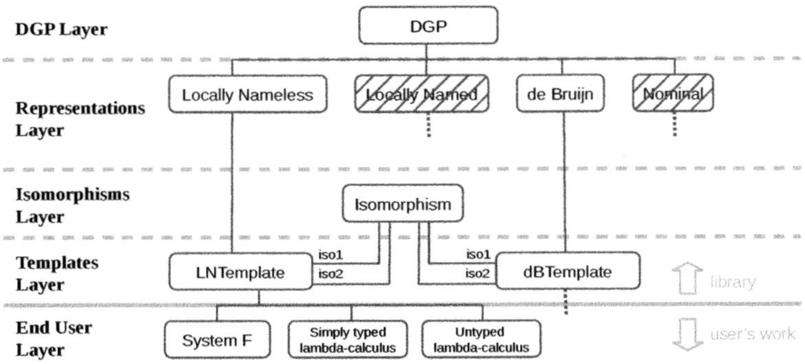

Fig. 4. A simplified modular structure overview of GMeta

- DGP Layer: The core DGP infrastructure is defined at the top-most layer. The main component is a universe that acts as a generic language that the lower-level modules use to define the infrastructure lemmas and definitions.
- Representation Layer: This layer is where the generic infrastructure lemmas and definitions for particular first-order representations are defined. GMeta currently supports locally nameless and de Bruijn representations. However, the DGP library can be extended to cover locally-named approaches (McKinna and Pollack 1993; Sato and Pollack 2010) and other representations.
- Isomorphism Layer: This layer provides simple module signatures for isomorphisms that serve as interfaces between the object language and its representation in the generic language. The adequacy of the object language representation follows from the isomorphism laws.
- Templates Layer: This layer provides templates for the basic infrastructure lemmas and definitions required by particular meta-theoretical developments. Templates are ML-style functors parameterized by isomorphisms between the syntactic sorts of object languages and their corresponding representations in the generic language. In Figure 4 we show only *LNTemplate* and *dBTemplate*, which are the fundamental templates providing reuse for the general infrastructure.
- End User Layer: End users will use GMeta's libraries to develop metatheory for particular object languages, for example, the simply typed lambda calculus (STLC) or System $F_{<:}$ used in our case studies.

The two top layers will be discussed in detail in Sections 4 and 5. They are the most interesting from a technical point of view. More information about other layers and a tutorial are available in GMeta's webpage.

3.1 Making GMeta Convenient to Use

To provide convenience to the user, GMeta employs several techniques. Although DGP plays a fundamental role in the definition of the core libraries of GMeta (at

$$fsubst_{\mathsf{term}\times\mathsf{term}} : \mathbb{N} \rightarrow \mathsf{term} \rightarrow \mathsf{term} \rightarrow \mathsf{term}$$
$$fsubst_{\mathsf{term}\times\mathsf{term}}\ k\ u\ t = to_{\mathsf{term}}\ ([k \ \rightarrow\ (from_{\mathsf{term}}\ u)]\ (from_{\mathsf{term}}\ t))$$
$$bsubst_{\mathsf{term}\times\mathsf{term}} : \mathbb{N} \rightarrow \mathsf{term} \rightarrow \mathsf{term} \rightarrow \mathsf{term}$$
$$bsubst_{\mathsf{term}\times\mathsf{term}}\ k\ u\ t = to_{\mathsf{term}}\ (\{k \ \rightarrow\ (from_{\mathsf{term}}\ u)\}\ (from_{\mathsf{term}}\ t))$$
$$fsubst_{\mathsf{term}\times\mathsf{type}} : \mathbb{N} \rightarrow \mathsf{type} \rightarrow \mathsf{term} \rightarrow \mathsf{term}$$
$$fsubst_{\mathsf{term}\times\mathsf{type}}\ k\ u\ t = to_{\mathsf{term}}\ ([k \ \rightarrow\ (from_{\mathsf{type}}\ u)]\ (from_{\mathsf{term}}\ t))$$
$$bsubst_{\mathsf{term}\times\mathsf{type}} : \mathbb{N} \rightarrow \mathsf{type} \rightarrow \mathsf{term} \rightarrow \mathsf{term}$$
$$bsubst_{\mathsf{term}\times\mathsf{type}}\ k\ u\ t = to_{\mathsf{term}}\ (\{k \ \rightarrow\ (from_{\mathsf{type}}\ u)\}\ (from_{\mathsf{term}}\ t))$$
$$bsubst_{\mathsf{type}\times\mathsf{type}} : \mathbb{N} \rightarrow \mathsf{type} \rightarrow \mathsf{type} \rightarrow \mathsf{type}$$
$$bsubst_{\mathsf{type}\times\mathsf{type}}\ k\ u\ t = to_{\mathsf{type}}\ ([k \ \rightarrow\ (from_{\mathsf{type}}\ u)]\ (from_{\mathsf{type}}\ t))$$
$$wf_{\mathsf{term}} : \mathsf{term} \rightarrow \mathsf{Prop}$$
$$wf_{\mathsf{type}} : \mathsf{type} \rightarrow \mathsf{Prop}$$
$$thbfsubst\_perm\_core : \forall (t : \mathsf{term})\ (u, v : \mathsf{type})\ (m\ k : \mathbb{N}),$$
$$wf_{\mathsf{type}}\ u \Rightarrow bsubst_{\mathsf{term}\times\mathsf{type}}\ k\ (bsubst_{\mathsf{type}\times\mathsf{type}}\ m\ u\ v)\ (fsubst_{\mathsf{term}\times\mathsf{type}}\ m\ u\ t)$$
$$= fsubst_{\mathsf{term}\times\mathsf{type}}\ m\ u\ (bsubst_{\mathsf{term}\times\mathsf{type}}\ k\ v\ t)$$

Fig. 5. Some representations of a template with two sorts: *terms* and *types*

the DGP and representation layers), end users should not need knowledge about DGP for uses of GMeta. However, this is not trivial to achieve because, among other things, end-user proofs generally require unfolding infrastructure operations like substitution, and those operations are written in a datatype-generic way, in a form which is alien to users that do not know about DGP.

Automatically Generated Isomorphisms. GMeta uses automatically generated isomorphisms between the user-defined object language and a corresponding representation of that language of the generic universe. Since information about the binding structure of the language is required to generate isomorphisms, GMeta uses a small annotation language. (see Figure 2 for an example of the annotation language).

Templates. GMeta uses templates to solve the problem of interfacing with the infrastructure DGP libraries.

As already illustrated in Figure 1, a simple language with two syntactic sorts (terms and types) needs two isomorphisms ($from_{\mathsf{term}}, to_{\mathsf{term}}$) and ($from_{\mathsf{type}}, to_{\mathsf{type}}$) between the generic language and the object language. What we mean by isomorphism is explained in the next paragraph about special tactics. In Figure 5, it is demonstrated how the two isomorphisms are used to get an instantiation where several variants of substitution, and well-formedness in the locally nameless style become available for free. The templates include also many lemmas about the operations and some of the lemmas may be true only for well-formedness expressions. For example, the lemma *thbfsubst_perm_core* describes a permutability of two kinds of substitutions where well-formed types (wf_{type}) are involved.

The general form of parameter substitution in the locally nameless template is as follows:

Module *LNTemplate* (iso_{S_1} : Iso, iso_{S_2} : Iso).

...

$$fsubst_{S_2 \times S_1} \quad : \mathbb{N} \to S_1 \to S_2 \to S_2$$
$$fsubst_{S_2 \times S_1}\ k\ u\ t = to_{S_2}\ (\{k \ \to\ (from_{S_1}\ u)\}\ (from_{S_2}\ t))$$

Essentially, S_1 and S_2 are supposed to be the types of the syntactic sorts used in object language. These types come from the isomorphisms iso_{S_1} and iso_{S_2}, which are the parameters of *LNTemplate*. Definitions like $\{\cdot \ \to\ \cdot\}_T \cdot$ are simply using the isomorphism (through the operations to_{S_1}, to_{S_2}, $from_{S_1}$ and $from_{S_2}$) to interface with generic operations like $\{\cdot \ \to\ \cdot\}\cdot$ (see Figure 9) defined in the representations layer.

Because of the isomorphisms between the user's object language and the representation of that language in the universe, users do not need to interact directly with the generic universe. Instead, all that a user needs to do is to instantiate the templates with the automatically generated isomorphisms. In Section 1.1, we already described how this technique is used to generate the infrastructure for System $F_{<:}$.

Special Tactics. When proving lemmas for their own formalizations, users may need to unfold operations which are defined in terms of corresponding generic operations. For example, the following lemma is a core lemma in formalization of in the solution to the POPLMark challenge by Aydemir et al. (2008).

Lemma *typing_subst* : $\forall E\ F\ U\ t\ T\ z\ u,$
  $(E \mathbin{++} (z, U) :: F) \vdash t : T \Rightarrow F \vdash u : U \Rightarrow$
  $(E \mathbin{++} F) \vdash ([z \ \to\ u]_T\ t) : T.$
Proof.
  intros; *dependent induction H*; *gsimpl*.
  ...
  grewrite tbfsubst_permutation_var_wf; *eauto*.
  ...
Qed.

The details of the Coq proof are not relevant. What is important to note is: 1) the key difference to the original proof by Aydemir et al. (2008) is that two different tactics (*gsimpl* and *grewrite*) are used; and 2) the lemma *tbfsubst_permutation_var_wf* and the operation $[\cdot \ \to\ \cdot]_T \cdot$ are provided by GMETA's templates.

If the user would try to use *simpl* (the standard Coq tactic to unfold and simplify definitions) directly, the definition of $[\cdot \ \to\ \cdot]_T \cdot$ would be unfolded and he would be presented with parts of the definition of $[\cdot \ \to\ \cdot]\cdot$ (See Figure 9). However, this is clearly undesirable since the expected definition at this point is one similar to a manually defined operation for the object language in hand.

Our solution to this problem is to define some Coq tactics (such as *gsimpl* and *grewrite*) that *specialize* operations and lemmas such as $[\cdot \ \to\ \cdot]_T \cdot$ and *tbfsubst_permutation_var_wf* using the isomorphisms provided by the user, and the isomorphism and adequacy laws shown in Figure 6.

$$
\begin{aligned}
to_{S_2}\ (from_{S_2}\ t) &= t \\
from_{S_2}\ (to_{S_2}\ t) &= t \\
from_{S_2}\ ([k \to u]_T\, t) &= [k \to (from_{S_2}\ u)]\ (from_{S_2}\ t)
\end{aligned}
$$

Fig. 6. Isomorphism and adequacy laws

4 DGP for Datatypes with First-Order Binders

This section briefly introduces DGP using inductive families to define universes of datatypes, and shows how to adapt a conventional universe of datatypes to support binders and variables. In our presentation we assume a type theory extended with inductive families, such as the Calculus of Inductive Constructions (CIC) (Paulin-Mohring 1996) or extensions of Martin-Löf type-theory (Martin-Löf 1984) with inductive families (Dybjer 1997).

4.1 Inductive Families

Inductive families are a generalization of conventional datatypes that has been introduced in dependently typed languages such as Epigram (McBride and McKinna 2004), Agda (Norell 2007) or the Coq theorem prover. They are also one of the inspirations for Generalized Algebraic Datatypes (GADTs) (Peyton Jones et al. 2006) in Haskell.

We adopt a notation similar to the one used by Epigram to describe inductive families. For example we can define a family of vectors of size n as follows:

$$
\textsc{Data}\ \frac{A : \star \qquad n : \mathsf{Nat}}{\mathsf{Vector}_A\ n : \star}\ \textsc{where}
$$

$$
\frac{}{\mathsf{vz} : \mathsf{Vector}_A\ \mathsf{z}} \qquad\qquad \frac{n : \mathsf{Nat} \qquad a : A \qquad as : \mathsf{Vector}_A\ n}{\mathsf{vs}\ a\ as : \mathsf{Vector}_A\ (\mathsf{s}\ n)}
$$

In this definition the type constructor for vectors has two type arguments. The first argument specifies the type A of elements of the vector, while the second argument n is the size of the vector. We write parametric type arguments in type constructors such as Vector_A using a subscript. Also, if a constructor is not explicitly applied to some arguments (for example $\mathsf{vs}\ a\ as$ is not applied to n), then those arguments are implicitly passed.

4.2 Datatype Generic Programming

The key idea behind DGP is that many functions can be defined generically for whole families of datatype definitions. Inductive families are useful to DGP because they allow us to define universes (Martin-Löf 1984) representing whole families of datatypes. By defining functions over this universe we obtain generic functions that work for any datatypes representable in that universe.

$\text{DATA } \mathsf{Rep} = 1 \mid \mathsf{Rep} + \mathsf{Rep} \mid \mathsf{Rep} \times \mathsf{Rep} \mid \mathsf{K}\ \mathsf{Rep} \mid \mathsf{R}$

$$\text{DATA } \frac{r, s : \mathsf{Rep}}{[\![s]\!]_r : \star} \text{ WHERE } \frac{}{() : [\![1]\!]_r} \qquad \frac{s : \mathsf{Rep} \quad v : [\![s]\!]}{\mathsf{k}\ v : [\![\mathsf{K}\ s]\!]_r}$$

$$\frac{s_1, s_2 : \mathsf{Rep} \quad v : [\![s_1]\!]_r}{\mathsf{i}_1\ v : [\![s_1 + s_2]\!]_r} \qquad \frac{s_1, s_2 : \mathsf{Rep} \quad v : [\![s_2]\!]_r}{\mathsf{i}_2\ v : [\![s_1 + s_2]\!]_r}$$

$$\frac{s_1, s_2 : \mathsf{Rep} \quad v_1 : [\![s_1]\!]_r \quad v_2 : [\![s_2]\!]_r}{(v_1, v_2) : [\![s_1 \times s_2]\!]_r} \qquad \frac{v : [\![r]\!]}{\mathsf{r}\ v : [\![\mathsf{R}]\!]_r}$$

$$\text{DATA } \frac{s : \mathsf{Rep}}{[\![s]\!] : \star} \text{ WHERE } \frac{s : \mathsf{Rep} \quad v : [\![s]\!]_s}{\mathsf{in}\ v : [\![s]\!]}$$

Fig. 7. A simple universe of types

A Simple Universe. The universe that underlies GMETA is based on a simplified version of the universe for regular tree types by Morris et al. (2004). Morris et al.'s universe is expressive enough to represent recursive types using μ-types (Pierce 2002). However, the presentation of the universe of regular tree types is complicated by the use of *telescopes* (Altenkirch and Reus 1999; McBride and McKinna 2004) for managing μ binders. For presentation purposes and to avoid distractions related to the use of telescopes (which are orthogonal to our purposes), we will use instead a simplified version of regular tree types in which only a single top-level recursive type binder is allowed. This precludes the ability to encode mutually recursive datatypes, which is possible in Morris et al.'s universe. Nevertheless, we have experimental versions of GMETA (both in Coq and Agda) on our online webpage that use the full universe and do support mutually recursive datatypes.

Figure 7 shows the simple universe that is the basis for GMETA. The datatype Rep (defined using the simpler ML-style notation for datatypes) describes the "grammar" of types that can be used to construct the datatypes representable in the universe. The three first constructs represent unit, sum and product types. The K constructor allows the representation of constants of some representable type. The R constructor is the most interesting construct: it is a reference to the recursive type that we are defining. For example, the type representations for naturals and lists of naturals are defined as follows:

$$\begin{array}{ll} \mathsf{RNat} : \mathsf{Rep} & \qquad \mathsf{RList} : \mathsf{Rep} \\ \mathsf{RNat} = 1 + \mathsf{R} & \qquad \mathsf{RList} = 1 + \mathsf{K}\ \mathsf{RNat} \times \mathsf{R} \end{array}$$

The interpretation of the universe is given by two mutually inductive families $[\![\cdot]\!]_r$ and $[\![\cdot]\!]$, while the data constructors of these two families provide the syntax to build terms of that universe. The parametric type r in the subscript in $[\![\cdot]\!]_r$, is the recursive type that is used when interpreting the constructor R. For illustrating the data constructors of terms of the universe, we first define the constructors nil and cons for lists:

$$\textsc{Data}\ \mathsf{Rep} = \ldots \mid \mathsf{E}\ \mathsf{Rep} \mid \mathsf{B}\ \mathsf{Rep}\ \mathsf{Rep}$$

$$Q : \star \qquad \text{(* Binder type *)} \qquad\qquad V : \star \qquad \text{(* Variable type *)}$$

$$\textsc{Data}\ \frac{r, s : \mathsf{Rep}}{[\![s]\!]_r : \star}\ \textsc{where}\ \ldots \quad \frac{s : \mathsf{Rep} \qquad v : [\![s]\!]}{\mathsf{e}\ v : [\![\mathsf{E}\ s]\!]_r} \qquad \frac{s_1, s_2 : \mathsf{Rep} \qquad q : Q \qquad v : [\![s_2]\!]_r}{\lambda_{s_1} q.v : [\![\mathsf{B}\ s_1\ s_2]\!]_r}$$

$$\textsc{Data}\ \frac{s : \mathsf{Rep}}{[\![s]\!] : \star}\ \textsc{where}\ \ldots \quad \frac{s : \mathsf{Rep} \qquad v : V}{\mathsf{var}\ v : [\![s]\!]}$$

Fig. 8. Extending universe with representations of binders and variables

$$\begin{array}{ll} \mathsf{nil} : [\![\mathsf{RList}]\!] & \mathsf{cons} : [\![\mathsf{RNat}]\!] \to [\![\mathsf{RList}]\!] \to [\![\mathsf{RList}]\!] \\ \mathsf{nil} = \mathsf{in}\ (\mathsf{i}_1\ ()) & \mathsf{cons}\ n\ ns = \mathsf{in}\ (\mathsf{i}_2\ (\mathsf{k}\ n, \mathsf{r}\ ns)) \end{array}$$

When interpreting $[\![\mathsf{RList}]\!]$, the representation type r in $[\![\cdot]\!]_\mathsf{r}$ stands for $1 + \mathsf{K}\ \mathsf{RNat}\ \times\ \mathsf{R}$. The constructor k takes a value of some interpretation for a type representation s and embeds it in the interpretation for representations of type r. For example, when building values of type $[\![\mathsf{RList}]\!]$, k is used to embed a natural number in the list. Similarly, the constructor r embeds list values in a larger list. The in constructor embeds values of type $[\![\mathsf{r}]\!]_\mathsf{r}$ into a value of inductive family $[\![\mathsf{r}]\!]$, playing the role of a fixpoint. The remaining data constructors (for representing unit, sums and products values) have the expected role, allowing sum-of-product values to be created.

Generic Functions. The key advantage of universes is that we can define (generic) functions that work for any representable datatypes. A simple example is a generic function counting the number of recursive occurrences on a term:

$$\begin{array}{ll} \mathit{size} : \forall (r : \mathsf{Rep}).\ [\![r]\!] \to \mathbb{N} & \mathit{size} : \forall (r, s : \mathsf{Rep}).\ [\![s]\!]_r \to \mathbb{N} \\ \mathit{size}\ (\mathsf{in}\ t) = \mathit{size}\ t & \mathit{size}\ () = 0 \\ & \mathit{size}\ (\mathsf{k}\ t) = 0 \\ & \mathit{size}\ (\mathsf{i}_1\ t) = \mathit{size}\ t \\ & \mathit{size}\ (\mathsf{i}_2\ t) = \mathit{size}\ t \\ & \mathit{size}\ (t, v) = \mathit{size}\ t + \mathit{size}\ v \\ & \mathit{size}\ (\mathsf{r}\ \ t) = 1 + \mathit{size}\ t \end{array}$$

To define such generic function, two-mutually inductive definitions are needed. Note that r and s (bound by $\forall$) are implicitly passed in the calls to *size*.

4.3 A Universe for Representing First-Order Binding

We enrich our universe to deal with binders and variables. Figure 7 is insufficient to define generic functions such as substitution and free variables requiring structural information about binders and variables. Figure 8 shows the additional definitions required to support representations of binders, variables, and also deeply embedded terms. The data constructor B of the datatype Rep provides the type for representations of binders. The type Rep is also extended with a constructor E which is the representation type for deeply embedded terms. This constructor is very similar to K. However, the fundamental difference is that generic functions should go inside the terms represented by deeply embedded terms, whereas terms built with K should be treated as constants by generic functions.

The abstract types Q and V represent the types of binders and variables. Depending on the particular first-order representations of binders these types will be instantiated differently.

We illustrate the instantiations of Q and V for 4 of the most popular first-order representations in a table. The last column of the table shows how the lambda term $\lambda x.\ x\ y$ can be encoded in the different approaches. For the nominal approach there is only one sort of variables, which can be represented by a natural number. In this representation, the binders hold information about the bound variables, thus the type Q is the same type as the type of variables V. In the de Bruijn style, the variables are denoted positionally with respect to the current enclosing binder. Thus the type Q is just the unit type and the type V is a natural number. The locally nameless approach can be viewed as a variant of the de Bruijn style. The difference to the de Bruijn style is that parameters and (bound) variables are distinguished. Therefore in the locally nameless style the type V is instantiated to a sum of two natural numbers. Finally, in the locally named style, there are also two sorts of variables and bound variables are represented as in the nominal style. Thus the type Q is a natural number and the type V is a sum type of two naturals. Note that we currently do not support the locally named and nominal style approaches in GMETA as these styles would require special care with issues like alpha-equivalence.

	Q	V	$\lambda x.\ x\ y$
Nominal	$\mathbb{N}$	$\mathbb{N}$	$\lambda x.\ x\ y$
De Bruijn	$\mathbb{1}$	$\mathbb{N}$	$\lambda.\ 0\ 1$
Locally nameless	$\mathbb{1}$	$\mathbb{N}+\mathbb{N}$	$\lambda.\ 0\ y$
Locally named	$\mathbb{N}$	$\mathbb{N}+\mathbb{N}$	$\lambda x.\ x\ a$

The inductive family $[\![\cdot]\!]_{\mathsf{r}}$ is extended with two new data constructors. The constructor e is similar to the constructor k and is used to build deeply embedded terms. The other constructor uses the standard lambda notation $\lambda_{s_1} q.v$ to denote the constructor for binders. The type representation s_1 is the representation of the syntactic sort of the variables that are bound by the binder, whereas the type representation s_2 is the representation of the syntactic sort of the body of the abstraction. We use $s_1 = \mathsf{R}$ to denote that the syntactic sort of the variables to be bound is the same as that of the body. This distinction is necessary because in certain languages the syntactic sorts of variables to be bound and the body of the abstraction are not the same. For example, in System F, type abstractions in terms such as $\Lambda X.e$ bind type variables X in a term e.

The inductive family $[\![\cdot]\!]$ is also extended with one additional data constructor for variables. This constructor allows terms to be constructed using a variable instead of a concretely defined term.

Instantiation of Q and V: $Q = \mathbb{1}$ and $V = \mathbb{N} + \mathbb{N}$.

Heterogeneous substitution for (bound) variables:

$$
\begin{array}{ll}
\{\cdot \rightarrow \cdot\}\ \cdot : \forall(r_1, r_2 : \mathsf{Rep}).\ \mathbb{N} \rightarrow [\![r_1]\!] \rightarrow [\![r_2]\!] \rightarrow [\![r_2]\!] & \\
\{k \rightarrow u\}\ (\mathsf{in}\ t) & = \mathsf{in}\ (\{k \rightarrow u\}\ t) \\
\{k \rightarrow u\}\ (\mathsf{var}\ (\mathsf{inl}\ x)) & = \mathsf{var}\ (\mathsf{inl}\ x) \\
\{k \rightarrow u\}\ (\mathsf{var}\ (\mathsf{inr}\ y)) & = \textbf{if}\ r_1 \equiv r_2 \wedge k \equiv y\ \textbf{then}\ u\ \textbf{else}\ (\mathsf{var}\ (\mathsf{inr}\ y))
\end{array}
$$

$$
\begin{array}{ll}
\{\cdot \rightarrow \cdot\}\ \cdot : \forall(r_1, r_2, s : \mathsf{Rep}).\ \mathbb{N} \rightarrow [\![r_1]\!] \rightarrow [\![s]\!]_{r_2} \rightarrow [\![s]\!]_{r_2} & \\
\{k \rightarrow u\}\ () & = () \\
\{k \rightarrow u\}\ (\mathsf{k}\ t) & = \mathsf{k}\ t \\
\{k \rightarrow u\}\ (\mathsf{e}\ t) & = \mathsf{e}\ (\{k \rightarrow u\}\ t) \\
\{k \rightarrow u\}\ (\mathsf{i}_1\ t) & = \mathsf{i}_1\ (\{k \rightarrow u\}\ t) \\
\{k \rightarrow u\}\ (\mathsf{i}_2\ t) & = \mathsf{i}_2\ (\{k \rightarrow u\}\ t) \\
\{k \rightarrow u\}\ (t, v) & = (\{k \rightarrow u\}\ t, \{k \rightarrow u\}\ v) \\
\{k \rightarrow u\}\ (\lambda_{r_3}\mathbb{1}.t) & = \textbf{if}\ (r_3 \equiv \mathsf{R} \wedge r_1 \equiv r_2) \vee (r_3 \not\equiv \mathsf{R} \wedge r_1 \equiv r_3) \\
 & \quad \textbf{then}\ \lambda_{r_3}\mathbb{1}.(\{(k+1) \rightarrow u\}\ t)\ \textbf{else}\ \lambda_{r_3}\mathbb{1}.(\{k \rightarrow u\}\ t) \\
\{k \rightarrow u\}\ (\mathsf{r}\ \ t) & = \mathsf{r}\ \ (\{k \rightarrow u\}\ t)
\end{array}
$$

Heterogeneous substitution for parameters in the following form are similarly defined:

$$[\cdot \rightarrow \cdot]\ \cdot : \forall(r_1\ r_2 : \mathsf{Rep}).\ \mathbb{N} \rightarrow [\![r_1]\!] \rightarrow [\![r_2]\!] \rightarrow [\![r_2]\!]$$

Example of a heterogeneous lemma:

$$\mathit{subst\_fresh} : \forall(r_1, r_2 : \mathsf{Rep})\ (t : [\![r_1]\!])\ (u : [\![r_2]\!])\ (m : \mathbb{N}),\ m \notin (fv_{r_2}\ t) \Rightarrow [m \rightarrow u]\ t = t$$

Fig. 9. Generic definitions for the locally nameless approach

5 Generic Operations and Lemmas

This section shows how generic operations and lemmas defined over the universe presented in Section 4 can be used to provide much of the basic infrastructure boilerplate for the languages representable in the universe.

5.1 Locally Nameless

Figure 9 presents generic definitions for the locally nameless approach. In this approach binders do not bind names, and (bound) variables and parameters (free variables) are distinguished. Thus, as discussed in Section 4.3, the types Q and V are, respectively, the unit type[3] and a sum of two naturals. Using these instantiations for Q and V, the operation for instantiating a (bound) variable with a term can be defined in a generic way. Also, generic lemmas can be defined using the generic operations. The statement for *subst_fresh* – which states that if a parameter does not occur in a term, then substitution of that parameter is the identity – is shown as an example of such generic lemmas.

As explained in Section 4, generic operations are defined over terms of the universe by two mutually-inductive operations defined over the $[\![\cdot]\!]$ and $[\![\cdot]\!]_r$

[3] For convenience, we use $\mathbb{1}$ for both the unit type and the unique term of that type.

(mutually-)inductive families. Note that our generic definition for substitution[4] effectively deals with all the possible combinations for defining a substitution in a multi-sorted syntax.

In the definition of substitutions the most interesting cases are variables and binders. In the case of variables, the condition $r_1 \equiv r_2$ is necessary to check whether the parameter (or variable) and the term to be substituted have the same representation. Note the use of $(\equiv)$ to compare type representations: the universe supports decidable equality, which is crutial for the definition of operations. The subscript r_3 keeps the information about which kind of variables is to be bound. When $r_3 = \mathsf{R}$, the binding is homogeneous, that is, the variable to be bound and the body of the binder have the same representation. For example, the term-level abstraction in terms $(\lambda x : T.e)$ of System F is homogeneous. An example of heterogeneous binding is the type-level abstraction in terms $(\Lambda X.e)$ of System F. In this case r_3 is the representation for System F types. Variable substitution happens when the bound variable and the terms to be substituted have the same representation. Note that, in the case of homogeneous binding $(r_3 \equiv \mathsf{R})$, we compare r_1 with r_2, not with r_3, because the bound variable and the body of the binder have the same representation r_2.

The main advantage of representing the syntax of languages with our generic universe is, of course, that all generic operations are immediately available. For instance, the 8 substitution operations mentioned in Section 1 can be recovered through suitable instantiations of the type representations r_1, r_2, r_3 in the two generic substitutions presented in this section.

5.2 De Bruijn

A key advantage of our modular approach is that we do not have to commit to using a particular first-order representation. Instead, by suitably instantiating the types Q and V, we can define the generic infrastructure for our own favored first-order representation. For example we can use GMETA to define the generic infrastructure for de Bruijn representations. In de Bruijn representations, binders do not bind any names, therefore the type Q is instantiated with the unit type. Also, because there is only one sort of (positional) variable, the type V is instantiated with the type of natural numbers. The implementation of heterogeneous generic shifting follows a pattern similar to that used in the generic operations for the locally nameless style for dealing with homogeneous and heterogeneous binders. The variable and binder cases implement the expected behavior for the de Bruijn indices operations and all the other cases are limited to traversal code. For more details we refer to the GMETA homepage.

6 Discussion and Evaluation

In this section we present the results of the case studies that we conducted. The discussion of these results is done in terms of three criteria proposed by

[4] Note that the notation for substitutions follows Aydemir et al. (2008).

		Definitions	Infrastructure (lemma + def.)	Core (lemma + def.)	Overall inf. overhead	total	ratio
STLC (locally nameless)	Aydemir et al.	**11**	**13** + 3	**4** + 0	17	31	55%
	GMETA	7	4 + 0	4 + 0	1	15	7%
System $F_{<:}$ (locally nameless)	Aydemir et al.	**20**	**48** + 7	**17** + 1	60	93	65%
	GMETA	13	26 + 1	17 + 1	25	58	43%
System $F_{<:}$ (de Bruijn)	Vouillon	27	24 + 0	50 + 0	41	101	41%
	GMETA	12	1 + 0	52 + 0	3	65	5%

Fig. 10. Formalization of POPLmark challenge (part 1A+2A) and STLC in Coq using locally nameless approach and de Bruijn approach with and without GMETA

Aydemir et al. (2005) (*reasonable overheads*, *cost of entry* and *transparency*) for evaluating mechanizations of formal metatheory.

Reasonable Overheads. The biggest benefit of GMETA is that it significantly lowers the overheads required in mechanical formalizations by providing reuse of the basic infrastructure. Figure 10 presents the detailed numbers obtained in our case studies. We follow Aydemir et al. by dividing the whole development into three parts: *definitions*, *infrastructure* and *core*. The numbers on those columns correspond to the number of definitions and lemmas used for each part. The definitions column presents the number of basic definitions about syntax, whereas the core column presents the number of main definitions and lemmas of the formalization (such as, for example, progress and preservation). The infrastructure column is the most interesting because this is where most of the tedious boilerplate lemmas and definitions are. The column boilerplate counts the number of such definitions and lemmas across the formalizations. Although, for the most part, boilerplate comes from the infrastructure part, some boilerplate also exists in the definitions part. This explains why GMETA is able to reduce the number of definitions and lemmas in the two parts. The numbers in bold face are the numbers that were presented by Aydemir et al. (2008). However those numbers did not reflect the real total number of definitions and lemmas in the solutions. For example, in the infrastructure part only the lemmas were counted. Since we are interested in all the boilerplate, our numbers reflect the total number of definitions and lemmas in each part.

In comparison with Aydemir et al.'s reference solutions, the proofs in our approach follow essentially the structure of the original proofs. One minor difference is that instead of some standard Coq tactics, a few more general tactics provided by GMETA should be used. Because this is the only significant difference, the proofs in the GMETA solution and Aydemir et al.'s solution have comparable sizes. This means that most proofs will still be comparable in size although a small number of proofs will be either shorter or longer.

Cost of Entry. One important criterion for evaluating mechanical formalizations of metatheory is the associated cost of entry. That is, how much does a user need to know in order to successfully develop a formalization? We believe that the associated cost of entry of GMETA is comparable to first-order approaches like the one by Aydemir et al. (2008).

One aspect of GMETA that (arguably) requires less knowledge when compared to Aydemir et al. (2008) is that the end-user does not need to know how to prove many basic infrastructure lemmas, since those are provided by GMETA's libraries.

Finally, we should mention that one advantage of generative approaches such as LNgen (Aydemir and Weirich 2009) is that the cost-of-entry, in terms of using the lemmas and definitions provided by LNgen, is a bit lower than in GMETA. This is because the generated infrastructure is directly defined in terms of the object language and the lemmas and definitions can be used as if they had been written by hand. In GMETA, the end-user, while not required to know about DGP, still needs to be aware of some special simplification tactics and, occasionally, he may need to apply adequacy lemmas by hand.

Transparency. The transparency criterion is intended to evaluate how easy it is for humans to understand particular formalization techniques. The issue of transparency is largely orthogonal to GMETA because it usually measures how particular representations of binding (such as locally nameless or de Bruijn), and lemmas and definitions using that approach, are easy to understand by humans. Since we do not introduce any new representation, transparency remains unchanged (the same representation, lemmas and definitions are used).

7 Related Work

Generative Approaches. Closest to our work are *generative* approaches like LNgen, which uses an external tool, based on Ott (Sewell et al. 2010) specifications, to generate the infrastructure lemmas and definitions for a particular language automatically. One advantage of generative approaches is that the generated infrastructure is directly defined in terms of the object language. In contrast, in GMETA, the infrastructure is indirectly defined in terms of generic definitions. This is not entirely ideal, but it is possible to handle the situation in a reasonably effective way in GMETA using tactics (see Section 3.1).

There are two main advantages of a DGP approach over generative approaches: *verifiability*; and *extensibility*. Although a generator allows defining once-and-for all the infrastructure, it would not be a simple task to verify once-and-for all that the generator always generates correct (well-typed) infrastructure. With a generator, we can only verify whether each particular generated set of infrastructure is correct. Another advantage of a libary-based approach is that it is easy to extend. If we wanted to add a new lemma, we would just need to extend a module with a new generic function. With a generator, this would amount to directly changing the generator code. Although there is also a cost to extending libraries, we believe that it is usually easier than changing the generator code.

It is also interesting to compare GMETA and LNgen in terms of which types of infrastructure they can reuse and how hard it is to reuse such infrastructure. The main advantage of LNgen is that dealing with inductive relations is easy. In GMETA, lemmas involving well-formedness require some more effort to be reused. A solution for this problem would be to extend the isomorphism generator to deal with inductive relations as well. On the other hand, the strength of GMETA lies in its extensibility. For example, sometimes there are domain-specific infrastructure lemmas like *thbfsubst_perm_core* in Figure 5. Dealing with such a infrastructure is in conflict with the general-purpose nature of LNgen.

DGP and Binding. DGP techniques have been used before for dealing with binders using a well-scoped de Bruijn index representation (Altenkirch and Reus 1999; McBride and McKinna 2004). Chlipala (2007) used an approach inspired by *proof by reflection techniques* (Boutin 1997) to provide several generic operations on well-typed terms represented by well-scoped de Bruijn indices. Licata and Harper (2009) proposed a universe in Agda that permits definitions that mix binding and computation. The obvious difference is that GMETA works with traditional (non-well-scoped) first-order representations instead of well-scoped de Bruijn indices. This difference of representation means that the universes and generic functions have to deal with significantly different issues and that they are quite different in nature. More fundamentally, Chlipala's (2007) and Licata and Harper's (2009) work can be viewed as trying to develop new ways to formalize metatheory in which many of the invariants hold by construction, that would have to be proved otherwise. This is different from our goal: we are not proposing new ways to formalize metatheory, rather we wish to make well-established ways to formalize metatheory with first-order representations less painful to use.

DGP techniques have also been widely used in conventional functional programming languages (Jansson and Jeuring 1997; Hinze and Jeuring 2003; Rodriguez et al. 2008), and Cheney (2005) explored how to provide generic operations such as substitution or collecting free variables using nominal abstract syntax.

Our work is inspired by the use of *universes* in type-theory (Martin-Löf 1984; Nordström et al. 1990). The basic universe construction presented in Figure 7 is a simple variation of the *regular tree types* universe proposed by Morris et al. (2004, 2009) in Epigram. Nevertheless the extensions for representing variables and binders presented in Figure 8 are new. Dybjer and Setzer (1999, 2001) showed universe constructions within a type-theory with an axiomatization of induction-recursion. Altenkirch and McBride (2003) proposed a universe capturing the datatypes and generic operations of Generic Haskell (Hinze and Jeuring 2003) and Norell (2008) shows how to do DGP with universes in Agda (Norell 2007).

Verbruggen et al. (2008, 2009) formalized a Generic Haskell (Hinze and Jeuring 2003) DGP style in Coq, which can also be used to do generic programming. This approach allows conventional datatypes to be expressed, but it cannot be used to express meta-theoretical generic operations since there are no representations for variables or binders.

Other Techniques for First-Order Approaches. Aydemir et al. (2009) investigated several variations of representing syntax with locally nameless representations aimed at reducing the amount of infrastructure overhead in languages like System $F_{<:}$. One advantage of these techniques is that they are very lightweight in nature and do not require additional tool support. However, while the proposed techniques are effective at achieving significant savings, they require the abstract syntax of the object language to be encoded in a way different from the traditional locally nameless style, potentially collapsing all syntactic sorts into one. In contrast, GMETA allows the syntax to be encoded in the traditional locally nameless style, while at the same time reducing the infrastructure overhead through its reusable libraries of infrastructure.

Higher-Order Approaches and Nominal Logic. Approaches based on higher-order abstract syntax (HOAS) (Pfenning and Elliot 1988; Harper et al. 1993) are used in logical frameworks such as Abella (Gacek 2008), Hybrid (Momigliano et al. 2008) or Twelf (Pfenning and Schürmann 1999). In HOAS, the object-language binding is represented using the binding of the metalanguage. This has the important advantage that facts about substitution or alpha-equivalence come for free since the binding infrastructure of the metalanguage is reused. It is well-known that in Coq it is not possible to use the usual HOAS encodings, although Despeyroux et al. (1995) and Chlipala (2008) have shown how weaker variations of HOAS can be encoded in Coq. Popescu et al. (2010) investigate how formalizations using HOAS can avoid standard problems by being encoded on top of first-order representations. Approaches like GMETA or LNgen are aimed at recovering many of the properties that one expects from a logical framework for free.

Nominal logic (Pitts 2003) is an extension of first-order logic that allows reasoning about alpha-equivalent abstract syntax in a generic way. Variants of nominal logic have been adopted in the Nominal Isabelle (Urban 2005). However, because Coq does not have a nominal variant, this approach cannot be used in Coq formalizations.

8 Conclusion

There are several techniques for formalizing metatheory using first-order representations, which typically involve developing the whole of the infrastructure by hand each time for a new formalization. GMETA improves on these techniques by providing reusable generic infrastructure in libraries, avoiding the repetition of definitions and lemmas for each new formalization. The DGP approach used by GMETA not only allows an elegant and verifiable formulation of the generic infrastructure which is appealing from the theoretical point of view, but also shows itself useful for conducting realistic formalizations of metatheory.

Acknowledgements. We are especially grateful to Sungwoo Park, which has provided us with many useful comments and suggestions. We thank Hugo Herbelin, Randy Pollack, Stephanie Weirich, the members of ROPAS and the anonymous reviewers for their useful comments and suggestions.

References

Altenkirch, T., McBride, C.: Generic programming within dependently typed programming. In: IFIP TC2/WG2.1 Working Conference on Generic Programming (2003)

Altenkirch, T., Reus, B.: Monadic Presentations of Lambda Terms Using Generalized Inductive Types. In: Flum, J., Rodríguez-Artalejo, M. (eds.) CSL 1999. LNCS, vol. 1683, pp. 453–468. Springer, Heidelberg (1999)

Aydemir, B., Weirich, S., Zdancewic, S.: Abstracting syntax. Technical Report MS-CIS-09-06, University of Pennsylvania (2009)

Aydemir, B.E., Weirich, S.: LNgen: Tool Support for Locally Nameless Representations (2009) (Unpublished manuscript)

Aydemir, B.E., Bohannon, A., Fairbairn, M., Foster, J.N., Pierce, B.C., Sewell, P., Vytiniotis, D., Washburn, G., Weirich, S., Zdancewic, S.: Mechanized Metatheory for the Masses: The PoplMark Challenge. In: Hurd, J., Melham, T. (eds.) TPHOLs 2005. LNCS, vol. 3603, pp. 50–65. Springer, Heidelberg (2005)

Aydemir, B.E., Charguéraud, A., Pierce, B.C., Pollack, R., Weirich, S.: Engineering formal metatheory. In: POPL 2008 (2008)

Boutin, S.: Using Reflection to Build Efficient and Certified Decision Procedures. In: Ito, T., Abadi, M. (eds.) TACS 1997. LNCS, vol. 1281, pp. 515–529. Springer, Heidelberg (1997)

Cheney, J.: Scrap your nameplate (functional pearl). In: ICFP 2005 (2005)

Chlipala, A.: A certified type-preserving compiler from lambda calculus to assembly language. In: PLDI 2007 (2007)

Chlipala, A.: Parametric higher-order abstract syntax for mechanized semantics. In: ICFP 2008 (2008)

The Coq Development Team. The Coq Proof Assistant Reference Manual, Version 8.2 (2009), `http://coq.inria.fr`

de Bruijn, N.G.: Lambda calculus notation with nameless dummies, a tool for automatic formula manipulation, with application to the church-rosser theorem. Indagationes Mathematicae (Proceedings) 75(5), 381–392 (1972)

Despeyroux, J., Felty, A.P., Hirschowitz, A.: Higher-Order Abstract Syntax in Coq. In: Dezani-Ciancaglini, M., Plotkin, G. (eds.) TLCA 1995. LNCS, vol. 902, pp. 124–138. Springer, Heidelberg (1995)

Dybjer, P.: Inductive families. Formal Aspects of Computing 6, 440–465 (1997)

Dybjer, P., Setzer, A.: A Finite Axiomatization of Inductive-Recursive Definitions. In: Girard, J.-Y. (ed.) TLCA 1999. LNCS, vol. 1581, pp. 129–146. Springer, Heidelberg (1999)

Dybjer, P., Setzer, A.: Indexed Induction-Recursion. In: Kahle, R., Schroeder-Heister, P., Stärk, R.F. (eds.) PTCS 2001. LNCS, vol. 2183, pp. 93–113. Springer, Heidelberg (2001)

Gacek, A.: The Abella Interactive Theorem Prover (System Description). In: Armando, A., Baumgartner, P., Dowek, G. (eds.) IJCAR 2008. LNCS (LNAI), vol. 5195, pp. 154–161. Springer, Heidelberg (2008)

Harper, R., Honsell, F., Plotkin, G.: A framework for defining logics. J. ACM 40(1), 143–184 (1993)

Hinze, R., Jeuring, J.: Generic Haskell: Practice and Theory. In: Backhouse, R., Gibbons, J. (eds.) Generic Programming SS 2002. LNCS, vol. 2793, pp. 1–56. Springer, Heidelberg (2003)

Jansson, P., Jeuring, J.: PolyP—a polytypic programming language extension. In: POPL 1997 (1997)

Licata, D.R., Harper, R.: A universe of binding and computation. In: ICFP 2009 (2009)
Martin-Löf, P.: Intuitionistic Type Theory. Bibliopolis (1984)
McBride, C., McKinna, J.: The view from the left. J. Funct. Program. 14(1), 69–111 (2004)
McKinna, J., Pollack, R.: Pure Type Systems Formalized. In: Bezem, M., Groote, J.F. (eds.) TLCA 1993. LNCS, vol. 664, pp. 289–305. Springer, Heidelberg (1993)
Momigliano, A., Martin, A.J., Felty, A.P.: Two-level hybrid: A system for reasoning using higher-order abstract syntax. Electron. Notes Theor. Comput. Sci. 196, 85–93 (2008)
Morris, P., Altenkirch, T., McBride, C.: Exploring the Regular Tree Types. In: Filliâtre, J.-C., Paulin-Mohring, C., Werner, B. (eds.) TYPES 2004. LNCS, vol. 3839, pp. 252–267. Springer, Heidelberg (2006)
Morris, P., Altenkirch, T., Ghani, N.: A universe of strictly positive families. Int. J. Found. Comput. Sci. 20(1), 83–107 (2009)
Nordström, B., Peterson, K., Smith, J.M.: Programming in Martin-Löf's Type Theory: An Introduction. Oxford Unversity Press (1990)
Norell, U.: Towards a practical programming language based on dependent type theory. PhD thesis, Chalmers University of Technology (2007)
Norell, U.: Dependently Typed Programming in Agda. In: Koopman, P., Plasmeijer, R., Swierstra, D. (eds.) AFP 2008. LNCS, vol. 5832, pp. 230–266. Springer, Heidelberg (2009)
Paulin-Mohring, C.: Définitions Inductives en Théorie des Types d'Ordre Supérieur. Habilitation à diriger les recherches, Université Claude Bernard Lyon I (1996)
Peyton Jones, S., Vytiniotis, D., Weirich, S., Washburn, G.: Simple unification-based type inference for GADTs. In: ICFP 2006 (2006)
Pfenning, F., Elliot, C.: Higher-order abstract syntax. In: PLDI 1988 (1988)
Pfenning, F., Schürmann, C.: System Description: Twelf - A Meta-Logical Framework for Deductive Systems. In: Ganzinger, H. (ed.) CADE 1999. LNCS (LNAI), vol. 1632, pp. 202–206. Springer, Heidelberg (1999)
Pierce, B.C.: Types and Programming Languages. The MIT Press (2002)
Pitts, A.M.: Nominal logic, a first order theory of names and binding. Inf. Comput. 186(2), 165–193 (2003)
Popescu, A., Gunter, E.L., Osborn, C.J.: Strong Normalization for System F by HOAS on top of FOAS. In: LICS, pp. 31–40 (2010)
Rodriguez, A., Jeuring, J., Jansson, P., Gerdes, A., Kiselyov, O., Oliveira, B.C.d.S.: Comparing libraries for generic programming in Haskell. In: Haskell 2008 (2008)
Rossberg, A., Russo, C.V., Dreyer, D.: F-ing modules. In: TLDI 2010 (2010)
Sato, M., Pollack, R.: External and internal syntax of the lambda-calculus. J. Symb. Comput. 45(5), 598–616 (2010)
Sewell, P., Nardelli, F.Z., Owens, S., Peskine, G., Ridge, T., Sarkar, S., Strniša, R.: Ott: Effective tool support for the working semanticist. J. Funct. Program. 20(01), 71–122 (2010)
Urban, C., Tasson, C.: Nominal Techniques in Isabelle/HOL. In: Nieuwenhuis, R. (ed.) CADE 2005. LNCS (LNAI), vol. 3632, pp. 38–53. Springer, Heidelberg (2005)
Verbruggen, W., de Vries, E., Hughes, A.: Polytypic programming in COQ. In: WGP 2008 (2008)
Verbruggen, W., de Vries, E., Hughes, A.: Polytypic properties and proofs in Coq. In: WGP 2009 (2009)
Vouillon, J.: Poplmark solutions using de bruijn indices (2007), `https://alliance.seas.upenn.edu/~plclub/cgi-bin/poplmark/`

Expansion for Universal Quantifiers

Sergueï Lenglet[1,*] and Joe B. Wells[2]

[1] University of Wrocław
[2] Heriot-Watt University

Abstract. *Expansion* is an operation on typings (i.e., pairs of typing environments and result types) defined originally in type systems for the λ-calculus with intersection types in order to obtain principal (i.e., most informative, strongest) typings. In a type inference scenario, expansion allows postponing choices for whether and how to use non-syntax-driven typing rules (e.g., intersection introduction) until enough information has been gathered to make the right decision. Furthermore, these choices can be equivalent to inserting uses of such typing rules at deeply nested positions in a typing derivation, without needing to actually inspect or modify (or even have) the typing derivation. Expansion has in recent years become simpler due to the use of *expansion variables* (e.g., in System E).

This paper extends expansion and expansion variables to systems with ∀-quantifiers. We present System F_s, an extension of System F with expansion, and prove its main properties. This system turns type inference into a constraint solving problem; this could be helpful to design a modular type inference algorithm for System F types in the future.

1 Introduction

1.1 Background and Motivation

Polymorphism and Principal Typings. Many practical uses of type systems require *polymorphism*, i.e., the possibility to reuse a generic piece of code with different types. Type systems most commonly provide polymorphism through ∀-*quantifiers*, like in the Hindley-Milner (HM) type system [16] and in System F [19,7], but can also use other methods like *intersection types* [3]. Systems with ∀-quantifiers assign general type schemes that can be instantiated to more specific types; for example, the identity function can be typed with $\forall a.(a \rightarrow a)$, and then used with types $\mathsf{int} \rightarrow \mathsf{int}$ or $\mathsf{real} \rightarrow \mathsf{real}$ when applied respectively to an integer or a real. Systems with intersection types list the different usage types of a term; if the identity function is applied exactly twice in a code fragment, once to an integer and once to a real, then its type will be $(\mathsf{int} \rightarrow \mathsf{int}) \sqcap (\mathsf{real} \rightarrow \mathsf{real})$.

Type systems with ∀-quantifiers are very popular, but they often lack *principal typings* [26], i.e., strongest, most informative typings (a typing is usually a pair of a type environments and a result type). Wells [26] proved that HM and System F do not have principal typings. It is important not to confuse this notion with

* The author is supported by the Alain Bensoussan Fellowship Programme.

H. Seidl (Ed.): ESOP 2012, LNCS 7211, pp. 456–475, 2012.

the (weaker) one of "principal types" defined for the HM type system in which typable terms admit a strongest result type for each fixed type environment. Principal typings are crucial for *compositional* type inference, where types for terms are found using only the analysis results of the immediate sub-components, which can be inspected independently and in any order. Compositional type inference helps in performing separate analysis of program modules, and therefore helps with separate compilation. Note that the Damas-Milner algorithm [4] for HM is not fully compositional: to give a type for a let-binding $\mathsf{let}\ x = e_1\ \mathsf{in}\ e_2$, the algorithm must infer first a type for e_1, and then use the result to type e_2.

Expansion and Expansion Variables. In contrast, type systems with intersection types usually have principal typings [3]. In such systems, admissible typings are obtained from a principal one using *expansion* (in addition to substitution and weakening). We present this mechanism through an example, taken from [2]. Consider the following λ-terms:

$$M_1 = \lambda x.x\ (\lambda y.y\ z) \qquad M_2 = \lambda g.\lambda x.g\ (g\ x)$$

One can compute the following principal typings for these terms in the type system of Coppo, Dezani, and Veneri [3].

$$M_1 : \langle z : a \vdash \underbrace{(((a \to b) \to b) \to c)}_{T_1} \to c\rangle$$

$$M_2 : \langle \emptyset \vdash \underbrace{((e \to f) \sqcap (d \to e)) \to (d \to f)}_{T_2}\rangle$$

Following [2], we write $M : \langle A \vdash T\rangle$ for the assignment of type T under type environment A (often written $A \vdash M : T$ in the literature). To type the application $M_1\ M_2$, we must somehow "unify" T_1 and T_2. We cannot do this by simple type substitutions, replacing type variables by types; we have a clash between type $(a \to b) \to b$ and type $(e \to f) \sqcap (d \to e)$. We cannot unify these types by removing the intersection, using idempotence $T \sqcap T = T$; we would have to solve the equation $a \to b = b$, which does not have a solution in absence of recursive types.

This inference problem can be solved by introducing an intersection in the typing of M_1, using *expansion*.

$$M_1 : \langle z : a_1 \sqcap a_2 \vdash (((a_1 \to b_1) \to b_1 \sqcap (a_2 \to b_2) \to b_2) \to c) \to c\rangle$$

We can then unify the two types as required by applying the substitution $e := a_1 \to b_1, f := b_1, d := a_2 \to a_1 \to b_1, b_2 := a_1 \to b_1, c := (a_2 \to a_1 \to b_1) \to b_1$

The expansion operation simulates on typings the use of an intersection introduction typing rule at a nested position in the typing derivation. The above expansion on the typing of M_1 transforms the typing derivation on the left in the figure below into the derivation on the right (we write @ for the application typing rule, λ and $\sqcap$ for respectively abstraction and intersection introductions),

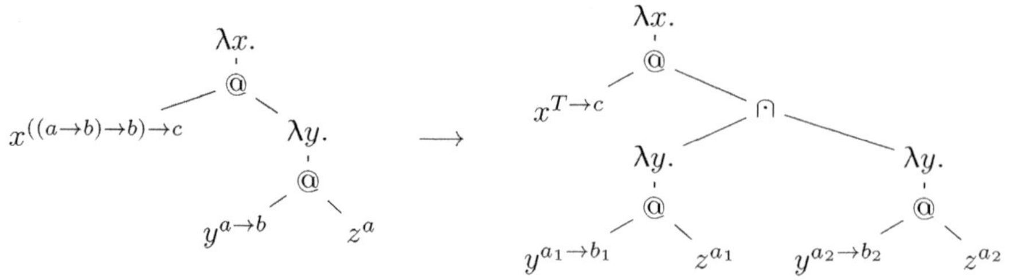

where $T = ((a_1 \to b_1) \to b_1) \cap ((a_2 \to b_2) \to b_2)$.

Earlier definitions of expansion [3,20] are quite difficult to follow and to implement. *Expansion variables* (or E-variables) were introduced by Kfoury and Wells in System I [8] to simplify expansion application. The construct has then been improved in System E [1]. An E-variable e is a placeholder for unknown uses of typing rules such as $\cap$-introduction. For example, the following typing derivation for M_1

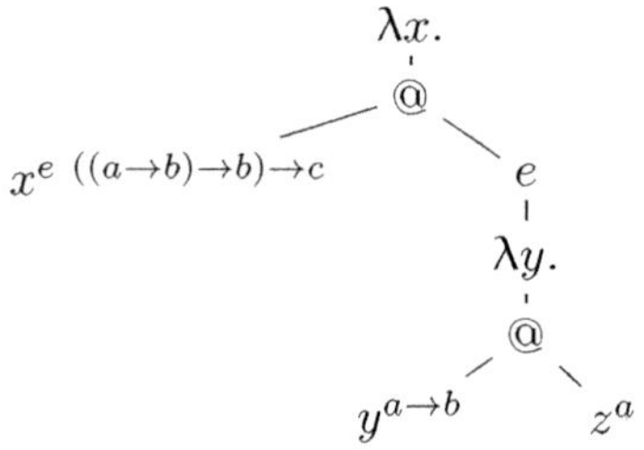

generates this typing:

$$M_1 : \langle z : e\ a \vdash (e\ ((a \to b) \to b) \to c) \to c \rangle$$

Note that the variable e is introduced in the result type as well as in the type environment. One can then perform the previous expansion by replacing e by the *expansion term* $(a := a_1, b := b_1) \cap (a := a_2, b := b_2)$, which introduces an intersection $\cap$ at the e position and applies a different substitution for each branch of the intersection. We then obtain the desired typing with intersection, given above.

Motivation. The idea behind expansion is fairly general, even if it has been defined only in systems with intersection types. It allows postponing the uses of non-syntactic typing rules, i.e., rules that are not driven by the syntax of terms, such as $\cap$-introduction, but also $\forall$-introduction and $\forall$-elimination. This is helpful in type inference scenarios: constructor introductions or eliminations can be delayed until all necessary information has been gathered. In the above example, we introduce an intersection in the typing of M_1 only when we have to, when applying M_1 to M_2. We want to bring this possibility of delaying the choice of uses of typing rules to type system with $\forall$-quantifiers, to see how (compositional) type inference could benefit from this property. We present an extension of System F with an expansion mechanism, called System F_s. Before going into the details of its syntax in Section 2, we first informally introduce System F_s and point out the main differences between its expansion mechanism and the one of System E.

1.2 Overview of System F_s

Quantifier Introduction. Assume that we have the following typings for the terms M_1 and M_2 given above.

$$M_1 : \langle z : a \vdash \underbrace{(((a \to b) \to b) \to c)}_{T_1} \to c \rangle$$

$$M_2 : \langle \emptyset \vdash \underbrace{(\forall e.((d \to e) \to e)) \to (d \to d \to f) \to f}_{T_2} \rangle$$

Suppose we have forgotten M_1 and M_2 (e.g., we have already compiled them and discarded the source code), and we want to type the application $M_1\ M_2$. We need to "unify" T_1 and T_2. We cannot unify $(a \to b) \to b$ and $\forall e.((d \to e) \to e)$ using only type substitutions, because of the $\forall$-quantifier. This $\forall$-quantifier is necessary, because the term g is used twice in M_2 with different usage types. We can solve this problem by introducing in T_1 a $\forall$-quantifier over b, the scope of which encompasses $(a \to b) \to b$. To this end, we introduce an *expansion variable* s at the required position in the typing of M_1 (we use s instead of e to avoid confusion with the E-variables of System E).

$$M_1 : \langle z : a \vdash (s^{\{a\}}\ ((a \to b) \to b) \to c) \to c \rangle$$

Unlike expansion variables in System E, s is not introduced in the type environment; the application of s to the typing is asymmetric. We discuss the role of the superscript $\{a\}$ below. A $\forall$-quantifier over b can be introduced at the position we want by replacing s by the *expansion term* $\forall b$. This operation corresponds to the following transformation on derivation trees

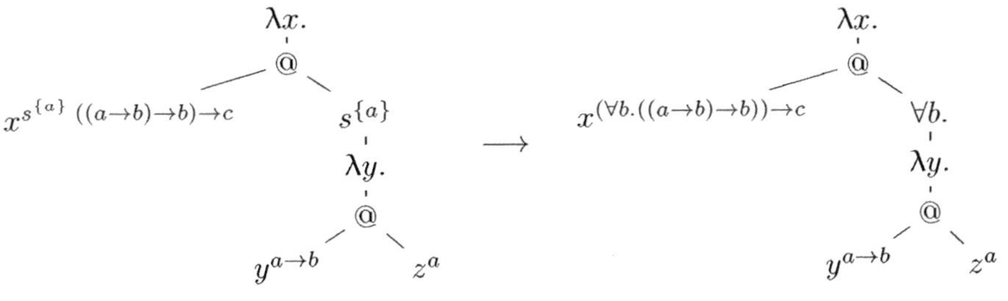

and generates the typing

$$M_1 : \langle z : a \vdash (\forall b.((a \to b) \to b) \to c) \to c \rangle$$

as wished. We can then unify $\forall b.((a \to b) \to b) \to c$ with T_2, by substituting d for a and $(d \to d \to f) \to f$ for c. The key point is we can get the new typing without needing to build the typing derivation (or have any memory of M_1).

When we introduce a ∀-quantifier, we forbid any quantification over type variables that are free in the type environment. To take this into account, we keep the set of free variables of the environment as a parameter of the E-variable. For example, when we introduce s in the typing of M_1, a is the only free variable occurring in the environment; we remember the set $\{a\}$ in $s^{\{a\}}$. This prevents any illegal quantification from happening; replacing s by the expansion $\forall a$ does not introduce a quantification over a in this case and leaves the typing judgement unchanged.

Subtyping. E-variables can be used to perform subtyping as well. Consider System F ∀-elimination as a subtyping relation: $\forall a.T_1 \leq [a := T_2]T_1$. Let $A = \text{choose} : \forall a.(a \to a \to a), \text{id} : \forall a.(a \to a)$ and suppose we want to type the application $M = \text{choose id}$ under A (this example is taken from [11]). We can derive the typing $\langle A \vdash (\forall a.(a \to a)) \to (\forall a.(a \to a))\rangle$ for M; however if we want to apply M to a term of type $b \to b$, we have to redo the type inference on M to obtain the needed typing $\langle A \vdash (b \to b) \to (b \to b)\rangle$.

To avoid this, we add an E-variable s on top of the type of id; we obtain the following typing derivation (nodes marked with a type represent uses of subtyping, i.e., in our case, instantiations of ∀-quantifiers)

$$
\begin{array}{c}
@ \\
\diagup \quad \diagdown \\
T \to T \to T \qquad \qquad s^{\emptyset} \\
\mid \qquad \qquad \qquad \mid \\
\text{choose}^{\forall a.(a \to a \to a)} \qquad \text{id}^{\forall a.(a \to a)}
\end{array}
$$

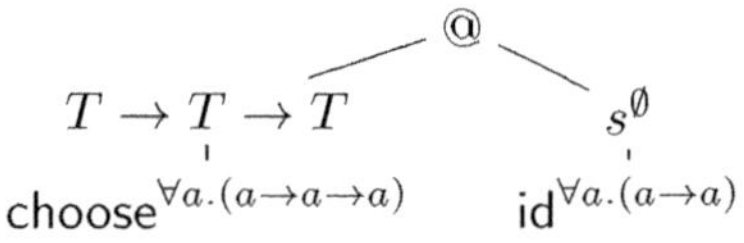

with $T = s^{\emptyset} \, \forall a.(a \to a)$, giving typing

$$M : \langle A \vdash (s^{\emptyset} \, \forall a.(a \to a)) \to (s^{\emptyset} \, \forall a.(a \to a))\rangle$$

If we want to apply M to a term M' of type $b \to b$, we utilize expansion to introduce the use of subtyping $\forall a.(a \to a) \leq b \to b$ at the s position in the typing tree. In the process, the type $T \to T \to T$ is updated into $(b \to b) \to (b \to b) \to (b \to b)$. We obtain

$$
\begin{array}{c}
@ \\
\diagup \quad \diagdown \\
(b \to b) \to (b \to b) \to (b \to b) \qquad b \to b \\
\mid \qquad \qquad \qquad \qquad \mid \\
\text{choose}^{\forall a.(a \to a \to a)} \qquad \qquad \text{id}^{\forall a.(a \to a)}
\end{array}
$$

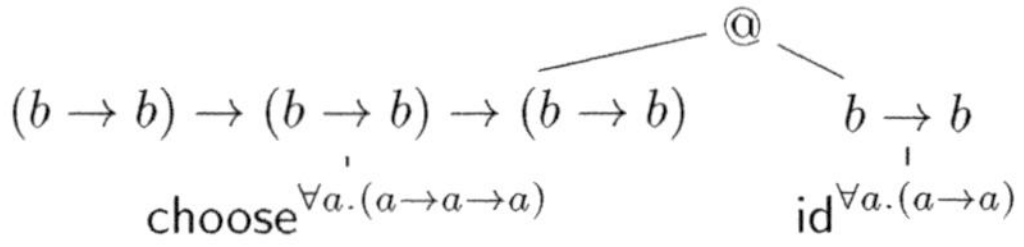

with typing $M : \langle A \vdash (b \to b) \to (b \to b)\rangle$, and we can then type $M\,M'$. In fact, the expansion mechanism for subtyping introduction does not depend on the definition of $\leq$, and therefore we keep System F_s parametric in its subtyping relation.

1.3   Summary of Contributions

We define System F_s and present its principal properties. Improvements over previous work are as follows:

$x \in \mathsf{TermVar} ::= \mathsf{x}_i$	$M \in \mathsf{Term}$	$::= x \mid \lambda x.M \mid M_1 \mathbin{@} M_2$
$a, b \in \mathsf{TypeVar} ::= \mathsf{a}_i$	$T \in \mathsf{Type}$	$::= a \mid T_1 \to T_2 \mid \forall a.T \mid s^B\, T$
$s \in \mathsf{ExpVar} ::= \mathsf{s}_i$	$S \in \mathsf{Substitution}$	$::= a := T, S \mid s := L, S \mid \boxdot$
$B \in \mathcal{P}_{\mathsf{fin}}(\mathsf{TypeVar})$	$L \in \mathsf{Expansion}$	$::= \Diamond \mid \forall a.L \mid s^B\, L \mid L^{:T}$
	$\Delta \in \mathsf{Constraint}$	$::= \top \mid T_1 \lessdot T_2 \mid \Delta_1 \wedge \Delta_2 \mid \exists a.\Delta \mid s^B_T\, \Delta$
	$A \in \mathsf{TypeEnv}$	$::= \emptyset \mid A, x : T$
	$Q \in \mathsf{Skeleton}$	$::= x^A \mid \lambda x.Q \mid Q_1 \mathbin{@} Q_2 \mid \forall a.Q \mid s^B\, Q \mid Q^{:T}$

Fig. 1. Syntax grammars and metavariable conventions

1. System $\mathrm{F_s}$ is the first type system with an expansion mechanism for $\forall$-quantifiers, where we can delay $\forall$-introduction and uses of subtyping with expansion.
2. System $\mathrm{F_s}$ extends the notion of expansion; we introduce a new expansion mechanism with its corresponding (asymmetric) E-variables, which differ greatly from the ones of System E [1].
3. We prove that we can generate all System $\mathrm{F_s}$ judgements from a *initial skeleton*, an incomplete typing derivation with constraints that need to be solved. This property is a (weaker) form of principality (Theorem 5.4).
4. System $\mathrm{F_s}$ is parametric in its subtyping relation; by using different subtyping relations (such as System F type application or Mitchell's relation [17]), one can change the typing power of System $\mathrm{F_s}$ without modifying the typing rules or judgements.
5. System $\mathrm{F_s}$ turns type inference into a type constraint solving problem. We believe it can be helpful to reason about modular type inference, even if we do not provide a constraint solving algorithm yet.

Proofs are available in an accompying research report [14].

2 Syntax

Fig. 1 defines the grammars and metavariable conventions of the entities used in this paper. Let i, j, m, n range over natural numbers. Given a set X, we write $\mathcal{P}_{\mathsf{fin}}(X)$ for the set of finite subsets of X. We distinguish between the metavariables x, a, s, and the concrete variables x_i, a_i, s_i. The (non-standard) symbol @ used for application helps in reading skeletons, and we keep it for terms for consistency. We explain the role of constraints (Δ) and skeletons (Q) in Section 3, and the syntax of expansion terms (L) and substitutions (S) in Section 4.

Precedence. To reduce parenthesis usage, we define precedence for operators and operations defined later (such as substitution and expansion applications $[S]T$ and $[\![L]\!]^B T$) in the following order, from highest to lowest: $s^B\, T$, $\forall a.T$, $[S]T$, $[\![L]\!]^B T$, $T_1 \to T_2$. For example, $[S]T_1 \to s^B\, T_2 = ([S]T_1) \to (s^B\, T_2)$ and $\forall a.a \to \forall a.a = (\forall a.a) \to (\forall a.a)$. Furthermore, the function type constructor is

$$x^A \triangleright x : \langle A \vdash A(x)\rangle/\top \quad (\mathsf{var}) \qquad \frac{Q \triangleright M : \langle A, x : T_1 \vdash T_2\rangle/\Delta}{\lambda x.Q \triangleright \lambda x.M : \langle A \vdash T_1 \to T_2\rangle/\Delta}\ (\mathsf{abs})$$

$$\frac{Q_1 \triangleright M_1 : \langle A \vdash T_1 \to T_2\rangle/\Delta_1 \qquad Q_2 \triangleright M_2 : \langle A \vdash T_1\rangle/\Delta_2}{Q_1 \mathbin{@} Q_2 \triangleright M_1 \mathbin{@} M_2 : \langle A \vdash T_2\rangle/(\Delta_1 \wedge \Delta_2)}\ (\mathsf{app})$$

$$\frac{Q \triangleright M : \langle A \vdash T\rangle/\Delta \qquad a \notin \mathsf{ftv}(A)}{\forall a.Q \triangleright M : \langle A \vdash \forall a.T\rangle/\exists a.\Delta}\ (\forall\text{-}\mathsf{I}) \qquad \frac{Q \triangleright M : \langle A \vdash T\rangle/\Delta \qquad \mathsf{ftv}(A) \subseteq B}{s^B\ Q \triangleright M : \langle A \vdash s^B\ T\rangle/s^B_T\ \Delta}\ (s\text{-}\mathsf{I})$$

$$\frac{Q \triangleright M : \langle A \vdash T_1\rangle/\Delta}{Q^{:T_2} \triangleright M : \langle A \vdash T_2\rangle/(\Delta \wedge (T_1 \lessdot T_2))}\ (\lessdot)$$

Fig. 2. Typing rules

right-associative, so that $T_1 \to T_2 \to T_3 = T_1 \to (T_2 \to T_3)$, and the application is left-associative, so that $M_1 \mathbin{@} M_2 \mathbin{@} M_3 = (M_1 \mathbin{@} M_2) \mathbin{@} M_3$.

Equalities and α-conversion. We allow α-conversion of bound variables in types (where $\forall a.T$ binds a), skeletons (where $\lambda x.Q$ binds x and $\forall a.Q$ binds a), and constraints (where $\exists a.\Delta$ binds a). Note that a is not bound in the expansion term $\forall a.L$, and therefore it cannot be α-converted.

We equate types up to reordering of adjacent $\forall$-quantifiers (so $\forall a_1.\forall a_2.{}_2T = \forall a_2.\forall a_1.T$), and suppression of dummy quantifiers (if a is not free in T, then $\forall a.T = T$). We also enforce the following equalities on constraints

$$\begin{array}{lll} \exists a.(\Delta_1 \wedge \Delta_2) = (\exists a.\Delta_1) \wedge (\exists a.\Delta_2) & \Delta \wedge \Delta = \Delta & \Delta \wedge \top = \Delta \\ s^B_T\ (\Delta_1 \wedge \Delta_2) = (s^B_T\ \Delta_1) \wedge (s^B_T\ \Delta_2) & \Delta_1 \wedge \Delta_2 = \Delta_2 \wedge \Delta_1 & \\ \Delta_1 \wedge (\Delta_2 \wedge \Delta_3) = (\Delta_1 \wedge \Delta_2) \wedge \Delta_3 & \multicolumn{2}{r}{\exists a.\Delta = \Delta \text{ if } a \text{ is not free in } \Delta} \end{array}$$

Auxiliary Notations and Functions. Let $\mathsf{fv}(M)$ be the set of free variables of M, defined in the usual way. The free type variables of a type, an expansion, and a substitution are defined as follows.

$$\begin{array}{llll} \mathsf{ftv}(a) & = \{a\} & \mathsf{ftv}(\diamond) & = \emptyset \\ \mathsf{ftv}(T_1 \to T_2) & = \mathsf{ftv}(T_1) \cup \mathsf{ftv}(T_2) & \mathsf{ftv}(L^{:T}) & = \mathsf{ftv}(L) \cup \mathsf{ftv}(T) \\ \mathsf{ftv}(\forall a.T) & = \mathsf{ftv}(T) \setminus \{a\} & \mathsf{ftv}(\forall a.L) & = \mathsf{ftv}(L) \cup \{a\} \\ \mathsf{ftv}(s^B\ T) & = \mathsf{ftv}(T) \cup B & \mathsf{ftv}(s^B\ L) & = \mathsf{ftv}(L) \cup B \end{array}$$

$$\begin{array}{ll} \mathsf{ftv}(\boxdot) & = \emptyset \\ \mathsf{ftv}(a := T, S) & = \{a\} \cup \mathsf{ftv}(T) \cup \mathsf{ftv}(S) \\ \mathsf{ftv}(s := L, S) & = \mathsf{ftv}(L) \cup \mathsf{ftv}(S) \end{array}$$

3 Typing Rules

A type environment A (defined in Fig. 1) is a list of assignments which maps term variables to types. When writing a non-empty environment, we allow omitting the leading symbols "$\emptyset$,". A type environment is *well-formed* iff it does not mention twice the same term variable. Henceforth, we consider only well-formed type environments. For $A = x_1 : T_1, \ldots, x_n : T_n$, we define $A(x_i) = T_i$ for $i \in \{1 \ldots n\}$, $\mathsf{ftv}(A) = \bigcup_{i \in \{1 \ldots n\}} \mathsf{ftv}(T_i)$, and $\mathsf{support}(A) = \{x_1 \ldots x_n\}$.

The typing rules of System $\mathrm{F_s}$ (Fig. 2) derive judgements of the form $Q \rhd M : \langle A \vdash T \rangle / \Delta$, where constraints that need to be solved (by type inference) are accumulated in Δ. A constraint of the form $T_1 \lessdot T_2$ is called *atomic*. By including constraints in judgements, we can use the same rules for type checking and type inference. If the constraint is *solved* w.r.t. some subtyping relation, then the judgement acts as a regular typing judgement, assigning *typing* $\langle A \vdash T \rangle$ to the untyped term M.

A skeleton Q is just a *proof term*, a compact piece of syntax which represents a complete typing derivation. A skeleton Q is *valid* iff there exist M, A, T, and Δ such that $Q \rhd M : \langle A \vdash T \rangle / \Delta$. Henceforth, we consider only valid skeletons. All components of a judgement $Q \rhd M : \langle A \vdash T \rangle / \Delta$ are uniquely determined by Q, therefore we can define functions rtype and tenv such that $\mathsf{rtype}(Q) = T$ and $\mathsf{tenv}(Q) = A$. Skeletons replace typing derivation trees in formal statements. For example, $\lambda x.(x^{x:\forall a.a})^{:(\forall a.a) \to b} \mathbin{@} x^{x:\forall a.a}$ represents the following derivation.

$$\dfrac{\dfrac{\dfrac{x : \langle x : \forall a.a \vdash \forall a.a \rangle / \top}{x : \langle x : \forall a.a \vdash (\forall a.a) \to b \rangle / (\forall a.a \lessdot (\forall a.a) \to b)} \qquad x : \langle x : \forall a.a \vdash \forall a.a \rangle / \top}{x \mathbin{@} x : \langle x : \forall a.a \vdash b \rangle / (\forall a.a \lessdot (\forall a.a) \to b)}}{\lambda x.x \mathbin{@} x : \langle \emptyset \vdash (\forall a.a) \to b \rangle / (\forall a.a \lessdot (\forall a.a) \to b)}$$

In examples, we sometimes omit skeletons and constraints when they are not relevant, writing $M : \langle A \vdash T \rangle$ iff there exists Q, Δ such that $Q \rhd M : \langle A \vdash T \rangle / \Delta$.

Remark 3.1. A variable skeleton x^A remembers a type environment A and not simply the type of x to be able to type a variable x in a term $\lambda x.M$ such that $x \notin \mathsf{fv}(M)$. For example, we have $\lambda x.y^{x:a,y:b} \rhd \lambda x.y : \langle y : b \vdash a \to b \rangle / \top$.

We could have used λ-terms with only type annotations on bindings, like many other systems, but our skeletons are also useful because they uniquely represent entire typing derivations (judgement trees). We also prefer our skeletons because a goal for future work is a system containing both System E and System $\mathrm{F_s}$ (cf. Section 8), and our format of skeleton is better suited for the intersection introduction typing rule of System E, as discussed in [27]. □

Rules (var), (abs), and (app) are classic. The subtyping rule ($\lessdot$) generates a new atomic constraint, the meaning of which depends on the chosen subtyping relation (cf. solvedness definition in Section 6.1). Rule ($\forall$-I) introduces a $\forall$-quantifier over a, provided that a is not free in A. Note that a may occur free in Δ; we use an existential quantifier $\exists a.\Delta$ to bind it, as solvedness requires Δ to be solved for some a (cf. Section 6.1), and not for all possible instantiations of a, as a $\forall$-binder would suggest.

Rule (s-I) introduces an expansion variable s to mark a position in the derivation tree where a $\forall$-quantifier can be added or where subtyping can be used.

$$\begin{array}{ll}
[\![\diamondsuit]\!]^B W = W & [\![\diamondsuit]\!]^B_T \Delta = \Delta \\
[\![s^{B'}\ L]\!]^B W = s^{B \cup B'}\ ([\![L]\!]^{B'} W) & [\![s^{B'}\ L]\!]^B_T \Delta = s^{B \cup B'}_{[\![L]\!]^B T}\ ([\![L]\!]^B_T \Delta) \\
[\![\forall a.L]\!]^B W = \begin{cases} \forall a.[\![L]\!]^B W \text{ if } a \notin B \\ [\![L]\!]^B W \quad \text{otherwise} \end{cases} & [\![\forall a.L]\!]^B_T \Delta = \begin{cases} \exists a.[\![L]\!]^B_T \Delta \text{ if } a \notin B \\ [\![L]\!]^B_T \Delta \quad \text{otherwise} \end{cases} \\
[\![L^{:T_2}]\!]^B T_1 = T_2 & [\![L^{:T_2}]\!]^B_{T_1} \Delta = ([\![L]\!]^B_{T_1} \Delta) \wedge (([\![L]\!]^B T_1) \lessdot T_2) \\
[\![L^{:T_2}]\!]^B Q = ([\![L]\!]^B Q)^{:T_2} &
\end{array}$$

Fig. 3. Expansion application

Because a quantification over a free variable of A is not allowed (rule ($\forall$-I)), the E-variable remembers an over-approximation B of $\mathsf{ftv}(A)$, which is used by the expansion mechanism to prevent any illegal $\forall$-introduction from happening. The type T mentioned in $s^B_T\ \Delta$ can be used during expansion to generate an atomic constraint $T \lessdot T'$ if needed. We explain the expansion mechanism in detail in the next section.

Remark 3.2. The rule (var) may also introduce E-variables, as for example in $x^{x:s^{\emptyset}\ a} \rhd x : \langle x : s^{\emptyset}\ a \vdash s^{\emptyset}\ a\rangle / \top$. In this case, performing expansion at the position of s does not correspond to a use of rules ($\forall$-I) or ($\lessdot$), and the set B of type variables remembered by s can be any set. Indeed we can derive $x^{x:s^B\ a} \rhd x : \langle x : s^B\ a \vdash s^B\ a\rangle / \top$ for any B. □

Remark 3.3. In rule (s-I), we can remember a set bigger than $\mathsf{ftv}(A)$ for subject reduction to hold. For example, consider the following judgement

$$Q \rhd (\lambda x.y) @ \lambda x.x : \langle y : b \vdash s^{\{a,b\}}\ b\rangle / s^{\{a,b\}}_b\ \top$$

with $Q = (\lambda x.s^{\{a,b\}}\ y^{x:a \to a, y:b}) @ \lambda x.x^{x:a,y:b}$. The term $(\lambda x.y) @ \lambda x.x$ reduces to y, and to derive

$$s^{\{a,b\}}\ y^{y:b} \rhd y : \langle y : b \vdash s^{\{a,b\}}\ b\rangle / s^{\{a,b\}}_b\ \top,$$

we have to be able to mention a even if it does not appear in $y : b$. □

4 Substitution and Expansion

4.1 Expansion Application

The syntax of expansion terms is given in Fig. 1. Let W range over types and skeletons. Fig. 3 defines the application of expansion to types, skeletons, and constraints. When applied to a type or a skeleton, the expansion mechanism relies on a set of type variables B, used in introductions of E-variable and $\forall$-quantifier; when applied to a constraint, it requires an extra parameter (a type) to generate an appropriate atomic constraint if needed. Each construct of expansion terms

Metavariables

$$v ::= a \mid s$$
$$\Phi ::= T \mid L$$

Substitution application

$$\begin{array}{lll}
[\boxdot]a & = a \\
[\boxdot]s & = s^{\emptyset}\ \Diamond \\
[v := \Phi, S]v & = \Phi \\
[v := \Phi, S]v' & = [S]v' \text{ if } v \neq v' \\
\\
[S](s^{B}\ T) & = [\![[S]s]\!]^{\mathsf{ftv}([S]B)}[S]T \\
[S]\forall a.T & = \forall a.[S]T \text{ if } a \notin \mathsf{ftv}(S) \\
[S](T_1 \to T_2) & = [S]T_1 \to [S]T_2
\end{array}$$

$$\begin{array}{ll}
[S]x^{A} & = x^{[S]A} \\
[S]\lambda x.Q & = \lambda x.[S]Q \\
[S](Q_1 @ Q_2) & = ([S]Q_1) @ ([S]Q_2) \\
[S](s^{B}\ Q) & = [\![[S]s]\!]^{\mathsf{ftv}([S]B)}[S]Q \\
[S]\forall a.Q & = \forall a.[S]Q \text{ if } a \notin \mathsf{ftv}(S) \\
[S](Q^{:T}) & = [S]Q^{:[S]T} \\
\\
[S](T_1 \lessdot T_2) & = [S]T_1 \lessdot [S]T_2 \\
[S]\top & = \top \\
[S](s^{B}_{T}\ \Delta) & = [\![[S]s]\!]^{\mathsf{ftv}([S]B)}_{[S]T}[S]\Delta \\
[S]\exists a.\Delta & = \exists a.[S]\Delta \text{ if } a \notin \mathsf{ftv}(S) \\
[S](\Delta_1 \wedge \Delta_2) & = ([S]\Delta_1) \wedge ([S]\Delta_2)
\end{array}$$

Fig. 4. Substitution application

corresponds to the application of a non-syntactic typing rule, except for the null expansion $\Diamond$, which leaves unchanged the entities it is applied to.

E-variable and $\forall$-quantifier expansions behave the same on types, skeletons, and constraints. Applied with parameter B, the expansions $s^{B'}\ L$ and $\forall a.L$ first execute L and then introduce an E-variable s (with set $B \cup B'$ of variables that cannot be quantified) and a quantifier over a (iff $a \notin B$), respectively. When applied to all parts of a judgement $Q \rhd M : \langle A \vdash T \rangle / \Delta$, we must have $\mathsf{ftv}(A) \subseteq B$ for these operations to be sound w.r.t. rules (s-I) and ($\forall$-I) (cf. Lemma 4.1).

The expansion $L^{:T_2}$ first applies L and then performs subtyping with T_2, as we can see in the skeleton case. When applied to a type, only the subtyping step matters, and we simply obtain T_2. Finally, the constraint case Δ requires an extra parameter T_1 to generate a new atomic constraint. In practice, T_1 will be the result type of the judgement $Q \rhd M : \langle A \vdash T_1 \rangle / \Delta$ from which Δ comes. When $L^{:T_2}$ is applied to the above judgement, L is applied first, in particular to the type T_1. To take this into account, the generated constraint is $([\![L]\!]^{B} T_1) \lessdot T_2$ (and not simply $T_1 \lessdot T_2$).

Expansion is sound w.r.t. to the type system of System $\mathrm{F_s}$.

Lemma 4.1. *If* $Q \rhd M : \langle A \vdash T \rangle / \Delta$ *and* $\mathsf{ftv}(A) \subseteq B$*, then* $[\![L]\!]^{B} Q \rhd M : \langle A \vdash [\![L]\!]^{B} T \rangle / [\![L]\!]^{B}_{T} \Delta$*.* $\square$

Expansion operates only at the top-level of the typing judgement in Lemma 4.1; in order to expand at a deeply nested position, we have to replace an E-variable s by an expansion L, as explained in the next section.

4.2 Substitution Application

Substitutions (defined in Fig. 1) are lists of assignments that map type variables to types ($a := T$) and E-variables to expansions ($s := L$), ended by the symbol $\boxdot$. Application of substitutions to type variable sets B and type environments A

is pointwise. Given a finite set of types $\{T_1 \dots T_n\}$, we define $\mathsf{ftv}(\{T_1 \dots T_n\})$ as $\bigcup_{i\in\{1\dots n\}} \mathsf{ftv}(T_i)$. Fig. 4 defines application of substitutions to variables, types, skeletons, and constraints.

A substitution S generates a type T (resp. an expansion L) when applied to a type variable a (resp. to an E-variable s). A substitution may contain several assignments for the same variable, as in $S = (a := T_1, a := T_2, \boxdot)$; in this case, only the first one is considered. We choose this design for simplicity; an alternate solution would be to syntactically prevent repetitions in the substitution definition, but the definition would then become more complex for no obvious gain.

The application of substitutions to types $s^B\,T$ is the most important case.

$$[S](s^B\,T) = [\![[S]s]\!]^{\mathsf{ftv}([S]B)}[S]T$$

The substitution S is first applied to s, which gives us an expansion $L = [S]s$, which is then applied to the type $[S]T$. We remember that B is (an over-approximation of) the set of free type variables that cannot be quantified over, because they appear in the type environment at the time the variable s is introduced. If S replaces a variable $a \in B$ by a type T', then T' now appears in the type environment, and its free variables cannot be quantified over. This explains why we have to apply the expansion $[\![[S]s]\!]^{\mathsf{ftv}([S]B)}[S]T$ with the set $\mathsf{ftv}([S]B)$ and not simply with the set B. The application of S to skeletons $s^B\,Q$ and to constraints $s^B_T\,\Delta$ follows the same pattern.

Example 4.2. Let $M = \lambda x.x \mathbin{@} y$. We have

$$M : \langle y : a \vdash s^{\{a\}}\,((a \to b) \to b)\rangle$$

Applying $S_1 = (a := a_1 \to a_2, \boxdot)$ to this typing gives us

$$M : \langle y : a_1 \to a_2 \vdash s^{\{a_1,a_2\}}\,(((a_1 \to a_2) \to b) \to b)\rangle$$

Then applying $S_2 = (s := \forall b.\diamondsuit, \boxdot)$ gives us

$$M : \langle y : a_1 \to a_2 \vdash \forall b.(((a_1 \to a_2) \to b) \to b)\rangle$$

Note that the substitution $(s := \forall a'.\diamondsuit, \boxdot)$ would have left the last judgement unchanged if $a' \in \{a_1, a_2\}$, and would have introduced a dummy quantifier if $a' \notin \{b, a_1, a_2\}$. We can achieve the same effect as doing S_1 before S_2 by applying the substitution $S = (a := a_1 \to a_2, s := \forall b.\diamondsuit, \boxdot)$ to the initial judgement. $\square$

Example 4.3. Let $T = \forall a.(a \to a)$. We have

$$\lambda x.s^{\emptyset}\,((x^{x:T})^{:T\to T} \mathbin{@} x^{x:T}) \rhd \lambda x.x \mathbin{@} x : \langle \emptyset \vdash T \to s^{\emptyset}\,T\rangle / s^{\emptyset}_T\,(T \lessdot T \to T)$$

Applying substitution $S = (s := \diamondsuit^{:b\to b}, \boxdot)$ gives us

$$\lambda x.((x^{x:T})^{:T\to T} \mathbin{@} x^{x:T})^{:b\to b} \rhd \lambda x.x \mathbin{@} x : \langle \emptyset \vdash T \to b \to b\rangle / \Delta$$

where $\Delta = (T \lessdot b \to b) \wedge (T \lessdot T \to T)$. Subtyping has been introduced at a nested position (under the λ), generating the expected constraint $T \lessdot b \to b$. $\square$

$$C \vdash x \triangleright s^{\mathsf{ftv}(C)}\, x^C \qquad \frac{C, x : a \vdash M \triangleright Q \qquad s \notin \mathsf{allvar}(Q) \qquad B = \mathsf{ftv}(\mathsf{tenv}(\lambda x.Q))}{C \vdash \lambda x.M \triangleright s^B\, (\lambda x.Q)}$$

$$\frac{\begin{array}{c}C \vdash M_1 \triangleright Q_1 \qquad C \vdash M_2 \triangleright Q_2 \qquad Q = Q_1^{:\mathsf{rtype}(Q_2) \to a} \,@\, Q_2 \qquad B = \mathsf{ftv}(\mathsf{tenv}(Q)) \\ (\mathsf{allvar}(Q_1) \cap \mathsf{allvar}(Q_2)) \setminus \mathsf{ftv}(C) = \emptyset \qquad \{a, s\} \cap (\mathsf{allvar}(Q_1) \cup \mathsf{allvar}(Q_2)) = \emptyset\end{array}}{C \vdash M_1 \,@\, M_2 \triangleright s^B\, Q}$$

$$\frac{C \vdash M \triangleright Q \qquad \mathsf{support}(C) = \mathsf{fv}(M)}{\vdash M \triangleright Q}$$

Fig. 5. Initial skeletons of a term

Substituting a variable s by an expansion L makes s disappear. As a result, one can use the null expansion $\diamondsuit$ to delete an E-variable s from a type $s^B\, T$. If $S = (s := \diamondsuit, \boxdot)$, then $[S](s^B\, T) = [\![\diamondsuit]\!]^B [S]T = [S]T$ (the occurrences of s in T are also removed). An expansion L can be applied at the location of a variable s without making s disappear using the substitution $S = (s := s^{\emptyset}\, L, \boxdot)$. Indeed we have $[S](s^B\, T) = [\![s^{\emptyset}\, L]\!]^B [S]T = s^B\, [\![L]\!]^B [S]T$. The substitution $\boxdot$ is the *identity* substitution; it leaves variables, types, skeletons, and constraints unchanged. For example, for E-variables, we have $[\boxdot](s^B\, T) = [\![s^{\emptyset}\, \diamondsuit]\!]^B [\boxdot]T = s^B\, [\boxdot]T$. The remaining cases of substitution application are straightforward descending cases. The resulting operation is sound w.r.t. System $\mathrm{F_s}$ type system.

Theorem 4.4. *If* $Q \triangleright M : \langle A \vdash T \rangle / \Delta$ *then* $[S]Q \triangleright M : \langle [S]A \vdash [S]T \rangle / [S]\Delta$. $\square$

5 Initial Skeletons

In this section, we prove that we can generate all System $\mathrm{F_s}$ judgements for a term M from an initial skeleton built from M.

We first show that we can obtain *relevant* skeletons; a skeleton Q such that $Q \triangleright M : \langle A \vdash T \rangle / \Delta$ is relevant if $\mathsf{fv}(M) = \mathsf{support}(A)$. In words, the type environment of a relevant skeleton does not mention more term variables than necessary. A *variable environment* C is a type environment which assigns type variables to expression variables and such that for all x, y such that $x \neq y$, we have $C(x) \neq C(y)$. We write $\mathsf{allvar}(Q)$ for the set of free type and E-variables occurring in Q. Fig. 5 defines a judgement $\vdash M \triangleright Q$, which means that Q is an *initial skeleton* for M. The main ideas behind this construct are as follows: first, we type each variable in $\mathsf{fv}(M)$ with a distinct type variable (using the environment C mentioned in the auxiliary judgement $C \vdash M \triangleright Q$). Then we introduce a (fresh) E-variable at every possible position in the skeleton. Finally, we use subtyping to ensure that a term in a function position in an application has an arrow type. Two initial skeletons for the same term are equivalent up to renaming of their variables, as stated in the lemma below (where we call an expansion of the form $s^B\, \diamondsuit$ an *E-expansion*).

Lemma 5.1. *Let Q_1, Q_2 such that $\vdash M \rhd Q_1$ and $\vdash M \rhd Q_2$. There exists a substitution S which maps type variables to type variables and E-variables to E-expansions such that $Q_1 = [S]Q_2$.* □

Example 5.2. Let $M = \lambda x.x \mathbin{@} x$. Then

$$Q = \mathsf{s}_3^{\emptyset}\, \lambda x.\mathsf{s}_2^{\{\mathsf{a}_0\}}\, ((\mathsf{s}_0^{\{\mathsf{a}_0\}}\, x^{x:\mathsf{a}_0})^{:(\mathsf{s}_1^{\{\mathsf{a}_0\}}\, \mathsf{a}_0 \to \mathsf{a}_1)} \mathbin{@} \mathsf{s}_1^{\{\mathsf{a}_0\}}\, x^{x:\mathsf{a}_0})$$

is an initial skeleton for M and we have

$$Q \rhd M : \langle \emptyset \vdash \mathsf{s}_3^{\emptyset}\, (\mathsf{a}_0 \to \mathsf{s}_2^{\{\mathsf{a}_0\}}\, \mathsf{a}_1)\rangle / \Delta$$

with $\Delta = {\mathsf{s}_3}^{\emptyset}_{\mathsf{a}_0 \to \mathsf{s}_2^{\{\mathsf{a}_0\}}\, \mathsf{a}_1}\ {\mathsf{s}_2}^{\{\mathsf{a}_0\}}_{\mathsf{a}_1}\, ((\mathsf{s}_0^{\{\mathsf{a}_0\}}\, \mathsf{a}_0 \lessdot \mathsf{s}_1^{\{\mathsf{a}_0\}}\, \mathsf{a}_0 \to \mathsf{a}_1) \wedge {\mathsf{s}_0}^{\{\mathsf{a}_0\}}_{\mathsf{a}_0}\, \top \wedge {\mathsf{s}_1}^{\{\mathsf{a}_0\}}_{\mathsf{a}_0}\, \top)$.
Roughly, the variables (s_i) can be used to introduce $\forall$-quantifiers or subtyping at their respective positions. For example, let $T = \forall a.(a \to a)$ and $S = (\mathsf{a}_0 := T, \mathsf{a}_1 := T, \mathsf{s}_0 := \diamondsuit, \mathsf{s}_1 := \diamondsuit, \mathsf{s}_2 := \diamondsuit^{:b \to b}, \mathsf{s}_3 := \forall b.\diamondsuit, \boxdot)$. Applying S to the above typing judgement, we obtain

$$\forall b.\lambda x.((x^{x:T})^{:T \to T} \mathbin{@} x^{x:T})^{:b \to b} \rhd M : \langle \emptyset \vdash \forall b.(T \to b \to b)\rangle / [S]\Delta$$

with $[S]\Delta = \exists b.((T \lessdot T \to T) \wedge (T \lessdot b \to b))$. □

In the following, we use a predicate refl to check that a constraint is built from atomic constraints of the form $T \lessdot T$. The formal definition is

$$\mathsf{refl}(\top) \qquad \mathsf{refl}(T \lessdot T) \qquad \frac{\mathsf{refl}(\Delta)}{\mathsf{refl}(\exists a.\Delta)} \qquad \frac{\mathsf{refl}(\Delta)}{\mathsf{refl}(s_T^B\ \Delta)} \qquad \frac{\mathsf{refl}(\Delta_1) \qquad \mathsf{refl}(\Delta_2)}{\mathsf{refl}(\Delta_1 \wedge \Delta_2)}$$

A reflexive constraint is always solved w.r.t. a reflexive subtyping relation (see solvedness definition in the next section). From any initial skeleton of M, we can obtain all relevant skeletons for M.

Lemma 5.3. *Let $\vdash M \rhd Q$. Let Q' relevant such that $Q' \rhd M : \langle A \vdash T\rangle/\Delta$. There exists S such that $[S]Q \rhd M : \langle A \vdash T\rangle/(\Delta \wedge \Delta')$ with Δ' reflexive.* □

Note that in the above lemma, we do not have $[S]Q = Q'$, and we obtain an approximation of Δ. By construction, an initial skeleton Q uses subtyping at each application node to generate an atomic constraint. Applying S turns these constraints into reflexive ones, but it cannot completely remove them. Therefore, $[S]Q$ is similar to Q' up to these uses of (reflexive) subtyping at application nodes.

To generate all possible typing derivations, we add a weakening rule to be able to extend a type environment.

$$\frac{Q \rhd M : \langle A_1 \vdash T\rangle/\Delta \qquad \mathsf{support}(A_1) \cap \mathsf{support}(A_2) = \emptyset}{Q^{A_2} \rhd M : \langle A_1, A_2 \vdash T\rangle/\Delta}$$

Theorem 5.4. *Let $\vdash M \rhd Q$. If $Q' \rhd M : \langle A \vdash T\rangle/\Delta$, then there exists S, A' such that $([S]Q)^{A'} \rhd M : \langle A \vdash T\rangle/(\Delta \wedge \Delta')$, with Δ' reflexive.* □

We emphasize that initial skeletons are quite different from principal typings: initial skeletons are not typing derivations, because they contain unsolved constraints, and all terms, even non typable ones, have an initial skeleton. To obtain a principal typing from the initial skeleton, we need to solve the constraints in a principal manner; we conjecture that it is not possible, i.e., System F_s does not have principal typings, for the same reason as for System F [26].

Nevertheless, we think that initial skeletons can be useful for modular type inference. First, note that we do not have to remember the skeleton itself or the term; the typing and constraint contain all the information we need. Besides, constraint solving can be divided into solution preserving steps, which produce an equivalent constraint, and solution reducing steps, where some information is lost. It is always possible to safely perform solution preserving steps, and one can periodically check if it is possible to apply solution reducing steps to find at least one solved typing. The best intermediate representation might be a typing on which all known solution preserving steps have been performed, together with (at least) one solution reducing step of that typing's constraint. We do not know in practice how many steps will be solution preserving versus solution reducing.

An example use of System F_s is to look for a subsystem of System F in which to do compositional type inference. System F_s is a good framework in which to perform such a search, by considering various different restrictions of System F_s until one is found with the right properties. Because all possible System F derivations can be obtained from System F_s initial skeletons, we know in advance that the framework has the right amount of power. Such subsystems could also be characterized by a constraint solving algorithm. Instead of searching for a subsystem by varying the typing rules, we could vary the constraint solving algorithm, and when a nice algorithm is found, we could try to find a corresponding restriction directly stated on the typing rules.

6 Solvedness and Subject Reduction

6.1 Solvedness and System F

A constraint Δ is solved w.r.t. a subtyping relation $\leq$ if its atomic constraints are solved w.r.t. $\leq$. Formally, we define the predicate solved, as follows.

$$\mathsf{solved}(\top, \leq) \qquad \frac{T_1 \leq T_2}{\mathsf{solved}(T_1 \lessdot T_2, \leq)} \qquad \frac{\mathsf{solved}(\Delta_1, \leq) \qquad \mathsf{solved}(\Delta_2, \leq)}{\mathsf{solved}(\Delta_1 \wedge \Delta_2, \leq)}$$

$$\frac{\mathsf{solved}(\Delta, \leq)}{\mathsf{solved}(\exists a.\Delta, \leq)} \qquad \frac{\mathsf{solved}(\Delta, \leq)}{\mathsf{solved}(s_T^B\ \Delta, \leq)}$$

A skeleton is solved if its constraint is solved. Solved skeletons correspond to typing derivations in the traditional sense.

We can express System F in System F_s by using the following relation $\leq_F$.

$$\forall a.T_1 \leq_F [a := T_2, \boxdot]T_1 \quad (\forall\text{-E})$$

Because of the equality involving dummy quantifiers, the relation $\leq$ is reflexive; indeed for $a \notin \mathsf{ftv}(T)$, we have $T = \forall a.T \leq_{\mathrm{F}} T$. Clearly, System $\mathrm{F_s}$ equipped with $\leq_{\mathrm{F}}$ extends System F. Conversely, it is easy to see that a term typable in System $\mathrm{F_s}$ is typable in F once we erase all the E-variables.

Proposition 6.1. *A term is typable in System F iff it is typable in System F_s with $\leq_{\mathrm{F}}$.* □

6.2 Subject Reduction

We now present the subject reduction result of System $\mathrm{F_s}$ with $\leq_{\mathrm{F}}$ w.r.t. call-by-value semantics. Let V range over values, i.e. $V ::= x \mid \lambda x.M$. We write $[x := M_1]M_2$ for the usual capture-avoiding substitution of terms. We define small-step call-by-value evaluation $M \xrightarrow{\mathsf{cbv}} M'$ as the smallest relation on terms verifying the following rules:

$$(\lambda x.M) @ V \xrightarrow{\mathsf{cbv}} [x := V]M \qquad \frac{M_1 \xrightarrow{\mathsf{cbv}} M_1'}{M_1 @ M_2 \xrightarrow{\mathsf{cbv}} M_1' @ M_2} \qquad \frac{M \xrightarrow{\mathsf{cbv}} M'}{V @ M \xrightarrow{\mathsf{cbv}} V @ M'}$$

Theorem 6.2. *If $Q \triangleright M : \langle A \vdash T\rangle/\Delta$, $\mathsf{solved}(\Delta, \leq_{\mathrm{F}})$, and $M \xrightarrow{\mathsf{cbv}} M'$, then there exists Q', Δ' such that $Q' \triangleright M' : \langle A \vdash T\rangle/\Delta'$ and $\mathsf{solved}(\Delta', \leq_{\mathrm{F}})$.* □

We prove Theorem 6.2 by defining a transformation on Q so that skeletons in a function position of an application, such as Q_1 in $Q_1 @ Q_2$, are turned into λ-abstraction skeletons. A substitution lemma then allows us to simulate β-reduction by replacing the occurrences of a variable skeleton x^A in a skeleton $\lambda x.Q_1'$ by Q_2. This proof technique depends on the subtyping relation being used. We conjecture it can be adapted to various relations (such as Mitchell's [17]), but nevertheless we look for a more generic proof technique (less dependant on the subtyping relation). We prove subject reduction only for call-by-value evaluation for simplicity; we conjecture that subject reduction also holds for call-by-need and call-by-name semantics, and for reduction in arbitrary contexts.

7 Related Work

7.1 Expansion

A full survey on expansion and expansion variables can be found in [2]; we only discuss here the main differences between System $\mathrm{F_s}$ and System E, the type system with expansion most closely related to our work. System E E-variables are introduced on top of skeletons, type environments, result types, and constraints, while System $\mathrm{F_s}$ E-variables are not inserted on top of type environments (rule (s-I)). System $\mathrm{F_s}$ expansion mechanism deals with subtyping, while System E expansion does not. In System E, an E-variable e defines a namespace. In type $T_1 = a \rightarrow e\ a$, the variable a outside e is not connected to the one in the scope of

e; applying substitution $(a := T_2, \boxdot)$ to T_1 gives $T_2 \to e\ a$. This is due to the fact that substitutions are a special case of System E expansions (see [2] for further details). It also makes composition of expansions and substitutions easier. In System F_s, substitutions cannot be considered as expansions, because they are applied to the whole typing judgement (Theorem 4.4), whereas the asymmetric expansions of System F_s are not applied to the type environments (Lemma 4.1). As a result, it would be unsound for System F_s E-variables to create namespaces. It is difficult to have a symmetric expansion in System F_s, because subtyping does not operate uniformly on typings (it is usually contravariant on the environment and covariant on the result type). It is possible to design System F_s with two kinds of E-variables (one, symmetric, to handle substitutions and $\forall$-introduction, and one, asymmetric, for subtyping), but it would make the system much more complex for no clear profit.

7.2 Type Inference in System F

Type inference in System F is undecidable [25]; however many different approaches have been conducted to circumvent this issue, by stratifying System F using a notion of rank, or by using type annotations to constrain type inference possibilities.

Giannini and Ronchi's Type Constraints. In [6], Giannini and Ronchi Della Rocca consider a syntax-directed version of System F. The authors define a notion of *typing scheme* σ, with a syntax similar to the one of System F types, except that quantifiers $\forall u.T$ contain placeholders u (called *sequence variables*), that can be replaced by a (possibly empty) set of type variables to give a System F type. For each term M, they also define a *principal typing scheme* $\Pi(M) = \langle D, \sigma, G, F \rangle$, where D is an environment that maps term variables to typing schemes, and G and F are constraints on the typing schemes occurring in σ or D that need to be satisfied. The set G contains subtyping constraints $\sigma_1 \leq_F \sigma_2$, and F prevents certain quantifications from happening by restricting the possible values for the sequence variables u.

The principal typing scheme $\Pi(M)$ is similar to our initial skeletons; if $\Pi(M) = \langle D, \sigma, G, F \rangle$ and $Q \rhd M : \langle A \vdash T \rangle / \Delta$ (with Q an initial skeleton for M), then D corresponds to A, σ to T, G to Δ, and F acts as the sets B that appear in E-variables $s^B T$. Any System F typing $\langle A \vdash T \rangle$ of M can be obtained from D, σ by applying a substitution (from type variables to types and sequence variables to set of type variables) which satisfies constraints G and F. This result corresponds to Theorem 5.4 in our system.

System F_s and the system of [6] differ mainly in their implementation. In particular, we have a mechanism to postpone subtyping (i.e., $\forall$-elimination), which does not have an equivalent in the system of Giannini and Ronchi. It seems that they do not need such mechanism, but to compensate for it, they have to generate more constraints when building their principal typing scheme $\Pi(M)$. We also believe that our system is easier to understand and easier to extend with other type constructors. Finally, Giannini and Ronchi define a notion of rank over system F types (distinct from Leivant's rank based on the presence of polymorphism on the left of function types [13]), and provide for all n an inference algorithm for each restriction of their system to types of rank lower than n. We conjecture that this algorithm can be adapted to System F_s.

ML^F *and Its Variants.* ML^F [10,11] is a conservative extension of ML at least as expressive as System F with principal types, i.e., result types whose instances (w.r.t. the ML^F type instance relation $\prec$) are exactly all possible result types for a term. The type system also enjoys decidable type inference (with a simple criterion on where type annotations are needed), and stability w.r.t. some program transformations, such as for example β-reduction and η-expansion.

ML^F types contain *flexible quantifiers* $\forall(a \succ \sigma)\sigma'$, which roughly represent sets of System F types of the form $[a := T]T'$, where T and T' are instances of the *type schemes* σ, σ'. For example, $\forall(a \succ \forall b(b \to b))(a \to a)$ represents the set $\{T \to T \mid \forall b(b \to b) \prec T\}$. With flexible quantifiers, terms that do not have a principal type in System F (w.r.t. the System F type instance relation) have a principal type in ML^F. Decidable type inference is obtained in ML^F by requiring type annotations on function parameters that are used two or more times with different type instances, so that the type inference algorithm never has to guess true polymorphism. *Rigid bindings* are used in ML^F types and typing rules to distinguish between inferred and annotated types. They are not necessary for decidable type inference, and can be removed at the cost of additional type annotations, as in HML [12].

Boxed Polymorphism. Boxed polymorphism [9,18] hides polymorphic types into boxes, considered as regular simple types. Several type systems follow this principle, such as PolyML [5], boxy types [24], and FPH [23]. We discuss only the most recent system, FPH. FPH is a type system based on System F, where boxes are used to mark where ∀-quantifiers have to be instantiated with polymorphic types. Provided that type annotations are given at these boxed positions, FPH type inference computes System F types (without any box) for terms. The system aims for simplicity for the programmer: only System F types are exposed, and writing type annotations does not require to think in term of boxes. Roughly, type annotations are necessary for λ-abstractions and let-bindings with *rich* types (i.e., types with quantifiers under arrow types). However, FPH is more restrictive than ML^F; more annotations are needed in general, and FPH terms admit principal types only for "box-free" types, not in general.

ML^F, FPH, and System F_s all aim for a modular type inference for System F types. It is difficult to compare our work to these two systems, because we do not propose a type inference algorithm for System F_s yet. In particular, assuming we follow their approach, we do not know how many annotations would be necessary to make System F_s type inference decidable. However, we can make the following observations. First, ML^F and FPH only infer result types, while our objective is to also infer complete typing, in order to have a fully compositional type inference algorithm. ML^F has principal types (w.r.t. to their instance relation), while System F_s have initial skeletons, and FPH has principal types only for box-free types (where ∀-quantified variables cannot be instantiated with polymorphic types). ML^F types more terms than System F, while FPH and System F_s type the same terms as System F. Finally, FPH and System F_s are direct extensions of System F, and the constructions specific to these systems (the boxes and E-variables) can be kept away from the programmer most of the time (except in type error reports). On the other hand, ML^F types and type instance relation $\prec$ can be hard to understand, even in its simpler version HML.

To illustrate the differences between the three type systems, we consider the following example (taken from [11,23]). Let $A = \mathsf{choose} : \forall a.(a \to a \to a), \mathsf{id} : \forall a.(a \to a)$ and $M = \mathsf{choose} \mathbin{@} \mathsf{id}$. We can derive the following typing judgement for M:

$$\begin{aligned} \mathrm{F_s} &: \langle A \vdash s_2^\emptyset\,((s_1^\emptyset\,\forall a.(a \to a)) \to (s_1^\emptyset\,\forall a.(a \to a)))\rangle \\ \mathsf{ML}^\mathsf{F} &: \langle A \vdash \forall(a \succ \forall b(b \to b))(a \to a)\rangle \\ \mathrm{FPH} &: \langle A \vdash \forall b((b \to b) \to (b \to b))\rangle \\ &\ \langle A \vdash \boxed{\forall b(b \to b)} \to \boxed{\forall b(b \to b)}\rangle \end{aligned}$$

FPH can infer two result types for M, depending on the presence or absence of type annotations. These two incomparable types can be obtained from the (principal) ML^F type (ignoring the boxes), and also from the System F_s type, by applying the substitution $(s_2 := \forall b.\diamondsuit, s_1 := \diamondsuit^{:b\to b}, \boxdot)$ for the first one, and by simply erasing the E-variables for the second one.

Both System F_s E-variables and ML^F flexible bindings factor several System F types and typing derivations that are incomparable in System F, as shown with the $\mathsf{choose} \mathbin{@} \mathsf{id}$ example. However, flexible bindings are more expressive and allow to type terms that are not typable in System F. Consider the example (taken from [11]) $\mathsf{let}\ x = (\mathsf{choose} \mathbin{@} \mathsf{id})\ \mathsf{in}\ \mathsf{let}\ z = x \mathbin{@} f\ \mathsf{in}\ x \mathbin{@} g$, where $f : \forall a.(a \to a) \to \forall a.(a \to a), g : (b \to b) \to (b \to b)$. The ML^F type for $\mathsf{choose} \mathbin{@} \mathsf{id}$ given above can be instantiated into the incomparable types of f and g. The term cannot be typed in System F nor in System F_s. Adding quantification over E-variables would allow System F_s to type this term; we could type $\mathsf{choose} \mathbin{@} \mathsf{id}$ with $\forall s.((s^\emptyset\,\forall a.(a \to a)) \to (s^\emptyset\,\forall a.(a \to a)))$ and instantiate s with different expansions to obtain the types of f and g. Adding quantification over E-variables should not raise any issue; we conjecture that it would allow System F_s to type as many terms as ML^F. It would be interesting to see if there exists an encoding of ML^F types into System F_s types extended with quantified E-variables, and conversely. We leave this topic to future work.

8 Conclusion and Future Work

System F_s is an extension of System F with expansion, an operation originally defined in systems with intersection types. Expansion allows postponing the introduction of ∀-quantifiers and subtyping uses at an arbitrary nested position in a typing derivation. For any term M, we can generate an initial skeleton, from which we can obtain any System F_s judgement for M. We now give some ideas of follow-up on this work.

Type Inference Algorithm. To obtain decidable type inference in System F_s, a first possibility is to use type annotations, as in ML^F or FPH. The question is then to know how many annotations are necessary compared to these two systems. Another idea is to study the link between constraints solving and semi-unification. Given a constraint $T_1 \leq T_2$, the semi-unification problem consists in finding S_1, S_2 so that $[S_2][S_1]T_1 = [S_1]T_2$. Vasconcellos et al. [22] used semi-unification to design and implement a type inference semi-algorithm for polymorphic recursion in Haskell. The authors claim that the algorithm terminates most of the time in practice. Maybe similar results can be obtained for System F_s as well. As discussed at the end of Section 5, System F_s can also be used to look for a subsystem of System F allowing for compositional type inference.

Mixing ∀-quantifiers and Intersection Types. A long-term goal is combining System E and System F into one system (called System EF), with both ∀-quantifiers and intersection types. With such a system, one could type a term with only intersection types, only System F types, or any combination of the two constructs, depending on the user's needs. Previous systems featuring both constructs (e.g. [15,21]) do not use expansion variables; the main difficulty in mixing System E and System F_s is to make precise the interactions between the symmetric and asymmetric expansions. Maybe it is possible to define a more general expansion mechanism which supersedes the existing ones, and combine the two kinds of expansion variables into a single construct. A goal would be for System EF to have principal typings.

Because System E types all strongly normalizing terms, ∀-quantified types would only be used when required by the user when performing type inference in System EF. To this end, we could imagine various kinds of type annotations to mark positions within terms where System F types are required. These annotations could be complete types, such as $\lambda x^{\forall a.(a \to a)}.M$, or just type templates, such as $\lambda x^{(\forall a.*) \to *}.M$, meaning that the inferred type for x should be an arrow type, and the type of the argument should be a System F type. One could imagine different kinds of annotations at various positions in the term; we would like to see under which conditions (on both the annotations language and the positions in the term) the inference for such a system becomes decidable. The inference algorithm would then use intersection types by default, except for the marked positions where ∀-quantified types are requested.

References

1. Carlier, S., Polakow, J., Wells, J.B., Kfoury, A.J.: System E: Expansion Variables for Flexible Typing with Linear and Non-linear Types and Intersection Types. In: Schmidt, D. (ed.) ESOP 2004. LNCS, vol. 2986, pp. 294–309. Springer, Heidelberg (2004)
2. Carlier, S., Wells, J.B.: Expansion: the crucial mechanism for type inference with intersection types: A survey and explanation. Electr. Notes Theor. Comput. Sci. 136, 173–202 (2005)
3. Coppo, M., Dezani-Ciancaglini, M., Venneri, B.: Principal type schemes and λ-calculus semantics. In: Hindley, J.R., Seldin, J.P. (eds.) To H. B. Curry: Essays on Combinatory Logic, Lambda Calculus, and Formalism, pp. 535–560. Academic Press (1980)

4. Damas, L., Milner, R.: Principal type-schemes for functional programs. In: POPL, pp. 207–212 (1982)
5. Garrigue, J., Rémy, D.: Semi-explicit first-class polymorphism for ML. Inf. Comput. 155(1-2), 134–169 (1999)
6. Giannini, P., Ronchi Della Rocca, S.: Type Inference in Polymorphic Type Discipline. In: Ito, T., Meyer, A.R. (eds.) TACS 1991. LNCS, vol. 526, pp. 18–37. Springer, Heidelberg (1991)
7. Girard, J.-Y.: Interprétation fonctionnelle et élimination des coupures de l'arithmétique d'ordre supérieur. PhD thesis, Université Paris VII (1972)
8. Kfoury, A.J., Wells, J.B.: Principality and type inference for intersection types using expansion variables. Theor. Comput. Sci. 311(1-3), 1–70 (2004)
9. Läufer, K., Odersky, M.: Polymorphic type inference and abstract data types. ACM Trans. Program. Lang. Syst. 16(5), 1411–1430 (1994)
10. Le Botlan, D., Rémy, D.: MLF: raising ML to the power of System F. In: ICFP, pp. 27–38. ACM (2003)
11. Le Botlan, D., Rémy, D.: Recasting MLF. Inf. Comput. 207(6), 726–785 (2009)
12. Leijen, D.: Flexible types: robust type inference for first-class polymorphism. In: POPL, pp. 66–77. ACM (2009)
13. Leivant, D.: Polymorphic type inference. In: POPL, pp. 88–98 (1983)
14. Lenglet, S., Wells, J.B.: Expansion for universal quantifiers (2012), `http://arxiv.org/abs/1201.1101`
15. Margaria, I., Zacchi, M.: Principal typing in a forall-and-discipline. J. Log. Comput. 5(3), 367–381 (1995)
16. Milner, R.: A theory of type polymorphism in programming. J. Comput. Syst. Sci. 17(3), 348–375 (1978)
17. Mitchell, J.C.: Polymorphic type inference and containment. Inf. Comput. 76(2/3), 211–249 (1988)
18. Rémy, D.: Programming Objects with ML-ART, an Extension to ML with Abstract and Record Types. In: Hagiya, M., Mitchell, J.C. (eds.) TACS 1994. LNCS, vol. 789, pp. 321–346. Springer, Heidelberg (1994)
19. Reynolds, J.C.: Towards a Theory of Type Structure. In: Loeckx, J. (ed.) ICALP 1974. LNCS, vol. 14, pp. 408–423. Springer, Heidelberg (1974)
20. Ronchi Della Rocca, S., Venneri, B.: Principal type schemes for an extended type theory. Theoretical Computer Science 28, 151–169 (1984)
21. van Bakel, S., Barbanera, F., Fernández, M.: Polymorphic Intersection Type Assignment for Rewrite Systems with Abstraction and β-Rule. In: Coquand, T., Nordström, B., Dybjer, P., Smith, J. (eds.) TYPES 1999. LNCS, vol. 1956, pp. 41–60. Springer, Heidelberg (2000)
22. Vasconcellos, C., Figueiredo, L., Camarão, C.: Practical type inference for polymorphic recursion: an implementation in haskell. J. UCS 9(8), 873–890 (2003)
23. Vytiniotis, D., Weirich, S., Peyton-Jones, S.: FPH: first-class polymorphism for Haskell. In: ICFP, pp. 295–306. ACM (2008)
24. Vytiniotis, D., Weirich, S., Peyton-Jones, S.: Boxy types: inference for higher-rank types and impredicativity. In: ICFP, pp. 251–262. ACM (2006)
25. Wells, J.B.: Typability and type checking in System F are equivalent and undecidable. Ann. Pure Appl. Logic 98(1-3), 111–156 (1999)
26. Wells, J.B.: The Essence of Principal Typings. In: Widmayer, P., Triguero, F., Morales, R., Hennessy, M., Eidenbenz, S., Conejo, R. (eds.) ICALP 2002. LNCS, vol. 2380, pp. 913–925. Springer, Heidelberg (2002)
27. Wells, J.B., Haack, C.: Branching Types. In: Le Métayer, D. (ed.) ESOP 2002. LNCS, vol. 2305, pp. 115–132. Springer, Heidelberg (2002)

Non-monotonic Self-Adjusting Computation

Ruy Ley-Wild[1], Umut A. Acar[2], and Guy Blelloch[3]

[1] IMDEA Software Institute
[2] Max-Planck Institute for Software Systems
[3] Carnegie Mellon University

Abstract. Self-adjusting computation is a language-based approach to writing programs that respond dynamically to input changes by maintaining a *trace* of the computation consistent with the input, thus also updating the output. For *monotonic* programs, i.e. where localized input changes cause localized changes in the computation, the trace can be repaired efficiently by insertions and deletions. However, non-local input changes can cause major reordering of the trace. In such cases, updating the trace can be asymptotically equal to running from scratch.

In this paper, we eliminate the monotonicity restriction by generalizing the update mechanism to use *trace slices*, which are partial fragments of the computation that can be reordered with some bookkeeping. We provide a high-level source language for pure programs, equipped with a notion of *trace distance* for comparing two runs of a program modulo reordering. The source language is translated into a low-level target language with intrinsic support for *non-monotonic* update (i.e., with reordering). We show that the translation asymptotically preserves the semantics and trace distance, that the cost of update coincides with trace distance, and that updating produces the same answer as a from-scratch run. We describe a concrete algorithm for implementing change-propagation with asymptotic bounds on running time. The concrete algorithm achieves running time bounds which are within $O(\log n)$ of the trace distance, where n is the trace length.

1 Introduction

In many applications, small changes to the input data cause proportionally small changes to the computation and output data. The broad goal of *incremental computation* is to exploit this correlation by efficiently updating the output when the input changes. *Dynamic* algorithms and data structures can be designed to take advantage of the particular problem structure [7,9].The manual approach often yields updates that are asymptotically faster than recomputing from scratch, but carries inherent complexity and non-compositionality that makes the algorithms difficult to design, analyze, and use.

Programming languages for incremental computation provide compile- and run-time support to (semi-)automatically derive incremental programs from static programs [8,16,17]. In particular, *self-adjusting computation* (SAC) is a language-based approach that provides a general-purpose *change-propagation*

H. Seidl (Ed.): ESOP 2012, LNCS 7211, pp. 476–496, 2012.

mechanism to update the output [1]. Previous work shows that SAC can be effective in a reasonably broad range of domains, such as computational geometry [3], invariant checking [18], and machine learning [5]. In many cases, self-adjusting programs closely match or improve the asymptotic complexity achieved by algorithmic techniques, and have even helped solve challenging open problems by providing high-level reasoning for complex computations [4].

Self-adjusting programs construct and maintain a *trace* that records data and control dependencies of the computation. The trace is initially built during a run from scratch, recording the operations (e.g., that depend on the input or identify possibility of reuse) in execution order. Change-propagation edits the trace of the first run into the trace of the second run: input changes identify parts of the computation affected that must be rebuilt, while unaffected parts can be reused. This update takes time proportional to performing the new work for the updated run and discarding stale work from the previous run; there is no cost for work that is reused between runs.

Previous semantics and implementation techniques for SAC critically relied on reusing subcomputations *monotonically*, i.e., in the same order that they appear in a trace. For input changes that reorder subcomputations, however, existing change-propagation mechanisms can be grossly inefficient. As an abstract example, consider a computation that initially performs $f(x); g(y)$. After a small input change, the execution order might swap, yielding $g(y); f(x)$ instead. Under monotonic change-propagation, we could only reuse one of these functions: we can reuse $g(y)$ but would have to re-run $f(x)$, or vice versa. If both calls are expensive, neither choice will have an efficient update. In Section 2, we discuss a concrete example where non-local input changes cause computation reordering, and compare monotonic and non-monotonic change-propagation.

All previous work on SAC critically relies on monotonicity of change-propagation to ensure correctness and efficiency. Relaxing this constraint would make the technique effective for a broader class of computations, but requires overcoming three key challenges: (1) Can change-propagation be generalized to correctly support reordering? (2) How can we reason about the complexity of non-monotonic change-propagation at the program level? (3) How can non-monotonic change-propagation be realized efficiently? In this paper, we generalize SAC to support *non-monotonic reuse* where subcomputations may be reused out of order and provide complete solutions to the three challenges.

We give a high-level, direct-style source language for pure programs (Src) (Section 3) with tree-shaped traces of their execution. A formal notion of *trace distance* quantifies dissimilarity between two runs modulo reordering and abstractly measures change-propagation time. Under monotonic reuse, *local* trace distance compares two runs head-to-head in execution order to account for their differences; intuitively this is edit distance under insertions and deletions. Under non-monotonic reuse, trace distance is supplemented by a *global* trace distance that decomposes each run into a set of *trace slices* (traces with holes), pairs subcomputations from each run, and adds their local trace distance; intuitively this is local trace distance modulo reordering, akin to set difference.

We translate the source languages into a low-level, continuation-passing target language (Tgt in Section 4) with intrinsic support for non-monotonic change-propagation. Since continuations capture the rest of the computation, a list-shaped trace overapproximates the scope of operations that must be re-run due to inconsistencies with input changes. Since a hole in a trace slice indicates computation that has been reused out of order and the hole is labeled with its continuation, the computation can resume by running the continuation. Therefore trace slices are essential for change-propagation to support non-monotonic (i.e., out-of-order) reuse while maintaining correctness. We prove the key consistency theorem that non-monotonic change-propagation always yields results that are consistent with a from scratch run. Moreover, we show that target-level global trace distance coincides with the cost of non-monotonic change-propagation. Finally, we also prove that greedy non-monotonic reuse yields asymptotically-optimal change-propagation for a particular class of programs.

We relate the source and target languages by translation and prove that the translation preserves the semantics and trace distance (Section 5).

Finally, we describe how to efficiently support non-monotonic SAC (Section 6). Specifically, we give algorithms and data structures to implement trace slices and non-monotonic change-propagation, such that the source-level trace distance can be realized with a logarithmic factor overhead in the size of the trace. We defer experimental evaluation to future work. Further discussion and technical details are in the first author's dissertation [11].

2 Overview

We illustrate how non-local input changes can cause computation reordering with a pure, self-adjusting map program on lists:

```
datatype 'a cell = nil | :: of 'a * 'a list
withtype 'a list = 'a cell ref

fun map (f : 'a -> 'b) (l : 'a list) : 'b list =
  case get l of nil   => put nil
              | h::t => put ((f h) :: (map f t))
```

We use write-once *modifiable references* (with put and get operations) for the tail to identify where input changes require new computation, and memoizing functions (declared by **fun**) to identify possible reuse across runs (Section 3). Here we explain its change-propagation and trace distance under monotonic and non-monotonic reuse. We revisit its formal trace distance in Section 3 and its performance under the change-propagation algorithm in Section 6.

A *trace* is a syntactic representation of a computation, which we depict with hierarchical box diagrams of the form: 

where the oval names the computation (e.g., $f(x)$), the inner rectangle is a hole to be filled with subtraces (e.g., recursive calls) capturing the call order, and the outer rectangle represents the local computation (i.e., between subcalls).

Monotonic SAC. Suppose we first map a function f on the list $[1, \ldots, n, k]$. Next, a meta-level mutator can change the input to $[k, 1, \ldots, n]$ by moving k to the front, and *change-propagate* the first run to be consistent with the new input.

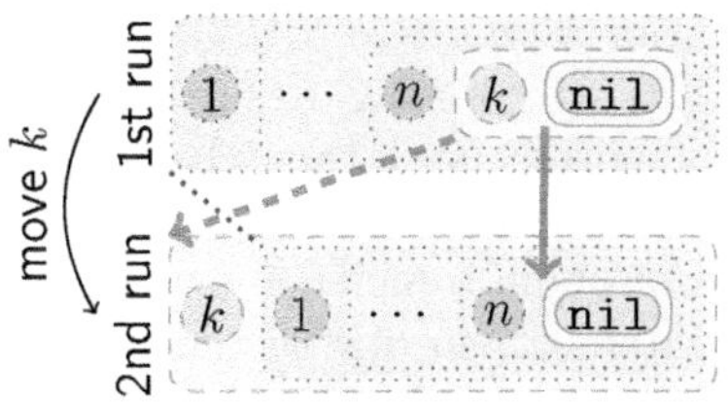

The obvious way to change the input is to splice k out of the list, reinsert it at the front, and change-propagate. The first run (top) is a from-scratch execution that constructs the trace: each rectangle represents the local work (dereference the location, apply the function to the element, place the result in a new reference) with its nested recursive call. After changing the input list, change-propagation (Subsection 4.1) uses the input change(s) to edit the trace of the first run into the trace of the second run (bottom). Since the list's head element is k instead of 1, change-propagation greedily steals the corresponding subtrace from the first run; this is a form of *partial reuse* (indicated by dashed/orange) between runs because it's the same local work but has different subcomputation. Assuming a monotonic reuse, change-propagation must discard the prefix trace $(1 \cdots n)$ from the first run in order to reuse the k subtrace, thus the work for $(1 \cdots n)$ must be done afresh for the second run; this work is *obstructed from (i.e., not available for) reuse* (indicated by dotted/red) between successive runs. Finally, the work for `nil` can be *fully reused* (indicated by solid/green) between runs. Thus change-propagation takes $O(n)$ time to update the computation, which is no more efficient than running from scratch.

Moving the last element to the front is a *non-local* change that swaps the relative order of execution between the computations for k and $(1 \cdots n)$. This is incompatible with monotonicity because work may only be reused if it occurs in the same order in both runs. Geometrically, the reuse arrows between the two traces cannot intersect.

Due to the complex semantics of change-propagation for the low-level Tgt language, we prefer to reason with an abstract *trace distance* [12] for the Src language, which quantifies the dissimilarities between runs. In Sections 4.3 and 5, we show that trace distance asymptotically coincides with the time for change-propagation. For monotonic reuse, *local* trace distance corresponds to an edit distance between traces. Intuitively, the distance between two traces is proportional to the partially reusable and discarded/fresh computation.

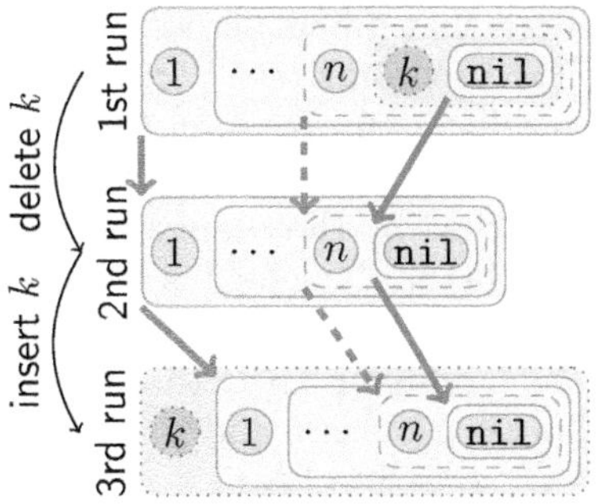

To improve change-propagation, we could employ a different reuse policy that instead performs the work for k afresh and reuses the work for $(1 \cdots n)$. Alternatively, we can factor the move into: (1) delete k from the list and change-propagate, then (2) reinsert it at the front and change-propagate again. Thus the bulk of the computation can be reused and change-propagation only requires $O(1)$ time to splice k out for the second run and perform the work afresh for the third run. Note that the work for $(1 \cdots n)$ and `nil` are reused monotonically. However, these solutions aren't robust enough to handle other changes such as swapping the first and second halves of the list.

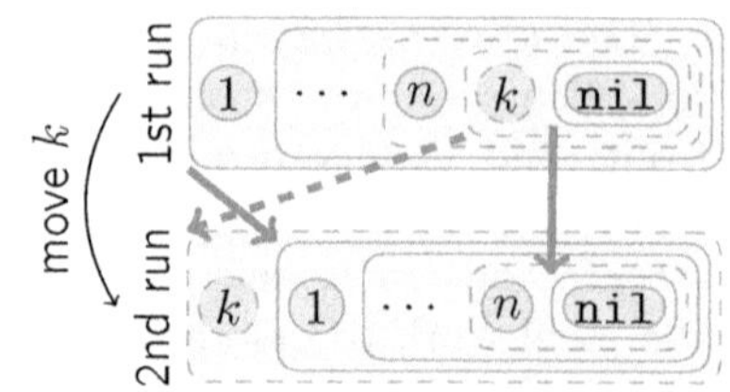

Non-Monotonic SAC. In the non-monotonic setting, reusing a subtrace doesn't discard its prefix and thus change-propagation can reuse work out of order. Geometrically, non-monotonicity allows the reuse arrows to intersect, so obstructed reuse lines from the monotonic illustration become full or partial reuse arrows.

Change-propagation can greedily steal the work for k without sacrificing the prefix trace $(1 \cdots n)$, again this is partial reuse because the element has a different tail computation ($(1 \cdots n)$ instead of `nil`). Next, the subtrace for $(1 \cdots n)$ from the first run can be (almost) fully reused, except for its differing tail list (`nil` instead of k). Finally, the trace for `nil` can also be fully reused. In this example reuse is maximized, thus change-propagation takes $O(1)$ time to update the computation, an asymptotic speedup over running from scratch. Unlike the alternatives suggested above, non-monotonicity make change-propagation robust enough to handle swapping larger list segments.

For non-monotonic reuse, trace distance is a hybrid of set difference and edit distance. In particular, *global* trace distance (Subsection 3.2) allows decomposing the trace of each run into *trace slices* (traces with holes) which are then compared pairwise with local trace distance. In Section 3, we revisit this example's formal trace distance derivation. Briefly, each trace can be decomposed into separate slices for $(1 \cdots n)$, k, and `nil`. The similar slices of each run have $O(1)$ local distance because the $(1 \cdots n)$ and k slices have to account for their differing tails between runs but are otherwise identical. Thus the global distance between runs is also $O(1)$. Finally, the algorithmic overhead of non-monotonic change-propagation (Section 6) is logarithmic in the size of the trace, so an implementation would require $O(\log n)$ time to update.

3 The Src Language

The Src language serves to write pure direct-style programs that depend on input data that differs across runs, and can be compiled into equivalent self-adjusting Tgt programs (see Sections 4 and 5). The dynamic and cost semantics of Src produces an *execution trace* that can be used to determine a *trace distance* that quantifies differences between runs modulo reordering, which is asymptotically matched by the change-propagation mechanism of Tgt.

The Src language is a pure call-by-value λ-calculus with ML-style references (without update) to represent data that may change across runs.[1] The following grammar gives the syntax of types τ, expressions e, and values v, using metavariables f and x for identifiers and ℓ for locations.

$$\tau ::= \mathbf{nat} \mid \tau_x \to \tau \mid \tau\ \mathbf{ref} \qquad e ::= v \mid \mathbf{caseN}\ v_n\ e_z\ x.e_s \mid e_f\ \$\ e_x \mid \mathbf{put}\ v \mid \mathbf{get}\ v_l$$
$$v ::= x \mid \mathbf{zero} \mid \mathbf{succ}\ v \mid \mathbf{fun}\ f.x.e \mid \ell$$

[1] Src (and Tgt of Section 4) includes natural numbers for didactic purposes and can easily be extended with products, sums, recursive types, etc..

Function application has the usual β-reduction semantics and is additionally recorded in the execution trace to help identify similarities between runs. The τ **ref** type classifies references: **put** v creates a reference; **get** v_l dereferences and identifies the need for re-computation by recording data dependencies.

3.1 Static, Dynamic, and Cost Semantics

The typing judgement $\Sigma; \Gamma \vdash e : \tau$ ascribes the type τ to the expression e in the store and variable typing contexts Σ and Γ. For brevity, we only give the types of the reference and suspension primitives: $\textbf{put} : \tau \rightarrow \tau\ \textbf{ref}$ and $\textbf{get} : \tau\ \textbf{ref} \rightarrow \tau$.

The dynamic and cost semantics of Src are defined by the large-step evaluation relation $\sigma; e \Downarrow T'; \sigma'; v'; c'$ to reduce expression e in store σ to value v' in updated store σ' and yields an execution *trace* T' and a *cost* c'. A store σ is a finite map from locations to values. The trace internalizes the *shape* of an evaluation derivation and will be used to identify the similarity of computations. The cost internalizes the *size* of a trace and will be used to relate the constant slowdown due to implementing suspensions with references and compiling Src programs to Tgt programs.

A *trace* T is a ε-terminated interleaving of *actions* A:

$$T ::= \varepsilon \mid A{\cdot}T \quad A ::= L \mid M(T) \quad L ::= \mathsf{put}^{v\uparrow\ell} \mid \mathsf{get}^{\ell\rightarrow v} \quad M ::= \mathsf{app}^{v_f \$ v_x \Downarrow v}$$

Local actions L identify where input changes cause two runs to differ because the operation yields a different result, while *memoizing actions* M delimit the trace T of an operation and identify where two runs perform similar computations. Therefore traces are necessary and sufficient to isolate the similarities and differences between program runs, without having to capture pure computation (e.g., case-analysis) because it is determined by the rest of the trace. Reference actions include allocation (put) and dereference (get) labeled with the location ℓ and value v involved in the operation. The function application action (app) is labeled with a function v_f, argument v_x, and result v.

For brevity, we only show the dynamic semantics of functions and references.

$$\frac{\sigma; e_f \Downarrow T_f; \sigma_f; \textbf{fun}\, f.x.e; c_f \quad \sigma_f; e_x \Downarrow T_x; \sigma_x; v_x; c_x \quad \sigma_x; [\textbf{fun}\, f.x.e/f][v_x/x]e \Downarrow T'; \sigma'; v'; c'}{\sigma; e_f \,\$\, e_x \Downarrow T_f{\cdot}T_x{\cdot}(\mathsf{app}^{(\textbf{fun}\, f.x.e)\$v_x \Downarrow v'}(T'){\cdot}\varepsilon); \sigma'; v'; c_f + c_x + 1 + c'}$$

$$\frac{\ell \notin \mathrm{dom}\, \sigma \quad \sigma' = \sigma[\ell \mapsto v]}{\sigma; \textbf{put}\, v \Downarrow \mathsf{put}^{v\uparrow\ell}{\cdot}\varepsilon; \sigma'; \ell; 1} \qquad \frac{\ell \in \mathrm{dom}\, \sigma \quad \sigma(\ell) = v}{\sigma; \textbf{get}\, \ell \Downarrow \mathsf{get}^{\ell\rightarrow v}{\cdot}\varepsilon; \sigma; v; 1}$$

Evaluation extends the trace and increments the cost counter according to the kind of reduction. A value reduces to itself, produces an empty trace, and has no cost. A case-analysis reduces according to the branch prescribed by the scrutinee; the trace and cost are unchanged since it is pure computation.

Function application reduces the function e_f and argument e_x to values and then evaluates the redex. An application concatenates the function, argument, and redex traces to represent the sequencing of work; the redex trace is delimited by the memoizing function action to identify the scope of the function call; the cost of the traces are added and incremented by 1 for the β-reduction.

Allocation extends the store with a fresh location that is initialized with the specified value and returns the location. Dereference returns the location's value. In each case, the trace is the singleton action of the primitive, and the work is 1.

3.2 Trace Distance

To reason about the effectiveness of *monotonic* self-adjusting computation, previous work developed a notion of *trace distance* to quantify the difference between two runs [12]. Since traces approximate the shape of an evaluation derivation, trace distance approximates a (higher-order) distance judgement on evaluation derivations that quantifies the dis/similarities between two runs (modulo the stores). Under monotonic reuse, the traces produced by the dynamic semantics are compared in execution order and thus trace distance intuitively captures their edit distance.

Under non-monotonic reuse, trace distance must be generalized to account for reordering and thus trace distance is a hybrid of set difference and edit distance. Intuitively, the difference between two runs can be obtained by globally decomposing each run into a set of subcomputations and locally comparing subcomputations pairwise under some matching. More specifically, the global decomposition of a computation slices a trace into a set of traces with holes, and the local comparison of two traces alternates between *searching* for a point where traces align (i.e., at memoizing actions) and *synchronizing* the two similar traces until they again differ (i.e., at local actions).

Action slices B and *trace slices* S represent (possibly) partial computations, analogous to how actions and traces represent full computations. Thus, memoizing action slices delimit an *optional trace slice* $\dot{S}$, which can be a present subcomputation or an absent subcomputation that was reordered.

$$B ::= L \mid M(\dot{S}) \quad S ::= \varepsilon \mid B{\cdot}S \quad \dot{S} ::= \square \mid S$$

Note that a trace is also a trace slice with no holes. The notation $\overline{S}$ denotes a list of slices and the metavariable U denotes a non-empty list of traces. A memoizing action $M(T)$ can be decomposed into a (skeleton) action slice with a hole $M(\square)$ and an extracted trace T. The slicing judgement $S \gg S', \overline{S}'$ (alternatively, $S \gg U'$) extends this operation to structurally traverse the slice S and decompose it into a (skeleton) slice S' with (nondeterministically) extracted slices $\overline{S}'$:

$$\frac{}{L \gg L, \bullet} \qquad \frac{S \gg S', \overline{S}'}{M(S) \gg M(S'), \overline{S}'} \qquad \frac{S \gg S', \overline{S}'}{M(S) \gg M(\square), (M(S'){\cdot}\varepsilon, \overline{S}')}$$

$$\frac{}{M(\square) \gg M(\square), \bullet} \qquad \frac{}{\varepsilon \gg \varepsilon, \bullet} \qquad \frac{B \gg B', \overline{S}'_1 \qquad S \gg S', \overline{S}'_2}{B{\cdot}S \gg B'{\cdot}S', (\overline{S}'_1, \overline{S}'_2)}$$

Intuitively, if $S \gg S', \overline{S}'$, then S' contains holes of the form $M_i(\square)$ and $\overline{S}'$ consists of trace slices $M_i(S_i){\cdot}\varepsilon$ representing the subcomputations of M_i extracted from S. Thus, replacing the corresponding holes in S' with S_i would reconsistute S.

Consider a trace slice $S[M(T)]$ that contains a deeply-nested trace $M(T)$ that could be stolen by non-monotonic memoization for out-of-order reuse. Intuitively, $S[M(T)]$ can be sliced into the trace $M(T)$ and a residual slice $S[M(\Box)]$, where the $M(\Box)$ indicates what computation was stolen. Formally, this is captured by the judgement $S[M(T)] \gg S[M(\Box)], M(T)\cdot\varepsilon$, which can be derived by using the first two rules to structurally traverse $S[M(T)]$ until reaching the trace $M(T)$, then using the third rule to extract the trace $M(T)$. Moreover, the premise of the third rule allows further decomposing the trace T into sub-slices $\overline{S}$.

The *global distance* $S_1 \boxminus^{\gg} S_2 = d$ between two slices S_1 and S_2 is obtained by decomposing each slice into the same number of sub-slices (e.g., the $M_i(S_si)$ above), matching sub-slices from each set (the notation $i \sim j$ is a bijective pairing of indices), and adding up the local distance between each pair of sub-slices:

$$\frac{S_1 \gg \overline{S'_{1i}} \quad S_2 \gg \overline{S'_{2j}} \quad i \sim j \quad S'_{1i} \boxminus S'_{2j} = d_{\mathrm{ij}} \quad d = \sum_{i \sim j} d_{\mathrm{ij}}}{S_1 \boxminus^{\gg} S_2 = d}$$

Local distance is formally captured by the search distance $S_1 \boxminus S_2 = d$ and synchronization distance $S_1 \ominus S_2 = d$ judgements:

search/l/L

$$\frac{}{\varepsilon \boxminus \varepsilon = \langle 0,0\rangle} \qquad \frac{S_1 \boxminus S_2 = d}{L\cdot S_1 \boxminus S_2 = \langle 1,0\rangle + d}$$

search/m/L

$$\frac{S_1\cdot S'_1 \boxminus S_2 = d}{M(S_1)\cdot S'_1 \boxminus S_2 = \langle 1,0\rangle + d}$$

search/none/L

$$\frac{S'_1 \boxminus S_2 = d}{M(\Box)\cdot S'_1 \boxminus S_2 = \langle 1,0\rangle + d}$$

search/synch

$$\frac{M_1 \approx M_2 \qquad S_1 \ominus S_2 = d \qquad S'_1 \boxminus S'_2 = d'}{M_1(S_1)\cdot S'_1 \boxminus M_2(S_2)\cdot S'_2 = \langle 1,1\rangle + d + d'}$$

synch/l

$$\frac{}{\varepsilon \ominus \varepsilon = \langle 0,0\rangle} \qquad \frac{S_1 \ominus S_2 = d}{L\cdot S_1 \ominus L\cdot S_2 = d}$$

synch/m

$$\frac{S_1 \ominus S_2 = d \qquad S'_1 \ominus S'_2 = d'}{M(S_1)\cdot S'_1 \ominus M(S_2)\cdot S'_2 = d + d'}$$

synch/search

$$\frac{S_1 \boxminus S_2 = d}{S_1 \ominus S_2 = d}$$

The search mode *can* switch to synchronization if it encounters similar program fragments (as identified by memoizing application actions), and the synchronization mode *must* switch to search mode if the trace actions differ at some point. Intuitively, the trace distance measures the symmetric difference between two traces (i.e., the size of trace segments that don't occur in both traces). Concretely, we quantify distance $d = \langle c_1, c_2\rangle$ between traces S_1 and S_2 as a pair of costs, where c_1 is the amount of work in S_1 that isn't shared with S_2 and c_2 is the amount of work in S_2 that isn't shared with S_1. We let $d + d'$ denote pointwise addition for distance.

The search distance $S_1 \boxminus S_2 = d$ accounts for traces that don't match, but switches to synchronization mode if it can align memoization actions. The search distance between empty traces is zero. Skipping an action in search mode incurs a cost of 1 in addition to the distance between the tail of the trace (**search/*/L** rules, the right rules are omitted). Upon simultaneously encountering similar memoizing actions $M_1(S_1)\cdot S'_1$ and $M_2(S_2)\cdot S'_2$ (**search/synch** rule), the search distance can switch to synchronizing the bodies S_1 and S_2, while separately searching for further synchronization of the tails S'_1 and S'_2. Two memoizing actions are *similar* $M_1 \approx M_2$ if they are both applications of the same function and argument ($M_i = \mathsf{app}^{v_f \$ v_x \Downarrow v_i}$); note that the return values need not coincide. The cost of the synchronization and search are added to the cost of 1 for the memoization match in each trace.

Turning to the synchronization distance, the $S_1 \ominus S_2 = d$ judgement attempts to structurally match the two traces. Identical work in both traces incurs no cost, but synchronization returns to search mode either nondeterministically or when work cannot be reused because traces don't match. Synchronization mode is only meant to be used on traces generated by the evaluation of the same expression under (possibly) different stores.

The synchronization distance between empty traces is zero. Encountering identical local actions allows distance to remain in synchronization mode without cost (**synch/l** rule). Synchronizing memoizing actions (**synch/m** rule) requires the actions to be identical; this allows the bodies as well as the tails to be synchronized separately and their distance compounded. Note that even if the bodies don't match completely and return to search mode, memoizing actions provide a degree of isolation because tails can be matched independently. Synchronization falls back to search mode (**synch/search** rule) nondeterministically or necessarily when the actions differ (e.g., because actions don't match).

The definition of Src trace distance is a relation because of nondeterminism in how global distance slices the traces and when local distance alternates between search and synchronization mode. While it is desirable to minimize the distance between runs (and thus the update time), the dynamic semantics of Tgt has nondeterministic allocation and memoization in order to avoid committing to an implementation. We show that any distance derivable for Src programs is preserved in Tgt (Corollary 1).

Example. Returning to the map example (Section 2), if ℓ contains $h::t$, the trace slice of $\mathtt{map}(\ell)$ has the form: $\mathsf{app}^{\mathtt{map}\$\ell\Downarrow\ell'}(\mathsf{get}^{\ell \to h::t}{\cdot}\mathsf{app}^{\mathtt{f}\$h\Downarrow h'}(T^{f(h)}){\cdot}\Box{\cdot}\mathsf{put}^{h'::t'\uparrow\ell'})$ where the trace $T^{f(h)}$ of $f(h)$ is assumed to have $O(1)$ size, and $\Box$ is a hole for the recursive call $\mathtt{map}(t) = t'$; we abbreviate such a slice as $\mathtt{m}^{h::t}(\Box)$. Thus the traces for the two runs from the example are, (abusing notation by confusing a location with its contents): $\mathtt{m}^{1..n::k}(\mathtt{m}^{k::\mathtt{nil}}(\mathtt{m}^{\mathtt{nil}}))$ and $\mathtt{m}^{k::1}(\mathtt{m}^{1..n::\mathtt{nil}}(\mathtt{m}^{\mathtt{nil}}))$, where $\mathtt{m}^{1..n::h}(\Box)$ abbreviates $\mathtt{m}^{1::2}(\cdots \mathtt{m}^{n::h}(\Box)\cdots)$.

Under monotonic reuse, change-propagation can only do as well as the local trace distance. We assume trace distance has a bias towards synchronizing the right-hand trace (which corresponds to greedy reuse). This derivation shows that trace distance is $O(n)$, with the relevant portions underlined with the same notation as in Section 2:

$$\dfrac{\dfrac{\dfrac{\dfrac{\dfrac{\dfrac{\dfrac{}{\underline{\mathtt{m}^{\mathtt{nil}}} \ominus \underline{\mathtt{m}^{\mathtt{nil}}} = \langle 0, 0\rangle}\ \textbf{synch}}{\mathtt{m}^{\mathtt{nil}} \boxminus \mathtt{m}^{\mathtt{nil}} = \langle O(1), O(1)\rangle}\ \textbf{search/synch}}{\mathtt{m}^{\mathtt{nil}} \boxminus \underline{\mathtt{m}^{1..n::\mathtt{nil}}}(\mathtt{m}^{\mathtt{nil}}) = \langle O(1), O(n)\rangle}\ \textbf{search/*/R}}{\mathtt{m}^{\mathtt{nil}} \ominus \mathtt{m}^{1..n::\mathtt{nil}}(\mathtt{m}^{\mathtt{nil}}) = \langle O(1), O(n)\rangle}\ \textbf{synch/search}}{\underline{\mathtt{m}^{k::\mathtt{nil}}}(\mathtt{m}^{\mathtt{nil}}) \ominus \underline{\mathtt{m}^{k::1}}(\mathtt{m}^{1..n::\mathtt{nil}}(\mathtt{m}^{\mathtt{nil}})) = \langle O(1), O(n)\rangle}\ \textbf{synch}}{\mathtt{m}^{k::\mathtt{nil}}(\mathtt{m}^{\mathtt{nil}}) \boxminus \mathtt{m}^{k::1}(\mathtt{m}^{1..n::\mathtt{nil}}(\mathtt{m}^{\mathtt{nil}})) = \langle O(1), O(n)\rangle}\ \textbf{search/synch}}{\underline{\mathtt{m}^{1..n::k}}(\mathtt{m}^{k::\mathtt{nil}}(\mathtt{m}^{\mathtt{nil}})) \boxminus \mathtt{m}^{k::1}(\mathtt{m}^{1..n::\mathtt{nil}}(\mathtt{m}^{\mathtt{nil}})) = \langle O(n), O(n)\rangle}\ \textbf{search/*/L}$$

Read bottom up: (1) search discards $\mathtt{m}^{1..n::k}$ with $O(n)$ cost on the left; (2) $\mathtt{m}^{k::\mathtt{nil}}$ and $\mathtt{m}^{k::1}$ match with $O(1)$ cost, the synchronization is partial because the tails differ; (3) search discards $\mathtt{m}^{1..n::\mathtt{nil}}$ with $O(n)$ cost on the right; (4) and finally $\mathtt{m}^{\mathtt{nil}}$ synchronizes with $O(1)$ cost. Note that the memoizing action for the application $\mathtt{map\$}k$ appears at the head of both $\mathtt{m}^{k::\mathtt{m}^{\mathtt{nil}}}$ and $\mathtt{m}^{k::1}$, which enables switching from search to synchronization mode (*cf.* rule **memo/match** in the evaluation semantics of Tgt, Subsection 4.1). On the other hand, the local action that fetches k from the store finds differing tails ($\mathtt{m}^{\mathtt{nil}}$ and 1), which require switching back to search mode (*cf.* rule **change** in the change-propagation semantics of Tgt, Subsection 4.1).

Under non-monotonic reuse, change-propagation can do as well as the global trace distance. This derivation decomposes each run into separate trace slices for $1..n$, k, and $\mathtt{nil}$. Since the slices are nearly identical, their distance is $O(1)$ to account for the initial synchronization and the return to search mode for the differing tails. Adding the local distances yields a global distance of $O(1)$.

$$\dfrac{\begin{array}{c}\mathtt{m}^{1..n::k}(\mathtt{m}^{k::\mathtt{nil}}(\mathtt{m}^{\mathtt{nil}})) \gg \mathtt{m}^{1..n::k}(\square), \mathtt{m}^{k::\mathtt{nil}}(\square), \mathtt{m}^{\mathtt{nil}} \\ \mathtt{m}^{k::1}(\mathtt{m}^{1..n::\mathtt{nil}}(\mathtt{m}^{\mathtt{nil}})) \gg \mathtt{m}^{k::1}(\square), \mathtt{m}^{1..n::\mathtt{nil}}(\square), \mathtt{m}^{\mathtt{nil}} \\ \underline{\mathtt{m}^{\mathtt{nil}}} \boxminus \underline{\mathtt{m}^{\mathtt{nil}}} = \langle O(1), O(1) \rangle \\ \underline{\mathtt{m}^{1..n::k}}(\square) \boxminus \underline{\mathtt{m}^{1..n::\mathtt{nil}}}(\square) = \langle O(1), O(1) \rangle \\ \mathtt{m}^{k::\mathtt{nil}}(\square) \boxminus \mathtt{m}^{k::1}(\square) = \langle O(1), O(1) \rangle \end{array}}{\mathtt{m}^{1..n::k}(\mathtt{m}^{k::\mathtt{nil}}(\mathtt{m}^{\mathtt{nil}})) \boxminus^{\gg} \mathtt{m}^{k::1}(\mathtt{m}^{1..n::\mathtt{nil}}(\mathtt{m}^{\mathtt{nil}})) = \langle O(1), O(1) \rangle}$$

4 The **Tgt** Language

The Tgt language is a call-by-value λ-calculus that enforces a continuation-passing style (CPS) discipline to help identify opportunities for reuse and computations for re-execution. The language includes *modifiable references* to track data dependencies and a *memoization* primitive to identify opportunities for computation reuse across runs.[2] The language is self-adjusting: its semantics includes evaluation to reduce expressions to values, and change-propagation to adapt computations to input changes. To support non-monotonic computation reuse, the dynamic semantics receives a trace of a previous run that can be sliced into subcomputations for reuse with reordering. Section 5 shows how Src programs are CPS-compiled into equivalent self-adjusting Tgt programs.

The following grammar gives the syntax of types τ, expressions e, values v, and adaptive commands κ.

$$\begin{array}{ll}\tau ::= \mathbf{res} \mid \mathbf{nat} \mid \tau_{\mathrm{x}} \to \tau \mid \tau\,\mathbf{mod} & e ::= v \mid \mathbf{caseN}\, v_{\mathrm{n}}\, e_{\mathrm{z}}\, (x.e_{\mathrm{s}}) \mid e_{\mathrm{f}}\, v_{\mathrm{x}} \\ v ::= x \mid \mathbf{zero} \mid \mathbf{succ}\, v \mid \mathbf{fun}\, f.x.e \mid \ell \mid \kappa & \kappa ::= \mathbf{halt}\, v \mid \mathbf{memo}\, e \mid \mathbf{put}\, v\, v_{\mathrm{k}} \mid \mathbf{get}\, v_{\mathrm{l}}\, v_{\mathrm{k}}\end{array}$$

Reference commands have an explicit continuation v_k identifying the computation that follows the command. The CPS discipline restricts a function application $e_f\ v_x$ to have a value argument. Modifiables $\tau\,\mathbf{mod}$ are mutable references

[2] Memoization in self-adjusting computation reuses computation between runs, whereas classical memoization [15] reuses results within a single run.

with commands **put** and **get** for allocation and dereference. The type **res** is an opaque answer type, while **halt** is a continuation that injects a final value into the **res** type. The dynamic semantics identifies opportunities for computation reuse at **memo** commands, which enable replaying the trace of a previous run.

4.1 Static, Dynamic, and Cost Semantics

The typing judgement $\Sigma; \Gamma \vdash e : \tau$ascribes the type τ to the expression e in the store and variable typing contexts Σ and Γ. For brevity, we only give the types of the adaptive commands:

$$\mathbf{halt} : \tau \to \mathbf{res} \qquad\qquad \mathbf{memo} : \mathbf{res} \to \mathbf{res}$$

$$\mathbf{put} : \tau \to (\tau\,\mathbf{mod} \to \mathbf{res}) \to \mathbf{res} \qquad\qquad \mathbf{get} : \tau\,\mathbf{mod} \to (\tau \to \mathbf{res}) \to \mathbf{res}$$

The following rules give the dynamic and cost semantics of evaluation $\overline{S}; \sigma; e \Downarrow_{\mathrm{E}} T'; \sigma'; v'; d'$(left) and change-propagation $\overline{S}; S; \sigma \curvearrowright T'; \sigma'; v'; d'$(right).

$$\frac{e \Downarrow \kappa \quad \overline{S}; \sigma; \kappa \Downarrow_{\mathrm{K}} T'; \sigma'; v'; d'}{\overline{S}; \sigma; e \Downarrow_{\mathrm{E}} T'; \sigma'; v'; d'} \qquad \frac{\lceil S \rceil = \kappa \quad S, \overline{S}; \sigma; \kappa \Downarrow_{\mathrm{K}} T'; \sigma'; v'; d'}{\overline{S}; S; \sigma \curvearrowright T'; \sigma'; v'; d'}\ \textbf{change}$$

$$\frac{|\overline{S}| = \mathrm{c}}{\overline{S}; \sigma; \mathbf{halt}\ v \Downarrow_{\mathrm{K}} \mathtt{halt}^{v}; \sigma; v; \langle \mathrm{c}, 1\rangle} \qquad \frac{|\overline{S}| = \mathrm{c}}{\overline{S}; \mathtt{halt}^{v}; \sigma \curvearrowright \mathtt{halt}^{v}; \sigma; v; \langle \mathrm{c}, 0\rangle}$$

$$\textbf{memo/miss}\ \frac{\overline{S}; \sigma; e \Downarrow_{\mathrm{E}} T'; \sigma'; v'; d'}{\overline{S}; \sigma; \mathbf{memo}\ e \Downarrow_{\mathrm{K}} \mathtt{memo}^{e} \cdot T'; \sigma'; v'; \langle 0, 1\rangle + d'} \qquad \frac{\overline{S}; S; \sigma \curvearrowright T'; \sigma'; v'; d'}{\overline{S}; \mathtt{memo}^{e} \cdot S; \sigma \curvearrowright \mathtt{memo}^{e} \cdot T'; \sigma'; v'; d'}$$

$$\textbf{memo/hit}\ \frac{\overline{S}; e \overset{\mathrm{m}}{\rightsquigarrow} \overline{S}'; S_{\mathrm{e}} \quad \overline{S}'; S_{\mathrm{e}}; \sigma \curvearrowright T'; \sigma'; v'; d'}{\overline{S}; \sigma; \mathbf{memo}\ e \Downarrow_{\mathrm{K}} \mathtt{memo}^{e} \cdot T'; \sigma'; v'; \langle 1, 1\rangle + d'}$$

$$\frac{\ell \notin \mathrm{dom}\,\sigma \quad \sigma_1 = \sigma[\ell \mapsto v] \quad \overline{S}; \sigma_1; v_{\mathrm{k}}\ \ell \Downarrow_{\mathrm{E}} T'; \sigma'; v'; d'}{\overline{S}; \sigma; \mathbf{put}\ v\ v_{\mathrm{k}} \Downarrow_{\mathrm{K}} \mathtt{put}_{v_{\mathrm{k}}}^{v \uparrow \ell} \cdot T'; \sigma'; v'; \langle 0, 1\rangle + d'} \qquad \frac{\ell \notin \mathrm{dom}\,\sigma \quad \sigma_1 = \sigma[\ell \mapsto v] \quad \overline{S}; S; \sigma_1 \curvearrowright T'; \sigma'; v'; d'}{\overline{S}; \mathtt{put}_{v_{\mathrm{k}}}^{v \uparrow \ell} \cdot S; \sigma \curvearrowright \mathtt{put}_{v_{\mathrm{k}}}^{v \uparrow \ell} \cdot T'; \sigma'; v'; d'}$$

$$\frac{\ell \in \mathrm{dom}\,\sigma \quad \sigma(\ell) = v \quad \overline{S}; \sigma; v_{\mathrm{k}}\ v \Downarrow_{\mathrm{E}} T'; \sigma'; v'; d'}{\overline{S}; \sigma; \mathbf{get}\ \ell\ v_{\mathrm{k}} \Downarrow_{\mathrm{K}} \mathtt{get}_{v_{\mathrm{k}}}^{\ell \to v} \cdot T'; \sigma'; v'; \langle 0, 1\rangle + d'} \qquad \frac{\ell \in \mathrm{dom}\,\sigma \quad \sigma(\ell) = v \quad \overline{S}; S; \sigma \curvearrowright T'; \sigma'; v'; d'}{\overline{S}; \mathtt{get}_{v_{\mathrm{k}}}^{\ell \to v} \cdot S; \sigma \curvearrowright \mathtt{get}_{v_{\mathrm{k}}}^{\ell \to v} \cdot T'; \sigma'; v'; d'}$$

The large-step evaluation relation $\overline{S}; \sigma; e \Downarrow_{\mathrm{E}} T'; \sigma'; v'; d'$ (resp. $\overline{S}; \sigma; \kappa \Downarrow_{\mathrm{K}} T'; \sigma'; v'; d'$) reduces the expression e (resp. the adaptive command κ) under the store σ, yielding the value v' and the updated store σ'. Evaluation also takes a list of trace slices $\overline{S}$ from a previous run which are available for reuse, and produces an execution trace T' of the current run and a pair of costs $d' = \langle c, c' \rangle$ for work c discarded from the reuse trace slices and new work c' performed for the current run. The auxiliary evaluation relation $e \Downarrow v'$ reduces an expression e to a value v' by the standard (and thus, elided) function and case-analysis β-reductions; such evaluation is pure and independent of the store.

A Tgt *trace* T is a sequence of reference and memo actions A, ending in a halt action. A *trace slice* S is a trace segment, possibly ending in a $\mathtt{hole}^{e}$ marker that indicates the rest of the trace (corresponding to the run of e) was stolen for out-of-order reuse. Note that a trace is also a trace slice without holes. $\overline{S}$ and U range over lists and non-empty lists of trace slices; concatenation extends to the first slice: $A \cdot (S, \overline{S}) = (A \cdot S, \overline{S})$.

$$A_s ::= \mathtt{put}^{v\uparrow\ell}_{v_k} \mid \mathtt{get}^{\ell\to v}_{v_k} \qquad A ::= A_s \mid \mathtt{memo}^e \quad T ::= \mathtt{halt}^v \mid A{\cdot}T$$
$$H ::= \mathtt{halt}^v \mid \mathtt{hole}^e \quad S ::= H \mid A{\cdot}S \quad \overline{S} ::= \bullet \mid S, \overline{S} \qquad U ::= S, \overline{S}$$

The **halt** v command yields a computation's final value, with a cost of 1 for the current run and a cost $c = |\overline{S}|$ summing the work discarded from the reuse trace slices $\overline{S}$, where the cost of a trace slice is the number of actions (except holes, which don't represent previous work) in the trace:

$$|\mathtt{hole}^e| = 0 \quad |\mathtt{halt}^v| = 1 \quad |A{\cdot}S| = 1 + |S|$$

An adaptive reference command uses the store (**put** and **get** rules) and passes the result to the continuation; the trace is extended with the corresponding action labeled by the location, value, and continuation, and incurs a cost of 1 for the current run. Note that it is acceptable (and, indeed, often desirable) for the location ℓ chosen by **put** to appear in the reuse trace slices because it can enable subsequent **memo**-matching on work from the previous run involving ℓ .

A memoized expression **memo** e in Tgt has no special behavior when evaluated from scratch (**memo/miss** rule): it evaluates the body e and extends the trace with a memo action $\mathtt{memo}^e$, incurring a cost of 1 for the current run. The **memo/hit** rule exploits the reuse trace from the previous evaluation and switches to change-propagation if the same expression was memoized and evaluated in the previous run.

The memoization judgement $S; e \overset{\text{m}}{\rightsquigarrow} S'_1; S'_e$ splits the reuse trace S into a suffix trace slice S'_e that corresponds to a (partial) previous run of e (under a (possibly) different store), and a prefix trace S'_1 of the work preceding S'_e with an explicit $\mathtt{hole}^e$ end marker to indicate the stolen tail.

$$\frac{S; e \overset{\text{m}}{\rightsquigarrow} S'; S'_e}{A{\cdot}S; e \overset{\text{m}}{\rightsquigarrow} A{\cdot}S'; S'_e} \qquad \textbf{hit}\ \frac{}{\mathtt{memo}^e{\cdot}S_e; e \overset{\text{m}}{\rightsquigarrow} \mathtt{hole}^e; S_e} \qquad \frac{\overline{S}; e \overset{\text{m}}{\rightsquigarrow} \overline{S}'; S'_e}{S, \overline{S}; e \overset{\text{m}}{\rightsquigarrow} S, \overline{S}'; S'_e} \qquad \frac{S; e \overset{\text{m}}{\rightsquigarrow} S'; S'_e}{S, \overline{S}; e \overset{\text{m}}{\rightsquigarrow} S', \overline{S}; S'_e}$$

Under monotonic memoization the prefix S'_1 would be discarded incurring a cost of $|S'_1|$, but under non-monotonicity it remains available for later reuse. Memoization extends to trace lists $\overline{S}; e \overset{\text{m}}{\rightsquigarrow} \overline{S}'; S'_e$ by memo-matching with one trace from the list.

The change-propagation relation $\overline{S}; S; \sigma \curvearrowright T'; \sigma'; v'; d'$ replays the partial execution trace S under the store σ, yielding the value v' and the updated store σ', with an updated execution trace T' and a pair of costs $d' = \langle c, c' \rangle$ for work c discarded from $S, \overline{S}$ (viz. the dotted/red work from the previous run's trace) and new work c' performed for T' (viz. the dotted/red and dashed/orange work for the new run's trace); the additional reuse traces $\overline{S}$ are other computations from the previous run that may be reused if change-propagation returns to evaluation. Any work that can be replayed from the previous run is free (viz. the solid/green work common to both traces). A halt action can be replayed to obtain the (unchanged) final value, incurring the cost of discarding the additional reuse traces. An adaptive action can be replayed without cost if the action is consistent with the current store, the tail of the trace can be recursively change-propagated and then extended with the same action. However, if a reference action is inconsistent with the store (e.g., a specific location can't be allocated or a dereference fetches a different value), then change-propagation must switch back to evaluation. A trace slice S can be *reified* back into an adaptive command $\kappa = \lceil S \rceil$, the tail trace slice S' (if any) can be ignored because adaptive actions capture the rest of the computation in the continuation:

$$\lceil \texttt{halt}^{v} \rceil = \mathbf{halt}\, v \qquad \lceil \texttt{hole}^{e} \rceil = \mathbf{memo}\, e \quad \lceil \texttt{memo}^{e} \cdot S' \rceil = \mathbf{memo}\, e$$
$$\lceil \texttt{put}^{v \uparrow \ell}_{v_k} \cdot S' \rceil = \mathbf{put}\, v\, v_k \quad \lceil \texttt{get}^{\ell \to v}_{v_k} \cdot S' \rceil = \mathbf{get}\, \ell\, v_k$$

Thus, change-propagation can reify an inconsistent trace slice S and re-evaluate the command, while keeping the trace S for possible reuse later (**change** rule). Note that the reified **put** (resp. **get**) forgets the (stale) location (resp. value). The **change** rule does *not*, however, require the action to be inconsistent; this nondeterminism intentionally avoids committing to particular allocation and memoization policies.

4.2 Consistency of Change-Propagation

Suppose we have a Tgt program e such that $\Sigma; \cdot \vdash e : \mathbf{res}$ and an initial store σ_1 of type $\Sigma \uplus \Sigma_1$. We can evaluate e under the store σ_1 and no reuse traces, yielding the initial result v'_1 and a trace T'_1: $\bullet; \sigma_1; e \Downarrow_{\mathrm{E}} \sigma'_1; v'_1; T'_1; d'_1$. After this initial evaluation, we can consider another store σ_2 of type $\Sigma \uplus \Sigma_2$ and update the output of the evaluation with respect to this store by applying change-propagation to T'_1 under the store σ_2: $\bullet; T'_1; \sigma_2 \curvearrowright T'_2; \sigma'_2; v'_2; d'_2$. The consistency of change-propagation asserts that the result and trace obtained by change-propagation are identical to those obtained by from-scratch evaluation (i.e., without any reuse traces). In the presence of non-monotonic memoization the reuse trace may be sliced, so consistency must be generalized to deal with trace slices and employs the auxiliary judgements S wfwrt e to mean S results from slicing a from-scratch execution of e ($\bullet; \_; e \Downarrow_{\mathrm{E}} T'; \_; \_; \_$ and $T'; e \overset{\mathrm{m}}{\leadsto} S; S'_{\mathrm{e}}$), and S wf to mean S wfwrt e for some e. Consistency is a corollary of the following theorem by instantiating $\overline{S}$ as the empty list and S'_1 as T'_1.

Theorem 1 (Consistency of Change-Propagation). *If* $\overline{S \text{ wf}}$, S'_1 wfwrt e, *and* $\overline{S}; S'_1; \sigma_2 \curvearrowright T'_2; \sigma'_2; v'_2; \_$, *then* $\bullet; \sigma_2; e \Downarrow_{\mathrm{E}} T'_2; \sigma'_2; v'_2; \_$.
If $\overline{S \text{ wf}}$ *and* $\overline{S}; \sigma_2; e \Downarrow_{\mathrm{E}} T'_2; \sigma'_2; v'_2; \_$, *then* $\bullet; \sigma_2; e \Downarrow_{\mathrm{E}} T'_2; \sigma'_2; v'_2; \_$.

4.3 Trace Distance

In this section, we introduce a notion of trace distance and show that the cost of change-propagation may be bounded by the distance between the input and the result traces. The definition of distance is similar to Src, in Section 5 we show that they are asymptotically the same.

The $S \gg U'$ judgement splits a Tgt trace slice S into a non-empty list of slices U' by (non-deterministically) replacing memo actions with holes.

$$\frac{}{H \gg H; \bullet} \qquad \frac{S \gg S'; \overline{S}'}{A \cdot S \gg A \cdot S'; \overline{S}'} \qquad \frac{S \gg S'; \overline{S}'}{\texttt{memo}^{e} \cdot S \gg \texttt{hole}^{e}; \texttt{memo}^{e} \cdot S', \overline{S}'}$$

The judgement extends to decomposing lists of slices $U \gg U'$ by appending the decomposition of each slice in the list. The judgement $U \overset{\pi}{\leadsto} U'$ means U' is a permutation of U.

The *global (search) distance* $U_1 \boxminus^{\gg} U_2 = d$ of two slice lists U_1 and U_2 results from slicing and permuting each list, and taking their local search distance.

$$\frac{U_1 \gg U_1' \qquad U_1' \overset{\pi}{\leadsto} U_1'' \qquad U_2 \gg U_2' \qquad U_2' \overset{\pi}{\leadsto} U_2'' \qquad U_1'' \boxminus U_2'' = d}{U_1 \boxminus^{\gg} U_2 = d}$$

Since global distance accounts for computation reordering, the *local search distance* $U_1 \boxminus U_2 = d$ accounts for differences between traces in order until it finds matching memoization actions, then it can use the *local synchronization distance* $U_1 \ominus U_2 = d$ to account for reuse between traces until they differ, at which point it must return to search distance. The distance $d = \langle c_1, c_2 \rangle$ quantifies the cost c_1 of work in U_1 that isn't shared with U_2 and the cost c_2 of work in U_2 that isn't shared with U_1. Analogous to the dynamic semantics of Tgt, search distance accounts for discarding old work on the left and performing new work on the right, while synchronization distance reuses work between runs.

$$\frac{|H_1| = c_1 \qquad |H_2| = c_2}{H_1; \bullet \boxminus H_2; \bullet = \langle c_1, c_2 \rangle} \qquad \frac{|H_1| = c_1 \qquad S_1; \overline{S}_1 \boxminus U_2 = d}{H_1; S_1, \overline{S}_1 \boxminus U_2 = \langle c_1, 0 \rangle + d}\ \textbf{h/L} \qquad \frac{}{\texttt{halt}^v; \bullet \ominus \texttt{halt}^v; \bullet = \langle 0, 0 \rangle}$$

$$\frac{S_1; \overline{S}_1 \boxminus U_2 = d}{A \cdot S_1; \overline{S}_1 \boxminus U_2 = \langle 1, 0 \rangle + d}\ \textbf{a/L} \qquad \frac{S_1; \overline{S}_1 \ominus S_2; \overline{S}_2 = d}{A \cdot S_1; \overline{S}_1 \ominus A \cdot S_2; \overline{S}_2 = d}$$

$$\frac{S_1; \overline{S}_1 \ominus S_2; \overline{S}_2 = d}{\texttt{memo}^e \cdot S_1; \overline{S}_1 \boxminus \texttt{memo}^e \cdot S_2; \overline{S}_2 = \langle 1, 1 \rangle + d}\ \textbf{memo/hit} \qquad \frac{U_1 \boxminus U_2 = d}{U_1 \ominus U_2 = d}$$

The search distance between halt or hole actions is the length of each action. Skipping an action incurs a cost of the length of the action for the corresponding trace and forces distance to remain in search mode (***/L** rules, the right rules are omitted). Two identical memo actions incur a cost of 1 each and enable switching from search to synchronization mode.

Synchronization distance, as in Src, is only meant to be used on traces generated by the evaluation of the same expression under (possibly) different stores (though synchronization distance exists between any two traces). The synchronization distance between halt actions is $\langle 0, 0 \rangle$, and assumes both actions return the same value. Identical adaptive actions match without cost and allow distance to continue synchronizing the tail. Synchronization may return to search mode, either nondeterministically or because adaptive actions don't match.

The following shows that the distance between a program's trace T and some traces $\overline{S}$ coincides with the cost of evaluating the program with reuse traces $\overline{S}$.

Theorem 2 (Dynamic Semantics Coincides with Distance). *If* $\overline{\overline{S}\ \mathsf{wf}}$*, and* $\bullet; \sigma; e \Downarrow_{\mathrm{E}} T'; \sigma'; v'; \_$*, then* $\overline{S} \boxminus^{\gg} T' = d$ *iff* $\overline{S}; \sigma; e \Downarrow_{\mathrm{E}} T'; \sigma'; v'; d$*.*

The following result shows that for pure computations with unique function calls, greedy non-monotonic reuse is optimal in the sense that it achieves minimal trace distance. The uniqueness condition means that an application $e_f \$ e_x$ with a given function e_f and argument e_x occurs at most once during the execution. This assumption is necessary because in the presence of duplicate calls and nondeterministic allocation, greedily stealing a computation may unnecessarily cause computation to become inconsistent. The purity assumption is necessary because effects can introduce dependencies between computations that incur an additional cost to reorder (see Section 6).

Theorem 3 (Optimality of Greediness). *Given two pure computations with unique function calls, greedy memo-matching is an optimal memoization policy that change-propagates with asymptotically minimal distance.*

Proof. By the uniqueness assumption, greedy memo-matching achieves maximal reuse of the computation, whence the Tgt-level distance is minimized and in turn the Src-level distance is minimized, up to a constant factor.

5 Translation

In this section, we describe a semantics- and trace distance-preserving translation from Src to Tgt

To translate from Src to Tgt, we use an *adaptive continuation-passing style* transformation. The explicit continuation helps identify the scope of inconsistent store actions that need to be re-executed as well as identical memoized computations that can be reused. That translation was previously used for monotonic self-adjusting computation with traces and local trace distance [12]; we exploit its robustness to extend it to the non-monotonic setting by generalizing to trace slices and global trace distance.

Program Translation. To establish the semantic connection, we define translation for types $[\![\tau^{\mathsf{src}}]\!] = \tau^{\mathsf{tgt}}$, expressions $[\![e^{\mathsf{src}}]\!]\ v_k^{\mathsf{tgt}} = e^{\mathsf{tgt}}$ with an explicit Tgt-level continuation v_k^{tgt}, values $[\![v^{\mathsf{src}}]\!] = v^{\mathsf{tgt}}$. The translation is a standard CPS conversion except that store primitives are translated into Tgt store commands with an explicit continuation v_k, and the function translation threads the continuation through the store and uses explicit **memo** operations before and after the function body to isolate the function call from the rest of the computation.

The correctness and efficiency of the translation is captured by the fact that well-typed Src programs are compiled into (statically and dynamically) equivalent well-typed Tgt programs with the same asymptotic complexity for initial runs (i.e., Tgt evaluation with an empty reuse trace), which are straightforward adaptations of the proofs for the monotonic variant of Tgt.

Theorem 4 (Static and Dynamic Preservation). *If* $\Sigma; \Gamma \vdash e : \tau$, *and* $[\![\Sigma]\!] ; [\![\Gamma]\!] , \Gamma' \vdash v_{\mathrm{k}} : [\![\tau]\!] \rightarrow \mathbf{res}$, *then* $[\![\Sigma]\!] ; [\![\Gamma]\!] , \Gamma' \vdash [\![e]\!]\ v_{\mathrm{k}} : \mathbf{res}$.
If $\sigma_0; e_0 \Downarrow T; \sigma_1; v_1; c_0$, *and* $\bullet; [\![\sigma_1]\!] \uplus \sigma_{\mathrm{k}}; v_{\mathrm{k}}\ [\![v_1]\!] \Downarrow_{\mathrm{E}} T_{\mathrm{k}}; \sigma_2; v_2; \langle \_, c_1 \rangle$, *then* $\bullet; [\![\sigma_0]\!] \uplus \sigma_{\mathrm{k}}; [\![e_0]\!]\ v_{\mathrm{k}} \Downarrow_{\mathrm{E}} T'; \sigma_2 \uplus \sigma_{\mathrm{e}}; v_2; \langle \_, \Theta(c_0 + c_1) \rangle$.

Trace Translation. To establish the trace distance connection, we define a *trace translation* $[\![S^{\mathsf{src}}]\!]\ v_k^{\mathsf{tgt}}\ U_k^{\mathsf{tgt}} = U^{\mathsf{tgt}}$ of a Src trace slice S^{src} using v_k^{tgt} as an initial continuation and suffix slice list U_k^{tgt} to produce a Tgt slice list U^{tgt} corresponding to the original computation (with explicit holes). The proof of global trace distance preservation requires establishing the preservation of local trace distance, which in turn requires auxiliary translations for a trace slice S^{src} extracted from a larger computation and for non-empty Src slice list U^{src}.

Corollary 1 (Src/Tgt **Distance Soundness).** *If* $S_1^{\mathsf{imp}} \boxminus\!\!\gg S_2^{\mathsf{imp}} = \langle \_, c\rangle$, *then* $[\![S_1^{\mathsf{imp}}]\!]\ \mathbf{id}_1\ U_{\mathbf{id}1}^{\mathsf{tgt}} \boxminus\!\!\gg [\![S_2^{\mathsf{imp}}]\!]\ \mathbf{id}_2\ U_{\mathbf{id}2}^{\mathsf{tgt}} = \langle \_, \Theta(c)\rangle$, *where* $U_{\mathbf{id}i}^{\mathsf{tgt}}$ *is the identity trace.*

Note that since Src and Tgt distance are quasi-symmetric, analogous results hold of the left component of distance. This means that change-propagation has the same asymptotic time-complexity as trace distance.

6 The Change Propagation Algorithm

Here we describe a concrete algorithm and associated data structures for efficiently supporting the reordering of the trace. This goes into a level more detail than the target semantics in Section 4 allowing an analysis of running time. We use CPA to refer to the change propagation algorithm in contrast to the abstract change propagation mechanism of Section 4. We use TDS to refer to the concrete data structure used for traces generated during the run of the program and updated by the CPA.

The main idea of the CPA is to traverse the trace in execution order while identifying the parts of the trace that need to be rerun (the $\Downarrow_{\mathrm{E}}$ and $\Downarrow_{\mathrm{K}}$ relations in Subsection 4.1) and the parts that can be reused (the $\curvearrowright$ relation in Subsection 4.1). In particular it is important to skip over the part that can be reused without incurring any cost. An important aspect is therefore to identify after a memo hit the next place in the trace that does not match the previous trace—i.e., the next inconsistency. Once this is identified the CPA also needs to splice the part between the match and the inconsistency out of the previous TDS and append it to the current TDS.

The TDS is based on a totally ordered timeline with a timestamp for each action in the trace—i.e., all memo and reference actions. This timeline therefore has a one-to-one correspondence to the trace in the target semantics. The TDS also maintains for each modifiable reference the timestamps for all actions on the reference, and for each **get** action it keeps the continuation that needs to be rerun if the value of the reference is changed. To support reordering this timeline needs to allow extraction and insertion of chunks of trace. As discussed below, this can be implemented reasonably efficiently. Finally the TDS needs to maintain a memo table mapping all memoized function calls and associated arguments to the timestamp at which the call is made. Here we assume that if there are multiple identical calls, only one is stored.

```
Algorithm CPA (S, T, Q, t_s)
  let t_i = find the next element in Q greater than t_s
  in if t_i is the end then T ++ S[t_s,end]
     else let T_r = S[t_s,t_i)
              S' = S − T_r
              (t_m, Q', T_n) = run continuation of t_i until memo match in S'
                t_m is the timestamp of the memo match
                Q' is Q extended such that every put(ℓ) during
                  the run adds all associated get(ℓ)s to the queue
                T_n is the new trace
              T' = T ++ T_r ++ T_n
          in if t_m is the end then T'
              else CPA (S', T', Q', t_m)
```

Fig. 1. The non-monotonic change propagation algorithm

Figure 1 describes the non-monotonic CPA. The algorithm starts with an input trace S (i.e., the list of trace slices $\overline{S}$ in the Tgt semantics, but the separation into pieces is implicit) and generates an output trace T for the updated run. The algorithm maintains a queue Q of the timestamps of inconsistent reads (**get** actions for which the value of the corresponding reference has changed), ordered by time. The queue is initialized to include all the **get** actions on any input references that have changed. The time t_s represents a finger (position) in S which is the start of a piece of trace that is being reused. Initially, t_s is at the start of S; at each step (recursive call), the algorithm finds the next inconsistent read past t_s. If there is none, then there are no more inconsistencies and the algorithm is done by appending the trace in S past the finger onto the end of T. If the next inconsistent read is at time t_i, CPA extracts the part of the trace between t_s (inclusive) and t_i (exclusive) because it hasn't changed since the last run and can be reused by simply appending it to the output trace (skipping the $\curvearrowright$ replay transitions). This chunk is also removed from the input trace since we don't want to use the same part of the input trace more than once.

Since the read at t_i is inconsistent (reads a different value from before) the algorithm needs to rerun the continuation for that read. While the continuation runs it looks for a memo match in S and stops when it finds one. This match could be anywhere in S, and in particular out of order with respect to matches found in previous steps. While running, whenever a change is made to a reference that existed in the previous run (a write with a new value), the timestamps for all the reads associated with that reference are added to Q'. Thus when the rerun is completed, all inconsistent reads caused by the run are properly marked in Q' and all memoized function calls are placed in the memo table for future reference. The rerun returns the timestamp t_m of the memo match, as well as the modified queue Q' and the new trace segment T_n for the computation that has just run. Now CPA can extend the original output trace T with the reusable trace T_r and the new trace T_n. Thus on every step (except perhaps the last), the algorithm adds one reused chunk of trace and one new chunk of trace to the output trace. Only the new chunks require work.

This algorithm implements the change propagation scheme described in Section 4 and is therefore correct as long as it properly identifies the **change** rule from the Tgt dynamic semantics—i.e., it properly identifies the next difference in the trace. This identification is correct since the only way a **get** of a pure reference from the source language can become inconsistent (read a different value) is if the original **put** has changed. These reference updates are all included in Q. The important property is that any reordering among the reads does not affect the values read since the write happens before all reads. Also the order of a read and write cannot swap since that would be an invalid program and would not be generated by any trace. This is not true for imperative source references, where there can be interleaving between writes and reads and a reordering of traces can swap the ordering of a read and write.

Now let's consider the running time of CPA. Certainly all new computation needs to be run but this is accounted for in the trace distance. The other costs of the algorithm include the time for extracting and appending chunks of the trace, the cost for the queue operations, and the cost for memo lookup and associated insertion into the memo table. We use $T_{splice}(n)$ to indicate the time to append or extract a chunk of trace for a trace of size n. Using balanced trees this can easily be implemented in $O(\log n)$ time, and with some work comparisons between timestamps in the trace can be made to work in $O(1)$ time. We use $T_{queue}(n)$ to indicate the time to insert or delete in the queue of size n. This is easy to implement in $O(\log n)$ time per operation as long as the comparison of time stamps is $O(1)$ time. We assume the memo lookup uses standard hash tables and therefore takes constant expected time per operation (either lookup or insertion). Consider a computation in which the total new computation is c, the total number of recursive calls of the CPA is l, the total trace distance just counting reads is r, and the maximum of the sizes of the input and output traces is n. The running time is then $O(c + lT_{splice}(n) + (r + l)T_{queue}(n))$. Relating this to the trace distance measured by the semantics, change propagation for two traces S_1 and S_2 such that $S_1 \ominus^{\gg} S_2 = \langle c_1, c_2 \rangle$ will run in time $O((c_1 + c_2)(1 + T_{splice}(n) + T_{queue}(n))) = O((c_1 + c_2) \log n)$.

Example. The Tgt trace of map has the form (abbreviations given below):

$$\underbrace{\texttt{call}^{\texttt{map}\$\ell\Downarrow\ell'}}_{\llcorner^{h}} \cdot \underbrace{\texttt{get}^{\ell\to h::t}}_{\texttt{g}} \cdot \underbrace{\texttt{call}^{f\$h\Downarrow h'} \cdot T^{f(h)} \cdot \texttt{ret}^{f\$h\Uparrow h'}}_{F^h} \cdot \underbrace{\square}_{\square} \cdot \underbrace{\texttt{put}^{h'::t'\uparrow\ell'}}_{\texttt{p}} \cdot \underbrace{\texttt{ret}^{\texttt{map}\$\ell\Uparrow\ell'}}_{\lrcorner^{h}}$$

where $T^{f(h)}$ is the body of $f(h)$ and $\square$ is a hole for the recursive call $\texttt{map}(t) = t'$.[3] The trace segments $\texttt{call}^{g\$x\Downarrow a}$ and $\texttt{ret}^{g\$x\Uparrow a}$ represent the *memoized* function call and return that result from translating a Src trace $\mathsf{app}^{g\$x\Downarrow a}(\_)$; they (1) enable reusing the subsequent trace up to the next inconsistent action and (2) identify an inconsistency (i.e., need to re-execute at the return) if the function is being reused in a different calling context (i.e., returning to a different continuation).

[3] For brevity, we omit the Tgt continuations on actions (e.g., a call has a continuation argument, a return passes the result to the continuation).

Next, we consider the CPA updating `map`. The table below shows the iterations of CPA with the reuse trace S and the trace T of the new run as it is built.

iteration	first run (S)	second run (T)
1	$\overset{1}{\llcorner}\mathtt{g}F^1\cdots\overset{n}{\llcorner}\mathtt{g}F^n\overset{k}{\llcorner}\mathtt{g}F^k\overset{\mathtt{nil}}{\llcorner}\mathtt{gp}\overset{\mathtt{nil}}{\lrcorner}\mathtt{p}\overset{k}{\lrcorner}\mathtt{p}\overset{n}{\lrcorner}\cdots\mathtt{p}\overset{1}{\lrcorner}$	$\overset{k}{\llcorner}\mathtt{g}$
2	$\overset{1}{\llcorner}\mathtt{g}F^1\cdots\overset{n}{\llcorner}\mathtt{g}F^n \quad F^k\overset{\mathtt{nil}}{\llcorner}\mathtt{gp}\overset{\mathtt{nil}}{\lrcorner}\mathtt{p}\overset{k}{\lrcorner}\mathtt{p}\overset{n}{\lrcorner}\cdots\mathtt{p}\overset{1}{\lrcorner}$	F^k
3	$\overset{1}{\llcorner}\mathtt{g}F^1\cdots\overset{n}{\llcorner}\mathtt{g}F^n \quad \overset{\mathtt{nil}}{\llcorner}\mathtt{gp}\overset{\mathtt{nil}}{\lrcorner}\mathtt{p}\overset{k}{\lrcorner}\mathtt{p}\overset{n}{\lrcorner}\cdots\mathtt{p}\overset{1}{\lrcorner}$	$\overset{1}{\llcorner}\mathtt{g}F^1\cdots\overset{n}{\llcorner}\mathtt{g}$
4	$F^n \quad \overset{\mathtt{nil}}{\llcorner}\mathtt{gp}\overset{\mathtt{nil}}{\lrcorner}\mathtt{p}\overset{k}{\lrcorner}\mathtt{p}\overset{n}{\lrcorner}\cdots\mathtt{p}\overset{1}{\lrcorner}$	F^n
5	$\overset{\mathtt{nil}}{\llcorner}\mathtt{gp}\overset{\mathtt{nil}}{\lrcorner}\mathtt{p}\overset{k}{\lrcorner}\mathtt{p}\overset{n}{\lrcorner}\cdots\mathtt{p}\overset{1}{\lrcorner}$	$\overset{\mathtt{nil}}{\llcorner}\mathtt{gp}\overset{\mathtt{nil}}{\lrcorner}\mathtt{p}$
6	$\mathtt{p}\overset{k}{\lrcorner}\mathtt{p}\overset{n}{\lrcorner}\cdots\mathtt{p}\overset{1}{\lrcorner}$	$\overset{n}{\lrcorner}\cdots\mathtt{p}\overset{1}{\lrcorner}\mathtt{p}\overset{k}{\lrcorner}$

The queue Q consists of inconsistent reads (e.g., `g`) due to input changes and inconsistent returns (e.g., $\overset{n}{\lrcorner}$ and the return at the end of F_n) because the calling context (i.e., caller) has changed. We use dotted/red in S for inconsistent actions and in T for new work (viz. T_n), dashed/orange in S for a partially inconsistent trace and in T for partially reused work (viz. T_r ++ T_n), and solid/green in S and T for the reused trace (viz. T_r).

The initial `map` on $[1, \ldots, n, k]$ produces the first trace S. Moving k to the front changes the input to $[k, 1, \ldots, n]$, and Q is initialized with the now-inconsistent `get` actions for k and n. In the first CPA iteration, $\overset{k}{\llcorner}$ is reused and the following `g` is re-run because it's inconsistent and immediately followed by a memo-match in F^k; in S, the return $\overset{k}{\lrcorner}$ is marked inconsistent because of the new caller (originally called from $\overset{n}{\llcorner}$, but now from the top-level) and the consumed trace segments are removed (indicated by blanks in the next iteration). In the second iteration, $F^k = \mathtt{call}^{f\$h\Downarrow h'}.T^{f(h)}.\mathtt{ret}^{f\$h\Uparrow h'}$ reuses the call and body, but re-runs the tail because of the different tail computation (`map`$[1, \ldots]$ instead of `map$nil`). The third and fourth iterations likewise reuse the `map` and f calls for $1..n$ and mark $\overset{1}{\lrcorner}$ inconsistent because of the different caller. The fifth iteration reuses the call and body for `nil`, but has to re-execute the return $\overset{\mathtt{nil}}{\lrcorner}$ and `p` of n because of the new caller. Finally, in the sixth iteration, the `map` returns of $n..2$ are reused, and the returns $\overset{1}{\lrcorner}$ and $\overset{k}{\lrcorner}$ are re-run because they have new callers. The reuse trace S is left over with unused remnants $\mathtt{p}\overset{k}{\lrcorner}$ and $\overset{1}{\lrcorner}$ which must be discarded.

7 Related Work

Self-adjusting computation has been realized through several formal languages and implementations. The first was a pure higher-order language with a modal type system that was implemented both as a Standard ML library with a monad and explicit destination-passing [2] and a Haskell library using several monads to enforce the modal constraints [6]. Subsequent proposals included a direct-style higher-order language compiled into a continuation-passing style (CPS) higher-order language implemented in the MLton Standard ML compiler [13], and a low-level imperative language implemented as a compiler for C [10]. All of these designs focus on *strict* languages with *call-by-value* (CBV) functions that *eagerly* evaluate function arguments[4] and none of them supported efficient reordering. Approaches based on pure memoization (function caching) alone [16,14] allow for incrementality with reordering; since they lack the fine-grained dependence tracking of modifiable references, they can only provide coarse-grained reuse and are inefficient for deeply-nested changes (e.g., changing the last element of a list). Previous work introduced a cost semantics for self-adjusting computation with updatable references and monotonic reuse, and showed analogous correctness properties of change-propagation and compilation [12].

8 Conclusion and Future Work

Self-adjusting computation (SAC) combines dynamic dependence tracking and memoization to effectively update a computation in response to input changes. However, since previous approaches are based on updating a timeline of the computation in monotonic (i.e., time-increasing) order and a greedy approach to memo matching, they perform inefficiently when subcomputations are reordered.

We generalize SAC with non-monotonic reuse to support input changes that affect the order of subcomputations. We give a high-level source language for expressing pure self-adjusting programs equipped with a notion of trace distance to quantify the dissimilarity of computations under an input change. We give a semantics- and trace distance-preserving translation to a low-level target language and show that trace distance coincides asymptotically with change-propagation (i.e., update). We also provide and analyze a new algorithm that realizes the semantics of change-propagation with reordering, which incurs a logarithmic overhead. In future work, we will evaluate the algorithm and extend non-monotonicity to other programming paradigms (e.g., updatable references and laziness).

References

1. Acar, U.A., Blelloch, G.E., Blume, M., Tangwongsan, K.: An experimental analysis of self-adjusting computation. In: PLDI (2006)
2. Acar, U.A., Blelloch, G.E., Harper, R.: Adaptive functional programming. ACM TOPLAS 28(6), 990–1034 (2006)
3. Acar, U.A., Blelloch, G.E., Tangwongsan, K., Türkoğlu, D.: Robust kinetic convex hulls in 3D. In: European Symposium on Algorithms (September 2008)
4. Acar, U.A., Cotter, A., Hudson, B., Türkoğlu, D.: Dynamic well-spaced point sets. In: Symposium on Computational Geometry (2010)
5. Acar, U.A., Ihler, A., Mettu, R., Sümer, Ö.: Adaptive Bayesian inference. In: Neural Information Processing Systems, NIPS (2007)

[4] Haskell is lazy, but the use of monads gives SAC primitives eager evaluation.

6. Carlsson, M.: Monads for incremental computing. In: ICFP (2002)
7. Chiang, Y.-J., Tamassia, R.: Dynamic algorithms in computational geometry. Proceedings of the IEEE 80(9), 1412–1434 (1992)
8. Demers, A., Reps, T., Teitelbaum, T.: Incremental evaluation of attribute grammars with application to syntax-directed editors. In: POPL (1981)
9. Eppstein, D., Galil, Z., Italiano, G.F.: Dynamic graph algorithms. In: Atallah, M.J. (ed.) Algorithms and Theory of Computation Handbook, ch.8, CRC Press (1999)
10. Hammer, M.A., Acar, U.A., Chen, Y.: CEAL: a C-based language for self-adjusting computation. In: PLDI (2009)
11. Ley-Wild, R.: Programmable Self-Adjusting Computation. PhD thesis, CSD, CMU (2010)
12. Ley-Wild, R., Acar, U.A., Fluet, M.: A cost semantics for self-adjusting computation. In: POPL (2009)
13. Ley-Wild, R., Fluet, M., Acar, U.A.: Compiling self-adjusting programs with continuations. In: ICFP (2008)
14. Liu, Y.A., Stoller, S., Teitelbaum, T.: Static caching for incremental computation. ACM TOPLAS 20(3), 546–585 (1998)
15. Michie, D.: "Memo" functions and machine learning. Nature 218, 19–22 (1968)
16. Pugh, W., Teitelbaum, T.: Incremental computation via function caching. In: POPL (1989)
17. Ramalingam, G., Reps, T.: A categorized bibliography on incremental computation. In: POPL (1993)
18. Shankar, A., Bodik, R.: DITTO: Automatic incrementalization of data structure invariant checks (in Java). In: PLDI (2007)

Java and the Java Memory Model — A Unified, Machine-Checked Formalisation*

Andreas Lochbihler

Karlsruher Institut für Technologie
andreas.lochbihler@kit.edu

Abstract. We present a machine-checked formalisation of the Java memory model and connect it to an operational semantics for Java source code and bytecode. This provides the link between sequential semantics and the memory model that has been missing in the literature. Our model extends previous formalisations by dynamic memory allocation, thread spawns and joins, infinite executions, the wait-notify mechanism and thread interruption. We prove the Java data race freedom guarantee for the complete formalisation in a modular way. This work makes the assumptions about the sequential semantics explicit and shows how to discharge them.

1 Introduction

A memory model (MM) specifies how shared memory behaves under concurrent programs. The most intuitive one is sequential consistency (SC) [15], which assumes interleaving semantics, i.e., threads execute one at a time and all threads immediately see all writes of all other threads. For efficiency reasons, modern hardware implements only MMs weaker than sequential consistency to allow for local caches and optimisations [1]. Similarly, many compiler optimisations that are correct for sequential code lead to unexpected results in concurrent code. Consider, e.g., the two threads in Fig. 1 that share locations x and y. Under sequential consistency, the result r1 == 2, r2 == 1 is impossible. However, if the compiler or the hardware reorders the independent statements in each thread — not being aware of the other thread — this outcome is in fact possible. Weak MMs relax interleaving semantics such that such optimisations become correct.

For the typical programmer, weak MMs like the Java Memory Model (JMM) [10,21] nevertheless provide intuitive SC semantics for an important class of programs – a property known as the data-race freedom (DRF) guarantee [2]: Two accesses to the same (non-volatile) location *conflict* if they originate from different threads and at least one is a write. A *data race* occurs if two conflicting accesses may happen concurrently, i.e., without synchronisation in between. Then, if no SC execution contains data races, the JMM promises that the program behaves like under SC semantics. In other words: If a programmer protects all accesses to shared data via locks or declares the locations volatile or in another way makes

* This work was partially funded by DFG grants Sn11/10-1,2.

H. Seidl (Ed.): ESOP 2012, LNCS 7211, pp. 497–517, 2012.

initially: x = y = 0;	
1: r1 = x;	3: r2 = y;
2: y = 1;	4: x = 2;

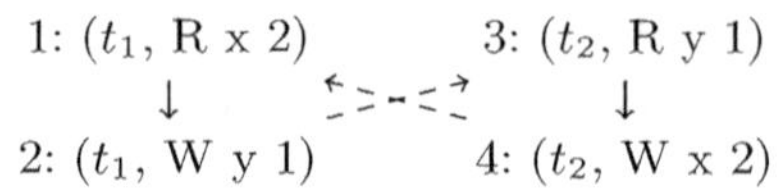

Fig. 1. Example program with data races from [21] (left) and (part of) its JMM execution for the result r1 == 2, r2 == 1 (right)

sure there are no data races, she can forget about the MM and assume interleaving semantics. In the above example, the read of x in l. 1 races with the write in l. 4 (and similarly l. 3 and l. 2 for y), i.e., the DRF guarantee does not apply.

In practice, the DRF guarantee is the most relevant part of the JMM. For type safety and security promises, the JMM also gives semantics to programs with data races, which is the main cause for its complexity. While the DRF guarantee is stated concisely and formally, only test cases [23] underpin these promises about type safety and security, and it is unclear whether the JMM actually provides the latter. Moreover, the JMM inadvertently and unnecessarily disallows certain program transformations that Java virtual machines (JVM) and the hardware regularly perform [9,26,29].[1] Hence, it fails to provide enough flexibility to compiler writers and implementors. Therefore, it is even more important that at least the DRF guarantee holds.

Given the technical complexity of the JMM and Java, it is crucial that all claims are mechanically checked – as a series of false claims about the JMM and their subsequent disproof demonstrates [21,9,26,29]. Moreover, such a JMM formalisation needs to be linked with a sequential semantics for Java, which several authors [4,9,11] have criticised as missing. Since the proof of the DRF guarantee makes assumptions about the sequential semantics, this is a prerequisite to show that Java actually provides it.

To that end, we extend our previous work JinjaThreads [16,17,20], a formalisation of multithreaded Java in the proof assistant Isabelle/HOL [22] as part of the Quis Custodiet project [25]. It models a substantial subset of multithreaded Java source code and bytecode, defines an interleaving semantics, and verifies a compiler from source code to bytecode — all assuming sequential consistency.

Contributions. In this work, we formalise the JMM in the proof assistant Isabelle/HOL [22], connect it to JinjaThreads, and prove the DRF guarantee. To our knowledge, this is the first unified, machine-checked model for Java and the JMM. All definitions and proofs have been checked by Isabelle and are available online in the Archive of Formal Proofs [18]. The accompanying technical report [19] contains high-level proofs for all theorems and further examples.

First, we present a *consistent* formalisation of the JMM based on the operational JinjaThreads semantics for Java source code and bytecode (§2). Our model covers dynamic memory allocation, thread spawns and joins, infinite

[1] It is inadvertent because the JMM's designers claimed that it allows such transformations [21], but were later proven wrong [9,26]. It is unnecessary as neither the DRF guarantee nor Java type safety nor its security promises would be broken.

executions, the wait-notify mechanism and interruption, all of which previous JMM formalisations [4,11] have omitted. Dynamic allocation and the special treatment of memory initialisation in the JMM force us to deal with infinite executions (see §1.1 for an informal JMM explanation).

Our model establishes a solid link between the semantics for sequential Java and the JMM by associating Java statements with their JMM inter-thread actions. In novel examples, we show that the Java Language Specification (JLS) [10] and the Java API define communication channels between threads that the JMM does not cover. Covert channels make the behaviour of one thread dependent on another thread's without synchronisation or memory access. We extend our model accordingly (§§2.1,2.2). Following [8,9], we interleave all threads and reconstruct the fundamental notions of the JMM a posteriori (§2.3).

Second, we prove the DRF guarantee (§3) for source code and bytecode. Our proof resolves the inconsistencies with initialisations of locations in previous proofs [21,11]. To bridge the gap between the axiomatic JMM and the operational semantics, we identify the assumptions of the DRF proof (§3.1) and prove that the semantics satisfies them (§3.2). Although these assumptions are intuitive, they surprisingly require a full subject reduction proof for sequentially consistent executions. In particular, we explicitly construct sequentially consistent executions for a given prefix by corecursion. Again, initialisations turn out to be the main complication in the proofs.

1.1 An Informal Introduction to the JMM

In this section, we informally explain the ideas of the JMM – see §2 for the formalisation. Aiming for independence from concrete hardware and implementations, the JMM [10, §17.4] consists of axiomatic rules that determine a posteriori whether a given execution is an allowed behaviour of a given program. To that end, it abstracts concrete thread operations to *(inter-thread) actions*:

- reading (R) from, writing (W) to and initialising (I) heap-based locations,
- locking (L) and unlocking (U) a monitor,
- thread start (S) and finish (F),
- interrupting (Ir) a thread and observing that it has been interrupted (Ird),
- spawning (Sp) of and joining (J) on a thread, and
- external actions (E) – for I/O, for example.

Actions in the JMM only deal with heap locations, i.e., object fields and array cells. Access to local variables, method parameters, and type information does not generate any inter-thread actions and is thus unaffected by the JMM.

In a given execution, the actions of a single thread are totally ordered by the sequence in which they would occur according to the intra-thread semantics, the so-called program order. Being consistent with this total order, the happens-before order provides a notion of time relative to a given action. It partitions the other actions into three groups: those that must have happened before it, those that must happen after it, and those that may happen concurrently. Synchronisation actions, which are all inter-thread actions except for external actions and reads from and writes to non-volatile locations, introduce happens-before relationships between actions of different threads.

The right-hand side of Fig. 1 shows the essential part of the execution with the unexpected result using the following notation (see [19, Fig. 5] for the complete execution): Statements are abstracted to their actions labelled with the thread ID. The solid arrows represent program order, transitive relationships are not shown. Dotted arrows used in later examples denote synchronisation (synchronises-with relationships); as there is no synchronisation, happens-before coincides with program order. Hence, l. 1 and l. 2 may happen "concurrently" with l. 3 and l. 4. The dashed arrows denote the flow of values from writes to reads. An execution assigns to each read action the write action it sees, e.g., l. 1 sees the write from l. 4.

The JMM requires that the write must not happen after the read. However, if only happens-before determines visibility of write actions, values may appear *out of thin air*. Consider, e.g.,

initially: x = y = 0;	
1: r1 = x;	3: r2 = y;
2: y = r1;	4: x = r2;

$$1: (t_1, \text{R x } 42) \qquad 3: (t_2, \text{R y } 42)$$
$$\downarrow \qquad\qquad \qquad \downarrow$$
$$2: (t_1, \text{W y } 42) \qquad 4: (t_2, \text{W x } 42)$$

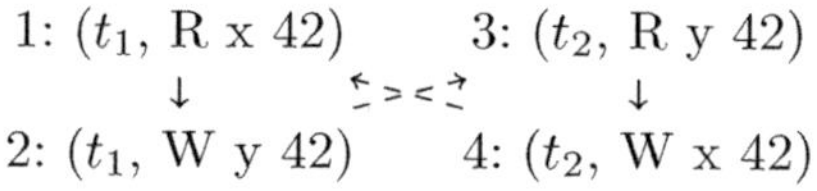

The reads in ll. 1 and 3 may see the writes in ll. 4 and 2, resp., as they may happen concurrently. If both writes write 42, both reads may read 42. Since the program cannot normally produce 42, 42 appears out of thin air.

For type safety and security guarantees, it is vital that values *do not* appear out of thin air [24]. To preclude this, the JMM adds a causality condition: Reads that see concurrent writes must be committed, i.e., there must be a justifying execution that writes the same value, but the read action sees a write that happens before it. We omit the technical details in the presentation, as they are not relevant for understanding this work, but we have formalised them similarly to previous work [4,11]. In the above example, causality forbids r1 == 42 because no execution can produce the value 42 without performing both reads from concurrent writes. The important thing to note is that at the basis of any sequence of justifying executions, there is one in which all reads see writes that happen before them.

This is where initialisations come into play. The JMM assumes that all locations are initialised to their default value at the start of the execution. By definition, these initialisations happen before any other action. Thus, there is always at least one suitable write that happens before a given read, which ensures that such a basis for justifying executions exists.

The requirement that the JMM initialises heap locations at the start (instead of when the location is allocated) has been one of the main complications in our DRF proof – which previous formalisations have omitted. Since initialisation actions originate from dynamic allocation, we must consider complete executions, which may be infinite, instead of finite prefixes [4] – at least for the single-thread semantics. Consider, e.g., the program and one of its (legal) executions in Fig. 2. Note that the initialisation for the field f of the object created in l. 3 at location l happens before all other actions although the single-thread semantics executes

class A { int f; }	initially: x = y = null
1: r1 = x; 2: if (r1 != null) r2 = r1.f; 3: r3 = new A(); 4: y = r3;	5: r4 = y; 6: x = r4;

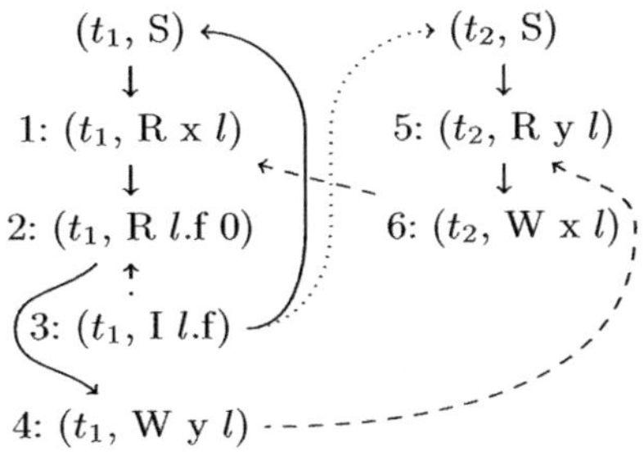

Fig. 2. Program with a legal execution in which a read sees the initialisation which occurs later in the program text

it only after ll. 1 and 2. Suppose we take the prefix of this execution up to l. 2. If (t_1, I l.f) is not part of the prefix, the prefix is an ill-formed execution because l. 2 sees no write. Hence, we must include the initialisation actions in prefixes. As the single-thread semantics produces initialisation actions only at allocations, we must run the program to completion, because we cannot decide at intermediate states whether we have collected all initialisation actions. Thus, our formalisation must deal with infinite executions.

1.2 Related Work

A lot of work has been devoted to hardware MMs, see [1] for an overview. Here, we focus on programming language MMs.

Huisman and Petri [11] have formalised the JMM and the proof of the DRF guarantee in Coq. They have already noted that initialisations break the proof, but added an axiom to avoid the problem. They set out at the abstract level of threads in isolation, without connection to an operational semantics.

Aspinall and Ševčík [4] have formalised parts of the JMM relevant for the DRF guarantee and proved the latter in Isabelle/HOL — which we have found very helpful in extending the DRF guarantee proof. Since they omit dynamic allocation, they need to consider only finite prefixes of executions, which considerably simplifies their proofs, as they do not need to assume that sequentially consistent continuations of executions exist. They do not provide an intra-thread semantics; instead, they model a program as an unspecified predicate that checks whether a trace of memory accesses and synchronisation operations represents a valid execution of the thread. This does not suffice to model the hidden communication channels between threads that the JLS specifies (see §§2.1, 2.2).

For a kernel language, Cenciarelli et al. [9] define an interleaving small-step semantics that generates configuration structures of actions which an axiomatic theory constrains. On paper, they show that they only generate behaviours that the JMM allows, but it is unknown if they produce every allowed behaviour.

Torlak et al. [29] developed a model checker for axiomatic memory models. Using whole-program analysis, they derive JMM executions from small Java programs that are restricted to a small (finite) number of heap locations and finite state; loops are unrolled. Thus, their algorithm can compute all actions and memory allocations in advance. They focus on checking small test cases rather than providing a full semantics and proofs.

Jagadeesan et al. [13] define an operational semantics for weak MMs with speculative computations similar to the JMM. Instead of validating executions a posteriori, their semantics explicitly encodes permitted reorderings and speculation. Yet, their model is neither machine-checked nor comparable to the JMM for programs with data races and synchronisation.

Boyland [8] formalises in Twelf a semantics for a simple language with allocation, synchronisation, volatiles, thread spawns and joins, which may raise an error upon a data race. He shows that a program never raises such errors iff it is data-race free in the JMM sense. For programs with data races, the semantics misses many behaviours that the JMM allows, e.g., reorderings as in Figs. 1,2, whereas our semantics deals with the full JMM.

The recent standard C++11 [12] considers programs with data races ill-formed and assigns undefined semantics to them, but it offers finer shades of synchronisation than Java. Boehm and Adve [7] describe the MM and prove the DRF guarantee for programs which use only strong synchronisation primitives. They show that such programs are characterised more intuitively as never having conflicting accesses adjacent in any interleaving. For the JMM, this equivalence does not hold since threads can communicate without introducing happens-before relationships (§2.1). Batty et al. [6] have formalised the MM with a focus on rigorously defining the semantics, but do not report on any proofs.

Ševčík et al. [27] have verified the CompCert compiler backend with respect to the formal MM for x86 processors by Sewell et al. [28], which is the first formal correctness proof for an optimising compiler backend w.r.t. a weak MM. They expose the x86-TSO model in the programming language, which is considerably stronger than the JMM and also provides a DRF guarantee.

2 From Sequential Java to the Java Memory Model

This section introduces JinjaThreads (§2.1) and connects it (§2.2) to our JMM formalisation (§2.3). We discuss deviations from and suggestions for the original JMM in §2.4.

2.1 Single-Thread Semantics

JinjaThreads is a complex model of Java that supports a broad spectrum of concepts: local variables, objects and fields, inheritance, dynamic dispatch, recursion, arrays and exception handling; for details see [14,16,17]. It uses a stack of small-step semantics to give meaning to programs (Fig. 3). As source code and bytecode share the same program structure except for method bodies, they share most of the levels. The stack falls into two parts: the multithreaded semantics at levels 4 to 6, which we defer to §2.2, and the sequential small-step semantics at levels 1 to 3. Source code and bytecode differ only on level 2, which defines the semantics of the language primitives. For bytecode, this level consists of three sub-levels 2a through 2c.

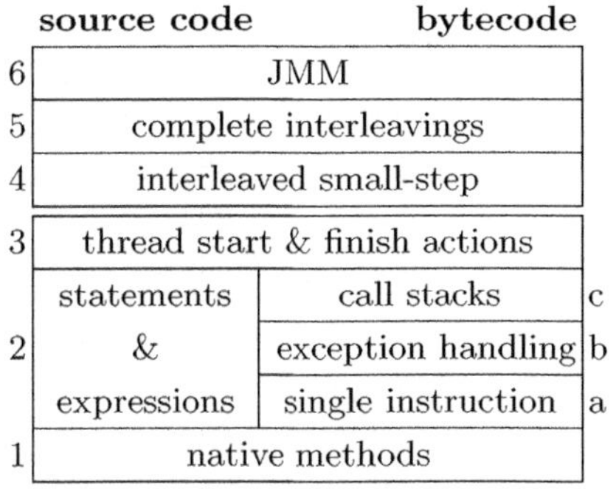
source code
bytecode
6
JMM
5
complete interleavings
4
interleaved small-step
3
thread start & finish actions
2
statements & expressions
call stacks
c
exception handling
b
single instruction
a
1
native methods

Fig. 3. Stack of JinjaThreads source code and bytecode semantics

Before we look at the individual levels, we discuss the general form $t \vdash \langle x, T\rangle \xrightarrow{as} \langle x', T'\rangle$ of the single-thread semantics. Local states of thread t are denoted by x and x', and T, T' are the (global) type information that all threads share (see §2.2). The multithreaded semantics abstracts from the concrete steps of the single-thread semantics and uses only lists as of inter-thread actions. Reductions can generate multiple actions in one step. When the `wait` method suspends the thread to the wait set, e.g., it also tests for the monitor lock and for not being interrupted. Reductions without actions, i.e., $as = []$, are called *τ-moves.*

Unfortunately, the actions from §1.1 are insufficient to correctly implement the JLS, because the JLS (and the Java API) introduce other communication channels between threads. Consider, e.g., the following program in which two threads race for spawning the same thread:

initially: x = null;

1: r1 = new Thread();	3: r2 = x;	5: r3 = x;
2: x = r1;	4: r2.start();	6: r3.start();

(P1)

Suppose both reads in ll. 3 and 5 see the write at l.2. Then, either l. 4 or l. 6 must throw an `IllegalThreadStateException`, but not both. Hence, both l. 4 and l. 6 must be allowed to fail in some executions. Thus, the two right-most threads may just start, read the address of the `Thread` object (then fail with the exception, but the JMM has no action for that), and then finish. Hence, if each thread were run in isolation, they both would be allowed to fail, too. Since this contradicts the specification of the `start` method, there is a *covert communication channel.*[2]

Therefore, we introduce the following additional inter-thread actions: (i) Detect that a thread has already been started (TS), (ii) wait in a monitor (Wait), (iii) notification (N, NA), (iv) clearing an interrupt (CIr), (v) testing for a thread not being interrupted (NIrd), and (vi) test whether the current thread does (not) hold a lock (HL, NL). Technically, the last group is only a convenience, because this way, a thread need not remember in its local state which locks it holds.

Now, let us return to the single-thread semantics. Most of Java concurrency hides in (native) library methods, in particular in classes `Thread` and `Object`.

[2] For `start`, the JMM specifies synchronisation only between a successful call and the first action of the spawned thread [10, §17.4.4]. A JVM implementation might add more synchronisation, but our semantics must not, since this might eliminate data races from programs, i.e., it could wrongly certify programs with data races as DRF.

$$t \vdash \langle (ad, \texttt{start}), T \rangle \xrightarrow{[\text{Sp } ad \ (method \ C \ run)]} \langle unit, T \rangle \qquad \text{SPAWN}$$

$$t \vdash \langle (ad, \texttt{start}), T \rangle \xrightarrow{[\text{TS } ad]} \langle throw \ \texttt{IllegalThreadStateException}, T \rangle \qquad \text{SPAWNF}$$

Fig. 4. Semantics of the methods `start` and `isInterrupted` for class Thread. All rules have the preconditions *typeof* T $ad = \lfloor C \rfloor$ and $C :\leq$ *Thread*, which have been omitted.

Hence, we provide at the bottom of the stack a hard-wired semantics for some native methods. We focus on concurrency-related methods such as `wait`, `notify`, `notifyAll` in `Object` or `start`, `join`, `interrupt` in `Thread`, but also include ordinary methods like `hashCode`.

Figure 4 gives a flavour of the semantics rules; the full definition can be found online [18]. If address *ad* has type C (notation *typeof* T $ad = \lfloor C \rfloor$) and C is a subtype of *Thread* (notation $C :\leq$ *Thread*), calling `start` on *ad* either (i) successfully spawns the new thread *ad* whose initial state becomes C's `run` method SPAWN, or (ii) fails with an `IllegalThreadStateException` SPAWNF. The single-thread semantics is non-deterministic here, but the reductions generate different actions; the concurrent semantics ensures which of these actions can actually happen. In particular, the new action TS in SPAWNF is necessary.

The second level specifies the semantics for the language primitives. In source code, this is a standard small-step semantics. In bytecode, sub-level 2a executes single instructions, calls to native methods are delegated to level 1. Sub-level 2b adds exception handling, 2c joins everything together into the semantics of a single thread.

All actions originate on level 2 except for thread start and finish actions and those generated by native methods. For example, `synchronized` blocks or `monitorenter` and `monitorexit` instructions generate lock and unlock actions, field accesses via `getfield` and `putfield` produce read and write actions. Field read expressions and instructions such as `getfield` non-deterministically read any value, irrespective of the dynamic location type. Primitives like `instanceof` that do not produce any action yield τ-moves. The shared type information grows when objects and arrays are allocated and remains unchanged otherwise.

On level 3, we add artificial start and finish actions to each thread. This ensures that the start action of a thread precedes all its other actions.

The semantics on level 3 defines the sequential small-step semantics, on which levels 4 to 6 build. In the remainder, we use $\rightarrow$ to refer to either source code or bytecode semantics of level 3.

2.2 Complete Interleavings

In this section, we build the multithreaded semantics on top of the sequential (levels 4 and 5 in Fig. 3).

The JMM is only concerned about values, not types and array lengths. Checked type casts, virtual method calls, and reading the length of an array are not part of the inter-thread actions and thus not affected by the JMM; reading types and array lengths must always return the correct data [10, §17.4.5].[3] However, since objects and arrays are dynamically allocated, the type of an object at a given address (or the type and length of an array at that address) is determined only after allocation. For types and array lengths, we adopt sequential consistency, i.e., allocations immediately update type information of all threads. This directly solves a problem pointed out by Aspinall and Ševčík [4]: What does it mean for an address being fresh for memory allocation?

Technically, the global type information T is like a global shared state that contains only type information and array lengths, but no data values. Then, an address is fresh in state T iff T contains no type information for it. Java's type safety then ensures that it has not yet been used in any thread, so we can safely use it when allocating new memory.

Threads also communicate via types and array lengths – unnoticed by the JMM. For example,

initially: x = 0; y = null;

1: r1 = x; 2: r2 = (r1 == 0 ? new A() : new B()); 3: y = r2;	4: x = 1;	5: r3 = y; 6: r4 = r3.f();

(P2)

Suppose that classes A and B inherit from an interface I which declares a method f() and that their objects may be allocated at the same address. Then, dynamic dispatch at l. 6 tells the thread on the right about the left thread's local variable r1. However, from the JMM point of view, the thread on the right only reads an address (in fact the same value in both cases), but behaves differently. An analogous problem occurs if we use array lengths instead of types or declare x and y as volatile.

Hence, threads cannot execute in isolation, as the JMM suggests. Instead, we compute their interleavings with type information as shared state, which guarantees sequential consistency. Our interleaving semantics also takes care of mutual exclusion for locks and manages the monitor wait sets and notifications.

In the rest of this section, we formally define the interleaved semantics (level 4) and complete interleavings (level 5). Remember that we must consider complete interleavings because the JMM treats initialisations specially (see §1.1). Since threads in the single-thread semantics can only communicate via type information or inter-thread actions, the following is independent of the concrete single-thread semantics.

A *thread pool* ts is a finite map from a thread's ID to its local state x, the multiset L of locks it holds, its interrupt status i, and its wait set status w (none, waiting in a monitor, notified, interrupted, reacquiring the locks). We define the *interleaved small-step semantics* $\langle ts, T\rangle \overset{(t,\, as)}{\Longrightarrow} \langle ts', T'\rangle$ as

$$\frac{ts(t) = \lfloor(x, L, i, w)\rfloor \qquad t \vdash \langle x, T\rangle \xrightarrow{as} \langle x', T'\rangle \qquad ts \vdash_t as\surd \qquad ts \xmapsto{t,\, as,\, x'} ts'}{\langle ts, T\rangle \overset{(t,\, as)}{\Longrightarrow} \langle ts', T'\rangle}$$

[3] Although the JLS specifies that every array has a final field `length` [10, §6.4.5] that stores its length, the JMM treats array lengths specially [10, §17.4.5].

where $\lfloor \_ \rfloor$ denotes definedness of a finite map. The predicate $ts \vdash_t as\surd$ checks whether t may perform all actions in as in the current system state ts. It implements the wait-notify and interruption mechanism, and ensures mutual exclusion for locks and that each thread is spawned at most once. $ts \xmapsto{t,\, as,\, x'} ts'$ inserts all threads spawned in as into ts and updates t's locks, wait set status, and local state to x', which yields ts'. For details, see [16,17].

A *complete interleaving* E is a potentially infinite list of pairs of thread ID and inter-thread action. The relation $\langle ts,\ T\rangle \Downarrow E$ characterises all complete interleavings E that start in $\langle ts,\ T\rangle$, which we define as

$$\langle ts,\ T\rangle \Downarrow E :\Leftrightarrow \exists E'.\ \langle ts,\ T\rangle \downarrow E' \wedge E = concat(E') \tag{1}$$

where $concat(E')$ concatenates all lists in E' and $\langle ts,\ T\rangle \downarrow E'$ (defined coinductively)[4] collects the list of lists of inter-thread actions.

$$\frac{\langle ts,\ T\rangle \not\Rightarrow}{\langle ts,\ T\rangle \downarrow []}\ \textsc{Stop} \qquad\qquad \frac{\langle ts,\ T\rangle \xRightarrow{(t,\, as)} \langle ts',\ T'\rangle \qquad \langle ts',\ T'\rangle \downarrow E'}{\langle ts,\ T\rangle \downarrow obs_t(as) : E'}\ \textsc{Step}$$

where $\langle \_,\ \_\rangle \not\Rightarrow$ characterises stuck configurations and $obs_t(as)$ collects all JMM inter-thread actions in as (as defined in §1.1) and pairs them with the thread ID t. That is, it removes the additional actions from above, as they are irrelevant for the JMM.

Note that the detour via a list of action lists is necessary. If we had defined $\langle ts,\ T\rangle \Downarrow E$ directly with the above coinductive rules Stop and Step (i.e., prepending $obs_t(as)$ to E instead of consing), we could have derived every trace E for a state $\langle ts,\ T\rangle$ that can perform an infinite sequence of τ-moves, because $obs_t(as) = []$ for all τ-moves. Our approach works fine since $obs_t(as) : E$ is productive and concatenating the infinite list of empty lists yields [].

The initial state $\langle ts_0,\ T_0\rangle$ for a program is specified by a class, a method name, and the list of parameters it takes. Its thread pool ts_0 consists of a single thread t_0 that holds no locks and is about to execute the specified method with the given parameters. T_0 has pre-allocated the t_0 `Thread` object and certain system exceptions. The list as_0 of start-up actions contains t_0's start action and initialisations for the fields of the pre-allocated objects.

For the JMM, we identify a program with the set $\mathcal{E}$ of complete interleavings that start in the initial state, prefixed with as_0. Formally:

$$\mathcal{E} = \{obs_{t_0}(as_0) +\!\!+\ E \mid \langle ts_0,\ T_0\rangle \Downarrow E\}$$

where ++ concatenates two lists. $\mathcal{E}$ contains many ill-formed executions, because read operations may read arbitrary values (see §2.1), even not type-conforming ones that no write operation of the program can ever produce. Since they have no write-seen function, the JMM on level 6 discards them.

[4] We use double bars to distinguish coinductive definitions from inductive ones.

2.3 The Java Memory Model

In this section, we formally derive the orders of the JMM (level 6) from a complete interleaving $E \in \mathcal{E}$. For the intuition behind them, see [21,10,11,4]. The JMM notions of well-formed and legal executions are standard [4,10], we only explain them informally; [19] shows their formal definitions.

Since an action can occur multiple times in E, we use the index in E to assign a unique identifier to an action. In the following, we identify an action with its index, i.e., $\mathcal{A}_E = \{a \in \mathbb{N} \mid a < |E|\}$ denotes the set of actions for E. This already provides the *induced total order* $\leq_E = \leq|_{\mathcal{A}_E}$ over $\mathcal{A}_E$, where $R|_A$ restricts the binary relation R to elements from A. Since the JMM requires initialisation actions[5] to be ordered before the threads' start actions, we introduce the (total) *execution order* $\leq^E_{\text{eo}}$ on $\mathcal{A}_E$:

$$a \leq^E_{\text{eo}} a' :\Leftrightarrow \text{if } \mathit{init}_E\, a \text{ then } \neg\, \mathit{init}_E\, a' \vee a \leq_E a' \text{ else } \neg\, \mathit{init}_E\, a' \wedge a \leq_E a'$$

where $\mathit{init}_E\, a$ predicates that a is an initialisation action in E.

The *program order* $\leq^E_{\text{po}}$ restricts $\leq^E_{\text{eo}}$ to actions of the same thread. The *synchronisation order* $\leq^E_{\text{so}}$ restricts $\leq^E_{\text{eo}}$ to synchronisation actions. *Synchronisation actions* are all initialisation actions, reads from and writes to volatile locations, locking and unlocking, thread spawns and joins, thread start and finish actions, and the interruption actions Ir and Ird. The *synchronises-with order* $\leq^E_{\text{sw}}$ restricts $\leq^E_{\text{so}}$ to release-acquire pairs of actions. (a, a') is a *release-acquire pair* iff

1. a unlocks monitor m and a' locks m,
2. a writes to a volatile location that a' reads,
3. a spawns a thread whose start action is a',
4. a is a thread's finish action on which a' joins,
5. a is an initialisation action and a' is a thread start action, or
6. a interrupts a thread t and a' observes that t has been interrupted.

The *happens-before order* $\leq^E_{\text{hb}}$ is the transitive closure of $\leq^E_{\text{po}}$ and $\leq^E_{\text{sw}}$. $\mathcal{V}_E\, a$ denotes the value that the write action $a \in \mathcal{A}_E$ writes – initialisation actions write default values (0, false, or null, resp.); for normal write actions, E contains the value written.

An *execution* (E, ws) consists of a complete interleaving E and a *write-seen function* ws on $\mathcal{A}_E$ that assigns to every read action in $\mathcal{A}_E$ the write action it sees. This yields the JMM notion of an execution [10, §17.4.6] as $(\mathcal{E}, \mathcal{A}_E, \leq^E_{\text{po}}, \leq^E_{\text{so}}, ws, \mathcal{V}_E, \leq^E_{\text{sw}}, \leq^E_{\text{hb}})$.

An execution is *well-formed* (written $\vdash (E, ws)\surd$) iff every thread has a thread start action that $\leq_E$-precedes its other actions except for initialisation actions (denoted $E\surd_{\text{start}}$) and ws is a proper write-seen functions for all reads in E as specified by the JMM well-formedness conditions 1 (each read sees a write to the same location), 4 ($\leq^E_{\text{hb}}$ consistency) and 5 ($\leq^E_{\text{so}}$ consistency for volatiles) in [10, §17.4.7]. (E, ws) meets conditions 2 ($\leq^E_{\text{hb}}$ is a partial order) and 3 (intra-thread consistency) by construction. E is *well-formed* iff $\vdash (E, ws)\surd$ for some ws.

[5] When the single-thread semantics allocates memory, it produces initialisation actions for the new locations. This records that the executing thread has generated them.

A *legal* execution is a well-formed execution (E, ws) that is justified by a sequence of justifying executions (E_i, ws_i). As §1.1 explains, it serves to ban values appearing out of thin air. The concrete definition is tedious, but uninteresting for the rest of this work. It can be found in [19].

2.4 Discussion of Our JMM Formalisation

Our formalisation shows how to connect a Java semantics with the JMM, which has been missing in the literature [4,9,11]. The main insight is that action traces of isolated threads do not suffice to obey the JLS and Java API. The examples (P1) and (P2) present hidden communication channels between threads that the JMM inter-thread actions do not capture – although they only use Java features that the JMM mentions. To expose these channels, we have introduced new actions – and our semantics shows that they suffice for the features that JinjaThreads models except for type information and array lengths. We conjecture that further actions for allocations would also lift this restriction (see below).

Most obviously, the JMM misses actions for thread interrupts. It predicates that `Thread.interrupt` "synchronises-with the point where any other thread [...] determines that [the thread] has been interrupted" [10, §17.4.4], but there are no designated actions for neither thread interruption nor "that point". Hence, we have added the synchronisation actions Ir and Ird (§1.1), and their duals for non-interruption CIr and NIrd (§2.1). Similarly, the API of class `Thread` requires new actions to query a thread's state, e.g., TS predicates that it has been started. Previous JMM formalisations [4,8,11] did without these new actions, because they omitted interruption and wait sets, but a realistic formalisation cannot.

The interesting question is which of these new actions should participate in synchronisation and happens-before order. We follow the original JMM in that only Ir synchronises with Ird; $obs_t(\_)$ removes the others. In particular, the others do not synchronise with any action and need not be committed or justified. Hence, they do not affect the writes that a read may see. We consider this sensible, because we have found it very hard to construct programs that can exploit such additional synchronisation to avoid data races (see, e.g., [19, P3]). Typically, other schedules exhibit races in such programs. Counter-intuitively, this may also disallow some behaviours, since adding synchronisation may allow new behaviours for programs with data races [3,21].

We do not use actions to broadcast type information, but interleave the execution to obtain sequential consistency for types. This also solves the problem of finding a fresh address for memory allocation, as the shared type information stores which addresses are fresh. Although complete interleavings introduce a global notion of time, we do not use it to constrain the write that each read sees, because the JMM order relations abstract from it.

However, we see two approaches to avoid the interleaving. One could include actions for producing and querying type information for locations and array lengths. In a well-formed execution, these actions have to be matched, but they do not interact with other thread actions. Alternatively, one could partition the address space by type and array length like in [13]. Then, however, every read of a reference value would implicitly transfer all type information associated with it, which is unrealistic for implementations. In either approach, allocation actions subsume initialisation actions such that allocation returns an arbitrary address and the JMM ensures that every address is allocated at most once.

There are also a few technical changes to the JMM that we briefly review: First, for the DRF guarantee, *all* initialisation actions must be synchronisation actions, not only those for volatile locations, which follows Aspinall and Ševčík [4]. In contrast to them [4], we do not need a special initialisation thread (which might run infinitely in the case of an infinite execution), but assign initialisation actions the thread's ID which created the object. This change is relevant for the final field semantics extension to the JMM, which requires to know which thread created which object [10, §17.5.1].

Second, happens-before for the `wait` method arises not only from the associated unlock and lock actions [10, §17.4.5], but also calling `interrupt` on the waiting thread synchronises with throwing the `InterruptedException`. When a thread in a wait set is both interrupted and notified, our semantics always respects happens-before, although the JLS does not require this [10, §17.8.1].

Third, we do not model thread divergence actions. The JMM introduces them to "model how a thread may cause all other threads to stall and fail to make progress" [10, §17.4.2]. Our construction achieves the same via the coinductive trace definition (Stop, Step), which then gets filtered for τ-moves (1). Thus, it handles terminating, non-terminating and diverging executions uniformly.

Finally, JinjaThreads models neither final fields nor garbage collection and finalisation. Hence, we do not model that part of the JMM [10, §17.5].

3 The Data Race Freedom Guarantee

The JMM promises that correctly synchronised programs exhibit only sequentially consistent behaviours. First, we recapitulate the definitions and identify the assumptions of this guarantee (§3.1). Next, we show that source code and bytecode indeed satisfy these assumptions (§3.2); the proofs can be found [19]. In §3.3, we discuss our formalisation and its implications.

3.1 The DRF Guarantee

In this section, we formally state the DRF guarantee and prove it. Two actions of an execution are *conflicting* if they are read or write actions to the same location with at least one being a write. Two conflicting actions constitute a *data race* if they are not ordered by happens-before.[6]

[6] As the happens-before order approximates time, it serves to identify data races. More intuitively, two conflicting actions race iff they can happen "concurrently" in an execution, i.e., they are adjacent in an interleaving and the location is not marked volatile. For simple models of happens-before, these are equivalent [7], but not for Java with implicit communication channels between threads, see, e.g., [19, P3]. Still, every data race in the latter sense is also one in the happens-before sense.

An execution (E, ws) is *sequentially consistent (SC)* iff every read action $a \in \mathcal{A}_E$ sees the most recent write action, i.e., $ws(a) \leq_{\text{eo}}^{E} a$, and $a' \leq_{\text{eo}}^{E} ws(a)$ or $a \leq_{\text{eo}}^{E} a'$ for all write actions a' to the location that a reads from.[7]

The program $\mathcal{E}$ is *correctly synchronised* (data race free, DRF) iff no SC execution in $\mathcal{E}$ contains a data race. Formally: Whenever $E \in \mathcal{E}, \vdash (E, ws)\surd$ and (E, ws) is SC, then $a \leq_{\text{hb}}^{E} a'$ or $a' \leq_{\text{hb}}^{E} a$ for all conflicting actions $a, a' \in \mathcal{A}_E$.

For the DRF guarantee, it is important that we only have to check that SC executions do not contain a data race. Otherwise, it would fail its purpose because the programmer would have to understand the whole JMM to see whether his program is correctly synchronised and the DRF guarantee applies to it.

Our proof of the DRF guarantee (Thm. 1) adapts the others' [21,4,11] to deal with memory allocation and initialisations (see §3.3 for a discussion). The key idea in all of them is that in a DRF program, a well-formed execution (E, ws) is SC if every read sees a write that happens before it (Lem. 1) – which includes program order. Then, the legality constraints ensure that all legal executions are SC.

Lemma 1. *Let $\mathcal{E}$ be correctly synchronised, $E \in \mathcal{E}$ such that $\vdash (E, ws)\surd$. If $ws(a) \leq_{hb}^{E} a$ for every read a in $\mathcal{A}_E$, then (E, ws) is sequentially consistent.*

To exploit correct synchronisation in a proof of Lem. 1 by contradiction, one first obtains a SC execution (E', ws') from (E, ws) as follows: E' starts like E until the first non-SC read a in E and continues SC from there on. Then, it suffices to find a data race between a, $ws(a)$, and $ws'(a)$ in E', and for this, we use Lem. 2 to transfer happens-before relationships between E and E' on their common prefix.

Lemma 2 ($\leq_{\text{hb}}$-prefix lemma). *Let E and E' be two complete interleavings such that their first n actions differ only in the values read or written, and let $a, a' < n$. If $E'\surd_{start}$ and $a \leq_{hb}^{E} a'$, then $a \leq_{hb}^{E'} a'$.*

Theorem 1 (DRF guarantee). *If the program P is correctly synchronised and (E, ws) a legal execution, then (E, ws) is sequentially consistent.*

The proof closely follows [4, Thm. 1], it uses Lem. 1. Both Thm. 1 and Lem. 1 implicitly rely on two assumptions about $\mathcal{E}$:

A1 For every sequentially-consistent prefix of a well-formed execution (E, ws) with $E \in \mathcal{E}$, there is a well-formed complete interleaving $E' \in \mathcal{E}$ with the same prefix and a write seen-function ws' such that (E', ws') is SC. If E immediately continues with a read after the prefix, E' also continues with a read from the same location.

A2 Every execution initialises every location at most once.

---

[7] The JMM only requires that $\leq_{\text{po}}$ is extended to a total order over all actions to determine most recent writes [10, §17.4.3]. Aspinall and Ševčík [4] showed that, to respect mutual exclusivity of locks, the total order must also extend $\leq_{\text{so}}$. Our execution order $\leq_{\text{eo}}$ extends both by construction.

The first assumption ensures that E' as required in the proof of Lem. 1 does exist, the second is a standard well-formedness condition. In §3.2, we prove that JinjaThreads source code and bytecode satisfy these by explicitly constructing SC executions. Moreover, Lem. 2 requires that *all* initialisation actions synchronise with thread start actions [19, P4], i.e., they are synchronisation actions.

3.2 Sequentially Consistent Completions

In the previous section, we have shown the DRF guarantee under two assumptions on the set $\mathcal{E}$ of complete interleavings. Now, we discharge them for source code and bytecode by descending the stack of semantics (Fig. 3) and adapting the assumptions. They act like an interface between the levels and ensure that we can share the proofs for all levels that source code and bytecode share.

We start with complete interleavings. The JMM definition of SC is not amenable to the coinductive definition of $\langle \_, \_\rangle \Downarrow \_$ as it relies on the notions of write-seen function and most recent write, which are only defined for complete interleavings. Therefore, we introduce a coinductive version of SC.

Let h denote a snapshot of a sequentially consistent heap, i.e., a finite map from locations to values. The function $mrw(h, a)$ updates the heap h if a is a write or initialisation action, else leaves h unchanged. The function $mrws$ folds mrw over action lists. An action list as is *sequentially consistent* (SC') for the heap h (denoted $h \vdash as\surd_{sc}$) iff

$$\frac{}{h \vdash [\,]\surd_{sc}} \qquad \frac{mrw(h,a) \vdash as\surd_{sc} \qquad a = \mathrm{R}\ l\ v \implies h(l) = \lfloor v \rfloor}{h \vdash a : as\surd_{sc}}$$

i.e., the empty list is SC' for all heaps, and $a : as$ is SC' for h iff as is SC' for the updated heap $mrw(h, a)$ and if a reads the value v from location l, then the heap h must store v at l.

The next theorem shows that $\emptyset \vdash \_\surd_{sc}$ adequately models SC, where $\emptyset$ denotes the empty map. Thus, we can use coinduction to show an execution being SC.

Theorem 2. *Let initialisations $\leq_E$-precede reads and $E\surd_{start}$. Then, $\emptyset \vdash E\surd_{sc}$ iff there is a ws such that $\vdash (E, ws)\surd$ and (E, ws) is SC.*

This equivalence holds only if the initialisation of any location l occurs before the first read from l in the complete interleaving. For example, the execution $[(t_1, \mathrm{S}), (t_1, \mathrm{R}\ l.\mathrm{x}\ 0), (t_1, \mathrm{I}\ l.\mathrm{x}\ 0)]$ is SC for $ws(t_1, \mathrm{R}\ l.\mathrm{x}\ 0) = (t_1, \mathrm{I}\ l.\mathrm{x}\ 0)$, but not SC'. The problem is real: Figure 2 shows a (non-SC) execution of a type-correct program that violates this assumption. In order to exploit this equivalence, we must show that initialisations $\leq_E$-precede reads in SC prefixes of complete interleaving (see below).

Prior to this, we construct a sequentially consistent completion $scc(\langle ts, T\rangle, h)$ that starts with a thread pool ts, global type information T, and a heap h. We define scc by corecursion as follows, where ε denotes Hilbert's choice operator.

$scc(\langle ts,\ T\rangle, h) :=$
if $\langle ts,\ T\rangle \not\Rightarrow$ then $[]$
else let $(t, as, ts', T') = \varepsilon(t, as, ts', T').\ \langle ts,\ T\rangle \xRightarrow{(t,\ as)} \langle ts',\ T'\rangle \wedge h \vdash as\surd_{sc}$
in $obs_t(as) : scc(\langle ts',\ T'\rangle, mrws(h, as))$

In order to prove anything about $scc(\langle ts,\ T\rangle, h)$, we must make sure that the predicate to the ε-operator is satisfiable for all reachable configurations. Hence, we presume for now that the interleaving semantics satisfies the *cut-and-update property* (C&U), namely whenever $\langle ts,\ T\rangle \xRightarrow{(t,as')} \langle ts',\ T'\rangle$ and $wf(\langle ts,\ T\rangle, h)$, then there are as'', ts'', and T'' such that (i) $\langle ts,\ T\rangle \xRightarrow{(t,as'')} \langle ts'',\ T''\rangle$, (ii) $h \vdash as''\surd_{sc}$, and (iii) $h \vdash as' \approx as''$. The predicate *wf* ensures well-formedness of the state and conformance of heap; for source code and bytecode, we define *wf* below and prove that their semantics satisfy C&U. Conditions (i) and (ii) predicate that non-stuck states always have a reduction with actions as that are SC' w.r.t. the current heap h; they suffice to prove that *scc* does compute an SC' interleaving (Lem. 3). Condition (iii) denotes that as' and as'' consist of the same actions upto the first SC' inconsistent read in as' and as'' continues with a read from the same location. With this condition, given a complete interleaving that is SC' up to a read r, we can cut the interleaving after r, change r to read the most recent value, and continue the interleaving SC'.

Let us further assume that $wf(\langle ts,\ T\rangle, h)$ holds for the initial state (ts_0, T_0) with the initial heap $h_0 := mrws(\emptyset, as_0)$, and is preserved by all SC' reductions. Then, *scc* computes an SC' execution (Lem. 3). By the equivalence of SC and SC' (Thm. 2), we can then discharge the main assumption of the DRF proof (Thm. 3).

Lemma 3.
If $wf(\langle ts,\ T\rangle, h)$, *then* $\langle ts,\ T\rangle \downarrow scc(\langle ts,\ T\rangle, h)$ *and* $h \vdash concat(scc(\langle ts,\ T\rangle, h))\surd_{sc}$.

Theorem 3 (SC completion). *Let* $E \in \mathcal{E}$, $\vdash (E, ws)\surd$, (E, ws) *be SC up to a read action* $(t, R\ l\ v)$, *say* $E = E_1 +\!\!+ (t, R\ l\ v) : E_2$ *with* $ws(r)$ *being the most recent write for all reads* $r \in \mathcal{A}_{E_1}$. *Then, there are* E_3, v', *and* ws' *such that* $E^* := E_1 +\!\!+ (t, R\ l\ v') : E_3 \in \mathcal{E}$, $\vdash (E^*, ws')\surd$, *and* (E^*, ws') *is SC.*

We have now replaced the assumptions A1 and A2 of §3.1 by the following, which are simpler and no longer refer to JMM notions.

B1 Every execution initialises every location at most once.
B2 If a complete interleaving has an SC' prefix as followed by a read from l, as must initialise l.
B3 *wf* is preserved by SC' reductions and $wf(\langle ts_0,\ T_0\rangle, h_0)$ holds.
B4 The interleaving semantics satisfies C&U.

Next, we tackle these proof obligations. They naturally translate to the levels below the interleaving semantics, so we do not expand on them in detail. The actual proofs decompose the semantics on levels 4 down to 1, perform induction on the semantics (source code) or case analysis on the individual instructions (bytecode), resp., and lift everything back to level 4. Here, we only present the main arguments.

For B1, remember that only memory allocations generate initialisation actions. When an allocation returns an address, it was fresh before, but afterwards, it is allocated, i.e., not fresh. Hence, it suffices to prove that the semantics correctly keeps track of all memory allocations in the inter-thread actions, as initialisation actions refer to the address.

For B2, not only must we show that the program cannot make up arbitrary addresses, but also that it accesses only the declared fields of objects. To that end, we define the well-formedness predicate $\mathit{wf}(\langle ts, T\rangle, h)$ to denote that

(i) for all allocated addresses a, T contains type information and h contains type-conforming values for all fields and array cells of a,
(ii) all addresses in thread-local states of ts and in h's range are allocated, and
(iii) all thread-local states in ts are language-specifically well-formed.

For source code, the latter states that all values in the local store are of correct type and the statement is runtime-typeable. For bytecode, the operand stack and registers must conform to the well-typing as computed by the bytecode verifier. Type correctness ensures that the semantics stays within the safe state space, e.g., it does not get unexpectedly stuck or yields undefined behaviour about which nothing can be proven.

Preservation for *wf* (assumption B3) relies on the JinjaThreads type safety proofs [16,17,14]. The subject reduction proofs require that reads only return type-conforming values. This holds because the semantics correctly keeps track of all reads in the inter-thread actions, which are by assumption SC', and the heap contains only type-conforming values. By the type safety proofs, all values written to the memory are type-conforming, too. Moreover, we show that the single-thread semantics cannot generate new addresses other than via memory allocation. Hence, *wf* ensures that addresses cannot appear out of thin air in an SC' execution. For the initial state, $\mathit{wf}(\langle ts_0, T_0\rangle, h_0)$ holds by construction.

From this, B2 follows. By preservation, *wf* holds for the state after the prefix as. Hence, type safety ensures that the read accesses an allocated location.

Finally, showing that the semantics satisfies C&U (assumption B4) is tedious, but uninteresting because reads may return arbitrary values.

Theorem 4. *The JMM DRF guarantee holds for source code and bytecode.*

This follows from Thm. 1, 3 by the above argument that their assumptions hold.

3.3 Discussion

The DRF guarantee for Java (§3.1) has been formalised before [4,11] – in fact, we employ the same key ideas in §3.1. The novel aspects are that (i) our JMM formalisation covers dynamic allocation with explicit initialisation actions and infinite executions, and (ii) we identify the assumptions of the DRF guarantee on the sequential semantics and discharge them for source code and bytecode. The key insights are the following:

1. Our new actions and different kinds of synchronisation do not affect the DRF proof. This suggests that other means of synchronisation that we do not cover, e.g., atomics in `java.util.concurrent`, do not affect it either.
2. We must find better ways to handle initialisations, as the JMM way severely complicates the proofs.
3. Our proofs show that the treatment of initialisations is irrelevant for the DRF guarantee, i.e., we are not constrained when searching for better ways.

Insight 3 a posteriori justifies Aspinall's and Ševčík's simpler approach of considering finite prefixes for the purpose of formalising the DRF guarantee. However, it is still insufficient when dealing with the full JMM. For example, the JMM allows the execution in Fig. 2, but not some of its prefixes.

Similarly, our DRF proof shows that it would be safe to restrict read operations to type-conforming values – for correctly synchronised programs. Subject reduction and preservation proofs would become significantly easier. However, it would disallow some legal executions of programs with data races such as Fig. 2.

Technical Considerations. Our work in §3.1 differs from [4,11,21] mainly in the proof of the key Lem. 1. We adapt the others' in two respects to deal with initialisation actions. First, the others topologically sort $\leq_{\mathrm{po}}^{E}$ [21] or $\leq_{\mathrm{hb}}$ [4,11] first to obtain $\leq_{\mathrm{eo}}$, and then take $\{a \mid a \leq_{\mathrm{eo}}^{E} r\}$ as the prefix for the SC execution. Instead of through sorting, we obtain the induced total order $\leq_E$ from the complete interleaving, which does not move initialisation actions to the program start.

Second, Manson et al. [21] and Huisman and Petri [11] require a sequentially consistent completion E'; so do we. However, the former ignore that different initialisation actions in the suffix might change the $\leq_{\mathrm{hb}}$ relation on the prefix. The latter note this problem, but add an axiom that $\leq_{\mathrm{hb}}$ remain unchanged. We solve the issue by using $\leq_E$ instead of $\leq_{\mathrm{eo}}^{E}$. Hence, $\leq_{\mathrm{hb}}$ on the prefix becomes independent of later initialisations (Lem. 2). Aspinall and Ševčík [4] completely avoid it by restricting their model to finite prefixes of executions – which causes problems when dynamic allocation creates initialisations (§1.1).

Initialisations also complicate the construction of sequentially consistent completions. We failed to construct them directly, as due to the special treatment of initialisations, ill-formed programs might not have such, see, e.g., [19, P5]. Hence, we would need appropriate constraints that the semantics preserves, but the JMM notion of execution is unsuitable for preservation proofs. Instead, we proved that sequential consistency w.r.t. happens-before is the same as for interleaving semantics – if initialisations do not interfere (Thm. 2).[8] Being operational, interleaving semantics is much more amenable to reduction invariants and their preservation proofs than the JMM. While it is still challenging to show properties about *scc*, most proofs follow the well-known pattern of preservation.

[8] Interestingly, Batty et al. [5, §4] found that initialisations of atomics cause problems in the DRF proof for C++11, too.

Faithfulness of the Semantics. Aspinall and Ševčík [4] suggested to weaken legality to enable more optimisation without sacrificing the DRF guarantee. Since our proof follows theirs, our proof also works for their weaker notion of legality. We have not formally checked that our semantics validates all JMM test cases by Pugh et. al. [23]. Torlak et. al. [29] have shown that the original JMM does not validate test cases 19 and 20, but the fix by Aspinall and Ševčík [4] does. Since none of the test cases uses dynamic allocation, spawning nor interruption of threads, nor `wait` and `notify`, our formalisation should perform equivalent to the original JMM. With the fix by Aspinall and Ševčík, our formalisation also validates test cases 19 and 20.

4 Conclusion and Future Work

Our machine-checked model of multithreaded Java spans from a realistic subset of Java source and bytecode via statement and instruction-level operational semantics to the axiomatic JMM. We have proven that our semantics provides the DRF guarantee, the most important property of the JMM for programmers.

Our DRF result is not limited to Java. The key lemma 1 plays a similar role in other DRF guarantee proofs, e.g., [2,7]. They all postulate sequentially consistent completions of prefixes, which we have constructed formally for a realistic language. For Java, this surprisingly requires a full subject reduction theorem, but this need not be a restriction for other languages. C and C++, e.g., assign such type-unsafe programs undefined semantics and exclude them from the guarantee.

For this work, it was essential to separate the MM from the operational semantics. This way, we were able to define the JMM and prove the DRF guarantee on the abstract level of complete interleavings in about 2.5kLoc of definitions and proof scripts. Similarly, this clear interface allows to reuse the same JMM formalisation for both source code and bytecode. Still, connecting the operational semantics to the JMM and discharging the DRF assumptions was tedious (7.2kLoc), since every lemma must be lifted over the whole stack of semantics. In particular, the complete interleavings from §2.2 turned out very unwieldy as they connect operational semantics with inductive and coinductive definition and proof principles to the world of abstract orders. Consequently, we achieved only little proof automation there; it was much better for the interleaving semantics and the abstract JMM specification.

Initialisations and the special way the JMM handles them caused most complications in our proofs. In this work, we willingly stayed as close to the JMM as possible, but we will investigate simpler ways of initialising locations. Moreover, we have shown type safety only for SC executions, i.e., correctly synchronised programs. Since the JinjaThreads compiler correctness proof relies on type safety, we hope to show that every legal execution is type safe. Type safety of the MM, when no explicit constraints trivially enforce it, is a necessary condition for the absence of out-of-thin-air values. This will hopefully provide a better understanding of this notion, which has so far only been illustrated by examples. Ultimately, it will be interesting to explore the tension between the safety guarantees that a MM provides and the compiler transformations it allows.

Acknowledgements. We thank M. Hecker, D. Lohner, and G. Snelting and the anonymous referees for valuable comments on earlier drafts.

References

1. Adve, S., Gharachaorloo, K.: Shared memory consistency models: A tutorial. IEEE Computer 29(12), 66–76 (1996)
2. Adve, S., Hill, M.D.: Weak ordering - a new definition. In: ISCA 1990, pp. 2–14. ACM (1990)
3. Adve, S.V., Boehm, H.J.: Memory models: A case for rethinking parallel languages and hardware. Commun. ACM 53, 90–101 (2010)
4. Aspinall, D., Ševčík, J.: Formalising Java's Data Race Free Guarantee. In: Schneider, K., Brandt, J. (eds.) TPHOLs 2007. LNCS, vol. 4732, pp. 22–37. Springer, Heidelberg (2007)
5. Batty, M., Memarian, K., Owens, S., Sarkar, S., Sewell, P.: Clarifying and compiling C/C++ concurrency: From C++11 to POWER. In: POPL 2012, pp. 509–520. ACM (2012)
6. Batty, M., Owens, S., Sarkar, S., Sewell, P., Weber, T.: Mathematizing C++ concurrency. In: POPL 2011, pp. 55–66. ACM (2011)
7. Boehm, H.J., Adve, S.V.: Foundations of the C++ concurrency memory model. In: PLDI 2008, pp. 68–78. ACM (2008)
8. Boyland, J.: An operational semantics including "volatile" for safe concurrency. Journal of Object Technology 8(4), 33–53 (2009); FTfJP 2008
9. Cenciarelli, P., Knapp, A., Sibilio, E.: The Java Memory Model: Operationally, Denotationally, Axiomatically. In: De Nicola, R. (ed.) ESOP 2007. LNCS, vol. 4421, pp. 331–346. Springer, Heidelberg (2007)
10. Gosling, J., Joy, B., Stelle, G., Bracha, G.: The Java Language Specification, 3rd edn. Addison-Wesley (2005)
11. Huisman, M., Petri, G.: The Java Memory Model: a formal explanation. In: VAMP 2007, pp. 81–96, Tech. Rep. ICIS-R07021, University of Nijmegen (2007)
12. International standard ISO/IEC 14882:2011. programming languages – C++. International Organization for Standardization (2011)
13. Jagadeesan, R., Pitcher, C., Riely, J.: Generative Operational Semantics for Relaxed Memory Models. In: Gordon, A.D. (ed.) ESOP 2010. LNCS, vol. 6012, pp. 307–326. Springer, Heidelberg (2010)
14. Klein, G., Nipkow, T.: A machine-checked model for a Java-like language, virtual machine and compiler. ACM TOPLAS 28(4), 619–695 (2006)
15. Lamport, L.: How to make a multiprocessor computer that correctly executes multiprocess programs. IEEE Trans. Comput. 28, 690–691 (1979)
16. Lochbihler, A.: Type safe nondeterminism - a formal semantics of Java threads. In: Foundations of Object-Oriented Languages, FOOL 2008 (2008)
17. Lochbihler, A.: Verifying a Compiler for Java Threads. In: Gordon, A.D. (ed.) ESOP 2010. LNCS, vol. 6012, pp. 427–447. Springer, Heidelberg (2010)
18. Lochbihler, A.: Jinja with threads. In: Klein, G., Nipkow, T., Paulson, L. (eds.) The Archive of Formal Proofs (2011), `http://afp.sourceforge.net/entries/JinjaThreads.shtml`, formal proof development

19. Lochbihler, A.: A unified, machine-checked formalisation of Java and the Java Memory Model. Tech. Rep. 2011-34, Karlsruhe Reports in Informatics (2011)
20. Lochbihler, A., Bulwahn, L.: Animating the Formalised Semantics of a Java-Like Language. In: van Eekelen, M., Geuvers, H., Schmaltz, J., Wiedijk, F. (eds.) ITP 2011. LNCS, vol. 6898, pp. 216–232. Springer, Heidelberg (2011)
21. Manson, J., Pugh, W., Adve, S.: The Java memory model. In: POPL 2005, pp. 378–391. ACM (2005)
22. Nipkow, T., Paulson, L.C., Wenzel, M.T.: Isabelle/HOL — A Proof Assistant for Higher-Order Logic. LNCS, vol. 2283. Springer, Heidelberg (2002)
23. Causality test cases for the Java memory model, `http://www.cs.umd.edu/~pugh/java/memoryModel/CausalityTestCases.html`
24. Pugh, W.: The Java memory model is fatally flawed. Concurrency: Practice and Experience 12, 445–455 (2000)
25. Quis custodiet, `http://pp.info.uni-karlsruhe.de/project.php?id=31`
26. Ševčík, J., Aspinall, D.: On Validity of Program Transformations in the Java Memory Model. In: Ryan, M. (ed.) ECOOP 2008. LNCS, vol. 5142, pp. 27–51. Springer, Heidelberg (2008)
27. Ševčík, J., Vafeiadis, V., Nardelli, F., Jagannathan, S., Sewell, P.: Relaxed-memory concurrency and verified compilation. In: POPL 2011. pp. 43–54. ACM (2011)
28. Sewell, P., Sarkar, S., Owens, S., Nardelli, F.Z., Myreen, M.O.: x86-TSO: a rigorous and usable programmer's model for x86 multiprocessors. Commun. ACM 53, 89–97 (2010)
29. Torlak, E., Vaziri, M., Dolby, J.: MemSAT: checking axiomatic specifications of memory models. In: PLDI 2010. pp. 341–350. ACM (2010)

A Type and Effect System for Determinism in Multithreaded Programs

Yi Lu[1], John Potter[1], Chenyi Zhang[2], and Jingling Xue[1]

[1] University of New South Wales
{ylu,potter,jingling}@cse.unsw.edu.au
[2] University of Queensland
chenyi@uq.edu.au

Abstract. There has been much recent interest in supporting deterministic parallelism in imperative programs. Structured parallel programming models have used type systems or static analysis to enforce determinism by constraining potential interference of lexically scoped tasks. But similar support for multithreaded programming, where threads may be ubiquitously spawned with arbitrary lifetimes, especially to achieve a modular and manageable combination of determinism and nondeterminism in multithreaded programs, remains an open problem.

This paper proposes a simple and intuitive approach for tracking thread interference and capturing both determinism and nondeterminism as computational effects. This allows us to present a type and effect system for statically reasoning about determinism in multithreaded programs. Our general framework may be used in multithreaded languages for supporting determinism, or in structured parallel models for supporting threads. Even more sophisticated concurrency models, such as actors, are often implemented on top of an underlying threading model, thus the underlying ideas presented here should be of value in reasoning about the correctness of such implementations.

1 Introduction

Concurrent programming is increasingly pervasive in mainstream software development as we attempt to exploit the full power of modern multicore processors. For developers working in heavily used languages such as C, C++, C# and Java, threads provide the dominant model for concurrent programming. Threads are a straightforward adaptation of the sequential model of computation to concurrent programs; programming languages require little or no syntactic changes to support them and modern computers and operating systems have evolved to efficiently support them. However, *they discard the most essential and appealing properties of sequential computation: understandability, predictability, and determinism* [13]. Threads may interact and share data in a myriad of ways; unanticipated thread interleavings and side effects can lead to subtle bugs and wrong results [24]. It is widely acknowledged that multithreaded programming is difficult and error-prone [21].

H. Seidl (Ed.): ESOP 2012, LNCS 7211, pp. 518–538, 2012.

Deterministic code is easier to debug and verify than nondeterministic code for both testing and formal methods [13,25]. Moreover, many computational algorithms are required to be deterministic—a given input is always expected to produce the same output—even when used in nondeterministic contexts. For example, most scientific computing, encryption/decryption, sorting, program analysis, and processor simulation algorithms exhibit deterministic behavior [1]. There has been much recent interest in supporting deterministic algorithms in multithreaded imperative programs. Programming models and type systems that support deterministic parallelism are emerging and have been proved to be useful in practice. Structured deterministic parallel models [1,26,2] enforce determinism statically at compile time by disallowing interference between concurrent computations (conflicting in their read and write sets); they typically rely on lexically scoped task parallelism (e.g., the fork/join style [12]) to localise and constrain potential interference of parallel tasks. While effective for applications where parallelism is often regular, structured parallelism may restrict programming styles thereby precluding many useful concurrency patterns which require irregular parallelism—*the world of client applications is not nearly as well structured and regular* [24]. Moreover, it may be difficult to support these models in mainstream programming languages where threads are used, because structured tasks can suffer interference from independent threads which may be ubiquitously spawned with arbitrary lifetimes. Reasoning statically about threads is a challenging problem, because we have to capture potential interference amongst all concurrent threads [13].

This paper proposes a simple and intuitive approach for type checking determinism in multithreaded imperative programs. By tracking and controlling what side effects may occur in parallel and how they may interfere with one another, our type system can check that deterministic behaviour is preserved in otherwise nondeterministic contexts. Programmers can freely assert that sections of code are deterministic, and have those assertions guaranteed by the type checker. Thus deterministic algorithms will assuredly produce deterministic results even in a nondeterministic context, making multithreaded programs more predictable and understandable. Our framework is general and may be used in existing multithreaded programming languages for supporting determinism, or in previous structured deterministic parallel models for supporting threads (e.g. Deterministic Parallel Java's region-based effect systems [1,2] can be extended with our approach to support multithreaded programming).

We formalise our approach in a novel type and effect system, called *Deterministic Effects*, as an extension to Nielson et al.'s effect systems [18,19]. Our small step operational semantics describes the concurrent behaviour of programs; crucially, the operational semantics preserves the relative nesting of thread creations. We prove that programmer-specified determinism for type correct multithreaded programs is indeed guaranteed. Deterministic effects can help improve the design and understanding of multithreaded software, such as in specifying or documenting concurrent behaviour for safety and optimisation. We envisage their use in interface specifications, facilitating modular development of large-scale concurrent programs. We also envisage static analyses for discovering determinism of expressions in existing multithreaded programs.

2 Deterministic Effects at a Glance

In this section, we introduce the basic ideas of deterministic effects with simple examples by showing how to track computational effects (specifically, side effects, though other effects may be possible, see Section 4.3) that may occur concurrently, how to capture determinism in nondeterministic code, and how to enforce programmer-specified deterministic expressions.

Deterministic effects capture the conflict between any two effects which may occur concurrently, by tracking the effects of forked threads in a form that mimics the tree structure of thread creation and then comparing these effects with the effects of any subsequent expressions to detect potential interference in a flow-sensitive manner. In general, earlier forks have more opportunity for interference than later forks. In Section 2.1, we introduce the syntax and demonstrate the use of deterministic effects to forbid all possible thread interference in a program. Programs that are well-typed have purely deterministic behaviours.

However, there are algorithms that may not have deterministic input-output behaviour. Real world applications are more likely composed of a mixture of deterministic and nondeterministic computations [2,25]. Achieving a manageable combination of determinism and nondeterminism is an important open problem in multithreaded programming. In Section 2.2, by reasoning about thread interference, we show how to infer determinism or nondeterminism of each expression in a possibly nondeterministic program. We extend our syntax with a programmer-specified deterministic construct, which is essentially the same as those used in [22,5], except that they check determinism dynamically at runtime while we enforce it statically at compile time (see discussion in Section 4.2). With this more liberal model, we show that we can allow arbitrary mixing of deterministic and nondeterministic computations in a safe way—guaranteeing desired determinism without unnecessarily restricting nondeterministic code.

2.1 Effects, Noninterference and Determinism

Our effect system extends Nielson et al.'s framework [18] for capturing interference between threads. We use a simple lambda calculus, similar to that used in [19,9,21,17], to provide the essential features of concurrent threads sharing access to memory including memory references and fork expressions. We describe the form of effects, and provide some simple examples to illustrate how to reason about thread interference. Memory reads and writes give rise to conventional sequential side effects based on regions determined by labels associated with memory allocation expressions. Threads are spawned by fork expressions, and their effects are represented separately from sequential side effects. By tracking the effects of threads spawned by a computation separately from its sequential continuation, we are able to use a flow-sensitive analysis to identify when the threads may interfere with the continuation. Despite its apparent simplicity, this approach appears to be novel.

The basic syntax is given by:

$$v ::= c \mid \mathbf{fn}\ x => e$$
$$e ::= v \mid x \mid e\ e \mid \mathbf{ref}_\pi\ e \mid !e \mid e := e \mid \mathbf{fork}\ e$$

The expression syntax e includes *values* v (a family of *integer constants* c and *functions*), a family of *variables* x, *function application* and the usual imperative operations on reference cells (*allocation*, *dereference* and *assignment*). The allocation expression $\mathbf{ref}_\pi\ e$ creates a new reference in memory and initialises it to the value of e, and the *label* (or *abstract location*) π uniquely identifies the creation point/allocation site. Common language constructs such as let, sequence or recursion are not directly defined, because they are easily encoded. The let expression $\mathbf{let}\ x = e_1\ \mathbf{in}\ e_2$ becomes $(\mathbf{fn}\ x => e_2)\ e_1$, and the sequence expression $e_1; e_2$ is $\mathbf{let}\ x = e_1\ \mathbf{in}\ e_2$ where x does not occur free in e_2. In examples, we will use explicit let and sequence expressions as shorthands. Like [18], which we extend, conditionals are omitted, as their treatment is standard. Recursive functions can be encoded by references as shown in [9,17] and in Section 4.1. Threads are introduced by $\mathbf{fork}\ e$, which spawns a new thread for the evaluation of e; the value of e is never used (this expression simply returns a zero when evaluated [9,3]), so a thread is only used for side effects.

The syntax for types and effects is given by:

$$\tau ::= int \mid \tau \xrightarrow{\varphi} \tau \mid ref_\rho\ \tau \qquad\qquad \varepsilon ::= !\rho \mid \rho :=$$
$$\varphi ::= \{\varepsilon\} \mid \{fork\ \varphi\} \mid \varphi \cup \varphi \mid \emptyset \qquad\qquad \rho ::= \{\pi\} \mid \rho \cup \rho \mid \emptyset$$

The syntax for types includes a primitive integer type, as well as function and reference type. The function type is annotated with effect information, φ, which captures concurrent effects that may occur during the execution of the function body. The reference type $ref_\rho\ \tau$ records the type τ of values that can be stored in the reference cell, and a *region* ρ where the cell may be created. The region syntax is used to denote finite sets of creation points or labels, which is a standard technique to distinguish cells created at different program points. The union operator $\cup$ is assumed to be commutative, associative and idempotent, with $\emptyset$ as its identity; $\{\pi_1\} \cup \ldots \cup \{\pi_n\}$ may be written as $\{\pi_1, \ldots \pi_n\}$. A *side effect* ε identifies a read $!\rho$ or a write $\rho :=$ to a region ρ.

A *fork effect*, *fork* φ, captures the effect of a forked thread. This allows us to syntactically distinguish the effect of the current expression from other fork effects arising from earlier forks, when determining thread interference. For example, the effect $\{!\{\pi_1\}, fork\ \{\{\pi_2\} :=\}\}$ describes a read effect $!\{\pi_1\}$ on the current thread, and a write effect $\{\pi_2\} :=$ on a thread spawned by the current thread, as identified by the keyword *fork*. The order of side effects and fork effects in an effect set (φ) is not important, but we track expression compositions flow-sensitively to identify potential interference between components (see examples below). In addition to π, we sometimes use ϖ, "var pi", to denote labels for program points in our examples.

We illustrate our ideas with a simple value setter example:

$$\begin{array}{l}\textbf{let}\ \ val = \textbf{ref}_\pi\ 0\ \ \textbf{in}\ \ \textbf{let}\ \ set = (\textbf{fn}\ x \Rightarrow val := x)\ \ \textbf{in}\\ \quad \textbf{fork}\ (set\ 2);\quad !val \qquad\qquad\qquad //\ error\end{array}$$

The types and effects for some of the expressions here, are

$$\begin{array}{ll} val : ref_\pi\ int & \&\ \emptyset \\ set : int \xrightarrow{\{\{\pi\} :=\}} int\ \&\ \emptyset & \end{array} \qquad \begin{array}{ll} set\ 2 & : int\ \&\ \{\{\pi\} :=\} \\ \textbf{fork}\ (set\ 2) & : int\ \&\ \{fork\ \{\{\pi\} :=\}\} \\ !val & : int\ \&\ \{!\{\pi\}\} \end{array}$$

The type of the variable *val* is determined by the allocation expression used to initialise it; the label π records the program point where the reference cell is allocated. Evaluating read-only variables has no memory effect, $\emptyset$. The function type of the variable *set* records its write effect on *val* for use in function application. This is manifested in the effect of the expression *set* 2. The effect of the dereference !*val* is the simple read effect $\{!\{\pi\}\}$.

In most type and effect systems, **fork** (*set* 2) has the same effect as *set* 2, namely $\{\{\pi\} :=\}$. Hence they may not tell if this code is safe. For example, if we swap the order of the dereference and fork above, as in

$$!val;\quad \textbf{fork}\ (set\ 2) \qquad //\ ok$$

there is no interference. This illustrates what we mean by our system being *flow sensitive*: in general, moving forks earlier in a sequential thread is more likely to make a program illegal.

Since our system distinguishes an effect on one thread from that on another, the effect of **fork** (*set* 2) is $\{fork\ \{\{\pi\} :=\}\}$—the fork effect captures the write effect on location $\{\pi\}$ and the *fork* indicates that it occurs on a different thread. For the original version of the example, the fork occurs before the dereference. Our flow-sensitive type and effect system recognises that the write effect $\{fork\ \{\{\pi\} :=\}\}$ for the fork may occur concurrently with the read effect $\{!\{\pi\}\}$ on the current thread, and considers this illegal. The second version of the example with reverse order of effects is legal in our system; we recognise that the read effect has completed before the conflicting fork. In our type system, this flow sensitivity is captured by checking sequential composition of effects for noninterference in Table 2 in Section 3.

Now consider an example with a thread forked inside a function:

$$\begin{array}{l}\textbf{let}\ \ x = \textbf{ref}_\pi\ 0\ \ \textbf{in}\ \ \textbf{let}\ \ y = \textbf{ref}_\varpi\ 0\ \ \textbf{in}\\ \textbf{let}\ \ f = (\textbf{fn}\ z \Rightarrow \textbf{fork}\ (x := 1);\ y := 1)\ \ \textbf{in}\\ \quad x := 2;\quad f\ 0;\quad y := 2 \qquad\qquad //\ ok\end{array}$$

This example shows no interference in our effect system, but may not pass, for example, type and effect systems for enforcing locking disciplines [9,3,21] which would conservatively dictate all memory accesses must be protected by a lock. Consider the effects recorded for the last three expressions. $x := 2$ is a sequential expression with effect $\{\{\pi\} :=\}$. It can never interfere with any later expressions.

$f\ 0$ may look like a sequential expression, but the body of f will fork a thread to access the shared variable x. Clearly $f\ 0$ writes to ϖ and creates a thread that writes to π; in our system its concurrent effect is $\{\{\varpi\}{:=}, \mathit{fork}\ \{\{\pi\}\ {:=}\}\}$. The effect of the third expression $y := 2$ is $\{\{\varpi\}\ {:=}\}$. The last two expressions do not interfere, because we only need to consider the concurrent part of the effect of the earlier expression, which is $\{\mathit{fork}\ \{\{\pi\}\ {:=}\}\}$, and the overall effect of the later expression, which is $\{\{\varpi\}\ {:=}\}$. (The sequential part of the second expression with effect $\{\{\varpi\}\ {:=}\}$ completes before the third expression starts.) The write effects $\{\mathit{fork}\ \{\{\pi\}\ {:=}\}\}$ and $\{\{\varpi\}\ {:=}\}$ do not interfere with each other since they access different reference cells.

Unsurprisingly, threads that concurrently read the same memory location do not interfere, as shown in the following example:

$$\begin{array}{l}\mathbf{let}\ x = \mathbf{ref}_\pi\ 1\ \ \mathbf{in}\ \ \mathbf{let}\ \ y = \mathbf{ref}_\varpi\ 2\ \ \mathbf{in}\\ \mathbf{let}\ \ \mathit{lim} = (\mathbf{fn}\ z => 100 - !z)\ \ \mathbf{in}\\ \quad \mathbf{fork}\ (\mathit{lim}\ x);\quad \mathbf{fork}\ (\mathit{lim}\ y);\quad \mathbf{fork}\ (\mathit{lim}\ x) \qquad //\ \mathit{ok}\end{array}$$

The function *lim* reverses a count from 100; its type and effect is:

$$\mathit{ref}_{\{\pi,\varpi\}}\ \mathit{int} \xrightarrow{\{!\{\pi,\varpi\}\}} \mathit{int}\ \&\ \emptyset$$

These threads do not interfere with each other because concurrent reads on the same memory region are considered safe. This example also shows the use of regions (rather than single labels) in reference types so that function arguments of reference type may be associated with multiple labels, in the absence of label polymorphism (see Section 4.1).

2.2 Deterministic Effects with Nondeterministism

We have seen how to enforce determinism by forbidding all thread interference. Programs which are well-typed, using our type rules, restrict concurrent computations to be purely deterministic. Now we introduce a more liberal model which allows arbitrary interleaving of threaded expressions, no matter what their potential interference may be. This provides a nondeterministic model of behaviour, typical of how threading works in current languages. However we allow (and enforce) explicit embedding of deterministic expressions. By tracking thread interference within expressions, we can capture the determinism or nondeterminism of expressions as effects.

If a stand-alone expression exhibits no interference in its evaluation, then its behaviour is deterministic. We say in that case the expression is *weakly deterministic*. However, if that deterministic expression is evaluated in a concurrent context in which other threads may interfere with it, the behaviour is no longer guaranteed to be deterministic. In other words, determinism of expression evaluation is not preserved by concurrent composition. This is partly in the nature of shared memory concurrency, but is unfortunate—if we have a deterministic algorithm we want to preserve its determinism even when it is embedded in a larger, possibly nondeterministic computation. Our solution is to allow a programmer to express this desire by declaring an expression to be deterministic using **det** (see extended syntax below). In that case, our system will firstly check that the expression is weakly deterministic. In addition, our system will enforce its determinism by insisting that any concurrent context where that expression appears cannot interfere with it. We say such expressions are *strongly deterministic.*

In this section we show how we can relax our earlier model, to allow both nondeterministic forms of expression, and also enforce strong determinism for expressions so declared with the following extended syntax:

$$e \quad ::= \quad ... \mid \textbf{det}\ e$$

Based on thread interference, the levels of determinism on expressions are distinguished by our effects system (from the weakest to the strongest): *nondeterministic*, *weakly deterministic* and *strongly deterministic.* A nondeterministic expression is allowed to contain interference, except that such interference does not affect any of its subexpressions which are asserted to be strongly deterministic. An expression is weakly deterministic if it does not contain interference, but may suffer interference from other threads; in other words, it is deterministic by itself, but may not be if used in a nondeterministic context. A strongly deterministic expression is weakly deterministic and must not be interfered with.

We start with a few examples before introducing our deterministic effect system in the next section.

$$\begin{array}{l}\textbf{let}\ \ x = \textbf{ref}_\pi\ 0\ \ \textbf{in}\ \ \textbf{let}\ \ y = \textbf{ref}_\varpi\ 1\ \ \textbf{in}\\ \quad \textbf{fork}(x := 1);\quad \textbf{fork}(x := !y);\quad \textbf{det}\ y := 2 \qquad \textit{// ok}\end{array}$$

The above program is nondeterministic, as it allows the value of y to interfere with the value of x. This is legal in our type and effect system, since the value of y, which is asserted as strongly deterministic, is not affected by its context. The following program is illegal.

$$\begin{array}{l}\textbf{let}\ \ x = \textbf{ref}_\pi\ 0\ \ \textbf{in}\ \ \textbf{let}\ \ y = \textbf{ref}_\varpi\ 1\ \ \textbf{in}\\ \quad \textbf{fork}(x := 1);\quad \textbf{fork}(x := !y);\quad \textbf{det}\ y := !x \qquad \textit{// error}\end{array}$$

We can also allow threads to be forked within **det** expressions. In both of the following examples, the fork expression may run concurrently with the last (nondeterministic) expression. In both examples, the value of x is guaranteed to be 2, and that of y may be 0 or 2. In the second example, because the computation for y is declared to be **det** this must be illegal. In that case the nondeterministic write to x interferes with the read of x inside the **det** expression. Note that in the first example, the read of x does not interfere with the write; this illustrates the asymmetry of the noninterference relation.

$$\begin{array}{l}\textbf{let}\ \ x = \textbf{ref}_\pi\ 0\ \ \textbf{in}\ \ \textbf{let}\ \ y = \textbf{ref}_\varpi\ 1\ \ \textbf{in}\\ \quad \textbf{det}\ \textbf{fork}(x := 2);\quad y := !x \qquad \textit{// ok}\end{array}$$

$$\begin{array}{l}\textbf{let}\ \ x = \textbf{ref}_\pi\ 0\ \ \textbf{in}\ \ \textbf{let}\ \ y = \textbf{ref}_\varpi\ 1\ \ \textbf{in}\\ \quad \textbf{det}\ \textbf{fork}(y := !x);\quad x := 2 \qquad \textit{// error}\end{array}$$

Any purely deterministic program is a special case of this more flexible system, in which the top-level program expression is declared to be **det**.

Table 1. Static Semantics

[CONSTANT] $\Gamma \vdash c : int \ \& \ \emptyset.\bot$

[VARIABLE] $\dfrac{\Gamma(x) = \tau}{\Gamma \vdash x : \tau \ \& \ \emptyset.\bot}$

[FUNCTION] $\dfrac{\Gamma, x \mapsto \tau_2 \vdash e : \tau_1 \ \& \ \Delta \qquad x \notin dom(\Gamma)}{\Gamma \vdash \mathbf{fn}\ x => e : \tau_2 \xrightarrow{\Delta} \tau_1 \ \& \ \emptyset.\bot}$

[APPLICATION] $\dfrac{\Gamma \vdash e_1 : \tau_2 \xrightarrow{\Delta_3} \tau_1 \ \& \ \Delta_1 \quad \Gamma \vdash e_2 : \tau_2 \ \& \ \Delta_2 \quad \Delta_1 \ ; \ \Delta_2 \ ; \ \Delta_3 = \Delta}{\Gamma \vdash e_1\ e_2 : \tau_1 \ \& \ \Delta}$

[REFERENCE] $\dfrac{\Gamma \vdash e : \tau \ \& \ \Delta}{\Gamma \vdash \mathbf{ref}_\pi\ e : ref_{\{\pi\}}\ \tau \ \& \ \Delta}$

[DEREFERENCE] $\dfrac{\Gamma \vdash e : ref_\rho\ \tau \ \& \ \Delta_1 \qquad \Delta_1 \ ; \ \{!\rho\}.\bot = \Delta}{\Gamma \vdash !e : \tau \ \& \ \Delta}$

[UPDATE] $\dfrac{\Gamma \vdash e_1 : ref_\rho\ \tau \ \& \ \Delta_1 \quad \Gamma \vdash e_2 : \tau \ \& \ \Delta_2 \quad \Delta_1 \ ; \ \Delta_2 \ ; \ \{\rho :=\}.\bot = \Delta}{\Gamma \vdash e_1 := e_2 : \tau \ \& \ \Delta}$

[FORK] $\dfrac{\Gamma \vdash e : \tau \ \& \ \varphi.\theta}{\Gamma \vdash \mathbf{fork}\ e : int \ \& \ \{fork\ \varphi\}.\theta}$

[DET] $\dfrac{\Gamma \vdash e : \tau \ \& \ \varphi.\bot}{\Gamma \vdash \mathbf{det}\ e : \tau \ \& \ \{det\ \varphi\}.\bot}$

[SUBSUMPTION] $\dfrac{\Gamma \vdash e : \tau' \ \& \ \Delta' \qquad \tau' <: \tau \qquad \Delta' \sqsubseteq \Delta}{\Gamma \vdash e : \tau \ \& \ \Delta}$

3 A Deterministic Effect System

In this section, we formalise our approach in a type and effect system by using the syntax introduced in the previous section. Since we now have the additional **det** e expression, we need to extend the syntax for types and effects:

$$\varphi ::= ... \mid \{det\ \varphi\} \qquad \Delta ::= \varphi.\theta$$
$$\tau ::= ... \mid \tau \xrightarrow{\Delta} \tau \qquad \theta ::= \bot \mid \top$$

The new form of effect for expressions is the *deterministic effect* Δ. We now refer to φ as *base effect*. The additional part of an effect, θ, refers to the inferred level of determinism for expressions—$\bot$ denotes a weakly deterministic effect and $\top$ denotes a nondeterministic effect with ordering, $\bot \leq \top$, so that weakly deterministic effects are more specific. An expression is strongly deterministic if it is syntactically annotated with the keyword **det**—it must have a qualified effect *det* φ which serves as a contract for the type system to ensure that any concurrent context where this expression appears cannot interfere with it.

3.1 Static Semantics

Effect systems [16] generally can be viewed as a type system where typing judgements have a more elaborate form, associating both a type and an effect with expressions. For the syntax defined in Section 2, Table 1 presents our type system for deterministic effects, using judgements of the form

$$\Gamma \vdash e : \tau \ \& \ \Delta$$

Table 2. Composition and Sequencing Rules

[COMPOSITION] $$\frac{\varphi_1 \hookrightarrow_\theta \varphi_2 \qquad \theta_1 \le \theta \qquad \theta_2 \le \theta}{\varphi_1.\theta_1 \ ; \ \varphi_2.\theta_2 = (\varphi_1 \cup \varphi_2).\theta}$$

[C-EMP] $$\emptyset \hookrightarrow_\theta \varphi$$

[C-EFF] $$\{\varepsilon\} \hookrightarrow_\theta \varphi$$

[C-UNI] $$\frac{\varphi_1 \hookrightarrow_\theta \varphi \qquad \varphi_2 \hookrightarrow_\theta \varphi}{\varphi_1 \cup \varphi_2 \hookrightarrow_\theta \varphi}$$

[C-DUN] $$\frac{\{det\ \varphi_1\} \hookrightarrow_\theta \varphi \qquad \{det\ \varphi_2\} \hookrightarrow_\theta \varphi}{\{det\ \varphi_1 \cup \varphi_2\} \hookrightarrow_\theta \varphi}$$

[C-DET-S] $$\frac{\varphi_1 \hookrightarrow_\bot \varphi_2}{\{det\ \varphi_1\} \hookrightarrow_\bot \varphi_2}$$

[C-FOK-S] $$\frac{\varphi_1 \not\twoheadrightarrow_\bot \varphi_2 \qquad \varphi_2 \not\twoheadrightarrow_\bot \varphi_1}{\{fork\ \varphi_1\} \hookrightarrow_\bot \varphi_2}$$

[C-FOK-W] $$\frac{\varphi_1 \not\twoheadrightarrow_\top \varphi_2 \qquad \varphi_2 \not\twoheadrightarrow_\top \varphi_1}{\{fork\ \varphi_1\} \hookrightarrow_\top \varphi_2}$$

[C-DET-W] $$\frac{\varphi_1 \not\twoheadrightarrow_\top \varphi_2 \qquad \varphi_2 \not\twoheadrightarrow_\bot \varphi_1}{\{det\ \{fork\ \varphi_1\}\} \hookrightarrow_\top \varphi_2}$$

Table 3. Noninterference Rules

[N-R/R] $$\{!\rho\} \not\twoheadrightarrow_\bot \varphi$$

[N-W/R] $$\frac{\rho_1 \cap \rho_2 = \emptyset}{\{\rho_1 :=\} \not\twoheadrightarrow_\bot \{!\rho_2\}}$$

[N-W/W] $$\frac{\rho_1 \cap \rho_2 = \emptyset}{\{\rho_1 :=\} \not\twoheadrightarrow_\bot \{\rho_2 :=\}}$$

[N-EFF] $$\{\varepsilon_1\} \not\twoheadrightarrow_\top \{\varepsilon_2\}$$

[N-DEL] $$\frac{\varphi_1 \not\twoheadrightarrow_\theta \varphi_2}{\{det\ \varphi_1\} \not\twoheadrightarrow_\theta \varphi_2}$$

[N-DER] $$\frac{\varphi_1 \not\twoheadrightarrow_\bot \varphi_2}{\varphi_1 \not\twoheadrightarrow_\theta \{det\ \varphi_2\}}$$

[N-FOL] $$\frac{\varphi_1 \not\twoheadrightarrow_\theta \varphi_2}{\{fork\ \varphi_1\} \not\twoheadrightarrow_\theta \varphi_2}$$

[N-FOR] $$\frac{\varphi_1 \not\twoheadrightarrow_\theta \varphi_2}{\varphi_1 \not\twoheadrightarrow_\theta \{fork\ \varphi_2\}}$$

[N-UNL] $$\frac{\varphi_1 \not\twoheadrightarrow_\theta \varphi \qquad \varphi_2 \not\twoheadrightarrow_\theta \varphi}{\varphi_1 \cup \varphi_2 \not\twoheadrightarrow_\theta \varphi}$$

[N-UNR] $$\frac{\varphi \not\twoheadrightarrow_\theta \varphi_1 \qquad \varphi \not\twoheadrightarrow_\theta \varphi_2}{\varphi \not\twoheadrightarrow_\theta \varphi_1 \cup \varphi_2}$$

[N-EMP] $$\emptyset \not\twoheadrightarrow_\theta \varphi$$

where τ is the type associated with the expression e relative to a type environment Γ which provides the type for each free variable as in a standard type system. The environment Γ is empty for top-level expressions which may therefore have no free variables; environment extension is written as $\Gamma, x \mapsto \tau$. The deterministic effect Δ describes the base effects that may take place during evaluation as well as its level of determinism (weakly deterministic or nondeterministic).

The rules in Table 1 infer typing judgements for each syntactic form of expression, together with the standard [SUBSUMPTION] rule using the definitions for subtyping and subeffects in Table 4. In Table 1, the inferred base effect φ is either empty, composed of effects of subexpressions, or generates new base effects. The rules [CONSTANT], [FUNCTION] and [VARIABLE] all have empty effect. The primitive side effects ($\{\varepsilon\}.\bot$) generated in [DEREFERENCE] and [UPDATE], as well as empty effects, are weakly deterministic.

In [FUNCTION], function abstraction records the (potential) deterministic effect of its body as an effect annotation in its type; it extends the environment for typing the body with a type for its variable (our types need not be unique).

Table 4. Subtype and Subeffect Rules

[T-RFL]	$\tau <: \tau$	[F-R/W]	$\dfrac{\rho_1 \subseteq \rho_2}{\{!\ \rho_1\} \sqsubseteq \{\rho_2 :=\}}$
[T-REF]	$\dfrac{\rho_1 \subseteq \rho_2}{ref_{\rho_1}\ \tau <: ref_{\rho_2}\ \tau}$	[F-W/W]	$\dfrac{\rho_1 \subseteq \rho_2}{\{\rho_1 :=\} \sqsubseteq \{\rho_2 :=\}}$
[T-FUN]	$\dfrac{\tau_1' <: \tau_1 \quad \tau_2 <: \tau_2' \quad \Delta \sqsubseteq \Delta'}{\tau_1 \xrightarrow{\Delta} \tau_2 <: \tau_1' \xrightarrow{\Delta'} \tau_2'}$	[F-FOK]	$\varphi \sqsubseteq \{fork\ \varphi\}$
[E-SUB]	$\dfrac{\varphi_1 \sqsubseteq \varphi_2 \quad \theta_1 \leq \theta_2}{\varphi_1.\theta_1 \sqsubseteq \varphi_2.\theta_2}$	[F-FOR]	$\dfrac{\varphi_1 \sqsubseteq \varphi_2}{\{fork\ \varphi_1\} \sqsubseteq \{fork\ \varphi_2\}}$
[E-DET]	$\dfrac{\varphi_1 \sqsubseteq \varphi_2}{\varphi_1.\bot \sqsubseteq \{det\ \varphi_2\}.\theta}$	[F-DET]	$\dfrac{\varphi_1 \sqsubseteq \varphi_2}{\{det\ \varphi_1\} \sqsubseteq \{det\ \varphi_2\}}$
[F-EMP]	$\emptyset \sqsubseteq \varphi$	[F-UNI]	$\dfrac{\varphi_1 \sqsubseteq \varphi_1' \quad \varphi_2 \sqsubseteq \varphi_2'}{\varphi_1 \cup \varphi_2 \sqsubseteq \varphi_1' \cup \varphi_2'}$
[F-R/R]	$\dfrac{\rho_1 \subseteq \rho_2}{\{!\ \rho_1\} \sqsubseteq \{!\ \rho_2\}}$		

The rules [APPLICATION], [REFERENCE], [DEREFERENCE], [UPDATE] and [FORK] inherit and sequentially compose deterministic effects from their subexpressions. For example, the overall deterministic effect of [APPLICATION] is the sequential composition of the deterministic effects of its function e_1 and argument e_2 evaluations, followed by the deterministic effect of the function body itself extracted from the function type. The composition of $\Delta_1;\ \Delta_2;\ \Delta_3 = \Delta$ is a shorthand for the composition of $\Delta_1;\ \Delta_2 = \Delta'$ and $\Delta';\ \Delta_3 = \Delta$. Sequential composition of effects is defined in [COMPOSITION] of Table 2 and requires sequential composability of the component effects. This is where the test for noninterference of concurrent effects arises in our system. In [REFERENCE], the labelled creation point π is recorded in the type of the introduced reference, so that later dereferences and assignments can track its use.

Only four rules are involved in base effect generation: [DEREFERENCE], [UPDATE], [FORK] and [DET]. The reference accessing expressions, dereference and update, compose the effect of the evaluation of their subexpressions, with the side effects generated by memory access (indicated by the read $!\rho$ or write $\rho :=$ in the rules). The effect of **fork** e is the effect of e qualified with the effect keyword *fork*. As discussed already, this distinguishes effects of concurrent threads from effects of the current thread; no other form of expression generates a fork effect. The rule [DET] asserts that an expression **det** e is strongly deterministic, provided that e is weakly deterministic and its inferred base effect $det\ \varphi$ ensures the expression cannot be interfered with by concurrent threads.

The type rules rely on effect composition, which in turn, as we shall see below, relies on a test of sequential composability which is asymmetric in its first and second effects. Consequently our type system is flow sensitive. In simple memory effect systems, the effect of $e_1; e_2$ and of $e_2; e_1$ are the same—simply the union of the two effects. For us, it is possible that $e_1; e_2$ is legal, whereas $e_2; e_1$ is not, as illustrated by the two versions of the first example in Section 2.1.

Sequential composition of deterministic effects, defined in Table 2, and the associated notion of noninterference, in Table 3, lie at the heart of the type system. We define the ordering $\bot \leq \top$, meaning that a deterministic expression can be considered as a nondeterministic expression. To reduce the number of rules, the symbol for sequential composition is parameterised with determinism: $\Delta_1 \hookrightarrow_\theta \Delta_2$ where θ could be either $\bot$ or $\top$. Now we define both *deterministic* and *nondeterministic compositions* in the [COMPOSITION] rule. If the composition is deterministic (i.e. the resulting effect is the union of effects $\varphi_1 \cup \varphi_2$ and $\bot$), then both expressions must be at least weakly deterministic and the $\hookrightarrow_\bot$ symbol is used to denote *strong sequential composability*. Otherwise, the $\hookrightarrow_\top$ symbol is used to denote *weak sequential composability* which allows interference between φ_1 and φ_2 and generates a nondeterministic combined effect $(\varphi_1 \cup \varphi_2).\top$.

The key role of [COMPOSITION] is to check that deterministic effects (thus expressions) are indeed sequentially composable. The rest of rules in Table 2 define strong and weak sequential composability as a binary relation over base effects φ. [C-EMP], [C-EFF], [C-UNI] and [C-DUN] are generic rules for both strong and weak sequential composability. By rule [C-EFF] we assert that side effects $\{\varepsilon\}$ associated solely with the current thread, are sequentially composable with any subsequent effect. This captures the idea that terminated computations cannot interfere with later ones. [C-UNI] allows the combination of effects on the left provided that each of them is sequentially composable with the effect on the right. The second union rule [C-DUN] preserves the *det* qualification over composition. Strong sequencing rules forbid thread interference between two effects; therefore it is safe to remove the *det* qualification in the strong sequencing rule [C-DET-S]. In another strong sequencing rule [C-FOK-S], composing a fork effect $\{fork\ \varphi_1\}$ with another φ_2 requires the effect φ_1 not to interfere ($\not\twoheadrightarrow_\bot$) with the overall effect of φ_2 and vice versa, because the thread may be running concurrently with the second expression. On the other hand, the weak sequencing rule [C-FOK-W] allows interference between threads by using $\not\twoheadrightarrow_\top$ (weak noninterference). [C-DET-W] is special, as it allows a deterministic concurrent effect $\{det\ \{fork\ \varphi_1\}\}$ to be composable with its following effect φ_2 only if φ_2 does not interfere with φ_1; the last pair of examples in Section 2 illustrate the use of this rule.

Table 3 defines strong and weak *noninterference* of concurrent effects; noninterference is asymmetric. We consider strong noninterference $\varphi_1 \not\twoheadrightarrow_\bot \varphi_2$ to mean that the effect φ_1 *does not affect* φ_2. So reading shared memory does not affect any writes to that memory, whereas a write can affect a read. [N-R/R] states that a read effect interferes with nothing; [N-W/R] and [N-W/W] state that a write effect does not interfere with other concurrent side-effect (read or write) only if they access distinct regions. Weak noninterference rules, on the other hand, are treated in a way that resembles weak sequencing; they are designed to allow arbitrary interference amongst expressions, except for deterministic expressions. [N-EFF] asserts that side effects do not weakly interfere with one another, implying they may occur in parallel. The remaining rules are generic for either strong or weak noninterference. The difference between [N-DEL] and [N-DER] is important. [N-DEL] asserts that a qualified *det* effect does not interfere with another

Table 5. Operational Semantics

[R-APP] $\langle \varsigma,\ (\mathbf{fn}\ x => e)\ v\rangle \xrightarrow{\emptyset} \langle \varsigma,\ [v/x]e\rangle$

[R-REF] $$\frac{\iota \notin dom(\varsigma) \qquad \varsigma' = \varsigma, \iota^{\pi} \mapsto v}{\langle \varsigma,\ \mathbf{ref}_{\pi}\ v\rangle \xrightarrow{\emptyset} \langle \varsigma',\ \iota\rangle}$$

[R-DRF] $\langle \varsigma,\ !\iota\rangle \xrightarrow{\{!\{\iota\}\}} \langle \varsigma,\ \varsigma(\iota)\rangle$

[R-UPD] $\langle \varsigma,\ \iota := v\rangle \xrightarrow{\{\{\iota\}:=\}} \langle \varsigma[\iota \mapsto v],\ v\rangle$

[R-FOK] $\langle \varsigma,\ \mathbf{fork}\ e\rangle \xrightarrow{\emptyset} \langle \varsigma,\ \widehat{e}\ 0\rangle$

[R-SEQ] $\langle \varsigma,\ \widehat{v}\ e\rangle \xrightarrow{\emptyset} \langle \varsigma,\ e\rangle$

[R-CON] $\langle \varsigma,\ E[\widehat{e}\ v]\rangle \xrightarrow{\emptyset} \langle \varsigma,\ \widehat{e}\ E[v]\rangle$

[R-DET] $$\frac{\langle \varsigma,\ e\rangle \xrightarrow{\varphi} \langle \varsigma,\ e'\rangle}{\langle \varsigma,\ \mathbf{det}\ e\rangle \xrightarrow{\{det\ \varphi\}} \langle \varsigma,\ \mathbf{det}\ e'\rangle}$$

[R-DER] $\langle \varsigma,\ \mathbf{det}\ v\rangle \xrightarrow{\emptyset} \langle \varsigma,\ v\rangle$

[R-CTX] $$\frac{\langle \varsigma,\ e\rangle \xrightarrow{\varphi} \langle \varsigma',\ e'\rangle}{\langle \varsigma,\ E[e]\rangle \xrightarrow{\varphi} \langle \varsigma',\ E[e']\rangle}$$

effect, providing the underlying effect does not. However, [N-DER] asserts that an effect does not (either strongly or weakly) interfere with a *det* effect only if it does not *strongly* interfere with it; this is essentially how strong determinism is enforced by using the *det* qualification. [N-FOL] and [N-FOR] state that a fork effect does not interfere with another effect provided their components do not and vice versa. [N-UNL] and [N-UNR] state that a union of effects does not interfere with another effect if its component do not and vice versa; [N-EMP] simply states that the empty effect interferes with no effect.

We complete this section with subtyping and subeffecting rules in Table 4. Subtyping is reflexive. As usual, function types are contravariant in arguments and covariant in results. Both function types and reference types allow broadening of effects or regions in moving to a supertype. [E-SUB] defines subeffecting for deterministic effects Δ. A deterministic expression can be considered as a nondeterministic expression. The [E-DET] rule is a special case, which states φ_1 cannot be a subeffect of $\{det\ \varphi_2\}$ unless it is deterministic (as suggested by $\perp$). The [F-] rules define subeffecting for base effects φ; those defining subeffecting for side effects are standard. [F-FOK] states that a fork effect is a supereffect of its component; it loses any information about effects being on the same thread. [F-FOR] states that a fork effect is monotonic on subeffecting, as does [F-DET] for *det*. For our purposes, the key property for subeffecting is that an effect inherits any noninterference enjoyed by a supereffect.

3.2 Dynamic Semantics and Properties

We define the dynamic behaviour of the core calculus, and demonstrate that the actual effects arising from the evaluation of a well-typed expression are consistent with its statically inferred effects. The syntax is extended to include features required for the dynamic semantics, as follows:

$$e \ ::= \ \ldots \mid \widehat{e}\ e \qquad\qquad v \ ::= \ \ldots \mid \iota^{\pi} \qquad\qquad \rho \ ::= \ \ldots \mid \{\iota\}$$

Unlike the more standard "list of threads" technique that does not preserve the relative nesting of thread creations [9], our extended syntax for runtime

Table 6. Auxiliary Definitions

[STORE]	$$\frac{dom(\Sigma) = dom(\varsigma) \qquad \forall \iota \in dom(\varsigma) \cdot \Gamma; \Sigma \vdash \varsigma(\iota) : \Sigma(\iota)\ \&\ \Delta}{\Gamma; \Sigma \vdash \varsigma}$$
[PARALLEL]	$$\frac{\Gamma; \Sigma \vdash e_1 : \tau_1\ \&\ \varphi_1.\theta_1 \quad \Gamma; \Sigma \vdash e_2 : \tau_2\ \&\ \Delta_2 \quad \{fork\ \varphi_1\}.\theta_1\ ; \Delta_2 = \Delta}{\Gamma; \Sigma \vdash \widehat{e_1}\ e_2 : \tau_2\ \&\ \Delta}$$
[REG-IN]	$\iota^\pi \in \{\pi\}$
[LOCATION]	$$\frac{\Sigma(\iota) = \tau}{\Gamma; \Sigma \vdash \iota : ref_{\{\iota\}}\ \tau\ \&\ \emptyset.\bot}$$
[REG-OUT]	$$\frac{\pi \neq \varpi}{\iota^\pi \notin \{\varpi\}}$$
[EQ-IDE]	$$\frac{for\ all\ \iota\ appears\ in\ e \cdot \varsigma(\iota) = \varsigma'(\iota)}{\langle \varsigma, e\rangle \cong \langle \varsigma', e\rangle}$$
[EQ-LOC]	$$\frac{\begin{array}{c}\langle \varsigma, \varsigma(\iota)\rangle \cong \langle \varsigma', \varsigma'(\iota')\rangle \\ [\iota''/\iota]\langle \varsigma, e\rangle \cong [\iota''/\iota']\langle \varsigma', e'\rangle \qquad \iota''\ does\ not\ appear\ in\ \varsigma,\ \varsigma',\ e\ or\ e'\end{array}}{\langle \varsigma, e\rangle \cong \langle \varsigma', e'\rangle}$$
[EQ-PAR]	$$\frac{\begin{array}{c}\forall i \in 1..n \cdot \langle \varsigma, e_i\rangle \cong \langle \varsigma', e_{\sigma(i)}\rangle \qquad where\ \sigma\ is\ a\ permutation\ of\ 1..n \\ \langle \varsigma, e\rangle \cong \langle \varsigma', e'\rangle\end{array}}{\langle \varsigma, \widehat{e_1}\ ..\ \widehat{e_n}\ e\rangle \cong \langle \varsigma', \widehat{e_{\sigma(1)}}\ ..\ \widehat{e_{\sigma(n)}}\ e'\rangle}$$

expressions introduces a novel parallel construct $\widehat{e}\ e$ to allow us to represent an expression together with its threading context, that is, the threads it has forked. This expression is right-associative, the sequential continuation e, after forking n threads $e_1 \ldots e_n$, is simply written as $\widehat{e_1}\ (\widehat{e_2} \ldots (\widehat{e_n}\ e))$ or just $\widehat{e_1}\ \widehat{e_2} \ldots \widehat{e_n}\ e$. This expression records the tree structure of forked threads. For example $\widehat{e_1}\ e_2$ may evaluate to $\widehat{\widehat{e_3}\ e_4}\ e_2$ if e_1 forks a thread e_3 and continues with e_4; again it may further evaluate to $\widehat{\widehat{e_3}\ e_4}\ \widehat{e_5}\ e_6$ if e_2 forks a thread e_5 and continues with e_6.

Values now include runtime store locations ι; these are annotated with the label π corresponding to the $\mathbf{ref}_\pi$ expression from where the location was allocated. For succinctness we omit the labels wherever they are not explicitly required. Runtime regions are sets of locations. Runtime effects correspond to accessing the store using locations; a runtime effect is a set of side effects on locations. The conventional form of evaluation contexts is used to define the order of evaluation of subexpressions in compound terms. Except for parallel expressions $\widehat{e}\ e$, the evaluation context is deterministic in its selection of subexpression.

$$E \ ::= \ [\,] \mid E\ e \mid (\mathbf{fn}\ x \Rightarrow e)\ E \mid \mathbf{ref}_\pi\ E \mid !E \mid E := e \mid \iota := E \mid \widehat{E}\ e \mid \widehat{e}\ E$$

The small step operational semantics in Table 5 uses this form of transition:

$$\langle \varsigma,\ e\rangle \xrightarrow{\varphi} \langle \varsigma',\ e'\rangle$$

where ς is the global store, e is the expression to be evaluated. A store ς maps locations to the values stored in them, and is initially empty at the beginning of evaluation. The store may be extended by [R-REF]; store extension is written as $\varsigma, \iota \mapsto v$. The effect of the evaluation φ identifies the effect of the small step transition, which is either empty, $\emptyset$, or a singleton side effect, $\{\varepsilon\}$.

All possible single step transitions between configurations are given, where the initial state for a top-level expression e has an empty store. Like conventional operational semantics for concurrent programs [9,1], each single step transition is atomic and thread interleaving is modelled by choice of step. The only non-determinism (modulo choice of new locations and structure on sequential terms; such equivalence is formally defined by the [EQ-] rules in Table 6) offered by these evaluation contexts arises from the two choices corresponding to the parallel construct $\widehat{e}\ e$, as either the concurrent part or the sequential part may undergo transitions, which is implicit in the rule [R-CTX], thus capturing thread interleaving.

The rules [R-APP] through [R-UPD] build up base cases on evaluation in a single thread. The [R-REF] transition captures the introduction of a new location into the store, with label annotations corresponding to the **ref** construct. The only transitions which directly have an effect are those for reads and writes of the store, namely [R-DRF] and [R-UPD]. New threads are introduced via [R-FOK]; it causes no direct effect but introduces a new thread ($\widehat{e}$) whose effect corresponds to the fork effect tracked in the static type system. The value that results from the **fork** step is arbitrarily chosen to be 0. If a concurrent thread $\widehat{e}$ reduces to a value $\widehat{v}$, there are no further reductions available for it. Such threads are effectively garbage and are easily eliminated with [R-SEQ]. Similarly, [R-DER] simply removes the keyword **det** from an expression when it finishes its evaluation. [R-DET] preserves **det** on expressions so that subsequent evaluation must also be deterministic; this is necessary in proving our determinism result, though it does not affect the evaluation. In [R-CON] a forked thread $\widehat{e}$ is relocated outside of its parent expression; this allows the return value to be used by the parent expression (e.g. a fork in an assignment needs to return a value for the assignment to progress). It preserves the nesting of thread creations in our syntax.

To help formalise and prove the safety properties, we use standard store typing for reference types [20] by extending the type judgements with an additional store typing Σ, which maps locations to their types; store typing extension is written as $\Sigma, \iota \mapsto \tau$. All expression typing judgements will have the form:

$$\Gamma; \Sigma \vdash e : \tau \,\&\, \varphi$$

The only rule that needs to use Σ is [LOCATION]. We do not rewrite other expression typing rules in Table 1, because they do not need to do anything interesting with the store typing—just pass it from premise to conclusion.

Table 6 provides auxiliary definitions used by the operational semantics and the theorems. The type rule for our intermediate form for concurrent expressions $\widehat{e_1}\ e_2$, is given by [PARALLEL]. This records the fact that concurrent threads have fork effects, and that their combined effect is given by the union of their effects. The standard definition [STORE] asserts that a store is well-typed if the value stored in every location has the type predicted by the store typing. In [STORE], we also capture the property that locations created at different program points must be different. We connect labels used in static semantics with the locations in dynamic semantics in [REG-IN] and [REG-OUT]. The [EQ-] rules define an equivalence on state: [EQ-IDE] is the induction base which allows us to restrict attention to just that part of the store which affects the value of the expression; [EQ-LOC] does location substitution which allows us to treat two locations holding the same value as being identical; [EQ-PAR] does shuffling which allows reordering of forked threads. For example, ι is regarded the same as ι' if they contain the same value, and $\widehat{e_1}\ \widehat{e_2}\ e_3$ is regarded the same as $\widehat{e_2}\ \widehat{e_1}\ e_3$, because the order of forked threads is not important.

We extend the transitions to multi-step, which have the form

$$\langle \varsigma,\ e\rangle \stackrel{\varphi}{\Longrightarrow} \langle \varsigma',\ e'\rangle$$

where φ is the union of effects of finitely many steps. We prove that for a terminating program, well-typedness implies determinism in its final value. The main result is a strong determinism theorem which states:

1. the evaluation of any deterministic sub-term (**det** e) cannot be affected by reductions in the external context.
2. without interleaving with its context, the result of the evaluation of **det** e is unique, independently of how the threads inside e interleave.

Theorem 1 (Strong determinism)
Given all reachable states $\langle \varsigma, E[\mathbf{det}\ e]\rangle$ *such that* $\Gamma; \Sigma \vdash E[\mathbf{det}\ e] : \tau \ \&\ \Delta$ *and* $\Gamma; \Sigma \vdash \varsigma$, *if* $\langle \varsigma,\ \mathbf{det}\ e\rangle \stackrel{\varphi_1}{\Longrightarrow} \langle \varsigma_1,\ v\rangle$ *and* $\langle \varsigma,\ E[\mathbf{det}\ e]\rangle \stackrel{\varphi_2}{\Longrightarrow} \langle \varsigma_2,\ E'[\mathbf{det}\ e]\rangle$, *then*

1. *there exists* $\langle \varsigma_2, E'[\mathbf{det}\ e]\rangle \stackrel{\varphi_3}{\Longrightarrow} \langle \varsigma_3, E'[v']\rangle$ *and* $\langle \varsigma_1, v\rangle \cong \langle \varsigma_3, v'\rangle$.
2. *for all* $\langle \varsigma,\ \mathbf{det}\ e\rangle \stackrel{\varphi_4}{\Longrightarrow} \langle \varsigma_4,\ v''\rangle$, *we have* $\langle \varsigma_1, v\rangle \cong \langle \varsigma_4, v''\rangle$.

4 Discussion

4.1 Extensions

This paper has presented a core calculus and effect system, based on the approach of Nielson et al., to allow a focus on the novel features of our approach and formal results. In this section, we review a number of existing techniques for improving precision and expressiveness of effect systems, and how they can be extended to our deterministic effects.

Thread-locality. Thread-local references cannot be aliased by other threads, thus effectively reducing interference between threads. Type systems can be used to restrict thread-local references. For example, the lexically scoped reference construct $\mathbf{new}_\pi\ x := e_1\ \mathbf{in}\ e_2$ in [18,19] creates a new reference variable x for use in e_2 and initialises it to the value of e_1. With such a construct we can confine the reference within its scope e_2 (incidentally, [18,19] do not explicitly impose such restrictions). Consider the following example adopted from [9]:

$$\begin{array}{l}\mathbf{let}\ \ f = (\mathbf{fn}\ x => \mathbf{new}_\pi\ y :=\ \ 0\ \mathbf{in}\ y := x)\ \ \mathbf{in}\\ \mathbf{let}\ \ rec = \mathbf{ref}_\varpi\ (\mathbf{fn}\ x => x)\ \ \mathbf{in}\\ \quad rec := \mathbf{fn}\ x => (\mathbf{fork}\ f\ 0;\ !rec\ 0);\quad !rec\ 0\end{array}$$

This example captures the essence of a server, which creates a thread to handle each incoming request. The core of this example is a recursive function that creates a new thread to allocate a reference cell y and use y in handling an incoming request (we simply use an assignment to represent the handling, and incoming requests are not modelled), and finally calls itself recursively to handle the next incoming request. We confine the references created at π within its lexical scope so that request handling threads have their own memory space isolated from one another. The effect of $!rec\ 0$ is $\{fork\ \{\{\pi\} :=\}, !\{\varpi\}\}$. Since references created at π are always thread-local, the visible effect of $!rec\ 0$ is $\{!\{\varpi\}\}$. There is no interference present in this example.

More expressive type systems such as uniqueness [10,7] or ownership [6,3,14] may be extended with our effect system to confine thread-local references in a more flexible way. Besides type systems, escape analysis [23] and thread sharing analysis [17] identify thread-local locations based on program analysis, and are often used in data race detection and other static analysis tools.

Structured Parallelism Previous type systems for deterministic parallelism [1,2] support structured parallel programs, which may be considered as a special case where lifetimes of threads are restricted to lexical scopes. It is easy to support such a fork/join construct, **forkjoin** $e_1\ e_2$, in our deterministic effect system, by a typing rule which simply checks if two tasks may interfere:

$$\text{[FORKJOIN]}\quad \frac{\Gamma \vdash e_1 : \tau_1 \ \&\ \varphi_1.\theta_1 \qquad \Gamma \vdash e_2 : \tau_2 \ \&\ \varphi_2.\theta_2 \qquad \varphi_1 \not\twoheadrightarrow_\bot \varphi_2 \qquad \varphi_2 \not\twoheadrightarrow_\bot \varphi_1 \qquad \theta_1 \leq \theta_3 \qquad \theta_2 \leq \theta_3}{\Gamma \vdash \mathbf{forkjoin}\ e_1\ e_2 : \tau_2 \ \&\ (\varphi_1 \cup \varphi_2).\theta_3}$$

For example, here is a Fibonacci function encoded in our calculus using the **forkjoin** expression (with conditionals and basic arithmetic):

$$\begin{array}{l}
\mathbf{let}\ \ fib = \mathbf{ref}\ (\mathbf{fn}\ n => n)\ \ \mathbf{in} \\
\quad fib := \mathbf{fn}\ n => (\ \mathbf{if}\ (n < 2)\ n \\
\qquad\qquad\qquad\qquad \mathbf{if}\ (n >= 2)\ (\ \mathbf{new}_\pi\ x := 0\ \ \mathbf{in}\ \ \mathbf{new}_\varpi\ y := 0\ \ \mathbf{in} \\
\qquad\qquad\qquad\qquad\quad \mathbf{forkjoin}\ (x := fib\ (n-1))\ (y := fib\ (n-2));\ x + y\ ) \\
\quad);\ \ !fib\ 10
\end{array}$$

Because task lifetime is constrained to the **forkjoin** construct, it does not introduce fork effects, unlike **fork**. The rule simply requires that the two parallel expressions do not interfere with one another (in this example, it is easy to see their effects are disjoint). Unlike [1,2], we can mix structured parallelism with threads; for example, the **forkjoin** expression may fork threads too. This generality does not compromise safety, because thread effects will be captured in the resulting effect of the **forkjoin** expression.

Polymorphism. Hindley/Milner polymorphism, as found in Standard ML and other functional languages, is a classical technique for increasing the precision of types and effects. It allows us to distinguish the effects of two applications of the same function. Let us consider the following example:

$$\begin{array}{l}
\mathbf{let}\ \ count1\ = \mathbf{ref}_\pi\ 0\ \ \mathbf{in}\ \ \mathbf{let}\ \ count2 = \mathbf{ref}_\varpi\ 0\ \ \mathbf{in} \\
\mathbf{let}\ \ inc = (\mathbf{fn}\ x => x := !x + 1)\ \ \mathbf{in} \\
\quad \mathbf{fork}\ (inc\ count1);\ \ \mathbf{fork}\ (inc\ count2)
\end{array}$$

According to the type rules presented in Section 3, the type of the function variable x of *inc* is $ref_{\{\pi,\varpi\}}\ int$, so that the effect of *inc* is $\{!\{\pi,\varpi\},\{\pi,\varpi\} :=\}$. This example cannot type check because the threads have the same effect $\{fork\ \{!\{\pi,\varpi\},\{\pi,\varpi\} :=\}\}$, which includes a write side-effect, so the threads are judged to interfere with one another. Of course we know that these threads access different reference cells and hence do not actually interfere at runtime.

The treatment of polymorphism for our type and effect is standard and has been given in [18,19], which allows us to achieve the extra precision required to type check this example. Using polymorphism in the previous example, the type of the variable x is $\forall\zeta.ref_{\zeta}\ int$ (where ζ is a region variable) and the effect of *inc* becomes $\forall\zeta.\{!\zeta,\zeta :=\}$. After instantiation of the region variable, the effects of the two threads can be distinguished as $\{fork\ \{!\{\pi\},\{\pi\} :=\}\}$ and $\{fork\ \{!\{\varpi\},\{\varpi\} :=\}\}$ respectively, which clearly do not interfere. Polymorphism also makes type checking modular, which is useful for checking incomplete programs. For example, without polymorphism, the type of *inc* may depend on how it is used in the last two expressions. With polymorphism, the type of *inc* is independent of its use so the function may be defined in a different module.

Effect Abstraction. Nielson et al.'s effect systems use simple abstraction to model shared locations—effectively the label of the program point at which the reference is created. Although our effect system extends their framework, the general approach presented in this paper is largely independent of the specific abstraction chosen. However in practice, stronger effect abstractions and specifications are needed for precision and modularity.

The precision of effect reasoning relies on aliasing reasoning, which is one of the main sources of imprecision in type and effect systems (in fact, any static analysis). Because any sound type system must make conservative choices about aliasing (for example, when two references may be aliases, we must conservatively consider them as aliases), some good programs may not type check or may signal false warnings. It is particularly difficult to distinguish references created from the same program point. Ownership [6,3,15] and region-based [16,1] effect systems parameterise object types with owners or regions to enrich the type structure. For instance, elements in a data structure may be distinguished if they have different types (parameterised with different owners/regions). DPJ [1] also suggests a special treatment for arrays, which relies on distinguishing element types by their array indices. Moreover, these effect systems support explicit effect specifications, which enhance program reasoning, enable separate compilation and facilitate modular software development. Our approach in this paper naturally supports modularity, as the effect of an expression can be inferred from only itself (i.e. independent to the context/environment, see more discussion in Section 4.2). Ownership or region-based effects may be extended in our framework to replace the simple label-based effects; we only need to adapt some noninterference rules for supporting these new forms of effects.

4.2 Related Work

Much work has addressed the challenges of shared-memory concurrent programming. In this section we restrict attention to directly related work, including determinism and effects systems. Traditionally, determinism can be guaranteed for some restricted styles of parallel programming, such as data parallel or pure functional. Recent times have seen increased support for deterministic parallelism in imperative programs. Examples include the use of dynamic analysis [22,5], type systems [25,1,2], static analysis [26] or separation logic [8].

Dynamic analysis allows programmers to assert desired deterministic sections and enforce determinism by runtime checks. Dynamic approaches are generally more flexible (e.g. [5] supports *semantic determinism* to tolerate some controlled nondeterminism inside a deterministic section) and precise (e.g. less or no false positives), but they often impose considerable runtime overhead and have limited test coverage. Type systems, on the other hand, enforce determinism statically at compile time; they typically capture errors earlier with no runtime cost, but may report more false warnings. Type systems require annotations, which may increase programming effort but are useful for program specification and documentation especially for modular development of large software.

Our type system is modelled on those of Nielson et al. [18,19]. In their systems they have provided separate effects for spawned expressions (like fork for us); their systems also track sequencing in effects. The key difference for our effects are that we explicitly prohibit unwanted concurrent behaviours; we only allow an effect sequence $\Delta_1; \Delta_2$ to be formed when the effects are sequentially composable. Our use of deterministic effects appears to be novel. Unlike related work on determinism for other concurrency models [1,2], as befits a threading model, our approach focuses on the effect of the current thread separately from the effect of the threads that it has forked. These approaches treat the components of a parallel expression symmetrically, and are flow-insensitive.

Type and effect systems for tracking noninterference in programs are useful for facilitating program reasoning and verification in sequential programs [6], for analysing behavior of concurrent processes in process algebras [11], and for enforcing determinism in structured parallel programs [1]. Fractional capabilities [4,25] provide similar support by treating a read capability as a fraction of the write capability and distributing capabilities on memory locations at synchronisation points to ensure that each thread must have sufficient capability to read/write these locations. They can support determinism and synchronisation but inherently lack modularity, because in order to type a function, for instance, the capability of the calling context (thread) must be known. On the other hand, deterministic effects may be described independently of the context in which they are used (flow-sensitivity is captured locally by sequential composability), thus making modular reasoning about incomplete programs (e.g. a function or a class) feasible. Furthermore, our approach can support a variety of computational effects (not just reads/writes) and check for different interference properties. For example, it may reason about deadlocks by capturing (ordered) lock sets as effects and the inconsistency in lock ordering as interference.

4.3 Future Work

With this work, we provide a sound and general framework which can be used as a basis for studying more kinds of computational effects and interference in multithreaded programs. Two interesting directions would be: higher level mechanisms for expressing effects, and incorporating synchronisation.

Understanding and writing multithreaded code is difficult, partly because of the lack of specification for concurrent behaviours. Programmers typically work with large libraries of code whose concurrent behaviours (e.g. threading, synchronisation, locks, etc.) are not precisely specified. Our framework may be extended with existing object-oriented effect systems (e.g. ownership or regions) to allow programmers to express their high-level design intentions via effect contracts on methods. Moreover, the ability to statically determine if two parallel computations may interfere is critical in the design of concurrent software, for instance, the degree of concurrency can be increased by reducing thread interference and removing redundant synchronisation.

In this paper, we have not been concerned with synchronisation/locking which adds little to the novelty of our model (deterministic and nondeterministic effects) and does not affect the results (strong and weak determinism). Instead we have aimed to present a foundation of a simple and general formalism for reasoning about multithreaded programming upon which we can build more elaborate models, including for synchronisation. For example, by capturing lock sets [9,21] as effects, our framework can be used to reason about data races [27] and deadlocks, which may be characterised as two kinds of thread interference. Type-based techniques for imposing locking disciplines can detect data races [9,3] or deadlocks [3] by requiring a shared location to be consistently guarded by a common lock, or locks to be acquired in a fixed order; typically they, pessimistically, assume maximal concurrency. With our thread-sensitive approach, it is possible to improve the precision of reasoning about concurrency vulnerabilities.

5 Conclusion

Threads are the dominant model in use today for general concurrent programming, but they are wildly nondeterministic and notoriously difficult to understand and predict, even for expert programmers. This paper proposes a novel approach for analysing thread interference and determinism in multithreaded programs, and presents a simple type and effect system to demonstrate our approach which can guarantee the preservation of desired deterministic behaviour. Deterministic effects may be used by tools or as interface specifications to assist with modular development of multithreaded software. We believe that deterministic effects are simple and easy enough to understand for average programmers, thus assisting them with difficult parts of multithreaded programming.

Acknowledgements. This research is supported by an Australian Research Council Grant DP0987236.

References

1. Bocchino Jr., R.L., Adve, V.S., Dig, D., Adve, S.V., Heumann, S., Komuravelli, R., Overbey, J., Simmons, P., Sung, H., Vakilian, M.: A type and effect system for Deterministic Parallel Java. In: OOPSLA (2009)
2. Bocchino Jr., R.L., Heumann, S., Honarmand, N., Adve, S.V., Adve, V.S., Welc, A., Shpeisman, T.: Safe nondeterminism in a deterministic-by-default parallel language. In: POPL (2011)
3. Boyapati, C., Lee, R., Rinard, M.: Ownership types for safe programming: Preventing data races and deadlocks. In: OOPSLA (2002)
4. Boyland, J.: Checking Interference with Fractional Permissions. In: Cousot, R. (ed.) SAS 2003. LNCS, vol. 2694, pp. 55–72. Springer, Heidelberg (2003)
5. Burnim, J., Sen, K.: Asserting and checking determinism for multithreaded programs. In: FSE (2009)
6. Clarke, D., Drossopoulou, S.: Ownership, encapsulation and disjointness of type and effect. In: OOPSLA (2002)
7. Clarke, D., Wrigstad, T.: External Uniqueness is Unique Enough. In: Cardelli, L. (ed.) ECOOP 2003. LNCS, vol. 2743, pp. 176–201. Springer, Heidelberg (2003)
8. Dodds, M., Jagannathan, S., Parkinson, M.J.: Modular reasoning for deterministic parallelism. In: POPL (2011)
9. Flanagan, C., Abadi, M.: Types for Safe Locking. In: Swierstra, S.D. (ed.) ESOP 1999. LNCS, vol. 1576, pp. 91–108. Springer, Heidelberg (1999)
10. Hogg, J.: Islands: aliasing protection in object-oriented languages. In: OOPSLA (1991)
11. Kobayashi, N.: Type Systems for Concurrent Programs. In: Aichernig, B.K. (ed.) Formal Methods at the Crossroads. From Panacea to Foundational Support. LNCS, vol. 2757, pp. 439–453. Springer, Heidelberg (2003)
12. Lea, D.: A Java fork/join framework. In: Java Grande (2000)
13. Lee, E.A.: The problem with threads. IEEE Computer 39(5) (2006)
14. Lu, Y., Potter, J.: On Ownership and Accessibility. In: Hu, Q. (ed.) ECOOP 2006. LNCS, vol. 4067, pp. 99–123. Springer, Heidelberg (2006)
15. Lu, Y., Potter, J.: Protecting representation with effect encapsulation. In: POPL (2006)
16. Lucassen, J.M., Gifford, D.K.: Polymorphic effect systems. In: POPL (1988)
17. Neamtiu, I., Hicks, M., Foster, J.S., Pratikakis, P.: Contextual effects for version-consistent dynamic software updating and safe concurrent programming. In: POPL (2008)
18. Nielson, F., Nielson, H.R.: Type and Effect Systems. In: Olderog, E.-R., Steffen, B. (eds.) Correct System Design. LNCS, vol. 1710, pp. 114–136. Springer, Heidelberg (1999)
19. Nielson, F., Nielson, H.R., Hankin, C.: Principles of Program Analysis. Springer, Heidelberg (1999)
20. Pierce, B.: Types and Programming Languages. The MIT Press (2002)
21. Pratikakis, P., Foster, J.S., Hicks, M.: Locksmith: context-sensitive correlation analysis for race detection. In: PLDI (2006)
22. Sadowski, C., Freund, S.N., Flanagan, C.: SingleTrack: A Dynamic Determinism Checker for Multithreaded Programs. In: Castagna, G. (ed.) ESOP 2009. LNCS, vol. 5502, pp. 394–409. Springer, Heidelberg (2009)
23. Salcianu, A., Rinard, M.C.: Pointer and escape analysis for multithreaded programs. In: PPOPP (2001)

24. Sutter, H., Larus, J.: Software and the concurrency revolution. Queue 3(7) (2005)
25. Terauchi, T., Aiken, A.: A capability calculus for concurrency and determinism. TOPLAS 30(5) (2008)
26. Vechev, M., Yahav, E., Raman, R., Sarkar, V.: Automatic Verification of Determinism for Structured Parallel Programs. In: Cousot, R., Martel, M. (eds.) SAS 2010. LNCS, vol. 6337, pp. 455–471. Springer, Heidelberg (2010)
27. Xie, X., Xue, J.: Acculock: Accurate and efficient detection of data races. In: CGO (2011)

Linear Logical Relations for Session-Based Concurrency

Jorge A. Pérez[1], Luís Caires[1], Frank Pfenning[2], and Bernardo Toninho[1,2]

[1] CITI and Departamento de Informática, FCT, Universidade Nova de Lisboa
[2] Computer Science Department, Carnegie Mellon University

Abstract. In prior work we proposed an interpretation of intuitionistic linear logic propositions as session types for concurrent processes. The type system obtained from the interpretation ensures fundamental properties of session-based typed disciplines—most notably, type preservation, session fidelity, and global progress. In this paper, we complement and strengthen these results by developing a theory of logical relations. Our development is based on, and is remarkably similar to, that for functional languages, extended to an (intuitionistic) linear type structure. A main result is that well-typed processes always terminate (strong normalization). We also introduce a notion of observational equivalence for session-typed processes. As applications, we prove that all proof conversions induced by the logic interpretation actually express observational equivalences, and explain how type isomorphisms resulting from linear logic equivalences are realized by coercions between interface types of session-based concurrent systems.

1 Introduction

Modern computing systems rely heavily on the concurrent communication of distributed software artifacts. Hence, to a large extent, guaranteeing their correctness amounts to ensuring consistent dialogues between these artifacts—an extremely challenging task given the complex interaction patterns they usually feature. *Session-based concurrency* has consolidated as a foundational approach to communication correctness: dialogues between participants are structured into *sessions*, the basic units of communication; descriptions of the interaction patterns are then abstracted as *session types* [11], which are statically checked against specifications. These specifications are usually given in the π-calculus [16], so we obtain *processes* communicating through so-called session channels connecting exactly two subsystems. The discipline of session types ensures session protocols in which actions always occur in dual pairs: when one partner sends, the other receives; when one partner offers a selection, the other chooses; when a session terminates, no further interaction may occur. New sessions may be dynamically created by invocation of shared servers. While *concurrency* arises in the simultaneous execution of sessions, *mobility* is present in the exchange of session and server names.

In session-based concurrency, typing disciplines usually guarantee communication correctness via (forms of) *subject reduction* and *progress* properties. The former states that well-typed processes always evolve to well-typed processes (a *safety* property); the latter says that well-typed processes will never run into a stuck state (a *liveness* property). In addition to ensure that sets of interactions adhere to their prescribed behavior, it is sensible to require such interactions to be *finite*: while from a global perspective systems are meant to run forever, at a local level we would like participants which always

H. Seidl (Ed.): ESOP 2012, LNCS 7211, pp. 539–558, 2012.

respond within a finite amount of time, and never engage into infinite internal computations. *Termination* (more commonly known as *strong normalization* in the functional setting) is indeed a most desirable liveness property; in session-based concurrency, it may substantially improve the correctness guarantees provided by subject reduction and progress. Ensuring termination in concurrent calculi, however, is known to be hard: in (variants of) the π-calculus, proofs require heavy constraints on the language and/or its types, often relying on ad-hoc machineries (see [8] for a survey).

In the first part of this paper, we study termination in session-based concurrency. The starting point is our interpretation of (intutionistic) linear logic propositions as session types [4], which has provided the first purely logical account of session types. In the interpretation, types are assigned to names (denoting communication channels) and describe their session protocol. This way, an object of type $A \multimap B$ denotes a session that first inputs a session channel of type A, and then behaves as B—another interactive behavior. An object of type $A \otimes B$ denotes a session that first sends a session channel of type A and then behaves as B. The $!A$ type is interpreted as a type of a shared server for sessions of type A. The additive product and sum are interpreted as branch and choice session type operators, respectively. The type system distinguishes two kinds of type environments: a *linear* part Δ and an *unrestricted* part Γ, where weakening and contraction principles hold for Γ but not for Δ. A type judgment is then of the form $\Gamma; \Delta \vdash P :: z{:}C$, with Γ, Δ, and $z{:}C$ having pairwise disjoint domains. We refer to $\Gamma; \Delta$ and $z{:}C$ as the left- and right-hand side typings, respectively. Such a judgment asserts: process P implements session C along channel z, provided it is placed in an environment offering the sessions declared in Γ and Δ. The classic duality of session types is retained via the multiplicative/additive nature of linear logic propositions. This way, e.g., $\otimes$ and $\multimap$ are dual in that *using* a session of one type (in the left-hand side typing) is equivalent to *implementing* a type of the other (in the right-hand side typing).

The interpretation establishes a tight correspondence between session types for the π-calculus and intuitionistic linear logic: typing rules correspond to linear sequent calculus proof rules and, moreover, process reduction may be simulated by proof conversions and reductions, and vice versa. As a result, we obtain subject reduction from which session fidelity follows. The type system ensures global progress, beyond the restricted progress on a single session property obtained in pure session type systems. Examples illustrating the expressiveness of the type system can be found in [5,4].

Our main contribution is a simple theory of logical relations for session types. The method of logical relations has proved to be extremely productive in the functional setting; in fact, properties such as termination, various forms of equivalence, confluence, parametricity can be established via logical relations. In this presentation, we use logical relations to prove termination for session-typed processes. Although our interpretation assigns types to names (and not to terms, as in the typed λ-calculus), quite remarkably, we are able to define *linear* logical relations which are truly defined on the structure of types—as in logical relations for the typed λ-calculus [23,24]. A salient aspect of our proof is that it closely follows the principles of the (linear) type system. As hinted at above, this is in sharp contrast with known proofs of termination in the π-calculus. To our knowledge, ours is the first proof of termination of its kind in the context of session-based concurrency.

Certifying termination of session-typed interacting programs is very important in practice. In server-client interactions, for instance, it is critical for clients to be sure that running some piece of code provided by a server (say, code embedded in web pages of a cloud application) will not cause it to get stuck indefinitely (as in a denial-of-service attack, or just due to some bug). Furthermore, strengthening session-based type disciplines with termination guarantees should be highly beneficial for the increasingly growing number of implementations (libraries, programming language extensions) based on session types foundations—see, e.g., [12,17,20].

In the second part of the paper, we present two applications of the basic theory, which bear witness to its complementarity with the other properties derived from the interpretation. The applications rely on a notion of *typed observational equivalence*, which we define following the intuitive meaning of type judgements. The first application concerns the *proof conversions* induced by the logic interpretation. In [4] a set of such conversions was shown to correspond to either structural congruence or reduction in the π-calculus. The conversions we study here (not considered in [4]) cannot be explained similarly: they induce forms of "prefix commutation" on typed processes which appear rather counterintuitive. We prove *soundness* of the proof conversions with respect to the observational equivalence, i.e., processes induced by proof conversions are shown to be observationally equivalent. This result thus elegantly explains subtle forms of causality that arise in the (interleaved) execution of concurrent sessions. In our second application, we explain how *type isomorphisms* resulting from linear logic equivalences are realized by coercions between interface types of session-based concurrent systems. We provide a simple behavioral characterization of these isomorphisms, by relying on typed observational equivalence. Type isomorphisms can be seen as a validation of our interpretation with respect to basic linear logic principles. For instance, the apparent asymmetry in the interpretation of $A \otimes B$ is clarified here via an appropriate isomorphism. The two applications thus shed further light on the relationship between linear logic propositions and structured communications. Termination is central to both of them, intuitively because in the bisimulation game strong transitions can be matched by weak transitions which are always finite.

The rest of the paper is structured as follows. Section 2 presents our process model, a synchronous π-calculus with guarded choice. Section 3 recalls the type system derived from the logical interpretation and main results from [4]. Section 4 presents linear logical relations and the termination result. Section 5 introduces a typed observational equivalence for processes. Section 6 discusses soundness of proof conversions and type isomorphisms. Section 7 discusses related work and Section 8 collects final remarks.

2 Process Model: Syntax and Semantics

We introduce the syntax and operational semantics of the synchronous π-calculus [22] extended with (binary) guarded choice.

Definition 2.1 (Processes). *Given an infinite set Λ of* names (x, y, z, u, v), *the set of* processes (P, Q, R) *is defined by*

$$P ::= \mathbf{0} \mid P \mid Q \mid (\boldsymbol{\nu} y)P \mid x\langle y\rangle.P \mid x(y).P \mid !x(y).P \mid [x \leftrightarrow y] \mid x.\mathtt{inl};P \mid x.\mathtt{inr};P \mid x.\mathtt{case}(P, Q)$$

The operators $\mathbf{0}$ (inaction), $P \mid Q$ (parallel composition), and $(\boldsymbol{\nu}y)P$ (name restriction) comprise the static fragment of any π-calculus. We then have $x\langle y\rangle.P$ (send name y on x and proceed as P), $x(y).P$ (receive a name z on x and proceed as P with parameter y replaced by z), and $!x(y).P$ which denotes replicated (persistent) input. The forwarding construct $[x \leftrightarrow y]$ equates names x and y; it is a primitive representation of a copycat process, akin to the link processes used in internal mobility encodings of name passing [3]. Also, this construct allows for a simple identity axiom in the type system [25]. The remaining three operators define a minimal labeled choice mechanism, comparable to the n-ary branching constructs found in standard session π-calculi (see, e.g., [11]). Without loss of generality we restrict our model to binary choice. In restriction $(\boldsymbol{\nu}y)P$ and input $x(y).P$ the distinguished occurrence of name y is binding, with scope P. The set of *free names* of a process P is denoted $\mathit{fn}(P)$. A process is *closed* if it does not contain free occurrences of names. We identify process up to consistent renaming of bound names, writing $\equiv_\alpha$ for this congruence. We write $P\{x/y\}$ for the capture-avoiding substitution of x for y in P. While *structural congruence* expresses basic identities on the structure of processes, *reduction* expresses the behavior of processes.

Definition 2.2. Structural congruence *($P \equiv Q$) is the least congruence relation on processes such that*

$$
\begin{array}{ll}
P \mid \mathbf{0} \equiv P & P \equiv_\alpha Q \Rightarrow P \equiv Q \\
P \mid Q \equiv Q \mid P & P \mid (Q \mid R) \equiv (P \mid Q) \mid R \\
(\boldsymbol{\nu}x)\mathbf{0} \equiv \mathbf{0} & x \notin \mathit{fn}(P) \Rightarrow P \mid (\boldsymbol{\nu}x)Q \equiv (\boldsymbol{\nu}x)(P \mid Q) \\
(\boldsymbol{\nu}x)(\boldsymbol{\nu}y)P \equiv (\boldsymbol{\nu}y)(\boldsymbol{\nu}x)P & [x \leftrightarrow y] \equiv [y \leftrightarrow x]
\end{array}
$$

Definition 2.3. Reduction *($P \to Q$) is the binary relation on processes defined by:*

$$
\begin{array}{ll}
x\langle y\rangle.Q \mid x(z).P \to Q \mid P\{y/z\} & x\langle y\rangle.Q \mid !x(z).P \to Q \mid P\{y/z\} \mid !x(z).P \\
(\nu x)([x \leftrightarrow y] \mid P) \to P\{y/x\} \;\; (x \neq y) & Q \to Q' \Rightarrow P \mid Q \to P \mid Q' \\
P \to Q \Rightarrow (\boldsymbol{\nu}y)P \to (\boldsymbol{\nu}y)Q & P \equiv P',\, P' \to Q',\, Q' \equiv Q \Rightarrow P \to Q \\
x.\mathtt{inr}; P \mid x.\mathtt{case}(Q, R) \to P \mid R & x.\mathtt{inl}; P \mid x.\mathtt{case}(Q, R) \to P \mid Q
\end{array}
$$

By definition, reduction is closed under $\equiv$. It specifies the computations a process performs on its own. To characterize the interactions of a process with its environment, we extend the early transition system for the π-calculus [22] with labels and transition rules for the choice and forwarding constructs. A transition $P \xrightarrow{\alpha} Q$ denotes that P may evolve to Q by performing the action represented by label α. Labels are given by

$$
\alpha ::= x(y) \mid \overline{x\langle y\rangle} \mid \overline{(\nu y)x\langle y\rangle} \mid x.\mathsf{inl} \mid \overline{x.\mathsf{inl}} \mid x.\mathsf{inr} \mid \overline{x.\mathsf{inr}} \mid \tau
$$

Actions are input $x(y)$, the left/right offers $x.\mathsf{inl}$ and $x.\mathsf{inr}$, and their matching co-actions, respectively the output $\overline{x\langle y\rangle}$ and bound output $\overline{(\boldsymbol{\nu}y)x\langle y\rangle}$ actions, and the left/right selections $\overline{x.\mathsf{inl}}$ and $\overline{x.\mathsf{inr}}$. The bound output $\overline{(\boldsymbol{\nu}y)x\langle y\rangle}$ denotes extrusion of a fresh name y along (channel) x. Internal action is denoted by τ. In general, an action α ($\overline{\alpha}$) requires a matching $\overline{\alpha}$ (α) in the environment to enable progress, as specified by the transition rules. For a label α, we define the sets $\mathit{fn}(\alpha)$ and $\mathit{bn}(\alpha)$ of free and bound names, respectively, as usual. We denote by $s(\alpha)$ the subject of α (e.g., x in $x\langle y\rangle$).

(out) $x\langle y\rangle.P \xrightarrow{x\langle y\rangle} P$ (in) $x(y).P \xrightarrow{x(z)} P\{z/y\}$ (id) $(\nu x)([x \leftrightarrow y] \mid P) \xrightarrow{\tau} P\{y/x\}$

(par) $$\frac{P \xrightarrow{\alpha} Q}{P \mid R \xrightarrow{\alpha} Q \mid R}$$ (com) $$\frac{P \xrightarrow{\overline{\alpha}} P' \quad Q \xrightarrow{\alpha} Q'}{P \mid Q \xrightarrow{\tau} P' \mid Q'}$$ (res) $$\frac{P \xrightarrow{\alpha} Q}{(\nu y)P \xrightarrow{\alpha} (\nu y)Q}$$

(open) $$\frac{P \xrightarrow{\overline{x\langle y\rangle}} Q}{(\nu y)P \xrightarrow{\overline{(\nu y)x\langle y\rangle}} Q}$$ (close) $$\frac{P \xrightarrow{\overline{(\nu y)x\langle y\rangle}} P' \quad Q \xrightarrow{x(y)} Q'}{P \mid Q \xrightarrow{\tau} (\nu y)(P' \mid Q')}$$ (rep) $!x(y).P \xrightarrow{x(z)} P\{z/y\} \mid !x(y).P$

(lout) $x.\mathtt{inl};P \xrightarrow{\overline{x.\mathsf{inl}}} P$ (rout) $x.\mathtt{inr};P \xrightarrow{\overline{x.\mathsf{inr}}} P$ (lin) $x.\mathsf{case}(P,Q) \xrightarrow{x.\mathsf{inl}} P$ (rin) $x.\mathsf{case}(P,Q) \xrightarrow{x.\mathsf{inr}} Q$

Fig. 1. π-calculus Labeled Transition System

Definition 2.4 (Labeled Transition System). *The relation* labeled transition *($P \xrightarrow{\alpha} Q$) is defined by the rules in Fig. 1, subject to the side conditions: in rule* (res), *we require $y \notin fn(\alpha)$; in rule* (par), *we require $bn(\alpha) \cap fn(R) = \emptyset$; in rule* (close), *we require $y \notin fn(Q)$. We omit the symmetric versions of rules* (par), (com), *and* (close).

We write $\rho_1\rho_2$ for the composition of relations ρ_1, ρ_2. Weak transitions are defined as usual: we write $\Longrightarrow$ for the reflexive, transitive closure of $\xrightarrow{\tau}$. Given $\alpha \neq \tau$, notation $\overset{\alpha}{\Longrightarrow}$ stands for $\Longrightarrow\xrightarrow{\alpha}\Longrightarrow$ and $\overset{\tau}{\Longrightarrow}$ stands for $\Longrightarrow$. We recall some basic facts about reduction, structural congruence, and labeled transition: closure of labeled transitions under structural congruence, and coincidence of τ-labeled transition and reduction [22]: (1) if $P \equiv\xrightarrow{\alpha} Q$ then $P \xrightarrow{\alpha}\equiv Q$, and (2) $P \to Q$ if and only if $P \xrightarrow{\tau}\equiv Q$.

3 Session Types as Dual Intutionistic Linear Logic Propositions

As anticipated in the introduction, the type structure coincides with intuitionistic linear logic [10,2], omitting atomic formulas and the additive constants $\top$ and $\mathbf{0}$.

Definition 3.1 (Types). *Types (A, B, C) are given by*

$$A, B ::= \mathbf{1} \mid !A \mid A \otimes B \mid A \multimap B \mid A \mathbin{\&} B \mid A \oplus B$$

Types are assigned to (channel) names, and are interpreted as a form of session types; an assignment $x{:}A$ enforces the use of name x according to discipline A. $A \otimes B$ types a session channel that first performs an output to its partner (sending a session channel of type A) before proceeding as specified by B. Similarly, $A \multimap B$ types a session channel that first performs an input from its partner (receiving a session channel of type A) before proceeding as specified by B. Type $\mathbf{1}$ means that the session terminated, no further interaction will take place on it; names of type $\mathbf{1}$ may still be passed around in sessions, as opaque values. $A \& B$ types a session channel that offers its partner a choice between an A behavior ("left" choice) and a B behavior ("right" choice). Dually, $A \oplus B$ types a session that either selects "left" and then proceeds as specified by A, or

$$\frac{}{\Gamma; x{:}A \vdash [x \leftrightarrow z] :: z{:}A}\ (\mathsf{Tid}) \qquad \frac{\Gamma; \Delta \vdash P :: T}{\Gamma; \Delta, x{:}\mathbf{1} \vdash P :: T}\ (\mathrm{T1L}) \qquad \frac{}{\Gamma; \cdot \vdash \mathbf{0} :: x{:}\mathbf{1}}\ (\mathrm{T1R})$$

$$\frac{\Gamma; \Delta, y{:}A, x{:}B \vdash P :: T}{\Gamma; \Delta, x{:}A \otimes B \vdash x(y).P :: T}\ (\mathrm{T}\otimes\mathrm{L}) \qquad \frac{\Gamma; \Delta \vdash P :: y{:}A \quad \Gamma; \Delta' \vdash Q :: x{:}B}{\Gamma; \Delta, \Delta' \vdash (\nu y)x\langle y\rangle.(P \mid Q) :: x{:}A \otimes B}\ (\mathrm{T}\otimes\mathrm{R})$$

$$\frac{\Gamma; \Delta \vdash P :: y{:}A \quad \Gamma; \Delta', x{:}B \vdash Q :: T}{\Gamma; \Delta, \Delta', x{:}A \multimap B \vdash (\nu y)x\langle y\rangle.(P \mid Q) :: T}\ (\mathrm{T}\multimap\mathrm{L}) \qquad \frac{\Gamma; \Delta, y{:}A \vdash P :: x{:}B}{\Gamma; \Delta \vdash x(y).P :: x{:}A \multimap B}\ (\mathrm{T}\multimap\mathrm{R})$$

$$\frac{\Gamma; \Delta \vdash P :: x{:}A \quad \Gamma; \Delta', x{:}A \vdash Q :: T}{\Gamma; \Delta, \Delta' \vdash (\nu x)(P \mid Q) :: T}\ (\mathsf{Tcut}) \qquad \frac{\Gamma; \cdot \vdash P :: y{:}A \quad \Gamma, u{:}A; \Delta \vdash Q :: T}{\Gamma; \Delta \vdash (\nu u)(!u(y).P \mid Q) :: T}\ (\mathsf{Tcut}^!)$$

$$\frac{\Gamma, u{:}A; \Delta, y{:}A \vdash P :: T}{\Gamma, u{:}A; \Delta \vdash (\nu y)u\langle y\rangle.P :: T}\ (\mathsf{Tcopy})$$

$$\frac{\Gamma, u{:}A; \Delta \vdash P\{u/x\} :: T}{\Gamma; \Delta, x{:}!A \vdash P :: T}\ (\mathrm{T!L}) \qquad \frac{\Gamma; \cdot \vdash Q :: y{:}A}{\Gamma; \cdot \vdash !x(y).Q :: x{:}!A}\ (\mathrm{T!R})$$

$$\frac{\Gamma; \Delta, x{:}A \vdash P :: T \quad \Gamma; \Delta, x{:}B \vdash Q :: T}{\Gamma; \Delta, x{:}A \oplus B \vdash x.\mathtt{case}(P, Q) :: T}\ (\mathrm{T}\oplus\mathrm{L}) \qquad \frac{\Gamma; \Delta \vdash P :: x{:}A \quad \Gamma; \Delta \vdash Q :: x{:}B}{\Gamma; \Delta \vdash x.\mathtt{case}(P, Q) :: x{:}A \,\&\, B}\ (\mathrm{T\&R})$$

$$\frac{\Gamma; \Delta, x{:}A \vdash P :: T}{\Gamma; \Delta, x{:}A \,\&\, B \vdash x.\mathtt{inl}; P :: T}\ (\mathrm{T\&L_1}) \qquad \frac{\Gamma; \Delta \vdash P :: x{:}A}{\Gamma; \Delta \vdash x.\mathtt{inl}; P :: x{:}A \oplus B}\ (\mathrm{T}\oplus\mathrm{R_1})$$

$$\frac{\Gamma; \Delta, x{:}B \vdash P :: T}{\Gamma; \Delta, x{:}A \,\&\, B \vdash x.\mathtt{inr}; P :: T}\ (\mathrm{T\&L_2}) \qquad \frac{\Gamma; \Delta \vdash P :: x{:}B}{\Gamma; \Delta \vdash x.\mathtt{inr}; P :: x{:}A \oplus B}\ (\mathrm{T}\oplus\mathrm{R_2})$$

Fig. 2. The Type System $\pi\mathtt{DILL}$

else selects "right", and then proceeds as specified by B. Type $!A$ types a shared (non-linearized) channel, to be used by a server for spawning an arbitrary number of new sessions (possibly none), each one conforming to type A.

A type environment is a collection of type assignments of the form $x{:}A$, where x is a name and A a type, the names being pairwise disjoint. Two kinds of type environments are subject to different structural properties: a *linear* part Δ and an *unrestricted* part Γ, where weakening and contraction principles hold for Γ but not for Δ. A type judgment is of the form $\Gamma; \Delta \vdash P :: z{:}C$ where name declarations in Γ are always propagated unchanged to all premises in the typing rules, while name declarations in Δ are handled multiplicatively or additively, depending on the nature of the type being defined. The domains of Γ, Δ and $z{:}C$ are required to be pairwise disjoint. Such a judgment asserts: P is ensured to safely provide a usage of name z according to the behavior specified by type C, whenever composed with any process environment providing usages of names according to the behaviors specified by names in $\Gamma; \Delta$. As shown in [4], in our case safety ensures that behavior is free of communication errors and deadlock. A client Q that relies on external services and does not provide any is typed as $\Gamma; \Delta \vdash Q :: -{:}\mathbf{1}$. In general, a process P such that $\Gamma; \Delta \vdash P :: z{:}C$ represents a system providing behavior C at channel z, building on "services" declared in $\Gamma; \Delta$. A system typed as $\Gamma; \Delta \vdash R :: z{:}!A$ represents a shared server. Interestingly, the asymmetry induced by the intuitionistic interpretation of $!A$ enforces locality of shared names but not of linear (session names), which exactly corresponds to the intended model of sessions.

The rules of our type system πDILL are given in Fig. 2. We use T, S for right-hand side singleton environments (e.g., $z{:}C$). Rule (Tid) defines identity in terms of the forwarding construct. Since in rule (T$\otimes$R) the sent name is always fresh, our typed calculus conforms to an internal mobility discipline [3], without loss of expressiveness. The composition rules (Tcut/Tcut$^!$) follow the "composition plus hiding" principle [1], extended to a name passing setting. Other linear typing rules for parallel composition (as in, e.g., [13]) are derivable—see [4]. As we consider π-calculus terms up to structural congruence, typability is closed under $\equiv$ by definition. πDILL enjoys the usual properties of equivariance, weakening, and contraction in Γ. The coverage property also holds: if $\Gamma; \Delta \vdash P :: z{:}A$ then $fn(P) \subseteq \Gamma \cup \Delta \cup \{z\}$. In the presence of type-annotated restrictions $(\nu x{:}A)P$, as usual in typed π-calculi [22], type-checking is decidable.

Session type constructors thus correspond directly to intuitionistic linear logic connectives. By erasing processes, typing judgments in πDILL correspond to DILL, a sequent formulation of Barber's dual intuitionistic linear logic [2,6]. Below we only provide some intuitions of this correspondence; see [4] for details.

DILL is equipped with a faithful proof term assignment, so sequents have the form $\Gamma; \Delta \vdash D : C$, where Γ is the unrestricted context, Δ the linear context, C a formula (= type), and D the proof term that faithfully represents the derivation of $\Gamma; \Delta \vdash C$. Given the parallel structure of the two systems, if $\Gamma; \Delta \vdash D{:}A$ is derivable in DILL then there is a process P and a name z such that $\Gamma; \Delta \vdash P :: z{:}A$ is derivable in πDILL. The converse also holds: if $\Gamma; \Delta \vdash P :: z{:}A$ is derivable in πDILL there is a derivation D that proves $\Gamma; \Delta \vdash D : A$. This correspondence is made explicit by a translation from faithful proof terms to processes: given $\Gamma; \Delta \vdash D : C$, we write $\hat{D}^z$ for the translation of D such that $\Gamma; \Delta \vdash \hat{D}^z :: z{:}C$. More precisely, we have *typed extraction*: we write $\Gamma; \Delta \vdash D \rightsquigarrow P :: z{:}A$, meaning "proof D extracts to P", whenever $\Gamma; \Delta \vdash D : A$ and $\Gamma; \Delta \vdash P :: z{:}A$ and $P \equiv \hat{D}^z$. Typed extraction is unique up to structural congruence. As processes are related by structural and computational rules, namely those involved in the definition of $\equiv$ and $\rightarrow$, derivations in DILL are related by structural and computational rules, that express certain sound proof transformations that arise in cut-elimination. Reductions generally take place when a right rule meets a left rule for the same connective, and correspond to reduction steps in the process term assignment. Similarly, structural conversions in DILL correspond to structural equivalences in the π-calculus, since they just change the order of cuts.

We now recall some main results from [4]: *subject reduction* and *progress*. For any P, define $live(P)$ iff $P \equiv (\nu \widetilde{n})(\pi.Q \mid R)$, for some sequence of names $\widetilde{n}$, a process R, and a *non-replicated* guarded process $\pi.Q$.

Theorem 3.2 (Subject Reduction). *If* $\Gamma; \Delta \vdash P{::}z{:}A$ *and* $P{\rightarrow}Q$ *then* $\Gamma; \Delta \vdash Q{::}z{:}A$.

Theorem 3.3 (Progress). *If* $\cdot; \cdot \vdash P{::}z{:}\mathbf{1}$ *and* $live(P)$ *then exists a* Q *such that* $P \rightarrow Q$.

4 Linear Logical Relations and Termination of Typed Processes

A process P *terminates* (written $P\Downarrow$) if there is no infinite reduction path from P. Here we introduce a theory of *linear* logical relations for session types, and use it to prove that well-typed processes always terminate. The proof can be summarized into two steps:

(i) Definition of a logical predicate on processes, by induction on the structure of types. Processes in the predicate are terminating by definition. (ii) Proof that every well-typed process is in the logical predicate.

We begin by stating an extension to $\equiv$, which will be useful in our developments.

Definition 4.1. *We write* $\equiv_!$ *for the least congruence relation on processes which results from extending structural congruence* $\equiv$ *(Def. 2.2) with the following axioms:*

1. $(\nu u)(!u(z).P \mid (\nu y)(Q \mid R)) \equiv_! (\nu y)((\nu u)(!u(z).P \mid Q) \mid (\nu u)(!u(z).P \mid R))$
2. $(\nu u)(!u(y).P \mid (\nu v)(!v(z).Q \mid R))$
   $\equiv_! (\nu v)((!v(z).(\nu u)(!u(y).P \mid Q)) \mid (\nu u)(!u(y).P \mid R))$
3. $(\nu u)(!u(y).Q \mid P) \equiv_! P$ *if* $u \notin fn(P)$

These axioms are called the *sharpened replication axioms* [22] and are known to express sound behavioral equivalences up to strong bisimilarity in our typed setting. Intuitively, (1) and (2) represent principles for the distribution of shared servers among processes, while (3) formalizes the garbage collection of shared servers which cannot be invoked by any process. Notice that $\equiv_!$ was defined in [4] (Def 4.3), and noted $\simeq_s$.

Proposition 4.2. *Let* P *and* Q *be well-typed processes.*

1. *If* $P \longrightarrow P'$ *and* $P \equiv_! Q$ *then there is* Q' *such that* $Q \longrightarrow Q'$ *and* $P' \equiv_! Q'$*.*
2. *If* $P \xrightarrow{\alpha} P'$ *and* $P \equiv_! Q$ *then there is* Q' *such that* $Q \xrightarrow{\alpha} Q'$ *and* $P' \equiv_! Q'$*.*

Proposition 4.3. *If* $P\Downarrow$ *and* $P \equiv_! Q$ *then* $Q\Downarrow$*.*

First Step: The Logical Predicate and its Closure Properties. We define a logical predicate on well-typed processes and establish a few associated closure properties. More precisely, we define a sequent-indexed family of sets of processes (process predicates) so that a set of processes $\mathcal{L}[\Gamma; \Delta \vdash T]$ enjoying certain closure properties is assigned to any sequent $\Gamma; \Delta \vdash T$. The logical predicate is defined by induction on the structure of sequents. The base case, given below, considers sequents with empty left-hand side typing, where we abbreviate $\mathcal{L}[\Gamma; \Delta \vdash T]$ by $\mathcal{L}[T]$. We write $P \not\longrightarrow$ to mean that P cannot reduce; it can perform visible actions, though.

Definition 4.4 (Logical Predicate - Base case). *For any type* $T = z{:}A$ *we inductively define* $\mathcal{L}[T]$ *as the set of all processes* P *such that* $P\Downarrow$ *and* $\cdot; \cdot \vdash P :: T$ *and*

$$P \in \mathcal{L}[z{:}\mathbf{1}] \text{ if } \forall P'.(P \Longrightarrow P' \wedge P' \not\longrightarrow) \Rightarrow P' \equiv_! \mathbf{0}$$

$$P \in \mathcal{L}[z{:}A \multimap B] \text{ if } \forall P' y.(P \overset{z(y)}{\Longrightarrow} P') \Rightarrow \forall Q \in \mathcal{L}[y{:}A].(\nu y)(P' \mid Q) \in \mathcal{L}[z{:}B]$$

$$P \in \mathcal{L}[z{:}A \otimes B] \text{ if } \forall P' y.(P \overset{\overline{(\nu y)z\langle y\rangle}}{\Longrightarrow} P') \Rightarrow$$
$$\exists P_1, P_2.(P' \equiv_! P_1 \mid P_2 \wedge P_1 \in \mathcal{L}[y{:}A] \wedge P_2 \in \mathcal{L}[z{:}B])$$

$$P \in \mathcal{L}[z{:}!A] \text{ if } \forall P'.(P \Longrightarrow P') \Rightarrow \exists P_1.(P' \equiv_! !z(y).P_1 \wedge P_1 \in \mathcal{L}[y{:}A])$$

$$P \in \mathcal{L}[z{:}A \,\&\, B] \text{ if } (\forall P'.(P \overset{z.\mathsf{inl}}{\Longrightarrow} P') \Rightarrow P' \in \mathcal{L}[z{:}A])$$
$$\wedge (\forall P'.(P \overset{z.\mathsf{inr}}{\Longrightarrow} P') \Rightarrow P' \in \mathcal{L}[z{:}B])$$

$$P \in \mathcal{L}[z{:}A \oplus B] \text{ if } (\forall P'.(P \overset{\overline{z.\mathsf{inl}}}{\Longrightarrow} P') \Rightarrow P' \in \mathcal{L}[z{:}A])$$
$$\wedge (\forall P'.(P \overset{\overline{z.\mathsf{inr}}}{\Longrightarrow} P') \Rightarrow P' \in \mathcal{L}[z{:}B])$$

Some comments are in order. First, observe how the definition of $\mathcal{L}[T]$ relies on both reductions and labeled transitions, and the fact that processes in the logical predicate are terminating by definition. Also, notice that the use of $\equiv_!$ in $\mathcal{L}[z{:}\mathbf{1}]$ is justified by the fact that a terminated process may be well the composition of a number of shared servers with no potential clients. Using suitable processes that "close" the derivative of the transition, in $\mathcal{L}[z{:}A \multimap B]$ and $\mathcal{L}[z{:}A \otimes B]$ we adhere to the linear logic interpretations for input and output types, respectively. In particular, in $\mathcal{L}[z{:}A \otimes B]$ it is worth observing how $\equiv_!$ is used to "split" the derivative of the transition, thus preserving consistency with the separate, non-interfering nature of the multiplicative conjunction. The definition of $\mathcal{L}[z{:}!A]$ is also rather structural, relying again on the distribution principles embodied in $\equiv_!$. The definition of $\mathcal{L}[z{:}A \,\&\, B]$ and $\mathcal{L}[z{:}A \oplus B]$ are self-explanatory.

Below, we extend the logical predicate to arbitrary typing environments. Observe how we adhere to the principles of rules (Tcut) and (Tcut!) for this purpose.

Definition 4.5 (Logical Predicate - Inductive case). *For any sequent $\Gamma; \Delta \vdash T$ with a non-empty left hand side environment, we define $\mathcal{L}[\Gamma; \Delta \vdash T]$ to be the set of processes inductively defined as follows:*

$$P \in \mathcal{L}[\Gamma; y{:}A, \Delta \vdash T] \text{ if } \forall R \in \mathcal{L}[y{:}A].(\nu y)(R \mid P) \in \mathcal{L}[\Gamma; \Delta \vdash T]$$
$$P \in \mathcal{L}[u{:}A, \Gamma; \Delta \vdash T] \text{ if } \forall R \in \mathcal{L}[y{:}A].(\nu u)(!u(y).R \mid P) \in \mathcal{L}[\Gamma; \Delta \vdash T]$$

We often rely on the following alternative characterization of the sets $\mathcal{L}[\Gamma; \Delta \vdash T]$.

Definition 4.6. *Let $\Gamma = u_1{:}B_1, \ldots, u_k{:}B_k$, and $\Delta = x_1{:}A_1, \ldots, x_n{:}A_n$ be a non-linear and a linear typing environment, resp. Letting $I = \{1, \ldots, k\}$ and $J = \{1, \ldots, n\}$, we define the sets of processes $\mathcal{C}_\Gamma$ and $\mathcal{C}_\Delta$ as:*

$$\mathcal{C}_\Gamma \stackrel{def}{=} \{\prod_{i \in I} !u_i(y_i).R_i \mid R_i \in \mathcal{L}[y_i{:}B_i]\} \qquad \mathcal{C}_\Delta \stackrel{def}{=} \{\prod_{j \in J} Q_j \mid Q_j \in \mathcal{L}[x_j{:}A_j]\}$$

Because of the rôle of left-hand side typing environments, processes in $\mathcal{C}_\Gamma$ and $\mathcal{C}_\Delta$ are then logical representatives of the behavior specified by Γ and Δ, respectively.

Proposition 4.7. *Let Γ and Δ be a non-linear and a linear typing environment, resp. Then, for all $Q \in \mathcal{C}_\Gamma$ and for all $R \in \mathcal{C}_\Delta$, we have $Q\Downarrow$ and $R\Downarrow$. Moreover, $Q \not\longrightarrow$.*

The proof of the following lemma is immediate from Definitions 4.5 and 4.6.

Lemma 4.8. *Let $\Gamma; \Delta \vdash P{::}T$, with $\Gamma{=}u_1{:}B_1, \ldots, u_k{:}B_k$ and $\Delta{=}x_1{:}A_1, \ldots, x_n{:}A_n$. We have: $P \in \mathcal{L}[\Gamma; \Delta \vdash T]$ iff $\forall Q \in \mathcal{C}_\Gamma, \forall R \in \mathcal{C}_\Delta, (\nu \widetilde{u}, \widetilde{x})(P \mid Q \mid R) \in \mathcal{L}[T]$.*

The following closure properties will be of the essence in the second step of the proof, when we will show that well-typed processes are in the logical predicate. We first state closure of $\mathcal{L}[T]$ with respect to substitution and structural congruence:

Proposition 4.9. *Let A be a type. If $P \in \mathcal{L}[z{:}A]$ then $P\{x/z\} \in \mathcal{L}[x{:}A]$.*

Proposition 4.10. *Let P, Q be well-typed. If $P \in \mathcal{L}[T]$ and $P \equiv Q$ then $Q \in \mathcal{L}[T]$.*

The next proposition provides a basic liveness guarantee for certain typed processes.

Proposition 4.11. *Let $P \in \mathcal{L}[z{:}T]$ with $T \in \{A \otimes B, A \multimap B, A \oplus B, A \,\&\, B\}$. Then, there exist α, P' such that (i) $P \stackrel{\alpha}{\Longrightarrow} P'$, and (ii) if $T{=}A \otimes B$ then $\alpha = \overline{(\nu y)z\langle y\rangle}$; if $T{=}A \multimap B$ then $\alpha = z(y)$; if $T{=}A \oplus B$ then $\alpha = \overline{z.\mathsf{inr}}$ or $\alpha = \overline{z.\mathsf{inl}}$; if $T{=}A \,\&\, B$ then $\alpha = z.\mathsf{inr}$ or $\alpha = z.\mathsf{inl}$.*

We now extend Proposition 4.10 so as to state closure of $\mathcal{L}[T]$ under $\equiv_!$.

Proposition 4.12. *Let P, Q be well-typed. If $P \in \mathcal{L}[T]$ and $P \equiv_! Q$ then $Q \in \mathcal{L}[T]$.*

We now state *forward* and *backward* closure of the logical predicate with respect to reduction; these are typical ingredients in the method of logical relations.

Proposition 4.13 (Forward Closure). *If $P \in \mathcal{L}[T]$ and $P \longrightarrow P'$ then $P' \in \mathcal{L}[T]$.*

Proposition 4.14 (Backward Closure). *If for all P_i such that $P \longrightarrow P_i$ we have $P_i \in \mathcal{L}[T]$ then $P \in \mathcal{L}[T]$.*

The final closure property concerns parallel composition of processes:

Proposition 4.15 (Weakening). *Let P, Q be processes such that $P \in \mathcal{L}[T]$ and $Q \in \mathcal{L}[-{:}\mathbf{1}]$. Then, $P \mid Q \in \mathcal{L}[T]$.*

Second Step: Well-typed Processes are in the Logical Predicate. We now prove that well-typed processes are in the logical predicate. Because of the definition of the predicate, termination of well-typed processes will follow as a consequence.

Lemma 4.16. *Let P be a process. If $\Gamma; \Delta \vdash P :: T$ then $P \in \mathcal{L}[\Gamma; \Delta \vdash T]$.*

Proof. By induction on the derivation of $\Gamma; \Delta \vdash P :: T$, with a case analysis on the last typing rule used. We have 18 cases to check; in all cases, we use Lemma 4.8 to show that every $M = (\nu \widetilde{u}, \widetilde{x})(P \mid G \mid D)$ with $G \in \mathcal{C}_\Gamma$ and $D \in \mathcal{C}_\Delta$, is in $\mathcal{L}[T]$. In case (Tid), we use Proposition 4.9 (closure wrt substitution) and Proposition 4.14 (backward closure). In cases (T⊗L), (T⊸L), (Tcopy), (T⊕L), (T&L$_1$), and (T&L$_2$), we proceed in two steps: first, using Proposition 4.13 (forward closure) we show that every M'' such that $M \Longrightarrow M''$ is in $\mathcal{L}[T]$; then, we use this result in combination with Proposition 4.14 (backward closure) to conclude that $M \in \mathcal{L}[T]$. In cases (T1R), (T⊗R), (T⊸R), (T!R), (T⊕R$_1$), and (T⊕R$_2$), we show that M conforms to a specific case of Definition 4.4. Case (T1L) uses Proposition 4.15 (weakening). Cases (T⊗L), (T⊸L), (T⊕L), and (T&L$_1$) use the liveness guarantee given by Proposition 4.11. Cases (Tcopy), (T!L), and (Tcut$^!$) use Proposition 4.10 (closure under $\equiv$). Cases (Tcut), (T⊸R), and (T!R) use Proposition 4.12 (closure under $\equiv_!$). See [18] for details. □

We now state the main result of this section: well-typed processes terminate.

Theorem 4.17 (Termination). *If $\Gamma; \Delta \vdash P :: T$ then $P\Downarrow$.*

Proof. Follows from previously proven facts. By assumption, we have $\Gamma; \Delta \vdash P :: T$. Using this and Lemma 4.16 we obtain $P \in \mathcal{L}[\Gamma; \Delta \vdash T]$. Pick any $G \in \mathcal{C}_\Gamma, D \in \mathcal{C}_\Delta$: combining $P \in \mathcal{L}[\Gamma; \Delta \vdash T]$ and Lemma 4.8 gives us $(\nu \widetilde{u}, \widetilde{x})(P \mid G \mid D) \in \mathcal{L}[T]$. By using this, together with Definition 4.4, we infer $(\nu \widetilde{u}, \widetilde{x})(P \mid G \mid D)\Downarrow$. Since Proposition 4.7 ensures that $G\Downarrow$ and $D\Downarrow$, this latter result allows us to conclude $P\Downarrow$. □

5 An Observational Equivalence for Typed Processes

Here we introduce *typed context bisimilarity*, an observational equivalence over typed processes. It is defined contextually, as a binary relation indexed over sequents. Roughly, typed context bisimilarity equates two processes if, once coupled with all of their requirements (as described by the left-hand side typing), they perform the same actions (as described by the right-hand side typing). To formalize this intuition, we rely on a combination of inductive and coinductive arguments. The base case of the definition covers the cases in which the left-hand side typing environment is empty (i.e., the process requires nothing from its context to execute): the bisimulation game is then defined by induction on the structure of the (right-hand side) typing, following the expected behavior in each case. The inductive case covers the cases in which the left-hand side typing environment is not empty: the tested processes are put in parallel with processes implementing the behaviors described in the left-hand side typing.

Below, we use $\mathcal{S}$ to range over sequents of the form $\Gamma; \Delta \vdash T$. In the following, we write $\vdash T$ to stand for $\cdot\,; \cdot \vdash T$. The definition of typed context bisimilarity relies on *type-respecting* relations, which are indexed by sequents $\mathcal{S}$.

Definition 5.1 (Type-respecting relations). *A* type-respecting binary relation *over processes, written $\{\mathcal{R}_\mathcal{S}\}_\mathcal{S}$, is defined as a family of relations over processes indexed by $\mathcal{S}$. We often write $\mathcal{R}$ to refer to the whole family. We write $\Gamma; \Delta \vdash P \,\mathcal{R}\, Q :: T$ to mean that (i) $\Gamma; \Delta \vdash P :: T$ and $\Gamma; \Delta \vdash Q :: T$, and (ii) $(P, Q) \in \mathcal{R}_{\Gamma;\Delta\vdash T}$.*

Definition 5.2 (Typed Context Bisimilarity). *A symmetric type-respecting binary relation over processes $\mathcal{R}$ is a* typed context bisimulation *if*
Base Cases

Tau $\vdash P \,\mathcal{R}\, Q :: T$ *implies that for all P' such that $P \xrightarrow{\tau} P'$, there exists a Q' such that $Q \Longrightarrow Q'$ and $\vdash P' \,\mathcal{R}\, Q' :: T$*

Input $\vdash P \,\mathcal{R}\, Q :: x{:}A \multimap B$ *implies that for all P' such that $P \xrightarrow{x(y)} P'$, there exists a Q' such that $Q \overset{x(y)}{\Longrightarrow} Q'$ and for all R such that $\vdash R :: y{:}A$, $\vdash (\nu y)(P' \mid R) \,\mathcal{R}\, (\nu y)(Q' \mid R) :: x{:}B$.*

Output $\vdash P \,\mathcal{R}\, Q :: x{:}A \otimes B$ *implies that for all P' such that $P \xrightarrow{\overline{(\nu y)x\langle y\rangle}} P'$, there exists a Q' such that $Q \overset{\overline{(\nu y)x\langle y\rangle}}{\Longrightarrow} Q'$ and for all R such that $\cdot; y{:}A \vdash R :: -{:}\mathbf{1}$, $\vdash (\nu y)(P' \mid R) \,\mathcal{R}\, (\nu y)(Q' \mid R) :: x{:}B$.*

Replication $\vdash P \,\mathcal{R}\, Q :: x{:}!A$ *implies that for all P' such that $P \xrightarrow{x(z)} P'$, there exists a Q' such that $Q \overset{x(z)}{\Longrightarrow} Q'$ and, for all R such that $\cdot; y{:}A \vdash R :: -{:}\mathbf{1}$, $\vdash (\nu z)(P' \mid R) \,\mathcal{R}\, (\nu z)(Q' \mid R) :: x{:}!A$.*

Choice $\vdash P \,\mathcal{R}\, Q :: x{:}A \mathbin{\&} B$ *implies both:*
- *If $P \xrightarrow{x.\mathsf{inl}} P'$ then $\vdash P' \,\mathcal{R}\, Q' :: x{:}A$, for some Q' such that $Q \overset{x.\mathsf{inl}}{\Longrightarrow} Q'$; and*
- *If $P \xrightarrow{x.\mathsf{inr}} P'$ then $\vdash P' \,\mathcal{R}\, Q' :: x{:}B$, for some Q' such that $Q \overset{x.\mathsf{inr}}{\Longrightarrow} Q'$.*

Selection $\vdash P \,\mathcal{R}\, Q :: x{:}A \oplus B$ *implies both:*
- *If $P \xrightarrow{\overline{x.\mathsf{inl}}} P'$ then $\vdash P' \,\mathcal{R}\, Q' :: x{:}A$ for some Q' such that $Q \overset{\overline{x.\mathsf{inl}}}{\Longrightarrow} Q'$; and*
- *If $P \xrightarrow{\overline{x.\mathsf{inr}}} P'$ then $\vdash P' \,\mathcal{R}\, Q' :: x{:}B$ for some Q' such that $Q \overset{\overline{x.\mathsf{inr}}}{\Longrightarrow} Q'$.*

Inductive Cases

Linear Names $\Gamma; \Delta, y{:}A \vdash P \,\mathcal{R}\, Q :: T$ *implies that for all* R *such that* $\vdash R :: y{:}A$, *then* $\Gamma; \Delta \vdash (\nu y)(P \mid R) \,\mathcal{R}\, (\nu y)(Q \mid R) :: T$.

Shared Names $\Gamma, u{:}A; \Delta \vdash P \,\mathcal{R}\, Q :: T$ *implies that for all* R *such that* $\vdash R :: z{:}A$, *then* $\Gamma; \Delta \vdash (\nu u)(!u(z).R \mid P) \,\mathcal{R}\, (\nu u)(!u(z).R \mid Q) :: T$.

We write $\approx$ *for the union of all typed context bisimulations, and call it* typed context bisimilarity.

In all cases, a strong action is matched with a weak transition. In proofs, we shall exploit the fact that by virtue of Theorem 4.17 such a weak transition is always finite. In the base case, the clauses for input, output, and replication decree the closure of the tested processes with a process R that "complements" the continuation of the tested behavior; observe the very similar treatment for output and replication (where R *depends* on some behavior), and contrast it with that for input (where R *provides* the behavior). Also, notice how all clauses but that for replication are defined coinductively for the tested processes (in the sense that closed evolutions should be in the relation), but inductively on the type indexing the relation—the clause for replication may be thus considered as the only fully coinductive one. Also worth noticing is how the closures defined in such clauses (and those defined by the clauses in the inductive case) follow closely the spirit of (Tcut/Tcut$^!$) rules in the type system.

Definition 5.2 immediately suggests a proof technique for typed context bisimilarity. First, close the processes with representatives of their context, applying repeatedly the inductive case until the left-hand side typing is empty. Then, following the usual co-inductive proof technique, show a type-respecting relation containing the processes obtained in the first step. The following results are useful to realize these intuitions.

We use K, K' to range over *(process) contexts*, i.e., processes with a hole $[\cdot]$. In particular, we use parallel contexts: contexts in which the hole can only occur in parallel.

Definition 5.3. *Let* Γ *and* Δ *be non-empty typing environments. The set of parallel contexts* $\mathcal{K}_{\Gamma;\Delta}$ *is defined by induction on the typing environments as follows:*

$$K \in \mathcal{K}_{\emptyset;\emptyset} \text{ if } K = [\cdot]$$
$$K \in \mathcal{K}_{\Gamma,u:B;\,\Delta} \text{ if } K \equiv (\nu u)(K' \mid !u(y).R) \quad \text{for some } K' \in \mathcal{K}_{\Gamma;\Delta} \text{ and } \vdash R :: y{:}B$$
$$K \in \mathcal{K}_{\Gamma;\,\Delta,x:A} \text{ if } K \equiv (\nu x)(K' \mid S) \quad \text{for some } K' \in \mathcal{K}_{\Gamma;\Delta} \text{ and } \vdash S :: x{:}A$$

Proposition 5.4. *Let* $\Gamma = u_1{:}B_1, \ldots, u_k{:}B_k$ *and* $\Delta = x_1{:}A_1, \ldots, x_n{:}A_n$ *be typing environments. Letting* $I = \{1, \ldots, k\}$ *and* $J = \{1, \ldots, n\}$, *we say that* $K \in \mathcal{K}_{\Gamma;\Delta}$ *if*

$$K \equiv (\nu \tilde{u}, \tilde{x})([\cdot] \mid \prod_{i \in I} !u_i(y_i).R_i \mid \prod_{j \in J} S_j) \quad \text{with } \vdash R_i :: y_i{:}B_i \text{ and } \vdash S_j :: x_j{:}A_j$$

The following proposition allows us to move from an (inductive) proof under non-empty typing environments Γ, Δ to a (coinductive) proof under empty environments, with pairs of processes within parallel contexts in $\mathcal{K}_{\Gamma;\Delta}$.

Proposition 5.5. $\Gamma; \Delta \vdash P \approx Q :: T$ *implies* $\vdash K[P] \approx K[Q] :: T$, *for every parallel context* $K \in \mathcal{K}_{\Gamma;\Delta}$.

$$
\begin{aligned}
(\nu x)(\hat{D} \mid (\nu y)z\langle y\rangle.(\hat{E} \mid \hat{F})) &\simeq_c (\nu y)z\langle y\rangle.((\nu x)(\hat{D} \mid \hat{E}) \mid \hat{F}) \\
(\nu x)(\hat{D} \mid y(z).\hat{E}) &\simeq_c y(z).(\nu x)(\hat{D} \mid \hat{E}) \\
(\nu x)(\hat{D} \mid y.\mathtt{inl}; \hat{E}) &\simeq_c y.\mathtt{inl}; (\nu x)(\hat{D} \mid \hat{E}) \\
(\nu x)(\hat{D} \mid (\nu y)u\langle y\rangle.\hat{E}) &\simeq_c (\nu y)u\langle y\rangle.(\nu x)(\hat{D} \mid \hat{E}) \\
(\nu x)(\hat{D} \mid y.\mathtt{case}(\hat{E}, \hat{F})) &\simeq_c y.\mathtt{case}((\nu x)(\hat{D} \mid \hat{E}), (\nu x)(\hat{D} \mid \hat{F})) \\
(\nu u)((!u(y).\hat{D}) \mid \mathbf{0}) &\simeq_c \mathbf{0} \\
(\nu u)((!u(y).\hat{D}) \mid (\nu z)x\langle z\rangle.(\hat{E} \mid \hat{F})) &\simeq_c (\nu z)x\langle z\rangle.((\nu u)((!u(y).\hat{D}) \mid \hat{E}) \mid (\nu u)((!u(y).\hat{D}) \mid \hat{F})) \\
(\nu u)((!u(y).\hat{D}) \mid y(z).\hat{E}) &\simeq_c y(z).(\nu u)((!u(y).\hat{D}) \mid \hat{E}) \\
(\nu u)((!u(z).\hat{D}) \mid y.\mathtt{inl}; \hat{E}) &\simeq_c y.\mathtt{inl}; (\nu u)((!u(z).\hat{D}) \mid \hat{E}) \\
(\nu u)((!u(z).\hat{D}) \mid y.\mathtt{case}(\hat{E}, \hat{F})) &\simeq_c y.\mathtt{case}((\nu u)((!u(z).\hat{D}) \mid \hat{E}), (\nu u)((!u(z).\hat{D}) \mid \hat{F})) \\
(\nu u)((!u(y).\hat{D}) \mid !x(z).\hat{E}) &\simeq_c !x(z).(\nu u)((!u(y).\hat{D}) \mid \hat{E}) \\
(\nu u)((!u(y).\hat{D}) \mid (\nu y)v\langle y\rangle.\hat{E}) &\simeq_c (\nu y)v\langle y\rangle.(\nu u)((!u(y).\hat{D}) \mid \hat{E})) \\
(\nu w)z\langle w\rangle.(R \mid (\nu y)x\langle y\rangle.(P \mid Q)) &\simeq_c (\nu y)x\langle y\rangle.(P \mid (\nu w)z\langle w\rangle.(R \mid Q)) \\
x(y).z(w).P &\simeq_c z(w).x(y).P
\end{aligned}
$$

Fig. 3. A sample of process equalities induced by proof conversions

Definition 5.6. *A type-respecting relation $\mathcal{R}$ is an* equivalence *if it enjoys the following three properties:*

- Reflexivity: $\Gamma; \Delta \vdash P :: T$ *implies* $\Gamma; \Delta \vdash P \mathcal{R} P :: T$*;*
- Symmetry: $\Gamma; \Delta \vdash P \mathcal{R} Q :: T$ *implies* $\Gamma; \Delta \vdash Q \mathcal{R} P :: T$*;*
- Transitivity: $\Gamma; \Delta \vdash P \mathcal{R} P' :: T$ *and* $\Gamma; \Delta \vdash P' \mathcal{R} Q :: T$ *imply* $\Gamma; \Delta \vdash P \mathcal{R} Q :: T$.

Proposition 5.7. $\approx$ *is an equivalence relation.*

In our setting, a notion of congruence for type-respecting relations turns out to be quite type-directed: both right- and left-hand side typings are quite explicit on the compositionality properties of processes. Defining such a notion is relatively straightforward: unsurprisingly, it mirrors the structure of the typing rules. For space reasons, we elide the details; see [18] for the definition and proof that $\approx$ is indeed a congruence.

6 Soundness of Proof Conversions and Type Isomorphisms

We use typed context bisimilarity—together with termination, subject reduction, and progress results—to clarify two issues derived from the logical interpretation: soundness of proof conversions and observational characterizations of type isomorphisms.

Soundness of Proof Conversions. Derivations in DILL are related by structural and computational rules that express sound proof transformations that arise in cut-elimination. As mentioned in Section 3 (and fully detailed in [4]), in our interpretation reductions and structural conversions in DILL correspond to reductions and structural congruence in the π-calculus. There is, however, a group of conversions in DILL not considered in [4] and which do not correspond to neither reduction or structural congruence in the process side. We call them *proof conversions*: they induce a congruence on typed processes, denoted $\simeq_c$. In this section, we show *soundness* of $\simeq_c$ with respect to $\approx$, that is, processes extracted from proof conversions are typed contextually bisimilar.

We illustrate the proof conversions and their associated π-calculus processes; Fig. 3 presents a sample of process equalities extracted from them. Each equality $M \simeq_c N$ is associated to appropriate right- and left-hand side typings; this way, e.g., the last equality in Fig. 3—associated to two applications of rule (T⊗L)—could be stated as

$$\cdot\,; x{:}A \otimes B, z{:}C \otimes D \vdash x(y).z(w).P \simeq_c z(w).x(y).P :: T$$

where A, B, C, D are types and T is a right-hand side typing. For the sake of illustration, however, in Fig. 3 these typings are elided, as we would like to stress on the consequences of conversions on the process side. Proof conversions describe the interplay of two rules in a type-preserving way: regardless of the order in which the rules are applied, they lead to typing derivations with the same right- and left-hand side typings, but with syntactically different processes. We consider two kinds of proof conversions. The first kind captures the interplay of left/right rules with Tcut/Tcut$^!$ rules; the first twelve rows in Fig. 3 are examples (the first five involve (Tcut), the other seven involve (Tcut$^!$)). The second kind captures the interplay of left and right rules with each other; typically they describe type-preserving transformations which commute actions from non-interfering sessions inside a process (the last two rows in Fig. 3 are examples).

Let us comment on the fifth process equality in Fig. 3. It corresponds to the interplay of rules (Tcut) and (T⊕L), under typing assumptions $\Gamma; \Delta_1 \vdash \hat{D} :: x{:}C$, $\Gamma; \Delta_2, y{:}A, x{:}C \vdash \hat{E}{::}T$, and $\Gamma; \Delta_2, y{:}A, x{:}C \vdash \hat{F}{::}T$. Letting $\Delta = \Delta_1, \Delta_2$, we have:

$$\Gamma; \Delta, y{:}A \oplus B \vdash \underbrace{(\nu x)(\hat{D} \,|\, y.\mathtt{case}(\hat{E}, \hat{F}))}_{(1)} \simeq_c \underbrace{y.\mathtt{case}((\nu x)(\hat{D} \,|\, \hat{E}), (\nu x)(\hat{D} \,|\, \hat{F}))}_{(2)} :: T$$

with types T, A, B, and C, linear environments Δ_1, Δ_2, and non-linear environment Γ.

Read from (1) to (2), this conversion can be interpreted as the "promotion" of the choice at y, which causes $\hat{D}$ to get "delayed" as a result. However, such a delay is seen to be only apparent once we examine the individual typing of $\hat{D}$ and the whole typing derivation. The first typing assumption says that $\hat{D}$ is able to offer behavior C at x (a free name in $\hat{D}$), as long as it is placed in a context in which the behaviors described by names in Γ, Δ_1 are available. The left-hand side typing for both processes says that they can offer some behavior T, as long as the behaviors declared in Γ, Δ and behavior $A \oplus B$ at y are provided. Crucially, since x is private to (1), type T cannot correspond to $x{:}C$. That is, even if $\hat{D}$ is at the top-level in (1) its behavior is not immediately available. Also because of the left-hand side typing, we know that (1) and (2) are only able to interact with some selection at y; only then, $\hat{D}$ will be able to interact with either $\hat{E}$ or $\hat{F}$, whose behavior depends on the presence of behavior C at x. A conversion of (1) into (2) could be seen as a "behavioral optimization" if one considers that (2) has only one available prefix, while (1) has two parallel components.

For all proof conversions, the apparent phenomenon of "prefix promotion" induced by proof conversions can be explained along the above lines. In our soundness result (Theorem 6.2 below), the crucial point is capturing the fact that some top-level processes may not be able to *immediately* exercise their behavior (cf. $\hat{D}$ in (1) above). We use the following notations on type-respecting relations. $\mathcal{I}_{\Gamma;\Delta \vdash T}$ stands for the relation

$\{(P, Q) : \Gamma; \Delta \vdash P :: T,\ \Gamma; \Delta \vdash Q :: T\}$ which collects pairs of processes with identical left- and right-hand side typings. Based on the logical interpretation of types, we introduce a notion of "continuation relation" for pairs of typed processes:

Definition 6.1. *Using* $\boxtimes$ *to range over* $\otimes, \multimap$ *and* $\boxplus$ *to range over* $\oplus, \&$*, we define the type-respecting relation* $\mathcal{W}_{\vdash x:A}$ *by induction on the right-hand side typing, as follows:*

$$\mathcal{W}_{\vdash x:\mathbf{1}} = \mathcal{I}_{\vdash x:\mathbf{1}} \qquad \mathcal{W}_{\vdash x:A \boxtimes B} = \mathcal{I}_{\vdash x:B} \cup \mathcal{W}_{\vdash x:B}$$
$$\mathcal{W}_{\vdash x:!A} = \mathcal{I}_{\vdash x:!A} \qquad \mathcal{W}_{\vdash x:A \boxplus B} = \mathcal{I}_{\vdash x:A} \cup \mathcal{W}_{\vdash x:A} \cup \mathcal{I}_{\vdash x:B} \cup \mathcal{W}_{\vdash x:B}$$

This way, e.g., the continuation relation for $\vdash x{:}A \otimes B$ is $\mathcal{I}_{\vdash x:B} \cup \mathcal{W}_{\vdash x:B}$: it contains all pairs typed by $\vdash x{:}B$ (as processes of type $x{:}A \otimes B$ are to be typed by $x{:}B$ after the output action) as well as those pairs in the continuation relation for $x{:}B$.

Theorem 6.2 (Soundness of Proof Conversions). *Let* P, Q *be processes such that (i)* $\Gamma; \Delta \vdash D \rightsquigarrow P :: T$*; (ii)* $\Gamma; \Delta \vdash E \rightsquigarrow Q :: T$*; (iii)* $P \simeq_c Q$*. Then,* $\Gamma; \Delta \vdash P \approx Q :: T$.

Proof. By coinduction, exhibiting appropriate typed context bisimulations for each proof conversion. In the bisimulation game, we exploit termination of well-typed processes (Theorem 4.17) to ensure that actions can be matched with finite weak transitions, and subject reduction (Theorem 3.2) to ensure type preservation under reductions.

We detail the case for the first proof conversion in Fig. 3—see [18] for other cases. This proof conversion corresponds to the interplay of rules (T⊗R) and (Tcut). We have to show that $\Gamma; \Delta \vdash M \approx N :: z{:}A \otimes B$ where

$$\Delta = \Delta_1, \Delta_2, \Delta_3 \quad \Gamma; \Delta_1 \vdash \hat{D} :: x{:}C \quad \Gamma; \Delta_2, x{:}C \vdash \hat{E} :: y{:}A \quad \Gamma; \Delta_3 \vdash \hat{F} :: z{:}B \quad (1)$$
$$M = (\nu x)(\hat{D} \mid (\nu y)z\langle y\rangle.(\hat{E} \mid \hat{F})) \quad N = (\nu y)z\langle y\rangle.((\nu x)(\hat{D} \mid \hat{E}) \mid \hat{F})$$

Using Proposition 5.5, we have to show that for every $K \in \mathcal{K}_{\Gamma;\Delta}$, we have $\vdash K[M] \approx K[N] :: z{:}A \otimes B$. In turn, this implies exhibiting a typed context bisimulation $\mathcal{R}$ containing the pair $(K[M], K[N])$. We define $\mathcal{R} = \mathcal{W}_{\vdash z:A\otimes B} \cup \mathcal{S} \cup \mathcal{S}^{-1}$, with

$$\mathcal{S} = \{(K_1[M'], K_2[N]) : M \Longrightarrow M',\ \ K_1, K_2 \in \mathcal{K}_{\Gamma;\Delta}\}$$

and $\mathcal{W}_{\vdash z:A\otimes B}$ is as in Definition 6.1. Notice that $\mathcal{S}$ is a type-respecting relation indexed by $\vdash z{:}A \otimes B$. In fact, using the typings in (1)—with $\Gamma = \Delta = \emptyset$—and exploiting subject reduction (Theorem 3.2), it can be checked that for all $(P, Q) \in \mathcal{S}$ both $\vdash P :: z{:}A \otimes B$ and $\vdash Q :: z{:}A \otimes B$ can be derived.

We now show that $\mathcal{R}$ is a typed context bisimulation. Pick any $K \in \mathcal{K}_{\Gamma;\Delta}$. Using Proposition 5.4, we can assume $K = (\nu\widetilde{u}, \widetilde{x})(K_\Gamma \mid K_\Delta \mid [\cdot])$ where

- $K_\Gamma \equiv \prod_{i\in I} !u_i(y_i).R_i$, with $\vdash R_i :: y_i{:}D_i$, for every $u_i{:}D_i \in \Gamma$;
- $K_\Delta \equiv \prod_{j\in J} S_j$, with $\vdash S_j :: x_j{:}C_j$, for every $x_j{:}C_j \in \Delta$.

Clearly, $(K[M], K[N]) \in \mathcal{S}$, and so it is in $\mathcal{R}$. Now, suppose $K[M]$ moves first: $K[M] \xrightarrow{\alpha} M_1^\star$. We have to find a matching action α from $K[N]$, i.e., $K[N] \stackrel{\alpha}{\Longrightarrow} N_1^\star$. Since $\vdash K[M] :: z{:}A \otimes B$, we have two possible cases for α:

1. Case $\alpha = \tau$. We consider the possibilities for the origin of the reduction:
   (a) $K_\Gamma \xrightarrow{\tau} K'_\Gamma$ and $K[M] \xrightarrow{\tau} K'[M]$. However, this cannot be the case, as by construction K_Γ corresponds to the parallel composition of input-guarded replicated processes which cannot evolve on their own.
   (b) $K_\Delta \xrightarrow{\tau} K'_\Delta$ and $K[M] \xrightarrow{\tau} K'[M]$. Then, for some $l \in J$, $S_l \xrightarrow{\tau} S'_l$:

$$K[M] \xrightarrow{\tau} (\nu\widetilde{u}, \widetilde{x})(K_\Gamma \mid K'_\Delta \mid M) = K'[M] = M_1^\star$$

   Now, context K is the same in $K[N]$. Then K_Δ occurs identically in $K[N]$, and this reduction can be matched by a *finite* weak transition (Theorem 4.17):

$$K[N] \Longrightarrow (\nu\widetilde{u}, \widetilde{x})(K_\Gamma \mid K''_\Delta \mid N) = K''[N] = N_1^\star$$

   By subject reduction (Theorem 3.2), $\vdash S'_l :: x_l{:}C_l$; hence, K', K'' are in $\mathcal{K}_{\Gamma;\Delta}$. Hence, the pair $(K'[M], K''[N])$ is in $\mathcal{S}$ (as $M \Longrightarrow M$) and so it is in $\mathcal{R}$.
   (c) $M \xrightarrow{\tau} M'$ and $K[M] \xrightarrow{\tau} K[M']$. Since $M = (\nu x)(\hat{D} \mid (\nu y)z\langle y\rangle.(\hat{E} \mid \hat{F}))$, the only possibility is that there is a $\hat{D}_1$ such that $\hat{D} \xrightarrow{\tau} \hat{D}_1$ and $M' = (\nu x)(\hat{D}_1 \mid (\nu y)z\langle y\rangle.(\hat{E} \mid \hat{F}))$. This way,

$$K[M] \xrightarrow{\tau} (\nu\widetilde{u}, \widetilde{x})(K_\Gamma \mid K_\Delta \mid M') = K[M'] = M_1^\star$$

   We observe that $K[N]$ cannot match this action, but $K[N] \Longrightarrow K[N]$ is a valid weak transition. Hence, $N_1^\star = K[N]$. By subject reduction (Theorem 3.2), we infer that $\vdash K[M'] :: z{:}A \otimes B$. We use this fact to observe that the pair $(K[M'], K[N])$ is included in $\mathcal{S}$. Hence, it is in $\mathcal{R}$.
   (d) There is an interaction between M and K_Γ or between M and K_Δ: this is only possible by the interaction of $\hat{D}$ with K_Γ or K_Δ on names in $\widetilde{u}, \widetilde{x}$. Again, the only possible weak transition from $K[N]$ matching this reduction is $K[N] \Longrightarrow K[N]$, and the analysis proceeds as in the previous case.
2. Case $\alpha \neq \tau$. Then the only possibility, starting from $K[M]$, is an output action of the form $\alpha = \overline{(\nu y)z\langle y\rangle}$. This action can only originate in M:

$$K[M] \xrightarrow{\overline{(\nu y)z\langle y\rangle}} (\nu\widetilde{x}, \widetilde{u})(K_\Gamma \mid K_\Delta \mid (\nu x)(\hat{D} \mid (\nu y)(\hat{E} \mid \hat{F}))) = M_1^\star$$

   Process $K[N]$ can match this action via the following finite weak transition:

$$K[N] \stackrel{\overline{(\nu y)z\langle y\rangle}}{\Longrightarrow} (\nu\widetilde{x}, \widetilde{u})(K'_\Gamma \mid K'_\Delta \mid (\nu y)((\nu x)(\hat{D}' \mid \hat{E}') \mid \hat{F}')) = N_1^\star$$

   Observe how $N_1^\star$ reflects the changes in $K[N]$ due to the possible reductions before and after the output action. By definition of $\approx$ (output case), we consider the composition of $M_1^\star$ and $N_1^\star$ with any V such that $y{:}A \vdash V :: -{:}1$. Using the typings in (1) and subject reduction (Theorem 3.2), we infer both

$$\vdash M_2^\star = (\nu\widetilde{x}, \widetilde{u})(K_\Gamma \mid K_\Delta \mid (\nu x)(\hat{D} \mid (\nu y)(\hat{E} \mid V \mid \hat{F}))) :: z{:}B$$
$$\vdash N_2^\star = (\nu\widetilde{x}, \widetilde{u})(K'_\Gamma \mid K'_\Delta \mid (\nu y)((\nu x)(\hat{D}' \mid \hat{E}' \mid V) \mid \hat{F}')) :: z{:}B$$

   Hence, the pair $(M_2^\star, N_2^\star)$ is in $\mathcal{W}_{\vdash z:A\otimes B}$ and so it is in $\mathcal{R}$.

Now suppose that $K[N]$ moves first: $K[N] \xrightarrow{\alpha} N_1^\star$. We have to find a matching action α from $K[M]$: $K[M] \stackrel{\alpha}{\Longrightarrow} M_1^\star$. Similarly as before, there are two cases: either $\alpha = \tau$ or $\alpha = (\nu y)z\langle y\rangle$. The former is as detailed before; the only difference is that reductions from $K[N]$ can only be originated in K_Δ; these are matched by $K[M]$ with finite weak transitions originating in both K and in M. We thus obtain pairs of processes in $\mathcal{S}^{-1}$. The analysis for the case for output mirrors the given above and is omitted. □

Type Isomorphisms. In type theory, types A and B are called *isomorphic* if there are morphisms (proofs in our case) π_A of $B \vdash A$ and π_B of $A \vdash B$ which compose to the identity in both ways—see, e.g., [9]. We adapt this notion to our setting, using typed context bisimilarity to account for *isomorphisms* in linear logic. (Below, we write $P^{\langle \widetilde{x} \rangle}$ for a process parametric on a sequence of names $x_1, \ldots, x_n$.)

Definition 6.3 (Isomorphism). *Two types A and B are called* isomorphic, *noted* $A \simeq B$, *if, for any names x, y, z, there exist processes $P^{\langle x,y\rangle}$ and $Q^{\langle y,x\rangle}$ such that:*
(i) $\cdot\,; x{:}A \vdash P^{\langle x,y\rangle} :: y{:}B$; *(ii)* $\cdot\,; y{:}B \vdash Q^{\langle y,x\rangle} :: x{:}A$;
(iii) $\cdot\,; x{:}A \vdash (\nu y)(P^{\langle x,y\rangle} \mid Q^{\langle y,z\rangle}) \approx [x \leftrightarrow z] :: z{:}A$; *and*
(iv) $\cdot\,; y{:}B \vdash (\nu x)(Q^{\langle y,x\rangle} \mid P^{\langle x,z\rangle}) \approx [y \leftrightarrow z] :: z{:}B$.

Thus, intuitively, if A, B are service specifications then by establishing $A \simeq B$ one can claim that having A is as good as having B, because we can build one from the other using an isomorphism. Isomorphisms in linear logic can then be used to simplify/transform service interfaces in the π-calculus. They can also help validating our interpretation with respect to basic linear logic principles. As an example, let us consider multiplicative conjunction $\otimes$. A basic linear logic principle is $A \otimes B \vdash B \otimes A$. Our interpretation of $A \otimes B$ may appear asymmetric as, in general, a channel of type $A \otimes B$ is not typable by $B \otimes A$. Theorem 6.4 below states the symmetric nature of $\otimes$ as a type isomorphism: symmetry is realized by a process which *coerces* any session of type $A \otimes B$ to a session of type $B \otimes A$. Other sensible isomorphisms, such as, e.g., $(A \oplus B) \multimap C \simeq (A \multimap C) \,\&\, (B \multimap C)$, can be handled similarly.

Theorem 6.4. *Let A, B be any type, as in Def 3.1. Then $A \otimes B \simeq B \otimes A$.*

Proof. We check conditions (i)-(iv) of Def. 6.3 for processes $P^{\langle x,y\rangle}, Q^{\langle y,x\rangle}$ defined as

$$\begin{aligned} P^{\langle x,y\rangle} &= x(u).(\nu n)y\langle n\rangle.([x \leftrightarrow n] \mid [u \leftrightarrow y]) \\ Q^{\langle y,x\rangle} &= y(w).(\nu m)x\langle m\rangle.([y \leftrightarrow m] \mid [w \leftrightarrow x]) \end{aligned}$$

Checking (i)-(ii), i.e., $\cdot\,; x{:}A \otimes B \vdash P^{\langle x,y\rangle} :: y{:}B \otimes A$ and $\cdot\,; y{:}B \otimes A \vdash Q^{\langle y,x\rangle} :: x{:}A \otimes B$ is easy; rule (Tid) ensures that both typings hold for any A, B.
We then show (iii) and (iv). We sketch only the proof of (iii); the proof of (iv) is analogous. Let $M = (\nu y)(P^{\langle x,y\rangle} \mid Q^{\langle y,z\rangle})$ and $N = [x \leftrightarrow z]$; we need to show $\cdot\,; x{:}A \otimes B \vdash M \approx N :: z{:}A \otimes B$. By Proposition 5.5, we have to show that for every $K \in \mathcal{K}_{\cdot\,; x:A \otimes B}$, we have $\vdash K[M] \approx K[N] :: z{:}A \otimes B$. In turn, this implies exhibiting a typed context bisimulation $\mathcal{R}$ containing $(K[M], K[N])$. Letting $\mathcal{S} = \{(R_1, R_2) : K[M] \Longrightarrow R_1,\ K[N] \Longrightarrow R_2\}$, we set $\mathcal{R} = \mathcal{W}_{\vdash z:A \otimes B} \cup \mathcal{S} \cup \mathcal{S}^{-1}$. Following expected lines, $\mathcal{R}$ can be shown to be a typed context bisimulation. □

7 Related Work

Termination in the π-calculus using logical relations has been studied in [26,21]. Neither of these works considers session types; hence, the technical details of the logical relations are very different, with semantic interpretations of types relying on constraints on the syntax and the types of processes. Here we started from a well-established type discipline for the π-calculus and showed termination of well-typed processes. In contrast, both [26,21] follow a somewhat opposite path, and aim at type disciplines that guarantee termination. The interpretation of intuitionistic linear logic as session types allows for intuitive logical relations, truly defined on the structure of types. In this sense, our approach is more principled than in [26,21], as it is not an adaptation of the method, but rather an instantiation of the method on our canonical linear type structure.

Another interpretation of session types as linear logic propositions is proposed in [7]. It is based on *soft* linear logic [15], and so the exponential "!" is treated following a non canonical discipline that uses two different typing environments. Hence, typing rules and judgements in [7] are rather different from ours. A bound on the length of reductions starting from well-typed-processes is obtained; the proof uses techniques from Implicit Computational Complexity. Notions of observational equivalence and their applications are not addressed in [7]. Although here we do not provide a similar bound, it is remarkable that our proof of termination follows *only* the principles and properties of [4]; in contrast to [7], our proof does not appeal to extraneous technical devices, and preserves a standard, intuitive treatment of "!". This is particularly desirable for extensions/generalizations of our framework, such as the proposed in [25,19].

Loosely related to typed context bisimilarity is [27], where a form of *linear bisimilarity* is proposed; following a linear type structure, it treats some visible actions as internal actions, thus leading to an equivalence larger than standard bisimilarity which is a congruence. The only work on behavioral equivalences for session-based concurrency we are aware of is [14]. It studies the behavioral theory of a π-calculus with asynchronous session communication and an event inspection primitive for buffered messages. The aim is to capture the distinction between order-preserving communications (inside already established connections) and non-order-preserving communications (outside established connections). Such a behavioral theory accounts for principles for prefix commutation that appear similar to those induced by our proof conversions. However, the origin and the nature of these commutations are quite different. In fact, while in [14] prefix commutation arises from the distinction mentioned above, commutations in our (synchronous) framework are due to causality relations captured by types.

8 Concluding Remarks

By relying on the principles established by an interpretation of linear logic as session types [4], we have introduced a theory of logical relations for session-typed disciplines. Our development is remarkably similar to that for functional languages; although in our setting types are assigned to names (and not to terms), our linear logical relations are defined on the structure of types, relying both on process reductions and labeled transitions. A main application of this theory is a proof that well-typed processes always terminate. This way, in addition to *safety* properties (nothing bad happens, cf. subject reduction), we have shown that session-typed processes also enjoy an important *liveness* property such as termination. Certifying termination of interacting concurrent systems is indeed important, from foundational and practical standpoints. We developed two applications of these results, which complement the results in [4]. Both of them rely on a novel observational equivalence for typed processes. First, we have shown soundness of *proof conversions* with respect to observational equivalence—an issue left open in [4]. Second, we studied *type isomorphisms* resulting from linear logic equivalences in our setting. The basic properties of the interpretation—especially, the combination of subject reduction and termination—were of the essence in both applications. Ongoing work concerns sound *and* complete axiomatizations of typed context bisilmilarity via proof conversions. Having introduced the method of logical relations for session types, we plan to explore it further for obtaining other results, such as parametricity.

Acknowledgments. This research was supported by the Fundação para a Ciência e a Tecnologia (Portuguese Foundation for Science and Technology) through the Carnegie Mellon Portugal Program, under grants INTERFACES NGN-44 / 2009 and SFRH / BD / 33763 / 2009, and CITI. We thank the anonymous reviewers for their useful comments.

References

1. Abramsky, S.: Computational interpretations of linear logic. Theor. Comput. Sci. 111, 3–57 (1993)
2. Barber, A.: Dual intuitionistic linear logic. Technical report, LFCS-96-347, Univ. of Edinburgh (1996)
3. Boreale, M.: On the expressiveness of internal mobility in name-passing calculi. Theor. Comput. Sci. 195, 205–226 (1998)
4. Caires, L., Pfenning, F.: Session Types as Intuitionistic Linear Propositions. In: Gastin, P., Laroussinie, F. (eds.) CONCUR 2010. LNCS, vol. 6269, pp. 222–236. Springer, Heidelberg (2010)
5. Caires, L., Pfenning, F., Toninho, B.: Towards concurrent type theory. In: Proc. of 7th Workshop on Types in Language Design and Implementation – TLDI 2012 (2012)
6. Chang, B.-Y.E., Chaudhuri, K., Pfenning, F.: A judgmental analysis of linear logic. Technical report, CMU-CS-03-131R, Carnegie Mellon University (2003)
7. Dal Lago, U., Di Giamberardino, P.: Soft session types. In: Proc. of 18th Workshop on Expressiveness in Concurrency – EXPRESS 2011. EPTCS, vol. 64, pp. 59–73 (2011)
8. Demangeon, R., Hirschkoff, D., Sangiorgi, D.: Mobile Processes and Termination. In: Palsberg, J. (ed.) Mosses Festschrift. LNCS, vol. 5700, pp. 250–273. Springer, Heidelberg (2009)
9. Di Cosmo, R.: A short survey of isomorphisms of types. Mathematical Structures in Computer Science 15(5), 825–838 (2005)
10. Girard, J.-Y., Lafont, Y.: Linear Logic and Lazy Computation. In: Ehrig, H., Levi, G., Montanari, U. (eds.) TAPSOFT 1987. LNCS, vol. 250, pp. 52–66. Springer, Heidelberg (1987)
11. Honda, K., Vasconcelos, V.T., Kubo, M.: Language Primitives and Type Discipline for Structured Communication-Based Programming. In: Hankin, C. (ed.) ESOP 1998. LNCS, vol. 1381, pp. 122–138. Springer, Heidelberg (1998)
12. Hu, R., Yoshida, N., Honda, K.: Session-Based Distributed Programming in Java. In: Ryan, M. (ed.) ECOOP 2008. LNCS, vol. 5142, pp. 516–541. Springer, Heidelberg (2008)

13. Kobayashi, N., Pierce, B.C., Turner, D.N.: Linearity and the pi-calculus. In: POPL, pp. 358–371 (1996)
14. Kouzapas, D., Yoshida, N., Honda, K.: On Asynchronous Session Semantics. In: Bruni, R., Dingel, J. (eds.) FORTE 2011 and FMOODS 2011. LNCS, vol. 6722, pp. 228–243. Springer, Heidelberg (2011)
15. Lafont, Y.: Soft linear logic and polynomial time. Theor. Comput. Sci. 318(1-2), 163–180 (2004)
16. Milner, R., Parrow, J., Walker, D.: A Calculus of Mobile Processes, part I/II. Inf. Comput. 100(1), 1–77 (1992)
17. Ng, N., Yoshida, N., Pernet, O., Hu, R., Kryftis, Y.: Safe Parallel Programming with Session Java. In: De Meuter, W., Roman, G.-C. (eds.) COORDINATION 2011. LNCS, vol. 6721, pp. 110–126. Springer, Heidelberg (2011)
18. Pérez, J.A., Caires, L., Pfenning, F., Toninho, B.: Linear Logical Relations for Session-Based Concurrency, Extended Version (2012), `http://goo.gl/iQVZu`
19. Pfenning, F., Caires, L., Toninho, B.: Proof-Carrying Code in a Session-Typed Process Calculus. In: Jouannaud, J.-P., Shao, Z. (eds.) CPP 2011. LNCS, vol. 7086, pp. 21–36. Springer, Heidelberg (2011)
20. Pucella, R., Tov, J.A.: Haskell session types with (almost) no class. In: Proc. of ACM SIGPLAN Symposium on Haskell, pp. 25–36. ACM (2008)
21. Sangiorgi, D.: Termination of processes. Mathematical Structures in Computer Science 16(1), 1–39 (2006)
22. Sangiorgi, D., Walker, D.: The π-calculus: A Theory of Mobile Processes. Cambridge University Press, New York (2001)
23. Statman, R.: Logical relations and the typed lambda-calculus. Information and Control 65(2/3), 85–97 (1985)
24. Tait, W.W.: Intensional Interpretations of Functionals of Finite Type I. J. Symbolic Logic 32, 198–212 (1967)
25. Toninho, B., Caires, L., Pfenning, F.: Dependent session types via intuitionistic linear type theory. In: Proc. of PPDP 2011, pp. 161–172. ACM Press, New York (2011)
26. Yoshida, N., Berger, M., Honda, K.: Strong normalisation in the pi -calculus. Inf. Comput. 191(2), 145–202 (2004)
27. Yoshida, N., Honda, K., Berger, M.: Linearity and bisimulation. J. Log. Algebr. Program. 72(2), 207–238 (2007)

Staged Computation with Staged Lexical Scope

Morten Rhiger

Roskilde University, P.O. Box 260, DK-4000 Roskilde, Denmark
mir@ruc.dk

Abstract. We present a simple core type system, $\lambda^{[]}$— pronounced "lambda open box" — for a statically typed, hygienic, and multi-stage lambda-calculus supporting evaluation under future-stage binders, open-code manipulation, a first-class eval function, and mutable state. The type system provides one type of lexically scoped code that precisely accounts for the contexts in which code values can be inserted. In particular, this type can distinguish between open and closed code. We show how to extend $\lambda^{[]}$ with subtype polymorphism over program contexts. The soundness and simplicity of $\lambda^{[]}$ demonstrate that the notion of staging is orthogonal to features that have been presented as instrumental in existing type systems for staged computation, such as polymorphism, nameless term representations, explicit substitutions, and delimited continuations.

1 Introduction

Staged computation enables programs to generate, combine, and execute code values at runtime. Its ability to delay the execution of code values induces a distinction between present-stage (or static) program parts (that are evaluated normally) and future-stage (or dynamic) program parts (that yield code values). Its ability to evaluate under future-stage binders makes staged computation ideal for partial evaluation and program specialization, compilation, runtime code generation, and macro expansion.

Code manipulation as a programming discipline dates back to the development of the first Fortran compiler in the late 1950s [1]. In the early 1960s, McCarthy proposed S-expressions as a uniform representation of code (and other data) in Lisp [15]. The work by the artificial-intelligence community in the 1970s then established *quasi quotations* as the preferred syntactic constructs for building such S-expressions [3]. The development of offline partial evaluation in the 1980s demonstrated that quasi quotations (or similar binding-time annotations) elegantly captures the notion of staged computation [5, 12]. In a couple of influential papers published in the mid 1990s, Davies [9] and Davies and Pfenning [10] established the type-theoretical foundation for staged computation via connections to temporal and modal logics. In the decade that has followed Davies and Pfenning's work, much research have been aimed at designing static type systems that combine general-purpose features with support for staged computation using quasi quotations as code-generation constructs [6, 14, 16, 22, 24, 26].

H. Seidl (Ed.): ESOP 2012, LNCS 7211, pp. 559–578, 2012.

1.1 The Challenge

Statically typed languages that support staged computation must guarantee that well-typed programs only generate, combine, and execute code values that are themselves well typed. Languages that evaluate under future-stage binders demand a careful treatment in the type system of potentially *open code* (that is, code that contains free variables). This is particularly challenging in the presence of an eval function and of assignments to mutable state since (1) an eval function must be passed closed code values only and (2) assignments enable code values to escape the scope in which they are generated, which in turn enables future-stage variables to escape their binder. Hence type systems for staged computation must distinguish between open and closed code values and must prevent future-stage variables from being captured by any binder but their own.

1.2 Our Contributions

We present $\lambda^{[]}$, a sound monomorphic type system for hygienic staged evaluation that supports *multiple stages*, *evaluation under future-stage binders*, and *open-code manipulation*. The type systems provides *one type of code*, which precisely distinguishes open from closed code. The type system supports a *first-class eval function* and *first-class mutable cells*. Mutable cells can contain (open as well as closed) code and assignments can pass (open as well as closed) code across binders. Yet, the type systems prevent future-stage variables from escaping their scope by the means of assignments. We then extend $\lambda^{[]}$ with subtype polymorphism and show that the result, $\lambda^{[]}_{<}$, is at least as expressive as the foundational multi-stage calculi $\lambda^{\bigcirc}$ [9] and $\lambda^{\Box}$ [10].

The type system of $\lambda^{[]}$ demonstrate that the notion of staging is orthogonal to features that are instrumental in existing type systems for staged computation, such as separate types for closed values [4, 16], polymorphism [25], nameless term representations [8], explicit substitutions [19], and delimited continuations [13]. $\lambda^{[]}$ is the first type system for multi-stage programming that makes an explicit eval function and mutable state coexist with hygienic evaluation under future binders.

2 The Staged Type System $\boldsymbol{\lambda}^{[]}$

$\lambda^{[]}$ is a type system for monomorphic staged λ-calculi. It extends the simply-typed λ-calculus with staging primitives $\uparrow e$ and $\downarrow e$ (similar to **next** and **prev** of $\lambda^{\bigcirc}$ [9] and to brackets $\langle\cdot\rangle$ and escape ˜ of the MetaML family of type systems, and reminiscent of `quasiquote` and `unquote` of Lisp and Scheme [3]) and with a single type of code $[\gamma]t$ parametrized over a type environment γ and a type t.

In $\lambda^{[]}$, values of type $[\gamma]t$ are code values: Intuitively, if an expression has type $[\gamma]t$ (and terminates), then it evaluates to (a representation of) a code fragment that has type t under type environment γ. Thus, the code type $[\gamma]t$ precisely characterizes the contexts that code values can be inserted into. Indeed, by varying γ, this code type is able to characterize both closed and (potentially) open code values. The code types of $\lambda^{[]}$ are *contextual modal types* but the typing rules are different from those of recently developed contextual modal type systems [19]. In terms of temporal logics, $\lambda^{[]}$ models linear (rather than branching) time.

To support hygienic evaluation under future-stage binders, the typing judgment of $\lambda^{[]}$ represents the context of a term by a linearly ordered sequence of type environments,

$$\gamma_0 \cdot \gamma_1 \cdot \cdots \cdot \gamma_{n-1} \cdot \gamma_n \,;\, \gamma_{n+1} \cdot \cdots \cdot \gamma_{m-1} \cdot \gamma_m,$$

of which the type environment to the left of the (unique) ";" is designated as the *current*. The *stage* (or *time*, in the vocabulary of temporal logic) of a bound variable equals the index of the environment that binds it. The stage of an expression is the index of the current type environment. (Lower stages are "more static" or "past"; higher stages are "more dynamic" or "future".) An expression can only access variables of the same stage. Hence variables at different stages live in different *namespaces*. We let Γ range over sequences of type environment not containing ";". We use a single "$\cdot$" to separate elements in a sequence.

When introducing a code value by $\uparrow e$ at stage n, e is typed at stage $n+1$: If $\uparrow e$ is typed in context $\Gamma\,;\gamma\cdot\Gamma'$, then e is typed in context $\Gamma\cdot\gamma\,;\Gamma'$. By the intuition above, if the type of e is t, then $\uparrow e$ has type $[\gamma]t$. Dually, when eliminating a code value by $\downarrow e$ at stage $n+1$, e is typed at stage n: If $\downarrow e$ is typed in context $\Gamma\cdot\gamma\,;\Gamma'$, then e is typed in context $\Gamma\,;\gamma\cdot\Gamma'$. Following intuition again, if the type of e is $[\gamma]t$, then $\downarrow e$ has type t. The typing rules for code introduction and elimination concisely sum up this explanation as follows.

$$\frac{\Gamma\cdot\gamma;\quad \Gamma' \vdash\ e:\ \ t}{\Gamma\quad ;\gamma\cdot\Gamma' \vdash \uparrow e : [\gamma]t} \qquad ([\,]\text{-I})$$

$$\frac{\Gamma\quad ;\gamma\cdot\Gamma' \vdash\ e : [\gamma]t}{\Gamma\cdot\gamma;\quad \Gamma' \vdash \downarrow e:\ \ t} \qquad ([\,]\text{-E})$$

The complete type system of $\lambda^{[]}$ is displayed in Fig. 1. The typing rules for variables, abstractions, and application closely mimic the simply-typed λ calculus. They access only the current type environment and pass the remaining sequence of past- and future-stage type environments unmodified to their subterms. The type rules for the staging primitives insist that each $\downarrow$ appears under at least one $\uparrow$. Without this requirement we would be forced to let a static occurrence of $\downarrow$ act as an eval function, but we prefer to study staging using $\uparrow$ and $\downarrow$ on one hand and an eval function on the other in isolation. We write ϵ for the empty sequence of type environments and we let b and c range over an unspecified set of base types and over type-indexed constants, respectively.

The typing rules of $\lambda^{[]}$ define a notion of *staged lexical scope:* A variable is bound by the nearest enclosing definition *at the same stage* of that variable. This notion extends to term variable that appears in type environments in types.

Syntax:

$$
\begin{aligned}
\text{(Types)}\ & t ::= b \mid t \to t \mid [\gamma]t \\
\text{(Terms)}\ & e ::= c_{\{t\}} \mid x \mid \lambda x\!:\!t.\,e \mid e\,e \mid \uparrow\! e \mid \downarrow\! e \\
\text{(Environments)}\ & \gamma ::= \emptyset \mid \gamma,\gamma \mid x : t \\
\text{(Sequences)}\ & \Gamma ::= \gamma \cdot \ldots \cdot \gamma
\end{aligned}
$$

Typing rules: $\boxed{\Gamma\ ;\ \Gamma' \vdash e : t}$

$$\frac{\Gamma\cdot\gamma\ ;\ \Gamma' \vdash t :: *}{\Gamma\cdot\gamma\ ;\ \Gamma' \vdash c_{\{t\}} : t}\ (\textsc{Const}) \qquad \frac{}{\Gamma\cdot(x:t,\gamma)\ ;\ \Gamma' \vdash x : t}\ (\textsc{Var})$$

$$\frac{\Gamma\cdot\gamma'\cdot\gamma;\quad \Gamma' \vdash\ e :\quad t}{\Gamma\cdot\gamma'\quad ;\gamma\cdot\Gamma' \vdash \uparrow\! e : [\gamma]t}\ ([\,]\mathrm{I}) \qquad \frac{\Gamma\cdot(x:t,\gamma)\ ;\ \Gamma' \vdash e : t' \quad \Gamma\cdot\gamma\ ;\ \Gamma' \vdash t :: *}{\Gamma\cdot\gamma\ ;\ \Gamma' \vdash \lambda x\!:\!t.\,e : t \to t'}\ (\to\mathrm{I})$$

$$\frac{\Gamma\cdot\gamma'\quad ;\gamma\cdot\Gamma' \vdash\ e : [\gamma]t}{\Gamma\cdot\gamma'\cdot\gamma;\quad \Gamma' \vdash \downarrow\! e :\quad t}\ ([\,]\mathrm{E}) \qquad \frac{\Gamma\cdot\gamma\ ;\ \Gamma' \vdash e_1 : t_2 \to t \quad \Gamma\cdot\gamma\ ;\ \Gamma' \vdash e_2 : t_2}{\Gamma\cdot\gamma\ ;\ \Gamma' \vdash e_1\,e_2 : t}\ (\to\mathrm{E})$$

Kinding rules: $\boxed{\Gamma\ ;\ \Gamma' \vdash t :: \kappa}$ $\boxed{\Gamma\ ;\ \Gamma' \vdash \gamma}$

$$\frac{}{\Gamma\ ;\ \Gamma' \vdash b :: *}\ (\mathrm{K}b) \qquad \frac{\Gamma\cdot\gamma\ ;\ \Gamma' \vdash \gamma' \quad \Gamma\cdot\gamma\ ;\ \Gamma' \vdash t :: *}{\Gamma\ ;\ \gamma\cdot\Gamma' \vdash [\gamma']t :: *}\ (\mathrm{K}[\,])$$

$$\frac{\left.\begin{array}{r}(x:t) \in \gamma,\ \ \text{and} \\ \Gamma\cdot\gamma\ ;\ \Gamma' \vdash t :: *\end{array}\right\}\ \text{for } (x:t) \in \gamma'}{\Gamma\cdot\gamma\ ;\ \Gamma' \vdash \gamma'}\ (\mathrm{K}\gamma) \qquad \frac{\Gamma\ ;\ \Gamma' \vdash t_0 :: * \quad \Gamma\ ;\ \Gamma' \vdash t_1 :: *}{\Gamma\ ;\ \Gamma' \vdash t_0 \to t_1 :: *}\ (\mathrm{K}\!\to)$$

Fig. 1. The Type System of $\lambda^{[\,]}$

Consequently, types that refer to unbound variables or that assert incorrect types for its variables are invalid. The type system of $\lambda^{[\,]}$ characterizes valid types using the kinding rules of Fig. 1. Most importantly, $[\gamma]t$ is valid at stage n when both γ and t are kind checked at stage $n+1$ since both the type t and any variable bound by γ are future stage entities. For example, $\lambda x\!:\!t.\,\lambda c\!:\![x:t]t.\,c$ is not well typed, since the x inside the asserted type of c is unbound. This x occurs at a stage different from the x bound at the surrounding λ.

2.1 Staged Lexical Scope

Before we present the semantics of $\lambda^{[\,]}$, we need to extend the definitions of free variables and substitution to a staged setting. This is particularly pertinent in the approach to staged computation we propose, where variables at different stages live in different namespaces.

Definition 1 (Free variables). *The set of free stage-n variables in stage-m terms, types, or environments are defined as follows.*

$$
\begin{aligned}
\mathrm{FV}^m_n(c_{\{t\}}) &= \mathrm{FV}^m_n(t)\\
\mathrm{FV}^m_m(x) &= \{x\}\\
\mathrm{FV}^m_n(x) &= \{\}, \quad \textit{if } m \neq n\\
\mathrm{FV}^m_m(\lambda x\!:\!t.\, e) &= \mathrm{FV}^m_m(t) \cup \left(\mathrm{FV}^m_m(e) - \{x\}\right)\\
\mathrm{FV}^m_n(\lambda x\!:\!t.\, e) &= \mathrm{FV}^m_n(t) \cup \mathrm{FV}^m_n(e), \quad \textit{if } m \neq n\\
\mathrm{FV}^m_n(e_1\, e_2) &= \mathrm{FV}^m_n(e_1) \cup \mathrm{FV}^m_n(e_2)\\
\mathrm{FV}^m_n(\uparrow e) &= \mathrm{FV}^{m+1}_n(e)\\
\mathrm{FV}^{m+1}_n(\downarrow e) &= \mathrm{FV}^m_n(e)\\
\\
\mathrm{FV}^m_n(b) &= \{\}\\
\mathrm{FV}^m_n(t_1 \to t_2) &= \mathrm{FV}^m_n(t_1) \cup \mathrm{FV}^m_n(t_2)\\
\mathrm{FV}^m_n([\gamma]t) &= \mathrm{FV}^{m+1}_n(\gamma) \cup \mathrm{FV}^{m+1}_n(t)\\
\\
\mathrm{FV}^m_n(\emptyset) &= \{\}\\
\mathrm{FV}^m_n(\gamma_1, \gamma_2) &= \mathrm{FV}^m_n(\gamma_1) \cup \mathrm{FV}^m_n(\gamma_2)\\
\mathrm{FV}^m_m(x : t) &= \{x\}\\
\mathrm{FV}^m_n(x : t) &= \{\}, \quad \textit{if } m \neq n
\end{aligned}
$$

The definition of free variables induces a notion of α-equivalence. $\lambda^{[\,]}$ then adheres to the following conventions. We occasionally state Convention 2 as an explicit side condition.

Convention 1 *α-equivalent terms (or types) are interchangeable in all contexts.*

Convention 2 (Barendregt [2]) *Bound and free variables are assumed to be different. (If necessary, Convention 1 can be used to rename the bound ones.)*

Definition 2 (Substitution). *The result of the capture-avoiding substitution of the stage-0 term e' for the stage-0 variable x in the stage-m term e is defined by*

$$
\begin{aligned}
(c_{\{t\}})^m\{e'/x\} &= c_{\{t\}}\\
(x)^0\{e'/x\} &= e'\\
(x)^m\{e'/x\} &= x, \qquad \textit{if } m \neq 0\\
(\lambda y\!:\!t.\, e)^m\{e'/x\} &= \lambda y\!:\!t.\, (e)^m\{e'/x\}\\
(e_1\, e_2)^m\{e'/x\} &= (e_1)^m\{e'/x\}\, (e_2)^m\{e'/x\}\\
(\uparrow e)^m\{e'/x\} &= \uparrow(e)^{m+1}\{e'/x\}\\
(\downarrow e)^{m+1}\{e'/x\} &= \downarrow(e)^m\{e'/x\}
\end{aligned}
$$

Notice that by Convention 2, x and y are different in the rule for substitution under lambdas.

The operational semantics of $\lambda^{[\,]}$ is presented in Sect. 3.4.

2.2 Properties of $\lambda^{[]}$

The type system of $\lambda^{[]}$ in Fig. 1 is sound with respect to a standard hygienic semantics of staging primitives. (The proof of soundness is outlined in Sect. 4.)

$\lambda^{[]}$ supports both a function run for immediate evaluation of code values and mutable state. We defer the detailed treatment of these to Sect. 3 and give just an outline here. We assume the existence of type-indexed families of constant symbols $\mathsf{run}_{\{[]t \to t\}}$, $\mathsf{ref}_{\{t \to t\,\mathsf{ref}\}}$, $\mathsf{get}_{\{t\,\mathsf{ref} \to t\}}$, and $\mathsf{set}_{\{t\,\mathsf{ref} \to t \to t\}}$. Given their usual semantics, these operations are type safe.

2.3 Examples

An implementation in $\lambda^{[]}$ of the classic staged power function is shown below. (In this implementation, we have taken the liberty to use standard integer arithmetic, monomorphic recursive let-expressions, and conditionals. They can all be added straightforwardly to $\lambda^{[]}$.)

$$
\begin{array}{l}
\mathsf{pow_{gen}} : \mathsf{int} \to [](\mathsf{int} \to \mathsf{int}) = \\
\quad \lambda n : \mathsf{int}. \\
\qquad \uparrow(\lambda x : \mathsf{int}. \\
\qquad\quad \downarrow(\mathsf{let\ rec\ pow_{bt}} : \mathsf{int} \to [x{:}\mathsf{int}]\mathsf{int} \to [x{:}\mathsf{int}]\mathsf{int} = \\
\qquad\qquad\qquad \lambda n : \mathsf{int}.\, \lambda c : [x{:}\mathsf{int}]\mathsf{int}. \\
\qquad\qquad\qquad\quad \mathsf{if}\ n = 0\ \mathsf{then}\ \uparrow 1\ \mathsf{else}\ \uparrow(\downarrow c \times \downarrow(\mathsf{pow_{bt}}\ (n-1)\ c)) \\
\qquad\quad\ \mathsf{in\ pow_{bt}}\ n\ \uparrow x))
\end{array}
$$

This example demonstrates the typical use of staged computation to implemented partial evaluation: The staging primitives are used to define a *binding-time separated* function $\mathsf{pow_{bt}}$ of type $\mathsf{int} \to [x : \mathsf{int}]\mathsf{int} \to [x : \mathsf{int}]\mathsf{int}$ and a *generating extension* $\mathsf{pow_{gen}}$ of type $\mathsf{int} \to [](\mathsf{int} \to \mathsf{int})$. Evaluating $\mathsf{pow_{gen}}\ n$ yields the textual representation of a function of type $\mathsf{int} \to \mathsf{int}$ that computes x^n. For example, $\mathsf{pow_{gen}}\ 3$ yields $\uparrow(\lambda x : \mathsf{int}.\, x \times x \times x \times 1)$ and $\mathsf{run}_{\{[](\mathsf{int} \to \mathsf{int}) \to \mathsf{int} \to \mathsf{int}\}}\ (\mathsf{pow_{gen}}\ 3)$ yields a function of type $\mathsf{int} \to \mathsf{int}$ that computes x^3.

The following shows an example where a code value ($\uparrow x$) with a free variable (x) is passed across the future-stage λ of another variable (y) by the means of an assignment. This example is well typed in $\lambda^{[]}$ since the free variable x does not escape its scope. (To ease readability, the types of the constants have been left out from this example.)

$$
\begin{array}{l}
\uparrow(\lambda x : \mathsf{int}. \\
\quad \downarrow(\mathsf{let}\, c : [x : \mathsf{int}]\mathsf{int} = \mathsf{ref}_{\{\dots\}}\ (\uparrow 1)\ \mathsf{in}\ \uparrow(\lambda y : t.\, \downarrow(\ \mathsf{set}_{\{\dots\}}\ c\ (\uparrow x)\ ;\ \cdots\ ))))
\end{array}
$$

On the other hand, the following classic attempt to pass a future-stage variable beyond its own scope is correctly rejected by the type system.

$$
\mathsf{let}\ c : t = \mathsf{ref}_{\{\dots\}}\ (\uparrow 1)\ \mathsf{in}\ \uparrow(\lambda x : \mathsf{int}.\, \downarrow(\ \mathsf{set}_{\{\dots\}}\ c\ (\uparrow x); \cdots\ ))
$$

In this example, the type of $\uparrow x$ is $[x : \mathsf{int}]\mathsf{int}$. Hence the type t of c must be $([x : \mathsf{int}]\mathsf{int})\ \mathsf{ref}$. But at the let-binding of c, this type is not well kinded since it refers to a unbound (future-stage) variable x.

3 The Staged Type System $\boldsymbol{\lambda}^{[]}_{<}$

As a type system for staged computation, $\lambda^{[]}$ is strikingly concise (as witnessed by its definition in Fig. 1). But $\lambda^{[]}$ lacks the expressive power required by general-purpose staged programming languages.

In this section, we first identify two examples representing lack of expressiveness in $\lambda^{[]}$. We argue that *subtype polymorphism* provide the expressiveness necessary to handle these examples. We therefore extend $\lambda^{[]}$ with a subtyping fragment, in Sect. 3.1. We then define the evaluation fragment and the imperative fragment of $\lambda^{[]}_{<}$, in Secs. 3.2 and 3.3. All fragments provide orthogonal features that can be added to $\lambda^{[]}$ independently of each other. Finally, in Sect. 3.4, we define the operational semantics of $\lambda^{[]}_{<}$.

Shortcoming 1. Consider the following term, which generates a closed code value and then splices that value into a context containing a variable x.

$$\mathsf{let}\ c = \uparrow 1\ \mathsf{in}\ \uparrow(\lambda x : t.\downarrow c)$$

This term in not typable in $\lambda^{[]}$: The typing rule for $\downarrow$ insists that the current type environment (in this example the one that declares x) must be identical to the type environment of the code spliced in (in this example an empty one). In $\lambda^{[]}$, a code value of type $[\gamma]t$ can only be spliced into a context that provides *exactly* the binding in γ. But recall the intuition that, if c has type $[\gamma]t$ then it denotes a representation of a term that has type t in type environment γ. Then it seems clear that c also has type $[\gamma']t$ for an extended environment γ' of γ. Similar reasoning is found within type systems for object calculi, record types, and other type systems with a built-in notion of subsumption.

To address this shortcoming, $\lambda^{[]}_{<}$ therefore extends $\lambda^{[]}$ with a rule of subsumption that allows us to *weaken* a code type (such as the type of $\downarrow c$ in the example above) by adding unused bindings to its environment. This idea is formalized in Sect. 3.1 below.

Shortcoming 2. Consider the following term that invokes run on a closed code value under a context containing a variable x: (The term is incomplete; we assume that the run is at stage 0.)

$$\uparrow(\lambda x : t.\downarrow(\cdots \mathsf{run}_{\{\ldots\}}\,(\uparrow 1)\cdots))$$

This term in not typable $\lambda^{[]}$: The $\uparrow 1$ has type $[x : t]\mathsf{int}$ but run expects a closed code value of type $[\,]\mathsf{int}$. The typing rule for $\uparrow$ insists that the type environment of the code generated is identical to the type environment used to type the future-stage term under the $\uparrow$ (in this example the one that declares x). But intuition tells us that if x is not used in the body of e, then the type of $\uparrow e$ need not mention x.

To address this shortcoming, $\lambda^{[]}_{<}$ also extends $\lambda^{[]}$ with a rule of subsumption that allows us to *strengthen* a typing context (such as the one used when typing

Additional Typing rules: $\boxed{\Gamma\ ;\ \Gamma' \vdash e : t}$

$$\frac{\Gamma_1\ ;\ \Gamma_1' \vdash \Gamma_2\ ;\Gamma_2' \quad \Gamma_1\ ;\ \Gamma_1' \vdash t_1 : * \quad \Gamma_2\ ;\ \Gamma_2' \vdash e : t_2 \quad \Gamma_1 ; \Gamma_1' \leq \Gamma_2 ; \Gamma_2' \quad t_2 \leq t_1}{\Gamma_1\ ;\ \Gamma_1' \vdash e : t_1}\ (\leq)$$

Subtyping rules: $\boxed{t \leq t'}$

$$\frac{}{t \leq t}\ (\text{S-Refl}) \qquad \frac{t_1 \leq t_2 \quad t_2 \leq t_3}{t_1 \leq t_3}\ (\text{S-Trans})$$

$$\frac{t_1 \leq t_2}{\forall T :: \kappa.\, t_1 \leq \forall T :: \kappa.\, t_2}\ (\text{S-All}) \qquad \frac{t_2 \leq t_1 \quad t_1' \leq t_2'}{t_1 \to t_1' \leq t_2 \to t_2'}\ (\text{S-Arrow})$$

$$\frac{t_1 \leq t_2}{\uparrow t_1 \leq \uparrow t_2}\ (\text{S-Up}) \qquad \frac{\gamma_2 \leq \gamma_1 \quad t_1 \leq t_2}{[\gamma_1]t_1 \leq [\gamma_2]t_2}\ (\text{S-Box})$$

$$\frac{t_1 \leq t_2}{\downarrow t_1 \leq \downarrow t_2}\ (\text{S-Down}) \qquad \frac{t_1 \leq t_2}{x : t_1 \leq x : t_2}\ (\text{S-Bind})$$

$$\frac{}{\gamma \leq \emptyset}\ (\text{S-Width}) \qquad \frac{\gamma_1 \leq \gamma_1' \quad \gamma_2 \leq \gamma_2'}{\gamma_1, \gamma_2 \leq \gamma_1', \gamma_2'}\ (\text{S-JoinCongr})$$

$$\frac{}{\gamma_1, (\gamma_2, \gamma_3) \leq (\gamma_1, \gamma_2), \gamma_3}\ (\text{S-JoinAssoc}) \qquad \frac{}{\gamma_1, \gamma_2 \leq \gamma_2, \gamma_1}\ (\text{S-JoinComm})$$

Fig. 2. The Subtype Fragment of $\lambda^{[]}_{<}$

$\uparrow 1$ in the example above) by removing unused bindings from its environments. This idea is also formalized in Sect. 3.1 below.

In the rest of this article, we let $\mathbf{V}$ and $\mathbf{L}$ denote disjoint sets of term variables and store locations, respectively. We let x and y range over $\mathbf{V}$ and ℓ over $\mathbf{L}$ (with primes and subscripts applied when necessary). We let ξ range over $\mathbf{V} \cup \mathbf{L}$.

3.1 Subtype Polymorphism

Figure 2 contains the subtype fragment of $\lambda^{[]}_{<}$. The subtype rules follows standard subtype rules for records and objects [20]. Notice that the code type is contravariant in the type environment and covariant in the type. The subsumption rule states that if we can type e with type environment γ, then we can also type it with type environment that provides more variable bindings than γ. This rule uses a pointwise extension of $\leq$ to sequences of type environments and the following iterative well kindedness rule for sequences of environments.

$$\frac{}{\ ;\ \Gamma_1' \vdash \Gamma_2} \qquad \frac{\Gamma_1\ ;\ \gamma_1 \cdot \Gamma_1' \vdash \gamma_2 \quad \Gamma_1\ ;\ \gamma_1 \cdot \Gamma_1' \vdash \Gamma_2}{\Gamma_1 \cdot \gamma_1\ ;\ \Gamma_1' \vdash \Gamma_2 \cdot \gamma_2}$$

Lemma 1. *If* $\Gamma\ ;\ \Gamma' \vdash t :: *$ *and* $t \leq t'$ *then also* $\Gamma\ ;\ \Gamma' \vdash t' :: *$

Additional syntax:

$$
\begin{aligned}
\text{(Terms) } e &::= \cdots \mid \rho\theta.\, e \\
\text{(Types) } t &::= \cdots \mid t\,\mathsf{ref} \\
\text{(Stores) } \theta &= \{\langle \ell_i, v_i^0 \rangle \mid 1 \le i \le k\}
\end{aligned}
$$

Additional typing rules: $\boxed{\Gamma \; ; \Gamma' \vdash e : t}$

$$
\frac{\begin{array}{l}(\gamma,\gamma') \; ; \Gamma \cdot \Gamma' \vdash v_i^0 : t_i \quad 1 \le i \le k \\ (\gamma,\gamma') \cdot \Gamma \; ; \Gamma' \vdash e : t\end{array}}{\gamma, \Gamma \; ; \Gamma' \vdash \rho\{\langle \ell_1, v_1^0\rangle, \ldots, \langle \ell_k, v_k^0\rangle\}.\, e : t} \; (\rho)
$$

$$
\text{where } \gamma' = (\ell_1 : t_1\,\mathsf{ref}, \ldots, \ell_k : t_k\,\mathsf{ref})
$$

Fig. 3. The imperative fragment of $\lambda_{<}^{[]}$

3.2 Evaluation and Lifting

The evaluation and lifting fragment of $\lambda_{<}^{[]}$ introduces two (type-indexed families of) constants, $\mathsf{run}_{\{[\,]t \to t\}}$ and $\mathsf{lift}_{\{t \to [\,]t\}}$, that serve dual purposes: run maps a future-stage value "back" to the present stage (called *demotion*) while lift maps a present-stage term "forward" to a future stage (called *promotion*).

The type of run guarantees that the argument is a *closed* future-stage term. It prevents, for example, the reduction $\mathsf{run}(\uparrow x) \longmapsto x$ in which a future-stage x percolates into the present stage. (See the reduction rule for run in Fig. 5 below.)

3.3 Mutable State

Figure 3 presents the type system for the imperative fragment of $\lambda_{<}^{[]}$. Mutable state is modeled syntactically using the approach pioneered by Felleisen and Hieb [11] and further developed by Wright and Felleisen [28]. Stores θ are finite sets of pairs containing cells and stage-0 values. As in Wright and Felleisen's work, we introduce a separate class of evaluation context, $\mathcal{R}$, that order the imperative operations according to left-to-right, call-by-value evaluation. Figure 4 below defines all evaluation contexts.

The syntactic approach to mutable state lets us express garbage collection on a store. Wright and Felleisen do not need to consider garbage collection, but the rule that we present is standard [17]. It is necessary in the proof of Progress (Lemma 11) for future-stage lambdas that contain ρ-terms. Here, garbage collection allows the reduction $\lambda x : t.\, \rho\theta.\, v^{n+1} \longmapsto \lambda x : t.\, v^{n+1}$, since the stage-$n+1$ value v^{n+1} cannot (by definition) contain cells ℓ.

The typing rule of ρ-terms is similar to that of Wright and Felleisen. Cells are treated as stage-0 variables and hence must be added to the left-most type environment in the type judgment. We use the usual invariant subtype rule for the type of references [20]:

$$\frac{t_1 \leq t_2 \quad t_2 \leq t_1}{t_1\ \mathsf{ref} \leq t_2\ \mathsf{ref}} \qquad \text{(S-REF)}$$

We use the following extensions of the definition of free variables and substitution for ρ-terms.

$$\begin{aligned}
\mathrm{FV}^m_m(\rho\theta.\,e) &= \mathrm{FV}^m_m(\mathrm{codom}\,\theta) \cup \big(\mathrm{FV}^m_m(e) - \mathrm{dom}\,\theta\big)\\
\mathrm{FV}^n_m(\rho\theta.\,e) &= \mathrm{FV}^n_m(\mathrm{codom}\,\theta) \cup \mathrm{FV}^n_m(e), \qquad \text{if } m \neq n
\end{aligned}$$

$$(\rho\theta.\,e)^m\{e'/x\} = \rho\theta.\,(e)^m\{e'/x\}$$

Notice that since the store contains stage-0 values only, it cannot contain free variables.

Figure 3 explicitly restricts reduction to situations that do not result in future-stage variables leaving their scope. For this purpose, we let $\mathrm{BV}^m_n(\mathcal{R}^m_{n'})$ denote the set of bound stage-n variables in the stage-m context $\mathcal{R}^m_{n'}$.

Definition 3 (Bound variables). $\mathrm{BV}^m_n(\mathcal{R}^m_{n'})$ *denotes the stage-n variables in* $\mathcal{R}^m_{n'}$ *bound by* λ*s that "surround" the hole* $\Box$*, defined as follows.*

$$\begin{aligned}
\mathrm{BV}^m_n(\Box) &= \{\}\\
\mathrm{BV}^m_n(\mathcal{R}^m_{n'}\ e) &= \mathrm{BV}^m_n(\mathcal{R}^m_{n'})\\
\mathrm{BV}^m_n(v^m\ \mathcal{R}^m_{n'}) &= \mathrm{BV}^m_n(\mathcal{R}^m_{n'})\\
\mathrm{BV}^m_n(\uparrow\mathcal{R}^{m+1}_{n'}) &= \mathrm{BV}^{m+1}_n(\mathcal{R}^{m+1}_{n'})\\
\mathrm{BV}^{m+1}_n(\downarrow\mathcal{R}^m_{n'}) &= \mathrm{BV}^m_n(\mathcal{R}^m_{n'})\\
\mathrm{BV}^{m+1}_{m+1}(\lambda x\!:\!t.\,\mathcal{R}^{m+1}_{n'}) &= \{x\} \cup \mathrm{BV}^{m+1}_{m+1}(\mathcal{R}^{m+1}_{n'})\\
\mathrm{BV}^{m+1}_n(\lambda x\!:\!t.\,\mathcal{R}^{m+1}_{n'}) &= \mathrm{BV}^{m+1}_n(\mathcal{R}^{m+1}_{n'}), \qquad \textit{if } m+1 \neq n
\end{aligned}$$

In the definition of bound variables, m denotes the stage of the context while n denotes the stage of the hole in that context.

3.4 Semantics of $\lambda^{[]}_{<}$

The reduction semantics of $\lambda^{[]}_{<}$ is defined by Figs. 4 and 5. Notice that the definition of values and contexts actually defines stage-indexed families of inductive terms. As remarked by Taha [23], the style of inductive definition is slightly unusual because it actually involves an infinite number of meta-variables. However, the values and contexts defined by these rules are still finite and admits inductive reasoning.

In the reduction rules in Fig. 5, $\oplus$ denotes a disjoint union.

4 Formal Properties

In this section we outline a formal proof of the soundness of the type system $\lambda^{[]}_{<}$ with respect to its reduction semantics. The proof follows the standard approach

$$
\begin{array}{rrl}
\text{(Values)} & v^0 & ::= \lambda x : t.\, e \mid c_{\{t\}} \mid \ell \\
 & v^m & ::= \uparrow v^{m+1} \\
 & v^{m+1} & ::= x \mid \lambda x : t.\, v^{m+1} \mid v^{m+1}\, v^{m+1} \\
 & v^{m+2} & ::= \downarrow v^{m+1} \\
(\mathcal{E}\text{-contexts}) & \mathcal{E}^m_m & ::= \Box \\
 & \mathcal{E}^m_n & ::= \mathcal{E}^m_n\, e \mid v^m\, \mathcal{E}^m_n \mid \uparrow \mathcal{E}^{m+1}_n \mid \rho\theta.\, \mathcal{E}^m_n \\
 & \mathcal{E}^{m+1}_n & ::= \downarrow \mathcal{E}^m_n \mid \lambda x : t.\, \mathcal{E}^{m+1}_n \\
(\mathcal{S}\text{-contexts}) & \mathcal{S}^m_m & ::= \Box \\
 & \mathcal{S}^m_n & ::= \lambda x : t.\, \mathcal{S}^m_n \mid \mathcal{S}^m_n\, e \mid v^{m+1}\, \mathcal{S}^m_n \mid \uparrow \mathcal{S}^{m+1}_n \\
 & \mathcal{S}^{m+1}_n & ::= \downarrow \mathcal{S}^m_n \\
(\mathcal{R}\text{-contexts}) & \mathcal{R}^m_n & ::= \Box \mid \mathcal{R}^m_n\, e \mid v^m\, \mathcal{R}^m_n \mid \uparrow \mathcal{R}^{m+1}_n \\
 & \mathcal{R}^{m+1}_n & ::= \downarrow \mathcal{R}^m_n \mid \lambda x : t.\, \mathcal{R}^{m+1}_n
\end{array}
$$

Fig. 4. Values and evaluation contexts of $\lambda^{[]}_{<}$

to soundness using a reduction semantics [28], but we need additional core results do deal with open terms. In particular, we need to deal with bound variables in addition to free variables, strengthening in addition to weakening, and with demotion and promotion.

4.1 Standard Results

Lemma 2 (Decomposition). *Let* $\mathrm{dom}_n(\gamma_0 \cdot \cdots \cdot \gamma_m) = \mathrm{dom}(\gamma_n)$.

(a) If D_0 is a derivation of $\gamma \cdot \Gamma$; $\Gamma' \vdash \mathcal{E}^{|\Gamma|}_0[e_1] : t$ then there exists an environment γ_1 with $\mathrm{dom}(\gamma_1) \subseteq \mathbf{L}$, a stack Γ'_1, a type t_1, and a derivation D_1 of (γ, γ_1) ; $\Gamma'_1 \vdash e_1 : t_1$ such that D_1 appears in D_0 at the location corresponding to the hole $\Box$ in $\mathcal{E}^{|\Gamma|}_0$.

(b) If D_0 is a derivation of $\gamma \cdot \gamma' \cdot \Gamma$; $\Gamma' \vdash \mathcal{S}^{|\Gamma|}_0[e_1] : t$ then there exists an environment γ'_1, a stack Γ'_1, a type t_1, and a derivation D_1 of $\gamma \cdot \gamma'_1$; $\Gamma'_1 \vdash e_1 : t_1$ such that D_1 appears in D_0 at the location corresponding to the hole $\Box$ in $\mathcal{S}^0_0$.

(c) If D_0 is a derivation of $\gamma \cdot \Gamma$; $\Gamma' \vdash \mathcal{R}^{|\Gamma|}_0[e_1] : t$ then there exists a stack $\Gamma'_1 \supseteq \Gamma'$, a type t_1, and a derivation D_1 of γ ; $\Gamma'_1 \vdash e_1 : t_1$ such that D_1 appears in D_0 at the location corresponding to the hole $\Box$ in $\mathcal{R}^{|\Gamma|}_0$ and for all n, $\mathrm{dom}_n(\Gamma'_1) - \mathrm{dom}_n(\Gamma') \subseteq \mathrm{BV}^0_n(\mathcal{R}^0_0)$.

The final part of case (c) states that the extra bindings in Γ'_1 required to type e_1 can be traced back to bindings in the context. This is used in the proof of Subject Reduction for case (Set), where it guarantees that the value to store can be typed using the outer type environment of the surrounding ρ-expression, which potentially provides fewer bindings.

The dual notion of decomposition is replacement:

Reduction rules: $\boxed{e \longmapsto e'}$

$$\frac{e \longmapsto e'}{\mathcal{E}_0^0[e] \longmapsto \mathcal{E}_0^0[e']} \qquad \text{(CTX)}$$

$$(\lambda x : t.\, e)\, v^0 \longmapsto (e)^0\{v^0/x\} \qquad (\beta)$$

$$\uparrow\mathcal{S}_0^0[\downarrow\uparrow v^1] \longmapsto \uparrow\mathcal{S}_0^0[v^1] \qquad (\downarrow\uparrow)$$

$$\mathsf{run}_{\{t\}}\,(\uparrow v^1) \longmapsto v^1 \qquad \text{(RUN)}$$

$$\mathsf{lift}_{\{t\}}\, v^0 \longmapsto \uparrow v^0 \qquad \text{(LIFT)}$$

$$\mathsf{ref}_{\{t\}}\, v^0 \longmapsto \rho\{\langle \ell, v^0\rangle\}.\, \ell \qquad \text{(REF)}$$

$$\rho\{\langle \ell, v^0\rangle\} \oplus \theta.\, \mathcal{R}_0^0[\mathsf{get}_{\{t\}}\, \ell] \longmapsto \rho\{\langle \ell, v^0\rangle\} \oplus \theta.\, \mathcal{R}_0^0[v^0] \qquad \text{(GET)}$$
$$\text{if } \mathrm{BV}_n^0(\mathcal{R}_0^0) \cap \mathrm{FV}_n^0(v^0) = \{\,\}$$

$$\rho\{\langle \ell, v_1^0\rangle\} \oplus \theta.\, \mathcal{R}_0^0[\mathsf{set}_{\{t\}}\, \ell\, v_2^0] \longmapsto \rho\{\langle \ell, v_2^0\rangle\} \oplus \theta.\, \mathcal{R}_0^0[v_2^0] \qquad \text{(SET)}$$
$$\text{if } \mathrm{BV}_n^0(\mathcal{R}_0^0) \cap \mathrm{FV}_n^0(v_2^0) = \{\,\}$$

$$\rho\theta_1.\, \rho\theta_2.\, e \longmapsto \rho\theta_1 \oplus \theta_2.\, e \qquad \text{(MERGE)}$$

$$\mathcal{R}_0^0[\rho\theta.\, e] \longmapsto \rho\theta.\, \mathcal{R}_0^0[e] \qquad (\rho\text{-LIFT})$$
$$\text{if } \mathrm{BV}_n^0(\mathcal{R}_0^0) \cap \mathrm{FV}_n(\theta) = \{\,\} \text{ and } \mathcal{R}_0^0 \neq \Box$$

$$\rho\theta_1 \oplus \theta_2.\, e \longmapsto \rho\theta_1.\, e \qquad \text{(GC)}$$
$$\text{if } \theta_2 \neq \{\,\} \text{ and } \mathrm{dom}(\theta_2) \cap \mathrm{FV}_0(\theta_1) = \{\,\}$$
$$\text{and } \mathrm{dom}(\theta_2) \cap \mathrm{FV}_0^0(e) = \{\,\}$$

Evaluation:

$$\mathrm{eval}(e) = v^0, \quad \text{if } e \longmapsto^* v^0$$

Convention 2 applies to case (REF), where it forces ℓ not to occur in v^0.

The side conditions of rules (GET) and (SET) prevent free variables in the contractum from being captured by the context. The side condition of (ρ-LIFT) prevents variables bound in the context from escaping their scope. These side conditions are explicit instances of Convention 2.

The rule (GC) allows part of the store to be *garbage collected*, if its cells are not referred to.

Fig. 5. Reduction semantics of $\lambda_<^{[]}$

Lemma 3 (Replacement).

(a) If D_0 is a derivation of $\gamma \cdot \Gamma\ ;\ \Gamma' \vdash \mathcal{E}_0^{|\Gamma|}[e_1] : t$, D_1 is a derivation of $\gamma_1\ ;\ \Gamma_1' \vdash e_1 : t_1$, D_1 appears in D_0 at the location corresponding to the hole, and $\gamma_1\ ;\ \Gamma_1' \vdash e_1' : t_1$, then $\gamma \cdot \Gamma\ ;\ \Gamma' \vdash \mathcal{E}_0^{|\Gamma|}[e_1'] : t$.

(b) If D_0 is a derivation of $\gamma \cdot \gamma' \cdot \Gamma ; \Gamma' \vdash \mathcal{S}_0^{|\Gamma|}[e_1] : t$, D_1 is a derivation of $\gamma_1 ; \Gamma_1' \vdash e_1 : t_1$, D_1 appears in D_0 at the location corresponding to the hole, and $\gamma_1\ ;\ \Gamma_1' \vdash e_1' : t_1$, then $\gamma \cdot \gamma' \cdot \Gamma\ ;\ \Gamma' \vdash \mathcal{S}_0^{|\Gamma|}[e_1'] : t$.

(c) If D_0 is a derivation of $\gamma \cdot \Gamma \,;\, \Gamma' \vdash \mathcal{R}_0^{|\Gamma|}[e_1] : t$, D_1 is a derivation of $\gamma_1 \,;\, \Gamma_1' \vdash e_1 : t_1$, D_1 appears in D_0 at the location corresponding to the hole, and $\gamma_1 \,;\, \Gamma_1' \vdash e_1' : t_1$, then $\gamma \cdot \Gamma \,;\, \Gamma' \vdash \mathcal{R}_0^{|\Gamma|}[e_1'] : t$.

Notice that we only ever substitute away stage-0 term variables (for a stage-0 values) in the evaluation rules.

Lemma 4 (Weakening). *If $\gamma_0 \cdot \cdots \cdot \gamma_m \,;\, \gamma_{m+1} \cdot \cdots \cdot \gamma_k \vdash e : t$ and for each $0 \leq i \leq k$, $\gamma_i \subseteq \gamma_i'$ and for each $\xi \in \mathrm{dom}(\gamma_i') - \mathrm{dom}(\gamma_i)$, $\xi \notin \mathrm{FV}_i^m(e)$ then $\gamma_0' \cdot \cdots \cdot \gamma_m' \,;\, \gamma_{m+1}' \cdot \cdots \cdot \gamma_k' \vdash e : t$.*

Lemma 5 (Strengthening). *If $\gamma_0' \cdot \cdots \cdot \gamma_m' \,;\, \gamma_{m+1}' \cdot \cdots \cdot \gamma_k' \vdash e : t$ and for each $0 \leq i \leq k$, $\gamma_i \subseteq \gamma_i'$ and for each $\xi \in \mathrm{dom}(\gamma_i') - \mathrm{dom}(\gamma_i)$, $\xi \notin \mathrm{FV}_i^m(e)$ then $\gamma_0 \cdot \cdots \cdot \gamma_m \,;\, \gamma_{m+1} \cdot \cdots \cdot \gamma_k \vdash e : t$.*

Strengthening is used in the proof of Subject Reduction, in the case (Set).

Lemma 6 (Substitution). *If $(x : t', \gamma) \cdot \Gamma \,;\, \Gamma' \vdash e : t$ and $\gamma \,;\, \Gamma \cdot \Gamma' \vdash e' : t'$ then $\gamma \cdot \Gamma \,;\, \Gamma' \vdash (e)^{|\Gamma|}\{e'/x\} : t$.*

4.2 Results for Staging

The following two lemmas show that demotion and promotion yield well-typed results: A well-typed value (but not necessarily an expression) at stage $m+1$ is also well-typed at stage m. And conversely, a well-typed value at stage m is also a well-typed value at stage $m+1$. These results are used in the proof of Subject Reduction (Lemma 9).

Lemma 7 (Demotion). *If $\Gamma \cdot \gamma \cdot \emptyset ; \Gamma' \vdash v^{|\Gamma|+1} : t$ then $\Gamma \cdot \gamma ; \emptyset \cdot \Gamma' \vdash v^{|\Gamma|+1} : t$.*

Lemma 8 (Promotion). *If $\Gamma \cdot \gamma \,;\, \emptyset \cdot \Gamma' \vdash v^{|\Gamma|} : t$ then $\Gamma \cdot \gamma \cdot \emptyset \,;\, \Gamma' \vdash v^{|\Gamma|} : t$.*

4.3 Subject Reduction

In the following statement of Subject Reduction, we need a general outer type environment γ (rather than an empty one) to account for cells in the store and we need the future-stage Γ' to account for future-stage variables.

Lemma 9 (Subject reduction). *If $\gamma \,;\, \Gamma' \vdash e : t$ and $e \longmapsto e'$ then $\gamma \,;\, \Gamma' \vdash e' : t$.*

Proof. by induction on $e \longmapsto e'$, with an induction case corresponding to reduction rule (Ctx), and with base cases for the remaining reduction rules. We make extensive use Decomposition (Lemma 2) and Replacement (Lemma 3). In each case, we apply a Typing Inversion lemma to deduce the types of subterms from the type of a term. This lemma is similar to that of Pierce [20, Sect. 15.3], but needs to account for stages. Substitution (Lemma 6) is used in case (β) and Demotion (Lemma 7) and Promotion (Lemma 8) are used in cases (Run) and (Lift).

4.4 Progress

We need the following definition of well-formed sequences of type environments.

Definition 4. *A sequence of type environments, $\Gamma\,;\Gamma'$, is well-formed if it satisfies the following rules.*

$$\vdash \epsilon\,;\Gamma' \qquad \frac{\Gamma\cdot\gamma\,;\,\Gamma'\vdash\gamma \qquad \vdash\Gamma\,;\gamma\cdot\Gamma'}{\vdash\Gamma\cdot\gamma\,;\Gamma'}$$

Lemma 10. *If $\vdash\Gamma\cdot\gamma\cdot\Gamma'\,;\epsilon$ and $\Gamma\cdot\gamma\,;\,\Gamma'\vdash t :: *$ then $\vdash\Gamma\cdot(x:t,\gamma)\cdot\Gamma'\,;\epsilon$.*

Lemma 11 (Progress). *If $\emptyset\,;\,\overline{\emptyset}\vdash e : t$ then either $e = v^0$, $e = \rho\theta.\,v^0$, or $e = \mathcal{E}_0^0[e']$ where $e' \longmapsto e''$. (Here $\overline{\emptyset}$ denotes a sufficiently long sequence of $\emptyset$s.)*

Proof. This follows as a corollary of a more general lemma that states that if $\gamma = (\ell_1 : t_1\,\mathsf{ref},\ldots,\ell_k : t_k\,\mathsf{ref})$ with $\gamma\,;\,\Gamma\cdot\Gamma'\vdash t_i :: *$ for any $1\le i\le l$ and $\vdash\gamma\cdot\Gamma\cdot\Gamma'\,;\epsilon$ and $\gamma\cdot\ ;\,\Gamma'\vdash e:t$ then either

(a) $e = v^{|\Gamma|}$ for some stage-$|\Gamma|$ value $v^{|\Gamma|}$,
(b) $e = \rho\theta.\,v^{|\Gamma|}$ for some θ and stage-$|\Gamma|$ value $v^{|\Gamma|}$,
(c) $e = \mathcal{E}_0^{|\Gamma|}[e']$ where $e'\longmapsto e''$ for some context $\mathcal{E}_0^{|\Gamma|}$ and terms e' and e'',
(d) $e = \mathcal{R}_0^{|\Gamma|}[\mathsf{get}_{\{t'\}}\,\ell]$,
(e) $e = \rho\theta.\,\mathcal{R}_0^{|\Gamma|}[\mathsf{get}_{\{t'\}}\,\ell]$ where $\ell\notin\mathrm{dom}\,\theta$,
(f) $e = \mathcal{R}_0^{|\Gamma|}[\mathsf{set}_{\{t'\}}\,\ell\,v^0]$, or
(g) $e = \rho\theta.\,\mathcal{R}_0^{|\Gamma|}[\mathsf{set}_{\{t'\}}\,\ell\,v^0]$ where $\ell\notin\mathrm{dom}\,\theta$.

Together, Subject Reduction and Progress establish type soundness of $\lambda^{[]}_{<}$.

5 Relation with Existing Type Systems

We show that $\lambda^{[]}$ types at least the terms typable in Davies's $\lambda^{\bigcirc}$ and that $\lambda^{[]}_{<}$ types at least the terms typable in Davies and Pfennings's λ^{S4}. (In the following subsections, we abuse notation by using the same meta variable for syntactic categories in different calculi.)

The next and prev of $\lambda^{\bigcirc}$ directly match $\uparrow$ and $\downarrow$ of $\lambda^{[]}_{<}$. Conversely, the unbox_n of λ^{S4} serves two purposes, namely as an iterated $\downarrow$ and as run. Hence the translation of λ^{S4} into $\lambda^{[]}_{<}$ is slightly more involved than translation of $\lambda^{\bigcirc}$ into $\lambda^{[]}_{<}$.

5.1 Relation to $\lambda^{\bigcirc}$

$\lambda^{\bigcirc}$ extends the simply-typed λ-calculus as follows.

Definition 5 **($\lambda^{\bigcirc}$).**

$$
\begin{aligned}
(\mathit{Types})\ & t ::= b \mid t_1 \to t_2 \mid \bigcirc t \\
(\mathit{Terms})\ & e ::= x \mid \lambda x{:}t.\, e \mid e_1\, e_2 \mid \mathsf{next}\, e \mid \mathsf{prev}\, e \\
(\mathit{Environments})\ & \Gamma ::= \emptyset \mid x : t^n, \Gamma
\end{aligned}
$$

The typing judgment of $\lambda^{\bigcirc}$, $\Gamma \vdash^n e : t$, is defined by the following typing rules.

$$
\frac{x : t^n \in \Gamma}{\Gamma \vdash^n x : t} \qquad \frac{\Gamma \vdash^{n+1} e : t}{\Gamma \vdash^n \mathsf{next}\, e : \bigcirc t} \qquad \frac{\Gamma \vdash^n e : \bigcirc t}{\Gamma \vdash^{n+1} \mathsf{prev}\, e : t}
$$

$$
\frac{x : t^n, \Gamma \vdash^n e : t'}{\Gamma \vdash^n \lambda x{:}t.\, e : t \to t'} \qquad \frac{\Gamma \vdash^n e_1 : t_2 \to t \quad \Gamma \vdash^n e_2 : t_2}{\Gamma \vdash^n e_1\, e_2 : t}
$$

The typing judgments of $\lambda^{\bigcirc}$ carry one type environment Γ that tracks the stage of variables by means of an integer staging annotation, $x : t^n$. In $\lambda^{[]}$, this staging information is implicitly given by the index into the stack where a variable is found. Hence, we parametrize the translation from $\lambda^{\bigcirc}$ into $\lambda^{[]}$ by a $\lambda^{\bigcirc}$ type environment and an integer that denotes the current stage.

Definition 6 (Translating $\lambda^{\bigcirc}$ into $\lambda^{[]}$). *Given a $\lambda^{\bigcirc}$ typing context Γ and a non-negative integer n, we generate a $\lambda^{[]}$ type environment containing the stage-n variables in Γ by*

$$
[\![\bigcirc]\!]^{\Gamma}_{m} = \left(x : [\![t]\!]^{\Gamma}_{m} \mid x : t^m \in \Gamma\right)
$$

and we then translate $\lambda^{\bigcirc}$ types and terms into $\lambda^{[]}$ types by

$$
\begin{aligned}
[\![b]\!]^{\Gamma}_{m} &= b & [\![x]\!]^{\Gamma}_{m} &= x \\
[\![t_1 \to t_2]\!]^{\Gamma}_{m} &= [\![t_1]\!]^{\Gamma}_{m} \to [\![t_2]\!]^{\Gamma}_{m} & [\![\lambda x{:}t.\, e]\!]^{\Gamma}_{m} &= \lambda x : [\![t]\!]^{\Gamma}_{m}.\, [\![e]\!]^{x:t^m,\Gamma}_{m} \\
[\![\bigcirc t]\!]^{\Gamma}_{m} &= [[\![\bigcirc]\!]^{\Gamma}_{m+1}][\![t]\!]^{\Gamma}_{m+1} & [\![e_1\, e_2]\!]^{\Gamma}_{m} &= [\![e_1]\!]^{\Gamma}_{m}\, [\![e_2]\!]^{\Gamma}_{m} \\
& & [\![\mathsf{next}\, e]\!]^{\Gamma}_{m} &= \uparrow [\![e]\!]^{\Gamma}_{m+1} \\
& & [\![\mathsf{prev}\, e]\!]^{\Gamma}_{m+1} &= \downarrow [\![e]\!]^{\Gamma}_{m}
\end{aligned}
$$

Given a $\lambda^{\bigcirc}$ typing context Γ and a pair of non-negative integers m, n, we generate a stack of $\lambda^{[]}$ type environment as follows.

$$
[\![\Gamma]\!]_{m,n} = \begin{cases} \epsilon, & \text{if } m > n \\ [\![\bigcirc]\!]^{\Gamma}_{m} \cdot [\![\Gamma]\!]_{m+1,n}, & \text{otherwise} \end{cases}
$$

Finally, $\lambda^{\bigcirc}$ type judgments are translated into $\lambda^{[]}$ as follows.

$$
\begin{aligned}
[\![\Gamma \vdash^m e : t]\!] = [\![\Gamma]\!]_{0,m}\ ;\ [\![\Gamma]\!]_{m+1,k} \vdash [\![e]\!]^{\Gamma}_{m} : [\![t]\!]^{\Gamma}_{m} \\
\text{where } k = \max\{m \mid x : t^m \in \Gamma\}
\end{aligned}
$$

This translation makes it evident that $\bigcirc t$ is a type of *open* code. The following lemma shows that the translation preserves typing. The proof follows by a straightforward induction on the derivation of the $\lambda^{\bigcirc}$ judgment using, in the case for abstractions, the observation that $[\![t]\!]_m^{x:t^m,\Gamma} = [\![t]\!]_m^{\Gamma}$ and hence also $[\![e]\!]_m^{x:t^m,\Gamma} = [\![e]\!]_m^{\Gamma}$.

Lemma 12. *If $\Gamma \vdash^m e : t$ is derivable in $\lambda^{\bigcirc}$ then $[\![\Gamma \vdash^m e : t]\!]$ is derivable in $\lambda^{[]}$.*

5.2 Relation to λ^{S4}

λ^{S4} is a variant of the modal type system $\lambda^{\Box}$ that replaces a combination of **unbox** with a number of **pop** operations by a single $\mathbf{unbox}_n$ operation [10].

Definition 7 (λ^{S4}).

$$\begin{aligned} (\mathit{Types})\ t &::= b \mid t_1 \to t_2 \mid \Box t \\ (\mathit{Terms})\ e &::= x \mid \lambda x{:}t.\,e \mid e_1\,e_2 \mid \mathsf{box}\,e \mid \mathsf{unbox}_n\,e \\ (\mathit{Environments})\ \Gamma &::= \emptyset \mid x : t, \Gamma \\ (\mathit{Stacks})\ \Psi &::= \epsilon \mid \Psi ; \Gamma \end{aligned}$$

The typing judgment of λ^{S4}, $\Psi;\Gamma \vdash e : t$, is defined by the following typing rules.

$$\frac{x : t \in \Gamma}{\Psi;\Gamma \vdash x : t}$$

$$\frac{\Psi;\Gamma;\emptyset \vdash e : t}{\Psi;\Gamma \vdash \mathsf{box}\,e : \Box t} \qquad \frac{\Psi;\Gamma \vdash e : \Box t}{\Psi;\Gamma;\Gamma_1;\cdots;\Gamma_n \vdash \mathsf{unbox}_n\,e : t}$$

$$\frac{\Psi;(x : t,\Gamma) \vdash e : t'}{\Psi;\Gamma \vdash \lambda x{:}t.\,e : t \to t'} \qquad \frac{\Psi;\Gamma \vdash e_1 : t_2 \to t \quad \Psi;\Gamma \vdash e_2 : t_2}{\Psi;\Gamma \vdash e_1\,e_2 : t}$$

We simplify the translation into $\lambda^{[]}_{<}$ by using constants run and lift that are not explicitly type annotated. (This can be avoided by defining the translation on typing judgments.) We also simplify lifting by assuming an implicit surrounding $\downarrow$. We thus write $\%e$ for $\downarrow(\mathsf{lift}\,e)$. More concretely, we use the following variants of the typing rules of run and lifting, both of which are admissible in $\lambda^{[]}_{<}$. The rule for lifting follows by a use of subsumption to strengthen the γ' to $\emptyset$.

$$\frac{\Gamma\cdot\gamma\,;\,\Gamma' \vdash e : [\,]t}{\Gamma\cdot\gamma\,;\,\Gamma' \vdash \mathsf{run}\,e : t} \qquad \frac{\Gamma\cdot\gamma\,;\,\emptyset\cdot\Gamma' \vdash e : t}{\Gamma\cdot\gamma\cdot\gamma'\,;\,\Gamma' \vdash \%e : t}$$

Definition 8 (Translating λ^{S4} into $\lambda^{[]}_{<}$). *We translate λ^{S4} types, terms, and judgments into $\lambda^{[]}_{<}$ by*

$$\begin{aligned} [\![b]\!] &= b & [\![x]\!] &= x \\ [\![t_1 \rightarrow t_2]\!] &= [\![t_1]\!] \rightarrow [\![t_2]\!] & [\![\lambda x : t.\, e]\!] &= \lambda x : [\![t]\!].\, [\![e]\!] \\ [\![\Box t]\!] &= [\,][\![t]\!] & [\![e_1\, e_2]\!] &= [\![e_1]\!]\, [\![e_2]\!] \\ & & [\![\mathsf{box}\, e]\!] &= \uparrow [\![e]\!] \\ & & [\![\mathsf{unbox}_0\, e]\!] &= \mathsf{run}\, [\![e]\!] \\ & & [\![\mathsf{unbox}_{n+1}\, e]\!] &= \%^n \downarrow [\![e]\!] \end{aligned}$$

$$[\![\Psi; \Gamma \vdash e : t]\!] = [\![\Psi]\!] \cdot [\![\Gamma]\!] \ ; \overline{\emptyset} \vdash [\![e]\!] : [\![t]\!]$$

This translation makes it evident that $\Box t$ is a type of *closed* code. The translation is similar to the translation of λ^{S4} into λ^{i}_{let} [6]. The following lemma shows that the $\lambda^{[]}_{<}$ variant of an unbox_n can remove the n topmost type environments. It follows by induction on n using the subsumption rule to discard the top-most assumptions.

Lemma 13. *If $\Gamma \cdot \gamma \ ; \overline{\emptyset} \vdash e : [\,]t$ then $\Gamma \cdot \gamma \cdot \gamma_1 \cdot \dots \cdot \gamma_{n+1} \ ; \overline{\emptyset} \vdash \%^{n+1} \downarrow e : t$.*

We can then show that the translation of λ^{S4} into $\lambda^{[]}$ preserves typing. The proof follows by induction on the derivation of the typing judgment in λ^{S4}.

Lemma 14. *If $\Psi; \Gamma \vdash e : t$ is derivable in λ^{S4} then $[\![\Psi; \Gamma \vdash e : t]\!]$ is derivable in $\lambda^{[]}_{<}$ with the above typing rules for the* run *and* %.

6 Related Work

Traditionally, type systems for staged programming are classified according to their ability to distinguish between open and closed code values. Davies's $\lambda^{\bigcirc}$ [9] and Davies and Pfenning's $\lambda^{\Box}$ [10] were the first type systems to introduce types of code values and the notion of multiple stages. The type system of $\lambda^{\bigcirc}$ cannot distinguish between open and closed code. Hence $\lambda^{\bigcirc}$ does not support an eval function.

The type system of MetaML is based on $\lambda^{\bigcirc}$ [26]. It provides a type of open code and hence cannot guarantee that only closed code is executed. Moggi et al. establish that guarantee by extending MetaML with an additional type of closed code [16]. Benaissa et al. generalize this type system by introducing a type that characterize closed *values*, not just closed *code values*, and then unifying the two code types into one of open code [4]. Neither of these type systems deal with mutable state. Calcagno et al. show that it is safe to store closed code values in reference cells [6].

The type system of $\lambda^{\Box}$ only allows closed code values [10]. An eval function can be encoded in $\lambda^{\Box}$. However, $\lambda^{\Box}$ does not support evaluation under future-stage λs. Hence, unlike approaches based on $\lambda^{\bigcirc}$, multi-stage programming in $\lambda^{\Box}$ leaves residual administrative redexes in code values.

Inspired by nominal logics, Nanevski proposes a variant of $\lambda^{\Box}$, called $\nu^{\Box}$, that allows code to contain free variables and that exposes these variables in the type of code [18]. This calculus introduces explicit substitutions to eliminate free variables. Nanevski et al. propose Contextual Modal Types in another variant of $\lambda^{\Box}$ with explicit substitutions [19]. Both of these calculi enable multi-stage programming that eliminates administrative redexes in code values.

Kim et al.'s λ^{sim}_{open} and λ^{poly}_{open} also extend $\lambda^{\Box}$ by parameterizing code types over type environments [14]. (Kim et al.'s type system generalizes a monomorphic type system previously presented by the present author [21].) But unlike the Contextual Modal Type system of Nanevski et al., λ^{sim}_{open} and λ^{poly}_{open} treats variables symbolically. This opens up for both a hygienic future-stage λ^* (via a capture-avoiding substitution) and a non-hygienic future-stage λ (via a capturing substitution). Unlike $\lambda^{[]}$, however, despite being hygienic λ^{sim}_{open} and λ^{poly}_{open} are not lexically scoped. For example, in these type systems a term such as $\uparrow(\lambda^* x : \mathsf{bool}. \downarrow(\mathsf{let}\ \_ = \uparrow(x + 1)\ \mathsf{in}\ \cdots))$ is well typed despite the mismatching types of x.

Taha and Nielsen's λ^{α} combine open-code manipulation with an eval function by introducing explicit classifiers that name type environments [25]. The code type of λ^{α} is annotated by the classifier for the environment in which code can be inserted. A type-level quantifier over classifiers is used to make (code) types parametric in classifiers. In subsequent work, Calcagno et al. define the variant λ^{i}_{let} which simplify this idea by eliminating explicit classifiers in terms [7]. Neither of these calculi supports mutable state. We have addressed the warnings of Taha and Nielsen [25, Sect. 1.4] by demonstrating that α-equivalence is compatible with types that carry environments and that no negative side conditions on environments are required.

Chen and Xi's λ_{code} introduce a code type parameterized over a type environment and a type [8]. λ_{code} is nameless: variables are represented by their de Bruijn indices, both in terms and in types. Although the precise connection between $\lambda^{[]}$ and λ_{code} remains to be established, it seems that λ_{code} is similar to a nameless variant of $\lambda^{[]}$. Chen and Xi do not discuss mutable state.

Kameyama et al.'s $\lambda_1^{\oslash}$ extends a simple variant of λ^{α} with control effects [13]. $\lambda_1^{\oslash}$ supports mutable state and an eval function. To prevent scope extrusion, $\lambda_1^{\oslash}$ prohibits the evaluation of future-state λs to have observable side effects. In recent work, Westbrook et al. relax this requirement by characterizing terms as *weakly separable* when they do not have observable side effects that involve code values [27]. By requiring that escaped terms (i.e., the $\downarrow e$ of $\lambda^{[]}$) are weakly separable, Westbrook et al. can guarantee that no code value (and hence no future-stage variable) can leave the scope in which it is generated. In contrast (as witnessed by the example at the end of Sect. 2.3), $\lambda^{[]}$ allows both escaped terms and future-stage λs to have observable effects involving open code.

7 Conclusions

We have defined $\lambda^{[]}$, a core type system for staged computation that is sound and hygienic and that supports open-code manipulation, a first-class eval function, and mutable state. We have also extended $\lambda^{[]}$ with subtype polymorphism. The result is $\lambda^{[]}_{<}$, a type system for staged computation that is at least as expressive as existing type systems for staged computation, but strikingly simpler.

References

[1] Backus, J.W., Beeber, R.J., Best, S., Goldberg, R., Haibt, L.M., Herrick, H.L., Nelson, R.A., Sayre, D., Sheridan, P.B., Stern, H., Ziller, I., Hughes, R.A., Nutt, R.: The Fortran automatic coding system. In: Techniques for Reliability, Proceedings of the Western Joint Computer Conference, pp. 188–198 (1957)

[2] Barendregt, H.: The Lambda Calculus — Its Syntax and Semantics. North-Holland (1984)

[3] Bawden, A.: Quasiquotation in Lisp. In: Proceedings of the ACM SIGPLAN Workshop on Partial Evaluation and Semantics-Based Program Manipulation, San Antonio, Texas (1999)

[4] Benaissa, Z.-E.-A., Moggi, E., Taha, W., Sheard, T.: Logical modalities and multi-stage programming. In: Proceedings of the Workshop on Intuitionistic Modal Logics and Applications, Trento, Italy (July 1999)

[5] Bondorf, A., Jones, N.D., Mogensen, T., Sestoft, P.: Binding time analysis and the taming of self-application. DIKU rapport, University of Copenhagen, Copenhagen, Denmark (1988)

[6] Calcagno, C., Moggi, E., Taha, W.: Closed Types as a Simple Approach to Safe Imperative Multi-stage Programming. In: Welzl, E., Montanari, U., Rolim, J.D.P. (eds.) ICALP 2000. LNCS, vol. 1853, pp. 25–36. Springer, Heidelberg (2000)

[7] Calcagno, C., Moggi, E., Taha, W.: ML-Like Inference for Classifiers. In: Schmidt, D. (ed.) ESOP 2004. LNCS, vol. 2986, pp. 79–93. Springer, Heidelberg (2004)

[8] Chen, C., Xi, H.: Meta-programming through typeful code representation. Journal of Functional Programming 15(6), 797–835 (2005)

[9] Davies, R.: A temporal-logic approach to binding-time analysis. In: Proceedings of the Eleventh Annual IEEE Symposium on Logic in Computer Science, pp. 184–195. IEEE Computer Society Press, New Brunswick (1996)

[10] Davies, R., Pfenning, F.: A modal analysis of staged computation. Journal of the ACM 48(3), 555–604 (2001)

[11] Felleisen, M., Hieb, R.: The revised report on the syntactic theories of sequential control and state. Technical Report Rice COMP TR89–100, Department of Computer Science, Rice University, Houston, Texas (June 1989)

[12] Jones, N.D., Gomard, C.K., Sestoft, P.: Partial Evaluation and Automatic Program Generation. International Series in Computer Science. Prentice-Hall (1993)

[13] Kameyama, Y., Kiselyov, O., Shan, C.C.: Shifting the stage: staging with delimited control. In: Proceedings of the ACM SIGPLAN Workshop on Partial Evaluation and Program Manipulation, pp. 111–120. ACM, Savannah (2009)

[14] Kim, I.-S., Yi, K., Calcagno, C.: A polymorphic modal type system for lisp-like multi-staged languages. In: Proceedings of the Thirty-Third Annual ACM Symposium on Principles of Programming Languages, pp. 257–268. ACM Press, Charleston (2006)

[15] McCarthy, J.: LISP 1.5 Programmer's Manual. The MIT Press, Cambridge (1962)

[16] Moggi, E., Taha, W., Benaissa, Z.-E.-A., Sheard, T.: An Idealized MetaML: Simpler, and More Expressive. In: Swierstra, S.D. (ed.) ESOP 1999. LNCS, vol. 1576, pp. 193–207. Springer, Heidelberg (1999)

[17] Morrisett, G., Felleisen, M., Harper, R.: Abstract models of memory management. In: Proceedings of the Seventh ACM Conference on Functional Programming and Computer Architecture, pp. 66–77. ACM Press, La Jolla (1995)
[18] Nanevski, A.: Meta-programming with names and necessity. In: Proceedings of the 2002 ACM SIGPLAN International Conference on Functional Programming, pp. 206–217. ACM Press, Pittsburgh (2002)
[19] Nanevski, A., Pfenning, F., Pientka, B.: Contextual modal type theory. ACM Transactions on Computational Logic 9(3), 1–49 (2008)
[20] Pierce, B.C.: Types and Programming Languages. The MIT Press, Cambridge (2002)
[21] Rhiger, M.: First-class open and closed code fragments. Trends in Functional Programming 6, 127–144 (2007), Intellect
[22] Taha, W.: Multi-Stage programming: Its Theory and Applications. PhD thesis, Oregon Graduate Institute of Science and Technology (1999)
[23] Taha, W.: A sound reduction semantics for untyped CBN multi-stage computations. or, the theory of MetaML is non-trivial. In: Proceedings of the ACM SIGPLAN Workshop on Partial Evaluation and Semantics-Based Program Manipulation. ACM Press, Boston (2000)
[24] Taha, W., Benaissa, Z.-E.-A., Sheard, T.: Multi-Stage Programming: Axiomatization and Type Safety. In: Larsen, K.G., Skyum, S., Winskel, G. (eds.) ICALP 1998. LNCS, vol. 1443, pp. 918–929. Springer, Heidelberg (1998)
[25] Taha, W., Nielsen, M.F.: Environment classifiers. In: Proceedings of the Thirtieth Annual ACM Symposium on Principles of Programming Languages, pp. 26–37. ACM Press, New Orleans (2003)
[26] Taha, W., Sheard, T.: Multi-stage programming with explicit annotations. In: Proceedings of the ACM SIGPLAN Symposium on Partial Evaluation and Semantics-Based Program Manipulation, pp. 203–217. ACM Press, Amsterdam (1997)
[27] Westbrook, E., Ricken, M., Inoue, J., Yao, Y., Abdelatif, T., Taha, W.: Mint: Java multi-stage programming using weak separability. In: Proceedings of the ACM SIGPLAN 2010 Conference on Programming Languages Design and Implementation, pp. 400–411. ACM Press, Toronto (2010)
[28] Wright, A.K., Felleisen, M.: A syntactic approach to type soundness. Information and Computation 115, 38–94 (1994)

Gradual Ownership Types

Ilya Sergey and Dave Clarke

IBBT-DistriNet, Department of Computer Science,
Katholieke Universiteit Leuven, Belgium
firstname.lastname@cs.kuleuven.be

Abstract. Gradual Ownership Types are a framework allowing programs to be partially annotated with ownership types, while providing the same encapsulation guarantees. The formalism provides a static guarantee of the desired encapsulation property for fully annotated programs, and dynamic guarantees for partially annotated programs via dynamic checks inserted by the compiler. This enables a smooth migration from ownership-unaware to ownership-typed code.

The paper provides a formal account of gradual ownership types. The theoretical novelty of this work is in adapting the notion of gradual type system with respect to *program heap properties*, which, unlike types in functional languages or object calculi, impose restrictions not only on data, but also on the environment the data is being processed in. From the practical side, we evaluate applicability of Gradual Ownership Types for Java 1.4 in the context of the Java Collection Framework and measure the necessary amount of annotations for ensuring the owners-as-dominators invariant.

1 Introduction

Type systems for ownership in object-oriented languages provide a declarative way to statically enforce a notion of object encapsulation in object-oriented programs. Object ownership ensures that objects cannot escape from the *scope* of the object or collection of objects that *own* them. Variants of ownership types allow a program to enjoy such computational properties as data race-freedom [4], disjointness of effects [8], various confinement properties [28] and effective memory management [5].

However, there are several obstacles to the adoption of ownership types. The first is verbosity. One way to overcome this problem is to omit annotations and use type inference instead. Unlike traditional type systems, ownership annotations are mostly design-driven, thus full inference of ownership types is not particularly useful, since a correct, trivial ownership typing always exists [12]. Therefore, inference is only practically applicable when some annotations are already provided to indicate the programmer's intention. But even in the case of partially-annotated programs, ownership type inference tends to produce an excessive amount of inferred annotations [21] or imprecise results due to the conservatism of the underlying analysis [20]. The second obstacle is that ownership types are often too rigid to capture the dynamic evolution of an object graph in real applications, and in some cases the imposed constraints need to be relaxed.

Adding ownership annotations into the code is similar to the migration from the untyped to typed code, a topic of much research nowadays [15,17,26,27]. Complete

H. Seidl (Ed.): ESOP 2012, LNCS 7211, pp. 579–599, 2012.

absence of types facilitates the fast prototyping and rapid evolution of the system, so one might need to introduce types into the code only when the demands for reliability and performance of the program are established. Ownership types provide more fine-grained safety guarantees. In this respect refactoring a program to employ them can be considered as a migration from typed to "even more typed" code. This observation leads to the idea of applying a *gradual* approach for an incremental migration.

This work is based on the ownership type system of Clarke and Drossopoulou [8], which ensures the *owners-as-dominators* invariant. It is expressive enough to investigate the concepts of interest and is close enough to a real language to guide the implementation. Nevertheless our approach is idiomatic and can be applied to many other ownership type systems. Overall, this paper makes the following contributions:

- A type system for a Java-like object-oriented language providing gradual ownership types, enabling the migration from ownership-unaware to ownership-annotated code.
- A type-directed program translation that ensures the dynamic preservation of the ownership invariant when insufficient type annotations are provided; soundness theorems and properties of the type-directed translation.
- An implementation of a translating compiler for full Java 1.4 that supports gradual ownership types and provides hints for smooth program migration.
- A report on migrating classes from Java's SDK to use gradual ownership types.
- A discussion on extending the described framework for different existing ownership policies and an overview of possible design choices of the implementation.

2 Intuition and Overview

This section gives the essence of ownership types enforcing the *owners-as-dominators* policy (OAD) and provides some intuition on the "gradualization" of the type system.

Ownership types are based on a *nesting* relation on objects ($\prec$). At run-time, each object o has an *owner*, i.e., another object o', such that $o \prec o'$. Nesting is a tree-shaped partial order on objects with greatest element **`world`**. The OAD invariant is as follows: *Given an object o and its* owner o', *every path in the object graph of a program from the* program roots *along object fields that ends in o, contains* o'. I.e., there are no fields referring to o that bypass o'. This means that one object cannot refer to a second object directly as a field, unless the first object is *inside* the second object's owner.

Figure 1 gives an example of the class `List` using ownership types. The class carries two *ownership parameters*: `owner` and `data`. The first parameter, `owner`, refers to the `List` instance's immediate, or *primary*, owner. The second parameter, `data`, refers, by conventions of the type system, to some object *outside* or equal to `owner`. As usual, **`this`** refers to the current instance itself. The same reasoning is applicable to two auxiliary classes, `Link` and `Iterator`. In the `List`'s method `add()`, the programmer indicates, by creating an instance of the class `Link` with owners **`this`** and `data` respectively, that this particular instance of `Link` is nested within its creator instance `List` and the content of the link can be accessed only through the owner referred to as `data` in `List`. The same is true for the instance of the class `Iterator`.

```
class List<owner, data> {
  Link <this, data> head;
  void add(Data <data> d) {
    head = new Link<this, data>(head, d);
  }
  Iterator <this,data> makeIterator() {
    return new Iterator<this, data>(head);
  }
}
class Link<owner,data> {
  Link <owner, data> next;
  Data <data> data;
  Link(Link <owner, data> next, Data <data> data) {
    this.next = next; this.data = data;
  }
}
class Iterator<owner, data> {
  Link <owner, data> current;
  Iterator(Link <owner, data> first) {
    current = first;
  }
  void next() { current = current.next; }
  Data <data> elem() { return current.data; }
  boolean done() { return (current == null); }
}
```

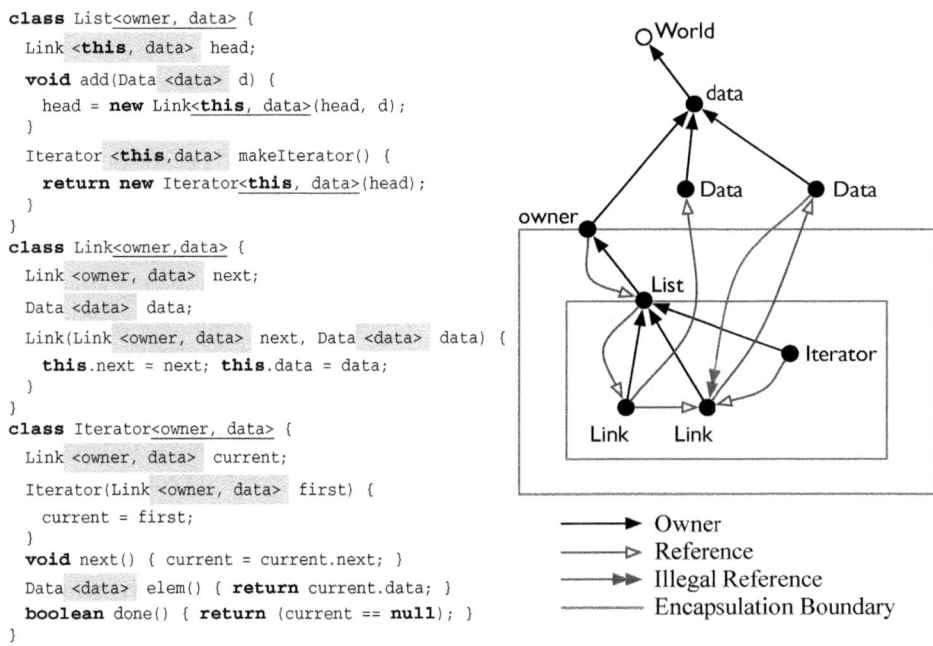

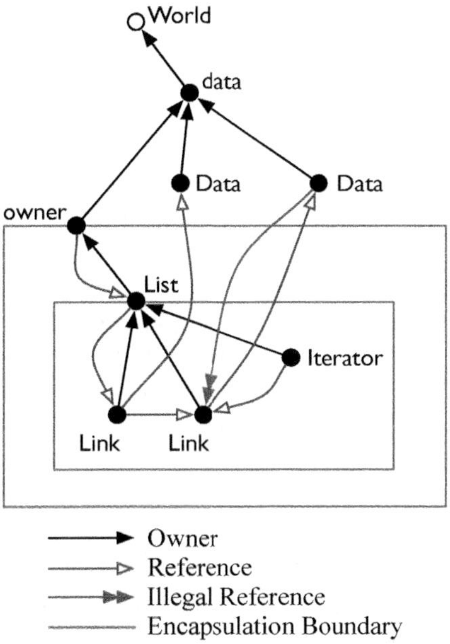

Fig. 1. A motivating example and the design intention: a list and its iterator code with structural (underlined) and constraint (grayed) ownership annotations

Ownership information for our list example can be provided by only five annotations. Three class parametrizations name the owners of the class instances and two allocation sites provide concrete owners for created objects. These annotations, underlined in Figure 1, are *structural*: they declare the information about nesting of objects involved (i.e., **this** $\prec$ owner $\prec$ data $\prec$ **world**) and define the owners of new instances. The remaining, *constraint*, annotations, grayed in the code, "propagate" ownership information through the program, since mutable variables and fields are traditionally annotated with types to keep information about objects they point to. We require the first kind of annotations to be explicitly specified, because it (a) reflects the programmer's intentions with respect to the invariant and (b) enables a simpler implementation of run-time dynamic checking—no ownership information needs to be inferred dynamically.

The runtime checking of conformance of an object's ownership structure to the expectation is performed via dynamic type casts. This technique is typical for gradual approaches: when an untyped value is coerced to a typed value, a dynamic check is performed to ensure that the further interactions through this particular reference conform to the target's type contract, in this setting, its ownership type. However, the preservation of the OAD invariant requires not only conformance of *actual* and *expected* types, but also checking that the *nesting* constraints are preserved—this information is lost when ownership information is lost.

The only place where the owners-as-dominators invariant can actually be broken is by a bad field assignment, which makes field assignments good candidates for extra run-time checks. Consider the following assignment:

```
receiver.f = result;
```

The correctness requirement for such an assignment demands that `receiver` $\prec$ `o`, where `o` is an owner of the object referred to by `result`. If the declaration of the field `f` lacks ownership information, there is a chance that the OAD invariant will be violated since the type of `f` may no longer impose any nesting between `receiver` and `result`. This is a sort of contract that should be checked dynamically. We call these *boundary checks*.

One can notice that dynamic type casts operate with objets' ownership structures, whereas boundary checks traverse a part of the heap and, therefore, are significantly more expensive. However, performing type casts *before* boundary checks might help to avoid most of them, since after the check we gain some extra knowledge of an object's structure. This observation leads us to a two-staged, typed-directed transformation, where each stage uses the available type information to perform one sort of check: *type conformance* and *nesting*. In the following sections we develop a staged algorithm for the correct translation. The first pass will insert dynamic casts and the second will handle possible OAD violations by inserting boundary checks.

Defined, Unknown and Dependent Owners. An important part of the ownership type system is the static representation of owners. The example in Figure 1 demonstrated one usage of ownership class parameters. The following example exhibits the concept of *dynamic aliasing* [8], which employs local final variables as local owners:

```
final List<p, world> list = new List<p, world>();
Iterator<list, world> iter = list.makeIterator();
```

Variable `list` denotes the owner of the iterator in `iter`. When `list` goes out of scope, the type `Iterator<list, world>` and other types containing owner `list` become illegal.

Following gradual types we introduce a notion of the special *unknown owner* "?". Types annotated with "?" in a gradually-typed language defer the checking of types to run-time via checks inserted by the compiler. In our system, types with no annotations are just syntactic sugar for types with all ownership annotations unknown, e.g., `List` $\equiv$ `List<?,?>`. The following code gives the essence of unknown owners:

```
List list; // ≡ List<?,?>
list = new List<p, world>();
list = new List<this, world>();
List<p, world> newList = list; // inserted cast (List<p, world>)list
```

The first two assignments are valid since the type of `list` does not specify which objects must own the instance referred by the variable. The last assignment is valid too; however, it requires a dynamic cast, due to the type refinement `List<?, ?>` $\Rightarrow$ `List<p, world>` to make sure that the owners of `list` matches the specification of `newList`.

Information lost due to unknown owners can be partially regained by tracking of dependencies between immutable references and owners of objects they refer to. For this purpose we introduce *dependent owners*, which record the origin of some owner arguments, allowing one to check them for equality without knowledge about the nesting.

```
1  class E<P> { D myD = ... }
2
3  class D<owner> {
4    E<owner> e;
5    void use(D<owner> arg) { ... }
6    void exploit(E<owner> arg) { this.e = arg; }
7    void test(E e) {
8      final D d = e.myD; // implicitly, d: D<d^{D.owner}>
9      d.use(d); // type refinement, but no type cast required
10     d.exploit(e); // type refinement, dynamic type cast required
11   }
12 }
```

Fig. 2. Dependent owners in action

Figure 2 provides and example with dependent owners. Class `E` declares a field of type `D`. However, information about the owner of the object referred to by field `myD` is lost due to the missing ownership annotation in the field declaration on line 1. As a consequence, the owner of variable `d` in line 8 is unknown. Nevertheless, since `d` is final, one can see that the owner of the object referred by `d` is the same as the one expected as of a parameter of the instance method `d.use()`. This knowledge is preserved by assigning the type $\texttt{D<d}^{D.owner}\texttt{>}$ to variable `d`. This should be read as "`d` has the type `D` and the owner of the object referred to is locally denoted as $\texttt{d}^{D.owner}$". The superscript `D.owner` refers to the particular ownership parameter of the statically known type `D`. Thus, by equality of owners, no extra dynamic check is required in line 9. Still, the owner of `e` remains unknown, so the method call `d.exploit()` on line 10 is potentially dangerous due to type refinement, and therefore the cast $\texttt{E<?>} \Rightarrow \texttt{E<d}^{D.owner}\texttt{>}$ is required.[1]

3 The Language $\mathsf{JO}_?$

To investigate the meta-theory of gradual ownership types we define $\mathsf{JO}_?$, an imperative Java-like language, extended with ownership types, and unknown and dependent owners, based on the system JOE_1 by Clarke and Drossopoulou [8].

3.1 Syntax

Figure 3 provides the full syntax of $\mathsf{JO}_?$. A program in $\mathsf{JO}_?$ is a collection of classes. A class definition describes a class named c, parametrized by the ownership parameters $\alpha_{i\in 1..n}$ with the superclass c', whose ownership parameters are instantiated with $p_{j\in 1..n'}$.[2] Methods have only one parameter for simplicity. Expressions in $\mathsf{JO}_?^+$ are a-normal form (ANF), i.e., all intermediate computations are named and assigned to the immutable variables. Local variables can be used as owners, as long as they do not escape the scope of a local stack frame.

[1] We have chosen the term "dependent owners" because of similarity of the idea to the notion of *path-dependent types* [22]—the value of the owner depends on the value of an object.

[2] More expressive possibilities exist in the literature, for example, by allowing the programmer to declare the expected relationship between owner parameters to a class [10].

P	$::= \mathit{class}_{j\in 1..m}$	***programs***
class	$::= \texttt{class}\ c\langle \alpha_{i\in 1..n}\rangle\ \texttt{extends}\ c'\langle p_{j\in 1..n'}\rangle\ \{\mathit{fd}_{k\in 1..m};\ \mathit{meth}_{l\in 1..u}\}$	***class declarations***
fd	$::= t\ f$	***field declarations***
meth	$::= t\ m(t\ x)\ \{e\}$	***method declarations***
e	$::= x \mid \texttt{let}\ x = b\ \texttt{in}\ e$	***expressions***
b	$::= x.f \mid x.f = x \mid x.m(x) \mid \texttt{new}\ c\langle p_{i\in 1..n}\rangle \mid \texttt{null}$	***computations***
v	$::= \iota \mid \texttt{null}$	***values***
E	$::= \emptyset \mid E, x : t \mid E, \iota : t \mid E, p \prec p'$	***typing environments***
B	$::= \emptyset \mid B, \alpha = k \mid B, x = v$	***bindings***

k	$::= \texttt{world} \mid \iota$	***run-time owners***	$x, y, z, \texttt{this}$	***variables***
p, q	$::= x \mid \texttt{this} \mid k \mid ? \mid \alpha$	***owners***	ι	***heap locations***
t, s	$::= c\langle p_{i\in 1..n}\rangle$	***types***	α	***formal owners***
o	$::= \langle c\langle k_{i\in 1..n}\rangle, \overline{f \mapsto v}\rangle$	***objects***	$x^{c.i}$	***dependent owners***
H	$::= \overline{\iota \mapsto o}$	***heaps***	$?$	***unknown owners***

$$\mathsf{defined}(p) \triangleq (p \neq ?) \wedge (p \neq x^{c.i}) \qquad \mathsf{owner}(c\langle\rangle) \triangleq \texttt{world}$$

$$\mathsf{undefined}(p) \triangleq \neg\mathsf{defined}(p) \qquad \mathsf{owner}(c\langle p_{i\in 1..n}\rangle) \triangleq p_1,\ \text{where } n > 0$$

$$\mathsf{actual}(p) \triangleq (p = \texttt{world}) \wedge (p = \iota) \qquad \mathsf{owner}_j(c\langle p_{i\in 1..n}\rangle) \triangleq p_j,\ \text{where } 0 < j \leq n$$

$$\mathsf{arity}(c) \triangleq n,\ \text{s.t. } \texttt{class}\ c\langle \alpha_{i\in 1..n}\rangle \in P \qquad \mathsf{owners}(c\langle p_{i\in 1..n}\rangle) \triangleq p_1 \ldots p_n$$

Fig. 3. Syntax of $\mathrm{JO}_?$ and syntactic helper functions

Types and Owners. A type $c\langle p_{i\in 1..n}\rangle$ consists of a class name c and a vector of ownership arguments $p_{i\in 1..n}$. Owners are represented syntactically by owner and term variables (α and x, respectively), *dependent* owners and *run-time* owners such as **`world`** and heap locations (i.e, run-time object identifiers). $x^{c.i}$ denotes the dependent owner corresponding to the i-th ownership parameter of the object referred to by the term variable x, whose statically known class type is c. Dependent owners are not supposed to be specified by the programmer. Instead, they are inferred by the compiler. We often use an alternative notation $c\langle\sigma\rangle$ for a type $c\langle p_{i\in 1..n}\rangle$, assuming σ to be a substitution $\{\alpha_i \mapsto p_i \mid i \in 1..\mathsf{arity}(c)\}$, and α_i are formal ownership parameters of the class c.

To distinguish between different kinds of owners when checking the well-formedness of types, we introduce several syntactic helper functions (Figure 3).

Objects and Heaps. In addition to having the class name and field values, an object also has a binding for its owner parameters, either `world` or some non-null heap locations. A heap H is a partially defined map from locations to objects.

3.2 Environments and Owners

A typing environment E binds variables and heap locations with types and defines ordering assumptions on owners with respect to the nesting relation $\prec$. The bindings B map formal owners to run-time owners and variables to values.

The dynamic semantics is defined in Section 5 in terms of an explicit binding of free variables, rather than via substitution. The presence of binding environment in the

$\boxed{E;B \vdash p}$

$$\text{(OWN-WORLD)}\ \frac{E;B \vdash \diamond}{E;B \vdash \texttt{world}} \qquad \text{(OWN-VAR)}\ \frac{E;B \vdash \diamond \quad E;B \vdash x:t}{E;B \vdash x} \qquad \text{(OWN-VAL)}\ \frac{E;B \vdash \diamond \quad E;B \vdash \iota:t}{E;B \vdash \iota}$$

$$\text{(OWN-?)}\ \frac{E;B \vdash \diamond}{E;B \vdash ?} \qquad \text{(OWN-DEPENDENT)}\ \frac{E;B \vdash x \quad i \in 1..\mathsf{arity}(c)}{E;B \vdash x^{c.i}} \qquad \text{(OWN-IN)}\ \frac{E;B \vdash \diamond \quad p \prec p' \in E}{E;B \vdash p, p'}$$

$\boxed{E;B \vdash p \prec p'}$ $\mathsf{defined}(p), \mathsf{defined}(p')$

$$\text{(IN-ENV)}\ \frac{p \prec p' \in E}{E;B \vdash p \prec p'} \qquad \text{(IN-REFL)}\ \frac{E;B \vdash p}{E;B \vdash p \prec p}$$

$$\text{(IN-TRANS)}\ \frac{E;B \vdash p \prec p' \quad E;B \vdash p' \prec p''}{E;B \vdash p \prec p''} \qquad \text{(IN-VAR)}\ \frac{E;B \vdash x:t \quad p = \mathsf{owner}(t)}{E;B \vdash x \prec p}$$

$\boxed{E;B \vdash p \lesssim p'}$

$$\text{(SUB-LEFT)}\ \frac{E;B \vdash p \quad E;B \vdash q \quad \mathsf{undefined}(q)}{E;B \vdash p \lesssim q} \qquad \text{(SUB-RIGHT)}\ \frac{E;B \vdash p \quad E;B \vdash q \quad \mathsf{undefined}(q)}{E;B \vdash q \lesssim p}$$

$$\text{(SUB-INCL)}\ \frac{E;B \vdash p \prec p'}{E;B \vdash p \lesssim p'} \qquad \text{(SUB-WORLD)}\ \frac{E;B \vdash p}{E;B \vdash p \lesssim \texttt{world}}$$

Fig. 4. Well-formed owners and owner nesting

typing judgements of the form $E;B \vdash \mathfrak{F}$ for some succedent $\mathfrak{F}$ does not affect the static semantics of JO$_?$, but we will need it to establish equalities between typing environments and dynamic bindings in the proof of the type preservation theorem.

A typing environment E is *well-formed* if $\prec$ is *antisymmetric* on $\{p \mid p \in \mathrm{dom}(E)\}$, i.e, the environment does not introduce cycles in ownership. Well-formed *environment-binding pairs* ($E;B \vdash \diamond$) are omitted and can be found in the companion technical report [25]. Informally, the pair $E;B$ enables owners and types in E to be used modulo equalities in the run-time binding environment B. To keep the presentation tractable, we omit explicit mentioning of the rules dealing with such equalities. The *well-formed owner* relation ($E;B \vdash p$) is shown in Figure 4. The rules (OWN-DEPENDENT) and (OWN-?) are novel for the gradual type system. A dependent owner is well-formed if the corresponding variable is in scope and if i does not exceed the ownership-arity of the class c. The definition of the nesting relation on owners (Figure 4, $E;B \vdash p \prec p'$) captures only defined owners. It is then embedded into a more general *consistent-inside* relation ($E;B \vdash p \lesssim p'$), which deals also with dependent and unknown owners. Informally, no precise information about nesting can be retrieved from unknown or dependent owners. Note that $\lesssim$ is not transitive, so $E;B \vdash q \lesssim ?$ and $E;B \vdash ? \lesssim p$ do not imply $E;B \vdash q \lesssim p$ for any *defined* p and q.

To state the OAD invariant we need a definition of a heap flattening. The notation $\widehat{H}$ is used also to *flatten* a heap H into a typing environment $\widehat{H}$.

Definition 1 (Heap flattening).

$$\widehat{H} \triangleq \{(\iota \prec o), (\iota : c\langle o, k_{i\in 2..n}\rangle) \mid (\iota \mapsto \langle c\langle o, k_{i\in 2..n}\rangle, \ldots\rangle) \in H\}$$

$\boxed{E;B \vdash p \sim p'}$ $\boxed{E;B \vdash t \sim t'}$

$$\frac{E;B \vdash p}{E;B \vdash p \sim p}\ (\text{CON-REFL}) \qquad \frac{E;B \vdash p \quad E;B \vdash q \quad \mathsf{undefined}(q)}{E;B \vdash q \sim p}\ (\text{CON-RIGHT}) \qquad \frac{E;B \vdash p \quad E;B \vdash q \quad \mathsf{undefined}(q)}{E;B \vdash p \sim q}\ (\text{CON-LEFT})$$

$$\frac{E;B \vdash c\langle p_{i\in 1..n}\rangle \quad E;B \vdash c\langle q_{i\in 1..n}\rangle \quad p_i \sim q_i\ \forall i \in 1..n}{E;B \vdash c\langle p_{i\in 1..n}\rangle \sim c\langle q_{i\in 1..n}\rangle}\ (\text{CON-TYPE})$$

$\boxed{E;B \vdash t}$ $\boxed{E;B \vdash t \lesssim t'}$

$$\frac{\mathsf{arity}(c) = n \quad E;B \vdash p_1 \lesssim p_i \quad \forall i \in 1..n}{E;B \vdash c\langle p_{i\in 1..n}\rangle}\ (\text{G-TYPE}) \qquad \frac{E;B \vdash c\langle\sigma\rangle \leq c'\langle\sigma'\rangle \quad E;B \vdash c'\langle\sigma'\rangle \sim c'\langle\sigma''\rangle}{E;B \vdash c\langle\sigma\rangle \lesssim c'\langle\sigma''\rangle}\ (\text{GRAD-SUB})$$

Fig. 5. Owner and type consistency; gradual subtyping

Definition 2 (Owners-as-Dominators Invariant [10]). $\mathsf{OAD}(H) \triangleq$ *for all locations* ι, ι' *and run-time owners* k,

$$\left.\begin{array}{c} H(\iota) = \langle c\langle k_{i\in 1..n}\rangle, \overline{f \mapsto v}\rangle \\ f_i \mapsto \iota' \ \ and\ \ H(\iota') = \langle t', \ldots\rangle \\ \mathsf{owner}(t') = k \end{array}\right\} \Rightarrow \widehat{H};\emptyset \vdash \iota \prec k$$

In words, if object ι references object ι' via a field, ι must be inside the owner of ι'.

3.3 Type Consistency and Subtyping

Types can be constructed from any class using any owner in scope (including an unknown owner "?"), as long as the correct number of arguments are supplied and the owner (the first parameter), if present, is provably consistently-inside all other parameters. The corresponding relation $E;B \vdash t$ is defined in Figure 5.

The type consistency relation answers the question: *which pairs of static types could possibly correspond to comparable run-time types?* It allows the type checker to compare types with dependent and unknown owners. We define the type consistency relation $\sim$ on types parametrized with partially known and dependent owners via the rules in Figure 5 (the relation $E;B \vdash t \sim t'$). The definition of the subtyping $E;B \vdash t \leq t'$ is is standard for parametrized object-oriented type systems, ownership parameters are invariant [8]. In order to eliminate non-determinacy from the type-checking algorithms we need to construct a relation that combines two kinds of subsumption of types: type consistency and subtyping. This relation is used then in type rules whenever an implicit upcast is necessary [23]. Siek and Taha suggest a way to design such *consistent-subtyping* relation ($\lesssim$) for the calculus $\mathbf{Ob}_{<:}$ of Abadi and Cardelli [1]. If two types $t = c\langle\sigma\rangle$ and $t' = c'\langle\sigma''\rangle$ are related via the consistent-subtyping relation, i.e., $t \lesssim t'$,

$\boxed{E;B \vdash b : t}$

$$\text{(T-NEW)}\quad \frac{E;B \vdash c\langle p_{i\in 1..n}\rangle \qquad \mathsf{defined}(p_i)\ \forall i \in 1..n}{E;B \vdash \texttt{new}\ c\langle p_{i\in 1..n}\rangle : c\langle p_{i\in 1..n}\rangle}$$

$$\text{(T-LKP)}\quad \frac{E;B \vdash z : c\langle\sigma\rangle \qquad \mathcal{F}_c(f) = t}{E;B \vdash z.f : \sigma_z(t)}$$

$$\text{(T-LET)}\quad \frac{E;B \vdash b : t \qquad E,x : \mathsf{fill}(x,t);B \vdash e : s}{E;B \vdash \texttt{let}\ x = b\ \texttt{in}\ e : s}$$

$\boxed{E \vdash t'\ m(t\ y)\{e\}}$

$$\text{(T-UPD)}\quad \frac{E;B \vdash z : c\langle\sigma\rangle \quad \mathcal{F}_c(f) = t \quad E;B \vdash y : s \quad E;B \vdash s \lesssim \sigma_z(t)}{E;B \vdash z.f = y : \sigma_z(t)}$$

$$\text{(T-CALL)}\quad \frac{E;B \vdash y : s \quad \mathcal{MT}_c(m) = (y', t \to t') \quad E;B \vdash z : c\langle\sigma\rangle \quad E;B \vdash s \lesssim \sigma_z(t) \quad \sigma' \equiv \sigma \uplus \{y' \mapsto y\}}{E;B \vdash z.m(y) : \sigma'_z(t')}$$

$$\text{(METHOD)}\quad \frac{E, y : \mathsf{fill}(y,t) \vdash e : s \qquad E \vdash s \lesssim t'}{E \vdash t'\ m(t\ y)\{e\}}$$

Fig. 6. Selected typing rules of $\mathsf{JO}_?$. Grayed parts mark explicit consistent-subtyping checks that may lead to the insertion of dynamic checks.

they can differ along both directions: the type consistency relation $\sim$ and the subtyping relation $\leq$. This is illustrated by the diagram on the left:

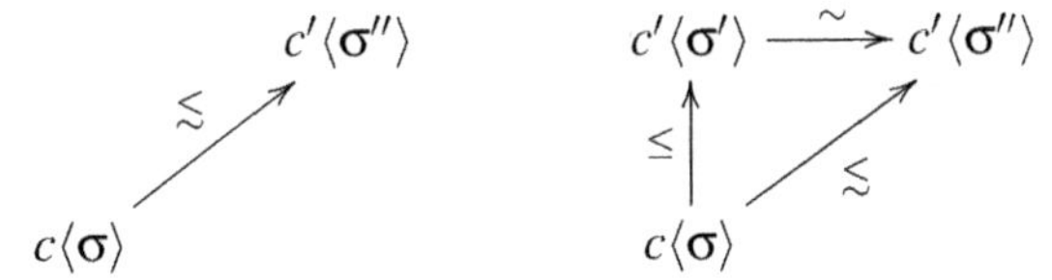

The "upper-left mediator" (the right part of the diagram) is a connecting link between two types. This intuition is formalized via the rule (GRAD-SUB) in Figure 5.

3.4 Expression, Method and Class Typing

Typing rules for expressions are described in Figure 6, following the standard approach [23]. Type rules for variables and values are standard. $m \uplus m'$ denotes the disjoint union of finite maps m and m', requiring that their domains are disjoint. σ_z is the substitution $\sigma \uplus \{\texttt{this} \mapsto z\}$ for any substitution σ. We use the mappings $\mathcal{F}_c$ and $\mathcal{MT}_c$ for retrieving types of fields and methods of a class c. In the rules (T-LET) and (METHOD), the helper function fill converts declared types with *unknown* owners to types with *dependent* owners to track owner dependencies.

$$\mathsf{fill}(x, c\langle p_{i\in 1..n}\rangle) \triangleq c\langle q_{i\in 1..n}\rangle, \text{ where } q_i = \begin{cases} x^{c.i} & \text{if } p_i = \ ? \\ p_i & \text{otherwise.} \end{cases}$$

The definition of well-formed classes ($\vdash c$) and programs ($\vdash P;e$) is standard.

4 Type-Directed Translation: The Language $\mathsf{JO}_?^+$

This section describes the type-based translation of programs in $\mathsf{JO}_?$ to an extended language, $\mathsf{JO}_?^+$, with run-time checks.

4.1 Syntax of $\mathsf{JO}_?^+$

The syntax is extended for dynamic type casts and boundary checks.

$$b \in \textbf{Comp} ::= \ldots \mid \langle t \rangle x \mid x.f \leftarrow y$$

The statement $\langle t \rangle x$ ensures that the run-time type of an object referred to by x *matches* the type t. The statement $x.f \leftarrow y$ performs the check that a field reference from x to y via the field f does not violate the ownership invariant and then performs the field update atomically. Casts and checks are not supposed to be inserted by the programmer. They are inserted instead by the compiler as described in Section 4.3.

4.2 Helper Relations

If two types are related via $\lesssim$, there is a freedom to choose the run-time semantics of type casts, moving along either $\sim$ or $\leq$ axis. Following the rule (GRAD-SUB), we compute the type $c'\langle\sigma'\rangle$ that is on the same class-level as the target type $c'\langle\sigma''\rangle$ for the upcast. The following lemma justifies this computation:

Lemma 1 (Inversion lemma for $\lesssim$). *If $E;B \vdash t \lesssim t''$, then there exists a type t' such that $E;B \vdash t \leq t'$ and $E;B \vdash t' \sim t''$.*

To construct an "upper-left" mediator type we use an extra helper function $t \uparrow c$ that computes a supertype of the type t at class c.

$$\begin{array}{l} c\langle\sigma\rangle \uparrow c \triangleq c\langle\sigma\rangle \\ c'\langle\sigma\rangle \uparrow c \triangleq d\langle\alpha_j \mapsto \sigma(p_j)_{j\in 1..m}\rangle \uparrow c \\ \qquad \text{where } \texttt{class } c'\langle\alpha_{i\in 1..n}\rangle \texttt{ extends } d\langle p_{j\in 1..m}\rangle \text{ and } \texttt{class } d\langle\alpha_{j\in 1..m}\rangle \in P. \\ t \uparrow c\langle\_\rangle \triangleq t \uparrow c. \end{array}$$

In words, the partially defined function $\uparrow$ pulls up the information from the substitution σ of the initial type $c\langle\sigma\rangle$ until it reaches the desired superclass c. If the class hierarchy `Object` is reached without making a match, the function is undefined.

Lemma 2 (Basic properties of $\uparrow$). *For all E, B, t, t',*

1. $(t \uparrow t) = t$
2. $(E;B \vdash t) \wedge (E;B \vdash t') \wedge (t \uparrow t' \neq \bot) \Rightarrow E;B \vdash t \leq (t \uparrow t')$
3. $E;B \vdash t \lesssim t' \Rightarrow E;B \vdash (t \uparrow t') \sim t'$.

The relation $E \vdash t \lhd t'$ states that t *satisfies all constraints imposed by known owners of* t'. It is used to detect where type casts should be inserted.

Definition 3 (t is more defined than t').

$$\begin{array}{l} E \vdash t \lhd t' \triangleq E \vdash t \lesssim t' \textit{ and } \forall i \;\; q_i \neq ? \vee p_i \neq q_i \\ \qquad\qquad \textit{where } (t \uparrow t') = c\langle p_{i\in 1..n}\rangle \textit{ and } t' = c\langle q_{i\in 1..n}\rangle \end{array}$$

$\boxed{E;B \vdash^{C} b : s}$

$$\text{(T-CAST)}\quad \frac{E;B \vdash y : s \quad E;B \vdash t \qquad E;B \vdash s \lesssim t}{E;B \vdash^{C} \langle t \rangle y : t} \qquad \text{(T-UPD')}\quad \frac{E;B \vdash z : c\langle\sigma\rangle \quad \mathcal{F}_c(f) = t \qquad E;B \vdash s \lhd \sigma_z(t) \quad E;B \vdash y : s}{E;B \vdash^{C} z.f = y : \sigma_z(t)}$$

$\boxed{E;B \vdash^{C}_{\mathcal{B}} b : s}$

$$\text{(T-CHECK)}\quad \frac{E;B \vdash z : c\langle\sigma\rangle \quad \mathcal{F}_c(f) = t \qquad E;B \vdash y : s \quad E;B \vdash s \lhd \sigma_z(t)}{E;B \vdash^{C}_{\mathcal{B}} z.f \leftarrow y : \sigma_z(t)} \qquad \text{(T-UPD'')}\quad \frac{E;B \vdash z : c\langle\sigma\rangle \quad \mathcal{F}_c(f) = t \quad E;B \vdash y : s \qquad E;B \vdash s \lhd \sigma_z(t) \quad \textbf{specified}(\sigma_z(t))}{E;B \vdash^{C}_{\mathcal{B}} z.f = y : \sigma_z(t)}$$

Fig. 7. Selected typing rules of $\vdash^{C}$ and $\vdash^{C}_{\mathcal{B}}$

If the information about the first owner parameter of the type t of some class field is not known statically, the OAD invariant cannot be guaranteed. In this case a boundary check should be inserted. The predicate **specified**(t) is true iff a type t provides enough static info about ist owners to ensure the OAD invariant preservation.

Definition 4 **(t specifies its owner).** **specified**$(t) \triangleq p_1 \neq\ ?$, *where* $t = c\langle p_{i \in 1..n}\rangle$

The type rules for type casts and boundary checks are present in Figure 7. For $\text{JO}_?^+$ we use different typing relations, namely, $\vdash^{C}$ and $\vdash^{C}_{\mathcal{B}}$. These two relations are similar to $\vdash$ for $\text{JO}_?$. The purpose of each of them is to ensure the specific safety conditions after the corresponding stage of the translation (type cast and boundary check insertion, respectively). One significant difference is that all the occurrences of $\lesssim$ in the typing of statements are now concentrated in the rule (T-CAST). In the rest of the $\lesssim$-rules are replaced by $\lhd$ (grayed parts). The rule (T-CHECK) ensures the type conformance via $\lhd$, but not the preservation of the OAD invariant: this is postponed until run-time. The rule (T-UPD") is targeted to ensure the OAD invariant.

4.3 Type-Directed Program Translation

We adopt the idea of Siek and Taha [27] to define a type-directed *type cast* insertions and extend it with the *boundary check* insertion relation (Figure 8, relations $\overset{C}{\rightsquigarrow}$ and $\overset{\mathcal{B}}{\rightsquigarrow}$, respectively). First, type casts are inserted into a program whenever additional information about types needs to be regained. Then the boundary check insertion translation works on the program with inserted casts, so each step of the translation eliminates an aspect of uncertainty caused by incomplete type annotations.

Figure 8 provides the definition of selected rules for the cast insertion relation that specifies the translation. It is written $E \vdash e_1 \overset{C}{\rightsquigarrow} e_2 : t$ for expressions and holds if, under the assumptions from E, expression e_1 is translated into expression e_2 and the type of e_1 is $\vdash$-determined as t. In the same way it is defined for methods. The rules for classes and a whole program are straightforward and omitted. No cast is inserted if the predicate $\lhd$ holds on types being compared. For conditional insertions we define the helper function

$$\boxed{E \vdash e \overset{C}{\rightsquigarrow} e' : t}$$

(C-UPD)
$$\frac{E \vdash z : c\langle\sigma\rangle \quad \mathcal{F}_c(f) = t \quad E \vdash s \lesssim \sigma_z(t) \quad E \vdash y : s \quad E, x : \mathsf{fill}(x, \sigma_z(t)) \vdash e_1 \overset{C}{\rightsquigarrow} e_2 : s'}{E \vdash \mathtt{let}\ x = (z.f = y)\ \mathtt{in}\ e_1 \overset{C}{\rightsquigarrow} C_E\langle s, \sigma_z(t)\rangle(\mathtt{let}\ x = (z.f = y)\ \mathtt{in}\ e_2) : s'}$$

(C-CALL)
$$\frac{E \vdash z : c\langle\sigma\rangle \quad \mathcal{MT}_c(m) = (y', t \to t') \quad E \vdash y : s \quad E \vdash s \lesssim \sigma_z(t) \quad \sigma' \equiv \sigma \uplus \{y' \mapsto y\} \quad E, x : \mathsf{fill}(x, \sigma'_z(t')) \vdash e_1 \overset{C}{\rightsquigarrow} e_2 : s'}{E \vdash \mathtt{let}\ x = z.m(y)\ \mathtt{in}\ e_1 \overset{C}{\rightsquigarrow} C_E\langle s, \sigma_z(t)\rangle(\mathtt{let}\ x = z.m(y)\ \mathtt{in}\ e_2) : s'}$$

$$\boxed{E \vdash t'\ m(t\ y)\{e\} \overset{C}{\rightsquigarrow} t'\ m(t\ y)\{e'\}}$$

(C-METHOD)
$$\frac{E \vdash e_1 : s \quad E \vdash s \lesssim t' \quad e_2 = F[z] \quad E, y : \mathsf{fill}(y, t) \vdash e_1 \overset{C}{\rightsquigarrow} e_2 : s}{E \vdash t'\ m(t\ y)\{e_1\} \overset{C}{\rightsquigarrow} t'\ m(t\ y)\{F[C_E\langle s, t'\rangle(z)]\}}$$

$$\boxed{E \vdash e \overset{\mathcal{B}}{\rightsquigarrow} e' : t}$$

(B-UPD)
$$\frac{E \vdash z : c\langle\sigma\rangle \quad \mathcal{F}_c(f) = t \quad E \vdash y : s \quad E \vdash s \lhd \sigma_z(t) \quad E, x : \mathsf{fill}(x, \sigma_z(t)) \vdash e_1 \overset{\mathcal{B}}{\rightsquigarrow} e_2 : s'}{E \vdash \mathtt{let}\ x = (z.f = y)\ \mathtt{in}\ e_1 \overset{\mathcal{B}}{\rightsquigarrow} \mathtt{let}\ x = \mathcal{B}\langle\sigma_z(t)\rangle(z.f = y)\ \mathtt{in}\ e_2 : s'}$$

Fig. 8. Compilation of $\mathsf{JO}_?$: type-directed translation

C, which uses non-recursive *local decomposition* of an expression e via the context G and optionally inserts type-casts:

$$\begin{aligned} C_E\langle t_1, t_2\rangle(e) &\triangleq \textbf{if}\ (E \vdash t_1 \lhd t_2)\ \textbf{then}\ e\ \textbf{else}\ (\mathtt{let}\ y' = \langle t_2\rangle y\ \mathtt{in}\ G[y']) \\ &\quad\ \textbf{where}\ y' \text{ is fresh},\ e = G[y] \\ G &::= [\,]\ |\ \mathtt{let}\ x = z.m([\,])\ \mathtt{in}\ e\ |\ \mathtt{let}\ x = (z.f = [\,])\ \mathtt{in}\ e \end{aligned}$$

Boundary check insertion $\overset{\mathcal{B}}{\rightsquigarrow}$ is of the second stage of the whole translation (Figure 8). The translation $\overset{\mathcal{B}}{\rightsquigarrow}$ works on top of the $\vdash^{C}$-well-typed program. The only type of the statement that can be affected by $\overset{\mathcal{B}}{\rightsquigarrow}$ is a *field update* since it is only one that can possibly break the OAD invariant. The helper function $\mathcal{B}$ is defined to optionally replace plain assignments with boundary-checked field assignments whenever insufficient type information about *primary* owners is provided. For the rest of the statements, expressions and methods, $\overset{\mathcal{B}}{\rightsquigarrow}$ is applied recursively.

$$\begin{aligned} \mathcal{B}\langle t\rangle(b) &\triangleq \textbf{let}\ (z.f = y) = b\ \textbf{in}\ (\textbf{if}\ \textbf{specified}(t)\ \textbf{then}\ b\ \textbf{else}\ z.f \leftarrow y) \\ F &::= [\,]\ |\ \mathtt{let}\ z = b\ \mathtt{in}\ F \end{aligned}$$

Definition 5. *$E \vdash e \rightsquigarrow e'' : t$ iff $E \vdash e \overset{C}{\rightsquigarrow} e' : t$ and $E \vdash e' \overset{\mathcal{B}}{\rightsquigarrow} e'' : t$ for some $e' \in \mathsf{JO}_?^+$.*

Theorem 1 (Program translation is $\vdash^{C}_{\mathcal{B}}$-sound.). *$E \vdash e : t$ implies $E \vdash e \rightsquigarrow e' : t$ for some e'. Furthermore, $E \vdash e \rightsquigarrow e' : t$ for some e implies $E \vdash^{C}_{\mathcal{B}} e' : t$.*

The translation relation $E \vdash e_1 \rightsquigarrow e_2 : t$ can be extended to classes and programs in a straightforward fashion. For instance, we denote $\vdash P_1; e_1 \rightsquigarrow P_2; e_2$ if a program $P_2; e_2$ is obtained from $P_1; e_1$ by the compositional type-directed translation.

$$\boxed{\langle H,B,e,K\rangle \Rightarrow \langle H',B',e',K'\rangle}$$

$$\text{(CAST-CHECK)}\quad \frac{H;B \vdash t \ltimes t' \quad B(y)=\iota \quad H(\iota)=\langle s,\ldots\rangle \quad \widehat{H} \vdash s \lhd t'}{H;B \vdash \mathsf{cast}(t,y)}$$

$$\text{(E-CAST1)}\quad \frac{B(y)=\mathtt{null} \lor H;B \vdash \mathsf{cast}(t,y) \quad B' = B[x \mapsto B(y)]}{\langle H,B,\mathtt{let}\ x{=}\langle t\rangle y\ \mathtt{in}\ e,K\rangle \Rightarrow \langle H,B',e,K\rangle}$$

$$\text{(E-CAST2)}\quad \frac{B(y)\neq\mathtt{null} \quad H;B \nvdash \mathsf{cast}(t,y) \quad K\neq\mathbf{fail}(\_) \quad e{=}(\mathtt{let}\ x{=}\langle t\rangle y\ \mathtt{in}\ e')}{\langle H,B,e,K\rangle \Rightarrow \langle H,B,e,\mathbf{fail}(K)\rangle}$$

$$\text{(BOUNDARY-CHECK)}\quad \frac{B(x)=\iota \quad B(y)=\iota' \quad H(\iota')=\langle c\langle k,\ldots\rangle,\ldots\rangle \quad \widehat{H};\emptyset \vdash \iota \prec k}{H;B \vdash \mathsf{boundary}(x,y)}$$

$$\text{(E-BOUNDARY1)}\quad \frac{(B(y')=\mathtt{null} \lor H;B \vdash \mathsf{boundary}(y,y')) \quad B(y)=\iota \quad B(y')=v \quad H(\iota)=o \quad H'=H[\iota \mapsto o[f \mapsto v]] \quad B'=B[x \mapsto v]}{\langle H,B,\mathtt{let}\ x{=}(y.f{\leftarrow}y')\ \mathtt{in}\ e,K\rangle \Rightarrow \langle H',B',e,K\rangle}$$

$$\text{(E-BOUNDARY2)}\quad \frac{B(y')\neq\mathtt{null} \quad H;B \nvdash \mathsf{boundary}(y,y') \quad K\neq\mathbf{fail}(\_) \quad e{=}(\mathtt{let}\ x{=}(y.f{\leftarrow}y')\ \mathtt{in}\ e')}{\langle H,B,e,K\rangle \Rightarrow \langle H,B,e,\mathbf{fail}(K)\rangle}$$

Fig. 9. Small-step operational semantics of $\mathsf{JO}_?^+$ (selected rules)

5 Operational Semantics of $\mathsf{JO}_?^+$

This section provides the definition of dynamic semantics of $\mathsf{JO}_?$. The selected rules of the small-step operational semantics of $\mathsf{JO}_?$ is presented in Figure 9 (the rest of the rules is standard and can be found in the companion technical report [25]). The semantics is in the form of a small-step CEK-like abstract machine with a single-threaded store H, binding environment B and explicit continuations K [14]. A continuation K is, informally, a serialized next step of computation.

$$K ::= \mathbf{mt} \ \mid\ \mathbf{call}(x:(t,\sigma),e,B,K) \ \mid\ \mathbf{fail}(K)$$

The *empty* continuation $\mathbf{mt}$ corresponds to the empty control stack which is a case at the beginning and at the correct end of program execution. $\mathbf{call}(x:(t,\sigma),e,B,K)$ describes the discipline of popping the stack when a method ends its execution and its caller's local environment B should be restored with a result assigned to a variable x. Finally, $\mathbf{fail}(K)$ denotes the result of failing casts and boundary checks.

To implement dynamic type casts, we first need a bit of machinery to relate *syntactic* types with *dynamic* types extracted from the object heap during the program execution. We define a helper relation $H;\ B \vdash t \ltimes t'$ to compute the dynamic type t' corresponding to a static type t in dynamic environments H and B by instantiating owners as follows:

$$\frac{\forall\, i \in 1..n \quad q_i = \begin{cases} k & \text{if } \begin{cases} p_i = x^{c.j} \\ H(B(x)) = \langle t,\ldots\rangle \\ k = \mathsf{owner}_j(t \uparrow c) \end{cases} & \textit{dependent owner} \\ p_i & \text{if } \mathsf{actual}(p_i) & \textit{run-time owner} \\ B(p_i) & \text{if } \mathsf{defined}(p_i) & \textit{formal owner or variable} \\ ? & \text{otherwise} & \textit{unknown owner} \end{cases}}{H;B \vdash c\langle p_{i\in 1..n}\rangle \ltimes c\langle q_{i\in 1..n}\rangle}$$

The test $\iota \prec o$ in the rule (BOUNDARY-CHECK) can be performed at run-time by checking whether o is ι or some transitive owner of ι—this information is retained via the flattened heap $\widehat{H}$.

6 Type Safety

In this section we sketch the type safety of $\mathsf{JO}_?$ as a corollary of the correctness of the type-guided program translation with respect to program typing and the type safety of the extended language $\mathsf{JO}_?^+$ with type casts and boundary checks. A complete formal treatment with the definition of well-formed run-time states and proofs of theorems is available in the accompanying technical report [25].

Proposition 1 (Compilation and gradual typing). $E \vdash P;e$ *iff* $\exists P',e'.\ E \vdash P;e \rightsquigarrow P';e'$.

The preservation of the OAD invariant relies on three facts: (1) an initial configuration of any program obeys the OAD invariant, (2) the subject reduction theorem guarantees the type preservation for subsequent configurations, and (3) making a step from any well-typed configuration obeying the OAD invariant, preserves the invariant. In the remainder of this section we formalize these statements.

The operational formalism we use is a stack-based abstract machine (continuations form a stack-like structure) with a heap, so we need to separate environments ro provide typing for heap objects and references in stack frames.

$$\begin{array}{ll} \mathcal{E} ::= \emptyset \mid \mathcal{E},\ \iota : c\langle k_{i\in 1..n}\rangle \mid \mathcal{E},\ \iota \prec k & \textbf{\textit{heap environments}} \\ \overline{E} ::= \mathbf{Nil} \mid E \bullet \overline{E} & \textbf{\textit{stack environments}} \end{array}$$

Below in this section we assume that static typing environments E defined in Section 3 contain only term and owner variables in their domain, but not heap locations. A stack environment is *well-formed* if all its constituents are well-formed. The definition of a well-formed run-time state ($\mathcal{E},\overline{E} \Vdash \langle H,B,e,K\rangle$), which is omitted, assumes the expression e to be well-typed ($\mathcal{E},E_0;B \vdash^{C}_{\mathcal{B}} e : t$) and environments $\mathcal{E}$ and $\overline{E}$ well-formed. The last ensures, in particular, that the heap H has no ownership-cycles ($\mathcal{E} \vdash H$).

Lemma 3 (Initial state typing). *$\mathcal{E},E;B \vdash^{C}_{\mathcal{B}} e : t$ iff $\mathcal{E},(E \bullet \mathbf{Nil}) \Vdash \langle H,B,e,\mathbf{mt}\rangle$ for some initial heap H such that $\mathcal{E} \vdash H$.*

Definition 6 (Heap environment extension). *An environment $\mathcal{E}'$ is an extension of $\mathcal{E}$ (written $\mathcal{E}' \gg \mathcal{E}$) if and only if $\mathcal{E} \subseteq \mathcal{E}'$.*

Definition 7 (Stack environment evolution). *We say that a stack environment $\overline{E}$ transforms to a stack environment $\overline{E}'$ (written $\overline{E} \rightsquigarrow \overline{E}'$) if one of the following holds:*

- $\overline{E}' = E' \bullet \overline{E}$ *for some* E' *(method call);*
- $\overline{E}' = (E_0,x:t) \bullet \mathsf{tail}(\overline{E})$ *for some t and $x \notin dom(E_0)$* *(variable assignment);*
- $\overline{E}' = (E_1,x:t) \bullet \mathsf{tail}(\mathsf{tail}(\overline{E}))$ *for some t and $x \notin dom(E_1)$* *(method return).*

Theorem 2 (Subject reduction in $\mathsf{JO}_?^+$). *If $e \in$ **Expr** in $\mathsf{JO}_?^+$, $\mathcal{S} = \langle H,B,e,K\rangle$, $\mathcal{E},\overline{E} \Vdash \mathcal{S}$ for some well-formed $\mathcal{E},\overline{E}$ and $\mathcal{S} \Rightarrow \mathcal{S}'$ then $\mathcal{E}',\overline{E}' \Vdash \mathcal{S}'$ for some well-formed $\mathcal{E}',\overline{E}'$ such that $\mathcal{E}' \gg \mathcal{E}$ and $\overline{E} \rightsquigarrow \overline{E}'$.*

Theorem 3 ensures that for all well-formed states, if it is possible to make a next step, then the OAD invariant is preserved for the heap component of the resulting state.

Theorem 3 (OAD **preservation in** $\mathsf{JO}_?^+$). *If* $e \in \mathbf{Expr}$ *in* $\mathsf{JO}_?^+$, $\mathcal{S} = \langle H, B, e, K \rangle$, $\mathcal{E}; \overline{E} \Vdash \mathcal{S}$, $\mathsf{OAD}(H)$ *and* $\mathcal{S} \Rightarrow \mathcal{S}'$ *for some* $\mathcal{S}' = \langle H', \_, \_, \_ \rangle$ *then* $\mathsf{OAD}(H')$.

Definition 8 (Initial state). *Assume* $P; e$ *to be a program in* $\mathsf{JO}_?^+$, $H = \{\mathtt{world} \mapsto \bullet\}$, $B = \{\mathtt{this} \mapsto \mathtt{world}\}$ *is an* initial binding environment. *Then the* initial configuration *of* $P; e$ *is* $\mathbf{init}(e) = \langle H, B, e, \mathbf{mt} \rangle$.

Following [11], we introduce a class `World` with no owner parameters to represent the object corresponding to the owner of `world`-annotated instances, and for the completeness we need to provide its type. Taking $\mathcal{E} = \{\mathtt{world} : \mathtt{World}\}$ and $\overline{E} = \{\mathtt{this} : \mathtt{World}\} \bullet \mathbf{Nil}$, we obtain $\emptyset \vdash_{\mathcal{B}}^{C} P; e \Rightarrow \mathcal{E}, \overline{E} \Vdash \mathbf{init}(e)$ by Lemma 3. Theorem 4 ends our chain of safety statements.

Theorem 4 (Static type safety of $\mathsf{JO}_?$**).** *If* $\vdash P; e \rightsquigarrow P'; e'$ *and* $\mathbf{init}(e') \Rightarrow^* \mathcal{S}$, *then one of the following statements holds:*

(a) $\mathcal{S} = \langle H, B, v, \mathbf{mt} \rangle$ *for some* H, B *and* v *(final state);*
(b) $\mathsf{NPE}(\mathcal{S})$ *(null-pointer error);*
(c) $\exists \mathcal{S}' : \mathcal{S} \Rightarrow \mathcal{S}'$ *(progress);*
(d) $\mathcal{S} = \langle H, B, b, \mathbf{fail}(K) \rangle$, *where* $b = \langle t \rangle y$ *or* $b = z.f \leftarrow y$ *for some* H, B, t, y, z, f *and* K *(*OAD *violation attempt).*

Combined Theorems 1, 3 and 4 state that the provided gradual type system ensures that (a) during a compiled program execution no ownership invariant will be violated, and (b) fully-annotated well-typed programs will be executed until the final or null-pointer error state with no ownership invariant violation.

7 Implementation

A prototype compiler for Gradual Ownership Types has been implemented in the JastAdd framework as a small syntactic extension of the JastAddJ compiler for Java [13]. The extension is about 2,600 lines of code, not including tests, blank lines and comments.[3] Although generics were introduced in Java 5, we have chosen Java 1.4 as a host language for the sake of simplicity. Parametric polymorphism is an orthogonal feature to the ownership parametrization, but they can be unified [24].

The type analysis and type-directed translation are implemented as attributes in the framework of reference attribute grammars [13]. The type analysis is built on top of the standard Java type-checking algorithm, which is augmented to handle ownership-parametrized types. The compiler uses several default conventions as well as *manifest ownership* [10] to seamlessly embed the *raw* Java code into an ownership-aware environment. To be parametrized by some owners, a class or an interface requires *all* its super classes and the interfaces it implements to carry ownership parameters. I.e., no casts of ownership-parametrized types to raw types is allowed, since it could lead to breakage of the OAD invariant [24]. The only one exception to this rule is handling of `Object` class. We assume that two `Object` classes exist: one is ownership-parametrized

[3] A prototype is available from `http://people.cs.kuleuven.be/ilya.sergey/gradual/`

and the other is owned by **world** and considered as a special case of the first one. Classes that inherit from parametrized classes or interfaces but do not declare ownership parameters are implicitly assumed to be owned by **world**, which is made the owner of the supertypes. The type-directed translation is implemented as a source-to-source transformation by erasing ownership types, augmenting classes with fields for owner parameters and inserting run-time checks into the code of expressions. The compiler might also need to modify code that interacts with owner-parametrized classes, i.e, some libraries might need to be recompiled.

Dependent Owners and Casts. Instead of transforming Java programs into ANF, we operate with dependent owners in terms of *source code locations* corresponding to the expression that computes an owned object. Any expression in the program can hereby give rise to dependent owners, which potentially can be used in further checks. To avoid management of all possible source locations, the compiler runs a simple static analysis to determine which dependent owners might be used in the current context.

Inner Classes and Manifest Ownership. In Java a non-static inner class is nested in the body of another class and contains an implicit reference to its enclosing class (*outer instance*). An instance of such a class can be leaked and referred to through a field by another object *outside* of its outer instance, which, again, breaks the desired invariant. There are multiple suggestions on the problem of interoperation of inner classes and different ownership policies [2,3]. We make outer instance's ownership parameters legal in the context of an inner class if the programmer passes them to the inner class as owner arguments, i.e., by a sort of closure-conversion. However, most of the time one does not intend an inner class to be parametrized, since it is something for the internal use, but it may be externally accessible. To solve this design problem, we employ *manifest ownership*, a mechanism to allow owned classes without explicit owner type parameters [10]. A manifest class does not have an explicit owner parameter, rather the class's owners are fixed, so all the objects of the class have the same owners.

8 Experience

We evaluated our approach by gradually porting several classes from the Java Collection Framework (Java SDK version 1.4.2) into Gradual Ownership Types. Most traditional collection classes that contain linked data structures implement internal logic to handle their entries in the way it is described in the example in Figure 1. We assume that internal entries should be dominated by their outer collection instances, so they are not supposed to be exposed to the external objects. It makes them a good possible candidate for ownership types and the owners-as-dominators policy. Our intention was to ensure the OAD invariant holds for inner classes such as `Entry` of collection classes such as `LinkedList` and `TreeMap`, without changing existing code, but only by adding annotations. The questions we were trying to answer are:

- How many annotations (i.e., lines of code changed) are needed minimally?
- What is the execution time overhead with minimal annotations?
- How many annotations are needed for full static checking?

The analysed code base consists of 46 source files, comprising about 8,200 lines of code, not including blank lines and comments. The compiler provides hints for easily migrating to ownership types by emitting static error messages and warnings. A static error message is emitted whenever necessary annotations are omitted. A warning message is displayed whenever dynamic casts or boundary checks are inserted.

LinkedList. The minimal amount of annotations to ensure the OAD invariant for instances of the inner class `Entry` of `LinkedList` is 17, comprising 7 annotations to the `LinkedList` class itself and 10 in five other classes. Class `Iterator` was owner-parametrized to preserve the OAD invariant, as the inner class `ListItr` has access to entries of the list. The correctly annotated class `ListItr` is defined as follows; the iterator is owned by the instance of `LinkedList` (employing the manifest ownership):

```
class ListItr implements ListIterator<LinkedList.this>
```

We implemented a series of simple benchmarks consisting of multiple list updates and iterations. These reveal that the minimal annotations cause average execution time per update to double. However, the implementation of `LinkedList` allows *full* annotation. By adding 17 extra annotations in the `LinkedList` class (i.e., 34 in total), one can reach zero execution overhead and full static preservation of the OAD invariant.

TreeMap. For the best result in terms of performance and the invariant preservation the `TreeMap` class requires 28 annotations, consisting of 26 annotations in the class itself and two extra annotations in the interfaces `Iterator` and `Map` respectively. Because of the static method `buildFromSorted`, which also operates with entries, it is impossible to provide full static ownership guarantee without modifying the original code. The possible solutions would be making the method non-static, or providing an extra final method parameter as an alias for the potential owner. Alternative solution is to use owner-polymorphic methods [9], which are not supported in the current formalism. According to the set of stress benchmarks involving multiple updates and iterations, even in the presence of some non-avoidable casts, the annotated `TreeMap` class exhibits only 30% average execution time overhead per update.

Detected Object Leaks. Our compiler has helped to detect a place in the Collection Framework with the possible "leak" of the inner `Entry` classes with respect to the OAD invariant. The class `ResourceBundleEnumeration` declares a package-protected field of type `Iterator`. Although this field is initialized with the iterator of the `Set` instance in the constructor, it can be reassigned elsewhere in client code, which will lead to an OAD invariant violation. Our compiler generates the code with necessary dynamic checks for updates of this field to ensure the invariant dynamically. However, for the static OAD guarantee a significant refactoring would be required.

9 Discussion

Several design choices were made in our approach to gradual ownership types. This section discusses other alternatives.

Alternative Ownership Disciplines. In our work we used the *owner-as-dominator* discipline as a base for applying the gradual technique. However, most of existing parametric ownership disciplines, such as *multiple ownership* [7] or *ownership domains* [2], can be "gradualized" using similar approach with *no changes* in the part related to type cast insertion. The difference between most of existing disciplines lies in the definition of the heap invariant and relation between owners that should be preserved. In the present work it is ensured by the boundary check, and for any other particular system it might require specific tweaks in the definitions of the consistent-inside relation, **specified** and the runtime semantics of boundary check.

Required Annotations. The present approach required that ownership parameters be specified (explicitly or via default conventions) at all allocation sites, hence object owners are all known at creation time. Two other possibilities were considered. The first was to annotate field and method types, thereby annotating the interface of the object. This approach unfortunately creates a significant overhead in the implementation, which would require run-time tracking of object aliasing: whenever an object owner becomes known, for example, by assignment into a field whose owners are specified, all other aliases to that object need to be checked for validity. Furthermore, the ownership of objects with the same owner as the assigned object also need to be updated—objects can have the same owner, even if this owner is not known; consider for example, the `Entry` objects in a linked list. The required run-time modifications are likely to introduce too much run-time overhead. The second approach was to allow annotations to occur anywhere in the code. This approach is clearly best suited for programmers, but it clearly also suffers the same problems as annotating just the interface.

Treatment of Libraries. Our approach essentially assumes that any library code that needs to be owner-aware must be rewritten, but rewriting the library is a significant overhead, the kind which gradual typing aims to avoid. Three alternative approaches are possible. One is to ignore leaks of an object into ownership-unaware code, and assume a weaker ownership invariant that amounts to saying that an object is protected only within code compiled by our compiler. With this more pragmatic approach, library code can more gradually be converted to owner-aware code and trusted library code can 'safely' be ignored. A second alternative is to implement the byte-code instrumentation procedure that inserts the run-time checks to monitor field assignments in the code. The third approach is to perform a static analysis of library (byte)code along the lines of Ma and Foster's work [19] to infer possible ownership annotations.

Boundary Checks. Boundary checks occur whenever an object is stored in a field of a type with an unknown primary owner of another object in order to preserve the OAD invariant. An alternative interpretation of such a type is that it does not care what the owners are. This would allow expensive boundary checks to be omitted, keeping only dynamic casts, at the expense of a weaker invariant. Such a system may be worth further investigation.

10 Related Work

Our work is strongly based on the idea of gradual types by Siek and Taha [26,27], which has been recently applied to Java-like generics [17] and modular typestate [30].

The notion of *blame control* is known in the context of gradual types to provide better debugging support [29]. Since dependent owners contain information about source code locations, the information from labels makes it easy to track back the flow dependencies and eliminate uncertainty by adding extra ownership annotations. This makes dependent owners similar to *blame labels*. The idea of combining static and dynamic type checking is also close to the work of Flanagan on *hybrid types* [15]. Hybrid types may contain refinements in the form arbitrary predicates on underlying data. The type checker attempts to satisfy the predicates statically using a theorem prover.

Gordon and Noble in the work on dynamic ownership introduce ConstraintedJava, a scripting language that provides dynamic ownership checking [16]. The authors suggest a dynamic ownership structure consisting of an owner pointer in every object. The semantics of the language relies on a message-passing protocol with a specific kind of monitoring, similar to our boundary checks.

Existential ownership types [18] offer variant subtyping of owners based on existential quantification [6]. This approach allows *owner-polymorphic methods* to be elegantly implemented and it distinguishes objects with different and equal *unknown* owners. Existential quantification also helps to implement effective run-time downcasts in the presence of ownership types: a subtype's inferred owners are treated as existentially quantified [32]. The key difference between these approaches and ours is that existential ownership expresses *don't care* whereas gradual types express *don't know* concerning the unknown owners.

Algorithms for *ownership inference* address a similar problem to ours: take a raw program and produce reasonable ownership annotations. The pioneering work on *dynamic* ownership types' inference is Wren's master's thesis [31]. The work provides a graph-theoretical background for run-time inference. The author formulates the system of equations to assign annotations to particular object allocation sites, based on an object graph's evolution history. However, no proof of correctness of these equations is provided. Milanova and Vitek [20] present a static analysis to infer ownership annotations for the OAD invariant. The analysis is based on the context-insensitive points-to analysis. A more general points-to analysis-based algorithm to infer ownership and uniqueness is presented by Ma and Foster [19] via constraint-based points-to analysis. The collected information about encapsulation properties is not however mapped to a type system. Dietl et al. [12] present a static analysis to infer *Universe Types*, a light-weight version of ownership types, according to a set of generated constraints. Constraints of the type system are encoded as a boolean satisfiability problem.

11 Conclusion

Introducing ownership types into real-life programs is a long-standing problem. The main causes are the verbosity of the formalism and its rigidity for some applications. In this work we applied the notion of gradual types to ownership type systems and the owners-as-dominators invariant for a Java-like language to seamlessly combine static and dynamic invariant checks. The developed framework has been formalized and proved to be correct [25]. We implemented Gradual Ownership Types as an extension of an existing Java compiler and evaluated it on a well-studied codebase.

Acknowledgements. We wish to acknowledge the detailed comments of Dominique Devriese, Frank Piessens and Jan Midtgaard. We are also grateful to Sophia Drossopoulou and José Proença for proof-reading an early draft version of the paper. Finally, we thank the anonymous reviewers of ESOP '12 for their feedback, which helped to make the motivation clearer.

References

1. Abadi, M., Cardelli, L.: A Theory of Objects. Springer-Verlag New York, Inc., Secaucus (1996)
2. Aldrich, J., Chambers, C.: Ownership Domains: Separating Aliasing Policy from Mechanism. In: Vetta, A. (ed.) ECOOP 2004. LNCS, vol. 3086, pp. 1–25. Springer, Heidelberg (2004)
3. Boyapati, C., Liskov, B., Shrira, L.: Ownership types for object encapsulation. In: POPL 2003, pp. 213–223. ACM (2003)
4. Boyapati, C., Rinard, M.: A parameterized type system for race-free Java programs. In: OOPSLA 2001, pp. 56–69. ACM (2001)
5. Boyapati, C., Salcianu, A., Beebee Jr., W., Rinard, M.: Ownership types for safe region-based memory management in real-time Java. In: PLDI 2003, pp. 324–337. ACM (2003)
6. Cameron, N., Drossopoulou, S.: Existential Quantification for Variant Ownership. In: Castagna, G. (ed.) ESOP 2009. LNCS, vol. 5502, pp. 128–142. Springer, Heidelberg (2009)
7. Cameron, N.R., Drossopoulou, S., Noble, J., Smith, M.J.: Multiple ownership. In: OOPSLA 2007, pp. 441–460. ACM (2007)
8. Clarke, D., Drossopoulou, S.: Ownership, encapsulation and the disjointness of type and effect. In: OOPSLA 2002, pp. 292–310. ACM (2002)
9. Clarke, D., Wrigstad, T.: External Uniqueness is Unique Enough. In: Cardelli, L. (ed.) ECOOP 2003. LNCS, vol. 2743, pp. 176–200. Springer, Heidelberg (2003)
10. Clarke, D.G.: Object ownership and containment. PhD thesis, University of New South Wales, New South Wales, Australia (2001)
11. Clarke, D.G., Potter, J.M., Noble, J.: Ownership types for flexible alias protection. In: OOPSLA 1998, pp. 48–64. ACM (1998)
12. Dietl, W., Ernst, M.D., Müller, P.: Tunable Static Inference for Generic Universe Types. In: Mezini, M. (ed.) ECOOP 2011. LNCS, vol. 6813, pp. 333–357. Springer, Heidelberg (2011)
13. Ekman, T., Hedin, G.: The JastAdd extensible Java compiler. In: OOPSLA 2007, pp. 1–18. ACM (2007)
14. Felleisen, M., Findler, R.B., Flatt, M.: Semantics Engineering with PLT Redex, 1st edn. The MIT Press (August 2009)
15. Flanagan, C.: Hybrid type checking. In: POPL 2006, pp. 245–256. ACM (2006)
16. Gordon, D., Noble, J.: Dynamic ownership in a dynamic language. In: DLS 2007, pp. 41–52. ACM (2007)
17. Ina, L., Igarashi, A.: Gradual typing for generics. In: OOPSLA 2011, pp. 609–624. ACM (2011)
18. Lu, Y., Potter, J.: On Ownership and Accessibility. In: Hu, Q. (ed.) ECOOP 2006. LNCS, vol. 4067, pp. 99–123. Springer, Heidelberg (2006)
19. Ma, K.-K., Foster, J.S.: Inferring aliasing and encapsulation properties for Java. In: OOPSLA 2007, pp. 321–336. ACM (2007)
20. Milanova, A., Vitek, J.: Static Dominance Inference. In: Bishop, J., Vallecillo, A. (eds.) TOOLS 2011. LNCS, vol. 6705, pp. 211–227. Springer, Heidelberg (2011)

21. Moelius III, S.E., Souter, A.L.: An object ownership inference algorithm and its applications. In: MASPLAS 2004 (2004)
22. Odersky, M., Cremet, V., Röckl, C., Zenger, M.: A Nominal Theory of Objects with Dependent Types. In: Cardelli, L. (ed.) ECOOP 2003. LNCS, vol. 2743, pp. 201–224. Springer, Heidelberg (2003)
23. Pierce, B.C.: Types and programming languages. MIT Press, Cambridge (2002)
24. Potanin, A., Noble, J., Clarke, D., Biddle, R.: Generic ownership for generic Java. In: OOPSLA 2006, pp. 311–324. ACM (2006)
25. Sergey, I., Clarke, D.: Gradual Ownership Types. Technical Report Report CW 613, Katholieke Universiteit Leuven (December 2011)
26. Siek, J., Taha, W.: Gradual typing for functional languages. In: Scheme 2006 (2006)
27. Siek, J., Taha, W.: Gradual Typing for Objects. In: Bateni, M. (ed.) ECOOP 2007. LNCS, vol. 4609, pp. 2–27. Springer, Heidelberg (2007)
28. Vitek, J., Bokowski, B.: Confined types. In: OOPSLA 1999, pp. 82–96. ACM (1999)
29. Wadler, P., Findler, R.B.: Well-Typed Programs Can't Be Blamed. In: Castagna, G. (ed.) ESOP 2009. LNCS, vol. 5502, pp. 1–16. Springer, Heidelberg (2009)
30. Wolff, R., Garcia, R., Tanter, É., Aldrich, J.: Gradual Typestate. In: Mezini, M. (ed.) ECOOP 2011. LNCS, vol. 6813, pp. 459–483. Springer, Heidelberg (2011)
31. Wren, A.: Inferring ownership. Master's thesis, Imperial College London, UK (June 2003)
32. Wrigstad, T., Clarke, D.: Existential owners for ownership types. Journal of Object Technology 6(4) (2007)

Author Index

GPSR Compliance

The European Union's (EU) General Product Safety Regulation (GPSR) is a set of rules that requires consumer products to be safe and our obligations to ensure this.

If you have any concerns about our products, you can contact us on ProductSafety@springernature.com

In case Publisher is established outside the EU, the EU authorized representative is:

Springer Nature Customer Service Center GmbH
Europaplatz 3
69115 Heidelberg, Germany

Batch number: 09490872

Printed by Printforce, the Netherlands